ROTHMA
RUGBY Y
1984-85

Editor: Stephen Jones
Technical Adviser: Vivian Jenkins

ROTHMANS
Queen Anne Press

A QUEEN ANNE PRESS BOOK

First published in Great Britain in 1984 by
Queen Anne Press
Macdonald & Co (Publishers) Ltd
London & Sydney

A BPCC plc Company

Front cover photograph: England's Maurice Colclough leaping in the line-out in the International against Ireland at Twickenham. (Colin Elsey, Colorsport)

Back cover photograph: Peter Winterbottom, England's wing forward, gaining possession at a loose maul in the France-England game at Parc des Princes. (Colin Elsey, Colorsport)

All photographs courtesy of Colorsport unless otherwise indicated.

British Library Cataloguing in Publication Data

Rothmans rugby yearbook—1984-85
1. Rugby football—Periodicals
796.33'3'05 GV944.8

ISBN 0-356-10447-8
ISBN 0-356-10448-6 Pbk

Photoset by Cylinder Typesetting Limited, London

Printed and bound in Great Britain by Hazell, Watson & Viney Limited,
Member of the BPCC Group, Aylesbury, Bucks.

CONTENTS

FOREWORD
FROM ROTHMANS PUBLICATIONS LTD

For the 13th time Rothmans Publications have the pleasure of welcoming a new issue of *Rothmans Rugby Yearbook*. With Stephen Jones now established in the Editor's chair, and with the wise counsel of Vivian Jenkins still available to us, the book can only continue to grow in stature. We feel that we can, with total justification, proudly describe the book as the definitive annual rugby publication.

Once again the pages which follow are an admirable mix of statistical information and editorial comment. Our thanks for the continuing excellence of this publication go to all involved in the compilation and production.

EDITORIAL PREFACE

This is the 13th appearance of the Yearbook and no Scot would ever forgive us if it did not contain a tribute to their Grand Slam team. To underline this achievement, David Leslie is our Player of the Year and the delightful pen of Norman Mair does justice herein to Leslie as a player and a character. In addition, David Norrie traces the remarkable year of Jim Telfer – all defeats with the Lions, all wins with Scotland.

There is also a fulsome tribute to the greatest try-scorer in rugby, Alan Morley, from John Mason, rugby correspondent of the *Daily Telegraph*, himself a proud Bristolian. Jim Woodward looks back at the remarkable Golden Oldies festival in Sydney, and Tim Glover conducts a rare interview with JPR Williams. There are full statistics of the 1983 Lions tour, full results coverage of the expanding, exotic Cathay Pacific-Hong Kong Bank Sevens, a new section on colt and youth rugby plus news of all the leading rugby from all over the world.

There are two main statistical changes this year. Firstly, every international match in the individual players' records is now given in chronological order, instead of in alphabetical order, as happened previously with matches prior to 1973.

Secondly, in the French records we have now recognised all internationals designated as 'full' internationals by the French Rugby Federation. There are several other improvements and additions throughout the book and this is an opportune time to thank all those readers who have written to us suggesting improvements or corrections. Your letters are warmly welcomed and will be acted upon in many cases.

Lastly, a publication of this sort often requires dedication beyond the call of duty from contributors and everyone else involved with the book. I would like to thank the ubiquitous Caroline North, our house editor, and everyone at Queen Anne Press; Mr John Prodger, rugby enthusiast and counsel and everyone at Carreras Rothmans; all the advisory panel; and John Griffiths and Vivian Jenkins, without whom these pages would be blank. Finally, my warmest thanks to each and every contributor. Like Scotland, they have been outstanding!

STEPHEN JONES

REVIEW OF THE SEASON

The Editor

Rugby remained in the glare of the spotlight throughout the season for many reasons; notably the astonishing threats of Mr David Lord, an Australian sports journalist, and the thorny, vexed question of sporting contacts with South Africa. There were miles of column inches and hours of television time on both counts. There were also drama and spectacle on the field, with the rare sights of New Zealand crashing to defeat against British teams and Scotland striding away with the International Championship to the surprise and utter delight of their own followers.

Lord was in many ways the most remarkable figure of the season. He had the breathtaking effrontery to inform rugby that he was taking over 200 of its best players from all the leading countries to play professional rugby for an organisation called World Championship Rugby. The whole circus was definitely to begin in mid-January in London, Mr Lord declared. He spoke of vast salaries for the players and large sponsorships from industry. No one was too staggered to learn from Mr Lord that he had overreached himself. The opening of World Championship Rugby was postponed. Then Mr Lord blithely announced that it would all start in March in Australia, and was quoted as saying that the 1984 International Championship was to be the last of its kind. Rugby people greeted this arrogance with a mixture of amusement and distaste. Needless to say, World Championship Rugby was still not launched long after Lord's deadlines for the death of amateur rugby had passed.

The South African question was far more important. The Rugby Football Union voted by an overwhelming margin to undertake the tour of South Africa which was on the schedule. They did it in the face of a virulent campaign by anti-apartheid groups, the British Government and Opposition, the World Council of Churches and leaders of the black and coloured communities either living in, or exiled from, South Africa. In favour of the tour were, it seemed, a vast majority of the British rugby community plus the Freedom in Sport organisation, formed in part to counter the propaganda of the anti-tour factions. The RFU were advised by those favouring a boycott that to tour would do all sorts of lasting damage to the lot of black people, not to mention the Commonwealth and Olympic Games movements. The RFU decided to retain their contacts in the hope that the undoubted progress towards multi-racial sport made by the South African rugby authorities would be further encouraged by a major tour. The threats and reaction from both sides continued to rumble on as England toured.

The International Championship once again provided tremendous entertainment and tension and there were signs of a more refreshing

Mr David Lord, an Australian journalist and businessman, who threatened to disrupt international rugby in 1984.

and skilful approach, especially from the talented French and the emerging Welsh team. But Scotland ruled the tournament. They began by winning in Cardiff while never playing at their best. They paralysed England's bid at Murrayfield by putting the finger on England's pack and taking their chances. Then, amid delight bordering on hysteria, they smashed Ireland's challenge to win their first Triple Crown for 46 years. They leaned heavily on a powerful scrummaging display from their front five and two sharp tries from Roy Laidlaw at scrum-half.

The Grand Slam match against France, who were also unbeaten, was the most exciting and controversial of the season. France had comfortably disposed of Romania, Ireland and England with wit and pace from their back division. They had struggled against Wales at Cardiff, and won because they took their kicking chances. They outplayed Scotland for the first 40 minutes, too. But Scotland improved dramatically after half-time and as they did so, France declined. The French had played with a rather suspect temperament all season and under pressure from the Scots and from Mr Winston Jones, who penalised them heavily, they crumbled. It was sad to see a talented team lacking the character to succeed.

While France were infringing, Scotland became ever stronger. They were superbly led throughout the season by Jim Aitken, and splendidly marshalled by Laidlaw and John Rutherford at half-back. They also had an excellent back row in Jim Calder, Iain Paxton and David Leslie, the latter making herculean efforts all over the field. Scotland moved on to victory and, perhaps blinking in the spotlight, sat at the top of the tree. Not even the followers of the other Championship teams begrudged the Scots their success. Typically, the team and its officials, including coach Jim Telfer, took their success with modesty and charm.

Charming was not the word for the French, however. They clearly believed that they had been victimised by the referee. It was a great pity that their season ended in acrimony because they certainly produced the most talented set of threequarters to emerge in the Championship for some years. Codorniou, for example, was an extremely efficient director of operations in the centre, Lescarboura was a siege-gun kicker but also an able tactician at fly-half, and Gallion was back to his magnificent best at scrum-half. Jean-Pierre Rives cast doubt on his future participation in the French team by declining to tour New Zealand with France in the close-season.

For all the efforts of Scotland and France it is probable that by the end of the Championship, Wales were the most accomplished all-round side. Their selectors began the season by choosing two hopelessly unbalanced and ineffective teams against Romania and Scotland and they got what they deserved – two defeats. However, the Irish match saw the introduction as captain of Mike Watkins, that engaging, inspiring character who was forgiven past indiscretions and helped transform the whole Welsh season. Ian Stephens, now the leading loose-head in Britain by a street, came back alongside Watkins and everything began to fall into place. By the time of their final match, which Wales comfortably won at Twickenham, they were a confident team. They were well-marshalled by the improving Malcolm Dacey at fly-half and drew considerable inspiration from the dazzling Titley on the wing. The Twickenham game also marked the return of the astonishing Terry Holmes, whose future was in doubt after a serious knee injury suffered on the Lions tour. Holmes came thundering back on to the scene with Cardiff and ended the international season back in the Welsh team, playing superbly. All Wales heaved a sigh of relief.

At the other end of the table were England and Ireland. The downfall of the latter was not exceptionally difficult to predict – their successful team of recent years was already showing signs of wear and tear and a large contingent of Irishmen suffered on the unsuccessful Lions tour. Sure enough, with their aging pack now clearly over the top, Ireland subsided to a melancholy whitewash and there was never a time during the season when they looked likely to avoid this. They played courageously against France, downright badly against Wales and Scotland and only showed snatches of their passionate best form in losing at Twickenham. Tony Ward and Moss Finn improved the team with their craft and footballing ability and Donal Lenihan occasionally won some clean line-out ball. But there was precious little to enthuse over. Willie John McBride now has to rebuild his team, with the forwards especially needing a complete overhaul.

England were favourites to win the Championship with a good few pundits and were encouraged by their win over New Zealand in the autumn. Tragically, far too many of their leading players failed to find their form. England quickly lost their momentum. They had a set-piece fixation and few ideas apart from attempting to dominate in the scrum. Their backs never functioned as an attacking force; they lacked possession from the line-out and close support and cover in the back row. Phil Blakeway and Peter Winterbottom were the outstanding forwards, Dusty Hare had an consistent season after a dose of the horrors with his poor kicking at Murrayfield. Bryan Barley made a useful centre. The rest finished nowhere. All those high hopes evaporated and Dick Greenwood, the new England coach, had a tough introduction.

The win over New Zealand was a false dawn for England, although claims that their victory was next to worthless were well wide of the mark. The All Blacks were lacking all their regular front five for their short but intensive tour, but they still fielded an aggressive, able side. They were at their best early in the tour when they crushed the South of Scotland at Gala, but they ran into trouble in the English divisional matches because each division prepared with commendable thoroughness. The Midlands reaped the benefits and on a passionate night at Welford Road they contained the All Blacks, made better use of their possession and, encouraged by heroism all over the field, especially from their back row of Gary Rees, Graham Robbins and Nick Jeavons, they moved to a famous win. It was sealed by a wonderful dropped goal from Dusty Hare, who picked up a stray kick in his own half and sent the ball soaring over to the thunderous delight of the packed stands. It was a night to remember.

Scotland actually out-rucked the All Blacks at Murrayfield but were slightly lucky to draw the match. England had a limited tactical plan but they stuck to it. Nick Youngs and his back row drove the ball close to the scrum and kept the pressure on the inexperienced New Zealand front five. England laid the ghost of Prince Obolensky, whose tries had given England their last win over New Zealand at Twickenham in 1936, with a clinching try from Maurice Colclough. It was a deeply satisfying experience for Peter Wheeler, at last promoted to the England captaincy which should have been his years before.

The domestic highlights of the season included a superb double by that enduring character Mike Rafter. He piloted both Gloucestershire and Bristol to Twickenham in the Thorn-EMI County Championship and John Player Cup respectively. Gloucestershire went on to win comfortably, while Bristol lost narrowly. He also insisted that his teams played open rugby. Yet before Bath and Bristol took over the club season was enlivened by the improvement of Wasps, Orrell and Nottingham, among others. In Scotland, Hawick and Gala had their annual fight for the Schweppes SRU League Division One title, which Hawick won once again.

In Wales, Cardiff and Neath powered through to their cup final, and Llanelli and the improving Newport enjoyed some excellent victories. But for all the excellence of Bristol and company in England and Hawick and company in Scotland, and for all the success of Cardiff and Neath, no one could really put their hand on their heart and say that Pontypool were not the outstanding club team in Britain last season. They faltered in the cup when they were without their ace, David Bishop, but at their best their forward play was unstoppable. They were again criticised for dirty play and some of the criticism was fully justified. They were a fearsome prospect.

Rugby suffered some sad losses during the season, notably in the deaths of Lord Wakefield, a great man in the game for so long, and Ricky Bartlett, the England fly-half of the late 1950s, to name just two. There were some illustrious retirements from international rugby too, with Jeff Squire, Graham Price, Mike Slemen, Maurice Colclough and Andy Irvine among those cutting down their commitments after long and honourable service at the top level.

There were still problem areas in rugby. There seemed to be a total reliance on forward play and the set pieces in particular by many teams. British rugby is still too static. And although the problem has probably been sensationalised, there was also still too much violence. There were some nasty incidents, two of the worst involving players from Rosslyn Park and Swansea. Brixham's appalling disciplinary problems led to the suspension of their first XV games, an extreme but welcome step. Bristol cancelled matches against Pontypool in protest at what they saw as continual violence in the fixture. There were still far too many competitions and far too much screaming from the touchlines in mini-rugby – although there was an enormous amount of fun and enjoyment, too. There were the perennial arguments about the structure of the English game and the merits – or lack of them – of the County Championship. Thankfully, it was a thoroughly enjoyable season too, in so many respects and in all areas of the game. The spectacle and entertainment once again outweighed all the problems.

ROTHMANS PLAYER OF THE YEAR – DAVID LESLIE

Norman Mair

'Victory is not as exhilarating,' ruminated David Leslie, amid the aftermath of Scotland's Grand Slam triumph at the expense of France, 'as defeat is depressing. But it is apt to be more lasting, and especially so in this instance.' Triple Crowns and Grand Slams go with you to the grave and Leslie will always have the additional pleasure of knowing that Scotland's Year was also his.

'The most important player in the side', declared no less a personage than Andy Irvine. 'Several others also had outstanding seasons, but to me his form and his contribution were the key to so much else.' Onllwyn Brace, erstwhile Welsh captain and brilliantly innovative scrum-half of the 'eighties, has one of the best rugby minds in these islands and he had no doubt who was his player of the Championship: 'David Leslie – and how they managed to leave that fellow out of the Lions' tour I shall never know'. Scotland's coach, Jim Telfer, reckoned Leslie had never played better: 'Our tactics suited him, but then you could put it the other way round and say he was just the player for our tactics'.

In particular, of course, Leslie was at once the best and most voracious winner of the ball on the floor in the Championship; a priceless asset to a team whose whole philosophy revolved heavily around dynamic rucking. A broken leg had kept Leslie out of Scotland's tour to Australia in 1982 and not the least significant of Jim Telfer's revelations on his return home was his typically honest admission that the team had missed Leslie's work on the deck far more than he had anticipated would be the case on the harder grounds of Australia.

The fearless, at times almost suicidally committed Leslie has had his share and more of injuries but he has his own answer to suggestions that he is injury-prone: 'If you are in the firing line, as a good flanker ought constantly to be, you're going to buy it now and then. It is the flanker who is virtually never injured of whom I should want to ask questions.'

Now 32, and a partner in a Dundee firm of architects, he is a governor of Glenalmond School, where he was head boy and for whom he played three seasons as a No 8, captaining the side in his last year and twice beating their Welsh counterparts in the course of winning three such caps. At Dundee High before Dalhousie Preparatory School, Leslie – who also had a summer in the Glenalmond cricket XI – is a sufficiently gifted all-round footballer to have played four matches for the Glenalmond First XV at fly-half while still eligible for the Under-15 team. When he was at Glenalmond, the coach was former Cambridge Blue

Bill Crow, who could be said to have had quite a bit of Jim Telfer in him. 'Both essentially hard drivers', as Leslie puts it feelingly but appreciatively.

Leslie remains grateful, too, for the fact that in his days with the Scottish North and Midlands, there was no small store of back-row lore on tap, what with Nairn MacEwan in the pack and both coaches, Jock Steven and Adam Robson, having been flankers themselves. He played third from the end in the line-out for North and Midlands and it was Ian McLauchlan who, as Scotland's captain, first cast him as a line-out tail-gunner.

His second international was against France at Parc des Princes and that afternoon Leslie tended to sell himself, too often leaving himself isolated in his anxiety to pressurise Lucien Paries, who was at fly-half for France. But since that now distant day he has learned an awful lot more about angles. Again, he is quick to point out that 'the change in the line-out law which allows a tail-gunner to take off from the 15 metres line has made it more difficult for the opposing fly-half to run outside him'.

Against France in Paris in 1983, in a match which, alas, no Lions' selector saw other than on video-tape, Leslie turned in an unforgettable display which had the watching Graham Mourie deeming him exactly the brand of flanker you need for a major tour of New Zealand. Time and again in that match Leslie outwitted the enfabled Jean-Pierre Rives in getting to the throw. Last season, again, when Wales inexplicably stationed their converted lock, Richard Moriarty, as the last man in their line-out, Leslie took devastating advantage in a match-winning performance.

Fascinatingly, he cites the old Scotland back row forward, Gordon Strachan, and the world of American football as his main sources of inspiration in the specialised business of playing off the back of the line-out. 'Gordon Strachan was a basketball player', he explains, 'and I saw how he brought his basketball skills into play by taking the longer throw on the move. Again, not only have I picked up something from American football about pressurising opponents, but there is much to be learned from their receivers when it comes to beating the opposition to a torpedo throw.'

Pringle Fisher, not particularly tall but spring-heeled and a lovely ball-player, won much invaluable possession for Scotland in the 'sixties, on occasion keeping them in the game by his work off the back of the line-out when the supply of ball had almost dried up elsewhere. In recent years, Leslie has come to mean as much to his country in that sphere and, of course, his aggressively dextrous jumping has had an additional dimension in the wonderfully perceptive support play of Jim Calder.

'When I first came into the Scottish team,' reflects Calder, 'we were much more concerned with stopping the opposition than with what we would do ourselves. Indeed, on my debut, which was at Parc des Princes in 1981, I actually found myself shunted to No 2 as we tried to come up with a counter to the French. Now the other countries, as far as the back of the line-out is concerned, are watching us, worrying about what we are going to do'.

Calder has boundless admiration for Leslie and especially for the way he builds himself up mentally for an international: 'He works himself up almost to a frenzy, yet he remains marvellously clear and concise in his more specific objectives. For instance, for the match with France, aside from his responsibilities with regard to the opposing halves and his contribution to scrum, ruck and line-out, he made it his business to impose himself physically upon Jean-Pierre Rives. Even in the heat of an international I was conscious of his always seeking to do so . . .'

Leslie has come to believe more and more in the importance of being mentally fresh and he himself would certainly consider it entirely relevant that, on one account or another, he did not once last season play on the Saturday before an international. He has always been to me the very antithesis of the one-pace forward who always seems to be on hand but never quite gets there, a quick-witted, selfless commitment giving him his sharpness rather than anything exceptional in the way of pace. He has been criticised in his time for being too fitful, for flashing in and out of a game. But Jim Telfer, who has always recognised Leslie's class, is convinced that his work-rate has never been higher. Moreover, as Leslie, who played for West of Scotland before Gala, has himself said of Border rugby, having the whole community behind you can add dramatically to the tempo of a man's play.

The notion that he is not a 'wide' player in the sense, say, of a Graham Mourie or a Peter Winterbottom probably cost him his Lions' tour. Suffice to remark that if a Lions' party had had to be selected at the end of the 1984 Championship, David George Leslie would have been a cast-iron certainty. As it is, his only tour of the front rank was with Scotland to New Zealand in 1981 when he captained the side against both Wellington and Mid-Canterbury. He led Gala to the Scottish Championship in 1982-83 and captained the Whites to their resounding 21-3 defeat of the senior team in last winter's national trial. However, even apart from the powerful counter-claims of Jim Aitken, I do not think that Leslie could have had the season he did had he been saddled with the cares of captaincy.

A player with very definite opinions of his own, who yet owes much to the influence of his older brother, Roger – a better rugby player *qua* rugby player than many who have worn their country's colours – Leslie owns to having thought vaguely in terms of retirement in each of the last four seasons. He knows, though, that when that day does finally come, he will not enjoy the withdrawal symptoms. 'There is a lot of truth,' he ponders, ruefully, 'in that tag about the body yearning for the adrenalin surge.' Never dropped, the 28 times capped Leslie – 6ft 1in and 14½ stones – missed out, at a quick calculation, on a possible further 24 caps either directly through injury or because he had not had time to work back to match fitness.

A married man with two children, Rodric aged two and Rebecca just a few months old, he finds his offspring help him to keep everything in perspective – not least Rodric who, a spectator at Murrayfield, found Scotland's tumultuous Grand Slam encounter with France so riveting he fell asleep for the last ten minutes. Afterwards, in the changing-room, he looked up at his father with the shining eyes of a small boy who had just been through a great experience. 'The pipers', he breathed, ecstatically, 'were very good.'

David Leslie, outnumbered but undaunted by the French in the thrilling Grand Slam decider at Murrayfield.

FROM WHITEWASH TO GRAND SLAM

David Norrie, of the *News of the World*, looks back on a remarkable year for Jim Telfer, coach of Scotland and the Lions

Jim Telfer celebrated his 44th birthday by seeing Scotland to their first Grand Slam for 59 years, but his customary caution would have balanced the euphoria with a backward glance to his 1983 summer of torture in New Zealand with the British Lions. Even now he refuses to allow Scotland's achievements to be inflated out of perspective: 'It's easier to win the International Championship than beat the All Blacks', he says. His experiences during the previous 12 months had taught him that, at least. Few sportsmen have suffered as Telfer did in New Zealand. The pain was all the more acute for him because his honesty and integrity make him a rarity in today's sporting jungle. At times in New Zealand he appeared intimidated and bemused by the various factions seeking to make capital out of his defeated rugby charges. But his good humour never left him, even at the final post-mortem press conference after the Lions had been completely annihilated at Eden Park. His admission of failure was not confused by pleas of mitigation – instead he merely produced a quiet, rhetorical: 'Is there life after death?'

Jim Aitken's Tartan Army revived Telfer in the most conclusive manner. Suddenly, he was a miracle worker, accepting the congratulatory pats on the back where only a few months earlier he had endured stabbing pains. But he is not a man to be diverted by the fickle finger, wherever it is pointing. Certainly, the gods conspired against him on the New Zealand expedition. But despite the injuries, the inconsiderate itinerary, the intransigence of some of his senior players and the customary intimidation from the New Zealand media, there was no shaking his resolve to sacrifice himself for the Lions' cause.

At times that strain took its toll, never more so than during a week's 'holiday' in the Bay of Islands after the second Test defeat in Wellington. The All Blacks were then dormie two – two up with two to play. A few days in the Bay of Islands concentrated Telfer's mind wonderfully on the undeniable truth that his party had reached the point of no return. 'I know you have to be prepared for anything', he said, 'but I never dreamed I would be in this position. I was sure we would win one of the first two Tests.' The prospect of a Test whitewash – which Telfer and Willie John McBride had experienced as players in New Zealand in 1966 – was alarmingly alive.

Small wonder then, that he thought of calling it a day on his return from New Zealand. Yet, although this Border Scot has always carefully assessed his own place on the rugby scene, it would have been a great

Jim Telfer makes a point to his charges during the ill-fated Lions tour to New Zealand.

surprise to those who had become acquainted with him during the previous summer if he had retired. After such a recent humiliation, that move might have been interpreted as throwing in the towel, and that is certainly not Jim Telfer's style. Still, the All Blacks provided a painful and almost immediate sense of *déjà vu* when they humbled the South of Scotland at Netherdale in the autumn. That same South side was to form the basis of Scotland's assault on the International Championship.

Even the national team's draw with the All Blacks at Murrayfield was overshadowed when England ended a 48-year Twickenham wait with a comfortable victory over Stuart Wilson's weakened All Black side the following Saturday. And when Scotland kicked off their international championship campaign in Cardiff, the bookies – no doubt after consulting rugby experts or perhaps a Scot looking for attractive odds – felt confident in making Jim Aitken's men the team least likely to succeed. Ironically, as Scotland made their historic march towards the Triple Crown, Grand Slam and Championship, the man who dominated from start to finish with total, Telfer-type commitment – Rothmans Player of the Year David Leslie – had not been considered good enough to be included in the eight British back row forwards required for service in New Zealand. His omission remains as puzzling today as it was then. 'David Leslie has been outstanding' was Telfer's verdict. 'He kept his enthusiasm throughout. I think he realised – like several others – that if he wanted something worthwhile out of his international career this might be his last chance. Also he may have had a point to prove to the 1983 Lions' selectors.'

There were other bonuses for Telfer. Aitken showed himself the captain Ciaran Fitzgerald had failed to be in New Zealand. Six Scottish Lions gained Test experience in 1983, and those who missed out, Iain Milne and Colin Deans, were no less deserving. 'There's no doubt that the Scots grew up on their trips abroad, especially after the Lions' tour', Telfer admits. 'Players like Deans, Paxton and Calder realised that rugby was easier in Britain and that some of their opponents in the championship were not that good.' The relentless humiliation in New Zealand made John Rutherford and company battle-hard and uncompromising disciples of Telfer. Without that at Murrayfield on 17 March the French would have gone back across the Channel in triumph. As it was Telfer eventually chalked up a balanced year in the limelight of the international scene – four losses, a draw, and finally four victories.

Telfer has been battling to beat the All Blacks for two decades now. The summer of 1983 provided him with the ideal opportunity. 'Being in charge of the Lions has to be the ultimate ambition of any British coach', he says. 'But it's no easy task. You have to make the best of it in a one-off situation for three months. You pick players on their reputations; you think you know them and their character, and then on a tour you find out differently as you are constantly having to rely on players of whom you know very little. I couldn't have asked the Lions' players for any greater effort or commitment, but in the end I was beaten by the system, which leaves the players too inflexible. The same criticism has been made of me. The trouble is that their style of play is in-bred by that stage of their careers and it's impossible to get them to change – but I don't blame the players for that. It's just that some of their rugby thinking had become too set.

'Another problem is keeping all 30 to 35 players happy, players from different countries with different temperaments. I realised that in 1966 – and 1983 was no different. Anyone who thinks a Scotsman is the same as an Englishman is living in cloud-cuckoo-land. You can't change that. As coach of Scotland I had to adapt my methods to suit my material.'

Telfer made the understandable error in thinking the wider net of the

Lions' selectors would give him enough talented material to defy that basic truth. Sadly, however, it still applied in New Zealand. Telfer is a great admirer of the best in All Black rugby. He spent half the Lions' tour looking for an inside centre to carry out the second fly-half duties that Jim Renwick fulfilled for Scotland. That quest was doomed while John Rutherford remained at fly-half. The midfield pairing for the first Test consisted of the two 'outside centres', Bob Ackerman and David Irwin, and even then Ackerman was not given the inside job he'd been doing so effectively for Wales the previous season. It was only when Rutherford moved to the midfield, as Mike Gibson had done outside David Watkins (1966) and Barry John (1971), did the Lions threaten the New Zealand try-line. Unfortunately, the heavens opened in Dunedin to drown the tourists' last lingering hopes in a muddy match.

By the fourth and final Test, the Lions had disintegrated completely – they were given the worst hiding in their history. Telfer deserved better than that, but was willing to take the blame the following morning. 'That final press conference was the lowest point of the trip as far as I was concerned', he says. 'There was no going back; we'd been beaten four-nil in the series and there was nothing more I could do about it.'

Telfer feels that maybe the job is too big for one man: 'After all, most national squads now have two coaches in reality. I've worked with Colin Telfer, and Wales have John Bevan and Terry Cobner in tandem. Two coaches, in other words, for 21 players. It's asking a lot for one man to take charge of 30 players, many of them unfamiliar, both as personalities and rugby players, and quickly make them into an effective unit against one of the top rugby nations in the world.'

It's a tribute to Telfer (or 'Creamy' as he's known in rugby circles) as an enduring personality – charisma is not a word which springs readily to mind in the borders of Scotland – that despite the many tribulations and the role of failures in today's competitive world, the 1983 British Lions remained an easy-going, friendly bunch. Yet that might have been part of their trouble. When the going got tough, Jim Telfer did not find too many kindred spirits ready to battle to put the pride back into British rugby – until, in the aftermath, he welded his Scots into Grand Slammers.

OLD GOLD IN AUSTRALIA

Jim Woodward looks back to Sydney's remarkable 'Golden Oldies' tournament, and ahead to a similar event planned for London

If rugby union's Golden Oldies tournament continues to grow at the present rate, London can look forward to hosting one of the biggest gatherings in sport in 1985. This is the happy prospect the tournament organisers face in the wake of the stunningly successful 1983 Golden Oldies carnival held in Sydney, Australia.

That event enticed 118 teams, easily surpassing the inaugural tournament in Auckland, New Zealand, which drew 17 teams in 1979; and the second one, held two years later at Long Beach, California, which 42 teams attended. With the competition deliberately staged in a different hemisphere every two years, the organisers are expecting an even greater entry when it moves to London in late September, 1985. Interest in Australia for the London tournament is already running high, with many teams saving money every week to cover costs.

Some 4,000 players and 2,000 supporters spent an estimated six million dollars at the Sydney Golden Oldies tournament, which boasted more competitors than the Commonwealth Games, held the previous year in Brisbane. The logistics of the event were obviously awesome, but excellent planning saw to it that everything functioned smoothly throughout, with the high point being the seating and feeding of 6,000 people at the farewell dinner at Randwick racecourse. The comradeship which permeated the 10-day celebration really overflowed that evening with 2,000 gallons of beer and 30,000 glasses of wine being consumed.

Tournament organiser John Howard, the Australian RU Hon Treasurer, was to say afterwards that the most important by-product of the venture was the willingness to become re-involved in the game of those who had previously drifted away from it.

'Since the tournament there has been a tremendous increase in the number of people making themselves available for a variety of administrative positions at all levels of rugby', Howard said. 'It's as if they have suddenly remembered how much fun they had during their rugby days and want to get involved again.'

By the time Sydney's Golden Oldies tournament began Howard found himself catering for players and supporters from 17 countries – Australia, New Zealand, Canada, USA, Cayman Islands, British West Indies, Mexico, Fiji, Japan, Hong Kong, England, Ireland, Scotland, Wales, Spain, Germany and the Bahamas. With 39 teams entered from

Tom Johnson (rear, left) was the founder of Golden Oldies. He plays for Crusaders – another Crusader (rear, right) is former All Black winger Malcolm Dick.
(Photograph by John Hall)

New Zealand, many Kiwis had to fly to Sydney up to five days before the tournament began just to be sure of finding a plane seat.

As had been the case at previous Golden Oldies events, the age categories in Sydney were over 35 and over 40, and to distinguish the ages of individual players, a colour coding of shorts was again implemented. Those aged between 35 and 40 wore club colour shorts, 40- to 50-year-olds wore white, 50- to 60-year-olds black, with red for ages 60- to 70, gold for ages 70- to 80 and purple for the over-80s.

The gold and purple shorts came in handy for 76-year-old Frank Griffiths and 83-year-old Mac Adams. Adams, who hails from the New South Wales resort of Port Macquarie was the oldest competitor, and seven men aged over 70 also took part.

When the tournament began there were certainly many players who recalled Oscar Wilde's words on advancing age: 'That period in life when a man has baldness, bridgework, bifocals, bay windows and bunions; when he believes the thinning of hair is only a temporary matter; when he'd rather not have a good time than have to get over it.'

The rules were certainly simple. There were no trophies for winners and no grand final which would destroy the very concept of the tournament. But while no awards were handed out for team effort, several players returned home with rare distinctions.

Mac Adams was, of course, the oldest player but who would have guessed that the tallest scrum-half would be 6ft 11ins – this honour belonged to David Klassen, who played with the Texas XXXs. Jack McLean qualified as the oldest referee at the age of 72, Naozo Hayashi (Wak-Sun), at the age of 76, was adjudged the oldest overseas visitor, and the most originally named club was deemed to be Coodabinawallabi.

It was a memorable experience to witness the final match at headquarters, Coogee Oval, between the Mihillians from Wairarapa in New Zealand and the Old Wicks, ex-Randwick players of considerable distinction. To see one-time Australian internationals John and Dick Thornett, Phil Hawthorne, and especially the former Lord Mayor of Sydney and current ARU president Sir Nicholas Shehadie on the field again was indeed something to savour. Sir Nicholas, who captained Australia in three of his 30 international matches; participated in games on all three days of the tournament, and in his own words: 'I scored a try and even attempted a dropped goal – I had a great time.' The tournament proved such a moving occasion for Dick Thornett, a veteran of 11 Tests, that he decided to return to an active role and was appointed third grade coach of premier club Randwick.

Thankfully injuries were minimal. The most serious reported were a broken leg, a broken arm and a few cases of cracked ribs. St John's Ambulanceman Fred Daniels said, 'That was because of the spirit of the festival. All the games were played in good heart. Nobody really cared about winning.' There were countless incidents which illustrated the mood in which the games – each of three sections of 20 minutes –

were played. One such involved leading New Zealand referee Graham Harrison, in town to take charge of the official Test match between Australia and the American Eagles. Harrison, as referee, suddenly found himself the 31st man in a Golden Oldies match when he was thrown the ball in a back line movement. He stuffed the whistle into his pocket and hared off for the try-line, where he duly scored and awarded himself the try. On another occasion a startled referee suddenly found himself confronted with a line-out consisting of 47 players, stretching across the entire width of the field. For some teams chilled champagne served during the breaks in play was commonplace.

It had been a fabulous few days and nobody disagreed with the words of president Shehadie when he said at the conclusion of the Sydney tournament; 'The way in which the 17 nations involved here played the game and mixed off the field is a lesson for all the world. Surely there would be no wars if we all played rugby like the Golden Oldies.'

Now it is London's turn!

TRY, TRY AND TRY AGAIN . . .

John Mason, Rugby Correspondent of the *Daily Telegraph*, talks to Alan Morley, of Bristol, who on 15 February 1984 became the world record-holder of the highest number of tries for one club in senior rugby, beating Andy Hill's 312 for Llanelli

Four days before Christmas in 1968 England were playing an international trial at Falmouth and the opposing captains were Dick Greenwood and Budge Rogers. A Bristol schoolboy had few thoughts about those august seniors – and none at all of making a late dash around the city shops to buy presents in the nick of time. The only dashing that Alan John George Morley had in mind would be reserved for that muddy morass, that energy-sapping swamp, known as the Memorial Ground, Bristol. On that dark, damp afternoon, Morley, then 18 years old and with one more term at Colston's School, Stapleton, to come, had a date against Abercarn, one of the senior junior clubs in the East Wales belt that assist generally in the education of those aspiring English club players fortunate enough to live immediately across the border. Morley was about to make his debut for Bristol – in the second team, the United.

Some 400 tries (overall), goodness knows how many matches and 16 years later, how does Morley feel about a career that, although it has explored the odd blind alley, shows few signs of flagging and has involved a succession of resounding personal achievements? The question is carefully considered and then, as if storming the opposition try-line from close quarters, the words come helter-skelter, forceful, with commitment in every breath.

'Still slightly surprised . . . but proud for all that; grateful for all the help I've received, the friendships made. Mindful, too, that games-playing at the level at which I've aimed is something more than just turning up with your kit. I really don't believe many are aware of the sacrifices, not even those you work with or the people in your own club – those whose playing days are either over or were not of that standard anyway. I'm not grumbling – far from it. I would change very little if I were starting out against Abercarn all over again, though like everyone else, I wish to goodness I knew then some of the things I know now. But that's life!

'I did my best then; I do my best now. I used to worry; I don't now . . . well, less than I did. I would have liked a longer run with England and in my heart of hearts, I'm certain I could have done at least as well as many who have appeared subsequently. I don't always agree with coaches, especially those who baffle themselves – and everyone else – with theory. Rugby's a simple game, honestly – look at me! But I did agree with Budge Rogers when he said about a year ago that a wing's job was to score tries. There's a lot more that's important, obviously. But the number one job, the priority, for a wing should be to score tries. Use the ball, support, call your set moves, kick for position, attack from close in when possible because that's the shortest path to the opposition line; yes, I agree with all of that, of course. I also ask that wings be kept fully employed doing the job they're best at: scoring tries.

'I regret getting injured at the wrong times and I'm sorry that assessments made of me a long time ago seem to have persisted, though I've done my best to alter them in my games for Bristol and Gloucestershire. About the time I was on the fringe of the England side, neither in nor out, it was said, mostly by those who knew my play well, that I didn't cope too easily with the ball in the air when defending, or with the one that comes over the shoulder, that my positioning defensively was all wrong anyway, and that ideally I should have played on the left. Some even suggested I should go back to the centre where I'd started – and those who said so loudest were those who'd clamoured for me to move in the first place. I would accept some of the criticisms and comments. But I don't agree one jot about playing on the left, which I know I can do. I'm most effective on the right, but in the interests of any team that will have me, I'll play where I'm chosen.

'You know, for a very long time, I wasn't sure enough about my own play, about what I could do and where I fitted into the scheme of things. A big match would come along and there would be all the squad business and pre-match training. I used to dread those journeys to London before an international – not that there were too many of them. At first, as an apprentice international, I would wonder whether I was good enough to be there, whether I'd let anyone down. I'd spend so much time bothering about that sort of thing, it never occurred to me that some opponents were probably going through the same agonies. Then suddenly, for no apparent reason, the trauma goes. You learn to relax, to apply your skills, you learn where you fit in and what can be done. However, by the time I got to that stage I was in the process of being dropped.

'Without being sour about it, I can tell you that for some years after being abandoned in England terms, I was playing far more effectively than when I was in the side. I'm not trying to be clever, but I could have done a job, of that I'm certain. That belief doesn't stop me enjoying my matches tremendously now, and didn't in the past. Rugby's my hobby, my relaxation, my enjoyment – didn't Mike Watkins say something like that around the time he was the 'B' team captain before Wales promoted him? The pressure bit is work, the fun is playing.

'I count myself very fortunate, and while records of one sort or another interest me, they don't dominate my thinking or, I hope, my rugby. You'd better ask others about that. But rugby's a team game. My job is to round off what 14 others have worked extremely hard to bring about. What I do is important to me, of course, but I regard it as

Another try for Morley is on its way as he prepares to break the tackle of Somerset's Charles Ralston in the county final.

being the logical part of a team effort; an attitude, I suppose, that has developed only gradually. You wrote something once about how my failure would not entail team failure: team failure almost certainly would mean that I had failed, too. I'm not sure I understood that at the time, but I do now.'

As Alan paused the 'phone rang. The caller was Peter Polledri, a friend and playing colleague at Bristol. The match that afternoon was an important one – another round in Bristol's defence of the John Player Special Cup at a time when the club, overall, had not been playing either well or consistently. Alan had a slightly sheepish grin as he returned to his lounge, the scrapbooks and programmes of 16 years, rescued that morning from the attic, scattered about the floor.

'I'm glad Pete rang,' he said. 'I have to pick him up on my way to the ground. I'd have forgotten otherwise. You see, I still worry about these games. You concentrate to such an extent that little else seems to get through. I can live with that now but when I was younger I spent so much time wondering how things were going to work out that the match was done and dusted before I'd properly got my bearings. Do you know, when we beat South Africa in Johannesburg in 1972, I don't think I played very well. I did score the only try but given what I know now, there were at least two more opportunities I should have taken. Now that would have been something, wouldn't it?'

I have known Alan for approaching 20 years. One of his masters at Colston's, an establishment that I attended many moons ago, was Dave Rollitt, who taught physics and mathematics. For Rollitt, rugby at Colston's was an extra-curricular activity in that he was immersed in a playing career with Bristol, Gloucestershire and England, so he hadn't much time. In any event he was not the rugby master, though he did lend a hand; a milk-and-water way of describing D M Rollitt's persuasive if critical tongue. He reckoned young Morley, and his brother, Chris, could *play* – and he told me so frequently in the course of my duties as the rugby man on the *Evening Post*, Bristol.

I had seen this young Colstonian – 'Alan will make it, probably on the wing, otherwise he's got me to answer to' said Rollitt very early on – in some of the school's representative matches during the Christmas and Easter holidays and even shared, vicariously, in the triumphs of an extremely successful School First XV over a couple of seasons. Austin Sheppard, a lock then, was the school captain and I wonder just how many times since these two have played in the same team. Counting schooldays, it must be approaching 800 matches. 'The Old Grey Fox, Rollitty, was right', says Shep. 'Alan can play – just a bit!' That, coming from a gnarled front-row forward for whom tries are crumbs from the rich man's table, is unstinting praise. The Colston's motto is 'Go and Do Thou Likewise'. The deeds of Alan Morley on the rugby field allow all Colstonians, old and new, to bask in reflected glory. Outsiders may join the club, too: the show is not closing just yet.

JPR WILLIAMS: CLASS AND CONTROVERSY

The game's outstanding full-back talks to *Tim Glover* about his contentious career

John Williams is probably the greatest all-round full-back the game has ever seen, but he ended his prodigious career amid controversy, acrimony and, subsequently, litigation. It sprang from his autobiography and, frankly, there are times when he wishes he'd never written the book: 'In many ways I regret it. I tried to do something constructive by opening a sports clinic with the proceeds and got criticised for it'.

Following publication of the autobiography five years ago he sued the *Daily Telegraph* for libel over an allegation that he had received money from the book. In 1982 he was awarded £20,000 damages but in 1983 the sum was withheld when an appeal court ruled that the jury had been misdirected. 'The money went to the trustees of a fund for the clinic and the rest to an agent. You can't write a book without signing a contract and if you sign a contract as an amateur player you get into trouble. I admit I'm a controversial figure and I won't back down from things. But as captain of Wales at the time I was put up to go to court over the book to defend not only myself but Welsh rugby and world rugby. Although the *Telegraph* won an appeal they had to pay most of the costs. The whole thing affected my family much more than me. I had my work to turn to.

'Other players have written books and carried on playing, Peter Wheeler for instance, but nobody said a word. I'm not paranoid about it but Welsh players, probably because they've been successful, are criticised more than others. You have only to look at the campaigns waged against Ringer and Moriarty.'

The world's most famous sports clinic duly opened this year in his home town of Bridgend. Incorporated in a leisure centre, it will not only treat sports injuries but conduct research into what is a neglected area of medicine. 'There will be nothing quite like this', says Williams, whose three brothers, Phil, Chris and Mike, all doctors in their father's practice, will run the clinic. 'I don't know how many copies the book sold or how much money it made', Williams says, 'but I never received a penny. As far as the book is concerned I'm absolutely clean.'

The decade of the dragon and of JPR – he helped Wales to six Triple Crowns in ten years – was to end in bitter anti-climax. He had been one of the most valuable, and one of the hardest, jewels in the crown. In the 1979-80 season, as sole survivor from the class of '69, he led Wales to another Triple Crown and Bridgend to the WRU Cup title in their centenary season despite having fallen victim at the Brewery Field to the boot of New Zealand prop John Ashworth during the All Blacks' tour. The handsome victory over England which gave Wales their fourth successive crown seemed to signal Williams' retirement. 'I was stale mentally and physically', he says.

But 18 months later he made a dramatic reappearance against the All Blacks in Wales's centenary season to win his 53rd cap and equal Gareth Edwards' record. The script was right and so was Williams, despite his lay off, but Wales were not. New Zealand gatecrashed the 100-year celebrations with a stunning 23-3 victory at the Arms Park. Williams recalls: 'I was asked by the selectors to be available and I had kept fit. I had trained very hard for six months. I wasn't in the squad to face the All Blacks and although they were supposed to be picking the team on the Saturday night, I had a call at 9 am on Sunday morning to attend training. When I turned up it was obvious I would be playing. What surprised me was the standard of fitness. It was pathetic. Only Terry Holmes and myself were match-fit.

'It's very difficult to make a come-back at international level but I had a particularly good game, which I regard as one of my finest performances, in a poor side. A lot of those players have never been heard of since. If it hadn't been for myself, Holmes and Bob Ackerman we'd have lost by 50 points.' The second heaviest home defeat in Wales' history prompted the WRU to send a letter to every squad member demanding a higher level of fitness.

Williams, never on the losing side against England, maintained that record and broke another. He passed Edwards' milestone by making his 54th appearance in a narrow win over England at Cardiff. He had already created a unique landmark by becoming the only player to take part in each of the special four countries matches to celebrate the centenaries of England, Scotland, Ireland and Wales. He won his 55th and final cap in a defeat against Scotland after which he was dropped for the first time in his career.

'The whole season went sour. We had a bad match at Murrayfield and they dropped seven of us including the skipper Steve Fenwick. You should never drop a captain in the middle of a season because it's bound to affect morale. We won no ball that day yet most of the backs went and the forwards stayed. The way I was treated was bad but then a lot of the older players were treated shabbily. I'm a great believer in horses for courses. If you are good enough it shouldn't matter whether you are 19 or 35. Allan Martin was the best line-out jumper in Wales. I started at 19, as did Keith Jarrett, but you don't find teenagers playing international rugby any more.

'There is a dearth of top class individuals with the result that entertainment value has decreased. British threequarter flair has gone and the French have really shown that up. We have become so obsessed with winning the ball that we have forgotten what to do with it. In many ways selectors and coaches are to blame. The last Lions tour was spoilt by poor selection. Why was Ciaran Fitzgerald the captain when he was fourth choice hooker? You don't pick a captain for his ability to speak. It's been the same problem with Wales. Eddie Butler was hardly even a first-class No 8, let alone a Welsh captain. So many players are picked who are not good enough. It's not their fault they don't perform well, but while they get dropped, the selectors who made the mistakes remain. Five selectors are too many and the coach has too much influence.

'England have been a prime example of over-coaching. You can see what they have been told to do and if it doesn't come off they're absolutely lost. When I was captain, the team would do what I wanted not what the coach said. Today's approach to the game is also wrong. The priority is not to lose and there's a vast difference between that and trying to win. Players, too, are less dedicated now. They expect to take a lot out of the game and put little in. Fitness is a personal thing but they don't train on their own any more, it's all done in squad sessions.'

Williams was junior Wimbledon tennis champion in 1966, and he has always prided himself on his fitness. 'I had to be especially fit to be able to play international rugby and work as a doctor,' he says. JPR hopes eventually to return to Bridgend and lend a helping hand at his clinic. At the age of 35 he is busy establishing himself as a top surgeon. He recently left the Royal Berks Hospital in Reading, where he was senior

John Williams makes a typical burst from defence in an international against Scotland.

registrar of orthopaedics, for the Royal National Orthopaedic Hospital in Stanmore, Middlesex. Earlier this year he was a member of a team which successfully sewed on a man's severed arm. 'That one', he says, 'got publicity but a similar operation which failed didn't.'

His wife Scilla, who is also a doctor, has just completed a two-year research programme into rugby injuries on behalf of the International Board. She did her work in Wales, because of the close concentration of clubs, and her report is due to be discussed this year. 'There have been no statistics available as to the number or nature of rugby injuries' says JPR. 'There has been a feeling in the game that neck injuries, for example, have been on the increase, and now the Board will have a register to see if that, in fact, is true.'

He has an intense distrust of what he seems to regard as third-rate fifth columnists from the fourth estate. 'I woke up one morning to hear on the radio that I was joining Kent Invicta Rugby League club. Not a semblance of truth. Nobody had checked with me but my name had been bandied about and no doubt Kent Invicta were delighted with the free publicity.' Also among his pet hates are aluminium studs. Many injuries, he believes, could be avoided if aluminium was replaced by rubber or polyurethane. 'All the top players wear aluminium studs and I have seen horrific head wounds as a result. If moves to outlaw aluminium studs had been introduced I wouldn't have suffered the injuries I did at the feet of Ashworth. The International Board need a kick up the backside. They rarely make any decisions and when they do they are usually detrimental to the game. They have been thinking about studs for years but nothing has happened.'

He hasn't changed much. His hair, once fashionably long, is now unfashionably long, and he is still as physically sharp as a scalpel although his face looks not so much like a boxer's, more the work of an overworked plastic surgeon. The greatest game he played in was the 1973 epic between the Baa-Baas and New Zealand. 'It was billed as the Lions v the All Blacks. It was 18 months after the tour of '71 but it was a sign of a great side that we knitted together again so well.' Gareth Edwards gets his vote as the finest all-round player he ever saw, and Pierre Villepreux the best full-back he faced. 'He had attacking flair and was sound in defence. The modern vogue is for attacking full-backs but their first requirement should be defence. I was always thought of as an attacking player but it was my defence I was proud of, particularly catching the high ball and tackling.'

He has three young daughters and there will be no JPR junior. 'I'm not sad about that. It would have been impossible for a son to follow in my footsteps. I don't think that's arrogant. People who know me don't think I'm arrogant. I was an arrogant rugby player but I had to be. I had no particular strengths, I wasn't the fastest or physically the most impressive or a great kicker. But I was very strong mentally. I never lacked confidence.'

NEW ZEALAND TO SCOTLAND AND ENGLAND 1983

New Zealand's impromptu eight-match tour of Scotland and England, replacing their cancelled Argentinian tour, gave some tortured British Lions an early chance for revenge and offered the ideal opportunity for other players to show Messrs McBride and Telfer – and the Lions selectors – that they shouldn't have been left behind. Both groups achieved some measure of success, but the tour was a special triumph for the Leicester hooker Peter Wheeler, who led the Midlands and then England to memorable victories over New Zealand in less than a fortnight. Such triumphs had evaded the Lions during their arduous summer campaign.

The All Blacks, however, had left some fairly hefty artillery at home. The front five of the Lions' whitewash – John Ashworth, skipper Andy Dalton, Gary Knight, Andy Haden and Gary Whetton – were all unable to travel, as was the man of that series, scrum-half David Loveridge. The absence of Haden and Loveridge was the biggest blow on a tour which, for the first time ever on a New Zealand visit to Britain, was led by a back, wing Stu Wilson.

Wilson found it tough going. After years of effective self-control, the All Blacks paid the price for an uncharacteristic lack of discipline. For those who had watched them deny Ollie Campbell a single penalty attempt at goal in 200 minutes of test rugby the previous summer, this turnaround was incredible. Wilson, among others, became visibly frustrated and gave vent to several outbursts on the field which, it is hoped, will not blemish a remarkable career. He did score his 50th try for the All Blacks, in the match against the South and South-West, but the final fortnight of the trip was a disappointing time for Wilson – he announced his retirement from international rugby after the tour.

The All Blacks won only one of their last four matches, and that was a boring affair in Bristol, and generally they found themselves on the rack, partly through their inability to keep within the laws. The Scottish Lions and coach Jim Telfer held their heads high after a nerve-racking 25-25 draw in the international at Murrayfield. England kept faith with an historic Midlands victory and six Leicester players plus prop Gary Pearce made it a double triumph by appearing also in England's 15-9 win at Twickenham.

The tour had started in gusty conditions in Edinburgh and had the home wing, Peter Steven, had his kicking boots on, the tourists would have been in trouble. In all coach Bryce Rope had 13 new All Blacks in his party and nine were playing in this match. The tourists took a while to settle and Scots had high hopes of the South's chances in the next game.

The home side boasted 13 caps, including five of Fitzgerald's Lions. Sadly, Scotland's captain Jim Aitken was forced out at the last minute with 'flu and it proved a bad omen for the South. They led 9-8 early in the second half, but were then taken to the cleaners as the All Blacks produced what was to be their best rugby of the tour. After this performance, it seemed odds-on that New Zealand's rugby supremacy was going to continue, at least as far as Britain was concerned.

The visitors were given a tough time by both the North and London, although neither team really looked like achieving victory. The Simpsons – hooker Andy and No 8 Paul – grabbed tries for the North from tapped penalties, making the All Blacks' defence look untypically vulnerable. London relied on the boot of full-back Nick Stringer to keep in touch. However, the All Blacks won both matches, 27-21 and 18-15 respectively.

The highlight of the tour was the Midlands' victory at Leicester. This was the first time the All Blacks had ever played under floodlights in Britain, and they went down to only their 14th defeat here in 231 matches, the first taking place as far back as 1905. Dusty Hare was crowned King of Welford Road as first his huge penalty and then an enormous dropped goal took the Midlands clear in the dying minutes. Not long before, the full-back had been the villain of the piece when he hooked a simple penalty attempt, but fate was ultimately kind to him.

The New Zealanders' indiscretions kept Scotland in the hunt at Murrayfield, when the tourists should have been well clear. The All Blacks' anger spilled over after the match when they were denied a late penalty near the posts after the French referee had consulted with the touch-judge and reversed his previous award.

The visitors were glad to be back on the winning trail at Bristol, but must have been worried the same evening when the new Chairman of the England selectors, Derek Morgan, announced that seven of the Midlands' team had been chosen for the international. England had waited 47 years to beat New Zealand at Twickenham; skipper and team made up for lost time with relish at Twickenham on the day.

It was not all gloom and despondency for the tourists. In Murray Mexted, at No 8, they have one of the outstanding forwards in world rugby, and he was an immense force on this trip. Peter Bush, the distinguished New Zealand photographer, rates Mexted as the most photogenic player in action he has ever come across and it is easy to see why. The other outstanding forward was hooker Hika Reid, eager to accept the chance offered by Dalton's unavailability.

Newcomers Andy Donald (scrum-half) and Craig Green (centre) showed promise, as did full-back Robbie Deans, who took full advantage of Alan Hewson's late withdrawal. Steve Pokere was a big disappointment in the centre and Bernie Fraser's kamikaze late charge, which put

John Carleton off the field in the international at Twickenham, epitomised the depths to which the All Blacks had been prepared to sink in search of victory.

THE TOURING PARTY

Captain S S Wilson **Manager** P W Mitchell
Assistant Manager D B Rope

FULL-BACKS
K J Crowley (Taranaki)
R M Deans (Canterbury)

THREEQUARTERS
S S Wilson (Wellington)
B G Fraser (Wellington)
B W Smith (Waikato)
C I Green (Canterbury)
S T Pokere (Southland)
W T Taylor (Canterbury)

HALF-BACKS
I T Dunn (North Auckland)
W R Smith (Canterbury)
A J Donald (Wanganui)
D E Kirk (Otago)

FORWARDS
M G Mexted (Wellington)
G H Old (Manawatu)
M W Shaw (Manawatu)
J M Hobbs (Canterbury)
F N K Shelford (Hawke's Bay)
A Anderson (Canterbury)
G J Braid (Bay of Plenty)
A Robinson (North Auckland)
M Davie (Canterbury)
S A Crichton (Wellington)
K G Boroevich (King Country)
B McGrattan (Wellington)
H R Reid (Bay of Plenty)
B H Wilson (Counties)

TOUR RECORD

All matches Played 8 Won 5 Lost 2 Drawn 1 Points for 162 Against 116
International matches Played 2 Lost 1 Drawn 1 Points for 34 Against 40

SCORING DETAILS

All matches

For:	19T	13C	20PG		162 Pts
Against:	6T	4C	23PG	5DG	116 Pts

International matches

For:	4T	3C	4PG		34 Pts
Against:	2T	1C	8PG	2DG	40 Pts

MATCH DETAILS

1983	OPPONENTS	VENUE	RESULTS
26 Oct	Edinburgh	Myreside	W 22-6
29 Oct	South of Scotland	Netherdale	W 30-9
2 Nov	Northern Division	Gateshead	W 27-21
5 Nov	London Division	Twickenham	W 18-15
8 Nov	Midland Division	Leicester	L 13-19
12 Nov	SCOTLAND	Murrayfield	D 25-25
15 Nov	South & SW Division	Bristol	W 18-6
19 Nov	ENGLAND	Twickenham	L 9-15

Deans was the top scorer for the tour with 52 points from eight conversions and 12 penalty goals in five appearances. Crowley came next with 38 points from one try, five conversions and eight penalty goals in three appearances. Skipper Wilson played in all eight matches, with his pack leader Shaw making seven appearances. Green, Anderson and Mexted played six times apiece.

MATCH 1 26 October, Myreside, Edinburgh

Edinburgh 6 (2PG) **New Zealanders 22** (2G 2PG 1T)
Edinburgh: A G Hastings (Watsonians); P D Steven (Heriot's FP), A E Kennedy (Watsonians) (*capt*), D I Johnston (Watsonians), J C W Beazley (Edinburgh Wands); D S Wylie (Stewart's-Melville FP), D Macdonald (Musselburgh); *No 8* F Calder (Stewart's-Melville FP); *Second Row* P N M Drennan (Edinburgh Acads), A L Dunlop (Heriot's FP), G P Millar (Heriot's FP), J H Calder (Stewart's-Melville FP); *Front Row* I G Milne (Heriot's FP), J C Munro (Heriot's FP), A K Brewster (Stewart's-Melville FP)
Scorers *Penalty Goals:* Steven, Hastings
New Zealanders: Deans; S S Wilson (*capt*), Pokere, Green, B W Smith; W R Smith, Kirk; *No 8* Old; *Second Row* Shaw, Braid, Anderson, Shelford; *Front Row* Crichton, B H Wilson, Boroevich
Scorers *Tries:* Shelford, B H Wilson, Green *Conversions:* Deans (2) *Penalty Goals:* Deans (2)
Referee L M Prideaux (England)

MATCH 2 29 October, Netherdale, Galashiels

South of Scotland 9 (2PG 1DG) **New Zealanders 30** (2G 2PG 3T)
South of Scotland: P W Dods (Gala); A Thomson (Kelso), G R T Baird (Kelso), K W Robertson (Melrose), I A Tukalo (Selkirk); J Y Rutherford (Selkirk), R J Laidlaw (Jedforest) (*capt*); *No 8* I A M Paxton (Selkirk); *Second Row* D G Leslie (Gala), T J Smith (Gala), A J Tomes (Hawick), D B White (Gala); *Front Row* R Cunningham (Gala), C T Deans (Hawick), K Sudlow (Jedforest)
Replacement: A J Campbell (Hawick) for Paxton (60 mins)
Scorers *Penalty Goals:* Dods (2) *Dropped Goal:* Rutherford
New Zealanders: Crowley; S S Wilson (*capt*), Pokere, Green, Fraser; Dunn, Donald; *No 8* Mexted; *Second Row* Shaw, Braid, Anderson, Hobbs; *Front Row* Davie, Reid, McGrattan
Scorers *Tries:* S S Wilson (2), Fraser, Hobbs, Crowley *Conversions:* Crowley (2) *Penalty Goals:* Crowley (2)
Referee F Howard (England)

MATCH 3 2 November, Gateshead International Stadium

Northern Division 21 (2G 2PG 1DG) **New Zealanders 27** (3G 3PG)
Northern Division: D M Norton (Headingley); J C Carleton (Orrell), S Townend (Wakefield), A M Bond (Sale), M A C Slemen (Liverpool); A G B Old (Sheffield), S J Smith (Sale) (*capt*); *No 8* P Simpson (Bath); *Second Row* P J Winterbottom (Headingley), S J Bainbridge (Gosforth), J P Syddall (Waterloo), S Hodgson (Vale of Lune); *Front Row* J Curry (Gosforth), A W Simpson (Sale), C White (Gosforth)
Scorers *Tries:* A W Simpson, P Simpson *Conversions:* Old (2) *Penalty Goals:* Old (2) *Dropped Goal:* Old
New Zealanders: Deans; S S Wilson (*capt*), Green, Taylor, Fraser; W R Smith, Donald; *No 8* Mexted; *Second Row* Shaw, Robinson, Anderson, Hobbs; *Front Row* Davie, Reid, McGrattan
Scorers *Tries:* Donald, Shaw, McGrattan *Conversions:* Deans (3) *Penalty Goals:* Deans (3)
Referee J M Fleming (Scotland)

MATCH 4 5 November, Twickenham

London Division 15 (5PG) **New Zealanders 18** (1G 4PG)

London Division: N C Stringer (Wasps); R M Cardus (Wasps), N J Preston (Richmond), M Williams (Wasps), M D Bailey (Cambridge U); G H Davies (Wasps), I K George (London Welsh); *No 8* C Butcher (Harlequins); *Second Row* D H Cooke (Harlequins), M J Colclough (Wasps) (*capt*), C Pinnegar (Wasps), F Emeruwa (Wasps); *Front Row* M F Claxton (Harlequins), A Simmons (Wasps), P A G Rendall (Wasps)
Scorer *Penalty Goals:* Stringer (5)
New Zealanders: Crowley; B W Smith, S S Wilson (*capt*), Green, Fraser; Dunn, Kirk; *No 8* Old; *Second Row* Shaw, Robinson, Braid, Shelford; *Front Row* Crichton, B H Wilson, Boroevich
Scorers *Try:* Shelford *Conversion:* Crowley *Penalty Goals:* Crowley (4)
Referee T E Allan (Scotland)

MATCH 5 8 November, Leicester

Midland Division 19 (1G 2PG 1DG 1T) **New Zealanders 13** (3PG 1T)
Midland Division: W H Hare (Leicester); S Holdstock (Nottingham), P W Dodge (Leicester), C R Woodward (Leicester), J Goodwin (Moseley); L Cusworth (Leicester), N C Youngs (Leicester); *No 8* G L Robbins (Coventry); *Second Row* G Rees (Nottingham), V Cannon (Northampton), R M Wilkinson (Bedford), N C Jeavons (Moseley); *Front Row* G S Pearce (Northampton), P J Wheeler (Leicester) (*capt*), Stuart Redfern (Leicester) *Replacement:* D Richards (Leicester) for Robbins (79 mins)
Scorers *Tries:* Robbins, Holdstock *Conversion:* Hare *Penalty Goals:* Hare (2) *Dropped Goal:* Hare
New Zealanders: Deans; S S Wilson (*capt*), Pokere, Taylor, B W Smith; W R Smith, Donald; *No 8* Mexted; *Second Row* Shaw, Anderson, Old, Hobbs; *Front Row* Davie, Reid, McGrattan
Scorers *Try:* Pokere *Penalty Goals:* Deans (3)
Referee W D Bevan (Wales)

MATCH 6 12 November, Murrayfield

SCOTLAND 25 (5PG 2DG 1T) **NEW ZEALAND 25** (2G 3PG 1T)

Until the Midlands game there were not too many who gave Scotland any chance, especially after the South of Scotland had been humiliated at Netherdale. But the tourists never really recovered from that Leicester set-back. Although this was an international match they let the game slip through their fingers. Scotland staged a thrilling fight-back in the closing stages and could have sneaked their first-ever win over the All Blacks; nevertheless, the New Zealanders' complaints lasted long into the Edinburgh night.

The Scots had dramatically levelled the scores with their only try just before the end when winger Jim Pollock, a late replacement for Steve Munro, dived on David Johnston's neat, diagonal kick-ahead over the line. Pollock was fast becoming Scotland's good luck charm. This was his third cap – the previous two had been on visits to Cardiff and Twickenham – and he was still to play on a losing Scotland side. His try made it 25-25 as full-back Peter Dods lined up the touch-line conversion. The Gala kicker had been in cracking form – he had notched up five penalty goals – but this final attempt just drifted wide.

There was still time for one last assault by the All Blacks and it brought frantic activity near the Scottish line. It seemed as if Mark Shaw had scored, but he was brought back by French referee Hourquet, who instead gave a penalty kick to the All Blacks for obstruction. However, after a consultation with the touch-judge, Brian Anderson, a Scottish international referee, he reversed his decision and the tourists' chance had gone. The All Blacks were not happy that Bernie Fraser, their wing, had been penalised for 'intent'.

Actually, the New Zealanders should have had the game sewn up long before that. John Rutherford had given the home side an early lead with a dropped goal, but this was quickly cancelled out by a penalty from Robbie Deans. Another Rutherford dropped goal regained the lead for Scotland before their opponents launched an all-out assault. Jock Hobbs and Fraser scored tries and Deans added a conversion to give New Zealand a 13-6 lead. Dods and Deans then swapped penalty goals, but two more from Dods left Scotland trailing by a single point, 15-16, at half-time. In the second half, Fraser grabbed another try, a carbon copy of his first, as he kicked ahead and won the chase with the Scottish defence. Dods' accurate boot kept chipping away at New Zealand's lead, but eventually it took Johnston's quick thinking to enable the Scots to gain their second draw with the All Blacks.

SCOTLAND: P W Dods (Gala); J A Pollock (Gosforth), A E Kennedy (Watsonians), D I Johnston (Watsonians), G R T Baird (Kelso); J Y Rutherford (Selkirk), R J Laidlaw (Jedforest); *No 8* I A M Paxton (Selkirk); *Second Row* J R Beattie (Glasgow Acads), T J Smith (Gala), W Cuthbertson (Harlequins), J H Calder (Stewart's-Melville FP); *Front Row* I G Milne (Heriot's FP), C T Deans (Hawick), J Aitken (Gala) (*capt*)
Scorers *Try:* Pollock *Penalty Goals:* Dods (5) *Dropped Goals:* Rutherford (2)
NEW ZEALAND: Deans; S S Wilson (*capt*), Pokere, Taylor, Fraser; W R Smith, Donald; *No 8* Mexted; *Second Row* Shaw, Anderson, Braid, Hobbs; *Front Row* Crichton, Reid, McGrattan *Replacement* Green for Taylor (40 mins)
Scorers *Tries:* Hobbs, Fraser (2) *Conversions:* Deans (2) *Penalty Goals:* Deans (3)
Referee R Hourquet (France)

MATCH 7 15 November, Bristol Memorial Ground

South & South-West Division 6 (2PG) **New Zealanders 18** (2G 2PG)
South & South-West Division: C Martin (Bath); D M Trick (Bath), J A Palmer (Bath), S Barnes (Oxford U), R Mogg (Gloucester); J P Horton (Bath), R Harding (Bristol); *No 8* M Teague (Gloucester); *Second Row* J Hall (Bath), S B Boyle (Gloucester), J Orwin (Gloucester), J Gadd (Gloucester); *Front Row* P J Blakeway (Gloucester) (*capt*), S G F Mills (Gloucester), M Preedy (Gloucester) *Replacements* A J Morley (Bristol) for Martin (51 mins), A Sheppard (Bristol) for Preedy (56 mins)
Scorer *Penalty Goals:* Barnes (2)
New Zealanders: Crowley; S S Wilson (*capt*), Pokere, Green, B W Smith; Dunn, Kirk; *No 8* Mexted; *Second Row* Shelford, Anderson, Robinson, Old; *Front Row* Davie, B H Wilson, Boroevich
Scorers *Tries:* S S Wilson, B W Smith *Conversions:* Crowley (2) *Penalty Goals:* Crowley (2)
Referee D I H Burnett (Ireland)

MATCH 8 19 November, Twickenham

ENGLAND 15 (1G 3PG) **NEW ZEALAND 9** (1G 1PG)

For nearly half a century the hero of England-New Zealand encounters at Twickenham had been the Russian Prince Obolensky, at least as far as the home side were concerned. England's only previous triumph on home soil over the All Blacks had been in 1936 when Obolensky's two tries sealed the tourists' fate. Now he is joined by a new English legend, 'the Marquis de Colclough', as victorious skipper Peter Wheeler described him after the game. Maurice Colclough has played most of his senior rugby in France; now he was back home playing for the Wasps and, as far as the Twickenham crowd was concerned, he couldn't have picked a better time to score his first try for his country.

This well-deserved success was the perfect start for England's new management – Chairman of selectors Derek Morgan, coach Dick Greenwood and skipper Peter Wheeler. In fact, England should have won more emphatically, but a winning result was something they had not managed in four outings in the 1983 Championship. While Peter Wheeler was showing what he could have done for the Lions as leader, scrum-half Nick Youngs was determined to prove himself as something more than Nigel Melville's stand-in.

All Black Brian McGrattan (1) fails to stop Maurice Colclough winning a line-out during New Zealand's historic 15-9 defeat at Twickenham.

The Leicester scrum-half gave a magnificent display and was easily the 'man of the match'. It was a memorable day, too, for Bath No 8 Paul Simpson, making his debut on the flank. Simpson was the victim of some rough handling, but nothing could knock the smile from his face.

In general, this was a tatty display by the All Blacks, who fell a long way short of their traditional standards of discipline. John Carleton limped off after a needlessly late tackle by Bernie Fraser. Simpson, Gary Pearce and John Scott all needed stitches and Mike Slemen, making a welcome reappearance after a year in the wilderness, had his back badly raked. England were no angels, but it was not a proud day for New Zealand rugby. Even skipper Stuart Wilson was drawn into the niggling incidents as he saw the All Blacks' first Test defeat in Britain since 1953 loom nearer.

Robbie Deans put the All Blacks ahead with a penalty, but two similar scores by Dusty Hare gave England a 6-3 half-time lead. Then Colclough powered over from a few yards out for Hare to convert. Replacement New Zealand prop Murray Davie matched Colclough's try, and Deans converted, but Hare's third penalty then put the result beyond doubt.

ENGLAND: W H Hare (Leicester); J Carleton (Orrell), C R Woodward (Leicester), P W Dodge (Leicester), M A C Slemen (Liverpool); L Cusworth (Leicester), N C Youngs (Leicester); *No 8* J P Scott (Cardiff); *Second Row* P J Winterbottom (Headingley), S Bainbridge (Gosforth), M J Colclough (Wasps), P D Simpson (Bath); *Front Row* G S Pearce (Northampton), P J Wheeler (Leicester) (*capt*), C White (Gosforth) *Replacement* N C Stringer (Wasps) for Carleton (38 mins)
Scorers *Try:* Colclough *Conversion:* Hare *Penalty Goals:* Hare (3)
NEW ZEALAND: Deans; S S Wilson (*capt*), Pokere, Green, Fraser; W R Smith, Donald; *No 8* Mexted; *Second Row* Shaw, Anderson, Braid, Hobbs; *Front Row* Crichton, Reid, McGrattan *Replacement* Davie for Crichton (15 mins)
Scorers *Try:* Davie *Conversion:* Deans *Penalty Goal:* Deans
Referee A M Hosie (Scotland)

BRITISH ISLES TO NEW ZEALAND 1983

An analysis of the tour appeared in last year's edition. The full match-by-match details are given here for the record.

THE TOURING PARTY

Captain C F Fitzgerald **Manager** W J McBride
Assistant Manager J Telfer

FULL-BACKS

H P MacNeill (Oxford U)
W H Hare (Leicester)

THREEQUARTERS

J Carleton (Orrell)
G R T Baird (Kelso)
T M Ringland (Ballymena)
G Evans (Maesteg)
D G Irwin (Instonians)
M J Kiernan (Dolphin)
R A Ackerman (London Welsh)
C R Woodward (Leicester)

HALF-BACKS

S O Campbell (Old Belvedere)
J Y Rutherford (Selkirk)
T D Holmes (Cardiff)
R J Laidlaw (Jedforest)
***N D Melville** (Wasps)
***S J Smith** (Sale)

FORWARDS

S T Jones (Pontypool)
I Stephens (Bridgend)
***G A J McLoughlin** (Shannon)
G Price (Pontypool)
I G Milne (Heriot's FP)
C T Deans (Hawick)
C F Fitzgerald (St Mary's Coll)
S B Boyle (Gloucester)
R L Norster (Cardiff)
M J Colclough (Angoulême)
***D G Lenihan** (Cork Const)
S Bainbridge (Gosforth)
J H Calder (Stewart's-Melville FP)
J B O'Driscoll (London Irish)
P J Winterbottom (Headingley)
J Squire (Pontypool)
N C Jeavons (Moseley)
J R Beattie (Glasgow Acad)
I A M Paxton (Selkirk)
***E T Butler** (Pontypool)

**denotes replacement during tour*

TOUR RECORD

All matches Played 18 Won 12 Lost 6 Points for 478 Against 276
International matches Played 4 Lost 4 Points for 26 Against 78

SCORING DETAILS

All matches

For:	58T	39C	44PG	12DG	478 Pts
Against:	30T	18C	34PG	6DG	276 Pts

International matches

For	2T	—	5PG	1DG	26 Pts
Against:	9T	6C	9PG	1DG	78 Pts

MATCH DETAILS

1983	OPPONENTS	VENUE	RESULTS
14 May	Wanganui	Wanganui	W 47-15
18 May	Auckland	Auckland	L 12-13
21 May	Bay of Plenty	Rotorua	W 34-16
25 May	Wellington	Wellington	W 27-19
28 May	Manawatu	Palmerston North	W 25-18

1983	OPPONENTS	VENUE	RESULTS
31 May	Mid Canterbury	Ashburton	W 26-6
4 June	NEW ZEALAND	Christchurch	L 12-16
8 June	West Coast	Greymouth	W 52-16
11 June	Southland	Invercargill	W 41-3
14 June	Wairarapa-Bush	Masterton	W 57-10
18 June	NEW ZEALAND	Wellington	L 0-9
25 June	North Auckland	Whangarei	W 21-12
28 June	Canterbury	Christchurch	L 20-22
2 July	NEW ZEALAND	Dunedin	L 8-15
6 July	Hawkes Bay	Napier	W 25-19
9 July	Counties	Pukekohe	W 25-16
12 July	Waikato	Hamilton	W 40-13
16 July	NEW ZEALAND	Auckland	L 6-38

APPEARANCES AND SCORERS

All matches	*App**	*T*	*C*	*PG*	*DG*	*Pts*		*App**	*T*	*C*	*PG*	*DG*	*Pts*
Ackerman	10(3R)	1	—	—	—	4	Kiernan	10	2	—	—	1	11
Bainbridge	11	—	—	—	—	0	Laidlaw	13(3R)	2	—	—	—	8
Baird	11	6	—	—	—	24	Lenihan	2	—	—	—	—	0
Beattie	9(2R)	4	—	—	—	16	McLoughlin	2	—	—	—	—	0
Boyle	6	—	—	—	—	0	MacNeill	9(2R)	—	1	2	—	8
Butler	1	—	—	—	—	0	Melville	2	2	—	—	—	8
Calder	7	3	—	—	—	12	Milne	8	1	—	—	—	4
Campbell	11	1	18	22	6	124	Norster	6	—	—	—	—	0
Carleton	11	9	—	—	—	36	O'Driscoll	8	—	—	—	—	0
Colclough	11	—	—	—	—	0	Paxton	9(1R)	4	—	—	—	16
Deans	7	2	—	—	—	8	Price	10	—	—	—	—	0
Evans	12(4R)	3	3	1	—	21	Ringland	9	5	—	—	—	20
Fitzgerald	11	—	—	—	—	0	Rutherford	10	2	—	—	5	23
Hare	6	—	17	18	—	88	Smith	2	—	—	—	—	0
Holmes	4	1	—	—	—	4	Squire	6	2	—	—	—	8
Irwin	11	6	—	—	—	24	Stephens	4	1	—	—	—	4
Jeavons	6	—	—	—	—	0	Winterbottom	12	1	—	—	—	4
Jones	13(1R)	—	—	—	—	0	Woodward	7	—	—	—	1	3

**Includes appearances as replacements* (R)

MATCH 1 14 May, Wanganui

Wanganui 15 (1G 3PG) **British Isles 47** (3G 5PG 2DG 2T)

Wanganui: T Fearn; D Brooks, S Crowley, S Gordon, M O'Connell; M Kendrick, A J Donald; *No 8* R Parsons; *Second Row* B Middleton *(capt)*, G Coleman, M Wild, P Stratton; *Front Row* R Kahukaka, L Graham, B Dallison

Scorers *Try:* Crowley *Conversion:* Fearn *Penalty Goals:* Fearn (3)

British Isles: Hare; Ringland, Ackerman, Kiernan, Evans; Rutherford, Laidlaw; *No 8* Beattie; *Second Row* Squire, Boyle, Norster, Winterbottom; *Front Row* Milne, Fitzgerald *(capt)*, Jones

Scorers *Tries:* Ringland, Squire (2), Beattie, Winterbottom *Conversions:* Hare (3) *Penalty Goals:* Hare (5) *Dropped Goals:* Rutherford (2)

Referee K Lawrence (Bay of Plenty)

MATCH 2 18 May, Auckland

Auckland 13 (2PG 1DG 1T) **British Isles 12** (1G 1PG 1DG)
Auckland: D Halligan; J Kirwin, J Stanley, M Mills, G Cunningham; G Fox, T Butcher; *No 8* G Rich; *Second Row* A Harvey *(capt)*, A M Haden, G W Whetton, A Whetton; *Front Row* J Drake, K Boyle, G Burgess
Scorers *Try:* Cunningham *Penalty Goals:* Fox (2) *Dropped Goal:* Fox
British Isles: MacNeill; Carleton, Woodward, Irwin, Baird; Campbell, Holmes; *No 8* Beattie; *Second Row* Calder, Boyle, Bainbridge, O'Driscoll; *Front Row* Price, Fitzgerald *(capt)*, Jones *Replacement* Evans for MacNeill (49 mins)
Scorers *Try:* Irwin *Conversion:* Campbell *Penalty Goal:* MacNeill *Dropped Goal:* Campbell
Referee G Harrison (Wellington)

MATCH 3 21 May, Rotorua

Bay of Plenty 16 (2G 1T) **British Isles 34** (4G 2PG 1T)
Bay of Plenty: A Sutherland; J Hanley, D Shelford, B McKillop, J Cameron; R Preston, M Basham; *No 8* G Elvin *(capt)*; *Second Row* C Ross, A De Jager, G J Braid, T Hohneck; *Front Row* B Cameron, H R Reid, S McDowell *Replacement* A Jayne for Basham (63 mins)
Scorers *Tries:* Cameron (2), Preston *Conversions:* Preston, Sutherland
British Isles: Hare; Carleton, Woodward, Ackerman, Ringland; Rutherford, Laidlaw; *No 8* Paxton; *Second Row* Squire *(capt)*, Colclough, Bainbridge, Calder; *Front Row* Stephens, Deans, Milne
Scorers *Tries:* Ringland, Carleton (2), Stephens, Paxton *Conversions:* Hare (4) *Penalty Goals:* Hare (2)
Referee C Gregan (Waikato)

MATCH 4 25 May, Wellington

Wellington 19 (1G 2PG 1DG 1T) **British Isles 27** (3G 3PG)
Wellington: A R Hewson; M Clamp, S S Wilson, J Salmon, B G Fraser; T Wyllie, N Sorenson; *No 8* M G Mexted; *Second Row* P B Quinn *(capt)*, G Wilkinson, D Archer, G Duffy; *Front Row* S Crichton, S Bryan, B McGrattan *Replacement* S Hinds for Wilkinson (44 mins)
Scorers *Tries:* Fraser, Quinn *Conversion:* Hewson *Penalty Goals:* Hewson (2) *Dropped Goal:* Hewson
British Isles: MacNeill; Carleton, Kiernan, Irwin, Baird; Campbell, Holmes; *No 8* Beattie; *Second Row* Squire, Colclough, Norster, Winterbottom; *Front Row* Price, Fitzgerald *(capt)*, Jones *Replacements* Laidlaw for Holmes (27 mins), Evans for Carleton (31 mins)
Scorers *Tries:* Baird (2), Kiernan *Conversions:* Campbell (3) *Penalty Goals:* Campbell (3)
Referee T Doocey (Canterbury)

MATCH 5 28 May, Palmerston North

Manawatu 18 (1G 2PG 2DG) **British Isles 25** (2G 2PG 1DG 1T)
Manawatu: M Finley; K Granger, P Drury, I Wood, P McElhinney; M Love, M Donaldson *(capt)*; *No 8* G H Old; *Second Row* M W Shaw, F J Oliver, M Rosenbrook, G Grant; *Front Row* T Clare, B Hemara, G A Knight
Scorers *Try:* Finley *Conversion:* Finley *Penalty Goals:* Finley (2) *Dropped Goals:* Finley, Love
British Isles: MacNeill; Baird, Kiernan, Ackerman, Ringland; Campbell, Laidlaw; *No 8* Paxton; *Second Row* Squire, Colclough, Norster, Winterbottom; *Front Row* Stephens, Fitzgerald *(capt)*, Price

Scorers *Tries:* Ringland (2), Paxton *Conversions:* Campbell (2)
Penalty Goals: Campbell (2) *Dropped Goal:* Campbell
Referee D Bishop (Southland)

MATCH 6 31 May, Ashburton

Mid Canterbury 6 (2PG) **British Isles 26** (1G 4PG 2T)
Mid Canterbury: M Holmes; P McLay, J Mudgway, M McLeod, G Frew; M Roulston, P Williams; *No 8* P Cunneen; *Second Row* A Morrison, A Hills, J Ross, W Frew; *Front Row* J McLay, G Perry *(capt)*, H Gordon *Replacement* A Edge for Holmes (70 mins)
Scorer *Penalty Goals:* Holmes (2)
British Isles: Hare; Ringland, Woodward, Irwin, Evans; Rutherford, Holmes; *No 8* Beattie; *Second Row* Jeavons, Colclough *(capt)*, Bainbridge, Calder; *Front Row* Jones, Deans, Milne *Replacement* Laidlaw for Holmes (70 mins)
Scorers *Tries:* Holmes, Calder, Evans *Conversion:* Hare *Penalty Goals:* Hare (4)
Referee R Soppert (Counties)

MATCH 7 4 June, Christchurch **1st International**

NEW ZEALAND 16 (3PG 1DG 1T) **BRITISH ISLES 12** (3PG 1DG)
NEW ZEALAND: A Hewson; S S Wilson, S T Pokere, W T Taylor, B G Fraser; I T Dunn, D S Loveridge; *No 8* M G Mexted *Second Row* M J B Hobbs, A M Haden, G W Whetton, M W Shaw; *Front Row* G A Knight, A G Dalton *(capt)*, J C Ashworth
Scorers *Try:* Shaw *Penalty Goals:* Hewson (3) *Dropped Goal:* Hewson
BRITISH ISLES: MacNeill; Ringland, Ackerman, Irwin, Baird; Campbell, Holmes; *No 8* Paxton; *Second Row* Winterbottom, Norster, Colclough, Squire; *Front Row* Price, Fitzgerald *(capt)*, Stephens *Replacement* Laidlaw for Holmes (31 mins)
Scorer *Penalty Goals:* Campbell (3) *Dropped Goal:* Campbell
Referee F Palmade (France)

MATCH 8 8 June, Greymouth

West Coast 16 (4PG 1T) **British Isles 52** (6G 4PG 1T)
West Coast: W Gugich; M MacIntosh, C Power, D Lynch, D King; G Cook, K Ford; *No 8* G McGurk; *Second Row* B Hopkins *(capt)*, I Forsyth, A Price, A Bruhn; *Front Row* J Walton, D Paterson, P Davidson
Scorers *Try:* Ford *Penalty Goals:* Gugich (4)
British Isles: Hare; Carleton, Woodward, Ackerman, Evans; Rutherford, Laidlaw *(capt)*; *No 8* Beattie; *Second Row* Jeavons, Boyle, Bainbridge, Calder; *Front Row* Jones, Deans, Milne
Scorers *Tries:* Carleton (4), Rutherford, Laidlaw, Beattie *Conversions:* Hare (6)
Penalty Goals: Hare (4)
Referee T Gresson (South Canterbury)

MATCH 9 11 June, Invercargill

Southland 3 (1PG) **British Isles 41** (4G 2PG 1DG 2T)
Southland: B McKenzie; J Cormack, S T Pokere, P Laidlaw, B Dickenson; B McKechnie *(capt)*, C Hilney; *No 8* B Robertson *Second Row* L M Rutledge, A Byrne, F Dermondy, P Henderson; *Front Row* D Murcott, L Chisholm, P Cosgrove
Replacement M Crowther for Chisholm (40 mins)
Scorers *Penalty Goal:* McKechnie
British Isles: Hare; Carleton, Irwin, Kiernan, Ringland; Rutherford, Melville; *No 8* Paxton; *Second Row* Calder, Colclough, Norster, O'Driscoll; *Front Row* Price,

Fitzgerald *(capt)*, Stephens *Replacements* Evans for Hare (17 mins), Jones for Stephens (55 mins)
Scorers *Tries:* Ringland, Kiernan, Melville (2), Calder, Irwin
Conversions: Evans (3), Hare *Penalty Goals:* Hare (2) *Dropped Goal:* Rutherford
Referee R Francis (Waikato)

MATCH 10 14 June, Masterton

Wairarapa-Bush 10 (1G 1T) **British Isles 57** (6G 2PG 1DG 3T)
Wairarapa-Bush: N Kjestrup; M Cornford, K Carter, C Kaka, G Karaitiana; P Rutene, B Anderson *(capt); No 8* C Baker; *Second Row* B Harvey, M McCool, D White, T Hullena; *Front Row* C Kupene, G McGlashen, W Rowlands
Scorers *Tries:* Cornford, Carter *Conversion:* Carter
British Isles: Evans; Carleton, Irwin, Kiernan, Baird; Campbell, Laidlaw *(capt); No 8* Beattie; *Second Row* Winterbottom, Bainbridge, Boyle, O'Driscoll; *Front Row* Milne, Deans, Jones *Replacement* Jeavons for Boyle (66 mins)
Scorers *Tries:* Evans (2), Carleton (2), Baird (2), Beattie (2), Irwin
Conversions: Campbell (6) *Penalty Goals:* Campbell (2) *Dropped Goal:* Kiernan
Referee K Henderson (Otago)

MATCH 11 18 June, Wellington **2nd International**

NEW ZEALAND 9 (1G 1PG) **BRITISH ISLES 0**
NEW ZEALAND: A R Hewson; S S Wilson, S T Pokere, W T Taylor, B G Fraser; W R Smith, D S Loveridge; *No 8* M G Mexted; *Second Row* M J B Hobbs, A M Haden, G W Whetton, M W Shaw; *Front Row* G A Knight, A G Dalton *(capt)*, J C Ashworth
Scorers *Try:* Loveridge *Conversion:* Hewson *Penalty Goal:* Hewson
BRITISH ISLES: MacNeill; Carleton, Irwin, Kiernan, Baird; Campbell, Laidlaw; *No 8* Paxton; *Second Row* Winterbottom, Norster, Colclough, O'Driscoll; *Front Row* Price, Fitzgerald *(capt)*, Jones *Replacement* Beattie for Paxton (53 mins)
Referee F Palmade (France)

MATCH 12 25 June, Whangerei

North Auckland 12 (1G 2PG) **British Isles 21** (2G 2PG 1DG)
North Auckland: G Valli; F Woodman, D Haynes, C Going, K Woodman; I T Dunn, C Hull; *No 8* N Ruddell; *Second Row* I Phillips, A G Robinson, J Reid, B Flavell; *Front Row* L Watene, P H Sloane *(capt)*, T Perkinson *Replacement* D Stevenson for Flavell (50 mins)
Scorers *Try:* Phillips *Conversion:* Valli *Penalty Goals:* Valli (2)
British Isles: Evans; Ringland, Rutherford, Kiernan, Ackerman; Campbell, Melville; *No 8* Squire; *Second Row* Jeavons, Boyle, Bainbridge, Calder; *Front Row* Price, Fitzgerald *(capt)*, Jones *Replacements* Laidlaw for Melville (6 mins), Beattie for Squire (25 mins)
Scorers *Tries:* Ackerman, Calder *Conversions:* Campbell (2)
Penalty Goals: Campbell (2) *Dropped Goal:* Campbell
Referee G Smith (Hawkes Bay)

MATCH 13 28 June, Christchurch

Canterbury 22 (1G 4PG 1T) **British Isles 20** (1G 1PG 1DG 2T)
Canterbury: R M Deans; C I Green, V Simpson, W T Taylor, G Hooper; W R Smith, B Deans; *No 8* D Atkins; *Second Row* M J B Hobbs, A Anderson, A Thorpe, D Haynes *(capt); Front Row* M G Davie, J Milne, J C Ashworth
Scorers *Tries:* Deans, Atkins *Conversion:* Deans *Penalty Goals:* Deans (4)

British Isles: MacNeill; Carleton, Irwin, Woodward, Baird; Rutherford, Laidlaw; *No 8* Paxton; *Second Row* Winterbottom, Bainbridge, Colclough, O'Driscoll *(capt); Front Row* Milne, Deans, Jones
Scorers *Tries:* Irwin, Baird, Paxton *Conversion:* MacNeill *Penalty Goal:* MacNeill *Dropped Goal:* Rutherford
Referee C Dainty (Wellington)

MATCH 14 2 July, Dunedin **3rd International**

NEW ZEALAND 15 (1G 3PG) **BRITISH ISLES** 8 (2T)
NEW ZEALAND: A R Hewson; S S Wilson, S T Pokere, W T Taylor, B G Fraser; W R Smith, D S Loveridge; *No 8* M G Mexted; *Second Row* M J B Hobbs, A M Haden, G W Whetton, M W Shaw; *Front Row* G A Knight, A G Dalton *(capt)*, J C Ashworth *Replacement* A Stone for Smith (37 mins)
Scorers *Try:* Wilson *Conversion:* Hewson *Penalty Goals:* Hewson (3)
BRITISH ISLES: Evans; Carleton, Kiernan, Rutherford, Baird; Campbell, Laidlaw; *No 8* Paxton; *Second Row* Winterbottom, Bainbridge, Colclough, Calder; *Front Row* Price, Fitzgerald *(capt)*, Jones
Scorers *Tries:* Baird, Rutherford
Referee R G Byres (Australia)

MATCH 15 6 July, Napier

Hawkes Bay 19 (2G 1DG 1T) **British Isles 25** (2G 2PG 1DG 1T)
Hawkes Bay: L Holmes; J Frost, R Allen, P Davis, P Dailey; P O'Shaughnessy, P Blake; *No 8* R Falcon; *Second Row* P Anson, P Fulford, G Higginson *(capt)*, F N K Shelford; *Front Row* J O'Connor, G Gregory, N Porter *Replacement* N Clapperton for Allen (37 mins)
Scorers *Tries:* Allen, Holmes, Porter *Conversions:* Holmes (2) *Dropped Goal:* O'Shaughnessy
British Isles: Hare; Ringland, Irwin, Woodward, Ackerman; Rutherford, Smith *(capt); No 8* Beattie; *Second Row* Winterbottom, Lenihan, Boyle, Jeavons; *Front Row* Milne, Deans, McLoughlin *Replacements* MacNeill for Hare (68 mins), Paxton for Beattie (12 mins)
Scorers *Tries:* Irwin, Deans, Paxton *Conversions:* Hare (2) *Penalty Goals:* Woodward, Hare *Dropped Goal:* Rutherford
Referee T Doocey (Canterbury)

MATCH 16 9 July, Pukehoke

Counties 16 (1G 2PG 1T) **British Isles 25** (5PG 2DG 1T)
Counties: A Walsh; R Kururangi, S Lineen, L Cameron, W Robertson; J Harvey, M Moore; *No 8* T Clarke; *Second Row* B Wilson, G Wright, P Tuoro, A Dawson; *Front Row* H Maxwell, A G Dalton *(capt)*, R Ketels
Scorers *Tries:* Dalton (2) *Conversion:* Harvey *Penalty Goals:* Harvey (2)
British Isles: Evans; Carleton, Kiernan, Rutherford, Baird; Campbell, Smith; *No 8* Jeavons; *Second Row* Winterbottom, Bainbridge, Lenihan, O'Driscoll; *Front Row* Price, Fitzgerald *(capt)*, Jones *Replacement* Ackerman for Rutherford (26 mins)
Scorers *Try:* Carleton *Penalty Goals:* Campbell (5) *Dropped Goals:* Campbell (2)
Referee K Lawrence (Bay of Plenty)

MATCH 17 12 July, Hamilton

Waikato 13 (1G 1PG 1T) **British Isles 40** (4G 4PG 1T)
Waikato: T Purcell; B Smith, A Stone, C Ellis, R Adam; J Boe, G Holmes; *No 8* G Tietjens; *Second Row* P Wills, J Fleming, W Bullot, M Melson;

Front Row K Searancke, P Bennett *(capt)*, P Koteka
Replacements B Parker for Purcell (24 mins), M Speight for Bullot (72 mins)
Scorers *Tries:* Stone, Smith *Conversion:* Adam *Penalty Goal:* Purcell
British Isles: MacNeill; Ringland, Irwin, Woodward, Baird; Campbell, Laidlaw; *No 8* Butler; *Second Row* Winterbottom, Bainbridge, Colclough, O'Driscoll *(capt)*; *Front Row* Milne, Deans, McLoughlin *Replacements* Ackerman for Woodward (45 mins), Evans for Campbell (72 mins)
Scorers *Tries:* Deans, Irwin, Laidlaw, Milne, Campbell *Conversions:* Campbell (4) *Penalty Goals:* Campbell (4)
Referee N Whittaker (Bay of Plenty)

MATCH 18 16 July, Auckland **4th International**

NEW ZEALAND 38 (4G 2PG 2T) **BRITISH ISLES 6** (2PG)
NEW ZEALAND: A R Hewson; S S Wilson, S T Pokere, W T Taylor, B G Fraser; I T Dunn, D S Loveridge; *No 8* M G Mexted; *Second Row* M N J Hobbs, A M Haden, G W Whetton, M W Shaw; *Front Row* G A Knight, A G Dalton *(capt)*, J C Ashworth
Scorers *Tries:* Wilson (3), Hewson, Hobbs, Haden *Conversions:* Hewson (4) *Penalty Goals:* Hewson (2)
BRITISH ISLES: Evans; Carleton, Irwin, Kiernan, Baird; Campbell, Laidlaw; *No 8* Paxton; *Second Row* Winterbottom, Bainbridge, Colclough, O'Driscoll; *Front Row* Price, Fitzgerald *(capt)*, Jones *Replacements* Ackerman for Baird (57 mins), MacNeill for Campbell (47 mins)
Scorers *Penalty Goals:* Evans (2)
Referee R G Byres (Australia)

JAPAN TO WALES 1983

The imaginative Japanese are always popular visitors and they gave a considerable boost to the early-season period in Wales. Nor did they collapse as Japanese teams have in the past against teams from Britain. They won two and drew one of their five matches, beating the powerful Newbridge team in the process, and in easily the best display of their tour they ran the Welsh XV spectacularly close in a marvellous game at Cardiff Arms Park.

With their customary attention to detail and enthusiasm, the Japanese have obviously taken to heart the lessons of previous tours. They have gone to a considerable amount of trouble to produce forwards of greater upper-body strength and endurance, so that they can compete to the end with the jumbo-sized packs of the other rugby countries. They also impressed with superb, quicksilver handling, outstanding support for the ball-carrier and clever variations in the line-out to offset the height advantage of the Welsh teams. However, they still had problems, a fact which was most evident in their heavy defeat by Pembrokeshire. This was the low point of the tour – they had beaten Abertillery comfortably and were to fight back well to draw with Neath.

All in all it was an immensely satisfying visit, giving the Japanese much on which to build. Shiggy Konno, their manager and a familiar figure on the world rugby scene, was delighted that his fear of crushing Japanese defeats, which have happened so often in the past, never looked like being realised.

The outstanding Japanese player was probably their captain, the quick-witted fly-half Yuji Matsuo. He was the hub of their attacks and the springboard for their marvellous fight-back in the international match. He struck up an impressive combination with Yoshimitsu Konishi, the team's experienced scrum-half. Kobayashi and Hirao were clever centres and Tanifuji a strong-running full-back.

The forwards fought bravely and showed astonishing mobility. Chida, at back row forward and Horaguchi, at tight-head prop, were the cornerstones and Oyagi and Hayashi often won clean line-out possession with precision jumping and expert synchronisation with their throwers. They could not hope to push back the home forwards in the tight but they often managed to lock the scrum sufficiently to make sure of winning their own ball.

All things considered, it was a memorable tour. The Japanese particularly delighted their Welsh RU hosts because their enterprise in the tour games attracted a very large crowd for the international. Receipts from 32,000 people paid for a good few rivets in the new grandstand at Cardiff Arms Park.

THE TOURING PARTY

Captain Y Matsuo **Manager** S Konno
Assistant Manager H Hibino

FULL-BACKS	FORWARDS
N Tanifuji	**K Sejimo**
M Yasuda	**T Ishizuka**
THREEQUARTERS	**K Takada**
H Toshima	**M Chida**
F Kanaya	**H Kawachi**
S Hirao	**K Kawachi**
T Yoshino	**Y Kawase**
K Honjo	**A Oyagi**
T Higashida	**T Hayashi**
HALF-BACKS	**Y Ikeda**
H Kobayashi	**M Inoue**
Y Matsuo	**T Fujita**
Y Konishi	**K Horaguchi**
T Okuwaki	**J Ishiyama**

TOUR RECORD

All matches Played 5 Won 2 Lost 2 Drawn 1 Points for 96 Against 105
International match Played 1 Lost 1 Points for 24 Against 29

SCORING DETAILS

All matches						**International match**				
For:	6G	12PG		6T	96 Pts	For:	1G	2PG	3T	24 Pts
Against:	5G	9PG	4DG	9T	105 Pts	Against:	3G	1PG	2T	29 Pts

MATCH DETAILS

1983	OPPONENTS	VENUE	RESULTS
8 Oct	Abertillery	Abertillery	W 17-13
12 Oct	Pembrokeshire	Haverfordwest	L 15-28
15 Oct	Neath	Neath	D 21-21
18 Oct	Newbridge	Newbridge	W 19-14
22 Oct	Wales XV	Cardiff Arms Park	L 24-29

Kobayashi was the leading points scorer on the tour with 32 (8PG 4C). Honjo scored 20 points (4PG 1T 2C). Yoshino, Matsuo and Konishi scored two tries apiece. Four players appeared in all five matches – Matsuo, Horaguchi, Chida and Oyagi (once as a replacement). Six players appeared in four matches – Konishi, Kobayashi, Hirao, Hayashi, Fujita and Kanaya (once as a replacement).

MATCH 1 8 October, Abertillery

Abertillery 13 (3PG 1T) **Japanese 17** (3PG 2T)
Abertillery: N Paul; D Owen, D George, J Davies, A Parry; K Clarke, R Moon (*capt*); *No 8* R Clark; *Second Row* R Preece, J Everett, M Baker, P Crane; *Front Row* H Gilson,

Bleddyn Bowen, the Welsh centre, gets in his pass under pressure during the Wales-Japan game.

D Gilson, M Pugh *Replacement* T Flower for Preece (70 mins)
Scorers *Try:* Owen *Penalty Goals:* Clarke (3)
Japanese: Tanifuji; Honjo, Kanaya, Kobayashi, Higashida; Matsuo (*capt*), Konishi; *No 8* Chida; *Second Row* Ishizuka, Oyagi, Hayashi, H Kawachi; *Front Row* Horaguchi, Fujita, Ishiyama
Scorers *Tries:* Higashida, Kanaya *Penalty Goals:* Honjo (3)
Referee R Parker (England)

MATCH 2 12 October, Haverfordwest

Pembrokeshire 28 (2G 3PG 1DG 1T) **Japanese 15** (2G 1PG)
Pembrokeshire: G Bowen (Narberth); H Forster (Cardigan), K Morgan (Haverfordwest), W Morgan (Haverfordwest), M Holding (Whitland); G John (S Glam Inst), E Phillips (Cardigan); *No 8* V Davies (Pembroke) (*capt*); *Second Row* R Price (Narberth), B Bennett (St David's), A Rose (Tenby Utd), N Morroney (Tenby Utd); *Front Row* G Evans (Tenby Utd), J Griffiths (Haverfordwest), B Williams (Narberth) *Replacement* R Thomas (St David's) for Morroney (75 mins)
Scorers *Tries:* Morroney, Phillips, Bowen *Conversions:* John (2) *Penalty Goals:* John (3) *Dropped Goal:* John
Japanese: Yasuda; Honjo, Yoshino, Hirao, Toshima; Matsuo (*capt*), Okuwaki; *No 8* Sejimo; *Second Row* Chida, Oyagi, K Kawachi, Kawase; *Front Row* Horaguchi, Inoue, Ikeda
Scorers *Tries:* Honjo, Yoshino *Conversions:* Honjo (2) *Penalty Goal:* Honjo
Referee D Templeton (Ireland)

MATCH 3 15 October, Neath

Neath 21 (3G 1PG) **Japanese 21** (1G 5PG)
Neath: N Harris; C Bridgewater, D Jacob, K Jones, S Powell; B Childs, C Gnojek; *No 8* D Glover; *Second Row* L Jones, J Willis, R Hughes (*capt*), G Jones; *Front Row* P Langford, M Richards, S Dando
Scorers *Tries:* L Jones, Gnojek, Childs *Conversions:* Harris (3) *Penalty Goal:* Harris
Japanese: Tanifuji; Kanaya, Kobayashi, Hirao, Higashida; Matsuo (*capt*), Konishi; *No 8* Kawase; *Second Row* Takada, Oyagi, Hayashi, Chida; *Front Row* Horaguchi, Fujita, Ishiyama *Replacement* Ikeda for Ishiyama (63 mins)
Scorers *Try:* Matsuo *Conversion:* Kobayashi *Penalty Goals:* Kobayashi (5)
Referee K Mott (England)

MATCH 4 18 October, Newbridge

Newbridge 14 (2PG 2T) **Japanese 19** (2G 1PG 1T)
Newbridge: W Bow; A Glasson, D Owen, P Evans, C Phillips; P Turner (*capt*), L Davies; *No 8* M Short; *Second Row* S Griffiths, S Harris, A Stimpson, P Jones; *Front Row* B Cripps, P Ransom, G Hewlett
Scorers *Tries:* Glasson, Short *Penalty Goals:* Turner (2)
Japanese: Yasuda; Yoshino, Kobayashi, Hirao, Toshima; Matsuo (*capt*), Konishi; *No 8* Sejimo; *Second Row* Takada, K Kawachi, Hayashi, Chida; *Front Row* Horaguchi, Fujita, Ikeda *Replacements:* Oyagi for Kawachi (22 mins) Kanaya for Yasuda (44 mins)
Scorers *Tries:* Konishi, Yoshino, Matsuo *Conversions:* Kobayashi (2) *Penalty Goal:* Kobayashi
Referee T E Allan (Scotland)

MATCH 5 22 October, Cardiff Arms Park

WALES XV 29 (3G 1PG 2T) **JAPAN 24** (1G 2PG 3T)

As this memorable encounter moved into the last quarter with Wales leading 29-10 it seemed as if the brave Japanese resistance was about to crumble. Their forwards had battled bravely and with great ingenuity to keep the heavier Welsh pack under control, but Wales had still managed five tries and for all their courage, Japan seemed to be out of the running. Shiggy Konno, their manager, admitted that he had fears at this stage of a huge Welsh score.

But just when Japan were assumed to be about to throw in the towel they came roaring back spectacularly into the game with three marvellous tries. Matsuo, the little general at fly-half, initiated a series of bewildering attacks and waves of Japanese support carried them on. In the end, the Welsh team must have been glad to hear the final whistle. There is no telling what indignities they might have suffered had the game gone on for another five minutes. Yet Wales contributed their share to a fast, exciting and thoroughly enjoyable match with some clever running from their new backs and powerful forward play from Billy James, John Perkins and skipper Eddie Butler.

A weaving run by Titley worked Hadley over to open the scoring for Wales but a breakdown in midfield then allowed Konishi to kick on and score an equalising try. Wales struck next with two tries in quick succession – from Brown, the tall flanker, and from Dacey, Wyatt converting the second. Before half-time, Konishi kicked two penalties for Japan.

Wales stretched away impressively after half-time. Wyatt kicked a penalty goal and converted tries by Bowen and Giles, both of which were initiated by clever work from Dacey, at fly-half. This made the score 29-10.

Japan's come-back brought tries from Tanifuji, Chida and Fujita, the last converted by Kobayashi, bringing Japan to within a converted try of victory. But time had run out, and there were to be no more shocks for Wales. The ovation which the crowd gave to the tourists as they left the field signified relief as much as admiration.

WALES XV: M A Wyatt (Swansea); M H Titley (Bridgend), K Hopkins (Swansea), B Bowen (South Wales Police), A M Hadley (Cardiff); M Dacey (Swansea), R Giles (Aberavon); *No 8* E T Butler (Pontypool) (*capt*); *Second Row* M Brown (Pontypool), S J Perkins (Pontypool), T W Shaw (Newbridge), M Davies (Swansea); *Front Row* I H Eidman (Cardiff), W J James (Aberavon), J Whitefoot (Cardiff)
Scorers *Tries:* Hadley, Brown, Dacey, Bowen, Giles *Conversions:* Wyatt (3)
Penalty Goal: Wyatt
JAPAN: Tanifuji; Kanaya, Kobayashi, Hirao, Higashida; Matsuo (*capt*), Konishi; *No 8* Kawase; *Second Row* H Kawachi, Oyagi, Hayashi, Chida; *Front Row* Horaguchi, Fujita, Ishiyama *Replacement:* Ikeda for Horaguchi (70 mins)
Scorers *Tries:* Konishi, Tanifuji, Chida, Fujita *Conversion:* Kobayashi
Penalty Goals: Kobayashi (2)
Referee J A F Trigg (England)

CANADA TO ENGLAND 1983

It was a major success on the part of Canadian rugby to send a team on tour at all. The sport in their country is beset by lack of funds and several of the leading players were unable to arrange time off from work to make the tour – notably the two experienced locks, Hindson and de Goede. There was a further disadvantage in the huge distances which have to be negotiated by players and selectors in trying to choose and prepare a tour party. Remarkably, Jennings, the touring team's lock from Newfoundland, lives nearer to London than he does to the party's manager, Alun Rees from British Columbia.

All in all, the Canadians were satisfied with their tour. Injuries as the tour progressed further depleted their resources; they beat only Oxford University and Combined Services in their five matches and they were bitterly disappointed to lose to Sussex in what should not have proved too testing a fixture. Yet they gave an heroic display against a powerful England XV at Twickenham and the tour gave impetus to 'missionary' work in Canada when the players returned. Generally, they did their country proud. If they could have played to form and beaten Sussex and then been awarded a try against England when their wing, Palmer, scored but had the effort disallowed, their memories of the tour would have been a great deal happier.

The Canadians had clever players in Wyatt, their goal-kicking full-back, in Palmer, the fast man on the wing and in Schieffler, the fly-half who missed the international through injury. MacMillan, the tour captain, was a clever, probing scrum-half. There were hard workers in the forwards, too. Jennings played in all five tour games and Dukelow was the best prop. Cvitak and the loose forwards always fought bravely. But the forwards lacked collective drive and urgency on occasions and were too often picked off by the superior ball-winning skills of the English packs. They rarely established a platform and lacked continuity.

The team's best display came, ironically, in their defeat by England, a game in which they were unlucky to concede a 27-point margin. The poor display against Sussex was undoubtedly the low point of the tour. They fought tenaciously to beat the Combined Services, scored a brilliant try in defeat at Headingley and showed some flashes of good play, but not consistency, in beating a limited Oxford University early in the latter's term. Off the field, they were friendly and well-behaved and their manager and coach, Alun Rees and Tillman Briggs respectively, coped manfully with problems logistical and technical alike.

Robin Russell, Canada's No 8, safely fields the ball after a line-out in the 'Test' against England.

THE TOURING PARTY

Captain I MacMillan **Manager** A Rees
Assistant Manager T A Briggs

FULL-BACKS

M Wyatt (British Columbia)
A McGann (Ontario)

THREEQUARTERS

J Delaney (Ontario)
F Forster (Ontario)
G Fraser (British Columbia)
J Hawthorn (British Columbia)
***C Jones** (British Columbia)
P Palmer (British Columbia)

HALF-BACKS

M Schieffler (Alberta)
I Stuart (British Columbia)
I MacMillan (British Columbia)
P MacLean (British Columbia)

FORWARDS

G Dukelow (British Columbia)
R Breen (British Columbia)
P Kyle (British Columbia)
M Murphy (Alberta)
D Spiers (Ontario)
J Vivian (Alberta)
G Jennings (Newfoundland)
J Kemp (Alberta)
Z Cvitak (Ontario)
R Frame (British Columbia)
A Godziek (Ontario)
R Russell (Ontario)
A A Stewart (British Columbia)
R Strang (British Columbia)

**Replacement during tour*

TOUR RECORD

All matches Played 5 Won 2 Lost 3 Points for 51 Against 82
International match Played 1 Lost 1 Points for 0 Against 27

SCORING DETAILS

All matches

For:	5T	2C	8PG	1DG	51 Pts
Against:	9T	5C	10PG	2DG	82 Pts

International match

For: nil

Against:	3T	3C	3PG	27 Pts

MATCH DETAILS

1983	OPPONENTS	VENUE	RESULTS
1 Oct	Combined Services	Portsmouth	W 17-14
5 Oct	Headingley	Headingley	L 9-16
8 Oct	Oxford University	Oxford	W 16-9
11 Oct	Sussex	Worthing	L 9-16
15 Oct	ENGLAND XV	Twickenham	L 0-27

Mark Wyatt, the Canadian full-back or fly-half, was top scorer with 35 points (1T, 2C, 8PG, 1DG). MacMillan, Palmer, McGann and MacLean scored a try apiece. Four players played in all five matches (Wyatt, Palmer, Jennings and Fraser); six played in four matches – MacLean, MacMillan, Cvitak, Russell, Strang, Stewart (including one as replacement); Hawthorn was injured in training and did not appear in any match.

MATCH 1 1 October, Portsmouth

Combined Services 14 (2PG 2T) **Canadians 17** (3PG 2T)
Combined Services: R Henderson (RN); D Johnson (Army), D Oakley (RN), P J Warfield (Army) *(capt)*, R Underwood (RAF); M Milburn (RAF), S Worrall (RAF); *No 8* C Christopher (Army); *Second Row* G Wood (Army), J Orwin (RAF), S Peacock (Army), M Sheldon (RN); *Front Row* M Whitcombe (RAF), R Joy (RN), J Hirst (RN)
Scorers *Tries:* Underwood, Sheldon *Penalty Goals:* Milburn, Henderson
Canadians: Wyatt; Palmer, Delaney, Fraser, Forster; Schieffler, MacMillan *(capt)*; *No 8* Stewart; *Second Row* Cvitak, Jennings, Strang, Russell; *Front Row* Breen, Vivian, Murphy *Replacement* A McGann for Delaney (42 mins)
Scorers *Tries:* Palmer, MacMillan *Penalty Goals:* Wyatt (3)
Referee R O P Jones (Wales)

MATCH 2 5 October, Headingley

Headingley 16 (1G 2PG 1T) **Canadians 9** (1G 1PG)
Headingley: D Norton; J Eagle, P Swales, J Mills, G Walker; J Howarth, J Turner; *No 8* M Winterbottom; *Second Row* P J Winterbottom, R France, M Reid, P Barker; *Front Row* A Machell, T Sinclair *(capt)*, P Huntsman
Scorers *Tries:* Eagle, Howarth *Conversion:* Swales *Penalty Goals:* Howarth (2)
Canadians: Wyatt *(capt)*; Palmer, Fraser, McGann, Schieffler; MacLean, Stuart; *No 8* Frame; *Second Row* Russell, Kemp, Jennings, Godziek; *Front Row* Kyle, Spiers, Murphy *Replacement* Stewart for Kemp (half-time)
Scorers *Try:* McGann *Conversion:* Wyatt *Penalty Goal:* Wyatt
Referee T Allen (Scotland)

MATCH 3 8 October, Iffley Road, Oxford

Oxford University 9 (2PG 1DG) **Canadians 16** (1G 1PG 1DG 1T)
Oxford University: H P MacNeill *(capt)*; T S O'Brien, D J Coleman, C J Millerchip, P J Crowe; S Barnes, S J Pearson; *No 8* M F Gargan *Second Row* R Morgan, J Rosier, J B Thomson, M Ashall; *Front Row* N J Herrod, J P Webster, D J Mills *Replacements* C Ewart for Barnes (75 mins) C Horner for Pearson (61 mins)
Scorers *Penalty Goals:* Barnes (2) *Dropped Goal:* O'Brien
Canadians: Wyatt; Palmer, MacLean, Fraser, Jones; Schieffler, MacMillan *(capt)*; *No 8* Stewart; *Second Row* Cvitak, Jennings, Strang, Frame; *Front Row* Breen, Vivian, Dukelow *Replacement* Stuart for MacMillan (20 mins)
Scorers *Tries:* Schieffler, Wyatt *Conversion:* Wyatt *Penalty Goal:* Wyatt *Dropped Goal:* Wyatt
Referee J Fleming (Scotland)

MATCH 4 11 October, Worthing

Sussex 16 (1G 1PG 1DG IT) **Canadians 9** (3PG)
Sussex: R Avery (London Welsh); B McLaughlin (Belfast Colleges), A Short (West London Inst), R Walshaw (East Grinstead), D Harrison (Lewes); P Coackley (Worthing), T Clarke (Worthing); *No 8* D Whiting (Lewes); *Second Row* R Herbie (Crawley), S Purdy (Worthing), M J Colclough (Wasps) *(capt)*, R Pearson (Lewes); *Front Row* T Borthwick (Cambridge U), N Grantham-Hill (Worthing), D Randall (Lewes) *Replacement* P Hornby (Worthing) for Borthwick (59 mins)
Scorers *Tries:* McLaughlin, Walshaw *Conversion:* Coackley *Penalty Goal:* Coackley *Dropped Goal:* Coackley
Canadians: Wyatt; Palmer, Delaney, Fraser, Forster, MacLean, MacMillan *(capt)*; *No 8* Stewart; *Second Row* Russell, Strang, Jennings, Cvitak; *Front Row* Kyle, Godziek, Dukelow

Scorers *Penalty Goals:* Wyatt (3)
Referee A W Bevan (Wales)

MATCH 5 15 October, Twickenham

ENGLAND XV 27 (3G 3PG) CANADA 0

The weather for this international at Twickenham was a foul combination of a strong, sometimes gale-force wind and driving rain and the fact that England and Canada provided such an enjoyable match was enormously to their credit, even though frequent mistakes robbed the proceedings of continuity. England gave a worthy if hardly brilliant performance. They kept grinding Canada down in the forwards, especially in the scrum. They also made brave attempts to run the ball to entertain the crowd when they could have been forgiven for kicking the leather off it.

Yet Canada played heroically. Deprived of some leading players through unavailability and injury they were expected to concede a cricket score but in fact were desperately unlucky to lose by the margin they did. It was only the brilliant goal-kicking of Dusty Hare which allowed England to pull away. Despite the wind and rain, Hare put over three penalty goals and three conversions from his six kicks – a marvellous exhibition of his talents.

There was further misfortune for Canada on one occasion when Slemen was caught in possession and Palmer hacked on the loose ball. The Canadian appeared to win the race for the touchdown and subsequent replays on television proved his contention that he should have been awarded a well-deserved try. But the referee ruled otherwise. Seconds later, Canada's other wing, Cliff Jones, narrowly failed to reach a ball rolling into touch-in-goal so the visitors' hopes of opening their account were finally dashed. But the brave efforts on the day of Cvitak, Russell and Godziek in their back row will long be remembered.

England scored three tries, two in the first half. The first was a penalty try, awarded when Canada collapsed the scrum near their own line with the England pack pushing forward. Skilful interpassing between Winterbottom, Youngs and Syddall sent Youngs over for the second try. A powerful drive from a tap penalty saw Winterbottom add a second-half try. Hare's three conversions and three penalty goals completed the scoring picture.

ENGLAND: W H Hare (Leicester); J Carleton (Orrell), P W Dodge (Leicester), S J Halliday (Bath), M A C Slemen (Liverpool); G H Davies (Wasps), N G Youngs (Leicester); *No 8* J P Scott (Cardiff); *Second Row* J D Gadd (Gloucester), J P Syddall (Waterloo), S Bainbridge (Gosforth), P J Winterbottom (Headingley); *Front Row* G S Pearce (Northampton), P J Wheeler (Leicester) *(capt)*, P A G Rendall (Wasps) *Replacement* N C Stringer (Wasps) for Carleton (41 mins)
Scorers *Tries:* Youngs, Winterbottom, penalty try *Conversions:* Hare (3)
Penalty Goals: Hare (3)
CANADA: Wyatt, Palmer, Delaney, Fraser, Jones; MacLean, MacMillan *(capt)*; *No 8* Russell; *Second Row* Cvitak, Jennings, Strang, Godziek; *Front Row* Breen, Vivian, Dukelow
Referee W Jones (Wales)

AUSTRALIA TO FRANCE 1983

Bob Donahue *International Herald Tribune*

Two ambitious sides struggling to achieve control – ball control, tactical control, self-control – but never really succeeding: this was the impression left by a Test series that disappointed Australia. Nevertheless, the Australians' 1983 tour to France was considerably more successful than their previous visit seven years earlier. In 1976, Geoff Shaw's tourists won only three of eight matches in France, losing five; the points tally was 98 for and 148 against, including a 34-6 Test defeat in Paris. This time the nine-match tally was four won, two drawn and three lost, with 135 points for and 150 against. The French margin in Paris was a mere nine points. If the preliminaries in Italy are included – defeats of Italy 'B', 26-0, and of Italy, 29-7 – the tour's full record becomes six victories and two draws in 11 matches, with 190 points for and 157 against.

From the French point of view, the tourists were notable for their strength in defence and a surprising failure to score tries. (They were outdone in this department, scoring 15 tries to 16 by French sides.) France had looked forward to an exciting Test series. After all, was not Bob Dwyer, the touring coach, an eloquent advocate of running rugby? When the first Test proved a sterile disappointment, President Albert Ferrasse berated both sides at the dinner. Sure enough, the Parc des Princes six days later was less than half full, despite the presence of thousands of non-paying schoolboy guests. Captain Mark Ella and coach Dwyer expressed regret, at the end, for having cramped their style, but it was clear that they did not have much choice. An extraordinary 36-6 defeat (six tries to nil) in Agen three days before the first Test determined what followed.

The Australians' victory in their first match, at Strasbourg against a powerful selection, earned them immediate respect. The draw against French Police could be attributed to refereeing decisions, but an emphatic victory in Grenoble confirmed the tourists' strength. They were upset in Perpignan, as sometimes happens on tour. But then came the traumatic rout in Agen.

Back row forwards Roche, Tuynman and Poidevin ultimately made the principal mark. Campese was the leading scorer with 43 points in eight matches in France. Mark Ella and Roche appeared in seven matches. Dwyer opined that with such pace it was a wonder France were ever defeated by anyone. Yet when the tourists let their hair down in Toulon against the French Barbarians, a thrilling match produced eight tries and a final victory for an Australian squad that clearly had much to offer.

THE TOURING PARTY

Captain M G Ella **Manager** Dr C Wilson
Assistant Manager R Dwyer

FULL-BACKS

R G Gould (Queensland)
Glen J Ella (New South Wales)

THREEQUARTERS

D I Campese (Australian Capital Territory)
B J Moon (Queensland)
R G Hanley (Queensland)
Gary A Ella (New South Wales)
M J Hawker (New South Wales)
A G Slack (Queensland)

HALF-BACKS

M G Ella (New South Wales)
M P Lynagh (Queensland)
***T A Lane** (Queensland)
A J Parker (Queensland)
D Vaughan (Queensland)

FORWARDS

J Coolican (New South Wales)
O B Hall (New South Wales)
M A Harding (New South Wales)
A J McIntyre (Queensland)
T Lawton (Queensland)
M I McBain (Queensland)
***R Crerar** (New South Wales)
S A Cutler (New South Wales)
D W Hillhouse (Queensland)
N C Holt (Queensland)
S A Williams (New South Wales)
J S Miller (Queensland)
S P Poidevin (New South Wales)
C Roche (Queensland)
D Hall (Queensland)
S N Tuynman (New South Wales)

**Replacement during tour*

TOUR RECORD

All matches Played 9 Won 4 Drawn 2 Lost 3 Points for 135 Against 150
International matches Played 2 Drawn 1 Lost 1 Points for 21 Against 30

MATCH DETAILS

1983	OPPONENTS	VENUE	RESULTS
26 Oct	French Selection	Strasbourg	W 18-16
29 Oct	French Police	Le Creusot	D 15-15
1 Nov	French Selection	Grenoble	W 27-7
5 Nov	French Selection	Perpignan	L 9-15
9 Nov	French Selection	Agen	L 6-36
13 Nov	FRANCE	Clermont-Ferrand	D 15-15
16 Nov	French Army	La Rochelle	W 16-10
19 Nov	FRANCE	Paris	L 6-15
23 Nov	French Barbarians	Toulon	W 23-21

MATCH 1 26 October, Strasbourg

French Selection 16 (1G 2PG 1T) **Australian XV 18** (2G 1PG 1DG)
French Selection: J-B Lafond; J Bégu, L Pardo, P Mothe, P Lagisquet; J-P Lescarboura, J Gallion; *No 8* E Champ; *Second Row* L Rodriguez, A Lorieux, J-P Wolff, E Buchet; *Front Row* P Ondarts, C Rizon, M Cremaschi
Replacements T Janeczek for Champ (21 mins), P-E Detrez for Rodriguez (41 mins)
Scorers *Tries:* Lafond, Pardo *Conversion:* Lescarboura
Penalty Goals: Mothe, Lescarboura
Australian XV: Gould; Campese, Gary Ella, Hawker, Hanley; M Ella *(capt)*, Parker; *No 8* Tuynman; *Second Row* Poidevin, Williams, Holt, Roche; *Front Row* McIntyre, Lawton, Coolican

Scorers *Tries:* Gary Ella, Hanley *Conversions:* Campese (2)
Penalty Goal: Campese *Dropped Goal:* Gould
Referee Y Bressy (Provence)

MATCH 2 29 October, Le Creusot

French Police 15 (5PG) **Australian XV 15** (1G 3PG)
French Police: T Ponel; D Porte, A Poujade, P Rougé-Thomas, G Portherat; P Mathias, P Ferrer; *No 8* D Erbani; *Second Row* J Gorgues, J-M Salvatge, C Bonnet, Y Allègre; *Front Row* J Bravo, C Prax *(capt),* J Brugiroux
Replacement D Athanase for Brugiroux (17 mins)
Scorer *Penalty Goals:* Mathias (5)
Australian XV: Glen Ella; Campese, Gary Ella, Hanley, Slack; Lynagh, Vaughan; *No 8* D Hall; *Second Row* Miller, Hillhouse, Holt, Roche; *Front Row* Harding, Lawton, O Hall
Scorers *Try:* D Hall *Conversion:* Lynagh *Penalty Goals:* Lynagh (3)
Referee G Maurette (Limousin)

MATCH 3 1 November, Grenoble

French Selection 7 (1DG 1T) **Australian XV 27** (4G 1PG)
French Selection: B Viviès; T Perrin, P Chadebech, P Mesny, S Malosse; D Camberabero, G Camberabero; *No 8* F Pepelnjak *(capt); Second Row* O Derghali, J-J Santos, P Occhini, B Delbreil; *Front Row* D Dubroca, B Gallion, J-M Romand
Replacement M Viatge for Derghali (52 mins)
Scorers *Try:* Malosse *Dropped Goal:* Viviès
Australian XV: Gould; Campese, Gary Ella, Hawker, Hanley; M Ella *(capt)*, Vaughan; *No 8* Tuynman; *Second Row* Poidevin, Williams, Hillhouse, Miller; *Front Row* McIntyre, McBain, O Hall *Replacement* Slack for Gould (78 mins)
Scorers *Tries:* Miller, M Ella, Gary Ella, Poidevin *Conversions:* Campese (4)
Penalty Goal: Campese
Referee O Doyle (Ireland)

MATCH 4 5 November, Perpignan

French Selection 15 (1G 3PG) **Australian XV 9** (1G 1PG)
French Selection: S Gabernet; D Bustaffa, P Fort, J-C Bourret, G Paulo; J-P Trille, G Ramon; *No 8* C Atcher; *Second Row* P Lacans *(capt)*, J-F Campredon, P Salas, T Janeczek; *Front Row* J-P Garuet, A Noguera, P-E Detrez
Replacement D Sanchez for Noguera (41 mins)
Scorers *Try:* Bourret *Conversion:* Trille *Penalty Goals:* Trille (3)
Australian XV: Glen Ella; Campese, Slack, Hawker, Moon; M Ella *(capt)*, Parker; *No 8* D Hall; *Second Row* Poidevin, Williams, Cutler, Roche; *Front Row* Harding, McBain, Coolican
Scorers *Try:* Coolican *Conversion:* Campese *Penalty Goal:* Campese
Referee J B Anderson (Scotland)

MATCH 5 9 November, Agen

French Selection 36 (3G 2PG 3T) **Australian XV 6** (2PG)
French Selection: J-M Lescure; J Bégu, P Perrier, P Barbotteau, B Lavigne; C Delage, J-P Sarrade *(capt); No 8* F Rongiéras; *Second Row* J Gratton, P Pujade, A Maleig, M Tonon; *Front Row* J-E Garat, C Rizon, J-L Tolot
Replacements B Delbreil for Tonon (65 mins), P Faget for Lavigne (71 mins)

Scorers *Tries:* Perrier (2), Lavigne (2), Barbotteau, Rizon *Conversions:* Lescure (3)
Penalty Goals: Lescure (2)
Australian XV: Glen Ella; Hanley, Slack, Gary Ella, Moon; Lynagh, Vaughan; *No 8* D Hall *(capt)*; *Second Row* Miller, Holt, Cutler, Tuynman; *Front Row* McIntyre, Lawton, O Hall *Replacement* M Ella for Lynagh (2 mins)
Scorer *Penalty Goals:* M Ella (2)
Referee R Hourquet (Provence)

MATCH 6 13 November, Clermont-Ferrand 1st International

FRANCE 15 (3PG 2DG) **AUSTRALIA 15** (1G 1PG 2DG)

The tireless Roche, scorer of the day's only try, later compared this match to a fiercely physical chess game – the tourists earned the draw with superior wit. In overcast but dry conditions, Australian pressure and spoiling nullified a superior French shove, made a lie of statistical parity in the line-out and prevailed at most of the breakdowns. Add memorable defence against seemingly triumphant French attacking in the first and last quarters, and it was left to kickers to settle matters. Seven men took 22 kicks at goal, not to mention incessant Australian up-and-unders and deep line-kicking by both sides.

Mark Ella's dropped goal after three minutes was offset by two Lescarboura penalty goals and a dropped goal by Lafond, but erratic finishing prevented France from breaking away. Instead, Campese narrowed the gap with his penalty goal just after the half-hour, and Roche's pounce-across try from a Hawker up-and-under, plus Campese's conversion, put Australia in the lead two minutes after the interval, 12-9.

Australia wheeled the French scrummage first one way and then the other. Rives' defence on Mark Ella was countered by having Hawker do the tactical kicking for Australia. Lescarboura replied at the end of the third quarter with a penalty goal followed immediately by a 51-metre dropped goal, but the quick-thinking Hawker, salvaging a mis-pass from Vaughan under pressure behind the scrum, stabbed a low-flying drop between the posts to even the score for good after 26 minutes. Australia had been absent in attack but present indeed in the gritty frustration of French ambitions.

FRANCE: J-B Lafond; P Lagisquet, P Sella, D Cordorniou, P Estève; J-P Lescarboura, J Gallion; *No 8* J-L Joinel; *Second Row* D Erbani, J-C Orso, J Condom, J-P Rives *(capt)*; *Front Row* J-P Garuet, P Dintrans, M Cremaschi
Replacements B Viviès for Lafond (42 mins), L Pardo for Viviès (78 mins)
Scorers *Penalty Goals:* Lescarboura (3) *Dropped Goals:* Lafond, Lescarboura
AUSTRALIA: Gould; Campese, Gary Ella, Hawker, Moon; M Ella *(capt)*, Vaughan; *No 8* Tuynman; *Second Row* Poidevin, Williams, Hillhouse, Roche;
Front Row McIntyre, McBain, Coolican *Replacement* Lawton for McBain (79 mins)
Scorers *Try:* Roche *Conversion:* Campese *Penalty Goal:* Campese
Dropped Goals: M Ella, Hawker
Referee G Harrison (New Zealand)

MATCH 7 16 November, La Rochelle

French Army 10 (1PG 1DG 1T) **Australian XV 16** (1G 1PG 1DG 1T)
French Army: J-M Magre; J Audabram, F Uthurry, P Séguret, L Sarraméa; D Camberabero, H Sanz; *No 8* K Janik; *Second Row* L Cabannes, W Pepelnjak, J Fourtane, M Delpoux; *Front Row* C Genton, D Pourpoint, L Armary
Replacement S Doumayrou for Janik (66 mins)
Scorers *Try:* Cabannes *Penalty Goal:* Camberabero *Dropped Goal:* Camberabero
Australian XV: Gould; Campese, Slack, Glen Ella, Hanley; Lane, Parker; *No 8* D Hall *(capt)*; *Second Row* Miller, Cutler, Holt, Roche; *Front Row* Harding, Lawton, O Hall
Scorers *Tries:* Gould, Glen Ella *Conversion:* Campese *Penalty Goal:* Campese *Dropped Goal:* Lane
Referee J-C Doulcet (Limousin)

MATCH 8 19 November, Paris 2nd International

FRANCE 15 (1G 3PG) **AUSTRALIA 6** (1PG 1DG)

This time Australia were outplayed at forward. Yet the scoring pattern looked for a long time like a re-run of the first Test: a mere three-point advantage for France at half-time despite lopsided territorial advantage, then an Australian come-back promptly after the interval when Mark Ella's dropped goal evened the score at 6-6. Again France soon restored a narrow lead (through Gabernet's penalty goal midway through the third quarter after a late tackle by Campese on Lescarboura), and again a late dropped goal threatened to secure a draw. But Gould and Mark Ella both missed. A converted try in injury time ultimately padded the French margin.

Whether that margin flattered France or Australia was debatable. All told, France spent more than an hour in Australia's half. The wheel was countered and French scrummage possession was clean. France won the rucks and mauls by a margin of more than two to one. Campese made good only once in four penalty attempts; but Lescarboura and Gabernet failed with six attempted dropped goals. Try-scoring opportunities created by the French outnumbered Australia's by more than three to one.

Gallion, Rives, Dintrans, Erbani, Codorniou and Sella came close to setting up tries in a torrid first half. Australia, looking episodically like the galloping Wallabies that the French had awaited, ran the ball with some success in the second half, but possession was lacking. As in Clermont-Ferrand, expert defences neutralised each other.

So it was that more than 160 minutes of Test rugby passed by before France's first and only try of the series brought a roar resembling a great sigh from the half-empty Parc des Princes. Behind a scrum on the left 40 metres out, Codorniou executed Rives' signal to scoot to the tight side while Lescarboura and Gabernet ran in diversion on the right, and Gallion's service to the centre was true. Codorniou straightened his run, half-drew Tuynman and Campese and flicked the ball leftward to Estève on the burst. With Gould yet to beat, the winger slackened his

Mark Ella, the Australian captain, who did his best to inspire Australia during their tour of mixed success to France.

pace, then accelerated outside the full-back and rounded yet another Wallaby before touching down. Lescarboura converted. Australia had undeniably lost a Test series that France barely won.

FRANCE: S Gabernet; P Lagisquet, P Sella, D Codorniou, P Estève; J-P Lescarboura, J Gallion; *No 8* J-L Joinel; *Second Row* D Erbani, J Condom, A Lorieux, J-P Rives *(capt)*; *Front Row* J-P Garuet, P Dintrans, M Cremaschi
Replacement P-E Detrez for Cremaschi (40 mins)
Scorers *Try:* Estève *Conversion:* Lescarboura
Penalty Goals: Lescarboura (2), Gabernet
AUSTRALIA: Gould; Campese, Gary Ella, Hawker, Moon; M Ella *(capt)*, Vaughan; *No 8* Tuynman; *Second Row* Poidevin, Williams, Hillhouse, Roche;
Front Row McIntyre, Lawton, Coolican
Scorers *Penalty Goal:* Campese *Dropped Goal:* M Ella
Referee G Harrison (New Zealand)

MATCH 9 23 November, Toulon

French Barbarians 21 (1G 1DG 3T) **Australian XV 23** (2G 1PG 2T)
French Barbarians: C Uthurriscq (Bayonne); P Sella (Agen), P Barbotteau (Angoulême), L Pardo (Montferrand), B Lavigne (Agen); G Laporte (Graulhet), P Elissalde (La Rochelle); *No 8* P Coulais (Toulon); *Second Row* J F Slattery (Blackrock College, Dublin), J-C Orso (Nice), J Condom (Le Boucau) J-P Rives (Racing Club de France); *Front Row* R Paparemborde (Racing Club de France) *(capt)*, P Dintrans (Tarbes), P-E Detrez (Nîmes) *Replacement* P Lacans (Béziers) for Rives (68 mins)
Scorers *Tries:* Rives, Sella, Barbotteau, Coulais *Conversion:* Laporte
Dropped Goal: Laporte
Australian XV: Glen Ella; Campese, Slack, Lane, Moon; M Ella *(capt)*, Parker; *No 8* D Hall; *Second Row* Poidevin, Williams, Hillhouse, Roche;
Front Row Harding, Crerar, Coolican
Scorers *Tries:* M Ella, Glen Ella, Slack (2) *Conversions:* Campese (2)
Penalty Goal: Campese
Referee M Puget (Limousin)

ARGENTINA TO AUSTRALIA 1983

Jim Woodward *Sydney Daily Telegraph*

Having been trounced by Argentina in the first international of a series in Buenos Aires in 1979, Australia were entitled to feel apprehensive when the Argentine captain, Hugo Porta, brought his Pumas 'down under' for the first time. That bleak day in Buenos Aires had seen Porta contribute 16 of his team's points from a penalty goal, two conversions and three dropped goals under pressure which had to be seen to be believed.

The Wallabies managed to square that series with a 17-12 win in the second Test, but only after hooker Billy Ross won a tight head in front of the Australian posts as the crowd chanted Porta's name in expectation of a clinching dropped goal.

Some of Australia's worst fears seemed to have been realised when, in the Pumas' opening game of the 1983 tour, Porta scored 15 points from a try, two penalty goals, a dropped goal and a conversion in Argentina's 19-7 defeat of New South Wales at the Sydney Cricket Ground.

However, when the tour was over Porta was judged not to have played the dominating role expected of him, and the Pumas, too, ultimately disappointed. True, Porta topped the tour's point-scoring aggregate with 79 points from the six games he played, but with injury, then lack of form, preventing the exciting and free-running Martin Sansot from playing full-back in the Tests, the Argentine back line did not warm to Porta's influence. Instead massive forward power, some of which had been seen earlier in Argentina, became the hallmark of the touring team.

Following the victory over a strong New South Wales side, the Argentine management decided to rest key players from the game against Australian Capital Territory in Canberra – in theory an easy game. But despite Porta contributing his team's nine points, Australian Capital Territory went on a six-try rampage to win 35-9. Coach Rudolfo O'Reilly did not experiment again and followed the Canberra debacle with a 34-28 win over Australia's provincial champions, Queensland, at Ballymore Park.

The visitors' international 'shake down' match against NSW Country in remote Narrabri resulted in a nine-try, 46-3 romp. For the Test, Sansot, injured in a collision with Wallaby Brendan Moon during the Queensland game, had to concede his place to Bernardo Miguens. But the Argentines' power lay in the pack. Although he was aware of the strength in the Pumas' forwards, Australian coach Bob Dwyer had no way of knowing exactly what lay ahead. In the event, the visitors' pack embarrassed Australia, with both tries coming from massive shoves against the head. After the first pushover try the Ballymore turf looked as though it had been raked by a plough as Australian skid-marks lay etched for all to see.

Porta took his team north to play Queensland Country in Townsville and although outscored by three tries to one, the Argentines comfortably defeated the home XV 22-12. Porta landed five penalty goals and a dropped goal.

With veteran loose-head prop John Meadows back in the Australian front row for the second Test, Argentine tight-head Enrique Rodriguez found himself unable to wreak the same havoc as in the first international. This time the Australian scrum stood firm and the home side managed to forge a 6-3 advantage.

Suddenly the whole complexion of the game changed when Welsh referee Clive Norling raced to the Argentine goal-posts and signalled a penalty try. An Australian movement had broken down, but there seemed no way a probable try had in any way been prevented by an Argentine offence.

Radio and TV commentators, including former champion half-back Ken Catchpole, were at a loss to explain Norling's decision. Unfortunately, Norling afterwards locked himself away instead of coming to the dressing-room door and explaining his decision to a bewildered press corps.

The try was the end of the road for the Pumas. They lost concentration as Australia ran in another four tries to win 29-13. Although to draw a series against a Board member country while on tour is a proud achievement, the Argentinians were not happy with their end result. Norling certainly didn't help them but to blame him entirely would be foolish. Perhaps the greatest failure of the tour was Porta's in not capitalising on available possession.

Matching Australia's back line brilliance is an awesome task but Porta seemed to have lost that little extra which had stamped him as one of the world's great fly-halves. Not so long ago Porta made the comment that he would retire on his own terms rather than set an advance date. As the 1983 Pumas left for home, it looked as though that time may not be far away.

THE TOURING PARTY

Captain H Porta **Manager** E Yanguella
Assistant Manager R O'Reilly

FULL-BACKS

M Sansot (Pueyrredón)
D Baetti (Rosario)
B Miguens (Club Universitario, Buenos Aires)

THREEQUARTERS

M Campo (Pueyrredón)
J Palma (Pucara)
R Madero (San Isidro Club)
M H Loffreda (San Isidro Club)
F Moran (Pucara)
G Varone (CA San Isidro)

HALF-BACKS

A Soares Gache (San Isidro Club)
M Larrubia (CA San Isidro)
H Porta (Banco Nación)

FORWARDS

B Minguez (Mar del Plata SC)
E Ure (Club Universitario, Buenos Aires)
R De Vedia (San Isidro Club)
C Neyra (Alumni)
T Petersen (San Isidro Club)
G T Travaglini (CA San Isidro)
G Milano (Jockey Club, Rosario)
E Branca (CA San Isidro)
E E Rodriguez (El Tala, Cordoba)
F Morel (CA San Isidro)
P Devoto (CA San Isidro)
S Dengra (San Martin)
J Baeck (Pueyrredón)
A Courreges (CA San Isidro)

TOUR RECORD

All matches Played 7 Won 5 Lost 2 Points for 161 Against 117
International matches Played 2 Won 1 Lost 1 Points for 31 Against 32

SCORING DETAILS

All matches

For:	19T	11C	15PG	6DG	161 Pts
Against:	18T*	9C	9PG	—	117 Pts

**Includes one penalty try*

International matches

For:	3T	2C	3PG	2DG	31 Pts
Against:	5T*	3C	2PG	—	32 Pts

MATCH DETAILS

1983	OPPONENTS	VENUE	RESULTS
16 July	New South Wales	Sydney	W 19-7
20 July	Australian Capital Territory	Canberra	L 9-35
24 July	Queensland	Brisbane	W 34-28
27 July	NSW Country	Narrabri	W 46-3
31 July	AUSTRALIA	Brisbane	W 18-3
3 August	Queensland Country	Townsville	W 22-12
7 August	AUSTRALIA	Sydney	L 13-29

Hugo Porta was top scorer for the tour with 79 points from a try, six conversisons, 15 penalty goals and six dropped goals in six appearances.

MATCH 1 16 July, Sydney

New South Wales 7 (1PG 1T) **Argentine XV 19** (1G 2PG 1DG 1T)
New South Wales *Try:* M Hawker *Penalty Goal:* Glen Ella
Argentine XV *Tries:* Porta, Palma *Conversion:* Porta *Penalty Goals:* Porta (2) *Dropped Goal:* Porta

MATCH 2 20 July, Canberra

Australian Capital Territory 35 (4G 1PG 2T) **Argentine XV 9** (2PG 1DG)
Australian Capital Territory *Tries:* D Campese (2), B Girvan, P McGrath, L Galvin, P O'Neill *Conversions:* D Campese (4) *Penalty Goal:* D Campese
Argentine XV *Penalty Goals:* Porta (2) *Dropped Goal:* Porta

MATCH 3 24 July, Brisbane

Queensland 28 (2G 4PG 1T) **Argentine XV 34** (3G 3PG 1DG 1T)
Queensland *Tries:* A Slack, M Lynagh, C Roche *Conversions:* M Lynagh (2) *Penalty Goals:* M Lynagh (3) *Dropped Goal:* M Lynagh
Argentine XV *Tries:* Campo (2), Minguez, Milano *Conversions:* Porta (3) *Penalty Goals:* Porta (3) *Dropped Goal:* Porta

MATCH 4 27 July, Narrabri

NSW Country 3 (1PG) **Argentine XV 46** (5G 4T)
NSW Country *Penalty Goal:* R Mercer
Argentine XV *Tries:* Madero (2), Campo (2), Baeck, Minguez, Ure, Loffreda, Varone
Conversions: Loffreda (5)

MATCH 5 31 July, Ballymore Park, Brisbane 1st International

AUSTRALIA 3 (1PG) **ARGENTINA 18** (2G 1PG 1DG)

With his confidence boosted by the nine-try 49-3 demolition of the United States a couple of weeks previously at the Sydney Cricket Ground, Australian coach Bob Dwyer confidently predicted that Argentina would have trouble in the first international against the Pumas in Brisbane. 'Collectively, they are a fast team, but I doubt if they have the pace of some of our men', Dwyer said before the Test match. 'I think that the Argentinians haven't ever in their lives been confronted with a game as fast as ours', he added.

That theory may well have held good but for one major factor that Dwyer had overlooked – possession. The Pumas simply smothered the Australian forwards with two massive eight-man shoves which brought tries and added two goals to the visitors' total. On the first occasion, the Australian scrum disintegrated, leaving deep skid-marks on the turf as a testimony to the shove which resulted in a breakaway try to Tomas Petersen. A second such try in the second half was not quite as embarrassing for the Australian forwards, but was just as effective, with No 8 Buenaventura Minguez getting the score.

Skipper Hugo Porta, as well as converting both tries, added a penalty goal and an almost inevitable dropped goal to complete Australia's humiliation. All the Australians could manage in reply was a penalty goal by David Campese, who had missed three attempts in the first half. The strong man of Argentina's scrum was tight-head prop Enrique Rodriguez, who was adjudged a legal scrummager despite Australian claims that he was boring.

AUSTRALIA: R G Gould (Queensland); D I Campese (Australian Capital Territory), A G Slack (Queensland), M J Hawker (NSW), B J Moon (Queensland); M G Ella (NSW) *(capt)*, D Vaughan (NSW); *No 8* D Codey (NSW); *Second Row* S P Poidevin (NSW), C Roche (Queensland), D W Hillhouse (Queensland), D Hall (Queensland); *Front Row* D J Curran (NSW), W S Ross (Queensland), S Pilecki (Queensland)
Replacement A J Parker (Queensland) for Vaughan
Scorers *Penalty Goal:* Campese

ARGENTINE: Miguens; Palma, Loffreda, Madero, Campo; Porta *(capt)*, Soares, Gache; *No 8* Minguez; *Second Row* Ure, Petersen, Milano, Branca;
Front Row Rodriguez, Courreges, Dengra
Scorers *Tries:* Petersen, Minguez *Conversions:* Porta (2) *Penalty Goal:* Porta
Dropped Goal: Porta
Referee C Norling (Wales)

MATCH 6 7 August, Townsville

Queensland Country 12 (3T) **Argentine XV** 22 (5PG 1DG 1T)
Queensland Country *Tries:* M Smee, S Wohler, R Burness
Argentine XV *Try:* Larrubia *Penalty Goals:* Porta (5) *Dropped Goal:* Porta

MATCH 7 7 August, Sydney Cricket Ground 2nd International

AUSTRALIA 29 (3G *1PG 2T) **ARGENTINA** 13 (2PG 1DG 1T)
(**includes one penalty try*)

Australian selectors made seven changes but dropped only tight-head prop Declan Curran as they sought to square the series. The old firm of Stan Pilecki and John Meadows was re-established in an effort to match the Pumas' props. Three changes were made because of injury with the other alterations being positional. Australian pride had been severely dented in the first Test; but it was never going to be easy and Australia had to work hard to establish a 6-3 advantage.

Suddenly they were sent a gift from heaven. Full-back David Campese made one of his electrifying bursts up the sideline before passing to skipper Mark Ella, who carried on until Petersen and Gache converged on him. Ella transferred to breakaway Simon Poideven who failed to take the pass cleanly, and the movement broke down. To the Pumas' horror Welsh referee Clive Norling raced straight between the posts and signalled a penalty try. He later refused to discuss his reason. Afterwards players from both sides and rival coaches could not explain Norling's actions. Argentine coach Rodolfo O'Reilly had reason to be the most bitter man at the ground, 'I don't understand the penalty try – one invention for the showman', he said in reference to Norling.

This score clearly knocked the wind out of the Pumas' sails and Australia went on to finish with four more tries. Porta tried his best to keep Argentina in sight with two penalty goals and a dropped goal, but Campese hit back with three conversions and a penalty goal. The Australian pack had been overwhelmed by the Argentine in Brisbane, but this time the home forwards did not give an inch. A measure of their improvement came close to half-time when, after four feeds to two scrums, the Pumas' pack never looked like repeating a pushover try.

AUSTRALIA: D I Campese (Australian Capital Territory); P C Grigg (Queensland), A G Slack (Queensland), M U Hawker (NSW), B J Moon (Queensland); M G Ella (NSW) *(capt)*, A J Parker (Queensland); *No 8* D Hall (Queensland); *Second row* S P Poidevin (NSW), S A Williams (NSW), D W Hillhouse (Queensland); *Front Row* C Roche (Queensland), S J Pilecki (Queensland), W S Ross (Queensland), J E C Meadows (Queensland)
Scorers *Tries:* Moon (2), Roche, Campese, penalty try *Conversions:* Campese (3) *Penalty Goal:* Campese

ARGENTINA: Miguens; Palma, Loffreda, Madero, Campo; Porta *(capt)*, Soares, Gache; *No 8* Minguez; *Second Row* Ure, Milano, Branca, Petersen; *Front Row* Rodriguez, Courreges, Dengra
Scorers *Try:* Milano *Penalty Goals:* Porta (2) *Dropped Goal:* Porta
Referee C Norling (Wales)

WALES TO SPAIN 1983

Robert Cole Western Mail

Many people scoffed at the Welsh for opting to tour one of the weaker countries, but despite the one-sided nature of the matches it proved a highly valuable experience for the party and the coach, John Bevan. As the British Lions required only eight Welshmen, the Welsh team that flew to Spain contained 12 internationals and a host of young talent. Six of the players blooded on the tour went on to win full caps in the 1984 season.

Before the tour, John Bevan said he wanted to find out who were the second and third best players in each position in his squad, and if nothing else the Spanish trip helped him to do that. He worked his players extremely hard and was rewarded with some fine displays. During the daily training sessions Bevan was able to put over his attacking philosophy and his young back division picked up his ideas enthusiastically. From this tour should spring a new, more adventurous Welsh attitude in the next few seasons. Indeed, the results of Bevan's attacking policy were evident in the 1984 International Championship.

South Wales Police fly-half Bleddyn Bowen was coaxed into a successful switch into the centre, where he formed a devastatingly skilful partnership with Cardiff's Mark Ring. Set up by the deft touches of Welsh fly-half Malcolm Dacey they became the tour's brightest stars and the Spaniards could find no answer to them. Left wing Adrian Hadley scored seven tries in his three appearances and was left out of the international side in Madrid only through lack of experience.

The tour began in northern Spain, where the party had a week's preparation before tackling a Basque XV. There were a few hiccups along the way – prop Gareth John cut his knee badly in a training accident and the game was allowed to go ahead only after the Guernica pitch had been cleared of stones and completely covered with sand and soil – but the Welsh side were off to a winning start. The Basque XV certainly made Wales work for victory and, in front of a crowd of 5,000, they put up a great fight. French international Laurent Pardo was the leading light in the Basque team, but the Welsh pack contained six full caps and proved too strong for them. The side continued to improve in the second game against the Spanish under-23 team. Six tries in that match set the Welshmen on the try-scoring trail for the rest of the tour. The 83 points and 15 tries scored against Castille/Leon were both record totals for a Welsh representative side, beating the previous best 82 points and 14 tries against Japan in Tokyo in 1975. The Welsh followed this with another 13 tries in their 71-point defeat of Valencia.

For the 'international' in Madrid, Hadley was kept out by the old firm wing pairing of Clive and Elgan Rees, Ray Giles upstaged Mark Douglas for the scrum-half berth and Cardiff's loose head prop, Jeff Whitefoot, confirmed his rapid rise by ousting the experienced Clive Williams. It was Ring who stole the show with 23 points, but the gallant Spaniards, whose tackling was one of their best features, hit back with some enterprising play and managed three tries.

A severe hamstring strain caused South Wales Police centre Richard Donovan to miss every match, although the management decided not to send for a replacement. Elgan Rees, too, suffered – with a kidney stone. It stopped him from playing in one of the games, but he recovered in time to play in the final two.

THE TOURING PARTY

Captain E T Butler **Manager** R H Williams
Coach J Bevan

FULL-BACK

H Davies (Bridgend)

THREEQUARTERS

C F W Rees (London Welsh)
H E Rees (Neath)
A M Hadley (Cardiff)
P Hopkins (Llanelli)
R Donovan (South Wales Police)
M Ring (Cardiff)

HALF-BACKS

M Dacey (Swansea)
B Bowen (South Wales Police)
R Giles (Aberavon)
M H J Douglas (Llanelli)

FORWARDS

C Williams (Swansea)
J Whitefoot (Cardiff)
I H Eidman (Cardiff)
G John (Swansea)
W James (Aberavon)
K Townley (Llanelli)
T Shaw (Newbridge)
S J Perkins (Pontypool)
R D Moriarty (Swansea)
G Roberts (Swansea)
M Davies (Swansea)
C Dennehy (Ebbw Vale)
J Thomas (Maesteg)
E T Butler (Pontypool)

TOUR RECORD

All matches Played 5 Won 5 Lost 0 Points for 275 Against 28

SCORING DETAILS

All matches

For: 51T 31C 2PG 1DG 275 Pts Against: 3T 2C 4PG 28 Pts

MATCH DETAILS

1983	OPPONENTS	VENUE	RESULTS
14 May	Basque Country XV	Guernica	W 24-3
17 May	Spain Under-23	Gijon	W 32-6
21 May	Castille/Leon XV	Valladolid	W 83-3
25 May	Valencia Select XV	Valencia	W 71-0
29 May	SPAIN	Madrid	W 65-16

Howell Davies was the only player to play in all of the five games and was the top points-scorer on the tour with 43. Mark Ring scored 39 points and his Cardiff club-mate Adrian Hadley was top try-scorer with 7 in three appearances.

MATCH 1 14 May, Guernica

Basque Country XV 3 (1PG) **Wales XV 24** (2G 3T)
Basque Country *Penalty Goal:* Javier Diaz Paternain
Wales XV *Tries:* Elgan Rees (2), Clive Rees, Hopkins, Dacey
Conversions: Howell Davies (2)
Team: Davies; E Rees, Ring, Hopkins, C Rees; Dacey, Giles; *No 8* Butler *(capt)*; *Second Row* Dennehy, Perkins, Moriarty, Davies; *Front Row* Williams, Townley, Eidman

MATCH 2 17 May, Gijon

Spain Under-23 6 (2PG) **Wales XV 32** (4G 2T)
Spain Under 23 *Penalty Goals:* Luis Nunez (2)
Wales XV *Tries:* Hopkins (2), James, Roberts, Hadley, Whitefoot
Conversions: Howell Davies (3), Ring
Team: Davies; Rees, Hopkins, Ring, Hadley; Bowen, Douglas; *No 8* Thomas; *Second Row* Dennehy, Moriarty, Shaw, Roberts; *Front Row* Whitefoot, James *(capt)*, Eidman

MATCH 3 21 May, Valladolid

Castille/Leon XV 3 (1PG) **Wales XV 83** (10G 1PG 5T)
Castille/Leon XV *Penalty Goal:* Francisco Lebrato
Wales XV *Tries:* Roberts (3), Hadley (3), Howell Davies (2), Dacey (2), Bowen, Butler, James, Mark Davies, Douglas *Conversions:* Howell Davies (5), Bowen (5)
Penalty Goal: Howell Davies
Team: Davies; Hadley, Bowen, Hopkins, C Rees; Dacey, Douglas; *No 8* Butler *(capt)*; *Second Row* Roberts, Perkins, Shaw, Davies; *Front Row* Williams, James, John
Replacement Ring for Hopkins (73 mins)

MATCH 4 25 May, Valencia

Valencia Select XV 0 **Wales XV 71** (8G 1DG 5T)
Wales XV *Tries:* Ring (3), Hadley (3), Howell Davies (2), Elgan Rees (2), Thomas (2), Dacey *Conversions:* Bowen (5), Howell Davies (2), Ring *Dropped Goal:* Dacey
Team: Davies; E Rees, Bowen, Ring, Hadley; Dacey, Giles; *No 8* Thomas; *Second Row* Dennehy, Shaw, Moriarty, Davies *(capt)*; *Front Row* Whitefoot, Townley, Eidman *Replacement* Roberts for M Davies (31 mins)

MATCH 5 29 May, Madrid

Spain 16 (2G 1T) **Wales 65** (7G 1PG 5T)
Spain *Tries:* Gabriel Rivero (2), Ricardo de la Cuesta *Conversions:* Manuel Moriche (2)
Wales XV *Tries:* Clive Rees (2), Ring (2), Giles (2), Moriarty, Perkins, Mark Davies, Bowen, Elgan Rees, penalty try *Conversions:* Ring (6), Bowen *Penalty Goal:* Ring
Team: Davies; H E Rees, Ring, Bowen, C Rees; Dacey, Giles; *No 8* Butler *(capt)*; *Second Row* Davies, Perkins, Moriarty, Roberts; *Front Row* Whitefoot, James, Eidman
Replacement Williams for Eidman (65 mins)

THE INTERNATIONAL CHAMPIONSHIP 1983-84

This was the most exciting Championship for some years and it ended with a thrilling 'shoot-out' for the Grand Slam between Scotland and France at Murrayfield. It was winner take all – Grand Slam and Championship. It is not often that the England-Wales clash is relegated to the status of a side-show, but the Murrayfield match claimed attention throughout the rugby-playing world. Scotland won the Championship amid tension, controversy and joy. The final table was:

	P	*W*	*D*	*L*	*F*	*A*	*Pts*
Scotland	4	4	0	0	86	36	8
France	4	3	0	1	90	67	6
Wales	4	2	0	2	67	60	4
England	4	1	0	3	51	83	2
Ireland	4	0	0	4	39	87	0

The consensus at the start of the international season was that France and England were the championship favourites; England because they had powered to an excellent win over New Zealand and France because they seemed to be harnessing their vast ability and had crushed the formidable Romanian team. As it turned out, the fortunes of France and England could hardly have varied more starkly – France played some successful and entertaining rugby while England were unsuccessful and their entertainment value was abysmal on occasions.

Scotland's team was less ambitious than some they have fielded in recent years. They improved in the forwards under the captaincy of Jim Aitken and the coaching of Jim Telfer, and this gave them the luxury of a platform to play off. Their back row of David Leslie, Jim Calder and Iain Paxton simply revelled in it and, chiefly through his long kicking, John Rutherford provided the perfect complement. The Scots improved throughout the season and crushed Ireland with an astonishing burst of points-scoring in the Triple Crown match at Lansdowne Road. The least efficient Scots performance of the season came at Cardiff, where, despite beating Wales, they never appeared Championship contenders. Yet the confidence which the win gave them galvanised the team for the rest of the season.

France were a maddening combination. They had a dazzling set of backs, easily the fastest in the Championship. And to set them moving they recalled the outstanding scrum-half, Jerome Gallion, from the international wilderness. They were at their best in the first quarter of the first match against Ireland and the last quarter of their match against England. They really should have beaten Scotland, given that they dominated the match for so long. But their failure showed up once again that temperamental edge to their game which dogged them throughout the season. Jean-Pierre Rives, the captain, was not firm enough, either with himself or with his side. In any case, French claims that they were robbed of a Grand Slam by what they saw as biased refereeing of the final match hardly stand up. They were beaten in most phases of the game against Wales in Cardiff, so it was only through good fortune that they were still unbeaten when they arrived at Murrayfield.

The Welsh selectors seemed to take time to get into their stride. Their selection for the Scottish match seemed odd in many areas. It was only with a new captain – the engaging Newport man, Mike Watkins – a re-cast pack and a new-found confidence that they improved, but then they played so efficiently that many sound judges felt they were the best team in the Championship at the end. Apart from France, they were the only team to attempt running rugby. They had superb runners in Mark Titley and Adrian Hadley, the new championship wings, and they had probably the best back of the season in Malcolm Dacey, the polished Swansea fly-half. Wales also provided a superb individual highlight when Bob Ackerman barged, sprinted, swerved and dummied his way to an amazing try against the Irish at Lansdowne Road. That marked the turning point of the Welsh season. But if Wales had able runners their effort was still based on a front five which bore comparison with any in Wales' recent history for effectiveness in the tight play.

England's high hopes evaporated when they lost the Calcutta Cup match in Scotland to a team which was quicker and which adapted better to the conditions. England's sole idea seemed to be domination at forward, but Scotland's pack were never going to allow that. England descended, in that match and throughout the season, into an uninspired, slow motion game with no authority from their front five and very little of a constructive nature throughout the team. It was all desperately disappointing, especially as that New Zealand win had nurtured false optimism.

The Irish suffered a whitewash and the team which was creaking at the joints last season simply caved in. They never looked likely to win a match. Their best display came in defeat at Twickenham, where Moss Finn and Mike Kiernan played well in the centre and Tony Ward – replacing the indisposed Ollie Campbell – revealed neat touches and kicked his goals. There was nothing else to savour and Willie John McBride, the Irish coach, is faced with a long, long period of rebuilding.

21 January, Parc des Princes
France 25 (1G 4PG 1DG 1T) **Ireland 12** (4PG)

France were overwhelming favourites for this match. They had impressed the rugby world with a superb early-season win over Romania and on a dry day in Paris the Irish old guard seemed to have little chance of checking French progress. As it turned out, Ireland fought bravely all around the field and France sank from early peaks of brilliance into inconsistency and indiscipline. In the end, however, they underlined the enormous gulf between the teams by winning comfortably.

Ireland's back row trio, Slattery, Duggan and O'Driscoll, played with amazing courage in the face of French fury. Both Duggan and Moss Keane, the veteran lock, were groggy with concussion in the second half, but they battled on. Ireland were fielding the oldest pack in their history but it became apparent only towards the end. Lenihan, the youngest member of the pack, performed expertly in the line-out.

But Ireland had nothing to offer in attack. They relied totally on Ollie Campbell's penalty goals. France had genius behind the scrum, especially in Sella and Gallion. They started in fearsome form, scoring two early tries, but they became frustrated when they found they could not quite keep it up. This frustration reached a peak when the referee sent off Garuet, the French prop, in the second half for gouging. Mr Norling controlled the game admirably and his decision could not be faulted.

Gallion opened the scoring for France, finishing off a breathtaking move with a try in the first two minutes. Lescarboura converted. Sella capped another brilliant back movement with a second try. Campbell, who had kicked one penalty goal between the French tries, brought the score to 10-9 to France with two more. Although Campbell added a fourth penalty goal late in the game Lescarboura, who had already dropped a goal, kicked four penalties to take France well out of Ireland's reach.

FRANCE: S Blanco (Biarritz); P Lagisquet (Bayonne), P Sella (Agen), D Cordorniou (Narbonne), P Estève (Narbonne); J-P Lescarboura (Dax), J Gallion (Toulon); *No 8* J-L Joinel (Brive); *Second Row* J-P Rives (Racing Club) (*capt*), J Condom (Boucau), A Lorieux (Grenoble), L Rodriguez (Mont-de-Marsan); *Front Row* J-P Garuet (Lourdes), P Dintrans (Tarbes), M Cremaschi (Lourdes)
Scorers *Tries:* Gallion, Sella *Conversion:* Lescarboura
Penalty Goals: Lescarboura (4) *Dropped Goal:* Lescarboura

IRELAND: H P MacNeill (Oxford U); T M Ringland (Ballymena), D G Irwin (Instonians), R J Moroney (Lansdowne), K D Crossan (Instonians); S O Campbell (Old Belvedere), R J M McGrath (Wanderers); *No 8* W P Duggan (Blackrock Coll); *Second Row* J B O'Driscoll (London Irish), M I Keane (Lansdowne), D G Lenihan (Cork Const), J F Slattery (Blackrock Coll); *Front Row* G A J McLoughlin (Shannon), C F Fitzgerald (St Mary's Coll) (*capt*), P A Orr (Old Wesley)
Scorer *Penalty Goals:* Campbell (4)
Referee C Norling (Wales)

21 January, Cardiff Arms Park
Wales 9 (1G 1PG) **Scotland 15** (2G 1PG)

The Welsh team had not been highly rated before this match and they gave few reasons for anyone to alter that judgement with a poor display in losing to Scotland. The Scots thus won at Cardiff for the second time in as many visits and gave themselves confidence for the matches ahead. Yet in truth they did not have to be world class to win and there were almost as many deficiencies in their performance as there were in that of Wales.

The outstanding figure in the match was Leslie, the Scottish flanker, who was so quick and competitive on the loose ball that he blotted out the experimental Welsh back row completely. Laidlaw, the Scots' scrum-half, gave his forwards superb backing and Aitken was a gritty, inspiring leader.

There were several flashes of excellence from the Welsh backs, especially from Ackerman and Titley, but the overall display was patchy. Norster had a fruitful day in the line-out but cohesion and continuity were absent from the Welsh side. There was an inconsistent display, too, from the half-back pairing of Douglas and Dacey.

Wales took the lead after half an hour when Howell Davies, the new full-back replacing the injured Mark Wyatt, kicked a penalty goal. Then Laidlaw, Rutherford and Leslie made the running for an excellent try for Scotland by Paxton, even though the two final passes seemed more than a fraction forward. Dods converted to put Scotland 6-3 ahead at the break.

In the second half, Titley restored the Welsh lead, squeezing into the corner for a try after Butler and Douglas had moved sharply from a scrum close to the Scottish line. Davies converted with a brilliant kick, but Dods replied with a penalty for Scotland and the visitors clinched the match, appropriately, when skipper Aitken forced his way over from a maul near the Welsh line for his first try for his country. Dods converted to seal a depressing afternoon for Wales.

WALES: H Davies (Bridgend); M H Titley (Bridgend), R A Ackerman (London Welsh), B Bowen (South Wales Police), A M Hadley (Cardiff); M Dacey (Swansea), M H J Douglas (Llanelli); *No 8* E T Butler (Pontypool) (*capt*); *Second Row* D F Pickering (Llanelli), R J Norster (Cardiff), S J Perkins (Pontypool), R D Moriarty (Swansea); *Front Row* R Morgan (Newport), W J James (Aberavon), S T Jones (Pontypool)
Scorers *Try:* Titley *Conversion:* Davies *Penalty Goal:* Davies

SCOTLAND: P W Dods (Gala); S Munro (Ayr), D I Johnston (Watsonians), A E Kennedy (Watsonians), G R T Baird (Kelso); J Y Rutherford (Selkirk), R J Laidlaw (Jedforest); *No 8* I A M Paxton (Selkirk); *Second Row* D G Leslie (Gala), A J Tomes (Hawick), W Cuthbertson (Harlequins), J H Calder (Stewart's-Melville FP); *Front Row* I G Milne (Heriot's FP), C T Deans (Hawick), J Aitken (Gala) (*capt*)
Scorers *Tries:* Paxton, Aitken *Conversions:* Dods (2) *Penalty Goal:* Dods
Referee O Doyle (Ireland)

Jim Aitken is congratulated by John Rutherford (left) and David Leslie after scoring the winning try for Scotland in their match against Wales.

4 February, Murrayfield
Scotland 18 (2G 2PG) **England 6** (2PG)

It took just one match, the hundredth between the two teams, for all the optimism which the win over New Zealand had generated for England to evaporate. They were easily defeated by a faster, more committed and more urgent Scotland team who put themselves within one match of their first Triple Crown for 46 years.

England's plan was to gain ascendancy in the front and then launch their scrum-half, Youngs, and their back row round the scrums, as they had done so effectively against the All Blacks. This time the forwards started well enough but it soon became apparent that the Scots were in no mood to be dominated. By the end, Scotland had gained the supremacy that their opponents had expected to achieve. England, thwarted up front, lacked the confidence and dexterity to change their game.

It might have been different if Hare had not had a miserable day with his goal-kicking. He put over only two penalty goals from eight attempts. Yet any result other than a Scotland win would have been a travesty. They had a superb general at fly-half in Rutherford, whose kicking tormented the England defence, and a quick-thinking, decisive back row in Leslie, Paxton and the brilliant Calder. Just as they had done against New Zealand, too, the Scots rucked impressively.

David Johnston opened the scoring for Scotland, dribbling a loose ball cleverly over the line for a try which Dods converted. Hare had kicked one goal by half-time to make it 6-3 to the Scots. After half-time came a killer blow. Scotland won a driving ruck down the right-hand side of the field and Rutherford picked up a low pass brilliantly from Laidlaw to put Kennedy through with a short pass for a try near the posts. Dods converted. Hare pulled it back to 12-6 with his second penalty, but English hopes were short-lived. The confident Dods kicked two more penalty goals to clinch Scotland's victory.

SCOTLAND: P W Dods (Gala); K W Robertson (Melrose), A E Kennedy (Watsonians), D I Johnston (Watsonians), G R T Baird (Kelso); J Y Rutherford (Selkirk), R J Laidlaw (Jedforest); *No 8* I A M Paxton (Selkirk); *Second Row* J H Calder (Stewart's-Melville FP), A J Tomes (Hawick), W Cuthbertson (Harlequins), D G Leslie (Gala); *Front Row* I G Milne (Heriot's FP), C T Deans (Hawick), J Aitken (Gala) (*capt*)
Replacements J R Beattie (Glasgow Acads) for Cuthbertson (40 mins); J A Pollock (Gosforth) for Kennedy (60 mins)
Scorers *Tries:* Johnston, Kennedy *Conversions:* Dods (2) *Penalty Goals:* Dods (2)

ENGLAND: W H Hare (Leicester); J Carleton (Orrell), C R Woodward (Leicester), G H Davies (Wasps), M A C Slemen (Liverpool); L Cusworth (Leicester), N C Youngs (Leicester); *No 8* J P Scott (Cardiff); *Second Row* P J Winterbottom (Headingley), M J Colclough (Wasps), S Bainbridge (Gosforth), P D Simpson (Bath); *Front Row* G S Pearce (Northampton), P J Wheeler (Leicester) (*capt*), C White (Gosforth) *Replacement* J P Hall (Bath) for Winterbottom (50 mins)
Scorer *Penalty Goals:* Hare (2)
Referee D I H Burnett (Ireland)

4 February, Dublin
Ireland 9 (3PG) Wales 18 (1G 4PG)

A vastly-improved Welsh performance under the captaincy of hooker Mike Watkins, a new cap, was sealed with a marvellous try by centre Robert Ackerman. Wales seemed to have the game under control going into the last quarter but they needed a score to clinch it. That score came in spectacular fashion. Ackerman received the ball a yard inside the Irish half, burst between Duncan and Duggan, wrong-footed the Irish backs and charged straight down the middle to MacNeill, at full-back. There Ackerman feinted to pass to Ian Stephens, who was galloping up in support, and MacNeill bought the dummy completely, leaving the Welsh man a clear path for the line. Howell Davies kicked the conversion and the contest was over.

Watkins' excellent leadership brought the best out of Norster, who ruled the line-out, and Moriarty, who gave a more disciplined, effective display than he had against Scotland. Stephens' return to the front row also helped Wales to ascendancy in the scrum.

Ireland's performance was desperately disappointing. They lost their captain, Fitzgerald, with a head wound after 14 minutes, and from then on they lacked power up front and imagination behind the scrum. Campbell never found his normally assured form although the indecision of McGrath at scrum-half did not help him.

Howell Davies opened the scoring for Wales with a penalty goal which was soon cancelled out by a similar effort from Campbell for Ireland. Bleddyn Bowen, the Welsh centre, then curled over two further penalty goals to put Wales 9-3 ahead at half-time. Campbell brought the score back to 9-6 with his second penalty, but Davies replied with another for Wales, and then converted Ackerman's try. Ireland had little left to offer but they did manage to set up another position for Campbell to kick his third penalty. The score remained at 18-9 to signal better days for Wales but much heart-searching for Ireland.

IRELAND: H P MacNeill (Oxford U); T M Ringland (Ballymena), D G Irwin (Instonians), R Moroney (Lansdowne), K D Crossan (Instonians); S O Campbell (Old Belvedere), R J M McGrath (Wanderers); *No 8* W P Duggan (Blackrock Coll); *Second Row* J B O'Driscoll (London Irish), D G Lenihan (Cork Const), M I Keane (Lansdowne), W Duncan (Malone); *Front Row* J McCoy (Dungannon), C F Fitzgerald (St Mary's Coll) (*capt*), P A Orr (Old Wesley)
Replacement H T Harbison (Bective Rangers) for Fitzgerald (14 mins)
Scorer *Penalty Goals:* Campbell (3)

WALES: H Davies (Bridgend); M H Titley (Bridgend), R A Ackerman (London Welsh), B Bowen (South Wales Police), A M Hadley (Cardiff); M Dacey (Swansea), M H J Douglas (Llanelli); *No 8* E T Butler (Pontypool); *Second Row* R D Moriarty (Swansea), R L Norster (Cardiff), J Perkins (Pontypool), D F Pickering (Llanelli); *Front Row* I Eidman (Cardiff), M J Watkins (Newport) (*capt*), I Stephens (Bridgend)
Scorers *Try:* Ackerman *Conversion:* Davies *Penalty Goals:* Davies (2), Bowen (2)
Referee R G Byres (Australia)

Bob Ackerman on his way to a splendid solo try for Wales in their match against Ireland. Willie Duncan (6) is the would-be tackler.

18 February, Twickenham
England 12 (3PG 1DG) **Ireland 9** (3PG)

There was much more adventure in the England performance following criticism of the sterility of their display against Scotland. Helped by an assured and accomplished display by Les Cusworth at fly-half England often spread the ball wide and occasionally looked dangerous. For all this, the final return was disappointing – there was only a narrow win and there were no tries. England failed to cash in on their new-found fluidity and the finishing was poor. John Carleton, the wing, was their most dangerous back but he was outshone by Moss Finn, the Ireland centre, who gave a superb display on his return to international rugby.

Another distinguished player returning to the international scene was Tony Ward, deputising at fly-half for the indisposed Ollie Campbell. Nor did he let his followers down. He played a nicely varied game, occasionally putting in chip-kicks over the defence to good effect. Yet like England, Ireland never built on what was a sound foundation. They were handicapped in the forwards where, although Donal Lenihan ruled the lines-out for them, they were badly beaten in the scrums. They went home fearing a championship whitewash, leaving England satisfied, but hardly overjoyed, with their first win.

After England had wasted a few early chances, Dusty Hare set the score-board moving with a penalty goal, but it was soon neutralised by a similar effort by Ward for Ireland. This was the result of a high tackle by Cusworth on Ward. Cusworth atoned shortly afterwards by dropping a goal and with Hare and Ward exchanging penalties again just before half-time, England led 9-6 at the interval. Hare's third penalty goal was the only score of the second half for England, but Ward had the last word with a superb penalty from 50 metres.

Of the new caps, England centre Bryan Barley was impressive and John Hall, the flanker, worked hard and often to good effect in the England back row.

ENGLAND: W H Hare (Leicester); J Carleton (Orrell), B Barley (Wakefield), C R Woodward (Leicester), R Underwood (Leicester); L Cusworth (Leicester), N C Youngs (Leicester); *No 8* J P Scott (Cardiff); *Second Row* J P Hall (Bath), M J Colclough (Wasps), S Bainbridge (Gosforth), D H Cooke (Harlequins); *Front Row* P J Blakeway (Gloucester), P J Wheeler (Leicester) (*capt*), C White (Gosforth)
Replacement S P Redfern (Leicester) for White (59 mins)
Scorers *Penalty Goals:* Hare (3) *Dropped Goal:* Cusworth

IRELAND: H P MacNeill (Oxford U); T M Ringland (Ballymena), M J Kiernan (Dolphin), M Finn (Cork Const), K D Crossan (Instonians); A J P Ward (St Mary's Coll), J A P Doyle (Greystones); *No 8* W P Duggan (Blackrock Coll) (*capt*); *Second Row* W R Duncan (Malone), M I Keane (Lansdowne), D G Lenihan (Cork Const), J B O'Driscoll (London Irish); *Front Row* D C Fitzgerald (Lansdowne), H T Harbison (Bective Rangers), P A Orr (Old Wesley)
Scorer *Penalty Goals:* Ward (3)
Referee R Hourquet (France)

18 February, Cardiff
Wales 16 (1G 2PG 1T) **France 21** (1G 4PG 1DG)

Even the French agreed that their championship challenge was lucky to survive this hurdle but they did gain their first win at Cardiff since 1968. The match was interesting without being spectacular for the first hour, but then it burst into life for the last 20 minutes, when there was some thrilling rugby.

The Welsh pack took an early grip and although France manufactured some possession from the line-out they were generally outgunned up front, and had to rely on the goal-kicking of Lescarboura. Wales were well-served by the powerful front row of Stephens, Watkins and Eidman, by the calm Dacey at fly-half and by the brilliant Titley on the wing. Sadly, they missed five kicks at goal and were also hindered by a poor service from the base of the scrum. France began in nervous mood and there was too much shoving and pushing off the ball, but when they did settle they played some quality rugby.

Howell Davies, the home full-back, opened the scoring with a well-struck penalty goal, but Davies and Bowen both misfired when trying to add further points with the boot. Lescarboura soon established a French lead with two penalty goals. A lovely move involving Lescarboura, Lagisquet and Blanco then brought the first try – scored for France by Sella. Lescarboura converted to make it 12-3 at half time, which was poor reward for a fairly encouraging half for Wales.

The home team then began to chip away at the French lead. Davies found the range with a penalty then Butler scored a try after clever work by Dacey and an opening provided by Titley. Davies could not convert and his failure was rubbed in by another Lescarboura penalty, which made it 15-10 to France, followed by a superb dropped goal, again by Lescarboura, in an isolated break-out by France. A try by Davies, which he himself converted, gave Wales hope, but Lescarboura drilled over another penalty goal to seal the match.

WALES: H Davies (Bridgend); M H Titley (Bridgend), R A Ackerman (London Welsh), B Bowen (South Wales Police), A M Hadley (Cardiff); M Dacey (Swansea), M H J Douglas (Llanelli); *No 8* E T Butler (Pontypool); *Second Row* D F Pickering (Llanelli), S J Perkins (Pontypool), R L Norster (Cardiff), R D Moriarty (Swansea); *Front Row* I Eidman (Cardiff), M J Watkins (Newport) (*capt*), I Stephens (Bridgend)
Scorers *Tries:* Davies, Butler *Conversion:* Butler *Penalty Goals:* Davies (2)

FRANCE: S Blanco (Biarritz); P Lagisquet (Bayonne), P Sella (Agen), D Codorniou (Narbonne), P Estève (Narbonne); J-P Lescarboura (Dax), J Gallion (Toulon); *No 8* J-L Joinel (Brive); *Second Row* D Erbani (Agen), A Lorieux (Grenoble), J Condom (Boucau), J-P Rives (Racing Club de France) (*capt*); *Front Row* D Dubroca (Agen), P Dintrans (Tarbes), M Cremaschi (Lourdes)
Scorers *Try:* Sella *Conversion:* Lescarboura *Penalty Goals:* Lescarboura (4)
Dropped Goal: Lescarboura
Referee R G Byers (Australia)

3 March, Paris
France 32 (3G 1PG 1DG 2T) **England 18** (2G 2PG)

Previous form during the season pointed strongly to a French victory, and if ever a match ran true to form, this was it. All the Gallic flair and brilliance was on view and all of England's limitations, which had become obvious earlier in the season, were again cruelly exposed.

England's one chance seemed to be to crush their opponents in the front five, where the French had been exposed against Wales. But the England pack, despite strenuous efforts from Blakeway, were never able to able to take a grip. Indeed, it was France who won more worthwhile possession. Outside the scrum the gulf in pace and class between the teams became ever more obvious. The French were given a lead by Gallion, a master at scrum-half, and by the strong-running back row, in which Erbani was outstanding. Lescarboura, at fly-half, was a perfect launch-pad and every threequarter scored a try. Three further touch-downs were disallowed.

Dusty Hare gave England the lead with a penalty goal and then equalised with a similar effort after Codorniou had scored a try for France, converted by Lescarboura. Then Lescarboura kicked a penalty goal and it was 9-6 to France at half-time – a narrow lead, but things already looked ominous for England. They had their most encouraging moment just after half-time. The forwards set up a rare drive and the ball squirted out to Underwood on the left wing. He dribbled cleverly, picked up and ghosted past Bégu and inside Blanco. Hare's goal made it 12-9 and, remarkably, England still saw a glimmer of hope.

It was quickly extinguished. At the other end, Underwood tried to minor a bouncing ball after a sweeping French attack but as he grasped it, Sella raced past and took it from him before diving for a try. Lescarboura converted and then added an astonishing dropped goal with his left foot. Estève, Bégu and Gallion completed the rout with a try apiece as France finished in breathtaking style. Lescarboura kicked one more conversion. Hare scored a late try which he converted himself, but it was small consolation.

FRANCE: S Blanco (Biarritz); J Bégu (Dax), D Codorniou (Narbonne), P Sella (Agen), P Estève (Narbonne); J-P Lescarboura (Dax), J Gallion (Toulon); *No 8* J-L Joinel (Brive); *Second Row* D Erbani (Agen), J Condom (Boucau), A Lorieux (Grenoble), J-P Rives (Racing Club de France) (*capt*); *Front Row* D Dubroca (Agen), P Dintrans (Tarbes), P Dospital (Bayonne) *Replacement* J-C Orso (Nice) for Lorieux (32 mins)
Scorers *Tries:* Codorniou, Sella, Estève, Bégu, Gallion *Conversions:* Lescarboura (3) *Penalty Goal:* Lescarboura *Dropped Goal:* Lescarboura

ENGLAND: W H Hare (Leicester); J Carleton (Orrell), C R Woodward (Leicester), B Barley (Wakefield), R Underwood (Leicester); L Cusworth (Leicester), N C Youngs (Leicester); *No 8* J P Scott (Cardiff); *Second Row* P J Winterbottom (Headingley), M J Colclough (Wasps), S Bainbridge (Gosforth), J P Hall (Bath); *Front Row* P J Blakeway (Gloucester), P J Wheeler (Leicester) (*capt*), C White (Gosforth)
Scorers *Tries:* Underwood, Hare *Conversions:* Hare (2) *Penalty Goals:* Hare (2)
Referee A M Hosie (Scotland)

The French team that hammered England in Paris. Back Row, L-R: *D Dubroca, P Dintrans, P Dospital, D Erbani, J Condom, J-L Joinel, A Lorieux* Front Row, L-R: *J Bégu, P Sella, S Blanco, J-P Lescarboura, J-P Rives (capt), J Gallion, D Codorniou, P Estève.*

3 March, Dublin
Ireland 9 (1G 1PG) Scotland 32 (3G 2PG 2T)

Scotland swept gloriously to the Triple Crown – the fact that it was their first for 46 years made it all the sweeter, and better still, they crushed Ireland with real style. It meant another championship whitewash for Ireland and they will be starting almost from scratch in their team-building. Scotland's back row of Paxton, Leslie and Calder was brilliant, but the front five lost nothing by comparison, with Alan Tomes shepherding his colleague, Alastair Campbell, expertly through his first international match. Scrum-half Roy Laidlaw had to leave the field with concussion at half-time but in the 40 minutes he played he virtually won the game with two superb tries. John Rutherford was the expert tactician and his towering punts broke Irish hearts.

Laidlaw opened the scoring with an individual dramatic try from side-stepping his way through the Ireland defence. Dods kicked the conversion then two penalties; then came a vital score. The Scots were driving the Irish over their own line with a drive and turn of the scrum when Duggan dived in offside to save. The referee gave a penalty try, and Dods converted. Then Laidlaw struck again with the third try – his own second – and almost before Ireland had begun they were 22-0 down.

Full-back John Murphy finally put Ireland on the score-board with a penalty goal after half-time, then Mike Kiernan knifed through for a try which Murphy goaled. But that was Ireland's limit. They lost Tony Ward after he was heavily tackled and Scotland then steadied the ship. Robertson and Dods scored late, clinching tries and Dods added one conversion before the field was invaded by hundreds of delirious Scots. The invasion, in fact provided the only sour note. A spectator collided with Gordon Hunter, Laidlaw's replacement, and Hunter suffered a fractured cheekbone. Otherwise, for the Scots, it was all joy.

IRELAND: J Murphy (Greystones); T M Ringland (Ballymena), M J Kiernan (Lansdowne), M Finn (Cork Const), K D Crossan (Instonians); A J P Ward (St Mary's Coll), J A P Doyle (Greystones); *No 8* W P Duggan (Blackrock Coll) (*capt*); Second Row J B O'Driscoll (London Irish), M I Keane (Lansdowne), D G Lenihan (Cork Const), D McGrath (UC, Dublin); *Front Row* D Fitzgerald (Lansdowne), H T Harbison (Bective Rangers), P A Orr (Old Wesley) *Replacement* H Condon (London Irish) for Ward (55 mins)
Scorers *Try:* Kiernan *Conversion:* Murphy *Penalty Goal:* Murphy

SCOTLAND: P W Dods (Gala); J M Pollock (Gosforth), K W Robertson (Melrose), D I Johnston (Watsonians), G R T Baird (Kelso); J Y Rutherford (Selkirk), R J Laidlaw (Jedforest); *No 8* I A M Paxton (Selkirk); *Second Row* D G Leslie (Gala), A Campbell (Hawick), A J Tomes (Hawick), J H Calder (Stewarts-Melville FP); *Front Row* I G Milne (Heriot's FP), C T Deans (Hawick), J Aitken (Gala) *Replacement* I G Hunter (Selkirk) for Laidlaw (half-time)
Scorers *Tries:* Laidlaw (2) penalty try, Robertson, Dods *Conversions:* Dods (3) *Penalty Goals:* Dods (2)
Referee F D Howard (England)

17 March, Murrayfield
Scotland 21 (1G 5PG) **France 12** (1G 1PG 1DG)

This Grand Slam decider provided little in the way of subtlety or invention – it was too tense and hard for that – but it did prove to be a wildly exciting, passionate and controversial match as Scotland, seemingly in grave difficulty against continual French pressure in the first half, held on and shifted the pressure on to France. The French had looked likely winners throughout the first half: the Scotland forwards were unable to establish themselves and John Rutherford and his backs showed uncharacteristic nervousness.

But France became rattled at their failure to draw away and also at a barrage of penalties which Mr Winston Jones, taking charge of his first international, awarded against them. The French were bitter about the refereeing afterwards but to the neutral it seemed that Mr Jones was merely doing his job. French discipline continued to suffer in the second half and Scotland's effort became all the stronger, with their back row and half-backs eventually getting on top.

Scotland took the lead with a penalty by Dods and the Scottish full-back went on to score 17 points, finishing the Championship with 50 points. This beat Andy Irvine's previous record for Scotland of 35. The only other score of the half was a try from Gallion. The brilliant French scrum-half, who was to leave the field concussed after an hour, received a pass from Orso after a five-yard scrum and evaded the Scots back row to score. Lescarboura converted. Following Gallion's departure France extended their lead with a penalty goal by Lescarboura. It was the start of a burst of kicking at goal. First, Dods found the range after earlier misses and two long goals made it 9-9. A wonderful dropped goal from Lescarboura edged France in front again, but Dods kicked his fourth goal bringing the score to 12-12. With France's defence struggling, Calder dived over for a historic try at a line-out near the French line, and Dods sealed the match. He goaled Calder's try and kicked his fifth penalty goal after a late tackle.

SCOTLAND: P W Dods (Gala); J A Pollock (Gosforth), K W Robertson (Melrose), D I Johnston (Watsonians), G R T Baird (Kelso); J Y Rutherford (Selkirk), R J Laidlaw (Jedforest); *No 8* I A M Paxton (Selkirk); *Second Row* J H Calder (Stewart's-Melville FP), A J Tomes (Hawick), A J Campbell (Hawick), D G Leslie (Gala); *Front Row* I G Milne (Heriot's FP), C T Deans (Hawick), J Aitken (Gala) *(capt)*
Scorers *Try:* Calder *Conversion:* Dods *Penalty Goals:* Dods (5)

FRANCE: S Blanco (Biarritz); J Bégu (Dax), P Sella (Agen), D Codorniou (Narbonne), P Estève (Narbonne); J-P Lescarboura (Dax), J Gallion (Toulon); *No 8* J-C Orso (Nice); *Second Row* J-L Joinel (Brive), J Condom (Boucau), F Haget (Biarritz), J-P Rives (Racing Club de France) *(capt)*; *Front Row* D Dubroca (Agen), P Dintrans (Tarbes), P Dospital (Bayonne) *Replacement* P Berbizier (Lourdes) for Gallion (60 mins)
Scorers *Try:* Gallion *Conversion:* Lescarboura *Penalty Goal:* Lescarboura *Dropped Goal:* Lescarboura
Referee W Jones (Wales)

17 March, Twickenham
England 15 (5PG) **Wales 24** (1G 4PG 2DG)

Throughout the Championship, England's fortunes had, if anything, been declining whereas by the time this fixture arrived Wales had much improved the team which began the Championship. They gave a powerful performance up front to put England on the rack, and they had an outstanding general at fly-half in Malcolm Dacey, who kicked and ran with assurance. Terry Holmes, who had been injured on the Lions tour, made a splendid return to international rugby at scrum-half. England had neither the forward base nor the authority at half-back that Wales enjoyed. Their only scoring weapon was Dusty Hare's goal-kicking.

It was another great day for the inspiring Welsh captain, Mike Watkins, and for his props and line-out men. Bob Norster and Richard Moriarty controlled the line-out and there was a loud, ironic cheer from the England followers in the second half when England at last won a ball from the line-out. Wales had clever runners in Mark Titley and Bleddyn Bowen and apart from the odd burst by John Carleton, England preferred to kick.

Hare gave England the lead three times, at 3-0, 6-3 and 9-6, but each time his opposite number Howell Davies kicked Wales level. Wales fashioned their try from a scything run from Bleddyn Bowen with excellent support from Eddie Butler. Butler interpassed with Adrian Hadley and Hadley scored. Davies converted and added a further penalty goal to make the score 18-9. This kick by Davies gave him a new record of 39 points for a Welsh player in the Championship.

Dusty Hare kicked two more goals for England but Malcolm Dacey sealed the Welsh win, with two clever dropped goals from the stream of possession he received. Although the final margin was only nine points it was certainly one of Wales' most conclusive wins ever over England.

ENGLAND: W H Hare (Leicester); J Carleton (Orrell), C R Woodward (Leicester), B Barley (Wakefield), R Underwood (Leicester); L Cusworth (Leicester), N C Youngs (Leicester); *No 8* J P Scott (Cardiff); *Second Row* P J Winterbottom (Headingley), M J Colclough (Wasps), S B Bainbridge (Gosforth), A Dun (Wasps); *Front Row* P J Blakeway (Gloucester), P J Wheeler (Leicester) *(capt)*, P A G Rendall (Wasps)
Scorer *Penalty Goals:* Hare (5)

WALES: H Davies (Bridgend); M H Titley (Bridgend), R A Ackerman (London Welsh), B Bowen (South Wales Police), A H Hadley (Cardiff); M Dacey (Swansea), T D Holmes (Cardiff); *No 8* E T Butler (Pontypool); *Second Row* D F Pickering (Llanelli), R L Norster (Cardiff), S J Perkins (Pontypool), R D Moriarty (Swansea); *Front Row* I Eidman (Cardiff), M J Watkins *(capt)*, I Stephens (Bridgend)
Scorers *Try:* Hadley *Conversion:* Davies *Penalty Goals:* Davies (4)
Dropped Goals: Dacey (2)
Referee J B Anderson (Scotland)

RESULTS OF INTERNATIONAL MATCHES *(up to 30 April 1984)*

Years for Five Nations' matches are for the second half of the season: eg 1972 means season 1971-72. Years for matches against touring teams from the Southern Hemisphere refer to the actual year of the match.

Points-scoring was first introduced in 1886, when an International Board was formed by Scotland, Ireland, and Wales. Points-values varied between countries until 1890, when England agreed to join the Board, and uniform values were adopted. The table below shows points-values from the 1890-91 season onwards.

Northern Hemisphere seasons	*Try*	*Conversion*	*Penalty goal*	*Dropped goal*	*Goal from mark*
1890-91	1	2	2	3	3
1891-92 to 1892-93	2	3	3	4	4
1893-94 to 1904-05	3	2	3	4	4
1905-06 to 1947-48	3	2	3	4	3
1948-49 to 1970-71	3	2	3	3	3
1971-72 onwards	4	2	3	3	3*

**The Goal from mark ceased to exist when Free kick clause was introduced, 1977-78.*

ENGLAND v SCOTLAND

Played 100 England won 47, Scotland won 37, Drawn 16

1871 Raeburn Place (Edinburgh)
Scotland 1G 1T to 1T

1872 The Oval (London)
England 1G 1DG 2T to 1DG

1873 Glasgow
Drawn no score

1874 The Oval
England 1DG to 1T

1875 Raeburn Place
Drawn no score

1876 The Oval
England 1G 1T to 0

1877 Raeburn Place
Scotland 1DG to 0

1878 The Oval
Drawn no score

1879 Raeburn Place
Drawn Scotland 1DG England 1G

1880 Manchester
England 2G 3T to 1G

1881 Raeburn Place
Drawn Scotland 1G 1T England 1DG 1T

1882 Manchester
Scotland 2T to 0

1883 Raeburn Place
England 2T to 1T

1884 Blackheath (London)
England 1G to 1T

1885 No Match

1886 Raeburn Place
Drawn no score

1887 Manchester
Drawn 1T each

1888 No Match

1889 No Match

1890 Raeburn Place
England 1G 1T to 0

1891 Richmond (London)
Scotland 2G 1DG (9) to 1G (3)

1892 Raeburn Place
England 1G (5) to 0

1893 Leeds
Scotland 2DG (8) to 0

1894 Raeburn Place
Scotland 2T (6) to 0

1895 Richmond
Scotland 1PG 1T (6) to 1PG (3)

1896 Glasgow
Scotland 1G 2T (11) to 0

1897 Manchester
England 1G 1DG 1T (12) to 1T (3)

1898 Powderhall (Edinburgh)
Drawn 1T (3) each

1899 Blackheath
Scotland 1G (5) to 0

1900 Inverleith (Edinburgh)
Drawn no score

1901 Blackheath
Scotland 3G 1T (18) to 1T (3)

1902 Inverleith
England 2T (6) to 1T (3)

1903 Richmond
Scotland 1DG 2T (10) to 2T (6)

1904 Inverleith
Scotland 2T (6) to 1T (3)

1905 Richmond
Scotland 1G 1T (8) to 0

1906 Inverleith
England 3T (9) to 1T (3)

1907 Blackheath
Scotland 1G 1T (8) to 1T (3)

1908 Inverleith
Scotland 1G 2DG 1T (16) to 2 G (10)

1909 Richmond
Scotland 3G 1T (18) to 1G 1T (8)

1910 Inverleith
England 1G 3T (14) to 1G (5)

1911 Twickenham
England 2G 1T (13) to 1G 1T (8)

1912 Inverleith
Scotland 1G 1T (8) to 1T (3)

1913 Twickenham
England 1T (3) to 0

1914 Inverleith
England 2G 2T (16) to 1G 1DG 2T (15)

1920 Twickenham
England 2G 1T (13) to 1DG (4)

1921 Inverleith
England 3G 1T (18) to 0

1922 Twickenham
England 1G 2T (11) to 1G (5)

1923 Inverleith
England 1G 1T (8) to 2T (6)

1924 Twickenham
England 3G 1DG (19) to 0

1925 Murrayfield
Scotland 2G 1DG (14)
to 1G 1PG 1T (11)

1926 Twickenham
Scotland 2G 1DG 1T (17) to 3T (9)

1927 Murrayfield
Scotland 1G 1DG 4T (21)
to 2G 1PG (13)

1928 Twickenham
England 2T (6) to 0

1929 Murrayfield
Scotland 4T (12) to 2T (6)

1930 Twickenham
Drawn no score

1931 Murrayfield
Scotland 5G 1T (28) to 2G 1PG 2T (19)

1932 Twickenham
England 2G 2T (16) to 1T (3)

1933 Murrayfield
Scotland 1T (3) to 0

1934 Twickenham
England 2T (6) to 1T (3)

1935 Murrayfield
Scotland 2G (10) to 1DG 1T (7)

1936 Twickenham
England 3T (9) to 1G 1PG (8)

1937 Murrayfield
England 2T (6) to 1PG (3)

1938 Twickenham
Scotland 2PG 5T (21)
to 1DG 3PG 1T (16)

1939 Murrayfield
England 3PG (9) to 2T (6)

1947 Twickenham
England 4G 1DG (24) to 1G (5)

1948 Murrayfield
Scotland 2T (6) to 1PG (3)

1949 Twickenham
England 2G 3T (19) to 1PG (3)

1950 Murrayfield
Scotland 2G 1T (13) to 1G 1PG 1T (11)

1951 Twickenham
England 1G (5) to 1T (3)

1952 Murrayfield
England 2G 1DG 2T (19) to 1T (3)

1953 Twickenham
England 4G 2T (26) to 1G 1T (8)

1954 Murrayfield
England 2G 1T (13) to 1T (3)

1955 Twickenham
England 1PG 2T (9) to 1PG 1T (6)

1956 Murrayfield
England 1G 2PG (11) to 1PG 1T (6)

1957 Twickenham
England 2G 1PG 1T (16) to 1PG (3)

1958 Murrayfield
Drawn 1PG (3) each

1959 Twickenham
Drawn 1PG (3) each

1960 Murrayfield
England 3G 1DG 1PG (21)
to 3PG 1T (12)

1961 Twickenham
England 1PG 1T (6) to 0

1962 Murrayfield
Drawn 1PG (3) each

1963 Twickenham
England 2G (10) to 1G 1DG (8)

1964 Murrayfield
Scotland 3G (15) to 1PG 1T (6)

1965 Twickenham
Drawn England 1T (3) Scotland 1DG (3)

1966 Murrayfield
Scotland 1PG 1T (6) to 1DG (3)

1967 Twickenham
England 3G 2PG 1DG 1T (27) to 1G 2PG 1T (14)

1968 Murrayfield
England 1G 1PG (8) to 1PG 1DG (6)

1969 Twickenham
England 1G 1T (8) to 1PG (3)

1970 Murrayfield
Scotland 1G 2PG 1T (14) to 1G (5)

1971 Twickenham
Scotland 2G 1DG 1T (16) to 3PG 2T (15)

*1971 Murrayfield
Scotland 4G 1PG 1T (26) to 1PG 1DG (6)

1972 Murrayfield
Scotland 4PG 1DG 2T (23) to 3PG (9)

1973 Twickenham
England 2G 2T (20) to 1G 1PG 1T (13)

1974 Murrayfield
Scotland 1G 2PG 1T (16) to 1DG 1PG 2T (14)

1975 Twickenham
England 1PG 1T (7) to 2PG (6)

1976 Murrayfield
Scotland 2G 2PG 1T (22) to 1G 2PG (12)

1977 Twickenham
England 2G 2PG 2T (26) to 2PG (6)

1978 Murrayfield
England 2G 1PG (15) to 0

1979 Twickenham
Drawn 1PG 1T (7) each

1980 Murrayfield
England 2G 2PG 3T (30) to 2G 2PG (18)

1981 Twickenham
England 1G 3PG 2T (23) to 1G 1PG 2T (17)

1982 Murrayfield
Drawn Scotland 2PG 1DG (9) England 3PG (9)

1983 Twickenham
Scotland 1G 3PG 1DG 1T (22) to 3PG 1DG (12)

1984 Murrayfield
Scotland 2G 2PG (18) to 2PG (6)

**Special Centenary match – non-championship*

ENGLAND v IRELAND

Played 96 England won 54, Ireland won 34, Drawn 8

1875 The Oval (London)
England 1G 1DG 1T to 0

1876 Dublin
England 1G 1T to 0

1877 The Oval
England 2G 2T to 0

1878 Dublin
England 2G 1T to 0

1879 The Oval
England 2G 1DG 2T to 0

1880 Dublin
England 1G 1T to 1T

1881 Manchester
England 2G 2T to 0

1882 Dublin
Drawn 2T each

1883 Manchester
England 1G 3T to 1T

1884 Dublin
England 1G to 0

1885 Manchester
England 2T to 1T

1886 Dublin
England 1T to 0

1887 Dublin
Ireland 2G to 0

1888 No Match

1889 No Match

1890 Blackheath (London)
England 3T to 0

1891 Dublin
England 2G 3T (9) to 0

1892 Manchester
England 1G 1T (7) to 0

1893 Dublin
England 2T (4) to 0

1894 Blackheath
Ireland 1DG 1T (7) to 1G (5)

1895 Dublin
England 2T (6) to 1T (3)

1896 Leeds
Ireland 2G (10) to 1DG (4)

1897 Dublin
Ireland 1GM 3T (13) to 2PG 1T (9)

1898 Richmond (London)
Ireland 1PG 2T (9) to 1PG 1T (6)

1899 Dublin
Ireland 1PG 1T (6) to 0

1900 Richmond
England 1G 1DG 2T (15) to 1DG (4)

1901 Dublin
Ireland 2G (10) to 1PG 1T (6)

1902 Leicester
England 2T (6) to 1T (3)

1903 Dublin
Ireland 1PG 1T (6) to 0

1904 Blackheath
England 2G 3T (19) to 0

1905 Cork
Ireland 1G 4T (17) to 1T (3)

1906 Leicester
Ireland 2G 2T (16) to 2T (6)

1907 Dublin
Ireland 1G 1GM 3T (17) to 1PG 2T (9)

1908 Richmond
England 2G 1T (13) to 1PG (3)

1909 Dublin
England 1G 2T (11) to 1G (5)

1910 Twickenham
Drawn no score

1911 Dublin
Ireland 1T (3) to 0

1912 Twickenham
England 5T (15) to 0

1913 Dublin
England 1PG 4T (15) to 1DG (4)

1914 Twickenham
England 1G 4T (17) to 1G 1DG 1T (12)

1920 Dublin
England 1G 3T (14) to 1G 1PG 1T (11)

1921 Twickenham
England 1G 1DG 2T (15) to 0

1922 Dublin
England 4T (12) to 1T (3)

1923 Leicester
England 2G 1DG 3T (23) to 1G (5)

1924 Belfast
England 1G 3T (14) to 1T (3)

1925 Twickenham
Drawn 2T (6) each

1926 Dublin
Ireland 2G 1PG 2T (19) to 3G (15)

1927 Twickenham
England 1G 1T (8) to 1PG 1T (6)

1928 Dublin
England 1DG 1T (7) to 2T (6)

1929 Twickenham
Ireland 2T (6) to 1G (5)

1930 Dublin
Ireland 1DG (4) to 1T (3)

1931 Twickenham
Ireland 1PG 1T (6) to 1G (5)

1932 Dublin
England 1G 2PG (11) to 1G 1PG (8)

1933 Twickenham
England 1G 4T (17) to 1PG 1T (6)

1934 Dublin
England 2G 1T (13) to 1T (3)

1935 Twickenham
England 1G 3PG (14) to 1T (3)

1936 Dublin
Ireland 2T (6) to 1T (3)

1937 Twickenham
England 1PG 2T (9) to 1G 1T (8)

1938 Dublin
England 6G 1PG 1T (36) to 1G 3T (14)

1939 Twickenham
Ireland 1G (5) to 0

1947 Dublin
Ireland 2G 1PG 3T (22) to 0

1948 Twickenham
Ireland 1G 2T (11) to 2G (10)

1949 Dublin
Ireland 1G 2PG 1T (14) to 1G (5)

1950 Twickenham
England 1T (3) to 0

1951 Dublin
Ireland 1PG (3) to 0

1952 Twickenham
England 1T (3) to 0

1953 Dublin
Drawn 2PG 1T (9) each

1954 Twickenham
England 1G 1PG 2T (14) to 1PG (3)

1955 Dublin
Drawn Ireland 1PG 1T (6)
England 2T (6)

1956 Twickenham
England 1G 3PG 2T (20) to 0

1957 Dublin
England 1PG 1T (6) to 0

1958 Twickenham
England 1PG 1T (6) to 0

1959 Dublin
England 1PG (3) to 0

1960 Twickenham
England 1G 1DG (8) to 1G (5)

1961 Dublin
Ireland 1G 2PG (11) to 1G 1T (8)

1962 Twickenham
England 2G 1PG 1T (16) to 0

1963 Dublin
Drawn no score

1964 Twickenham
Ireland 3G 1T (18) to 1G (5)

1965 Dublin
Ireland 1G (5) to 0

1966 Twickenham
Drawn 1PG 1T (6) each

1967 Dublin
England 1G 1PG (8) to 1PG (3)

1968 Twickenham
Drawn England 2PG 1DG (9)
Ireland 3PG (9)

1969 Dublin
Ireland 1G 2PG 1DG 1T (17)
to 4PG 1T (15)

1970 Twickenham
England 2DG 1T (9) to 1PG (3)

1971 Dublin
England 3PG (9) to 2T (6)

1972 Twickenham
Ireland 1G 1DG 1PG 1T (16)
to 1G 2PG (12)

1973 Dublin
Ireland 2G 1PG 1DG (18) to 1G 1PG (9)

1974 Twickenham
Ireland 2G 1PG 1DG 2T (26)
to 1G 5PG (21)

1975 Dublin
Ireland 2G (12) to 1G 1DG (9)

1976 Twickenham
Ireland 2PG 1DG 1T (13) to 4PG (12)

1977 Dublin
England 1T (4) to 0

1978 Twickenham
England 2G 1PG (15) to 2PG 1DG (9)

1979 Dublin
Ireland 1G 1PG 1DG (12) to 1PG 1T (7)

1980 Twickenham
England 3G 2PG (24) to 3PG (9)

1981 Dublin
England 1G 1T (10) to 2 DG (6)

1982 Twickenham
Ireland 1G 2PG 1T (16) to 1G 3PG (15)

1983 Dublin
Ireland 1G 5PG 1T (25) to 5PG (15)

1984 Twickenham
England 1DG 3PG (12) to 3PG (9)

ENGLAND v WALES

Played 89 England won 35, Wales won 42, Drawn 12

1881 Blackheath (London)
England 7G 1DG 6T to 0

1882 No Match

1883 Swansea
England 2G 4T to 0

1884 Leeds
England 1G 2T to 1G

1885 Swansea
England 1G 4T to 1G 1T

1886 Blackheath
England 1GM 2T to 1G

1887 Llanelli
Drawn no score

1888 No Match

1889 No Match

1890 Dewsbury
Wales 1T to 0

1891 Newport
England 2G 1T (7) to 1G (3)

1892 Blackheath
England 3G 1T (17) to 0

1893 Cardiff
Wales 1G 1PG 2T (12) to 1G 3T (11)

1894 Birkenhead
England 4G 1GM (24) to 1T (3)

1895 Swansea
England 1G 3T (14) to 2T (6)

1896 Blackheath
England 2G 5T (25) to 0

1897 Newport
Wales 1G 2T (11) to 0

1898 Blackheath
England 1G 3T (14) to 1DG 1T (7)

1899 Swansea
Wales 4G 2T (26) to 1T (3)

1900 Gloucester
Wales 2G 1PG (13) to 1T (3)

1901 Cardiff
Wales 2G 1T (13) to 0

1902 Blackheath
Wales 1PG 2T (9) to 1G 1T (8)

1903 Swansea
Wales 3G 2T (21) to 1G (5)

1904 Leicester
Drawn England 1G 1PG 2T (14)
Wales 2G 1GM (14)

1905 Cardiff
Wales 2G 5T (25) to 0

1906 Richmond (London)
Wales 2G 2T (16) to 1T (3)

1907 Swansea
Wales 2G 4T (22) to 0

1908 Bristol
Wales 3G 1DG 1PG 2T (28)
to 3G 1T (18)

1909 Cardiff
Wales 1G 1T (8) to 0

1910 Twickenham
England 1G 1PG 1T (11) to 2T (6)

1911 Swansea
Wales 1PG 4T (15) to 1G 2T (11)

1912 Twickenham
England 1G 1T (8) to 0

1913 Cardiff
England 1G 1DG 1T (12) to 0

1914 Twickenham
England 2G (10) to 1G 1DG (9)

1920 Swansea
Wales 1G 2DG 1PG 1T (19) to 1G (5)

1921 Twickenham
England 1G 1DG 3T (18) to 1T (3)

1922 Cardiff
Wales 2G 6T (28) to 2T (6)

1923 Twickenham
England 1DG 1T (7) to 1T (3)

1924 Swansea
England 1G 4T (17) to 3T (9)

1925 Twickenham
England 1PG 3T (12) to 2T (6)

1926 Cardiff
Drawn 1T (3) each

1927 Twickenham
England 1G 1PG 1GM (11)
to 1PG 2T (9)

1928 Swansea
England 2G (10) to 1G 1T (8)

1929 Twickenham
England 1G 1T (8) to 1T (3)

1930 Cardiff
England 1G 1PG 1T (11) to 1T (3)

1931 Twickenham
Drawn England 1G 2PG (11)
Wales 1G 1GM 1T (11)

1932 Swansea
Wales 1G 1DG 1PG (12) to 1G (5)

1933 Twickenham
Wales 1DG 1T (7) to 1T (3)

1934 Cardiff
England 3T (9) to 0

1935 Twickenham
Drawn England 1PG (3) Wales 1T (3)

1936 Swansea
Drawn no score

1937 Twickenham
England 1DG (4) to 1T (3)

1938 Cardiff
Wales 1G 2PG 1T (14) to 1G 1T (8)

1939 Twickenham
England 1T (3) to 0

1947 Cardiff
England 1G 1DG (9) to 2T (6)

1948 Twickenham
Drawn England 1PG (3) Wales 1T (3)

1949 Cardiff
Wales 3T (9) to 1DG (3)

1950 Twickenham
Wales 1G 1PG 1T (11) to 1G (5)

1951 Swansea
Wales 4G 1T (23) to 1G (5)

1952 Twickenham
Wales 1G 1T (8) to 2T (6)

1953 Cardiff
England 1G 1PG (8) to 1PG (3)

1954 Twickenham
England 3T (9) to 1PG 1T (6)

1955 Cardiff
Wales 1PG (3) to 0

1956 Twickenham
Wales 1G 1T (8) to 1PG (3)

1957 Cardiff
England 1PG (3) to 0

1958 Twickenham
Drawn England 1T (3) Wales 1PG (3)

1959 Cardiff
Wales 1G (5) to 0

1960 Twickenham
England 1G 2PG 1T (14) to 2PG (6)

1961 Cardiff
Wales 2T (6) to 1T (3)

1962 Twickenham
Drawn no score

1963 Cardiff
England 2G 1DG (13) to 1PG 1T (6)

1964 Twickenham
Drawn 2T (6) each

1965 Cardiff
Wales 1G 1DG 2T (14) to 1PG (3)

1966 Twickenham
Wales 1G 2PG (11) to 1PG 1T (6)

1967 Cardiff
Wales 5G 2PG 1DG (34) to 4PG 3T (21)

1968 Twickenham
Drawn England 1G 1PG 1T (11)
Wales 1G 1DG 1T (11)

1969 Cardiff
Wales 3G 2PG 1DG 2T (30) to 3PG (9)

1970 Twickenham
Wales 1G 1DG 3T (17) to 2G 1PG (13)

1971 Cardiff
Wales 2G 2DG 1PG 1T (22)
to 1PG 1T (6)

1972 Twickenham
Wales 1G 2PG (12) to 1PG (3)

1973 Cardiff
Wales 1G 1PG 4T (25) to 2PG 1DG (9)

1974 Twickenham
England 1G 2PG 1T (16)
to 1G 2PG (12)

1975 Cardiff
Wales 1G 2PG 2T (20) to 1T (4)

1976 Twickenham
Wales 3G 1PG (21) to 3PG (9)

1977 Cardiff
Wales 2PG 2T (14) to 3PG (9)

1978 Twickenham
Wales 3PG (9) to 2PG (6)

1979 Cardiff
Wales 2G 1DG 3T (27) to 1PG (3)

1980 Twickenham
England 3PG (9) to 2T (8)

1981 Cardiff
Wales 1G 4PG 1DG (21) to 5PG 1T (19)

1982 Twickenham
England 3PG 2T (17) to 1DG 1T (7)

1983 Cardiff
Drawn 1DG 2PG 1T (13) each

1984 Twickenham
Wales 1G 2DG 4PG (24) to 5PG (15)

ENGLAND v FRANCE

Played 59 England won 32, France won 21, Drawn 6

1906 Paris
England 4G 5T (35) to 1G 1T (8)

1907 Richmond (London)
England 5G 1DG 4T (41)
to 2G 1PG (13)

1908 Paris
England 2G 3T (19) to 0

1909 Leicester
England 2G 4T (22) to 0

1910 Paris
England 1G 2T (11) to 1T (3)

1911 Twickenham
England 5G 2PG 2T (37) to 0

1912 Paris
England 1G 1DG 3T (18) to 1G 1T (8)

1913 Twickenham
England 1G 5T (20) to 0

1914 Paris
England 6G 3T (39) to 2G 1T (13)

1920 Twickenham
England 1G 1PG (8) to 1T (3)

1921 Paris
England 2G (10) to 2PG (6)

1922 Twickenham
Drawn England 1G 2PG (11)
France 1G 2T (11)

1923 Paris
England 1G 1DG 1T (12) to 1PG (3)

1924 Twickenham
England 2G 3T (19) to 1DG 1T (7)

1925 Paris
England 2G 1GM (13) to 1G 2T (11)

1926 Twickenham
England 1G 2T (11) to 0

1927 Paris
France 1T (3) to 0

1928 Twickenham
England 3G 1T (18) to 1G 1T (8)

1929 Paris
England 2G 2T (16) to 2T (6)

1930 Twickenham
England 1G 2T (11) to 1G (5)

1931 Paris
France 2DG 2T (14) to 2G 1T (13)

1947 Twickenham
England 2T (6) to 1PG (3)

1948 Paris
France 1G 1DG 2T (15) to 0

1949 Twickenham
England 1G 1DG (8) to 1DG (3)

1950 Paris
France 2T (6) to 1T (3)

1951 Twickenham
France 1G 1DG 1T (11) to 1T (3)

1952 Paris
England 2PG (6) to 1T (3)

1953 Twickenham
England 1G 2T (11) to 0

1954 Paris
France 1G 1DG 1T (11) to 1T (3)

1955 Twickenham
France 2G 2DG (16) to 2PG 1T (9)

1956 Paris
France 1G 2PG 1T (14) to 2PG 1T (9)

1957 Twickenham
England 3T (9) to 1G (5)

1958 Paris
England 1G 1PG 2T (14) to 0

1959 Twickenham
Drawn 1PG (3) each

1960 Paris
Drawn France 1PG (3) England 1T (3)

1961 Twickenham
Drawn 1G (5) each

1962 Paris
France 2G 1T (13) to 0

1963 Twickenham
England 2PG (6) to 1G (5)

1964 Paris
England 1PG 1T (6) to 1T (3)

1965 Twickenham
England 2PG 1T (9) to 1PG 1T (6)

1966 Paris
France 2G 1T (13) to 0

1967 Twickenham
France 2G 1DG 1PG (16)
to 3PG 1DG (12)

1968 Paris
France 1G 2DG 1PG (14)
to 1DG 2PG (9)

1969 Twickenham
England 2G 3PG 1T (22)
to 1G 1DG (8)

1970 Paris
France 4G 2DG 1PG 2T (35)
to 2G 1PG (13)

1971 Twickenham
Drawn England 1G 3PG (14)
France 1G 1PG 1DG 1T (14)

1972 Paris
France 5G 1PG 1T (37) to 1G 2PG (12)

1973 Twickenham
England 2PG 2T (14) to 1G (6)

1974 Paris
Drawn 1G 1PG 1DG (12) each

1975 Twickenham
France 4G 1PG (27) to 4PG 2T (20)

1976 Paris
France 3G 3T (30) to 1G 1PG (9)

1977 Twickenham
France 1T (4) to 1PG (3)

1978 Paris
France 2G 1PG (15) to 2DG (6)

1979 Twickenham
England 1PG 1T (7) to 1G (6)

1980 Paris
England 1PG 2DG 2T (17)
to 1G 1PG 1T (13)

1981 Twickenham
France 1G 2DG 1T (16) to 4 PG (12)

1982 Paris
England 2G 5PG (27) to
1G 2PG 1DG (15)

1983 Twickenham
France 2G 1PG 1T (19)
to 4PG 1DG (15)

1984 Paris
France 3G 1DG 1PG 2T (32)
to 2G 2PG (18)

ENGLAND v NEW ZEALAND

Played 13 England won 3, New Zealand won 10, Drawn 0

1905 Crystal Palace (London)
New Zealand 5T (15) to 0

1925 Twickenham
New Zealand 1G 1PG 3T (17)
to 1G 1PG 1T (11)

1936 Twickenham
England 1DG 3T (13) to 0

1954 Twickenham
New Zealand 1G (5) to 0

1963 *1* Auckland
New Zealand 3G 1DG 1PG (21)
to 1G 2PG (11)

2 Christchurch
New Zealand 1GM 2T (9)
to 1PG 1T (6)
New Zealand won series 2-0

1964 Twickenham
New Zealand 1G 2PG 1T (14) to 0

1967 Twickenham
New Zealand 4G 1T (23)
to 1G 1PG 1T (11)

1973 Twickenham
New Zealand 1G 1DG (9) to 0

1973 Auckland
England 2G 1T (16) to 1G 1T (10)

1978 Twickenham
New Zealand 1G 2PG 1T (16)
to 1PG 1DG (6)

1979 Twickenham
New Zealand 2PG 1T (10) to 3PG (9)

1983 Twickenham
England 1G 3PG (15) to 1G 1PG (9)

ENGLAND v SOUTH AFRICA

Played 7 England won 2, South Africa won 4, Drawn 1

1906 Crystal Palace (London)
Drawn 1T (3) each

1913 Twickenham
South Africa 2PG 1T (9) to 1T (3)

1932 Twickenham
South Africa 1DG 1T (7) to 0

1952 Twickenham
South Africa 1G 1PG (8) to 1T (3)

1961 Twickenham
South Africa 1G (5) to 0

1969 Twickenham
England 1G 1PG 1T (11) to 1G 1PG (8)

1972 Johannesburg
England 1G 4PG (18) to 3PG (9)

ENGLAND v AUSTRALIA

Played 10 England won 4, Australia won 6, Drawn 0

1909 Blackheath (London)
Australia 3T (9) to 1T (3)

1948 Twickenham
Australia 1G 2T (11) to 0

1958 Twickenham
England 1PG 2T (9) to 1DG 1PG (6)

1963 Sydney
Australia 3G 1T (18) to 3T (9)

1967 Twickenham
Australia 1G 3DG 2PG 1T (23)
to 1G 2PG (11)

1973 Twickenham
England 1G 2PG 2T (20) to 1PG (3)

1975 *1* Sydney
Australia 2PG 2DG 1T (16)
to 1G 1PG (9)

2 Brisbane
Australia 2G 2PG 3T (30)
to 2G 3PG (21)
Australia won series 2-0

1976 Twickenham
England 1G 3PG 2T (23) to 2PG (6)

1982 Twickenham
England 1G 3PG (15) to 1PG 2T (11)

SCOTLAND v IRELAND

Played 94 Scotland won 47, Ireland won 43, Drawn 4

1877 Belfast
Scotland 4G 2DG 2T to 0

1878 No Match

1879 Belfast
Scotland 1G 1DG 1T to 0

1880 Glasgow
Scotland 1G 2DG 2T to 0

1881 Belfast
Ireland 1DG to 1T

1882 Glasgow
Scotland 2T to 0

1883 Belfast
Scotland 1G 1T to 0

1884 Raeburn Place (Edinburgh)
Scotland 2G 2T to 1T

1885 Raeburn Place
Scotland 1G 2T to 0

1886 Raeburn Place
Scotland 3G 1DG 2T to 0

1887 Belfast
Scotland 1G 1GM 2T to 0

1888 Raeburn Place
Scotland 1G to 0

1889 Belfast
Scotland 1DG to 0

1890 Raeburn Place
Scotland 1DG 1T to 0

1891 Belfast
Scotland 3G 1DG 2T (14) to 0

1892 Raeburn Place
Scotland 1T (2) to 0

1893 Belfast
Drawn no score

1894 Dublin
Ireland 1G (5) to 0

1895 Raeburn Place
Scotland 2T (6) to 0

1896 Dublin
Drawn no score

1897 Powderhall (Edinburgh)
Scotland 1G 1PG (8) to 1T (3)

1898 Belfast
Scotland 1G 1T (8) to 0

1899 Inverleith (Edinburgh)
Ireland 3T (9) to 1PG (3)

1900 Dublin
Drawn no score

1901 Inverleith (Edinburgh)
Scotland 3T (9) to 1G (5)

1902 Belfast
Ireland 1G (5) to 0

1903 Inverleith
Scotland 1T (3) to 0

1904 Dublin
Scotland 2G 3T (19) to 1T (3)

1905 Inverleith
Ireland 1G 2T (11) to 1G (5)

1906 Dublin
Scotland 2G 1GM (13) to 2T (6)

1907 Inverleith
Scotland 3G (15) to 1PG (3)

1908 Dublin
Ireland 2G 2T (16) to 1G 1PG 1T (11)

1909 Inverleith
Scotland 3T (9) to 1PG (3)

1910 Belfast
Scotland 1G 3T (14) to 0

1911 Inverleith
Ireland 2G 2T (16) to 1DG 2T (10)

1912 Dublin
Ireland 1DG 1PG 1T (10) to 1G 1T (8)

1913 Inverleith
Scotland 4G 3T (29) to 2G 1DG (14)

1914 Dublin
Ireland 2T (6) to 0

1920 Inverleith
Scotland 2G 1PG 2T (19) to 0

1921 Dublin
Ireland 3T (9) to 1G 1T (8)

1922 Inverleith
Scotland 2T (6) to 1T (3)

1923 Dublin
Scotland 2G 1T (13) to 1T (3)

1924 Inverleith
Scotland 2G 1T (13) to 1G 1T (8)

1925 Dublin
Scotland 2G 1DG (14) to 1G 1PG (8)

1926 Murrayfield
Ireland 1T (3) to 0

1927 Dublin
Ireland 2T (6) to 0

1928 Murrayfield
Ireland 2G 1T (13) to 1G (5)

1929 Dublin
Scotland 2G 2T (16) to 1DG 1T (7)

1930 Murrayfield
Ireland 1G 3T (14) to 1G 2T (11)

1931 Dublin
Ireland 1G 1T (8) to 1G (5)

1932 Murrayfield
Ireland 4G (20) to 1G 1T (8)

1933 Dublin
Scotland 2DG (8) to 2T (6)

1934 Murrayfield
Scotland 2G 1PG 1T (16) to 3T (9)

1935 Dublin
Ireland 4T (12) to 1G (5)

1936 Murrayfield
Ireland 1DG 2T (10) to 1DG (4)

1937 Dublin
Ireland 1G 2T (11) to 1DG (4)

1938 Murrayfield
Scotland 2G 1DG 1PG 2T (23)
to 1G 3T (14)

1939 Dublin
Ireland 1PG 1GM 2T (12) to 1T (3)

1947 Murrayfield
Ireland 1T (3) to 0

1948 Dublin
Ireland 2T (6) to 0

1949 Murrayfield
Ireland 2G 1PG (13) to 1PG (3)

1950 Dublin
Ireland 3G 2PG (21) to 0

1951 Murrayfield
Ireland 1DG 1T (6) to 1G (5)

1952 Dublin
Ireland 1PG 3T (12) to 1G 1PG (8)

1953 Murrayfield
Ireland 4G 2T (26) to 1G 1PG (8)

1954 Belfast
Ireland 2T (6) to 0

1955 Murrayfield
Scotland 2PG 1DG 1T (12) to 1PG (3)

1956 Dublin
Ireland 1G 3T (14) to 2G (10)

1957 Murrayfield
Ireland 1G (5) to 1PG (3)

1958 Dublin
Ireland 2PG 2T (12) to 2T (6)

1959 Murrayfield
Ireland 1G 1PG (8) to 1PG (3)

1960 Dublin
Scotland 1DG 1T (6) to 1G (5)

1961 Murrayfield
Scotland 2G 1PG 1T (16) to 1G 1T (8)

1962 Dublin
Scotland 1G 1DG 2PG 2T (20)
to 1PG 1T (6)

1963 Murrayfield
Scotland 1PG (3) to 0

1964 Dublin
Scotland 2PG (6) to 1PG (3)

1965 Murrayfield
Ireland 2G 1DG 1T (16) to 1DG 1PG (6)

1966 Dublin
Scotland 1G 2T (11) to 1PG (3)

1967 Murrayfield
Ireland 1G (5) to 1PG (3)

1968 Dublin
Ireland 1G 1PG 2T (14) to 2PG (6)

1969 Murrayfield
Ireland 2G 2T (16) to 0

1970 Dublin
Ireland 2G 2T (16) to 1G 1DG 1T (11)

1971 Murrayfield
Ireland 1G 2PG 2T (17) to 1G (5)

1972 No Match

1973 Murrayfield
Scotland 2PG 3DG 1T (19)
to 2PG 2T (14)

1974 Dublin
Ireland 1G 1PG (9) to 2PG (6)

1975 Murrayfield
Scotland 2PG 2DG 2T (20)
to 1G 1PG 1T (13)

1976 Dublin
Scotland 4PG 1DG (15) to 2PG (6)

1977 Murrayfield
Scotland 2PG 1DG 3T (21)
to 1G 3PG 1DG (18)

1978 Dublin
Ireland 1G 2PG (12) to 3PG (9)

1979 Murrayfield
Drawn 1PG 2T (11) each

1980 Dublin
Ireland 1G 3PG 1DG 1T (22)
to 2G 1PG (15)

1981 Murrayfield
Scotland 1PG 1DG 1T (10)
to 1G 1PG (9)

1982 Dublin
Ireland 6PG 1DG (21) to 1G 2PG (12)

1983 Murrayfield
Ireland 1G 3PG (15)
to 2PG 1DG 1T (13)

1984 Dublin
Scotland *3G 2PG 2T (32) to 1G 1PG (9)
**includes one penalty try*

SCOTLAND v WALES

Played 88 Scotland won 37, Wales won 49, Drawn 2

1883 Raeburn Place (Edinburgh)
Scotland 3G to 1G

1884 Newport
Scotland 1DG 1T to 0

1885 Glasgow
Drawn no score

1886 Cardiff
Scotland 2G 1T to 0

1887 Raeburn Place
Scotland 4G 8T to 0

1888 Newport
Wales 1T to 0

1889 Raeburn Place
Scotland 2T to 0

1890 Cardiff
Scotland 1G 2T to 1T

1891 Raeburn Place
Scotland 1G 2DG 6T (15) to 0

1892 Swansea
Scotland 1G 1T (7) to 1T (2)

1893 Raeburn Place
Wales 1PG 3T (9) to 0

1894 Newport
Wales 1DG 1T (7) to 0

1895 Raeburn Place
Scotland 1G (5) to 1GM (4)

1896 Cardiff
Wales 2T (6) to 0

1897 No Match

1898 No Match

1899 Inverleith (Edinburgh)
Scotland 1GM 2DG 3T (21) to 2G (10)

1900 Swansea
Wales 4T (12) to 1T (3)

1901 Inverleith
Scotland 3G 1T (18) to 1G 1T (8)

1902 Cardiff
Wales 1G 3T (14) to 1G (5)

1903 Inverleith
Scotland 1PG 1T (6) to 0

1904 Swansea
Wales 3G 1PG 1T (21) to 1T (3)

1905 Inverleith
Wales 2T (6) to 1T (3)

1906 Cardiff
Wales 3T (9) to 1PG (3)

1907 Inverleith
Scotland 2T (6) to 1PG (3)

1908 Swansea
Wales 2T (6) to 1G (5)

1909 Inverleith
Wales 1G (5) to 1PG (3)

1910 Cardiff
Wales 1G 3T (14) to 0

1911 Inverleith
Wales 2G 1DG 6T (32)
to 1DG 2T (10)

1912 Swansea
Wales 2G 2DG 1T (21) to 2T (6)

1913 Inverleith
Wales 1G 1T (8) to 0

1914 Cardiff
Wales 2G 2DG 1PG 1T (24) to 1G (5)

1920 Inverleith
Scotland 2PG 1T (9) to 1G (5)

1921 Swansea
Scotland 1G 1PG 2T (14) to 2DG (8)

1922 Inverleith
Drawn Scotland 1PG 2T (9)
Wales 1G 1DG (9)

1923 Cardiff
Scotland 1G 2T (11) to 1G 1PG (8)

1924 Inverleith
Scotland 4G 1PG 4T (35) to 2G (10)

1925 Swansea
Scotland 1G 1DG 5T (24)
to 1G 1PG 2T (14)

1926 Murrayfield
Scotland 1G 1PG (8) to 1G (5)

1927 Cardiff
Scotland 1G (5) to 0

1928 Murrayfield
Wales 2G 1T (13) to 0

1929 Swansea
Wales 1G 3T (14) to 1DG 1PG (7)

1930 Murrayfield
Scotland 1G 1DG 1T (12)
to 1G 1DG (9)

1931 Cardiff
Wales 2G 1T (13) to 1G 1T (8)

1932 Murrayfield
Wales 1PG 1T (6) to 0

1933 Swansea
Scotland 1G 1PG 1T (11) to 1T (3)

1934 Murrayfield
Wales 2G 1T (13) to 1PG 1T (6)

1935 Cardiff
Wales 1DG 2T (10) to 2T (6)

1936 Murrayfield
Wales 2G 1T (13) to 1T (3)

1937 Swansea
Scotland 2G 1T (13) to 2T (6)

1938 Murrayfield
Scotland 1G 1PG (8) to 2T (6)

1939 Cardiff
Wales 1G 1PG 1T (11) to 1PG (3)

1947 Murrayfield
Wales 2G 1PG 3T (22) to 1G 1PG (8)

1948 Cardiff
Wales 1G 1PG 2T (14) to 0

1949 Murrayfield
Scotland 2T (6) to 1G (5)

1950 Swansea
Wales 1DG 1PG 2T (12) to 0

1951 Murrayfield
Scotland 2G 1DG 1PG 1T (19) to 0

1952 Cardiff
Wales 1G 2PG (11) to 0

1953 Murrayfield
Wales 1PG 3T (12) to 0

1954 Swansea
Wales 1PG 4T (15) to 1T (3)

1955 Murrayfield
Scotland 1G 1DG 1PG 1T (14)
to 1G 1T (8)

1956 Cardiff
Wales 3T (9) to 1PG (3)

1957 Murrayfield
Scotland 1DG 1PG 1T (9)
to 1PG 1T (6)

1958 Cardiff
Wales 1G 1T (8) to 1PG (3)

1959 Murrayfield
Scotland 1PG 1T (6) to 1G (5)

1960 Cardiff
Wales 1G 1PG (8) to 0

1961 Murrayfield
Scotland 1T (3) to 0

1962 Cardiff
Scotland 1G 1T (8) to 1DG (3)

1963 Murrayfield
Wales 1DG 1PG (6) to 0

1964 Cardiff
Wales 1G 1PG 1T (11) to 1T (3)

1965 Murrayfield
Wales 1G 2PG 1T (14) to 2DG 2PG (12)

1966 Cardiff
Wales 1G 1T (8) to 1PG (3)

1967 Murrayfield
Scotland 1G 1DG 1T (11) to 1G (5)

1968 Cardiff
Wales 1G (5) to 0

1969 Murrayfield
Wales 1G 2PG 2T (17) to 1PG (3)

1970 Cardiff
Wales 3G 1T (18) to 1DG 1PG 1T (9)

1971 Murrayfield
Wales 2G 1PG 2T (19) to 4PG 2T (18)

1972 Cardiff
Wales 3G 3PG 2T (35) to 1G 2PG (12)

1973 Murrayfield
Scotland 1G 1T (10) to 3PG (9)

1974 Cardiff
Wales 1G (6) to 0

1975 Murrayfield
Scotland 3PG 1DG (12) to 2PG 1T (10)

1976 Cardiff
Wales 2G 3PG 1DG 1T (28) to 1G (6)

1977 Murrayfield
Wales 2G 2PG (18) to 1G 1DG (9)

1978 Cardiff
Wales 1PG 1DG 4T (22) to 2PG 2T (14)

1979 Murrayfield
Wales 1G 3PG 1T (19) to 3PG 1T (13)

1980 Cardiff
Wales 1G 1PG 2T (17) to 1G (6)

1981 Murrayfield
Scotland *2G 1PG (15) to 2PG (6)
includes one penalty try

1982 Cardiff
Scotland 4G 2DG 1T (34)
to 1G 4PG (18)

1983 Murrayfield
Wales 1G 3PG 1T (19) to 1G 3PG (15)

1984 Cardiff
Scotland 2G 1PG (15) to 1G 1PG (9)

SCOTLAND v FRANCE

Played 54 Scotland won 26, France won 26, Drawn 2

1910 Inverleith (Edinburgh)
Scotland 3G 4T (27) to 0

1911 Paris
France 2G 2T (16) to 1G 1DG 2T (15)

1912 Inverleith
Scotland 5G 1PG 1T (31) to 1T (3)

1913 Paris
Scotland 3G 2T (21) to 1T (3)

1914 No Match

1920 Paris
Scotland 1G (5) to 0

1921 Inverleith
France 1T (3) to 0

1922 Paris
Drawn 1T (3) each

1923 Inverleith
Scotland 2G 2T (16) to 1GM (3)

1924 Paris
France 4T (12) to 1DG 1PG 1T (10)

1925 Inverleith
Scotland 2G 5T (25) to 1DG (4)

1926 Paris
Scotland 1G 1PG 4T (20) to 1PG 1T (6)

1927 Murrayfield
Scotland 4G 1PG (23) to 2T (6)

1928 Paris
Scotland 5T (15) to 2T (6)

1929 Murrayfield
Scotland 1PG 1T (6) to 1T (3)

1930 Paris
France 1DG 1T (7) to 1T (3)

1931 Murrayfield
Scotland 2PG (6) to 1DG (4)

1947 Paris
France 1G 1T (8) to 1PG (3)

1948 Murrayfield
Scotland 2PG 1T (9) to 1G 1PG (8)

1949 Paris
Scotland 1G 1T (8) to 0

1950 Murrayfield
Scotland 1G 1T (8) to 1G (5)

1951 Paris
France 1G 2PG 1T (14) to 2PG 2T (12)

1952 Murrayfield
France 2G 1PG (13) to 1G 2PG (11)

1953 Paris
France 1G 1DG 1PG (11) to 1G (5)

1954 Murrayfield
France 1T (3) to 0

1955 Paris
France 1PG 4T (15) to 0

1956 Murrayfield
Scotland 2PG 2T (12) to 0

1957 Paris
Scotland 1DG 1PG (6) to 0

1958 Murrayfield
Scotland 1G 1PG 1T (11) to 2PG 1T (9)

1959 Paris
France 2DG 1T (9) to 0

1960 Murrayfield
France 2G 1T (13) to 1G 1PG 1T (11)

1961 Paris
France 1G 1DG 1PG (11) to 0

1962 Murrayfield
France 1G 2PG (11) to 1PG (3)

1963 Paris
Scotland 1G 1DG 1PG (11)
to 1DG 1PG (6)

1964 Murrayfield
Scotland 2G (10) to 0

1965 Paris
France 2G 2T (16) to 1G 1T (8)

1966 Murrayfield
Drawn Scotland 1T (3) France 1PG (3)

1967 Paris
Scotland 2PG 1DG (9) to 1G 1T (8)

1968 Murrayfield
France 1G 1T (8) to 1PG 1T (6)

1969 Paris
Scotland 1PG 1T (6) to 1PG (3)

1970 Murrayfield
France 1G 1DG 1T (11) to 2PG 1T (9)

1971 Paris
France 2G 1PG (13) to 1G 1PG (8)

1972 Murrayfield
Scotland 1G 1PG 1DG 2T (20)
to 1G 1PG (9)

1973 Paris
France 3PG 1DG 1T (16)
to 2PG 1DG 1T (13)

1974 Murrayfield
Scotland 1G 3PG 1T (19) to 1PG 1DG (6)

1975 Paris
France 1PG 1DG 1T (10) to 3PG (9)

1976 Murrayfield
France 3PG 1T (13) to 1PG 1DG (6)

1977 Paris
France 2G 1PG 2T (23) to 1PG (3)

1978 Murrayfield
France 1G 3PG 1T (19)
to 1G 1PG 1DG 1T (16)

1979 Paris
France 2PG 1DG 3T (21)
to 1G 1PG 2T (17)

1980 Murrayfield
Scotland 2G 2PG 1T (22)
to 1PG 1DG 2T (14)

1981 Paris
France 1G 2PG 1T (16)
to 1G 1PG (9)

1982 Murrayfield
Scotland 3PG 1DG 1T (16)
to 1PG 1T (7)

1983 Paris
France 1G 1T 3PG (19)
to 1G 2DG 1PG (15)

1984 Murrayfield
Scotland 1G 5PG (21)
to 1G 1DG 1PG (12)

SCOTLAND v NEW ZEALAND

Played 12 Scotland won 0, New Zealand won 10, Drawn 2

1905 Inverleith (Edinburgh)
New Zealand 4T (12) to 1DG 1T (7)

1935 Murrayfield
New Zealand 3G 1T (18) to 1G 1T (8)

1954 Murrayfield
New Zealand 1PG (3) to 0

1964 Murrayfield
Drawn no score

1967 Murrayfield
New Zealand 1G 2PG 1T (14)
to 1DG (3)

1972 Murrayfield
New Zealand 1G 2T (14) to 1DG 2PG (9)

1975 Auckland
New Zealand 4G (24) to 0

1978 Murrayfield
New Zealand 2G 2PG (18) to 1G
1DG (9)

1979 Murrayfield
New Zealand 2G 2T (20) to 2PG (6)

1981 *1* Dunedin
New Zealand 1PG 2T (11) to 1T (4)

2 Auckland
New Zealand 6G 1T (40) to 1G 2PG
1DG (15)
**New Zealand won series 2-0*

1983 Murrayfield
Drawn Scotland 5PG 2DG 1T (25)
New Zealand 2G 3PG 1T (25)

SCOTLAND v SOUTH AFRICA

Played 8 Scotland won 3, South Africa won 5, Drawn 0

1906 Glasgow
Scotland 2T (6) to 0

1912 Inverleith
South Africa 2G 2T (16) to 0

1932 Murrayfield
South Africa 2T (6) to 1T (3)

1951 Murrayfield
South Africa 7G 1DG 2T (44) to 0

1960 Port Elizabeth
South Africa 3G 1T (18) to 2G (10)

1961 Murrayfield
South Africa 2PG 2T (12) to 1G (5)

1965 Murrayfield
Scotland 1G 1DG (8) to 1G (5)

1969 Murrayfield
Scotland 1PG 1T (6) to 1PG (3)

SCOTLAND v AUSTRALIA

Played 9 Scotland won 6, Australia won 3, Drawn 0

1947 Murrayfield
Australia 2G 2T (16) to 1DG 1PG (7)

1958 Murrayfield
Scotland 2PG 2T (12) to 1G 1T (8)

1966 Murrayfield
Scotland 1G 1PG 1T (11) to 1G (5)

1968 Murrayfield
Scotland 2PG 1T (9) to 1PG (3)

1970 Sydney
Australia 1G 1PG 5T (23) to 1PG (3)

1975 Murrayfield
Scotland 1G 1T (10) to 1PG (3)

1981 Murrayfield
Scotland 1G 5PG 1DG (24)
to 1PG 3T (15)

1982 *1* Brisbane
Scotland 1G 1PG 1DG (12) to 1PG 1T (7)

2 Sydney
Australia 3G 5PG (33) to 3PG (9)
**Series drawn 1-1*

IRELAND v WALES

Played 86 Ireland won 28, Wales won 53, Drawn 5

1882 Dublin
Wales 2G 2T to 0

1883 No Match

1884 Cardiff
Wales 1DG 2T to 0

1885 No Match

1886 No Match

1887 Birkenhead
Wales 1DG 1T to 3T

1888 Dublin
Ireland 1G 1DG 1T to 0

1889 Swansea
Ireland 2T to 0

1890 Dublin
Drawn 1G each

1891 Llanelli
Wales 1G 1DG (6) to 1DG 1T (4)

1892 Dublin
Ireland 1G 2T (8) to 0

1893 Llanelli
Wales 1T (2) to 0

1894 Belfast
Ireland 1PG (3) to 0

1895 Cardiff
Wales 1G (5) to 1T (3)

1896 Dublin
Ireland 1G 1T (8) to 1DG (4)

1897 No Match

1898 Limerick
Wales 1G 1PG 1T (11) to 1PG (3)

1899 Cardiff
Ireland 1T (3) to 0

1900 Belfast
Wales 1T (3) to 0

1901 Swansea
Wales 2G (10) to 3T (9)

1902 Dublin
Wales 1G 1DG 2T (15) to 0

1903 Cardiff
Wales 6T (18) to 0

1904 Belfast
Ireland 1G 3T (14) to 4T (12)

1905 Swansea
Wales 2G (10) to 1T (3)

1906 Belfast
Ireland 1G 2T (11) to 2T (6)

1907 Cardiff
Wales 2G 1DG 1PG 4T (29) to 0

1908 Belfast
Wales 1G 2T (11) to 1G (5)

1909 Swansea
Wales 3G 1T (18) to 1G (5)

1910 Dublin
Wales 1DG 5T (19) to 1T (3)

1911 Cardiff
Wales 2G 1PG 1T (16) to 0

1912 Belfast
Ireland 1G 1DG 1T (12) to 1G (5)

1913 Swansea
Wales 2G 1PG 1T (16) to 2G 1PG (13)

1914 Belfast
Wales 1G 2T (11) to 1T (3)

1920 Cardiff
Wales 3G 1DG 3T (28) to 1DG (4)

1921 Belfast
Wales 1PG 1T (6) to 0

1922 Swansea
Wales 1G 2T (11) to 1G (5)

1923 Dublin
Ireland 1G (5) to 1DG (4)

1924 Cardiff
Ireland 2G 1T (13) to 1DG 2T (10)

1925 Belfast
Ireland 2G 1PG 2T (19) to 1T (3)

1926 Swansea
Wales 1G 2T (11) to 1G 1PG (8)

1927 Dublin
Ireland 2G 1PG 2T (19) to 1G 1DG (9)

1928 Cardiff
Ireland 2G 1T (13) to 2G (10)

1929 Belfast
Drawn 1G (5) each

1930 Swansea
Wales 1PG 3T (12) to 1DG 1PG (7)

1931 Belfast
Wales 1G 1DG 2T (15) to 1T (3)

1932 Cardiff
Ireland 4T (12) to 1DG 2T (10)

1933 Belfast
Ireland 1DG 1PG 1T (10) to 1G (5)

1934 Swansea
Wales 2G 1T (13) to 0

1935 Belfast
Ireland 2PG 1T (9) to 1PG (3)

1936 Cardiff
Wales 1PG (3) to 0

1937 Belfast
Ireland 1G (5) to 1PG (3)

1938 Swansea
Wales 1G 1PG 1T (11) to 1G (5)

1939 Belfast
Wales 1DG 1T (7) to 0

1947 Swansea
Wales 1PG 1T (6) to 0

1948 Belfast
Ireland 2T (6) to 1T (3)

1949 Swansea
Ireland 1G (5) to 0

1950 Belfast
Wales 2T (6) to 1PG (3)

1951 Cardiff
Drawn Wales 1PG (3) to Ireland 1T (3)

1952 Dublin
Wales 1G 1PG 2T (14) to 1PG (3)

1953 Swansea
Wales 1G (5) to 1T (3)

1954 Dublin
Wales 1DG 3PG (12) to 2PG 1T (9)

1955 Cardiff
Wales 3G 1PG 1T (21) to 1PG (3)

1956 Dublin
Ireland 1G 1DG 1PG (11) to 1PG (3)

1957 Cardiff
Wales 2PG (6) to 1G (5)

1958 Dublin
Wales 3T (9) to 1PG 1T (6)

1959 Cardiff
Wales 1G 1T (8) to 1PG 1T (6)

1960 Dublin
Wales 2G (10) to 2PG 1T (9)

1961 Cardiff
Wales 2PG 1T (9) to 0

1962 Dublin
Drawn Ireland 1DG (3) Wales 1PG (3)

1963 Cardiff
Ireland 1G 1DG 2PG (14)
to 1DG 1T (6)

1964 Dublin
Wales 3G (15) to 2PG (6)

1965 Cardiff
Wales 1G 1DG 1PG 1T (14)
to 1G 1PG (8)

1966 Dublin
Ireland 1DG 1PG 1T (9) to 1PG 1T (6)

1967 Cardiff
Ireland 1T (3) to 0

1968 Dublin
Ireland 1PG 1DG 1T (9) to 1PG 1DG (6)

1969 Cardiff
Wales 3G 1DG 1PG 1T (24)
to 1G 2PG (11)

1970 Dublin
Ireland 1G 1DG 1PG 1T (14) to 0

1971 Cardiff
Wales 1G 2PG 1DG 3T (23) to 3PG (9)

1972 No Match

1973 Cardiff
Wales 1G 2PG 1T (16) to 1G 2PG (12)

1974 Dublin
Drawn Ireland 3PG (9)
Wales 1G 1PG (9)

1975 Cardiff
Wales 3G 2PG 2T (32) to 1T (4)

1976 Dublin
Wales 3G 4PG 1T (34) to 3PG (9)

1977 Cardiff
Wales 2G 2PG 1DG 1T (25) to 3PG (9)

1978 Dublin
Wales 4PG 2T (20) to 3PG 1DG 1T (16)

1979 Cardiff
Wales 2G 4PG (24) to 2G 3PG (21)

1980 Dublin
Ireland 3G 1PG (21) to 1PG 1T (7)

1981 Cardiff
Wales 2PG 1DG (9) to 2T (8)

1982 Dublin
Ireland 1G 2PG 2T (20)
to 1G 1PG 1DG (12)

1983 Cardiff
Wales 1G 3PG 2T (23) to 3PG (9)

1984 Dublin
Wales 1G 4PG (18) to 3PG (9)

IRELAND v FRANCE

Played 57 Ireland won 25, France won 28, Drawn 4

1909 Dublin
Ireland 2G 1PG 2T (19) to 1G 1T (8)

1910 Paris
Ireland 1G 1T (8) to 1T (3)

1911 Cork
Ireland 3G 1DG 2T (25) to 1G (5)

1912 Paris
Ireland 1G 2T (11) to 2T (6)

1913 Cork
Ireland 3G 3T (24) to 0

1914 Paris
Ireland 1G 1T (8) to 2T (6)

1920 Dublin
France 5T (15) to 1DG 1T (7)

1921 Paris
France 4G (20) to 2G (10)

1922 Dublin
Ireland 1G 1PG (8) to 1T (3)

1923 Paris
France 1G 3T (14) to 1G 1T (8)

1924 Dublin
Ireland 2T (6) to 0

1925 Paris
Ireland 1PG 2T (9) to 1T (3)

Ireland's Donal Lenihan disputes a line-out with Jean Condom during the 1984 International Championship match against France.

1926 Belfast
Ireland 1G 1PG 1T (11) to 0

1927 Paris
Ireland 1G 1PG (8) to 1T (3)

1928 Belfast
Ireland 4T (12) to 1G 1T (8)

1929 Paris
Ireland 2T (6) to 0

1930 Belfast
France 1G (5) to 0

1931 Paris
France 1T (3) to 0

1947 Dublin
France 4T (12) to 1G 1PG (8)

1948 Paris
Ireland 2G 1T (13) to 2T (6)

1949 Dublin
France 2G 2PG (16) to 3PG (9)

1950 Paris
Drawn France 1DG (3) Ireland 1PG (3)

1951 Dublin
Ireland 1PG 2T (9) to 1G 1T (8)

1952 Paris
Ireland 1G 1PG 1T (11) to 1G 1PG (8)

1953 Belfast
Ireland 2G 2T (16) to 1DG (3)

1954 Paris
France 1G 1T (8) to 0

1955 Dublin
France 1G (5) to 1PG (3)

1956 Paris
France 1G 2DG 1T (14) to 1G 1PG (8)

1957 Dublin
Ireland 1G 1PG 1T (11) to 2PG (6)

1958 Paris
France 1G 1DG 1PG (11) to 2PG (6)

1959 Dublin
Ireland 1DG 1PG 1T (9) to 1G (5)

1960 Paris
France 1G 3DG 3T (23) to 2T (6)

1961 Dublin
France 2DG 2PG 1T (15) to 1PG (3)

1962 Paris
France 1G 2T (11) to 0

1963 Dublin
France 3G 2DG 1T (24) to 1G (5)

1964 Paris
France 3G 1DG 3T (27) to 1DG 1T (6)

1965 Dublin
Drawn 1T (3) each

1966 Paris
France 1G 1PG 1T (11) to 1DG 1PG (6)

1967 Dublin
France 1G 2DG (11) to 1PG 1T (6)

1968 Paris
France 2G 1PG 1DG (16) to 2PG (6)

1969 Dublin
Ireland 1G 1DG 3PG (17) to 2PG 1T (9)

1970 Paris
France 1G 1DG (8) to 0

1971 Dublin
Drawn Ireland 2PG 1T (9)
France 2PG 1DG (9)

1972 Paris
Ireland 2PG 2T (14) to 1G 1PG (9)

*1972 Dublin
Ireland 3G 2PG (24) to 1G 2T (14)

1973 Dublin
Ireland 2PG (6) to 1T (4)

1974 Paris
France 1G 1PG (9) to 2PG (6)

1975 Dublin
Ireland 2G 1PG 2DG 1T (25)
to 1PG 1DG (6)

1976 Paris
France 2G 2PG 2T (26) to 1PG (3)

1977 Dublin
France 1G 3PG (15) to 2PG (6)

1978 Paris
France 2PG 1T (10) to 3PG (9)

1979 Dublin
Drawn Ireland 3PG (9)
France 1G 1PG (9)

1980 Paris
France 1G 2PG 1DG 1T (19)
to 1G 3PG 1DG (18)

1981 Dublin
France 3PG 2DG 1T (19)
to 3PG 1T (13)

1982 Paris
France 1G 4PG 1T (22) to 3PG (9)

1983 Dublin
Ireland 1G 4PG 1T (22)
to 1G 2PG 1T (16)

1984 Paris
France 1G 4PG 1DG 1T (25) to 4PG (12)

**Non-championship match*

IRELAND v NEW ZEALAND

Played 9 Ireland won 0, New Zealand won 8, Drawn 1

1905 Dublin
New Zealand 3G (15) to 0

1924 Dublin
New Zealand 1PG 1T (6) to 0

1935 Dublin
New Zealand 1G 2PG 2T (17)
to 2PG 1T (9)

1954 Dublin
New Zealand 1G 1DG 1PG 1T (14)
to 1PG (3)

1963 Dublin
New Zealand 1PG 1T (6) to 1G (5)

1973 Dublin
Drawn Ireland 2PG 1T (10)
New Zealand 1G 1T (10)

1974 Dublin
New Zealand 1G 3PG (15) to 2PG (6)

1976 Wellington
New Zealand 1PG 2T (11) to 1PG (3)

1978 Dublin
New Zealand 2DG 1T (10) to 2PG (6)

IRELAND v SOUTH AFRICA

Played 10 Ireland won 1, South Africa won 8, Drawn 1

1906 Belfast
South Africa 1PG 4T (15)
to 1PG 3T (12)

1912 Dublin
South Africa 4G 6T (38) to 0

1931 Dublin
South Africa 1G 1T (8) to 1PG (3)

1951 Dublin
South Africa 1G 1DG 3T (17) to 1G (5)

1960 Dublin
South Africa 1G 1T (8) to 1PG (3)

1961 Cape Town
South Africa 3G 1PG 2T (24)
to 1G 1PG (8)

1965 Dublin
Ireland 2PG 1T (9) to 1PG 1T (6)

1970 Dublin
Drawn 1G 1PG (8) each

1981 *1* Cape Town
South Africa 1G 3PG 2T (23)
to 2G 1PG (15)

2 Durban
South Africa 1PG 3DG (12)
to 2PG 1T (10)
South Africa won series 2-0

IRELAND v AUSTRALIA

Played 9 Ireland won 6, Australia won 3, Drawn 0

1947 Dublin
Australia 2G 2T (16) to 1PG (3)

1958 Dublin
Ireland 1PG 2T (9) to 2T (6)

1967 Dublin
Ireland 2DG 1PG 2T (15) to 1G 1DG (8)

1967 Sydney
Ireland 1G 1DG 1T (11) to 1G (5)

1968 Dublin
Ireland 2G (10) to 1T (3)

1976 Dublin
Australia 1G 2PG 2T (20)
to 2PG 1T (10)

1979 *1* Brisbane
Ireland 2G 4PG 1DG (27)
to 1G 2PG (12)

2 Sydney
Ireland 1PG 2DG (9) to 1PG (3)
Ireland won series 2-0

1981 Dublin
Australia 3PG 1DG 1T (16) to 4PG (12)

WALES v FRANCE

Played 57 Wales won 36, France won 18, Drawn 3

1908 Cardiff
Wales 3G 1PG 6T (36) to 1DG (4)

1909 Paris
Wales 7G 4T (47) to 1G (5)

1910 Swansea
Wales 8G 1PG 2T (49)
to 1G 2PG 1T (14)

1911 Paris
Wales 3G (15) to 0

1912 Newport
Wales 1G 3T (14) to 1G 1T (8)

1913 Paris
Wales 1G 2T (11) to 1G 1T (8)

1914 Swansea
Wales 5G 2T (31) to 0

1920 Paris
Wales 2T (6) to 1G (5)

1921 Cardiff
Wales 2PG 2T (12) to 1DG (4)

1922 Paris
Wales 1G 2T (11) to 1T (3)

1923 Swansea
Wales 2G 1PG 1T (16) to 1G 1T (8)

1924 Paris
Wales 1DG 2T (10) to 2T (6)

1925 Cardiff
Wales 1G 2T (11) to 1G (5)

1926 Paris
Wales 1DG 1T (7) to 1G (5)

1927 Swansea
Wales 2G 5T (25) to 1DG 1T (7)

1928 Paris
France 1G 1T (8) to 1T (3)

1929 Cardiff
Wales 1G 1T (8) to 1T (3)

1930 Paris
Wales 2DG 1T (11) to 0

1931 Swansea
Wales 5G 1DG 2T (35) to 1T (3)

1947 Paris
Wales 1PG (3) to 0

1948 Swansea
France 1G 2T (11) to 1PG (3)

1949 Paris
France 1G (5) to 1T (3)

1950 Cardiff
Wales 3G 1PG 1T (21) to 0

1951 Paris
France 1G 1PG (8) to 1T (3)

1952 Swansea
Wales 1DG 2PG (9) to 1G (5)

1953 Paris
Wales 2T (6) to 1PG (3)

1954 Cardiff
Wales 2G 3PG (19) to 2G 1PG (13)

1955 Paris
Wales 2G 2PG (16) to 1G 1DG 1PG (11)

1956 Cardiff
Wales 1G (5) to 1T (3)

1957 Paris
Wales 2G 1PG 2T (19) to 2G 1T (13)

1958 Cardiff
France 2G 2DG (16) to 1PG 1T (6)

1959 Paris
France 1G 1PG 1T (11) to 1PG (3)

1960 Cardiff
France 2G 2T (16) to 1G 1PG (8)

1961 Paris
France 1G 1T (8) to 2T (6)

1962 Cardiff
Wales 1PG (3) to 0

1963 Paris
France 1G (5) to 1PG (3)

1964 Cardiff
Drawn 1G 2PG (11) each

1965 Paris
France 2G 1PG 1DG 2T (22) to 2G 1T (13)

1966 Cardiff
Wales 2PG 1T (9) to 1G 1T (8)

1967 Paris
France 1G 2DG 1PG 2T (20) to 1G 2PG 1DG (14)

1968 Cardiff
France 1G 1PG 1DG 1T (14) to 2PG 1T (9)

1969 Paris
Drawn France 1G 1PG (8) Wales 1G 1T (8)

1970 Cardiff
Wales 1G 2PG (11) to 2T (6)

1971 Paris
Wales 1PG 2T (9) to 1G (5)

1972 Cardiff
Wales 4PG 2T (20) to 2PG (6)

1973 Paris
France 3PG 1DG (12) to 1DG (3)

1974 Cardiff
Drawn 3PG 1DG 1T (16) each

1975 Paris
Wales 1G 1PG 4T (25) to 2PG 1T (10)

1976 Cardiff
Wales 5PG 1T (19) to 1G 1PG 1T (13)

1977 Paris
France 1G 2PG 1T (16) to 3PG (9)

1978 Cardiff
Wales 1G 2DG 1T (16) to 1DG 1T (7)

1979 Paris
France 2PG 2T (14) to 3PG 1T (13)

1980 Cardiff
Wales 1G 3T (18) to 1DG (9)

1981 Paris
France 5PG 1T (19) to 1G 3PG (15)

1982 Cardiff
Wales 6PG 1T (22) to 1G 2PG (12)

1983 Paris
France 1DG 3PG 1T (16) to 1G 1PG (9)

1984 Cardiff
France 1G 4PG 1DG (21) to 1G 2PG 1T (16)

WALES v NEW ZEALAND

Played 11 Wales won 3, New Zealand won 8, Drawn 0

1905 Cardiff
Wales 1T (3) to 0

1924 Swansea
New Zealand 2G 1PG 2T (19) to 0

1935 Cardiff
Wales 2G 1T (13) to 1G 1DG 1T (12)

1953 Cardiff
Wales 2G 1PG (13) to 1G 1PG (8)

1963 Cardiff
New Zealand 1DG 1PG (6) to 0

1967 Cardiff
New Zealand 2G 1PG (13) to 1DG 1PG (6)

1969 *1* Christchurch
New Zealand 2G 1PG 2T (19) to 0

2 Auckland
New Zealand 3G 1DG 5PG (33) to 2PG 2T (12)
New Zealand won series 2-0

1972 Cardiff
New Zealand 5PG 1T (19) to 4PG 1T (16)

1978 Cardiff
New Zealand 3PG 1T (13) to 4PG (12)

1980 Cardiff
New Zealand 2G 1PG 2T (23) to 1PG (3)

WALES v SOUTH AFRICA

Played 7 Wales won 0, South Africa won 6, Drawn 1

1906 Swansea
South Africa 1G 2T (11) to 0

1912 Cardiff
South Africa 1PG (3) to 0

1931 Swansea
South Africa 1G 1T (8) to 1T (3)

1951 Cardiff
South Africa 1DG 1T (6) to 1T (3)

1960 Cardiff
South Africa 1PG (3) to 0

1964 Durban
South Africa 3G 1DG 2PG (24) to 1PG (3)

1970 Cardiff
Drawn 1PG 1T (6) each

WALES v AUSTRALIA

Played 10 Wales won 7, Australia won 3, Drawn 0

1908 Cardiff
Wales 1PG 2T (9) to 2T (6)

1947 Cardiff
Wales 2PG (6) to 0

1958 Cardiff
Wales 1DG 1PG 1T (9) to 1T (3)

1966 Cardiff
Australia 1G 1DG 1PG 1T (14) to 1G 1PG 1T (11)

1969 Sydney
Wales 2G 2PG 1T (19) to 2G 2PG (16)

1973 Cardiff
Wales 4PG 3T (24) to 0

1975 Cardiff
Wales 3G 1PG 1DG 1T (28) to 1PG (3)

1978 *1* Brisbane
Australia 1G 4PG (18) to 2T (8)

2 Sydney
Australia 3PG 2DG 1T (19) to 2PG 1DG 2T (17)
Australia won series 2-0

1981 Cardiff
Wales 1G 3PG 1DG (18) to 1G 1PG 1T (13)

FRANCE v NEW ZEALAND

Played 18 France won 4, New Zealand won 14, Drawn 0

1906 Paris
New Zealand 4G 6T (38) to 1G 1T (8)

1925 Toulouse
New Zealand 3G 5T (30) to 2T (6)

1954 Paris
France 1T (3) to 0

1961 *1* Auckland
New Zealand 2G 1DG (13) to 2DG (6)

2 Wellington
New Zealand 1G (5) to 1T (3)

3 Christchurch
New Zealand 4G 3PG 1T (32) to 1T (3)
New Zealand won series 3-0

1964 Paris
New Zealand 1DG 1PG 2T (12)
to 1PG (3)

1967 Paris
New Zealand 3G 1PG 1T (21)
to 3PG 1DG 1T (15)

1968 *1* Christchurch
New Zealand 3PG 1T (12)
to 1DG 2PG (9)

2 Wellington
New Zealand 3PG (9) to 1PG (3)

3 Auckland
New Zealand 2G 1DG 2PG (19)
to 1DG 3T (12)
New Zealand won series 3-0

1973 Paris
France 1G 1PG 1T (13) to 2PG (6)

1977 *1* Toulouse
France 1G 1DG 3PG (18)
to 1DG 2PG 1T (13)

2 Paris
New Zealand 1G 1DG 2PG (15)
to 1PG (3)
Series drawn 1-1

1979 *1* Christchurch
New Zealand 1G 3PG 2T (23)
to 1G 1DG (9)

2 Auckland
France 1G 1PG 1DG 3T (24)
to 1G 3PG 1T (19)
Series drawn 1-1

1981 *1* Toulouse
New Zealand 2PG 1DG 1T (13)
to 2PG 1DG (9)

2 Paris
New Zealand 2G 2PG (18) to 2PG (6)
New Zealand won series 2-0

FRANCE v SOUTH AFRICA

Played 19 France won 3, South Africa won 12, Drawn 4

1913 Bordeaux
South Africa 4G 1PG 5T (38) to 1G (5)

1952 Paris
South Africa 2G 1PG 4T (25)
to 1DG (3)

1958 *1* Cape Town
Drawn South Africa 1T (3)
France 1DG (3)

2 Johannesburg
France 2DG 1PG (9) to 1G (5)
France won series 1-0, with 1 draw

1961 Paris
Drawn no score

1964 Springs (SA)
France 1G 1PG (8) to 1PG 1T (6)

1967 *1* Durban
South Africa 4G 1PG 1T (26) to 1T (3)

2 Bloemfontein
South Africa 2G 1PG 1T (16) to 1PG (3)

3 Johannesburg
France 2G 2DG 1PG (19)
to 1G 2PG 1T (14)

4 Cape Town
Drawn South Africa 1DG 1PG (6)
France 1PG 1T (6)
South Africa won series 2-1, with 1 draw

1968 *1* Bordeaux
South Africa 4PG (12) to 3T (9)

2 Paris
South Africa 2G 1PG 1T (16)
to 1G 2DG (11)
South Africa won series 2-0

1971 *1* Bloemfontein
South Africa 2G 1DG 3PG (22)
to 2PG 1T (9)

2 Durban
Drawn 1G 1DG (8) each
South Africa won series 1-0, with 1 draw

1974 *1* Toulouse
South Africa 3PG 1T (13) to 1T (4)

2 Paris
South Africa 2PG 1T (10) to 2T (8)
South Africa won series 2-0

1975 *1* Bloemfontein
South Africa 3G 4PG 2T (38)
to 3G 1PG 1T (25)

2 Pretoria
South Africa 2G 7PG (33)
to 1G 3PG 1DG (18)
South Africa won series 2-0

1980 Pretoria
South Africa 4G 3PG 1T (37)
to 1G 3PG (15)

FRANCE v AUSTRALIA

Played 15 France won 9, Australia won 4, Drawn 2

1948 Paris
France 2G 1T (13) to 2PG (6)

1958 Paris
France 2G 2DG 1T (19) to 0

1961 Sydney
France 2DG 3T (15) to 1G 1PG (8)

1967 Paris
France 1G 1DG 4PG (20)
to 1G 1DG 1PG 1T (14)

1968 Sydney
Australia 1G 1DG 1PG (11) to 2G (10)

1971 *1* Toulouse
Australia 1G 1PG 1T (13) to 1PG 2T (11)

2 Paris
France 1G 4PG (18) to 3PG (9)
Series drawn 1-1

1972 *1* Sydney
Drawn Australia 2PG 2T (14)
France 1G 2T (14)

2 Brisbane
France 2G 1T (16) to 5PG (15)
France won series 1-0, with 1 draw

1976 *1* Bordeaux
France 3G (18) to 4PG 1DG (15)

2 Paris
France 2G 1PG 1DG 4T (34) to 2PG (6)
France won series 2-0

1981 *1* Brisbane
Australia 1G 1PG 2T (17)
to 1G 2PG 1DG (15)

2 Sydney
Australia 2G 4PG (24) to 2DG 2T (14)
Australia won series 2-0

1983 *1* Clermont-Ferrand
Drawn France 3PG 2DG (15)
Australia 1G 1PG 2DG (15)

2 Paris
France 1G 3PG (15) to 1PG 1DG (6)
France won series 1-0, with 1 draw

NEW ZEALAND v SOUTH AFRICA

Played 37 New Zealand won 15, South Africa won 20, Drawn 2

1921 *1* Dunedin
New Zealand 2G 1T (13) to 1G (5)

2 Auckland
South Africa 1G 1DG (9) to 1G (5)

3 Wellington
Drawn no score
Series drawn 1-1, with 1 draw

1928 *1* Durban
South Africa 2DG 2PG 1T (17) to 0

2 Johannesburg
New Zealand 1DG 1PG (7)
to 1PG 1GM (6)

3 Port Elizabeth
South Africa 1G 2T (11) to 2T (6)

4 Cape Town
New Zealand 1DG 2PG 1T (13)
to 1G (5)
Series drawn 2-2

1937 *1* Wellington
New Zealand 1DG 2PG 1T (13)
to 1DG 1T (7)

2 Christchurch
South Africa 2G 1PG (13) to 2T (6)

3 Auckland
South Africa 1G 4T (17) to 2PG (6)
South Africa won series 2-1

1949 *1* Cape Town
South Africa 5PG (15)
to 1G 1DG 1PG (11)

2 Johannesburg
South Africa 1DG 1PG 2T (12)
to 1DG 1PG (6)

3 Durban
South Africa 3PG (9) to 1T (3)

4 Port Elizabeth
South Africa 1G 1DG 1PG (11)
to 1G 1T (8)
South Africa won series 4-0

1956 *1* Dunedin
New Zealand 2G (10) to 1PG 1T (6)

2 Wellington
South Africa 1G 1T (8) to 1T (3)

3 Christchurch
New Zealand 1G 2PG 2T (17)
to 2G (10)

4 Auckland
New Zealand 1G 2PG (11) to 1G (5)
New Zealand won series 3-1

1960 *1* Johannesburg
South Africa 2G 1PG (13) to 0

2 Cape Town
New Zealand 1G 1DG 1PG (11)
to 1T (3)

3 Bloemfontein
Drawn 1G 2PG (11) each

4 Port Elizabeth
South Africa 1G 1PG (8) to 1PG (3)
South Africa won series 2-1, with 1 draw

1965 *1* Wellington
New Zealand 2T (6) to 1DG (3)

2 Dunedin
New Zealand 2G 1T (13) to 0

3 Christchurch
South Africa 2G 1PG 2T (19)
to 2G 1PG 1T (16)

4 Auckland
New Zealand 1G 1DG 4T (20)
to 1PG (3)
New Zealand won series 3-1

1970 *1* Pretoria
South Africa 1G 2PG 1DG 1T (17) to 1PG 1T (6)

2 Cape Town
New Zealand 1PG 2T (9) to 1G 1PG (8)

3 Port Elizabeth
South Africa 1G 2PG 1T (14) to 1PG (3)

4 Johannesburg
South Africa 1G 4PG 1T (20) to 1G 4PG (17)
South Africa won series 3-1

1976 *1* Durban
South Africa 1G 1PG 1DG 1T (16) to 1PG 1T (7)

2 Bloemfontein
New Zealand 1G 2PG 1DG (15) to 3PG (9)

3 Cape Town
South Africa 1G 2PG 1DG (15) to 2PG 1T (10)

4 Johannesburg
South Africa 1G 2PG 1DG (15) to 1PG 1DG 2T (14)
South Africa won series 3-1

1981 *1* Christchurch
New Zealand 1G 2T (14) to 1G 1DG (9)

2 Wellington
South Africa 1G 5PG 1DG (24) to 4PG (12)

3 Auckland
New Zealand 1G 4PG 1DG 1T (25) to 2G 2PG 1T (22)
New Zealand won series 2-1

NEW ZEALAND v AUSTRALIA

Played 75 New Zealand won 53, Australia won 18, Drawn 4

1903 Sydney
New Zealand 1G 1PG 2GM 2T (22) to 1PG (3)

1905 Dunedin
New Zealand 1G 3T (14) to 1T (3)

1907 *1* Sydney
New Zealand 4G 2T (26) to 1PG 1GM (6)

2 Brisbane
New Zealand 1G 3T (14) to 1G (5)

3 Sydney
Drawn 1G (5) each
New Zealand won series 2-0, with 1 draw

1910 *1* Sydney
New Zealand 2T (6) to 0

2 Sydney
Australia 1G 2T (11) to 0

3 Sydney
New Zealand 2G 6T (28) to 2G 1PG (13)
New Zealand won series 2-1

1913 *1* Wellington
New Zealand 3G 5T (30) to 1G (5)

2 Dunedin
New Zealand 3G 1DG 2T (25) to 2G 1T (13)

3 Christchurch
Australia 2G 2T (16) to 1G (5)
New Zealand won series 2-1

1914 *1* Sydney
New Zealand 1G (5) to 0

2 Brisbane
New Zealand 1G 4T (17) to 0

3 Sydney
New Zealand 2G 4T (22) to 1DG 1T (7)
New Zealand won series 3-0

1929 *1* Sydney
Australia 2PG 1T (9) to 1G 1PG (8)

2 Brisbane
Australia 1G 2PG 2T (17) to 1PG 2T (9)

3 Sydney
Australia 3PG 2T (15) to 2G 1T (13)
Australia won series 3-0

1931 Auckland
New Zealand 1G 4PG 1T (20) to 2G 1T (13)

1932 *1* Sydney
Australia 2G 2PG 2T (22) to 2G 1DG 1T (17)

2 Brisbane
New Zealand 1G 1DG 1PG 3T (21) to 1T (3)

3 Sydney
New Zealand 3G 2T (21) to 2G 1T (13)
New Zealand won series 2-1

1934 *1* Sydney
Australia 2G 3PG 2T (25) to 1G 2T (11)

2 Sydney
Drawn 1T (3) each
Australia won series 1-0, with 1 draw

1936 *1* Wellington
New Zealand 1G 2T (11) to 1PG 1T (6)

2 Dunedin
New Zealand 4G 1PG 5T (38) to 2G 1PG (13)
New Zealand won series 2-0

1938 *1* Sydney
New Zealand 3G 2PG 1T (24) to 3PG (9)

2 Brisbane
New Zealand 2G 1DG 2T (20) to 1G 1PG 2T (14)

3 Sydney
New Zealand 1G 2PG 1T (14)
to 1PG 1T (6)
New Zealand won series 3-0

1946 *1* Dunedin
New Zealand 5G 2T (31) to 1G 1T (8)

2 Auckland
New Zealand 1G 3PG (14) to 2G (10)
New Zealand won series 2-0

1947 *1* Brisbane
New Zealand 2G 1T (13) to 1G (5)

2 Sydney
New Zealand 3G 4PG (27)
to 1G 3PG (14)
New Zealand won series 2-0

1949 *1* Wellington
Australia 1G 2T (11) to 1PG 1T (6)

2 Auckland
Australia 2G 1PG 1T (16)
to 1DG 1PG 1T (9)
Australia won series 2-0

1951 *1* Sydney
New Zealand 1G 1PG (8) to 0

2 Sydney
New Zealand 1G 1DG 3T (17)
to 1G 1PG 1T (11)

3 Brisbane
New Zealand 2G 2T (16) to 2PG (6)
New Zealand won series 3-0

1952 *1* Christchurch
Australia 1G 1DG 2T (14) to 1PG 2T (9)

2 Wellington
New Zealand 1DG 2PG 2T (15)
to 1G 1PG (8)
Series drawn 1-1

1955 *1* Wellington
New Zealand 2G 1PG 1T (16)
to 1G 1PG (8)

2 Dunedin
New Zealand 1G 1DG (8) to 0

3 Auckland
Australia 1G 1T (8) to 1T (3)
New Zealand won series 2-1

1957 *1* Sydney
New Zealand 2G 3PG 2T (25)
to 1G 2PG (11)

2 Brisbane
New Zealand 2G 1DG 1GM 2T (22)
to 2PG 1T (9)
New Zealand won series 2-0

1958 *1* Wellington
New Zealand 2G 5T (25) to 1T (3)

2 Christchurch
Australia 1PG 1T (6) to 1T (3)

3 Auckland
New Zealand 1G 4PG (17)
to 1G 1PG (8)
New Zealand won series 2-1

1962 *1* Brisbane
New Zealand 1G 1DG 1PG 3T (20)
to 2PG (6)

2 Sydney
New Zealand 1G 2PG 1T (14) to 1G (5)
New Zealand won series 2-0

1962 *1* Wellington
Drawn New Zealand 2PG 1T (9)
Australia 3PG (9)

2 Dunedin
New Zealand 1PG (3) to 0

3 Auckland
New Zealand 2G 1DG 1T (16)
to 1G 1PG (8)
New Zealand won series 2-0, with 1 draw

1964 *1* Dunedin
New Zealand 1G 1DG 2PG (14)
to 2PG 1T (9)

2 Christchurch
New Zealand 3G 1T (18) to 1T (3)

3 Wellington
Australia 1G 1DG 3PG 1T (20) to 1G (5)
New Zealand won series 2-1

1967 Wellington
New Zealand 4G 1DG 2PG (29)
to 1PG 2T (9)

1968 *1* Sydney
New Zealand 3G 1PG 3T (27)
to 1G 2PG (11)

2 Brisbane
New Zealand 2G 2PG 1T (19)
to 5PG 1T (18)
New Zealand won series 2-0

1972 *1* Wellington
New Zealand 3G 1DG 2T (29)
to 2PG (6)

2 Christchurch
New Zealand 2G 2PG 3T (30)
to 1G 1DG 2T (17)

3 Auckland
New Zealand 4G 2PG 2T (38)
to 1PG (3)
New Zealand won series 3-0

1974 *1* Sydney
New Zealand 1PG 2T (11) to 1G (6)

2 Brisbane
Drawn 1G 2PG 1T (16) each

3 Sydney
New Zealand 2G 1T (16) to 2PG (6)
New Zealand won series 2-0, with 1 draw

1978 *1* Wellington
New Zealand 3PG 1T (13)
to 1G 2PG (12)

2 Christchurch
New Zealand 2G 1PG 1DG 1T (22)
to 1PG 1DG (6)

3 Auckland
Australia 2G 1PG 1DG 3T (30)
to 1G 2PG 1T (16)
New Zealand won series 2-1

1979 Sydney
Australia 3PG 1DG (12)
to 1PG 1DG (6)

1980 *1* Sydney
Australia 1G 1DG 1T (13) to 3PG (9)

2 Brisbane
New Zealand 1G 2PG (12)
to 1G 1PG (9)

3 Sydney
Australia 2G 1PG 1DG 2T (26)
to 2PG 1T (10)
Australia won series 2-1

1982 *1* Christchurch
New Zealand 2G 1PG 2T (23)
to 1G 2PG 1T (16)

2 Wellington
Australia 1G 3PG 1T (19)
to 1G 2PG 1T (16)

3 Auckland
New Zealand 2G 5PG 2DG (33)
to 1G 3PG 1DG (18)
New Zealand won series 2-1

1983 Sydney
New Zealand 1G 4PG (18) to 2T (8)

SOUTH AFRICA v AUSTRALIA

Played 28 South Africa won 21, Australia won 7, Drawn 0

1933 *1* Cape Town
South Africa 1G 1PG 3T (17) to 1PG (3)

2 Durban
Australia 3G 1PG 1T (21) to 1PG 1T (6)

3 Johannesburg
South Africa 1G 1DG 1T (12) to 1T (3)

4 Port Elizabeth
South Africa 1G 1PG 1T (11) to 0

5 Bloemfontein
Australia 1G 1DG 2T (15) to 1DG (4)
South Africa won series 3-2

1937 *1* Sydney
South Africa 1PG 2T (9) to 1G (5)

2 Sydney
South Africa 4G 2T (26)
to 1G 2PG 2T (17)
South Africa won series 2-0

1953 *1* Johannesburg
South Africa 2G 2PG 3T (25) to 1PG (3)

2 Cape Town
Australia 3G 1T (18) to 1G 3T (14)

3 Durban
South Africa 3G 1T (18) to 1G 1PG (8)

4 Port Elizabeth
South Africa 2G 2DG 2PG (22)
to 2PG 1T (9)
South Africa won series 3-1

1956 *1* Sydney
South Africa 1PG 2T (9) to 0

2 Brisbane
South Africa 1DG 2T (9) to 0
South Africa won series 2-0

1961 *1* Johannesburg
South Africa 2G 6T (28) to 1PG (3)

2 Port Elizabeth
South Africa 1G 1DG 3PG 2T (23)
to 1G 2PG (11)
South Africa won series 2-0

1963 *1* Pretoria
South Africa 1G 2PG 1T (14) to 1T (3)

2 Cape Town
Australia 1DG 1PG 1T (9) to 1G (5)

3 Johannesburg
Australia 1G 1DG 1PG (11) to 3PG (9)

4 Port Elizabeth
South Africa 2G 3PG 1T (22)
to 1DG 1PG (6)
Series drawn 2-2

1965 *1* Sydney
Australia 4PG 2T (18) to 1G 1PG 1T (11)

2 Brisbane
Australia 4PG (12) to 1G 1T (8)
Australia won series 2-0

1969 *1* Johannesburg
South Africa 3G 3PG 2T (30)
to 1G 2PG (11)

2 Durban
South Africa 2G 1PG 1T (16) to 3PG (9)

3 Cape Town
South Africa 1G 1PG 1T (11) to 1PG (3)

4 Bloemfontein
South Africa 2G 2PG 1T (19)
to 1G 1PG (8)
South Africa won series 4-0

1971 *1* Sydney
South Africa 2G 1DG 1PG 1T (19)
to 1G 2PG (11)

2 Brisbane
South Africa 1G 1PG 2T (14) to 1DG (6)

3 Sydney
South Africa 3G 1PG (18) to 1PG 1T (6)
South Africa won series 3-0

GRAND SLAM WINNERS

Wales 8 times: 1908, 1909, 1911, 1950, 1952, 1971, 1976, 1978.
England 8 times: 1913, 1914, 1921, 1923, 1924, 1928, 1957, 1980.
France 3 times: 1968, 1977, 1981. **Scotland** twice: 1925, 1984. **Ireland** once: 1948.

TRIPLE CROWN WINNERS

Wales 16 times: 1893, 1900, 1902, 1905, 1908, 1909, 1911, 1950, 1952, 1965, 1969, 1971, 1976, 1977, 1978, 1979. **England** 15 times: 1883, 1884, 1892, 1913, 1914, 1921, 1923, 1924, 1928, 1934, 1937, 1954, 1957, 1960, 1980. **Scotland** 9 times: 1891, 1895, 1901, 1903, 1907, 1925, 1933, 1938 1984. **Ireland** 5 times: 1894, 1899, 1948, 1949, 1982.

INTERNATIONAL CHAMPIONSHIP WINNERS

1883	**England**
1884	**England**
1885*	———
1886	**England**
	Scotland
1887	**Scotland**
1888*	———
1889*	———
1890	**England**
	Scotland
1891	**Scotland**
1892	**England**
1893	**Wales**
1894	**Ireland**
1895	**Scotland**
1896	**Ireland**
1897*	———
1898*	———
1899	**Ireland**
1900	**Wales**
1901	**Scotland**
1902	**Wales**
1903	**Scotland**
1904	**Scotland**
1905	**Wales**
1906	**Ireland**
	Wales
1907	**Scotland**
1908	**Wales**
1909	**Wales**
1910	**England**
1911	**Wales**
1912	**England**
	Ireland
1913	**England**
1914	**England**
1920	**England**
	Scotland
	Wales
1921	**England**
1922	**Wales**
1923	**England**
1924	**England**
1925	**Scotland**
1926	**Scotland**
	Ireland
1927	**Scotland**
	Ireland
1928	**England**
1929	**Scotland**
1930	**England**
1931	**Wales**
1932	**England**
	Wales
	Ireland
1933	**Scotland**
1934	**England**
1935	**Ireland**
1936	**Wales**
1937	**England**
1938	**Scotland**
1939	**England**
	Wales
	Ireland
1947	**Wales**
	England
1948	**Ireland**
1949	**Ireland**
1950	**Wales**
1951	**Ireland**
1952	**Wales**
1953	**England**
1954	**England**
	France
	Wales
1955	**France**
	Wales
1956	**Wales**
1957	**England**
1958	**England**
1959	**France**
1960	**France**
	England
1961	**France**
1962	**France**
1963	**England**
1964	**Scotland**
	Wales
1965	**Wales**
1966	**Wales**
1967	**France**
1968	**France**
1969	**Wales**
1970	**France**
	Wales
1971	**Wales**
1972*	———
1973	**Quintuple tie**
1974	**Ireland**
1975	**Wales**
1976	**Wales**
1977	**France**
1978	**Wales**
1979	**Wales**
1980	**England**
1981	**France**
1982	**Ireland**
1983	**France**
	Ireland
1984	**Scotland**

**Matches not completed, for various reasons*

Wales have won the title outright most times, 21; England have won it 18 times, Scotland 12, Ireland 9, and France 7.

'B' INTERNATIONALS 1983-84

3 December, Bourg-en-Bresse
France 'B' 11 (1PG 2T) Wales 'B' 23 (2G 1DG 2T)

France 'B': J-M Lescure (Albi); J Bégu (Dax), P Trautmann (Vienne), P Barboteau (Angoulême), B Lavigne (Agen); J-P Trille (Tarbes), J-P Sarrade (Dax) *(capt); No 8* F Pepelnjak (Grenoble); *Second Row* T Janeczek (Tarbes), P Atcher (Nîmes), C Pujade (Agen), J Gratton (Agen); *Front Row* J-L Tolot (Agen), A Noguera (Perpignan), P Ondarts (Biarritz)
Scorers *Tries:* Bégu, Sarrade *Penalty Goal:* Trille
Wales 'B': H Davies (Bridgend); M Batten (Newport), K Hopkins (Swansea), R Griffiths (Bridgend), P Lewis (Llanelli); G John (South Glamorgan Inst), M Douglas (Llanelli); *No 8* C Dennehy (Ebbw Vale); *Second Row* M Morris (South Wales Police), J Williams (Ebbw Vale), D Waters (Newport), G Roberts (Swansea); *Front Row* R Morgan (Newport), M J Watkins (Newport) *(capt),* J Whitefoot (Cardiff)
Scorers *Tries:* Griffiths, Morris, Dennehy, Hopkins *Conversions:* John (2) *Dropped Goal:* John
Referee J Fleming (Scotland)

3 December, Melrose
Scotland 'B' 22 (1PG 1DG 4T) Ireland 'B' 13 (3PG 1T)

Scotland 'B': A G Hastings (Watsonians); P D Steven (Heriot's FP), C J Williamson (West of Scotland), D R M Bruce-Lockhart (London Scottish), I Tukalo (Selkirk); D S Wyllie (Stewart's-Melville FP), I G Hunter (Selkirk); *No 8* F Calder (Stewart's-Melville FP); *Second Row* R W Murray (Hawick), I D McKie (Sale), A J Campbell (Hawick), J Jeffrey (Kelso); *Front Row* J A Fraser (London Scottish), R Cunningham (Bath) *(capt),* D M B Sole (Exeter University)
Scorers *Tries:* Steven, Tukalo (2), Wyllie *Penalty Goal:* Steven *Dropped Goal:* Hunter
Ireland 'B': J P K Barry (Cork Const); J M McGeady (Lansdowne), B J Mullin (Dublin U), R J M Moroney (Lansdowne), R V Palmer (Collegians); H C Condon (London Irish), M T Bradley (Cork Const); *No 8* D P Fanning (St Mary's Coll) *(capt); Second Row* D G McGrath (University Coll, Dublin), M M Moylett (Shannon), B W McCall (London Irish), W Sexton (Garryowen); *Front Row* D C Fitzgerald (Lansdowne), H T Harbison (Bective Rangers), J Langbroek (Blackrock Coll)
Scorers *Try:* Condon *Penalty Goals:* Palmer (3)
Referee R Parker (England)

Mark Douglas in action for Wales against Scotland. He first made his mark last season in the 'B' match against France.

19 February, Albi
France 'B' 10 (2PG 1T) Scotland 'B' 13 (2PG 1DG 1T)

France 'B': J-M Lescure (Albi); P Peytavin (Bayonne), E Bonneval (Toulouse), P Mothe (Agen) *(capt)*, J Bégu (Dax); S Cazaban (Mont-de-Marsan), H Sanz (Graulhet); *No 8* E Champ (Toulon); *Second Row* M Tonon (Montferrand), B Larroussinie (Graulhet), J-P Pelloux (Nice), J Gratton (Agen); *Front Row* J-E Garat (Bayonne), D Sanchez (Albi), P Ondarts (Biarritz)
Scorers *Try:* Lescure *Penalty Goals:* Lescure (2)
Scotland 'B': A G Hastings (Watsonians); P D Steven (Heriot's FP), D R M Bruce-Lockhart (London Scottish), S W McAslan (Heriot's FP), I Tukalo (Selkirk); D S Wyllie (Stewart's-Melville FP), I G Hunter (Selkirk); *No 8* F Calder (Stewart's-Melville FP); *Second Row* S K McGaughey (Hawick), I D McKie (Sale), A J Campbell (Hawick), J Jeffrey (Kelso); *Front Row* J A Fraser (London Scottish), R Cunningham (Bath) *(capt)*, D M B Sole (Exeter University)
Replacement R W Murray (Hawick) for McGaughey (73 mins)
Scorers *Try:* Jeffrey *Penalty Goals:* Steven (2) *Dropped Goal:* Wyllie
Referee K Parfitt (Wales)

NATIONAL TRIAL MATCHES 1983-84

ENGLAND

7 January, Twickenham
England 18 (1G 3PG 1DG) The Rest 15 (5PG)

England: W H Hare (Leicester); J Carleton (Orrell), C R Woodward (Leicester), G H Davies (Wasps), M A C Slemen (Liverpool); L Cusworth (Leicester), N C Youngs (Leicester); *No 8* J P Scott (Cardiff); *Second Row* P J Winterbottom (Headingley), M J Colclough (Wasps) (*capt*), S Bainbridge (Gosforth), P D Simpson (Bath); *Front Row* G S Pearce (Northampton), A Simpson (Sale), C White (Gosforth)
Replacement G Rees (Nottingham) for Winterbottom (47 mins)
Scorers *Try:* Davies *Conversion:* Hare *Penalty Goals:* Hare (3)
Dropped Goal: Cusworth
The Rest: N C Stringer (Wasps); A H Swift (Swansea), J A Palmer (Bath), N J Preston (Richmond), M D Bailey (Cambridge U); S Barnes (Bristol), R Hill (Bath); *No 8* M Teague (Gloucester); *Second Row* J Gadd (Gloucester), J H Fidler (Gloucester), J P Syddall (Waterloo), D H Cooke (Harlequins); *Front Row* P J Blakeway (Gloucester) (*capt*), S G F Mills (Gloucester), G A F Sargent (Gloucester)
Replacement B Barley (Wakefield) for Palmer (48 mins)
Scorer *Penalty Goals:* Stringer (5)
Referee J A F Trigg (London Society)

Gloucester No 8 Mike Teague, playing for The Rest, beats England triallist John Scott to the ball.

IRELAND

17 December, Dublin (Lansdowne Road)
Whites 21 (2G 3PG) Blues 12 (1G 2PG)

Whites: J J Murphy (Greystones); T M Ringland (Ballymena), D G Irwin (Instonians), M J Kiernan (Lansdowne), M C Finn (Cork Const); S O Campbell (Old Belvedere), R J M McGrath (Wanderers); *No 8* W P Duggan (Blackrock Coll); *Second Row* J B O'Driscoll (London Irish), D G Lenihan (Cork Const), M I Keane (Lansdowne), J F Slattery (Blackrock Coll); *Front Row* J McCoy (Dungannon), C F Fitzgerald (St Mary's Coll) (*capt*), P A Orr (Old Wesley)
Scorers *Tries:* Ringland, penalty try *Conversions:* Murphy (2)
Penalty Goals: Murphy (3)
Blues: R V Palmer (Collegians); P Haycock (Terenure Coll), B J Mullin (Dublin U), R J Moroney (Lansdowne), J M P McGeady (Lansdowne); A J P Ward (St Mary's Coll), J A P Doyle (Greystones); *No 8* D E Spring (Bagnères); *Second Row* D A G McGrath (UC Dublin), B W McCall (London Irish), J J Glennon (Skerries), R K Kearney (Wanderers); *Front Row* M P Fitzpatrick (Wanderers) (*capt*), H T Harbison (Bective Rangers), J G Langbroek (Blackrock Coll)
Scorers *Try:* Kearney *Conversion:* Ward *Penalty Goals:* Palmer, Ward
Referee D I H Burnett (Leinster)

SCOTLAND

7 January, Murrayfield
Blues 3 (1PG) Whites 21 (1G 1PG 3T)

Blues: P W Dods (Gala); J A Pollock (Gosforth), J M Renwick (Hawick), D I Johnston (Watsonians), G R T Baird (Kelso); J Y Rutherford (Selkirk), I G Hunter (Selkirk); *No 8* J R Beattie (Glasgow Acads); *Second Row* J H Calder (Stewart's-Melville FP), W Cuthbertson (Harlequins), T J Smith (Gala), J Jeffrey (Kelso); *Front Row* I G Milne (Heriot's FP), C T Deans (Hawick), J Aitken (Gala) (*capt*)
Scorer *Penalty Goal:* Dods
Whites: G Hastings (Watsonians); S Munro (Ayr), K W Robertson (Melrose), R J Gordon (London Scottish), I Tukalo (Selkirk); D Wyllie (Stewart's-Melville FP), R J Laidlaw (Jedforest); *No 8* I A M Paxton (Selkirk); *Second Row* S McGaughey (Hawick), A Campbell (Hawick), A J Tomes (Hawick), D G Leslie (Gala) (*capt*); *Front Row* N A Rowan (Boroughmuir), R Cunningham (Bath), G MacKenzie (Highland)
Replacement F Calder (Stewart's-Melville FP) for McGaughey (27 mins)
Scorers *Tries:* Robertson, Tukalo, F Calder, Campbell *Conversion:* Hastings
Penalty Goal: Hastings
Referee A M Hosie (Glasgow)

OTHER INTERNATIONAL MATCHES 1983-84

12 November, Bucharest
Romania 24 (1G 2PG 3T) **Wales 6** (2PG)

The Welsh selectors were castigated in some quarters before the match for putting out what appeared to be a dangerously unbalanced and untried team. The criticism knew no bounds after Wales suffered a humiliating defeat, in which the Romanians dominated the line-out, roamed largely unchecked in the back row and needed no heroics from their back division. Wales fumbled through the match and conceded four tries. Granted there were a few promising touches from their backs, but these provided little consolation.

For Romania, it was one of the greatest days in their rugby history. Their back row of Constantin, Murariu and Radulescu was in tremendous form, and although they were hardly a spectacular team no one could doubt their effectiveness. They caused Wales considerable heart-searching.

ROMANIA: V Ion; M Aldea, A Lungu, M Marghescu, S Fuicu; D Alexandru, M Paraschiv *(capt); No 8* S Constantin; *Second Row* F Murariu, G Dumitru, G Caragea, A Radulescu; *Front Row* I Bucan, M Munteanu, V Pascu
Scorers *Tries:* Carageua, Murariu, Aldea, Lungu *Conversion:* Alexandru
Penalty Goals: Alexandru (2)
WALES: G Evans (Maesteg); M H Titley (Bridgend), R A Ackerman (London Welsh), B Bowen (South Wales Police), A H Hadley (Cardiff); M Dacey (Swansea), R Giles (Aberavon); *No 8* E T Butler (Pontypool) *(capt); Second Row* D Pickering (Llanelli), T Shaw (Newbridge), S J Perkins (Pontypool), M Brown (Pontypool);
Front Row I Eidman (Cardiff), W James (Aberavon), S T Jones (Pontypool)
Replacement D S Richards (Swansea) for Dacey (60 mins)
Scorer *Penalty Goals:* Evans (2)
Referee: J-C Yché (France)

7 April, Cardiff
Wales XV 27 (2G 5PG) **WRU President's XV 17** (1G 1PG 2T)

This match brought together some of the greatest players of the era to celebrate the completion of the Cardiff Arms Park complex. The ground had been completely rebuilt by the WRU, under the guidance of its treasurer, Ken Harris. As costs spiralled the WRU faced dark days of financial difficulty but they pulled through and now have the most envied sporting stadium in sport.

The President's XV played a lively game at Llanelli against Captain Crawshay's XV and the team moved on to the 'international' in no mood to be used as a plaything by Wales. Under their captain, the Springbok Rob Louw, the visitors combined well and played bravely. They scored, three lovely tries, two through that master in the centre, Steve Pokere. The match featured prodigious work from the President's

XV back row of Louw, Rafter and Leslie, a few surging runs by Whetton and wise play from Rutherford.

Wales were hard-pressed to win, and did so, rather disappointingly, with five penalties and just two tries. Terry Holmes was outstanding, and even at threequarter pace the front five still proved their worth. Despite the controversy caused by the presence of three South Africans in the visiting squad, it was a famous occasion.

WALES: H Davies (Bridgend); M H Titley (Bridgend), R A Ackerman (London Welsh), B Bowen (South Wales Police), A H Hadley (Cardiff); M Dacey (Swansea), T D Holmes (Cardiff); *No 8* E T Butler (Pontypool); *Second Row* D Pickering (Llanelli), S J Perkins (Pontypool), R L Norster (Cardiff), R D Moriarty (Swansea); *Front Row* I Eidman (Cardiff), M J Watkins (Newport) *(capt)*, I Stephens (Bridgend)
Scorers *Tries:* Ackerman, Holmes *Conversions:* Davies (2)
Penalty Goals: Davies (3), Bowen (2)
WRU PRESIDENT'S XV: R Gould (Australia); P Grigg (Australia), W Cupido (South Africa), S T Pokere (New Zealand), P Estève (France); J Y Rutherford (Selkirk), J Gallion (France); *No 8* R J Louw (South Africa); *Second Row* M J Rafter (England), G Whetton (New Zealand), M J Colclough (Wasps), D G Leslie (Scotland); *Front Row* M Harding (Australia), C T Deans (Scotland), H van Aswegen (South Africa)
Scorers *Tries:* Pokere (2), Leslie *Conversion:* Rutherford *Penalty Goal:* Rutherford
Referee: C Norling (Wales)

Gary Whetton, the outstanding New Zealand lock, makes a powerful burst while playing for the WRU President's XV against Wales at Cardiff Arms Park. Whetton's run almost led to a try.

THE FIRA CHAMPIONSHIP 1983-84

Chris Rhys

In a season full of interest and improving standards, France regained the FIRA championship from Romania, largely as a result of a 26-15 win at Toulouse in December. Italy finished the campaign in style, but the Soviet Union showed that their win against France last season was an exceptional achievement, rather than evidence of a sharp improvement in the Soviet team's general standard of play.

The early season results were predictable. Romania were far too strong for Poland, and scored four tries in their 31-0 win. In defeating Italy 16-7 at Kiev the Soviet Union registered three tries, from Igor Mironov, Mikhail Parshin and Sergei Feshenko. The two winners then met in Bucharest, shortly after Romania had beaten Wales. The Soviets conceded only one try, but Dinu Alexandru added 5 penalty goals for Romania. The half-time score of 19-3 was not improved upon in the second half. On the same day, Italy beat Poland 6-0. At least, that was the score awarded on default. The Poles claimed that they couldn't fulfil the fixture due to the deaths of two of their players. One was known to have died after the match in Bucharest, having been taken ill, but the fate of the other remains a mystery. Italy arranged a match with their own 'B' XV and lost comfortably.

The side which wins the France versus Romania match frequently wins the championship. Romania came to Toulouse, and there became the latest country to suffer from the boot of Jean Lescarboura. He contributed 14 points, including a try, to the French win, to which Jerome Gallion, Patrick Estève and Patrick Lagisquet added further fine tries. The Romanians replied with tries from Podarescu and Radelescu, and a further seven points from Podarescu, but this was not enough.

Two more French wins, in quick succession, cemented their effort at Toulouse. Italy came to Chalon-sur-Saône and were soundly beaten, 38-16, by a side fielding 10 full internationals. Didier Camberabero contributed 18 points, the French ran in six tries to two, and the nearest Italy came to closing the gap was 28-16 after 67 minutes. The attendance, down to 2,400, was affected by the jam of strike-bound lorries on the nearby motorway. France then defeated Morocco 45-10 at Libourne, near Bordeaux. The Moroccans had held the full French team to 25-15 at the Mediterranean Games at the start of the season, a result which persuaded the selectors to field a useful team containing seven full internationals under the captaincy of Gerald Martinez. Cold and dispirited, the Moroccans subsided by eight tries to one, though they trailed only 13-6 at half-time. A fortnight later Morocco went to Piacenza and were beaten 27-0 by Italy, an outcome which rather saved the season for the home side. But the Moroccans only folded in the last five minutes, to tries by Gizzoni, Zanon and Screnci. Morocco, fearing another hammering, withdrew from their game against Romania, and set about constructing a 10 team league in their own country. Finances and pitches are a difficulty, but the enthusiasm is there.

Italy and Romania met at L'Aquila, the Italians defending an extraordinary record of not having been beaten at home by Romania in their nine previous games, stretching back to 1934. Italy surprised everyone except themselves by winning again, 12-6, before a crowd of nearly 10,000. There were no tries in the match, but the Italians were full value for their win. They had three outstanding players in key positions, the Mogliano fly-half Stefano Bettarello, who scored all 12 points, and who has attracted the attention of most leading French clubs; the lock forward Antonio Colella, at 6ft 7ins capable of dominating even the Romanian line-out giants, and Gianni Zanon, the 24-year-old flanker from the Treviso club. Romania, like most Communist sporting teams, are poor travellers, and could manage only a couple of Dinu Alexandru penalties in reply.

The way was now clear for France to coast to the championship. Their biennial trip to Moscow looked a little more difficult on this occasion – France were short of their New Zealand tourists and there was only a sparse representation from Agen and Béziers, the championship finalists – whilst the Soviets fancied another match to rank alongside last season's memorable 12-6 win over France at Merignac. To cut expenses, France called in at Warsaw on the way to Moscow. Poland had just beaten Morocco 7-6 to avoid last place, and they held France, surprisingly, to a penalty each at half-time. Three second-half tries from Jacques Bégu, Dalla Riva and Faugeron gave France a 19-3 victory.

On to Moscow, and a strengthened team with new half-backs Henri Sanz, the Graulhet scrum-half who was called into the New Zealand tour for the injured Gallion, and Didier Camberabero. Both had been 'dropped' from the Warsaw match because they were doing National Service. The unfortunate Bégles back Yves Foulgot was not allowed anywhere near the place simply because he had decided on a career in the Armed Forces! The Soviet Union, who had also beaten Morocco in a warm-up match – by 23-9 in Rabat – could, mathematically, still have won the championship. But their assumptions went sadly adrift. They began well with a penalty from captain and centre Yuri Korpukhin, but the French had secured a narrow lead by half-time with a try from Pierre Peytavin and a Didier Camberabero penalty goal. Two early second-half tries from Bégu began the downfall of the Russians; Lescure and Bertolucci added further tries, both converted by Camberabero, who added a penalty goal en route to a 32-3 victory. The Soviet problems were compounded when Karpukhin was carried off, and their frustrations were complete when prop Alexander Epifanov was sent off five minutes from the end with the Nice lock Jean-Paul Pelloux.

MATCH DETAILS (GROUP A)

1983	VENUE	RESULT
30 October	Kiev	Soviet Union 16 Italy 7
30 October	Bucharest	Romania 31 Poland 0
20 November	Padua	Italy 6 Poland 0 (default)
20 November	Bucharest	Romania 19 Soviet Union 3
4 December	Toulouse	France 26 Romania 15

1984		
19 February	Chalon	France 38 Italy 16
4 March	Libourne	France 45 Morocco 10
18 March	Piacenza	Italy 27 Morocco 0
8 April	Bucharest	Romania 6 Morocco 0 (default)
22 April	L'Aquila	Italy 12 Romania 6
29 April	Rabat	Morocco 6 Poland 7
6 May	Rabat	Morocco 9 Soviet Union 23
16 May	Warsaw	Poland 3 France 19
20 May	Moscow	Soviet Union 3 France 32
27 May	Warsaw	Poland 3 Soviet Union 22

FINAL TABLE

	P	*W*	*D*	*L*	*F*	*A*	*Pts*
France	5	5	0	0	160	47	15
Romania	5	3	0	2	77	41	11
Italy	5	3	0	2	68	60	11
Soviet Union	5	3	0	2	67	70	11
Poland	5	1	0	4	13	84	7
Morocco	5	0	0	5	25	108	5

Winners		*Runners Up*	*Third*
1973-4	**France**	Romania	Spain
1974-5	**Romania**	France	Italy
1975-6	**France**	Italy	Romania
1976-7	**Romania**	France	Italy
1977-8	**France**	Romania	Spain
1978-9	**France**	Romania	Soviet Union
1979-80	**France**	Romania	Italy
1980-1	**Romania**	France	Soviet Union
1981-2	**France**	Italy	Romania
1982-3	**Romania**	Italy	Soviet Union
1983-4	**France**	Romania	Italy

For the start of the season the system in the lower divisions was changed. Instead of promotion and relegation via Group B and Group C, Group B has been divided into two sections, B1 and B2. The winners in each section now replace the bottom two countries in Group A.

The strength of Group B1 was in Iberia, and both Spain and Portugal had similar victories over the Benelux countries, Holland and Belgium. Between those games Spain drew 6-6 in Portugal. All depended on the last series of matches against the unhappy Danes. Portugal set the target by winning 40-3, and Spain needed 23 points to gain promotion.

They did so in style, winning 53-13. Spain had overcome a wretched start to their season. Their New Year training camp had ended in chaos, with trainer Luis Linares resigning and only three of the team keeping their places. Javire Diaz and Luis Nunez proved capable half-backs, and Loghneye and Amunariz useful threequarters. Gabriel Rivero, the Lourdes threequarter was a class player, but suffered from the common club/country conflict.

GROUP B1

Holland 6, Belgium 6; Holland 28, Denmark 3; Belgium 31, Denmark 9; Spain 32, Holland 6; Portugal 6, Spain 6; Portugal 21, Holland 3; Spain 12, Belgium 3; Belgium 9, Portugal 13; Denmark 3, Portugal 40; Spain 53, Denmark 13

FINAL TABLE

	P	*W*	*D*	*L*	*F*	*A*	*Pts*
Spain	4	3	1	0	103	28	11
Portugal	4	3	1	0	79	21	11
Belgium	4	1	1	2	49	39	7
Holland	4	1	1	2	43	62	7
Denmark	4	0	0	4	28	152	4

In Group B2 the surprise was that West Germany failed to return to the elite. Both Tunisia and Czechoslovakia beat the Germans, Tunisia's game being shown live on television. Tunisia had to travel to Prague in May to play Czechoslovakia in what was to prove the crucial game in the group. They went into a 16-6 half time lead, and although each side added only a try apiece in the second half, Tunisia were promoted.

GROUP B2

Czechoslovakia 20, Sweden 10; Tunisia 25, Sweden 6; Tunisia 23, West Germany 9; Yugoslavia 16, Czechoslovakia 20; West Germany 38, Yugoslavia 0; West Germany 3, Czechoslovakia 15; Yugoslavia 12, Tunisia 22; Sweden 15, West Germany 13; Czechoslovakia 10, Tunisia 20; Sweden 6, Yugoslavia 0 Default

FINAL TABLE

	P	*W*	*D*	*L*	*F*	*A*	*Pts*
Tunisia	4	4	0	0	90	37	12
Czechoslovakia	4	3	0	1	65	49	10
Sweden	4	2	0	2	37	58	8
West Germany	4	0	0	4	63	53	4
Yugoslavia	4	1	0	3	28	86	3

For the first time since 1974, France failed to win the FIRA Junior Under-19 Championship losing 18-13 to Italy. It completed a marvellous spring for Italy in which their senior team beat Romania, the under-15 team beat Wales 11-9 at Pembroke, and the under-16 side beat England 14-9 at Brescia.

OTHER INTERNATIONAL TOURNAMENTS 1983-84

Cathay Pacific – Hong Kong Bank Invitation Sevens 1984

Pool A
Australia 30, Kwang Hua-Taipei 0; Canada 24, Kwang Hua-Taipei 0; Australia 12, Canada 12
**Canada qualified for the Cup championship as pool winners on the toss of a coin after scoring same number of tries as Australia.*

Pool B
Irish Wolfhounds 32, Thailand 0; Solomon Islands 20, Thailand 6; Irish Wolfhounds 40, Solomon Islands 6

Pool C
New Zealand 32, Indonesia 4; Hong Kong 24, Indonesia 6; New Zealand 38, Hong Kong 0

Pool D
French Barbarians 34, Malaysia 4; Korea 28, Malaysia 10; French Barbarians 28, Korea 0

Pool E
Public School Wanderers 28, Singapore 0; Tonga 22, Singapore 0;
Public School Wanderers 20, Tonga 4

Clive Rees, playing for Captain Crawshay's VII, tries to break away from Papua New Guinea's Martin Taumau in a group match.

Pool F
Crawshays 22, Papua New Guinea 10; American Eagles 18, Papua New Guinea 4; Crawshays 14, American Eagles 10

Pool G
Western Samoa 44, Brunei 0; Bahrain 18, Brunei 4; Western Samoa 36, Bahrain 4

Pool H
Fiji 26, Sri Lanka 6; Japan 22, Sri Lanka 6; Fiji 26, Japan 6

Bowl Championship
(for third-placed teams in pool)
Quarter-final
Kwang Hua-Taipei 10, Thailand 16; Indonesia 22, Malaysia 10; Singapore 0, Papua New Guinea 22; Brunei 0, Sri Lanka 26
Semi-final
Thailand 14, Indonesia 6; Papua New Guinea 4, Sri Lanka 10
FINAL
Thailand 10, Sri Lanka 16
Teams in the Bowl Final:
Thailand: S Lamsam, C Thongplub, T Patamasingh, C Chan Ruddit; C Kumfung, S Phekpan, P Nakpuang
Sri Lanka: H Abdeen, C Dharmadasa, C Abeygunawardena, L de Silva; R Pieris, N de Silva, P Perera

Plate Championship
(for second-placed teams in pool)
Quarter-final
Australia 18, Solomon Islands 9; Hong Kong 0, Korea 8; Tonga 0, American Eagles 18; Bahrain 0, Japan 18

Paulo Nawalu, the Fijian, outstrips New Zealand's John Mills in the thrilling final of the Sevens.

Semi-final
Australia 16, Korea 0; American Eagles 8, Japan 10
FINAL
Australia 26, Japan 20
Teams in Plate Final:
Australia: B Moon, G Ella, M Ella, J Maxwell; P Lucas, C Roche, G Pearce
Japan: Y Konishi, S Hirao, K Honjo, Y Matsuo; Y Koshiyama, H Kawachi, M Chida

Competition Proper

(for pool winners)
Quarter-final
Canada 4, Irish Wolfhounds 20; New Zealand 20, French Barbarians 0; Public School Wanderers 22, Crawshays 6; Western Samoa 6, Fiji 22
Semi-final
Irish Wolfhounds 20, New Zealand 12; Public School Wanderers 4, Fiji 12
FINAL
New Zealand 0, Fiji 26
Teams in Final:
New Zealand: M Clamp, W Smith, R Fry, J Kirwan; G Rich, J Mills, D Kirk
Fiji: A Waqaliti, S Laulau, D Manaseitava, A Niuqila; E Gusuivalu, P Nawalu, S Gutugutuwai

THE 1983-84 SEASON IN ENGLAND

David Frost *The Guardian*

England once again raised hopes in the first half of the season, only to finish with a disappointing International Championship campaign. At the start there was a feeling abroad that England would turn over a new leaf – with a new chairman of selectors, Derek Morgan, a fresh coach, Richard Greenwood, and a new and much admired captain, Peter Wheeler. Moreover, morale was increased by the recall of Mike Slemen, who had been omitted the previous season without a trial.

An England XV played a warm-up international against the touring Canadians, and then the hopes of English supporters rose sky-high with the clear-cut victory over the All Blacks in November. This was the first time England had defeated New Zealand at Twickenham since Obolensky's match in 1936. The game was notable, not for the kind of open play seen in 1936, but rather for the guts and determination England showed in sticking to their plan to drive at the All Blacks from scrum-half and loose forward. Nick Youngs at scrum-half and Paul Simpson on the flank had much to do with England's successful scheme, and Youngs' punting also played a vital part.

Then came the England trial, for which the selectors fielded a host of experienced Gloucester forwards in The Rest's pack. These tough Rest forwards gave the England pack plenty to think about, but for the first Championship match of the season, against Scotland at Murrayfield, the selectors decided to stay loyal to the side who had defeated the All Blacks. This decision was criticised later, but at the time it was the right one. It would have been most ungrateful, and demoralising for the team, if changes had been made at that stage. Moreover Scotland, in drawing their game against the All Blacks, had played very much in the New Zealand style, putting the emphasis on rucking in the loose. There was therefore reason to hope that the side who had beaten the All Blacks would be the best bet for a game against Scotland.

In the event, Scotland won 18-6 in the 100th match between the two countries and thoroughly deserved to do so. England, this time, were criticised for re-employing the tactics which had undone the All Blacks, but in difficult weather conditions they were probably right, at least initially, to continue in the same style of play. The simple answer was that England's forwards, more than one of whom were not 100 per cent fit, were not good enough, and the consuming desire to win that had been so evident in the England-All Blacks match appeared to have gone. It could be said that England reached a peak against the All Blacks but could not similarly raise their game at Murrayfield. This was not so much the fault of the players as of the environment in which they

The England team which met Ireland at Twickenham. Back Row, L-R: *S Barnes (replacement), R Hill (replacement), P Simpson (replacement), W H Hare, C White, D H Cooke, J Hall, S B Bainbridge, M J Colclough, J P Scott, C R Woodward, B Barley, N C Stringer (replacement), S P Redfearn (replacement), S G F Mills (replacement)* Front Row L-R: *L Cusworth, N C Youngs, J Carleton, P J Wheeler (capt), P J Blakeway, R Underwood.*

play their domestic rugby. In the weeks leading up to the international against the All Blacks the English players had had their reactions sharpened and their competitiveness awakened by a series of regional fixtures against the New Zealanders. It seems that if the England team, in any one season, are to raise their game to several peaks, they need regular competitive rugby of a high standard to increase and maintain their mental and physical stamina.

Just as the regional matches against the All Blacks produced the desired effects and result, so would an inter-regional tournament in the weeks leading up to the International Championship campaign. If there was also a system of regular club league fixtures in the early part of each season, as there is in New Zealand, there would be a natural progression from competitive club games to competitive inter-regional matches and then to the International Championship itself. Scotland and Ireland have continuing competitions at club and representative levels and so make far better use of their relatively meagre resources than England do of their much more substantial ones.

Against Ireland at Twickenham England did try to play a more expansive game. They did not play it very well, but they did win the match and gave their supporters some dashing runs to applaud. Here it is worth recalling that England, once again, did not have the best of luck with injuries. Colin Smart, who would have brought stability to the front row and technique to the middle of the line-out, and Paul Dodge, who might have lent a sense of direction to the centre, both missed the whole of the Championship campaign, as indeed did scrum-half Nigel Melville, whose quick passing would surely have given the team's mid-field a more promising springboard. England went on to lose both their remaining games, against France in Paris and against Wales at Twickenham. They did, however, blood two very promising newcomers in Bryan Barley in the centre and Rory Underwood on the left wing, and one win from their four Championship matches was a better record than they had achieved the previous season.

There was a lot of controversy about the RFU's decision to make Twickenham the permanent home of the final of the Thorn EMI County Championship. The arguments increased when two West Country sides, Gloucestershire and Somerset, reached the final. Why, it was asked, should these two teams and their supporters travel all the way to Twickenham for the final? In the event the staging of the final at Twickenham proved a success. The supporters looked on the occasion as a day out in the capital; Gloucestershire, with their forwards going great guns, won handsomely 36-18; and the gate receipts of £60,000 could not have been matched on any ground in Gloucestershire or Somerset. Many people felt, however, that it was wrong for there to be a gap of four months – from November to 31 March – between the semi-finals and the final. Surely room could be found for the final in future years to be held in December. A December date would give the players the added incentive of knowing that they were showing their paces to the national selectors before the choosing of England's team for the International Championship.

The County Championship final marked the first leg of what had become known as the Rafter Spring Double. The previous season, Mike Rafter had led Gloucestershire to victory in the final of the Championship and then gone on to captain his club, Bristol, to their triumph over Leicester in the final of the John Player Cup. Here he was again, taking Gloucestershire to success. This time, however, the second leg of the double eluded him, Bristol being beaten 10-9 by their near neighbours, Bath, in the John Player final. The 1984 Cup final did not produce the spectacular play of the 1983 match, but the Bath forwards, ably supported by Richard Hill and John Horton at half-back, rose to the occasion with a mighty display which prevented Bristol from showing their best form. It was really a typical local derby transposed to Twickenham. Before the day many people felt that the previous year's record attendance of 34,000 would in no way be approached. In the event 32,000 people turned up at Twickenham, which made an interesting comparison with the crowd of 25,000 for the Schweppes Cup final at Cardiff the same fine afternoon.

The appearance of Bath and Bristol in the final showed the current strength of club rugby in the West Country. In addition Gloucester, who as usual had some notable victories in their normal club programmes to their credit, were kept out of the season's John Player Cup. During the previous season they had failed to pick up enough points in the anomalous South-West merit table to qualify.

Bath had a more impressive record in the Cup than Bristol. They beat a promising Nottingham side 12-3 in their semi-final, and before that had defeated Headingley 17-0, Blackheath 41-12, and Wasps 26-12. Bristol's most convincing Cup performance was their thrashing of London Welsh by 36-8 in the fourth round. Thereafter they scraped home against Waterloo 12-9 and against Harlequins 21-18 in the semi-final. Harlequins and Wasps were probably the most consistent sides in the London area, and they both did well in the Cup before being knocked out by eventual finalists. Harlequins were notably well led by David Cooke, the England flanker, and the all-round ability of Alex Woodhouse at scrum-half enabled them to vary their game intelligently. Wasps were unlucky that their chosen captain, Nigel Melville, scarcely played at all because of injury, and for the same reason they had for a long period to do without the services of Huw Davies, the England mid-field player, who had joined them from Coventry.

In the North, Orrell, like Wasps, remained unbeaten in the early months of the season. They fell away later, leaving West Hartlepool to win the Northern Merit Table for the first time. Waterloo had a highly impressive season and were perhaps unlucky to lose 9-12 to Bristol in the quarter-final of the John Player Cup. Nottingham's progress to the semi-final of the Cup was a reward for a club who have worked very hard to improve themselves both on and off the field. Their young side should do even better in the years to come. Coventry had the distinction of knocking Leicester out of the Cup 13-9 in the third round, but Leicester still had a successful season in spite of injuries to key players like Paul Dodge, Ian Smith, Nick Youngs, Nigel Gillingham, and the Redfern brothers.

RFU CLUB MERIT TABLES 1983-84

Northern Division

	P	W	D	L	F	A	%
W Hartlepool	11	9	1	1	152	100	86.36
Sale	12	10	0	2	295	117	83.33
Waterloo	8	6	0	2	133	84	75.00
Gosforth	12	8	1	3	222	134	70.83
Orrell	12	6	2	4	258	150	58.33
Headingley	12	6	1	5	225	149	54.17
Sheffield	14	7	1	6	162	237	53.57
Vale of Lune	11	5	1	5	119	169	50.00
Liverpool	13	5	2	6	213	152	46.15
Wakefield	13	6	0	7	167	192	46.15
Hartlepool R	11	4	0	7	96	170	36.36
Roundhay	14	4	2	8	122	172	35.71
Fylde	12	3	1	8	139	242	29.17
Harrogate	12	2	1	9	104	240	20.83
Otley	13	2	1	10	124	223	19.23

Northern Division Qualifying Table

	P	W	D	L	%
Morley	12	8	1	3	70.83
Broughton Pk	13	8	1	4	65.38
Preston G	10	6	0	4	60.00
Hull & ER	10	4	1	5	45.00
Birkenhead Pk	12	4	0	8	33.33
Northern	9	2	0	7	22.22
Bradford & B	11	2	0	9	18.18
Halifax	10	1	1	8	15.00
Wilmslow	12	1	1	10	12.50
Huddersfield	7	0	0	7	—
Middlesbrough	8	0	0	8	—
Manchester	11	0	0	11	—
New Brighton	12	0	0	12	—

South and South-West

	P	W	D	L	F	A	%
Gloucester	7	6	0	1	219	66	85.71
Bath	6	5	0	1	156	55	83.33
Bristol	3	2	0	1	96	37	66.66
Plymouth	9	5	0	4	131	129	55.55
Camborne	7	2	1	4	50	99	35.71
Exeter	9	3	0	6	104	218	33.33
Launceston	9	1	1	7	88	240	16.66

Midlands Division

	P	W	D	L	F	A	%
Leicester	5	5	0	0	237	41	100
Coventry	8	6	1	1	155	95	81.25
Nottingham	6	4	1	1	141	48	75.00
Moseley	8	5	0	3	142	95	62.50
Northampton	7	4	0	3	132	94	57.15
Nuneaton	8	4	0	4	109	163	50.00
Bedford	8	2	0	6	91	162	25.00
Birmingham	7	1	0	6	48	178	14.30
Rugby	7	0	0	7	64	243	—

London Division

	P	W	D	L	F	A	%
Harlequins	7	7	0	0	135	53	100
Wasps	5	4	1	0	97	38	90.00
Saracens	7	4	1	2	79	70	64.29
London Welsh	8	5	0	3	138	90	62.50
L. Scottish	7	4	0	3	98	103	57.14
Richmond	9	5	0	4	117	138	55.55
Rosslyn Park	7	3	1	3	91	75	50.00
London Irish	9	2	1	6	99	155	27.78
Met Police	8	1	0	7	94	142	12.50
Blackheath	9	0	2	7	73	157	11.11

ENGLISH INTERNATIONAL PLAYERS
(up to 30 April 1984)

ABBREVIATIONS

A	Australia
Arg	Argentina
F	France
I	Ireland
M	Maoris
NSW	New South Wales
NZ	New Zealand
S	Scotland
SA	South Africa
W	Wales
(C)	Centenary match v Scotland at Murrayfield, 1971 (non-championship)
P	England v President's Overseas XV, at Twickenham, in RFU's Centenary season, 1970-71
(R)	Replacement
Note:	Years given for Five Nations' matches are for second half of season; eg 1972 means season 1971-72. Years for all other matches refer to the actual year of the match.

Aarvold, C D (Cambridge U, W Hartlepool, Headingley, Blackheath) 1928 *NSW, W, I, F, S*, 1929 *W, I, F*, 1931 *W, S, F*, 1932 *SA, W, I, S*, 1933 *W*
Adams, A A (London Hospital) 1910 *F*
Adams, F R (Richmond) 1875 *I, S*, 1876 *S*, 1877 *I*, 1878 *S*, 1879 *S, I*
Adey, G J (Leicester) 1976 *I, F*
Adkins, S J (Coventry) 1950 *I, F, S*, 1953 *W, I, F, S*
Agar, A E (Harlequins) 1952 *SA, W, S, I, F*, 1953 *W, I*
Alcock, A (Guy's Hospital) 1906 *SA*
Alderson, F H R (Hartlepool R) 1891 *W, I, S*, 1892 *W, S*, 1893 *W*
Alexander, H (Richmond) 1900 *I, S*, 1901 *W, I, S*, 1902 *W, I*
Alexander, W (Northern) 1927 *F*
Allison, D F (Coventry) 1956 *W, I, S, F*, 1957 *W*, 1958 *W, S*
Allport, A (Blackheath) 1892 *W*, 1893 *I*, 1894 *W, I, S*
Anderson, S (Rockcliff) 1899 *I*
Anderson, W F (Orrell) 1973 *NZ*
Anderton, C (Manchester FW) 1889 *M*
Archer, H (Bridgwater A) 1909 *W, F, I*
Armstrong, R (Northern) 1925 *W*
Arthur, T G (Wasps) 1966 *W, I*
Ashby, R C (Wasps) 1966 *I, F*, 1967 *A*
Ashcroft, A (Waterloo) 1956 *W, I, S, F*, 1957 *W, I, F, S*, 1958 *W, A, I, F, S*, 1959 *I, F, S*
Ashcroft, A H (Birkenhead Park) 1909 *A*
Ashford, W (Richmond) 1897 *W, I*, 1898 *S, W*
Ashworth, A (Oldham) 1892 *I*
Askew, J G (Cambridge U) 1930 *W, I, F*
Aslett, A R (Richmond) 1926 *W, I, F, S*, 1929 *S, F*
Assinder, E W (O Edwardians) 1909 *A, W*
Aston, R L (Blackheath) 1890 *S, I*
Auty, J R (Headingley) 1935 *S*

Bainbridge, S (Gosforth) 1982 *F, W*, 1983 *F, W, S, I, NZ*, 1984 *S, I, F, W*
Baker, D G S (OMTs) 1955 *W, I, F, S*
Baker, E M (Moseley) 1895 *W, I, S*, 1896 *W, I, S*, 1897 *W*
Baker, H C (Clifton) 1887 *W*
Bance, J F (Bedford) 1954 *S*
Barley, B (Wakefield) 1984 *I, F, W*
Barr, R J (Leicester) 1932 *SA, W, I*
Barrett, E I M (Lennox) 1903 *S*
Barrington, T J M (Bristol) 1931 *W, I*
Barrington-Ward, L E (Edinburgh U) 1910 *W, I, F, S*
Barron, J H (Bingley) 1896 *S*, 1897 *W, I*
Bartlett, J T (Waterloo) 1951 *W*
Bartlett, R M (Harlequins) 1957 *W, I, F, S*, 1958 *I, F, S*
Barton, J (Coventry) 1967 *I, F, W*, 1972 *F*
Batchelor, T B (Oxford U) 1907 *F*
Bateson, A H (Otley) 1930 *W, I, F, S*
Bateson, H D (Liverpool) 1879 *I*
Batson, T (Blackheath) 1872 *S*, 1874 *S*, 1875 *I*
Batten, J M (Cambridge U) 1874 *S*
Baume, J L (Northern) 1950 *S*
Baxter, J (Birkenhead Park) 1900 *W, I, S*
Bazley, R C (Waterloo) 1952 *I, F*, 1953 *W, I, F, S*, 1955 *W, I, F, S*
Beaumont, W B (Fylde) 1975 *I, A*, (2[1R]), 1976 *A, W, S, I, F*, 1977 *S, I, F, W*, 1978 *F, W, S, I, NZ*, 1979 *S, I, F, W, NZ*, 1980 *I, F, W, S*, 1981 *W, S, I, F, Arg* (2), 1982 *A, S*
Bedford, H (Morley) 1889 *M*, 1890 *S, I*
Bedford, L L (Headingley) 1931 *W, I*
Beer, I D S (Harlequins) 1955 *F, S*
Beese, M C (Liverpool) 1972 *W, I, F*
Bell, F J (Northern) 1900 *W*
Bell, H (New Brighton) 1884 *I*
Bell, J L (Darlington) 1878 *I*
Bell, P J (Blackheath) 1968 *W, I, F, S*
Bell, R W (Northern) 1900 *W, I, S*
Bendon, G J (Wasps) 1959 *W, I, F, S*
Bennett, N O (St Mary's Hospital, Waterloo) 1947 *W, S, F*, 1948 *A, W, I, S*
Bennett, W N (Bedford, London Welsh) 1975 *S, A*, 1976 *S* (R), 1979 *S, I, F, W*
Bennetts, B B (Penzance) 1909 *A, W*
Bentley, J E (Gipsies) 1871 *S*, 1872 *S*
Berridge, M J (Northampton) 1949 *W, I*
Berry, H (Gloucester) 1910 *W, I, F, S*
Berry, J (Tyldesley) 1891 *W, I, S*
Berry, J T W (Leicester) 1939 *W, I, S*
Beswick, E (Swinton) 1882 *I, S*
Biggs, J M (UCH) 1878 *S*, 1879 *I*
Birkett, J G G (Harlequins) 1906 *S, F, SA*, 1907 *F, W, S*, 1908 *F, W, I, S*, 1910 *W, I, S*, 1911 *W, F, I, S*, 1912 *W, I, S, F*
Birkett, L (Clapham R) 1875 *S*, 1877 *I, S*
Birkett, R H (Clapham R) 1871 *S*, 1875 *S*, 1876 *S*, 1877 *I*
Bishop, C C (Blackheath) 1927 *F*
Black, B H (Blackheath) 1930 *W, I, F, S*, 1931 *W, I, S, F*, 1932 *S*, 1933 *W*
Blacklock, J H (Aspatria) 1898 *I*, 1899 *I*
Blakeway, P J (Gloucester) 1980 *I, F, W, S*, 1981 *W, S, I, F*, 1982 *I, F, W*, 1984 *I, F, W*
Blakiston, A F (Northampton) 1920 *S*, 1921 *W, I, S, F*, 1922 *W*, 1923 *S, F*, 1924 *W, I, F, S*, 1925 *NZ, W, I, S, F*
Blatherwick, T (Manchester) 1878 *I*
Body, J A (Gipsies) 1872 *S*, 1873 *S*

Steve Bainbridge palms the ball for England against France in Paris. John Hall, a new cap during the year, is also airborne.

Bolton, C A (United Services) 1909 *F*
Bolton, R (Harlequins) 1933 *W*, 1936 *S*, 1937 *S*, 1938 *W*, *I*
Bolton, W N (Blackheath) 1882 *I*, *S*, 1883 *W*, *I*, *S*, 1884 *W*, *I*, *S*, 1885 *I*, 1887 *I*, *S*
Bonaventura, M S (Blackheath) 1931 *W*
Bond, A M (Sale) 1978 *NZ*, 1979 *S*, *I*, *NZ*, 1980 *I*, 1982 *I*
Bonham-Carter, E (Oxford U) 1891 *S*
Bonsor, F (Bradford) 1886 *W*, *I*, *S*, 1887 *W*, *S*, 1889 *M*
Boobbyer, B (Rosslyn Park) 1950 *W*, *I*, *F*, *S*, 1951 *W*, *F*, 1952 *S*, *I*, *F*
Booth, L A (Headingley) 1933 *W*, *I*, *S*, 1934 *S*, 1935 *W*, *I*, *S*
Botting, I J (Oxford U) 1950 *W*, *I*
Boughton, H J (Gloucester) 1935 *W*, *I*, *S*
Boyle, C W (Oxford U) 1873 *S*
Boyle, S B (Gloucester) 1983 *W*, *S*, *I*
Boylen, F (Hartlepool R) 1908 *F*, *W*, *I*, *S*
Bradby, M S (United Services) 1922 *I*, *F*
Bradley, R (W Hartlepool) 1903 *W*
Bradshaw, H (Bramley) 1892 *S*, 1893 *W*, *I*, *S* 1894 *W*, *I*, *S*
Braithwaite, J (Leicester) 1905 *NZ*
Braithwaite-Exley, B (Headingley) 1949 *W*
Brettargh, A T (Liverpool OB) 1900 *W*, 1903 *I*, *S*, 1904 *W*, *I*, *S*, 1905 *I*, *S*
Brewer, J (Gipsies) 1876 *I*
Briggs, A (Bradford) 1892 *W*, *I*, *S*
Brinn, A (Gloucester) 1972 *W*, *I*, *S*
Broadley, T (Bingley) 1893 *W*, *S*, 1894 *W*, *I*, *S*, 1896 *S*
Bromet, W E (Richmond) 1891 *W*, *I*, 1892 *W*, *I*, *S*, 1893 *W*, *I*, *S*, 1895 *W*, *I*, *S*, 1896 *I*
Brook, P W P (Harlequins) 1930 *S*, 1931 *F*, 1936 *S*
Brooke, T J (Richmond) 1968 *F*, *S*
Brooks, F G (Bedford) 1906 *SA*
Brooks, M J (Oxford U) 1874 *S*
Brophy, T J (Liverpool) 1964 *I*, *F*, *S*, 1965 *I*, *W*, 1966 *W*, *I*, *F*
Brough, J W (Silloth) 1925 *NZ*, *W*
Brougham, H (Harlequins) 1912 *W*, *I*, *S*, *F*
Brown, A A (Exeter) 1938 *S*
Brown, L G (Blackheath) 1911 *W*, *F*, *I*, *S*, 1913 *SA*, *W*, *F*, *I*, *S*, 1914 *W*, *I*, *S*, *F*, 1921 *W*, *I*, *S*, *F*, 1922 *W*
Brown, T W (Bristol) 1928 *S*, 1929 *W*, *I*, *S*, *F*, 1932 *S*, 1933 *W*, *I*, *S*
Brunton, J (N Durham) 1914 *W*, *I*, *S*
Brutton, E B (Cambridge U) 1886 *S*
Bryden, C C (Clapham R) 1876 *I*, 1877 *S*
Bryden, H A (Clapham R) 1874 *S*
Buckingham, R A (Leicester) 1927 *F*
Bucknall, A L (Richmond) 1969 *SA*, 1970 *I*, *W*, *S*, *F*, 1971 *W*, *I*, *F*, *S* (2[1C])
Budd, A (Blackheath) 1878 *I*, 1879 *S*, *I*, 1881 W, S
Budworth, R T D (Blackheath) 1890 *W*, 1891 *W*, *S*
Bull, A G (Northampton) 1914 *W*
Bullough, E (Wigan) 1892 *W*, *I*, *S*
Bulpitt, M P (Blackheath) 1970 *S*
Bulteel, A J (Manchester) 1876 *I*
Bunting, W L (Moseley) 1897 *I*, *S*, 1898 *I*, *S*, *W*, 1899 *S*, 1900 *S*, 1901 *I*, *S*
Burland, D W (Bristol) 1931 *W*, *I*, *F*, 1932 *I*, *S*, 1933 *W*, *I*, *S*
Burns, B H (Blackheath) 1871 *S*
Burton, G W (Blackheath) 1879 *S*, *I*, 1880 *S*, 1881 *I*, *W*, *S*
Burton, H C (Richmond) 1926 *W*
Burton, M A (Gloucester) 1972 *W*, *I*, *F*, *S*, *SA*, 1974 *F*, *W*, 1975 *S*, *A* (2), 1976 *A*, *W*, *S*, *I*, *F*, 1978 *F*, *W*
Bush, J A (Clifton) 1872 *S*, 1873 *S*, 1875 *S*, 1876 *I*, *S*

Butcher, W V (Streatham) 1903 *S*, 1904 *W*, *I*, *S*, 1905 *W*, *I*, *S*
Butler, A G (Harlequins) 1937 *W*, *I*
Butler, P E (Gloucester) 1975 *A*, 1976 *F*
Butterfield, J (Northampton) 1953 *F*, *S*, 1954 *W*, *NZ*, *I*, *S*, *F*, 1955 *W*, *I*, *F*, *S*, 1956 *W*, *I*, *S*, *F*, 1957 *W*, *I*, *F*, *S*, 1958 *W*, *A*, *I*, *F*, *S*, 1959 *W*, *I*, *F*, *S*
Byrne, F A (Moseley) 1897 *W*
Byrne, J F (Moseley) 1894 *W*, *I*, *S*, 1895 *I*, *S*, 1896 *I*, 1897 *W*, *I*, *S*, 1898 *I*, *S*, *W*, 1899 *I*

Cain, J J (Waterloo) 1950 *W*
Campbell, D A (Cambridge U) 1937 *W*, *I*
Candler, P L (St Bart's Hospital) 1935 *W*, 1936 *NZ*, *W*, *I*, *S*, 1937 *W*, *I*, *S*, 1938 *W*, *S*
Cannell, L B (Oxford U, St Mary's Hospital) 1948 *F*, 1949 *W*, *I*, *F*, *S*, 1950 *W*, *I*, *F*, *S*, 1952 *SA*, *W*, 1953 *W*, *I*, *F*, 1956 *I*, *S*, *F*, 1957 *W*, *I*
Caplan, D W N (Headingley) 1978 *S*, *I*
Cardus, R M (Roundhay) 1979 *F*, *W*
Carey, G M (Blackheath) 1895 *W*, *I*, *S*, 1896 *W*, *I*
Carleton, J (Orrell) 1979 *NZ*, 1980 *I*, *F*, *W*, *S*, 1981 *W*, *S*, *I*, *F*, *Arg* (2), 1982 *A*, *S*, *I*, *F*, *W*, 1983 *F*, *W*, *S*, *I*, *NZ*, 1984 *S*, *I*, *F*, *W*
Carpenter, A D (Gloucester) 1932 *SA*
Carr, R S L (Manchester) 1939 *W*, *I*, *S*
Cartwright, V H (Nottingham) 1903 *W*, *I*, *S*, 1904 *W*, *S*, 1905 *W*, *I*, *S*, *NZ*, 1906 *W*, *I*, *S*, *F*, *SA*
Catcheside, H C (Percy Park) 1924 *W*, *I*, *F*, *S*, 1926 *W*, *I*, 1927 *I*, *S*
Cattell, R H B (Blackheath) 1895 *W*, *I*, *S*, 1896 *W*, *I*, *S*, 1900 *W*
Cave, J W (Richmond) 1889 *M*
Cave, W T C (Blackheath) 1905 *W*
Challis, R (Bristol) 1957 *I*, *F*, *S*
Chambers, E L (Bedford) 1908 *F*, 1910 *W*, *I*
Chantrill, B S (Bristol) 1924 *W*, *I*, *F*, *S*
Chapman, C E (Cambridge U) 1884 *W*
Chapman, F E (Hartlepool) 1910 *W*, *I*, *F*, *S*, 1912 *W*, 1914 *W*, *I*
Cheesman, W I (OMTs) 1913 *SA*, *W*, *F*, *I*
Cheston, E C (Richmond) 1873 *S*, 1874 *S*, 1875 *I*, *S*, 1876 *S*
Christopherson, P (Blackheath) 1891 *W*, *S*
Clark, C W H (Liverpool) 1876 *I*
Clarke, A J (Coventry) 1935 *W*, *I*, *S*, 1936 *NZ*, *W*, *I*
Clarke, S J S (Cambridge U, Blackheath) 1963 *W*, *I*, *F*, *S*, *NZ* (2), *A*, 1964 *NZ*, *W*, *I*, 1965 *I*, *F*, *S*
Clayton, J H (Liverpool) 1871 *S*
Clements, J W (O Cranleighans) 1959 *I*, *F*, *S*
Cleveland, C R (Blackheath) 1887 *W*, *S*
Clibborn, W G (Richmond) 1886 *W*, *I*, *S*, 1887 *W*, *I*, *S*
Coates, C H (Yorkshire W) 1880 *S*, 1881 *S*, 1882 *S*
Coates, V H M (Bath) 1913 *SA*, *W*, *F*, *I*, *S*
Cobby, W (Hull) 1900 *W*
Cockerham, A (Bradford Olicana) 1900 *W*
Colclough, M J (Angoulême, Wasps) 1978 *S*, *I*, 1979 *NZ*, 1980 *F*, *W*, *S*, 1981 *W*, *S*, *I*, *F*, 1982 *A*, *S*, *I*, *F*, *W*, 1983 *F*, *NZ*, 1984 *S*, *I*, *F*, *W*
Coley, E (Northampton) 1929 *F*, 1932 *W*
Collins, P J (Camborne) 1952 *S*, *I*, *F*
Collins, W E (O Cheltonians) 1874 *S*, 1875 *I*, *S*, 1876 *I*, *S*
Considine, S G U (Bath) 1925 *F*
Conway, G S (Hartlepool R) 1920 *F*, *I*, *S*, 1921 *F*, 1922 *W*, *I*, *F*, *S*, 1923 *W*, *I*, *S*, *F*, 1924 *W*, *I*, *F*, *S*, 1925 *NZ*, 1927 *W*
Cook, J G (Bedford) 1937 *S*
Cook, P W (Richmond) 1965 *I*, *F*
Cooke, D A (Harlequins) 1976 *W*, *S*, *I*, *F*
Cooke, D H (Harlequins) 1981 *W*, *S*, *I*, *F*, 1984 *I*
Cooke, P (Richmond) 1939 *W*, *I*
Coop, T (Leigh) 1892 *S*
Cooper, J G (Moseley) 1909 *A*, *W*
Cooper, M J (Moseley) 1973 *F*, *S*, *NZ* (R), 1975 *F*, *W*, 1976 *A*, *W*, 1977 *S*, *I*, *F*, *W*
Coopper, S F (Blackheath) 1900 *W*, 1902 *W*, *I*, 1905 *W*, *I*, *S*, 1907 *W*
Corbett, L J (Bristol) 1921 *F*, 1923 *W*, *I*, 1924 *W*, *I*, *F*, *S*, 1925 *NZ*, *W*, *I*, *S*, *F*, 1927 *W*, *I*, *S*, *F*
Corless, B J (Coventry, Moseley) 1976 *A*, *I* (R), 1977 *S*, *I*, *F*, *W*, 1978 *F*, *W*, *S*, *I*
Cotton, F E (Loughborough Colls, Coventry, Sale) 1971 *S* (2[1C]), *P*, 1973 *W*, *I*, *F*, *S*, *NZ*, *A*, 1974 *S*, *I*, 1975 *I*, *F*, *W*, 1976 *A*, *W*, *S*, *I*, *F*, 1977 *S*, *I*, *F*, *W*, 1978 *S*, *I*, 1979 *NZ*, 1980 *I*, *F*, *W*, *S*, 1981 *W*
Coulman, M J (Moseley) 1967 *A*, *I*, *F*, *S*, *W*, 1968 *W*, *I*, *F*, *S*
Coulson, T J (Coventry) 1927 *W*, 1928 *NSW*, *W*
Court, E D (Blackheath) 1885 *W*
Coverdale, H (Blackheath) 1910 *F*, 1912 *I*, *F*, 1920 *W*
Cove-Smith, R (OMTs) 1921 *S*, *F*, 1922 *I*, *F*, *S*, 1923 *W*, *I*, *S*, *F*, 1924 *W*, *I*, *S*, *F*, 1925 *NZ*, *W*, *I*, *S*, *F*, 1927 *W*, *I*, *S*, *F*, 1928 *NSW*, *W*, *I*, *F*, *S*, 1929 *W*, *I*
Cowling, R J (Leicester) 1977 *S*, *I*, *F*, *W*, 1978 *F*, *NZ*, 1979 *S*, *I*
Cowman, A R (Loughborough Colls, Coventry) 1971 *S* (2[1C]), *P*, 1973 *W*, *I*
Cox, N S (Sunderland) 1901 *S*
Cranmer, P (Moseley) 1934 *W*, *I*, *S*, 1935 *W*, *I*, *S*, 1936 *NZ*, *W*, *I*, *S*, 1937 *W*, *I*, *S*, 1938 *W*, *I*, *S*
Creed, R N (Coventry) 1971 *P*
Cridlan, A G (Blackheath) 1935 *W*, *I*, *S*
Crompton, C A (Blackheath) 1871 *S*
Crosse, C W (Oxford U) 1874 *S*, 1875 *I*
Cumberlege, B S (Blackheath) 1920 *W*, *I*, *S*, 1921 *W*, *I*, *S*, *F*, 1922 *W*
Cumming, D C (Blackheath) 1925 *S*, *F*
Cunliffe, F L (RMA) 1874 *S*
Currey, F I (Marlborough N) 1872 *S*
Currie, J D (Bristol) 1956 *W*, *I*, *S*, *F*, 1957 *W*, *I*, *F*, *S*, 1958 *W*, *A*, *I*, *F*, *S*, 1959 *W*, *I*, *F*, *S*, 1960 *W*, *I*, *F*, *S*, 1961 *SA*, 1962 *W*, *I*, *F*
Cusworth, L (Leicester) 1979 *NZ*, 1982 *F*, *W*, 1983 *F*, *W*, *NZ*, 1984 *S*, *I*, *F*, *W*

D'Aguilar, F B G (Royal Engineers) 1872 *S*
Dalton, T J (Coventry) 1969 *S* (R)
Danby, T (Harlequins) 1949 *W*
Daniell, J (Richmond) 1899 *W*, 1900 *I*, *S*, 1902 *I*, *S*, 1904 *I*, *S*
Darby, A J L (Birkenhead Park) 1899 *I*
Davenport, A (Ravenscourt Park) 1871 *S*
Davey, J (Redruth) 1908 *S*, 1909 *W*
Davey, R F (Teignmouth) 1931 *W*
Davidson, Jas (Aspatria) 1897 *S*, 1898 *S*, *W*, 1899 *I*, *S*
Davidson, Jos (Aspatria) 1899 *W*, *S*
Davies, G H (Cambridge U, Coventry) 1981 *S*, *I*, *F*, *Arg* (2), 1982 *A*, *S*, *I*, 1983 *F*, *W*, *S*, 1984 *S*
Davies, P H (Sale) 1927 *I*
Davies, V G (Harlequins) 1922 *W*, 1925 *NZ*
Davies, W J A (United Services, RN) 1913 *SA*, *W*, *F*, *I*, *S*, 1914 *I*, *S*, *F*, 1920 *F*, *I*, *S*, 1921 *W*, *I*, *S*, *F*, 1922 *I*, *F*, *S*, 1923 *W*, *I*, *S*, *F*
Davies, W P C (Harlequins) 1953 *S*, 1954 *NZ*, *I*, 1955 *W*, *I*, *F*, *S*, 1956 *W*, 1957 *F*, *S*, 1958 *W*
Davis, A M (Harlequins) 1963 *W*, *I*, *S*, *NZ* (2), 1964 *NZ*, *W*, *I*, *F*, *S*, 1966 *W*, 1967 *A*, 1969 *SA*, 1970 *I*, *W*, *S*
Dawson, E F (RIEC) 1878 *I*
Day, H L V (Leicester) 1920 *W*, 1922 *W*, *F*, 1926 *S*
Dean, G J (Harlequins) 1931 *I*
Dee, J M (Hartlepool R) 1962 *S*, 1963 *NZ*
Devitt, Sir T G (Blackheath) 1926 *I*, *F*, 1928 *NSW*, *W*
Dewhurst, J H (Richmond) 1887 *W*, *I*, *S*, 1890 *W*
De Winton, R F C (Marlborough N) 1893 *W*
Dibble, R (Bridgwater A) 1906 *S*, *F*, *SA*, 1908 *F*, *W*, *I*, *S*, 1909 *A*, *W*, *F*, *I*, *S*, 1910 *S*, 1911 *W*, *F*, *S*, 1912 *W*, *I*, *S*
Dicks, J (Northampton) 1934 *W*, *I*, *S*, 1935 *W*, *I*, *S*, 1936 *S*, 1937 *I*
Dillon, E W (Blackheath) 1904 *W*, *I*, *S*, 1905 *W*
Dingle, A J (Hartlepool R) 1913 *I*, 1914 *S*, *F*
Dixon, P J (Harlequins, Gosforth) 1971 *P*, 1972 *S*, *I*, *W*, *F*, 1973 *I*, *F*, *S*, 1974 *S*, *I*, *F*, *W*, 1975 *I*, 1976 *F*, 1977 *S*, *I*, *F*, *W*, 1978 *F*, *S*, *I*, *NZ*
Dobbs, G E B (Devonport A) 1906 *W*, *I*
Doble, S A (Moseley) 1972 *SA*, 1973 *NZ*, *W*
Dobson, D D (Newton Abbot) 1902 *W*, *I*, *S*, 1903 *W*, *I*, *S*
Dobson, T H (Bradford) 1895 *S*
Dodge, P W (Leicester) 1978 *W*, *S*, *I*, *NZ*, 1979 *S*, *I*, *F*, *W*, 1980 *W*, *S*, 1981 *W*, *S*, *I*, *F*, *Arg* (2), 1982 *A*, *S*, *F*, *W*, 1983 *F*, *W*, *S*, *I*, *NZ*
Donnelly, M P (Oxford U) 1947 *I*
Dovey, B A (Rosslyn Park) 1963 *W*, *I*
Down, P J (Bristol) 1909 *A*

Dowson, A O (Moseley) 1899 *S*
Drake-Lee, N J (Cambridge U, Leicester) 1963 *W*, *I*, *F*, *S*, 1964 *NZ*, *W*, *I*, 1965 *W*
Duckett, H (Bradford) 1893 *I*, *S*
Duckham, D J (Coventry) 1969 *I*, *F*, *S*, *W*, *SA*, 1970 *I*, *W*, *S*, *F*, 1971 *W*, *I*, *F*, *S* (2[1C]), *P*, 1972 *W*, *I*, *F*, *S*, 1973 *NZ*, *W*, *I*, *F*, *S*, *NZ*, *A*, 1974 *S*, *I*, *F*, *W*, 1975 *I*, *F*, *W*, 1976 *A*, *W*, *S*
Dudgeon, H W (Richmond) 1897 *S*, 1898 *I*, *S*, *W*, 1899 *W*, *I*, *S*
Dugdale, J M (Ravenscourt Park) 1871 *S*
Dun, A F (Wasps) 1984 *W*
Duncan, R F H (Guy's Hospital) 1922 *F*, *I*, *S*
Dunkley, P E (Harlequins) 1931 *I*, *S*, 1936 *NZ*, *W*, *I*, *S*
Duthie, J (W Hartlepool) 1903 *W*
Dyson, J W (Huddersfield) 1890 *S*, 1892 *S*, 1893 *I*, *S*

Ebdon, P J (Wellington) 1897 *W*, *I*
Eddison, J H (Headingley) 1912 *W*, *I*, *S*, *F*
Edgar, C S (Birkenhead Park) 1901 *S*
Edwards, R (Newport) 1921 *W*, *I*, *S*, *F*, 1922 *W*, *F*, 1923 *W*, 1924 *W*, *F*, *S*, 1925 *NZ*
Elliot, C H (Sunderland) 1886 *W*
Elliot, E W (Sunderland) 1901 *W*, *I*, *S*, 1904 *W*
Elliot, W (United Services, RN) 1932 *I*, *S*, 1933 *W*, *I*, *S*, 1934 *W*, *I*
Elliott, A E (St Thomas's Hospital) 1894 *S*
Ellis, J (Wakefield) 1939 *S*
Ellis, S S (Queen's House) 1880 *I*
Emmott, C (Bradford) 1892 *W*
Enthoven, H J (Richmond) 1878 *I*
Estcourt, N S D (Blackheath) 1955 *S*
Evans, E (Sale) 1948 *A*, 1950 *W*, 1951 *I*, *F*, *S*, 1952 *SA*, *W*, *S*, *I*, *F*, 1953 *I*, *F*, *S*, 1954 *W*, *NZ*, *I*, *F*, 1956 *W*, *I*, *S*, *F*, 1957 *W*, *I*, *F*, *S*, 1958 *W*, *A*, *I*, *F*, *S*
Evans, G W (Coventry) 1972 *S*, 1973 *W* (R), *F*, *S*, *NZ*, 1974 *S*, *I*, *F*, *W*
Evans, N L (RNEC) 1932 *W*, *I*, *S*, 1933 *W*, *I*
Evanson, A M (Richmond) 1883 *W*, *I*, *S*, 1884 *S*
Evanson, W A D (Richmond) 1875 *S*, 1877 *S*, 1878 *S*, 1879 *S*, *I*
Evershed, F (Blackheath) 1889 *M*, 1890 *W*, *S*, *I*, 1892 *W*, *I*, *S*, 1893 *W*, *I*, *S*
Eyres, W C T (Richmond) 1927 *I*

Fagan, A R St L (Richmond) 1887 *I*
Fairbrother, K E (Coventry) 1969 *I*, *F*, *S*, *W*, *SA*, 1970 *I*, *W*, *S*, *F*, 1971 *W*, *I*, *F*
Faithfull, C K T (Harlequins) 1924 *I*, 1926 *F*, *S*
Fallas, H (Wakefield T) 1884 *I*
Fegan, J H C (Blackheath) 1895 *W*, *I*, *S*
Fernandes, C W L (Leeds) 1881 *I*, *W*, *S*
Fidler, J H (Gloucester) 1981 *Arg* (2)
Field, E (Middlesex W) 1893 *W*, *I*
Fielding, K J (Moseley, Loughborough Colls) 1969 *I*, *F*, *S*, *SA*, 1970 *I*, *F*, 1972 *W*, *I*, *F*, *S*
Finch, R T (Cambridge U) 1880 *S*
Finlan, J F (Moseley) 1967 *I*, *F*, *S*, *W*, *NZ*, 1968 *W*, *I*, 1969 *I*, *F*, *S*, *W*, 1970 *F*, 1973 *NZ*
Finlinson, H W (Blackheath) 1895 *W*, *I*, *S*
Finney, S (RIE Coll) 1872 *S*, 1873 *S*
Firth, F (Halifax) 1894 *W*, *I*, *S*
Fletcher, N C (OMTs) 1901 *W*, *I*, *S*, 1903 *S*
Fletcher, T (Seaton) 1897 *W*
Fletcher, W R B (Marlborough N) 1873 *S*, 1875 *S*
Fookes, E F (Sowerby Bridge) 1896 *W*, *I*, *S*, 1897 *W*, *I*, *S*, 1898 *I*, *W*, 1899 *I*, *S*
Ford, P J (Gloucester) 1964 *W*, *I*, *F*, *S*
Forrest, J W (United Services, RN) 1930 *W*, *I*, *F*, *S*, 1931 *W*, *I*, *S*, *F*, 1934 *I*, *S*
Forrest, R (Wellington) 1899 *W*, 1900 *S*, 1902 *I*, *S*, 1903 *I*, *S*
Foulds, R T (Waterloo) 1929 *W*, *I*
Fowler, F D (Manchester) 1878 *S*, 1879 *S*
Fowler, H (Oxford U) 1878 *S*, 1881 *W*, *S*
Fowler, R H (Leeds) 1877 *I*
Fox, F H (Wellington) 1890 *W*, *S*
Francis, T E S (Cambridge U) 1926 *W*, *I*, *F*, *S*
Frankcom, G P (Cambridge U, Bedford) 1965 *W*, *I*, *F*, *S*
Fraser, E C (Blackheath) 1875 *I*
Fraser, G (Richmond) 1902 *W*, *I*, *S*, 1903 *W*, *I*
Freakes, H D (Oxford U) 1938 *W*, 1939 *W*, *I*
Freeman, H (Marlborough N) 1872 *S*, 1873 *S*, 1874 *S*
French, R J (St Helens) 1961 *W*, *I*, *F*, *S*
Fry, H A (Liverpool) 1934 *W*, *I*, *S*
Fry, T W (Queen's House) 1880 *I*, *S*, 1881 *W*
Fuller, H G (Bath) 1882 *I*, *S*, 1883 *W*, *I*, *S*, 1884 *W*

Gadney, B C (Leicester, Headingley) 1932 *I*, *S*, 1933 *I*, *S*, 1934 *W*, *I*, *S*, 1935 *S*, 1936 *NZ*, *W*, *I*, *S*, 1937 *S*, 1938 *W*
Gamlin, H T (Blackheath) 1899 *W*, *S*, 1900 *W*, *I*, *S*, 1901 *S*, 1902 *W*, *I*, *S*, 1903 *W*, *I*, *S*, 1904 *W*, *I*, *S*
Gardner, E R (Devonport Services) 1921 *W*, *I*, *S*, 1922 *W*, *I*, *F*, 1923 *W*, *I*, *S*, *F*
Gardner, H P (Richmond) 1878 *I*
Garnett, H W T (Bradford) 1877 *S*
Gavins, M N (Leicester) 1961 *W*
Gay, D J (Bath) 1968 *W*, *I*, *F*, *S*
Gent, D R (Gloucester) 1905 *NZ*, 1906 *W*, *I*, 1910 *W*, *I*
Genth, J S M (Manchester) 1874 *S*, 1875 *S*
George, J T (Falmouth) 1947 *S*, *F*, 1949 *I*
Gerrard, R A (Bath) 1932 *SA*, *W*, *I*, *S*, 1933 *W*, *I*, *S*, 1934 *W*, *I*, *S*, 1936 *NZ*, *W*, *I*, *S*
Gibbs, G A (Bristol) 1947 *F*, 1948 *I*
Gibbs, J C (Harlequins) 1925 *NZ*, *W*, 1926 *F*, 1927 *W*, *I*, *S*, *F*
Gibbs, N (Harlequins) 1954 *S*, *F*
Giblin, L F (Blackheath) 1896 *W*, *I*, 1897 *S*
Gibson, A S (Manchester) 1871 *S*
Gibson, C O P (Northern) 1901 *W*
Gibson, G R (Northern) 1899 *W*, 1901 *S*
Gibson, T A (Northern) 1905 *W*, *S*
Gilbert, F G (Devonport Services) 1923 *W*, *I*
Gilbert, R (Devonport A) 1908 *W*, *I*, *S*
Giles, J L (Coventry) 1935 *W*, *I*, 1937 *W*, *I*, 1938 *I*, *S*
Gittings, W J (Coventry) 1967 *NZ*
Glover, P B (Bath) 1967 *A*, 1971 *F*, *P*
Godfray, R E (Richmond) 1905 *NZ*
Godwin, H O (Coventry) 1959 *F*, *S*, 1963 *S*, *NZ* (2), *A*, 1964 *NZ*, *I*, *F*, *S*, 1967 *NZ*
Gordon-Smith, G W (Blackheath) 1900 *W*, *I*, *S*
Gotley, A L H (Oxford U) 1910 *F*, *S*, 1911 *W*, *F*, *I*, *S*
Graham, D (Aspatria) 1901 *W*
Graham, H J (Wimbledon H) 1875 *I*, *S*, 1876 *I*, *S*
Graham, J D G (Wimbledon H) 1876 *I*
Gray, A (Otley) 1947 *W*, *I*, *S*
Green, J (Skipton) 1905 *I*, 1906 *S*, *F*, *SA*, 1907 *F*, *W*, *I*, *S*
Green, J F (West Kent) 1871 *S*
Greenwell, J H (Rockcliff) 1893 *W*, *I*
Greenwood, J E (Cambridge U) 1912 *F*, 1913 *SA*, *W*, *F*, *I*, *S*, 1914 *W*, *S*, *F*, 1920 *W*, *F*, *I*, *S*
Greenwood, J R H (Waterloo) 1966 *I*, *F*, *S*, 1967 *A*, 1969 *I*
Greg, W (Manchester) 1876 *I*, *S*
Gregory, G G (Bristol) 1931 *I*, *S*, *F*, 1932 *SA*, *W*, *I*, *S*, 1933 *W*, *I*, *S*, 1934 *W*, *I*, *S*
Gregory, J A (Blackheath) 1949 *W*
Grylls, W M (Redruth) 1905 *I*
Guest, R H (Waterloo) 1939 *W*, *I*, *S*, 1947 *W*, *I*, *S*, *F*, 1948 *A*, *W*, *I*, *S*, 1949 *F*, *S*
Guillemard, A G (West Kent) 1871 *S*, 1872 *S*
Gummer, C H A (Plymouth A) 1929 *F*
Gunner, C R (Marlborough N) 1876 *I*
Gurdon, C (Richmond) 1880 *I*, *S*, 1881 *I*, *W*, *S*, 1882 *I*, *S*, 1883 *S*, 1884 *W*, *S*, 1885 *I*, 1886 *W*, *I*, *S*
Gurdon, E T (Richmond) 1878 *S*, 1879 *I*, 1880 *S*, 1881 *I*, *W*, *S*, 1882 *S*, 1883 *W*, *I*, *S*, 1884 *W*, *I*, *S*, 1885 *W*, *I*, 1886 *S*

Haigh, L (Manchester) 1910 *W*, *I*, *S*, 1911 *W*, *F*, *I*, *S*
Hale, P M (Moseley) 1969 *SA*, 1970 *I*, *W*
Hall, C (Gloucester) 1901 *I*, *S*
Hall, J (N Durham) 1894 *W*, *I*, *S*
Hall, J P (Bath) 1984 *S* (R), *I*, *F*
Hall, N M (Richmond) 1947 *W*, *I*, *S*, *F*, 1949 *W*, *I*, 1952 *SA*, *W*, *S*, *I*, *F*, 1953 *W*, *I*, *F*, *S*, 1955 *W*, *I*
Hamersley, A St G (Marlborough N) 1871 *S*, 1872 *S*, 1873 *S*, 1874 *S*
Hamilton-Hill, Σ A (Harlequins) 1936 *NZ*, *W*, *I*
Hamilton-Wickes, R H (Cambridge U) 1924 *I*, 1925 *NZ*, *W*, *I*, *S*, *F*, 1926 *W*, *I*, *S*, 1927 *W*
Hammett, E D G (Newport) 1920 *W*, *F*, *S*, 1921 *W*, *I*, *S*, *F*, 1922 *W*
Hammond, C E L (Harlequins) 1905 *S*, *NZ*, 1906 *W*, *I*,

S, *F*, 1908 *W*, *I*
Hancock, A W (Northampton) 1965 *F*, *S*, 1966 *F*
Hancock, G E (Birkenhead Park) 1939 *W*, *I*, *S*
Hancock, J H (Newport) 1955 *W*, *I*
Hancock, P F (Blackheath) 1886 *W*, *I*, 1890 *W*
Hancock, P S (Richmond) 1904 *W*, *I*, *S*
Handford, F G (Manchester) 1909 *W*, *F*, *I*, *S*
Hands, R H M (Blackheath) 1910 *F*, *S*
Hanley, J (Plymouth A) 1927 *W*, *S*, *F*, 1928 *W*, *I*, *F*, *S*
Hannaford, R C (Bristol) 1971 *W*, *I*, *F*
Hanvey, R J (Aspatria) 1926 *W*, *I*, *F*, *S*
Harding, E H (Devonport Services) 1931 *I*
Harding, V S J (Saracens) 1961 *F*, *S*, 1962 *W*, *I*, *F*, *S*
Hardwick, P F (Percy Park) 1902 *I*, *S*, 1903 *W*, *I*, *S*, 1904 *W*, *I*, *S*
Hardy, E M P (Blackheath) 1951 *I*, *F*, *S*
Hare, W H (Nottingham, Leicester) 1974 *W*, 1978 *F*, *NZ*, 1979 *NZ*, 1980 *I*, *F*, *W*, *S*, 1981 *W*, *S*, *Arg* (2), 1982 *F*, *W*, 1983 *F*, *W*, *S*, *I*, *NZ*, 1984 *S*, *I*, *F*, *W*
Harper, C H (Exeter) 1899 *W*
Harris, S W (Blackheath) 1920 *I*, *S*
Harris, T W (Northampton) 1929 *S*, 1932 *I*
Harrison, A C (Hartlepool R) 1931 *I*, *S*
Harrison, A L (United Services, RN) 1914 *I*, *F*
Harrison, G (Hull) 1877 *I*, *S*, 1879 *S*, *I*, 1880 *S*, 1885 *W*, *I*
Harrison, H C (United Services, RN) 1909 *S*, 1914 *I*, *S*, *F*
Hartley, B C (Blackheath) 1901 *S*, 1902 *S*
Haslett, L W (Birkenhead Park) 1926 *I*, *F*
Hastings, G W D (Gloucester) 1955 *W*, *I*, *F*, *S*, 1957 *W*, *I*, *F*, *S*, 1958 *W*, *A*, *I*, *F*, *S*
Havelock, H (Hartlepool R) 1908 *F*, *W*, *I*
Hawcridge, J J (Bradford) 1885 *W*, *I*
Hayward, L W (Cheltenham) 1910 *I*
Hazell, D St G (Leicester) 1955 *W*, *I*, *F*, *S*
Hearn, R D (Bedford) 1966 *F*, *S*, 1967 *I*, *F*, *S*, *W*
Heath, A H (Oxford U) 1876 *S*
Heaton, J (Waterloo) 1935 *W*, *I*, *S*, 1939 *W*, *I*, *S*, 1947 *I*, *S*, *F*
Henderson, A P (Edinburgh Wands) 1947 *W*, *I*, *S*, *F*, 1948 *I*, *S*, *F*, 1949 *W*, *I*
Henderson, R S F (Blackheath) 1883 *W*, *S*, 1884 *W*, *S*, 1885 *W*
Heppell, W G (Devonport A) 1903 *I*
Herbert, A J (Wasps) 1958 *F*, *S*, 1959 *W*, *I*, *F*, *S*
Hesford, R (Bristol) 1981 *S* (R), 1982 *A*, *S*, *F* (R), 1983 *F* (R)
Hetherington, J G G (Northampton) 1958 *A*, *I*, 1959 *W*, *I*, *F*, *S*
Hewitt, E N (Coventry) 1951 *W*, *I*, *F*
Hewitt, W W (Queen's House) 1881 *I*, *W*, *S*, 1882 *I*
Hickson, J L (Bradford) 1887 *W*, *I*, *S*, 1890 *W*, *S*, *I*
Higgins, R (Liverpool) 1954 *W*, *NZ*, *I*, *S*, 1955 *W*, *I*, *F*, *S*, 1957 *W*, *I*, *F*, *S*, 1959 *W*
Hignell, A J (Cambridge U, Bristol) 1975 *A*, 1976 *A*, *W*, *S*, *I*, 1977 *S*, *I*, *F*, *W*, 1978 *W*, 1979 *S*, *I*, *F*, *W*
Hill, B A (Blackheath) 1903 *I*, *S*, 1904 *W*, *I*, 1905 *W*, *NZ*, 1906 *SA*, 1907 *F*, *W*
Hillard, R J (Oxford U) 1925 *NZ*
Hiller, R (Harlequins) 1968 *W*, *I*, *F*, *S*, 1969 *I*, *F*, *S*, *W*, *SA*, 1970 *I*, *W*, *S*, 1971 *I*, *F*, *S* (2[1C]), *P*, 1972 *W*, *I*
Hind, A E (Leicester) 1905 *NZ*, 1906 *W*
Hind, G R (Blackheath) 1910 *S*, 1911 *I*
Hobbs, R F A (Blackheath) 1899 *S*, 1903 *W*
Hobbs, R G S (Richmond) 1932 *SA*, *W*, *I*, *S*
Hodges, H A (Nottingham) 1906 *W*, *I*
Hodgson, J Mc D (Northern) 1932 *SA*, *W*, *I*, *S*, 1934 *W*, *I*, 1936 *I*
Hodgson, S A M (Durham City) 1960 *W*, *I*, *F*, *S*, 1961 *SA*, *W*, 1962 *W*, *I*, *F*, *S*, 1964 *W*
Hofmeyr, M B (Oxford U) 1950 *W*, *F*, *S*
Hogarth, T B (Hartlepool R) 1906 *F*
Holford, G (Gloucester) 1920 *W*, *F*
Holland, D (Devonport A) 1912 *W*, *I*, *S*
Holliday, T E (Aspatria) 1923 *S*, *F*, 1925 *I*, *S*, *F*, 1926 *F*, *S*
Holmes, C B (Manchester) 1947 *S*, 1948 *I*, *F*
Holmes, E (Manningham) 1890 *S*, *I*
Holmes, W A (Nuneaton) 1950 *W*, *I*, *F*, *S*, 1951 *W*, *I*, *F*, *S*, 1952 *SA*, *S*, *I*, *F*, 1953 *W*, *I*, *F*, *S*
Holmes, W B (Cambridge U) 1949 *W*, *I*, *F*, *S*
Hook, W G (Gloucester) 1951 *S*, 1952 *SA*, *W*
Hooper, C A (Middlesex W) 1894 *W*, *I*, *S*
Hopley, F J V (Blackheath) 1907 *F*, *W*, 1908 *I*
Hordern, P C (Gloucester) 1931 *I*, *S*, *F*, 1934 *W*
Horley, C H (Swinton) 1885 *I*
Hornby, A N (Manchester) 1877 *I*, *S*, 1878 *S*, *I*, 1880 *I*, 1881 *I*, *S*, 1882 *I*, *S*
Horrocks-Taylor, J P (Middlesbrough) 1958 *W*, *A*, 1961 *S*, 1962 *S*, 1963 *NZ* (2), *A*, 1964 *NZ*, *W*
Horsfall, E L (Harlequins) 1949 *W*
Horton, A L (Blackheath) 1965 *W*, *I*, *F*, *S*, 1966 *F*, *S*, 1967 *NZ*
Horton, J P (Bath) 1978 *W*, *S*, *I*, *NZ*, 1980 *I*, *F*, *W*, *S*, 1981 *W*, 1983 *S*, *I*
Horton, N E (Moseley, Toulouse) 1969 *I*, *F*, *S*, *W*, 1971 *I*, *F*, *S*, 1974 *S*, 1975 *W*, 1977 *S*, *I*, *F*, *W*, 1978 *F*, *W*, 1979 *S*, *I*, *F*, *W*, 1980 *I*
Hosen, R W (Bristol, Northampton) 1963 *NZ* (2), *A*, 1964 *F*, *S*, 1967 *A*, *I*, *F*, *S*, *W*
Hosking, G R d'A (Devonport Services) 1949 *W*, *I*, *F*, *S*, 1950 *W*
Houghton, S (Runcorn) 1892 *I*, 1896 *W*
Howard, P D (O Millhillians) 1930 *W*, *I*, *F*, *S*, 1931 *W*, *I*, *S*, *F*
Hubbard, G C (Blackheath) 1892 *W*, *I*
Hubbard, J C (Harlequins) 1930 *S*
Hudson, A (Gloucester) 1906 *W*, *I*, *F*, 1908 *F*, *W*, *I*, *S*, 1910 *F*
Hughes, G E (Barrow) 1896 *S*
Hulme, F C (Birkenhead Park) 1903 *W*, *I*, 1905 *W*, *I*
Hunt, J T (Manchester) 1882 *I*, *S*, 1884 *W*
Hunt, R (Manchester) 1880 *I*, 1881 *W*, *S*, 1882 *I*
Hunt, W H (Manchester) 1876 *S*, 1877 *I*, *S*, 1878 *I*
Hurst, A C B (Wasps) 1962 *S*
Huskisson, T F (OMTs) 1937 *W*, *I*, *S*, 1938 *W*, *I*, 1939 *W*, *I*, *S*
Hutchinson, F (Headingley) 1909 *F*, *I*, *S*
Hutchinson, J E (Durham City) 1906 *I*
Hutchinson, W C (RIE Coll) 1876 *S*, 1877 *I*
Hutchinson, W H H (Hull) 1875 *I*, 1876 *I*
Huth, H (Huddersfield) 1879 *S*
Hyde, J P (Northampton) 1950 *F*, *S*
Hynes, W B (United Services, RN) 1912 *F*

Ibbitson, E D (Headingley) 1909 *W*, *F*, *I*, *S*
Imrie, H M (Durham City) 1906 *NZ*, 1907 *I*
Inglis, R E (Blackheath) 1886 *W*, *I*, *S*
Irvin, S H (Devonport A) 1905 *W*
Isherwood, F W (Ravenscourt Park) 1872 *S*

Jackett, E J (Leicester) 1905 *NZ*, 1906 *W*, *I*, *S*, *F*, *SA*, 1907 *W*, *I*, *S*, 1909 *W*, *F*, *I*, *S*
Jackson, A H (Blackheath) 1878 *I*, 1880 *I*
Jackson, B S (Broughton Park) 1970 *S* (R), *F*
Jackson, P B (Coventry) 1956 *W*, *I*, *F*, 1957 *W*, *I*, *F*, *S*, 1958 *W*, *A*, *F*, *S*, 1959 *W*, *I*, *F*, *S*, 1961 *S*, 1963 *W*, *I*, *F*, *S*
Jackson, W J (Halifax) 1894 *S*
Jacob, F (Cambridge U) 1897 *W*, *I*, *S*, 1898 *I*, *S*, *W*, 1899 *W*, *I*
Jacob, H P (Blackheath) 1924 *W*, *I*, *F*, *S*, 1930 *F*
Jacob, P G (Blackheath) 1898 *I*
Jacobs, C R (Northampton) 1956 *W*, *I*, *S*, *F*, 1957 *W*, *I*, *F*, *S*, 1958 *W*, *A*, *I*, *F*, *S*, 1960 *W*, *I*, *F*, *S*, 1961 *SA*, *W*, *I*, *F*, *S*, 1963 *NZ* (2), *A*, 1964 *W*, *I*, *F*, *S*
Jago, R A (Devonport A) 1906 *W*, *I*, *SA*, 1907 *W*, *I*
Janion, J P A G (Bedford) 1971 *W*, *I*, *F*, *S* (2[1C]), *P*, 1972 *W*, *S*, *SA*, 1973 *A*, 1975 *A* (2)
Jarman, J W (Bristol) 1900 *W*
Jeavons, N C (Moseley) 1981 *S*, *I*, *F*, *Arg* (2), 1982 *A*, *S*, *I*, *F*, *W*, 1983 *F*, *W*, *S*, *I*
Jeeps, R E G (Northampton) 1956 *W*, 1957 *W*, *I*, *F*, *S*, 1958 *W*, *A*, *I*, *F*, *S*, 1959 *I*, 1960 *W*, *I*, *F*, *S*, 1961 *SA*, *W*, *I*, *F*, *S*, 1962 *W*, *I*, *F*, *S*
Jeffery, G L (Blackheath) 1886 *W*, *I*, *S*, 1887 *W*, *I*, *S*
Jennins, C R (Waterloo) 1967 *A*, *I*, *F*
Jewitt, J (Hartlepool R) 1902 *W*
Johns, W A (Gloucester) 1909 *W*, *F*, *I*, *S*, 1910 *W*, *I*, *F*
Johnston, W R (Bristol) 1910 *W*, *I*, *S*, 1912 *W*, *I*, *S*, *F*, 1913 *SA*, *W*, *F*, *I*, *S*, 1914 *W*, *I*, *S*, *F*
Jones, F P (N Brighton) 1893 *S*
Jones, H A (Barnstaple) 1950 *W*, *I*, *F*
Jorden, A M (Cambridge U, Blackheath, Bedford) 1970 *F*, 1973 *I*, *F*, *S*, 1974 *F*, 1975 *W*, *S*

Jowett, D (Heckmondwike) 1889 *M*, 1890 *S*, *I*, 1891 *W*, *I*, *S*
Judd, P E (Coventry) 1962 *W*, *I*, *F*, *S*, 1963 *S*, *NZ* (2), *A*, 1964 *NZ*, 1965 *I*, *F*, *S*, 1966 *W*, *I*, *F*, *S*, 1967 *A*, *I*, *F*, *S*, *W*, *NZ*

Kayll, H E (Sunderland) 1878 *S*
Keeling, J H (Guy's Hospital) 1948 *A*, *W*
Keen, B W (Newcastle U) 1968 *W*, *I*, *F*, *S*
Keeton, G H (Leicester) 1904 *W*, *I*, *S*
Kelly, G A (Bedford) 1947 *W*, *I*, *S*, 1948 *W*
Kelly, T S (London Devonians) 1906 *W*, *I*, *S*, *F*, *SA*, 1907 *F*, *W*, *I*, *S*, 1908 *F*, *I*, *S*
Kemble, A T (Liverpool) 1885 *W*, *I*, 1887 *I*
Kemp, D T (Blackheath) 1935 *W*
Kemp, T A (Richmond) 1937 *W*, *I*, 1939 *S*, 1948 *A*, *W*
Kendall, P D (Birkenhead Park) 1901 *S*, 1902 *W*, 1903 *S*
Kendall-Carpenter, J MacG K (Oxford U, Bath) 1949 *I*, *F*, *S*, 1950 *W*, *I*, *F*, *S*, 1951 *I*, *F*, *S*, 1952 *SA*, *W*, *S*, *I*, *F*, 1953 *W*, *I*, *F*, *S*, 1954 *W*, *NZ*, *I*, *F*
Kendrew, D A (Leicester) 1930 *W*, *I*, 1933 *I*, *S*, 1934 *S*, 1935 *W*, *I*, 1936 *NZ*, *W*, *I*
Kennedy, R D (Camborne S of M) 1949 *I*, *F*, *S*
Kent, C P (Rosslyn Park) 1977 *S*, *I*, *F*, *W*, 1978 *F* (R)
Kent, T (Salford) 1891 *W*, *I*, *S*, 1892 *W*, *I*, *S*
Kershaw, C A (United Services, RN) 1920 *W*, *F*, *I*, *S*, 1921 *W*, *I*, *S*, *F*, 1922 *W*, *I*, *F*, *S*, 1923 *W*, *I*, *S*, *F*
Kewley, E (Liverpool) 1874 *S*, 1875 *S*, 1876 *I*, *S*, 1877 *I*, *S*, 1878 *S*
Kewney, A L (Leicester) 1906 *W*, *I*, *S*, *F*, 1909 *A*, *W*, *F*, *I*, *S*, 1911 *W*, *F*, *I*, *S*, 1912 *I*, *S*, 1913 *SA*
Key, A (O Cranleighans) 1930 *I*, 1933 *W*
Keyworth, M (Swansea) 1976 *A*, *W*, *S*, *I*
Kilner, B (Wakefield T) 1880 *I*
Kindersley, R S (Exeter) 1883 *W*, 1884 *S* 1885 *W*
King, I (Harrogate) 1954 *W*, *NZ*, *I*
King, J A (Headingley) 1911 *W*, *F*, *I*, *S*, 1912 *W*, *I*, *S*, 1913 *SA*, *W*, *F*, *I*, *S*
King, Q E M A (Army) 1921 *S*
Kingston, P (Gloucester) 1975 *A* (2), 1979 *I*, *F*, *W*
Kitching, A E (Blackheath) 1913 *I*
Kittermaster, H J (Harlequins) 1925 *NZ*, *W*, *I*, 1926 *W*, *I*, *F*, *S*
Knight, F (Plymouth) 1909 *A*
Knight, P M (Bristol) 1972 *F*, *S*, *SA*
Knowles, E (Millom) 1896 *S*, 1897 *S*
Knowles, T C (Birkenhead Park) 1931 *S*
Krige, J A (Guy's Hospital) 1920 *W*

Labuschagne, N A (Harlequins, Guy's Hospital) 1953 *W*, 1955 *W*, *I*, *F*, *S*
Lagden, R O (Richmond) 1911 *S*
Laird, H C C (Harlequins) 1927 *W*, *I*, *S*, 1928 *NSW*, *W*, *I*, *F*, *S*, 1929 *W*, *I*
Lambert, D (Harlequins) 1907 *F*, 1908 *F*, *W*, *S*, 1911 *W*, *F*, *I*
Lampkowski, M S (Headingley) 1976 *A*, *W*, *S*, *I*
Lapage, W N (United Services, RN) 1908 *F*, *W*, *I*, *S*
Larter, P J (Northampton, RAF) 1967 *A*, *NZ*, 1968 *W*, *I*, *F*, *S*, 1969 *I*, *F*, *S*, *W*, *SA*, 1970 *I*, *W*, *F*, *S*, 1971 *W*, *I*, *F*, *S* (2[1C]), *P*, 1972 *SA*, 1973 *NZ*, *W*
Law, A F (Richmond) 1877 *S*
Law, D E (Birkenhead Park) 1927 *I*
Lawrence, Hon H A (Richmond) 1873 *S*, 1874 *S*, 1875 *I*, *S*
Lawrie, P W (Leicester) 1910 *S*, 1911 *S*
Lawson, R G (Workington) 1928 *NSW*, *W*
Lawson, T M (Workington) 1925 *I*
Leadbetter, M M (Broughton Park) 1970 *F*
Leadbetter, V H (Edinburgh Wands) 1954 *S*, *F*
Leake, W R M (Harlequins) 1891 *W*, *I*, *S*
Leather, G (Liverpool) 1907 *I*
Lee, F H (Marlborough N) 1876 *S*, 1877 *I*
Lee, H (Blackheath) 1907 *F*
Le Fleming, J (Blackheath) 1887 *W*
Leslie-Jones, F A (Richmond) 1895 *W*, *I*
Lewis, A O (Bath) 1952 *SA*, *W*, *S*, *I*, *F*, 1953 *W*, *I*, *F*, *S*, 1954 *F*
Leyland, R (Waterloo) 1935 *W*, *I*, *S*
Livesay, R O'H (Blackheath) 1898 *W*, 1899 *W*
Lloyd, R H (Harlequins) 1967 *NZ*, 1968 *W*, *I*, *F*, *S*
Locke, H M (Birkenhead Park) 1923 *S*, *F*, 1924 *W*, *F*, *S*, 1925 *W*, *I*, *S*, *F*, 1927 *W*, *I*, *S*
Lockwood, R E (Heckmondwike) 1887 *W*, *I*, *S*, 1889 *M*, 1891 *W*, *I*, *S*, 1892 *W*, *I*, *S*, 1893 *W*, *I*, 1894 *W*, *I*
Login, S H M (RN Coll) 1876 *I*
Lohden, F C (Blackheath) 1893 *W*
Longland, R J (Northampton) 1932 *S*, 1933 *W*, *S*, 1934 *W*, *I*, *S* 1935 *W*, *I*, *S*, 1936 *NZ*, *W*, *I*, *S*, 1937 *W*, *I*, *S*, 1938 *W*, *I*, *S*
Lowe, C N (Blackheath) 1913 *SA*, *W*, *F*, *I*, *S*, 1914 *W*, *I*, *S*, *F*, 1920 *W*, *F*, *I*, *S*, 1921 *W*, *I*, *S*, *F*, 1922 *W*, *I*, *F*, *S*, 1923 *W*, *I*, *S*, *F*
Lowrie, F (Wakefield T) 1889 *M*, 1890 *W*
Lowry, W M (Birkenhead Park) 1920 *F*
Luddington, W G E (Devonport Services) 1923 *W*, *I*, *S*, *F*, 1924 *W*, *I*, *F*, *S*, 1925 *W*, *I*, *S*, *F*, 1926 *W*
Luscombe, F (Gipsies) 1872 *S*, 1873 *S*, 1875 *I*, *S*, 1876 *I*, *S*
Luscombe, J H (Gipsies) 1871 *S*
Luxmoore, A F C C (Richmond) 1900 *S*, 1901 *W*
Luya, H F (Waterloo, Headingley) 1948 *W*, *I*, *S*, *F*, 1949 *W*
Lyon, A (Liverpool) 1871 *S*
Lyon, G H d'O (United Services, RN) 1908 *S*, 1909 *A*

McCanlis, M A (Gloucester) 1931 *W*, *I*
McFadyean, C W (Moseley) 1966 *I*, *F*, *S*, 1967 *A*, *I*, *F*, *S*, *W*, *NZ*, 1968 *W*, *I*
MacIlwaine, A H (United Services, Hull, E Riding) 1912 *W*, *I*, *S*, *F*, 1920 *I*
Mackie, O G (Wakefield T, Cambridge U) 1897 *S*, 1898 *I*
Mackinlay, J E H (St George's Hospital) 1872 *S*, 1873 *S*, 1875 *I*
MacLaren, W (Manchester) 1871 *S*
MacLennan, R R F (OMTs) 1925 *I*, *S*, *F*
McLeod, N F (RIE Coll) 1879 *S*, *I*
Madge, R J P (Exeter) 1948 *A*, *W*, *I*, *S*
Malir, F W S (Otley) 1930 *W*, *I*, *S*
Mangles, R H (Richmond) 1897 *W*, *I*
Manley, D C (Exeter) 1963 *W*, *I*, *F*, *S*
Mann, W E (United Services, Army) 1911 *W*, *F*, *I*
Mantell, N D (Rosslyn Park) 1975 *A*
Markendale, E T (Manchester R) 1880 *I*
Marques, R W D (Harlequins) 1956 *W*, *I*, *S*, *F*, 1957 *W*, *I*, *F*, *S*, 1958 *W*, *A*, *I*, *F*, *S*, 1959 *W*, *I*, *F*, *S*, 1960 *W*, *I*, *F*, *S*, 1961 *SA*, *W*
Marquis, J C (Birkenhead Park) 1900 *I*, *S*
Marriott, C J B (Blackheath) 1884 *W*, *I*, *S*, 1886 *W*, *I*, *S*, 1887 *I*
Marriott, E E (Manchester) 1876 *I*
Marriott, V R (Harlequins) 1963 *NZ* (2), *A*, 1964 *NZ*
Marsden, G H (Morley) 1900 *W*, *I*, *S*
Marsh, H (RIE Coll) 1873 *S*
Marsh, J (Swinton) 1892 *I*
Marshall, H (Blackheath) 1893 *W*
Marshall, M W (Blackheath) 1873 *S*, 1874 *S*, 1875 *I*, *S*, 1876 *I*, *S*, 1877 *I*, *S*, 1878 *S*, *I*
Marshall, R M (Oxford U) 1938 *I*, *S*, 1939 *W*, *I*, *S*
Martin, N O (Harlequins) 1972 *F* (R)
Martindale, S A (Kendal) 1929 *F*
Massey, E J (Leicester) 1925 *W*, *I*, *S*
Mathias, J L (Bristol) 1905 *W*, *I*, *S*, *NZ*
Matters, J C (RNE Coll) 1899 *S*
Matthews, J R C (Harlequins) 1949 *F*, *S*, 1950 *I*, *F*, *S*, 1952 *SA*, *W*, *S*, *I*, *F*
Maud, P (Blackheath) 1893 *W*, *I*
Maxwell, A W (New Brighton, Headingley) 1975 *A*, 1976 *A*, *W*, *S*, *I*, *F*, 1978 *F*
Maxwell-Hyslop, J E (Oxford U) 1922 *I*, *F*, *S*
Maynard, A F (Cambridge U) 1914 *W*, *I*, *S*
Meikle, G W C (Waterloo) 1934 *W*, *I*, *S*
Meikle, S S C (Waterloo) 1929 *S*
Mellish, F W (Blackheath) 1920 *W*, *F*, *I*, *S*, 1921 *W*, *I*
Merriam, L P B (Blackheath) 1920 *W*, *F*
Michell, A T (Oxford U) 1875 *I*, *S*, 1876 *I*
Middleton, B B (Birkenhead Park) 1882 *I*, 1883 *I*
Middleton, J A (Richmond) 1922 *S*
Miles, J H (Leicester) 1903 *W*
Millett, H (Richmond) 1920 *F*
Mills, F W (Marlborough N) 1872 *S*, 1873 *S*
Mills, S G F (Gloucester) 1981 *Arg* (2), 1983 *W*
Mills, W A (Devonport A) 1906 *W*, *I*, *S*, *F*, *SA*, 1907

F, W, I, S, 1908 *F, W*
Milman, D L K (Bedford) 1937 *W,* 1938 *W, I, S*
Milton, C H (Camborne S of M) 1906 *I*
Milton, J G (Camborne S of M) 1904 *W, I, S,* 1905 *S,* 1907 *I*
Milton, W H (Marlborough N) 1874 *S,* 1875 *I*
Mitchell, F (Blackheath) 1895 *W, I, S,* 1896 *W, I, S*
Mitchell, W G (Richmond) 1890 *W, S, I,* 1891 *W, I, S,* 1893 *S*
Mobbs, E R (Northampton) 1909 *A, W, F, I, S,* 1910 *I, F*
Moberly, W O (Ravenscourt Park) 1872 *S*
Moore, E J (Blackheath) 1883 *I, S*
Moore, N J N H (Bristol) 1904 *W, I, S*
Moore, P B C (Blackheath) 1951 *W*
Moore, W K T (Leicester) 1947 *W, I,* 1949 *F, S,* 1950 *I, F, S*
Mordell, R J (Rosslyn Park) 1978 *W*
Morfitt, S (W Hartlepool) 1894 *W, I, S,* 1896 *W, I, S*
Morgan, J R (Hawick) 1920 *W*
Morgan, W G D (Medicals, Newcastle) 1960 *W, I, F, S,* 1961 *SA, W, I, F, S*
Morley, A J (Bristol) 1972 *SA,* 1973 *NZ, W, I,* 1975 *S, A* (2)
Morris, A D W (United Services, RN) 1909 *A, W, F*
Morrison, P H (Cambridge U) 1890 *W, S, I,* 1891 *I*
Morse, S (Marlborough N) 1873 *S,* 1874 *S,* 1875 *S*
Mortimer, W (Marlborough N) 1899 *W*
Morton, H J S (Blackheath) 1909 *I, S,* 1910 *W, I*
Moss, F (Broughton) 1885 *W, I,* 1886 *W*
Mycock, J (Sale) 1947 *W, I, S, F,* 1948 *A*
Myers, E (Bradford) 1920 *I, S,* 1921 *W, I,* 1922 *W, I, F, S,* 1923 *W, I, S, F,* 1924 *W, I, F, S,* 1925 *S, F*
Myers, H (Keighley) 1898 *I*

Nanson, W M B (Carlisle) 1907 *F, W*
Nash, E H (Richmond) 1875 *I*
Neale, B A (Rosslyn Park) 1951 *I, F, S*
Neale, M E (Blackheath) 1912 *F*
Neame, S (O Cheltonians) 1879 *S, I,* 1880 *I, S*
Neary, A (Broughton Park) 1971 *W, I, F, S* (2[1C]), *P,* 1972 *W, I, F, S, SA,* 1973 *NZ, W, I, F, S, NZ, A,* 1974 *S, I, F, W,* 1975 *I, F, W, S, A,* 1976 *A, W, S, I, F,* 1977 *I,* 1978 *F* (R), 1979 *S, I, F, W, NZ,* 1980 *I, F, W, S*
Nelmes, B G (Cardiff) 1975 *A* (2), 1978 *W, S, I, NZ*
Newbold, C J (Blackheath) 1904 *W, I, S,* 1905 *W, I, S*
Newman, S C (Oxford U) 1947 *F,* 1948 *A, W*
Newton, A W (Blackheath) 1907 *S*
Newton, P A (Blackheath) 1882 *S*
Newton-Thompson, J O (Oxford U) 1947 *S, F*
Nichol, W (Brighouse R) 1892 *W, S*
Nicholas, P L (Exeter) 1902 *W*
Nicholson, B E (Harlequins) 1938 *W, I*
Nicholson, E S (Leicester) 1935 *W, I, S,* 1936 *NZ, W*
Nicholson, E T (Birkenhead Park) 1900 *W, I*
Nicholson, T (Rockcliff) 1893 *I*
Ninnes, B F (Coventry) 1971 *W*
Norman, D J (Leicester) 1932 *SA, W*
North, E H G (Blackheath) 1891 *W, I, S*
Northmore, S (Millom) 1897 *I*
Novak, M J (Harlequins) 1970 *W, S, F*
Novis, A L (Blackheath) 1929 *S, F,* 1930 *W, I, F,* 1933 *I, S*

Oakeley, F E (United Services, RN) 1913 *S,* 1914 *I, S, F*
Oakes, R F (Hartlepool R) 1897 *W, I, S,* 1898 *I, S, W,* 1899 *W, S*
Oakley, L F L (Bedford) 1951 *W*
Obolensky, A (Oxford U) 1936 *NZ, W, I, S*
Old, A G B (Middlesbrough, Leicester, Sheffield) 1972 *W, I, F, S, SA,* 1973 *NZ, A,* 1974 *S, I, F, W,* 1975 *I, A,* 1976 *S, I,* 1978 *F*
Oldham, W L (Coventry) 1908 *S,* 1909 *A*
O'Neill, A (Teignmouth, Torquay A) 1901 *W, I, S*
Openshaw, W E (Manchester) 1879 *I*
Osborne, R R (Manchester) 1871 *S*
Osborne, S H (Oxford U) 1905 *S*
Oughtred, B (Hartlepool R) 1901 *S,* 1902 *W, I, S,* 1903 *W, I*
Owen, J E (Coventry) 1963 *W, I, F, S, A,* 1964 *NZ,* 1965 *W, I, F, S,* 1966 *I, F, S,* 1967 *NZ*
Owen-Smith, H G O (St Mary's Hospital) 1934 *W, I, S,* 1936 *NZ, W, I, S,* 1937 *W, I, S*

Page, J J (Bedford, Northampton) 1971 *W, I, F, S,* 1975 *S*
Pallant, J N (Notts) 1967 *I, F, S*
Palmer, A C (London Hospital) 1909 *I, S*
Palmer, F H (Richmond) 1905 *W*
Palmer, G V (Richmond) 1928 *I, F, S*
Pargetter, T A (Coventry) 1962 *S,* 1963 *F, NZ*
Parker, G W (Gloucester) 1938 *I, S*
Parker, Hon S (Liverpool) 1874 *S,* 1875 *S*
Parsons, E J (RAF) 1939 *S*
Parsons, M J (Northampton) 1968 *W, I, F, S*
Patterson, W M (Sale) 1961 *SA, S*
Pattisson, R M (Blackheath) 1883 *I, S*
Paul, J E (RIE Coll) 1875 *S*
Payne, A T (Bristol) 1935 *I, S*
Payne, C M (Harlequins) 1964 *I, F, S,* 1965 *I, F, S,* 1966 *W, I, F, S*
Payne, J H (Broughton) 1882 *S,* 1883 *W, I, S,* 1884 *I,* 1885 *W, I*
Pearce, G S (Northampton) 1979 *S, I, F, W,* 1981 *Arg* (2), 1982 *A, S,* 1983 *F, W, S, I, NZ,* 1984 *S*
Pearson, A W (Blackheath) 1875 *I, S,* 1876 *I, S,* 1877 *S,* 1878 *S, I*
Peart, T G A H (Hartlepool R) 1964 *F, S*
Pease, F E (Hartlepool R) 1887 *I*
Penny, S H (Leicester) 1909 *A*
Penny, W J (United Hospitals) 1878 *I,* 1879 *S, I*
Percival, L J (Rugby) 1891 *I,* 1892 *I,* 1893 *S*
Periton, H G (Waterloo) 1925 *W,* 1926 *W, I, F, S,* 1927 *W, I, S, F,* 1928 *NSW, I, F, S,* 1929 *W, I, S, F,* 1930 *W, I, F, S*
Perrott, E S (O Cheltonians) 1875 *I*
Perry, D G (Bedford) 1963 *F, S, NZ* (2), *A,* 1964 *NZ, W, I,* 1965 *W, I, F, S,* 1966 *W, I, F*
Perry, S V (Cambridge U, Waterloo) 1947 *W, I,* 1948 *A, W, I, S, F*
Peters, J (Plymouth) 1906 *S, F,* 1907 *I, S,* 1908 *W*
Phillips, C (Birkenhead Park) 1880 *S,* 1881 *I, S*
Phillips, M S (Fylde) 1958 *A, I, F, S,* 1959 *W, I, F, S,* 1960 *W, I, F, S,* 1961 *W,* 1963 *W, I, F, S, NZ* (2), *A,* 1964 *NZ, W, I, F, S*
Pickering, A S (Harrogate) 1907 *I*
Pickering, R D A (Bradford) 1967 *I, F, S, W,* 1968 *F, S*
Pickles, R C W (Bristol) 1922 *I, F*
Pierce, R (Liverpool) 1898 *I,* 1903 *S*
Pilkington, W N (Cambridge U) 1898 *S*
Pillman, C H (Blackheath) 1910 *W, I, F, S,* 1911 *W, F, I, S,* 1912 *W, F,* 1913 *SA, W, F, I, S,* 1914 *W, I, S*
Pillman, R L (Blackheath) 1914 *F*
Pinch, J (Lancaster) 1896 *W, I,* 1897 *S*
Pinching, W W (Guy's Hospital) 1872 *S*
Pitman, I J (Oxford U) 1922 *S*
Plummer, K C (Bristol) 1969 *W,* 1976 *S, I, F*
Poole, F O (Oxford U) 1895 *W, I, S*
Poole, R W (Hartlepool R) 1896 *S*
Pope, E B (Blackheath) 1931 *W, S, F*
Portus, G V (Blackheath) 1908 *F, I*
Poulton, R W (later **Poulton Palmer**) (Oxford U, Harlequins, Liverpool) 1909 *F, I, S,* 1910 *W,* 1911 *S,* 1912 *W, I, S,* 1913 *SA, W, F, I, S,* 1914 *W, I, S, F*
Powell, D L (Northampton) 1966 *W, I,* 1969 *I, F, S, W,* 1971 *W, I, F, S* (2[1C])
Pratten, W E (Blackheath) 1927 *S, F*
Preece, I (Coventry) 1948 *I, S, F,* 1949 *F, S,* 1950 *W, I, F, S,* 1951 *W, I, F*
Preece, P S (Coventry) 1972 *SA,* 1973 *NZ, W, I, F, S, NZ,* 1975 *I, F, W, A,* 1976 *W* (R)
Prentice, F D (Leicester) 1928 *I, F, S*
Prescott, R E (Harlequins) 1937 *W, I,* 1938 *I,* 1939 *W, I, S*
Preston, N J (Richmond) 1979 *NZ,* 1980 *I, F*
Price, H L (Harlequins) 1922 *I, S,* 1923 *W, I*
Price, J (Coventry) 1961 *I*
Price, P L A (RIE Coll) 1877 *I, S,* 1878 *S*
Price, T W (Cheltenham) 1948 *S, F,* 1949 *W, I, F, S*
Prout, D H (Northampton) 1968 *W, I*
Pullin, J V (Bristol) 1966 *W,* 1968 *W, I, F, S,* 1969 *I, F, S, W, SA,* 1970 *I, W, S, F,* 1971 *W, I, F, S* (2[1C]), *P,* 1972 *W, I, F, S, SA,* 1973 *NZ, W, I, F, S, NZ, A,* 1974 *S, I, F, W,* 1975 *I, W* (R), *S, A* (2), 1976 *F*
Purdy, S J (Rugby) 1962 *S*
Pyke, J (St Helens Recreation) 1892 *W*
Pym, J A (Blackheath) 1912 *W, I, S, F*

Quinn, J P (New Brighton) 1954 *W, NZ, I, S, F*

Rafter, M (Bristol) 1977 *S, F, W*, 1978 *F, W, S, I, NZ*, 1979 *S, I, F, W, NZ*, 1980 *W* (R), 1981 *W, Arg* (2)
Ralston, C W (Richmond) 1971 *S* (C), *P*, 1972 *W, I, F, S, SA*, 1973 *NZ, W, I, F, S, NZ, A*, 1974 *S, I, F, W*, 1975 *I, F, W, S*
Ramsden, H E (Bingley) 1898 *W, S*
Ranson, J M (Rosslyn Park) 1963 *NZ* (2), *A*, 1964 *W, I, F, S*
Raphael, J E (OMTs) 1902 *W, I, S*, 1905 *W, S, NZ*, 1906 *W, S, F*
Ravenscroft, J (Birkenhead Park) 1881 *I*
Rawlinson, W C W (Blackheath) 1876 *S*
Redfern, S (Leicester) 1984 *I* (R)
Redmond, G F (Cambridge U) 1970 *F*
Redwood, B W (Bristol) 1968 *W, I*
Reeve, J S R (Harlequins) 1929 *F*, 1930 *W, I, F, S*, 1931 *W, I, S*
Regan, M (Liverpool) 1953 *W, I, F, S*, 1954 *W, NZ, I, S, F*, 1956 *I, S, F*
Rendall, P A G (Wasps) 1984 *W*
Rew, H (Blackheath) 1929 *S, F*, 1930 *F, S*, 1931 *W, S, F*, 1934 *W, I, S*
Reynolds, F J (O Cranleighans) 1937 *S*, 1938 *I, S*
Reynolds, S (Richmond) 1900 *W, I, S*, 1901 *I*
Rhodes, J (Castleford) 1896 *W, I, S*
Richards, E E (Plymouth A) 1929 *S, F*
Richards, J (Bradford) 1891 *W, I, S*
Richards, S B (Richmond) 1965 *W, I, F, S*, 1967 *A, I, F, S, W*
Richardson, J V (Birkenhead Park) 1928 *NSW, W, I, F, S*
Richardson, W R (Manchester) 1881 *I*
Rickards, C H (Gipsies) 1873 *S*
Rimmer, G (Waterloo) 1949 *W, I*, 1950 *W*, 1951 *W, I, F*, 1952 *SA, W*, 1954 *W, NZ, I, S*
Rimmer, L I (Bath) 1961 *SA, W, I, F, S*
Ripley, A G (Rosslyn Park) 1972 *W, I, F, S, SA*, 1973 *NZ, W, I, F, S, NZ, A*, 1974 *S, I, F, W*, 1975 *I, F, S, A* (2), 1976 *A, W, S*
Risman, A B W (Loughborough Colls) 1959 *W, I, F, S*, 1961 *SA, W, I, F*
Ritson, J A S (Northern) 1910 *F, S*, 1912 *F*, 1913 *SA, W, F, I, S*
Rittson-Thomas, G C (Oxford U) 1951 *W, I, F*
Robbins, P G D (Moseley) 1956 *W, I, S, F*, 1957 *W, I, F, S*, 1958 *W, A, I, S*, 1960 *W, I, F, S*, 1961 *SA, W*, 1962 *S*
Roberts, A D (Northern) 1911 *W, F, I, S*, 1912 *I, S, F*, 1914 *I*
Roberts, E W (RNE Coll) 1901 *W, I*, 1905 *NZ*, 1906 *W, I*, 1907 *S*
Roberts, G D (Harlequins) 1907 *S*, 1908 *F, W*
Roberts, J (Sale) 1960 *W, I, F, S*, 1961 *SA, W, I, F, S*, 1962 *W, I, F, S*, 1963 *W, I, F, S*, 1964 *NZ*
Roberts, R S (Coventry) 1932 *I*
Roberts, S (Swinton) 1887 *W, I*
Roberts, V G (Harlequins) 1947 *F*, 1949 *W, I, F, S*, 1950 *I, F, S*, 1951 *W, I, F, S*, 1956 *W, I, S, F*
Robertshaw, A R (Bradford) 1886 *W, I, S*, 1887 *W, S*
Robinson, A (Blackheath) 1889 *M*, 1890 *W, S, I*
Robinson, E F (Coventry) 1954 *S*, 1961 *I, F, S*
Robinson, G C (Percy Park) 1897 *I, S*, 1898 *I*, 1899 *W*, 1900 *I, S*, 1901 *I, S*
Robinson, J J (Headingley) 1893 *S*, 1902 *W, I, S*
Robson, A (Northern) 1924 *W, I, F, S*, 1926 *W*
Robson, M (Oxford U) 1930 *W, I, F, S*
Rogers, D P (Bedford) 1961 *I, F, S*, 1962 *W, I, F*, 1963 *W, I, F, S, NZ* (2), *A*, 1964 *NZ, W, I, F, S*, 1965 *W, I, F, S*, 1966 *W, I, F, S*, 1967 *A, S, W, NZ*, 1969 *I, F, S, W*
Rogers, J H (Moseley) 1890 *W, S, I*, 1891 *S*
Rogers, W L Y (Blackheath) 1905 *W, I*
Rollit, D M (Bristol) 1967 *I, F, S, W*, 1969 *I, F, S, W*, 1975 *S, A* (2)
Roncoroni, A D S (West Herts, Richmond) 1933 *W, I, S*
Rose, W M H (Cambridge U, Coventry) 1981 *I, F*, 1982 *A, S, I*
Rossborough, P A (Coventry) 1971 *W*, 1973 *NZ, A*, 1974 *S, I*, 1975 *I, F*
Rosser, D W A (Wasps) 1965 *W, I, F, S*, 1966 *W*
Rotherham, Alan (Richmond) 1883 *W, S*, 1884 *W, S*, 1885 *W, I*, 1886 *W, I, S*, 1887 *W, I, S*
Rotherham, Arthur (Richmond) 1898 *S, W*, 1899 *W, I, S*
Roughley, D (Liverpool) 1973 *A*, 1974 *S, I*
Rowell, R E (Leicester) 1964 *W*, 1965 *W*
Rowley, A J (Coventry) 1932 *SA*
Rowley, H C (Manchester) 1879 *S, I*, 1880 *I, S*, 1881 *I, W, S*, 1882 *I, S*
Royds, P M R (Blackheath) 1898 *S, W*, 1899 *W*
Royle, A V (Broughton R) 1889 *M*
Rudd, E L (Liverpool) 1965 *W, I, S*, 1966 *W, I, S*
Russell, R F (Leicester) 1905 *NZ*
Rutherford, D (Gloucester) 1960 *W, I, F, S*, 1961 *SA*, 1965 *W, I, F, S*, 1966 *W, I, F, S*, 1967 *NZ*
Ryalls H J (N Brighton) 1885 *W, I*
Ryan, P H (Richmond) 1955 *W, I*

Sadler, E H (Army) 1933 *I, S*
Sagar, J W (Cambridge U) 1901 *W, I*
Sample, C H (Cambridge U) 1884 *I*, 1885 *I*, 1886 *S*
Sanders, D L (Harlequins) 1954 *W, NZ, I, S, F*, 1956 *W, I, S, F*
Sanders, F W (Plymouth A) 1923 *I, S, F*
Sandford, J R P (Marlborough N) 1906 *I*
Sangwin, R D (Hull and E Riding) 1964 *NZ, W*
Sargent, G A F (Gloucester) 1981 *I* (R)
Savage, K F (Northampton) 1966 *W, I, F, S*, 1967 *A, I, F, S, W, NZ*, 1968 *W, F, S*
Sawyer, C M (Broughton) 1880 *S*, 1881 *I*
Saxby, L E (Gloucester) 1932 *SA, W*
Schofield, J W (Manchester) 1880 *I*
Scholfield, J A (Preston Grasshoppers) 1911 *W*
Schwarz, R O (Richmond) 1899 *S*, 1901 *W, I*
Scorfield, E S (Percy Park) 1910 *F*
Scott, C T (Blackheath) 1900 *W, I*, 1901 *I, W*
Scott, E K (St Mary's Hospital, Redruth) 1947 *W*, 1948 *A, W, I, S*
Scott, F S (Bristol) 1907 *W*
Scott, H (Manchester) 1955 *F*
Scott, J P (Rosslyn Park, Cardiff) 1978 *F, W, S, I, NZ*, 1979 *S* (R), *I, F, W, NZ*, 1980 *I, F, W, S*, 1981 *W, S, I, F, Arg* (2), 1982 *I, F, W*, 1983 *F, W, S, I, NZ*, 1984 *S, I, F, W*
Scott, J S M (Oxford U) 1958 *F*
Scott, M T (Cambridge U) 1887 *I*, 1890 *S, I*
Scott, W M (Cambridge U) 1889 *M*
Seddon, R L (Broughton R) 1887 *W, I, S*
Sellar, K A (United Services, RN) 1927 *W, I, S*, 1928 *NSW, W, I, F*
Sever, H S (Sale) 1936 *NZ, W, I, S*, 1937 *W, I, S*, 1938 *W, I, S*
Shackleton, I R (Cambridge U) 1969 *SA*, 1970 *I, W, S*
Sharp, R A W (Oxford U, Wasps, Redruth) 1960 *W, I, F, S*, 1961 *I, F*, 1962 *W, I, F*, 1963 *W, I, F, S*, 1967 *A*
Shaw, C H (Moseley) 1906 *S, SA*, 1907 *F, W, I, S*
Shaw, F (Cleckheaton) 1898 *I*
Shaw, J F (RNE Coll) 1898 *S, W*
Sheppard, A (Bristol) 1981 *W* (R)
Sherrard, C W (Blackheath) 1871 *S*, 1872 *S*
Sherriff, G A (Saracens) 1966 *S*, 1967 *A, NZ*
Shewring, H E (Bristol) 1905 *I, NZ*, 1906 *W, S, F, SA*, 1907 *F, W, I, S*
Shooter, J H (Morley) 1899 *I, S*, 1900 *I, S*
Shuttleworth, D W (Headingley) 1951 *S*, 1953 *S*
Sibree, H J H (Harlequins) 1908 *F*, 1909 *I, S*
Silk, N (Harlequins) 1965 *W, I, F, S*
Simpson, C P (Harlequins) 1965 *W*
Simpson, P D (Bath) 1983 *NZ*, 1984 *S*
Simpson, T (Rockcliff) 1902 *S*, 1903 *W, I, S*, 1904 *I, S*, 1905 *I, S*, 1906 *S, SA*, 1909 *F*
Sladen, G M (United Services, RN) 1929 *W, I, S*
Slemen, M A C (Liverpool) 1976 *I, F*, 1977 *S, I, F, W*, 1978 *F, W, S, I, NZ*, 1979 *S, I, F, W, NZ*, 1980 *I, F, W, S*, 1981 *W, S, I, F*, 1982 *A, S, I, F, W*, 1983 *NZ*, 1984 *S*
Slocock, L A N (Liverpool) 1907 *F, W, I, S*, 1908 *F, W, I, S*
Slow, C F (Leicester) 1934 *S*
Small, H D (Oxford U) 1950 *W, I, F, S*
Smallwood, A M (Leicester) 1920 *F, I*, 1921 *W, I, S,*

F, 1922 *I*, *S*, 1923 *W*, *I*, *S*, *F*, 1925 *I*, *S*
Smart, C E (Newport) 1979 *F*, *W*, *NZ*, 1981 *S*, *I*, *F*, *Arg* (2), 1982 *A*, *S*, *I*, *F*, *W*, 1983 *F*, *W*, *S*, *I*
Smart, S (Gloucester) 1913 *SA*, *W*, *F*, *I*, *S*, 1914 *W*, *I*, *S*, *F*, 1920 *W*, *I*, *S*
Smeddle, R W (Cambridge U) 1929 *W*, *I*, *S*, 1931 *F*
Smith, C C (Gloucester) 1901 *W*
Smith, D F (Richmond) 1910 *W*, *I*
Smith, J V (Cambridge U, Rosslyn Park) 1950 *W*, *I*, *F*, *S*
Smith, K (Roundhay) 1974 *F*, *W*, 1975 *W*, *S*
Smith, M J K (Oxford U) 1956 *W*
Smith, S J (Sale) 1973 *I*, *F*, *S*, *A*, 1974 *I*, *F*, 1975 *W* (R), 1976 *F*, 1977 *F* (R), 1979 *NZ*, 1980 *I*, *F*, *W*, *S*, 1981 *W*, *S*, *I*, *F*, *Arg* (2), 1982 *A*, *S*, *I*, *F*, *W*, 1983 *F*, *W*, *S*
Smith, S R (Richmond) 1959 *W*, *F*, *S*, 1964 *F*, *S*
Smith, T A (Northampton) 1951 *W*
Soane, F (Bath) 1893 *S*, 1894 *W*, *I*, *S*
Sobey, W H (O Millhillians) 1930 *W*, *F*, *S*, 1932 *SA*, *W*
Solomon, B (Redruth) 1910 *W*
Sparks, R H W (Plymouth A) 1928 *I*, *F*, *S*, 1929 *W*, *I*, *S*, 1931 *I*, *S*, *F*
Speed, H (Castleford) 1894 *W*, *I*, *S*, 1896 *S*
Spence, F W (Birkenhead Park) 1890 *I*
Spencer, J (Harlequins) 1966 *W*
Spencer, J S (Cambridge U, Headingley) 1969 *I*, *F*, *S*, *W*, *SA*, 1970 *I*, *W*, *S*, *F*, 1971 *W*, *I*, *S* (2[1C]), *P*
Spong, R S (O Millhillians) 1929 *F*, 1930 *W*, *I*, *F*, *S*, 1931 *F*, 1932 *SA*, *W*
Spooner, R H (Liverpool) 1903 *W*
Springman, H H (Liverpool) 1879 *S*, 1887 *S*
Spurling, A (Blackheath) 1882 *I*
Spurling, N (Blackheath) 1886 *I*, *S*, 1887 *W*
Squires, P J (Harrogate) 1973 *F*, *S*, *NZ*, *A*, 1974 *S*, *I*, *F*, *W*, 1975 *I*, *F*, *W*, *S*, *A* (2), 1976 *A*, *W*, 1977 *S*, *I*, *F*, *W*, 1978 *F*, *W*, *S*, *I*, *NZ*, 1979 *S*, *I*, *F*, *W*
Stafford, R C (Bedford) 1912 *W*, *I*, *S*, *F*
Stafford, W F H (RE) 1874 *S*
Stanbury, E (Plymouth A) 1926 *W*, *I*, *S*, 1927 *W*, *I*, *S*, *F*, 1928 *NSW*, *W*, *I*, *F*, *S*, 1929 *W*, *I*, *S*, *F*
Standing, G (Blackheath) 1883 *W*, *I*
Stanger-Leathes, C F (Northern) 1905 *I*
Stark, K J (O Alleynians) 1927 *W*, *I*, *S*, *F*, 1928 *NSW*, *W*, *I*, *F*, *S*
Starks, A (Castleford) 1896 *W*, *I*
Starmer-Smith, N C (Harlequins) 1969 *SA*, 1970 *I*, *W*, *S*, *F*, 1971 *S* (C), *P*
Start, S P (United Services, RN) 1907 *S*
Steeds, J H (Saracens) 1949 *F*, *S*, 1950 *I*, *F*, *S*
Steele-Bodger, M R (Cambridge U) 1947 *W*, *I*, *S*, *F*, 1948 *A*, *W*, *I*, *S*, *F*
Steinthal, F E (Ilkley) 1913 *W*, *F*
Stevens, C B (Penzance-Newlyn, Harlequins) 1969 *SA*, 1970 *I*, *W*, *S*, 1971 *P*, 1972 *W*, *I*, *F*, *S*, *SA*, 1973 *NZ*, *W*, *I*, *F*, *S*, *NZ*, *A*, 1974 *S*, *I*, *F*, *W*, 1975 *I*, *F*, *W*, *S*
Still, E R (Oxford U, Ravenscourt P) 1873 *S*
Stirling, R V (Wasps) 1951 *W*, *I*, *F*, *S*, 1952 *SA*, *W*, *S*, *I*, *F*, 1953 *W*, *I*, *F*, *S*, 1954 *W*, *NZ*, *I*, *S*, *F*
Stoddart, A E (Blackheath) 1885 *W*, *I*, 1886 *W*, *I*, *S*, 1889 *M*, 1890 *W*, *I*, 1893 *W*, *S*
Stoddart, W B (Liverpool) 1897 *W*, *I*, *S*
Stokes, F (Blackheath) 1871 *S*, 1872 *S*, 1873 *S*
Stokes, L (Blackheath) 1875 *I*, 1876 *S*, 1877 *I*, *S*, 1878 *S*, 1879 *S*, *I*, 1880 *I*, *S*, 1881 *I*, *W*, *S*
Stone, F le S (Blackheath) 1914 *F*
Stoop, A D (Harlequins) 1905 *S*, 1906 *S*, *F*, *SA*, 1907 *F*, *W*, 1910 *W*, *I*, *S*, 1911 *W*, *F*, *I*, *S*, 1912 *W*, *S*
Stoop, F M (Harlequins) 1910 *S*, 1911 *F*, *I*, 1913 *SA*
Stout, F M (Richmond) 1897 *W*, *I*, 1898 *I*, *S*, *W*, 1899 *I*, *S*, 1903 *S*, 1904 *W*, *I*, *S*, 1905 *W*, *I*, *S*
Stout, P W (Richmond) 1898 *S*, *W*, 1899 *W*, *I*, *S*
Stringer, N C (Wasps) 1982 *A* (R), 1983 *NZ* (R)
Strong, E L (Oxford U) 1884 *W*, *I*, *S*
Summerscales, G E (Durham City) 1906 *NZ*
Sutcliffe, J W (Heckmondwike) 1889 *M*
Swarbrick, D W (Oxford U) 1947 *W*, *I*, *F*, 1948 *A*, *W*, 1949 *I*
Swayne, D H (Oxford U) 1931 *W*
Swayne, J W R (Bridgwater) 1929 *W*
Swift, A H (Swansea) 1981 *Arg* (2), 1983 *F*, *W*, *S*
Syddall, J P (Waterloo) 1982 *I*
Sykes, A R V (Blackheath) 1914 *F*
Sykes, F D (Northampton) 1955 *F*, *S*, 1963 *NZ*, *A*
Sykes, P W (Wasps) 1948 *F*, 1952 *S*, *I*, *F*, 1953 *W*, *I*, *F*
Syrett, R E (Wasps) 1958 *W*, *A*, *I*, *F*, 1960 *W*, *I*, *F*, *S*, 1962 *W*, *I*, *F*

Tallent, J A (Cambridge U, Blackheath) 1931 *S*, *F*, 1932 *SA*, *W*, 1935 *I*
Tanner, C C (Cambridge U, Gloucester) 1930 *S*, 1932 *SA*, *W*, *I*, *S*
Tarr, F N (Leicester) 1909 *A*, *W*, *F*, 1913 *S*
Tatham, W M (Oxford U) 1882 *S*, 1883 *W*, *I*, *S*, 1884 *W*, *I*, *S*
Taylor, A S (Blackheath) 1883 *W*, *I*, 1886 *W*, *I*
Taylor, E W (Rockcliff) 1892 *I*, 1893 *I*, 1894 *W*, *I*, *S*, 1895 *W*, *I*, *S*, 1896 *W*, *I*, 1897 *W*, *I*, *S* 1899 *I*
Taylor, F (Leicester) 1920 *F*, *I*
Taylor, F M (Leicester) 1914 *W*
Taylor, H H (Blackheath) 1879 *S*, 1880 *S*, 1881 *I*, *W*, 1882 *S*
Taylor, J T (W Hartlepool) 1897 *I*, 1899 *I*, 1900 *I*, 1901 *W*, *I*, 1902 *W*, *I*, *S* 1903 *W*, *I*, 1905 *S*
Taylor, P J (Northampton) 1955 *W*, *I*, 1962 *W*, *I*, *F*, *S*
Taylor, R B (Northampton) 1966 *W*, 1967 *I*, *F*, *S*, *W*, *NZ*, 1969 *F*, *S*, *W*, *SA*, 1970 *I*, *W*, *S*, *F*, 1971 *S* (2[1C])
Taylor, W J (Blackheath) 1928 *NSW*, *W*, *I*, *F*, *S*
Teden, D E (Richmond) 1939 *W*, *I*, *S*
Teggin, A (Broughton R) 1884 *I*, 1885 *W*, 1886 *I*, *S*, 1887 *I*, *S*
Tetley, T S (Bradford) 1876 *S*
Thomas, C (Barnstaple) 1895 *W*, *I*, *S*, 1899 *I*
Thompson, P H (Headingley, Waterloo) 1956 *W*, *I*, *S*, *F*, 1957 *W*, *I*, *F*, *S*, 1958 *W*, *A*, *I*, *F*, *S*, 1959 *W*, *I*, *F*, *S*
Thomson, G T (Halifax) 1878 *S*, 1882 *I*, *S*, 1883 *W*, *I*, *S*, 1884 *I*, *S*, 1885 *I*
Thomson, W B (Blackheath) 1892 *W*, 1895 *W*, *I*, *S*
Thorne, J D (Bristol) 1963 *W*, *I*, *F*
Tindall, V R (Liverpool U) 1951 *W*, *I*, *F*, *S*
Tobin, F (Liverpool) 1871 *S*
Todd, A F (Blackheath) 1900 *I*, *S*
Todd, R (Manchester) 1877 *S*
Toft, H B (Waterloo) 1936 *S*, 1937 *W*, *I*, *S*, 1938 *W*, *I*, *S*, 1939 *W*, *I*, *S*
Toothill, J T (Bradford) 1890 *S*, *I*, 1891 *W*, *I*, 1892 *W*, *I*, *S*, 1893 *W*, *I*, *S*, 1894 *W*, *I*
Tosswill, L R (Exeter) 1902 *W*, *I*, *S*
Touzel, C J C (Liverpool) 1877 *I*, *S*
Towell, A C (Bedford) 1948 *F*, 1951 *S*
Travers, B H (Harlequins) 1947 *W*, *I*, 1948 *A*, *W*, 1949 *F*, *S*
Treadwell, W T (Wasps) 1966 *I*, *F*, *S*
Trick, D M (Bath) 1983 *I*
Tristram, H B (Oxford U) 1883 *S*, 1884 *W*, *S*, 1885 *W*, 1887 *S*
Troop, C L (Aldershot S) 1933 *I*, *S*
Tucker, J S (Bristol) 1922 *W*, 1925 *NZ*, *W*, *I*, *S*, *F*, 1926 *W*, *I*, *F*, *S*, 1927 *W*, *I*, *S*, *F*, 1928 *NSW*, *W*, *I*, *F*, *S*, 1929 *W*, *I*, *F*, 1930 *W*, *I*, *F*, *S*, 1931 *W*
Tucker, W E (Blackheath) 1894 *W*, *I*, 1895 *W*, *I*, *S*
Tucker, W E (Blackheath) 1926 *I*, 1930 *W*, *I*
Turner, D P (Richmond) 1871 *S*, 1872 *S*, 1873 *S*, 1874 *S*, 1875 *I*, *S*
Turner, E B (St George's Hospital) 1876 *I*, 1877 *I*, 1878 *I*
Turner, G R (St George's Hospital) 1876 *S*
Turner, H J C (Manchester) 1871 *S*
Turner, M F (Blackheath) 1948 *S*, *F*
Turquand-Young, D (Richmond) 1928 *NSW*, *W*, 1929 *I*, *S*, *F*
Twynam, H T (Richmond) 1879 *I*, 1880 *I*, 1881 *W*, 1882 *I*, 1883 *I*, 1884 *W*, *I*, *S*

Underwood, A M (Exeter) 1962 *W*, *I*, *F*, *S*, 1964 *I*
Underwood, R (Leicester, RAF) 1984 *I*, *F*, *W*
Unwin, E J (Rosslyn Park, Army) 1937 *S*, 1938 *W*, *I*, *S*
Unwin, G T (Blackheath) 1898 *S*
Uren, R (Waterloo) 1948 *I*, *S*, *F*, 1950 *I*
Uttley, R M (Gosforth) 1973 *I*, *F*, *S*, *NZ*, *A*, 1974 *I*, *F*, *W*, 1975 *F*, *W*, *S*, *A* (2), 1977 *S*, *I*, *F*, *W*, 1978 *NZ*, 1979 *S*, 1980 *I*, *F*, *W*, *S*

Valentine, J (Swinton) 1890 *W*, 1896 *W*, *I*, *S*
Vanderspar, C H R (Richmond) 1873 *S*
Van Ryneveld, C B (Oxford U) 1949 *W*, *I*, *F*, *S*
Varley, H (Liversedge) 1892 *S*

Vassall, H (Blackheath) 1881 *W, S*, 1882 *I, S*, 1883 *W*
Vassall, H H (Blackheath) 1908 *I*
Vaughan, D B (Headingley) 1948 *A, W, I, S*, 1949 *I, F, S*, 1950 *W*
Vaughan-Jones, A (Army) 1932 *I, S*, 1933 *W*
Verelst, C L (Liverpool) 1876 *I*, 1878 *I*
Vernon, G F (Blackheath) 1878 *S, I*, 1880 *I, S*, 1881 *I*
Vickery, G (Aberavon) 1905 *I*
Vivyan, E J (Devonport A) 1901 *W*, 1904 *W, I, S*
Voyce, A T (Gloucester) 1920 *I, S*, 1921 *W, I, S, F*, 1922 *W, I, F, S*, 1923 *W, I, S, F*, 1924 *W, I, F, S*, 1925 *NZ, W, I, S, F*, 1926 *W, I, F, S*

Wackett, J A S (Rosslyn Park) 1959 *W, I*
Wade, C G (Richmond) 1883 *W, I, S*, 1884 *W, S*, 1885 *W*, 1886 *W, I*
Wade, M R (Cambridge U) 1962 *W, I, F*
Wakefield, W W (Harlequins) 1920 *W, F, I, S*, 1921 *W, I, S, F*, 1922 *W, I, F, S*, 1923 *W, I, S, F*, 1924 *W, I, F, S*, 1925 *NZ, W, I, S, F*, 1926 *W, I, F, S*, 1927 *S, F*
Walker, G A (Blackheath) 1939 *W, I*
Walker, H W (Coventry) 1947 *W, I, S, F*, 1948 *A, W, I, S, F*
Walker, R (Manchester) 1874 *S*, 1875 *I*, 1876 *S*, 1879 *S*, 1880 *S*
Wallens, J N S (Waterloo) 1927 *F*
Walton, E J (Castleford) 1901 *W, I*, 1902 *I, S*
Walton, W (Castleford) 1894 *S*
Ward, G (Leicester) 1913 *W, F, S*, 1914 *W, I, S*
Ward, H (Bradford) 1895 *W*
Ward, J I (Richmond) 1881 *I*, 1882 *I*
Ward, J W (Castleford) 1896 *W, I, S*
Wardlow, C S (Northampton) 1969 *SA* (R), 1971 *W, I, F, S* (2[1C])
Warfield, P J (Rosslyn Park, Durham U) 1973 *NZ, W, I*, 1975 *I, F, S*
Warr, A L (Oxford U) 1934 *W, I*
Watkins, J A (Gloucester) 1972 *SA*, 1973 *NZ, W, NZ, A*, 1975 *F, W*
Watkins, J K (United Services, RN) 1939 *W, I, S*
Watson, F B (United Services, RN) 1908 *S*, 1909 *S*
Watson, J H D (Blackheath) 1914 *W, S, F*
Watt, D E J (Bristol) 1967 *I, F, S, W*
Webb, C S H (Devonport Services, RN) 1932 *SA, W, I, S*, 1933 *W, I, S*, 1935 *S*, 1936 *NZ, W, I, S*
Webb, J W G (Northampton) 1926 *F, S*, 1929 *S*
Webb, R E (Coventry) 1967 *S, W, NZ*, 1968 *I, F, S*, 1969 *I, F, S, W*, 1972 *I, F*
Webb, St L H (Bedford) 1959 *W, I, F, S*
Webster, J G (Moseley) 1972 *W, I, SA*, 1973 *NZ, W, NZ*, 1974 *S, W*, 1975 *I, F, W*
Wedge, T G (St Ives) 1907 *F*, 1909 *W*
Weighill, R H G (RAF, Harlequins) 1947 *S, F*, 1948 *S, F*
Wells, C M (Cambridge U, Harlequins) 1893 *S*, 1894 *W, S*, 1896 *S*, 1897 *W, S*
West, B R (Loughborough Colls, Northampton) 1968 *W, I, F, S*, 1969 *SA*, 1970 *I, W, S*
Weston, H T F (Northampton) 1901 *S*
Weston, L E (W of Scotland) 1972 *F, S*
Weston, M P (Richmond, Durham City) 1960 *W, I, F, S*, 1961 *SA, W, I, F, S*, 1962 *W, I, F*, 1963 *W, I, F, S, NZ* (2), *A*, 1964 *NZ, W, I, F, S*, 1965 *F, S*, 1966 *S*, 1968 *F, S*
Weston, W H (Northampton) 1933 *I, S*, 1934 *I, S*, 1935 *W, I, S* 1936 *NZ, W, S*, 1937 *W, I, S*, 1938 *W, I, S*
Wheatley, A A (Coventry) 1937 *W, I, S*, 1938 *W, S*
Wheatley, H F (Coventry) 1936 *I*, 1937 *S*, 1938 *W, S*, 1939 *W, I, S*
Wheeler, P J (Leicester) 1975 *F, W*, 1976 *A, W, S, I*, 1977 *S, I, F, W*, 1978 *F, W, S, I, NZ*, 1979 *S, I, F, W, NZ*, 1980 *I, F, W, S*, 1981 *W, S, I, F*, 1982 *A, S, I, F, W*, 1983 *F, S, I, NZ*, 1984 *S, I, F, W*
White, C (Gosforth) 1983 *NZ*, 1984 *S, I, F*
White, D F (Northampton) 1947 *W, I, S*, 1948 *I, F*, 1951 *S*, 1952 *SA, W, S, I, F*, 1953 *W, I, S*
Whiteley, E C P (O Alleynians) 1931 *S, F*
Whiteley, W (Bramley) 1896 *W*
Whitley, H (Northern) 1929 *W*
Wightman, B J (Moseley, Coventry) 1959 *W*, 1963 *W, I, NZ, A*
Wigglesworth, H J (Thornes) 1884 *I*
Wilkins, D T (United Services, RN, Roundhay) 1951 *W, I, F, S*, 1952 *SA, W, S, I, F*, 1953 *W, I, F, S*
Wilkinson, E (Bradford) 1886 *W, I, S*, 1887 *W, S*
Wilkinson, H J (Halifax) 1889 *M*
Wilkinson, H (Halifax) 1929 *W, I, S*, 1930 *F*
Wilkinson, P (Law Club) 1872 *S*
Wilkinson, R M (Bedford) 1975 *A*, 1976 *A, W, S, I, F*
Willcocks, T J (Plymouth) 1902 *W*
Willcox, J G (Oxford U, Harlequins) 1961 *I, F, S*, 1962 *W, I, F, S*, 1963 *W, I, F, S*, 1964 *NZ, W, I, F, S*
William-Powlett, P B R W (United Services, RN) 1922 *S*
Williams, C G (Gloucester, RAF) 1976 *F*
Williams, C S (Manchester) 1910 *F*
Williams, J E (O Millhillians and Sale) 1954 *F*, 1955 *W, I, F, S*, 1956 *I, S, F*, 1965 *W*
Williams, J M (Penzance-Newlyn) 1951 *I, S*
Williams, S G (Devonport A) 1902 *W, I, S* 1903 *I, S*, 1907 *I, S*
Williams, S H (Newport) 1911 *W, F, I, S*
Williamson, R H (Oxford U) 1908 *W, I, S*, 1909 *A, F*
Wilson, A J (Camborne S of M) 1909 *I*
Wilson, C E (Blackheath) 1898 *I*
Wilson, C P (Cambridge U, Marlborough N) 1881 *W*
Wilson, D S (Met Police, Harlequins) 1953 *F*, 1954 *W, NZ, I, S, F*, 1955 *F, S*
Wilson, G S (Tyldesley) 1929 *W, I*
Wilson, K J (Gloucester) 1963 *F*
Wilson, R P (Liverpool OB) 1891 *W, I, S*
Wilson, W C (Richmond) 1907 *I, S*
Winn, C E (Rosslyn Park) 1952 *SA, W, S, I, F*, 1954 *W, S, F*
Winterbottom, P J (Headingley) 1982 *A, S, I, F, W*, 1983 *F, W, S, I, NZ*, 1984 *S, F, W*
Wintle, T C (Northampton) 1966 *S*, 1969 *I, F, S, W*
Wodehouse, N A (United Services, RN) 1910 *F*, 1911 *W, F, I, S*, 1912 *W, I, S, F*, 1913 *SA, W, F, I, S*
Wood, A (Halifax) 1884 *I*
Wood, A E (Gloucester, Cheltenham) 1908 *F, W, I*
Wood, G W (Leicester) 1914 *W*
Wood, R (Liversedge) 1894 *I*
Wood, R D (Liverpool OB) 1901 *I*, 1903 *W, I*
Woodgate, E E (Paignton) 1952 *W*
Woodhead, E (Huddersfield) 1880 *I*
Woodruff, C G (Harlequins) 1951 *W, I, F, S*
Woods, S M J (Cambridge U, Wellington) 1890 *W, S, I*, 1891 *W, I, S*, 1892 *I, S*, 1893 *W, I*, 1895 *W, I, S*
Woods, T (Bridgwater) 1908 *S*
Woods, T (United Services, RN) 1920 *S*, 1921 *W, I, S, F*
Woodward, C R (Leicester) 1980 *I* (R), *F, W, S*, 1981 *W, S, I, F, Arg* (2), 1982 *A, S, I, F, W*, 1983 *I, NZ*, 1984 *S, I, F, W*
Woodward, J E (Wasps) 1952 *SA, W, S*, 1953 *W, I, F, S*, 1954 *W, NZ, I, S, F*, 1955 *W, I*, 1956 *S*
Wooldridge, C S (Oxford U, Blackheath) 1883 *W, I, S*, 1884 *W, I, S*, 1885 *I*
Wordsworth, A J (Cambridge U) 1975 *A* (R)
Worton, J R B (Harlequins, Army) 1926 *W*, 1927 *W*
Wrench, D F B (Harlequins) 1964 *F, S*
Wright, C C G (Cambridge U, Blackheath) 1909 *I, S*
Wright, F T (Edinburgh Acads, Manchester) 1881 *S*
Wright, I D (Northampton) 1971 *W, I, F, S*, (R)
Wright, J C (Met Police) 1934 *W*
Wright, J F (Bradford) 1890 *W*
Wright, T P (Blackheath) 1960 *W, I, F, S*, 1961 *SA, W, I, F, S*, 1962 *W, I, F, S*
Wright, W H G (Plymouth) 1920 *W, F*
Wyatt, D M (Bedford) 1976 *S* (R)

Yarranton, P G (RAF, Wasps) 1954 *W, NZ, I*, 1955 *F, S*
Yiend, W (Hartlepool R, Gloucester) 1889 *M*, 1892 *W, I, S*, 1893 *I, S*
Young, A T (Cambridge U, Blackheath, Army) 1924 *W, I, F, S*, 1925 *NZ, F*, 1926 *I, F, S*, 1927 *I, S, F*, 1928 *NSW, W, I, F, S*, 1929 *I*
Young, J R C (Oxford U, Harlequins) 1958 *I*, 1960 *W, I, F, S* 1961 *SA, W, I, F*
Young, M (Gosforth) 1977 *S, I, F, W*, 1978 *F, W, S, I, NZ*, 1979 *S*
Young, P D (Dublin Wands) 1954 *W, NZ, I, S, F*, 1955 *W, I, F, S*
Youngs, N G (Leicester) 1983 *I, NZ*, 1984 *S, I, F, W*

ENGLISH INTERNATIONAL RECORDS

From 1890-91, when uniform points-scoring was first adopted by International Board countries, to 30 April 1984. Both team and individual records are against International Board countries only, except for the match against the RFU President's XV in the 1970-71 centenary season. Where caps have been awarded for other matches, this is recorded, in the case of the most capped players, in the notes.

TEAM RECORDS

Highest score
41 v France (41-13) 1907 Richmond
v individual countries
30 v Scotland (30-18) 1980 Murrayfield
36 v Ireland (36-14) 1938 Dublin
25 v Wales (25-0) 1896 Blackheath (London)
41 v France (41-13) 1907 Richmond
16 v N Zealand (16-10) 1973 Auckland
18 v S Africa (18-9) 1972 Johannesburg
23 v Australia (23-6) 1976 Twickenham

Biggest winning points margin
37 v France (37-0) 1911 Twickenham
v individual countries
20 v Scotland (26-6) 1977 Twickenham
22 v Ireland (36-14) 1938 Dublin
25 v Wales (25-0) 1896 Blackheath
37 v France (37-0) 1911 Twickenham
13 v N Zealand (13-0) 1936 Twickenham
9 v S Africa (18-9) 1972 Johannesburg
17 v Australia { (20-3) 1973 Twickenham; (23-6) 1976 Twickenham }

Highest score by opposing team
37 France (12-37) 1972 Colombes (Paris)
by individual countries
28 Scotland (19-28) 1931 Murrayfield
26 Ireland (21-26) 1974 Twickenham
34 Wales (21-34) 1967 Cardiff
37 France (12-37) 1972 Colombes
23 N Zealand (11-23) 1967 Twickenham
9 S Africa { (3-9) 1913 Twickenham; (18-9) 1972 Johannesburg }
30 Australia (21-30) 1975 Brisbane

Biggest losing points margin
25 { v Wales (0-25) 1905 Cardiff; v France (12-37) 1972 Colombes }
v individual countries
20 v Scotland (6-26) 1971 Murrayfield
22 v Ireland (0-22) 1947 Dublin
25 v Wales (0-25) 1905 Cardiff
25 v France (12-37) 1972 Colombes
15 v N Zealand (0-15) 1905 Crystal Palace (London)
7 v S Africa (0-7) 1932 Twickenham
12 v Australia (11-23) 1967 Twickenham

Most points by England in International Championship in a season – 82
(in season 1913-14)

Most tries by England in International Championship in a season – 20
(in season 1913-14)

Most tries by England in an international
9 { v France (35-8) 1906 Parc des Princes (Paris); v France (41-13) 1907 Richmond; v France (39-13) 1914 Colombes }
England scored 13 tries v Wales at Blackheath in 1881, before uniform scoring was adopted.

Most tries against England in an international
8 by Wales (6-28) 1922 Cardiff

INDIVIDUAL RECORDS

Most capped player
A Neary 43 1971-80
in individual positions
Full-back
W H Hare 21(23)† 1974-84

Wing
M A C Slemen 31* 1976-84
Centre
J Butterfield 28* 1953-59
Fly-half
W J A Davies 22 1913-23
Scrum-half
S J Smith 26(28)† 1973-83
Prop
F E Cotton 31 1971-81
Hooker
J V Pullin 42 1966-76
Lock
W B Beaumont 32(34)† 1975-82
Flanker
A Neary 43 1971-80
No 8
J P Scott 29(32)‡ 1978-84

**David Duckham, England's most capped back, played 14 times at centre, and 22 times on the wing, making a total of 36 caps.*
M P Weston won 5 of his 29 caps as a fly-half, and 24 in the centre.
†Smith, Hare and Beaumont have played twice each against Argentina.
‡Scott has played twice against Argentina and was capped once as a lock.

Most internationals as captain – 19*
W B Beaumont 1978-82
**Excludes 2 games as captain in matches against Argentina.*

Most points in internationals – 204*
W H Hare (21 appearances)
**Excludes 15 points in two matches against Argentina.*

Most points in an international – 22
D Lambert v France 1911 Twickenham

Most tries in internationals – 18
C N Lowe (25 appearances) 1913-23

Most tries in an international – 5
D Lambert v France 1907 Richmond (on first appearance)

Most conversions in an international – 6
J E Greenwood v France 1914 Paris
G W Parker v Ireland 1938 Dublin
L Stokes kicked 6 v Wales at Blackheath in 1881, before uniform scoring was adopted.

Most points in International Championship in a season – 44
W H Hare (4 appearances) 1983-84

Most tries in International Championship in a season – 8
C N Lowe (4 appearances) 1913-14

Most conversions in International Championship in a season – 7
G S Conway (4 appearances) 1923-24

Most penalty goals in International Championship in a season – 14
W H Hare (4 appearances) 1982-83

Most points on overseas tour – 48
W N Bennett (4 appearances) Australia 1975

Most points in any tour match – 36
W N Bennett v Western Australia 1975 Perth

Most tries in any tour match – 4
A J Morley v Western Australia 1975 Perth
P S Preece v New South Wales 1975 Sydney

THORN-EMI COUNTY CHAMPIONSHIP 1983-84

Michael Heal

31 March, Twickenham
Gloucestershire 36 (3G 2PG 3T) **Somerset 18** (1G 4PG)

A superb team performance by Gloucestershire won them many new admirers and, fittingly, the Thorn-EMI trophy before a crowd of 26,000 at Twickenham. The game was full of movement throughout but once Gloucestershire had overcome the early onslaught from Somerset in the first half, they controlled possession and emphasised their superiority by outscoring their neighbours by six tries to one.

Some concern had been voiced about the wisdom of staging the final at Twickenham and as long as four months after the semi-finals. Happily the West Country support was fervent enough to overcome these logistical irritants and as the two counties were selected from just three clubs there was no barrier to teamwork. Somerset were forced to contest the final without the services of scrum-half Richard Hill, an England squad member, Rob Cunningham, the Scotland reserve hooker, and Gareth Williams, the Bristol wing. However, with Bath crushing all opposition in the preceding months they were confident they could do the same in the shirts of Somerset.

In the first quarter they forced Gloucestershire onto the defensive but they had only three penalty goals from Palmer to show for it. By half-time Gloucestershire were showing signs of regaining their composure and had scored a try through Knibbs and two penalty goals by Barnes. Then in the second half Gloucestershire moved into top gear. Monopolising possession, they scored tries through Morley (2), Barnes, Harding and Hogg with Barnes kicking three conversions. The Gloucestershire half-backs kept Somerset on the rack. Barnes, in particular, confirmed that he is ready for higher honours. He had all the individual skills in abundance and displayed a tactical awareness rare in one so young. Furthermore, his goal-kicking was in the Dusty Hare class and he finished the match with 16 points.

Somerset were forced to run the ball away from the predatory Gloucestershire pack at every opportunity in an effort to create space for the speedy Trick. But this was always a risky business, especially as several of their backs were not at their best. Knibbs, Hogg and Morley took full advantage as Somerset became increasingly desperate. The back row battle was also won by the Gloucestershire trio of Rafter, Gadd and Hesford. Somerset's Spurrell took an early knock and finally retired after 55 minutes and this hindered his team's attempts to provide the vital loose possession. Only occasionally did Simpson, at No 8, prove a threat with his powerful running but even then he was often unsupported.

Gloucestershire had the match won early in the second half and from then on they played with complete assurance. They have now won the title a record 15 times and seem to be in danger of claiming permanent possession.

Several players, neglected by the England selectors, had a few points to make, especially with the trip to South Africa in the offing. Given England's poor showing in the Championship it was not difficult to feel sympathy for the men from Gloucestershire.

Mike Rafter's record as a captain is truly exceptional. In 1983 he led both Gloucestershire and Bristol to victory in the premier competitions. In 1984 he was to narrowly fail to retain the John Player Cup but on his 32nd birthday he deservedly claimed the Thorn-EMI trophy for Gloucestershire.

A moment of triumph for Alan Morley as he holds aloft the Thorn-EMI trophy after Gloucestershire's win over Somerset.

TEAMS IN THE FINAL

Gloucestershire: P C Cue (Bristol); A J Morley (Bristol), R A Knibbs (Bristol), S T Hogg (Bristol), R Mogg (Gloucester); S Barnes (Gloucester), R M Harding (Bristol); *No 8* R Hesford (Bristol); *Second Row* M J Rafter (Bristol) *(capt)*, J Fidler (Bristol), J Orwin (Bristol), J Gadd (Gloucester); *Front Row* M Preedy (Gloucester), S G F Mills (Gloucester), P J Blakeway (Gloucester)
Scorers *Tries:* Morley (2), Knibbs, Barnes, Harding, Hogg *Conversions:* Barnes (3) *Penalty Goals:* Barnes (2)
Somerset: C Ralston (Bath); D M Trick (Bath), J A Palmer (Bath), A Rees (Bath), P Simmons (Bath); J P Horton (Bath) *(capt)*, C Stanley (Bath); *No 8* P D Simpson (Bath); *Second Row* R Spurrell (Bath), R H Hakin (Bath), P J Stiff (Bristol), J P Hall (Bath); *Front Row* C C Lilley (Bath), G Bess (Bath), R M Lee (Bath) *Replacements* P Turner (Bath) for Spurrell (55 mins) N Hopkins (Weston-super-Mare) for Trick (79 mins)
Scorers *Try:* Rees *Conversion:* Palmer *Penalty Goals:* Palmer (4)
Referee F Howard (Liverpool)

In their semi-final, Gloucestershire defeated Middlesex by 13-12, recovering from being 12-0 down. The basis of victory was predictably their forward domination with the Gloucestershire pack depriving Middlesex of both possession and territorial advantage for long periods of the game. Consequently, Gloucestershire's true superiority was not reflected in the narrow margin of victory.

In the other semi-final Somerset snatched victory from Yorkshire in the dying minutes with a try from a line-out by their lock, Hakin. Somerset were fortunate to be awarded a dropped goal in the first half when all but the referee thought that Horton's attempt was wide. However, Yorkshire squeezed ahead and seemed to be in control until that last desperate fling by Somerset.

TEAMS IN THE SEMI-FINALS

26 November, Gloucester RFC (Kingsholm)
Gloucestershire 13 (3PG 1T) Middlesex 12 (1G 1PG 1DG)

Gloucestershire: S Hogg (Bristol); A J Morley (Bristol), R Mogg (Gloucester), R Knibbs (Bristol), N Price (Gloucester); S Barnes (Bristol), R Harding (Bristol); *No 8* R Hesford (Bristol); *Second Row* J Gadd (Gloucester), J Orwin (Gloucester), J Fidler (Gloucester), M J Rafter (Bristol) *(capt)*; *Front Row* M Preedy (Gloucester), S G F Mills (Gloucester), P J Blakeway (Gloucester)
Scorers *Try:* Morley *Penalty Goals:* Barnes (3)
Middlesex: N Stringer (Wasps); R M Cardus (Wasps), A Dent (Harlequins), R Gordon (London Scottish), S O'Reilly (Met Police); M Williams (Wasps), J Cullen (Wasps); *No 8* C Butcher (Harlequins); *Second Row* K Bowring (London Welsh), R Riddell (Harlequins), W Cuthbertson (Harlequins), D H Cooke (Harlequins) *(capt)*: *Front Row* P Curtis (Rosslyn Park), J Olver (Harlequins), M Claxton (Harlequins) *Replacement* T Bryan (Met Police) for Williams (65 mins)
Scorers *Try:* Claxton *Conversion:* Stringer *Dropped Goal:* Williams *Penalty Goal:* Stringer
Referee D Thomas (North Midlands)

26 November, Bath RFC
Somerset 15 (1G 2PG 1DG) Yorkshire 12 (1G 2PG)

Somerset: C Ralston (Bath); D M Trick (Bath), J A Palmer (Bath), G Williams (Bristol), P Simmons (Bath); J P Horton (Bath) *(capt)*, R Hill (Bath); *No 8* P Simpson (Bath); *Second Row* J Hall (Bath), R Hakin (Bath), P Stiff (Bristol), R Spurrell (Bath); *Front Row* G Chillcott (Bath), R Cunningham (Bath), R Lee (Bath)
Scorers *Try:* Hakin *Conversion:* Palmer *Dropped Goal:* Horton
Penalty Goals: Palmer (2)
Yorkshire: D Norton (Headingley); M Harrison (Wakefield), B Barley (Wakefield), S Townend (Wakefield), R Underwood (Leicester); A G B Old (Sheffield) *(capt)*, H Jarzyna (Morley); *No 8* P Buckton (Liverpool); *Second Row* S Tipping (Sale), P Jones (Rotherham), R Walters (Huddersfield), P Winterbottom (Headingley), *Front Row* P Huntsman (Headingley), B Coyne (Middlesbrough), J Tinker (Harrogate)
Scorers *Try:* Tipping *Conversion:* Old *Penalty Goals:* Old (2)
Referee R Russell (London)

DIVISIONAL ROUNDS

Division 1 (Group A)

Gloucestershire beat Surrey 22-3, Northumberland 19-16, and Yorkshire 23-6
Yorkshire beat Northumberland 14-10, Surrey 24-8; lost to Gloucestershire 6-23
Northumberland beat Surrey 20-6; lost to Yorkshire 10-14 and Gloucestershire 16-19
Surrey lost to Gloucestershire 3-22, Yorkshire 8-24 and Northumberland 6-20

	P	*W*	*D*	*L*	*F*	*A*	*Pts*
Gloucestershire	3	3	0	0	64	25	6
Yorkshire	3	2	0	1	44	41	4
Northumberland	3	1	0	2	46	39	2
Surrey	3	0	0	3	17	66	0

Division 1 (Group B)

Somerset beat Lancashire 15-12, Devon 27-18 and Middlesex 10-9
Middlesex beat Devon 33-7 and Lancashire 30-13; lost to Somerset 9-10
Lancashire beat Devon 30-14; lost to Somerset 12-15 and Middlesex 13-30
Devon lost to Middlesex 7-33, Somerset 18-27 and Lancashire 14-30

	P	*W*	*D*	*L*	*F*	*A*	*Pts*
Somerset	3	3	0	0	52	39	6
Middlesex	3	2	0	1	72	30	4
Lancashire	3	1	0	2	55	59	2
Devon	3	0	0	3	39	90	0

Division 2 (Group A)

Notts, Lincs & Derbys beat Durham 15-9 and Warwickshire 21-9; drew with North Midlands 9-9
Durham beat North Midlands 13-3 and Warwickshire 25-9; lost to Notts, Lincs & Derbys 9-15
North Midlands beat Warwickshire 6-3; drew with Notts, Lincs & Derbys 9-9; lost to Durham 3-13
Warwickshire lost to North Midlands 3-6, Notts, Lincs & Derbys 9-21 and Durham 9-25

Charles Ralston of Somerset attempts to secure the loose ball under pressure from Gloucestershire's Ralph Knibbs during the county final at Twickenham.

	P	W	D	L	F	A	Pts
Notts, Lincs & Derbys	3	2	1	0	45	27	5
Durham	3	2	0	1	47	27	4
North Midlands	3	1	1	1	18	25	3
Warwickshire	3	0	0	3	21	52	0

Division 2 (Group B)

Kent beat Hertfordshire 18-8, Cornwall 8-6 and Cheshire 35-18
Cornwall beat Cheshire 20-0, Hertfordshire 10-4; lost to Kent 6-8
Hertfordshire beat Cheshire 22-16; lost to Kent 8-18 and Cornwall 4-10
Cheshire lost to Cornwall 0-20, Hertfordshire 16-22 and Kent 18-35

	P	W	D	L	F	A	Pts
Kent	3	3	0	0	61	32	6
Cornwall	3	2	0	1	36	12	4
Hertfordshire	3	1	0	2	34	44	2
Cheshire	3	0	0	3	34	77	0

Division 3 (Group A)

Leicestershire beat Staffordshire 9-0, Sussex 15-7 and Oxfordshire 36-9
Staffordshire beat Oxfordshire 41-0 and Sussex 10-7; lost to Leicestershire 0-9
Sussex beat Oxfordshire 15-3; lost to Leicestershire 7-15 and Staffordshire 7-10
Oxfordshire lost to Sussex 3-15, Staffordshire 0-41 and Leicestershire 9-36

	P	W	D	L	F	A	Pts
Leicestershire	3	3	0	0	61	16	6
Staffordshire	3	2	0	1	51	16	4
Sussex	3	1	0	2	29	29	2
Oxfordshire	3	0	0	3	12	92	0

Division 3 (Group B)

Cumbria beat Buckinghamshire 13-3, East Midlands 20-8 and Eastern Counties 16-6
Eastern Counties beat East Midlands 24-9; drew with Buckinghamshire 3-3; lost to Cumbria 6-16
Buckinghamshire drew with Eastern Counties 3-3 and East Midlands 7-7; lost to Cumbria 3-13
East Midlands drew with Buckinghamshire 3-3; lost to Eastern Counties 9-24 and Cumbria 3-13

	P	W	D	L	F	A	Pts
Cumbria	3	3	0	0	49	17	6
Eastern Counties	3	1	1	1	33	28	3
Buckinghamshire	3	0	2	1	13	23	2
East Midlands	3	0	1	2	24	51	1

Division 4

Hampshire beat Dorset & Wilts 21-4 and Berkshire 20-4; lost to Berkshire 13-16 and Dorset & Wilts 3-10
Dorset & Wilts beat Hampshire 10-3 and Berkshire 18-6; lost to Hampshire 4-21 and Berkshire 10-22

Berkshire beat Hampshire 16-13 and Dorset & Wilts 22-10; lost to Dorset & Wilts 6-18 and Hampshire 4-20

	P	*W*	*D*	*L*	*F*	*A*	*Pts*
Hampshire	4	2	0	2	57	34	4
Dorset & Wilts	4	2	0	2	42	52	4
Berkshire	4	2	0	2	48	61	4

Semi-finals
Gloucester beat Middlesex 13-12; Somerset beat Yorkshire 15-12
Division 1 Relegation
Northumberland beat Devon 19-11; Lancs drew with Surrey 6-6
Division 2 Promotion
Kent beat Durham 17-15; Notts, Lincs & Derbys beat Cornwall 18-13
Division 2 Relegation
Warwickshire beat Hertfordshire 17-7; Cheshire beat North Midlands 17-3
Division 3 Promotion
Cumbria beat Staffordshire 7-0; Eastern Counties beat Leicestershire 21-16
Division 3 Relegation
Buckinghamshire beat Oxfordshire 11-3; Sussex beat East Midlands 21-10

JOHN PLAYER SPECIAL CUP 1983-84

(RFU Club competition)

Michael Austin *The Daily Telegraph*

28 April, Twickenham
Bath 10 (1PG 1DG 1T) **Bristol 9** (1G 1PG)

After being in the shadow of West Country clubs Gloucester and Bristol for so long, Bath won the competition for the first time, beating Bristol, the holders and favourites, before a crowd of 25,000 basking in hot sunshine. A gruelling match, limited by the safety-first restraints befitting such an important game between rivals separated by only 13 miles, it was nevertheless a compelling cup contest. The Cup was won by Bath's forwards and especially by their bigger back row.

While Bristol lacked their traditional commitment and offered only fleeting moments of excellence, Bath's combination of Spurrell, Simpson and Hall, the most impressive players on the field, dominated the loose ball and allowed Horton to force Bristol into defensive positions. Bristol, trailing 3-10 at half time and struggling unexpectedly in the scrums, had scarcely won enough possession to feed even their centres and the only time they looked possible winners was in the final scoreless 25 minutes.

Such was the tension that Jack Rowell, Bath's coach, could not bear to watch the last five minutes and retired to the Twickenham car park. Rowell did not see the crucial missed penalty attempt by Bristol's Barnes with the final kick of the match – neither did Spurrell, Bath's captain, who turned his back and knelt on the ground. Trevaskis, Bath's left wing, had tackled Morley without the ball as Bristol launched a last desperate move. Barnes, who scored 48 of his side's 102 cup points during the season, took the kick but booted wide from near the right touchline on Bath's 22-metre line. A case for a penalty try could have been made if Morley had been impeded five metres nearer to Bath's line.

Palmer, Bath's goalkicker, could sympathise with Barnes; he missed his first five attempts in a testing wind, blowing from the south-east corner. But Palmer's successful penalty goal from 28 metres just before half-time opened a vital, seven-point lead. This situation stemmed from Horton's angled dropped goal from the left after four minutes and Simpson's try. Barnes responded with a penalty goal for Bristol, Spurrell having obstructed the resourceful Harding, who had kicked ahead. Horton's dropped goal was engineered by his own high punt, which had pressurised Bristol, and Simpson scored his try from a driving run around the blind-side of a scrum, using Hall as a foil. All Bristol expected Simpson to pass, but he drove onwards and over the line.

Both sides were without an international forward – Bath by choice, with 19-year-old Redman, a strong and mobile lock, chosen ahead of

Hakin, the Ireland cap and Bristol out of necessity, when Hesford's eve-of-match withdrawal through a poisoned elbow brought in Chidgey at No 8. Chidgey's industrious efforts could not compensate for the loss of continuity caused by Hesford's absence, but at least Bristol showed increasing appetite for the game and challenged Bath's lead by tapping a highly kickable penalty. From it, Bath halted Pomphrey's charge for the line, but from the next scrum, Harding achieved the notable feat of deceiving Bath's back row, Spurrell and Horton in particular, for a try. Barnes' conversion, after 55 minutes, was the final score of the match.

Horton missed a dropped goal attempt five minutes from the end and Bristol twice relied on the generosity of the bounce to avoid conceding a second try. Cue, for Bristol, lost sight of Horton's high kick in the sun, Horton and Hill challenged him and Horton's cross kick narrowly escaped Trevaskis.

Spurrell had told Jack Simpkins, Bath's president, before Christmas that his side would win the cup. Unwavering confidence during Bath's training sessions in the lead-up to the final strengthened Spurrell's assertion, but even he could not have anticipated such a commanding first-half performance.

Defeat ended Mike Rafter's hopes of leading his club and county, Gloucestershire, to titles in successive seasons. The 'double double' had eluded him and, two days after the final, Rafter announced he was stepping down from Bristol's captaincy – in a decision he had taken before his team lost at Twickenham. Peter Polledri succeeds him.

Bath: C R Martin; D M Trick, J A Palmer, A Rees, B Trevaskis; J P Horton, R Hill; *No 8* P D Simpson; *Second Row* R A Spurrell *(capt)*, N Gaymond, N Redman, J P Hall; *Front Row* G Chilcott, R Cunningham, M R Lee
Scorers *Try:* Simpson *Penalty Goal:* Palmer *Dropped Goal:* Horton
Bristol: P C Cue; A J G Morley, R A Knibbs, S T Hogg, J F Carr; S Barnes, R M Harding; *No 8* D L Chidgey; *Second Row* P Polledri, N J C Pomphrey, P J Stiff, M Rafter *(capt)*; *Front Row* R J Doubleday, D J Palmer, A Sheppard
Scorers *Try:* Harding *Conversion:* Barnes *Penalty Goal:* Barnes
Referee R C Quittenton (London and Sussex Societies)

Some of the more fancied clubs, notably Leicester, Orrell, West Hartlepool and Gosforth, who all enjoyed an excellent season, had disappeared from the competition by the quarter-final stage. Wasps, Coventry and Waterloo promptly joined them and Gloucester, who had failed to qualify for the competition because of their fifth placing in the 1982-83 South and South West Merit Table, looked on sadly, especially with West Country rivals contesting the final.

Bath, who failed to qualify for the competition at all in the previous season, rose from 12 years of oblivion, having won only six of 17 cup matches, to reaching their first final. Their previous pinnacles were quarter-final appearances in 1975 and 1980. This curious lack of success became a spur for Bath, who dismissed Blackheath 41-12 at the Rectory Field in the first meeting between the clubs for almost 50 years. Under John Horton's benign guidance, they beat Wasps 26-12 before defeating Nottingham 12-3, watched by a capacity crowd of 5,000 in a dour semi-final deferred for a fortnight because of a waterlogged pitch.

Simpson, Hall and Spurrell, a balanced back row, inspired Bath's victory, though Nottingham had led by Hodgkinson's 32nd-minute penalty goal and retained their advantage until the last 15 minutes when Ralston, a replacement, kicked the first of two penalty goals and converted a try by Trick – from a chip ahead by Lilley, a prop. Trick scored five of Bath's 13 tries in their advance to the final while Bristol, a side they had beaten 12-10 in a club match the previous October, relished the influence of Barnes, England's reserve fly-half.

After scoring five tries at Norwich and six against London Welsh, Bristol relied on Barnes' four penalty goals – the last of these in injury time – to beat Waterloo in the quarter-finals at Blundellsands. Barnes landed five penalty goals and was successful with six kicks from seven attempts in the 21-18 defeat of Harlequins, who scored three tries to one in the semi-final at the Memorial Ground.

Harlequins, the competition's enigma, had overwhelmed Camborne, and then struggled to win by a point at Plymouth Albion with a try in the ninth minute of injury time by Ball. Next, they ruined Coventry's hopes of reaching their eighth semi-final by beating them 24-15.

After contesting the quarter-finals three time in the previous four years, Nottingham confirmed their progress by qualifying for their first semi-final. They had begun in the first round six months earlier, won five games and had the longest cup run in the competition's history. Hodgkinson, at full-back, scored 56 of their 111 points.

Moseley, ultimately knocked out by Nottingham at The Reddings, had previously achieved a 10-9 win at Sale. Coventry eliminated Leicester 13-9 in the third round with the assistance of Fairn's left-footed goal-kicking and Bevan's try, from Lander's break in his final game as Coventry's scrum-half before joining Exeter.

Leicester failed to reach the semi-finals for the first time in seven years, a powerful statistic underlining their previous achievements, while the Wasps, ill-treated by the fates of the draw, added to the competition's growing folklore by being the first club to qualify for the quarter-finals without winning a game. They drew 12-12 in a delayed third-round match at Gosforth where the only try of the game, by Emeruwa, qualified them for an equally demanding visit to Orrell. This time, two tries to nil in a 15-15 draw put Wasps into the quarter-finals at Bath. Having been unbeaten in their first 24 games of the season, Wasps could rue their cup travels.

Twelve clubs were new to the competition, including Old Redcliffians, a Bristol Combination club, who went down bravely to London Scottish; Devon and Cornwall Police, founded in 1967 and the youngest first round entrants, and Newark, who lost at Nottingham. Features of the earlier round were High Wycombe's defeat of Launceston, Plymouth Albion's comprehensive win at Stroud and Southend's staunch efforts in holding Blackheath to 10-14. West Hartlepool were unfortunate to be drawn away to Orrell but the Northern clubs failed to fulfil their initial promise in the competition.

Meanwhile, competing clubs have gained welcome financial benefits in these inflationary times. In 1983-84, John Player increased sponsorship from the previous season by £10,000 to £95,000, bringing the total provided by Imperial Tobacco Limited to over half a million pounds (£500,000) since sponsorship began in 1975-76. The finalists received £3,375, an increase of £375 per club, and there were rises in all other categories with the losing semi-finalists each being allocated £2,700, compared with £2,400 the previous season. In all, 130 clubs benefited financially, with first round losers earning £785 for which many clubs, including Alnwick, of Northumberland, were very grateful. This sum covered half of their travelling costs for the whole season.

RESULTS

First round

Aspatria 3 West Hartlepool 20
Betteshanger Colliery 11 Worthing 20
Fyle 43 Alnwick 21
*Henley 12 Maidenhead 12
High Wycombe 6 Launceston 0
Morley 38 Alsager College 4
Newark 28 Dudley Kingswinford 6
Norwich 9 Guildford and Godalming 3
Nottingham 29 Solihull 3
Nuneaton 19 Walsall 6
Old Redcliffians 7 Devon and Cornwall Police 6
Richmond 22 Saracens 16
Stroud 15 Bournemouth 0
Tabard 9 US Portsmouth 15
Vipers 18 Bedford Athletic 9

**Henley won on 'more tries' rule*

Second round

High Wycombe 16 †Lydney 28
Norwich 21 Henley 15
Nottingham 34 Newark 3
Nuneaton 33 Fylde 21
Richmond 43 US Portsmouth 0
†Southend 24 †KCS Old Boys 3
Stroud 18 †Dartfordians 4
Vipers 3 †Stourbridge 13
West Hartlepool 6 Morley 4
Worthing 6 Old Redcliffians 25

†indicates entry of qualifiers from Gloucestershire, Eastern Counties, Kent, Surrey and North Midlands Cups

Third round

Bath 17 †Headingley 0
Coventry 13 Leicester 9
Gosforth 12 *Wasps 12
†Harlequins 46 Camborne 4
Liverpool 9 Waterloo 13
London Irish 15 Bedford 7
London Welsh 17 Lydney 9
Norwich 3 Bristol 24
Nottingham 13 Stourbridge 3
Nuneaton 6 Richmond 9
†Orrell 13 West Hartlepool 6
Old Redcliffians 15 London Scottish 24
Rosslyn Park 6 Northampton 20
Sale 9 Moseley 10
Southend 10 Blackheath 14
Stroud 0 Plymouth Albion 23

†indicates entry of winners of Middlesex, Yorkshire and Lancashire Cups
**Wasps won on 'more tries' rule*

Fourth round

Blackheath 12 Bath 41
Bristol 36 London Welsh 8
Coventry 16 London Irish 7
London Scottish 34 Northampton 6
Moseley 3 Nottingham 10
Orrell 15 *Wasps 15
Plymouth Albion 16 Harlequins 17
Waterloo 26 Richmond 19

**Wasps won on 'more tries' rule*

Quarter finals

Bath 26 Wasps 12
Coventry 16 Harlequins 24

Nottingham 22 London Scottish 16
Waterloo 9 Bristol 12

Semi-finals
Bristol 21 Harlequins 18
Nottingham 3 Bath 12

Previous finals *(all at Twickenham)*
1972 Gloucester 17 Moseley 6
1973 Coventry 27 Bristol 15
1974 Coventry 26 London Scottish 6
1975 Bedford 28 Rosslyn Park 12
1976 Gosforth 23 Rosslyn Park 14
1977 Gosforth 27 Waterloo 11
1978 Gloucester 6 Leicester 3
1979 Leicester 15 Moseley 12
1980 Leicester 21 London Irish 9
1981 Leicester 22 Gosforth 15
1982 Gloucester 12 Moseley 12 (Title shared)
1983 Bristol 28 Leicester 22

COUNTY CUP WINNERS 1983-84

Berkshire	**Maidenhead**
Buckinghamshire	**Bletchley**
Cheshire	**Sale**
Cornwall	**Redruth**
Cumbria	**Aspatria**
Devon	**Plymouth Albion**
Dorset-Wilts	**Swindon**
Durham	**West Hartlepool**
Eastern Counties	**North Walsham**
East Midlands	**Rushden & Higham**
Gloucestershire	**Berry Hill**
Hampshire	**Havant**
Hertfordshire	**Fullerians**
Kent	**Blackheath**
Lancashire	**Liverpool**
Leicestershire	**Loughborough Students**
Middlesex	**Wasps**
North Midlands	**Stourbridge**
Northumberland	**Alnwick**
Notts/Lincs/Derbys	**Paviors**
Oxfordshire	**Oxford Old Boys**
Somerset	**Old Redcliffians**
Staffordshire	**Lichfield**
Surrey	**Sutton and Epsom**
Sussex	**Crawley**
Warwickshire	**Barkers' Butts**
Yorkshire	**Headingley**

Roger Spurrell, the Bath captain, hoists the John Player Cup skywards in joy following the final.

THE BARBARIANS 1983-84

The Barbarians started the season in style with a comfortable victory over Cornwall in their Centenary match at Redruth. It was the first time the Baa-Baas had travelled to Cornwall and a large appreciative crowd enjoyed a fine match with the visitors scoring six tries. A strong pack – in which Rafter, Wheeler and Hesford all played particularly well – gradually took control, and the light Cornish forwards had to work hard in the mauls to produce any reasonable possession.

The inevitable result was that as the game progressed the county's breakaway forwards were increasingly tied in and the Baa-Baas' backs were given more freedom to attack. With the exception of a final try by Perkins all the Barbarian tries were scored by the backs. Cardus scored two tries and other scores were made by Swift, Richards and Evans with Wyatt kicking four conversions. For Cornwall, the hard-working Trevaskis produced a fine piece of running in scoring Cornwall's only try, and Champion added a penalty goal.

On a windy, wet evening at Newport, a late Hesford try and a Dudman conversion enabled the Baa-Baas to equalise in an 18-18 drawn match, only the fourth in the 77-match series. In an enterprising match Newport led at half-time 15-12, mainly through resourceful forward power and good teamwork. Dudman kicked two penalty goals and also converted a try by Mark Douglas.

The traditional Christmas holiday fixture at Leicester produced a thrilling match in which the home team gained a narrow win in front of a capacity 17,000 crowd. Although the Baa-Baas led three times during the game, they could not maintain the wholehearted approach that Leicester displayed. The home team matched the visitors in terms of attacking rugby and made full use of their team skills, and this probably decided the result. Both sides had scored tries within the first five minutes. Viviès, who with Dupont provided the French element in the Barbarian team, was caught under his posts and Richards freed the ball for Youngs to score. Then Gareth Davies, following an impressive forward surge by the visitors, dummied the defence to put the New Zealander, Green, in to score, and then added the conversion.

In a fast and sometimes hectic match, it was interesting to see another All Black, Donald, pit his wits against Youngs, and both players produced outstanding displays. The duel at No 8 between Richards and Gargan, the Oxford University player, was also fascinating to watch, and the performance by Clive Woodward was also a timely reminder to the English selectors. As Holdstock and Bailey were opposite Leicester's Evans and Underwood, a quartet of England's top wings were on view, and with the ball running well for him, Underwood showed the potential which was to win him a place in the national team later in the season. Barbarian tries were also scored by Gargan, direct from a line-out;

Donald, from close quarters, and Holdstock, with Davies kicking two penalty goals and two conversions.

The Baa-Baas won an exciting victory at Northampton against East Midlands in the annual Edgar Mobbs memorial match. After only a quarter of an hour, Ian George replaced the injured Mark Douglas, and enjoyed a fruitful afternoon on his own home ground. Quinn distributed the ball well at fly-half, and with Hare always wanting to join the attack the Baa-Baas produced some splendid moves. East Midlands produced their best display for some years, and won good possession through Cannon and the evergreen Wilkinson, which was energetically supported by a fast and effective back row.

Bob Ackerman scored two tries, his second score being the result of a 75-yard interception, and Ian George showed his paces with a 30-yard dash from the back of the scrum to score a fine try. Mark Bailey, having been starved of the ball for much of the afternoon, was then released on the half way line and made a fine, swerving run, beating the defence to score under the posts. Hare kicked a penalty goal and converted two of the tries.

Penarth, rising to the occasion for their annual match against the Baa-Baas, made the visitors battle all the way for their 32-21 win, and provided a good match for a full house at the Athletic Ground. The Baa-Baas took time in settling to the task and allowed an improved Penarth to compete in all phases of the play. It was not until Underwood, receiving the ball from a tapped penalty move, raced away to score the first try that the Baa-Baas relaxed and started to produce attacking rugby, often initiated by Didier Camberabero and David Richards, the acting captain for the day.

Gwyn Evans scored a fine try coming through the middle of the field and well supported by a hard-working back row of Jeffrey, Bowring and Connor, the Baa-Baas gradually gained the upper hand. Simon Smith then outflanked the defence with Camberabero converting a fine try. Early in the second half the French fly-half lofted a delicate short punt to the left which Underwood caught and raced away to score. Evans and Richards then combined for the latter to score, and Camberabero finally sealed the match by intercepting a Penarth pass for a try which he converted himself.

On a fine Spring Easter Saturday, Cardiff, with Holmes and Gareth Davies at the heels of a tremendous pack, beat the tourists by the biggest total of points ever recorded in the series of these matches. They scored six goals and four tries against two goals and a try, and the Welsh Cup winners were dominant in every phase of the game.

The current front five of the Cardiff pack can be compared with those of any team who have played for the Club, and with the guiding hand of John Scott, Crothers and Golding especially in tremendous form, the match was virtually over just before half-time. To make matters worse for the Baa-Baas, they lost Baird and Bowen and then flanker Gary Rees had to go on the wing, Terry Holmes expanded his game with full effect. For the Baa-Baas Jeffrey, Harding and Rees, all uncapped players, strived to the end and tries by Smith, Salmon and Squires helped to restore some of the spirit, but it was well and truly Cardiff's day.

After a weekend of raising morale within the Barbarian party, and with some trepidation, the tourists took the field against Swansea under Ian George with Ian Stephens leading the forwards. The team looked steady and confident from the start and although failing to take some early chances of scoring the pack, with Shaw and Waters winning the line-out and an Irish-Welsh combination in the front row, had the stability which was so important. Rees, Gadd and Connor contributed to the task in hand and gained valuable possession for the Baa-Baas when it mattered. Ian George controlled the game at scrum-half with a fine display, and his calming attitude did much to restore confidence to the team.

Swansea took the lead through a Wyatt penalty goal and then the Baa-Baas replied with a try by Hopkins, and Underwood, using all his pace and strength scored twice, to be followed by a Smith try which put the Baa-Baas into a good lead. After half-time the Baa-Baas maintained their improvement and scored tries through Hopkins and Camberabero. After a Thomas try for Swansea and a conversion by Wyatt, George, for the Baa-Baas, scored an opportunist try. Finally, Underwood escaped the defence, and with Rees up in support, Shaw went over for a Swansea try, to which Evans added another conversion. Thus, against the odds, the Barbarians won by 40-13 and produced much the better display.

The Barbarians were pleased with the performance and Swansea were at the receiving end of a severe backlash, following the result at Cardiff. It is always significant if the Baa-Baas lose heavily, and after Cardiff this year and Swansea the previous season, various comments have been made as to the future of the Easter Tour by the club. The Baa-Baas are determined to stick to their traditional style of play which can be a refreshing tonic to an increasing amount of stereotyped rugby.

With an ever-increasing number of rugby commitments for leading players at the end of April, a Barbarian Easter Tour inevitably means that there are problems of availability. Perhaps it is an omen that the next time Easter is so late will be in the year 2011 – but if the response is anything to go by, and the tries which are scored year after year to the delight of the large home crowds, the Baa-Baa tour helps to provide a fitting finale to the season.

PLAYERS 1983-84

Abbreviations C — Cornwall; EM — East Midlands; L — Leicester; N — Newport; SW1 — Penarth; SW2 — Cardiff; SW3 — Swansea; (R) — Replacement; * — New Barbarian

Full-backs M A Wyatt (Swansea & Wales) [C]; *R Dudman (Harlequins) [N]; *B Vivies (Agen & France) [L]; W H Hare (Leicester & England) [EM]; G Evans (Maesteg & Wales) [SW1, SW3]; N C Stringer (Wasps & England) [SW2]

Threequarters B Evans (Leicester) [C]; R M Cardus (Wasps & England) [C, N, L]; D S Richards (Swansea & Wales) [C, SW1]; A H Swift (Swansea & England) [C]; J A Pollock (Gosforth & Scotland) [N]; K W Robertson (Melrose & Scotland) [N]; C F W Rees (London Welsh & Wales) [N]; *S Holdstock (Nottingham) [L]; *C Green (Canterbury & New Zealand) [L]; M D Bailey (Cambridge University) [L, EM]; H E Rees (Neath & Wales) [EM]; *M C Finn (Cork Const & Ireland) [EM]; R A Ackerman (London Welsh & Wales) [EM]; *S T Smith (Wasps) [SW1, SW2, SW3]; *J L B Salmon (Harlequins & New Zealand) [SW1, SW2, SW3]; *R Underwood (Leicester & England) [SW1, SW3]; D I Johnston (Watsonians & Scotland) [SW2]; G R T Baird (Kelso & Scotland) [SW2]; *R Moon (Abertillery) [SW3(R)]; *K Hopkins (South Glam Inst & Swansea) [SW3]

Half-backs *P M Dean (St Mary's College & Ireland) [C]; *G Williams (Bridgend & Wales) [C]; *M Dacey (Swansea & Wales) [N]; M Douglas (Llanelli & Wales) [N, EM]; W G Davies (Cardiff & Wales) [L]; *A Donald (Wanganui & New Zealand) [L]; M A M Quinn (Lansdowne & Ireland) [EM]; *D Camberabero (La Voulte & France) [SW1, SW3]; I George (Northampton) [EM(R), SW1, SW2(R), SW3]; *B Bowen (S W Police & Wales) [SW2]; *R M Harding (Bristol) [SW2]

Forwards R J Doubleday (Bristol) [C]; P J Wheeler (Leicester & England) [C, EM]; I H Eidman (Cardiff & Wales) [C]; R Hesford (Bristol & England) [C, N]; S J Perkins (Pontypool & Wales) [C]; M Rafter (Bristol & England) [C]; D F Pickering (Llanelli & Wales) [C]; D Richards (Leicester) [C]; S T Jones (Pontypool & Wales) [N]; K Townley (Llanelli) [N]; I G Milne (Heriot's FP & Scotland) [N, SW2]; S B Boyle (Gloucester & England) [N]; W Cuthbertson (Harlequins & Scotland) [N, SW2]; *J Jeffrey (Kelso) [N, SW1, SW2]; D H Cooke (Harlequins & England) [N, EM]; I G Stephens (Bridgend & Wales) [L, SW3]; *J-L Dupont (Agen & France) [L]; P J Blakeway (Gloucester & England) [L]; *K Bowring (London Welsh) [L, SM]; M J Colclough (Wasps & England) [L]; S Bainbridge (Gosforth & England) [L]; P J Winterbottom (Headingley & England) [L]; *M F Gargan (Oxford University) [L]; *C White (Gosforth & England) [EM, SW1]; *R H Morgan (Newport & Wales) [EM]; *T Shaw (Newbridge & Wales) [EM, SW1, SW3]; *D Waters (Newport) [EM, SW3]; *P J Hendy (St Ives) [EM]; P D Simpson (Bath & England) [EM]; J Herdman (Swansea) [SW1]; *D C Fitzgerald (Lansdowne) [SW1, SW2(R), SW3]; R M Wilkinson (Bedford & England) [SW1]; *L Connor (Waterloo) [SW1, SW3]; *H T Harbison Bective Rangers & Ireland) [SW1(R), SW2, SW3]; *M Preedy (Gloucester) [SW2]; *J H Fidler (Gloucester & England) [SW2]; J Squire (Pontypool & Wales) [SW2]; *G Rees (Nottingham) [SW2, SW3]; *J Gadd (Gloucester) [SW3]

RESULTS 1983-84

Played 7 Won 4 Drawn 1 Lost 2 For 187 Against 157

1983	
21 Sept	**Beat Cornwall** at Redruth 4G 2T (32) to 1PG 1T (7)
4 Oct	**Drew with Newport** at Newport 2G 2PG (18) to 2G 1PG 1DG (18)
28 Dec	**Lost to Leicester** at Leicester 2G 2PG 2T (26) to 2G 3PG 1DG 2T (30)
1984	
7 March	**Beat East Midlands** at Northampton 2G 1PG 2T (23) to 1G 2PG 1T (16)
20 April	**Beat Penarth** at Penarth 4G 2T (32) to 3G 1PG (21)
21 April	**Lost to Cardiff** at Cardiff 2G 1T (16) to 6G 4T (52)
23 April	**Beat Swansea** at Swansea 4G 4T (40) to 1G 1PG 1T (13)

THE 'VARSITY MATCH 1983

6 December, Twickenham
Oxford University 9 (3PG)
Cambridge University 20 (4PG 2T)

Oxford's limited team held out bravely for an hour in an entertaining match but throughout there was the probability that Cambridge's more extensive all-round talents would win through. So it proved. Two tries in the last quarter finally destroyed the Dark Blues' resistance and Cambridge duly moved to their fourth successive win in the fixture. Oxford have won only twice in the last 12 years.

Cambridge's two outstanding players were the northerners Simms, in the centre, and Ellison at No 8. Ellison inspired his side's pack to ward off the Oxford challenge and eventually come out on top. Simms, when he finally had some possession, ran cleverly and showed he has a sound rugby brain. Making a break after a long run by Bailey and a ruck on the left, Simms found Smith outside him, and the wing put full-back Martin over for a vital score. It was 9-9 before Martin's try, with Barnes for Oxford and Andrew for Cambridge having kicked three penalty goals each.

The match was decided soon afterwards. MacNeill, the Oxford captain, tackled Andrew high as he desperately tried to snuff out a move and Andrew kicked his fourth penalty goal. A late try from Bailey, the Cambridge captain, after a misdirected pass from MacNeill was the icing on the Cambridge cake.

MacNeill's match therefore ended unhappily. He was suffering from a knee ligament injury before the game and although he played with great courage was obviously not fully fit. His team had not enjoyed a successful term's rugby but they fought back courageously. There were flashes of excellence from all their backs, especially from Crowe and O'Brien. The latter became the first player to win a blue at each university – he had played for Cambridge in the 1981 and 1982 matches.

In the Oxford pack Gargan, at No 8, persevered magnificently with Morgan a worthy assistant in the back row. Pearson, the scrum-half, did not have a snappy service but he made up for his limitations with sheer enthusiasm, taking on and tackling the big men of the Cambridge pack. His effort typified the new spirit of the 'Varsity Match – making the most of resources which are a little limited compared to those of the past – and a large crowd appreciated this.

Oxford University: H P MacNeill (Trinity Coll, Dublin & St Edmund Hall) (*capt*); A C Findlay (Marlborough & St Edmund Hall), T S O'Brien (Bradford GS & University), D J Coleman (St Edward's, Liverpool & University), P J Crowe (Sydney & University); S Barnes (Bassaleg & St Edmund Hall), S B Pearson (Uppingham & Trinity); *No 8* M F Gargan (St Peter's, York & St Edmund Hall); *Second Row* R de R Morgan (Christ's Coll, Brecon & Worcester), J R H Rosier (Keble), J B Thomson (Collyers & Keble), A S J McQuaid (Bradford GS & Keble); *Front Row* N J Herrod (King Henry VIII, Coventry & St John's), J P Webster (Bradford GS & Queen's), D J Mills (Maritzburg Coll & St Catherine's)
Scorer *Penalty Goals:* Barnes (3)
Cambridge University: A W Martin (Cardiff HS & St Edmund's House); S T Smith (King Henry VIII, Lichfield & Magdalene), K G Simms (West Park GS & Emmanuel), T Paterson-Brown (Glenalmond & Magdalene), M D Bailey (Ipswich & Corpus Christi) (*capt*); C R Andrew (Barnard Castle and St John's), S N J Roberts (Manchester GS & Christ's); *No 8* J F Ellison (St Peter's, York & Corpus Christi); *Second Row* A G R Harper (Sydney U & Downing), P W David (RGS Guildford & Trinity Hall), C F Ewbank (Felsted & St John's), I R Morrison (Glenalmond & Pembroke); *Front Row* J D Bush (Batley GS & Pembroke), F J Timmons (Wimbledon Coll & Magdalene), R C Bailey (Lancaster RGS & Fitzwilliam)
Scorers *Tries:* Bailey, Martin *Penalty Goals:* Andrew (4)
Referee J A F Trigg (London)

Mark Bailey, the Cambridge captain, hoists the Bowring Bowl skywards. Bailey leads Cambridge again in 1984.

'VARSITY MATCH RESULTS

102 Matches played Oxford 43 wins Cambridge 46 wins 13 Draws

Match played at Oxford 1871-72; Cambridge 1872-73; The Oval 1873-74 to 1879-80; Blackheath 1880-81 to 1886-87; Queen's Club 1887-88 to 1920-21; then Twickenham.

Season		
1871-72	**Oxford**	1G 1T to 0
1872-73	**Cambridge**	1G 2T to 0
1873-74	Drawn	1T each
1874-75*	Drawn	Oxford 2T to 0
1875-76	**Oxford**	1T to 0
1876-77	**Cambridge**	1G 2T to 0
1877-78	**Oxford**	2T to 0
1878-79	Drawn	No score
1879-80	**Cambridge**	1G 1DG to 1DG
1880-81	Drawn	1T each
1881-82	**Oxford**	2G 1T to 1G
1882-83	**Oxford**	1T to 0
1883-84	**Oxford**	3G 4T to 1G
1884-85	**Oxford**	3G 1T to 1T
1885-86	**Cambridge**	2T to 0
1886-87	**Cambridge**	3T to 0
1887-88	**Cambridge**	1DG 2T to 0
1888-89	**Cambridge**	1G 2T to 0
1889-1890	**Oxford**	1G 1T to 0
1890-91	Drawn	1G each
1891-92	**Cambridge**	2T to 0
1892-93	Drawn	No score
1893-94	**Oxford**	1T to 0
1894-95	Drawn	1G each
1895-96	**Cambridge**	1G to 0
1896-97	**Oxford**	1G 1DG to 1G 1T
1897-98	**Oxford**	2T to 0
1898-99	**Cambridge**	1G 2T to 0
1899-1900	**Cambridge**	2G 4T to 0
1900-01	**Oxford**	2G to 1G 1T
1901-02	**Oxford**	1G 1T to 0
1902-03	Drawn	1G 1T each
1903-04	**Oxford**	3G 1T to 2G 1T
1904-05	**Cambridge**	3G to 2G
1905-06	**Cambridge**	3G (15) to 2G 1T (13)
1906-07	**Oxford**	4T (12) to 1G 1T (8)
1907-08	**Oxford**	1G 4T (17) to 0
1908-09	Drawn	1G (5) each
1909-10	**Oxford**	4G 5T (35) to 1T (3)
1910-11	**Oxford**	4G 1T (23) to 3G 1T (18)
1911-12	**Oxford**	2G 3T (19) to 0
1912-13	**Cambridge**	2G (10) to 1T (3)
1913-14	**Cambridge**	1DG 3T (13) to 1T (3)
1914-18	*No matches*	
1919-20	**Cambridge**	1DG 1PG (7) to 1G (5)
1920-21	**Oxford**	1G 4T (17) to 1G 3T (14)
1921-22	**Oxford**	1G 2T (11) to 1G (5)
1922-23	**Cambridge**	3G 2T (21) to 1G 1T (8)
1923-24	**Oxford**	3G 2T (21) to 1G 1PG 2T (14)
1924-25	**Oxford**	1G 2T (11) to 2T (6)
1925-26	**Cambridge**	3G 6T (33) to 1T (3)
1926-27	**Cambridge**	3G 5T (30) to 1G (5)
1927-28	**Cambridge**	2G 2PG 2T (22) to 1G 3T (14)
1928-29	**Cambridge**	1G 3T (14) to 1DG 1PG 1T (10)
1929-30	**Oxford**	1G 1DG (9) to 0
1930-31	Drawn	Oxford 1PG (3) Cambridge 1T (3)
1931-32	**Oxford**	1DG 2T (10) to 1T (3)
1932-33	**Oxford**	1G 1T (8) to 1T (3)
1933-34	**Oxford**	1G (5) to 1T (3)
1934-35	**Cambridge**	2G 1DG 1PG 4T (29) to 1DG (4)
1935-36	Drawn	No score
1936-37	**Cambridge**	2T (6) to 1G (5)
1937-38	**Oxford**	1G 4T (17) to 1DG (4)
1938-39	**Cambridge**	1G 1PG (8) to 2PG (6)
1939-45	*War-time series*	
1945-46	**Cambridge**	1G 2T (11) to 1G 1PG (8)
1946-47	**Oxford**	1G 1DG 2T (15) to 1G (5)
1947-48	**Cambridge**	2PG (6) to 0
1948-49	**Oxford**	1G 1DG 2T (14) to 1G 1PG (8)
1949-50	**Oxford**	1T (3) to 0
1950-51	**Oxford**	1G 1PG (8) to 0
1951-52	**Oxford**	2G 1T (13) to 0
1952-53	**Cambridge**	1PG 1T (6) to 1G (5)
1953-54	Drawn	Oxford 1PG 1T (6) Cambridge 2PG (6)
1954-55	**Cambridge**	1PG (3) to 0
1955-56	**Oxford**	1PG 2T (9) to 1G (5)
1956-57	**Cambridge**	1G 1DG 1PG 1T (14) to 2PG 1T (9)
1957-58	**Oxford**	1T (3) to 0
1958-59	**Cambridge**	1G 1PG 3T (17) to 1PG 1T (6)
1959-60	**Oxford**	3PG (9) to 1PG (3)
1960-61	**Cambridge**	2G 1T (13) to 0
1961-62	**Cambridge**	1DG 2T (9) to 1DG (3)
1962-63	**Cambridge**	1G 1DG 1PG 1T (14) to 0
1963-64	**Cambridge**	2G 1PG 2T (19) to 1G 1DG 1PG (11)
1964-65	**Oxford**	2G 1PG 2T (19) to 1PG 1GM (6)
1965-66	Drawn	1G each
1966-67	**Oxford**	1G 1T (8) to 1DG 1T (6)
1967-68	**Cambridge**	1T 1PG (6) to 0
1968-69	**Cambridge**	1T 1PG 1DG (9) to 2T (6)
1969-70	**Oxford**	3PG (9) to 2PG (6)
1970-71	**Oxford**	1G 1DG 2T (14) to 1PG (3)
1971-72	**Oxford**	3PG 3T (21) to 1PG (3)
1972-73	**Cambridge**	1G 1PG 1DG 1T (16) to 2PG (6)
1973-74	**Cambridge**	1DG 1PG 2T (14) to 1G 2PG (12)
1974-75	**Cambridge**	1G 2PG 1T (16) to 5PG (15)
1975-76	**Cambridge**	2G 5PG 1DG 1T (34) to 3PG 1DG (12)
1976-77	**Cambridge**	1G 3PG (15) to 0
1977-78	**Oxford**	4PG 1T (16) to 2PG 1T (10)
1978-79	**Cambridge**	2G 3PG 1T (25) to 1PG 1T (7)
1979-80	**Oxford**	2PG 1DG (9) to 1PG (3)
1980-81	**Cambridge**	3PG 1T (13) to 3PG (9)
1981-82	**Cambridge**	3PG (9) to 2PG (6)
1982-83	**Cambridge**	3PG 1DG 2T (20) to 1G 1PG 1T (13)
1983-84	**Cambridge**	4PG 2T (20) to 3PG (9)

**At this date no match could be won unless a goal was scored.*

THE WAR-TIME MATCHES

Season		
1939-40	**Oxford**	1G 1DG 2T (15) to 1T (3) (at Cambridge)
1940-41	**Cambridge**	1G 2T (11) to 1G 1DG (9) (at Oxford)
	Cambridge	2G 1T (13) to 0 (at Cambridge)
1941-42	**Cambridge**	1PG 2T (9) to 1PG 1T (6) (at Cambridge)
	Cambridge	1G 2PG 2T (17) to 1G 1T (8) (at Oxford)
1942-43	**Cambridge**	1G 1DG (9) to 0 (at Oxford)
	Cambridge	1G 3T (14) to 2G 1T (13) (at Oxford)
	Cambridge	2G 2T (16) to 1T (3) (at Cambridge)
1943-44	**Cambridge**	2G 1T (13) to 1DG (4) (at Cambridge)
	Oxford	2T (6) to 1G (5) (at Oxford)
1944-45	Drawn	1T (3) each (at Oxford)
	Cambridge	2G 2T (16) to 1DG (4) (at Cambridge)

OXFORD and CAMBRIDGE BLUES 1872-1983

(Each year indicates a separate appearance)

OXFORD

Abbott, J S	1954-55
Abell, G E B	1923-24-25-26
Adamson, J A	1928-29-31
Adcock, J R L	1961
Aitken, G G	1922-24
Aldridge, J E	1888
Alexander, H	1897-98
Alexander, P C	1930
Allaway, R C P	1953-54-55
Allen, C P	1881-82-83
Allen, T	1909
Allen, W C	1910
Allison, M G	1955
Almond, R G P	1937
Ashby, C J	1973
Asher, A G G	1881-82-83-84
Asquith, P R	1974
Atkinson, C C	1876
Back, A	1878
Badenoch, D F	1971
Baden-Powell, F S	1873
Baggaley, J C	1953-54
Bain, D McL	1910-11-12-13
Bainbrigge, J H	1874-76-77
Baird, J S	1966-67
Baiss, R S H	1894-95
Baker, C D	1891-93
Baker, D G S	1951-52
Baker, E M	1893-94-95-96
Baker, P	1980 (R)
Baker, R T	1968
Balfour, E R	1893-94-95
Bannerman, J MacD	1927-28
Barker, A C	1966-67
Barnes, S	1981-82-83
Barr, D C A	1980
Barry, C E	1897-98-99
Barry, D M	1968-69-70
Barwick, W M	1880-81
Bass, R G	1961
Batchelor, T B	1906
Bateson, H D	1874-75-77
Baxter, T J	1958-59
Beamish, S H	1971
Beare, A	1982
Bedford, T P	1965-66-67
Behn, A R	1968-69
Bell, D L	1970
Benson, E T	1928
Bentley, P J	1960
Berkeley, W V	1924-25-26
Berry, C W	1883-84
Bettington, R H B	1920-22
Bevan, J H	1946
Bibby, A J	1980-81
Binham, P A	1971
Birrell, H B	1953
Black, B H	1929
Blair, A S	1884
Blencowe, L C	1907-08
Bloxham, C T	1934-35-36-37
Blyth, P H	1885-86
Bolton, W H	1873-74-75
Bonham-Carter, E	1890-91
Boobbyer, B	1949-50-51
Booker, J L	1880
Booth, J L	1956
Bos, F H ten	1958-59-60
Boswell, J D	1885-86-87
Botfield, A S G	1871
Botting, I J	1949-50
Bourdillon, H	1873-74-75
Bourns, C	1903
Bowers, J B	1932-34
Boyce, A W	1952-53
Boyd, A de H	1924
Boyd, E F	1912
Boyle, D S	1967-68-69
Brace, D O	1955-56
Bradby, G F	1882-85
Bradford, C C	1887
Branfoot, E P	1878-79
Bray, C N	1979
Bremridge, H	1876-77
Brett, J A	1935-36-37
Brett, P V	1978
Brewer, R J	1965
Brewer, T J	1951
Bridge, D J W	1946-47-48
Brierley, H	1871
Britton, R B	1963-64
Bromet, W E	1889
Brooks, A W	1980-81-82
Brooks, M J	1873
Brooks, W	1872
Broster, L R	1912
Broughton, R C	1965
Brown, L G	1910-11-12
Brunskill, R F	1873-74
Bryan, T A	1975-76-77
Bryer, L W	1953
Buchanan, F G	1909-10
Bucknall, A L	1965-66
Budge, K J	1977-78-79
Budworth, R T D	1887-88-89
Bullard, G L	1950-51
Bullock, H	1910-11
Bulpett, C W L	1871
Burnet, P J	1960
Burrow, K C	1933
Burse, R M	1974
Bush, A	1934
Bussell, J G	1903-04
Butcher, W M	1954
Butler, F E R	1959-60
Button, E L	1936
Byers, R M	1926
Caccia, H A	1926
Cadell, P R	1890
Cairns, A G	1899-1900-01
Campbell, E	1919-20-21
Cannell, L B	1948-49-50
Cardale, C F	1929-30
Carey, G M	1891-92-94
Carey, W J	1894-95-96-97
Carlyon, H B	1871
Carroll, B M	1970-71
Carroll, P R	1968-69-70
Carter, C R	1885
Cartwright, V H	1901-02-03-04
Cass, T	1961
Castens, H H	1886-87
Cattell, R H B	1893
Cave, H W	1881
Cawkwell, G L	1946-47
Chadwick, A J	1898-99
Chambers, J C	1921
Champain, F H B	1897-98-99
Champneys, F W	1874-75-76
Charles, A E S	1932
Cheesman, W I	1910-11
Cheyne, H	1903-04
Cholmondeley, F G	1871-73
Christopherson, P	1886-87-88
Clark, R B	1978-79
Clarke, E J D	1973
Clarke, I A	1913
Clauss, P R	1889-90-91
Clements, B S	1975
Cleveland, C R	1885-86
Cochran, P C	1889-91
Cohen B A	1884
Coker, J B H	1965
Cole, B W	1945
Coleman, D J	1982-83
Coles, D G G	1937-38
Coles, P	1884-85-86
Coles, S C	1954-56-57
Collingwood, J A	1961-62
Colville, A H	1892-93
Conway-Rees, J	1891-92-93
Cooke, J L	1968-69
Cooke, P	1936-37
Cooke, W R	1976
Cookson, G H F	1891-92
Cooper, A H	1951
Cooper, M McG	1934-35-36
Cooper, R A	1937
Cooper, R M	1946
Cornish, W H	1876
Couper, T	1899-1900
Court, E D	1882-83
Cousins, F C	1885-86
Coutts, I D F	1951
Coventry, R G T	1889-90-91
Cowen, T J	1938
Cowlishaw, F I	1890-91
Cox, G V	1878
Cozens-Hardy, B	1904-05-06
Crabbie, J E	1898-99-1900-01
Craig, F J R	1963-64-65
Cranmer, P	1933-34
Crawfurd, J W F A	1900
Creese, N A H	1951
Cridlan, A G	1928-29-30
Croker, J R	1966-67
Crole, G B	1913-19
Cronje, S N	1907-08
Crosse, C W	1874
Crowe, P J	1981-82-83
Crump, L M	1896
Cuff, T W	1945
Cunningham, G	1907-08-09
Currie, J D	1954-55-56-57
Curry, J A H	1961
Curtis, A B	1949
Dalby, C	1923
Davey, P	1967
Davey, R A E	1972
David, A M	1921-22
Davies, D B	1905-06-07
Davies, D E	1951
Davies, D M	1958-59-60
Davies, J A B	1920
Davies, L L J	1927
Davies, R	1969
Davies, R H	1955-56-57
Davies S J T	1972-73
Davies, W G	1977
Davis, R A	1974-75
Davis, T M E	1978-79-80
Dawkins, P M	1959-60-61
Deacon, E A	1871-72
De Winton, R F C	1888-89-90
Dew, C J	1978
Diamond, A J	1957
Dickson, M R	1903
Dickson, W M	1912
Diggle, P R	1908-09
Dingle, A J	1911
Disney, P C W	1935
Dixon, P J	1967-68-69-70

Dobson, D D	1899-1900-01
Donald, D G	1911-12-13
Donaldson, C L	1895
Donaldson, D W	1893
Donaldson, W P	1892-93-94
Donnelly, M P	1946
Donovan, T J	1971
Douglas, A I	1970-71
Dorman, J M A	1964
Dowson, A O	1896
Druitt, W A H	1929-30-31
Dryburgh, D J W	1926
Drysdale, D	1925
Dunbar, I T	1970-71-73
Duncan, D D	1919-20
Dunn, L B	1897
Eberle, G S J F	1901-02
Edgell, E M R	1871-73
Edmiston, J H F	1926-27
Edmonds, J N	1978
Ellis, A W	1975
Elwes, A C	1892-93
Emms, D A	1949-50
Enevoldson, T P	1976-77-78-79-80
Evans, A H	1877-78
Evans, C H	1919-20
Evans, D P	1959
Evans, D W	1887-88
Evanson, A M	1880-81
Evers, C P	1897-98
Evers, R W	1909
Ewart, C B	1982
Ewing, M H O	1886
Faktor, S J	1977
Fallon, T J	1953-55
Farquharson, J C L	1903
Fearenside, E	1903
Fellows-Smith, J P	1953-54
Fergusson, E A J	1952-53
Field, H	1873
Filby, L L	1960
Fildes, D G	1922-25
Finch, C J	1978
Findlay, A C	1983
Fisher, C D C	1902
Fisher, S J	1976
Fleming, C J N	1887-88-89-90
Flemmer, W K	1906
Fletcher, K R	1871
Fletcher, W R B	1871-73-74
Forman, J	1875-76
Forsayth, H H	1920-21
Forster, F M McL	1937
Fowler, H	1877-78
Francis, C K	1871
Francis, D G	1919
Franklin, H W F	1923
Fraser, E C	1872-73-74-75
Freakes, H D	1936-37-38
Gabitass, J R	1965-66
Gaisford, R B	1876
Galbraith, J H	1947
Game, W H	1872-73-74
Gardner, C J	1905-06
Gardner, J W	1871
Gargan, M F	1980-82-83
Gedge, H T S	1893
Geen, W P	1910-11-12
Gent, G N	1949
German, G J	1922
Gibson, A G	1894-95
Gibson, C H	1927
Gill, R D	1947-48
Gilmour, A	1911
Gilray, C M	1908-09
Gilthorpe, C G	1946-47
Glover, J	1959-60
Glover, T R	1973-74
Glubb, J M	1887
Gooding, W F	1872-73
Goold, A N	1927
Gordon, P F C	1970
Gotley, A L H	1909
Gould, E J H	1963-64-65-66
Grant, A D	1922
Grant, A H	1892
Green, R	1948-49-50
Gregson, R E S	1903
Grellet, R C	1899-1900-01-02
Grenfell, W T	1888
Grieve, C F	1934-35-36
Griffith, C J L	1950-51-52
Griffiths, D A	1969-70
Griffiths, R L	1969
Grischotti, W	1899
Gubb, T W	1926-27-28-29
Guy, J C	1934
Gush, E P	1963
Habergham, W D R	1980-82
Hadman, W G	1964-65-66
Hall, J D	1885-86
Halliday, S J	1979-80-81
Hamilton, C W	1872
Hammond, C E L	1899-1900
Hands, K C M	1912
Hands, P A M	1910
Hands, R H M	1908-09
Harcourt, A B	1945-46
Harding, R F	1935
Harper, C H	1897-98
Harrison, C F	1873-74-75
Hartley, J C	1894-95-96
Harvey, R C M	1886
Havard, W T	1919
Hawkesworth, C J	1970-71-72
Heal, M G	1971
Hearn, R D	1964
Heath, A H	1875-77-78-79
Hefer, W J	1949-50
Henderson, J H	1952
Henderson, N F	1886
Henley, W E	1929-30-31
Heppenstall, A F	1926-27
Herring, D G	1909
Herrod, N J	1981-82-83
Higham, J R S	1959
Hillard, R J	1923-24
Hiller, R	1965
Hines, G W	1961-62
Hirst, E T	1877-78-79
Hoadley, A A	1905-06
Hoare, A H M	1956-57
Hobart, A H	1981
Hockley, M	1975
Hodges, H A	1905-06-07-08
Hodgson, F W	1881
Hofmeyr, K de J	1927
Hofmeyr, M B	1948-49-50
Hofmeyr, S J	1928-29-30
Hofmeyr, S M	1979
Hollis, G	1938
Holroyd, C A	1966
Honey, R	1909-10
Hood, R K	1976
Hoolahan, R M C	1976-77-78
Hopkins, K M	1977
Hordern, P C	1928
Horne, E C	1975-76-77
Hoskin, W W	1904-05-06-07
Houston, K J	1964
Hovde, F L	1931
Howard, A	1907
Howard, P D	1929-30
Howe-Browne, N R F G	1905-06
Hoyer-Millar, G C	1952
Hughes, H M	1935-36
Hughes, R A	1978
Hugo-Hamman, C T	1981-82
Hume, J W G	1927-28
Humfrey, L C	1892-93
Humphrey, M W	1923
Hunt, R W	1890
Hunter, R S	1888-89
Hutchinson, J M	1972-73
Hutchison, R O	1902
Ilett, N L	1947
Inglis, R E	1883-84
Irwin, H	1880
Isherwood, F W	1871
Jackson, K L T	1932-33
Jackson, W M	1938
Jacob, G O	1878-79
Jacob, H P	1923-24-25
Jacot, B L	1920
James, A I	1934
James, J	1875-76-77
James, S	1970-71
James, S J B	1966
Jenkin, J M	1952
Jenkins, A	1971
Jenkins, O	1913-19
Jenkins, P	1980
Jenkins, V G J	1930-31-32
Jesson, D	1957-58-59
Johnson, P M	1968-70
Johnson, T F	1875
Johnstone, P G	1952-53-54
Jones, D R R	1972
Jones, D K	1963
Jones, G S A	1896
Jones, I C	1962-63-64
Jones, K W J	1931-32
Jones, R O P	1969-70-71
Jones, T O	1898
Jones, T W	1978-79
Jones, V W	1954
Jupp, H B	1873
Kay, A R	1889-90-91
Kay, D C	1972-73
Kelly, H M	1932
Kendall-Carpenter, J MacG K	1948-49-50
Kennedy, N	1901
Kennedy, W D	1904
Kent, C P	1972-73-74-75
Kent, P C	1970
Kershaw, F	1898-99-1900-01
Key, K J	1885-86
Kindersley, R S	1882-83
King, B B H	1963
King, P E	1975
King, T W	1929
Kininmonth, P W	1947-48
Kitson, J A	1895
Kittermaster, H J	1922-24
Kitto, R C M	1884-85-86-87
Knight, R L	1879
Knott, F H	1910-11-12-13
Koe, A P	1886
Kyrke, G V	1902-03
Kyrke-Smith, P St L	1973-74-75 (R)
Lagden, R O	1909-10-11
Laidlaw, C R	1968-69
Lamb, R H	1962-63-64
Lamport, N K	1930-31-32
Landale, D F	1925-26
Lane, R O B	1887-88-89
Langley, P J	1949
Latham, H E	1907
Latter, A	1892
Law, A F	1875
Lawrence, W S	1954-56
Lawrie, A A	1903-05
Lawton, T	1921-22-23
Lee, F H	1874-75-76-77
Lee, J W	1973-74
Lee, R J	1972
Legge, D	1897
Lennox-Cook, J M	1945
Leslie, C F H	1880-81

Leslie, R E	1954
Leslie-Jones, F A	1894-95-96
Lewin, A J A	1962-63
Lewis, A K	1888
Lewis, D J	1950
Lewis, S M	1973
Light, B	1977
Lindsay, G C	1882-83-84-85
Littlechild, E J F	1972
Littlewood, R B	1893
Lloyd, E A	1964-65-66
Lloyd, J E	1872-74
Lloyd, R	1908
Lombard, L T	1956-57-58
Longdon, J S	1889
Lorraine, H D B	1932-33-34
Loudoun-Shand, E G	1913-19
Love, R D	1972
Low, R C S	1933
Luce, F M	1899-1900
Luddington, R S	1980-81-82
Lusty, W	1927
Luyt, R E	1938
Lyle, A M P	1902-04-05
McCanlis, M A	1926-27
McClure, R N	1973
Macdonald, D A	1975-76
Macdonald, D S M	1974-75-76
Macdonald, G E	1922
Macdonald, N L	1926
MacEwen, G L	1895
McFarland, P R E	1967
MacGibbon, R R	1930-31
McGlashan, J R C	1945
McGrath, N F	1934-35-36
MacGregor, A	1871
Mackenzie, A O M	1880-81
Mackenzie, D W	1974
Mackenzie, F J C	1882-83
Mackintosh, C E W C	1925
MacLachlan, L P	1953
Maclachlan, N	1879-80
Macmillan, M	1876
McNeill, A	1884
MacNeill, H P	1982-83
McPartlin, J L	1960-61-62
Macpherson, G P S	1922-23-24
Macpherson, N M S	1928
McQuaid, A S J	1983
McShane, J M S	1933-35
Maddock, W P	1972
Mallalieu, J P W	1927
Mallett, N V H	1979
Marshall, H P	1921
Marshall, R M	1936-37-38
Martin, H	1907-08-09
Mather, E G S	1933
Maxwell-Hyslop, J E	1920-21-22
Mayhew, P K	1937
Mead, B D	1972-73
Meadows, H J	1948
Merivale, G M	1874
Merriam, L P B	1913
Michell, A T	1871-72-73-74
Millerchip, C J	1981-82
Mills, D J	1983
Milton, N W	1905-06-07
Minns, P C	1930-31-32
Mitchell, M D	1977
Moberly, W O	1871-72-73
Moir, M J P	1977
Molohan, M J B	1928
Monteath, J G	1912
Montgomery, J R	1958
Moorcroft, E K	1966
Moore, E J	1882-83
Moore, H B	1912-13
Moore, H R	1956
Moore, P B C	1945-46
Moresby-White, J M	1913-19
Morgan, A K	1963-64
Morgan, D J	1979

Morgan, F	1888
Morgan, R de R	1983
Morris, E G	1904
Morrison, W E A	1979-80
Mortimer, L	1892
Moubray, J J	1876-77-78
Muller, H	1938
Mullins, R C	1894
Mulvey, R S	1968
Munro, P	1903-04-05
Murray, G C	1959
Nash, E H	1874-75
Nelson, T A	1897-98
Nesbitt, J V	1904-05
Neser, V H	1919-20
Neville, T B	1971-72
Newman, A P	1973
Newman, S C	1946-47
Newton, H F	1895-96-97
Newton, P A	1879-80
Newton-Thompson, J O	1945-46
Nicholas, P L	1897-98-99
Nicholson, E S	1931-32-33-34
North, E G H	1888-89-90
Novis, A L	1927
Nunn, J A	1925-26
Obolensky, A	1935-37
O'Brien, T S	1983
O'Connor, A	1958
Odgers, W B	1901-02
Orpen, L J J	1898
Osborn, E C	1969
Osborne, S H	1900-01-02
Osler, S G	1931
Owen-Smith, H G O	1932-33
Page, H V	1884-85
Painter, P A	1967
Palmer, M S	1960
Parker, L	1905
Parker, T	1888
Parkin, W H	1890
Paterson, A M	1889-90
Patterson, A R	1879-80-81
Patterson, L R	1886-87
Payne, C M	1960
Peacock, M B	1880
Peacock, M F	1932-33
Peake, H W	1871
Pearce, J K	1945
Pearson, S	1983
Pearson, T S	1871
Peat, W H	1898
Peck, A Q	1981
Pennington, H H	1937-38
Percival, L J	1889-91
Percy, H R G	1936-38
Pether, S	1938
Phillips, C	1876-77-78-79
Phillips, E L	1933
Phillips, M S	1956-57-58-59
Phillips, P C	1938
Phillips, R H	1966-67-68
Pienaar, J H	1933-34-35
Pitman, I J	1921
Plant, W I	1958
Pleydell-Bouverie, Hon B	1923
Plumbridge, R A	1954-55-56
Podmore, G	1872
Pollard, D	1952
Poole, F O	1891-92-93-94
Poulton, R W	1909-10-11
Prescott, A E C	1928
Prescott, R E	1932
Preston, B W	1925
Price, H L	1920-21
Price, V R	1919-20-21
Prodger, J A	1955
Quinnen, P N	1974-75
Quist-Arcton, E A K	1978-79

Rahmatallah, F J	1976
Ramsay, A W	1952-53
Ramsden, J E	1945
Raphael, J E	1901-02-03-04
Rashleigh, W	1887-88
Ravenscroft, J	1877-78
Raymond, R L	1924
Rayner-Wood, A C	1895-96
Read, R F	1965
Reeler, I L	1955-56
Rees, H	1930
Rees, H J V	1913
Rees, P S	1974-75-78
Rees-Jones, G R	1933-34-35
Reid, C J	1896
Reid, G A	1935-36
Reid, N	1912-13
Renwick, W N	1936-37
Rice-Evans, W	1890
Richards, C A L	1932
Richards, S B	1962
Richardson, J V	1925
Richardson, W R	1881
Rigby, J P	1955-56
Rimmer, L I	1958
Rittson-Thomas, G C	1949-50
Robbins, P G D	1954-55-56-57
Roberts, G D	1907-08
Roberts, M G	1968
Roberts, N T	1979-80-81
Roberts, W	1928-29-30-31
Robertson, A M	1903
Robertson, J W	1921
Robertson, M A	1894-96
Robinson, D A B	1952-53
Robinson, R G	1976-77
Robson, M	1929
Rogers, W L Y	1898-1900
Roos, G D	1936
Rosier, J R H	1983
Ross, W S	1980
Rotherham, A	1882-83-84
Roughead, W N	1924-25-26
Rousseau, W P	1929
Row, A W L	1921
Rowley, J V D'A	1929
Rucker, R W	1874-76
Rudd, E L	1963-64
Russell, H	1872-73-74-75
Russell, J H	1929
Russell-Roberts, F D	1931
Sachs, D M	1962
Sampson, D H	1945
Sampson, H F	1910-11
Sanctuary, C F S	1879-80
Sandford, J R P	1902-03
Saunders, C J	1951
Sawtell, P R	1972
Sayer, J	1871
Sayer, J B	1887
Scholefield, B G	1920-21
Scott, J S M	1957-58
Searle, J P	1981-82
Seccombe, L S	1925
Selby, E	1891
Sexton, C M	1976
Seymour, T M	1971-73
Shacksnovis, A	1922-23
Sharp, H S	1910-11
Sharp, R A W	1959-60-61
Sharp, R G	1919
Shaw, C	1974-75
Shearman, M	1878-79
Sheffield, R W	1873-74
Sheil, A G R	1958
Shillito, G V	1930
Sidgwick, A	1872
Siepmann, C A	1921
Silk, N	1961-62-63
Sim, A C	1876
Simmie, M S	1965-66
Simpson, E P	1887

Simpson, H B 1920
Skipper, D J 1952
Slater, N T 1960
Sloan, T 1908
Sloane, A D 1902
Small, H D 1949-50
Smith, A R 1894-95-96-97
Smith, I S 1923
Smith, J A 1892-93
Smith, M J K 1954-55
Southee, E A 1913
Speed, R R 1967-68-69
Spence, K M 1951-52
Spencer, B L 1960
Spragg, F F 1926
Springman, P 1877-78
Squire, W H S 1882-83-84
Stagg, P K 1961-62
Stafford, P M W 1961-62
Starmer-Smith, N C 1965-66
Steel, J J 1953
Steinthal, F E 1906
Stevens, D T 1959
Stewart, A 1947-48
Stewart, W B 1892
Steyn, S S L 1911-12
Still, E R 1871-73
Stobie, A M 1945
Stobie, W D K 1947
Stone, T 1897
Stoneman, B M 1962
Stoop, A D 1902-03-04
Strand-Jones, J 1899-1900-01
Stratton, J W 1897
Strong, E L 1881-83
Strong, W I N 1924-25
Stuart-Watson, J L 1935
Summerskill, W H J 1945
Surtees, E A 1885
Sutherland, I W 1938
Sutherland, J G B 1885
Sutton, M A 1945-46
Swan, M W 1957
Swanston, J F A 1897-98-99-1900
Swanzy, A J 1901-02
Swarbrick, D W 1946-47-48
Swayne, D H 1930-31
Sweatman, E A 1927

Taberer, H M 1892
Tahany, M P 1945
Tanner, T L 1931
Tarr, F N 1907-08-09
Tatham, W M 1881-82-83
Taylor, E G 1926-27-28
Taylor, J A 1974
Terry, H F 1900-01
Theron, T P 1923
Thomas, A C 1979
Thomas, T R 1938
Thomas, W E 1911-12
Thomas, W L 1893-94
Thomson, B E 1951-52
Thomson, C 1896
Thomson, F W 1912-13
Thomson, J B 1983
Thomson, W J 1895-96
Thorburn, C W 1964
Thorniley-Walker, M J 1967
Tongue, P K 1975
Torry, P J 1968-69
Travers, B H 1946-47
Tristram, H B 1882-83-84
Troup, D S 1928
Tudor, H A 1878-79-80-81
Turcan, H H 1928
Turner, A B 1884
Turner, F H 1908-09-10

Unwin, G T 1894-95-96

Valentine, A C 1923-24-25
Van Der Riet, E F 1920-21
Van Ryneveld, A J 1946-47-48
Van Ryneveld, C B 1947-48-49
Vassall, H 1879-80-81-82
Vassall, H H 1906-07-08
Vecqueray, A H 1877-78
Vecqueray, G C 1873
Vidal, R W S 1872
Vincent, A N 1948-49

Wade, C G 1882-83-84
Waide, S L 1932
Wake, H B L 1922
Wakefield, W H 1891-92
Wakelin, W S 1964
Waldock, F A 1919
Waldock, H F 1919-20
Waldron, O C 1965-67
Walford, M M 1935-36-37
Walker, A 1880
Walker, J C 1955
Walker, J G 1879-80-81
Walker, M 1950-51
Wall, T W 1875-76-77
Wallace, A C 1922-23-24-25
Walton, E J 1900-01
Ward, J M 1972
Ware, M A 1961-62
Warr, A L 1933-34
Waterman, J S 1974
Wates, C S 1961
Watkins, L 1879
Watkinson, A F 1977-78
Watson, P W 1954-55
Watt, K A 1976
Watts, I H 1937-38
Watts, L D 1957-58
Webster, J G M 1980-81
Webster, J P 1982-83
Wesche, V V G 1924
Weston, B A G 1957
Weston, J W 1871
White, G L 1976-77
White, N T 1905-06
Whyte, A G D 1963
Whyte, D J 1963
Wilcock, R M 1962
Wilcock, S H 1957-58-59
Willcox, J G 1959-60-61-62
Wilkinson, J V S 1904
Wilkinson, W E 1891
Williams, C D 1945
Williams, J R 1969
Williamson, A C 1913
Williamson, R H 1906-07-08
Willis, D C 1975-76-77
Wilson, C T M 1948
Wilson, D B 1874
Wilson, G A 1946-48
Wilson, J 1967-68
Wilson, J H G 1888-89-90
Wilson, N G C 1967
Wilson, R W 1956
Wilson, S 1963-64
Wilson, S E 1890
Wilson, W G 1887
Wimperis, E J 1951
Winn, C E 1950
Winn, R R 1953
Witney, N K-J 1970-71
Wix, R S 1904-05-06-07
Wood, A E 1904
Wood, D E 1952-53
Wood, G F 1919
Woodhead, P G 1974
Woodrow, D K 1978-79-80
Wooldridge, C S 1882
Wordsworth, C R 1922-23-24
Wordsworth, C W 1902
Wordsworth, J R 1885
Wray, M O 1933-34
Wyatt, D M 1981
Wydell, H A 1951
Wynter, E C C 1947

Young, J R C 1957-58

CAMBRIDGE

Aarvold, C D 1925-26-27-28
Ackford, P J 1979
Adams, G C A 1929
Adams, H F S 1884-85
Agnew, C M 1875-76
Agnew, G W 1871-72-73
Agnew, W L 1876-77-78
Albright, G S 1877
Alderson, F H R 1887-88
Alexander, E P 1884-85-86
Alexander, J W 1905-06
Allan, C J 1962
Allan, J L F 1956
Allen, A D 1925-26-27
Allen, D B 1975
Allen, J 1875-76
Allchurch, T J 1980-81
Anderson, W T 1931-32
Andrew, C R 1982-83
Anthony, A J 1967
Archer, G M D 1950-51
Arthur, T G 1962
Ashcroft, A H 1908-09
Ashford, C L 1929
Askew, J G 1929-30-31
Asquith, J P K 1953
Aston, R L 1889-90
Atkinson, M L 1908-09
Attfield, S J W 1982

Back, F F 1871-72
Bailey, G H 1931
Bailey, M D 1982-83
Bailey, R C 1982-83
Balding, I A 1961
Balfour, A 1896-97
Bance, J F 1945
Barker, R E 1966
Barlow, C S 1923-24-25-26
Barlow, R M M 1925
Barrow, C 1950
Barter, A F 1954-55-56
Bartlett, R M 1951
Bateman-Champain, P J C 1937
Batten, J M 1871-72-73-74
Batty, P A 1919-20
Baxter, R 1871-72-73
Baxter, W H B 1912-13
Bealey, R J 1874
Bearne, K R F 1957-58-59
Beazley, T A G 1971
Bedell-Sivright, D R 1899-1900-01-02
Bedell-Sivright, J V 1900-01-02-03
Beer, I D S 1952-53-54
Bell, R W 1897-98-99
Bell, S P 1894-95-96
Bennett, G M 1897-98
Bennett, N J 1981

Benthall, E C	1912
Beringer, F R	1951-52
Beringer, G G	1975-76
Berman, J V	1966
Berry, S P	1971
Bevan, G A J	1951
Bevan, J A	1877-80
Bevan, W	1887
Biddell, C W	1980-81
Biggar, M A	1971
Bird, D R J	1958-59
Birdwood, C R B	1932
Bishop, C C	1925
Black, M A	1897-98
Blair, P C B	1910-11-12-13
Blake, W H	1875
Boggon, R P	1956
Bole, E	1945-46-47
Bonham-Carter, J	1873
Bordass, J H	1923-24
Boughton-Leigh, C E W	1878
Boulding, P V	1975-76
Bowcott, H M	1927-28
Bowcott, J E	1933
Bowen, R W	1968
Bowhill, J W	1888-89
Bowman, J H	1933-34
Boyd, C W	1909
Boyd-Moss, R J	1980-81-82
Brandram, R A	1896
Brash, J C	1959-60-61
Brathwaite, G A	1934
Breakey, J N F	1974-75(R)-77
Bree-Frink, F C	1888-89-90
Briggs, P D	1962
Bromet, E	1887-88
Brook, P W P	1928-29-30-31
Brookstein, R	1969
Brooman, R J	1977-78
Browell, H H	1877-78
Brown, A C	1920-21
Brown, S L	1975-76
Browning, O C	1934
Bruce Lockhart, J H	1910
Bruce Lockhart, L	1945-46
Bruce Lockhart, R B	1937-38
Brutton, E B	1883-85-86
Bryce, R D H	1965
Bull, H A	1874-75
Bunting, W L	1894-95
Burt-Marshall, J	1905
Burton, B C	1882-83
Bush, J D	1983
Bussey, W M	1960-61-62
Butler, E T	1976-77-78
Campbell, D A	1936
Campbell, H H	1946
Campbell, J A	1897-98-99
Campbell, J D	1927
Campbell, J W	1973-74
Campbell, R C C	1907
Candler, P L	1934
Cangley, B T G	1946
Carey, G V	1907-08
Carpmael, W P	1885
Carris, H E	1929
Carter, C P	1965
Cave, J W	1887-88
Cave, W T C	1902-03-04
Chadwick, W O	1936-37-38
Chalmers, P S	1979
Chambers, E L	1904
Chapman, C E	1881-84
Chapman, E S	1879-80
Chapman, G M	1907-08-09
Chapman, J M	1873
Chilcott, E W	1883
Child, H H	1875-76
Clarke, B D F	1978
Clarke, S J S	1962-63
Clayton, H R	1876-77-78
Clayton, J R W	1971
Clements, J W	1953-54-55
Clifford, P H	1876-77-78
Coates, C H	1877-78-79
Coates, V H M	1907
Cobby, W	1900
Cock, T A	1899
Cocks, F W	1935
Coghlan, G B	1926-27-28
Cohen, A S	1922
Colbourne, G L	1883
Coley, M	1964
Collett, G F	1898
Collier, R B	1960-61
Collin, T	1871
Collins, W O H	1931
Collis, W R F	1919-20
Collison, L H	1930
Considine, W C D	1919
Conway, G S	1919-20-21
Cook, D D B	1920-21
Cook, S	1920-21
Cooke, S J	1981
Cooper, H S	1881
Cooper, P T	1927-28
Cope, W	1891
Corry, T M	1966
Cosh, N J	1966
Covell, G A B	1949
Cove-Smith, R	1919-20-21
Cox, F L	1879
Craig, H J	1891
Craigmile, H W C	1920
Crichton-Miller, D	1928
Crothers, G	1977(R)
Crow, W A M	1961-62
Cullen, J C	1980-81-82
Cumberlege, B S	1910-11-12-13
Cumberlege, R F	1897
Cumming, D C	1922-23-24
Currie, W C	1905
Dalgleish, K J	1951-52-53
Dalton, E R	1872-73-74
Dalton, W L T	1875-76
Daniell, J	1898-99-1900
Darby, A J L	1896-97-98
Darch, W J	1875
David, P W	1983
Davies, G	1948-49-50
Davies, G H	1980-81
Davies, H J	1958
Davies, J C	1949
Davies, J S	1977
Davies, P M	1952-53-54
Davies, T G R	1968-69-70
Davies, W G	1946-47
Deakin, J E	1871
Delafield, G E	1932
De Nobriga, A P	1948
De Villiers, D I	1913
Devitt, Sir T G	1923-24-25
Dewhurst, J H	1885-86
Dick, R C S	1933
Dickins, J P	1972-73
Dickson, J W	1881
Dinwiddy, H P	1934-35
Dixon, A M	1928
Dixon, C	1894
Dods, M	1938
Doherty, H D	1950
Doherty, W D	1913
Don Wauchope, A R	1880-81
Dorwood, A F	1947-48-49
Douglas, E A	1882-83-84
Douglas, R N	1891
Douty, P S	1924
Dovey, B A	1960
Downes, K D	1936-37-38
Downey, W J	1954-55-56-57
Doyle, M G	1965
Drake-Lee, N J	1961-62-63
Drake, T R	1965
Druce, W G	1893-94
Drummond, N W	1971
Drysdale, T	1900-01
Dudgeon, R F	1871
Duncan, C	1966
Duncan, M M	1885-86-87
Dutson, C S	1963
Edlmann, S R R	1974-75
Edmonds, G A	1976
Edwards, E F	1971
Edwards, R J	1971-72
Elliott, A E	1891
Ellis, P R	1975
Ellison, J F	1983
Embleton, J J E	1928-29-30
Evans, A E	1906-07
Evans, D P	1922
Evans, E D	1903-04
Evans, M R M	1955
Evans, W R	1955
Ewbank, C F	1983
Fairbanks, W	1873-74
Fairgrieve, J	1945
Falcon, W	1894-95
Fasson, F H	1897-98-99
Fforde, A B	1891
Fiddian, J V	1908-09
Field, E	1892-93-94
Finch, R T	1876-77-78-79
Fitch, C E	1889
Fleming, R S	1964
Fletcher, N C	1897-98-99
Fogg-Elliott, J W	1887
Folker, E L A	1937
Folwell, A J S	1967-68
Forbes, A S	1873
Ford, J N	1977-78-79
Fordham, J G	1898
Forman, A	1904-05
Forrest, J G S	1936-37-38
Fosh, M K	1977-78
Fowler, T G	1911-12
Fox, S	1945
Francis, T E S	1922-23-24-25
Frankcom, G P	1961-63-64
Fraser, R	1908-09-10
French, N J	1973
French, R B	1969
Fuller, H G	1878-79-80-81-82-83
Fyfe, K C	1932-33-34-35
Gardiner, F A	1921-22-23
Gatford, H J H	1946
Geddes, K I	1938
Geoghegan, K F	1977
Gethin, D	1965-66
Gibbins, R B	1905-06
Gibbons, J F	1882
Gibbs, J D	1965
Giblin, L F	1894-95-96
Gibson, C M H	1963-64-65
Gibson, E	1925-26
Gibson, T A	1901-02
Gill, S M	1980-81
Gilliland, W D	1979
Glanvill, S F	1977-79-80
Gloag, I S	1949-50-52
Gloag, L G	1948
Godby, T A	1906-07
Godson, A	1959-60
Golightly, C H	1879
Goodhue, F W J	1885-86
Gover, J J	1879
Gowans, J J	1892-93
Grant, A R	1975-76
Grant, J J H	1978
Green, M J	1965-66-67
Greenlees, J R C	1898-99-1900-01
Greenwood, G M	1929-30
Greenwood, J E	1910-11-12-13-19

Greenwood, J R H	1962-63
Greg, A H	1893
Greig, I A	1977-78
Griffith, J M	1933
Griffith, R	1894-95
Griffiths, H B	1953
Gurdon, C	1877
Gurdon, E T	1874-75-76
Guthrie, G B	1883
Gwilliam, J A	1947-48
Hacking, A	1898-99
Hamilton, G A C	1925-26
Hamilton, H A	1871-73
Hamilton-Smythe, A F	1926
Hamilton-Wickes, R H	1920-21-22-23
Hammond, J	1881
Hampel, A K R	1982
Hamp-Ferguson, A J C	1964-65
Hannaford, C	1967
Harding, R	1973-74
Harding, V S J	1958-59-60
Harding, W R	1924-25-26-27
Harper, A G R	1983
Harris, B G	1904-05-06
Harrison, R B	1951
Hartley, B C	1900
Hartley, J J	1974
Harvey, M J	1957
Harvey, J R W	1963-64
Hearfield, J	1901
Hearson, H F P	1904-06
Heath, F M N	1936-37
Heath, N R M	1977-78
Henderson, A P	1945-46-47
Herbert, A J	1954-55-56
Heslip, M R	1967
Hetherington, J G G	1955
Hewett, B J	1963
Heywood, F M	1928
Higham, C F W	1961-62
Hignell, A J	1974-75-76-77
Hill, D B	1892
Hind, A E	1900
Hinton, N P	1969-70
Hockey, J R	1957
Hodges, E C	1903-04-05
Hodgson, J T	1955
Hodgson, M E	1973
Holloway, B H	1907-09
Holmes, W B	1947-48
Hooper, C A	1890
Hopkins, A A	1874
Hopkins, W D B	1929
Hopper, L B	1897
Hornby, J J	1873-74-76
Horner, P J	1982
Horrocks-Taylor, J P	1956-57
Horsfall, J	1903-04
Horsley, S	1901-02-03
Howard, J M	1971-72
Howell, R G B	1924
Hughes, K	1968-69
Hull, F M	1871-72-73
Hunter, J M	1946
Illingworth, P H	1889-90
Inglis, F C	1959
Inglis, W M	1935-36
Irving, K G	1935
Jackson, A L	1889
Jackson, T L	1892
Jacob, F	1895-96
Jacob, P G	1894-95-96
Jagger, D	1954
James, A M	1948-49
James, J H H	1962-63-64
James, S R	1876-77-78
Jameson, A	1874
Jeffcock, C E	1877
Jeffery, G L	1884-85
Jenkins, J D	1964
Jenkins, J M	1949-51
Jenkins, W G	1948
Jessop, A W	1972
Johnson, J N	1981
Johnston, D	1897
Johnston, W G S	1932-33-34
Johnstone, H B L	1931
Jolliffe, R L K	1965
Jones, B M	1949
Jones, C W	1933-34-35
Jones, D G H	1951-52
Jones, E A A	1895
Jones, F H	1898-99-1900
Jones, J S	1908-09
Jones, R B	1931-32-33
Jones, S E	1878
Jones, T R K	1921
Jones, W W A	1968-69-70-72
Jones, W I	1923-24-25
Jorden, A M	1968-69
Juckes, R	1913
Juckes, T R	1938
Keeton, G H	1899-1900
Keith-Roach, P d'A	1969-70-71
Kemp, T A	1936
Kennedy, C M	1877-78
Kennedy, R S	1907-09
Kershaw, M E	1955
Killick, S E	1978
Kimberley, H M	1945-46-47-48
King, R H	1950
Kingston, C J	1980-81-82
Kirby, T K M	1945
Kitchin, P A	1965
Kitching, A E	1910-11
Koop, G G	1905
Laborde, C D	1933-34-35-36
Laing, H	1893
Lambert, I C	1871
Langton, E C	1888-89
Lawry, S J	1894-95
Laxon, H	1903-04
Laycock, A M	1979
Leadbetter, V H	1951-52
Leake, W R M	1885-86-87
Leather, W H	1931-32
Leather, W J	1931-32-33-34
Lee, H	1904
Lees, J	1883
Le Fanu, V C	1884-85-86
Le Fleming, J	1884-85-86
Leishman, F J	1938
Lely, W G	1906-07-08
Leonard, R J N	1957
Lewis, A D	1975-76
Lewis, A R	1875
Lewis, A R	1959
Lewis, B R	1909-10-11
Lewis, G A	1872-73-74-75
Lewis, G G	1976
Lewis, G W	1956-57-58
Lewis, J M C	1913-19
Lewis, W H	1926-27
Lewthwaite, W	1872-73
Lillington, P M	1981-82
Lindsay, P A R	1937-38
Linnecar, R J D	1970
Lintott, T M R	1974
Lister, R C	1969
Lloyd-Davies, R H	1947
Lord, J R C	1933-34-35
Lord, M	1960
Loveday, B R	1956-57
Low, J D	1935-36-37
Lowden, G S	1945
Lowe, C N	1911-12-13
Lowry, R H W	1923
Loxdale, J W	1874
Lucas, P M	1882
Luscombe, R P	1871-72-73-74
Lushington, A J	1872
Luxmoore, A F C C	1896-97
Lyon, C E	1871
Lyon, D W	1967-68
McAfee, L A	1910
McClung, T	1954
McCosh, E	1910
McCosh, R	1905-06-07
McMorris, L	1963
MacDonald, A	1871
MacDonald, J A	1936-37
MacDonnell, J C	1889
MacEwen, D L	1887
MacEwen, R K G	1953-54
McGahey, A M J	1979-80-81
McGown, T M W	1896
MacGregor, G	1889-90
McIlwaine, G A	1926-27-28
Mackenzie, W G B	1922
McKenzie, M R	1968
Mackie, O G	1895-96-97
Macklin, A J	1979-80-82
Maclay, J P	1920
MacLeod, K G	1905-06-07-08
MacLeod, L M	1903-04-05
Macleod, W M	1880-82
MacMyn, D J	1921-22-23-24
McNeill, A H	1902-03
McRoberts, T S	1946-47-48
MacSweeney, D A	1957-58-59
Mainprice, H	1902-03-04-05
Makin, R L	1959
Malik, N A	1975
Mann, F T	1910
Marburg, C L H	1909-10
Margerison, R	1871-72-73
Marques, R W D	1954-55-56-57
Marr, D M	1929-30-31-32
Marr, T C K	1945
Marsden, E W	1950
Marriott, C J B	1881-82-83
Marshall, T R	1950
Martin, A W	1983
Martin, N O	1965-66-67
Martin, S A	1961-62-63
Massey, D G	1952
Massey, M J O	1951-52-53
Maxwell, D M W	1922
Mayfield, E	1891
Maynard, A F	1912-13
Mayne, W N	1888
Mellor, J E	1906
Melluish, R K	1922
Metcalfe, I R	1978-79
Methuen, A	1886-87-88
Michaelson, R C B	1960-61-62
Michell, W G	1873-75-76
Middlemas, P	1912
Miliffe, M J	1964
Millard, D E S	1956
Miller, J L H	1920
Mills, D C	1958
Mills, H H	1947-48
Mills, P R	1958-59
Milne, C J B	1882-83-84
Mitchell, F	1893-94-95
Mitchell, W G	1886
Monahan, J D	1967-68
Monro, A H	1973
Monteith, H G	1903-04-05
Montgomery, R	1891
Moore, A W	1874
Moore, P J de A	1947-48
Morel, T E	1920-22
Morgan, H P	1952-53
Morgan, W G	1926-27-28-29
Moriarty, S P	1980
Morpeth, G	1925
Morrison, B J	1965
Morrison, I R	1983
Morrison, P H	1887-88-89-90
Morse, E St J	1871

Mortimer, W	1895-96
Morton, H J S	1908
Moyes, J L	1974-75
Mulligan, A A	1955-56-57
Murray, R A	1982
Murray, R O	1933-34
Napier, Hon M F	1871
Neild, W C	1911-12
Neilson, H	1884
Neilson, W	1891-92-93
Nelson, W E	1892
Newbold, C J	1902-03
Newman, C H	1882
Newton-Thompson, C L	1937-38
Nicholl, C B	1890-91-92-93
Nixon, P J L	1976
O'Brien, T S	1981-82
O'Callaghan, C	1978
O'Callaghan, M W	1974-75-76-77
Odgers, F W	1901
Ogilvy, F J L	1887
Onyett, P S	1966-67
Orr, J C S	1891
Orr-Ewing, D	1919
Oswald, G B R	1945
Oulton, E V	1901
Ovens, A B	1910-11
Owen, A V	1945
Owen, J E	1961
Page, J J	1968-69-70
Page, R S	1972-73
Palmer, H R	1899
Parker, G W	1932-33-34-35
Parr, M F	1978
Parry, T R	1936-37-38
Parsons, J	1938
Pater, S	1880-81
Paterson, L R	1886-87
Paterson-Brown, T	1983
Patterson, H W T	1890
Patterson, W M	1956
Pattisson, R M	1881-82
Payne, J H	1879
Payne, O V	1900
Pearce, D	1873-74
Pearson, T C	1952-53
Peck, I G	1979
Pender, A R	1963
Penny, W M	1906
Perry, D G	1958
Perry, S V	1946-47
Phillips, G P	1971-72
Phillips, J H L	1930-32
Phillips, R J	1964
Pienaar, L L	1911
Pilkington, L E	1893-94
Pilkington, W N	1896-97
Pinkham, C	1910
Pitt, T G	1905-06
Plews, W J	1884
Pope, E B	1932
Powell, P	1900
Pratt, S R G	1973-74
Price, P R	1967
Pringle, A S	1897-98
Pringle, J S	1902
Prosser-Harries, A	1957
Pumphrey, C E	1902
Purves, W D C L	1907-08-09
Pyman, F C	1907-08
Rae, A J	1901
Raffle, N C G	1954-55
Raikes, W A	1872-74
Raine, J B	1947
Rainforth, J J	1958-59
Ramsay, A R	1930
Ransome, H F	1882-83-84
Rawlence, J R	1935-36
Raybould, W H	1966
Redmond, G F	1969-70-71
Reed, E D E	1937
Rees, A M	1933-34
Rees, B I	1963-64-65-66
Rees, G	1972-73
Rees, J I	1931-32
Reeve, P B	1950-51
Reid, J L P	1932
Rendall, H D	1892-93
Reynolds, E P	1909
Rice, E	1880-81
Richards, T B	1955
Richardson, W P	1883
Rigby, J C A	1982
Riley, H	1871-72-73
Ritchie, W T	1903-04
Robbie, J C	1977-78
Roberts, A F	1901-02
Roberts, A J R	1901-02
Roberts, J	1952-53-54
Roberts, J	1927-28
Roberts, S N J	1983
Robertson, D D	1892
Robertson, I	1967
Robinson, A	1886-87
Robinson, B F	1891-92-93
Robinson, J J	1892
Robinson, P J	1962
Rocyn-Jones, D N	1923
Roden, W H	1936-37
Rodgers, A K	1968-69-70
Roffey, D B	1874-75
Rose, H	1872
Rose, W M H	1979-80-81
Rosser, D W A	1962-63-64
Rosser, M F	1972-73
Ross-Skinner, W M	1924
Rotherham, A	1890-91
Rottenburg, H	1898
Rowell, W I	1890
Ryan, C J	1966
Ryan, P H	1952-53
Ryder, D C D	1921-23
Salmon, W B	1883
Sagar, J W	1899-1900
Sample, C H	1882-83-84
Sample, H W	1884
Sanderson, A B	1901
Saunders-Jacobs, S M	1929
Saville, C D	1967-68-69-70
Sawyer, B T C	1910
Saxon, K R J	1919-21
Scholfield, J A	1909-10
Schwarz, R O	1893
Scotland, K J F	1958-59-60
Scott, A W	1945-48
Scott, C T	1899
Scott, J M	1927
Scott, M T	1885-86-87
Scott, R R F	1957
Scott, W B	1923-24
Scott, W M	1888
Scoular, J G	1905-06
Seddon, E R H	1921
Shackleton, I R	1968-69-70
Shaw, P A V	1977
Shepherd, J K	1950
Sherrard, P	1938
Shipsides, J	1970
Shirer, J A	1885
Silk, D R W	1953-54
Sim, R G	1966-67
Simms, K G	1983
Simpson, C P	1890
Simpson, F W	1930-31
Sisson, J P	1871
Skinner, R C O	1970-71
Slater, K J P	1964
Smallwood, A M	1919
Smeddle, R W	1928-29-30-31
Smith, A F	1873-74
Smith, A R	1954-55-56-57
Smith, H K P	1920
Smith, H Y L	1878-79-80-81
Smith, J	1889
Smith, J J E	1926
Smith, J M	1972
Smith, J V	1948-49-50
Smith, K P	1919
Smith, M A	1966-67
Smith, P K	1970
Smith, S R	1958-59
Smith, S T	1982-83
Sobey, W H	1925-26
Spencer, J S	1967-68-69
Spicer, N	1901-02
Spray, K A N	1946-47
Sprot, A	1871
Staunton, H	1891
Stead, R J	1977
Steeds, J H	1938
Steel, D Q	1877
Steele, H K	1970
Steele, J T	1879-80
Steele-Bodger, M R	1945-46
Stevenson, H J	1977(R)-79
Stevenson, L E	1884-85
Steward, R	1875-76
Stewart, A A	1975-76
Stewart, J R	1935
Stokes, R R	1921
Stone, R J	1901
Storey, E	1878-79-80
Storey, L H T	1909
Storey, T W P	1889-90-91-92
Stothard, N A	1979
Style, H B	1921
Surtees, A A	1886
Sutherland, J F	1908
Swanson, J C	1938
Swayne, F G	1884-85-86
Symington, A W	1911-12-13
Synge, J S	1927
Tait, J G	1880-82
Talbot, S C	1900
Tallent, J A	1929-30-31
Tanner, C C	1930
Tarsh, D N	1955
Taylor, A S	1879-80-81
Taylor, D G	1982
Taylor, H B J	1894-96
Taylor, W J	1926
Templer, J L	1881-82
Thomas, B	1960-61-62
Thomas, D R	1972-73-74
Thomas, H W	1912
Thomas, J	1945
Thomas, N B	1966
Thomas, R C C	1949
Thomas, T J	1895-96
Thomas, W H	1886-87
Thompson, M J M	1950
Thompson, R	1890
Thompson, R V	1948-49
Thorman, W H	1890
Thorne, C	1911
Thornton, J F	1976-78-79
Threlfall, R	1881-83
Timmons, F J	1983
Todd, A F	1893-94-95
Todd, T	1888
Touzel, C J C	1874-75-76
Tredwell, J R	1968
Trethewy, A	1888
Trubshaw, A R	1919
Tucker, W E	1892-93-94
Tucker, W E	1922-23-24-25
Tudsbery, F C T	1907-08
Turnbull, B R	1924-25
Turner, J A	1956
Turner, M F	1946
Tyler, R H	1978-79-80
Umbers, R H	1954
Ure, C McG	1911

Valentine, G E	1930
Van Schalkwijk, J	1906
Vaughan, G P	1949
Vaux, J G	1957
Vincent, C A	1913
Vivian, J M	1976
Wace, H	1873-74
Wade, M R	1958-59-60-61
Waddell, G H	1958-60-61
Wainwright, J F	1956
Wainwright, M A	1980
Wakefield, W W	1921-22
Walker, A W	1929-30
Walker, D R	1980-81
Walker, E E	1899-1900
Walker, R M	1963
Walkey, J R	1902
Wallace, W M	1912-13
Waller, G S	1932
Wallis, H T	1895-96
Ward, R O C	1903
Ware, C H	1882
Warfield, P J	1974
Warlow, S	1972-74
Waters, F H	1927-28-29
Waters, J B	1902-03-04
Watherston, J G	1931
Watson, C F K	1919-20
Watt, J R	1970
Webb, G K M	1964-65
Webster, A P	1971
Wells, C M	1891-92
Wells, T U	1951
Wetson, M T	1958-59-60
Wheeler, P J F	1951-52-53
White, J B	1922
White, W N	1947
Whiteway, S E A	1893
Wiggins, C E M	1928
Wiggins, C M	1964
Wilkinson, R M	1971-72-73
Will, J G	1911-12-13
Williams, A G	1926-27
Williams, C C U	1950
Williams, C H	1930
Williams, C R	1971-72-73
Williams, D B	1973
Williams, E J H	1946
Williams, H A	1876
Williams, J M	1949
Williams, L T	1874-75
Williams, N E	1950
Williams, P T	1888-89
Williamson, I S	1972
Willis, H	1949-50-51
Wilson, A H	1911-12-13
Wilson, C P	1877-78-79-80
Wilton, C W	1936
Winthrop, W Y	1871
Wintle, T C	1960-61
Wood, G E	1974-75-76
Wood, G E C	1919
Woodall, B J C	1951
Woodroffe, O P	1952
Woods, S M J	1888-89-90
Wooller, W	1933-34-35
Wordsworth, A J	1973-75
Wotherspoon, W	1888-89
Wrench, D F B	1960
Wright, C C G	1907-08
Wrigley, P T	1877-78-79-80
Wynne, E H	1887
Yetts, R M	1879-80-81
Young, A B S	1919-20
Young, A T	1922-23-24
Young, J S	1935
Young, J V	1906
Young, P D	1949
Young, S K	1974
Young, W B	1935-36-37

Simon Smith, the Cambridge wing, sets off through the middle in the 1983 'Varsity match with his team in close support.

UAU CHAMPIONSHIP 1983-84

7 March, Twickenham
Loughborough University 23 (2G 1PG 2T)
Nottingham University 10 (2PG 1T)

It is sometimes better to travel in hope than to arrive. Nottingham learned the bitter truth of this adage when the quest for their first UAU Championship ended in comprehensive defeat. Loughborough's heavy pack was suitably complemented by a talented back division, and though Nottingham stretched them to the end, they were always in control of the match.

Loughborough made their intentions known as early as the third minute, when sustained pressure on the Nottingham line at last provided Williams with room to score on the blindside, Llewellyn converting the try. Nottingham's half-backs were effectively bottled up, and with Nottingham's Friend having an off-day in kicking, the main scoring threat came from Loughborough. However, sound defence from Nottingham and their own poor finishing prevented Loughborough adding to the score. Then, in the final minute of the half, Friend scored a penalty goal to bring the East Midlands team back into the game.

Their dream was quickly shattered, when Loughborough created a glorious try in the second minute of the second half. Scrum-half Williams gathered deep in his own half, the ball was moved to the right where Burnhill beat three men along the touch-line for a try converted by Llewellyn. Nottingham had not given up, although they obtained little enough ball from the line-out, but they rarely moved the ball along the line and could not escape the clutches of the opposing back row. Friend kicked another penalty to revive their hopes, but Loughborough quickly countered with a penalty by Llewellyn. The victors conceded a number of penalties, but Nottingham's set moves were easily stifled, and Loughborough in turn showed how to use the width of the pitch, as first Reid and then Allen scored unconverted tries to put them out of reach. Nottingham had the last word, when prop forward Ward found himself unmarked close to the line from a simple penalty kick. He promptly passed to Yates, who scored an unconverted try. It was the last move of the match, and they deserved that consolation for helping to create one of the better finals, but Loughborough were excellent value in achieving a record 18th Championship win.

Loughborough University: S Reid; I McMillan, S Burnhill, P Coles, C Allen; D Llewellyn, C Williams; *No 8* N Castleton; *Second Row* J Wells *(capt)*, J Morrison, D Egerton, T Waldron; *Front Row* M Freer, A Rogerson, M Hayes
Scorers *Tries:* Williams, Burnhill, Reid, Allen *Conversions:* Llewellyn (2)
Penalty Goal: Llewellyn

Nottingham University: J Lomas; N George, M Clarke, R Thame, D Yates; N Friend, H Jones *(capt); No 8* N Robinson; *Second Row* A Reason, P Daniell, I Brennan, P Collins; *Front Row* G Mudge, B Moore, J Ward
Scorers *Try:* Yates *Penalty Goals:* Friend (2)
Referee: R C Quittenton (London & Sussex)
Loughborough have won the title 18 times, Durham, Liverpool and Swansea 7, Bristol 5, Manchester 4, Cardiff 3, Bangor and UWIST 2, Aberystwyth, Birmingham, Leeds and Newcastle once each

After a period in the shadow, the traditional rugby strongholds dominated the UAU Championship, the destiny of the title probably having been decided in the quarter-finals when the holders, Durham, fell at Loughborough in a match which presaged the pattern of the Final, and when Exeter failed to take home advantage against Nottingham to the right conclusion.

The representative programme was restored to full strength and indicated a levelling of talent around the country. However, the English Universities were rarely at full strength because of postponements in the Championship and the subsequent unavailability of key players. That the talent was there was shown by the subsequent international recognition of Stephen Burnhill, the Loughborough centre, by England, and the selection of several UAU players for the England Under-23 tour of Spain. The arrangement of fixtures will always be a problem with the varying length of university terms, but the presence of players of high quality was reassuring and certainly was reflected in an improvement in standards in the Championship.

Results of representative matches: Scottish Universities 23, Welsh Universities 16 (Edinburgh); Scottish Universities 11, English Universities 11 (Edinburgh); English Universities 10, Welsh Universities 12 (London); UAU 10, Irish Universities 28 (Liverpool); French Universities 16, UAU 12 (Paris); UAU 21, British Polytechnics 14 (Loughborough)

DIVISIONAL RESULTS

Eastern Division

NORTH-EAST GROUP

	P	*W*	*D*	*L*	*F*	*A*	*Pts*
Durham	2	2	0	0	74	28	4
Newcastle	2	1	0	1	19	35	2
Hull	2	0	0	2	18	48	0

EAST MIDLANDS GROUP

	P	*W*	*D*	*L*	*F*	*A*	*Pts*
Nottingham	3	3	0	0	89	10	6
Leeds	3	2	0	1	50	44	4
Bradford	3	1	0	2	44	68	2
Sheffield	3	0	0	3	21	82	0

Winners and Runners-up in each group go through to Challenge Round

Western Division

NORTH-WEST GROUP

	P	*W*	*D*	*L*	*F*	*A*	*Pts*
UMIST	5	5	0	0	112	32	10
Manchester	5	4	0	1	105	34	8

WEST MIDLANDS GROUP

	P	*W*	*D*	*L*	*F*	*A*	*Pts*
Loughbor'gh	4	4	0	0	140	13	8
Leicester	4	2	0	2	42	67	4

	P	W	D	L	F	A	Pts
Lancaster	5	3	0	2	80	56	6
Liverpool	5	2	0	3	63	89	4
Keele	5	1	0	4	51	101	2
Salford	5	0	0	5	22	121	0

	P	W	D	L	F	A	Pts
Warwick	4	2	0	2	54	97	4
Birmingham	4	1	0	4	39	51	2
Aston	4	1	0	3	35	82	2

Winners and Runners-up in each group go through to Challenge Round, plus winners of play-off between third-placed teams

PLAY-OFF
Lancaster beat Warwick 23-13 at Lancaster

Southern Division

SOUTH-EAST GROUP

(a) North Thames

	P	W	D	L	F	A	Pts
East Anglia	4	3	0	1	80	45	6
Brunel	4	2	1	1	81	29	5
Essex	4	2	0	2	45	106	4
The City	3	1	0	2	26	32	2
UC London	3	0	1	2	28	48	0

(b) South Thames

	P	W	D	L	F	A	Pts
Surrey	3	3	0	0	60	19	6
LSE	3	2	0	1	61	28	4
Kent	3	1	0	2	50	59	2
Sussex	3	0	0	3	18	83	0

Winners in each section go through to Challenge Round. Runners-up play off to meet third-placed team in South West Group for place in Challenge Round

South-East Group title match
Surrey beat East Anglia 26-13 at Guildford

Play-off between runners-up
Brunel beat LSE 12-10 at New Malden

SOUTH-WEST GROUP

	P	W	D	L	F	A	Pts
Exeter	4	4	0	0	122	9	8
Bristol	4	3	0	1	89	40	6
Bath	4	1	0	3	33	58	2
Reading	4	1	0	3	25	84	2
Southampton	4	1	0	3	45	123	2

Winners and Runners-up go through to Challenge Round. Third-placed team plays winner of match between runners-up in South East Group for place in Challenge Round

PLAY-OFF
Brunel beat Bath 20-16 at Uxbridge

Welsh Division

	P	W	D	L	F	A	Pts
Swansea	5	5	0	0	182	31	10
Cardiff	5	4	0	1	116	60	8
Aberystwyth	5	3	0	2	80	99	6
Bangor	5	2	0	3	45	66	4
Cardiff Med	5	1	0	4	57	103	2
UWIST	5	0	0	5	38	159	0

Winners and Runners-up go through to Challenge Round

Challenge Round
Surrey 6 Leicester 17
Cardiff 11 Leeds 6
Loughborough 48 Manchester 6
Durham wo East Anglia scr.
Swansea 32 Lancaster 0
UMIST 13 Newcastle 0
Exeter 36 Brunel 9
Nottingham 12 Bristol 9

Quarter-finals
Leicester 0 Cardiff 6
Loughborough 10 Durham 3
Swansea 45 UMIST 0
Exeter 3 Nottingham 6

Semi-finals
Loughborough 17 Cardiff 3
(at Cheltenham)
Nottingham 19 Swansea 6 (at Stroud)

FINAL (at Twickenham)
Loughborough 23 Nottingham 10

UAU Sevens Tournament

(at Liverpool University)
Quarter-finals: Loughborough I 32, Liverpool 0; Bangor 14, Imperial 6; Loughborough II 22, Leeds 6; Cardiff 12, Exeter 6
Semi-finals: Loughborough I 18, Bangor 6; Loughborough II 16, Cardiff 6
Final: Loughborough I 22, Loughborough II 6

BRITISH POLYTECHNICS CUP 1984
(for the Rugby World Trophy)

14 March, London Irish RFC
Kingston Polytechnic 21 (2G 3DG) **Bristol Polytechnic 6** (2PG)

For the first time in five years, Wales Poly did not contest the final of the British Polys tournament. Once again they fielded a powerful side, but succumbed to a fighting Kingston team 6-9 in the first knock-out round. It was fitting therefore, that Kingston should go on to win the trophy, eventually crushing Bristol in a pulsating final at Sunbury.

Kingston's inspiration was Ian Skinner, a former England Colts fly-half. Skinner dropped three remarkable goals to give Kingston a 9-3 lead at half-time and his genius had a hand in clinching the tries, by Brosch and Pearson, in the second half. He also kicked both conversions. Skinner played for the English Students' XV later in the season.

Bristol, the favourites, were hampered by a lack of continuity behind the scrum. They had strong forwards in Chris Mills and John Willis and Edmunds, at scrum-half, kicked their points with two penalty goals. It was Bristol's fourth losing final in five years.

Kingston Polytechnic: R Cramb; G Pearson, R Brosch, D Evans, D Parkes; I Skinner, M Wallace; *No 8* K Withey; *Second Row* G Birt, T Lishman, P Ashworth, S Hayter; *Front Row* M Howell, J Meadowcroft, M Vellacott
Replacement D Campbell for Cramb (69 mins)
Scorers *Tries:* Brosch, Pearson *Conversions:* Skinner (2) *Dropped Goals:* Skinner (3)
Bristol Polytechnic: S Dyble; R Powell, R Evans, T Pike, G Jones; R Pinnell, R Edmunds; *No 8* D Ridler; *Second Row* M Crooks, J Willis, M Case, P Meades; *Front Row* M Thomas, A Jones, C Mills
Scorer *Penalty Goals:* Edmunds
Referee R C Quittenton (London & Sussex)

Quarter-finals
Trent 21, North Staffs 0; Bristol 7, South Bank 0; Thames 6, Kingston 10; Wolverhampton 4, Newcastle 9
Semi-finals
Kingston 9, Newcastle 6; Bristol 17, Trent 7

Wales (formerly Glamorgan Poly) have won the title six times; Kingston have won three times and Liverpool have won twice; Lanchester, Leeds, Middlesex and Bristol have all won once.

Roger Brosch of Kingston Poly scores in the final of the British Polytechnics Cup. Steve Dyble of Bristol is too late with the tackle.

HOSPITALS' CHALLENGE CUP 1984

Rupert Cherry

14 March, Roehampton (Rosslyn Park RFC)
St Mary's Hospital 22 (1G 4T) **Royal Free Hospital 3** (1PG)
Replay after drawn final, St Mary's 9 (1G 1PG) Royal Free 9 (3PG)

St Mary's won the Hospitals' Cup for the 24th time by beating the Royal Free in a replayed final. For seven years, the Royal Free have managed to reach the second round. In 1984 they reached the final for the first time, and gave a splendid performance to hold St Mary's to a draw. They had three outstanding players in Dave Walsh of London Irish and latterly of Richmond, Tony Watkinson, an Oxford Blue also of London Irish, and Otto Chan, a Chinese flanker who was on the fringe of the England Under-23 side.

St Mary's had a very strong pack, but until the replay they lacked the assistance of Paul Jackson, who has played many games for Harlequins. The forwards carried them through to the final but the backs did not run well enough to score tries and Walsh kicked a third penalty goal for Royal Free in injury time to force them to a replay.

Jackson came into the Mary's side at No 8 for the replay, his sixth final, and the difference was amazing. Mary's had a great deal of good ball, their backs ran with imagination, and most important of all, Jackson stole three tries, two from scrums and one from a line-out. Robinson in the centre scored two tries and Miles, the fly-half, converted one. Walsh kicked a penalty goal for Royal Free who went down bravely, running what little possession they could get.

St Mary's: J Hobart; D Grant, R Robinson, R Harvey, P Longden; J Miles, A Williams; *No 8* P D Jackson; *Second Row* C Hayward, S Kemp, C Guest, P Horner; *Front Row* M Emberton, M Kenny, P Enevoldson
Replacement J Booth for Harvey (74 mins)
Royal Free: J Hare; J McGann, A Watkinson, D Hughes, J Jackson; D Walsh, R Woodbaker; *No 8* J Morris; *Second Row* A Manktelow, T O'Kelly, H Sansom, O Chan; *Front Row* G Steinberg, T Wistow, A MacDonald
Referee G Crawford (London Society)

Full Results
First Round: King's Cross 11, Middlesex 6; St Thomas's 0, Royal Free 23; Charing Cross 8, St George's 4; St Bartholomew's 19, Guy's 13
Second Round: King's College 0, Westminster 31; Royal Free 23, The London 9; Charing Cross 6, University College 0; St Bartholomew's 0, St Mary's 12
Semi-finals: Westminster 9, Royal Free 12; Charing Cross 0, St Mary's 16
Final: Royal Free 9, St Mary's 9
Replay: Royal Free 3, St Mary's 22

Guy's have won the Cup 30 times, St Mary's 24, St Thomas's 17, The London 10, St Bartholomew's 9, St George's and Westminster 3 times each, and Middlesex once.

THE INTER-SERVICES TOURNAMENT 1983-84

Rupert Cherry

For only the eighth time in 64 years there was a triple tie in the Inter-Services Championship, each team winning one match and losing one. The Army might have been expected to retain the championship they had won in 1983 for they had a good pack, an effective fly-half in Geoffrey Nield, and two good runners on the wings, Kevin Bassom and David Johnson.

Their solid defence and the astuteness of their scrum-half Gareth Davies, who snatched a try in a pushover, accounted for the Navy, and when they came to play the RAF they seemed to have the match won by half-time. They led 12-6, but after that everything seemed to go against them. Rory Underwood on the RAF left wing, now an England international, scored a brilliant try in the corner which gave the RAF the lead and settled the result of the whole tournament.

3 March, Twickenham
Army 13 (2PG 1DG 1T) **Royal Navy 6** (2PG)
for the Stewart Wrightson Trophy

Army: Sgt M Blomquist (RE); Sgt D Johnson (RWF), Cpl I Shaw (RAOC), Capt P Warfield (RAEC) *(capt)*, Cpl K Bassom (RE); Lt G Nield (RE), Sgt/Instr G Davies (APTC); *No 8* Capt B McCall (REME); *Second Row* Sgt C Christopher (RAOC), Sgt/Instr S Peacock (APTC), Sgt R Travers (RAOC), Dvr B McFarlane (RCT); *Front Row* Capt C Harvey (DWR), Lt R Bedford (RE), L/Cpl J Brown (RAOC) *Replacement* Cpl P Lockitt (REME) for Warfield (26 mins)
Scorers *Try:* Davies *Penalty Goals:* Nield (2) *Dropped Goal:* Nield
Royal Navy: LAEM (WL) R Henderson (HMS Seahawk); Mid P Barcilon (BRNC Dartmouth), Sub Lt C Alcock (HMS Seahawk), MEM (L) G Price (HMS Otus), Lt T Newson (NWTAA); Mne S Barnett (42 Commando), WEA1 C Youldon (HMS Tireless); *No 8* AEM (M) G Wood (HMS Daedalus); *Second Row* Sgt R Tinson (RM) *(capt)*, Sgt D Hadlow (RM), Cpl A Turner (RM), PO WEA M Sheldon (HMS Cardiff); *Front Row* L/Wrtr J Hirst (HMS Warrior), Lt I Thompson (HMS Collingwood), AEM (M) S Lord (HMS Seahawk)
Scorers *Penalty Goals:* Henderson, Barnett
Referee C J High (Lancashire)

24 March, Twickenham
Royal Navy 10 (2PG 1T) **Royal Air Force 9** (1G 1PG)
for the Windsor Life Trophy

Royal Navy: Mne S Lawrence (Cdo Log Regt); LPT R Penfold (HMS Drake), MEM G Price (HMS Otus), MEM T Andrews (HMS Drake), Lt T Newson (NWTAA); WEA1 C Youldon (HMS Tireless), Sub Lt M Durkin (BRNC Dartmouth); *No 8* AEM (M) G Wood (HMS Daedalus); *Second Row* Sgt R Tinson (RM) *(capt)*, Sgt D Hadlow (RM), Cpl A Turner (RM), PO WEA M Sheldon (HMS Cardiff); *Front Row* L/Wrtr J Hirst (HMS Warrior), Lt I Thompson (HMS Collingwood),

AEM (M) S Lord (HMS Seahawk) *Replacement* PO AEM (M) H Williams (HMS Heron) for Hirst (35 mins)
Scorers *Try:* Hadlow *Penalty Goals:* Lawrence (2)
RAF: Off Cdt P Bate (Cranwell); F/Lt R Allison (Brize Norton), Off Cdt I Gosling (Cranwell), Cpl L Bruckner (Brize Norton), P O R Underwood (Swinderby); Cpl M Evans (Odiham), Cpl R Owen (Odiham); *No 8* Cpl G Still (Innsworth); *Second Row* F/O R Lamb (St Mawgan), Cpl J Orwin (Brize Norton) *(capt)*, F/Lt N Gillingham (Cottesmore), F/Lt M Coptcoat (Wroughton); *Front Row* Cpl M Whitcombe (N Luffenham), Cpl P Wheeler (St Athan), Sgt S Turner (Brize Norton) *Replacement* Cpl P Aherne (Newton) for Bruckner (28 mins)
Scorers *Try:* Underwood *Conversion:* Evans *Penalty Goal:* Evans
Referee D L Thomas (N Midlands)

7 April, Twickenham
Royal Air Force 19 (1G 1PG 2DG 1T) Army 15 (1G 3PG)
for the Windsor Life Challenge Cup

RAF: Off Cdt P Bate (Cranwell); F/Lt R Allison (Brize Norton), Off Cdt I Gosling (Cranwell), Cpl P Aherne (Newton), P/O R Underwood (Cranwell); Cpl M Evans (Odiham), Cpl R Owen (Odiham); *No 8* Cpl D Parsonage (Finningley); *Second Row* F/O R Lamb (St Mawgan), Cpl J Orwin (Brize Norton) *(capt)*, F/Lt N Gillingham (Cottesmore), F/Lt M Coptcoat (Wroughton); *Front Row* Cpl M Whitcombe (N Luffenham), Cpl M Wheeler (St Athan), Cpl C Stephenson (Abingdon)
Scorers *Tries:* Allison, Underwood *Conversion:* Evans *Penalty Goal:* Evans *Dropped Goals:* Evans (2)
Army: Lt A MacKay (RCT); Sgt D Johnson (RWF), Cpl P Lockitt (REME), Capt P J Warfield (RAEC) *(capt)*, Cpl K Bassom (RE); Lt G Nield (RE), Sgt Instr G Davies (APTC); *No 8* Capt P C McCall (REME); *Second Row* Sgt C Christopher (RAOC), Sgt Instr S Peacock (APTC), Major J M Bowles (RCT), Dvr B McFarlane (RCT); *Front Row* Capt C Harvey (DWR), Sgt J P Byrne (REME), L/Cpl J K Brown (RAOC) *Replacement* Sgt M Blomquist for Nield (52 mins)
Scorers *Try:* Lockitt *Conversion:* Nield *Penalty Goals:* Nield (2), Blomquist
Referee D J Wilson (Yorkshire)

Inter-Services Tournament Champions

The Army have won the Tournament outright 25 times, the Royal Navy 15 times, and the RAF 9 times.

1920 **Navy**	1931 **Navy**	1949 **Army** / **RAF**	1960 **Army**	1972 **Army**
1921 **Navy**	1932 **Army**		1961 **Navy**	1973 **Navy**
1922 **Navy**	1933 **Army**	1950 **Army**	1962 **RAF**	1974 **Navy**
1923 **RAF**	1934 **Army**	1951 **Navy**	1963 **Army**	1975 Triple Tie
1924 Triple Tie	1935 Triple Tie	1952 **Army**	1964 **Army**	1976 **Army**
1925 **Army** / **RAF**	1936 **Army**	1953 **Army**	1965 **Army**	1977 **Navy**
	1937 **Army**	1954 Triple Tie	1966 **Navy**	1978 Triple Tie
1926 **Army**	1938 **Navy**	1955 **RAF**	1967 **Army**	1979 **Army**
1927 **Navy**	1939 **Navy**	1956 Triple Tie	1968 **Army**	1980 **Army**
1928 **Army**	1946 **Army**	1957 **Army**	1969 **Army**	1981 **Navy**
1929 **Army**	1947 **RAF**	1958 **RAF**	1970 **Navy**	1982 **RAF**
1930 **Army**	1948 Triple Tie	1959 **RAF**	1971 **RAF**	1983 **Army**
				1984 Triple Tie

Royal Navy v Army Royal Navy have won 29, Army 35, and 3 matches have been drawn
Royal Navy v RAF Royal Navy have won 35, RAF 20, and 4 matches have been drawn
Army v RAF Army have won 35, RAF 17, and 7 matches have been drawn

THE MIDDLESEX SEVENS 1984

Rupert Cherry

The Welsh apititude for sevens overcame traditional Scottish skills in this specialised version of the game with an overwhelming victory in the Middlesex Final at Twickenham. It seems that London Welsh can usually find the man to rise to the occasion, and this time it was a young player who is half English. Matthew Ebsworth's name first appeared in the sporting columns when he was a schoolboy at Millfield, and since then he had played for Northampton, which was his father's club, and London Welsh. The Exiles had been playing him at full-back in their XV, but on the great day of the Sevens final he was able to show his pace and his kicking ability in his true position at fly-half. The Welsh, at the top of the draw as the previous season's losing finalists, had a comparatively easy run throughout the tournament. They overcame Rosslyn Park almost as easily as they did the junior club Cheshunt, and with the strong-running Robert Ackerman and Ebsworth scoring fine tries they beat a very useful Blackheath seven in the semi-final.

The other finalists were the guest side, Heriot's FP, who after comfortable victories over Exeter University and Old Kingsburians, at Twickenham for the first time, nearly stumbled to defeat against Richmond second team. They had plenty of chances to make sure of winning, but wasted most of them by not passing quickly enough. Richmond led 10-6, and would have won if Mackaness had succeeded with a penalty kick at goal in the last second. Richmond had overcome their senior side by 16-12 in a most exciting match, raising visions of 33 years ago when 'Nim' Hall led a Richmond second team to victory in the final.

Heriot's tried to pull themselves together in the final, Doucherty snatching a try early on when the Welsh fumbled behind their line. Then Ebsworth got into his stride, scored a try, converted it, and went on to convert a try by Ackerman and a couple more by the evergreen Clive Rees. He finished an excellent performance by converting another of his own tries. Near the end Heriot's brought on that celebrated full-back, Andy Irvine, as a replacement and he made the last kick of the day, the conversion of a try from wide out. On the whole the standard of play has not improved, but the popularity of the event grows every year.

RESULTS

Sixth round: London Welsh I 28, Cheshunt 6; London Welsh II 12, Rosslyn Park 16; Blackheath I 12, Harlequins 10; Blackheath II 12, Bridgend 22; Heriot's FP 18, Exeter University 10; Old Kingsburians 11, London Irish 6; Richmond II 12, London Scottish 8; Saracens 6, Richmond I 20

Seventh round: London Welsh I 22, Rosslyn Park 4; Blackheath I 22, Bridgend 18;

Heriot's FP 36, Old Kingsburians 6; Richmond II 16, Richmond I 12
Semi-finals: London Welsh I 16, Blackheath I 6; Heriot's FP 12, Richmond II 10
Final: London Welsh I 34, Heriot's FP 18

TEAMS IN THE FINAL

London Welsh I: C F W Rees; R A Ackerman, M Ebsworth; M Douglas; K Bowring *(capt)*, R John, B Morgan
Scorers *Tries:* Ebsworth (2), Rees (2), Ackerman, John *Conversions:* Ebsworth (5)
Heriot's FP: P Hewitt; S Doucherty, N Marshall; A J M Lawson *(capt)*; P T O'Neill, K Milne, D Livingstone *Replacement* A R Irvine for Marshall (18 mins)
Scorers *Tries:* Doucherty (2), Livingstone *Conversions:* Marshall, Hewitt, Irvine
Referee P J Wakefield (London Society)

WINNERS

1926	**Harlequins**
1927	**Harlequins**
1928	**Harlequins**
1929	**Harlequins**
1930	**London Welsh**
1931	**London Welsh**
1932	**Blackheath**
1933	**Harlequins**
1934	**Barbarians**
1935	**Harlequins**
1936	**Sale**
1937	**London Scottish**
1938	**Metropolitan Police**
1939	**Cardiff**
1940	**St Mary's Hospital**
1941	**Cambridge University**
1942	**St Mary's Hospital**
1943	**St Mary's Hospital**
1944	**St Mary's Hospital**
1945	**Notts**
1946	**St Mary's Hospital**
1947	**Rosslyn Park**
1948	**Wasps**
1949	**Heriot's FP**
1950	**Rosslyn Park**
1951	**Richmond II**
1952	**Wasps**
1953	**Richmond**
1954	**Rosslyn Park**
1955	**Richmond**
1956	**London Welsh**
1957	**St Luke's College**
1958	**Blackheath**
1959	**Loughborough Colleges**
1960	**London Scottish**
1961	**London Scottish**
1962	**London Scottish**
1963	**London Scottish**
1964	**Loughborough Colleges**
1965	**London Scottish**
1966	**Loughborough Colleges**
1967	**Harlequins**
1968	**London Welsh**
1969	**St Luke's College**
1970	**Loughborough Colleges**
1971	**London Welsh**
1972	**London Welsh**
1973	**London Welsh**
1974	**Richmond**
1975	**Richmond**
1976	**Loughborough Colleges**
1977	**Richmond**
1978	**Harlequins**
1979	**Richmond**
1980	**Richmond**
1981	**Rosslyn Park**
1982	**Stewart's Melville FP**
1983	**Richmond**
1984	**London Welsh**

Richmond have won the title 9 times (including once by Richmond II) which is more than any other club. Harlequins and London Welsh have won it 8 times each, London Scottish 6, St Mary's Hospital and Loughborough Colleges 5, Rosslyn Park 4, Blackheath, Wasps, and St Luke's College (now Exeter University) twice, Barbarians, Sale, Met Police, Cardiff, Cambridge University, Notts (now Nottingham), Heriot's FP and Stewart's-Melville FP once each

SCHOOLS RUGBY 1983-84

George Abbott

In the 18 Group Internationals England began on a high note, playing at the top of their form to inflict a comprehensive defeat on Wales. Yet an uneasy feeling persisted that this was too good to be true and, sure enough, the English boys were brought down to earth three days later, when the commitment and scrummaging power of a rampaging Irish pack destroyed them – as it had already shattered Scotland. The superior English backs scored one fine try to add to their three against Wales, but Irish pressure was rewarded with five penalty goals. England's third and last match, in France, again showed the limitations of their fowards, but their admirable spirit in fighting back after France had taken an eight-point lead was good to see, even though the winning try did not come until injury time. All six of England's tries in their three games were scored by the three-quarters, for which the centres, W D C Carling (Sedbergh) and J M Priestley (Bradford GS), can take considerable credit.

The Welsh captain, Robert Jones, who played several times with distinction at senior club level for Swansea, was a scrum-half of high class and their backs as a whole were a talented combination. England frustrated them by denying them good possession and by sound defence, but against France, although the Welsh forwards were again out-scrummaged, the midfield players found chances to show their ability and skilful running produced three exciting tries. The result of this match at last brought Wales on level terms with France in the series of junior internationals, which started in 1924. France took a clear lead in the early years, but the score now stands at France 21, Wales 21, with six draws.

Ireland, who limit their international engagements to two games each season won both for the first time since 1978. They owed much to their forwards, but the backs brought off some fine movements and two of their five tries against Scotland came from classic passing along the line. Moreover, six of the Irish team were under 17 when the season began and will therefore be still within the 18 Group age limit for the 1984-85 season.

Although Scotland had an edge in experience over their rivals (the team included six players who had been capped the previous season, whereas Wales had two and England and Ireland just one each), their only success was against Zimbabwe. On that occasion they kept the game tight, a wise policy, since Zimbabwe had some mature and talented backs; notably David Curtis, the captain and fly-half and son of an Irish international, who at 18½ looked quite ready to step straight into first class rugby.

Devotees of the running game might like to note that, as in the last three seasons, the international 18 Group matches produced more tries than penalty goals. The ratio, 22 to 18, was not as great as some would like, but nevertheless it presented a striking and welcome contrast to the norm in senior internationals nowadays. The lower age groups suffered from the fact that England and Wales could not agree on a common age level. Consequently the junior fixture between those two countries (which was inaugurated in 1904) was discontinued, with Wales playing 15 Group matches against Scotland and Italy and England's 16 Group opposition coming from Holland, Portugal and Italy. The Welsh boys beat Scotland 16-9 and then entertained a visiting party from Italy, winning the full international 30-7 and losing the 'B' match 11-9. England scored nine tries in defeating Holland 40-3 at Ipswich, added a further ten in a rather hollow 53-0 victory over Portugal at Twickenham, and then toured in Italy, where they played three games. After two victories, over Venice Region 50-3 and Italy 'B' 24-9, the English boys faced the full Italian team (who had beaten Wales at 15 Group level a year before) and lost 14-9 to fast and skilful opponents.

Although northern players did not dominate the international teams as heavily as in the last two seasons, the North of England still produced some of the strongest sides in England. In particular, *West Park* (St Helens) and *Sedbergh* ranked alongside *Epsom* and *Millfield* among the best and most successful in the country.

West Park, blessed with a number of talented players, completed their season with the remarkable figures of 28 wins and one draw in 29 matches, following a 1982-83 season in which they had won 25 out of 28. They gave many displays of very high quality, as did *Sedbergh*, who finish their First XV inter-school fixtures before Christmas and who overcame all rivals for the second year running, conceding only one try in ten games. *Ampleforth*, as usual, enjoyed a fine contest with Sedbergh and won ten of their 12 school fixtures. *Cowley*, who are West Park's keenest rivals, fielded a very young XV which suffered a number of reverses, but which showed spirit and promise. The *Royal Grammar School, Lancaster,* who have played consistently good rugby for a number of years, won nine and drew two of their 13 inter-school matches. Their defeats came from *Sedbergh* and *Rossall,* whose results, creditable as they were (W9, L4) would have been better but for a series of crippling injuries.

Two Lancashire schools with very different backgrounds produced teams which compared well with any in the North. *Winstanley College* (Wigan), comparative newcomers to the rugby scene, recorded 21 victories and lost only to West Park, while *Hutton GS*, who have been playing the game since 1866, were highly regarded in their circuit, although injuries to key players proved a handicap. After losing seven of their pre-Christmas matches *Wirral GS* finished well with ten wins in the last 11, bringing their figures to W18, D1, L8. *Birkenhead's* three defeats were by narrow margins and to set against them they had 13 victories in a strong fixture list. The strength of the *King's, Macclesfield* forwards ensured a hard test for all opponents and they won ten out of 18 games, only once losing by more than five points.

Strong forward play by *Austin Friars* (Carlisle) provided a flow of good possession; after an unbeaten first term they finished with 12 wins, one draw and three losses. *Durham*'s backs were probably the most exciting combination in England; they lost to three very strong opponents, Ampleforth, Sedbergh and Sherborne, but won their other 12 matches and scored no less than 627 points. Yorkshire had good and successful teams in *Bradford GS* (W16, L6), *Hymers, Hull* (W17, D1, L2), *Leeds GS* (W15, D1, L5) and *Queen Elizabeth GS, Wakefield* (W14, L4).

Playing a fast and fluid game, the *Royal Grammar School, Worcester* moved the ball well and secured excellent results, scoring 69 tries and winning 16 of their 18 matches. They drew with *Warwick*, (who celebrated their centenary season with a number of successes) and lost to *King Henry VIII, Coventry*, who continued their fine results of recent seasons, recording 20 wins in 24 fixtures. *Rugby*'s main strength lay in the forwards and their team performances were uneven, resulting in a fair record of seven victories, one draw and four defeats; three of the four games lost were decided by a single-point margin. A succession of low-scoring contests for *Uppingham* included three draws in a row; their other results were five wins and two losses.

When *Nottingham HS*'s young team lost two of their first three games the outlook was not particularly bright, but consistently sound work by the pack then brought an unbroken run of 15 successes. They were one of three sides to overcome *Trent*, who drew with Uppingham and won their other nine school matches. *Millfield* followed an unbeaten 1982-83 season with another in which they won 11 and drew one of their 12 fixtures with schools. After drawing with Gowerton in Wales they won the return match 17-0. They were the only side to beat *Sherborne*, whose highly competent XV recorded nine victories, and draws with Taunton and Radley. *Blundell*'s, with a light but mobile pack and speedy, talented backs, enjoyed their best season for some time; they had 14 wins, two draws and one defeat, by Sherborne.

A 14-13 defeat in the last match of the season deprived *Queen Elizabeth's Hospital* (Bristol) of another unbeaten record; they won all 19 games in 1982-83 and in 1983-84 they had 16 victories in succession before going down to Bristol GS. *St Brendan*'s again provided formidable opposition for all rivals; they lost four times to schools, but won 14 matches. Forward strength was mainly responsible for *Clifton* finishing in credit (W5, D1, L4).

King's, Taunton, who possessed pace and thrust in the backs, started with five wins in a row, but suffered some reverses later; their final figures were W7, D1, L4. *Taunton*'s scoreless draw with Sherborne was their best performance, but they also recorded good victories over Downside and *Bryanston*, who in a year of rebuilding had seven successes and five defeats. Four setbacks running in mid-term made a low point in *Marlborough*'s season; of their other school fixtures they won eight and drew one.

A series of competent and sometimes spectacular displays made 1983 a memorable year for *Epsom*, who won all 13 matches against schools. They had two particularly close contests, with Cranleigh and Wellington, both of whom had XVs of well above average quality. *Cranleigh*, hardened by a tour in New Zealand and Australia before the season started, beat all but three of their domestic rivals, while *Wellington's* sole defeat in 10 fixtures was by Epsom.

Radley's team of all-round competence lost only to Wellington, although both Sherborne and Harrow held them to draws. With only 300 boys in the school *Douai* did well to record ten victories. *Harrow* continued their revival, which started in 1982, with seven wins, one draw and four losses, finishing their season on a high note. *Haberdashers' Aske's, Elstree* (W12, L2) had a back division which few schools could match for pace and scoring power. Their defeats came from Dulwich and *Berkhamsted*, whose eight victories from 11 fixtures were due mainly to the talent and experience they possessed in the back row and behind the scrum.

Bishop's Stortford, with five county players among their backs, were supreme in their circuit in East Anglia. They played 13 matches against schools, winning 12, scoring nearly 400 points and losing only to Blundell's, who visited Essex on tour. *Campion* (Hornchurch) maintained their customary high standard and their figures were again impressive (W20, D2, L3). An experienced *Gresham's* side did not allow an early setback to unsettle them and went on to record 12 successes, broken only by three defeats against strong opposition on a mid-term tour in the North-West.

A workmanlike *St Paul's* XV won all but three of their 12 fixtures against schools. Their most notable triumph was gained at the expense of their old rivals, *Dulwich*, who proved hard to beat as usual, never conceding more than a single try in their 12 games, of which they won nine and drew one. Fourteen victories and six defeats represented another good season for *John Fisher* (Purley). They were the only team to master *Trinity* (Croydon), who recorded 16 wins and a draw, gaining in confidence as the term progressed. *Reigate GS* (W12, D3, L3) fully upheld their position as one of the leading schools in the South-East.

Tonbridge, a sound defensive combination, enjoyed their best season for some time. They were unbeaten up to the end of November, but then lost narrowly to Wellington and Dulwich. *Judd* (Tonbridge) suffered only one defeat, by Tonbridge, before Christmas, but lost four of their six fixtures in the Easter Term. *St Joseph's Academy* (Blackheath) had an even longer run of success, winning 16, drawing one and losing one of their first 18 matches, but four losses in February rather spoilt their record. In a different circuit *Kent College* (Canterbury) were again a dominant force; they won all 12 games, going through the season unbeaten for the third time in five years.

An experienced *Brighton* XV secured eight victories from 11 school fixtures and recorded a rare triumph over *Christ's Hospital*, who suffered from lack of experience after two seasons of unbroken success and won only four games out of 11. *Portsmouth GS* proved too strong for most local rivals; in 20 fixtures their only defeats came from Bryanston, St Brendan's and, in the Hampshire Cup final, from Peter Symonds, Winchester.

In Scotland *Strathallan* had the best record, going through unbeaten with 13 victories and a draw with Edinburgh Academy. *Dollar Academy* had an excellent season; they lost to Strathallan and Watson's, but won their remaining 19 matches, scoring more than 800 points. They also had five representatives in the Scottish 18 Group international XV. *George Watson's* enjoyed another good season to follow their impressive results of 1982-83. A hard side to beat, their figures were W14, D1, L2, the defeats coming from Edinburgh Academy and Merchiston Castle. *Edinburgh Academy*, *Fettes*, *Glenalmond* and *Stewart's-Melville* had satisfactory records, but all suffered an occasional reverse.

Monmouth included Christ, Brecon and Llandovery (both of whom had undistinguished seasons) among their seven victims; they lost three times, to Marlborough, Millfield and Ampleforth. Monmouth also ended their winter activities by touring in the USA, where they played and won six matches against school or university teams. Several Welsh schools whose XVs are seldom seen outside the Principality did extremely well – notably *St Cyres*, Penarth (W24, L2) and *Barry* (W22, L4). Barry shared with Cwmtawe the distinction of supplying four players for the Welsh 18 Group squad, and *Cwmtawe* were only once able to field their strongest side, because of trials, representative games and calls from first class clubs. Best of all statistically were *Ystalyfera*, who won all 21 matches, extending to 37 an unbroken run of successes which begun in October 1982.

Royal Belfast Academical Institution were the popular favourites for the Ulster Schools Cup on the strength of their consistently strong play. But they went out in the second round to Coleraine Academical Institution, suffering only their third defeat of the season, in which they recorded 27 victories. The final was contested by *Methodist College, Belfast* and *Belfast Royal Academy* and MCB's 13-9 win gave them a record 24th capture of the title, for which the Ulster schools have been competing since 1876.

School tours to distant areas are now too numerous to mention individually, with Canada, New Zealand, Australia, Hong Kong and Zimbabwe among the more ambitious destinations. On the national scene there were two of major importance. Wales, after completing the junior grand slam in the 1982-83 season, sent their 18 Group party to Canada in August 1983. There they won five matches, including both internationals, 27-3 in Vancouver and 20-15 in Toronto, but they lost narrowly (16-13) to British Columbia, a result that must form a landmark as well as give a boost for the junior game in that province. Following visits by five different school parties from Zimbabwe in the last three seasons the national Schools team of that country toured in Britain in December 1983. They played four matches in England and three in Scotland, breaking even with three victories, one draw and three defeats. The one international was won 13-10 by Scotland. As the season ended preparations were being made for a first visit by New Zealand Schools in the 1984-85 season, with fixtures in all four home countries.

In the most important seven-a-side tournaments honours were shared by *West Park*, *Millfield* and *Ampleforth*, with *Rossall* pressing them hard. *West Park* won four of the seven competitions that they entered, including the most prestigious of all, the National Schools Open run by Rosslyn Park. *Millfield* had a similar record, four successes out of seven starts, with the Oxfordshire event as the most significant. *Ampleforth* performed the remarkable feat of winning Rosslyn Park's Festival event (for schools playing rugby for one term only) for a third year in succession. And the *Rossall* VII, coming to Roehampton unbeaten with three victories in the North, were denied a fourth only by a fine Ampleforth team at the top of their form in the final of the Festival.

The sixth Preston Grasshoppers 15-a-side Festival, blessed with fine weather in the first week-end of April, provided a feast of open rugby, more tries than ever before and yet another triumph for *West Park*'s remarkable team. Undismayed at losing their opening match on the first day of the tournament, they went on to win their other two games and qualify for the later stages as runners-up in their group. On the second and third days they made no mistake, winning five more matches in fine style thanks to the running, passing and support play that had marked them throughout the season as an exceptional side. Their opponents in the final were *Arnold* (Blackpool), who although they could not compare with West Park in scoring power, held on tenaciously and gave their opponents some anxious moments before going down 7-3.

The following players took part in the 18 Group international matches. (Countries played against are shown in square brackets).

Abbreviations: *E* – England, *F* – France, *I* – Ireland, *S* – Scotland, *W* – Wales, *Z* – Zimbabwe, (R) – Replacement.

ENGLAND

Full-back A M B Hobbs (Cranleigh) [*W, I, F*]
Threequarters P J Hamer (Lancaster RGS) [*W, I, F*], W D C Carling (Sedbergh) [*W, I, F*], J M Priestley (Bradford GS) [*W, I, F*], R A Bennett (Bristol Cathedral) [*W, I, F*]
Half-backs A J Buzza (Redruth) [*W, I, F*], G D Sephton (Cowley) [*W, I, F*]
Forwards J B Wilby (QEGS, Wakefield) [*W, I, F*], S S Bryant (Sherborne) [*W, I, F*], A G Blackmore (Bedminster Down, Bristol) [*W, I, F*], D A Hay (Lyndhurst, Gateshead) [*W, I, F*], M D Sweett (Sutton HS, Plymouth) [*W, I, F*], N A Banbury (Arnold Hill, Notts) [*W, I, F*], D W Haley (John Willmott, Sutton Coldfield) [W, I, F], R A Hunt (Trent) [*W, I, F*]
W D C Carling was captain in all three matches

SCOTLAND

Full-back N M Fisher (Edinburgh Academy) [*Z, W, I*]
Threequarters M Wright (Dollar Academy) [*Z, W, I*], G Swann (Glenalmond) [*I*], A C Glasgow (Dollar Academy) [*Z, W, I*], J H Jeavons-Fellows (Gordonstoun) [*Z, W*], N H McKee (Strathallan) [*Z, W, I*]
Half-backs A Donaldson (Currie HS) [*Z, W, I*(R)], I C Glasgow (Dollar Academy) [*I*], G A Parker (Galashiels Academy) [*Z, W*], J G A Frost (Stewart's-Melville) [*I*]
Forwards A C Murray (George Watson's) [*Z, W, I*], G R Brown (Galashiels Academy) [*Z, W*], J D Busby (Hillhead HS) [*I*], R Scott (Lomond, Glasgow) [*Z, W, I*], J R C Main (Dollar Academy) [*Z, W, I*], D R Milne (Harris Academy, Dundee) [*Z, W*], J Robertson (Dollar Academy) [*I*], S J McIrvine (Kelvinside Academy) [*Z, W, I*], K J Burnett (Dundee HS) [*Z, W*], G K Affleck (Dunbar GS) [*I*], I C Donnelly (St Aloysius, Glasgow) [*Z, W, I*]
N M Fisher was captain in all three matches

IRELAND

Full-back D P Larkin (St Munchin's, Limerick) [*S, E*]
Threequarters M T Costello (Terenure) [*S, E*], B T Glennon (De La Salle, Churchtown) [*S, E*], A P Archer (Royal School, Dungannon) [*S, E*], J C Riordan (Rockwell) [*S, E*]
Half-backs R M Cullen (Royal Belfast Academical Institution) [*S, E*], R J Montford (Presentation Bros, Bray) [*S, E*]
Forwards K T Leahy (Crescent, Limerick) [*S, E*], D G G Madigan (Gonzaga, Dublin) [*S, E*], L M Dinneen (Crescent, Limerick) [*S, E*], P L R Coleman (Christian Bros, Cork) [*S, E*], R McFarland (Belfast Royal Academy) [*S, E*], B J Rhodes (Ballymena Academy) [*S, E*], P D Madden (Christian Bros, Cork) [*S, E*], G F Halpin (Rockwell) [*S, E*]
B J Rhodes was captain in both matches

WALES

Full-backs C Bradshaw (Dyffryn, Port Talbot) [*S, E*], J Callard (Bassaleg, Newport) [*E*(R), *F*]
Threequarters O Fahiya (Barry) [*S, E*], G Phillips (Lewis, Pengam) [*F*], S Parfitt (Bryntirion, Bridgend) [*S, E, F*], A Summers (St Cyres, Penarth) [*S*], S R Jones (Cwmtawe) [*E*], W Evans (Heolddu, Blackwood) [*F*], G Davies (Pencoed, Bridgend) [*S, E, F*]
Half-backs D W Evans (Aberdare) [*S, E, F*], R Jones (Cwmtawe) [*S, E, F*]
Forwards D Bryant (Bryntirion) [*S, E, F*], M R Francis (Pentrehafod, Swansea) [*S, E, F*], S H Reed (Barry) [*S, E, F*], C Crane (Pontypool Tertiary) [*S, E, F*], M L Howell (Whitland GS) [*S*], S Davies (Bishop Gore, Swansea) [*E, F*], A D Williams (Fishguard) [*S, E*], A O'Brien (Bryncelynnog, Beddau) [*F*], A Lewis (Bedwas, Caerphilly) [*S, E, F*], G E Bundock (Amman Valley) [*S, E*], P Riley (Archbishop McGrath) [*F*]
R Jones was captain in all three matches

MATCH DETAILS (18 Group)

10 December, Edinburgh

SCOTLAND 13 (2PG 1DG 1T) **ZIMBABWE 10** (1G 1T)
Scotland *Try:* Scott *Dropped Goal:* Donaldson *Penalty Goals:* Donaldson (2)
Zimbabwe *Tries:* Viljoen, Letcher *Conversion:* Pohl
Referee J M Fleming (Boroughmuir)

7 January, Wrexham

WALES 9 (1G 1PG) **SCOTLAND 3** (1PG)
Wales *Try:* Bryant *Conversion:* D Evans *Penalty Goal:* D Evans
Scotland *Penalty Goal:* Donaldson
Referee F A Howard (England)

7 April, Glasgow

SCOTLAND 13 (1G 1PG 1T) **IRELAND 26** (1PG 1DG 5T)
Scotland *Tries:* Murray, Robertson *Conversion:* I C Glasgow *Penalty Goal:* I C Glasgow
Ireland *Tries:* Costello (2), Riordan, Rhodes, Montford *Penalty Goal:* Larkin
Dropped Goal: Cullen
Referee A W Bevan (Wales)

11 April, Cambridge

ENGLAND 18 (2PG 3T) **WALES 0**
England *Tries:* Hamer (3) *Penalty Goals:* Hobbs (2)
Referee D H Burnett (Ireland)

14 April, Belfast

IRELAND 15 (5PG) **ENGLAND 7** (1PG 1T)
Ireland *Penalty Goals:* Larkin (5)
England *Try:* Bennett *Penalty Goal:* Hobbs
Referee R Megson (Scotland)

21 April, St Nazaire

FRANCE 12 (2G) **ENGLAND** (2PG 2T)
France *Tries:* Loubet, Clavier *Conversions:* Clavier (2)
England *Tries:* Carling, Bennett *Penalty Goals:* Hobbs (2)
Referee O Jones (Wales)

25 April, Bridgend

WALES 20 (1G 2PG 2T) **FRANCE 0**
Wales *Tries:* Riley, D Evans (2) *Conversion:* D Evans *Penalty Goals:* D Evans (2)
Referee T Allan (Scotland)

COLTS AND YOUTH RUGBY 1983-84

Since its formation in 1949 the Welsh Youth Rugby Union has proved an integral and important part of the game in the Principality. Organised to foster the rugby welfare of boys under 19 years of age, who are in, or registered for, employment, the Union's objective has long been to provide the opportunity to play the amateur code and to prepare the individual for the senior game.

In England, Colts football is in its infancy. It has evolved rapidly to fill a major gap in the changing pattern of 'youth' rugby overseen by the RFU. In little more than a decade its influence has approached that of its Wales Youth counterpart.

The 1983-84 Youth-Colts season was far from being a classic. Although domestically sound, and aided in Wales by the financial support of Esso, and in England by the sponsorship of the Colts County Championship by the National Westminster Bank, neither country can really gain solace from their international performances. However the intensity of the different systems employed, which exhausts all but the cream of young players, has again brought to the fore a small number who show the potential to become outstanding rugby footballers.

The record of Welsh Youth in producing future full internationals and British Lions is excellent. Indeed the present national squad contains no less than 11 former Youth caps, nine of whom have played either against Romania or in the Five Nations' Championship.

Though the England Colts cannot hope to match such an impressive record, five of their number were capped this season.

ENGLAND COLTS

21 January, Torquay
Devon 16 (1G 2PG 1T) **Lancashire 22** (1G 4T)

Dominated throughout by the Lancashire eight, the Colts County Championship was effectively won minutes after half-time when Ashurst scored his second try to add to the Northern county's already commanding 12-point lead. To Devon's credit, they were able to summon the spirit shown in earlier matches and came within an ace of upsetting the favourites.

Devon: *Tries:* Martin, Vanstone *Conversion:* Allen *Penalty Goals:* Kift (2)
Lancashire: *Tries:* Halsall, Ashurst (2), O'Toole, Stott *Conversion:* Wakefield

16 March, Honor Oak Park, London
England Colts 28 (2G 4PG 1T) **Italy Youth 0**

Concluding a three match visit, the Italians displayed a vigorous style and certainly helped disrupt the England eight at the set piece, particularly during the second half when they restricted the scoring to just nine points. Fly-half Stuart Wakefield gave a mature performance, and Jeremy Chadwick impressed at centre.

England Colts: *Tries:* Hargreaves, Halsall, Chadwick *Conversions:* Wakefield (2)
Penalty Goals: Wakefield (4)
Referee J Roberts (Wales)

24 March, Pontypridd
Wales Youth 21 (1G 1PG 3T) **England Colts 10** (1G 1T)

This was by no means a vintage performance by the young dragons but it did enable them to salvage something from what had been a disappointing season. The Welsh dominated the exchanges, exerting relentless pressure, and looked set to easily stop the English recording a fourth successive victory.

But it was to the Colts' credit that their back division, arguably the most confident and purposeful unit seen in England colours at this level, were able to live off the scraps offered them.

Solid scrummaging and dominance at the line-out by Wales finally exposed the inherent weakness of the England pack. Only indecision and the indifferent play of some of the Welsh threequarters restricted the score to ten second half points.

Wales Youth: *Tries:* K Lee (2), I Williams, F Setaro *Conversion:* G Prosser
Penalty Goal: M Watts
England Colts: *Tries:* C Ashurst, A Parsons *Conversion:* S Wakefield
Referee J Fleming (Scotland)

7 April, Fylde
England Colts 9 (3PG) **France Youth 10** (1G 1T)

Without a win in the previous eight meetings, the Colts appeared unable to match the speed of the French, particularly in defence.

The scores were level at half-time, but it took the French just four minutes to conjure what proved to be the winning try. A change in direction gave wing Dominique Dalpos all the time and room to beat off two challenges on his way to the in-goal area.

England Colts: *Penalty Goals:* S Wakefield (2), M Tainton
France Youth: *Tries:* C Delandes, D Dalpos *Conversions:* P Peso
Referee A Hosie (Scotland)

WALES YOUTH

South African Schools to Wales 1983-84

MATCH DETAILS

1983	OPPONENTS	VENUE	RESULTS
23 Dec	Aberavon and Bridgend	Llandybie	W 10-9
24 Dec	Mid Wales and Rhondda	Brecon	W 20-9

28 Dec	Gwent Federation	Monmouth	L 7-13
31 Dec	Neath, Loughor and Swansea	Pontarddulais	W 15-6
1984			
3 Jan	Amman, Llanelli and Pembroke	Whitland	L 12-13
7 Jan	WALES YOUTH	Llanelli	W 9-6

18 March, Rodez
France Youth 31 (3G 3PG 1T) **Wales Youth 3** (1PG)

Despite weathering an early offensive, the Welsh, showing indiscipline at vital moments, succumbed to a team comprised almost entirely of players already competing in the first division of the French Championship. Orchestrated by Didier Farenq, France demonstrated all their traditional threequarter skills.

France Youth: *Tries:* P Jehl (2), D Dalpos, E Leconte *Conversions:* D Farenq (3) *Penalty Goals:* (3)
Wales Youth: *Penalty Goal:* G Prosser
Referee A Welsby (England)

PLAYERS 1983-84

Abbreviations: E – England Colts, W – Wales Youth, F – France Youth, SA – South African Schools, I – Italy Youth

England Colts

Full-back J Rogers (Hereford) [I, W, F]
Threequarters A Parsons (Moseley) [I, W, F], M Tainton (Bristol) [I, W, F], J Chadwick (Roundhay) [I, W, F], P Halsall (Orrell) [I, W, F]
Half-backs S Wakefield (St Helens) [I, W, F], C Read (Westcombe Park) [I, W, F, (R)], R Field (Northampton) [W, (R), F]
Forwards G Holmes (Wasps) [W, F], G Kell (Gateshead Fell) [I, W, F], M Walton (Ainwick) [I, W, F], S Croft (Harrogate) [I, W], P Bowman (Hinkley) [I, W, F], N Hargreaves (Bramley) [I, W, F], C Ashurst (Orrell) [I, W, F], C Fearns (Newport) [I, W, F], G Cole (Wasps) [I], K Ferdinand (Bedworth) [I]
M Tainton was captain in all three matches

Welsh Youth

Full-backs M Rayer (Llandaff North) [SA, F], M Watts (Bridgend) [F (R), E]
Threequarters S Hanson (Pontypool) [SA, F, E], F Setaro (Whitland) [E], A Bateman (Maesteg) [SA, F, E], N Diplock (BSC Port Talbot) [F, E], D O'Driscoll (Llandaff North) [SA, F], C Norman (St Peters, Cardiff) [SA]
Half-backs N Davies (Trimsaren) [SA, F, E], K Lee (Rumney) [SA, F, E], R Downes (Pontypridd) [E, (R)], A Parry (Cardiff) [E (R)]
Forwards R Fussell (Whitland) [SA], A Langford (Neath Colts) [SA, F], K Jones (Pontypridd) [SA], N Jones (Cardiff) [SA], M Jones (Glanhowy) [SA], W Wilkinson (Rumney) [SA], D Jones (Abertillery) [SA], S Foster (Pontrhydyfen) [F, E], D Roberts (Llanelli) [E], D Conway (Cardiff) [F, E], P Jackson (Neath Colts) [F, E], A Sutton (Abergavenny) [F (R), E], I Williams (Glanhowy) [SA, F, E], G Jenkins (Abertillery) [F, E], G Prosser (SW Police) [F, E]
M Rayer was captain against South Africa and France
M Watts was captain against England

THE 1983-84 SEASON IN SCOTLAND

Bill McMurtrie *Glasgow Herald*

At last it was Scotland's year: the first Triple Crown and championship since 1938, the first Grand Slam since 1925, and the vindication of Jim Telfer as coach after the disappointments of the Lions' tour in New Zealand in 1983. Telfer had nurtured and developed the Scottish team since 1980, with one season off while he concentrated on the Lions' selection, but not only in the coaching had the basis for the Grand Slam been laid down in those four years. The selecting policy directed by Ian MacGregor, convener of selectors, and his committee was of much importance in the building of the championship triumph.

In 1980 the Scots went on a short tour in France without their Lions. Their opposition included a French Barbarians team, which was essentially the French 1977 Grand Slam side. The competition in the three matches on that tour initiated the newer members of the Scots party in the demands they would have to face in the future, and it is significant that only two of the uncapped players on that trip have failed to win caps since. That was Telfer's first time in charge, and during the next two British summers he took the Scots on even more testing tours, first to New Zealand and then to Australia.

Scotland shared the 1982 Test series against the Wallabies, winning the international in Brisbane. This was the start of a successful run for the Scots away from home. Beginning with the win against Wales in 1982 and running up to the Triple Crown match two years later, Scotland won five out of seven away internationals. The victories came in Cardiff, Brisbane, Twickenham, Cardiff again, and Lansdowne Road, and the only defeats were in Sydney and Paris. Scotland's 21-12 win at Twickenham in 1983 was Jim Aitken's first international as captain, and it was the first of six successive matches without defeat with him in charge. The Twickenham victory was followed by the 25-25 draw with the All Blacks at Murrayfield in November, 1983, and then the Grand Slam foursome.

Through all those pressure matches has grown an effervescent spirit within the Scottish squad, and the results of this are obvious. Scotland's composure was at its most fragile at the beginning of the Grand Slam season in the match against England. They survived despite their aberrations because England's Dusty Hare was off target. Scotland's temperament was at its best against France. Enough penalties were conceded for Scotland to have lost to England but the count went the other way in the match against France, the Scots refusing to stoop to the ball-killing game that eventually proved the visitors' undoing.

Earlier, the draw with the All Blacks was less than Scotland had hoped for. New Zealand, without so many big names, were by no means as strong as they had been in whitewashing the Lions in the summer, and the November international was as good a chance as any Scotland had had of beating the All Blacks for the first time.

A fortnight before the international Scottish hopes took a hefty dent at Galashiels. The All Blacks won by 30-9, scoring five tries to nil against the South of Scotland, seven of whose players were to go on to take part in the international. Aitken missed the Galashiels match because of 'flu, but 12 days before his thirty-sixth birthday Scotland, under his command, put the Borderers' defeat out of their minds and played with persistence, even though they conceded three tries. John Rutherford's two dropped goals and Peter Dods' five penalty goals kept Scotland in the match, and Jim Pollock's late try from David Johnston's kick through tied the scores. From well out on the right, however, Dods failed with the conversion that would have given Scotland their first victory over the All Blacks.

England's win against New Zealand put Scotland's draw in perspective but two months later, the Scots came home from Cardiff with their second successive victory there. Iain Paxton and Aitken scored the tries, each his first in international rugby, but the crucial factor was the way that Aitken's Gala colleague, David Leslie, dominated the line-out tail and gathered in a hoard of breakdown possession. It was then that Scotland had the first scent of the big prizes. Victory away from home gave them the boost they needed, and they followed the Cardiff success with an 18-6 win over England, with tries by Euan Kennedy and David Johnston, the Watsonian centres.

Scotland conceded too many penalties in that match – in sharp contrast to their previous game. In Cardiff they were penalised only once in the second half whereas over the whole Calcutta Cup match the Scots gave away no fewer than 20 penalties. Fortunately Hare missed with six of his kicks, but it was a major point of concern for the visit to Ireland, the last leg of the Triple Crown.

No one need have worried. The Scots had a dream start. They were given the advantage of the strong wind in the first half by Willie Duggan, Ireland's captain, and by the interval they led by 22-0. Roy Laidlaw scored two tries, then Duggan helped Scotland again by conceding a penalty try dived into the Scottish scrum to deny the Scots a pushover. Peter Dods notched up four goals. Laidlaw, however, was injured in that first half, and retired at the interval with what was later diagnosed as 'footballer's migraine'. Gordon Hunter took over for his first cap, joining his Selkirk half-back partner, John Rutherford, and in the final flourish the replacement scrum-half made the lateral break for a Keith Robertson try. Dods finished off with an overlap try for a total of 16 points, one short of Andy Irvine's record in an international for Scotland. Scotland's score in the 32-9 victory and the margin, too, were records for the international series against Ireland. It was a truly emphatic way to win the Triple Crown for the first time in 46 years.

Laidlaw was back for the final international, which was just as well for Scotland as Hunter's left cheekbone had been fractured in a collision with a spectator as the new cap ran from the field at the end of the Dublin match. In the game at Murrayfield against the French, who were also unbeaten, Dods equalled Irvine's record, kicking five penalty goals and converting the try that Jim Calder snapped up at a line-out on the visitors' goal-line. On each side of that try Dods kicked a penalty goal. It all helped Scotland to finish off with 12 points in seven minutes as Murrayfield echoed to delirious voices celebrating the Grand Slam even before it was won. Thus ended 59 years of waiting.

Over the four matches Scotland scored 10 tries, the most since 1927, and conceded just three, and Dods had 50 points, far and away a Scottish record for the championship. On top of that, he could add his 15 against the All Blacks. The team total of 86 points was also a record in the championship.

Scotland's 'B' team also had a successful season, beating Ireland by 22-13 at Melrose and France by 13-10 in Albi, emulating the 1979-80 side which won at Lansdowne Road and Aurillac. Campbell and Hunter came out of the 1983-84 'B' team for their first caps, joining Kennedy as

Scotland prepare for their Triple Crown match against Ireland in Dublin. Back Row, L-R: *F A Howard (referee), O E Doyle (deputy touch-judge), D G Leslie, I Milne, I A M Paxton, A J Tomes, A Campbell, J H Calder, D I Johnston, J A F Trigg (touch-judge), R Quittenton (touch-judge),* Front Row, L-R: *J Pollock, K Robertson, J Rutherford, J Aitken, R J Laidlaw, C T Deans, G R T Baird, P Dods.*

Scotland's new internationals of the season.

Scotland's Grand Slam was not the only clean sweep led by Jim Aitken. The Gala prop also captained the South of Scotland to victory in the district championship, the Borderers beating North and Midlands 44-6, the Anglo-Scots 15-0, Edinburgh 29-15, and Glasgow 32-9, the second successive season in which they defeated all four other districts.

Over the whole season the South played eight matches, winning six. They lost to Ulster 21-22 and to the All Blacks. Their scoring was dominated by Peter Dods, who was responsible for no fewer than 97 of the Borderers' 245 points. In his 42 games for the district the Gala full-back has now scored 303 points, a figure that has been exceeded for any Scottish district only by his predecessor in the international XV, Andy Irvine.

Edinburgh, the Anglo-Scots and Glasgow were joint second in the district championship, each with two wins. Glasgow beat Edinburgh by 14-12, the Anglos defeated Glasgow 20-16, Edinburgh won by 12-7 against the Anglos, and all three beat North and Midlands, who have now lost 24 successive championship matches.

Hawick, like Scotland and the South, had a clean sweep, taking the Schweppes Trophy club championship from Gala. It was Hawick's seventh championship in the 11 years of the competition, and they also took the Border League, winning all but one match. In all matches Hawick passed 1,000 points for the first time in their history, reaching four figures in the game in which they completed their national championship campaign with a 52-9 win over Selkirk. They scored 167 tries, and Colin Gass had 323 points for the club. Two Hawick players were top of the scoring lists in the championship first division, Gass with 178 points and Keith Mitchell with 12 tries. Two of their colleagues also finished with double figures in the try count: Keith Murray had 11 and Billy Murray the Hawick captain, 10.

Peter Dods was Scottish rugby's top scorer overall in the season with 403 points, 210 of them for Gala. His club, however, had to settle for second place in the championship, beaten only by Hawick.

Kilmarnock and Haddington were relegated to the second division, the latter losing all 12 of the games they played in the championship. Glasgow Academicals and their Edinburgh namesakes stepped up as champions and runners-up in the second division. The Glasgow club had been in the first division in the championship's first season, 1973-74, while Edinburgh Academicals had been in the second throughout the 11 seasons of the competition.

Another of the original first division clubs, Edinburgh Wanderers, were champions of the third division, losing only to Madras College FP, and that was once the title was settled.

Kelso won five of the eight Border sevens tournaments, Hawick took two of the others, Richmond won Gala's centenary event, and London Welsh lifted the Haig Trophy at Murrayfield.

Also on the international pitch Stewart's-Melville FP beat Heriot's FP 15-9 in the final of the Murrayfield Cup competition, which was extended to include the major east clubs for the first time. Ayr won the Glasgow and District Cup, beating Hutchesons' in the final, but lost to Kilmarnock in the Ayrshire Cup. Howe of Fife took the Midlands Cup, beating Dundee High School FP by just 10-9 in the final.

INTER-DISTRICT CHAMPIONSHIP

	P	*W*	*D*	*L*	*F*	*A*	*Pts*
South	4	4	0	0	120	30	8
Edinburgh	4	2	0	2	107	59	4
Anglo-Scots	4	2	0	2	46	43	4
Glasgow	4	2	0	2	57	77	4
North & Midlands	4	0	0	4	28	149	0

SCHWEPPES CLUB CHAMPIONSHIP

Division 1	*P*	*W*	*D*	*L*	*F*	*A*	*Pts*
Hawick	13	13	0	0	477	53	26
Gala	13	12	0	1	299	75	24
Stewart's-Melville FP	13	9	0	4	327	151	18
Kelso	13	9	0	4	266	161	18
Heriot's FP	12	8	1	3	258	145	17
Watsonians	13	8	0	5	203	190	16
Boroughmuir	12	7	0	5	215	205	14
Selkirk	13	5	0	8	215	222	10
West of Scotland	13	4	0	9	194	303	8
Jedforest	13	3	1	9	142	216	7
Melrose	13	3	1	9	118	243	7
Ayr	12	3	1	8	87	310	7
Kilmarnock	13	2	2	9	155	286	6
Haddington	12	0	0	12	64	460	0

Champions: Hawick
Relegated: Kilmarnock, Haddington
Previous champions: Hawick 6 times, 1973-74 to 1977-78, 1981-82; Heriot's FP 1978-79; Gala 3 times, 1979-80, 1980-81, 1982-83

Division 2	*P*	*W*	*D*	*L*	*F*	*A*	*Pts*
Glasgow Acads	12	10	1	1	268	114	21
Edinburgh Acads	13	10	0	3	172	102	20
Portobello FP	13	9	0	4	198	121	18
Stirling County	13	8	0	5	210	155	16
Preston Lodge FP	13	6	1	6	165	143	13
Gordonians	13	6	1	6	162	174	13
Langholm	12	6	1	5	110	182	13
Highland	13	6	0	7	160	164	12
Clarkston	13	5	1	7	194	193	11
Jordanhill	13	5	1	7	128	168	11
Royal High	13	5	0	8	147	207	10
Howe of Fife	13	4	1	8	133	159	9
Glasgow High/ Kelvinside	13	3	1	9	140	209	7
Aberdeen GSFP	13	3	0	10	107	194	6

Promoted: Glasgow Academicals, Edinburgh Academicals
Relegated: Glasgow High/Kelvinside, Aberdeen GSFP

Division 3	*P*	*W*	*D*	*L*	*F*	*A*	*Pts*
Edinburgh Wands	13	12	0	1	245	91	24
Dunfermline	13	10	1	2	240	64	21
Musselburgh	13	10	1	2	182	95	21
Cambuslang	13	7	0	6	131	162	14
Dalziel HSFP	13	6	0	7	119	138	12
Greenock Wands	13	6	0	7	112	196	12
Hutchesons'	13	5	1	7	115	132	11
Hillhead	13	5	1	7	156	178	11
Leith Acads	13	5	1	7	101	131	11
Kirkcaldy	13	5	0	8	105	127	10
Madras College FP	13	5	0	8	87	122	10
Trinity Acads	13	5	0	8	140	178	10
Aberdeen U	13	4	1	8	163	200	9
Glenrothes	13	3	0	10	135	217	6

Promoted: Edinburgh Wanderers, Dunfermline
Relegated: Aberdeen University, Glenrothes

Division 4	P	W	D	L	F	A	Pts
Perthshire	13	11	0	2	205	92	22
Morgan Academy FP	13	10	0	3	263	104	20
Alloa	13	10	0	3	199	119	20
Corstorphine	13	8	2	3	164	115	18
Grangemouth	13	6	1	6	151	114	13
Dumfries	13	6	1	6	147	123	13
Harris Academy FP	12	5	2	5	135	123	12
Broughton	13	6	0	7	131	185	12
Marr	13	4	3	6	127	144	11
Currie	11	5	0	6	156	139	10
Edinburgh U	12	5	0	7	141	137	10
Allan Glen's	13	4	1	8	101	212	9
Ardrossan Acads	13	3	0	10	104	275	6
Old Aloysians	13	1	0	12	73	215	2

Promoted: Perthshire, Morgan Academy FP
Relegated: Ardrossan Academicals, Old Aloysians

Division 5	P	W	D	L	F	A	Pts
Dundee HSFP	13	12	1	0	329	40	25
Lenzie	13	11	0	2	211	131	22
Peebles	13	9	1	3	183	114	19
Stewartry	13	7	0	6	146	162	14
Penicuik	13	7	0	6	145	189	14
Cartha QP	13	6	1	6	157	152	13
Drumpellier	13	6	1	6	123	158	13
Livingston	13	6	0	7	125	145	12
Lismore	13	6	0	7	145	175	12
East Kilbride	13	5	1	7	143	196	11
Moray	13	4	1	8	130	151	9
Hamilton Acads	13	4	0	9	106	177	8
Garnock	13	2	2	9	132	191	6
North Berwick	13	1	2	10	82	176	4

Promoted: Dundee HSFP, Lenzie
Relegated: Garnock, North Berwick

Division 6	P	W	D	L	F	A	Pts
Panmure	13	11	1	1	242	89	23
Hillfoots	13	11	0	2	253	134	22
Linlithgow	12	8	2	2	277	86	18
Crieff	12	8	0	4	210	104	16
Dalkeith	13	7	1	5	198	193	15
Strathclyde Police	13	6	0	7	129	178	12
Dunbar	12	5	0	7	107	124	10
Cumbernauld	12	5	0	7	119	147	10
Stobswell FP	13	5	0	8	171	210	10
Dundee U	11	5	0	6	111	202	10
Walkerburn	13	5	0	8	114	217	10
Paisley	13	4	1	8	143	226	9
Wigtownshire	13	4	0	9	120	157	8
Uddingston	13	1	1	11	108	235	3

Promoted: Panmure, Hillfoots
Relegated: Wigtownshire, Uddingston

Division 7	P	W	D	L	F	A	Pts
Earlston	13	12	0	1	210	66	24
Biggar	13	11	1	1	276	68	23
Waysiders	13	9	1	3	223	142	19
Montrose	12	8	0	4	174	110	16
Edinburgh Northern	13	7	1	5	142	160	15
Waid Academy FP	13	5	3	5	144	104	13
Hyndland FP	13	5	3	5	105	106	13
Aberdeenshire	13	5	1	7	207	128	11
Falkirk	13	5	1	7	150	202	11
Stirling U	13	5	0	8	125	248	10
Strathmore	13	4	1	8	116	186	9
Cumnock	13	4	0	9	123	174	8
St Andrews U	13	3	1	9	113	262	7
Strathendrick	12	0	1	11	75	227	1

Promoted: Earlston, Biggar
Relegated: Cumnock, St Andrews University, Strathendrick
District champions (promoted to Division 7 of the Schweppes championship): Murrayfield (East), Clydebank (West), Rosyth and District (Midlands)

BORDER LEAGUE

	P	W	D	L	F	A	Pts
Hawick	12	11	0	1	354	79	22
Gala	11	9	0	2	231	101	18
Kelso	10	5	0	5	187	105	10
Selkirk	10	5	0	5	166	167	10
Jedforest	10	4	0	6	112	159	8
Melrose	11	3	0	8	84	255	6
Langholm	10	0	0	10	43	311	0

SCOTTISH INTERNATIONAL PLAYERS
(up to 30 April 1984)

ABBREVIATIONS

A	Australia	*W*	Wales
E	England	(C)	Centenary match v England at Murrayfield, 1971 (non-championship)
F	France	P	Scotland v President's Overseas XV, at Murrayfield, in SFU's Centenary season, 1972-73
I	Ireland	(R)	Replacement
NSW	New South Wales	Note:	Years given for Five Nations' matches are for second half of season; eg 1972 means season 1971-72. Years for all other matches refer to the actual year of the match.
NZ	New Zealand		
R	Romania		
SA	South Africa		

Abercrombie, C H (United Services) 1910 *I, E,* 1911 *F, W,* 1913 *F, W*
Abercrombie, J G (Edinburgh U) 1949 *F, W, I,* 1950 *F, W, I, E*
Agnew, W C C (Stewart's Coll FP) 1930 *W, I*
Ainslie, R (Edinburgh Inst FP) 1879 *I, E,* 1880 *I, E,* 1881 *E,* 1882 *I, E*
Ainslie, T (Edinburgh Inst FP) 1881 *E,* 1882 *I, E,* 1883 *W, I, E,* 1884 *W, I, E,* 1885 *W, I*
Aitchison, G R (Edinburgh Wands) 1883 *I*
Aitchison, T G (Gala) 1929 *W, I, E*
Aitken, A I (Edinburgh Inst FP) 1889 *I*
Aitken, G G (Oxford U) 1924 *W, I, E,* 1925 *F, W, I, E,* 1929 *F*
Aitken, J (Gala) 1977 *E, I, F,* 1981 *F, W, E, I, NZ* (2), *R, A,* 1982 *E, I, F, W,* 1983 *F, W, E, NZ,* 1984 *W, E, I, F*
Aitken, R (London Scottish) 1947 *W*
Allan, B (Glasgow Acads) 1881 *I*
Allan, J L (Melrose) 1952 *F, W, I,* 1953 *W*
Allan, J L F (Cambridge U) 1957 *I, E*
Allan, J W (Melrose) 1927 *F,* 1928 *I,* 1929 *F, W, I, E,* 1930 *F, E,* 1931 *F, W, I, E,* 1932 *SA, W, I,* 1934 *I, E*
Allan, R C (Hutchesons' GSFP) 1969 *I*
Allardice, W D (Aberdeen GSFP) 1948 *A, F, W, I,* 1949 *F, W, I, E*
Allen, H W (Glasgow Acads) 1873 *E*
Anderson, A H (Glasgow Acads) 1894 *I*
Anderson, D G (London Scottish) 1889 *I,* 1890 *W, I, E,* 1891 *W, E,* 1892 *W, E*
Anderson, E (Stewart's Coll FP) 1947 *I, E*
Anderson, J W (W of Scotland) 1872 *E*
Anderson, T (Merchiston) 1882 *I*
Angus, A W (Watsonians) 1909 *W,* 1910 *F, W, E,* 1911 *W, I,* 1912 *F, W, I, E, SA,* 1913 *F, W,* 1914 *E,* 1920 *F, W, I, E*
Anton, P A (St Andrew's U) 1873 *E*
Arneil, R J (Edinburgh Acads, Leicester and Northampton) 1968 *I, E, A,* 1969 *F, W, I, E, SA,* 1970 *F, W, I, E, A,* 1971 *F, W, I, E* (2[1C]), 1972 *F, W, E,* 1973 *NZ*
Arthur, A (Glasgow Acads) 1875 *E,* 1876 *E*
Arthur, J W (Glasgow Acads) 1871 *E,* 1872 *E*
Asher, A G G (Oxford U) 1882 *I,* 1884 *W, I, E,* 1885 *W,* 1886 *I, E*
Auld, W (W of Scotland) 1889 *W,* 1890 *W*
Auldjo, L J (Abertay) 1878 *E*

Bain, D McL (Oxford U) 1911 *E,* 1912 *F, W, E, SA,* 1913 *F, W, I, E,* 1914 *W, I*
Baird, G R T (Kelso) 1981 *A,* 1982 *E, I, F, W, A* (2), 1983 *I, F, W, E, NZ,* 1984 *W, E, I, F*
Balfour, A (Watsonians) 1896 *W, I, E,* 1897 *E*
Balfour, L M (Edinburgh Acads) 1872 *E*
Bannerman, E M (Edinburgh Acads) 1872 *E,* 1873 *E*
Bannerman, J M (Glasgow HSFP) 1921 *F, W, I, E,* 1922 *F, W, I, E,* 1923 *F, W, I, E,* 1924 *F, W, I, E,* 1925 *F, W, I, E,* 1926 *F, W, I, E,* 1927 *F, W, I, E, NSW,* 1928 *F, W, I, E,* 1929 *F, W, I, E*
Barnes, I A (Hawick) 1972 *W,* 1974 *F* (R), 1975 *E* (R), *NZ,* 1977 *I, F, W*
Barrie, R W (Hawick) 1936 *E*
Bearne, K R F (Cambridge U, London Scottish) 1960 *F, W*
Beattie, J A (Hawick) 1929 *F, W,* 1930 *W,* 1931 *F, W, I, E,* 1932 *SA, W, I, E,* 1933 *W, E, I,* 1934 *I, E,* 1935 *W, I, E, NZ,* 1936 *W, I, E*
Beattie, J R (Glasgow Acads) 1980 *I, F, W, E,* 1981 *F, W, E, I,* 1983 *F, W, E, NZ,* 1984 *E* (R)
Bedell-Sivright, D R (Cambridge U, Edinburgh U) 1900 *W,* 1901 *W, I, E,* 1902 *W, I, E,* 1903 *W, I,* 1904 *W, I, E,* 1905 *NZ,* 1906 *W, I, E, SA,* 1907 *W, I, E,* 1908 *W, I*
Bedell-Sivright, J V (Cambridge U) 1902 *W*
Begbie, T A (Edinburgh Wands) 1881 *I, E*
Bell, D L (Watsonians) 1975 *I, F, W, E*
Bell, J A (Clydesdale) 1901 *W, I, E,* 1902 *W, I, E*
Bell, L H I (Edinburgh Acads) 1900 *E,* 1904 *W, I*
Berkeley, W V (Oxford U) 1926 *F,* 1929 *F, W, I*
Berry, C W (Fettesian-Lorettonians) 1884 *I, E,* 1885 *W,* 1887 *I, W, E,* 1888 *W, I*
Bertram, D M (Watsonians) 1922 *F, W, I, E,* 1923 *F, W, I, E,* 1924 *W, I, E*
Biggar, A G (London Scottish) 1969 *SA,* 1970 *F, I, E, A,* 1971 *F, W, I, E* (2[1C]), 1972 *F, W*
Biggar, M A (London Scottish) 1975 *I, F, W, E,* 1976 *W, E, I,* 1977 *I, F, W,* 1978 *I, F, W, E, NZ,* 1979 *W, E, I, F, NZ,* 1980 *I, F, W, E*
Birkett, G A (Harlequins, London Scottish) 1975 *NZ*
Bishop, J M (Glasgow Acads) 1893 *I*
Bisset, A A (RIE Coll) 1904 *W*
Black, A W (Edinburgh U) 1947 *F, W,* 1948 *E,* 1950 *W, I, E*
Black, W P (Glasgow HSFP) 1948 *F, W, I, E,* 1951 *E*
Blackadder, W F (W of Scotland) 1938 *E*
Blaikie, C F (Heriot's FP) 1963 *I, E,* 1966 *E,* 1968 *A,* 1969 *F, W, I, E*
Blair, P C B (Cambridge U) 1912 *SA,* 1913 *F, W, I, E*
Bolton, W H (W of Scotland) 1876 *E*
Borthwick, J B (Stewart's Coll FP) 1938 *W, I*
Bos, F H ten (Oxford U, London Scottish) 1959 *E,* 1960 *F, W, SA,* 1961 *F, SA, W, I, E,* 1962 *F, W, I, E,* 1963 *F, W, I, E*
Boswell, J D (W of Scotland) 1889 *W, I,* 1890 *W, I, E,* 1891 *W, I, E,* 1892 *W, I, E,* 1893 *I, E,* 1894 *I, E*
Bowie, T C (Watsonians) 1913 *I, E,* 1914 *I, E*
Boyd, G M (Glasgow HSFP) 1926 *E*
Boyd, J L (United Services) 1912 *E, SA*
Boyle, A C W (London Scottish) 1963 *F, W, I*

Boyle, A H W (St Thomas's Hospital, London Scottish) 1966 *A*, 1967 *F*, *NZ*, 1968 *F*, *W*, *I*
Brash, J C (Cambridge U) 1961 *E*
Breakey, R W (Gosforth) 1978 *E*
Brewis, N T (Edinburgh Inst FP) 1876 *E*, 1878 *E*, 1879 *I*, *E*, 1880 *I*, *E*
Brewster, A K (Stewart's-Melville FP) 1977 *E*, 1980 *I*, *F*
Brown, A H (Heriot's FP) 1928 *E*, 1929 *F*, *W*
Brown, A R (Gala) 1971 *E* (2[1C]), 1972 *F*, *W*, *E*
Brown, C H C (Dunfermline) 1929 *E*
Brown, D I (Cambridge U) 1933 *W*, *E*, *I*
Brown, G L (W of Scotland) 1969 *SA*, 1970 *F*, *W* (R), *I*, *E*, *A* 1971 *F*, *W*, *I*, *E* (2[1C]), 1972 *F*, *W*, *E*, *NZ*, 1973 *E* (R), *P*, 1974 *W*, *E*, *I*, *F*, 1975 *I*, *F*, *W*, *E*, *A*, 1976 *F*, *W*, *E*, *I*
Brown, J A (Glasgow Acads) 1908 *W*, *I*
Brown, J B (Glasgow Acads) 1879 *I*, *E*, 1880 *I*, *E*, 1881 *I*, *E*, 1882 *I*, *E*, 1883 *W*, *E*, 1884 *W*, *I*, *E*, 1885 *I*, 1886 *W*, *I*, *E*
Brown, P C (W of Scotland, Gala) 1964 *F*, *NZ*, *W*, *I*, *E*, 1965 *I*, *E*, *SA*, 1966 *A*, 1969 *I*, *E*, 1970 *W*, *E*, 1971 *F*, *W*, *I*, *E* (2[1C]), 1972 *F*, *W*, *E*, *NZ*, 1973 *F*, *W*, *I*, *E*, *P*
Brown, T G (Heriot's FP) 1929 *W*
Brown, W D (Glasgow Acads) 1871 *E*, 1872 *E*, 1873 *E*, 1874 *E*, 1875 *E*
Brown, W S (Edinburgh Inst FP) 1880 *I*, *E*, 1882 *I*, *E*, 1883 *W*, *I*, *E*
Browning, A (Glasgow HSFP) 1920 *I*, 1922 *F*, *W*, *I*, 1923 *W*, *I*, *E*
Bruce, C R (Glasgow Acads) 1947 *F*, *W*, *I*, *E*, 1949 *F*, *W*, *I*, *E*
Bruce, N S (Blackheath, Army and London Scottish) 1958 *F*, *A*, *I*, *E*, 1959 *F*, *W*, *I*, *E*, 1960 *F*, *W*, *I*, *E*, *SA*, 1961 *F*, *SA*, *W*, *I*, *E*, 1962 *F*, *W*, *I*, *E*, 1963 *F*, *W*, *I*, *E*, 1964 *F*, *NZ*, *W*, *I*, *E*
Bruce, R M (Gordonians) 1947 *A*, 1948 *F*, *W*, *I*
Bruce-Lockhart, J H (London Scottish) 1913 *W*, 1920 *E*
Bruce-Lockhart, L (London Scottish) 1948 *E*, 1950 *F*, *W*, 1953 *I*, *E*
Bruce-Lockhart, R B (Cambridge U and London Scottish) 1937 *I*, 1939 *I*, *E*
Bryce, C C (Glasgow Acads) 1873 *E*, 1874 *E*
Bryce, R D H (W of Scotland) 1973 *I* (R)
Bryce, W E (Selkirk) 1922 *W*, *I*, *E*, 1923 *F*, *W*, *I*, *E*, 1924 *F*, *W*, *I*, *E*
Brydon, W R C (Heriot's FP) 1939 *W*
Buchanan, A (Royal HSFP) 1871 *E*
Buchanan, F G (Kelvinside Acads and Oxford U) 1910 *F*, 1911 *F*, *W*
Buchanan, J C R (Stewart's Coll, FP) 1921 *W*, *I*, *E*, 1922 *W*, *I*, *E*, 1923 *F*, *W*, *I*, *E*, 1924 *F*, *W*, *I*, *E*, 1925 *F*, *I*
Bucher, A M (Edinburgh Acads) 1897 *E*
Budge, G M (Edinburgh Wands) 1950 *F*, *W*, *I*, *E*
Bullmore, H H (Edinburgh U) 1902 *I*
Burnet, P J (London Scottish and Edinburgh Acads) 1960 *SA*
Burnet, W (Hawick) 1912 *E*
Burnet, W A (W of Scotland) 1934 *W*, 1935 *W*, *I*, *E*, *NZ* 1936 *W*, *I*, *E*
Burnett, J N (Heriot's FP) 1980 *I*, *F*, *W*, *E*
Burrell, G (Gala) 1950 *F*, *W*, *I*, 1951 *SA*

Cairns, A G (Watsonians) 1903 *W*, *I*, *E*, 1904 *W*, *I*, *E*, 1905 *W*, *I*, *E*, 1906 *W*, *I*, *E*
Calder, J H (Stewart's-Melville FP) 1981 *F*, *W*, *E*, *I*, *NZ* (2), *R*, *A*, 1982 *E*, *I*, *F*, *W*, *A* (2), 1983 *I*, *F*, *W*, *E*, *NZ*, 1984 *W*, *E*, *I*, *F*
Cameron, A (Glasgow HSFP) 1948 *W*, 1950 *I*, *E*, 1951 *F*, *W*, *I*, *E*, *SA*, 1953 *I*, *E*, 1955 *F*, *W*, *I*, *E*, 1956 *F*, *W*, *I*
Cameron, A D (Hillhead HSFP) 1951 *F*, 1954 *F*, *W*
Cameron, A W (Watsonians) 1887 *W*, 1893 *W*, 1894 *I*
Cameron, D (Glasgow HSFP) 1953 *I*, *E*, 1954 *F*, *NZ*, *I*, *E*
Cameron, N W (Glasgow U) 1952 *E*, 1953 *F*, *W*
Campbell, A J (Hawick) 1984 *I*, *F*
Campbell, G T (London Scottish) 1892 *W*, *I*, *E*, 1893 *I*, *E*, 1894 *W*, *I*, *E*, 1895 *W*, *I*, *E*, 1896 *W*, *I*, *E*, 1897 *I*, 1899 *I*, 1900 *E*
Campbell, H H (Cambridge U, London Scottish) 1947 *I*, *E*, 1948 *I*, *E*
Campbell, J A (W of Scotland) 1878 *E*, 1879 *I*, *E*, 1881 *I*, *E*
Campbell, J A (Cambridge U) 1900 *I*
Campbell, N M (London Scottish) 1956 *F*, *W*
Campbell-Lamerton, M J (Halifax, Army, London Scottish) 1961 *F*, *SA*, *W*, *I*, 1962 *F*, *W*, *I*, *E*, 1963 *F*, *W*, *I*, *E*, 1964 *I*, *E*, 1965 *F*, *W*, *I*, *E*, *SA*, 1966 *F*, *W*, *I*, *E*
Carmichael, A B (W of Scotland) 1967 *I*, *NZ*, 1968 *F*, *W*, *I*, *E*, *A*, 1969 *F*, *W*, *I*, *E*, *SA*, 1970 *F*, *W*, *I*, *E*, *A*, 1971 *F*, *W*, *I*, *E* (2[1C]), 1972 *F*, *W*, *E*, *NZ*, 1973 *F*, *W*, *I*, *E*, *P*, 1974 *W*, *E*, *I*, *F*, 1975 *I*, *F*, *W*, *E*, *NZ*, *A*, 1976 *F*, *W*, *E*, *I*, 1977 *E*, *I* (R), *F*, *W*, 1978 *I*
Carmichael, J H (Watsonians) 1921 *F*, *W*, *I*
Carrick, J S (Glasgow Acads) 1876 *E*, 1877 *E*
Cassels, D Y (W of Scotland) 1880 *E*, 1881 *I*, 1882 *I*, *E*, 1883 *W*, *I*, *E*
Cathcart, C W (Edinburgh U) 1872 *E*, 1873 *E*, 1876 *E*
Cawkwell, G L (Oxford U) 1947 *F*
Chalmers, T (Glasgow Acads) 1871 *E*, 1872 *E*, 1873 *E*, 1874 *E*, 1875 *E*, 1876 *E*
Chambers, H F T (Edinburgh U) 1888 *W*, *I*, 1889 *W*, *I*
Charters, R G (Hawick) 1955 *W*, *I*, *E*
Chisholm, D H (Melrose) 1964 *I*, *E*, 1965 *E*, *SA*, 1966 *F*, *I*, *E*, *A*, 1967 *F*, *W*, *NZ*, 1968 *F*, *W*, *I*
Chisholm, R W T (Melrose) 1955 *I*, *E*, 1956 *F*, *W*, *I*, *E*, 1958 *F*, *W*, *A*, *I*, 1960 *SA*
Church, W C (Glasgow Acads) 1906 *W*
Clark, R L (Edinburgh Wands, Royal Navy) 1972 *F*, *W*, *E*, *NZ*, 1973 *F*, *W*, *I*, *E*, *P*
Clauss, P R A (Oxford U) 1891 *W*, *I*, *E*, 1892 *W*, *E*, 1895 *I*
Clay, A T (Edinburgh Acads) 1886 *W*, *I*, *E*, 1887 *I*, *W*, *E*, 1888 *W*
Clunies-Ross, A (St Andrews U) 1871 *E*
Coltman, S (Hawick) 1948 *I*, 1949 *F*, *W*, *I*, *E*
Colvile, A G (Merchistonians, Blackheath) 1871 *E*, 1872 *E*
Connell, G C (Trinity Acads and London Scottish) 1968 *E*, *A*, 1969 *F*, *E*, 1970 *F*
Cooper, M McG (Oxford U) 1936 *W*, *I*
Cordial, I F (Edinburgh Wands) 1952 *F*, *W*, *I*, *E*
Cotter, J L (Hillhead HSFP) 1934 *I*, *E*
Cottington, G S (Kelso) 1934 *I*, *E*, 1935 *W*, *I*, 1936 *E*
Coughtrie, S (Edinburgh Acads) 1959 *F*, *W*, *I*, *E*, 1962 *W*, *I*, *E*, 1963 *F*, *W*, *I*, *E*
Couper, J H (W of Scotland) 1896 *W*, *I*, 1899 *I*
Coutts, F H (Melrose, Army) 1947 *W*, *I*, *E*
Coutts, I D F (Old Alleynians) 1951 *F*, 1952 *E*
Cowan, R C (Selkirk) 1961 *F*, 1962 *F*, *W*, *I*, *E*
Cowie, W L K (Edinburgh Wands) 1953 *E*
Cownie, W B (Watsonians) 1893 *W*, *I*, *E*, 1894 *W*, *I*, *E*, 1895 *W*, *I*, *E*
Crabbie, G E (Edinburgh Acads) 1904 *W*
Crabbie, J E (Edinburgh Acads, Oxford U) 1900 *W*, 1902 *I*, 1903 *W*, *I*, 1904 *E*, 1905 *W*
Craig, J B (Heriot's FP) 1939 *W*
Cranston, A G (Hawick) 1976 *W*, *E*, *I*, 1977 *E*, *W*, 1978 *F* (R), *W*, *E*, *NZ*, 1981 *NZ* (2)
Crawford, J A (Army, London Scottish) 1934 *I*
Crawford, W H (United Services, RN) 1938 *W*, *I*, *E*, 1939 *W*, *E*
Crichton-Miller, D (Gloucester) 1931 *W*, *I*, *E*
Crole, G B (Oxford U) 1920 *F*, *W*, *I*, *E*
Cross, M (Merchistonians) 1875 *E*, 1876 *E*, 1877 *I*, *E*, 1878 *E*, 1879 *I*, *E*, 1880 *I*, *E*
Cross, W (Merchistonians) 1871 *E*, 1872 *E*
Cumming, R S (Aberdeen U) 1921 *F*, *W*
Cunningham, G (Oxford U) 1908 *W*, *I*, 1909 *W*, *E*, 1910 *F*, *I*, *E*, 1911 *E*
Cunningham, R F (Gala) 1978 *NZ*, 1979 *W*, *E*
Currie, L R (Dunfermline) 1947 *A*, 1948 *F*, *W*, *I*, 1949 *F*, *W*, *I*, *E*
Cuthbertson, W (Kilmarnock, Harlequins) 1980 *I*, 1981 *W*, *E*, *I*, *NZ* (2), *R*, *A*, 1982 *E*, *I*, *F*, *W*, *A* (2), 1983 *I*, *F*, *W*, *NZ*, 1984 *W*, *E*

Dalgleish, A (Gala) 1890 *W*, *E*, 1891 *W*, *I*, 1892 *W*, 1893 *W*, 1894 *W*, *I*
Dalgleish, K J (Edinburgh Wands, Cambridge U) 1951 *I*, *E*, 1953 *F*, *W*
Dallas, J D (Watsonians) 1903 *E*
Davidson, J A (London Scottish, Edinburgh Wands) 1959 *E*, 1960 *I*, *E*

Davidson, J N G (Edinburgh U) 1952 *F, W, I, E*, 1953 *F, W*, 1954 *F*
Davidson, J P (RIE Coll) 1873 *E*, 1874 *E*
Davidson, R S (Royal HSFP) 1893 *E*
Davies, D S (Hawick) 1922 *F, W, I, E*, 1923 *F, W, I, E*, 1924 *F, E*, 1925 *W, I, E*, 1926 *F, W, I, E*, 1927 *F, W, I*
Dawson, J C (Glasgow Acads) 1947 *A*, 1948 *F, W*, 1949 *F, W, I*, 1950 *F, W, I, E*, 1951 *F, W, I, E, SA*, 1952 *F, W, I, E*, 1953 *E*
Deans, C T (Hawick) 1978 *F, W, E, NZ*, 1979 *W, E, I, F, NZ*, 1980 *I, F*, 1981 *F, W, E, I, NZ* (2), *R, A*, 1982 *E, I, F, W, A* (2), 1983 *I, F, W, E, NZ*, 1984 *W, E, I, F*
Deans, D T (Hawick) 1968 *E*
Deas, D W (Heriot's FP) 1947 *F, W*
Dick, L G (Loughborough Colls, Jordanhill, Swansea) 1972 *W* (R), *E*, 1974 *W, E, I, F*, 1975 *I, F, W, E, NZ, A*, 1976 *F*, 1977 *E*
Dick, R C S (Cambridge U, Guy's Hospital) 1934 *W, I, E*, 1935 *W, I, E, NZ*, 1936 *W, I, E*, 1937 *W*, 1938 *W, I, E*
Dickson, G (Gala) 1978 *NZ*, 1979 *W, E, I, F, NZ*, 1980 *W*, 1981 *F*, 1982 *W* (R)
Dickson, M R (Edinburgh U) 1905 *I*
Dickson, W M (Blackheath, Oxford U) 1912 *F, W, E, SA*, 1913 *F, W, I*
Dobson, J (Glasgow Acads) 1911 *E*, 1912 *F, W, I, E, SA*
Dobson, J D (Glasgow Acads) 1910 *I*
Dobson, W G (Heriot's FP) 1922 *W, I, E*
Docherty, J T (Glasgow HSFP) 1955 *F, W*, 1956 *E*, 1958 *F, W, A, I, E*
Dods, F P (Edinburgh Acads) 1901 *I*
Dods, J H (Edinburgh Acads) 1895 *W, I, E*, 1896 *W, I, E*, 1897 *I, E*
Dods, P W (Gala) 1983 *I, F, W, E, NZ*, 1984 *W, E, I, F*
Donald, D G (Oxford U) 1914 *W, I*
Donald, R L H (Glasgow HSFP) 1921 *W, I, E*
Donaldson, W P (Oxford U, W of Scotland) 1893 *I*, 1894 *I*, 1895 *E*, 1896 *I, E*, 1899 *I*
Don-Wauchope, A R (Fettesian-Lorettonians) 1881 *E*, 1882 *E*, 1883 *W*, 1884 *W, I, E*, 1885 *W, I*, 1886 *W, I, E*, 1888 *I*
Don-Wauchope, P H (Fettesian-Lorettonians) 1885 *I*, 1886 *W*, 1887 *I, W, E*,
Dorward, A F (Cambridge U, Gala) 1950 *F*, 1951 *SA*, 1952 *W, I, E*, 1953 *F, W, E*, 1955 *F*, 1956 *I, E*, 1957 *F, W, I, E*
Dorward, T F (Gala) 1938 *W, I, E*, 1939 *I, E*
Douglas, G (Jedforest) 1921 *W*
Douglas, J (Stewart's Coll FP) 1961 *F, SA, W, I, E*, 1962 *F, W, I, E*, 1963 *F, W, I*
Douty, P S (London Scottish) 1927 *NSW*, 1928 *F, W*
Drew, D (Glasgow Acads) 1871 *E*, 1876 *E*
Druitt, W A H (London Scottish) 1936 *W, I, E*
Drummond, A H (Kelvinside Acads) 1938 *W, I*
Drummond, C W (Melrose) 1947 *F, W, I, E*, 1948 *F, I, E*, 1950 *F, W, I, E*
Drybrough, A S (Edinburgh Wands, Merchistonians) 1902 *I*, 1903 *I*
Dryden, R H (Watsonians) 1937 *E*
Drysdale, D (Heriot's FP) 1923 *F, W, I, E*, 1924 *F, W, I, E*, 1925 *F, W, I, E*, 1926 *F, W, I, E*, 1927 *F, W, I, E, NSW*, 1928 *F, W, I, E*, 1929 *F*
Duff, P L (Glasgow Acads) 1936 *W, I*, 1938 *W, I, E*, 1939 *W*
Duffy, H (Jedforest) 1955 *F*
Duke, A (Royal HSFP) 1888 *W, I*, 1889 *W, I*, 1890 *W, I*
Duncan, A W (Edinburgh U) 1901 *W, I, E*, 1902 *W, I, E*
Duncan, D D (Oxford U) 1920 *F, W, I, E*
Duncan, M M (Fettesian-Lorettonians) 1888 *W*
Dunlop, J W (W of Scotland) 1875 *E*
Dunlop, Q (W of Scotland) 1971 *E* (2[1C])
Dykes, A S (Glasgow Acads) 1932 *E*
Dykes, J C (Glasgow Acads) 1922 *F, E*, 1924 *I*, 1925 *F, W, I*, 1926 *F, W, I, E*, 1927 *F, W, I, E, NSW*, 1928 *F, I*, 1929 *F, W, I*
Dykes, J M (Clydesdale, Glasgow HSFP) 1898 *I, E*, 1899 *W, E*, 1900 *W, I*, 1901 *W, I, E*, 1902 *E*

Edwards, D B (Heriot's FP) 1960 *I, E, SA*
Elgie, M K (London Scottish) 1954 *NZ, I, E, W*, 1955 *F, W, I, E*
Elliot, C (Langholm) 1958 *E*, 1959 *F*, 1960 *F*, 1963 *E*, 1964 *F, NZ, W, I, E*, 1965 *F, W, I*
Elliot, M (Hawick) 1895 *W*, 1896 *E*, 1897 *I, E*, 1898 *I, E*
Elliot, T (Gala) 1905 *E*
Elliot, T (Gala) 1955 *W, I, E*, 1956 *F, W, I, E*, 1957 *F, W, I, E*, 1958 *W, A, I*
Elliot, T G (Langholm) 1968 *W, A*, 1969 *F, W*, 1970 *E*
Elliot, W I D (Edinburgh Acads) 1947 *F, W, E, A*, 1948 *F, W, I, E*, 1949 *F, W, I, E*, 1950 *F, W, I, E*, 1951 *F, W, I, E, SA*, 1952 *F, W, I, E*, 1954 *NZ, I, E, W*
Emslie, W D (Royal HSFP) 1930 *F*, 1932 *I*
Evans, H L (Edinburgh U) 1885 *I*
Ewart, E N (Glasgow Acads) 1879 *E*, 1880 *I, E*

Fahmy, Dr E C (Abertillery) 1920 *F, W, I, E*
Fasson, F H (London Scottish, Edinburgh Wands) 1900 *W*, 1901 *W, I*, 1902 *W, E*
Fell, A N (Edinburgh U) 1901 *W, I, E*, 1902 *W, E*, 1903 *W, E*
Ferguson, J H (Gala) 1928 *W*
Ferguson, W G (Royal HSFP) 1927 *NSW*, 1928 *F, W, I, E*
Fergusson, E A J (Oxford U) 1954 *F, NZ, I, E, W*
Finlay, A B (Edinburgh Acads) 1875 *E*
Finlay, J F (Edinburgh Acads) 1871 *E*, 1872 *E*, 1874 *E*, 1875 *E*
Finlay, N J (Edinburgh Acads) 1875 *E*, 1876 *E*, 1878 *E*, 1879 *I, E*, 1880 *I, E*, 1881 *I, E*
Finlay, R (Watsonians) 1948 *E*
Fisher, A T (Waterloo, Watsonians) 1947 *I, E*
Fisher, C D (Waterloo) 1975 *NZ, A*, 1976 *W, E, I*
Fisher, D (W of Scotland) 1893 *I*
Fisher, J P (Royal HSFP, London Scottish) 1963 *E*, 1964 *F, NZ, W, I, E*, 1965 *F, W, I, E, SA*, 1966 *F, W, I, E, A*, 1967 *F, W, I, E, NZ*, 1968 *F, W, I, E*
Fleming, C J N (Edinburgh Wands) 1896 *I, E*, 1897 *I*
Fleming, G R (Glasgow Acads) 1875 *E*, 1876 *E*
Fletcher, H N (Edinburgh U) 1904 *E*, 1905 *W*
Flett, A B (Edinburgh U) 1901 *W, I, E*, 1902 *W, I*
Forbes, J L (Watsonians) 1905 *W*, 1906 *I, E*
Ford, D St C (United Services, RN) 1930 *I, E*, 1931 *E*, 1932 *W, I*
Ford, J R (Gala) 1893 *I*
Forrest, J E (Glasgow Acads) 1932 *SA*, 1935 *E, NZ*
Forrest, J G S (Cambridge U) 1938 *W, I, E*
Forrest, W T (Hawick) 1903 *W, I, E*, 1904 *W, I, E*, 1905 *W, I*
Forsayth, H H (Oxford U) 1921 *F, W, I, E*, 1922 *W, I, E*
Forsyth, I, W (Stewart's Coll FP) 1972 *NZ*, 1973 *F, W, I, E, P*
Forsyth, J (Edinburgh U) 1871 *E*
Foster, R A (Hawick) 1930 *W*, 1932 *SA, I, E*
Fox, J (Gala) 1952 *F, W, I, E*
Frame, J N M (Edinburgh U, Gala) 1967 *NZ*, 1968 *F, W, I, E*, 1969 *W, I, E, SA*, 1970 *F, W, I, E, A*, 1971 *F, W, I, E* (2[1C]), 1972 *F, W, E*, 1973 *P* (R)
France, C (Kelvinside Acads) 1903 *I*
Fraser, C F P (Glasgow U) 1888 *W*, 1889 *W*
Fraser, J W (Edinburgh Inst FP) 1881 *E*
Fraser, R (Cambridge U) 1911 *F, W, I, E*
French, J (Glasgow Acads) 1886 *W*, 1887 *I, W, E*
Frew, A (Edinburgh U) 1901 *W, I, E*
Frew, G M (Glasgow HSFP) 1906 *SA*, 1907 *W, I, E*, 1908 *W, I, E*, 1909 *W, I, E*, 1910 *F, W, I*, 1911 *I, E*
Friebe, J P (Glasgow HSFP) 1952 *E*
Fulton, A K (Edinburgh U, Dollar Acads) 1952 *F*, 1954 *F*
Fyfe, K C (Cambridge U, Sale, London Scottish) 1933 *W, E*, 1934 *E*, 1935 *W, I, E, NZ*, 1936 *W, E*, 1939 *I*

Gallie, G H (Edinburgh Acads) 1939 *W*
Gallie, R A (Glasgow Acads) 1920 *F, W, I, E*, 1921 *F, W, I, E*
Gammell, W B B (Edinburgh Wands) 1977 *I, F, W*, 1978 *W, E*
Geddes, I C (London Scottish) 1906 *SA*, 1907 *W, I, E*, 1908 *W, E*
Geddes, K I (London Scottish) 1947 *F, W, I, E*
Gedge, H T S (Oxford U, London Scottish, Edinburgh Wands) 1894 *W, I, E*, 1896 *E*, 1899 *W, E*

Gedge, P M S (Edinburgh Wands) 1933 *I*
Gemmill, R (Glasgow HSFP) 1950 *F, W, I, E*, 1951 *F, W, I*
Gibson, W R (Royal HSFP) 1891 *I, E*, 1892 *W, I, E*, 1893 *W, I, E*, 1894 *W, I, E*, 1895 *W, I, E*
Gilbert-Smith, D S (London Scottish) 1952 *E*
Gilchrist, J (Glasgow Acads) 1925 *F*
Gill, A D (Gala) 1973 *P*, 1974 *W, E, I, F*
Gillespie, J I (Edinburgh Acads) 1899 *E*, 1900 *W, E*, 1901 *W, I, E*, 1902 *W, I*, 1904 *I, E*
Gillies, A C (Watsonians) 1924 *W, I, E*, 1925 *F, W, E*, 1926 *F, W*, 1927 *F, W, I, E*
Gilray, C M (Oxford U, London Scottish) 1908 *E*, 1909 *W, E*, 1912 *I*
Glasgow, R J C (Dunfermline) 1962 *F, W, I, E*, 1963 *I, E*, 1964 *I, E*, 1965 *W, I*
Glen, W S (Edinburgh Wands) 1955 *W*
Gloag, L G (Cambridge U) 1949 *F, W, I, E*
Goodfellow, J (Langholm) 1928 *W, I, E*
Goodhue, F W J (London Scottish) 1890 *W, I, E*, 1891 *W, I, E*, 1892 *W, I, E*
Gordon, R (Edinburgh Wands) 1951 *W*, 1952 *F, W, I, E*, 1953 *W*
Gordon, R E (Royal Artillery) 1913 *F, W, I*
Gordon, R J (London Scottish) 1982 *A* (2)
Gore, A C (London Scottish) 1882 *I*
Gossman, B M (W of Scotland) 1980 *W*, 1983 *F, W*
Gossman, J S (W of Scotland) 1980 *E* (R)
Gowans, J J (Cambridge U, London Scottish) 1893 *W*, 1894 *W, E*, 1895 *W, I, E*, 1896 *I, E*
Gowland, G C (London Scottish) 1908 *W*, 1909 *W, E*, 1910 *F, W, I, E*
Gracie, A L (Harlequins) 1921 *F, W, I, E*, 1922 *F, W, I, E*, 1923 *F, W, I, E*, 1924 *F*
Graham, I N (Edinburgh Acads) 1939 *I, E*
Graham, J (Kelso) 1926 *I, E*, 1927 *F, W, I, E, NSW*, 1928 *F, W, I, E*, 1930 *I, E*, 1932 *SA, W*
Graham, J H S (Edinburgh Acads) 1876 *E*, 1877 *I, E*, 1878 *E*, 1879 *I, E*, 1880 *I, E*, 1881 *I, E*
Grant, D (Hawick) 1965 *F, E, SA*, 1966 *F, W, I, E, A*, 1967 *F, W, I, E, NZ*, 1968 *F*
Grant, D M (East Midlands) 1911 *W, I*
Grant, M L (Harlequins) 1955 *F*, 1956 *F, W*, 1957 *F*
Grant, T O (Hawick) 1960 *I, E, SA*, 1964 *F, NZ, W*
Grant, W St C (Craigmount) 1873 *E*, 1874 *E*
Gray, D (W of Scotland) 1978 *E*, 1979 *I, F, NZ*, 1980 *I, F, W, E*, 1981 *F*
Gray, G L (Gala) 1935 *NZ*, 1937 *W, I, E*
Gray, T (Northampton, Heriot's FP) 1950 *E*, 1951 *F, E*
Greenlees, H D (Leicester) 1927 *NSW*, 1928 *F, W*, 1929 *I, E*, 1930 *E*
Greenlees, J R C (Cambridge U, Kelvinside Acads) 1900 *I*, 1902 *W, I, E*, 1903 *W, I, E*
Greenwood, J T (Dunfermline and Perthshire Acads) 1952 *F*, 1955 *F, W, I, E*, 1956 *F, W, I, E*, 1957 *F, W, E*, 1958 *F, W, A, I, E*, 1959 *F, W, I*
Greig, A (Glasgow HSFP) 1911 *I*
Greig, L L (Glasgow Acads, United Services) 1905 *NZ*, 1906 *SA*, 1907 *W*, 1908 *W, I*
Greig, R C (Glasgow Acads) 1893 *W*, 1897 *I*
Grieve, C F (Oxford U) 1935 *W*, 1936 *E*
Grieve, R M (Kelso) 1935 *W, I, E, NZ*, 1936 *W, I, E*
Gunn, A W (Royal HSFP) 1912 *F, W, I, SA*, 1913 *F*

Hamilton, A S (Headingley) 1914 *W*, 1920 *F*
Hamilton, H M (W of Scotland) 1874 *E*, 1875 *E*
Hannah, R S M (W of Scotland) 1971 *I*
Harrower, P R (London Scottish) 1885 *W*
Hart, J G M (London Scottish) 1951 *SA*
Hart, T M (Glasgow U) 1930 *W, I*
Hart, W (Melrose) 1960 *SA*
Harvey, L (Greenock Wands) 1899 *I*
Hastie, A J (Melrose) 1961 *W, I, E*, 1964 *I, E*, 1965 *E, SA*, 1966 *F, W, I, E, A*, 1967 *F, W, I, NZ*, 1968 *F, W*
Hastie, I R (Kelso) 1955 *F*, 1958 *F, E*, 1959 *F, W, I*
Hastie, J D H (Melrose) 1938 *W, I, E*
Hay, B H (Boroughmuir) 1975 *NZ, A*, 1976 *F*, 1978 *I, F, W, E, NZ*, 1979 *W, E, I, F, NZ*, 1980 *I, F, W, E*, 1981 *F, W, E, I, NZ* (2)
Hay-Gordon, J R (Edinburgh Acads) 1875 *E*, 1877 *I, E*
Hegarty, C B (Hawick) 1978 *I, F, W, E*
Hegarty, J J (Hawick) 1951 *F*, 1953 *F, W, I, E*, 1955 *F*
Henderson, B C (Edinburgh Wands) 1963 *E*, 1964 *F, I, E*, 1965 *F, W, I, E*, 1966 *F, W, I, E*
Henderson, F W (London Scottish) 1900 *W, I*
Henderson, I C (Edinburgh Acads) 1939 *I, E*, 1947 *F, W, E, A*, 1948 *I, E*
Henderson, J H (Oxford U, Richmond) 1953 *F, W, I, E*, 1954 *F, NZ, I, E, W*
Henderson, J M (Edinburgh Acads) 1933 *W, E, I*
Henderson, J Y M (Watsonians) 1911 *E*
Henderson, M M (Dunfermline) 1937 *W, I, E*
Henderson, N F (London Scottish) 1892 *I*
Henderson, R G (Newcastle Northern) 1924 *I, E*
Hendrie, K G P (Heriot's FP) 1924 *F, W, I*
Hendry, T L (Clydesdale) 1893 *W, I, E*, 1895 *I*
Henriksen, E H (Royal HSFP) 1953 *I*
Hepburn, D P (Woodford) 1947 *A*, 1948 *F, W, I, E*, 1949 *F, W, I, E*
Heron, G (Glasgow Acads) 1874 *E*, 1875 *E*
Hill, C C P (St Andrew's U) 1912 *F, I*
Hinshelwood, A J W (London Scottish) 1966 *F, W, I, E, A*, 1967 *F, W, I, E, NZ*, 1968 *F, W, I, E, A*, 1969 *F, W, I, SA*, 1970 *F, W*
Hodgson, C G (London Scottish) 1968 *I, E*
Hogg, C G (Boroughmuir) 1978 *F* (R), *W* (R)
Holms, W F (RIE Coll) 1886 *W, E*, 1887 *I, E*, 1889 *W, I*
Horsburgh, G B (London Scottish) 1937 *W, I, E*, 1938 *W, I, E*, 1939 *W, I, E*
Howie, D D (Kirkcaldy) 1912 *F, W, I, E, SA*, 1913 *F, W*
Howie, R A (Kirkcaldy) 1924 *F, W, I, E*, 1925 *W, I, E*
Hoyer-Millar, G C (Oxford U) 1953 *I*
Huggan, J L (London Scottish) 1914 *E*
Hume, J (Royal HSFP) 1912 *F*, 1920 *F*, 1921 *F, W, I, E*, 1922 *F*
Hume, J W G (Oxford U, Edinburgh Wands) 1928 *I*, 1930 *F*
Hunter, F (Edinburgh U) 1882 *I*
Hunter, I G (Selkirk) 1984 *I* (R)
Hunter, J M (Cambridge U) 1947 *F*
Hunter, M D (Glasgow High) 1974 *F*
Hunter, W J (Hawick) 1964 *F, NZ, W*, 1967 *F, W, I, E*
Hutchison, W R (Glasgow HSFP) 1911 *E*
Hutton, A H M (Dunfermline) 1932 *I*
Hutton, J E (Harlequins) 1930 *E*, 1931 *F*

Inglis, H M (Edinburgh Acads) 1951 *F, W, I, E, SA*, 1952 *W, I*
Inglis, J M (Selkirk) 1952 *E*
Inglis, W M (Cambridge U, Royal Engineers) 1937 *W, I, E*, 1938 *W, I, E*
Innes, J R S (Aberdeen GSFP) 1939 *W, I, E*, 1947 *A*, 1948 *F, W, I, E*
Ireland, J C H (Glasgow HSFP) 1925 *W, I, E*, 1926 *F, W, I, E*, 1927 *F, W, I, E*
Irvine, A R (Heriot's FP) 1972 *NZ*, 1973 *F, W, I, E, P*, 1974 *W, E, I, F*, 1975 *I, F, W, E, NZ, A*, 1976 *F, W, E, I*, 1977 *E, I, F, W*, 1978 *I, F, E, NZ*, 1979 *W, E, I, F, NZ*, 1980 *I, F, W, E*, 1981 *F, W, E, I, NZ* (2), *R, A*, 1982 *E, I, F, W, A* (2)
Irvine, D R (Edinburgh Acads) 1878 *E*, 1879 *I, E*
Irvine, R W (Edinburgh Acads) 1871 *E*, 1872 *E*, 1873 *E*, 1874 *E*, 1875 *E*, 1876 *E*, 1877 *I, E*, 1878 *E*, 1879 *I, E*, 1880 *I, E*
Irvine, T W (Edinburgh Acads) 1885 *I*, 1886 *W, I, E*, 1887 *I, W, E*, 1888 *W, I*, 1889 *I*

Jackson, K L T (Oxford U) 1933 *W, E, I*, 1934 *W*
Jackson, T G H (Army) 1947 *F, W, E, A*, 1948 *F, W, I, E*, 1949 *F, W, I, E*
Jackson, W D (Hawick) 1964 *I*, 1965 *E, SA*, 1968 *A*, 1969 *F, W, I, E*
Jamieson, J (W of Scotland) 1883 *W, I, E*, 1884 *W, I, E*, 1885 *W, I*
Johnston, D I (Watsonians) 1979 *NZ*, 1980 *I, F, W, E*, 1981 *R, A*, 1982 *E, I, F, W, A* (2), 1983 *I, F, W, NZ*, 1984 *W, E, I, F*
Johnston, H H (Edinburgh Collegian FP) 1877 *I, E*
Johnston, J (Melrose) 1951 *SA*, 1952 *F, W, I, E*
Johnston, W G S (Cambridge U) 1935 *W, I*, 1937 *W, I, E*
Johnston, W C (Glasgow HSFP) 1922 *F*
Junor, J E (Glasgow Acads) 1876 *E*, 1877 *I, E*, 1878 *E*, 1879 *E*, 1881 *I*

Keddie, R R (Watsonians) 1967 *NZ*
Keith, G J (Wasps) 1968 *F, W*
Keller, D H (London Scottish) 1949 *F, W, I, E*, 1950 *F, W, I*
Kelly, R F (Watsonians) 1927 *NSW*, 1928 *F, W, E*
Kemp, J W Y (Glasgow HSFP) 1954 *W*, 1955 *F, W, I, E*, 1956 *F, W, I, E*, 1957 *F, W, I, E*, 1958 *F, W, A, I, E*, 1959 *F, W, I, E*, 1960 *F, W, I, E, SA*
Kennedy, A E (Watsonians) 1983 *NZ*, 1984 *W, E*
Kennedy, F (Stewart's Coll FP) 1920 *F, W, I, E*, 1921 *E*
Kennedy, N (W of Scotland) 1903 *W, I, E*
Ker, H T (Glasgow Acads) 1887 *I, W, E*, 1888 *I*, 1889 *W*, 1890 *I, E*
Kerr, D S (Heriot's FP) 1923 *F, W*, 1924 *F*, 1926 *I, E*, 1927 *W, I, E*, 1928 *I, E*
Kerr, G C (Old Dunelmians, Edinburgh Wands) 1898 *I, E*, 1899 *I, W, E*, 1900 *W, I, E*
Kerr, J M (Heriot's FP) 1935 *NZ*, 1936 *I, E*, 1937 *W, I*
Kerr, W (London Scottish) 1953 *E*
Kidston, D W (Glasgow Acads) 1883 *W, E*
Kidston, W H (W of Scotland) 1874 *E*
Kilgour, I J (RMC Sandhurst) 1921 *F*
King, J H F (Selkirk) 1953 *F, W, E*, 1954 *E*
Kininmonth, P W (Oxford U, Richmond) 1949 *F, W, I, E*, 1950 *F, W, I, E*, 1951 *F, W, I, E, SA*, 1952 *F, W, I*, 1954 *F, NZ, I, E, W*
Kinnear, R M (Heriot's FP) 1926 *F, W, I*
Knox, J (Kelvinside Acads) 1903 *W, I, E*
Kyle, W E (Hawick) 1902 *W, I, E*, 1903 *W, I, E*, 1904 *W, I, E*, 1905 *W, I, E, NZ*, 1906 *W, I, E*, 1908 *E*, 1909 *W, I, E*, 1910 *W*

Laidlaw, A S (Hawick) 1897 *I*
Laidlaw, F A L (Melrose) 1965 *F, W, I, E, SA*, 1966 *F, W, I, E, A*, 1967 *F, W, I, E, NZ*, 1968 *F, W, I, A*, 1969 *F, W, I, E, SA*, 1970 *F, W, I, E, A*, 1971 *F, W, I*
Laidlaw, R J (Jedforest) 1980 *I, F, W, E*, 1981 *F, W, E, I, NZ* (2), *R, A*, 1982 *E, I, F, W, A* (2), 1983 *I, F, W, E, NZ*, 1984 *W, E, I, F*
Laing, A D (Royal HSFP) 1914 *W, I, E*, 1920 *F, W, I*, 1921 *F*
Lambie, I K (Watsonians) 1978 *NZ* (R), 1979 *W, E, NZ*
Lambie, L B (Glasgow HSFP) 1934 *W, I, E*, 1935 *W, I, E, NZ*
Lamond, G A W (Kelvinside Acads) 1899 *W, E*, 1905 *E*
Lang, D (Paisley) 1876 *E*, 1877 *I*
Langrish, R W (London Scottish) 1930 *F*, 1931 *F, W, I*
Lauder, W (Neath) 1969 *I, E, SA*, 1970 *F, W, I, A*, 1973 *F*, 1974 *W, E, I, F*, 1975 *I, F, NZ, A*, 1976 *F*, 1977 *E*
Laughland, I H P (London Scottish) 1959 *F*, 1960 *F, W, I, E*, 1961 *SA, W, I, E*, 1962 *F, W, I, E*, 1963 *F, W, I*, 1964 *F, NZ, W, I, E*, 1965 *F, W, I, E, SA*, 1966 F, W, I, E, 1967 *E*
Lawrie, J R (Melrose) 1922 *F, W, I, E*, 1923 *F, W, I, E*, 1924 *W, I, E*
Lawrie, K G (Gala) 1980 *F* (R), *W, E*
Lawson, A J M (Edinburgh Wands, London Scottish) 1972 *F* (R), *E*, 1973 *F*, 1974 *W, E*, 1976 *E, I*, 1977 *E*, 1978 *NZ*, 1979 *W, E, I, F, NZ*, 1980 *W* (R)
Lawther, T H B (Old Millhillians) 1932 *SA, W*
Ledingham, G A (Aberdeen GSFP) 1913 *F*
Lees, J B (Gala) 1947 *I, A*, 1948 *F, W, E*
Leggatt, H T O (Watsonians) 1891 *W, I, E*, 1892 *W, I*, 1893 *W, E*, 1894 *I, E*
Lely, W G (Cambridge U, London Scottish) 1909 *I*
Leslie, D G (Dundee HSFP, W of Scotland, Gala) 1975 *I, F, W, E, NZ, A*, 1976 *F, W, E, I*, 1978 *NZ*, 1980 *E*, 1981 *W, E, I, NZ* (2), *R, A*, 1982 *E*, 1983 *I, F, W, E*, 1984 *W, E, I, F*
Liddell, E H (Edinburgh U) 1922 *F, W, I*, 1923 *F, W, I, E*
Lind, H (Dunfermline) 1928 *I*, 1931 *F, W, I, E*, 1932 *SA, W, E*, 1933 *W, E, I*, 1934 *W, I, E*, 1935 *I*, 1936 *E*
Lindsay, A B (London Hospital) 1910 *I*, 1911 *I*
Lindsay, G C (London Scottish) 1884 *W*, 1887 *W, E*
Lindsay-Watson, R H (Hawick) 1909 *I*
Little, A W (Hawick) 1905 *W*
Logan, W R (Edinburgh U, Edinburgh Wands) 1931 *E*, 1932 *SA, W, I*, 1933 *W, E, I*, 1934 *W, I, E*, 1935 *W, I, E, NZ*, 1936 *W, I, E*, 1937 *W, I, E*
Lorraine, H D B (Oxford U) 1933 *W, E, I*
Loudoun-Shand, E G (Oxford U) 1913 *E*
Lowe, J D (Heriot's FP) 1934 *W*
Lumsden, I J M (Bath, Watsonians) 1947 *F, W, A*, 1949 *F, W, I, E*
Lyall, G G (Gala) 1947 *A*, 1948 *F, W, I, E*
Lyall, W J C (Edinburgh Acads) 1871 *E*

Mabon, J T (Jedforest) 1898 *I, E*, 1899 *I*, 1900 *I*
Macarthur, J P (Waterloo) 1932 *E*
MacCallum, J C (Watsonians) 1905 *E, NZ*, 1906 *W, I, E, SA*, 1907 *W, I, E*, 1908 *W, I, E*, 1909 *W, I, E*, 1910 *F, W, I, E*, 1911 *F, I, E*, 1912 *F, W, I, E*
McClung, T (Edinburgh Acads) 1956 *I, E*, 1957 *W, I, E*, 1959 *F, W, I*, 1960 *W*
McClure, G B (W of Scotland) 1873 *E*
McClure, J H (W of Scotland) 1872 *E*
McCowan, D (W of Scotland) 1880 *I, E*, 1881 *I, E*, 1882 *I, E*, 1883 *I, E*, 1884 *I, E*
McCowat, R H (Glasgow Acads) 1905 *I*
McCrae, I G (Gordonians) 1967 *E*, 1968 *I*, 1969 *F* (R), *W*, 1972 *F, NZ*
McCrow, J W S (Edinburgh Acads) 1921 *I*
McDonald, C (Jedforest) 1947 *A*
Macdonald, D C (Edinburgh U) 1953 *F, W*, 1958 *I, E*
Macdonald, D S M (Oxford U, London Scottish, W of Scotland) 1977 *E, I, F, W*, 1978 *I, W, E*
Macdonald, J D (London Scottish, Army) 1966 *F, W, I, E*, 1967 *F, W, I, E*
Macdonald, J M (Edinburgh Wands) 1911 *W*
Macdonald, J S (Edinburgh U) 1903 *E*, 1904 *W, I, E*, 1905 *W*
Macdonald, K R (Stewart's Coll FP) 1956 *F, W, I*, 1957 *W, I, E*
Macdonald, R (Edinburgh U) 1950 *F, W, I, E*
McDonald, W A (Glasgow U) 1889 *W*, 1892 *I, E*
Macdonald, W G (London Scottish) 1969 *I* (R)
Macdougall, J B (Greenock Wands, Wakefield) 1913 *F*, 1914 *I*, 1921 *F, I, E*
McEwan, M C (Edinburgh Acads) 1886 *E*, 1887 *I, W, E*, 1888 *W, I*, 1889 *W, I*, 1890 *W, I, E*, 1891 *W, I, E*, 1892 *E*
MacEwan, N A (Gala, Highland) 1971 *F, W, I, E* (2[1C]), 1972 *F, W, E, NZ*, 1973 *F, W, I, E, P*, 1974 *W, E, I, F*, 1975 *W, E*
McEwan, W M C (Edinburgh Acads) 1894 *W, E*, 1895 *W, E*, 1896 *W, I, E*, 1897 *I, E*, 1898 *I, E*, 1899 *I, W, E*, 1900 *W, E*
MacEwen, R K G (Cambridge U, London Scottish) 1954 *F, NZ, I, W*, 1956 *F, W, I, E*, 1957 *F, W, I, E*, 1958 *W*
Macfarlan, D J (London Scottish) 1883 *W*, 1884 *W, I, E*, 1886 *W, I*, 1887 *I*, 1888 *I*
McFarlane, J L H (Edinburgh U) 1871 *E*, 1872 *E*, 1873 *E*
McGeechan, I R (Headingley) 1972 *NZ*, 1973 *F, W, I, E, P*, 1974 *W, E, I, F*, 1975 *I, F, W, E, NZ, A*, 1976 *F, W, E, I*, 1977 *E, I, F, W*, 1978 *I, F, W, NZ*, 1979 *W, E, I, F*
McGlashan, T P L (Royal HSFP) 1947 *F, I, E*, 1954 *F, NZ, I, E, W*
MacGregor, D G (Watsonians, Pontypridd) 1907 *W, I, E*
MacGregor, G (Cambridge U) 1890 *W, I, E*, 1891 *W, I, E*, 1893 *W, I, E*, 1894 *W, I, E*, 1896 *E*
MacGregor, I A A (Hillhead HSFP, Llanelli) 1955 *I, E*, 1956 *F, W, I, E*, 1957 *F, W, I*
MacGregor, J R (Edinburgh U) 1909 *I*
McGuinness, G M (W of Scotland) 1982 *A* (2), 1983 *I*
McHarg, A F (W of Scotland, London Scottish) 1968 *I, E, A*, 1969 *F, W, I, E*, 1971 *F, W, I, E* (2(1C]), 1972 *F, E, NZ*, 1973 *F, W, I, E, P*, 1974 *W, E, I, F*, 1975 *I, F, W, E, NZ, A*, 1976 *F, W, E, I*, 1977 *E, I, F, W*, 1978 *I, F, W, NZ*, 1979 *W, E*
McIndoe, F (Glasgow Acads) 1886 *W, I*
MacIntyre, I (Edinburgh Wands) 1890 *W, I, E*, 1891 *W, I, E*
Mackay, E B (Glasgow Acads) 1920 *W*, 1922 *E*
McKeating, E (Heriot's FP) 1957 *F, W*, 1961 *SA, W, I, E*
Mckendrick, J G (W of Scotland) 1889 *I*
Mackenzie, C J G (United Services) 1921 *E*
Mackenzie, D D (Edinburgh U) 1947 *W, I, E*, 1948 *F, W, I*
Mackenzie, D K A (Edinburgh, Wands) 1939 *I, E*

Mackenzie, J M (Edinburgh U) 1905 *NZ*, 1909 *W*, *I*, *E*, 1910 *W*, *I*, *E*, 1911 *W*, *I*
Mackenzie, R C (Glasgow Acads) 1877 *I*, *E*, 1881 *I*, *E*
Mackie, G Y (Highland) 1975 *A*, 1976 *F*, *W*, 1978 *F*
MacKinnon, A (London Scottish) 1898 *I*, *E*, 1899 *I*, *W*, *E*, 1900 *E*
Mackintosh, C E W C (London Scottish) 1924 *F*
Mackintosh, H S (Glasgow U, W of Scotland) 1929 *F*, *W*, *I*, *E*, 1930 *F*, *W*, *I*, *E*, 1931 *F*, *W*, *I*, *E*, 1932 *SA*, *W*, *I*, *E*
MacLachlan, L P (Oxford U, London Scottish) 1954 *NZ*, *I*, *E*, *W*
Maclagan, W E (Edinburgh Acads) 1878 *E*, 1879 *I*, *E*, 1880 *I*, *E*, 1881 *I*, *E*, 1882 *I*, *E*, 1883 *W*, *I*, *E*, 1884 *W*, *I*, *E*, 1885 *W*, *I*, 1887 *I*, *W*, *E*, 1888 *W*, *I*, 1890 *W*, *I*, *E*
McLaren, A (Durham County) 1931 *F*
McLaren, E (London Scottish, Royal HSFP) 1923 *F*, *W*, *I*, *E*, 1924 *F*
McLauchlan, J (Jordanhill) 1969 *E*, *SA*, 1970 *F*, *W*, 1971 *F*, *W*, *I*, *E* (2[1C]), 1972 *F*, *W*, *E*, *NZ*, 1973 *F*, *W*, *I*, *E*, *P*, 1974 *W*, *E*, *I*, *F*, 1975 *I*, *F*, *W*, *E*, *NZ*, *A*, 1976 *F*, *W*, *E*, *I*, 1977 *W*, 1978 *I*, *F*, *W*, *E*, *NZ*, 1979 *W*, *E*, *I*, *F*, *NZ*
McLean, D I (Royal HSFP) 1947 *I*, *E*
Maclennan, W D (Watsonians) 1947 *F*, *I*
MacLeod, D A (Glasgow U) 1886 *I*, *E*
MacLeod, G (Edinburgh Acads) 1878 *E*, 1882 *I*
McLeod, H F (Hawick) 1954 *F*, *NZ*, *I*, *E*, *W*, 1955 *F*, *W*, *I*, *E*, 1956 *F*, *W*, *I*, *E*, 1957 *F*, *W*, *I*, *E*, 1958 *F*, *W*, *A*, *I*, *E*, 1959 *F*, *W*, *I*, *E*, 1960 *F*, *W*, *I*, *E*, *SA*, 1961 *F*, *SA*, *W*, *I*, *E*, 1962 *F*, *W*, *I*, *E*
MacLeod, K G (Cambridge U) 1905 *NZ*, 1906 *W*, *I*, *E*, *SA*, 1907 *W*, *I*, *E*, 1908 *I*, *E*
MacLeod, L M (Cambridge U) 1904 *W*, *I*, *E*, 1905 *W*, *I*, *NZ*
Macleod, W M (Fettesian-Lorettonians, Edinburgh Wands) 1886 *W*, *I*
McMillan, K H D (Sale) 1953 *F*, *W*, *I*, *E*
MacMillan, R G (London Scottish) 1887 *W*, *I*, *E*, 1890 *W*, *I*, *E*, 1891 *W*, *E*, 1892 *W*, *I*, *E*, 1893 *W*, *E*, 1894 *W*, *I*, *E*, 1895 *W*, *I*, *E*, 1897 *I*, *E*
MacMyn, D J (Cambridge U, London Scottish) 1925 *F*, *W*, *I*, *E*, 1926 *F*, *W*, *I*, *E*, 1927 *E*, *NSW*, 1928 *F*
McNeil, A S B (Watsonians) 1935 *I*
McPartlin, J J (Harlequins, Oxford U) 1960 *F*, *W*, 1962 *F*, *W*, *I*, *E*
Macphail, J A R (Edinburgh Acads) 1949 *E*, 1951 *SA*
Macpherson, D G (London Hospital) 1910 *I*, *E*
Macpherson, G P S (Oxford U, Edinburgh Acads) 1922 *F*, *W*, *I*, *E*, 1924 *W*, *E*, 1925 *F*, *W*, *E*, 1927 *F*, *W*, *I*, *E*, 1928 *F*, *W*, *E*, 1929 *I*, *E*, 1930 *F*, *W*, *I*, *E*, 1931 *W*, *E*, 1932 *SA*, *E*
Macpherson, N C (Newport, Mon) 1920 *W*, *I*, *E*, 1921 *F*, *E*, 1923 *I*, *E*
McQueen, S B (Waterloo) 1923 *F*, *W*, *I*, *E*
Macrae, D J (St Andrews U) 1937 *W*, *I*, *E*, 1938 *W*, *I*, *E*, 1939 *W*, *I*, *E*
Madsen, D F (Gosforth) 1974 *W*, *E*, *I*, *F*, 1975 *I*, *F*, *W*, *E* 1976 *F*, 1977 *E*, *I*, *F*, *W*, 1978 *I*
Mair, N G R (Edinburgh U) 1951 *F*, *W*, *I*, *E*
Maitland, G (Edinburgh Inst FP) 1885 *W*, *I*
Maitland, R (Edinburgh Inst FP) 1881 *E*, 1882 *I*, *E*, 1884 *W*, 1885 *W*
Maitland, R P (Royal Artillery) 1872 *E*
Malcolm, A G (Glasgow U) 1888 *I*
Marsh, J (Edinburgh Inst FP) 1889 *W*, *I*
Marshall, A (Edinburgh Acads) 1875 *E*
Marshall, J C (London Scottish) 1954 *F*, *NZ*, *I*, *E*, *W*
Marshall, K W (Edinburgh Acads) 1934 *W*, *I*, *E*, 1935 *W*, *I*, *E*, 1936 *W*, 1937 *E*
Marshall, T R (Edinburgh Acads) 1871 *E*, 1872 *E*, 1873 *E*, 1874 *E*
Marshall, W (Edinburgh Acads) 1872 *E*
Martin, H (Edinburgh Acads, Oxford U) 1908 *W*, *I*, *E*, 1909 *W*, *E*
Masters, W H (Edinburgh Inst FP) 1879 *I*, 1880 *I*, *E*
Maxwell, G H H P (Edinburgh Acads, RAF, London Scottish) 1913 *I*, *E*, 1914 *W*, *I*, *E*, 1920 *W*, *E*, 1921 *F*, *W*, *I*, *E*, 1922 *F*, *E*
Maxwell, F T (Royal Engineers) 1872 *E*
Maxwell, J M (Langholm) 1957 *I*
Mein, J (Edinburgh Acads) 1871 *E*, 1872 *E*, 1873 *E*, 1874 *E*, 1875 *E*
Melville, C L (Army) 1937 *W*, *I*, *E*
Menzies, H F (W of Scotland) 1893 *W*, *I*, 1894 *W*, *E*
Methuen, A (London Scottish) 1889 *W*, *I*
Michie, E J S (Aberdeen U, Aberdeen GSFP) 1954 *F*, *NZ*, *I*, *E*, 1955 *W*, *I*, *E*, 1956 *F*, *W*, *I*, *E*, 1957 *F*, *W*, *I*, *E*
Millar, J N (W of Scotland) 1892 *W*, *I*, *E*, 1893 *W*, 1895 *I*, *E*
Millar, R K (London Scottish) 1924 *I*
Millican, J G (Edinburgh U) 1973 *W*, *I*, *E*
Milne, C J B (Fettesian-Lorettonians, W of Scotland) 1886 *W*, *I*, *E*
Milne, I G (Heriot's FP) 1979 *I*, *F*, *NZ*, 1980 *I*, *F*, 1981 *NZ* (2), *R*, *A*, 1982 *E*, *I*, *F*, *W*, *A* (2), 1983 *I*, *F*, *W*, *E*, *NZ*, 1984 *W*, *E*, *I*, *F*
Milne, W M (Glasgow Acads) 1904 *I*, *E*, 1905 *W*, *I*
Milroy, E (Watsonians) 1910 *W*, 1911 *E*, 1912 *W*, *I*, *E*, *SA*, 1913 *F*, *W*, *I*, *E*, 1914 *I*, *E*
Mitchell, G W E (Edinburgh Wands) 1967 *NZ*, 1968 *F*, *W*
Mitchell, J G (W of Scotland) 1885 *W*, *I*
Moncreiff, F J (Edinburgh Acads) 1871 *E*, 1872 *E*, 1873 *E*
Monteith, H G (Cambridge U, London Scottish) 1905 *E*, 1906 *W*, *I*, *E*, *SA*, 1907 *W*, *I*, 1908 *E*
Monypenny, D B (London Scottish) 1899 *I*, *W*, *E*
Moodie, A R (St Andrew's U) 1909 *E*, 1910 *F*, 1911 *F*
Morgan, D W (Stewart's-Melville FP) 1973 *W*, *I*, *E*, *P*, 1974 *I*, *F*, 1975 *I*, *F*, *W*, *E*, *NZ*, *A*, 1976 *F*, *W*, 1977 *I*, *F*, *W*, 1978 *I*, *F*, *W*, *E*
Morrison, M C (Royal HSFP) 1896 *W*, *I*, *E*, 1897 *I*, *E*, 1898 *I*, *E*, 1899 *I*, *W*, *E*, 1900 *W*, *E*, 1901 *W*, *I*, *E*, 1902 *W*, *I*, *E*, 1903 *W*, *I*, 1904 *W*, *I*, *E*
Morrison, R H (Edinburgh U) 1886 *W*, *I*, *E*
Morrison, W H (Edinburgh Acads) 1900 *W*
Morton, D S (W of Scotland) 1887 *I*, *W*, *E*, 1888 *W*, *I*, 1889 *W*, *I*, 1890 *I*, *E*
Mowat, J G (Glasgow Acads) 1883 *W*, *E*
Muir, D E (Heriot's FP) 1950 *F*, *W*, *I*, *E*, 1952 *W*, *I*, *E*
Munnoch, N M (Watsonians) 1952 *F*, *W*, *I*
Munro, P (Oxford, London Scottish) 1905 *W*, *I*, *E*, *NZ*, 1906 *W*, *I*, *E*, *SA*, 1907 *I*, *E*, 1911 *F*, *W*, *I*
Munro, R (St Andrews U) 1871 *E*
Munro, S (Ayr, W of Scotland) 1980 *I*, *F*, 1981 *F*, *W*, *E*, *I*, *NZ* (2), *R*, 1984 *W*
Munro, W H (Glasgow HSFP) 1947 *I*, *E*
Murdoch, W C W (Hillhead HSFP) 1935 *E*, *NZ*, 1936 *W*, *I*, 1939 *E*, 1948 *F*, *W*, *I*, *E*
Murray, G M (Glasgow Acads) 1921 *I*, 1926 *W*
Murray, H M (Glasgow U) 1936 *W*, *I*
Murray, R O (Cambridge U) 1935 *W*, *E*
Murray, W A K (London Scottish) 1920 *F*, *I*, 1921 *F*

Napier, H M (W of Scotland) 1877 *I*, *E*, 1878 *E*, 1879 *I*, *E*
Neill, J B (Edinburgh Acads) 1963 *E*, 1964 *F*, *NZ*, *W*, *I*, *E*, 1965 *F*
Neill, R M (Edinburgh Acads) 1901 *E*, 1902 *I*
Neilson, G T (W of Scotland) 1891 *W*, *I*, *E*, 1892 *W*, *E*, 1893 *W*, 1894 *W*, *I*, 1895 *W*, *I*, *E*, 1896 *W*, *I*, *E*
Neilson, J A (Glasgow Acads) 1878 *E*, 1879 *E*
Neilson, R T (W of Scotland) 1898 *I*, *E*, 1899 *I*, *W*, 1900 *I*, *E*
Neilson, T (W of Scotland) 1874 *E*
Neilson, W (Merchiston, Cambridge U, London Scottish) 1891 *W*, *E*, 1892 *W*, *I*, *E*, 1893 *I*, *E*, 1894 *E*, 1895 *W*, *I*, *E*, 1896 *I*, 1897 *I*, *E*
Neilson, W G (Merchistonians) 1894 *E*
Nelson, J B (Glasgow Acads) 1925 *F*, *W*, *I*, *E*, 1926 *F*, *W*, *I*, *E*, 1927 *F*, *W*, *I*, *E*, 1928 *I*, *E*, 1929 *F*, *W*, *I*, *E*, 1930 *F*, *W*, *I*, *E*, 1931 *F*, *W*, *I*
Nelson, T A (Oxford U) 1898 *E*
Nichol, J A (Royal HSFP) 1955 *W*, *I*, *E*
Nimmo, C S (Watsonians) 1920 *E*

Ogilvy, C (Hawick) 1911 *I*, *E*, 1912 *I*
Oliver, G K (Gala) 1970 *A*
Orr, C E (W of Scotland) 1887 *I*, *E*, *W*, 1888 *W*, *I*, 1889 *W*, *I*, 1890 *W*, *I*, *E*, 1891 *W*, *I*, *E*, 1892 *W*, *I*, *E*
Orr, H J (London Scottish) 1903 *W*, *I*, *E*, 1904 *W*, *I*
Orr, J E (W of Scotland) 1889 *I*, 1890 *W*, *I*, *E*, 1891 *W*, *I*, *E*, 1892 *W*, *I*, *E*, 1893 *I*, *E*
Orr, J H (Edinburgh City Police) 1947 *F*, *W*

Osler, F L (Edinburgh U) 1911 *F, W*

Park, J (Royal HSFP) 1934 *W*
Paterson, D S (Gala) 1969 *SA*, 1970 *I, E, A*, 1971 *F, W, I, E* (2[1C]), 1972 *W*
Paterson, G Q (Edinburgh Acads) 1876 *E*
Paterson, J R (Birkenhead Park) 1924 *F, W, I, E*, 1926 *F, W, I, E*, 1927 *F, W, I, E, NSW*, 1928 *F, W, I, E*, 1929 *F, W, I, E*
Patterson, D (Hawick) 1896 *W*
Pattullo, G L (Panmure) 1920 *F, W, I, E*
Paxton, I A M (Selkirk) 1981 *NZ* (2), *R, A*, 1982 *E, I, F, W, A* (2), 1983 *I, E, NZ*, 1984 *W, E, I, F*
Paxton, R E (Kelso) 1982 *I, A* (R)
Pearson, J (Watsonians) 1909 *I, E*, 1910 *F, W, I, E*, 1911 *F*, 1912 *F, W, SA*, 1913 *I, E*
Pender, I M (London Scottish) 1914 *E*
Pender, N E K (Hawick) 1977 *I*, 1978 *F, W, E*
Penman, W M (RAF) 1939 *I*
Peterkin, W A (Edinburgh U) 1881 *E*, 1883 *I*, 1884 *W, I, E*, 1885 *I, W*
Petrie, A G (Royal HSFP) 1873 *E*, 1874 *E*, 1875 *E*, 1876 *E*, 1877 *I, E*, 1878 *E*, 1879 *I, E*, 1880 *I, E*
Philp, A (Edinburgh Inst FP) 1882 *E*
Pocock, E I (Edinburgh Wands) 1877 *I, E*
Pollock, J A (Gosforth) 1982 *W*, 1983 *E, NZ*, 1984 *E* (R), *I, F*
Polson, A H (Gala) 1930 *E*
Purdie, W (Jedforest) 1939 *W, I, E*
Purves, A B H L (London Scottish) 1906 *W, I, E, SA*, 1907 *W, I, E*, 1908 *W, I, E*
Purves, W D C L (London Scottish) 1912 *F, W, I, SA*, 1913 *I, E*

Rea, C W W (W of Scotland, Headingley) 1968 *A*, 1969 *F, W, I, SA*, 1970 *F, W, I, A*, 1971 *F, W, E* (2[1C])
Reid, C (Edinburgh Acads) 1881 *I, E*, 1882 *I, E*, 1883 *W, I, E*, 1884 *W, I, E*, 1885 *W, I*, 1886 *W, I, E*, 1887 *I, W, E*, 1888 *W, I*
Reid, J (Edinburgh Wands) 1874 *E*, 1875 *E*, 1876 *E*, 1877 *I, E*
Reid, J M (Edinburgh Acads) 1898 *I, E*, 1899 *I*
Reid, M F (Loretto) 1883 *I, E*
Reid-Kerr, J (Greenock Wand) 1909 *E*
Ralph, W K L (Stewart's Coll FP) 1955 *F, W, I, E*
Renny-Tailyour, H W (Royal Engineers) 1872 *E*
Renwick, J M (Hawick) 1972 *F, W, E, NZ*, 1973 *F*, 1974 *W, E, I, F*, 1975 *I, F, W, E, NZ, A*, 1976 *F, W, E*, (R), 1977 *I, F, W*, 1978 *I, F, W, E, NZ*, 1979 *W, E, I, F, NZ*, 1980 *I, F, W, E*, 1981 *F, W, E, I, NZ* (2), *R, A*, 1982 *E, I, F, W*, 1983 *I, F, W, E*
Renwick, W N (London Scottish, Edinburgh Wands) 1938 *E*, 1939 *W*
Ritchie, G (Merchistonians) 1871 *E*
Ritchie, G F (Dundee HSFP) 1932 *E*
Ritchie, J M (Watsonians) 1933 *W, E, I*, 1934 *W, I, E*
Ritchie, W T (Cambridge U) 1905 *I, E*
Robb, G H (Glasgow U) 1881 *I*, 1885 *W*
Roberts, G (Watsonians) 1938 *W, I, E*, 1939 *W, E*
Robertson, A H (W of Scotland) 1871 *E*
Robertson, A W (Edinburgh Acads) 1897 *E*
Robertson, D (Edinburgh Acads) 1875 *E*
Robertson, D D (Cambridge U) 1893 *W*
Robertson, I (London Scottish, Watsonians) 1968 *E*, 1969 *E, SA*, 1970 *F, W, I, E, A*
Robertson, I P M (Watsonians) 1910 *F*
Robertson, J (Clydesdale) 1908 *E*
Robertson, K W (Melrose) 1978 *NZ*, 1979 *W, E, I, F, NZ*, 1980 *W, E*, 1981 *F, W, E, I, R, A*, 1982 *E, I, F, A* (2), 1983 *I, F, W, E*, 1984 *E, I, F*
Robertson, L (London Scottish, United Services) 1908 *E*, 1911 *W*, 1912 *W, I, E, SA*, 1913 *W, I, E*
Robertson, M A (Gala) 1958 *F*
Robertson, R D (London Scottish) 1912 *F*
Robson, A (Hawick) 1954 *F*, 1955 *F, W, I, E*, 1956 *F, W, I, E*, 1957 *F, W, I, E*, 1958 *W, A, I, E*, 1959 *F, W, I, E*, 1960 *F*
Rodd, J A T (United Services, RN, London Scottish) 1958 *F, W, A, I, E*, 1960 *F, W*, 1962 *F*, 1964 *F, NZ, W*, 1965 *F, W, I*
Rogerson, J (Kelvinside Acads) 1894 *W*
Roland, E T (Edinburgh Acads) 1884 *I, E*
Rollo, D M D (Howe of Fife) 1959 *E*, 1960 *F, W, I, E, SA*, 1961 *F, SA, W, I, E*, 1962 *F, W, E*, 1963 *F, W, I, E*, 1964 *F, NZ, W, I, E*, 1965 *F, W, I, E, SA*, 1966 *F, W, I, E, A*, 1967 *F, W, E, NZ*, 1968 *F, W, I*
Rose, D M (Jedforest) 1951 *F, W, I, E, SA*, 1953 *F, W*
Ross, A (Kilmarnock) 1924 *F, W*
Ross, A (Royal HSFP) 1905 *W, I, E*, 1909 *W, I*
Ross, A R (Edinburgh U) 1911 *W*. 1914 *W, I, E*
Ross, E J (London Scottish) 1904 *W*
Ross, G T (Watsonians) 1954 *NZ, I, E, W*
Ross, I A (Hillhead HSFP) 1951 *F, W, I, E*
Ross, J (London Scottish) 1901 *W, I, E*, 1902 *W*, 1903 *E*
Ross, K I (Boroughmuir FP) 1961 *SA, W, I, E*, 1962 *F, W, I, E*, 1963 *F, W, E*
Ross, W A (Hillhead HSFP) 1937 *W, E*
Rottenburg, H (Cambridge U, London Scottish) 1899 *W, E*, 1900 *W, I, E*
Roughead, W N (Edinburgh Acads, London Scottish) 1927 *NSW*, 1928 *F, W, I, E*, 1930 *I, E*, 1931 *F, W, I, E*, 1932 *W*
Rowan, N A (Boroughmuir) 1980 *W, E*, 1981 *F, W, E, I*
Rowand, R (Glasgow HSFP) 1930 *F, W*, 1932 *E*, 1933 *W, E, I*, 1934 *W*
Roy, A (Waterloo) 1938 *W, I, E*, 1939 *W, I, E*
Russell, W L (Glasgow Acads) 1905 *NZ*, 1906 *W, I, E*
Rutherford, J Y (Selkirk) 1979 *W, E, I, F, NZ*, 1980 *I, F, E*, 1981 *F, W, E, I, NZ* (2), *A*, 1982 *E, I, F, W, A* (2), 1983 *E, NZ*, 1984 *W, E, I, F*

Sampson, R W F (London Scottish) 1939 *W*, 1947 *W*
Sanderson, G A (Royal HSFP) 1907 *W, I, E*, 1908 *I*
Sanderson, J L P (Edinburgh Acads) 1873 *E*
Schulze, D G (London Scottish) 1905 *E*, 1907 *I, E*, 1908 *W, I, E*, 1909 *W, I, E*, 1910 *W, I, E*, 1911 *W*
Scobie, R M (Royal Military Coll) 1914 *W, I, E*
Scotland, K J F (Heriot's FP, Cambridge U, Leicester) 1957 *F, W, I, E*, 1958 *E*, 1959 *F, W, I, E*, 1960 *F, W, I, E*, 1961 *F, SA, W, I, E*, 1962 *F, W, I, E*, 1963 *F, W, I, E*, 1965 *F*
Scott, D M (Langholm, Watsonians) 1950 *I, E*, 1951 *W, I, E, SA*, 1952 *F, W, I*, 1953 *F*
Scott, J M B (Edinburgh Acads) 1907 *E*, 1908 *W, I, E*, 1909 *W, I, E*, 1910 *F, W, I, E*, 1911 *F, W, I*, 1912 *W, I, E, SA*, 1913 *W, I, E*
Scott, J S (St Andrews U) 1950 *E*
Scott, J W (Stewart's Coll FP) 1925 *F, W, I, E*, 1926 *F, W, I, E*, 1927 *F, W, I, E, NSW*, 1928 *F, W, E*, 1929 *E*, 1930 *F*
Scott, R (Hawick) 1898 *I*, 1900 *I, E*
Scott, T (Langholm, Hawick) 1896 *W*, 1897 *I, E*, 1898 *I, E*, 1899 *I, W, E*, 1900 *W, I, E*
Scott, T M (Hawick) 1893 *E*, 1895 *W, I, E*, 1896 *W, E*, 1897 *I, E*, 1898 *I, E*, 1900 *W, I*
Scott, W P (W of Scotland) 1900 *I, E*, 1902 *I, E*, 1903 *W, I, E*, 1904 *W, I, E*, 1905 *W, I, E, NZ*, 1906 *W, I, E, SA*, 1907 *W, I, E*
Scoular, J G (Cambridge U) 1905 *NZ*, 1906 *W, I, E, SA*
Selby, J A R (Watsonians) 1920 *W, I*
Shackleton, J A P (London Scottish) 1959 *E*, 1963 *F, W*, 1964 *NZ, W*, 1965 *I, SA*
Sharp, G (Stewart's FP, Army) 1960 *F*, 1964 *F, NZ, W*
Shaw, G D (Sale) 1935 *NZ*, 1936 *W*, 1937 *W, I, E*, 1939 *I*
Shaw, I (Glasgow HSFP) 1937 *I*
Shaw, J N (Edinburgh Acads) 1921 *W, I*
Shaw, R W (Glasgow HSFP) 1934 *W, I, E*, 1935 *W, I, E, NZ*, 1936 *W, I, E*, 1937 *W, I, E*, 1938 *W, I, E*, 1939 *W, I, E*
Shedden, D (W of Scotland) 1972 *NZ*, 1973 *F, W, I, E, P*, 1976 *W, E, I*, 1977 *I, F, W*, 1978 *I, F, W*
Shillinglaw, R B (Gala, Army) 1960 *I, E, SA*, 1961 *F, SA*
Simmers, B M (Glasgow Acads) 1965 *F, W*, 1966 *A*, 1967 *F, W, I*, 1971 *F* (R)
Simmers, W M (Glasgow Acads) 1926 *W, I, E*, 1927 *F, W, I, E, NSW*, 1928 *F, W, I, E*, 1929 *F, W, I, E*, 1930 *F, W, I, E*, 1931 *F, W, I, E*, 1932 *SA, W, I, E*
Simpson, J W (Royal HSFP) 1893 *I, E*, 1894 *W, I, E*, 1895 *W, I, E*, 1896 *W, I*, 1897 *E*, 1899 *W, E*
Simpson, R S (Glasgow Acads) 1923 *I*
Simson, E D (Edinburgh U, London Scottish) 1902 *E*, 1903 *W, I, E*, 1904 *W, I, E*, 1905 *W, I, E, NZ*, 1906 *W*,

I, *E*, 1907 *W*, *I*, *E*
Simson, J T (Watsonians) 1905 *NZ*, 1909 *W*, *I*, *E*, 1910 *F*, *W*, 1911 *I*
Simson, R F (London Scottish) 1911 *E*
Sloan, A T (Edinburgh Acads) 1914 *W*, 1920 *F*, *W*, *I*, *E*, 1921 *F*, *W*, *I*, *E*
Sloan, D A (Edinburgh Acads, London Scottish) 1950 *F*, *W*, *E*, 1951 *W*, *I*, *E*, 1953 *F*
Sloan, T (Glasgow Acads, Oxford U) 1905 *NZ*, 1906 *W*, *SA*, 1907 *W*, *E*, 1908 *W*, 1909 *I*
Smeaton, P W (Edinburgh Acads) 1881 *I*, 1883 *I*, *E*
Smith, A R (Oxford U) 1895 *W*, *I*, *E*, 1896 *W*, *I*, 1897 *I*, *E*, 1898 *I*, *E*, 1900 *I*, *E*
Smith, A R (Cambridge U, Gosforth, Ebbw Vale, Edinburgh Wands) 1955 *W*, *I*, *E*, 1956 *F*, *W*, *I*, *E*, 1957 *F*, *W*, *I*, *E*, 1958 *F*, *W*, *A*, *I*, 1959 *F*, *W*, *I*, *E*, 1960 *F*, *W*, *I*, *E*, *SA*, 1961 *F*, *SA*, *W*, *I*, *E*, 1962 *F*, *W*, *I*, *E*
Smith, D W C (London Scottish) 1949 *F*, *W*, *I*, *E*, 1950 *F*, *W*, *I*, 1953 *I*
Smith, E R (Edinburgh Acads) 1879 *I*
Smith, G K (Kelso) 1957 *I*, *E*, 1958 *F*, *W*, *A*, 1959 *F*, *W*, *I*, *E*, 1960 *F*, *W*, *I*, *E*, 1961 *F*, *SA*, *W*, *I*, *E*
Smith, H O (Watsonians) 1895 *W*, 1896 *W*, *I*, *E*, 1898 *I*, *E*, 1899 *W*, *I*, *E*, 1900 *E*, 1902 *E*
Smith, I S (Oxford U, Edinburgh U) 1924 *W*, *I*, *E*, 1925 *F*, *W*, *I*, *E*, 1926 *F*, *W*, *I*, *E*, 1927 *F*, *I*, *E*, 1929 *F*, *W*, *I*, *E*, 1930 *F*, *W*, *I*, 1931 *F*, *W*, *I*, *E*, 1932 *SA*, *W*, *I*, *E*, 1933 *W*, *E*, *I*
Smith, I S G (London Scottish) 1969 *SA*, 1970 *F*, *W*, *I*, *E*, 1971 *F*, *W*, *I*
Smith, M A (London Scottish) 1970 *W*, *I*, *E*, *A*
Smith, R T (Kelso) 1929 *F*, *W*, *I*, *E*, 1930 *F*, *W*, *I*
Smith, S H (Glasgow Acads) 1877 *I*, 1878 *E*
Smith, T J (Gala) 1983 *E*, *NZ*
Somerville, D (Edinburgh Inst FP) 1879 *I*, 1882 *I*, 1883 *W*, *I*, *E*, 1884 *W*
Speirs, L M (Watsonians) 1906 *SA*, 1907 *W*, *I*, *E*, 1908 *W*, *I*, *E*, 1910 *F*, *W*, *E*
Spence, K M (Oxford U) 1953 *I*
Spencer, E (Clydedale) 1898 *I*
Stagg, P K (Sale) 1965 *F*, *W*, *E*, *SA*, 1966 *F*, *W*, *I*, *E*, *A*, 1967 *F*, *W*, *I*, *E*, *NZ*, 1968 *F*, *W*, *I*, *E*, *A*, 1969 *F*, *W*, *I* (R), *SA*, 1970 *F*, *W*, *I*, *E*, *A*
Steele, W C C (Langholm, Bedford, RAF, London Scottish) 1969 *E*, 1971 *F*, *W*, *I*, *E* (2(1C]), 1972 *F*, *W*, *E*, *NZ*, 1973 *F*, *W*, *I*, *E*, 1975 *I*, *F*, *W*, *E*, *NZ* (R), 1976 *W*, *E*, *I*, 1977 *E*
Stephen, A E (W of Scotland) 1885 *W*, 1886 *I*
Steven, R (Edinburgh Wands) 1962 *I*
Stevenson, A K (Glasgow Acads) 1922 *F*, 1923 *F*, *W*, *E*
Stevenson, A M (Glasgow U) 1911 *F*
Stevenson, G D (Hawick) 1956 *E*, 1957 *F*, 1958 *F*, *W*, *A*, *I*, *E*, 1959 *W*, *I*, *E*, 1960 *W*, *I*, *E*, *SA*, 1961 *F*, *SA*, *W*, *I*, *E*, 1963 *F*, *W*, *I*, 1964 *E*, 1965 *F*
Stevenson, H J (Edinburgh Acads) 1888 *W*, *I*, 1889 *W*, *I*, 1890 *W*, *I*, *E*, 1891 *W*, *I*, *E*, 1892 *W*, *I*, *E*, 1893 *I*, *E*
Stevenson, L E (Edinburgh U) 1888 *W*
Stevenson, R C (London Scottish) 1897 *I*, *E*, 1898 *E*, 1899 *I*, *W*, *E*
Stevenson, R C (St Andrews U) 1910 *F*, *I*, *E*, 1911 *F*, *W*, *I*
Stevenson, W H (Glasgow Acads) 1925 *F*
Stewart, A K (Edinburgh U) 1874 *E*, 1876 *E*
Stewart, A M (Edinburgh Acads) 1914 *W*
Stewart, C A R (W of Scotland) 1880 *I*, *E*
Stewart, C E B (Kelso) 1960 *W*, 1961 *F*
Stewart, J (Glasgow HSFP) 1930 *F*
Stewart, J L (Edinburgh Acads) 1921 *I*
Stewart, M S (Stewart's Coll FP) 1932 *SA*, *W*, *I*, 1933 *W*, *E*, *I*, 1934 *W*, *I*, *E*
Stewart, W A (London Hospital) 1913 *F*, *W*, *I*, 1914 *W*
Steyn, S S L (Oxford U) 1911 *E*, 1912 *I*
Strachan, G M (Jordanhill) 1971 *E* (C) (R), 1973 *W*, *I*, *E*, *P*

Alan Tomes, the long-serving Scots lock, is tackled by Les Cusworth and Nick Youngs of England.

Stronach, R S (Glasgow Acads) 1901 *W, E*, 1905 *W, I, E*
Stuart, C D (W of Scotland) 1909 *I*, 1910 *F, W, I, E*, 1911 *I, E*
Stuart, L M (Glasgow HSFP) 1923 *F, W, I, E*, 1924 *F*, 1928 *E*, 1930 *I, E*
Suddon, N (Hawick) 1965 *W, I, E, SA*, 1966 *A*, 1968 *E, A*, 1969 *F, W, I*, 1970 *I, E, A*
Sutherland, W R (Hawick) 1910 *W, E*, 1911 *F, E*, 1912 *F, W, E, SA*, 1913 *F, W, I, E*, 1914 *W*
Swan, J S (Army, London Scottish, Leicester) 1953 *E*, 1954 *F, NZ, I, E, W*, 1955 *F, W, I, E*, 1956 *F, W, I, E*, 1957 *F, W*, 1958 *F*
Swan, M W (Oxford U, London Scottish) 1958 *F, W, A, I, E*, 1959 *F, W, I*
Sweet, J B (Glasgow HSFP) 1913 *E*, 1914 *I*
Symington, A W (Cambridge U) 1914 *W, E*

Tait, J G (Edinburgh Acads) 1880 *I*, 1885 *I*
Tait, P W (Royal HSFP) 1935 *E*
Taylor, E G (Oxford U) 1927 *W, NSW*
Taylor, R C (Kelvinside-West) 1951 *W, I, E, SA*
Telfer, C M (Hawick) 1968 *A*, 1969 *F, W, I, E*, 1972 *F, W, E*, 1973 *W, I, E, P*, 1974 *W, E, I*, 1975 *A*, 1976 *F*
Telfer, J W (Melrose) 1964 *F, NZ, W, I, E*, 1965 *F, W, I*, 1966 *F, W, I, E*, 1967 *W, I, E*, 1968 *E, A*, 1969 *F, W, I, E, SA*, 1970 *F, W, I*
Tennent, J M (W of Scotland) 1909 *W, I, E*, 1910 *F, W, E*
Thom, D A (London Scottish) 1934 *W*, 1935 *W, I, E, NZ*
Thom, G (Kirkcaldy) 1920 *F, W, I, E*
Thom, J R (Watsonians) 1933 *W, E, I*
Thomson, A E (United Services) 1921 *F, W, E*
Thomson, A M (St Andrews U) 1949 *I*
Thomson, B E (Oxford U) 1953 *F, W, I*
Thomson, I H M (Heriot's FP, Army) 1951 *W, I*, 1952 *F, W, I*, 1953 *I, E*
Thomson, J S (Glasgow Acads) 1871 *E*
Thomson, R H (London Scottish) 1960 *I, E, SA*, 1961 *F, SA, W, I, E*, 1963 *F, W, I, E*, 1964 *F, NZ, W*
Thomson, W H (W of Scotland) 1906 *SA*
Thomson, W J (W of Scotland) 1899 *W, E*, 1900 *W*
Timms, A B (Edinburgh U, Edinburgh Wands) 1896 *W*, 1900 *W, I*, 1901 *W, I, E*, 1902 *W, E*, 1903 *W, E*, 1904 *I, E*, 1905 *I, E*
Tod, H B (Gala) 1911 *F*
Tod, J (Watsonians) 1884 *W, I, E*, 1885 *W, I*, 1886 *W, I, E*
Todd, J K (Glasgow Acads) 1874 *E*, 1875 *E*
Tolmie, J M (Glasgow HSFP) 1922 *E*
Tomes, A J (Hawick) 1976 *E, I*, 1977 *E*, 1978 *I, F, W, E, NZ*, 1979 *W, E, I, F, NZ*, 1980 *F, W, E*, 1981 *F, W, E, I, NZ* (2), *R, A*, 1982 *E, I, F, W, A* (2), 1983 *I, F, W*, 1984 *W, E, I, F*
Torrie, T J (Edinburgh Acads) 1877 *E*
Turk, A S (Langholm) 1971 *E* (R)
Turnbull, F O (Kelso) 1951 *F, SA*
Turnbull, G O (W of Scotland) 1896 *I, E*, 1897 *I, E*, 1904 *W*
Turnbull, P (Edinburgh Acads) 1901 *W, I, E*, 1902 *W, I, E*
Turner, F H (Oxford U, Liverpool) 1911 *F, W, I, E*, 1912 *F, W, I, E, SA*, 1913 *F, W, I, E*, 1914 *I, E*
Turner, J W C (Gala) 1966 *W, A*, 1967 *F, W, I, E, NZ*, 1968 *F, W, I, E, A*, 1969 *F*, 1970 *E, A*, 1971 *F, W, I, E* (2[1C])

Usher, C M (United Services, Edinburgh Wands) 1912 *E*, 1913 *F, W, I, E*, 1914 *E*, 1920 *F, W, I, E*, 1921 *W, E*, 1922 *F, W, I, E*

Valentine, A R (RNAS, Anthorn) 1953 *F, W, I*
Valentine, D D (Hawick) 1947 *I, E*
Veitch, J P (Royal HSFP) 1882 *E*, 1883 *I*, 1884 *W, I, E*, 1885 *I*, 1886 *E*
Villar, C (Edinburgh Wands) 1876 *E*, 1877 *I, E*

Waddell, G H (London Scottish, Cambridge U) 1957 *E*, 1958 *F, W, A, I, E*, 1959 *F, W, I, E*, 1960 *I, E, SA*, 1961 *F*, 1962 *F, W, I, E*
Waddell, H (Glasgow Acads) 1924 *F, W, I, E*, 1925 *I, E*, 1926 *F, W, I, E*, 1927 *F, W, I, E*, 1930 *W*
Wade, A L (London Scottish) 1908 *E*
Walker, A (W of Scotland) 1881 *I*, 1882 *E*, 1883 *W, I, E*
Walker, A W (Cambridge U, Birkenhead Park) 1931 *F, W, I, E*, 1932 *I*
Walker, J G (W of Scotland) 1882 *E*, 1883 *W*
Walker, M (Oxford U) 1952 *F*
Wallace, A C (Oxford U) 1923 *F*, 1924 *F, W, E*, 1925 *F, W, I, E*, 1926 *F*
Wallace, W M (Cambridge U) 1913 *E*, 1914 *W, I, E*
Walls, W A (Glasgow Acads) 1882 *E*, 1883 *W, I, E*, 1884 *W, I, E*, 1886 *W, I, E*
Walter, M W (London Scottish) 1906 *I, E, SA*, 1907 *W, I*, 1908 *W, I*, 1910 *I*
Warren, J R (Glasgow Acads) 1914 *I*
Warren, R C (Glasgow Acads) 1922 *W, I*, 1930 *W, I, E*
Waters, F H (Cambridge U, London Scottish) 1930 *F, W, I, E*, 1932 *SA, W, I*
Waters, J A (Selkirk) 1933 *W, E, I*, 1934 *W, I, E*, 1935 *W, I, E, NZ*, 1936 *W, I, E*, 1937 *W, I, E*
Waters, J B (Cambridge U) 1904 *I, E*
Watherston, J G (Edinburgh Wands) 1934 *I, E*
Watherston, W R A (London Scottish) 1963 *F, W, I*
Watson, D H (Glasgow Acads) 1876 *E*, 1877 *I, E*
Watson, W S (Boroughmuir) 1974 *W, E, I, F*, 1975 *NZ*, 1977 *I, F, W*, 1979 *I, F*
Watt, A G M (Edinburgh Acads) 1947 *F, W, I, A*, 1948 *F, W*
Weatherstone, T G (Stewart's Coll FP) 1952 *E*, 1953 *I, E*, 1954 *F, NZ, I, E, W*, 1955 *F*, 1958 *W, A, I, E*, 1959 *W, I, E*
Welsh, R (Watsonians) 1895 *W, I, E*, 1896 *W*
Welsh, R B (Hawick) 1967 *I, E*
Welsh, W B (Hawick) 1927 *NSW*, 1928 *F, W, I*, 1929 *I, E*, 1930 *F, W, I, E*, 1931 *F, W, I, E*, 1932 *SA, W, I, E*, 1933 *W, E, I*
Welsh, W H (Edinburgh U) 1900 *I, E*, 1901 *W, I, E*, 1902 *W, I, E*
Wemyss, A (Gala, Edinburgh Wands) 1914 *W, I*, 1920 *F, E*, 1922 *F, W, I*
West, L (Edinburgh U, West Hartlepool) 1903 *W, I, E*, 1905 *I, E, NZ*, 1906 *W, I, E*
Weston, V G (Kelvinside Acads) 1936 *I, E*
White, D B (Gala) 1982 *F, W, A* (2)
White, D M (Kelvinside Acads) 1963 *F, W, I, E*
White, T B (Edinburgh Acads) 1888 *W, I*, 1889 *W*
Whittington, T P (Merchistonians) 1873 *E*
Whitworth, R J E (London Scottish) 1936 *I*
Whyte, D J (Edinburgh Wands) 1965 *W, I, E, SA*, 1966 *F, W, I, E, A*, 1967 *F, W, I, E*
Will, J G (Cambridge U) 1912 *F, W, I, E*, 1914 *W, I, E*
Wilson, A W (Dunfermline) 1931 *F, I, E*
Wilson, G A (Oxford U) 1949 *F, W, E*
Wilson, G R (Royal HSFP) 1886 *E*, 1890 *W, I, E*, 1891 *I*
Wilson, J H (Watsonians) 1953 *I*
Wilson, J S (St Andrews U) 1931 *F, W, I, E*, 1932 *E*
Wilson, J S (United Services, London Scottish) 1908 *I*, 1909 *W*
Wilson, R (London Scottish) 1976 *E, I*, 1977 *E, I, F*, 1978 *I, F*, 1981 *R*, 1983 *I*
Wilson, R L (Gala) 1951 *F, W, I, E, SA*, 1953 *F, W, E*
Wilson, R W (W of Scotland) 1873 *E*, 1874 *E*
Wilson, S (Oxford U, London Scottish) 1964 *F, NZ, W, I, E*, 1965 *W, I, E, SA*, 1966 *F, W, I, A*, 1967 *F, W, I, E, NZ*, 1968 *F, W, I, E*
Wood, A (Royal HSFP) 1873 *E*, 1874 *E*, 1875 *E*
Wood, G (Gala) 1931 *W, I*, 1932 *W, I, E*
Woodburn, J C (Kelvinside Acads) 1892 *I*
Woodrow, A N (Glasgow Acads) 1887 *I, W, E*
Wotherspoon, W (W of Scotland) 1891 *I*, 1892 *I*, 1893 *W, E*, 1894 *W, I, E*
Wright, F A (Edinburgh Acads) 1932 *E*
Wright, H B (Watsonians) 1894 *W*
Wright, K M (London Scottish) 1929 *F, W, I, E*
Wright, R W J (Edinburgh Wands) 1973 *F*
Wright, S T H (Stewart's Coll FP) 1949 *E*
Wright, T (Hawick) 1947 *A*

Young, A H (Edinburgh Acads) 1874 *E*
Young, E T (Glasgow Acads) 1914 *E*
Young, R G (Watsonians) 1970 *W*
Young, T E B (Durham) 1911 *F*
Young, W B (Cambridge U, London Scottish) 1937 *W, I, E*, 1938 *W, I, E*, 1939 *W, I, E*, 1948 *E*

SCOTTISH INTERNATIONAL RECORDS

From 1890-91, when uniform points-scoring was first adopted by International Board countries, to 30 April 1984. Both team and individual records are against International Board countries, only, except for the match against the SRU President's XV in the 1972-73 centenary season. Where caps have been awarded for other matches, this is recorded, in the case of the most capped players, in the notes.

TEAM RECORDS

Highest score
35 v Wales (35-10) 1924 Inverleith (Edinburgh)
v individual countries
28 v England (28-19) 1931 Murrayfield
32 v Ireland (32-9) 1984 Dublin
35 v Wales (35-10) 1924 Inverleith
31 v France (31-3) 1912 Inverleith
25 v N Zealand (25-25) 1983 Murrayfield
10 v S Africa (10-18) 1960 Port Elizabeth
24 v Australia (24-15) 1981 Murrayfield

Biggest winning points margin
28 v France (31-3) 1912 Inverleith
v individual countries
20 v England (26-6) 1971 Murrayfield
23 v Ireland (32-9) 1984 Dublin
25 v Wales (35-10) 1924 Inverleith
28 v France (31-3) 1912 Inverleith
No win v N Zealand
6 v S Africa (6-0) 1906 Hampden Park (Glasgow)
9 v Australia (24-15) 1981 Murrayfield

Highest score by opposing team
44 S Africa (0-44) 1951 Murrayfield
by individual countries
30 England (18-30) 1980 Murrayfield
26 Ireland (8-26) 1953 Murrayfield
35 Wales (12-35) 1972 Cardiff
23 France (3-23) 1977 Paris (Parc des Princes)
40 New Zealand (15-40) 1981 Auckland
44 S Africa (0-44) 1951 Murrayfield
33 Australia (9-33) 1982 Sydney

Biggest losing points margin
44 v S Africa (0-44) 1951 Murrayfield
v individual countries
20 v England (6-26) 1977 Twickenham
21 v Ireland (0-21) 1950 Dublin
23 v Wales (12-35) 1972 Cardiff
20 v France (3-23) 1977 Parc des Princes
25 v N Zealand (15-40) 1981 Auckland
44 v S Africa (0-44) 1951 Murrayfield
24 v Australia (9-33) 1982 Sydney

Most points by Scotland in International Championship in a season – 86
(in season 1983-84)

Most tries by Scotland in International Championship in a season – 17
(in season 1924-25)

Most tries by Scotland in an international
8 v Wales (35-10) 1924 Inverleith
Scotland scored 12 tries v Wales at Raeburn Place in 1887, but this was before uniform scoring was adopted.

Most tries against Scotland in an international
9 by S Africa (0-44) 1951 Murrayfield

INDIVIDUAL RECORDS

Most capped player
A B Carmichael 50 1967-78
J M Renwick 50 (51) 1972-83
A R Irvine 50 (51) 1972-82
Renwick and Irvine played once v Romania
in individual positions
Full-back
A R Irvine 46(51)* 1972-82
**Irvine has been chosen 4 times as a wing and once v Romania*

Wing
A R Smith 33 1955-62
Centre
J M Renwick 49(51)** 1972-83
Fly-half
J Y Rutherford 27*** 1979-84
Scrum-half
R J Laidlaw 26§ 1980-84
Prop
A B Carmichael 50 1967-78
Hooker
C T Deans 33§ 1978-84
Lock
A F McHarg 42(44)‡ 1968-79
Flanker
W I D Elliot 29 1947-54
No 8
J W Telfer 22(25)† 1964-70

***Renwick has played once on the wing, as a replacement, and once v Romania*
****I R McGeechan, 32 caps, won 20 as a centre and 12 as a fly-half*
†Telfer won 3 caps as a flanker
‡McHarg has won 2 caps at No 8
§Laidlaw and Deans have also played v Romania

Most internationals as captain – 19
J McLauchlan 1973-79

Most points in international – 261*
A R Irvine (50 appearances) 1972-82
**Includes one penalty try and excludes 12 points against Romania*

Most points in an international – 17
A R Irvine v Australia 1981 Murrayfield
P W Dods v France 1984 Murrayfield

Most tries in internationals – 24
I S Smith (32 appearances) 1924-33

Most tries in an international – 4
W A Stewart v Ireland 1913 Inverleith
I S Smith v France 1925 Inverleith
I S Smith v Wales 1925 Swansea

G C Lindsay scored 5 tries v Wales at Raeburn Place in 1887, but this was before uniform scoring was adopted. In 1925 I S Smith scored 6 tries in succession – the last 3 of the match v France, and the first 3 of the next match v Wales

---

Most conversions in an international – 5
F H Turner v France 1912 Inverleith
J W Allan v England 1931 Murrayfield

Most points in International Championship in a season – 50
P W Dods (4 appearances) 1983-84

Most tries in International Championship in a season – 8
I S Smith (4 appearances) 1924-25

Most conversions in International Championship in a season – 8
P W Dods (4 appearances) 1983-84

Most penalty goals in International Championship in a season – 10
P W Dods (4 appearances) 1983-84

Most points on overseas tour – 56
W Lauder (5 appearances) Australia 1970
A R Irvine (4 appearances) New Zealand 1981

Most points in any match on tour – 24
D W Morgan v Wellington 1975 Wellington, NZ
A R Irvine v King Country 1981 Taumarunui, NZ
A R Irvine v Wairarapa-Bush 1981 Masterton, NZ

Most tries in any match on tour – 3
A R Smith v Eastern Transvaal 1960 Springs, SA

THE 1983-84 SEASON IN IRELAND

Sean Diffley *The Irish Independent*

Back in 1981-82 when Ireland was winning the Triple Crown and International Championship, the harbingers of doom were already predicting the awful fate which awaited the seasoned team that had brought such distinction to the green jersey. In 1984 the prophecies came true with a resounding and doleful thud. The Irish hit rock-bottom, registering the 13th 'whitewash' in their history. It wasn't really unexpected – the signs had been there from early in the season. Many of the older forwards revealed all the symptoms of stress and strain and few of the younger fry demonstrated that they were ready to move up a niche or two.

The Irish selectors, chaired by a former national coach, Roly Meates, and including the new coach, Willie John McBride – lately back from the traumas of managing the 1983 Lions in New Zealand – let it be known that they intended to make some changes in the 1984 Irish team, but nothing really drastic. They knew – as everybody did – that changes would have to be made very astutely. The dangers of making wholesale alterations, and of disrupting the team by bringing in inexperienced players, were pointed out. But it must be said that the selectors did not follow their own counsel all that well and they must stand indicted for some strange, unproductive and indiscreet selections. They began by picking the first side of the season, against France in Paris, on the most negative of principles. The selectors' plan was to concentrate almost wholly on defence. It was a disaster at the Parc des Princes and the season continued in that vein.

The same pack and the same leader, hooker Ciaran Fitzgerald, were chosen for the French match but the selectors ignored flair for the middle of the field and chose in the centre David Irwin, clearly out of form, and a new cap in Rory Moroney, a solid performer. France ran riot in the opening moments of the match, to the total discomfiture of the Irish. It wasn't primarily the fault, of course, of the centres: the whole side, clearly not well organised, was caught napping. All Ireland could garner was four penalty goals from Ollie Campbell. The French eased off in the second half but still managed a grand total of 25 points.

There had been much muttering about the poor preparation the Irish team were given for the International Championship. The mutterings grew in volume after the Paris debacle and, if anything, the decibel-level increased as the defeats continued in the remaining matches. There is no doubt that the IRFU has been lax in organising tours to and from Ireland for the top players. In the lead-up to the 1984 Inter-

The Irish team which lost narrowly to England at Twickenham. Back row, L-R: *J-C Yché (touch-judge), W R Duncan, T M Ringland, D C Fitzgerald, M I Keane, D G Lenihan, J B O'Driscoll, H P MacNeill, P A Orr, H T Harbison, R Hourquet (referee), F Palmade (touch-judge)* Front row, L-R: *K D Crossan, M C Finn, M J Kiernan, W P Duggan (capt), A J P Ward, J A P Doyle.*

national Championship, Scotland and England played the touring New Zealanders. England also had the touring Canadians to help their preparations, and Wales had their matches with the Japanese and Romania. The French, too, had a busy build-up with games against Romania and Australia. Ireland, in vivid contrast, had nothing to aid their build-up except a 'B' international against Scotland at Melrose. It was known that Willie John McBride was concerned about this state of affairs. In a sense, the four defeats in 1984 may have been some sort of a blessing – the IRFU admitted afterwards that they had been slow in arranging decent extra fixtures for Irish teams.

Policy, I gather, has now been changed and the Irish Union now considers itself in the market-place for worthwhile tours. There is also a move afoot to found an all-Ireland competition for clubs. Ireland is the only major country which confines its club competitions to its various regions. It is generally felt that in this instance, too, the Irish have been lagging behind the other countries.

For Ireland's second match last season, against Wales in Dublin, the selectors shocked followers by dropping Fergus Slattery and bringing in Willie Duncan as flanker. Not only was Slattery (who had been having virus problems) not forgiven for a rather ordinary performance against France, but his replacement was not recognised as an openside flanker, which seemed to ensure that Duncan would hardly be a success. Gerry McLoughlin was dropped from tight-head prop and Jim McCoy from Dungannon was awarded his first cap. The consensus outside the selectors' rooms was that the nettle had not been grasped. The match against Wales underlined the point. Wales were far from their best form but won 18-9, with all Ireland's points coming once again from the place-kicking boot of Ollie Campbell. But on this occasion the Irish lost their captain, Ciaran Fitzgerald, with a nasty head gash. Willie Duggan took over the captaincy on the field when Fitzgerald retired from the match, and held the post until the end of the season.

That was Fitzgerald's last involvement of the season and it caused a furore. He was not picked for the match against England at Twickenham. The reason, it was announced, was that although he had been passed fit by the doctors, the selectors feared it would be a risk to play him; that the face wound would reopen and that Ireland would, for the second time, lose their captain. Instead, Harry Harbison of Bective Rangers was chosen as hooker, Duggan as captain, Moss Finn and Michael Kiernan as the centres and Tony Ward and Tony Doyle as the half-backs, replacing the indisposed Ollie Campbell and the discarded Robbie McGrath. Slattery returned to action and Des Fitzgerald was a new cap at tight-head prop. The Finn-Kiernan combination brought a glimmer of skill into midfield but the creaking bones elsewhere meant that England, although not playing with distinction, still won by 12-9.

Tony Ward kicked Ireland's three penalty goals at Twickenham and the only question left was whether Ireland would go through the campaign without scoring a try. To the relief of all, a 'record' was not set. At Lansdowne Road, against Scotland, Michael Kiernan did get over for a try, which John Murphy, at full-back, converted. Murphy had already kicked a penalty goal. In the meantime, of course, Scotland were making their own bit of history, scoring four tries in their 32-9 Triple Crown victory.

It was a victory that was not begrudged in the slightest. Most Irish supporters were pleased that Scotland had at last won a distinction they so richly deserved. But Ireland ended the season by scoring a mere 39 points (only England's poor total of 36 points was worse), and conceded 78 points, proving that their defence was the most porous of all.

In the Inter-provincial Championship the honours went to Leinster, who won the title for the fourth time in five years – the best dividend in the history of the event, which spans more than 100 years. But Ulster, who had a very young side, won plaudits for their enterprise. They arranged several matches against opposition from abroad, including a visiting team from Sydney, Australia. The IRFU were most appreciative of Ulster, who were the one side to adopt enthusiastically the policy of diversifying the fixture list outside Ireland.

Bangor, who scored 558 points in 30 matches, must again be considered the top side in Ireland, followed by Blackrock College, who led the 15 Leinster clubs. Cork Constitution were the best in Munster. However, all such assessments must be viewed in the context of the lack of a real country-wide competition. It is to be hoped that this situation will be remedied shortly.

INTER-PROVINCIAL MATCHES

Leinster 22, Munster 13; Connacht 9, Ulster 4; Leinster 20, Ulster 16; Munster 29, Connacht 7; Ulster 13, Munster 12; Leinster 29, Connacht 6

WINNERS OF PROVINCIAL TOURNAMENTS

LEINSTER
Senior Cup: Wanderers
Senior League: Terenure College
Provincial Towns Cup: Athy
Schools Senior Cup: Terenure College
Schools Junior Cup: Blackrock College
Old Belvedere Sevens: Lansdowne

MUNSTER
Senior Cup: Young Munster
Senior League: Cork Constitution
Junior Cup: Young Munster
Schools Senior Cup: CBC Cork
Schools Junior Cup: PBC Cork

ULSTER
Senior Cup: Malone
Senior League: Ards
Bass Boston Cup: Bangor
Schools Senior Cup: Methodist College
Schools Medallion: Campbell College

CONNACHT
Senior Cup: Corinthians
Senior League: Galwegians
Junior Cup: Corinthians
Schools Senior Cup: Garbally
Schools Junior Cup: Garbally

IRISH INTERNATIONAL PLAYERS
(up to 30 April 1984)

ABBREVIATIONS

A	Australia
E	England
F	France
M	Maoris
NSW	New South Wales
NZ	New Zealand
S	Scotland
SA	South Africa
P	Ireland v IRFU President's XV at Lansdowne Road in IRFU centenary season, 1974-75
W	Wales
(R)	Replacement
NIFC	North of Ireland Football Club
CIYMS	Church of Ireland Young Men's Society
KCH	King's College Hospital
Note:	Years given for Five Nations' matches are for second half of season; eg 1972 means season 1971-72. Years for all other matches refer to the actual year of the match
NB	The second of Ireland's two matches against France in 1972 was a non-championship match

Abraham, M (Bective Rangers) 1912 *E, S, W, SA,* 1914 *W*
Adams, C (Old Wesley) 1908 *E,* 1909 *E, F,* 1910 *F,* 1911 *E, S, W, F,* 1912 *S, W, SA,* 1913 *W, F,* 1914 *F, E, S*
Agar, R D (Malone) 1947 *F, E, S, W,* 1948 *F,* 1949 *S, W,* 1950 *F, E, W*
Agnew, P J (CIYMS) 1974 *F* (R), 1976 *A*
Ahearn, T (Queen's Coll, Cork) 1899 *E*
Alexander, R (NIFC, Police Union) 1936 *E, S, W,* 1937 *E, S, W,* 1938 *E, S,* 1939 *E, S, W*
Allen, C E (Derry, Liverpool) 1900 *E, S, W,* 1901 *E, S, W,* 1903 *S, W,* 1904 *E, S, W,* 1905 *E, S, W, NZ,* 1906 *E, S, W, SA,* 1907 *S, W*
Allen, G G (Derry, Liverpool) 1896 *E, S, W,* 1897 *E, S,* 1898 *E, S,* 1899 *E, W*
Allen, T C (NIFC) 1885 *E, S*
Allen, W S (Wanderers) 1875 *E*
Allison, J B (Edinburgh U) 1899 *E, S,* 1900 *E, S, W,* 1901 *E, S, W,* 1902 *E, S, W,* 1903 *S*
Anderson, F E (Queen's U, Belfast, NIFC) 1953 *F, E, S, W,* 1954 *NZ, F, E, S, W,* 1955 *F, E, S, W*
Anderson, H J (Old Wesley) 1903 *E, S,* 1906 *E, S*
Andrews, G (NIFC) 1875 *E,* 1876 *E*
Andrews, H W (NIFC) 1888 *M,* 1889 *S, W*
Archer, A M (Dublin U, NIFC) 1879 *S*
Arigho, J E (Lansdowne) 1928 *F, E, W,* 1929 *F, E, S, W,* 1930 *F, E, S, W,* 1931 *F, E, S, W, SA*
Armstrong, W K (NIFC) 1960 *SA,* 1961 *E*
Arnott, D T (Lansdowne) 1876 *E*
Ash, W H (NIFC) 1875 *E,* 1876 *E,* 1877 *S*
Aston, H R (Dublin U) 1908 *E, W*
Atkins, A P (Bective Rangers) 1924 *F*
Atkinson, J M (NIFC) 1927 *F, NSW*
Atkinson, J R (Dublin U) 1882 *W, S*

Bagot, J C (Dublin U, Lansdowne) 1879 *S, E,* 1880 *E, S,* 1881 *S*
Bailey, A H (UC Dublin, Lansdowne) 1934 *W,* 1935 *E, S, W, NZ,* 1936 *E, S, W,* 1937 *E, S, W,* 1938 *E, S*
Bailey, N (Northampton) 1952 *E*
Bardon, M E (Bohemians) 1934 *E*
Barlow, M (Wanderers) 1875 *E*
Barnes, R J (Dublin U, Armagh) 1933 *W*
Barr, A (Methodist Coll, Belfast) 1898 *W,* 1899 *S,* 1901 *E, S,*
Beamish, C E St J (RAF, Leicester) 1933 *W, S,* 1934 *S, W,* 1935 *E, S, W, NZ,* 1936 *E, S, W,* 1938 *W*
Beamish, G R (RAF, Leicester) 1925 *E, S, W,* 1928 *F, E, S, W,* 1929 *F, E, S, W,* 1930 *F, S, W,* 1931 *F, E, S, W, SA,* 1932 *E, S, W,* 1933 *E, W, S*
Beatty, W J (NIFC, Richmond) 1910 *F,* 1912 *F, W*
Becker, V (Lansdowne) 1974 *F, W*
Beckett, G G P (Dublin U) 1908 *E, S, W*
Bell, R J (NIFC) 1875 *E,* 1876 *E*
Bell, W E (Belfast Collegians) 1953 *F, E, S, W*
Bennett, F (Belfast Collegians) 1913 *S*
Bent, G C (Dublin U) 1882 *W, E*
Berkery, P J (Lansdowne) 1954 *W,* 1955 *W,* 1956 *S, W,* 1957 *F, E, S, W,* 1958 *A, E, S*
Bermingham, J J (Blackrock Coll) 1921 *E, S, W, F*
Blackham, J C (Queen's Coll, Cork) 1909 *S, W, F,* 1910 *E, S, W*
Blake-Knox, S E F (NIFC) 1976 *E, S,* 1977 *F* (R)
Blayney, J (Wanderers) 1950 *S*
Bond, A T W (Derry) 1894 *S, W*
Bornemann, W W (Wanderers) 1960 *E, S, W, SA*
Bowen, D St J (Cork Const) 1977 *W, E, S*
Boyd, C A (Dublin U) 1900 *S,* 1901 *S, W*
Boyle, C V (Dublin U) 1935 *NZ,* 1936 *E, S, W,* 1937 *E, S, W,* 1938 *W,* 1939 *W*
Brabazon, H M (Dublin U) 1884 *E,* 1886 *E*
Bradley, M J (Dolphin) 1920 *W, F,* 1922 *E, S, W, F,* 1923 *E, S, W, F,* 1925 *F, S, W,* 1926 *F, E, S, W,* 1927 *F, W*
Bradshaw, G (Belfast Collegians) 1903 *W*
Bradshaw, R M (Wanderers) 1885 *E, S*
Brady, A M (UC Dublin, Malone) 1966 *S,* 1968 *E, S, W*
Brady, J A (Wanderers) 1976 *E, S*
Brady, J R (CIYMS) 1951 *S, W,* 1953 *F, E, S, W,* 1954 *W,* 1956 *W,* 1957 *F, E, S, W*
Bramwell, T (NIFC) 1928 *F*
Brand, T N (NIFC) 1924 *NZ*
Brennan, J I (CIYMS) 1957 *S, W*
Bresnihan, F P K (UC Dublin, Lansdowne, London Irish) 1966 *E, W,* 1967 *A, E, S, W, F,* 1968 *F, E, S, W, A,* 1969 *F, E, S, W,* 1970 *SA, F, E, S, W,* 1971 *F, E, S, W*
Brett, J T (Monkstown) 1914 *W*
Bristow, J R (NIFC) 1879 *E*
Brophy, N H (Blackrock Coll, UC Dublin) 1957 *F, E,* 1959 *E, S, W, F,* 1960 *F, SA,* 1961 *S, W,* 1962 *E, S, W,* 1963 *E, W,* 1967 *E, S, W, F, A*
Brown, E L (Instonians) 1958 *F*
Brown, G S (Monkstown, United Services) 1912 *S, W, SA*
Brown, H (Windsor) 1877 *E*
Brown, T (Windsor) 1877 *E, S*
Brown, W H (Dublin U) 1899 *E*
Brown, W J (Malone) 1970 *SA, F, S, W*
Brown, W S (Dublin U) 1893 *S, W,* 1894 *E, S, W*
Browne, A W (Dublin U) 1951 *SA*
Browne, D (Blackrock Coll) 1920 *F*
Browne, H C (United Services and RN) 1929 *E, S, W*
Browne, W F (United Services and Army) 1925 *E, S, W,* 1926 *S, W,* 1927 *F, E, S, W, NSW,* 1928 *E, S*
Browning, D R (Wanderers) 1881 *E, S*
Bruce, S A M (NIFC) 1883 *E, S,* 1884 *E*
Brunker, A A (Lansdowne) 1895 *E, W*

Bryant, C H (Cardiff) 1920 *E*, *S*
Buchanan, A McM (Dublin U) 1926 *E*, *S*, *W*, 1927 *S*, *W*, *NSW*
Buchanan, J B (Dublin U) 1882 *S*, 1884 *E*, *S*
Buckley, J H (Sunday's Well) 1973 *E*, *S*
Bulger, L Q (Lansdowne) 1896 *E*, *S*, *W*, 1897 *E*, *S*, 1898 *E*, *S*, *W*
Bulger, M J (Dublin U) 1888 *M*
Burges, J H (Rosslyn Park) 1950 *F*, *E*
Burgess, R B (Dublin U) 1912 *SA*
Burkitt, J C S (Queen's Coll, Cork) 1881 *E*
Burns, I J (Wanderers) 1980 *E* (R)
Butler, L (Blackrock Coll) 1960 *W*
Butler, N (Bective Rangers) 1920 *E*
Byers, R M (NIFC) 1928 *S*, *W*, 1929 *E*, *S*, *W*
Byrne, E M J (Blackrock Coll) 1977 *S*, *F*, 1978 *F*, *W*, *E*, *NZ*
Byrne, F (UC Dublin) 1962 *F*
Byrne, S J (UC Dublin, Lansdowne) 1953 *S*, *W*, 1955 *F*
Byron, W G (NIFC) 1896 *E*, *S*, *W*, 1897 *E*, *S*, 1898 *E*, *S*, *W*, 1899 *E*, *S*, *W*

Caddell, E D (Dublin U, Wanderers) 1904 *S*, 1905 *E*, *S*, *W*, *NZ*, 1906 *E*, *S*, *W*, *SA*, 1907 *E*, *S*, 1908 *S*, *W*
Cagney, S J (London Irish) 1925 *W*, 1926 *F*, *E*, *S*, *W*, 1927 *F*, 1928 *E*, *S*, *W*, 1929 *F*, *E*, *S*, *W*
Callan, C P (Lansdowne) 1947 *F*, *E*, *S*, *W*, 1948 *F*, *E*, *S*, *W*, 1949 *F*, *E*
Cameron, E D (Bective Rangers) 1891 *S*, *W*
Campbell, C E (Old Wesley) 1970 *SA*
Campbell, E F (Monkstown) 1899 *S*, *W*, 1900 *E*, *W*
Campbell, S B B (Derry) 1911 *E*, *S*, *W*, *F*, 1912 *F*, *E*, *S*, *W*, *SA*, 1913 *E*, *S*, *F*
Campbell, S O (Old Belvedere) 1976 *A*, 1979 *A* (2), 1980 *E*, *S*, *F*, *W*, 1981 *F*, *W*, *E*, *S*, *SA*, 1982 *W*, *E*, *S*, *F*, 1983 *S*, *F*, *W*, *E*, 1984 *F*, *W*
Canniffe, D M (Lansdowne) 1976 *W*, *E*
Cantrell, J L (UC Dublin, Blackrock Coll) 1976 *A*, *F*, *W*, *E*, *S*, 1981 *S*, *SA* (2), *A*
Carpendale, M J (Monkstown) 1886 *S*, 1887 *W*, 1888 *W*, *S*
Carroll, C (Bective Rangers) 1930 *F*
Carroll, R (Lansdowne) 1947 *F*, 1950 *S*, *W*
Casement, B N (Dublin U) 1875 *E*, 1876 *E*, 1879 *E*
Casement, F (Dublin U) 1906 *E*, *S*, *W*
Casey, P J (Lansdowne) 1963 *F*, *E*, *S*, *W*, *NZ*, 1964 *E*, *S*, *W*, *F*, 1965 *F*, *E*, *S*
Casey, T C (Young Munster) 1930 *S*, 1932 *E*
Chambers, J (Dublin U) 1886 *E*, *S*, 1887 *E*, *S*, *W*
Chambers, R R (Instonians) 1951 *F*, *E*, *S*, *W*, 1952 *F*, *W*
Clarke, J A B (Bective Rangers) 1922 *S*, *W*, *F*, 1923 *F*, 1924 *E*, *S*, *W*
Clegg, R J (Bangor) 1973 *F*, 1975 *E*, *S*, *F*, *W*
Clifford, T (Young Munster) 1949 *F*, *E*, *S*, *W*, 1950 *F*, *E*, *S*, *W*, 1951 *F*, *E*, *SA*, 1952 *F*, *S*, *W*
Clinch, A D (Dublin U, Wanderers) 1892 *S*, 1893 *W*, 1895 *E*, *S*, *W*, 1896 *E*, *S*, *W*, 1897 *E*, *S*
Clinch, J D (Wanderers, Dublin U) 1923 *W*, 1924 *F*, *E*, *S*, *W*, *NZ*, 1925 *F*, *E*, *S*, 1926 *E*, *S*, *W*, 1927 *F*, 1928 *F*, *E*, *S*, *W*, 1929 *F*, *E*, *S*, *W*, 1930 *F*, *E*, *S*, *W*, 1931 *F*, *E*, *S*, *W*, *SA*
Clune, J J (Blackrock Coll) 1912 *SA*, 1913 *W*, *F*, 1914 *F*, *E*, *W*
Coffey, J J (Lansdowne) 1900 *E*, 1901 *W*, 1902 *E*, *S*, *W*, 1903 *E*, *S*, *W*, 1905 *E*, *S*, *W*, *NZ*, 1906 *E*, *S*, *W*, *SA*, 1907 *E*, 1908 *W*, 1910 *F*
Cogan, W St J (Queen's Coll, Cork) 1907 *E*, *S*
Collier, S R (Queen's Coll, Belfast) 1883 *S*
Collis, W R F (KCH, Harlequins) 1924 *F*, *W*, *NZ*, 1925 *F*, *E*, *S*, 1926 *F*
Collis, W S (Wanderers) 1884 *W*
Collopy, G (Bective Rangers) 1891 *S*, 1892 *S*
Collopy, R (Bective Rangers) 1923 *E*, *S*, *W*, *F*, 1924 *F*, *E*, *S*, *W*, *NZ*, 1925 *F*, *E*, *S*, *W*
Collopy, W P (Bective Rangers) 1914 *F*, *E*, *S*, *W*, 1921 *E*, *S*, *W*, *F*, 1922 *E*, *S*, *W*, *F*, 1923 *S*, *W*, *F*, 1924 *F*, *E*, *S*, *W*
Combe, A (NIFC) 1875 *E*
Condon, H C (London Irish) 1984 *S* (R)
Cook, H G (Lansdowne) 1884 *W*
Coote, P B (RAF, Leicester) 1933 *S*
Corcoran, J C (London Irish) 1947 *A*, 1948 *F*
Corken, T S (Belfast Collegians) 1937 *E*, *S*, *W*
Corley, H H (Dublin U, Wanderers) 1902 *E*, *S*, *W*, 1903 *E*, *S*, *W*, 1904 *E*, *S*
Cormac, H S T (Clontarf) 1921 *E*, *S*, *W*
Costello, P (Bective Rangers) 1960 *F*
Cotton, J (Wanderers) 1889 *W*
Coulter, H H (Queen's U, Belfast) 1920 *E*, *S*, *W*
Courtney, A W (UC Dublin) 1920 *S*, *W*, *F*, 1921 *E*, *S*, *W*, *F*
Cox, H L (Dublin U) 1875 *E*, 1876 *E*, 1877 *E*, *S*
Craig, R G (Queen's U, Belfast) 1938 *S*, *W*
Crawford, E C (Dublin U) 1885 *E*
Crawford, W E (Lansdowne) 1920 *E*, *S*, *W*, *F*, 1921 *E*, *S*, *W*, *F*, 1922 *E*, *S*, 1923 *E*, *S*, *W*, *F*, 1924 *F*, *E*, *W*, *NZ*, 1925 *F*, *E*, *S*, *W*, 1926 *F*, *E*, *S*, *W*, 1927 *F*, *E*, *S*, *W*
Crean, T J (Wanderers) 1894 *E*, *S*, *W*, 1895 *E*, *S*, *W*, 1896 *E*, *S*, *W*
Crichton, R Y (Dublin U) 1920 *E*, *S*, *W*, *F*, 1921 *F*, 1922 *E*, 1923 *W*, *F*, 1924 *F*, *E*, *S*, *W*, *NZ*, 1925 *E*, *S*
Croker, E W D (Limerick) 1878 *E*
Cromey, G E (Queen's U, Belfast) 1937 *E*, *S*, *W*, 1938 *E*, *S*, *W*, 1939 *E*, *S*, *W*
Cronyn, A P (Dublin U, Lansdowne) 1875 *E*, 1876 *E*, 1880 *S*
Crossan, K D (Instonians) 1982 *S*, 1984 *F*, *W*, *E*, *S*
Crowe, J (UC Dublin) 1974 *NZ*
Crowe, L (Old Belvedere) 1950 *E*, *S*, *W*
Crowe, M P (Lansdowne) 1929 *W*, 1930 *E*, *S*, *W*, 1931 *F*, *S*, *W*, *SA*, 1932 *S*, *W*, 1933 *W*, *S*, 1934 *E*
Crowe, P (Blackrock Coll) 1935 *E*, 1938 *E*
Cullen, T J (UC Dublin) 1949 *F*
Cullen, W J (Monkstown and Manchester) 1920 *E*
Culliton, M G (Wanderers) 1959 *E*, *S*, *W*, *F*, 1960 *E*, *S*, *W*, *F*, *SA*, 1961 *E*, *S*, *W*, *F*, 1962 *S*, *F*, 1964 *E*, *S*, *W*, *F*
Cummins, W E A (Queen's Coll, Cork) 1879 *S*, 1881 *E*, 1882 *E*
Cunningham, D McC (NIFC) 1923 *E*, *S*, *W*, 1925 *F*, *E*, *W*
Cunningham, M J (UC Cork) 1955 *F*, *E*, *S*, *W*, 1956 *F*, *S*, *W*
Cunningham, W A (Lansdowne) 1920 *W*, 1921 *E*, *S*, *W*, *F*, 1922 *E*, 1923 *S*, *W*
Cuppaidge, J L (Dublin U) 1879 *E*, 1880 *E*, *S*
Currell, J (NIFC) 1877 *S*
Curtis, A B (Oxford U) 1950 *F*, *E*, *S*
Cuscaden, W A (Dublin U, Bray) 1876 *E*
Cussen, D J (Dublin U) 1921 *E*, *S*, *W*, *F*, 1922 *E*, 1923 *E*, *S*, *W*, *F*, 1926 *F*, *E*, *S*, *W*, 1927 *F*, *E*

Daly, J C (London Irish) 1947 *F*, *E*, *S*, *W*, 1948 *E*, *S*, *W*
Daly, M J (Harlequins) 1938 *E*
Dargan, M (Old Belvedere) 1952 *S*, *W*
Davidson, C T (NIFC) 1921 *F*
Davidson, I G (NIFC) 1899 *E*, 1900 *S*, *W*, 1901 *E*, *S*, *W*, 1902 *E*, *S*, *W*
Davidson, J C (Dungannon) 1969 *F*, *E*, *S*, *W*, 1973 *NZ*, 1976 *NZ*
Davies, F E (Lansdowne) 1892 *S*, *W*, 1893 *E*, *S*, *W*
Davis, J L (Monkstown) 1898 *E*, *S*
Davis, W J N (Edinburgh U, Bessbrook) 1890 *S*, *W*, *E*, 1891 *E*, *S*, *W*, 1892 *E*, *S*, 1895 *S*
Davison, W (Belfast Academy) 1887 *W*
Davy, E O'D (UC Dublin, Lansdowne) 1925 *W*, 1926 *F*, *E*, *S*, *W*, 1927 *F*, *E*, *S*, *W*, *NSW*, 1928 *F*, *E*, *S*, *W*, 1929 *F*, *E*, *S*, *W*, 1930 *F*, *E*, *S*, *W*, 1931 *F*, *E*, *S*, *W*, *SA*, 1932 *E*, *S*, *W*, 1933 *E*, *W*, *S*, 1934 *E*
Dawson, A R (Wanderers) 1958 *A*, *E*, *S*, *W*, *F*, 1959 *E*, *S*, *W*, *F*, 1960 *F*, *SA*, 1961 *E*, *S*, *W*, *F*, *SA*, 1962 *S*, *F*, *W*, 1963 *F*, *E*, *S*, *W*, *NZ*, 1964 *E*, *S*, *F*
Dean, P M (St Mary's Coll) 1981 *SA* (2), *A*, 1982 *W*, *E*, *S*, *F*
Deane, E C (Monkstown) 1909 *E*
Deering, M (Bective Rangers) 1929 *W*
Deering, S J (Bective Rangers) 1935 *E*, *S*, *W*, *NZ*, 1936 *E*, *S*, *W*, 1937 *E*, *S*
Deering, S M (Garryowen, St Mary's Coll) 1974 *W*, 1976 *F*, *W*, *E*, *S*, 1977 *W*, *E*, 1978 *NZ*
de Lacy, H (Harlequins) 1948 *E*, *S*
Delany, M G (Bective Rangers) 1895 *W*
Dennison, J P (Garryowen) 1973 *F*, 1975 *E*, *S*
Dick, C J (Ballymena) 1961 *W*, *F*, *SA*, 1962 *W*, 1963 *F*, *E*, *S*, *W*
Dick, J S (Queen's U, Belfast) 1962 *E*
Dick, J S (Queen's Coll, Cork) 1887 *E*, *S*, *W*
Dickson, J A N (Dublin U) 1920 *E*, *W*, *F*

Doherty, A (Old Wesley) 1974 *P* (R)
Doherty, W D (Guy's Hospital) 1920 *E, S, W*, 1921 *E, S, W, F*
Donaldson, J A (Belfast Collegians) 1958 *A, E, S, W*
Donovan, T M (Queen's Coll, Cork) 1889 *S*
Dooley, J F (Galwegians) 1959 *E, S, W*
Doran, B R W (Lansdowne) 1900 *S, W*, 1901 *E, S, W*, 1902 *E, S, W*
Doran, E F (Lansdowne) 1890 *S, W*
Doran, G P (Lansdowne) 1899 *S, W*, 1900 *E, S*, 1902 *S, W*, 1903 *W*, 1904 *E*
Douglas, A C (Instonians) 1923 *F*, 1924 *E, S*, 1927 *NSW*, 1928 *S*
Downing, A J (Dublin U) 1882 *W*
Dowse, J C A (Monkstown) 1914 *F, S, W*
Doyle, J A P (Greystones) 1984 *E, S*
Doyle, J I (Bective Rangers) 1935 *W*
Doyle, M G (Blackrock Coll, UC Dublin) 1965 *F, E, S, W, SA*, 1966 *F, E, S, W*, 1967 *A, E, S, W, F, A*, 1968 *F, E, S, W, A*
Doyle, T J (Wanderers) 1968 *E, S, W*
Duggan, A T A (Lansdowne) 1963 *NZ*, 1964 *F*, 1966 *W*, 1967 *A, S, W, A*, 1968 *F, E, S, W*, 1969 *F, E, S, W*, 1970 *SA, F, E, S, W*, 1971 *F, E, S, W*, 1972 *F*
Duggan, W (UC Cork) 1920 *S, W*
Duggan, W P (Blackrock Coll) 1975 *E, S, F, W*, 1976 *A, F, W, S, NZ*, 1977 *W, E, S, F*, 1978 *S, F, W, E, NZ*, 1979 *E, S, A* (2), 1980 *E*, 1981 *F, W, E, S, SA* (2), *A*, 1982 *W, E, S*, 1983 *S, F, W, E*, 1984 *F, W, E, S*
Duncan, W R (Malone) 1984 *W, E*
Dunlop, R (Dublin U) 1889 *W*, 1890 *S, W, E*, 1891 *E, S, W*, 1892 *E, S*, 1893 *W*, 1894 *W*
Dunn, P E F (Bective Rangers) 1923 *S*
Dunn, T B (NIFC) 1935 *NZ*
Dunne, M J (Lansdowne) 1929 *F, E, S*, 1930 *F, E, S, W*, 1932 *E, S, W*, 1933 *E, W, S*, 1934 *E, S, W*
Dwyer, P J (UC Dublin) 1962 *W*, 1963 *F, NZ*, 1964 *S, W*

Edwards, H G (Dublin U) 1877 *E*, 1878 *E*
Edwards, R W (Malone) 1904 *W*
Edwards, T (Lansdowne) 1888 *M*, 1890 *S, W, E*, 1892 *W*, 1893 *E*
Edwards, W V (Malone) 1912 *F, E*
Egan, J D (Bective Rangers) 1922 *S*
Egan, J T (Cork Constitution) 1931 *F, E, SA*
Egan, M S (Garryowen) 1893 *E*, 1895 *S*
Ekin, W (Queen's Coll, Belfast) 1888 *W, S*
Elliott, W R J (Bangor) 1979 *S*
English, M A F (Lansdowne, Limerick Bohemians) 1958 *W, F*, 1959 *E, S, F*, 1960 *E, S*, 1961 *S, W, F*, 1962 *F, W*, 1963 *E, S, W, NZ*
Ennis, F N G (Wanderers) 1979 *A* (R)
Ensor, A H (Wanderers) 1973 *W, F*, 1974 *F, W, E, S, P, NZ*, 1975 *E, S, F, W*, 1976 *A, F, W, E, NZ*, 1977 *E*, 1978 *S, F, W, E*
Entrican, J C (Queen's U, Belfast) 1931 *S*

Fagan, C (Wanderers) 1956 *F, E, S*
Fagan, G L (Kingstown School) 1878 *E*
Farrell, J L (Bective Rangers) 1926 *F, E, S, W*, 1927 *F, E, S, W, NSW*, 1928 *F, E, S, W*, 1929 *F, E, S, W*, 1930 *F, E, S, W*, 1931 *F, E, S, W, SA*, 1932 *E, S, W*
Feddis, N (Lansdowne) 1956 *E*
Feighery, C F P (Lansdowne) 1972 *F, E, F*
Feighery, T A O (St Mary's Coll) 1977 *W, E*
Ferris, J H (Queen's Coll, Belfast) 1900 *E, S, W*, 1901 *W*
Finlay, J E (Queen's Coll, Belfast) 1913 *E, S, W*, 1920 *E, S, W*
Finlay, W (NIFC) 1876 *E*, 1877 *E, S*, 1878 *E*, 1879 *S, E*, 1880 *S*, 1882 *S*
Finn, M C (UC Cork, Cork Constitution) 1979 *E*, 1982 *W, E, S, F*, 1983 *S, F, W, E*, 1984 *E, S*
Finn, R (UC Dublin) 1977 *F*
Fitzgerald, C C (Glasgow U, Dungannon) 1902 *E*, 1903 *E, S*
Fitzgerald, C F (St Mary's Coll) 1979 *A* (2), 1980 *E, S, F, W*, 1982 *W, E, S, F*, 1983 *S, F, W, E*, 1984 *F, W*
Fitzgerald, D C (Lansdowne) 1984 *E, S*
Fitzgerald, J (Wanderers) 1884 *W*
Fitzpatrick, M P (Wanderers) 1978 *S*, 1980 *S, F, W*, 1981 *F, W, E, S, A*

Fletcher, W W (Kingstown) 1882 *W, S*, 1883 *E*
Flood, R S (Dublin U) 1925 *W*
Flynn, M K (Wanderers) 1959 *F*, 1960 *F*, 1962 *E, S, F, W*, 1964 *E, S, W, F*, 1965 *F, E, S, W, SA*, 1966 *F, E, S*, 1972 *F, E, F*, 1973 *NZ*
Fogarty, T (Garryowen) 1891 *W*
Foley, B O (Shannon) 1976 *F, E*, 1977 *W* (R), 1980 *F, W*, 1981 *F, E, S, SA* (2), *A*
Forbes, R E (Malone) 1907 *E*
Forrest, A J (Wanderers) 1880 *E, S*, 1881 *E, S*, 1882 *W, E*, 1883 *E*
Forrest, E G (Wanderers) 1888 *M*, 1889 *S, W*, 1890 *S, E*, 1891 *E*, 1893 *S*, 1894 *E, S, W*, 1895 *W*, 1897 *E, S*
Forrest, H (Wanderers) 1893 *S, W*
Fortune, J J (Clontarf) 1963 *NZ*, 1964 *E*
Foster, A R (Derry) 1910 *E, S, F*, 1911 *E, S, W, F*, 1912 *F, E, S, W*, 1914 *E, S, W*, 1921 *E, S, W*
Franks, J G (Dublin U) 1898 *E, S, W*
Frazer, E F (Bective Rangers) 1891 *S*, 1892 *S*
Freer, A E (Lansdowne) 1901 *E, S, W*
Fulton, J (NIFC) 1895 *S, W*, 1896 *E*, 1897 *E*, 1898 *W*, 1899 *E*, 1900 *W*, 1901 *E*, 1902 *E, S, W*, 1903 *E, S, W*, 1904 *E, S*

Gaffikin, W (Windsor) 1875 *E*
Gage, J H (Queen's U, Belfast) 1926 *S, W*, 1927 *S, W*
Galbraith, E (Dublin U) 1875 *E*
Galbraith, H T (Belfast Acad) 1890 *W*
Galbraith, R (Dublin U) 1875 *E*, 1876 *E*, 1877 *E*
Ganly, J B (Monkstown) 1927 *F, E, S, W, NSW*, 1928 *F, E, S, W*, 1929 *F, S*, 1930 *F*
Gardiner, F (NIFC) 1900 *E, S*, 1901 *E, W*, 1902 *E, S, W*, 1903 *E, W*, 1904 *E, S, W*, 1906 *E, S, W*, 1907 *S, W*, 1908 *S, W*, 1909 *E, S, F*
Gardiner, J B (NIFC) 1923 *E, S, W, F*, 1924 *F, E, S, W, NZ*, 1925 *F, E, S, W*
Gardiner, S (Belfast Albion) 1893 *E, S*
Gardiner, W (NIFC) 1892 *E, S*, 1893 *E, S, W*, 1894 *E, S, W*, 1895 *E, S, W*, 1896 *E, S, W*, 1897 *E, S*, 1898 *W*
Garry, M G (Bective Rangers) 1909 *E, S, W, F*, 1911 *E, S, W*
Gaston, J T (Dublin U) 1954 *NZ, F, E, S, W*, 1955 *W*, 1956 *F, E*
Gavin, T J (Moseley, London Irish) 1949 *F, E*
Gibson, C M H (Cambridge U, NIFC) 1964 *E, S, W, F*, 1965 *F, E, S, W, SA*, 1966 *F, E, S, W*, 1967 *A, E, S, W, F, A*, 1968 *E, S, W, A*, 1969 *E, S, W*, 1970 *SA, F, E, S, W*, 1971 *F, E, S, W*, 1972 *F, E, F*, 1973 *NZ, E, S, W, F*, 1974 *F, W, E, S, P*, 1975 *E, S, F, W*, 1976 *A, F, W, E, S, NZ*, 1977 *W, E, S, F*, 1978 *F, W, E, NZ*, 1979 *S, A* (2)
Gibson, M E (Lansdowne) 1979 *F, W, E, S*, 1981 *W* (R)
Gifford, H P (Wanderers) 1890 *S*
Gillespie, J C (Dublin U) 1922 *W, F*
Gilpin, F G (Queen's U, Belfast) 1962 *E, S, F*
Glass, D C (Belfast Collegians) 1958 *F*, 1960 *W*, 1961 *W, SA*
Glennon, J J (Skerries) 1980 *E, S*
Godfrey, R P (UC Dublin) 1954 *S, W*
Goodall, K G (City of Derry and Newcastle U) 1967 *A, E, S, W, F, A*, 1968 *F, E, S, W, A*, 1969 *F, E, S*, 1970 *SA, F, E, S, W*
Gordon, A (Dublin U) 1884 *S*
Gordon, T G (NIFC) 1877 *E, S*, 1878 *E*
Gotto, R P C (NIFC) 1906 *SA*
Goulding, W J (Cork) 1879 *S*
Grace, T O (UC Dublin, St Mary's Coll) 1972 *F, E*, 1973 *NZ, E, S, W*, 1974 *E, S, P, NZ*, 1975 *E, S, F, W*, 1976 *A, F, W, E, S, NZ*, 1977 *W, E, S, F*, 1978 *S*
Graham, R I (Dublin U) 1911 *F*
Grant, E L (CIYMS) 1971 *F, E, S, W*
Grant, P J (Bective Rangers) 1894 *S, W*
Graves, C R A (Wanderers) 1934 *E, S, W*, 1935 *E, S, W, NZ*, 1936 *E, S, W*, 1937 *E, S*, 1938 *E, S, W*
Gray, R D (Old Wesley) 1923 *E, S*, 1925 *F*, 1926 *F*
Gregg, R J (Queen's U, Belfast) 1953 *F, E, S, W*, 1954 *F, E, S*
Greene, E H (Dublin U, Kingstown) 1882 *W*, 1884 *W*, 1885 *E, S*, 1886 *E*
Greer, R (Kingstown) 1876 *E*
Greeves, T J (NIFC) 1907 *E, S, W*, 1909 *W, F*
Griffin, C S (London Irish) 1951 *F, E*
Griffin, J L (Wanderers) 1949 *S, W*

Griffiths, W (Limerick) 1878 *E*
Grimshaw, C (Queen's U, Belfast) 1969 *E* (R)
Guerin, B N (Galwegians) 1956 *S*
Gwynn, A P (Dublin U) 1895 *W*
Gwynn, L H (Dublin U) 1893 *S*, 1894 *E, S, W*, 1897 *S*, 1898 *E, S*

Hakin, R F (CIYMS) 1976 *W, S, NZ*, 1977 *W, E, F*
Hall, R O N (Dublin U) 1884 *W*
Hall, W H (Instonians) 1923 *E, S, W, F*, 1924 *F, S*
Hallaran, C F G T (Royal Navy) 1921 *E, S, W*, 1922 *E, S, W*, 1923 *E, F*, 1924 *F, E, S, W*, 1925 *F*, 1926 *F, E*
Halpin, T (Garryowen) 1909 *S, W, F*, 1910 *E, S, W*, 1911 *E, S, W, F*, 1912 *F, E, S*
Hamilton, A J (Lansdowne) 1884 *W*
Hamilton, R L (NIFC) 1926 *F*
Hamilton, R W (Wanderers) 1893 *W*
Hamilton, W J (Dublin U) 1877 *E*
Hamlet, G T (Old Wesley) 1902 *E, S, W*, 1903 *E, S, W*, 1904 *S, W*, 1905 *E, S, W, NZ*, 1906 *SA*, 1907 *E, S, W*, 1908 *E, S, W*, 1909 *E, S, W, F*, 1910 *E, S, F*, 1911 *E, S, W, F*
Hanrahan, C J (Dolphin) 1926 *S, W*, 1927 *E, S, W, NSW*, 1928 *F, E, S*, 1929 *F, E, S, W*, 1930 *F, E, S, W*, 1931 *F*, 1932 *S, W*
Harbison, H T (Bective Rangers) 1984 *W* (R), *E, S*
Hardy, G G (Bective Rangers) 1962 *S*
Harman, G R A (Dublin U) 1899 *E, W*
Harper, J (Instonians) 1947 *F, E, S*
Harpur, T G (Dublin U) 1908 *E, S, W*
Harrison, T (Cork) 1879 *S*, 1880 *S*, 1881 *E*
Harvey, F M W (Wanderers) 1907 *W*, 1911 *F*
Harvey, G A D (Wanderers) 1903 *E, S*, 1904 *W*, 1905 *E, S*
Harvey, T A (Dublin U) 1900 *W*, 1901 *S, W*, 1902 *E, S, W*, 1903 *E, W*
Headon, T A (UC Dublin) 1939 *S, W*
Healey, P (Limerick) 1901 *E, S, W*, 1902 *E, S, W*, 1903 *E, S, W*, 1904 *S*
Heffernan, M R (Cork Constitution) 1911 *E, S, W, F*
Hemphill, R (Dublin U) 1912 *F, E, S, W*
Henderson, N J (Queen's U, Belfast, NIFC) 1949 *S, W*, 1950 *F*, 1951 *F, E, S, W, SA*, 1952 *F, S, W, E*, 1953 *F, E, S, W*, 1954 *NZ, F E, S, W*, 1955 *F, E, S, W*, 1956 *S, W*, 1957 *F, E, S, W*, 1958 *A, E, S, W, F*, 1959 *E, S, W, F*
Henebrey, G J (Garryowen) 1906 *E, S, W, SA*, 1909 *W, F*
Heron, A G (Queen's Coll, Belfast) 1901 *E*
Heron, J (NIFC) 1877 *S*, 1879 *E*
Heron, W T (NIFC) 1880 *E, S*
Herrick, R W (Dublin U) 1886 *S*
Heuston, F S (Kingstown) 1882 *W*, 1883 *E, S*
Hewitt, D (Queen's U, Belfast, Instonians) 1958 *A, E, S, F*, 1959 *S, W, F*, 1960 *E, S, W, F*, 1961 *E, S, W, F*, 1962 *S, F*, 1965 *W*
Hewitt, F S (Instonians) 1924 *W, NZ*, 1925 *F, E, S*, 1926 *E*, 1927 *E, S, W*
Hewitt, J A (NIFC) 1981 *SA* (2[2R])
Hewitt, T R (Queen's U, Belfast) 1924 *W, NZ*, 1925 *F, E, S*, 1926 *F, E, S, W*
Hewitt, V A (Instonians) 1935 *S, W, NZ*, 1936 *E, S, W*
Hewitt, W J (Instonians) 1954 *E*, 1956 *S*, 1959 *W*, 1961 *SA*
Hewson, F T (Wanderers) 1875 *E*
Hickie, D J (St Mary's Coll) 1971 *F, E, S, W*, 1972 *F, E*
Higgins, J A D (Civil Service) 1947 *S, W, A*, 1948 *F, S, W*
Higgins, W W (NIFC) 1884 *E, S*
Hillary, M (UC Dublin) 1952 *E*
Hingerty, D (UC Dublin) 1947 *F, E, S, W*
Hinton, W P (Old Wesley) 1907 *W*, 1908 *E, S, W*, 1909 *E, S*, 1910 *E, S, W, F*, 1911 *E, S, W*, 1912 *F, E, W*
Hipwell, M L (Terenure Coll) 1962 *E, S*, 1968 *F, A*, 1969 *F* (R), *S* (R), *W*, 1971 *F, E, S, W*, 1972 *F*
Hobbs, T H M (Dublin U) 1884 *S*, 1885 *E*
Hobson, E W (Dublin U) 1876 *E*
Hogg, W (Dublin U) 1885 *S*
Holland, J J (Wanderers) 1981 *SA* (2)
Holmes, G W (Dublin U) 1912 *SA*, 1913 *E, S*
Holmes, L J (Lisburn) 1889 *S, W*
Hooks, K J (Queen's U, Belfast) 1981 *S*
Horan, A K (Blackheath) 1920 *E, W*
Houston, K J (Oxford U, London Irish) 1961 *SA*, 1964 *S, W*, 1965 *F, E, SA*
Hughes, R W (NIFC) 1878 *E*, 1880 *E, S*, 1881 *S*, 1882 *E, S*, 1883 *E, S*, 1884 *E, S*, 1885 *E*, 1886 *E*
Hunt, E W F de Vere (Army, Rosslyn Park) 1930 *F*, 1932 *E, S, W*, 1933 *E*
Hunter, D V (Dublin U) 1885 *S*
Hunter, L (Civil Service) 1968 *W, A*
Hunter, W R (CIYMS) 1962 *E, S, W, F*, 1963 *F, E, S*, 1966 *F, E, S*
Hutton, S A (Malone) 1967 *S, W, F, A*

Ireland, J (Windsor) 1876 *E*, 1877 *E*
Irvine, H A S (Collegians) 1901 *S*
Irwin, D G (Queen's U, Belfast) 1980 *F, W*, 1981 *F, W, E, S, SA* (2), *A*, 1982 *W*, 1983 *S, F, W, E*, 1984 *F, W*
Irwin, J W S (NIFC) 1938 *E, S*, 1939 *E, S, W*
Irwin, S T (Queen's Coll, Belfast) 1900 *E, S, W*, 1901 *E, W*, 1902 *E, S, W*, 1903 *S*

Jack, H W (UC Cork) 1914 *S, W*, 1921 *W*
Jackson, A R V (Wanderers) 1911 *E, S, W, F*, 1913 *W, F*, 1914 *F, E, S, W*
Jackson, F (NIFC) 1923 *E*
Jackson, H W (Dublin U) 1877 *E*
Jameson, J S (Lansdowne) 1888 *M*, 1889 *S, W*, 1891 *W*, 1892 *E, W*, 1893 *S*
Jeffares, E W (Wanderers) 1913 *E, S*
Johnston, J (Belfast Acad) 1881 *S*, 1882 *S*, 1884 *S*, 1885 *S*, 1886 *E*, 1887 *E, S, W*
Johnston, M (Dublin U) 1880 *E, S*, 1881 *E, S*, 1882 *E*, 1884 *E, S*, 1886 *E*
Johnston, R (Wanderers) 1893 *E, W*
Johnston, R W (Dublin U) 1890 *S, W, E*
Johnston, T J (Queen's Coll, Belfast) 1892 *E, S, W*, 1893 *E, S*, 1895 *E*
Johnstone, W E (Dublin U) 1884 *W*
Johnstone-Smyth, T R (Lansdowne) 1882 *E*

Kavanagh, J R (UC Dublin, Wanderers) 1953 *F, E, S, W*, 1954 *NZ, S, W*, 1955 *F, E*, 1956 *E, S, W*, 1957 *F, E, S, W*, 1958 *A, E, S, W*, 1959 *E, S, W, F*, 1960 *E, S, W, F, SA*, 1961 *E, S, W, F, SA*, 1962 *F*
Kavanagh, P (UC Dublin, Wanderers) 1952 *E*, 1955 *W*
Keane, M I (Lansdowne) 1974 *F, W, E, S, P, NZ*, 1975 *E, S, F, W*, 1976 *A, F, W, E, S, NZ*, 1977 *W, E, S, F*, 1978 *S, F, W, E, NZ*, 1979 *F, W, E, S, A* (2), 1980 *E, S, F, W*, 1981 *F, W, E, S*, 1982 *W, E, S, F*, 1983 *S, F, W, E*, 1984 *F, W, E, S*
Kearney, R K (Wanderers) 1982 *F*
Keeffe, E (Sunday's Well) 1947 *F, E, S, W, A*, 1948 *F*
Kelly, H C (NIFC) 1877 *E, S*, 1878 *E*, 1879 *S*, 1880 *E, S*
Kelly, J C (UC Dublin) 1962 *F, W*, 1963 *F, E, S, W, NZ*, 1964 *E, S, W, F*
Kelly, S (Lansdowne) 1954 *S, W*, 1955 *S*, 1960 *W, F*
Kelly, W (Wanderers) 1884 *S*
Kennedy, A G (Belfast Collegians) 1956 *F*
Kennedy, F (Wanderers) 1880 *E*, 1881 *E*, 1882 *W*
Kennedy, F A (Wanderers) 1904 *E, W*
Kennedy, H (Bradford) 1938 *S, W*
Kennedy, J M (Wanderers) 1882 *W*, 1884 *W*
Kennedy, K W (Queen's U, Belfast, London Irish) 1965 *F, E, S, W, SA*, 1966 *F, E, W*, 1967 *A, E, S, W, F, A*, 1968 *F, A*, 1969 *F, E, S, W*, 1970 *SA, F, E, S, W*, 1971 *F, E, S, W*, 1972 *F, E, F*, 1973 *NZ, E, S, W, F*, 1974 *F, W, E, S, P, NZ*, 1975 *F, W*
Kennedy, T J (St Mary's Coll) 1978 *NZ*, 1979 *F, W, E* (R), *A* (2), 1980 *E, S, F, W*, 1981 *SA* (2), *A*
Keogh, F S (Bective Rangers) 1964 *W, F*
Keon, J J (Limerick) 1879 *E*
Kidd, F W (Dublin U, Lansdowne) 1877 *E, S*, 1878 *E*
Kiely, M D (Lansdowne) 1962 *W*, 1963 *F, E, S, W*
Kiernan, M J (Dolphin, Lansdowne) 1982 *W* (R), *E, S, F*, 1983 *S, F, W, E*, 1984 *E, S*
Kiernan, T J (UC Cork, Cork Const) 1960 *E, S, W, F, SA*, 1961 *E, S, W, F, SA*, 1962 *E, W*, 1963 *F, S, W, NZ*, 1964 *E, S*, 1965 *F, E, S, W, SA*, 1966 *F, E, S, W*, 1967 *A, E, S, W, F, A*, 1968 *F, E, S, W, A*, 1969 *F, E, S, W*, 1970 *SA, F, E, S, W*, 1971 *F*, 1972 *F, E, F*, 1973 *NZ, E, S*
Killeen, G V (Garryowen) 1912 *E, S, W*, 1913 *E, S, W, F*, 1914 *E, S, W*
King, H (Dublin U) 1883 *E, S*
Knox, J H (Dublin U, Lansdowne) 1904 *W*, 1905 *E, S,*

W, *NZ*, 1906 *E*, *S*, *W*, 1907 *W*, 1908 *S*
Kyle, J W (Queen's U, Belfast, NIFC) 1947 *F*, *E*, *S*, *W*, *A*, 1948 *F*, *E*, *S*, *W*, 1949 *F*, *E*, *S*, *W*, 1950 *F*, *E*, *S*, *W*, 1951 *F*, *E*, *S*, *W*, *SA*, 1952 *F*, *S*, *W*, *E*, 1953 *F*, *E*, *S*, *W*, 1954 *NZ*, *F*, 1955 *F*, *E*, *W*, 1956 *F*, *E*, *S*, *W*, 1957 *F*, *E*, *S*, *W*, 1958 *A*, *E*, *S*

Lambert, N H (Lansdowne) 1934 *S*, *W*
Lamont, R A (Instonians) 1965 *F*, *E*, *SA*, 1966 *F*, *E*, *S*, *W*, 1970 *SA*, *F*, *E*, *S*, *W*
Landers, M F (Cork Const) 1904 *W*, 1905 *E*, *S*, *W*, *NZ*
Lane, D (UC Cork) 1934 *S*, *W*, 1935 *E*, *S*
Lane, M F (UC Cork) 1947 *W*, 1949 *F*, *E*, *S*, *W*, 1950 *F*, *E*, *S*, *W*, 1951 *F*, *S*, *W*, *SA*, 1952 *F*, *S*, 1953 *F*, *E*
Lane, P (Old Crescent) 1964 *W*
Langan, D J (Clontarf) 1934 *W*
Lavery, P (London Irish) 1974 *W*, 1976 *W*
Lawler, P J (Clontarf) 1951 *S*, *SA*, 1952 *F*, *S*, *W*, *E*, 1953 *F*, 1954 *NZ*, *E*, *S*, 1956 *F*, *E*
Lawlor, P J (Bective Rangers) 1935 *E*, *S*, *W*, 1937 *E*, *S*, *W*
Leahy, M W (UC Cork) 1964 *W*
Lee, S (NIFC) 1891 *E*, *S*, *W*, 1892 *E*, *S*, *W*, 1893 *E*, *S*, *W*, 1894 *E*, *S*, *W*, 1895 *E*, *W*, 1896 *E*, *S*, *W*, 1897 *E*, 1898 *E*
Le Fanu, V C (Cambridge U, Lansdowne) 1886 *E*, *S*, 1887 *E*, *W*, 1888 *S*, 1889 *W*, 1890 *E*, 1891 *E*, 1892 *E*, *S*, *W*
Lenihan, D G (UC Cork, Cork Const) 1981 *A*, 1982 *W*, *E*, *S*, *F*, 1983 *S*, *F*, *W*, *E*, 1984 *F*, *W*, *E*, *S*
L'Estrange, L P F (Dublin U) 1962 *E*
Levis, F H (Wanderers) 1884 *E*
Lightfoot, E J (Lansdowne) 1931 *F*, *E*, *S*, *W*, *SA*, 1932 *E*, *S*, *W*, 1933 *E*, *W*, *S*
Lindsay, H (Dublin U, Armagh) 1893 *E*, *S*, *W*, 1894 *E*, *S*, *W*, 1895 *E*, 1896 *E*, *S*, *W*, 1898 *E*, *S*, *W*
Little, T J (Bective Rangers) 1898 *W*, 1899 *S*, *W*, 1900 *S*, *W*, 1901 *E*, *S*
Lloyd, R A (Dublin U, Liverpool) 1910 *E*, *S*, 1911 *E*, *S*, *W*, *F*, 1912 *F*, *E*, *S*, *W*, *SA*, 1913 *E*, *S*, *W*, *F*, 1914 *F*, *E*, 1920 *E*, *F*
Lydon, C (Galwegians) 1956 *S*
Lyle, R K (Dublin U) 1910 *W*, *F*
Lyle, T R (Dublin U) 1885 *E*, *S*, 1886 *E*, 1887 *E*, *S*
Lynch, J F (St Mary's Coll) 1971 *F*, *E*, *S*, *W*, 1972 *F*, *E*, *F*, 1973 *NZ*, *E*, *S*, *W*, 1974 *F*, *W*, *E*, *S*, *P*, *NZ*
Lynch, L (Lansdowne) 1956 *S*
Lytle, J H (NIFC) 1894 *E*, *S*, *W*, 1895 *S*, *W*, 1896 *E*, *S*, *W*, 1897 *E*, *S*, 1898 *E*, *S*, 1899 *S*
Lytle, J N (NIFC) 1888 *M*, 1889 *W*, 1890 *E*, 1891 *E*, *S*, 1894 *E*, *S*, *W*
Lyttle, V J (Collegians, Bedford) 1938 *E*, 1939 *E*, *S*

McAllan, G H (Dungannon) 1896 *S*, *W*
Macaulay, J (Limerick) 1887 *E*, *S*
McBride, W J (Ballymena) 1962 *E*, *S*, *F*, *W*, 1963 *F*, *E*, *S*, *W*, *NZ*, 1964 *E*, *S*, *F*, 1965 *F*, *E*, *S*, *W*, *SA*, 1966 *F*, *E*, *S*, *W*, 1967 *A*, *E*, *S*, *W*, *F*, *A*, 1968 *F*, *E*, *S*, *W*, *A*, 1969 *F*, *E*, *S*, *W*, 1970 *SA*, *F*, *E*, *S*, *W*, 1971 *F*, *E*, *S*, *W*, 1972 *F*, *E*, *F*, 1973 *NZ*, *E*, *S*, *W*, *F*, 1974 *F*, *W*, *E*, *S*, *P*, *NZ*, 1975 *E*, *S*, *F*, *W*
McCallan, B (Ballymena) 1960 *E*, *S*
McCarten, R J (London Irish) 1961 *E*, *W*, *F*
McCarthy, E A (Kingstown) 1882 *W*
McCarthy, J S (Dolphin) 1948 *F*, *E*, *S*, *W*, 1949 *F*, *E*, *S*, *W*, 1950 *W*, 1951 *F*, *E*, *S*, *W*, *SA*, 1952 *F*, *S*, *W*, *E*, 1953 *F*, *E*, *S*, 1954 *NZ*, *F*, *E*, *S*, *W*, 1955 *F*, *E*
MacCarthy, St G (Dublin U) 1882 *W*
McCarthy, T (Cork) 1898 *W*
McClelland, T A (Queen's U, Belfast) 1921 *E*, *S*, *W*, *F*, 1922 *E*, *W*, *F*, 1923 *E*, *S*, *W*, *F*, 1924 *F*, *E*, *S*, *W*, *NZ*
McClenahan, R O (Instonians) 1923 *E*, *S*, *W*
McClinton, A N (NIFC) 1910 *W*, *F*
McCombe, W McM (Dublin U, Bangor) 1968 *F*, 1975 *E*, *S*, *F*, *W*
McConnell, A A (Collegians) 1947 *A*, 1948 *F*, *E*, *S*, *W*, 1949 *F*, *E*
McConnell, G (Derry, Edinburgh U) 1912 *F*, *E*, 1913 *W*, *F*
McConnell, J W (Lansdowne) 1913 *S*
McCormac, F M (Wanderers) 1909 *W*, 1910 *W*, *F*
McCormick, W J (Wanderers) 1930 *E*
McCoull, H C (Belfast Albion) 1895 *E*, *S*, *W*, 1899 *E*
McCourt, D (Queen's U, Belfast) 1947 *A*
McCoy, J J (Dungannon) 1984 *W*
McCracken, H (NIFC) 1954 *W*
McDermott, S J (London Irish) 1955 *S*, *W*
Macdonald, J A (Methodist Coll, Belfast) 1875 *E*, 1876 *E*, 1877 *S*, 1878 *E*, 1879 *S*, 1880 *E*, 1881 *S*, 1882 *E*, *S*, 1883 *E*, *S*, 1884 *E*, *S*
McDonnell, A C (Dublin U) 1889 *W*, 1890 *S*, *W*, 1891 *E*
McDowell, J C (Instonians) 1924 *F*, *NZ*
McFarland, B A T (Derry) 1920 *S*, *W*, *F*, 1922 *W*
McGann, B J (Lansdowne) 1969 *F*, *E*, *S*, *W*, 1970 *SA*, *F*, *E*, *S*, *W*, 1971 *F*, *E*, *S*, *W*, 1972 *F*, *E*, *F*, 1973 *NZ*, *E*, *S*, *W*, 1976 *F*, *W*, *E*, *S*, *NZ*
McGown, T M W (NIFC) 1899 *E*, *S*, 1901 *S*
McGrath, D G (UC Dublin) 1984 *S*
McGrath, N F (Oxford U, London Irish) 1934 *W*
McGrath, T (Garryowen) 1956 *W*, 1958 *F*, 1960 *E*, *S*, *W*, *F*, 1961 *SA*
McGrath, P J (UC Cork) 1965 *E*, *S*, *W*, *SA*, 1966 *F*, *E*, *S*, *W*, 1967 *A* (2)
McGrath, R J M (Wanderers) 1977 *W*, *E*, *F* (R), 1981 *SA* (2), *A*, 1982 *W*, *E*, *S*, *F*, 1983 *S*, *F*, *W*, *E*, 1984 *F*, *W*
McGuire, E P (UC Galway) 1963 *E*, *S*, *W*, *NZ*, 1964 *E*, *S*, *W*, *F*
MacHale, S (Lansdowne) 1965 *F*, *E*, *S*, *W*, *SA*, 1966 *F*, *E*, *S*, *W*, 1967 *S*, *W*, *F*
McIldowie, G (Malone) 1906 *SA*, 1910 *E*, *S*, *W*
McIlrath, J A (Ballymena) 1976 *A*, *F*, *NZ*, 1977 *W*, *E*
McIlwaine, E H (NIFC) 1895 *S*, *W*
McIlwaine, E N (NIFC) 1875 *E*, 1876 *E*
McIlwaine, J E (NIFC) 1897 *E*, *S*, 1898 *E*, *S*, *W*, 1899 *E*, *W*
McIntosh, L M (Dublin U) 1884 *S*
MacIvor, C V (Dublin U) 1912 *F*, *E*, *S*, *W*, 1913 *E*, *S*, *F*
McKay, J W (Queen's U, Belfast) 1947 *F*, *E*, *S*, *W*, *A*, 1948 *F*, *E*, *S*, *W*, 1949 *F*, *E*, *S*, *W*, 1950 *F*, *E*, *S*, *W*, 1951 *F*, *E*, *S*, *W*, *SA*, 1952 *F*
McKee, W D (NIFC) 1947 *A*, 1948 *F*, *E*, *S*, *W*, 1949 *F*, *E*, *S*, *W*, 1950 *F*, *E*, 1951 *SA*
McKelvey, J M (Queen's U, Belfast) 1956 *F*, *E*
McKibbin, A R (Instonians, London Irish) 1977 *W*, *E*, *S*, 1978 *S*, *F*, *W*, *E*, *NZ*, 1979 *F*, *W*, *E*, *S*, 1980 *E*, *S*
McKibbin, C H (Instonians) 1976 *S* (R)
McKibbin, D (Instonians) 1950 *F*, *E*, *S*, *W*, 1951 *F*, *E*, *S*, *W*
McKibbin, H R (Queen's U, Belfast) 1938 *W*, 1939 *E*, *S*, *W*
McKinney, S A (Dungannon) 1972 *F*, *E*, *F*, 1973 *W*, *F*, 1974 *F*, *E*, *S*, *P*, *NZ*, 1975 *E*, *S*, 1976 *A*, *F*, *W*, *E*, *S*, *NZ*, 1977 *W*, *E*, *S*, 1978 *S* (R), *F*, *W*, *E*
McLaughlin, J H (Derry) 1887 *E*, *S*, 1888 *W*, *S*
McLean, R E (Dublin U) 1881 *S*, 1882 *W*, *E*, *S*, 1883 *E*, *S*, 1884 *E*, *S*, 1885 *E*
Maclear, B (Cork County, Monkstown) 1905 *E*, *S*, *W*, *NZ*, 1906 *E*, *S*, *W*, *SA*, 1907 *E*, *S*, *W*
McLennan, A C (Wanderers) 1977 *F*, 1978 *S*, *F*, *W*, *E*, *NZ*, 1979 *F*, *W*, *E*, *S*, 1980 *E*, *F*, 1981 *F*, *W*, *E*, *S*, *SA* (2)
McLoughlin, F M (Northern) 1976 *A*
McLoughlin, G A J (Shannon) 1979 *F*, *W*, *E*, *S*, *A* (2), 1980 *E*, 1981 *SA* (2), 1982 *W*, *E*, *S*, *F*, 1983 *S*, *F*, *W*, *E*, 1984 *F*
McLoughlin, R J (Blackrock Coll) 1962 *E*, *S*, *F*, 1963 *E*, *S*, *W*, *NZ*, 1964 *E*, *S*, 1965 *F*, *E*, *S*, *W*, *SA*, 1966 *F*, *E*, *S*, *W*, 1971 *F*, *E*, *S*, *W*, 1972 *F*, *E*, *F*, 1973 *NZ*, *E*, *S*, *W*, *F*, 1974 *F*, *W*, *E*, *S*, *P*, *NZ*, 1975 *E*, *S*, *F*, *W*
McMahon, L B (Blackrock Coll, UC Dublin) 1931 *E*, *SA*, 1933 *E*, 1934 *E*, 1936 *E*, *S*, *W*, 1937 *E*, *S*, *W*, 1938 *E*, *S*
McMaster, A W (Ballymena) 1972 *F*, *E*, *F*, 1973 *NZ*, *E*, *S*, *W*, *F*, 1974 *F*, *E*, *S*, *P*, 1975 *F*, *W*, 1976 *A*, *F*, *W*, *NZ*
McMordie, J (Queen's Coll, Belfast) 1886 *S*
McMorrow, A (Garryowen) 1951 *W*
McMullen, A R (Cork) 1881 *E*, *S*
McNamara, V (UC Cork) 1914 *E*, *S*, *W*
McNaughton, P P (Greystones) 1978 *S*, *F*, *W*, *E*, 1979 *F*, *W*, *E*, *S*, *A* (2), 1980 *E*, *S*, *F*, *W*, 1981 *F*
MacNeill, H P (Dublin U, Oxford U) 1981 *F*, *W*, *E*, *S*, *A*, 1982 *W*, *E*, *S*, *F*, 1983 *S*, *F*, *W*, *E*, 1984 *F*, *W*, *E*
MacSweeney, D A (Blackrock Coll) 1955 *S*
McVicker, H (Army, Richmond) 1927 *E*, *S*, *W*, *NSW*, 1928 *F*
McVicker, J (Collegians) 1924 *F*, *E*, *S*, *W*, *NZ*, 1925 *F*, *E*, *S*, *W*, 1926 *F*, *E*, *S*, *W*, 1927 *F*, *E*, *S*, *W*, *NSW*, 1928 *W*, 1930 *F*
McVicker, S (Queen's U, Belfast) 1922 *E*, *S*, *W*, *F*

Madden, M N (Sunday's Well) 1955 *E, S, W*
Magee, J T (Bective Rangers) 1895 *E*
Magee, A M (Louis) (Bective Rangers, London Irish) 1895 *E, S, W*, 1896 *E, S W*, 1897 *E, S*, 1898 *E, S, W*, 1899 *E, S, W*, 1900 *E, S, W*, 1901 *E, S, W*, 1902 *E, S, W*, 1903 *E, S, W*, 1904 *W*
Maginiss, R M (Dublin U) 1875 *E*, 1876 *E*
Magrath, R M (Cork Constitution) 1909 *S*
Maguire, J F (Cork) 1884 *S*
Mahony, J (Dolphin) 1923 *E*
Malcolmson, G L (RAF, NIFC) 1935 *NZ*, 1936 *E, S, W*, 1937 *E, S, W*
Maloney, J (UC Dublin) 1950 *S*
Marshall, B D E (Queen's U, Belfast) 1963 *E*
Massey-Westropp, R H (Limerick, Monkstown) 1886 *E*
Matier, R N (NIFC) 1878 *E*, 1879 *S*
Mattsson, J (Wanderers) 1948 *E*
Mays, K M A (UC Dublin) 1973 *NZ, E, S, W*
Mayne, R B (Queen's U, Belfast) 1937 *W*, 1938 *E, W*, 1939 *E, S, W*
Mayne, R H (Belfast Academy) 1888 *W, S*
Mayne, T (NIFC) 1921 *E, S, F*
Meares, A W D (Dublin U) 1899 *S, W*, 1900 *E, W*
Megaw, J (Richmond, Instonians) 1934 *W*, 1938 *E*
Millar, A (Kingstown) 1880 *E, S*, 1883 *E*
Millar, H J (Monkstown) 1904 *W*, 1905 *E, S, W*
Millar, S (Ballymena) 1958 *F*, 1959 *E, S, W, F*, 1960 *E, S, W, F, SA*, 1961 *E, S, W, F, SA*, 1962 *E, S, F*, 1963 *F, E, S, W*, 1964 *F*, 1968 *F, E, S, W, A*, 1969 *F, E, S, W*, 1970 *SA, F, E, S, W*
Millar, W H J (Queen's U, Belfast) 1951 *E, S, W*, 1952 *S, W*
Miller, F H (Wanderers) 1886 *S*
Milliken, R A (Bangor) 1973 *E, S, W, F*, 1974 *F, W, E, S, P, NZ*, 1975 *E, S, F, W*
Millin, T J (Dublin) 1925 *W*
Minch, J B (Bective Rangers) 1912 *SA*, 1913 *E, S*, 1914 *E, S*
Moffat, J (Belfast Academy) 1888 *W, S, M*, 1889 *S*, 1890 *S, W*, 1891 *S*
Moffatt, J E (Old Wesley) 1904 *S*, 1905 *E, S, W*
Moffett, J W (Ballymena) 1961 *E, S*
Molloy, M G (UC Galway, London Irish) 1966 *F, E*, 1967 *A, E, S, W, F, A*, 1968 *F, E, S, W, A*, 1969 *F, E, S, W*, 1970 *F, E, S, W*, 1971 *F, E, S, W*, 1973 *F*, 1976 *A*
Moloney, J J (St Mary's Coll) 1972 *F, E, F*, 1973 *NZ, E, S, W, F*, 1974 *F, W, E, S, P, NZ*, 1975 *E, S, F, W*, 1976 *S*, 1978 *S, F, W, E*, 1979 *A* (2), 1980 *S, W*
Moloney, L A (Garryowen) 1976 *W* (R), *S*, 1978 *S* (R), *NZ*
Monteith, J D E (Queen's U, Belfast) 1947 *E, S, W*
Montgomery, A (NIFC) 1895 *S*
Montgomery, F P (Queen's U, Belfast) 1914 *E, S, W*
Montgomery, R (Cambridge U) 1887 *E, S, W*, 1891 *E*, 1892 *W*
Moore, C M (Dublin U) 1887 *S*, 1888 *W, S*
Moore, D F (Wanderers) 1883 *E, S*, 1884 *E, W*
Moore, F W (Wanderers) 1884 *W*, 1885 *E, S*, 1886 *S*
Moore, H (Windsor) 1876 *E*, 1877 *S*
Moore, H (Queen's U, Belfast) 1910 *S*, 1911 *W, F*, 1912 *F, E, S, W, SA*
Moore, T A P (Highfield) 1967 *A*, 1973 *NZ, E, S, W, F*, 1974 *F, W, E, S, P, NZ*
Moore, W D (Queen's Coll, Belfast) 1878 *E*
Moran, F G (Clontarf) 1936 *E*, 1937 *E, S, W*, 1938 *S, W*, 1939 *E, S, W*
Morell, H B (Dublin U) 1881 *E, S*, 1882 *W, E*
Morgan, G J (Clontarf) 1934 *E, S, W*, 1935 *E, S, W, NZ*, 1936 *E, S, W*, 1937 *E, S, W*, 1938 *E, S, W*, 1939 *E, S, W*
Moriarty, C C H (Monkstown) 1899 *W*
Moroney, J C M (Garryowen) 1968 *W, A*, 1969 *F, E, S, W*
Moroney, R J (Lansdowne) 1984 *F, W*
Moroney, T A (UC Dublin) 1964 *W*, 1976 *A, E*
Morphy, E McG (Dublin U) 1908 *E*
Morris, D P (Bective Rangers) 1931 *W*, 1932 *E*, 1935 *E, S, W, NZ*
Morrow, J W R (Queen's Coll, Belfast) 1882 *S*, 1883 *E, S*, 1884 *E, W*, 1885 *S*, 1886 *E, S*, 1888 *S*
Mortell, M (Dolphin) 1953 *F, E, S, W*, 1954 *NZ, F, E, S, W*
Morton, W A (Dublin U) 1888 *S*
Moyers, L W (Dublin U) 1884 *W*
Mulcahy, W A (Bective Rangers) 1958 *A, E, S, W, F*, 1959 *E, S, W, F*, 1960 *E, S, W, SA*, 1961 *E, S, W, SA*, 1962 *E, S, F, W*, 1963 *F, E, S, W, NZ*, 1964 *E, S, W, F*, 1965 *F, E, S, W, SA*
Mullan, B (Clontarf) 1947 *F, E, S, W*, 1948 *F, E, S, W*
Mullane, J P (Limerick Bohemians) 1928 *W*, 1929 *F*
Mullen, K D (Old Belvedere) 1947 *F, E, S, W, A*, 1948 *F, E, S, W*, 1949 *F, E, S, W*, 1950 *F, E, S, W*, 1951 *F, E, S, W, SA*, 1952 *F, S, W*
Mulligan, A A (Wanderers) 1956 *F, E*, 1957 *F, E, S, W*, 1958 *A, E, S, F*, 1959 *E, S, W, F*, 1960 *E, S, W, F, SA*, 1961 *W, F, SA*
Murphy, C J (Lansdowne) 1939 *E, S, W*, 1947 *F, E*
Murphy, J G M W (London Irish) 1951 *SA*, 1952 *S, W, E*, 1954 *NZ*, 1958 *W*
Murphy, J J (Greystones) 1981 *SA*, 1982 *W* (R), 1984 *S*
Murphy, N F (Cork Constitution) 1930 *E, W*, 1931 *F, E, S, W, SA*, 1932 *E, S, W*, 1933 *E*
Murphy, N A A (Cork Constitution) 1958 *A, E, S, W, F*, 1959 *E, S, W, F*, 1960 *E, S, W, F, SA*, 1961 *E, S, W*, 1962 *E*, 1963 *NZ*, 1964 *E, S, W, F*, 1965 *F, E, S, W, SA*, 1966 *F, E, S, W*, 1967 *A, E, S, W, F*, 1969 *F, E, S, W*
Murphy-O'Connor, J (Bective Rangers) 1954 *E*
Murray, H W (Dublin) 1877 *S*, 1878 *E*, 1879 *E*
Murray, J B (UC Dublin) 1963 *F*
Murray, P F (Wanderers) 1927 *F*, 1929 *F, E, S*, 1930 *F, E, S, W*, 1931 *F, E, S, W, SA*, 1932 *E, S, W*, 1933 *E, W, S*
Murtagh, C W (Portadown) 1977 *S*
Myles, J (Dublin U) 1875 *E*

Nash, L C (Queen's Coll, Cork) 1889 *S*, 1890 *W, E*, 1891 *E, S, W*
Neely, M R (Collegians) 1947 *F, E, S, W*
Neill, H J (NIFC) 1885 *E, S*, 1886 *S*, 1887 *E, S, W*, 1888 *W, S*
Neill, J McF (Instonians) 1926 *F*
Nelson, J E (Malone) 1947 *A*, 1948 *E, S, W*, 1949 *F, E, S, W*, 1950 *F, E, S, W*, 1951 *F, E, W*, 1954 *F*
Nelson, R (Queen's Coll, Belfast) 1882 *E, S*, 1883 *S*, 1886 *S*
Nesdale, T J (Garryowen) 1961 *F*
Neville, W C (Dublin U) 1879 *S, E*
Nicholson, P C (Dublin U) 1900 *E, S, W*
Norton, G W (Bective Rangers) 1949 *F, E, S, W*, 1950 *F, E, S, W*, 1951 *F, E, S*
Notley, J R (Wanderers) 1952 *F, S*

O'Brien, B (Derry) 1893 *S, W*
O'Brien, B A P (Shannon) 1968 *F, E, S*
O'Brien, D J (London Irish, Cardiff, Old Belvedere) 1948 *E, S, W*, 1949 *F, E, S, W*, 1950 *F, E, S, W*, 1951 *F, E, S, W, SA*, 1952 *F, S, W, E*
O'Brien, K A (Broughton Park) 1980 *E*, 1981 *SA* (2[1R])
O'Brien-Butler, P E (Monkstown) 1897 *S*, 1898 *E, S*, 1899 *S, W*, 1900 *E*
O'Callaghan, C T (Carlow) 1910 *W, F*, 1911 *E, S, W, F*, 1912 *F*
O'Callaghan, M P (Sunday's Well) 1962 *W*, 1964 *E, F*
O' Callaghan, P (Dolphin) 1967 *A, E, A*, 1968 *F, E, S, W*, 1969 *F, E, S, W*, 1970 *SA, F, E, S, W*, 1976 *F, W, E, S, NZ*
O'Connell, P (Bective Rangers) 1913 *W, F*, 1914 *F, E, S, W*
O'Connell, W J (Lansdowne) 1955 *F*
O'Connor, H S (Dublin U) 1957 *F, E, S, W*
O'Connor, J (Garryowen) 1895 *S*
O'Connor, J H (Bective Rangers) 1888 *M*, 1890 *S, W, E*, 1891 *E, S*, 1892 *E, W*, 1893 *E, S*, 1894 *E, S, W*, 1895 *E*, 1896 *E, S, W*
O'Connor, J J (Garryowen) 1909 *F*
O'Connor, J J (UC Cork) 1933 *S*, 1934 *E, S, W*, 1935 *E, S, W, NZ*, 1936 *S, W*, 1938 *S*
O'Connor, P J (Lansdowne) 1887 *W*
O'Donnell, R C (St Mary's Coll) 1979 *A* (2), 1980 *S, F, W*
O'Donoghue, P J (Bective Rangers) 1955 *F, E, S, W*, 1956 *W*, 1957 *F, E*, 1958 *A, E, S, W*
Odbert, R V M (RAF) 1928 *F*
O'Driscoll, B J (Manchester) 1971 *F* (R), *E, S, W*

O'Driscoll, J B (London Irish, Manchester) 1978 *S*, 1979 *A* (2), 1980 *E, S, F, W*, 1981 *F, W, E, S, SA* (2), *A*, 1982 *W, E, S, F*, 1983 *S, F, W, E*, 1984 *F, W, E, S*
O'Flanagan, K P (London Irish) 1947 *A*
O'Flanagan, M (Lansdowne) 1948 *S*
O'Hanlon, B (Dolphin) 1947 *E, S, W*, 1948 *F, E, S, W*, 1949 *F, E, S, W*, 1950 *F*
O'Leary, A (Cork Constitution) 1952 *S, W, E*
O'Loughlin, D B (UC Cork) 1938 *E, S, W*, 1939 *E, S, W*
O'Meara, J A (UC Cork, Dolphin) 1951 *F, E, S, W, SA*, 1952 *F, S, W, E*, 1953 *F, E, S, W*, 1954 *NZ, F, E, S*, 1955 *F, E*, 1956 *S, W*, 1958 *W*
O'Neill, H O'H (Queen's U, Belfast, UC Cork) 1930 *E, S, W*, 1933 *E, S, W*
O'Neill, J B (Queen's U, Belfast) 1920 *S*
O'Neill, W A (UC Dublin) 1952 *E*, 1953 *F, E, S, W*, 1954 *NZ*
O'Reilly, A J F (Old Belvedere, Leicester) 1955 *F, E, S, W*, 1956 *F, E, S, W*, 1957 *F, E, S, W*, 1958 *A, E, S, W, F*, 1959 *E, S, W, F*, 1960 *E*, 1961 *E, F, SA*, 1963 *F, S, W*, 1970 *E*
Orr, P A (Old Wesley) 1976 *F, W, E, S, NZ*, 1977 *W, E, S, F*, 1978 *S, F, W, E, NZ*, 1979 *F, W, E, S, A* (2), 1980 *E, S, F, W*, 1981 *F, W, E, S, SA* (2), *A*, 1982 *W, E, S, F*, 1983 *S, F, W, E*, 1984 *F, W, E, S*
O'Sullivan, A C (Dublin U) 1882 *S*
O'Sullivan, J M (Limerick) 1884 *S*, 1887 *S*
O'Sullivan, P J A (Galwegians) 1957 *F, E, S, W*, 1959 *E, S, W, F*, 1960 *SA*, 1961 *E, S*, 1962 *F, W*, 1963 *F, NZ*
O'Sullivan, W (Queen's Coll, Cork) 1895 *S*
Owens, R H (Dublin U) 1922 *E, S*

Parfrey, P (UC Cork) 1974 *NZ*
Parke, J C (Monkstown) 1903 *W*, 1904 *E, S, W*, 1905 *W, NZ*, 1906 *E, S, W, SA*, 1907 *E, S, W*, 1908 *E, S, W*, 1909 *E, S, W, F*
Parr, J S (Wanderers) 1914 *F, E, S, W*
Patterson, C S (Instonians) 1978 *NZ*, 1979 *F, W, E, S, A* (2), 1980 *E, S, F, W*
Patterson, R d'A (Wanderers) 1912 *F, S, W, SA*, 1913 *E, S, W, F*
Payne, C T (NIFC) 1926 *E*, 1927 *F, E, S, NSW*, 1928 *F, E, S, W*, 1929 *F, E, W*, 1930 *F, E, S, W*
Pedlow, A C (CIYMS) 1953 *W*, 1954 *NZ, F, E*, 1955 *F, E, S, W*, 1956 *F, E, S, W*, 1957 *F, E, S, W*, 1958 *A, E, S, W, F*, 1959 *E*, 1960 *E, S, W, F, SA*, 1961 *S*, 1962 *W*, 1963 *F*
Pedlow, J (Bessbrook) 1882 *S*, 1884 *W*
Pedlow, R (Bessbrook) 1891 *W*
Pedlow, T B (Queen's Coll, Belfast) 1889 *S, W*
Peel, T (Limerick) 1892 *E, S, W*
Peirce, W (Cork) 1881 *E*
Phipps, G C (Army) 1950 *E, W*, 1952 *F, W, E*
Pike, T O (Lansdowne) 1927 *E, S, W, NSW*, 1928 *F, E, S, W*
Pike, V J (Lansdowne) 1931 *E, S, W, SA*, 1932 *E, S, W*, 1933 *E, W, S*, 1934 *E, S, W*
Pike, W W (Kingstown) 1879 *E*, 1881 *E, S*, 1882 *E*, 1883 *S*
Pinion, G (Belfast Collegians) 1909 *E, S, W, F*
Piper, O J S (Cork Constitution) 1909 *E, S, W, F*, 1910 *E, S, W, F*
Polden, S E (Clontarf) 1913 *W, F*, 1914 *F*, 1920 *F*
Popham, I (Cork Constitution) 1922 *S, W, F*, 1923 *F*
Potterton, H N (Wanderers) 1920 *W*
Pratt, R H (Dublin U) 1933 *E, W, S*, 1934 *E, S*
Price, A H (Dublin U) 1920 *S, F*
Pringle, J C (NIFC) 1902 *S, W*
Purcell, N M (Lansdowne) 1921 *E, S, W, F*
Purdon, H (NIFC) 1879 *S, E*, 1880 *E*, 1881 *E, S*
Purdon, W B (Queen's Coll, Belfast) 1906 *E, S, W*
Purser, F C (Dublin U) 1898 *E, S, W*

Quinlan, S V J (Blackrock Coll) 1956 *F, E, W*, 1958 *W*
Quinn, B T (Old Belvedere) 1947 *F*
Quinn, F P (Old Belvedere) 1981 *F, W, E*
Quinn, J P (Dublin U) 1910 *E, S*, 1911 *E, S, W, F*, 1912 *E, S, W*, 1913 *E, W, F*, 1914 *F, E, S*
Quinn, K (Old Belvedere) 1947 *F, A*, 1953 *F, E, S*
Quinn, M A M (Lansdowne) 1973 *F*, 1974 *F, W, E, S, P, NZ*, 1977 *S, F*, 1981 *SA*
Quirke, J T M (Blackrock Coll) 1962 *E, S*, 1968 *S*

Rambaut, D F (Dublin U) 1887 *E, S, W*, 1888 *W*
Rea, H H (Edinburgh U) 1967 *A*, 1969 *F*
Read, H M (Dublin U) 1910 *E, S*, 1911 *E, S, W, F*, 1912 *F, E, S, W, SA*, 1913 *E, S*
Rearden, J V (Cork Constitution) 1934 *E, S*
Reid, C (NIFC) 1899 *S, W*, 1900 *E*, 1903 *W*
Reid, J L (Richmond) 1934 *S, W*
Reid, P J (Garryowen) 1947 *A*, 1948 *F, E, W*
Reid, T E (Garryowen) 1953 *E, S, W*, 1954 *F, NZ*, 1955 *E, S*, 1956 *F, E*, 1957 *F, E, S, W*
Reidy, C J (London Irish) 1937 *W*
Reidy, G F (Dolphin, Lansdowne) 1953 *W*, 1954 *F, E, S, W*
Richey, H A (Dublin U) 1889 *W*, 1890 *S*
Ridgeway, E C (Wanderers) 1932 *S, W*, 1935 *E, S, W*
Ringland, T M (Queen's U, Belfast, Ballymena) 1981 *A*, 1982 *W, E, F*, 1983 *S, F, W, E*, 1984 *F, W, E, S*
Riordan, W F (Cork Constitution) 1910 *E*
Ritchie, J S (London Irish) 1956 *F, E*
Robb, C G (Queen's Coll, Belfast) 1904 *E, S, W*, 1905 *NZ*, 1906 *S*
Robbie, J C (Dublin U) 1976 *A, F, NZ*, 1977 *S, F*, 1981 *F, W, E, S*
Robinson, T T H (Wanderers) 1904 *E, S*, 1905 *E, S, W, NZ*, 1906 *SA*, 1907 *E, S, W*
Roche, J (Wanderers) 1890 *S, W, E*, 1891 *E, S, W*, 1892 *W*
Roche, R E (UC Galway) 1955 *E, S*, 1957 *S, W*
Roche, W J (UC Cork) 1920 *E, S, F*
Roddy, P J (Bective Rangers) 1920 *S, F*
Roe, R (Lansdowne) 1952 *E*, 1953 *F, E, S, W*, 1954 *F, E, S, W*, 1955 *F, E, S, W*, 1956 *F, E, S, W*, 1957 *F, E, S, W*
Rooke, C V (Dublin U) 1891 *E, W*, 1892 *E, S, W*, 1893 *E, S, W*, 1894 *E, S, W*, 1895 *E, S, W*, 1896 *E, S, W*, 1897 *E, S*
Ross, D J (Belfast Academy) 1884 *E*, 1885 *S*, 1886 *E, S*
Ross, G R P (CIYMS) 1955 *W*
Ross, J F (NIFC) 1886 *S*
Ross, J P (Lansdowne) 1885 *E, S*, 1886 *E, S*
Ross, N G (Malone) 1927 *F, E*
Ross, W McC (Queen's U, Belfast) 1932 *E, S, W*, 1933 *E, W, S*, 1934 *E, S*, 1935 *NZ*
Russell, J (UC Cork) 1931 *F, E, S, W, SA*, 1933 *E, W, S*, 1934 *E, S, W*, 1935 *E, S, W*, 1936 *E, S, W*, 1937 *E, S*
Rutherford, W G (Tipperary) 1884 *E, S*, 1885 *E*, 1886 *E*, 1888 *W*
Ryan, E (Dolphin) 1937 *W*, 1938 *E, S*
Ryan, J (Rockwell Coll) 1897 *E*, 1898 *E, S, W*, 1899 *E, S, W*, 1900 *S, W*, 1901 *E, S, W*, 1902 *E*, 1904 *E*
Ryan, J G (UC Dublin) 1939 *E, S, W*
Ryan, M (Rockwell Coll) 1897 *E, S*, 1898 *E, S, W*, 1899 *E, S, W*, 1900 *E, S, W*, 1901 *E, S, W*, 1903 *E*, 1904 *E, S*

Sayers, H J M (Lansdowne) 1935 *E, S, W*, 1936 *E, S, W*, 1938 *W*, 1939 *E, S, W*
Schute, F (Wanderers) 1878 *E*, 1879 *E*
Schute, F G (Dublin U) 1912 *SA*, 1913 *E, S*
Scott, D (Malone) 1961 *F, SA*, 1962 *S*
Scott, R D (Queen's U, Belfast) 1967 *E, F*, 1968 *F, E, S*
Scovell, R H (Kingstown) 1883 *E*, 1884 *E*
Scriven, G (Dublin U) 1879 *S, E*, 1880 *E, S*, 1881 *E*, 1882 *S*, 1883 *E, S*
Sealy, J (Dublin U) 1896 *E, S, W*, 1897 *S*, 1899 *E, S, W*, 1900 *E, S*
Shanahan, T (Lansdowne) 1885 *E, S*, 1886 *E*, 1888 *S, W*
Shaw, G M (Windsor) 1877 *S*
Sheehan, M D (London Irish) 1932 *E*
Sherry, B F (Terenure Coll) 1967 *A, E, S, A*, 1968 *F, E*
Sherry, M J A (Lansdowne) 1975 *F, W*
Siggins, J A E (Belfast Collegians) 1931 *F, E, S, W, SA*, 1932 *E, S, W*, 1933 *E, W, S*, 1934 *E, S, W*, 1935 *E, S, W, NZ*, 1936 *E, S, W*, 1937 *E, S, W*
Slattery, J F (UC Dublin, Blackrock Coll) 1970 *SA, F, E, S, W*, 1971 *F, E, S, W*, 1972 *F, E, F*, 1973 *NZ, E, S, W, F*, 1974 *F, W, E, S, P, NZ*, 1975 *E, S, F, W*, 1976 *A*, 1977 *S, F*, 1978 *S, F, W, E, NZ*, 1979 *F, W, E, S, A* (2), 1980 *E, S, F, W*, 1981 *F, W, E, S, SA* (2), *A*, 1982 *W, E, S, F*, 1983 *S, F, W, E*, 1984 *F*
Smartt, F N B (Dublin U) 1908 *E, S*, 1909 *E*
Smith, J H (London Irish) 1951 *F, E, S, W, SA*, 1952

F, S, W, E, 1954 *NZ, W, F*
Smith, R E (Lansdowne) 1892 *E*
Smithwick, F F S (Monkstown) 1898 *S, W*
Smyth, J T (Queen's U, Belfast) 1920 *F*
Smyth, P J (Belfast Collegians) 1911 *E, S, F*
Smyth, R S (Dublin U) 1903 *E, S,* 1904 *E*
Smyth, T (Malone, Newport) 1908 *E, S, W,* 1909 *E, S, W* 1910 *E, S, W, F,* 1911 *E, S, W,* 1912 *E*
Smyth, W S (Belfast Collegians) 1910 *W, F,* 1920 *E*
Solomons, B A H (Dublin U) 1908 *E, S, W,* 1909 *E, S, W, F,* 1910 *E, S, W*
Spain, A W (UC Dublin) 1924 *NZ*
Sparrow, W (Dublin U) 1893 *W,* 1894 *E*
Spring, D E (Dublin U) 1978 *S, NZ,* 1979 *S,* 1980 *S, F, W,* 1981 *W*
Spring, R M (Lansdowne) 1979 *F, W, E*
Spunner, H F (Wanderers) 1881 *E, S,* 1884 *W*
Stack, C R R (Dublin U) 1889 *S*
Stack, G H (Dublin U) 1875 *E*
Steele, H W (Ballymena) 1976 *E,* 1977 *F,* 1978 *F, W, E,* 1979 *F, W, E, A* (2)
Stephenson, G V (Queen's U, Belfast, London Hosp) 1920 *F,* 1921 *E, S, W, F,* 1922 *E, S, W, F,* 1923 *E, S, W, F,* 1924 *F, E, S, W, NZ,* 1925 *F, E, S, W,* 1926 *F, E, S, W,* 1927 *F, E, S, W, NSW,* 1928 *F, E, S, W,* 1929 *F, E, W,* 1930 *F, E, S, W*
Stephenson, H W V (United Services) 1922 *S, W, F,* 1924 *F, E, S, W, NZ,* 1925 *F, E, S, W,* 1927 *NSW,* 1928 *E*
Stevenson, J (Dungannon) 1888 *M,* 1889 *S*
Stevenson, J B (Instonians) 1958 *A, E, S, W, F*
Stevenson, R (Dungannon) 1887 *E, S, W,* 1888 *M,* 1889 *S, W,* 1890 *S, W, E,* 1891 *W,* 1892 *W,* 1893 *E, S, W*
Stevenson, T H (Belfast Acad) 1895 *E, W,* 1896 *E, S, W,* 1897 *E, S*
Stewart, A L (NIFC) 1913 *W, F,* 1914 *F*
Stewart, W J (Queen's U, Belfast, NIFC) 1922 *F,* 1924 *S,* 1928 *F, E, S, W,* 1929 *F, E, S, W*
Stoker, E W (Wanderers) 1888 *W, S*
Stoker, F O (Wanderers) 1886 *S,* 1888 *W, M,* 1889 *S,* 1891 *W*
Stokes, O S (Cork Bankers) 1882 *E,* 1884 *E*
Stokes, P (Garryowen) 1913 *E, S,* 1914 *F,* 1920 *E, S, W, F,* 1921 *E, S, F,* 1922 *W, F*
Stokes, R D (Queen's Coll, Cork) 1891 *S, W*
Strathdee, E (Queen's U, Belfast) 1947 *E, S, W, A,* 1948 *W, F,* 1949 *E, S, W*
Stuart, C P (Clontarf) 1912 *SA*
Stuart, I M B (Dublin U) 1924 *E, S*
Sugars, H S (Dublin U) 1905 *NZ,* 1906 *SA,* 1907 *S*
Sugden, M (Wanderers) 1925 *F, E, S, W,* 1926 *F, E, S, W,* 1927 *E, S, W, NSW,* 1928 *F, E, S, W,* 1929 *F, E, S, W,* 1930 *F, E, S, W,* 1931 *F, E, S, W*
Sullivan, D B (UC Dublin) 1922 *E, S, W, F*
Sweeney, J A (Blackrock Coll) 1907 *E, S, W*
Symes, G R (Monkstown) 1895 *E*
Synge, J S (Lansdowne) 1929 *S*

Taggart, T (Dublin U) 1887 *W*
Taylor, A S (Queen's Coll, Belfast) 1910 *E, S, W,* 1912 *F*
Taylor, D R (Queen's Coll, Belfast) 1903 *E*
Taylor, J (Belfast Collegians) 1914 *E, S, W*
Taylor, J W (NIFC) 1879 *S,* 1880 *E, S,* 1881 *S,* 1882 *E, S,* 1883 *E, S*
Tector, W R (Wanderers) 1955 *F, E, S*
Tedford, A (Malone) 1902 *E, S, W,* 1903 *E, S, W,* 1904 *E, S, W,* 1905 *E, S, W, NZ,* 1906 *E, S, W, SA,* 1907 *E, S, W,* 1908 *E, S, W*
Teehan, C (UC Cork) 1939 *E, S, W*
Thompson, C (Belfast Collegians) 1907 *E, S,* 1908 *E, S, W,* 1909 *E, S, W, F,* 1910 *E, S, W, F*
Thompson, J A (Queen's Coll, Belfast) 1885 *S*
Thompson, J K S (Dublin U) 1921 *W,* 1922 *E, S, F,* 1923 *E, S, W, F*
Thompson, R G (Lansdowne) 1882 *W*
Thompson, R H (Instonians) 1951 *SA,* 1952 *F,* 1954 *NZ, F, E, S, W,* 1955 *F, S, W,* 1956 *W*
Thornhill, T (Wanderers) 1892 *E, S, W,* 1893 *E*
Thrift, H (Dublin U) 1904 *W,* 1905 *E, S, W, NZ,* 1906 *E, W, SA,* 1907 *E, S, W,* 1908 *E, S, W,* 1909 *E, S, W, F*
Tierney, D (UC Cork) 1938 *S, W,* 1939 *E*
Tillie, C R (Dublin U) 1887 *E, S,* 1888 *W, S*
Todd, A W P (Dublin U) 1913 *W, F,* 1914 *F*
Torrens, J D (Bohemians) 1938 *W,* 1939 *E, S, W*
Tucker, C C (Shannon) 1979 *F, W,* 1980 *F* (R)
Tuke, B B (Bective Rangers) 1890 *E,* 1891 *E, S,* 1892 *E,* 1894 *E, S, W,* 1895 *E, S*
Turley, N (Blackrock Coll) 1962 *E*
Tydings, J (Young Munster) 1968 *A*
Tyrrell, W (Queen's U, Belfast) 1910 *F,* 1913 *E, S, W, F,* 1914 *F, E, S, W*

Uprichard, R J H (Harlequins, RAF) 1950 *S, W*

Waide, S L (Oxford U, NIFC) 1932 *E, S, W,* 1933 *E, W*
Waites, J (Bective Rangers) 1886 *S,* 1888 *M,* 1889 *W,* 1890 *S, W, E,* 1891 *E*
Waldron, O C (Oxford U, L. Irish) 1966 *S, W,* 1968 *A*
Walker, S (Instonians) 1934 *E, S,* 1935 *E, S, W, NZ,* 1936 *E, S, W,* 1937 *E, S, W,* 1938 *E, S, W*
Walkington, D B (NIFC) 1887 *E, W,* 1888 *W,* 1890 *W, E,* 1891 *E, S, W*
Walkington, R B (NIFC) 1875 *E,* 1876 *E,* 1877 *E, S,* 1878 *E,* 1879 *S,* 1880 *E, S,* 1882 *E, S*
Wall, H (Dolphin) 1965 *S, W*
Wallace, Jas (Wanderers) 1904 *E, S*
Wallace, Jos (Wanderers) 1903 *S, W,* 1904 *E, S, W,* 1905 *E, S, W, NZ,* 1906 *W*
Wallace, T H (Cardiff) 1920 *E, S, W*
Wallis, A K (Wanderers) 1892 *E, S, W,* 1893 *E, W*
Wallis, C O'N (Old Cranleighans, Wanderers) 1935 *NZ*
Wallis, T G (Wanderers) 1921 *F,* 1922 *E, S, W, F*
Wallis, W A (Wanderers) 1880 *S,* 1881 *E, S,* 1882 *W,* 1883 *S*
Walmsley, G (Bective Rangers) 1894 *E*
Walpole, A (Dublin U) 1888 *S, M*
Walsh, E J (Lansdowne) 1887 *E, S, W,* 1892 *E, S, W,* 1893 *E*
Walsh, H D (Dublin U) 1875 *E,* 1876 *E*
Walsh, J C (UC Cork, Sunday's Well) 1960 *S, SA,* 1961 *E, S, F, SA,* 1963 *E, S, W, NZ,* 1964 *E, S, W, F,* 1965 *F, S, W, SA,* 1966 *F, S, W,* 1967 *E, S, W, F, A*
Ward, A J P (Garryowen, St Mary's Coll) 1978 *S, F, W, E, NZ,* 1979 *F, W, E, S,* 1981 *W, E, S, A,* 1983 *E* (R), 1984 *E, S*
Warren, J P (Kingstown) 1883 *E*
Warren, R G (Lansdowne) 1884 *W,* 1885 *E, S,* 1886 *E,* 1887 *E, S, W,* 1888 *W, S, M,* 1889 *S, W,* 1890 *S, W, E*
Watson, R (Wanderers) 1912 *SA*
Wells, H G (Bective Rangers) 1891 *S, W,* 1894 *E, S*
Westby, A J (Dublin U) 1876 *E*
Wheeler, G H (Queen's Coll, Belfast) 1884 *S,* 1885 *E*
Wheeler, J R (Queen's U, Belfast) 1922 *E, S, W, F,* 1924 *E*
Whelan, P C (Garryowen) 1975 *E, S,* 1976 *NZ,* 1977 *W, E, S, F,* 1978 *S, F, W, E, NZ,* 1979 *F, W, E, S,* 1981 *F, W, E*
White, M (Queen's Coll, Cork) 1906 *E, S, W, SA,* 1907 *E, W*
Whitestone, A M (Dublin U) 1877 *E,* 1879 *S, E,* 1880 *E,* 1883 *S*
Wilkinson, R W (Wanderers) 1947 *A*
Williamson, F W (Dolphin) 1930 *E, S, W*
Willis, W J (Lansdowne) 1879 *E*
Wilson, F (CIYMS) 1977 *W, E, S*
Wilson, H G (Glasgow U) 1905 *E, S, W, NZ,* 1906 *E, S, W, SA,* 1907 *E, S, W,* 1908 *E, S, W,* 1909 *E, S, W,* 1910 *W*
Wilson, W H (Bray) 1877 *E, S*
Withers, H H C (Army, Blackheath) 1931 *F, E, S, W, SA*
Wolfe, E J (Armagh) 1882 *E*
Wood, G H (Dublin U) 1913 *W,* 1914 *F*
Wood, B G M (Garryowen) 1954 *E, S,* 1956 *F, E, S, W,* 1957 *F, E, S, W,* 1958 *A, E, S, W, F,* 1959 *E, S, W, F,* 1960 *E, S, W, F, SA,* 1961 *E, S, W, F, SA*
Woods, D C (Bessbrook) 1888 *M,* 1889 *S*
Wright, R A (Monkstown) 1912 *S*

Yeates, R A (Dublin U) 1889 *S, W*
Young, G (UC Cork) 1913 *E*
Young, R M (Collegians) 1965 *F, E, S, W, SA,* 1966 *F, E, S, W,* 1967 *W, F,* 1968 *W, A,* 1969 *F, E, S, W,* 1970 *SA, F, E, S, W,* 1971 *F, E, S, W*

IRISH INTERNATIONAL RECORDS

From 1890-1, when uniform point-scoring was first adopted by International Board Countries, to 30 April 1984. Both team and individual records are against International Board countries only, except for the match against the IRFU President's XV in the 1974-75 centenary season. Where caps have been awarded for other matches, this is recorded, in the case of the most capped players, in the notes.

TEAM RECORDS

Highest score

26 { v Scotland (26-8) 1953 Murrayfield
v England (26-21) 1974 Twickenham }

v individual countries

26 v England (26-21) 1974 Twickenham
26 v Scotland (26-8) 1953 Murrayfield
21 v Wales { (21-24) 1979 Cardiff
(21-7) 1980 Dublin }
25 v France { (25-5) 1911 Cork
(25-6) 1975 Dublin }
10 v N Zealand (10-10) 1973 Dublin
15 v S Africa (15-23) 1981 Cape Town
27 v Australia (27-12) 1979 Brisbane

Biggest winning points margin

24 v France (24-0) 1913 Cork

v individual countries

22 v England (22-0) 1947 Dublin
21 v Scotland (21-0) 1950 Dublin
16 v Wales (19-3) 1925 Belfast
24 v France (24-0) 1913 Cork
No win v N Zealand
3 v S Africa (9-6) 1965 Dublin
15 v Australia (27-12) 1979 Brisbane

Highest score by opposing team

38 S Africa (0-38) 1912 Dublin

by individual countries

36 England (14-36) 1938 Dublin
32 Scotland (9-32) 1984 Dublin
34 Wales (9-34) 1976 Dublin
27 France (6-27) 1964 Paris
17 N Zealand (9-17) 1935 Dublin
38 S Africa (0-38) 1912 Dublin
20 Australia (10-20) 1976 Dublin

Biggest losing points margin

38 v S Africa (0-38) 1912 Dublin

v individual countries

22 v England (14-36) 1938 Dublin
23 v Scotland (9-32) 1984 Dublin
29 v Wales (0-29) 1907 Cardiff
23 v France (3-26) 1976 Paris
15 v N Zealand (0-15) 1905 Dublin
38 v S Africa (0-38) 1912 Dublin
13 v Australia (3-16) 1947 Dublin

Most points by Ireland in International Championship in a season – 71

(in season 1982-83)

Most tries by Ireland in International Championship in a season – 12

(in seasons 1927-28 and 1952-53)

Most tries by Ireland in an international

6 { v France (24-0) 1913 Cork
v Scotland (26-8) 1953 Murrayfield }

Most tries against Ireland in an international

10 by S Africa (0-38) 1912 Dublin

INDIVIDUAL RECORDS

Most capped player

C M H Gibson 69 1964-79

in individual positions

Full-back

T J Kiernan 54 1960-73

Wing

A T A Duggan } 25 { 1964-72
T O Grace } 25 { 1972-78

Centre

C M H Gibson 40(69)* 1964-79

Fly-half

J W Kyle 46 1947-58

Scrum-half

M Sugden 27(28)† 1925-31

Prop

P A Orr 43 1976-84

Hooker

K W Kennedy 45 1965-75

Lock
W J McBride 63 1962-75
Flanker
J F Slattery 61 1970-84
No 8
W P Duggan 39(41)‡ 1975-84

**Gibson won 40 caps as a centre, 25 at fly-half and four as a wing*
G V Stephenson, 42 caps, won 37 as a centre (including one against New South Wales) and five on the wing
N J Henderson, 40 caps, won 35 as a centre and five at full-back
†Sugden played once against New South Wales
J J Moloney, 27 caps, won 23 at scrum-half and four on the wing
‡Duggan has won 39 caps at No 8 and two as a flanker

Most internationals as captain – 24
T J Kiernan 1963-73

Most points in internationals – 217
S O Campbell (22 appearances) 1976-84

Most points in an international – 21
S O Campbell v Scotland 1982 Dublin
S O Campbell v England 1983 Dublin

Most tries in internationals – 14
G V Stephenson (41 appearances) 1920-30
(Stephenson also played once against NSW)

Most tries in an international – 3
J P Quinn v France 1913 Cork
E O'D Davy v Scotland 1930 Murrayfield
S Byrne v Scotland 1953 Murrayfield

Most conversions in an international – 4
P F Murray v Scotland 1932 Murrayfield
R J Gregg v Scotland 1953 Murrayfield

Most points in International Championship in a season – 52
S O Campbell (4 appearances) 1982-83

Most tries in International Championship in a season – 5
J E Arigho (3 appearances) 1927-28

Most conversions in International Championship in a season – 7
R A Lloyd (4 appearances) 1912-13

Most penalty goals in International Championship in a season – 14
S O Campbell (4 appearances) 1982-83

Most points for Ireland on overseas tour – 60
S O Campbell (5 appearances) 1979 Australia

Most points in any match on tour – 19
A J P Ward v Australian Capital Territory 1979 Canberra
S O Campbell v Australia 1979 Brisbane

Most tries in any match on tour – 3
A T A Duggan v Victoria 1967 Melbourne
J F Slattery v SA President's XV 1981 East London
M J Kiernan v Gold Cup XV 1981 Oudtshoorn, SA

THE 1983-84 SEASON IN WALES

John Billot *Western Mail*

Wales have registered just one victory from their last five full international matches at the Arms Park. It is a stark statistic following the unforgettable record sequence of invincibility during 27 International Championship matches there between 1969 and 1982. Standards, of course, have declined since the decade of Welsh supremacy in the 'seventies, but searching self-criticism will never admit that a team could not be fielded capable of defending national honour more successfully amid the uplifting sound of home supporters. For Wales to lose at Cardiff is to know the discredit of failure in its most savage form.

Events began to go wrong against Japan in October. Though Wales won 29-24, the lead was 29-10 when the home defence fell apart. The Japanese stole back 14 points in a sensational finish and spectators were quick to offer the highest praise for the visitors' positive attacking measures. 'Lucky we did not have to play another five minutes' was an expression widely heard. Alas, the WRU selectors could not have been within earshot because they persisted in playing Terry Shaw, the excellent Newbridge front jumper, in the middle of the line in the next match in Bucharest. It was a decision that astonished every coach in Wales and an important factor in undermining the confidence of the team even before they arrived behind the Iron Curtain.

All the critics had commented that a specialist middle jumper was essential after the need had been exposed by Japan. Romania's line-out would present an awesome challenge. But the lesson went unheeded in the absence of the injured Robert Norster. Unbelievably, the selectors sent Shaw to jump in the middle again.

That November day in the August 23 Stadium branded a horrible scar on Welsh rugby: humiliation by 24 points to six without a try in answer to the four by the home country. Romania's forward power proved overwhelming. They poured through the line-out, especially the tail, virtually without hindrance. There was no real colour from Romania as attackers behind the scrum. Expression and invention belonged to the Welsh backs; but without the ball theirs was a severely restricted operation. With six new caps, Wales slumped to their heaviest away defeat for 14 years. It was a nightmare occasion for Gwyn Evans, the Maesteg full-back, who was uncertain under the high ball but by no means the only unhappy man in a scarlet jersey.

It was evident to everyone except – apparently – the selectors, that a change of captaincy was necessary. One critic bewailed the intransigence of the Big Five, who stubbornly refused to appoint Mike Watkins, the Newport hooker, as captain, and in doing so defied the urgings of responsible writers on the game. Not until Scotland had won at the Arms Park did they grudgingly admit the error of their ways and name Watkins as successor to Eddie Butler. The controversies over the captaincy, the back row composition, and the middle line jumper had done incalculable harm to the credibility of the selectors and opened a wide gulf between them and the media. Had they been soccer managers, the Big Five would have been sacked *en bloc* and with every justification.

Watkins's behavioural patterns originally had been unacceptable with a track record that, as he frankly admitted, left much to be desired; yet he settled down to the responsibilities of captaincy at Newport. With maturity had come a new Watkins. He had natural powers of motivation that Butler could never produce. Watkins drove his pack with a primitive passion that invoked immediate and sustained response. Butler's play improved considerably once he had been relieved of the leadership and the No 8 was especially diligent with his speedy support work. Watkins – 'Spike' to his team-mates and the Welsh rugby fraternity at large – enjoyed the distinction of captaining Wales on his debut, against Ireland, and to a notable victory in the process. It was only the second instance of a new cap leading Wales to victory. On the first occasion, Charles Lewis (Llandovery) captained his side against Ireland as far back as 1882.

The Welsh pack dominated with tremendous scrum drive in Dublin to win there for the first time in six years, and Richard Moriarty, the Swansea lock, performed particularly effectively in his unaccustomed role of blindside flanker. Few agreed with this drastic experiment, but the 6 ft 6 ins, aggressive Moriarty undeniably added a significant dimension to ball-winning at the tail of the line-out.

He proved a little too physical on occasions and the French, in particular, were resentful of his style of play. The letters columns of some Welsh newspapers also gave extensive exposure to the Moriarty method and here again the Welsh selectors were under fire for selecting players with allegedly rough inclinations. Other countries possessed them, to be sure, but not in such abundance, or so it was suggested.

The Welsh team were robbed of nearly £800 by a sneak thief who climbed down a ventilator shaft into the dressing-room while the match was being played at Lansdowne Road on the occasion of the official opening of the £4 million Triple Crown Stand, but the Irish RFU reimbursed every player before they left for home – an especially worthy effort considering the banks were closed. Irish generosity was perhaps too much in evidence, though, in the way in which they permitted Robert Ackerman to find his way through to score the game's only try.

The stranglehold that penalty kicks have on rugby were emphasised in Wales' two remaining games. Wales outscored France on tries by two

The Welsh team which won at Twickenham. Back Row, L-R: *M Brown (replacement), J D Bevan (coach), J Whitefoot (replacement), M Douglas (replacement), I H Eidman, I Stephens, S J Perkins, R D Moriarty, R L Norster, E T Butler, D F Pickering, A M Hadley, W James (replacement), G Evans* Front Row, L-R: *H E Rees, B Bowen, M H Titley, M Dacey, M J Watkins (capt), T D Holmes, R A Ackerman, H Davies*

to one, but Jean-Patrick Lescarboura landed four penalty goals in supplying 17 of his side's 21 points to register a fortunate victory in Cardiff. For the first time in 21 years Wales had lost both their championship home matches. However, Jean-Pierre Rives had no regrets at this state of affairs: it saw him lead his Tricolours to their first Cardiff victory since 1968. Howell Davies, for Wales, missed two 'sitters' with penalty shots, but the Bridgend full-back finished the season in triumph, breaking the Welsh record of most championship points in a season with 39. Previously Phil Bennett (1976) and Steve Fenwick (1979) had totalled 38. Howell came in originally as deputy for the injured Mark Wyatt, and retained his place on merit as a consistent goal-kicker who also nipped in for a very good try against France.

Twickenham seemed sure to be a goal-kicking duel between Howell Davies and Dusty Hare. The England full-back pipped Davies by five penalty goals to four, but the Welshman converted the game's only try, beautifully set up for Adrian Hadley by Bleddyn Bowen's dummy and break. This game saw the return to international rugby of Terry Holmes following the serious knee ligament injury he had suffered in the first Test in New Zealand eight months earlier. After just three games for Cardiff's first team, Holmes was hurriedly included in the Welsh XV and played a key role in this second away victory of the season.

Malcolm Dacey, the Swansea fly-half, finished his second championship season with a suitable flourish, dropping two Twickenham goals in the closing stages and giving a convincing reply to those who made critical comparison with Gareth Davies, of Cardiff, whom Dacey had replaced. Against Ireland and England, Dacey revealed his acquired control as a kicker for position. Though not a stylist in the Cardiff man's manner of kicking, Dacey fitted into the Welsh team's scheme of spinning the ball, and it was not his fault that the wings did not receive as many opportunities as were intended. Mark Titley, on the right wing, emerged as the most exciting attacker in the team; deservedly compared with the legendary Gerald Davies. Adrian Hadley, the long-striding Cardiff wing, did not develop quite so successfully, but obviously is a player of considerable potential. Wales gave clear warning that they have match-winners behind the scrum, particularly with Holmes back to impose his all-consuming authority.

The drive of the front five – Ian Stephens, Watkins, Ian Eidman, John Perkins and Robert Norster – was irresistible, even though at times the Welsh line-out was less dominating than the previous year. Certainly Scotland had destroyed the Welsh belief that their ruck technique was improving; but at long last the lessons of defeat by the Scots were accepted and acted upon. To end the season and mark the completion of the £9 million Arms Park development project, Wales recorded their only home success, a 27-17 win over the WRU President's World XV on 7 April. John Bevan, the Welsh coach, explained that his team were going on the field to win, without frills if need be: this was no fun game. The outcome was that penalty goals decided the issue yet again. Howell Davies (3) and Bleddyn Bowen (2) were responsible for five for Wales, who were outscored on tries 3-2. The match saw Gary Whetton, the New Zealander, in such form that he forced us to consider him the world's best lock forward; and also gave us the opportunity to witness another player of the highest class, South African No 8 Rob Louw, who captained the World XV.

One result during the season should not be allowed to escape attention. It was the 23-11 success by Wales 'B' over France 'B' at Bourg-en-Bresse on December 3, the first time Wales had won on French territory in this annual fixture since the exchange began in March 1970 in Paris. Significantly, Mike Watkins captained the Wales 'B' team, which included Howell Davies at full-back and the most promising player on the Welsh scene, South Glamorgan Institute fly-half Geraint John. John figured in emergency as fly-half for the WRU President's World XV against Crawshay's Welsh at Stradey Park, deputising for the absent Tony Ward, of Ireland, and scored 24 points, including two tries, in the World's 36-13 victory.

The Japanese tour during October proved eventful in as much as a marked improvement was evident in the rugby standards of the visitors, especially in the tenacity of their tackling. Manager Shiggy Konno explained that they had concentrated on the development of upper body strength to prevent opponents breaking out of tackles. They defeated Abertillery and Newbridge, drew at Neath and lost only to Pembrokeshire and Wales.

Sanctions were imposed by Mid-Glamorgan County Council as a result of South Africans playing for the WRU President's XV in a match to mark the completion of the Arms Park redevelopment. The Welsh team could not train at the South Wales Police sports ground, Waterton Cross, as a consequence. The WRU called a general meeting for 2 June, so that the clubs could decide if sporting links were to be maintained with South Africa.

The 'Boot Money' scandal that had blown up over Adidas payments to players was countered by the WRU signing a contract with the same company for the kit supplies for the whole Welsh squad. Other important sponsorships continued, notably with Schweppes supporting the WRU Cup competition and Welsh Brewers promoting the cup competition for the Welsh Districts RU. This latter event was won again by Baglan, who beat Cimla 12-6 at the national ground with, unfortunately, the first instance of a player being sent off in a Welsh Brewers Cup Final. Cimla No 8 Howell Griffiths was the guilty party: he was dismissed in the last 10 minutes for illegal use of a knee.

Cardiff, winning the Schweppes Cup for the third time in four years, completed the season with a record aggregate of points while Gareth Davies broke his own record for the club with 383. Hooker Alan

Phillips scored more tries in a season for the club than any forward, with 24. Pontypool won the Western Mail Welsh club championship with only two defeats (by Cardiff and Neath) and a draw at Maesteg in 40 games. They also topped the Whitbread Merit Table with just one defeat. On the last day of the season Pontypool defeated Llanelli 54-16 to set a world record aggregate of 1,607 points for a season, with Peter Lewis's contribution of 472 the second-highest individual figure ever recorded in Welsh rugby. Only Pontypool record-holder Robin Williams (517 points in 1974-75) has exceeded that. The tremendous motivation of Ray Prosser, their coach, drove Pontypool to these new heights.

Bridgend scored a record total for a first-class match in Wales by beating Penarth 100-7 on 26 April and their aggregate of 1,596 points became a world record – but for less than a week – until Pontypool relieved them of the distinction. Newport were another club to set record points and tries aggregates for a season while South Wales Police wing Mark Brinkworth scored a remarkable total of 54 tries, the most since Dan Jones scored 59 for Neath in 1928-29.

Glamorgan regained the Welsh Counties Cup, toppling North Wales 20-10; South Wales Police retained the British Police Cup and Cardiff won the Snelling Sevens after Abertillery, celebrating their centenary season, had battled their way unexpectedly to the final.

WESTERN MAIL CLUB CHAMPIONSHIP 1983-84

	W	*D*	*L*	*F*	*A*	*Avge*
Pontypool	37	1	2	1220	390	93.75
Bridgend	32	3	8	1157	487	77.90
Cardiff	29	1	10	993	606	73.75
Newbridge	32	2	11	916	597	73.33
S W Police	25	0	10	748	535	71.42
Newport	26	2	16	876	652	61.36
Llanelli	25	1	16	906	672	60.71
Swansea	26	0	18	1036	699	59.09
Neath	22	2	18	636	617	54.76
Tredegar	17	1	15	539	434	53.03
Aberavon	18	2	18	569	611	50.00
Maesteg	19	3	21	700	738	48.83
Glam Wands	20	0	21	635	756	48.78
London Welsh	16	3	18	480	599	47.29
Abertillery	15	4	23	514	605	40.47
Cross Keys	13	0	22	447	572	37.14
Ebbw Vale	14	1	31	529	879	31.52
Pontypridd	13	0	31	493	876	29.54
Penarth	8	1	30	420	1022	21.79

WHITBREAD MERIT TABLE 1983-84

(Only matches against other teams in the table count)

	W	*D*	*L*	*F*	*A*	*Avge*
Pontypool	23	1	1	846	219	94.00
Bridgend	20	3	5	696	305	76.78
Newbridge	18	2	6	469	353	73.07
Neath	15	0	8	381	302	65.21
Newport	16	0	10	443	372	61.53
Llanelli	11	0	9	420	328	55.00
Swansea	12	0	10	389	282	54.54
Maesteg	12	1	12	428	332	50.00
Aberavon	11	1	12	305	357	47.91
Abertillery	10	1	14	303	338	42.00
Ebbw Vale	8	1	18	254	538	31.84
Cross Keys	7	0	17	248	426	29.16
Pontypridd	7	0	19	261	515	26.92
Glam Wands	6	0	17	297	451	26.00
Penarth	3	0	21	228	744	12.50

(Cardiff do not participate)

WELSH INTERNATIONAL PLAYERS
(up to 30 April 1984)

ABBREVIATIONS

A	Australia
E	England
F	France
I	Ireland
M	Maoris
NSW	New South Wales
NZ	New Zealand
NZA	New Zealand Army
R	Romania
S	Scotland
SA	South Africa
(R)	Replacement – (2[1R]) denotes two appearances, one as a replacement
Note:	Years given for Five Nations' matches are for second half of season; eg 1972 means season 1971-72. Years for all other matches refer to the actual year of the match

Ackerman, R A (Newport) 1980 *NZ*, 1981 *E, S, A*, 1982 *I, F, E, S*, 1983 *S, I, F, R*, 1984 *S, I, F, E*
Alexander, E P (Llandovery Coll, Cambridge U) 1885 *S*, 1886 *E, S*, 1887 *E, I*
Alexander, W H (Llwynpia) 1898 *I, E*, 1899 *E, S, I*, 1901 *S, I*
Allen, C P (Oxford U, Beaumaris) 1884 *E, S*
Andrews, F G (Swansea) 1884 *E, S*
Andrews, F (Pontypool) 1912 *SA*, 1913 *E, S, I*
Andrews, G (Newport) 1926 *E, S*, 1927 *E, F, I*
Anthony, L (Neath) 1948 *E, S, F*
Arnold, W (Swansea) 1903 *S*
Arthur, C S (Cardiff) 1888 *I, M*, 1891 *E*
Arthur, T (Neath) 1927 *S, F, I*, 1929 *E, S, F, I*, 1930 *E, S, I, F*, 1931 *E, S, F, I, SA*, 1933 *E, S*
Ashton, C (Aberavon) 1959 *E, S, I*, 1960 *E, S, I*, 1962 *I*
Attewell, L (Newport) 1921 *E, S, F*

Badger, O (Llanelli) 1895 *E, S, I*, 1896 *E*
Baker, A (Neath) 1921 *I*, 1923 *E, S, F, I*
Baker, A M (Newport) 1909 *S, F*, 1910 *S*
Bancroft, J (Swansea) 1909 *E, S, F, I*, 1910 *F, E, S, I*, 1911 *E, F, I*, 1912 *E, S, I*, 1913 *I*, 1914 *E, S, F*
Bancroft, W J (Swansea) 1890 *S, E, I*, 1891 *E, S, I*, 1892 *E, S, I*, 1893 *E, S, I*, 1894 *E, S, I*, 1895 *E, S, I*, 1896 *E, S, I*, 1897 *E*, 1898 *I, E*, 1899 *E, S, I*, 1900 *E, S, I*, 1901 *E, S, I*
Barlow, T M (Cardiff) 1884 *I*
Barrell, R (Cardiff) 1929 *S, F, I*, 1933 *I*
Bartlett, J D (Llanelli) 1927 *S*, 1928 *E, S*
Bassett, A (Cardiff) 1934 *I*, 1935 *E, S, I*, 1938 *E, S*
Bassett, J (Penarth) 1929 *E, S, F, I*, 1930 *E, S, I*, 1931 *E, S, F, I, SA*, 1932 *E, S, I*
Bayliss, G (Pontypool) 1933 *S*
Bebb, D I E (Carmarthen TC, Swansea) 1959 *E, S, I, F*, 1960 *E, S, I, F, SA*, 1961 *E, S, I, F*, 1962 *E, S, F, I*, 1963 *E, F, NZ*, 1964 *E, S, F, SA*, 1965 *E, S, I, F*, 1966 *F, A*, 1967 *S, I, F, E*
Beckingham, G (Cardiff) 1953 *E, S*, 1958 *F*
Bennett, I (Aberavon) 1937 *I*
Bennett, P (Cardiff Harlequins) 1891 *E, S*, 1892 *S, I*
Bennett, P (Llanelli) 1969 *F* (R), 1970 *SA, S, F*, 1972 *S* (R), *NZ*, 1973 *E, S, I, F, A*, 1974 *S, I, F, E*, 1975 *S* (R), *I*, 1976 *E, S, I, F*, 1977 *I, F, E, S*, 1978 *E, S, I, F*
Bergiers, R T E (Cardiff Coll of Ed, Llanelli) 1972 *E, S, F, NZ*, 1973 *E, S, I, F, A*, 1974 *E*, 1975 *I*
Bevan, G (Llanelli) 1947 *E*
Bevan, J A (Cambridge U) 1881 *E*
Bevan, J C (Cardiff, Cardiff Coll of Ed) 1971 *E, S, I, F*, 1972 *E, S, F, NZ*, 1973 *E, S*
Bevan, J D (Aberavon) 1975 *F, E, S, A*
Bevan, S (Swansea) 1904 *I*
Beynon, B (Swansea) 1920 *E, S*
Beynon, E (Swansea) 1925 *F, I*
Biggs, N (Cardiff) 1888 *M*, 1889 *I*, 1892 *I*, 1893 *E, S, I*, 1894 *E, I*
Biggs, S (Cardiff) 1895 *E, S*, 1896 *S*, 1897 *E*, 1898 *I, E*, 1899 *S, I*, 1900 *I*
Birch, J (Neath) 1911 *S, F*
Birt, F W (Newport) 1911 *E, S*, 1912 *E, S, I, SA*, 1913 *E*
Bishop, E H (Swansea) 1889 *S*
Blackmore, J (Abertillery) 1909 *E*
Blake, J (Cardiff) 1899 *E, S, I*, 1900 *E, S, I*, 1901 *E, S, I*
Blakemore, R E (Newport) 1947 *E*
Bland, A F (Cardiff) 1887 *E, S, I*, 1888 *S, I, M*, 1890 *S, E, I*
Blyth, L (Swansea) 1951 *SA*, 1952 *E, S*
Blyth, W R (Swansea) 1974 *E*, 1975 *S* (R), 1980 *F, E, S, I*
Boon, R W (Cardiff) 1930 *S, F*, 1931 *E, S, F, I, SA*, 1932 *E, S, I*, 1933 *E, I*
Booth, J (Pontymister) 1898 *I*
Boots, G (Newport) 1898 *I, E*, 1899 *I*, 1900 *E, S, I*, 1901 *E, S, I*, 1902 *E, S, I*, 1903 *E, S, I*, 1904 *E*
Boucher, A W (Newport) 1892 *E, S, I*, 1893 *E, S, I*, 1894 *E*, 1895 *E, S, I*, 1896 *E, I*, 1897 *E*
Bowcott, H M (Cardiff, Cambridge U) 1929 *S, F, I*, 1930 *E*, 1931 *E, S*, 1933 *E, I*
Bowdler, F A (Cross Keys) 1927 *NSW*, 1928 *E, S, I, F*, 1929 *E, S, F, I*, 1930 *E*, 1931 *SA*, 1932 *E, S, I*, 1933 *I*
Bowen, B (S Wales Police) 1983 *R*, 1984 *S, I, F, E*
Bowen, C (Llanelli) 1896 *E, S, I*, 1897 *E*
Bowen D H (Llanelli) 1883 *E*, 1886 *E, S*, 1887 *E*
Bowen, G E (Swansea) 1887 *S, I*, 1888 *S, I*
Bowen, W (Swansea) 1921 *S, F*, 1922 *E, S, F, I*
Bowen, Wm (Swansea) 1886 *E, S*, 1887 *E, S, I*, 1888 *M*, 1889 *S, I*, 1890 *S, E, I*, 1891 *E, S*
Brace, D O (Llanelli, Oxford U) 1956 *E, S, I, F*, 1957 *E*, 1960 *S, I, F*, 1961 *I*
Braddock, K J (Newbridge) 1966 *A*, 1967 *S, I*
Bradshaw, K (Bridgend) 1964 *E, S, I, F, SA*, 1966 *E, S, I, F*
Brewer, T J (Newport) 1950 *E*, 1955 *E, S*
Brice, A (Aberavon) 1899 *E, S, I*, 1900 *E, S, I*, 1901 *E, S, I*, 1902 *E, S, I*, 1903 *E, S, I*, 1904 *E, S, I*
Bridie, R H (Newport) 1882 *I*
Britton, G (Newport) 1961 *S*
Broughton, A (Treorchy) 1927 *NSW*, 1929 *S*
Brown, A (Newport) 1921 *I*
Brown, J (Cardiff) 1907 *E, S, I*, 1908 *E, S, F*, 1909 *E*
Brown, J (Cardiff) 1925 *I*
Brown, M (Pontypool) 1983 *R*
Burcher, D H (Newport) 1977 *I, F, E, S*
Burgess, R C (Ebbw Vale) 1977 *I, F, E, S*, 1981 *I, F*, 1982 *F, E, S*
Burnett, R (Newport) 1953 *E*
Burns, J (Cardiff) 1927 *F, I*
Bush, P F (Cardiff) 1905 *NZ*, 1906 *E, SA*, 1907 *I*, 1908 *E, S*, 1910 *S, I*
Butler, E T (Pontypool) 1980 *F, E, S, I, NZ* (R), 1982 *S*, 1983 *E, S, I, F, R*, 1984 *S, I, F, E*

Cale, W R (Newbridge, Pontypool) 1949 *E, S, I*, 1950 *E, S, I, F*
Cattell, A (Llanelli) 1883 *E, S*
Challinor, C (Neath) 1939 *E*
Clapp, T J S (Newport) 1882 *I*, 1883 *E, S*, 1884 *E, S, I*, 1885 *E, S*, 1886 *S*, 1887 *E, S, I*, 1888 *S, I*
Clare, J (Cardiff) 1883 *E*
Clark, S S (Neath) 1882 *I*, 1887 *I*
Cleaver, W B (Cardiff) 1947 *E, S, F, I, A*, 1948 *E, S, F, I*, 1949 *I*, 1950 *E, S, I, F*
Clegg, B G (Swansea) 1979 *F*
Clement, W H (Llanelli) 1937 *E, S, I*, 1938 *E, S, I*
Cobner, T J (Pontypool) 1974 *S, I, F, E*, 1975 *F, E, S, I, A*, 1976 *E, S*, 1977 *F, E, S*, 1978 *E, S, I, F, A*
Coldrick, A P (Newport) 1911 *E, S, I*, 1912 *E, S, F*
Coleman, E (Newport) 1949 *E, S, I*
Coles, F C (Pontypool) 1960 *S, I, F*
Collins, J (Aberavon) 1958 *A, E, S, F*, 1959 *E, S, I, F*, 1960 *E*, 1961 *F*
Collins, T (Mountain Ash) 1923 *I*
Conway-Rees, J (Llanelli) 1892 *S*, 1893 *E*, 1894 *E*
Cook, T (Cardiff) 1949 *S, I*
Cope, W (Cardiff, Blackheath) 1896 *S*
Cornish, F H (Cardiff) 1897 *E*, 1898 *I, E*, 1899 *I*
Cornish, R A (Cardiff) 1923 *E, S*, 1924 *E*, 1925 *E, S, F*, 1926 *E, S, I, F*
Coslett, K (Aberavon) 1962 *E, S, F*
Cowey, B T V (Welch Regt, Newport) 1934 *E, S, I*, 1935 *E*
Cresswell, B (Newport) 1960 *E, S, I, F*
Cummins, W (Treorchy) 1922 *E, S, I, F*
Cunningham, L J (Aberavon) 1960 *E, S, I, F*, 1962 *E, S, F, I*, 1963 *NZ*, 1964 *E, S, I, F, SA*

Dacey, M (Swansea) 1983 *E, S, I, F, R*, 1984 *S, I, F, E*
Daniel, D J (Llanelli) 1891 *S*, 1894 *E, S, I*, 1898 *I, E*, 1899 *E, I*
Daniel, L T D (Newport) 1970 *S*
Daniels, P C T (Cardiff) 1981 *A*, 1982 *I*
Darbishire, G (Bangor) 1881 *E*
Dauncey, F H (Newport) 1896 *E, S, I*
Davey, E C (Swansea) 1930 *F*, 1931 *E, S, F, I, SA*, 1932 *E, S, I*, 1933 *E, S*, 1934 *E, S, I*, 1935 *E, S, I, NZ*, 1936 *S*, 1937 *E, I*, 1938 *E, I*
David, R (Cardiff) 1907 *I*
David, T P (Llanelli, Pontypridd) 1973 *F, A*, 1976 *I, F*
Davidge, G D (Newport) 1959 *F*, 1960 *S, I, F, SA*, 1961 *E, S, I*, 1962 *F*
Davies, A C (London Welsh) 1889 *I*
Davies, B (Llanelli) 1895 *E*, 1896 *E*
Davies, C H A (Llanelli, Cardiff) 1957 *I*, 1958 *A, E, S, I*, 1960 *SA*, 1961 *E*
Davies, C L (Cardiff) 1956 *E, S, I*
Davies, C R (Bedford, RAF) 1934 *E*
Davies, C (Cardiff) 1947 *S, F, I, A*, 1948 *E, S, F, I*, 1949 *F*, 1950 *E, S, I, F*, 1951 *E, S, I*
Davies, D (Bridgend) 1921 *I*, 1925 *I*
Davies, D B (Llanelli) 1907 *E*
Davies, D B (Llanelli) 1962 *I*, 1963 *E, S*
Davies, D G (Cardiff) 1923 *E, S*
Davies, D H (Neath) 1904 *S*
Davies, D H (Aberavon) 1924 *E*
Davies, D I (Swansea) 1939 *E*
Davies, D J (Neath) 1962 *I*
Davies, D M (Somerset Police) 1950 *E, S, I, F*, 1951 *E, S, I, F, SA*, 1952 *E, S, I, F*, 1953 *I, F, NZ*, 1954 *E*
Davies, E (Aberavon) 1947 *A*, 1948 *I*
Davies, E (Maesteg) 1919 *NZA*
Davies, E (Cardiff) 1912 *E, F*
Davies, G (Swansea) 1900 *E, S, I*, 1901 *E, S, I*, 1905 *E, S, I*
Davies, G (Cambridge U, Pontypridd) 1947 *S, A*, 1948 *E, S, F, I*, 1949 *E, S, F*, 1951 *E, S*
Davies, G (Llanelli) 1921 *F, I*, 1925 *F*

Wales' new full-back, Howell Davies, about to score against France at Cardiff.

Davies, G (Cardiff) 1928 *F*, 1929 *E*, 1930 *S*
Davies, H (Swansea) 1898 *I, E*, 1901 *S, I*
Davies, H (Newport) 1924 *S*
Davies, H (Swansea, Llanelli) 1939 *S, I*, 1947 *E, S, F, I*
Davies, H (Neath) 1912 *E, S*
Davies, H (Bridgend) 1984 *S, I, F, E*
Davies, H J (Cambridge U, Aberavon) 1959 *E, S*
Davies, I T (Llanelli) 1914 *S, F, I*
Davies, Rev J A (Swansea) 1913 *S, F, I*, 1914 *E, S, F, I*
Davies, J H (Aberavon) 1923 *I*
Davies, L (Llanelli) 1954 *F, S*, 1955 *I*
Davies, L (Swansea) 1939 *S, I*
Davies, L (Bridgend) 1966 *E, S, I*
Davies, M (Swansea) 1981 *A*, 1982 *I*
Davies, M J (Blackheath) 1939 *S, I*
Davies, N G (London Welsh) 1955 *E*
Davies, R H (Oxford U, London Welsh) 1957 *S, I, F*, 1958 *A*, 1962 *E, S*
Davies, S (Treherbert) 1923 *I*
Davies, T J (Devonport Services, Swansea, Llanelli) 1953 *E, S, I, F*, 1957 *E, S, I, F*, 1958 *A, E, S, F*, 1959 *E, S, I, F*, 1960 *E, SA*, 1961 *E, S, F*
Davies, T G R (Cardiff, London Welsh) 1966 *A*, 1967 *S, I, F, E*, 1968 *E, S*, 1969 *S, I, F, NZ* (2), *A*, 1971 *E, S, I, F*, 1972 *E, S, F, NZ*, 1973 *E, S, I, F, A*, 1974 *S, F, E*, 1975 *F, E, S, I*, 1976 *E, S, I, F*, 1977 *I, F, E, S*, 1978 *E, S, I, A* (2)
Davies, T M (London Welsh, Swansea) 1969 *S, I, F, E, NZ* (2), *A*, 1970 *SA, S, E, I, F*, 1971 *E, S, I, F*, 1972 *E, S, F, NZ*, 1973 *E, S, I, F, A*, 1974 *S, I, F, E*, 1975 *F, E, S, I, A*, 1976 *E, S, I, F*
Davies, W (Cardiff) 1896 *S*
Davies, W (Swansea) 1931 *SA*, 1932 *E, S, I*
Davies, W (Aberavon) 1912 *S, I*
Davies, W G (Cardiff) 1978 *A* (2), *NZ*, 1979 *S, I, F, E*, 1980 *F, E, S, NZ*, 1981 *E, S, A*, 1982 *I, F, E, S*
Davies, W T H (Swansea) 1936 *I*, 1937 *E, I*, 1939 *E, S, I*
Davis, C E (Newbridge) 1978 *A*, 1981 *E, S*
Davis, W E N (Cardiff) 1939 *E, S, I*
Dawes, S J (London Welsh) 1964 *I, F, SA*, 1965 *E, S, I, F*, 1966 *A*, 1968 *I, F*, 1969 *E, NZ, A*, 1970 *SA, S, E, I, F*, 1971 *E, S, I, F*
Day, H C (Newport) 1930 *S, I, F*, 1931 *E, S*
Day, H T (Newport) 1892 *I*, 1893 *E, S*, 1894 *S, I*
Day, T (Swansea) 1931 *E, S, F, I, SA*, 1932 *E, S, I*, 1934 *S, I*, 1935 *E, S, I*
Deacon, T (Swansea) 1891 *I*, 1892 *E, S, I*
Delahay, W J (Bridgend) 1922 *E, S, I, F*, 1923 *E, S, I, F*, 1924 *NZ*, 1925 *E, S, F, I*, 1926 *E, S, I, F*, 1927 *S*
Devereux, D (Neath) 1958 *A, E, S*
Dobson, G (Cardiff) 1900 *S*
Dobson, T (Cardiff) 1898 *I, E*, 1899 *E, S*
Donovan, A J (Swansea) 1978 *A*, 1981 *I* (R), *A*, 1982 *E, S*
Donovan, R (S Wales Police) 1983 *F* (R)
Douglas, M H J (Llanelli) 1984 *S, I, F*
Douglas, W M (Cardiff) 1886 *E, S*, 1887 *E, S*
Dowell, W (Newport) 1907 *E, S, I*, 1908 *E, S, F, I*
Dyke, J C M (Penarth) 1906 *SA*
Dyke, L M (Penarth, Cardiff) 1910 *I*, 1911 *S, F, I*

Edwards, A B (London Welsh, Army) 1955 *E, S*
Edwards, B (Newport) 1951 *I*
Edwards, D (Glynneath) 1921 *E*
Edwards, G O (Cardiff, Cardiff Coll of Ed) 1967 *F, E, NZ*, 1968 *E, S, I, F*, 1969 *S, I, F, E, NZ* (2), *A*, 1970 *SA, S, E, I, F*, 1971 *E, S, I, F*, 1972 *E, S, F, NZ*, 1973 *E, S, I, F, A*, 1974 *S, I, F, E*, 1975 *F, E, S, I, A*, 1976 *E, S, I, F*, 1977 *I, F, E, S*, 1978 *E, S, I, F*
Eidman, I H (Cardiff) 1983 *S, R*, 1984 *I, F, E*
Elliott, J E (Cardiff) 1894 *I*, 1898 *I, E*
Elsey, W J (Cardiff) 1895 *E*
Evans, A C (Pontypool) 1924 *E, I, F*
Evans, B (Swansea) 1933 *S*
Evans, B (Llanelli) 1933 *E, S*, 1936 *E, S, I*, 1937 *E*
Evans, B S (Llanelli) 1920 *E*, 1922 *E, S, I, F*
Evans, C (Pontypool) 1960 *E*
Evans, D (Penygraig) 1896 *S, I*, 1897 *E*, 1898 *E*
Evans, D B (Swansea) 1926 *E*
Evans, D D (Cheshire, Cardiff U) 1934 *E*
Evans, D P (Llanelli) 1960 *SA*
Evans, D W (Cardiff) 1889 *S, I*, 1890 *E, I*, 1891 *E*
Evans, E (Llanelli) 1937 *E*, 1939 *S, I*
Evans, F (Llanelli) 1921 *S*
Evans, G (Cardiff) 1947 *E, S, F, I, A*, 1948 *E, S, F, I*, 1949 *E, S, I*
Evans, G (Maesteg) 1981 *S* (R), *I, F, A*, 1982 *I, F, E, S*, 1983 *F, R*
Evans, G L (Newport) 1977 *F* (R), 1978 *F, A* (R)
Evans, I (London Welsh) 1934 *S, I*
Evans, I (Swansea) 1922 *E, S, I, F*
Evans, J (Llanelli) 1896 *S, I*, 1897 *E*
Evans, J (Blaina) 1904 *E*
Evans, J (Pontypool) 1907 *E, S, I*
Evans, J D (Cardiff) 1958 *I, F*
Evans, J E (Llanelli) 1924 *S*
Evans, J R (Newport) 1934 *E*
Evans, O J (Cardiff) 1887 *E, S*, 1888 *S, I*
Evans, P (Llanelli) 1951 *E, F*
Evans, R (Cardiff) 1889 *S*
Evans, R (Bridgend) 1963 *S, I, F*
Evans, R T (Newport) 1947 *F, I*, 1950 *E, S, I, F*, 1951 *E, S, I, F*
Evans, T (Llanelli) 1906 *I*, 1907 *E, S, I*, 1908 *I, A*, 1909 *E, S, F, I*, 1910 *F, E, S, I*, 1911 *E, S, F, I*
Evans, T (Swansea) 1924 *I*
Evans, T G (London Welsh) 1970 *SA, S, E, I*, 1972 *E, S, F*
Evans, T P (Swansea) 1975 *F, E, S, I, A*, 1976 *E, S, I, F*, 1977 *I*
Evans, V (Neath) 1954 *I, F, S*
Evans, W (Llanelli) 1958 *A*
Evans, W F (Rhymney) 1882 *I*, 1883 *S*
Evans, W G (Brynmawr) 1911 *I*
Evans, W H (Llwynypia) 1914 *E, S, F, I*
Evans, W J (Pontypool) 1947 *S*
Evans, W R (Bridgend) 1958 *A, E, S, I, F*, 1960 *SA*, 1961 *E, S, I, F*, 1962 *E, S, I*
Everson, W A (Newport) 1926 *S*

Faulkner, A G (Pontypool) 1975 *F, E, S, I, A*, 1976 *E, S, I, F*, 1978 *E, S, I, F, A* (2), *NZ*, 1979 *S, I, F*
Faull, J (Swansea) 1957 *I, F*, 1958 *A, E, S, I, F*, 1959 *E, S, I*, 1960 *E, F*
Fear, A (Newport) 1934 *S, I*, 1935 *S, I*
Fender, N (Cardiff) 1930 *I, F*, 1931 *E, S, F, I*
Fenwick, S P (Bridgend) 1975 *F, E, S, A*, 1976 *E, S, I, F*, 1977 *I, F, E, S*, 1978 *E, S, I, F, A* (2), *NZ*, 1979 *S, I, F, E*, 1980 *F, E, S, I, NZ*, 1981 *E, S*
Finch, E (Llanelli) 1924 *F, NZ*, 1925 *F, I*, 1926 *F*, 1927 *NSW*, 1928 *I*
Finlayson, A A J (Cardiff) 1974 *I, F, E*
Fitzgerald, D (Cardiff) 1894 *S, I*
Ford, F J V (Welch Regt, Newport) 1939 *E*
Ford, I (Newport) 1959 *E, S*
Forward, A (Pontypool, Mon Police) 1951 *S, SA*, 1952 *E, S, I, F*
Fowler, I (Llanelli) 1919 *NZA*
Francis, D G (Llanelli) 1919 *NZA* 1924 *S*

Gabe, R T (Cardiff, Llanelli) 1901 *I*, 1902 *E, S, I*, 1903 *E, S, I*, 1904 *E, S, I*, 1905 *E, S, I, NZ*, 1906 *E, I, SA*, 1907 *E, S, I*, 1908 *E, S, F, I*
Gale, N R (Swansea, Llanelli) 1960 *I*, 1963 *E, S, I, NZ*, 1964 *E, S, I, F, SA*, 1965 *E, S, I, F*, 1966 *E, S, I, F, A*, 1967 *E, NZ*, 1968 *E*, 1969 *NZ* (2[1R]), *A*
Gallacher, I S (Llanelli) 1970 *F*
Garrett, R M (Penarth) 1888 *M*, 1889 *S*, 1890 *S, E, I*, 1891 *S, I*, 1892 *E*
Geen, W P (Oxford U, Newport) 1912 *SA*, 1913 *E, I*
George, E (Pontypridd) 1895 *S, I*, 1896 *E*
Gething, G I (Neath) 1913 *F*
Gibbs, R A (Cardiff) 1906 *S, I*, 1907 *E, S*, 1908 *E, S, F, I*, 1910 *F, E, S, I*, 1911 *E, S, F, I*
Giles, R (Aberavon) 1983 *R*
Girling, B E (Cardiff) 1881 *E*
Goldsworthy, S (Swansea) 1884 *I*, 1885 *E, S*
Gore, J (Blaina) 1924 *I, F, NZ*, 1925 *E*
Gore, W (Newbridge) 1947 *S, F, I*
Gould, A J (Newport) 1885 *E, S*, 1886 *E, S*, 1887 *E, S, I*, 1888 *S*, 1889 *I*, 1890 *S, E, I*, 1892 *E, S, I*, 1893 *E, S, I*, 1894 *E, S*, 1895 *E, S, I*, 1896 *E, S, I*, 1897 *E*
Gould, G H (Newport) 1892 *I*, 1893 *S, I*
Gould, R (Newport) 1882 *I*, 1883 *E, S*, 1884 *E, S, I*,

1885 *E*, *S*, 1886 *E*, 1887 *E*, *S*
Graham, T C (Newport) 1890 *I*, 1891 *S*, *I*, 1892 *E*, *S*, 1893 *E*, *S*, *I*, 1894 *E*, *S*, 1895 *E*, *S*
Gravell, R W R (Llanelli) 1975 *F*, *E*, *S*, *I*, *A*, 1976 *E*, *S*, *I*, *F*, 1978 *E*, *S*, *I*, *F*, *A* (2), *NZ*, 1979 *S*, *I*, 1981 *I*, *F*, 1982 *F*, *E*, *S*
Gray, A J (London Welsh) 1968 *E*, *S*
Greenslade, D (Newport) 1962 *S*
Greville, H (Llanelli) 1947 *A*
Griffin, Dr A (Edinburgh U) 1883 *S*
Griffiths, C (Llanelli) 1979 *E* (R)
Griffiths, D (Llanelli) 1888 *M*, 1889 *I*
Griffiths, G (Llanelli) 1889 *I*
Griffiths, G M (Cardiff) 1953 *E*, *S*, *I*, *F*, *NZ*, 1954 *I*, *F*, *S*, 1955 *I*, *F*, 1957 *E*, *S*
Griffiths, V M (Newport) 1924 *S*, *I*, *F*
Gronow, B (Bridgend) 1910 *F*, *E*, *S*, *I*
Gwilliam, J A (Cambridge U, Newport) 1947 *A*, 1948 *I*, 1949 *E*, *S*, *I*, *F*, 1950 *E*, *S*, *I*, *F*, 1951 *E*, *S*, *I*, *SA*, 1952 *E*, *S*, *I*, *F*, 1953 *E*, *I*, *F*, *NZ*, 1954 *E*
Gwynn, D (Swansea) 1883 *E*, 1887 *S*, 1890 *E*, *I*, 1891 *E*, *S*
Gwynn, W H (Swansea) 1884 *E*, *S*, *I*, 1885 *E*, *S*

Hadley, A M (Cardiff) 1983 *R*, 1984 *S*, *I*, *F*, *E*
Hall, I (Aberavon) 1967 *NZ*, 1970 *SA*, *S*, *E*, 1971 *S*, 1974 *S*, *I*, *F*
Hancock, F E (Cardiff) 1884 *I*, 1885 *E*, *S*, 1886 *S*
Hannan, J (Newport) 1888 *M*, 1889 *S*, *I*, 1890 *S*, *E*, *I*, 1891 *E*, 1892 *E*, *S*, *I*, 1893 *E*, *S*, *I*, 1894 *E*, *S*, *I*, 1895 *E*, *S*, *I*
Harding, A F (London Welsh) 1902 *E*, *S*, *I*, 1903 *E*, *S*, *I*, 1904 *E*, *S*, *I*, 1905 *E*, *S*, *I*, *NZ*, 1906 *E*, *S*, *I*, *SA*, 1907 *I*, 1908 *E*, *S*
Harding, G F (Newport) 1881 *E*, 1882 *I*, 1883 *E*, *S*
Harding, T (Newport) 1888 *M*, 1889 *S*, *I*
Harding, W R (Swansea, Cambridge U) 1923 *E*, *S*, *F*, *I*, 1924 *I*, *F*, *NZ*, 1925 *F*, *I*, 1926 *E*, *I*, *F*, 1927 *E*, *S*, *F*, *I*, 1928 *E*
Harris, D J E (Pontypridd, Cardiff) 1959 *I*, *F*, 1960 *S*, *I*, *F*, *SA*, 1961 *E*, *S*
Harris, T (Aberavon) 1927 *NSW*
Hathway, G (Newport) 1924 *I*, *F*
Havard, Rev W T (Llanelli) 1919 *NZA*
Hawkins, F (Pontypridd) 1912 *I*, *F*
Hayward, D (Newbridge) 1949 *E*, *F*, 1950 *E*, *S*, *I*, *F*, 1951 *E*, *S*, *I*, *F*, *SA*, 1952 *E*, *S*, *I*, *F*
Hayward, D J (Cardiff) 1963 *E*, *NZ*, 1964 *S*, *I*, *F*, *SA*
Hayward, G (Swansea) 1908 *S*, *F*, *I*, *A*, 1909 *E*
Hellings, R (Llwynypia) 1897 *E*, 1898 *I*, *E*, 1899 *S*, *I*, 1900 *E*, *I*, 1901 *E*, *S*
Herrerá, R (Cross Keys) 1925 *S*, *F*, *I*, 1926 *E*, *S*, *I*, *F*, 1927 *E*
Hiams, H (Swansea) 1912 *I*, *F*
Hickman, A (Neath) 1930 *E*, 1933 *S*
Hiddlestone, D (Neath) 1922 *E*, *S*, *I*, *F*, 1924 *NZ*
Hill, A F (Cardiff) 1885 *S*, 1886 *E*, *S*, 1888 *S*, *I*, *M*, 1889 *S*, 1890 *S*, *I*, 1893 *E*, *S*, *I*, 1894 *E*, *S*, *I*
Hinam, S (Cardiff) 1925 *I*, 1926 *E*, *S*, *I*, *F*
Hinton, J T (Cardiff) 1884 *I*
Hirst, G L (Newport) 1912 *S*, 1913 *S*, 1914 *E*, *S*, *F*, *I*
Hodder, W (Pontypool) 1921 *E*, *S*, *F*
Hodges, J J (Newport) 1899 *E*, *S*, *I*, 1900 *E*, *S*, *I*, 1901 *E*, *S*, 1902 *E*, *S*, *I*, 1903 *E*, *S*, *I*, 1904 *E*, *S*, 1905 *E*, *S*, *I*, *NZ*, 1906 *E*, *S*, *I*
Hodgson, G T R (Neath) 1962 *I*, 1963 *E*, *S*, *I*, *F*, *NZ*, 1964 *E*, *S*, *I*, *F*, *SA*, 1966 *S*, *I*, *F*, 1967 *I*
Hollingdale, B (Swansea) 1912 *SA*, 1913 *E*
Hollingdale, T (Neath) 1927 *NSW*, 1928 *E*, *S*, *I*, *F*, 1930 *E*
Holmes, T D (Cardiff) 1978 *A*, *NZ*, 1979 *S*, *I*, *F*, *E*, 1980 *F*, *E*, *S*, *I*, *NZ*, 1981 *A*, 1982 *I*, *F*, *E*, 1983 *E*, *S*, *I*, *F*, 1984 *E*
Hopkins, W H (Newport) 1937 *S*
Hopkins, P (Swansea) 1908 *A*, 1909 *E*, *I*, 1910 *E*
Hopkins, R (Maesteg) 1970 *E* (R)
Hopkins, T (Swansea) 1926 *E*, *S*, *I*, *F*
Hopkins, W J (Aberavon) 1925 *E*, *S*
Howells, B (Llanelli) 1934 *E*
Howells, G (Llanelli) 1957 *E*, *S*, *I*, *F*
Howells, W H (Swansea) 1888 *S*, *I*
Hughes, D (Newbridge) 1967 *NZ*, 1969 *NZ*, 1970 *SA*, *S*, *E*, *I*
Hughes, G (Penarth) 1934 *E*, *S*, *I*
Hughes, H (Cardiff) 1887 *S*, 1889 *S*
Hughes, K (Cambridge U, London Welsh) 1970 *I*, 1973 *A*, 1974 *S*
Hullin, W (Cardiff) 1967 *S*
Hurrell, J (Newport) 1959 *F*
Hutchinson, F (Neath) 1894 *I*, 1896 *S*, *I*
Huxtable, R (Swansea) 1920 *F*, *I*
Huzzey, V (Cardiff) 1898 *I*, *E*, 1899 *E*, *S*, *I*
Hybart, A J (Cardiff) 1887 *E*

Ingledew, H M (Cardiff) 1890 *I*, 1891 *E*, *S*
Isaacs, I (Cardiff) 1933 *E*, *S*

Jackson, T H (Swansea) 1895 *E*
James, B (Bridgend) 1968 *E*
James, C R (Llanelli) 1958 *A*, *F*
James, D (Swansea) 1891 *I*, 1892 *S*, *I*, 1899 *E*
James, D R (Treorchy) 1931 *F*, *I*
James, E (Swansea) 1890 *S*, 1891 *I*, 1892 *S*, *I*, 1899 *E*
James, M (Cardiff) 1947 *A*, 1948 *E*, *S*, *F*, *I*
James, T O (Aberavon) 1935 *I*, 1937 *S*
James, W J (Aberavon) 1983 *E*, *S*, *I*, *F*, *R*, 1984 *S*
James, W P (Aberavon) 1925 *E*, *S*
Jarman, H (Newport) 1910 *E*, *S*, *I*, 1911 *E*
Jarrett, K S (Newport) 1967 *E*, 1968 *E*, *S*, 1969 *S*, *I*, *F*, *E*, *NZ* (2), *A*
Jeffery, J J (Cardiff Coll of Ed, Newport) 1967 *NZ*
Jenkin, A M (Swansea) 1895 *I*, 1896 *E*
Jenkins, A (Llanelli) 1920 *E*, *S*, *F*, *I*, 1921 *S*, *F*, 1922 *F*, 1923 *E*, *S*, *F*, *I*, 1924 *NZ*, 1928 *S*, *I*
Jenkins, D (Treorchy) 1926 *E*, *S*, *I*, *F*
Jenkins, D R (Swansea) 1927 *NSW*, 1929 *E*
Jenkins, E (Newport) 1910 *S*, *I*
Jenkins, E M (Aberavon) 1927 *S*, *F*, *I*, *NSW*, 1928 *E*, *S*, *I*, *F*, 1929 *F*, 1930 *E*, *S*, *I*, *F*, 1931 *E*, *S*, *F*, *I*, *SA*, 1932 *E*, *S*, *I*
Jenkins, J C (London Welsh) 1906 *SA*
Jenkins, L (Aberavon) 1923 *S*, *F*
Jenkins, L (Mon TC, Newport) 1954 *I*, 1956 *E*, *S*, *I*, *F*
Jenkins, V G J (Oxford U, Bridgend, London Welsh) 1933 *E*, *I*, 1934 *S*, *I*, 1935 *E*, *S*, *NZ*, 1936 *E*, *S*, *I*, 1937 *E*, 1938 *E*, *S*, 1939 *E*
Jenkins, W (Cardiff) 1912 *I*, *F*, 1913 *S*, *I*
John, A (Llanelli) 1925 *I*, 1928 *E*, *S*, *I*
John, B (Llanelli, Cardiff) 1966 *A*, 1967 *S*, *NZ*, 1968 *E*, *S*, *I*, *F*, 1969 *S*, *I*, *F*, *E*, *NZ* (2), *A*, 1970 *SA*, *S*, *E*, *I*, 1971 *E*, *S*, *I*, *F*, 1972 *E*, *S*, *F*
John D E (Llanelli) 1923 *F*, *I*, 1928 *E*, *S*, *I*
John, E R (Neath) 1950 *E*, *S*, *I*, *F*, 1951 *E*, *S*, *I*, *F*, *SA*, 1952 *E*, *S*, *I*, *F*, 1953 *E*, *S*, *I*, *F*, *NZ*, 1954 *E*
John, G (St Luke's Coll, Exeter) 1954 *E*, *F*
John, J H (Swansea) 1926 *E*, *S*, *I*, *F*, 1927 *E*, *S*, *F*, *I*
Johnson, T (Cardiff) 1921 *E*, *F*, *I*, 1923 *E*, *S*, *F*, 1924 *E*, *S*, *NZ*, 1925 *E*, *S*, *F*
Johnson, W D (Swansea) 1953 *E*
Jones, A H (Cardiff) 1933 *E*, *S*
Jones, B (Abertillery) 1914 *E*, *S*, *F*, *I*
Jones, Bert (Llanelli) 1934 *S*, *I*
Jones, Bob (Llwynypia) 1901 *I*
Jones, B J (Newport) 1960 *I*, *F*
Jones, B Lewis (Devonport Services, Llanelli) 1950 *E*, *S*, *I*, *F*, 1951 *E*, *S*, *SA*, 1952 *E*, *I*, *F*
Jones, C W (Cambridge U, Cardiff) 1934 *E*, *S*, *I*, 1935 *E*, *S*, *I*, *NZ*, 1936 *E*, *S*, *I*, 1938 *E*, *S*, *I*
Jones, C W (Bridgend) 1920 *E*, *S*, *F*
Jones, D (Neath) 1927 *NSW*
Jones, D (Aberavon) 1897 *E*
Jones, D (Swansea) 1947 *E*, *F*, *I*, 1949 *E*, *S*, *I*, *F*
Jones, D (Treherbert) 1902 *E*, *S*, *I*, 1903 *E*, *S*, *I*, 1905 *E*, *S*, *I*, *NZ*, 1906 *E*, *S*, *SA*
Jones, D (Newport) 1926 *E*, *S*, *I*, *F*, 1927 *E*
Jones, D (Llanelli) 1948 *E*
Jones, D K (Llanelli, Cardiff) 1962 *E*, *S*, *F*, *I*, 1963 *E*, *F*, *NZ*, 1964 *E*, *S*, *SA*, 1966 *E*, *S*, *I*, *F*
Jones, D P (Pontypool) 1907 *I*
Jones, E (Llanelli) 1930 *F*, 1933 *E*, *S*, *I*, 1935 *E*
Jones, Elvet (Llanelli) 1939 *S*
Jones, G (Cardiff) 1930 *S*, 1933 *I*
Jones, G (Ebbw Vale) 1963 *S*, *I*, *F*
Jones, H (Penygraig) 1902 *S*, *I*
Jones, H (Neath) 1904 *I*
Jones, H (Neath) 1929 *E*, *S*

Jones, H (Swansea) 1930 *I, F*
Jones, Iorwerth (Llanelli) 1927 *NSW*, 1928 *E, S, I, F*
Jones, Ivor (Llanelli) 1924 *E, S*, 1927 *S, F, I, NSW*, 1928 *E, S, I, F*, 1929 *E, S, F, I*, 1930 *E, S*
Jones, I C (London Welsh) 1968 *I*
Jones, J (Aberavon) 1901 *E*
Jones, J A (Cardiff) 1883 *S*
Jones, Jim (Aberavon) 1919 *NZA*, 1920 *E, S*, 1921 *S, F, I*
Jones, J (Swansea) 1924 *F*
Jones, J P (Pontypool) 1908 *A*, 1909 *E, S, F, I*, 1910 *F, E*, 1912 *E, F*, 1913 *F, I*, 1920 *F, I*, 1921 *E*
Jones, K D (Cardiff) 1960 *SA*, 1961 *E, S, I*, 1962 *E, F*, 1963 *E, S, I, NZ*
Jones, K J (Newport) 1947 *E, S, F, I, A*, 1948 *E, S, F, I*, 1949 *E, S, I, F*, 1950 *E, S, I, F*, 1951 *E, S, I, F, SA*, 1952 *E, S, I, F*, 1953 *E, S, I, F, NZ*, 1954 *E, I, F, S*, 1955 *E, S, I, F*, 1956 *E, S, I, F*, 1957 *S*
Jones, K W J (Oxford U, London Welsh) 1934 *E*
Jones, P B (Newport) 1921 *S*
Jones, P (Newport) 1912 *SA*, 1913 *E, S, F*, 1914 *E, S, F, I*
Jones, R (Swansea) 1901 *I*, 1902 *E*, 1904 *E, S, I*, 1905 *E*, 1908 *F, I, A*, 1909 *E, S, F, I*, 1910 *F, E*
Jones, R (London Welsh) 1929 *E*
Jones, R B (Cambridge U) 1933 *E, S*
Jones, R E (Coventry) 1967 *F, E*, 1968 *S, I, F*
Jones, R (Northampton) 1926 *E, S, F*
Jones, R (Swansea) 1927 *NSW*, 1928 *F*
Jones, S T (Pontypool) 1983 *S, I, F, R*, 1984 *S*
Jones, T B (Newport) 1882 *I*, 1883 *E, S*, 1884 *S*, 1885 *E, S*
Jones, Tom (Newport) 1922 *E, S, I, F*, 1924 *E, S*
Jones, T (Pontypool) 1913 *S*
Jones, W (Cardiff) 1898 *I, E*
Jones, W I (Llanelli, Cambridge U) 1925 *E, S, F, I*
Jones, W J (Llanelli) 1924 *I*
Jones, W K (Cardiff) 1967 *NZ*, 1968 *E, S, I, F*
Jones, W (Mountain Ash) 1905 *I*
Jones-Davies, T E (London Welsh) 1930 *E, I*, 1931 *E, S*
Jordan, H M (Newport) 1885 *E, S*, 1889 *S*
Joseph, W (Swansea) 1902 *E, S, I*, 1903 *E, S, I*, 1904 *E, S*, 1905 *E, S, I, NZ*, 1906 *E, S, I, SA*
Jowett, W F (Swansea) 1903 *E*
Judd, S (Cardiff) 1953 *E, S, I, F, NZ*, 1954 *E, F, S*, 1955 *E, S*
Judson, J H (Llanelli) 1883 *E, S*

Kedzlie, Q D (Cardiff) 1888 *S, I*
Keen, L (Aberavon) 1980 *F, E, S, I*
Knill, F M D (Cardiff) 1976 *F* (R)

Lane, S M (Cardiff) 1978 *A* (2[1R]), 1979 *I* (R), 1980 *S, I*
Lang, J (Llanelli) 1931 *F, I*, 1934 *S, I*, 1935 *E, S, I, NZ*, 1936 *E, S, I*, 1937 *E*
Lawrence, S (Bridgend) 1925 *S, I*, 1926 *S, I, F*, 1927 *E*
Law, V J (Newport) 1939 *I*
Legge, W G (Newport) 1937 *I*, 1938 *I*
Leleu, J (London Welsh, Swansea) 1959 *E, S*, 1960 *F, SA*
Lemon, A (Neath) 1929 *I*, 1930 *S, I, F*, 1931 *E, S, F, I, SA*, 1932 *E, S, I*, 1933 *I*
Lewis, A J (Ebbw Vale) 1970 *F*, 1971 *E, I, F*, 1972 *E, S, F*, 1973 *E, S, I, F*
Lewis, A R (Abertillery) 1966 *E, S, I, F, A*, 1967 *I*
Lewis, B (Swansea) 1912 *I*, 1913 *I*
Lewis, C P (Llandovery Coll) 1882 *I*, 1883 *E, S*, 1884 *E, S*
Lewis, D H (Cardiff) 1886 *E, S*
Lewis, E J (Llandovery) 1881 *E*
Lewis, G W (Richmond) 1960 *E, S*
Lewis, H (Swansea) 1913 *S, F, I*, 1914 *E*
Lewis, J (Llanelli) 1887 *I*
Lewis, J M C (Cardiff, Cambridge U) 1912 *E*, 1913 *S, F, I*, 1914 *E, S, F, I*, 1921 *I*, 1923 *E, S*
Lewis, J R (S Glam Inst, Cardiff) 1981 *E, S, I, F*, 1982 *F, E, S*
Lewis, M (Treorchy) 1913 *F*
Lewis, T (Cardiff) 1926 *E*, 1927 *E, S*
Lewis, W H (London Welsh, Cambridge U) 1926 *I*, 1927 *E, F, I, NSW*, 1928 *F*
Lewis, W (Llanelli) 1925 *F*
Llewellyn, P D (Swansea) 1973 *I, F, A*, 1974 *S, E*
Llewellyn, W (Llwynypia) 1899 *E, S, I*, 1900 *E, S, I*, 1901 *E, S, I*, 1902 *E, S, I*, 1903 *I*, 1904 *E, S, I*, 1905 *E, S, I, NZ*
Llewelyn, D B (Newport, Llanelli) 1970 *SA, S, E, I, F*, 1971 *E, S, I, F*, 1972 *E, S, F, NZ*
Lloyd, D J (Bridgend) 1966 *E, S, I, F, A*, 1967 *S, I, F, E*, 1968 *S, I, F*, 1969 *S, I, F, E, NZ, A*, 1970 *F*, 1972 *E, S, F*, 1973 *E, S*
Lloyd, E (Llanelli) 1895 *S*
Lloyd, G L (Newport) 1896 *I*, 1899 *S, I*, 1900 *E, S*, 1901 *E, S*, 1902 *S, I*, 1903 *E, S, I*
Lloyd, P (Llanelli) 1890 *S, E*, 1891 *E, I*
Lloyd, R (Pontypool) 1913 *S, F, I*, 1914 *E, S, F, I*
Lloyd, T (Maesteg) 1953 *I, F*
Lloyd, T C (Neath) 1909 *F*, 1913 *F, I*, 1914 *E, S, F, I*
Lockwood, T W (Newport) 1887 *E, S, I*
Long, E (Swansea) 1936 *E, S, I*, 1937 *E, S*, 1939 *S, I*
Lyne, H S (Newport) 1883 *S*, 1884 *E, S, I*, 1885 *E*

Maddocks, H T (London Welsh) 1906 *E, S, I*, 1907 *E, S*, 1910 *F*
Maddocks, K (Neath) 1957 *E*
Main, D R (London Welsh) 1959 *E, S, I, F*
Mainwaring, H J (Swansea) 1961 *F*
Mainwaring, W T (Aberavon) 1967 *S, I, F, E, NZ*, 1968 *E*
Major, W (Maesteg) 1949 *F*, 1950 *S*
Male, B O (Cardiff) 1921 *F*, 1923 *S*, 1924 *S, I*, 1927 *E, S, F, I*, 1928 *S, I, F*
Manfield, L (Mountain Ash, Cardiff) 1939 *S, I*, 1947 *A*, 1948 *E, S, F, I*
Mann, B B (Cardiff) 1881 *E*
Mantle, J T (Loughborough Colls, Newport) 1964 *E, SA*
Margrave, F L (Llanelli) 1884 *E, S*
Marsden-Jones, D (Cardiff) 1921 *E*, 1924 *NZ*
Martin, A J (Aberavon) 1973 *A*, 1974 *S, I*, 1975 *F, E, S, I, A*, 1976 *E, S, I, F*, 1977 *I, F, E, S*, 1978 *E, S, I, F, A* (2), *NZ*, 1979 *S, I, F, E*, 1980 *F, E, S, I, NZ*, 1981 *I, F*
Martin, W J (Newport) 1912 *I, F*, 1919 *NZA*
Mathews, Rev A A (Lampeter) 1886 *S*
Mathias, R (Llanelli) 1970 *F*
Matthews, C (Bridgend) 1939 *I*
Matthews, J (Cardiff) 1947 *E, A*, 1948 *E, S, F*, 1949 *E, S, I, F*, 1950 *E, S, I, F*, 1951 *E, S, I, F*
McCall, B E W (Welch Regt, Newport) 1936 *E, S, I*
McCarley, A (Neath) 1938 *E, S, I*
McCutcheon, W (Swansea) 1891 *S*, 1892 *E, S*, 1893 *E, S, I*, 1894 *E*
Meredith, A (Devonport Services) 1949 *E, S, I*
Meredith, B V (St Luke's Coll, London Welsh, Newport) 1954 *I, F, S*, 1955 *E, S, I, F*, 1956 *E, S, I, F*, 1957 *E, S, I, F*, 1958 *A, E, S, I*, 1959 *E, S, I, F*, 1960 *E, S, F, SA*, 1961 *E, S, I*, 1962 *E, S, F, I*
Meredith, C C (Neath) 1953 *S, NZ*, 1954 *E, I, F, S*, 1955 *E, S, I, F*, 1956 *E, I*, 1957 *E, S*
Meredith, J (Swansea) 1888 *S, I*, 1890 *S, E*
Merry, G E (Pill Harriers) 1912 *I, F*
Michael, G (Swansea) 1923 *E, S, F*
Michaelson, R C B (Aberavon, Cambridge U) 1963 *E*
Miller, F (Mountain Ash) 1896 *I*, 1900 *E, S, I*, 1901 *E, S, I*
Mills, F (Swansea) 1892 *E, S, I*, 1893 *E, S, I*, 1894 *E, S, I*, 1895 *E, S, I*, 1896 *E*
Moore, W J (Bridgend) 1933 *I*
Morgan, C H (Llanelli) 1957 *I, F*
Morgan, C I (Cardiff) 1951 *I, F, SA*, 1952 *E, S, I*, 1953 *S, I, F, NZ*, 1954 *E, I, S*, 1955 *E, S, I, F*, 1956 *E, S, I, F*, 1957 *E, S, I, F*, 1958 *E, S, I, F*
Morgan, D (Swansea) 1885 *S*, 1886 *E, S*, 1887 *E, S, I*, 1889 *I*
Morgan, D (Llanelli) 1895 *I*, 1896 *E*
Morgan, D R (Llanelli) 1962 *E, S, F, I*, 1963 *E, S, I, F, NZ*
Morgan, E (Llanelli) 1920 *I*, 1921 *E, S, F*
Morgan, E T (London Welsh) 1902 *E, S, I*, 1903 *I*, 1904 *E, S, I*, 1905 *E, S, I, NZ*, 1906 *E, S, I, SA*, 1908 *F*
Morgan, Edgar (Swansea) 1914 *E, S, F, I*
Morgan, F L (Llanelli) 1938 *E, S, I*, 1939 *E*
Morgan, H J (Abertillery) 1958 *E, S, I, F*, 1959 *I, F*,

1960 *E*, 1961 *E*, *S*, *I*, *F*, 1962 *E*, *S*, *F*, *I*, 1963 *S*, *I*, *F*, 1965 *E*, *S*, *I*, *F*, 1966 *E*, *S*, *I*, *F*, *A*
Morgan, H P (Newport) 1956 *E*, *S*, *I*, *F*
Morgan, I (Swansea) 1908 *A*, 1909 *E*, *S*, *F*, *I*, 1910 *F*, *E*, *S*, *I*, 1911 *E*, *F*, *I*, 1912 *S*
Morgan, J (Llanelli) 1912 *SA*, 1913 *E*
Morgan, M E (Swansea) 1938 *E*, *S*, *I*, 1939 *E*
Morgan, N (Newport) 1960 *S*, *I*, *F*
Morgan, P (Aberavon) 1961 *E*, *S*, *F*
Morgan, P J (Llanelli) 1980 *S* (R), *I*, *NZ* (R), 1981 *I*
Morgan, R (Newport) 1984 *S*
Morgan, T (Llanelli) 1889 *I*
Morgan, W G (Cambridge U) 1927 *F*, *I*, 1929 *E*, *S*, *F*, *I*, 1930 *I*, *F*
Morgan, W L (Cardiff) 1910 *S*
Moriarty, R D (Swansea) 1981 *A*, 1982 *I*, *F*, *E*, *S*, 1983 *E*, 1984 *S*, *I*, *F*, *E*
Morley, J C (Newport) 1929 *E*, *S*, *F*, *I*, 1930 *E*, *I*, 1931 *E*, *S*, *F*, *I*, *SA*, 1932 *E*, *S*, *I*
Morris, G L (Swansea) 1882 *I*, 1883 *E*, *S*, 1884 *E*, *S*
Morris, H T (Cardiff) 1951 *F*, 1955 *I*, *F*
Morris, I (Swansea) 1924 *E*, *S*
Morris, R R (Swansea, Bristol) 1933 *S*, 1937 *S*
Morris, S (Cross Keys) 1920 *E*, *S*, *F*, *I*, 1922 *E*, *S*, *I*, *F*, 1923 *E*, *S*, *F*, *I*, 1924 *E*, *S*, *F*, *NZ*, 1925 *E*, *S*, *F*
Morris, W (Abertillery) 1919 *NZA*, 1920 *F*, 1921 *I*
Morris, W (Llanelli) 1896 *S*, *I*, 1897 *E*
Morris, W D (Neath) 1967 *F*, *E*, 1968 *E*, *S*, *I*, *F*, 1969 *S*, *I*, *F*, *E*, *NZ* (2), *A*, 1970 *SA*, *S*, *E*, *I*, *F*, 1971 *E*, *S*, *I*, *F*, 1972 *E*, *S*, *F*, *NZ*, 1973 *E*, *S*, *I*, *A*, 1974 *S*, *I*, *F*, *E*
Morris, W J (Newport) 1965 *S*, 1966 *F*
Morris, W J (Pontypool) 1963 *S*, *I*
Murphy, C (Cross Keys) 1935 *E*, *S*, *I*

Nash, D (Ebbw Vale) 1960 *SA*, 1961 *E*, *S*, *I*, *F*, 1962 *F*
Neill, W (Cardiff) 1904 *S*, *I*, 1905 *E*, *S*, *I*, 1907 *E*, *I*, 1908 *E*, *S*, *F*, *I*
Newman, C H (Newport) 1881 *E*, 1882 *I*, 1883 *E*, *S*, 1884 *E*, *S*, 1885 *E*, *S*, 1886 *E*, 1887 *E*
Nicholas, D L (Llanelli) 1981 *E*, *S*, *I*, *F*
Nicholas, T J (Cardiff) 1919 *NZA*
Nicholl, C B (Cambridge U, Llanelli) 1891 *I*, 1892 *E*, *S*, *I*, 1893 *E*, *S*, *I*, 1894 *E*, *S*, 1895 *E*, *S*, *I*, 1896 *E*, *S*, *I*
Nicholl, D W (Llanelli) 1894 *I*
Nicholls, E G (Cardiff) 1896 *S*, *I*, 1897 *E*, 1898 *I*, *E*, 1899 *E*, *S*, *I*, 1900 *S*, *I*, 1901 *E*, *S*, *I*, 1902 *E*, *S*, *I*, 1903 *I*, 1904 *E*, 1905 *I*, *NZ*, 1906 *E*, *S*, *I*, *SA*
Nicholls, F E (Cardiff Harlequins) 1892 *I*
Nicholls, H (Cardiff) 1958 *I*
Nicholls, S H (Cardiff) 1888 *M*, 1889 *S*, *I*, 1891 *S*
Norris, C H (Cardiff) 1963 *F*, 1966 *F*
Norster, R L (Cardiff) 1982 *S*, 1983 *E*, *S*, *I*, *F*, 1984 *S*, *I*, *F*, *E*
Norton, W B (Cardiff)) 1882 *I*, 1883 *E*, *S*, 1884 *E*, *S*, *I*

O'Connor, A (Aberavon) 1960 *SA*, 1961 *E*, *S*, 1962 *F*, *I*
O'Connor, R (Aberavon) 1957 *E*
O'Shea, J P (Cardiff) 1967 *S*, *I*, 1968 *S*, *I*, *F*
Oliver, G (Pontypool) 1920 *E*, *S*, *F*, *I*
Osborne, W T (Mountain Ash) 1902 *E*, *S*, *I*, 1903 *E*, *S*, *I*
Ould, W J (Cardiff) 1924 *E*, *S*
Owen, A (Swansea) 1924 *E*
Owen, G (Newport) 1955 *I*, *F*, 1956 *E*, *S*, *I*, *F*
Owen, R M (Swansea) 1901 *I*, 1902 *E*, *S*, *I*, 1903 *E*, *S*, *I*, 1904 *E*, *S*, *I*, 1905 *E*, *S*, *I*, *NZ*, 1906 *E*, *S*, *I*, *SA*, 1907 *E*, *S*, 1908 *F*, *I*, *A*, 1909 *E*, *S*, *F*, *I*, 1910 *F*, *E*, 1911 *E*, *S*, *F*, *I*, 1912 *E*, *S*

Packer, H (Newport) 1891 *E*, 1895 *S*, *I*, 1896 *E*, *S*, *I*, 1897 *E*
Palmer, F (Swansea) 1922 *E*, *S*, *I*
Parfitt, F C (Newport) 1893 *E*, *S*, *I*, 1894 *E*, *S*, *I*, 1895 *S*, 1896 *S*, *I*
Parker, D (Swansea) 1924 *I*, *F*, *NZ*, 1925 *E*, *S*, *F*, *I*, 1929 *F*, *I*, 1930 *E*
Parker, T (Swansea) 1919 *NZA*, 1920 *E*, *S*, *I*, 1921 *E*, *S*, *F*, *I*, 1922 *E*, *S*, *I*, *F*, 1923 *E*, *S*, *F*
Parker, W (Swansea) 1899 *E*, *S*
Parsons, G (Newport) 1947 *E*
Pascoe, D (Bridgend) 1923 *F*, *I*
Pask, A E I (Abertillery) 1961 *F*, 1962 *E*, *S*, *F*, *I*, 1963 *E*, *S*, *I*, *F*, *NZ*, 1964 *E*, *S*, *I*, *F*, *SA*, 1965 *E*, *S*, *I*, *F*, 1966 *S*, *I*, *F*, *E*, *A*, 1967 *S*, *I*
Payne, G W (Army, Pontypridd) 1960 *E*, *S*, *I*
Payne, H (Swansea) 1935 *NZ*
Peacock, H (Newport) 1929 *S*, *F*, *I*, 1930 *S*, *I*, *F*
Peake, E (Chepstow) 1881 *E*
Pearce, G P (Bridgend) 1981 *I*, *F*, 1982 *I* (R)
Pearson, T W (Cardiff, Newport) 1891 *E*, *I*, 1892 *E*, *S*, 1894 *S*, *I*, 1895 *E*, *S*, *I*, 1897 *E*, 1898 *I*, *E*, 1903 *E*
Pegge, E V (Neath) 1891 *E*
Perkins, S J (Pontypool) 1983 *S*, *I*, *F*, *R*, 1984 *S*, *I*, *F*, *E*
Perrett, F (Neath) 1912 *SA*, 1913 *E*, *S*, *F*, *I*
Perrins, V C (Newport) 1970 *SA*, *S*
Perry, W (Neath) 1911 *E*
Phillips, A J (Cardiff) 1979 *E*, 1980 *F*, *E*, *S*, *I*, *NZ*, 1981 *E*, *S*, *I*, *F*, *A*, 1982 *I*, *F*, *E*, *S*
Phillips, B (Aberavon) 1925 *E*, *S*, *F*, *I*, 1926 *E*
Phillips, H (Newport) 1927 *E*, *S*, *F*, *I*, *NSW*, 1928 *E*, *S*, *I*, *F*
Phillips, H (Swansea) 1952 *F*
Phillips, L A (Newport) 1900 *E*, *S*, *I*, 1901 *S*
Phillips, P (Newport) 1892 *E*, 1893 *E*, *S*, *I*, 1894 *E*, *S*
Phillips, W D (Cardiff) 1881 *E*, 1882 *I*, 1884 *E*, *S*, *I*
Pickering, D F (Llanelli) 1983 *E*, *S*, *I*, *F*, *R*, 1984 *S*, *I*, *F*, *E*
Plummer, R C S (Newport) 1912 *S*, *I*, *F*, *SA*, 1913 *E*
Pook, T (Newport) 1895 *S*
Powell, G (Ebbw Vale) 1957 *I*, *F*
Powell, J (Cardiff) 1906 *I*
Powell, J (Cardiff) 1923 *I*
Powell, R W (Newport) 1888 *S*, *I*
Powell, W C (London Welsh) 1926 *S*, *I*, *F*, 1927 *E*, *F*, *I*, 1928 *S*, *I*, *F*, 1929 *E*, *S*, *F*, *I*, 1930 *S*, *I*, *F*, 1931 *E*, *S*, *F*, *I*, *SA*, 1932 *E*, *S*, *I*, 1935 *E*, *S*, *I*
Powell, W J (Cardiff) 1920 *E*, *S*, *F*, *I*
Price, B (Newport) 1961 *I*, *F*, 1962 *E*, *S*, 1963 *E*, *S*, *F*, *NZ*, 1964 *E*, *S*, *I*, *F*, *SA*, 1965 *E*, *S*, *I*, *F*, 1966 *E*, *S*, *I*, *F*, *A*, 1967 *S*, *I*, *F*, *E*, 1969 *S*, *I*, *F*, *NZ* (2), *A*
Price, G (Pontypool) 1975 *F*, *E*, *S*, *I*, *A*, 1976 *E*, *S*, *I*, *F*, 1977 *I*, *F*, *E*, *S*, 1978 *E*, *S*, *I*, *F*, *A* (2), *NZ*, 1979 *S*, *I*, *F*, *E*, 1980 *F*, *E*, *S*, *I*, *NZ*, 1981 *E*, *S*, *I*, *F*, *A*, 1982 *I*, *F*, *E*, *S*, 1983 *E*, *I*, *F*
Price, M J (Pontypool, RAF) 1959 *E*, *S*, *I*, *F*, 1960 *E*, *S*, *I*, *F*, 1962 *E*
Price, R E (Weston) 1939 *S*, *I*
Price, T G (Llanelli) 1965 *E*, *S*, *I*, *F*, 1966 *E*, *A*, 1967 *S*, *F*
Priday, A J (Cardiff) 1958 *I*, 1961 *I*
Pritchard, C (Pontypool) 1928 *E*, *S*, *I*, *F*, 1929 *E*, *S*, *F*, *I*
Pritchard, C C (Newport, Pontypool) 1904 *S*, *I*, 1905 *NZ*, 1906 *E*, *S*
Pritchard, C M (Newport) 1904 *I*, 1905 *E*, *S*, *NZ*, 1906 *E*, *S*, *I*, *SA*, 1907 *E*, *S*, *I*, 1908 *E*, 1910 *F*, *E*
Prosser, D R (Neath) 1934 *S*, *I*
Prosser, G (Neath) 1934 *E*, *S*, *I*, 1935 *NZ*
Prosser, J (Cardiff) 1921 *I*
Prosser, R (Pontypool) 1956 *S*, *F*, 1957 *E*, *S*, *I*, *F*, 1958 *A*, *E*, *S*, *I*, *F*, 1959 *E*, *S*, *I*, *F*, 1960 *E*, *S*, *I*, *F*, *SA*, 1961 *I*, *F*
Prothero, G J (Bridgend) 1964 *S*, *I*, *F*, 1965 *E*, *S*, *I*, *F*, 1966 *E*, *S*, *I*, *F*
Pryce-Jenkins, T J (London Welsh) 1888 *S*, *I*
Pugh, C (Maesteg) 1924 *E*, *S*, *I*, *F*, *NZ*, 1925 *E*, *S*
Pugsley, J (Cardiff) 1910 *E*, *S*, *I*, 1911 *E*, *S*, *F*, *I*
Pullman, J (Neath) 1910 *F*
Purdon, F (Newport) 1881 *E*, 1882 *I*, 1883 *E*, *S*

Quinnell, D L (Llanelli) 1972 *F* (R), *NZ*, 1973 *E*, *S*, *A*, 1974 *S*, *F*, 1975 *E* (R), 1977 *I* (R), *F*, *E*, *S*, 1978 *E*, *S*, *I*, *F*, *A*, *NZ*, 1979 *S*, *I*, *F*, *E*, 1980 *NZ*

Radford, W J (Newport) 1923 *I*
Ralph, A R (Newport) 1931 *F*, *I*, *SA*, 1932 *E*, *S*, *I*
Ramsey, S H (Treorchy) 1896 *E*, 1904 *E*
Randell, R (Aberavon) 1924 *I*, *F*
Raybould, W H (London Welsh, Cambridge U, Newport) 1967 *S*, *I*, *F*, *E*, *NZ*, 1968 *I*, *F*, 1970 *SA*, *E*, *I*, *F* (R)
Rees, Aaron (Maesteg) 1919 *NZA*
Rees, Alan (Maesteg) 1962 *E*, *S*, *F*
Rees, A M (London Welsh) 1934 *E*, 1935 *E*, *S*, *I*, *NZ*, 1936 *E*, *S*, *I*, 1937 *E*, *S*, *I*, 1938 *E*, *S*

Rees, B I (London Welsh) 1967 *S, I, F*
Rees, C F W (London Welsh) 1974 *I*, 1975 *A*, 1978 *NZ*, 1981 *F, A*, 1982 *I, F, E, S*, 1983 *E, S, I, F*
Rees, D (Swansea) 1968 *S, I, F*
Rees, Dan (Swansea) 1900 *E*, 1903 *E, S*, 1905 *E, S*
Rees, E B (Swansea) 1919 *NZA*
Rees, H (Cardiff) 1937 *S, I*, 1938 *E, S, I*
Rees, H E (Neath) 1979 *S, I, F, E*, 1980 *F, E, S, I, NZ*, 1983 *E, S, I, F*
Rees, J I (Swansea) 1934 *E, S, I*, 1935 *S, NZ*, 1936 *E, S, I*, 1937 *E, S, I*, 1938 *E, S, I*
Rees, J (Swansea) 1920 *E, S, F, I*, 1921 *E, S, I*, 1922 *E*, 1923 *E, F, I*, 1924 *E*
Rees, L (Cardiff) 1933 *I*
Rees, P (Llanelli) 1947 *F, I*
Rees, P M (Newport) 1961 *E, S, I*, 1964 *I*
Rees, T (Newport) 1935 *S, I, NZ*, 1936 *E, S, I*, 1937 *E, S*
Rees, T A (Llandovery) 1881 *E*
Rees, T E (London Welsh) 1926 *I, F*, 1927 *NSW*, 1928 *E*
Rees-Jones, G R (Oxford U, London Welsh) 1934 *E, S*, 1935 *I, NZ*, 1936 *E*
Reeves, F (Cross Keys) 1920 *F, I*, 1921 *E*
Rhapps, J (Penygraig) 1897 *E*
Rice-Evans, W (Swansea) 1890 *S*, 1891 *E, S*
Richards, B (Swansea) 1960 *F*
Richards, C (Pontypool) 1922 *E, S, I, F*, 1924 *I*
Richards, D S (Swansea) 1979 *F, E*, 1980 *F, E, S, I, NZ*, 1981 *E, S, I, F*, 1982 *I, F*, 1983 *E, S, I, R* (R)
Richards, E S (Swansea) 1885 *E*, 1887 *S*
Richards, G (Cardiff) 1927 *S*
Richards, I (Cardiff) 1925 *E, S, F*
Richards, K (Bridgend) 1960 *SA*, 1961 *E, S, I, F*
Richards, M C R (Cardiff) 1968 *I, F*, 1969 *S, I, F, E, NZ* (2), *A*
Richards, R (Aberavon) 1913 *S, F, I*
Richards, R (Cross Keys) 1956 *F*
Richards, T L (Maesteg) 1923 *I*
Richardson, S J (Aberavon) 1978 *A* (R), 1979 *E*
Rickards, A R (Cardiff) 1924 *F*
Ring, J (Aberavon) 1921 *E*
Ring, M G (Cardiff) 1983 *E*
Ringer, P (Ebbw Vale, Llanelli) 1978 *NZ*, 1979 *S, I, F, E*, 1980 *F, E, NZ*
Roberts, C (Neath) 1958 *I, F*
Roberts, D E A (London Welsh) 1930 *E*
Roberts, E (Llanelli) 1886 *E*, 1887 *I*
Roberts, E J (Llanelli) 1888 *S, I*, 1889 *I*
Roberts, H M (Cardiff) 1960 *SA*, 1961 *E, S, I, F*, 1962 *S, F*, 1963 *I*
Roberts, J (Cardiff) 1927 *E, S, F, I, NSW*, 1928 *E, S, I, F*, 1929 *E, S, F, I*
Roberts, M G (London Welsh) 1971 *E, S, I, F*, 1973 *I, F*, 1975 *S*, 1979 *E*
Roberts, T (Newport) 1921 *S, F, I*, 1922 *E, S, I, F*, 1923 *E, S*
Roberts, W (Cardiff) 1929 *E*
Robins, J D (Birkenhead Park) 1950 *E, S, I, F*, 1951 *E, S, I, F*, 1953 *E, I, F*
Robins, R J (Pontypridd) 1953 *S*, 1954 *F, S*, 1955 *E, S, I, F*, 1956 *E, F*, 1957 *E, S, I, F*
Robinson, I R (Cardiff) 1974 *F, E*
Rocyn-Jones, D N (Cambridge U) 1925 *I*
Roderick, W B (Llanelli) 1884 *I*
Rosser, M (Penarth) 1924 *S, F*
Rowlands, C F (Aberavon) 1926 *I*
Rowlands, D C T (Pontypool) 1963 *E, S, I, F, NZ*, 1964 *E, S, I, F, SA*, 1965 *E, S, I, F*
Rowlands, G (RAF, Cardiff) 1953 *NZ*, 1954 *E, F*, 1956 *F*
Rowlands, J (Lampeter) 1885 *E*
Rowlands, K A (Cardiff) 1962 *F, I*, 1963 *I*, 1965 *I, F*
Rowles, G R (Penarth) 1892 *E*

Samuel, D (Swansea) 1891 *I*, 1893 *I*
Samuel, F (Mountain Ash) 1922 *S, I, F*
Samuel, J (Swansea) 1891 *I*
Scourfield, T (Torquay) 1930 *F*
Scrine, F (Swansea) 1899 *E, S*, 1901 *I*
Shanklin, J L (London Welsh) 1970 *F*, 1972 *NZ*, 1973 *I, F*
Shaw, G (Neath) 1972 *NZ*, 1973 *E, S, I, F, A*, 1974 *S, I, F, E*, 1977 *I, F*
Shaw, T W (Newbridge) 1983 *R*
Shea, J (Newport) 1919 *NZA*, 1920 *E, S*, 1921 *E*
Shell, R C (Aberavon) 1973 *A* (R)
Simpson, H J (Cardiff) 1884 *E, S, I*
Skrimshire, R T (Newport) 1899 *E, S, I*
Skym, A (Llanelli) 1928 *E, S, I, F*, 1930 *E, S, I, F*, 1931 *E, S, F, I, SA*, 1932 *E, S, I*, 1933 *E, S, I*, 1935 *E*
Smith, J S (Cardiff) 1884 *E, I*, 1885 *E*
Sparks, B (Neath) 1954 *I*, 1955 *E, F*, 1956 *E, S, I*, 1957 *S*
Spiller, W (Cardiff) 1910 *S, I*, 1911 *E, S, F, I*, 1912 *E, F, SA*, 1913 *E*
Squire, J (Newport, Pontypool) 1977 *I, F*, 1978 *E, S, I, F, A, NZ*, 1979 *S, I, F, E*, 1980 *F, E, S, I, NZ*, 1981 *E, S, I, F, A*, 1982 *I, F, E*, 1983 *E, S, I, F*
Stadden, W H (Cardiff) 1884 *I*, 1886 *E, S*, 1887 *I*, 1888 *S, M*, 1890 *S, E*
Stephens, G (Neath) 1912 *E, S, I, F, SA*, 1913 *E, S, F, I*, 1919 *NZA*
Stephens, I (Bridgend) 1981 *E, S, I, F, A*, 1982 *I, F, E, S*, 1984 *I, F, E*
Stephens, Rev J G (Llanelli) 1922 *E, S, I, F*
Stephens, J R G (Neath) 1947 *E, S, F, I*, 1948 *I*, 1949 *S, I, F*, 1951 *F, SA*, 1952 *E, S, I, F*, 1953 *E, S, I, F, NZ*, 1954 *E, I*, 1955 *E, S, I, F*, 1956 *S, I, F*, 1957 *E, S, I, F*
Stock, A (Newport) 1924 *F, NZ*, 1926 *E, S*
Stone, P (Llanelli) 1949 *F*
Strand-Jones, J (Llanelli) 1902 *E, S, I*, 1903 *E, S*
Summers, R H B (Haverfordwest) 1881 *E*
Sutton, S (Pontypool) 1982 *F, E*
Sweet-Escott, R B (Cardiff) 1891 *S*, 1894 *I*, 1895 *I*

Tamplin, W E (Cardiff) 1947 *S, F, I, A*, 1948 *E, S, F*
Tanner, H (Swansea, Cardiff) 1935 *NZ*, 1936 *E, S, I*, 1937 *E, S, I*, 1938 *E, S, I*, 1939 *E, S, I*, 1947 *E, S, F, I*, 1948 *E, S, F, I*, 1949 *E, S, I, F*
Tarr, D J (Swansea, Royal Navy) 1935 *NZ*
Taylor, A R (Cross Keys) 1937 *I*, 1938 *I*, 1939 *E*
Taylor, C G (Ruabon) 1884 *E, S, I*, 1885 *E, S*, 1886 *E, S*, 1887 *E, I*
Taylor, J (London Welsh) 1967 *S, I, F, E, NZ*, 1968 *I, F*, 1969 *S, I, F, E, NZ, A*, 1970 *F*, 1971 *E, S, I, F*, 1972 *E, S, F, NZ*, 1973 *E, S, I, F*
Thomas, A (Newport) 1963 *NZ*, 1964 *E*
Thomas, A G (Swansea, Cardiff) 1952 *E, S, I, F*, 1953 *S, I, F*, 1954 *E, I, F*, 1955 *S, I, F*
Thomas, Bob (Swansea) 1900 *E, S, I*, 1901 *E*
Thomas, Brian (Neath, Cambridge U) 1963 *E, S, I, F, NZ*, 1964 *E, S, I, F, SA*, 1965 *E*, 1966 *E, S, I*, 1967 *NZ*, 1969 *S, I, F, E, NZ* (2)
Thomas, C (Bridgend) 1925 *E, S*
Thomas, C J (Newport) 1888 *I, M*, 1889 *S, I*, 1890 *S, E, I*, 1891 *E, I*
Thomas, D (Aberavon) 1961 *I*
Thomas, D (Swansea) 1930 *S, I*, 1932 *E, S, I*, 1933 *E, S*, 1934 *E*, 1935 *E, S, I*
Thomas, D (Llanelli) 1954 *I*
Thomas, Dick (Mountain Ash) 1906 *SA*, 1908 *F, I*, 1909 *S*
Thomas, D J (Swansea) 1904 *E*, 1908 *A*, 1910 *E, S, I*, 1911 *E, S, F, I*, 1912 *E*
Thomas, D L (Neath) 1937 *E*
Thomas, E (Newport) 1904 *S, I*, 1909 *S, F, I*, 1910 *F*
Thomas, G (Llanelli) 1923 *E, S, F, I*
Thomas, G (Newport) 1888 *M*, 1890 *I*, 1891 *S*
Thomas, H (Llanelli) 1912 *F*
Thomas, H (Neath) 1936 *E, S, I*, 1937 *E, S, I*
Thomas, H W (Swansea) 1912 *SA*, 1913 *E*
Thomas, I (Bryncethin) 1924 *E*
Thomas, L C (Cardiff) 1885 *E, S*
Thomas, M C (Newport, Devonport Services) 1949 *F*, 1950 *E, S, I, F*, 1951 *E, S, I, F, SA*, 1952 *E, S, I, F*, 1953 *E*, 1956 *E, S, I, F*, 1957 *E, S*, 1958 *E, S, I, F*, 1959 *I, F*
Thomas, M (St Bart's Hospital) 1919 *NZA*, 1921 *S, F, I*, 1923 *F*, 1924 *E*
Thomas, R (Pontypool) 1909 *F, I*, 1911 *S, F*, 1912 *E, S, SA*, 1913 *E*
Thomas, R C C (Swansea) 1949 *F*, 1952 *I, F*, 1953 *S, I, F, NZ*, 1954 *E, I, F, S*, 1955 *S, I*, 1956 *E, S, I*, 1957 *E*, 1958 *A, E, S, I, F*, 1959 *E, S, I, F*
Thomas, R L (London Welsh) 1889 *S, I*, 1890 *I*, 1891

E, S, I, 1892 *E*
Thomas, S (Llanelli) 1890 *S, E,* 1891 *I*
Thomas, W (Llanelli, Waterloo, Swansea) 1927 *E, S, F, I,* 1929 *E,* 1931 *E, S, SA,* 1932 *E, S, I,* 1933 *E, S, I*
Thomas, W D (Llanelli) 1966 *A,* 1968 *S, I, F,* 1969 *E, NZ, A,* 1970 *SA, S, E, I, F,* 1971 *E, S, I, F,* 1972 *E, S, F, NZ,* 1973 *E, S, I, F,* 1974 *E*
Thomas, W H (Llandovery Coll, Cambridge U) 1885 *S,* 1886 *E, S,* 1887 *E, S,* 1888 *S, I,* 1890 *E, I,* 1891 *S, I*
Thomas, W J (Cardiff) 1961 *F,* 1963 *F*
Thomas, W L (Newport) 1894 *S,* 1895 *E, I*
Thomas, W T (Abertillery) 1930 *E*
Thompson, J F (Cross Keys) 1923 *E*
Titley, M H (Bridgend) 1983 *R,* 1984 *S, I, F, E*
Towers, W H (Swansea) 1887 *I,* 1888 *M*
Travers, G (Pill Harriers) 1903 *E, S, I,* 1905 *E, S, I, NZ,* 1906 *E, S, I, SA,* 1907 *E, S, I,* 1908 *E, S, F, I, A,* 1909 *E, S, I,* 1911 *S, F, I*
Travers, W H (Newport) 1937 *S, I,* 1938 *E, S, I,* 1939 *E, S, I,* 1949 *E, S, I, F*
Treharne, E (Pontypridd) 1881 *E,* 1883 *E*
Trew, W J (Swansea) 1900 *E, S, I,* 1901 *E, S,* 1903 *S,* 1905 *S,* 1906 *S,* 1907 *E, S,* 1908 *E, S, F, I, A,* 1909 *E, S, F, I,* 1910 *F, E, S,* 1911 *E, S, F, I,* 1912 *S,* 1913 *S, F*
Trott, R F (Cardiff) 1948 *E, S, F, I,* 1949 *E, S, I, F*
Truman, H (Llanelli) 1934 *E,* 1935 *E*
Trump, L (Newport) 1912 *E, S, I, F*
Turnbull, B R (Cardiff) 1925 *I,* 1927 *E, S,* 1928 *E, F,* 1930 *S*
Turnbull, M J (Cardiff) 1933 *E, I*

Uzzell, H (Newport) 1912 *E, S, I, F,* 1913 *S, F, I,* 1914 *E, S, F, I,* 1920 *E, S, F, I*
Uzzell, J (Newport) 1963 *NZ,* 1965 *E, S, I, F*

Vickery, W (Aberavon) 1938 *E, S, I,* 1939 *E*
Vile, T H (Newport) 1908 *E, S,* 1910 *I,* 1912 *I, F, SA,* 1913 *E,* 1921 *S*
Vincent, H C (Bangor) 1882 *I*

Waldron, R (Neath) 1965 *E, S, I, F*
Waller, P D (Newport) 1908 *A,* 1909 *E, S, F, I,* 1910 *F*
Walters, D (Llanelli) 1902 *E*
Wanbon, R (Aberavon) 1968 *E*
Ward, W (Cross Keys) 1934 *S, I*
Warlow, J (Llanelli) 1962 *I*
Watkins, D (Newport) 1963 *E, S, I, F, NZ,* 1964 *E, S, I, F, SA,* 1965 *E, S, I, F,* 1966 *E, S, I, F,* 1967 *I, F, E*
Watkins, E (Neath) 1924 *E, S, I, F*
Watkins, E (Blaina) 1926 *S, I, F*
Watkins, E (Cardiff) 1935 *NZ,* 1937 *S, I,* 1938 *E, S, I,* 1939 *E, S*
Watkins, H (Llanelli) 1904 *S, I,* 1905 *E, S, I,* 1906 *E*
Watkins, L (Oxford U, Llandaff) 1881 *E*
Watkins, M J (Newport) 1984 *I, F, E*
Watkins, S J (Newport, Cardiff) 1964 *S, I, F,* 1965 *E, S, I, F,* 1966 *E, S, I, F, A,* 1967 *S, I, F, E, NZ,* 1968 *E, S,* 1969 *S, I, F, E, NZ,* 1970 *E, I*
Watkins, W (Newport) 1959 *F*
Watts, D (Maesteg) 1914 *E, S, F, I*
Watts, J (Llanelli) 1907 *E, S, I,* 1908 *E, S, F, I, A,* 1909 *S, F, I*
Watts, W (Llanelli) 1914 *E*
Watts, W H (Newport) 1892 *E, S, I,* 1893 *E, S, I,* 1894 *E, S, I,* 1895 *E, I,* 1896 *E*
Weaver, D (Swansea) 1964 *E*
Webb, J (Abertillery) 1907 *S,* 1908 *E, S, F, I, A,* 1909 *E, S, F, I,* 1910 *F, E, S, I,* 1911 *E, S, F, I,* 1912 *E, S*
Webb, J E (Newport) 1888 *M,* 1889 *S*
Wells, G (Cardiff) 1955 *E, S,* 1957 *I, F,* 1958 *A, E, S*
Westacott, D (Cardiff) 1906 *I*
Wetter, H (Newport) 1912 *SA,* 1913 *E*
Wetter, J (Newport) 1914 *S, F, I,* 1920 *E, S, F, I,* 1921 *E,* 1924 *I, NZ*
Wheel, G A D (Swansea) 1974 *I, E* (R), 1975 *F, E, I, A,* 1976 *E, S, I, F,* 1977 *I, E, S,* 1978 *E, S, I, F, A* (2), *NZ,* 1979 *S, I,* 1980 *F, E, S, I,* 1981 *E, S, I, F, A,* 1982 *I*
Wheeler, P J (Aberavon) 1967 *NZ,* 1968 *E*
Whitfield, J (Newport) 1919 *NZA,* 1920 *E, S, F, I,* 1921 *E,* 1922 *E, S, I, F,* 1924 *S, I*
Whitson, G (Newport) 1956 *F,* 1960 *S, I*
Williams, B (Llanelli) 1920 *S, F, I*
Williams, B L (Cardiff) 1947 *E, S, F, I, A,* 1948 *E, S, F, I,* 1949 *E, S, I,* 1951 *I, SA,* 1952 *S,* 1953 *E, S, I, F, NZ,* 1954 *S,* 1955 *E*
Williams, C (Llanelli) 1924 *NZ,* 1925 *E*
Williams, C (Aberavon, Swansea) 1977 *E, S,* 1980 *F, E, S, I, NZ,* 1983 *E*
Williams, C D (Cardiff, Neath) 1955 *F,* 1956 *F*
Williams, D (Ebbw Vale) 1963 *E, S, I, F,* 1964 *E, S, I, F, SA,* 1965 *E, S, I, F,* 1966 *E, S, I, A,* 1967 *F, E, NZ,* 1968 *E,* 1969 *S, I, F, E, NZ* (2), *A,* 1970 *SA, S, E, I,* 1971 *E, S, I, F*
Williams, D B (Newport, Swansea) 1978 *A,* 1981 *E, S*
Williams, E (Neath) 1924 *NZ,* 1925 *F*
Williams, E (Aberavon) 1925 *E, S*
Williams, F L (Cardiff) 1929 *S, F, I,* 1930 *E, S, I, F,* 1931 *F, I, SA,* 1932 *E, S, I,* 1933 *I*
Williams G (Aberavon) 1936 *E, S, I*
Williams G (London Welsh) 1950 *I, F,* 1951 *E, S, I, F, SA,* 1952 *E, S, I, F,* 1953 *NZ,* 1954 *E*
Williams, G (Bridgend) 1981 *I, F,* 1982 *E* (R), *S*
Williams, G P (Bridgend) 1980 *NZ,* 1981 *E, S, A,* 1982 *I*
Williams, J (Blaina) 1920 *E, S, F, I,* 1921 *S, F, I*
Williams, J F (London Welsh) 1905 *I, NZ,* 1906 *S, SA*
Williams, J J (Llanelli) 1973 *F* (R), *A,* 1974 *S, I, F, E,* 1975 *F, E, S, I, A,* 1976 *E, S, I, F,* 1977 *I, F, E, S,* 1978 *E, S, I, F, A* (2), *NZ,* 1979 *S, I, F, E*
Williams, J L (Cardiff) 1906 *SA,* 1907 *E, S, I,* 1908 *E, S, I, A,* 1909 *E, S, F, I,* 1910 *I,* 1911 *E, S, F, I*
Williams, J P R (London Welsh, Bridgend) 1969 *S, I, F, E, NZ* (2), *A,* 1970 *SA, S, E, I, F,* 1971 *E, S, I, F,* 1972 *E, S, F, NZ,* 1973 *E, S, I, F, A,* 1974 *S, I, F,* 1975 *F, E, S, I, A,* 1976 *E, S, I, F,* 1977 *I, F, E, S,* 1978 *E, S, I, F, A* (2), *NZ,* 1979 *S, I, F, E,* 1980 *NZ,* 1981 *E, S*
Williams, L (Cardiff) 1957 *S, I, F,* 1958 *E, S, I, F,* 1959 *E, S, I,* 1961 *F,* 1962 *E, S*
Williams, L (Llanelli, Cardiff) 1947 *E, S, F, I, A,* 1948 *I,* 1949 *E*
Williams, M (Newport) 1923 *F*
Williams, O (Llanelli) 1947 *E, S, A,* 1948 *E, S, F, I*
Williams, R (Llanelli) 1954 *S,* 1957 *F,* 1958 *A*
Williams, R D G (Newport) 1881 *E*
Williams, R F (Cardiff) 1912 *SA,* 1913 *E, S,* 1914 *I*
Williams, R H (Llanelli) 1954 *I, F, S,* 1955 *S, I, F,* 1956 *E, S, I,* 1957 *E, S, I, F,* 1958 *A, E, S, I, F,* 1959 *E, S, I, F,* 1960 *E*
Williams, S (Aberavon) 1939 *E, S, I*
Williams, S (Llanelli) 1947 *E, S, F, I,* 1948 *S, F*
Williams, T (Pontypridd) 1882 *I*
Williams, T (Swansea) 1888 *S, I*
Williams, T (Swansea) 1912 *I,* 1913 *F,* 1914 *E, S, F, I*
Williams, T (Cross Keys) 1935 *S, I, NZ,* 1936 *E, S, I,* 1937 *S, I*
Williams, Tudor (Swansea) 1921 *F*
Williams, W (Crumlin) 1927 *E, S, F, I*
Williams, W A (Newport) 1952 *I, F,* 1953 *E*
Williams, W E O (Cardiff) 1887 *S, I,* 1889 *S,* 1890 *S, E*
Williams, W H (Pontymister) 1900 *E, S, I,* 1901 *E*
Williams, W O G (Swansea, Devonport Services) 1951 *F, SA,* 1952 *E, S, I, F,* 1953 *E, S, I, F, NZ,* 1954 *E, I, F, S,* 1955 *E, S, I, F,* 1956 *E, S, I*
Williams, W P J (Neath) 1974 *I, F*
Willis, W R (Cardiff) 1950 *E, S, I, F,* 1951 *E, S, I, F, SA,* 1952 *E, S,* 1953 *S, NZ,* 1954 *E, I, F, S,* 1955 *E, S, I, F*
Wiltshire, M L (Aberavon) 1967 *NZ,* 1968 *E, S, F*
Windsor, R W (Pontypool) 1973 *A,* 1974 *S, I, F, E,* 1975 *F, E, S, I, A,* 1976 *E, S, I, F,* 1977 *I, F, E, S,* 1978 *E, S, I, F, A* (2), *NZ,* 1979 *S, I, F*
Winfield, H B (Cardiff) 1903 *I,* 1904 *E, S, I,* 1905 *NZ,* 1906 *E, S, I,* 1907 *S, I,* 1908 *E, S, F, I, A*
Winmill, S (Cross Keys) 1921 *E, S, F, I*
Wooller, W (Sale, Cambridge U, Cardiff) 1933 *E, S, I,* 1935 *E, S, I, NZ,* 1936 *E, S, I,* 1937 *E, S, I,* 1938 *S, I,* 1939 *E, S, I*
Wyatt, M A (Swansea) 1983 *E, S, I, F*

Young, G A (Cardiff) 1886 *E, S*
Young, J (Harrogate, RAF, London Welsh) 1968 *S, I, F,* 1969 *S, I, F, E, NZ,* 1970 *E, I, F,* 1971 *E, S, I, F,* 1972 *E, S, F, NZ,* 1973 *E, S, I, F*

WELSH INTERNATIONAL RECORDS

From 1890-91, when uniform points-scoring was first adopted by International Board countries, to 30 April 1984. Both team and individual records are for matches against International Board countries only.

TEAM RECORDS

Highest score
49 v France (49-14) 1910 Swansea
v individual countries
34 v England (34-21) 1967 Cardiff
35 v Scotland (35-12) 1972 Cardiff
34 v Ireland (34-9) 1976 Dublin
49 v France (49-14) 1910 Swansea
16 v N Zealand (16-19) 1972 Cardiff
6 v S Africa (6-6) 1970 Cardiff
28 v Australia (28-3) 1975 Cardiff

Biggest winning points margin
42 v France (47-5) 1909 Colombes (Paris)
v individual countries
25 v England (25-0) 1905 Cardiff
23 v Scotland (35-12) 1972 Cardiff
29 v Ireland (29-0) 1907 Cardiff
42 v France (47-5) 1909 Colombes
5 v N Zealand (13-8) 1953 Cardiff
No win v S Africa
25 v Australia (28-3) 1975 Cardiff

Highest score by opposing team
35 Scotland (10-35) 1924 Inverleith (Edinburgh)
by individual countries
25 England (0-25) 1896 Blackheath
35 Scotland (10-35) 1924 Inverleith
21 Ireland { (24-21) 1979 Cardiff; (7-21) 1980 Dublin }
22 France (13-22) 1965 Colombes
33 N Zealand (12-33) 1969 Auckland
24 S Africa (3-24) 1964 Durban
19 Australia (17-19) 1978 Sydney

Biggest losing points margin
25 { v England (0-25) 1896 Blackheath; v Scotland (10-35) 1924 Inverleith }
v individual countries
25 v England (0-25) 1896 Blackheath
25 v Scotland (10-35) 1924 Inverleith
16 v Ireland (3-19) 1925 Belfast
10 v France (6-16) 1958 Cardiff
21 v N Zealand (12-33) 1969 Auckland
21 v S Africa (3-24) 1964 Durban
10 v Australia (8-18) 1978 Brisbane

Most points by Wales in International Championship in a season – 102
(in season 1975-76)

Most tries by Wales in International Championship in a season – 21
(in season 1909-10)

Most tries by Wales in an international
11 v France (47-5) 1909 Colombes

Most tries against Wales in an international
8 by Scotland (10-35) 1924 Inverleith
England scored 13 tries v Wales in 1881 and Scotland 12 tries in 1887, but this was before uniform scoring was adopted.

INDIVIDUAL RECORDS

Most capped player
J P R Williams 55 1969-81
in individual positions
Full-back
J P R Williams 54(55)* 1969-81
Wing
K J Jones 44** 1947-57
Centre
S P Fenwick 30 1975-81
Fly-half
C I Morgan 29† 1951-58

Scrum-half
G O Edwards 53 1967-78
Prop
G Price 41 1975-83
Hooker
B V Meredith 34 1954-62
**Williams won one cap as a flanker.*
***T G R Davies, 46 caps, won 35 as a wing, and 11 as a centre.*
†P Bennett, 29 caps, won one at full-back, as a replacement, one on the wing and two at centre, once as a replacement.
Lock
A J Martin 34 1973-81
Flanker
W D Morris 32(34)‡ 1967-74
No 8
T M Davies 38 1969-76
‡Morris won his first two caps at No 8

Most internationals as captain – 18
A J Gould 1889-97

Most points in internationals – 166
P Bennett (29 appearances) 1969-78

Most points in an international – 19
J Bancroft v France 1910 Swansea
K S Jarrett v England 1967 Cardiff
P Bennett v Ireland 1976 Dublin

Most tries in internationals – 20
G O Edwards (53 appearances) 1967-78
T G R Davies (46 appearances) 1966-78

Most tries in an international – 4
W Llewellyn* v England 1899 Swansea
R A Gibbs v France 1908 Cardiff
M C R Richards v England 1969 Cardiff
**on first appearance*

Most conversions in an international – 8
J Bancroft v France 1910 Swansea

Most points in International Championship in a season – 39
H Davies (4 appearances) 1983-84

Most tries in International Championship in a season – 6
R A Gibbs 1907-08
M C R Richards 1968-69

Most conversions in International Championship in a season – 11
J Bancroft (4 appearances) 1908-09

Most penalty goals in International Championship in a season – 11
G Evans (4 appearances) 1981-82

Most points on overseas tour – 55
S P Fenwick (7 appearances) Australia 1978

Most points in any match on tour – 15
K S Jarrett v Otago 1969 Dunedin, NZ

Most tries in any match on tour – 3
M C R Richards v Otago 1969 Dunedin, NZ

SCHWEPPES CHALLENGE CUP 1983-84

John Billot *Western Mail*

28 April, Cardiff (National Ground)
Cardiff 24 (2G 4PG) **Neath 19** (2G 1PG 1T)

Few teams had been made more comprehensive favourites for the Welsh final than Cardiff, whose opponents, Neath, had recorded just one victory in six matches (over Leicester, 28-24) after putting Aberavon out in the semi-final stage. The consensus of opinion, therefore was heavily in favour of Cardiff – Neath were going along to make up the numbers. Such an attitude was just what Brian Thomas, the demanding Neath team-manager, welcomed as an extra incentive for his players. A lot of people were going to have to revise their viewpoint – and with unseemly haste, Thomas reckoned.

The Gnoll club's forwards fought with unforgettable pride and passion, their tireless back row unit of Lyn Jones, Dai Morgan and Gareth Jones outshining the Cardiff trio of Lakin, Scott and Golding, while Gareth Jones, the scrum-half, stole the Lloyd Lewis Award as the Man of the Match. This was an amazing feat against such an adversary as Terry Holmes. Yet the 20-year-old pit-worker, on strike at the time due to the mining dispute, skipped away to score a try shortly after making an 80-yard interception, and he and tenacious flanker Lyn Jones were symbolic in all they did of Neath's refusal to submit. Ironically, in defeat they outscored Cardiff on tries by three to two.

As in so many games nowadays, the outcome was settled by penalty goals. Gareth Davies, for Cardiff, kicked four of them and converted the tries by Owen Golding and Gerald Cordle; Neale Harris, unfortunately, was below his best as Neath's kicker and managed only one penalty goal. He converted two of the three tries, by David Jacob (2) and Gareth Jones. Cardiff, for all their scrummaging superiority and line-out possession, could not match Neath's forward pace about the field and failed to spread the ball among their backs with the polish and panache expected of them.

'Neath played far better than I expected', confessed Cardiff skipper John Scott. 'We knew they would be fully committed and keep coming at us. But we did not really get to grips with the game at all'. Nevertheless, this was the best cup final of them all and again both finalists received £12,000.

Cardiff: P Rees; G Cordle, A Donovan, M Ring, A Hadley; W G Davies, T D Holmes; *No 8* J P Scott *(capt); Second Row* R Lakin, K Edwards, R L Norster, O Golding; *Front Row* J Whitefoot, A J Phillips, I Eidman *Replacement* N Humphreys for Hadley (48 mins)

Scorers *Tries:* Golding, Cordle *Conversions:* Davies (2) *Penalty Goals:* Davies (4)
Neath: N Harris; H E Rees *(capt);* D Jacob, K Jones, C Bridgwater; J Davies, Gareth Jones; *No 8* D Morgan; *Second Row* G Jones, S Dando, H Richards, L Jones; *Front Row* B Williams, M Richards, P Langford
Scorers *Tries:* Jacob (2), Gareth Jones *Conversions:* Harris (2) *Penalty Goal:* Harris
Referee C Norling (Swansea)

Cardiff registered their expected success against Llanelli in the semi-final, in front of almost 20,000 spectators at Swansea. They scored five tries in a result of 26-6. Neath, the dark horses of the competition, disrupted Aberavon at Bridgend to win 12-3, but there were no tries to excite 8,000 onlookers. Four penalty goals by Neale Harris took the Gnoll club to the final while the disappointed Wizards had only one penalty goal by Mike Lewis to show for all their endeavours. Two poor teams contributed little in the way of positive measures, though Neath's forwards could not be faulted for their tenacity and commitment.

Llanelli were fearful of Cardiff's scrummaging superiority and the immense presence of Terry Holmes, playing only his fourth first team game since his knee injury in the Lions' first Test in New Zealand in June. Inevitably, he scored a try and others came from Owen Golding, Gerald Cordle, Paul Rees and Alun Donovan. Gareth Davies, strangely out of form, converted three. The Scarlets' only points came from a drop-shot and penalty goal by Gary Pearce. There were some heated moments in the first half, notably a flare-up between Robert Norster and Llanelli captain Phil May, who again demonstrated his line-out command.

The Llanelli-Pontypool tie was the highlight of the quarter-final stage and 17,000 spectators were totally absorbed by the thrilling contest at Stradey. Pontypool, the holders, went out because Llanelli scored the only try in a 15-15 draw. This was Pontypool's first visit to Stradey for 13 years. Their chances were seriously reduced by the absence of David Bishop, sent off for stamping against Saracens a fortnight earlier. Pontypool caused considerable controversy by inviting the former England scrum-half, 32-year-old Peter Kingston, then in semi-retirement, to fill Bishop's place. However, it was not the first instance of a club bringing in a guest player for a cup-tie though the WRU competitions committee are to take a closer look at cup regulations in this context. Kingston, however, could not inject the urgency in attack and enterprise of Bishop, who had scored 28 tries by that stage. Peter Lewis kicked five penalty goals for the losers. Injuries meant Llanelli were without Ray Gravell and David Pickering, but they snapped up their try after just four minutes when a punt ahead by wing Phil Lewis bounced over the goal-line and Anthony Buchanan, a lively prop, dived on the ball.

Holmes was the inspiring influence in his first game of the season for Cardiff, crossing for a try in a 29-9 victory at Newbridge. Aberavon triumphed 16-7 at Ebbw Vale, where two forwards were sent off – John Williams, the home line-out jumper, and Aberavon prop David Joseph. Neath's forwards controlled matters at the Gnoll to force the exit of Newport by 25-11. Jonathan Davies, in his first appearance for 14 months, dropped a goal for the winners and played expertly at fly-half.

The third round featured a thrilling duel at Pontypool Park, in which the holders went into injury time trailing 16-15 against Bridgend, the lead having switched four times during the final 10 minutes. Then a high tackle gave Peter Lewis an easy sixth penalty goal and Pontypool an 18-16 verdict. Cardiff retained their ground record against Swansea, whose schoolboy scrum-half, Robert Jones, looked a player of tremendous potential.

There were violent scenes in the second round at Treorchy, and referee Clive Norling sent off Jeff Whitefoot, the Cardiff prop, and three home forwards after fighting early in the game. Treorchy, beaten 31-4, announced they had suspended Chris Jones, one of the dismissed three, for five years. He had only recently returned following a 28-week suspension and this was his third sending off in five years. Two players also were sent off at Stradey in this round: Llanelli prop Anthony Buchanan and Carmarthen Athletic wing forward Steve Thomas, who had joined them from Aberavon. Swansea had a nail-biting, 15-12 last-minute win at Cross Keys.

No giant-killers emerged among the smaller clubs in the first round, but Taffs Well, specially coached by British Lion prop Ian Stephens, of Bridgend, knocked Penarth out 14-3 in the second preliminary round stage. In the first preliminary round, Glamorgan Wanderers were grateful to win 16-14 at Cowbridge.

RESULTS

First round

Aberavon 10 Nantyffyllon 9
Abercynon 13 Llanharan 9
Abergavenny 6 Newport Saracens 9
Abertillery 32 Tonna 3
Blackwood 20 Llanhilleth 3
Bonymaen 9 Aberavon Quins 16
Bridgend 32 Glamorgan Wands 6
Bryncoch 6 Newport 20
Caerleon 12 Tenby United 16
Cardigan 4 Pontypool United 12
Carmarthen 12 Maesteg 24
Cross Keys 27 Bargoed 0
Ebbw Vale 33 Bangor 9
Gowerton 24 Ynysddu 3
Llandaff 6 Ammanford 9
Llanelli 72 Rumney 3
Llantwit Fardre 15 Furnace 18
Narberth 0 South Glam Inst 11
Neath 15 Vardre 9
Old Illtydians 0 Swansea 53
Penclawdd 18 Newbridge 30
Pontypool 80 Blaengarw 10
Pontypridd 24 Dunvant 3
S W Police 18 Kidwelly 14
Senghenydd 3 Cardiff 43
Seven Sisters 12 Mountain Ash 4
Taffs Well 0 Waunarlwydd 9
Tredegar 24 Skewen 3
Treorchy 4 Pyle 3
Whitland 3 Carmarthen Athletic 14
Wrexham 35 Cardiff HSOB 7
Ystradgynlais 20 Pontarddulais 9

Second round
Aberavon Quins 11 Pontypool 38
Abercynon 6 Maesteg 17
Abertillery 13 Blackwood 11
Cross Keys 12 Swansea 15
Gowerton 13 Ebbw Vale 19
Llanelli 56 Carmarthen Athletic 3
Newport 67 Ammanford 9
Newport Saracens 6 S W Police 39
Pontypool United 4 Newbridge 21
Pontypridd 29 Waunarlwydd 8
Seven Sisters 14 South Glam Inst 20
Tenby United 3 Aberavon 35
Tredegar 37 Furnace 3
Treorchy 4 Cardiff 31
Wrexham 7 Neath 18
Ystradgynlais 6 Bridgend 19

Third round
Aberavon 18 Pontypridd 3
Cardiff 12 Swansea 7
Maesteg 18 Newbridge 21
Neath 10 Abertillery 6
Newport 34 South Glam Inst 13
Pontypool 18 Bridgend 16
S W Police 16 Llanelli 47
Tredegar 9 Ebbw Vale 10

Fourth round
Ebbw Vale 7 Aberavon 16
*Llanelli 15 Pontypool 15
Neath 25 Newport 11
Newbridge 9 Cardiff 29

**Denotes winners on tries ruling*

Semi-finals
Cardiff 26 Llanelli 6
(at Swansea)
Neath 12 Aberavon 3
(at Bridgend)

Final *(at Cardiff, National Ground)*
Cardiff 24 Neath 19

Previous finals
(all at Cardiff, National Ground)
1972 Neath 15 Llanelli 9
1973 Llanelli 30 Cardiff 7
1974 Llanelli 12 Aberavon 10
1975 Llanelli 15 Aberavon 6
1976 Llanelli 15 Swansea 4
1977 Newport 16 Cardiff 15
1978 Swansea 13 Newport 9
1979 Bridgend 18 Pontypridd 12
1980 Bridgend 15 Swansea 9
1981 Cardiff 14 Bridgend 6
1982 †Cardiff 12 Bridgend 12
1983 Pontypool 18 Swansea 6

†Won by Cardiff on 'most tries' rule

SNELLING SEVENS 1983-84

27 August 1983 (Rodney Parade, Newport)

Pool A: Pontypridd 22, Cross Keys 6; Bridgend 16, Swansea 8; Bridgend 34, Cross Keys 0; Swansea 18, Pontypridd 10; Swansea 36, Cross Keys 4; Bridgend 22, Pontypridd 6
Pool B: Cardiff 24, Bath 0; Glamorgan Wanderers 16, Penarth 0; Glamorgan Wanderers 14, Bath 10; Cardiff 18, Penarth 4; Bath 24, Penarth 6; Cardiff 20, Glamorgan Wanderers 14
Pool C: Llanelli 22, Neath 4; Abertillery 12, Aberavon 10; Neath 22, Aberavon 6; Abertillery 16, Llanelli 12; Abertillery 8, Neath 6; Llanelli 22, Aberavon 12
Pool D: Newport 4, Ebbw Vale 0; Maesteg 10, Newbridge 4; Maesteg 18, Ebbw Vale 0; Newbridge 14, Newport 6; Newbridge 18, Ebbw Vale 10; Newport 12, Maesteg 10
Semi-finals: Cardiff 30, Bridgend 0; Abertillery 20, Maesteg 12
Final: Cardiff 44, Abertillery 6

TEAMS IN THE FINAL

Cardiff: G Cordle, D Preece, M Ring, G Williams; T Charles *(capt)*, O Golding, H Stone
Abertillery: D Owen, D George, M Rossiter, A Parry (capt); R Preece, A Thomas, J Everett
Referee W D Bevan (Clydach)

THE 1983-84 SEASON IN FRANCE

Bob Donahue *International Herald Tribune*

The national side had a unanimously-supported purpose: to develop an ambitious attacking style. The goal was well-nigh achieved. France improved from match to match yet faltered each time in one respect or another, so that work always remained to be done before the next attempt and there would be no complacency. Attacking rugby was being mastered, in fact, instead of being merely talked about. It was a season of achievement and enduring suspense.

Didier Codorniou, Philippe Sella, Patrick Estève, Jean-Patrick Lescarboura, Jérôme Gallion, Philippe Dintrans, Jean Condom, Jean-Luc Joinel and Jean-Pierre Rives appeared in all seven major matches, starting with the two Australian Tests and the 26-15 defeat of Romania. Flanker Dominique Erbani and right wing Patrice Lagisquet, a new cap, made their mark in five appearances. Serge Blanco recovered from renal surgery in time for the Championship. The tight forwards were a problem area; five props were tried, and Condom had three different partners at lock.

Senior officials, freshly converted to sponsorship and worried by the heavy media coverage of soccer, wanted try-scoring rugby. So did players and supporters. Coach Jacques Fouroux, still only 36 but already influential among his fellow selectors, promised to comply.

France drew the season-opener against Australia, won five times and lost the controversial Championship final to Scotland. Ninety points in the Championship bettered the previous French record of 82 (1976). The totals for the full season were 146 points for (all scored by backs) to 103 against: 14 tries to 7, 9 conversions to 6, 7 dropped goals to 3, 17 penalty goals to 18. (Like Wales and Ireland, France conceded 13 penalty goals in the Championship.) However, the totals fail to convey the real achievement, which was the creation of scoring opportunities. For every try scored, two seemed to go begging. Erratic finishing was sometimes the cause, but often the trouble was inspired defence. It was understandable that defence against France should be the priority in 1983-84, and French success in creating try-scoring chances was all the more noteworthy for this.

Outplayed in the set pieces by Wales, the pack recovered against England and then played a full part, during the first half at Murrayfield, in what veteran French rugby writers called the most dominant French team performance in memory. Ultimate defeat by a strong Scottish side that day, and failure for the second consecutive year to secure a likely Grand Slam, was attributed to several factors that included Scottish fitness and French muddle under the high ball. President Albert Ferrasse alluded to another possible cause when he was asked on television a

Jerome Gallion, the French scrum-half, who made a brilliant return to the national side after a three-year absence.

month later whether he regarded the Murrayfield match as a great one. 'It would have been greater', he replied, 'if the refereeing had been better.' Having outrucked Australia in Paris under the watchful eye of a New Zealand referee, France had awaited Murrayfield with interest; but the expected rucking duel failed to happen, in part because referee Winston Jones apparently regarded it as too dangerous. Scots held this to be regrettable, but expressions of regret were also heard in the French camp.

Half-backs Gallion and Lescarboura had a good first season together but rarely achieved the degree of tactical control they sought. Meanwhile, Gallion scored four tries, of which three in the Championship recalled his 1978 debut. And young Lescarboura (he turned 23 on 12 March) totalled 88 points from a try, nine conversions, six dropped goals (including one in each Championship match) and 16 penalty goals. Against Ireland and Wales he equalled the French record of 17 points in an international, and his 54 Championship points erased Ollie Campbell's record of 52. A curiosity of the season was Blanco's failure to register a score of any sort after setting up a French record with 36 points in the 1983 Championship. Another oddity was the sending off of a French player – tight head prop Jean-Pierre Garuet, against Ireland – for the first time in an international match. Yet another was the 20 minutes spent by 23-year-old flanker Laurent Rodriguez at loose head (Michel Crémaschi having switched sides) after Gauret's exit. Rodriguez had worn the No 6 shirt against New Zealand at the start of the 1981-82 season and then turned up in the Championship wearing numbers 8, 5, 4 and 7. His stint in the front row meant that he had now played against International Board countries at six different positions.

With his 26th IB cap (at Murrayfield), Dintrans passed Alain Paco as France's most-capped hooker. It was no surprise, Rives having declined to tour New Zealand in the close season, when the Tarbes man was named captain of the touring squad. Pierre Lacans, the Béziers captain, was named to take Rives' place in the squad.

Among his other records, Rives had now equalled Wilson Whineray's world record of 30 internationals as captain against IB countries. Was that the end? Rives was not saying. In any case, as England's president Ron Jacobs put it in Paris, he had been 'an extraordinary ambassador'. At Murrayfield the Rives spirit of enterprise was illustrated from the start when France kicked off to right wing Jacques Bégu. Attack then followed attack, with the French display during the first half representing the high point of the season. It was sad it was not maintained, and that controversy should break out afterwards, but Rives was later to say that he felt he had no lessons yet to learn as regards courtesy or fair play.

FRENCH CLUB CHAMPIONSHIP WINNERS

(First Division)

1892 Racing Club de France
1893 Stade Français
1894 Stade Français
1895 Stade Framçais
1896 Olympique de Paris
1897 Stade Français
1898 Stade Français
1899 Bordeaux UC
1900 Racing Club de France
1901 Stade Français
1902 Racing Club de France
1903 Stade Français
1904 Bordeaux UC
1905 Bordeaux UC
1906 Bordeaux UC
1907 Bordeaux UC
1908 Stade Français
1909 Bordeaux UC
1910 FC Lyon
1911 Bordeaux UC
1912 Stade Toulousain
1913 Bayonne
1914 Perpignan
1915 *No competition*
1916-19*
1920 Tarbes
1921 Perpignan
1922 Stade Toulousain
1923 Stade Toulousain
1924 Stade Toulousain
1925 Perpignan
1926 Stade Toulousain
1927 Stade Toulousain
1928 Pau
1929 Quillan
1930 Agen
1931 Toulon
1932 Lyon Olympique U
1933 Lyon Olympique U
1934 Bayonne
1935 Biarritz
1936 Narbonne
1937 Vienne
1938 Perpignan
1939 Biarritz
1940-42 *No competition*
1943 Bayonne
1944 Perpignan
1945 Agen
1946 Pau
1947 Stade Toulousain
1948 Lourdes
1949 Castres
1950 Castres
1951 Carmaux
1952 Lourdes
1953 Lourdes
1954 Grenoble
1955 Perpignan
1956 Lourdes
1957 Lourdes
1958 Lourdes
1959 Racing Club de France
1960 Lourdes
1961 Béziers
1962 Agen
1963 Mont-de-Marsan
1964 Pau
1965 Agen
1966 Agen
1967 Montauban
1968 Lourdes†
1969 Bègles
1970 La Voulte
1971 Béziers
1972 Béziers
1973 Tarbes
1974 Béziers
1975 Béziers
1976 Agen
1977 Béziers
1978 Béziers
1979 Narbonne
1980 Béziers
1981 Béziers
1982 Agen
1983 Béziers
1984 Béziers

**from 1916 to 1919 the Championship was replaced by the 'Coupe de L'Esperance'.*
†Lourdes beat Toulon on tries, in a final drawn 9-9.

FRENCH INTERNATIONAL PLAYERS
(up to 30 April 1984)

ABBREVIATIONS

A – Australia; *Arg* – Argentina; *B* – British Forces Teams; *Cz* – Czechoslovakia; *E* – England; *Fj* – Fiji; *G* – Germany; *I* – Ireland; *It* – Italy; *J* – Japan; *K* – New Zealand Services; *M* – Maoris; *NSW* – New South Wales; *NZ* – New Zealand; *R* – Romania; *S* – Scotland; *SA* – South Africa; *US* – United States of America; *W* – Wales; (R) – Replacement.

Club Abbreviations: ASF-Association Sportive Française; BEC-Bordeaux Etudiants Club; CASG-Club Athlétique des Sports Généraux; PUC-Paris Université Club; RCF-Racing Club de France; SBUC-Stade Bordelais Université Club; SCUF-Sporting Club Universitaire de France; SF-Stade Français; SOE-Stade Olympien des Etudiants; TOEC-Toulouse Olympique Employés Club.

Note: Years given for Five Nations' matches are for second half of season, eg 1972 refers to season 1971-72. Years for all other matches refer to the actual year of the match. When a series has taken place, or more than one match has been played against a country in the same year, figures have been used to denote the particular matches in which players have featured. Thus 1967 *SA* 2,4 indicates that a player appeared in the second and fourth Tests of the 1967 series against South Africa. This list includes only those players who have appeared in FFR International Matches '*donnant droit au titre d'international*'.

Abadie, A (Pau) 1964 *I*
Abadie, A (Graulhet) 1965 *R*, 1967 *SA* 1, 3, 4, *NZ*, 1968 *S*, *I*
Abadie, L (Tarbes) 1963 *R*
Aguerre, R (Biarritz O) 1979 *S*
Aguilar, D (Pau) 1937 *G*
Aguirre, J-M (Bagnères) 1971 *A* 2, 1972 *S*, 1973 *W*, *I*, *J*, *R*, 1974 *I*, *W*, *Arg* 2, *R*, *SA* 1, 1976 *W* (R), *E*, *US*, *A* 2, *R*, 1977 *W*, *E*, *S*, *I*, *Arg* 1, 2, *NZ* 1, 2, *R*, 1978 *E*, *S*, *I*, *W*, *R*, 1979 *I*, *W*, *E*, *S*, *NZ*, 1, 2, *R*, 1980 *W*, *I*
Ainciart, E (Bayonne) 1933 *G*, 1934 *G*, 1935 *G*, 1937 *G*, *It*, 1938 *G* 1
Albaladejo, P (Dax) 1954 *E*, *It*, 1960 *W*, *I*, *It*, *R*, 1961 *S*, *SA*, *E*, *W*, *I*, *NZ* 1, 2, *A*, 1962 *S*, *E*, *W*, *I*, 1963 *S*, *I*, *E*, *W*, *It*, 1964 *S*, *NZ*, *W*, *It*, *I*, *SA*, *Fj*
Alvarez, A (Tyrosse) 1945 *B* 2, 1946 *B*, *I*, *K*, *W*, 1947 *S*, *I*, *W*, *E*, 1948 *I*, *A*, *S*, *W*, *E*, 1949 *I*, *E*, *W*, 1951 *S*, *E*, *W*
Amand, H (SF) 1906 *NZ*
Ambert, A (Toulouse) 1930 *S*, *I*, *E*, *G*, *W*
Amestoy, J-B (Mont-de-Marsan) 1964 *NZ*, *E*
André, G (RCF) 1913 *SA*, *E*, *W*, *I*, 1914 *I*, *W*, *E*
Anduran, J (SCUF) 1910 *W*
Araou, R (Narbonne) 1924 *R*
Arcalis, R (Brive) 1950 *S*, *I*, 1951 *I*, *E*, *W*
Arino, M (Agen) 1962 *R*
Aristouy, P (Pau) 1948 *S*, 1949 *Arg* 2, 1950 *S*, *I*, *E*, *W*
Arnal, J-M (RCF) 1914 *I*, *W*
Arnaudet, M (Lourdes) 1964 *I*, 1967 *It*, *W*
Arotca, R (Bayonne) 1938 *R*
Arrieta, J (SF) 1953 *E*, *W*
Astre, R (Béziers) 1971 *R*, 1972 *I* 1, 1973 *E* (R), 1975 *E*, *S*, *I*, *SA* 1, 2, *Arg* 2, 1976 *A* 2, *R*
Augé, J (Dax) 1929 *S*, *W*
Augras, L (Agen) 1931 *I*, *S*, *W*
Averous, J-L (La Voulte) 1975 *S*, *I*, *SA* 1, 2, 1976 *I*, *W*, *E*, *US*, *A* 1, 2, *R*, 1977 *W*, *E*, *S*, *I*, *Arg* 1, *R*, 1978 *E*, *S*, *I*, 1979 *NZ* 1, 2, 1980 *E*, *S*, 1981 *A* 2
Azarete, J-L (Dax, St Jean-de-Luz) 1969 *W*, *R*, 1970 *S*, *I*, *W*, *R*, 1971 *S*, *I*, *E*, *SA* 1, 2, *A* 1, 1972 *E*, *W*, *I* 2, *A* 1, *R*, 1973 *NZ*, *W*, *I*, *R*, 1974 *I*, *R*, *SA* 1, 2, 1975 *W*

Bader, E (Primevères) 1926 *M*, 1927 *I*, *S*
Badin, C (Chalon) 1973 *W*, *I*, 1975 *Arg* 1
Baillette, M (Perpignan) 1925 *I*, *NZ*, *S*, 1926 *W*, *M*, 1927 *I*, *W*, *G* 2, 1929 *G*, 1930 *S*, *I*, *E*, *G*, 1931 *I*, *S*, *E*, 1932 *G*
Baladie, G (Agen) 1945 *B* 1, 2, *W*, 1946 *B*, *I*, *K*
Ballarin, J (Tarbes) 1924 *E*, 1925 *NZ*, *S*
Baquet, J (Toulouse) 1921 *I*
Barbazanges, A (Roanne) 1932 *G*, 1933 *G*
Barrau, M (Beaumont, Toulouse) 1971 *S*, *E*, *W*, 1972 *E*, *W*, *A* 1, 2, 1973 *S*, *NZ*, *E*, *I*, *J*, *R*, 1974 *I*, *S*
Barrère, P (Toulon) 1929 *G*, 1931 *W*
Barrière, R (Béziers) 1960 *R*
Barthe, E (SBUC) 1925 *W*, *E*
Barthe, J (Lourdes) 1954 *Arg* 1, 2, 1955 *S*, 1956 *I*, *W*, *It*, *E*, *Cz*, 1957 *S*, *I*, *E*, *W*, *R* 1, 2, 1958 *S*, *E*, *A*, *W*, *It*, *I*, *SA* 1, 2, 1959 *S*, *E*, *It*, *W*
Basauri, R (Albi) 1954 *Arg* 1
Bascou, P (Bayonne) 1914 *E*
Basquet, G (Agen) 1945 *W*, 1946 *B*, *I*, *K*, *W*, 1947 *S*, *I*, *W*, *E*, 1948 *I*, *A*, *S*, *W*, *E*, 1949 *S*, *I*, *E*, *W*, *Arg* 1, 1950 *S*, *I*, *E*, *W*, 1951 *S*, *I*, *E*, *W*, 1952 *S*, *I*, *SA*, *W*, *E*, *It*
Bastiat, J-P (Dax) 1969 *R*, 1970 *S*, *I*, *W*, 1971 *S*, *I*, *SA* 2, 1972 *S*, *A* 1, 1973 *E*, 1974 *Arg* 1, 2, *SA* 2, 1975 *W*, *Arg* 1, 2, *R*, 1976 *S*, *I*, *W*, *E*, *A* 1, 2, *R*, 1977 *W*, *E*, *S*, *I*, 1978 *E*, *S*, *I*, *W*
Baudry, N (Montferrand) 1949 *S*, *I*, *W*, *Arg* 1, 2
Baulon, R (Vienne, Bayonne) 1954 *S*, *NZ*, *W*, *E*, *It*, 1955 *I*, *E*, *W*, *It*, 1956 *S*, *I*, *W*, *It*, *E*, *Cz*, 1957 *S*, *I*, *It*
Baux, J-P (Lannemezan) 1968 *NZ* 1, 2, *SA* 1, 2
Bavozet, J (Lyon) 1911 *S*, *E*, *W*
Bayard, J (Toulouse) 1923 *S*, *W*, *E*, 1924 *W*, *R*, *US*
Bayardon, J (Chalon) 1964 *S*, *NZ*, *E*
Beaurin, C (SF) 1907 *E*, 1908 *E*
Bégu, J (Dax) 1982 *Arg* 2 (R), 1984 *E*, *S*
Béguerie, C (Agen) 1979 *NZ* 1
Beguet, L (RCF) 1922 *I*, 1923 *S*, *W*, *E*, *I*, 1924 *S*, *I*, *E*, *R*, *US*
Behoteguy, A (Bayonne, Cognac) 1923 *E*, 1924 *S*, *I*, *E*, *W*, *R*, *US*, 1926 *E*, 1927 *E*, *G* 1, 2, 1928 *NSW*, *I*, *E*, *G*, *W*, 1929 *S*, *W*, *E*
Behoteguy, H (RCF, Cognac) 1923 *W*, 1928 *NSW*, *I*, *E*, *G*, *W*
Belascain, C (Bayonne) 1977 *R*, 1978 *E*, *S*, *I*, *W*, *R*, 1979 *I*, *W*, *E*, *S*, 1982 *W*, *E*, *S*, *I*, 1983 *E*, *S*, *I*, *W*
Belletante, G (Nantes) 1951 *I*, *E*, *W*
Bénésis, R (Narbonne) 1969 *W*, *R*, 1970 *S*, *I*, *W*, *E*, *R*, 1971 *S*, *I*, *E*, *W*, *A* 2, *R*, 1972 *S*, *I* 1, *E*, *W*, *I* 2, *A* 1, *R*, 1973 *NZ*, *E*, *W*, *I*, *J*, *R*, 1974 *I*, *W*, *E*, *S*
Benetière, J (Roanne) 1954 *It*, *Arg* 1
Berbizier, P (Lourdes) 1981 *S*, *I*, *W*, *E*, *NZ* 1, 2, 1982 *I*, *R*, 1983 *S*, *I*, 1984 *S* (R)
Berejnoi, J-C (Tulle) 1963 *R*, 1964 *S*, *W*, *It*, *I*, *SA*, *Fj*, *R*, 1965 *S*, *I*, *E*, *W*, *It*, *R*, 1966 *S*, *I*, *E*, *W*, *It*, *R*, 1967 *S*, *A*, *E*, *It*, *W*, *I*, *R*
Berges, B (Toulouse) 1926 *I*
Berges-Cau, R (Lourdes) 1976 *E* (R)
Bergeze, F (Bayonne) 1936 *G* 2, 1937 *G*, *It*, 1938 *G* 1, *R*, *G* 2
Bergougnan, Y (Toulouse) 1945 *B* 1, *W*, 1946 *B*, *I*, *K*, *W*, 1947 *S*, *I*, *W*, *E*, 1948 *S*, *W*, *E*, 1949 *S*, *E*, *Arg* 1, 2
Bernard, R (Bergerac) 1951 *S*, *I*, *E*, *W*
Bernon, J (Lourdes) 1922 *I*, 1923 *S*
Berot, J-L (Toulouse) 1968 *NZ* 3, *A*, 1969 *S*, *I*, 1970 *E*, *R*, 1971 *S*, *I*, *E*, *W*, *SA* 1, 2, *A* 1, 2, *R*, 1972 *S*, *I* 1, *E*, *W*, *A* 1, 1974 *I*
Bertrand, P (Bourg) 1951 *I*, *E*, *W*, 1953 *S*, *I*, *E*, *W*, *It*
Bertranne, R (Bagnères) 1971 *E*, *W*, *SA* 2, *A* 1, 2, 1972 *S*, *I* 1, 1973 *NZ*, *E*, *J*, *R*, 1974 *I*, *W*, *E*, *S*, *Arg* 1, 2, *R*, *SA* 1, 2, 1975 *W*, *E*, *S*, *I*, *SA* 1, 2, *Arg* 1, 2, *R*, 1976 *S*, *I*, *W*, *E*, *US*, *A* 1, 2, *R*, 1977 *W*, *E*, *S*, *I*, *Arg* 1, 2, *NZ* 1, 2, *R*, 1978 *E*, *S*, *I*, *W*, *R*, 1979 *I*, *W*, *E*, *S*, *R*, 1980 *W*, *E*, *S*, *I*, *SA*, *R*, 1981 *S*, *I*, *W*, *E*, *R*, *NZ* 1, 2
Besset, E (Grenoble) 1924 *S*
Besset, L (SCUF) 1914 *W*, *E*
Besson, M (CASG) 1924 *I*, 1925 *I*, *E*, 1926 *S*, *W*, 1927 *I*
Besson, P (Brive) 1963 *S*, *I*, *E*, 1965 *R*, 1968 *SA* 1
Bichendaritz, J (Biarritz O) 1954 *It*, *Arg* 1, 2
Bidart, L (La Rochelle) 1953 *W*
Biemouret, P (Agen) 1969 *E*, *W*, 1970 *I*, *W*, *E*, 1971 *W*,

SA 1, 2, *A* 1, 1972 *E*, *W*, *I* 2, *A* 2, *R*, 1973 *S*, *NZ*, *E*, *W*, *I*
Biénès, R (Cognac) 1950 *S*, *I*, *E*, *W*, 1951 *S*, *I*, *E*, *W*, 1952 *S*, *I*, *SA*, *W*, *E*, *It*, 1953 *S*, *I*, *E*, 1954 *S*, *I*, *NZ*, *W*, *E*, *Arg* 1, 2, 1956 *S*, *I*, *W*, *It*, *E*
Bigot, C (Quillan) 1930 *S*, *E*, 1931 *I*, *S*
Bilbao, L (St Jean de Luz) 1978 *I*, 1979 *I*
Billac, E (Bayonne) 1920 *S*, *E*, *W*, *I*, *US*, 1921 *S*, *W*, 1922 *W*, 1923 *E*
Billière, M (Toulouse) 1968 *NZ* 3
Bioussa, A (Toulouse) 1924 *W*, *US*, 1925 *I*, *NZ*, *S*, *E*, 1926 *S*, *I*, *E*, 1928 *E*, *G*, *W*, 1929 *I*, *S*, *W*, *E*, 1930 *S*, *I*, *E*, *G*, *W*
Bioussa, C (Toulouse) 1913 *W*, *I*, 1914 *I*
Biraben, M (Dax) 1920 *W*, *I*, *US*, 1921 *S*, *W*, *E*, *I*, 1922 *S*, *E*, *I*
Blain, A (Carcassonne) 1934 *G*
Blanco, S (Biarritz O) 1980 *SA*, *R*, 1981 *S*, *W*, *E*, *A* 1, 2, *R*, *NZ* 1, 2, 1982 *W*, *E*, *S*, *I*, *R*, *Arg* 1, 2, 1983 *E*, *S*, *I*, *W*, 1984 *I*, *W*, *E*, *S*
Blond, J (SF) 1935 *G*, 1936 *G* 2, 1937 *G*, 1938 *G* 1, *R*, *G* 2
Boffelli, V (Aurillac) 1971 *A* 2, *R*, 1972 *S*, *I* 1, 1973 *J*, *R*, 1974 *I*, *W*, *E*, *S*, *Arg* 1, 2, *R*, *SA* 1, 2, 1975 *W*, *S*, *I*
Bonal, J-M (Toulouse) 1968 *E*, *W*, *Cz*, *NZ* 2, 3, *SA* 1, 2, *R*, 1969 *S*, *I*, *E*, *R*, 1970 *W*, *E*
Bonamy, R (SB) 1928 *NSW*, *I*
Boniface, A (Mont-de-Marsan) 1954 *I*, *NZ*, *W*, *E*, *It*, *Arg* 1, 2, 1955 *S*, *I*, 1956 *S*, *I*, *W*, *It*, *Cz*, 1957 *S*, *I*, *W*, *R* 2, 1958 *S*, *E*, 1959 *E*, 1961 *NZ* 1, 3, *A*, *R*, 1962 *E*, *W*, *I*, *It*, *R*, 1963 *S*, *I*, *E*, *W*, *It*, *R*, 1964 *S*, *NZ*, *E*, *W*, *It*, 1965 *W*, *It*, *R*, 1966 *S*, *I*, *E*, *W*
Boniface, G (Mont-de-Marsan) 1960 *W*, *I*, *It*, *R*, *Arg* 1, 2, 3, 1961 *S*, *SA*, *E*, *W*, *It*, *I*, *NZ* 1, 2, 3, *R*, 1962 *R*, 1963 *S*, *I*, *E*, *W*, *It*, *R*, 1964 *S*, 1965 *S*, *I*, *E*, *W*, *It*, *R*, 1966 *S*, *I*, *E*, *W*
Bonnes, E (Narbonne) 1924 *W*, *R*, *US*
Bonnus, F (Toulon) 1950 *S*, *I*, *E*, *W*
Bonnus, M (Toulon) 1937 *It*, 1938 *G* 1, *R*, *G* 2, 1940 *B*
Bontemps, D (La Rochelle) 1968 *SA* 2
Borchard, G (RCF) 1908 *E*, 1909 *E*, *W*, *I*, 1911 *I*
Borde, F (RCF) 1920 *I*, *US*, 1921 *S*, *W*, *E*, 1922 *S*, *W*, 1923 *S*, *I*, 1924 *E*, 1925 *I*, 1926 *E*
Bordenave, L (Toulon) 1948 *A*, *S*, *W*, *E*, 1949 *S*
Boubee, J (Tarbes) 1921 *S*, *E*, *I*, 1922 *E*, *W*, 1923 *E*, *I*, 1925 *NZ*, *S*
Boudreau, R (SCUF) 1910 *W*, *S*
Bouguyon, G (Grenoble) 1961 *SA*, *E*, *W*, *It*, *I*, *NZ* 1, 2, 3, *A*
Boujet, C (Grenoble) 1968 *NZ* 2, *A* (R), *SA* 1
Bouquet, J (Bourgoin, Vienne) 1954 *S*, 1955 *E*, 1956 *S*, *I*, *W*, *It*, *E*, *Cz*, 1957 *S*, *E*, *W*, *R* 2, 1958 *S*, *E*, 1959 *S*, *It*, *W*, *I*, 1960 *S*, *E*, *W*, *I*, *R*, 1961 *S*, *SA*, *E*, *W*, *It*, *I*, *R*, 1962 *S*, *E*, *W*, *I*
Bourdeu, J R (Lourdes) 1952 *S*, *I*, *SA*, *W*, *E*, *It*, 1953 *S*, *I*, *E*
Bourgarel, R (Toulouse) 1969 *R*, 1970 *S*, *I*, *E*, *R*, 1971 *W*, *SA* 1, 2, 1973 *S*
Bousquet, A (Béziers) 1921 *E*, *I*, 1924 *R*
Bousquet, R (Albi) 1926 *M*, 1927 *I*, *S*, *W*, *E*, *G* 1, 1929 *W*, *E*, 1930 *W*
Boyau, M (SBUC) 1912 *I*, *S*, *W*, *E*, 1913 *W*, *I*
Boyer, P (Toulon) 1935 *G*
Branca, G (SF) 1928 *S*, 1929 *I*, *S*
Branlat, A (RCF) 1906 *NZ*, *E*, 1908 *W*
Brejassou, R (Tarbes) 1952 *S*, *I*, *SA*, *W*, *E*, 1953 *W*, *E*, 1954 *S*, *I*, *NZ*, 1955 *S*, *I*, *E*, *W*, *It*
Brethes, R (St Sever) 1960 *Arg* 2
Bringeon, A (Biarritz O) 1925 *W*
Brun, G (Vienne) 1950 *E*, *W*, 1951 *S*, *E*, *W*, 1952 *S*, *I*, *SA*, *W*, *E*, *It*, 1953 *E*, *W*, *It*
Bruneau, M (SBUC) 1910 *W*, *E*, 1913 *SA*, *E*
Brunet, Y (Perpignan) 1975 *SA* 1, 1977 *Arg* 1
Buchet, E (Nice) 1980 *R*, 1982 *E*, *R* (R), *Arg* 1, 2
Buisson, H (Béziers) 1931 *E*, *G*
Buonomo, Y (Béziers) 1971 *A* 2, *R*, 1972 *I* 1
Burgun, M (RCF) 1909 *I*, 1910 *W*, *S*, *I*, 1911 *S*, *E*, 1912 *I*, *S*, 1913 *S*, *E*, 1914 *E*
Bustaffa, D (Carcassonne) 1977 *Arg* 1, 2, *NZ* 1, 2, 1978 *W*, *R*, 1980 *W*, *E*, *S*, *SA*, *R*
Buzy E (Lourdes) 1946 *K*, *W*, 1947 *S*, *I*, *W*, *E*, 1948 *I*, *A*, *S*, *W*, *E*, 1949 *S*, *I*, *E*, *W*, *Arg* 1, 2

Cabanier, J-M (Montauban) 1963 *R*, 1964 *S*, *Fj*, 1965 *S*, *I*, *W*, *It*, *R*, 1966 *S*, *I*, *E*, *W*, *It*, *R*, 1967 *S*, *A*, *E*, *It*, *W*, *I*, *SA* 1, 3, *NZ*, *R*, 1968 *S*, *I*
Cabrol, H (Béziers) 1972 *A* 1 (R), *A* 2, 1973 *J*, 1974 *SA* 2
Cadenat, J (SCUF) 1910 *S*, *E*, 1911 *W*, *I*, 1912 *W*, *E*, 1913 *I*
Cahuc, F (St Girons) 1922 *S*
Cals, R (RCF) 1938 *G* 1
Calvo, G (Lourdes) 1961 *NZ* 1, 3
Camberabero, D (La Voulte) 1982 *R*, *Arg* 1, 2, 1983 *E*, *W*
Camberabero, G (La Voulte) 1961 *NZ* 3, 1962 *R*, 1964 *R*, 1967 *A*, *E*, *It*, *W*, *I*, *SA* 1, 3, 4, 1968 *S*, *E*, *W*
Camberabero, L (La Voulte) 1964 *R*, 1965 *S*, *I*, 1966 *E*, *W*, 1967 *A*, *E*, *It*, *W*, *I*, 1968 *S*, *E*, *W*
Cambré, T (Oloron) 1920 *E*, *W*, *I*, *US*
Camel, A (Toulouse) 1928 *S*, *NSW*, *I*, *E*, *G*, *W*, 1929 *W*, *E*, *G*, 1930 *S*, *I*, *E*, *G*, *W*, 1935 *G*
Camel, M (Toulouse) 1929 *S*, *W*, *E*
Camicas, F (Tarbes) 1927 *G* 2, 1928 *S*, *I*, *E*, *G*, *W*, 1929 *I*, *S*, *W*, *E*
Camo, E (Villeneuve) 1931 *I*, *S*, *W*, *E*, *G*, 1932 *G*
Campaes, A (Lourdes) 1965 *W*, 1967 *NZ*, 1968 *S*, *I*, *E*, *W*, *Cz*, *NZ* 1, 2, *A*, 1969 *S*, *W*, 1972 *R*, 1973 *NZ*
Cantoni, J (Béziers) 1970 *W*, *R*, 1971 *S*, *I*, *E*, *W*, *SA* 1, 2, *A* 1, *R*, 1972 *S*, *I* 1, 1973 *S*, *NZ*, *W*, *I*, 1975 *W* (R)
Capdouze, J (Pau) 1964 *SA*, *Fj*, *R*, 1965 *S*, *I*, *E*
Capendeguy, J-M (Begles) 1967 *NZ*, *R*
Capitani, P (Toulon) 1954 *Arg* 1, 2
Capmau, (Toulouse) 1914 *E*
Carabignac, J (Agen) 1951 *S*, *I*, 1952 *SA*, *W*, *E*, 1953 *S*, *I*
Carbonne, P (Perpignan) 1927 *W*
Caron, L (Lyon O, Castres) 1947 *E*, 1948 *I*, *A*, *W*, *E*, 1949 *S*, *I*, *E*, *W*, *Arg* 1
Carpentier, M (Lourdes) 1980 *E*, *SA*, *R*, 1981 *S*, *I*, *A* 1, 1982 *E*, *S*
Carrère, C (Toulon) 1966 *R*, 1967 *S*, *A*, *E*, *W*, *I*, *SA* 1, 3, 4, *NZ*, *R*, 1968 *S*, *I*, *E*, *W*, *Cz*, *NZ* 3, *A*, *R*, 1969 *S*, *I*, 1970 *S*, *I*, *W*, *E*, 1971 *E*, *W*
Carrère, J (Vichy, Toulon) 1956 *S*, 1957 *E*, *W*, *R* 2, 1958 *S*, *SA* 1, 2, 1959 *I*
Carrère, R (Mont-de-Marsan) 1953 *E*, *It*
Casaux, L (Tarbes) 1959 *I*, *It*, 1962 *S*
Cassagne, P (Pau) 1957 *It*
Cassayet, A (Tarbes, Narbonne) 1920 *S*, *E*, *W*, *US*, 1921 *W*, *E*, *I*, 1922 *S*, *E*, *W*, 1923 *S*, *W*, *E*, *I*, 1924 *S*, *E*, *W*, *R*, *US*, 1925 *I*, *NZ*, *S*, *W*, 1926 *S*, *I*, *E*, *W*, *M*, 1927 *I*, *S*, *W*
Cassiède, M (Dax) 1961 *NZ* 3, *A*, *R*
Castets, J (Toulon) 1923 *W*, *E*, *I*
Caujolle, J (Tarbes) 1909 *E*, 1913 *SA*, *E*, 1914 *W*, *E*
Caunègre, R (SB) 1938 *R*, *G* 2
Caussade, A (Lourdes) 1978 *R*, 1979 *I*, *W*, *E*, *NZ* 1, 2, *R*, 1980 *W*, *E*, *S*, 1981 *S* (R), *I*
Caussarieu, G (Pau) 1929 *I*
Cayrefourcq, E (Tarbes) 1921 *E*
Cazals, P (Mont-de-Marsan) 1961 *NZ* 1, *A*, *R*
Cazenave, A (Pau) 1927 *E*, *G* 1, 1928 *S*, *NSW*, *G*
Cazenave, F (RCF) 1950 *E*, 1952 *S*, 1954 *I*, *NZ*, *W*, *E*
Celaya, M (Biarritz O, SBUC) 1953 *E*, *W*, *It*, 1954 *I*, *E*, *It*, *Arg* 1, 2, 1955 *S*, *I*, *E*, *W*, *It*, 1956 *S*, *I*, *W*, *It*, *E*, *Cz*, 1957 *S*, *I*, *E*, *W*, *R* 2, 1958 *S*, *E*, *A*, *W*, *It*, 1959 *S*, *E*, 1960 *S*, *E*, *W*, *I*, *R*, *Arg* 1, 2, 3, 1961 *S*, *SA*, *E*, *W*, *It*, *I*, *NZ* 1, 2, 3, *A*, *R*
Celhay, M (Bayonne) 1935 *G*, 1936 *G* 1, 1937 *G*, *It*, 1938 *G* 1, 1940 B
Cessieux, J (Lyon) 1906 *NZ*
Cester, E (TOEC, Valence) 1966 *S*, *I*, *E*, 1967 *W*, 1968 *S*, *I*, *E*, *W*, *Cz*, *NZ* 1, 3, *A*, *SA* 1, 2, *R*, 1969 *S*, *I*, *E*, *W*, 1970 *S*, *I*, *W*, *E*, 1971 *A* 1, 1972 *R*, 1973 *S*, *NZ*, *W*, *I*, *J*, *R*, 1974 *I*, *W*, *E*, *S*
Chaban-Delmas, J (CASG) 1945 *B* 2
Chadebach, P (Brive) 1982 *R*, *Arg* 1, 2
Chapuy, L (SF) 1926 *S*
Charpentier, G (SF) 1911 *E*, 1912 *W*, *E*
Charton, P (Montferrand) 1940 *B*
Chassagne, J (Montferrand) 1938 *G* 1
Chateau, A (Bayonne) 1913 *SA*
Chaud, E (Toulon) 1932 *G*, 1934 *G*, 1935 *G*
Chenevay, C (Grenoble) 1968 *SA* 1
Chevallier, B (Montferrand) 1952 *S*, *I*, *SA*, *W*, *E*, *It*, 1953 *E*, *W*, *It*, 1954 *S*, *I*, *NZ*, *W*, *Arg* 1, 1955 *S*, *I*, *E*, *W*, *It*, 1956 *S*, *I*, *W*, *It*, *E*, *Cz*, 1957 *S*

Chiberry, J (Chambéry) 1955 *It*
Chilo, A (RCF) 1920 *S, W*, 1925 *I, NZ*
Cholley, G (Castres) 1975 *E, S, I, SA* 1, 2, *Arg* 1, 2, *R*, 1976 *S, I, W, E, A* 1, 2, *R*, 1977 *W, E, S, I, Arg* 1, 2, *NZ* 1, 2, *R*, 1978 *E, S, I, W, R*, 1979 *I, S*
Choy, J (Narbonne) 1930 *S, I, E, G, W*, 1931 *I*, 1933 *G*, 1934 *G*, 1935 *G*, 1936 *G* 2
Cimarosti, J (Castres) 1976 *US* (R)
Clady, A (Lezignan) 1929 *G*, 1931 *I, S, E, G*
Clarrac, H (St Girons) 1938 *G* 1
Claudel, R (Lyon) 1932 *G*, 1934 *G*
Clauzel, F (Béziers) 1924 *E, W*, 1925 *W*
Clave, J (Agen) 1936 *G* 2, 1938 *R, G* 2
Claverie, H (Lourdes) 1954 *NZ, W*
Clement, J (RCF) 1921 *S, W, E*, 1922 *S, E, W, I*, 1923 *S, W, I*
Clement, P (RCF) 1931 *W*
Clemente, M (Oloron) 1978 *R*, 1980 *S, I*
Cluchague, L (Biarritz O) 1924 *S*, 1925 *E*
Coderc, J (Chalon) 1932 *G*, 1933 *G*, 1934 *G*, 1935 *G*, 1936 *G* 1
Codorniou, D (Narbonne) 1979 *NZ* 1, 2, *R*, 1980 *W, E, S, I*, 1981 *S, W, E, A* 2, 1983 *E, S, I, W, A* 1, 2, *R*, 1984 *I, W, E, S*
Cognet, L (Montferrand) 1932 *G*, 1936 *G* 1, 2, 1937 *G, It*
Colombier, J (St Junien) 1952 *SA, W, E*
Colomine, G (Narbonne) 1979 *NZ* 1
Combe, J (SF) 1910 *S, E, I*, 1911 *S*
Combes, G (Fumel) 1945 *B* 2
Communeau, M (SF) 1906 *NZ, E*, 1907 *E*, 1908 *E, W*, 1909 *E, W, I*, 1910 *S, E, I*, 1911 *S, E, I*, 1912 *I, S, W, E*, 1913 *SA, E, W*
Condom, J (Boucau) 1982 *R*, 1983 *E, S, I, W, A* 1, 2, *R*, 1984 *I, W, E, S*
Conil de Beyssac, J (SBUC) 1912 *I, S*, 1914 *I, W, E*
Constant, G (Perpignan) 1920 *W*
Coscoll, G (Béziers) 1921 *S, W*
Costantino, J (Montferrand) 1973 *R*
Costes, F (Montferrand) 1979 *E, S, NZ* 1, 2, *R*, 1980 *W, I*
Coulon, J (Grenoble) 1928 *S*
Crabos, R (RCF) 1920 *S, E, W, I, US*, 1921 *S, W, E, I*, 1922 *S, E, W, I*, 1923 *S, I*, 1924 *S, I*
Crampagne, J (Begles) 1967 *SA* 4
Crancee, R (Lourdes) 1960 *Arg* 3, 1961 *S*
Crauste, M (RCF, Lourdes) 1957 *R* 1, 2, 1958 *S, E, A, W, It, I*, 1959 *E, It, W, I*, 1960 *S, E, W, I, It, R, Arg* 1, 3, 1961 *S, SA, E, W, It, I, NZ* 1, 2, 3, *A, R*, 1962 *S, E, W, I, It, R*, 1963 *S, I, E, W, It, R*, 1964 *S, NZ, E, W, It, I, SA, Fj, R*, 1965 *S, I, E, W, It, R*, 1966 *S, I, E, W, It*
Cremaschi, M (Lourdes) 1980 *R*, 1981 *R, NZ* 1, 2, 1982 *W, S*, 1983 *A* 1, 2, *R*, 1984 *I, W*
Crichton, W H (Le Havre) 1906 *NZ, E*
Cristina, J (Montferrand) 1979 *R*
Cussac, P (Biarritz O) 1934 *G*
Cutzach, A (Quillan) 1929 *G*

Daguerre, F (Biarritz O) 1936 *G* 1
Daguerre, J (CASG) 1933 *G*
Danion, J (Toulon) 1924 *I*
Danos, P (Toulon, Béziers) 1954 *Arg* 1, 2, 1957 *R* 2, 1958 *S, E, W, It, I, SA* 1, 2, 1959 *S, E, It, W, I*, 1960 *S, E*
Darbos, P (Dax) 1969 *R*
Darracq, R (Dax) 1957 *It*
Darrieussecq, A (Biarritz O) 1973 *E*
Darrieussecq, J (Mont-de-Marsan) 1953 *It*
Darrouy, C (Mont-de-Marsan) 1957 *I, E, W, It, R* 1, 1959 *E*, 1961 *R*, 1963 *S, I, E, W, It*, 1964 *NZ, E, W, It, I, SA, Fj, R*, 1965 *S, I, E, It, R*, 1966 *S, I, E, W, It, R*, 1967 *S, A, E, It, W, I, SA* 1, 2, 4
Daudignon, G (SF) 1928 *S*
Dauga, B (Mont-de-Marsan) 1964 *S, NZ, E, W, It, I, SA, Fj, R*, 1965 *S, I, E, W, It, R*, 1966 *S, I, E, W, It, R*, 1967 *S, A, E, It, W, I, SA* 1, 2, 3, 4, *NZ, R*, 1968 *S, I, NZ* 1, 2, 3, *A, SA* 1, 2, *R*, 1969 *S, I, E, R*, 1970 *S, I, W, E, R*, 1971 *S, I, E, W, SA* 1, 2, *A* 1, 2, *R*, 1972 *S, I* 1, *W*
Dauger, J (Bayonne) 1945 *B* 1, 2, 1953 *S*
Daulouede, P (Tyrosse) 1937 *G, It*, 1938 *G* 1, 1940 *B*
Decamps, P (RCF) 1911 *S*
Dedet, J (SF) 1910 *S, E, I*, 1911 *W, I*, 1912 *S*, 1913 *E, I*
Dedeyn, P (RCF) 1906 *NZ*
Dedieu, P (Béziers) 1963 *E, It*, 1964 *W, It, I, SA, Fj, R*, 1965 *S, I, E, W*
De Gregorio, J (Grenoble) 1960 *S, E, W, I, It, R, Arg* 1, 2, 1961 *S, SA, E, W, It, I*, 1962 *S, E, W*, 1963 *S, W, It*, 1964 *NZ, E*
Dehez, J-L (Agen) 1967 *SA* 2, 1969 *R*
De Jouvencel, E (SF) 1909 *W, I*
De Laborderie, M (RCF) 1921 *I*, 1922 *I*, 1925 *W, E*
Delage, C (Agen) 1983 *S, I*
De Malherbe, H (CASG) 1932 *G*, 1933 *G*
De Malmann, R (RCF) 1908 *E, W*, 1909 *E, W, I*, 1910 *E, I*
De Muison, J (SF) 1910 *I*
Delaigue, G (Toulon) 1973 *J, R*
Delque, A (Toulouse) 1937 *It*, 1938 *G* 1, *R, G* 2
Descamps, (SB) 1927 *G* 2
Desclaux, F (RCF) 1949 *Arg* 1, 2, 1953 *It*
Desclaux, J (Perpignan) 1934 *G*, 1935 *G*, 1936 *G* 1, 2, 1937 *G, It*, 1938 *G* 1, *R, G* 2, 1945 *B* 1
Desnoyer, L (Brive) 1974 *R*
Destarac, L (Tarbes) 1926 *S, I, E, W, M*, 1927 *W, E, G* 1, 2
Desvouges, R (SF) 1914 *W*
Detrez, P-E (Nîmes) 1983 *A* 2 (R)
Deygas, M (Vienne) 1937 *It*
Dintrans, P (Tarbes) 1979 *NZ* 1, 2, *R*, 1980 *E, S, I, SA, R*, 1981 *S, I, W, E, A* 1, 2, *R, NZ* 1, 2, 1982 *W, E, S, I, R, Arg* 1, 2, 1983 *E, W, A* 1, 2, *R*, 1984 *I, W, E, S*
Dizabo, P (Tyrosse) 1948 *A, S, E*, 1949 *S, I, E, W, Arg* 2, 1950 *S, I*, 1960 *Arg* 1, 2, 3
Domec, A (Carcassonne) 1929 *W*
Domec, H (Lourdes) 1953 *W, It*, 1954 *S, I, NZ, W, E, It*, 1955 *S, I, E, W*, 1956 *I, W, It*, 1958 *E, A, W, It, I*
Domenech, A (Vichy, Brive) 1954 *W, E, It*, 1955 *S, I, E, W*, 1956 *S, I, W, It, E, Cz*, 1957 *S, I, E, W, It, R* 1, 2, 1958 *S, E, It*, 1959 *It*, 1960 *S, E, W, I, It, R, Arg* 1, 2, 3, 1961 *S, SA, E, W, It, I, NZ* 1, 2, 3, *A, R*, 1962 *S, E, W, I, It, R*, 1963 *W, It*
Domercq, J (Bayonne) 1912 *I, S*
Dorot, J (RCF) 1935 *G*
Dospital, P (Bayonne) 1977 *R*, 1980 *I*, 1981 *S, I, W, E*, 1982 *I, R, Arg* 1, 2, 1983 *E, S, I, W*, 1984 *E, S*
Dourthe, C (Dax) 1966 *R*, 1967 *S, A, E, W, I, SA* 1, 2, 3, *NZ*, 1968 *W, NZ* 3, *SA* 1, 2, 1969 *W*, 1971 *SA* 2 (R), *R*, 1972 *I* 1, 2, *A* 1, 2, *R*, 1973 *S, NZ, E*, 1974 *I, Arg* 1, 2, *SA* 1, 2, 1975 *W, E, S*
Dousseau, E (Angoulême) 1938 *R*
Droitecourt, M (Montferrand) 1972 *R*, 1973 *NZ* (R), *E*, 1974 *E, S, Arg* 1, *SA* 2, 1975 *SA* 1, 2, *Arg* 1, 2, *R*, 1976 *S, I, W, A* 1, 1977 *Arg* 2
Dubertrand, A (Montferrand) 1971 *A* 2, *R*, 1972 *I* 2, 1974 *I, W, E, SA* 2, 1975 *Arg* 1, 2, *R*, 1976 *S, US*
Dubois, D (Begles) 1971 *S*
Dubroca, D (Agen) 1979 *NZ* 2, 1981 *NZ* 2 (R), 1982 *E, S*, 1984 *W, E, S*
Duche, A (Limoges) 1929 *G*
Duclos, A (Lourdes) 1931 *S*
Ducousso, J (Tarbes) 1925 *S, W, E*
Dufau, G (RCF) 1948 *I, A*, 1949 *I, W*, 1950 *S, E, W*, 1951 *S, I, E, W*, 1952 *SA, W*, 1953 *S, I, E, W*, 1954 *S, I, NZ, W, E, It*, 1955 *S, I, E, W, It*, 1956 *S, I, W, It*, 1957 *S, I, E, W, It, R* 1
Dufau, J (Biarritz) 1912 *I, S, W, E*
Duffaut, Y (Agen) 1954 *Arg* 1, 2
Dufourcq, J (SBUC) 1906 *NZ, E*, 1907 *E*, 1908 *W*
Dufour, R (Tarbes) 1911 *W*
Duhard, Y (Bagnères) 1980 *E*
Duhau, J (SF) 1928 *I*, 1930 *I, G*, 1931 *I, S, W*, 1933 *G*
Dulaurans, C (Toulouse) 1926 *I*, 1928 *S*, 1929 *W*
Duluc, A (Béziers) 1934 *G*
Du Manoir, Y (RCF) 1925 *I, NZ, S, W, E*, 1926 *S*, 1927 *I, S*
Dupont, C (Lourdes) 1923 *S, W, I*, 1924 *S, I, W, R, US*, 1925 *S*, 1927 *E, G* 1, 2, 1928 *NSW, G, W*, 1929 *I*
Dupont, J-L (Agen) 1983 *S*
Dupont, L (RCF) 1934 *G*, 1935 *G*, 1936 *G* 1, 2, 1938 *R, G* 2
Dupouy, A (SB) 1924 *W, R*
Duprat, B (Bayonne) 1966 *E, W, It, R*, 1967 *S, A, E, SA* 2, 3, 1968 *S, I*, 1972 *E, W, I* 2, *A* 1
Dupré, P (RCF) 1909 *W*

Dupuy, J (Tarbes) 1956 *S, I, W, It, E, Cz*, 1957 *S, I, E, W, It, R* 2, 1958 *S, E, SA* 1, 2, 1959 *S, E, It, W, I*, 1960 *W, I, It, Arg* 1, 3, 1961 *S, SA, E, NZ* 2, *R*, 1962 *S, E, W, I, It*, 1963 *W, It, R*, 1964 *S*
Du Souich, C (SCUF) 1911 *W, I*
Dutin, B (Mont-de-Marsan) 1968 *NZ* 2, *A, SA* 2, *R*
Dutour, F (Toulouse) 1911 *E, I*, 1912 *S, W, E*, 1913 *S*
Dutrain, H (Toulouse) 1945 *W*, 1946 *B, I*, 1947 *E*, 1949 *I, E, W, Arg* 1
Dutrey, J (Lourdes) 1940 *B*
Duval, R (SF) 1908 *E, W*, 1909 *E*, 1911 *E, W, I*

Echave, L (Agen) 1961 *S*
Elissalde, E (Bayonne) 1936 *G* 2, 1940 *B*
Elissalde, J-P (La Rochelle) 1980 *SA, R*, 1981 *A* 1, 2, *R*
Erbani, D (Agen) 1981 *A* 1, 2, *NZ* 1, 2, 1982 *Arg* 1, 2, 1983 *S* (R), *I, W, A* 1, 2, *R*, 1984 *W, E*
Escaffre, P (Narbonne) 1933 *G*, 1934 *G*
Escommier, M (Montelimar) 1955 *It*
Esponda, J-M (RCF) 1967 *SA* 1, 2, *R*, 1968 *NZ* 1, 2, *SA* 2, *R*, 1969 *S, I* (R), *E*
Estève, A (Béziers) 1971 *SA* 1, 1972 *I* 1, *E, W, I* 2, *A* 2, *R*, 1973 *S, NZ, E, I*, 1974 *I, W, E, S, R, SA* 1, 2, 1975 *W, E*
Estève, P (Narbonne) 1982 *R, Arg* 1, 2, 1983 *E, S, I, W, A* 1, 2, *R*, 1984 *I, W, E, S*
Etcheberry, J (Rochefort, Cognac) 1923 *W, I*, 1924 *S, I, E, W, R, US*, 1926 *S, I, E, M*, 1927 *I, S, W, G* 2
Etchenique, J (Biarritz O) 1974 *R, SA* 1, 1975 *E, Arg* 2
Etchepare, J (Bayonne) 1922 *I*
Etcheverry, M (Pau) 1971 *S, I*
Eutrope, A (SCUF) 1913 *I*

Fabre, E (Toulouse) 1937 *It*, 1938 *G* 1, 2
Fabre, J (Toulouse) 1963 *S, I, E, W, It*, 1964 *S, NZ, E*
Fabre, L (Lezignan) 1930 *G*
Fabre, M (Béziers) 1981 *A* 1, *R, NZ* 1, 2, 1982 *I, R*
Failliot, P (RCF) 1911 *S, W, I*, 1912 *I, S, E*, 1913 *E, W*
Fargues, H (Dax) 1923 *I*
Faure, F (Tarbes) 1914 *I, W, E*
Fauvel, J-P (Tulle) 1980 *R*
Favre, M (Lyon) 1913 *E, W*
Ferrand, L (Chalon) 1940 *B*
Ferrien, R (Tarbes) 1950 *S, I, E, W*
Finat, R (CASG) 1932 *G*, 1933 *G*
Fite, R (Brive) 1963 *W, It*
Forestier, J (SCUF) 1912 *W*
Forgues, F (Bayonne) 1911 *S, E, W*, 1912 *I, W, E*, 1913 *S, SA, W*, 1914 *I, E*
Fort, J (Agen) 1967 *It, W, I, SA* 1, 2, 3, 4
Fourcade, G (BEC) 1909 *E, W*
Foures, H (Toulouse) 1951 *S, I, E, W*
Fournet, F (Montferrand) 1950 *W*
Fouroux, J (La Voulte) 1972 *I* 2, *R*, 1974 *W, E, Arg* 1, 2, *R, SA* 1, 2, 1975 *W, Arg* 1, *R*, 1976 *S, I, W, E, US, A* 1, 1977 *W, E, S, I, Arg* 1, 2, *NZ* 1, 2, *R*
Franquenelle, A (Vaugirard) 1911 *S*, 1913 *W, I*
Furcade, R (Perpignan) 1952 *S*

Gabernet, S (Toulouse) 1980 *E, S*, 1981 *S, I, W, E, A* 1, 2, *R, NZ* 1, 2, 1982 *I*, 1983 *A* 2, *R*
Gachassin, J (Lourdes) 1961 *S, I*, 1963 *R*, 1964 *S, NZ, E, W, It, I, SA, Fj, R*, 1965 *S, I, E, W, It, R*, 1966 *S, I, E, W*, 1967 *S, A, It, W, I, NZ*, 1968 *I, E*, 1969 *S, I*
Galau, H (Toulouse) 1924 *S, I, E, W, US*
Galia, J (Quillan) 1927 *E, G* 1, 2, 1928 *S, NSW, I, E, W*, 1929 *I, E, G*, 1930 *S, I, E, G, W*, 1931 *S, W, E, G*
Gallion, J (Toulon) 1978 *E, S, I, W*, 1979 *I, W, E, S, NZ* 2, *R*, 1980 *W, E, S, I*, 1983 *A* 1, 2, *R*, 1984 *I, W, E, S*
Galy, J (Perpignan) 1953 *W*
Garuet, J-P (Lourdes) 1983 *A* 1, 2, *R*, 1984 *I*
Gasc, J (Graulhet) 1977 *NZ* 2
Gasparotto, G (Montferrand) 1976 *A* 2, *R*
Gauby, G (Perpignan) 1956 *Cz*
Gaudermen, P (RCF) 1906 *E*
Gayraud, W (Toulouse) 1920 *I*
Geneste, R (BEC) 1945 *B* 1, 1949 *Arg* 2
Gensanne, R (Béziers) 1962 *S, E, W, I, It, R*, 1963 *S*
Gerald, G (RCF) 1927 *E, G* 2, 1928 *S*, 1929 *I, S, W, E, G*, 1930 *S, I, E, G, W*, 1931 *I, S, E, G*
Gerintes, G (CASG) 1924 *R*, 1925 *I*, 1926 *W*
Geschwind, P (RCF) 1936 *G* 1, 2

Giaccardy, M (SBUC) 1907 *E*
Gommes, J (RCF) 1909 *I*
Gonnet, C-A (Albi) 1921 *E, I*, 1922 *E, W*, 1924 *S, E*, 1926 *S, I, E, W, M*, 1927 *I, S, W, E, G* 1
Got, R (Perpignan) 1920 *I, US*, 1921 *S, W*, 1922 *S, E, W, I*, 1924 *I, E, W, R, US*
Gourdon, J-F (RCF, Bagnères) 1974 *S, Arg* 1, 2, *R, SA* 1, 2, 1975 *W, E, S, I, R*, 1976 *S, I, W, E*, 1978 *E, S*, 1979 *W, E, S, R*, 1980 *I*
Goyard, A (Lyon U) 1936 *G* 1, 2, 1937 *G, It*, 1938 *G* 1, *R, G* 2
Graciet, R (SBUC) 1926 *I, W*, 1927 *S, G* 1, 1929 *E*, 1930 *W*
Graule, V (Arl Perpignan) 1926 *I, E, W*, 1927 *S, W*, 1931 *G*
Greffe, M (Grenoble) 1968 *W, Cz, NZ* 1, 2, *SA* 1
Griffard, J (Lyon U) 1932 *G*, 1933 *G*, 1934 *G*
Gruarin, A (Toulon) 1964 *W, It, I, SA, Fj, R*, 1965 *S, I, E, W, It*, 1966 *S, I, E, W, It, R*, 1967 *S, A, E, It, W, I, NZ*, 1968 *S, I*
Guelorget, P (RCF) 1931 *E, G*
Guichemerre, A (Dax) 1920 *E*, 1921 *E, I*, 1923 *S*
Guilbert, A (Toulon) 1975 *E, S, I, SA* 1, 2, 1976 *A* 1, 1977 *Arg* 1, 2, *NZ* 1, 2, *R*, 1979 *I, W, E*
Guillemin, P (RCF) 1908 *E, W*, 1909 *E, I*, 1910 *W, S, E, I*, 1911 *S, E, W*
Guilleux, P (Agen) 1952 *SA, It*
Guiral, M (Agen) 1931 *G*, 1932 *G*, 1933 *G*

Haget, A (PUC) 1953 *E*, 1954 *I, NZ, E, Arg* 2, 1955 *E, W, It*, 1957 *I, E, It, R* 1, 1958 *It, SA* 2
Haget, F (Agen) 1974 *Arg* 1, 2, 1975 *SA* 2, *Arg* 1, 2, *R*, 1976 *S*, 1978 *S, I, W, R*, 1979 *I, W, E, S, NZ* 1, 2, *R*, 1980 *W, S, I*, 1984 *S*
Haget, H (CASG) 1928 *S*, 1930 *G*
Halet, (Strasbourg) 1925 *NZ, S, W*
Harize, D (Cahors, Toulouse) 1975 *SA* 1, 2, 1976 *A* 1, 2, *R*, 1977 *W, E, S, I*
Hauc, J (Toulon) 1928 *E, G*, 1929 *I, S, G*
Hauser, M (Lourdes) 1969 *E*
Hedembaigt, M (Bayonne) 1913 *S, SA*, 1914 *W*
Herice, D (Begles) 1950 *I*
Herrero, A (Toulon) 1963 *R*, 1964 *NZ, E, W, It, I, SA, Fj, R*, 1965 *S, I, E, W*, 1966 *W, It, R*, 1967 *S, A, E, It, I, R*
Herrero, B (Nice) 1983 *I*
Hiquet, J-C (Agen) 1964 *E*
Hoche, M (PUC) 1957 *I, E, W, It, R* 1
Hortoland, J-P (Béziers) 1971 *A* 2
Houblain, H (SCUF) 1909 *E*, 1910 *W*
Houdet, R (SF) 1927 *S, W, G* 1, 1928 *G, W*, 1929 *I, S, E*, 1930 *S, E*
Hourdebaigt, (SBUC) 1909 *I*, 1910 *W, S, E, I*
Hubert, A (ASF) 1906 *E*, 1907 *E*, 1908 *E, W*, 1909 *E, W, I*
Hutin, R (CASG) 1927 *I, S, W*

Icard, J (SF) 1909 *E, W*
Iguinitz, E (Bayonne) 1914 *E*
Ihingoué, D (BEC) 1912 *I, S*
Imbernon, J-F (Perpignan) 1976 *I, W, E, US, A* 1, 1977 *W, E, S, I, Arg* 1, 2, *NZ* 1, 2, 1978 *E, R*, 1979 *I*, 1981 *S, I, W, E*, 1982 *I*, 1983 *I, W*
Iraçabal, J (Bayonne) 1968 *NZ* 1, 2, *SA* 1, 1969 *S, I, W, R*, 1970 *S, I, W, E, R*, 1971 *W, SA* 1, 2, *A* 1, 1972 *E, W, I* 2, *A* 2, *R*, 1973 *S, NZ, E, W, I, J*, 1974 *I, W, E, S, Arg* 1, 2, *SA* 2 (R)
Isaac, H (RCF) 1907 *E*, 1908 *E*
Ithurra, E (Biarritz O) 1936 *G* 1, 2, 1937 *G*

Janeczek, T (Tarbes) 1982 *Arg* 1, 2
Jarasse, A (Brive) 1945 *B* 1
Jardel, J (SB) 1928 *I, E*
Jaureguy, A (RCF, Toulouse, SF) 1920 *S, E, W, I, US*, 1922 *S, W*, 1923 *S, W, E, I*, 1924 *S, W, R, US*, 1925 *I, NZ*, 1926 *S, E, W, M*, 1927 *I, E*, 1928 *S, NSW, E, G, W*, 1929 *I, S, E*
Jaureguy, P (Toulouse) 1913 *S, SA, W, I*
Jeangrand, H (Tarbes) 1921 *I*
Jeanjean, P (Toulon) 1948 *I*
Jérôme, G (SF) 1906 *NZ, E*
Joinel, J-L (Brive) 1977 *NZ* 1, 1978 *R*, 1979 *I, W, E, S, NZ* 1, 2, *R*, 1980 *W, E, S, I, SA*, 1981 *S, I, W, E, R*,

NZ 1, 2, 1982 *E, S, I, R*, 1983 *E, S, I, W, A* 1, 2, *R*, 1984 *I, W, E, S*
Jol, M (Biarritz O) 1947 *S, I, W, E*, 1949 *S, I, E, W, Arg* 1, 2
Junquas, L (Tyrosse) 1945 *B* 1, 2, *W*, 1946 *B, I, K, W*, 1947 *S, I, W, E*, 1948 *S, W*

Kaczorowksi, D (Le Creusot) 1974 *I* (R)
Kaempf, A (St Jean-de-Luz) 1946 *B*

Labadie, P (Bayonne) 1952 *S, I, SA, W, E, It*, 1953 *S, I, It*, 1954 *S, I, NZ, W, E, Arg* 2, 1955 *S, I, E, W*, 1956 *I*, 1957 *I*
Labartl.ete, R (Pau) 1952 *S*
Labazuy, A (Lourdes) 1952 *I*, 1954 *S, W*, 1956 *E*, 1958 *A, W, I*, 1959 *S, E, It, W*
Laborde, C (RCF) 1962 *It, R*, 1963 *R*, 1964 *SA*, 1965 *E*
Lacans, P (Béziers) 1980 *SA*, 1981 *W, E, A* 2, *R*, 1982 *W*
Lacassagne, A (SBUC) 1906 *NZ*, 1907 *E*
Lacaussade, R (Begles) 1948 *A, S*
Lacaze, C (Lourdes, Angoulême) 1961 *NZ* 2, 3, *A, R*, 1962 *E, W, I, It*, 1963 *W, R*, 1964 *S, NZ, E*, 1965 *It, R*, 1966 *S, I, E, W, It, R*, 1967 *S, E, SA* 1, 3, 4, *R*, 1968 *S, E, W, Cz, NZ* 1, 1969 *E*
Lacaze, H (Périgueux) 1928 *I, G, W*, 1929 *I, W*
Lacaze, P (Lourdes) 1958 *SA* 1, 2, 1959 *S, E, It, W, I*
Lacazedieu, C (Dax) 1923 *W, I*, 1928 *NSW, I*, 1929 *S*
Lacome, M (Pau) 1960 *Arg* 2
Lacoste, R (Tarbes) 1914 *I, W, E*
Lacrampe, F (Béziers) 1949 *Arg* 2
Lacroix, P (Mont-de-Marsan, Agen) 1958 *A*, 1960 *W, I, It, R, Arg* 1, 2, 3, 1961 *S, SA, E, W, I, NZ* 1, 2, 3, *A, R*, 1962 *S, E, W, I, R*, 1963 *S, I, E, W*
Lafarge, Y (Montferrand) 1978 *R*, 1979 *NZ* 1, 1981 *I* (R)
Laffond, A (Bayonne) 1922 *E*
Laffont, H (Narbonne) 1926 *W*
Lafitte, L (SCUF) 1910 *W, S*
Lafond, J-B (RCF) 1983 *A* 1
Lagisquet, P (Bayonne) 1983 *A* 1, 2, *R*, 1984 *I, W*
Lagrange, J-C (RCF) 1966 *It*
Lalande, M (RCF) 1923 *S, W, I*
Lane, G (RCF) 1906 *NZ, E*, 1907 *E*, 1908 *E, W*, 1909 *E, W, I*, 1910 *W, E*, 1911 *S, W*, 1912 *I, W, E*, 1913 *S*
Laporte, G (Graulhet) 1981 *I, W, E, R, NZ* 1, 2
Larreguy, P (Bayonne) 1954 *It*
Larribeau, L (Périgueux) 1912 *I, S, W, E*, 1913 *S*, 1914 *I, E*
Larrieu, J (Tarbes) 1920 *I, US*, 1921 *W*, 1923 *S, W, E, I*
Larrieu, M (SB) 1927 *G* 2
Larrue, H (Carmaux) 1960 *W, I, It, R, Arg* 1, 2, 3
Lasâosa, P (Dax) 1950 *I*, 1952 *S, I, E, It*, 1955 *It*
Lassegue, J (Toulouse) 1946 *W*, 1947 *S, I, W*, 1948 *W*, 1949 *I, E, W, Arg* 1
Lasserre, J-C (Dax) 1963 *It*, 1964 *S, NZ, E, W, It, I, Fj*, 1965 *W, It, R*, 1966 *R*, 1967 *S*
Lasserre, M (Agen) 1967 *SA* 2, 3, 1968 *E, W, Cz, NZ* 3, *A, SA* 1, 2, 1969 *S, I, E*, 1970 *E*, 1971 *E, W*
Lasserre, R (Bayonne, Cognac, Grenoble) 1914 *I*, 1920 *S*, 1921 *S, W, I*, 1922 *S, E, W, I*, 1923 *W, E*, 1924 *S, I, R, US*
Laterrade, G (Tarbes) 1910 *E, I*, 1911 *S, E, I*
Laudouar, J (Soustons, SBUC) 1961 *NZ* 1, 2, *R*, 1962 *I, R*
Lauga, P (Vichy) 1950 *S, I, E, W*
Laurent, A (Biarritz O) 1925 *NZ, S, W, E*, 1926 *W*
Laurent, J (Bayonne) 1920 *S, E, W*
Laurent, M (Auch) 1932 *G*, 1933 *G*, 1934 *G*, 1935 *G*, 1936 *G* 1
Lavail, G (Perpignan) 1937 *G*, 1940 *B*
Lavaud, (Carcassonne) 1914 *I, W*
Lavergne, P (Limoges) 1950 *S*
Lavigne, B (Dax) 1920 *E, W*
Lazies, H (Auch) 1954 *Arg* 2, 1955 *It*, 1956 *E*, 1957 *S*
Le Bourhis, R (La Rochelle) 1961 *R*
Lecointre, M (Nantes) 1952 *It*
Le Droff, J (Auch) 1963 *It, R*, 1964 *S, NZ, E*, 1970 *E, R*, 1971 *S, I*
Lefevre, R (Brive) 1961 *NZ* 2
Lefort, J-B (Biarritz O) 1938 *G* 1
Le Goff, R (Métro) 1938 *R, G* 2
Legrain, M (SF) 1909 *I*, 1910 *I*, 1911 *S, E, W, I*, 1913 *S, SA, E, I*, 1914 *I, W*
Lenient, J-J (Vichy) 1967 *R*
Lepatey, J (Mazamet) 1954 *It*, 1955 *S, I, E, W*
Lepatey, L (Mazamet) 1924 *S, I, E*
Lescarboura, J-P (Dax) 1982 *W, E, S, I*, 1983 *A* 1, 2, *R*, 1984 *I, W, E, S*
Lesieur, E (SF) 1906 *E*, 1908 *E, W*, 1909 *E, W, I*, 1910 *S, E, I*, 1911 *E, I*, 1912 *W*
Leuvielle, M (SBUC) 1908 *W*, 1913 *S, SA, E, W*, 1914 *W, E*
Levasseur, R (SF) 1925 *W, E*
Levee, H (RCF) 1906 *NZ*
Lewis, E W (Le Havre) 1906 *E*
Libaros, G (Tarbes) 1936 *G* 1, 1940 *B*
Lira, M (La Voulte) 1962 *R*, 1963 *I, E, W, It, R*, 1964 *W, It, I, SA*, 1965 *S, I, R*
Llary, (Carcassonne) 1926 *S*
Lobies, J (RCF) 1921 *S, W, E*
Lombard, F (Narbonne) 1934 *G*, 1937 *It*
Lombarteix, R (Montferrand) 1938 *R, G* 2
Londios, J (Montauban) 1967 *SA* 3
Lorieux, A (Grenoble) 1981 *A* 1, *R, NZ* 1, 2, 1982 *W*, 1983 *A* 2, *R*, 1984 *I, W, E*
Loury, A (RCF) 1927 *E, G* 1, 2, 1928 *S, NSW, I*
Lousteau, M (Dax) 1923 *E*
Lubin-Lebrère, M-F (Toulouse) 1914 *I, W, E*, 1920 *S, E, W, I, US*, 1921 *S*, 1922 *S, E, W*, 1924 *W, US*, 1925 *I*
Lubrano, A (Béziers) 1972 *A* 2, 1973 *S*
Lux, J-P (Tyrosse, Dax) 1967 *E, It, W, I, SA* 1, 2, 4, *R*, 1968 *I, E, Cz, NZ* 3, *A, SA* 1, 2, 1969 *S, I, E*, 1970 *S, I, W, E, R*, 1971 *S, I, E, W, A* 1, 2, 1972 *S, I* 1, *E, W, I* 2, *A* 1, 2, *R*, 1973 *S, NZ, E*, 1974 *I, W, E, S, Arg* 1, 2, 1975 *W*

Maclos, P (SF) 1906 *E*, 1907 *E*
Magnanou, C (RCF) 1923 *E*, 1925 *W, E*, 1926 *S*, 1929 *S, W*, 1930 *S, I, E, W*
Magnol, L (Toulouse) 1928 *S*, 1929 *S, W, E*
Magois, H (La Rochelle) 1968 *SA* 1, 2, *R*
Majerus, R (SF) 1928 *W*, 1929 *I, S*, 1930 *S, I, E, G, W*
Malbet, J-C (Agen) 1967 *SA* 2, 4
Maleig, A (Oloron) 1979 *W, E, NZ* 2, 1980 *W, E, SA, R*
Malquier, Y (Narbonne) 1979 *S*
Manterola, T (Lourdes) 1955 *It*, 1957 *R* 1
Mantoulan, C (Pau) 1959 *I*
Marcet, J (Albi) 1925 *I, NZ, S, W, E*, 1926 *I, E*
Marchal, J-F (Lourdes) 1979 *S, R*, 1980 *W, S, I*
Marchand, R (Poitiers) 1920 *S, W*
Marot, A (Brive) 1969 *R*, 1970 *S, I, W*, 1971 *SA* 1, 1972 *I* 2, 1976 *A* 1
Marquesuzaa, A (RCF) 1958 *It, SA* 1, 2, 1959 *S, E, It, W*, 1960 *S, E, Arg* 1
Marracq, H (Pau) 1961 *R*
Martin, C (Lyon) 1909 *I*, 1910 *W, S*
Martin, H (SBUC) 1907 *E*, 1908 *W*
Martin, J-L (Béziers) 1971 *A* 2, *R*, 1972 *S, I* 1
Martin, L (Pau) 1948 *I, A, S, W, E*, 1950 *S*
Martine, R (Lourdes) 1952 *S, I, It*, 1953 *It*, 1954 *S, I, NZ, W, E, It, Arg* 2, 1955 *S, I, W*, 1958 *A, W, It, I, SA* 1, 2, 1960 *S, E, Arg* 3, 1961 *S, It*
Martinez, G (Toulouse) 1982 *W, E, S, Arg* 1, 2, 1983 *E, W*
Mas, F (Béziers) 1962 *R*, 1963 *S, I, E, W*
Maso, J (Perpignan, Narbonne) 1966 *It, R*, 1967 *S, R*, 1968 *S, W, Cz, NZ* 1, 2, 3, *A, R*, 1969 *S, I, W*, 1971 *SA* 1, 2, *R*, 1972 *E, W, A* 2, 1973 *W, I, J, R*
Massare, J (PUC) 1945 *B* 1, 2, *W*, 1946 *B, I, W*
Masse, A (SBUC) 1908 *W*, 1909 *E, W*, 1910 *W, S, E, I*
Masse, H (Grenoble) 1937 *G*
Matheu, J (Agen) 1945 *W*, 1946 *B, I, K, W*, 1947 *S, I, W, E*, 1948 *I, A, S, W, E*, 1949 *S, I, E, W, Arg* 1, 2, 1950 *E, W*, 1951 *S, I*
Mauduy, G (Périgueux) 1957 *It, R* 1, 2, 1958 *S, E*, 1961 *W, It*
Mauran, J (Castres) 1952 *SA, W, E, It*, 1953 *I, E*
Mauriat, P (Lyon) 1907 *E*, 1908 *E, W*, 1909 *W, I*, 1910 *W, S, E, I*, 1911 *S, E, W, I*, 1912 *I, S*, 1913 *S, SA, W, I*
Maurin, (ASF) 1906 *E*
Maury, A (Toulouse) 1925 *I, NZ, S, W, E*, 1926 *S, I, E*
Maysonnie, A (Toulouse) 1908 *E, W*, 1910 *W*
Menrath, (SCUF) 1910 *W*

Menthiller, Y (Romans) 1964 *W, It, SA, R,* 1965 *E*
Meret, F (Tarbes) 1940 *B*
Mericq, S (Agen) 1959 *I,* 1960 *S, E, W,* 1961 *I*
Merquey, J (Toulon) 1950 *S, I, E, W*
Mesny, P (RCF) 1979 *NZ* 1, 2, 1980 *SA, R,* 1981 *I, W* (R), *A* 1, 2, *R, NZ* 1, 2, 1982 *I, Arg* 1, 2
Meyer, S (Périgueux) 1960 *S, E, It, R, Arg* 2
Meynard, J (Cognac) 1954 *Arg* 1, 1956 *Cz*
Mias, L (Mazamet) 1951 *S, I, E, W,* 1952 *I, SA, W, E, It,* 1953 *S, I, W, It,* 1954 *S, I, NZ, W,* 1957 *R* 2, 1958 *S, E, A, W, I, SA* 1, 2, 1959 *S, It, W, I*
Milliand, P (Grenoble) 1936 *G* 2, 1937 *G, It*
Minjat, R (Lyon) 1945 *B* 1
Mir, J-H (Lourdes) 1967 *R,* 1968 *I*
Mir, J-P (Lourdes) 1967 *A*
Moga, A (Begles) 1945 *B* 1, 2, *W,* 1946 *B, I, K, W,* 1947 *S, I, W, E,* 1948 *I, A, S, W, E,* 1949 *S, I, E, W, Arg* 1, 2
Mommejat, B (Cahors) 1958 *It, I, SA* 1, 2, 1959 *S, E, It, W, I,* 1960 *S, E, I, R,* 1962 *S, E, W, I, It, R,* 1963 *S, I, W*
Moncla, F (RCF, Pau) 1956 *Cz,* 1957 *I, E, W, It, R* 1, 1958 *SA* 1, 2, 1959 *S, E, It, W, I,* 1960 *S, E, W, I, It, R, Arg* 1, 2, 3, 1961 *S, SA, E, W, It, I, NZ* 1, 2, 3
Monie, R (Perpignan) 1956 *Cz,* 1957 *E*
Monnier, R (SBUC) 1911 *I,* 1912 *S*
Monniot, M (RCF) 1912 *W, E*
Montade, A (Perpignan) 1925 *I, NZ, S, W,* 1926 *W*
Moraitis, B (Toulon) 1969 *E, W*
Morel, A (Grenoble) 1954 *Arg* 2
Morere, J (Toulouse) 1927 *E, G* 1, 1928 *S, NSW*
Mounicq, P (Toulouse) 1911 *S, E, W, I,* 1912 *I, E,* 1913 *S, SA, E*
Moure, H (SCUF) 1908 *E*
Moureu, P (Béziers) 1920 *I, US,* 1921 *W, E, I,* 1922 *S, W, I,* 1923 *S, W, E, I,* 1924 *S, I, E, W,* 1925 *E*
Mournet, A (Bagnères) 1981 *A* 1 (R)
Mouronval, F (SF) 1909 *I*
Muhr, A H (RCF) 1906 *NZ, E,* 1907 *E*
Murillo, G (Dijon) 1954 *It, Arg* 1

Namur, R (Toulon) 1931 *E, G*
Noble, J-C (La Voulte) 1968 *E, W, Cz, NZ* 3, *A, R*
Normand, A (Toulouse) 1957 *R* 1
Novès, G (Toulouse) 1977 *NZ* 1, 2, *R,* 1978 *W, R,* 1979 *I, W*

Olive, D (Montferrand) 1951 *I,* 1952 *I*
Orso, J-C (Nice) 1982 *Arg* 1, 2, 1983 *E, S, A* 1, 1984 *E* (R), *S*
Othats, J (Dax) 1960 *Arg* 2, 3

Paco, A (Béziers) 1974 *Arg* 1, 2, *R, SA* 1, 2, 1975 *W, E, Arg* 1, 2, *R,* 1976 *S, I, W, E, US, A* 1, 2, *R,* 1977 *W, E, S, I, NZ* 1, 2, *R,* 1978 *E, S, I, W, R,* 1979 *I, W, E, S,* 1980 *W*
Palat, J (Perpignan) 1938 *G* 2
Palmié, M (Béziers) 1975 *SA* 1, 2, *Arg* 1, 2, *R,* 1976 *S, I, W, E, US,* 1977 *W, E, S, I, Arg* 1, 2, *NZ* 1, 2, *R,* 1978 *E, S, I, W*
Paoli, R (SF) 1911 *I,* 1912 *I, S*
Paparemborde, R (Pau) 1975 *SA* 1, 2, *Arg* 1, 2, *R,* 1976 *S, I, W, E, US, A* 1, 2, *R,* 1977 *W, E, S, I, Arg* 1, *NZ* 1, 2, 1978 *E, S, I, W, R,* 1979 *I, W, E, S, NZ* 1, 2, *R,* 1980 *W, E, S, SA, R,* 1981 *S, I, W, E, A* 1, 2, *R, NZ* 1, 2, 1982 *W, I, R, Arg* 1, 2, 1983 *E, S, I, W*
Pardo, L (Hendaye) 1924 *I, E*
Pardo, L (Bayonne) 1980 *SA, R,* 1981 *S, I, W, E, A* 1, 1982 *W, E, S,* 1983 *A* 1 (R)
Pargade, J-H (Lyon U) 1953 *It*
Paries, L (Biarritz O) 1968 *SA* 2, *R,* 1970 *S, I, W,* 1975 *E, S, I*
Pascalin, P (Mont-de-Marsan) 1950 *I, E, W,* 1951 *S, I, E, W*
Pascarel, A (TOEC) 1912 *W, E,* 1913 *S, SA, E, I*
Pascot, J (Perpignan) 1922 *S, E, I,* 1923 *S,* 1926 *I,* 1927 *G* 2
Paul, R (Montferrand) 1940 *B*
Pauthe, G (Graulhet) 1956 *E*
Pebeyre, E (Fumel, Brive) 1945 *W,* 1946 *I, K, W,* 1947 *S, I, W, E*
Pebeyre, M (Vichy, Montferrand) 1970 *E, R,* 1971 *I, SA* 1, 2, *A* 1, 1973 *W*
Pecune, J (Tarbes) 1974 *W, E, S,* 1975 *Arg* 1, 2, *R,* 1976 *I, W, E, US*
Pedeutour, P (Begles) 1980 *I*
Pellissier, L (RCF) 1928 *NSW, I, E, G, W*
Peron, P (RCF) 1975 *SA* 1, 2
Perrier, P (Bayonne) 1982 *W, E, S, I* (R)
Pesteil, J-P (Béziers) 1975 *SA* 1, 1976 *A* 2, *R*
Petit, C (Lorrain) 1931 *W*
Peyrelade, H (Tarbes) 1940 *B*
Peyroutou, (Périgueux) 1911 *S, E*
Phliponneau, J-F (Montferrand) 1973 *W, I*
Piazza, A (Montauban) 1968 *NZ* 1, *A*
Pierrot, G (Pau) 1914 *I, W, E*
Pilon, J (Périgueux) 1949 *E,* 1950 *E*
Piqué, J (Pau) 1961 *NZ* 2, 3, *A,* 1962 *S, It,* 1964 *NZ, E, W, It, I, SA, Fj, R,* 1965 *S, I, E, W, It*
Piquemal, M (Tarbes) 1927 *I, S,* 1929 *I, G,* 1930 *S, I, E, G, W*
Piquiral, E (RCF) 1924 *S, I, E, W, R, US,* 1925 *E,* 1926 *S, I, E, W, M,* 1927 *I, S, W, E, G* 1, 2, 1928 *E*
Piteu, R (Pau) 1921 *S, W, E, I,* 1922 *S, E, W, I,* 1923 *E,* 1924 *E,* 1925 *I, NZ, W, E,* 1926 *E*
Plantefol, A (RCF) 1967 *SA* 2, 3, 4, *NZ, R,* 1968 *E, W, Cz, NZ* 2, 1969 *E, W*
Plantey, S (RCF) 1961 *A,* 1962 *It*
Podevin, G (SF) 1913 *W, I*
Poirier, G (SCUF) 1907 *E*
Pomathios, M (Agen, Lyon U, Bourg) 1948 *I, A, S, W, E,* 1949 *S, I, E, W, Arg* 1, 2, 1950 *S, I, W,* 1951 *S, I, E, W,* 1952 *W, E,* 1953 *S, I, W,* 1954 *S*
Pons, P (Toulouse) 1920 *S, E, W,* 1921 *S, W,* 1922 *S*
Porra, M (Lyon) 1931 *I*
Porthault, A (RCF) 1951 *S, E, W,* 1952 *I,* 1953 *S, I, It*
Potel, A (Begles) 1932 *G*
Poydebasque, F (Bayonne) 1914 *I, W*
Prat, J (Lourdes) 1945 *B* 1, 2, *W,* 1946 *B, I, K, W,* 1947 *S, I, W, E,* 1948 *I, A, S, W, E,* 1949 *S, I, E, W, Arg* 1, 2, 1950 *S, I, E, W,* 1951 *S, E, W,* 1952 *S, I, SA, W, E, It,* 1953 *S, I, E, W, It,* 1954 *S, I, NZ, W, E, It,* 1955 *S, I, E, W, It*
Prat, M (Lourdes) 1951 *I,* 1952 *S, I, SA, W, E,* 1953 *S, I, E,* 1954 *I, NZ, W, E, It,* 1955 *S, I, E, W, It,* 1956 *I, W, It, Cz,* 1957 *S, I, W, It, R* 1, 1958 *A, W, I*
Prevost, A (Albi) 1926 *M,* 1927 *I, S, W*
Prin-Clary, J (Cavaillon, Brive) 1945 *B* 1, 2, *W,* 1946 *B, I, K, W,* 1947 *S, I, W*
Puech, L (Toulouse) 1920 *S, E, I,* 1921 *E, I*
Puget, M (Toulouse) 1961 *It,* 1966 *S, I, It,* 1967 *SA* 1, 3, 4, *NZ,* 1968 *Cz, NZ* 1, 2, *SA* 1, 2, *R,* 1969 *E, R,* 1970 *W*
Puig, A (Perpignan) 1926 *S, E*
Pujol, T (SOE Toulouse) 1906 *NZ*

Quaglio, A (Mazamet) 1957 *R* 2, 1958 *S, E, A, W, I, SA* 1, 2, 1959 *S, E, It, W, I*
Quilis, A (Narbonne) 1967 *SA* 1, 4, *NZ,* 1970 *R,* 1971 *I*

Ramis, R (Perpignan) 1922 *E, I,* 1923 *W*
Rancoule, H (Lourdes, Toulon, Tarbes) 1955 *E, W, It,* 1958 *A, W, It, I, SA* 1, 1959 *S, It, W,* 1960 *I, It, R, Arg* 1, 2, 1961 *SA, E, W, It, NZ* 1, 2, 1962 *S, E, W, I, It*
Rapin, A (SBUC) 1938 *R*
Raymond, F (Toulouse) 1925 *S,* 1927 *W,* 1928 *I*
Raynal, F (Perpignan) 1935 *G,* 1936 *G* 1, 2, 1937 *G, It*
Raynaud, F (Carcassonne) 1933 *G*
Razat, J-P (Agen) 1962 *R,* 1963 *S, I, R*
Rebujent, R (RCF) 1963 *E*
Revallier, D (Graulhet) 1981 *S, I, W, E, A* 1, 2, *R, NZ* 1, 2, 1982 *W, S, I, R, Arg* 1
Revillon, J (RCF) 1926 *I, E,* 1927 *S*
Ribère, E (Perpignan, Quillan) 1924 *I,* 1925 *I, NZ, S,* 1926 *S, I, W, M,* 1927 *I, S, W, E, G* 1, 2, 1928 *S, NSW, I, E, G, W,* 1929 *I, E, G,* 1930 *S, I, E, W,* 1931 *I, S, W, E, G,* 1932 *G,* 1933 *G*
Rives, J-P (Toulouse, RCF) 1975 *E, S, I, Arg* 1, 2, *R,* 1976 *S, I, W, E, US, A* 1, 2, *R,* 1977 *W, E, S, I, Arg* 1, 2, *R,* 1978 *E, S, I, W, R,* 1979 *I, W, E, S, NZ* 1, 2, *R,* 1980 *W, E, S, I, SA,* 1981 *S, I, W, E, A* 2, 1982 *W, E, S, I, R,* 1983 *E, S, I, W, A* 1, 2, *R,* 1984 *I, W, E, S*
Rochon, A (Montferrand) 1936 *G* 1
Rodrigo, M (Mauléon) 1931 *I, W*
Rodriguez, L (Mont-de-Marsan) 1981 *A* 1, 2, *R, NZ* 1, 2, 1982 *W, E, S, I, R,* 1983 *E, S,* 1984 *I*

Rogé, L (Béziers) 1952 *It*, 1953 *E, W, It*, 1954 *S, Arg* 1, 2, 1955 *S, I*, 1956 *W, It, E*, 1957 *S*, 1960 *S, E*
Rollet, J (Bayonne) 1960 *Arg* 3, 1961 *NZ* 3, *A*, 1962 *It*, 1963 *I*
Romero, H (Montauban) 1962 *S, E, W, I, It, R*, 1963 *E*
Romeu, J-P (Montferrand) 1972 *R*, 1973 *S, NZ, E, W, I, R*, 1974 *W, E, S, Arg* 1, 2, *R, SA* 1, 2 (R), 1975 *W, SA* 2, *Arg* 1, 2, *R*, 1976 *S, I, W, E, US*, 1977 *W, E, S, I, Arg* 1, 2, *NZ* 1, 2, *R*
Roques, A (Cahors) 1958 *A, W, It, I, SA* 1, 2, 1959 *S, E, W, I*, 1960 *S, E, W, I, It, Arg* 1, 2, 3, 1961 *S, SA, E, W, It, I*, 1962 *S, E, W, I, It*, 1963 *S*
Roques, J-C (Brive) 1966 *S, I, It, R*
Rossignol, J-C (Brive) 1972 *A* 2
Rouan, J (Narbonne) 1953 *S, I*
Roucaries, G (Perpignan) 1956 *S*
Rouffia, L (Narbonne) 1945 *B* 2, *W*, 1946 *W*, 1948 *I*
Rougerie, J (Montferrand) 1973 *J*
Roujas, R (Tarbes) 1910 *I*
Rousie, M (Villeneuve) 1931 *S, G*, 1932 *G*, 1933 *G*
Rousset, G (Béziers) 1975 *SA* 1, 1976 *US*
Ruiz, A (Tarbes) 1968 *SA* 2, *R*
Rupert, J-J (Tyrosse) 1963 *R*, 1964 *S, Fj*, 1965 *E, W, It*, 1966 *S, I, E, W, It*, 1967 *It, R*, 1968 *S*

Sagot, R (SF) 1906 *NZ*, 1908 *E*, 1909 *W*
Sahuc, A (Métro) 1945 *B* 1, 2
Sahuc, F (Toulouse) 1936 *G* 2
Saisset, O (Béziers) 1971 *R*, 1972 *S, I* 1, *A* 1, 2, 1973 *S, NZ, E, W, I, J, R*, 1974 *I, Arg* 2, *SA* 1, 2, 1975 *W*
Salas, P (Narbonne) 1979 *NZ* 1, 2, *R*, 1980 *W, E*, 1981 *A* 1, 1982 *Arg* 2
Salinie, R (Perpignan) 1923 *E*
Sallefranque, M (Dax) 1981 *A* 2, 1982 *W, E, S*
Salut, J (TOEC) 1966 *R*, 1967 *S*, 1968 *I, E, Cz, NZ* 1, 1969 *I*
Samatan, R (Agen) 1930 *S, I, E, G, W*, 1931 *I, S, W, E, G*
Sanac, A (Perpignan) 1952 *It*, 1953 *S, I*, 1954 *E*, 1956 *Cz*, 1957 *S, I, E, W, It*
Sangalli, F (Narbonne) 1975 *I, SA* 1, 2, 1976 *S, A* 1, 2, *R*, 1977 *W, E, S, I, Arg* 1, 2, *NZ* 1, 2
Sappa, M (Nice) 1973 *J, R*, 1977 *R*
Sarrade, R (Pau) 1929 *I*
Saux, J-P (Pau) 1960 *W, It, Arg* 1, 2, 1961 *SA, E, W, It, I, NZ* 1, 2, 3, *A*, 1962 *S, E, W, I, It*, 1963 *S, I, E, It*
Savitsky, M (La Voulte) 1969 *R*
Savy, M (Montferrand) 1931 *I, S, W, E*, 1936 *G* 1
Sayrou, J (Perpignan) 1926 *W, M*, 1928 *E, G, W*, 1929 *S, W, E, G*
Scohy, R (BEC) 1931 *S, W, E, G*
Sébedio, J (Tarbes) 1913 *S, E*, 1914 *I*, 1920 *S, I, US*, 1922 *S, E*, 1923 *S*
Seguier, N (Béziers) 1973 *J, R*
Sella, P (Agen) 1982 *R, Arg* 1, 2, 1983 *E, S, I, W, A* 1, 2, *R*, 1984 *I, W, E, S*
Semmartin, J (SCUF) 1913 *W, I*
Senal, G (Béziers) 1974 *Arg* 1, 2, *R, SA* 1, 2, 1975 *W*
Sentilles, J (Tarbes) 1912 *W, E*, 1913 *S, SA*
Serin, L (Béziers) 1928 *E*, 1929 *W, E, G*, 1930 *S, I, E, G, W*, 1931 *I, W, E*
Serre, P (Perpignan) 1920 *S, E*
Servole, L (Toulon) 1931 *I, S, W, E, G*, 1934 *G*, 1935 *G*
Sicart, N (Perpignan) 1922 *I*
Sillières, J (Tarbes) 1968 *R*, 1970 *S, I*, 1971 *S, I, E*, 1972 *E, W*
Siman, M (Montferrand) 1948 *E*, 1949 *S*, 1950 *S, I, E, W*
Sitjar, M (Agen) 1964 *W, It, I, R*, 1965 *It, R*, 1967 *A, E, It, W, I, SA* 1, 2
Skréla, J-C (Toulouse) 1971 *SA* 2, *A* 1, 2, 1972 *I* 1 (R), *E, W, I* 2, *A* 1, 1973 *W, J, R*, 1974 *W, E, S, Arg* 1, *R*, 1975 *W* (R), *E, S, I, SA* 1, 2, *Arg* 1, 2, *R*, 1976 *S, I, W, E, US, A* 1, 2, *R*, 1977 *W, E, S, I, Arg* 1, 2, *NZ* 1, 2, *R*, 1978 *E, S, I, W*
Soler, (Quillan) 1929 *G*
Soro, R (Lourdes, Romans) 1945 *B* 1, 2, *W*, 1946 *B, I, K*, 1947 *S, I, W, E*, 1948 *I, A, S, W, E*, 1949 *S, I, E, W, Arg* 1, 2
Sorrondo, M (Montauban) 1946 *K*, 1947 *S, I, W, E*, 1948 *I*
Soulié, E (CASG) 1920 *E, I, US*, 1921 *S, E, I*, 1922 *E, W, I*
Sourgens, J (Begles) 1926 *M*
Spanghero, C (Narbonne) 1971 *E, W, SA* 1, 2, *A* 1, 2, *R*, 1972 *S, E, W, I* 2, *A* 1, 2, 1974 *I, W, E, S, R, SA* 1, 1975 *E, S, I*
Spanghero, W (Narbonne) 1964 *SA, Fj, R*, 1965 *S, I, E, W, It, R*, 1966 *S, I, E, W, It, R*, 1967 *S, A, E, SA* 1, 2, 3, 4, *NZ*, 1968 *S, I, E, W, NZ* 1, 2, 3, *A, SA* 1, 2, *R*, 1969 *S, I, W*, 1970 *R*, 1971 *E, W, SA* 1, 1972 *E, I* 2, *A* 1, 2, *R*, 1973 *S, NZ, E, W, I*
Stener, G (PUC) 1956 *S, I, E*, 1958 *SA* 1, 2
Struxiano, P (Toulouse) 1913 *W, I*, 1920 *S, E, W, I, US*
Sutra, G (Narbonne) 1967 *SA* 2, 1969 *W*, 1970 *S, I*
Swierczinski, C (Begles) 1969 *E*, 1977 *Arg* 2

Taffary, M (RCF) 1975 *W, E, S, I*
Taillantou, J (Pau) 1930 *I, G, W*
Tarricq, P (Lourdes) 1958 *A, W, It, I*
Tavernier, (Toulouse) 1913 *I*
Terreau, M (Bourg) 1945 *W*, 1946 *B, I, K, W*, 1947 *S, I, W, E*, 1948 *I, A, W, E*, 1949 *S, Arg* 1, 2, 1951 *S*
Theuriet, A (SCUF) 1909 *E, W*, 1910 *S*, 1911 *W*, 1913 *E*
Thevenot, G (SCUF) 1910 *W, E, I*
Thierry, R (RCF) 1920 *S, E, W, US*
Thiers, P (Montferrand) 1936 *G* 1, 2, 1937 *G, It*, 1938 *G* 1, 2, 1940 *B*, 1945 *B* 1, 2
Thil, P (Nantes) 1912 *W, E*, 1913 *S, SA, E, W*
Tignol, P (Toulouse) 1953 *S, I*
Torreilles, S (Perpignan) 1956 *S*
Tourte, R (St Girons) 1940 *B*
Trillo, J (Begles) 1967 *SA* 3, 4, *NZ, R*, 1968 *S, I, NZ* 1, 2, 3, *A*, 1969 *I, E, W, R*, 1970 *E, R*, 1971 *S, I, SA* 1, 2, *A* 1, 2, 1972 *S, A* 1, 2, *R*, 1973 *S, E*
Triviaux, R (Cognac) 1931 *E, G*
Tucoo-Chalat, M (PUC) 1940 *B*

Ugartemendia, J-L (St Jean-de-Luz) 1975 *S, I*

Vaills, G (Perpignan) 1928 *NSW*, 1929 *G*
Vallot, E (SCUF) 1912 *S*
Vannier, M (RCF, Chalon) 1953 *W*, 1954 *S, I, Arg* 1, 2, 1955 *S, I, E, W, It*, 1956 *S, I, W, It, E*, 1957 *S, I, E, W, It, R* 1, 2, 1958 *S, E, A, W, It, I*, 1960 *S, E, W, I, It, R, Arg* 1, 3, 1961 *SA, E, W, It, I, NZ* 1, *A*
Vaquer, F (Perpignan) 1921 *S, W*, 1922 *W*
Vaquerin, A (Béziers) 1971 *R*, 1972 *S, I* 1, *A* 1, 1973 *S*, 1974 *W, E, S, Arg* 1, 2, *R, SA* 1, 2, 1975 *W, E, S, I*, 1976 *US, A* 1 (R), 2, *R*, 1977 *Arg* 2, 1979 *W, E*, 1980 *S, I*
Vareilles, C (SF) 1907 *E*, 1908 *E, W*, 1910 *S, E*
Varenne, F (RCF) 1952 *S*
Varvier, T (RCF) 1906 *E*, 1909 *E, W*, 1911 *E, W*, 1912 *I*
Vassal, G (Carcassonne) 1938 *R, G* 2
Vaysse, J (Albi) 1924 *US*, 1926 *M*
Vellat, E (Grenoble) 1927 *I, E, G* 1, 2, 1928 *NSW*
Verger, A (SF) 1927 *W, E, G* 1, 1928 *I, E, G, W*
Verges, (SF) 1906 *NZ, E*, 1907 *E*
Viard, G (Narbonne) 1969 *W*, 1970 *S, R*, 1971 *S, I*
Vigerie, M (Agen) 1931 *W*
Vigier, R (Montferrand) 1956 *S, W, It, E, Cz*, 1957 *S, E, W, It, R* 1, 2, 1958 *S, E, A, W, It, I, SA* 1, 2, 1959 *S, E, It, W, I*
Vigneau, A (Bayonne) 1935 *G*
Vignes, C (RCF) 1957 *R* 1, 2, 1958 *S, E*
Villa, E (Tarbes) 1926 *M*
Villagra, J (Vienne) 1945 *B* 2
Villepreux, P (Toulouse) 1967 *It, I, SA* 2, *NZ*, 1968 *I, Cz, NZ* 1, 2, 3, *A*, 1969 *S, I, E, W, R*, 1970 *S, I, W, E, R*, 1971 *S, I, E, W, A* 1, 2, *R*, 1972 *S, I* 1, *E, W, I* 2, *A* 1, 2
Viviès, B (Agen) 1978 *E, S, I, W*, 1980 *SA, R*, 1981 *S, A* 1, 1983 *A* 1 (R)
Volot, M (SF) 1945 *W*, 1946 *B, I, K, W*

Wolff, J-P (Béziers) 1980 *SA, R*, 1981 *A* 2, 1982 *E*

Yachvili, M (Tulle, Brive) 1968 *E, W, Cz, NZ* 3, *A, R*, 1969 *S, I, R*, 1971 *E, SA* 1, 2, *A* 1, 1972 *R*, 1975 *SA* 2

Zago, F (Montauban) 1963 *I, E*

FRENCH INTERNATIONAL RECORDS

From 1890-91, when uniform points-scoring was first adopted by International Board countries, to 30 April 1984. Both team and individual records are against International Board countries only, unless otherwise stated.

TEAM RECORDS

Highest score
37 v England (37-12) 1972 Colombes (Paris)
v individual countries
37 v England (37-12) 1972 Colombes
23 v Scotland (23-3) 1977 Parc des Princes (Paris)
27 v Ireland (27-6) 1964 Colombes
22 v Wales (22-13) 1965 Colombes
24 v N Zealand (24-19) 1979 Auckland
25 v S Africa (25-38) 1975 Bloemfontein
34 v Australia (34-6) 1976 Parc des Princes

Biggest winning points margin
28 v Australia (34-6) 1976 Parc des Princes
v individual countries
25 v England (37-12) 1972 Colombes
20 v Scotland (23-3) 1977 Parc des Princes
23 v Ireland (26-3) 1976 Parc des Princes
10 v Wales (16-6) 1958 Cardiff
7 v N Zealand (13-6) 1973 Parc des Princes
5 v S Africa (19-14) 1967 Johannesburg
28 v Australia (34-6) 1976 Parc des Princes

Highest score by opposing team
49 Wales (14-49) 1910 Swansea
S Africa beat 'France' 55-6 at Parc des Princes on 3 January 1907, but it is not regarded as an official international match
by individual countries
41 England (13-41) 1907 Richmond
31 Scotland (3-31) 1912 Inverleith (Edinburgh)
25 Ireland { (5-25) 1911 Cork; (6-25) 1975 Dublin }
49 Wales (14-49) 1910 Swansea
38 N Zealand (8-38) 1906 Parc des Princes
38 S Africa { (5-38) 1913 Bordeaux; (25-38) 1975 Bloemfontein }
24 Australia (14-24) 1981 Sydney

Biggest losing points margin
42 v Wales (5-47) 1909 Colombes
The 6-55 defeat by S Africa in Paris in 1907 is regarded as unofficial
v individual countries
37 v England (0-37) 1911 Twickenham
28 v Scotland (3-31) 1912 Inverleith
24 v Ireland (0-24) 1913 Cork
42 v Wales (5-47) 1909 Colombes
30 v N Zealand (8-38) 1906 Parc des Princes
33 v S Africa (5-38) 1913 Bordeaux
10 v Australia (14-24) 1981 Sydney

Most points by France in International Championship in a season – 90
(in season 1983-84)

Most tries by France in International Championship in a season – 13
(in season 1975-76)

Most tries by France in an international
6 {
v Ireland (27-6) 1964 Colombes
v England (35-13) 1970 Colombes
v England (37-12) 1972 Colombes
v England (30-9) 1976 Parc des Princes
v Australia (34-6) 1976 Parc des Princes
}

Most tries against France in an international
11 by Wales (5-47) 1909 Colombes
S Africa's 13 tries in the 1907 match in Paris are regarded as unofficial

Most points on a tour (all matches)
282 in South Africa (11 matches) 1975

INDIVIDUAL RECORDS

Most capped player
R Bertranne 52 1971-81
in individual positions
Full-back
M Vannier 30 1953-61
Wing
J Dupuy 28 1956-64
C Darrouy 28 1957-67
Centre
R Bertranne 39(52)* 1971-81
Fly-half
P Albaladejo 23(24)† 1954-64
Scrum-half
G Dufau 33 1948-57
Prop
R Paparemborde 42 1975-83
Hooker
P Dintrans 26 1979-84
Lock
E Cester 30** 1966-74
Flanker
J-P Rives 47‡ 1975-84
No 8
G Basquet 26†† 1947-52

**Bertranne played 13 times on the wing*
†Albaladejo won his first cap at full-back
***B Dauga, 50 caps, won 29 as lock and 21 at No 8*
M Celaya, 35 caps, won 18 as lock, 15 at No 8, and 2 as flanker
‡M Crauste, 43 caps, won 39 as flanker, 4 at No 8
††W Spanghero, 42 caps, won 21 at No 8, 16 at lock and 5 as flanker. J-L Joinel, 31 caps, has won 17 as flanker and 14 at No 8

Most internationals as captain – 30*
J-P Rives 1979-84
**Excludes 4 games as captain in official French internationals against non-IB teams*

Most points in internationals – 139
J-P Romeu (22 appearances) 1973-77

Most points in an international – 17
G Camberabero v Australia 1967 Colombes
J-P Lescarboura v Ireland 1984 Paris
J-P Lescarboura v Wales 1984 Cardiff

Most tries in internationals – 14
C Darrouy (28 appearances) 1957-67

Most tries in an international – 3
M Crauste v England 1962 Colombes
C Darrouy v Ireland 1963 Dublin

Most conversions in an international – 5
P Villepreux v England 1972 Paris

Most points in International Championship in a season – 54
J-P Lescarboura (4 appearances) 1983-84

Most tries in International Championship in a season – 5
P Estève (4 appearances) 1982-83
Estève scored in each championship match, a feat performed only twice before: by A C Wallace of Scotland in 1925, and by H C Catcheside of England in 1924

Most conversions in International Championship in a season – 7
P Villepreux (4 appearances) 1971-72

Most penalty goals in International Championship in a season – 10
J-P Lescarboura (4 appearances) 1983-84

Most points on overseas tour – 71
J-P Romeu (7 appearances) 1975 S Africa

Most points in any match on tour – 19
J L Dehez v SW Districts (SA) 1967 George

Most tries in any match on tour – 4
R Bertranne v W Transvaal 1971 Potchefstroom
M Bruel v Australian Capital Territory 1981 Canberra

THE 1983 SEASON IN SOUTH AFRICA

Reg Sweet

It was entirely fitting that Western Province should host the prime event of the 1983 South African season, the match at Newlands, Cape Town, against the Invitation Centenary XV. This was the true climax of 1983, the season in which Western Province became the first of the provincial Unions to reach its centenary.

Circumstances had made the visit of the Centenary XV an even more significant event than it would otherwise have been. By government decree in Paris, Albert Ferrasse, the FFR President, had been denied the right to send the national team to South Africa. However, in the event French players were not prevented from accepting for the Centenary XV, and they formed an important component of that side.

The three-match tour set an impressive seal on the Western Province celebrations. Under the management of Ireland's Syd Millar and coached by the former All Black mentor Ivan Vodanovich, the Centenary side included seven All Blacks fresh from their home series with the British Lions.

It assembled as follows: Stu Wilson, Bernie Fraser, Steve Pokere, Gary Knight, John Ashworth, Mark Shaw, Gary Whetton (New Zealand), Jerome Gallion, Jean-Patrick Lescarboura, Roland Bertranne, Jean-Baptiste Lafond, Robert Paparemborde (France), Billy James, John Perkins, Richard Moriarty, Gareth Davies, Mark Ring (Wales), Peter Wheeler, Mike Slemen, Les Cusworth, Nick Youngs (England), John Murphy, Willie Duggan (Ireland), and David Leslie (Scotland).

There were inevitable problems, as there must be with invitation sides; yet coach Vodanovich achieved a degree of teamwork within a couple of days that could only be marvelled at – notably in the cohesion and drive of a splendid pack, making possible as it did a feast of mobile rugby. Unhappily Stuart Wilson, attempting to start the tour where he had left off against the Lions a week earlier with his record-breaking Eden Park display, damaged a rib in the opening game and could not play again.

The Centenary XV beat Natal 30-23 at King's Park, Durban, lost 22-17 to Western Province at Newlands, Cape Town after holding the lead six minutes from the end, and finally went down 37-35 to the SA Board President's XV at Newlands after leading at half-time. The margin was seven tries to five. As it happened, the SA selectors named a side for the final match which may not have differed in more than a couple of positions from a Springbok XV on the season's form. Uncapped players selected were the Federation and Western Province centre Wilfred Cupido, lock forward Rudi Visagie of Orange Free State and No 8 Jannie Breedt, of Northern Transvaal. There was a late change when the injured Danie Gerber was replaced at centre by John Villet of

Western Province. Significantly Errol Tobias, 1981 Springbok against Ireland and in New Zealand, was named at fly-half with the controversial Naas Botha already overseas, preparing to start his new career as a 'gridiron' player in America.

To cap their season of celebration, Western Province retained the Currie Cup with a 9-3 victory over Northern Transvaal in the final at Pretoria. Not to put too fine a point on it, both sides had performed better by far when they contested the 1982 final. The 1983 final lacked imagination, finesse and other qualities.

The lesser competitions produced new winners. Stellenbosch University lost their Toyota national club championship at Easter, failing for the first time to reach the final after winning the event six times in the previous eight years. Western Province had one last effort to make in their centenary season, and they wound it up with a flourish at King's Park in Durban, winning the Elastoplast National Sevens title, in its second year, by beating Transvaal 14-12 in the final.

New on the South African scene was the inter-provincial Lion Cup knock-out, sponsored by SA Breweries. It produced some extraordinary results, including the elimination of Western Province and Northern Transvaal (Province by a completely unfancied side, South-Eastern Transvaal), before Free State won the final 24-12 against Transvaal at Ellis Park, Johannesburg.

Visitors to South Africa included Chile, on their first such tour, and a club side from West Germany. A multi-racial team sponsored by the Chamber of Mines made its second tour to the USA, and a South African Schools team's visit to Wales at the year's end went off so well that there are high hopes that a reciprocal tour may be arranged.

Final placings in the 1983 Currie Cup competition were:

Section A	*P*	*W*	*D*	*L*	*F*	*A*	*Pts*
Western Province	10	8	1	1	276	131	17
Northern Transvaal	10	7	1	2	233	144	15
Orange Free State	10	5	1	4	252	218	11
Transvaal	10	4	1	5	235	182	9
Eastern Province	10	4	0	6	203	227	8
Eastern Transvaal	10	0	0	10	106	403	0

Section B	*P*	*W*	*D*	*L*	*F*	*A*	*Pts*
Northern OFS	10	9	0	1	193	115	18
Natal	10	7	0	3	191	152	14
Griqualand West	10	6	0	4	210	171	12
Western Transvaal	10	5	0	5	187	147	10
Boland	10	2	0	8	140	184	4
South-Western Districts	10	1	0	9	122	274	2

Semi-finals
Natal 3, Western Province 7; Northern Transvaal 32, Northern OFS 15
FINAL (at Loftus Versfeld, Pretoria)
Northern Transvaal 3, Western Province 9

SOUTH AFRICAN INTERNATIONAL PLAYERS *(up to 30 April 1984)*

ABBREVIATIONS

A	Australia
BI	British Isles teams
E	England
F	France
I	Ireland
NZ	New Zealand
S	Scotland
S Am	South America
US	United States of America
W	Wales
Wld	World Invitation XV
(T)	Tour to Northern Hemisphere
(ST)	Short overseas tour
(R)	Replacement—(2[1R]) denotes two appearances, one as a replacement

Ackermann, D S P (Western Province) 1955 *BI* (3), 1956 *A* (2), *NZ* (2), 1958 *F*
Albertyn, P K (South Western Districts) 1924 *BI* (4)
Alexander, E (Griqualand West) 1891 *BI* (2)
Allen, PB (Eastern Province) 1960 *S*
Allport, P (Western Province) 1910 *BI* (2)
Anderson, J A (Western Province) 1903 *BI*
Anderson, J H (Western Province), 1896 *BI* (3)
Andrew, J B (Transvaal) 1896 *BI*
Antelme, M J G (Transvaal) 1960 *NZ* (4), 1960-61 (T) *F*
Apsey, J T (Western Province) 1933 *A* (2), 1938 *BI*
Ashley, S (Western Province) 1903 *BI*
Aston, F T D (Transvaal) 1896 *BI* (4)
Aucamp, J (Western Transvaal) 1924 *BI* (2)

Baard, A P (Western Province) 1960-61 (T) *I*
Babrow, L (Western Province) 1937 *A* (2), *NZ* (3)
Barnard, J H (Transvaal) 1964-65 (ST) *S*, 1965 *A* (2), *NZ* (2)
Barnard, R W (Transvaal) 1970 *NZ* (R)
Barnard, W H M (Northern Transvaal) 1949 *NZ*, 1951-52 (T) *W*
Barry, J (Western Province) 1903 *BI* (3)
Bastard, W E (Natal) 1937 *A*, *NZ* (3), 1938 *BI* (2)
Bates, A J (Western Transvaal) 1969-70 (T) *E*, 1970 *NZ* (2), 1972 *E*
Bayvel, P C R (Transvaal) 1974 *BI* (2), 1974 (ST) *F* (2), 1975 *F* (2), 1976 *NZ* (4)
Beck, J J (Western Province) 1981 *NZ* (2[2R]), *US*
Bedford, T P (Natal) 1963 *A* (4), 1964 *W*, *F*, 1964-65 (ST) *I*, 1965 *A* (2), 1968 *BI* (4), 1968-69 (ST) *F* (2), 1969 *A* (4), 1969-70 (T) *S*, *E*, *I*, *W*, 1971 *F* (2)
Bekker, H J (Western Province) 1981 *NZ* (2)
Bekker, H P J (Northern Transvaal) 1951-52 (T) *E*, *F*, 1953 *A* (4), 1955 *BI* (3), 1956 *A* (2), *NZ* (4)
Bekker, M J (Northern Transvaal) 1960 *S*
Bekker, R P (Northern Transvaal) 1953 *A* (2)
Bergh, W F (South Western Districts) 1931-32 (T) *W*, *I*, *E*, *S*, 1933 *A* (5), 1937 *A* (2), *NZ* (3), 1938 *BI* (3)
Bestbier, A (Orange Free State) 1974 (ST) *F* (R)
Bester, J J N (Western Province) 1924 *BI* (2)
Bester, J L A (Western Province) 1938 *BI* (2)
Beswick, A M (Border), 1896 *BI* (3)
Bezuidenhoudt, C E (Northern Transvaal) 1962 *BI* (3)
Bezuidenhoudt, N S E (Northern Transvaal) 1972 *E* 1974 *BI* (3), 1974 (ST) *F* (2), 1975 *F* (2), 1977 Wld
Bierman, J N (Transvaal) 1931-32 (T) *I*
Bisset, W M (Western Province) 1891 *BI* (2)
Blair, R (Western Province) 1977 Wld
Bosch, G R (Transvaal) 1974 *BI*, 1974 (ST) *F* (2), 1975 *F* (2), 1976 *NZ* (4)
Bosman, N J S (Transvaal) 1924 *BI* (3)
Botha, D S (Northern Transvaal) 1981 *NZ*
Botha, H E (Northern Transvaal) 1980 *S Am* (2), *BI* (4), *S Am* (ST) (2), *F*, 1981 *I* (2), *NZ* (3), *US*, 1982 *S Am* (2)
Botha, J (Transvaal) 1903 *BI*
Botha, J P F (Northern Transvaal) 1962 *BI* (3)
Botha, P H (Transvaal) 1965 *A* (2)
Boyes, H C (Griqualand West) 1891 *BI* (2)
Brand, G H (Western Province) 1928 *NZ* (2), 1931-32 (T) *W*, *I*, *E*, *S*, 1933 *A* (5), 1937 *A* (2), *NZ* (2), 1938 *BI*
Bredenkamp, M (Griqualand West) 1896 *BI* (2)
Brewis, J D (Northern Transvaal) 1949 *NZ* (4) 1951-52 (T) *S*, *I*, *W*, *E*, *F*, 1953 *A*
Briers, T P D (Western Province) 1955 *BI* (4), 1956 *NZ* (3)
Brink, D J (Western Province) 1906-07 (T) *S*, *W*, *E*,
Brooks, D (Border) 1906-07 (T) *S*
Brown, C (Western Province) 1903 *BI* (3)
Brynard, G S (Western Province) 1965 *A*, *NZ* (4) 1968 *BI* (2)
Buchler, J U (Transvaal) 1951-52 (T) *S*, *I*, *W*, *E*, *F*, 1953 *A* (4), 1956 *A*
Burdett, A F (Western Province) 1906-07 (T) *S*, *I*
Burger, M B (Northern Transvaal) 1980 *BI* (R), (ST) *S Am*, 1981 *US* (R)
Burger, W A G (Border), 1906-07 (T) *S*, *I*, *W*, 1910 *BI*

Carelse, G (Eastern Province) 1964 *W*, *F*, 1964-65 (ST) *I*, *S*, 1967 *F* (3), 1968-69 (ST) *F* (2), 1969 *A* (4), 1969-70 (T) *S*
Carlson, R A (Western Province) 1972 *E*
Carolin, H W (Western Province) 1903 *BI*, 1906-07 (T) *S*, *I*
Castens, H H (Western Province) 1891 *BI*
Chignell, T W (Western Province) 1891 *BI*
Cilliers, G D (Orange Free State) 1963 *A* (3)
Claassen, J T (Western Transvaal) 1955 *BI* (4), 1956 *A* (2), *NZ* (4), 1958 *F* (2), 1960 *S*, *NZ* (3), 1960-61 (T) *W*, *I*, *E*, *S*, *F*, 1961 *I*, *A* (2), 1962 *BI* (4)
Claassen, W (Natal) 1981 *I* (2), *NZ* (2), *US*, 1982 *S Am* (2)
Clark, W H (Transvaal) 1933 *A*
Clarkson, W A (Natal) 1921 *NZ* (2), 1924 *BI*
Cloete, H A (Western Province), 1896 *BI*
Cockrell, C H (Western Province) 1969-70 (T) *S*, *I*, *W*
Cockrell, R J (Western Province) 1974 (ST) *F* (2), 1975 *F* (2), 1976 *NZ* (2), 1977 Wld, 1981 *NZ* (3[1R]), *US*
Coetzee, J H H (Western Province) 1974 *BI*, 1975 *F* (R), 1976 *NZ* (4)
Cope, D (Transvaal) 1896 *BI*
Cotty, W (Griqualand West) 1896 *BI*
Crampton, G (Griqualand West) 1903 *BI*
Craven, D H (Western Province) 1931-32 (T) *W*, *I*, *S*, 1933 *A* (5), 1937 *A* (2), *NZ* (3), 1938 *BI* (3)
Cronje, P A (Transvaal) 1971 *F* (2), *A* (3), 1974 *BI* (2)
Crosby, J H (Transvaal) 1896 *BI*
Crosby, N (Transvaal) 1910 *BI* (2)
Currie, C (Griqualand West) 1903 *BI*

D'Alton, G (Western Province) 1933 *A*
Daneel, G M (Western Province) 1928 *NZ* (4), 1931-32 (T) *W*, *I*, *E*, *S*
Daneel, H J (Western Province) 1906-07 (T) *S*, *I*, *W*, *E*
Davidson, M (Eastern Province) 1910 *BI*
De Bruyn, J (Orange Free State) 1974 *BI*

De Jongh, H P K (Western Province) 1928, *NZ*
De Klerk, I J (Transvaal) 1969-70 (T) *E, I, W*
De Klerk, K B H (Transvaal) 1974 *BI* (3[1R]), 1975 *F* (2), 1976 *NZ* (3[1R]), 1980 *S Am* (2), *BI* 1981 *I* (2)
De Kock, A (Griqualand West) 1891 *BI*
De Kock, J S (Western Province) 1921 *NZ*, 1924 *BI*
Delport, W H (Eastern Province) 1951-52 (T) *S, I, W, E, F*, 1953 *A* (4)
De Melker, S C (Griqualand West) 1903 *BI*, 1906-07 (T) *E*
Devenish, C (Griqualand West) 1896 *BI*
Devenish, G St L (Transvaal) 1896 *BI*
Devenish, M (Transvaal) 1891 *BI*
De Villiers, D I (Transvaal) 1910 *BI* (3)
De Villiers, D J (Western Province) 1962 *BI* (2), 1964-65 (ST) *I*, 1965 *NZ* (3), 1967 *F* (4), 1968 *BI* (4), 1968-69 (ST) *F* (2), 1969 *A* (2), 1969-70 (T) *E, I, W*, 1970 *NZ* (4)
De Villiers, H A (Western Province) 1906-07 (T) *S, W, E*
De Villiers, H O (Western Province) 1967 *F* (4), 1968-69 (ST) *F* (2), 1969 *A* (4), 1969-70 (T) *S, E, I, W*
De Villiers, P du P (Western Province) 1928 *NZ* (3), 1931-32 (T) *E*, 1933 *A*, 1937 *A* (2), *NZ*
Devine, D (Transvaal) 1924 *BI*, 1928 *NZ*
De Vos, D J J (Western Province) 1964-65 (ST) *S*, 1969 *A*, 1969-70 (T) *S*
De Waal, A N (Western Province) 1967 *F* (4)
De Waal, P (Western Province) 1896 *BI*
De Wet, A E (Western Province) 1969 *A* (2), 1969-70 (T) *E*
De Wet, P (Western Province) 1938 *BI* (3)
Dinkelmann, E E (Northern Transvaal) 1951-52 (T) *S, I, E, F*, 1953 *A* (2)
Dirksen, C W (Northern Transvaal) 1963 *A*, 1964 *W*, 1964-65 (ST) *I, S*, 1967 *F* (4), 1968 *BI* (2)
Dobbin, F J (Griqualand West) 1903 *BI* (2), 1906-07 (T) *S, W, E*, 1910 *BI*, 1912-13 (T) *S, I, W*
Dobie, J A R (Transvaal) 1928 *NZ*
Dormehl, P J (Western Province) 1896 *BI* (2)
Douglass, F W (Eastern Province) 1896 *BI*
Dryburgh, R G (Western Province) 1955 *BI* (3), 1956 *A, NZ* (2), 1960 *NZ* (2)
Duff, B (Western Province) 1891 *BI* (3)
Duffy, B A (Border) 1928 *NZ*
Du Plessis, C J (Western Province) 1982 *S Am* (2)
Du Plessis, D C (Northern Transvaal) 1977 Wld, 1980 *S Am*
Du Plessis, F (Transvaal) 1949 *NZ* (3)
Du Plessis, M (Western Province) 1971 *A* (3), 1974 *BI* (2), 1974 (ST) *F* (2), 1975 *F* (2), 1976 *NZ* (4), 1977 Wld, 1980 *S Am* (2), *BI* (4), *S Am* (ST), *F*
Du Plessis, N J (Western Transvaal) 1921 *NZ* (2), 1924 *BI* (3)
Du Plessis, P G (Northern Transvaal) 1972 *E*
Du Plessis, T D (Northern Transvaal) 1980 *S Am* (2)
Du Plessis, W (Western Province) 1980 *S Am* (2), *BI* (4), *S Am* (ST) (2), *F*, 1981 *NZ* (3), 1982 *S Am* (2)
Du Plooy, A J J (Eastern Province) 1955 *BI*
Du Preez, F C H (Northern Transvaal) 1960-61 (T) *E, S*, 1961 *A* (2), 1962 *BI* (4), 1963 *A*, 1964 *W, F*, 1965 *A* (2), *NZ* (4), 1967 *F*, 1968 *BI* (4), 1968-69 (ST) *F* (2), 1969 *A* (2), 1969-70 (T) *S, I, W*, 1970 *NZ* (4), 1971 *F* (2), *A* (3)
Du Preez, J G H (Western Province) 1956 *NZ*
Du Rand, J A (Rhodesia, Northern Transvaal) 1949 *NZ* (2), 1951-52 (T) *S, I, W, E, F*, 1953 *A* (4), 1955 *BI* (4), 1956 *A* (2), *NZ* (4)
Du Toit, A F (Western Province) 1928 *NZ* (2)
Du Toit, B A (Transvaal) 1938 *BI* (3)
Du Toit, P A (Northern Transvaal) 1949 *NZ* (3), 1951-52 (T) *S, I, W, E, F*
Du Toit, P G (Western Province) 1981 *NZ*, 1982 *S Am* (2)
Du Toit, P S (Western Province) 1958 *F* (2), 1960 *NZ* (4), 1960-61 (T) *W, I, E, S, F*, 1961 *I, A* (2)
Duvenage, F P (Griqualand West) 1949 *NZ* (2)

Edwards, P (Northern Transvaal) 1980 *S Am* (2)
Ellis, J H (South West Africa) 1965 *NZ* (4), 1967 *F* (4), 1968 *BI* (4), 1968-69 (ST) *F* (2), 1969 *A* (4), 1969-70 (T) *S, I, W*, 1970 *NZ* (4), 1971 *F* (2), *A* (3), 1972 *E*, 1974 *BI* (4), 1974 (ST) *F* (2), 1976 *NZ*
Ellis, M (Transvaal) 1921 *NZ* (2), 1924 *BI* (4)
Engelbrecht, J P (Western Province) 1960 *S*, 1960-61 (T) *W, I, E, S, F*, 1961 *A* (2), 1962 *BI* (3), 1963 *A* (2), 1964 *W, F*, 1964-65 (ST) *I, S*, 1965 *A* (2), *NZ* (4), 1967 *F* (4), 1968 *BI* (2), 1968-69 (ST) *F* (2), 1969 *A* (2)
Etlinger, T E (Western Province) 1896 *BI*

Ferris, H H (Transvaal) 1903 *BI*
Forbes, H H (Transvaal) 1896 *BI*
Fourie, C (Eastern Province) 1974 (ST) *F* (2), 1975 *F* (2)
Fourie, T T (South-East Transvaal) 1974 *BI*
Fourie, W L (South-West Africa) 1958 *F* (2)
Francis, J A J (Transvaal) 1912-13 (T) *S, I, W, E, F*
Frederickson, C A (Transvaal) 1974 *BI*, 1980 *S Am* (2)
Frew, A (Transvaal) 1903 *BI*
Froneman, D C (Orange Free State) 1977 Wld
Froneman, I L (Border) 1933 *A*
Fry, S P (Western Province) 1951-52 (T) *S, I, W, E, F*, 1953 *A* (4), 1955 *BI* (4)

Gage, J H (Orange Free State) 1933 *A*
Gainsford, J L (Western Province) 1960 *S, NZ* (4) 1960-61 (T) *W, I, E, S, F*, 1961 *A* (2), 1962 *BI* (4) 1963 *A* (4), 1964 *W, F*, 1964-65 (ST) *I, S*, 1965 *A* (2), *NZ* (4), 1967 *F* (3)
Geel, P J (Orange Free State) 1949 *NZ*
Geere, V (Transvaal) 1933 *A* (5)
Geffin, A (Transvaal) 1949 *NZ* (4), 1951-52 (T) *S, I, W*
Geldenhuys, S B (Northern Transvaal) 1981 *NZ* (2), *US*, 1982 *S Am* (2)
Gentles, T A (Western Province) 1955 *BI* (3), 1956 *NZ* (2), 1958 *F*
Geraghty, E M (Border) 1949 *NZ*
Gerber, D M (Eastern Province) 1980 *S Am* (ST) (2), *F*, 1981 *I* (2), *NZ* (3), *US*, 1982 *S Am* (2)
Gerber, M C (Eastern Province) 1958 *F* (2), 1960 *S*
Gericke, F W (Transvaal) 1960 *S*
Germishuys, J S (Orange Free State, Transvaal) 1974 *BI*, 1976 *NZ* (4), 1977 Wld, 1980 *S Am* (2), *BI* (4), *S Am* (ST) (2), *F*, 1981 *I* (2), *NZ* (2), *US*
Gibbs, B (Griqualand West) 1903 *BI*
Goosen, C P (Orange Free State) 1965 *NZ*
Gorton, H C (Transvaal) 1896 *BI*
Gould, R L (Natal) 1968 *BI* (4)
Gray, B G (Western Province) 1931-32 (T) *W, E, S*, 1933 *A*
Greenwood, C M (Western Province) 1961 *I*
Greyling, P J F (Orange Free State) 1967 *F* (4), 1968 *BI* 1968-69 (ST) *F* (2), 1969 *A* (4), 1969-70 (T) *S, E, I, W*, 1970 *NZ* (4), 1971 *F* (2), *A* (3), 1972 *E*
Grobler, C J (Orange Free State) 1971 *BI*, 1975 *F* (2)
Guthrie, F H (Western Province) 1891 *BI* (2), 1896 *BI*

Hahn, C H L (Transvaal) 1910 *BI* (3)
Hamilton, F (Eastern Province) 1891 *BI*
Harris, T A (Transvaal) 1937 *NZ* (2), 1938 *BI* (3)
Hartley, A J (Western Province) 1891 *BI*
Hattingh, L B (Orange Free State) 1933 *A*
Heatlie, B H (Western Province) 1891 *BI* (2), 1896 *BI* (2), 1903 *BI* (2)
Hepburn, T (Western Province) 1896 *BI*
Heunis, J W (Northern Transvaal) 1981 *NZ* (R), *US*, 1982 *S Am* (2)
Hill, R A (Rhodesia) 1960-61 (T) *W, I*, 1961 *I, A* (2), 1962 *BI*, 1963 *A*
Hirsch, J G (Eastern Province) 1906-07 (T) *I*, 1910 *BI*
Hobson, T E C (Western Province) 1903 *BI*
Hoffman, R S (Boland) 1953 *A*
Holton, D N (Eastern Province) 1960 *S*
Hopwood, D J (Western Province) 1960 *S, NZ* (2), 1960-61 (T) *W, E, S, F*, 1961 *I, A*, (2), 1962 *BI* (4), 1963 *A* (3), 1964 *W, F*, 1964-65 (ST) *S*, 1965 *NZ* (2)
Howe, B F (Border) 1956 *NZ* (2)
Howe-Browne, N R F G (Western Province) 1910 *BI* (3)

Immelman, J H (Western Province) 1912-13 (T) *F*

Jackson, D C (Western Province) 1906-07 (T) *I, W, E*
Jackson, J S (Western Province) 1903 *BI*
Jansen, E (Orange Free State) 1981 *NZ*
Jansen, J S (Orange Free State) 1970 *NZ* (4), 1971 *F*

Danie Gerber, the brilliant Springbok centre, seen here in the colours of the Barbarians.

(2), *A* (3), 1972 *E*
Jennings, C B (Border) 1937 *NZ*
Johnstone, P G A (Western Province) 1951-52 (T) *S*, *I*, *W*, *E*, *F*, 1956 *A*, *NZ* (3)
Jones, C H (Transvaal) 1903 *BI* (2)
Jones, P S T (Western Province) 1896 *BI* (3)
Jordaan, R P (Northern Transvaal) 1949 *NZ* (4)
Joubert, S J (Western Province) 1906-07 (T) *I*, *W*, *E*

Kahts, W J H (Northern Transvaal) 1980 *BI* (3), *S Am* (ST) (2), *F*, 1981 *I* (2), *NZ*, 1982 *S Am* (2)
Kaminer, J (Transvaal) 1958 *F*
Kelly, E W (Griqualand West) 1896 *BI*
Kenyon, B J (Border), 1949 *NZ*
Kipling, H G (Griqualand West) 1931-32 (T) *W*, *I*, *E*, *S*, 1933 *A* (5)
Kirkpatrick, A I (Griqualand West) 1953 *A*, 1956 *NZ*, 1958 *F*, 1960 *S*, *NZ* (4), 1960-61 (T) *W*, *I*, *E*, *S*, *F*
Knight, A S (Transvaal) 1912-13 (T) *S*, *I*, *W*, *E*, *F*
Koch, A C (Boland) 1949 *NZ* (3), 1951-52 (T) *S*, *I*, *W*, *E*, *F*, 1953 *A* (3), 1955 *BI* (4), 1956 *A*, *NZ* (2), 1958 *F* (2), 1960 *NZ* (2)
Koch, H W (Western Province) 1949 *NZ* (4)
Kotze, G J M (Western Province) 1967 *F* (4)
Krantz, E F W (Orange Free State) 1976 *NZ* 1981 *I*
Krige, J D (Western Province) 1903 *BI* (2), 1906-07 (T) *S*, *I*, *W*
Kritzinger, J L (Transvaal) 1974 *BI* (2), 1974 (ST) *F* (2), 1975 *F* (2), 1976 *NZ*
Kroon, C M (Eastern Province) 1955 *BI*
Kruger, T L (Transvaal) 1921 *NZ* (2), 1924 *BI* (4), 1928 *NZ* (2)
Kuhn, S P (Transvaal) 1960 *NZ* (2), 1960-61 (T) *W*, *I*, *E*, *S*, *F*, 1961, *I*, *A*, (2), 1962 *BI* (4), 1963 *A* (3), 1964-65 (ST) *I*, *S*

La Grange, J B (Western Province) 1924 *BI* (2)
Larard, A (Transvaal) 1896 *BI* (2)
Lategan, M T (Western Province) 1949 *NZ* (4), 1951-52 (T) *S*, *I*, *W*, *E*, *F*, 1953 *A* (2)
Lawless, M J (Western Province) 1964 *F*, 1969-70 (T) *E* (R), *I*, *W*
Ledger, S H (Griqualand West) 1912-13 (T) *S*, *I*, *E*, *F*
Le Roux, M (Orange Free State) 1980 *BI* (4), *S Am* (ST) (2), *F*, 1981 *I*
Le Roux, P A (Western Province) 1906-07 (T) *I*, *W*, *E*
Little, E M M (Griqualand West) 1891 *BI* (2)
Lochner, G P 'Butch' (Western Province) 1955 *BI*, 1956 *A* (2), *NZ* (4), 1958 *F* (2)
Lochner, G P (Eastern Province) 1937 *NZ*, 1938 *BI* (2)
Lockyear, R J (Griqualand West) 1960 *NZ* (4), 1960-61 (T) *I*, *F*
Lombard, A C (Eastern Province) 1910 *BI*
Lotz, J W (Transvaal) 1937 *A* (2), *NZ* (3) 1938 *BI* (3)
Loubser, J A (Western Province) 1903 *BI*, 1906-07 (T) *S*, *I*, *W*, *E*, 1910 *BI* (2)
Lourens, M J (Northern Transvaal) 1968 *BI* (3)
Louw, J S (Transvaal) 1891 *BI* (3)
Louw, M J (Transvaal) 1971 *A* (2)
Louw, M M (Western Province) 1928 *NZ* (2), 1931-32 (T) *W*, *I*, *E*, *S*, 1933 *A* (5), 1937 *A* (2), *NZ* (2), 1938 *BI* (3)
Louw, R J (Western Province) 1980 *S Am* (2), *BI* (4), *S Am* (ST) (2), *F* 1981 *I* (2), *NZ* (2), 1982 *S Am* (2)
Louw, S C (Western Province) 1933 *A* (5), 1937 *A*, *NZ* (3), 1938 *BI* (3)
Luyt, F P (Western Province) 1910 *BI* (3), 1912-13 (T) *S*, *I*, *W*, *E*
Luyt, J D (Eastern Province) 1912-13 (T) *S*, *W*, *E*, *F*
Luyt, R R (Western Province) 1910 *BI* (2), 1912-13 (T) *S*, *I*, *W*, *E*, *F*
Lyons, D (Eastern Province) 1896 *BI*
Lyster, P J (Natal) 1933 *A* (2), 1937 *NZ*

MacDonald, A W (Rhodesia), 1965 *A*, *NZ* (4)
Macdonald, D A (Western Province) 1974 *BI*
Malan, A S (Transvaal) 1960 *NZ* (4), 1960-61 (T) *W*, *I*, *E*, *S*, *F*, 1962 *BI*, 1963 *A* (3), 1964 *W*, 1964-65 (ST) *I*, *S*
Malan, E (Northern Transvaal) 1980 *BI* (2[1R])
Malan, G F (Western Province) 1958 *F*, 1960 *NZ* (3), 1960-61 (T) *E*, *S*, *F*, 1962 *BI* (3), 1963 *A* (3), 1964 *W*, 1965 *A* (2), *NZ* (2)

Malan, P (Transvaal) 1949 *NZ*
Mans, W J (Western Province) 1964-65 (ST) *I, S*
Marais, F P (Boland) 1949 *NZ* (2), 1951-52 (T) *S*, 1953 *A* (2)
Marais, J F K (Western Province) 1963 *A*, 1964 *W, F*, 1964-65 (ST) *I, S*, 1965 *A*, 1968 *BI* (4), 1968-69 (ST) *F* (2), 1969 *A* (4), 1969-70 (T) *S, E, I, W*, 1970 *NZ* (4), 1971 *F* (2), *A* (3), 1974 *BI* (4), 1974 (ST) *F* (2)
Mare, D S (Transvaal) 1906-07 (T) *S*
Marsberg, A F W (Griqualand West) 1906-07 (T) *S, W, E*
Marsberg, P A (Griqualand West) 1910 *BI*
Martheze, W C (Griqualand West) 1903 *BI*, 1906-07 (T) *I, W*
Martin, H J (Transvaal) 1937 *A*
McCallum, I D (Western Province) 1970 *NZ* (4), 1971 *F* (2), *A* (3), 1974 *BI* (2)
McCallum, R J (Western Province) 1974 *BI*
McCulloch, J D (Griqualand West) 1912-13 (T) *E, F*
McDonald, J A J (Western Province) 1931-32 (T) *W, I, E, S*
McEwan, W M C (Transvaal) 1903 *BI* (2)
McHardy, E E (Orange Free State) 1912-13 (T) *S, I, W, E, F*
McKendrick, J A (Western Province) 1891 *BI*
Mellett, T (Griqualand West) 1896 *BI*
Mellish, F W (Western Province) 1921 *NZ* (2), 1924 *BI* (4)
Merry, J (Eastern Province) 1891 *BI*
Metcalf, H D (Border) 1903 *BI*
Meyer, C du P (Western Province) 1921 *NZ* (3)
Meyer, P J (Griqualand West) 1896 *BI*
Michau, J M (Transvaal) 1921 *NZ*
Michau, J P (Western Province) 1921 *NZ* (3)
Millar, W A (Western Province) 1906-07 (T) *E*, 1910 *BI* (2), 1912-13 (T) *I, W, F*
Mills, W J (Western Province) 1910 *BI*
Molls, T (Transvaal) 1910 *BI*
Montini, P E (Western Province) 1956 *A* (2)
Moolman, L C (Northern Transvaal) 1977 Wld, 1980 *S Am* (2), *BI* (4), *S Am* (ST) (2), *F*, 1981 *I* (2), *NZ* (3), *US*, 1982 *S Am* (2)
Mordt, R H (Zimbabwe-Rhodesia) 1980 *S Am* (2), *BI* (4), *S Am* (ST) (2), *F* 1981 *I, NZ* (3), *US*, 1982 *S Am* (2)
Morkel, A O (Transvaal) 1903 *BI*
Morkel, D F T (Transvaal) 1906-07 (T) *I, E*, 1910 *BI* (2), 1912-13 (T) *S, I, W, E, F*
Morkel, H J (Western Province) 1921 *NZ*
Morkel, H W (Western Province) 1921 *NZ* (2)
Morkel, J A (Western Province) 1921 *NZ* (2)
Morkel, J W H (Western Province) 1912-13 (T) *S, I, W, E, F*
Morkel, P G (Western Province) 1912-13 (T) *S, I, W, E, F*, 1921 *NZ* (3)
Morkel, P K (Western Province) 1928 *NZ*
Morkel, W H (Western Province) 1910 *BI*, 1912-13 (T) *S, I, W, E, F*, 1921 *NZ* (3)
Morkel, W S (Transvaal), 1906-07 (T) *S, I, W, E*
Moss, C (Natal) 1949 *NZ* (4)
Mostert, P J (Western Province) 1921 *NZ* (3), 1924 *BI* (3), 1928 *NZ* (4), 1931-32 (T) *W, I, E, S*
Muller, G H (Western Province) 1969 *A* (2), 1969-70 (T) *S, W*, 1970 *NZ* (4), 1971 *F* (2), 1972 *E*, 1974 *BI* (3)
Muller, H S V (Transvaal) 1949 *NZ* (4), 1951-52 (T) *S, I, W, E, F*, 1953 *A* (4)
Myburgh, F R (Eastern Province) 1896 *BI*
Myburgh, J L (Northern Transvaal) 1962 *BI*, 1963 *A*, 1964 *W, F*, 1968 *BI* (3), 1968-69 (ST) *F* (2), 1969 *A* (4), 1969-70 (T) *E, I, W*, 1970 *NZ* (2)
Myburgh, W H (Western Transvaal) 1924 *BI*

Naude, J P (Western Province) 1963 *A*, 1965 *A* (2), *NZ* (3), 1967 *F* (4), 1968 *BI* (4)
Neethling, J B (Western Province) 1967 *F* (4), 1968 *BI*, 1969-70 (T) *S*, 1970 *NZ* (2)
Nel, J A (Transvaal), 1960 *NZ* (2), 1963 *A* (2), 1965 *A*, *NZ* (4), 1970 *NZ* (2)
Nel, J J (Western Province) 1956 *A* (2), *NZ* (4), 1958 *F* (2)
Nel, P A R O (Transvaal) 1903 *BI* (3)
Nel, P J (Natal) 1928 *NZ* (4), 1931-32 (T) *W, I, E, S*, 1933 *A* (4), 1937 *A* (2), *NZ* (2)
Nimb, C F (Western Province) 1961 *I*
Nomis, S H (Transvaal) 1967 *F*, 1968 *BI* (4), 1968-69 (ST) *F* (2), 1969 *A* (4), 1969-70 (T) *S, E, I, W*, 1970 *NZ* (4), 1971 *F* (2), *A* (3), 1972 *E*
Nykamp, J L (Transvaal) 1933 *A*

Ochse, J K (Western Province) 1951-52 (T) *I, W, E, F*, 1953 *A* (3)
Oelofse, J S A (Transvaal) 1953 *A* (4)
Oliver, J F (Transvaal) 1928 *NZ* (2)
Olivier, E (Western Province) 1967 *F* (4), 1968 *BI* (4), 1968-69 (ST) *F* (2), 1969 *A* (4), 1969-70 (T), *S, E*,
Olver, E (Eastern Province) 1896 *BI*
Oosthuizen, J J (Western Province) 1974 *BI*, 1974 (ST) *F* (2), 1975 *F* (2), 1976 *NZ* (4)
Oosthuizen, O W (Northern Transvaal) 1981 *I* (2[1R]), *NZ* (2), *US*, 1982 *S Am* (2)
Osler, B L (Western Province) 1924 *BI* (4), 1928 *NZ* (4), 1931-32 (T) *W, I, E, S*, 1933 *A* (5)
Osler, S G (Western Province) 1928 *NZ*
Oxlee, K (Natal) 1960 *NZ* (4), 1960-61 (T) *W, I, S*, 1961 *A* (2), 1962 *BI* (4), 1963 *A* (3), 1964 *W*, 1965 *NZ* (2)

Parker, W H (Eastern Province) 1965 *A* (2)
Partridge, J E C (Transvaal) 1903 *BI*
Payn, C (Natal) 1924 *BI* (2)
Pelser, H J M (Transvaal) 1958 *F*, 1960 *NZ* (4), 1960-61 (T) *W, I, F*, 1961 *I, A* (2)
Pfaff, B D (Western Province) 1956 *A*
Pickard, J A J (Western Province) 1953 *A* (2), 1956 *NZ*, 1958 *F*
Pienaar, Z M J (Orange Free State) 1980 *S Am* (R), *BI* (4), *S Am* (ST) (2), *F* 1981 *I* (2), *NZ* (3)
Pitzer, G (Northern Transvaal) 1967 *F* (4), 1968 *BI* (4), 1968-69 (ST) *F* (2), 1969 *A* (2)
Pope, C F (Western Province) 1974 *BI* (4), 1975 *F* (2), 1976 *NZ* (3)
Potgieter, H J (Orange Free State) 1928 *NZ* (2)
Potgieter, H L (Orange Free State) 1977 Wld
Powell, A W (Griqualand West) 1896 *BI*
Powell, J M (Griqualand West) 1891 *BI*, 1896 *BI*, 1903 *BI* (2)
Prentis, R B (Transvaal) 1980 *S Am* (2), *BI* (4), *S Am* (ST) (2), *F* 1981 *I* (2)
Pretorius, N F (Transvaal) 1928 *NZ* (4)
Prinsloo, J (Transvaal) 1958 *F* (2)
Prinsloo, J (Northern Transvaal) 1963 *A*
Prinsloo, J P (Transvaal) 1928 *NZ*
Putter, D J (Western Transvaal) 1963 *A* (3)

Raaff, J W E (Griqualand West) 1903 *BI* (2), 1906-07 (T), *S, W, E*, 1910 *BI*
Ras, W J de Wet (Orange Free State) 1976 *NZ* (R), 1980 *S Am* (R)
Reid, A (Western Province) 1903 *BI*
Reid, B C (Border) 1933 *A*
Rens, I J (Transvaal) 1953 *A* (2)
Retief, D F (Northern Transvaal) 1955 *BI* (3), 1956 *A* (2), *NZ* (4)
Reynecke, H J (Western Province) 1910 *BI*
Richards, A (Western Province) 1891 *BI* (3)
Riley, N (Eastern Transvaal) 1963 *A*
Riordan, C E (Transvaal) 1910 *BI* (2)
Robertson, I W (Rhodesia) 1974 (ST) *F* (2), 1976 *NZ* (3)
Roos, G D (Western Province) 1910 *BI* (2)
Roos, P J (Western Province) 1903 *BI*, 1906-07 (T) *I, W, E*,
Rosenberg, W (Transvaal) 1955 *BI* (3), 1956 *NZ*, 1958 *F*
Rossouw, D H (Western Province) 1953 *A* (2)
Rousseau, W P (Western Province) 1928 *NZ* (2)
Roux, F du T (Western Province) 1960-61 (T) *W*, 1961 *A* (2), 1962 *BI* (4), 1963 *A*, 1965 *A* (2), *NZ* (4), 1968 *BI* (2), 1968-69 (ST) *F* (2), 1969 *A* (4), 1969-70 (T) *I*, 1970 *NZ* (4)
Roux, O A (Northern Transvaal) 1969-70 (T) *S, E, I, W*, 1972 *E*, 1974 *BI* (2)

Samuels, T A (Griqualand West) 1896 *BI* (3)
Sauermann, J T (Transvaal) 1971 *F* (2), *A*, 1972 *E*, 1974 *BI*
Schlebusch, J J J (Orange Free State) 1974 *BI* (2), 1975 *F*
Schmidt, L U (Northern Transvaal) 1958 *F*, 1962 *BI*

Schoeman, J (Western Province) 1963 *A* (2), 1964-65 (ST) *I*, *S*, 1965 *A*, *NZ* (2)
Scholtz, H H (Western Province) 1921 *NZ* (2)
Scott, P (Transvaal) 1896 *BI* (4)
Sendin, W D (Griqualand West) 1921 *NZ*
Serfontein, D J (Western Province) 1980 *BI* (4), *S Am* (ST) (2), *F*, 1981 *I* (2), *NZ* (3), *US*, 1982 *S Am* (2)
Shand, R (Griqualand West) 1891 *BI* (2)
Sheriff, A R (Transvaal) 1938 *BI* (3)
Shum, E H (Transvaal) 1912-13 (T) *E*
Sinclair, D J (Transvaal) 1955 *BI* (4)
Sinclair, J H (Transvaal) 1903 *BI*
Skene, A L (Western Province) 1958 *F*
Slater, J T (Eastern Province) 1924 *BI* (2), 1928 *NZ*
Smith, C M (Orange Free State) 1963 *A* (2), 1964 *W*, *F*, 1965 *A* (2), *NZ*
Smith, C W (Griqualand West) 1891 *BI*, 1896 *BI* (2)
Smith, D (Griqualand West) 1891 *BI*
Smith, D J (Zimbabwe-Rhodesia) 1980 *BI* (4)
Smith, G A C (Eastern Province) 1938 *BI*
Smollan, F C (Transvaal) 1933 *A* (3)
Snedden, R C (Griqualand West) 1891 *BI*
Snyman, D S L (Western Province) 1972 *E*, 1974 *BI* (2[1R]), 1974 (ST) *F* (2), 1975 *F* (2), 1976 *NZ* (2), 1977 Wld
Snyman, J C P (Orange Free State) 1974 *BI* (3)
Sonnekus, G (Orange Free State) 1974 *BI*
Spies, J J (Northern Transvaal) 1970 *NZ* (4)
Stander, J C J (Orange Free State) 1974 *BI* (R), 1976 *NZ* (4)
Stapelberg, W P (Northern Transvaal) 1974 (ST) *F* (2)
Starke, J J (Western Province) 1956 *NZ*
Starke, K T (Western Province) 1924 *BI* (4)
Steenekamp, J G A (Transvaal) 1958 *F*
Stegmann, A C (Western Province) 1906-07 (T) *S*, *I*
Stegmann, J A (Transvaal) 1912-13 (T) *S*, *I*, *W*, *E*, *F*
Stewart, D A (Western Province) 1960 *S*, 1960-61 (T) *E*, *S*, *F*, 1961 *I*, 1963 *A* (3), 1964 *W*, *F*, 1964-65 (ST) *I*
Stofberg, M T S (Orange Free State, Northern Transvaal) 1976 *NZ* (2), 1977 Wld, 1980 *S Am* (2), *BI* (4), *S Am* (ST) (2), *F*, 1981 *I* (2), *NZ* (2), *US*, 1982 *S Am* (2)
Strachan, L C (Transvaal) 1931-32 (T) *E*, *S*, 1937 *A* (2), *NZ* (3), 1938 *BI* (3)
Strauss, J H P (Transvaal) 1976 *NZ* (2), 1980 *S Am*
Strauss, S S F (Griqualand West) 1921 *NZ*
Strydom, C F (Orange Free State) 1955 *BI*, 1956 *A* (2), *NZ* (2), 1958 *F*
Strydom, L J (Northern Transvaal) 1949 *NZ* (2)
Suter, M R (Natal) 1964-65 (ST) *I*, *S*
Swart, J J N (South West Africa) 1955 *BI*

Taberer, W S (Griqualand West) 1896 *BI*
Taylor, O B (Natal) 1962 *BI*
Theunissen, D J (Griqualand West) 1896 *BI*
Thompson, G (Western Province) 1912-13 (T), *S*, *I*, *W*
Tindall, J C (Western Province) 1924 *BI*, 1928 *NZ* (4)
Tobias, E G (SARF, Boland) 1981 *I* (2)
Tod, N S (Natal) 1928 *NZ*
Townsend, W H (Natal) 1921 *NZ*
Trenery, W (Griqualand West) 1891 *BI*
Truter, D R (Western Province) 1924 *BI* (2)
Truter, J T (Natal) 1963 *A*, 1964 *F*, 1965 *A*
Turner, F G (Eastern Province) 1933 *A* (3), 1937 *A* (2), *NZ* (3), 1938 *BI* (3)
Twigge, R J (Northern Transvaal) 1960 *S*

Van Aswegen, H J (Western Province) 1981 *NZ*
Van Broekhuizen, H D (Western Province) 1896 *BI*
Van Buuren, M C (Transvaal) 1891 *BI*
Van De Vyver, D F (Western Province) 1937 *A*
Van Den Berg, D S (Natal) 1975 *F* (2), 1976 *NZ* (2)
Van Den Berg, M A (Western Province) 1937 *A*, *NZ* (3)
Van Der Merwe, A J (Boland) 1955 *BI* (3), 1956 *A* (2), *NZ* (4), 1958 *F*, 1960 *S*, *NZ*
Van Der Merwe, A J (Western Province) 1931-32 (T) *W*
Van Der Merwe, B S (Northern Transvaal) 1949 *NZ*
Van Der Merwe, H S (Northern Transvaal) 1960 *NZ*, 1963 *A* (3), 1964 *F*
Van Der Merwe, J P (Western Province) 1969-70 (T) *W*
Van Der Merwe, P R (South Western Districts) 1981 *NZ* (2), *US*
Vanderplank, B E (Natal) 1924 *BI* (2)
Van Der Schyff, J H (Griqualand West) 1949 *NZ* (4), 1955 *BI*
Van Der Watt, A E (Western Province) 1969-70 (T) *S* (R), *E*, *I*
Van Der Westhuizen, J C (Western Province) 1928 *NZ* (3), 1931-32 (T) *I*
Van Der Westhuizen, J H (Western Province) 1931-32 (T) *I*, *E*, *S*
Van Druten, N J V (Transvaal) 1924 *BI* (4), 1928 *NZ* (4)
Van Heerden, A J (Transvaal) 1921 *NZ* (2)
Van Heerden, J L (Northern Transvaal, Transvaal) 1974 *BI* (2), 1974 (ST) *F* (2), 1975 *F* (2), 1976 *NZ* (4), 1977 Wld, 1980 *BI* (3), *S Am* (ST) (2), *F*
Van Jaarsveld, C J (Transvaal) 1949 *NZ*
Van Jaarsveldt, D C (Rhodesia) 1960 *S*
Van Niekerk, J A (Western Province) 1928 *NZ*
Van Reenen, G L (Western Province) 1937 *A*, *NZ*
Van Renen, C G (Western Province) 1891 *BI*, 1896 *BI* (2)
Van Renen, W (Western Province) 1903 *BI* (2)
Van Rooyen, G W (Transvaal) 1921 *NZ* (2)
Van Ryneveld, R C B (Western Province) 1910 *BI* (2)
Van Schoor, R A M (Rhodesia) 1949 *NZ* (3), 1951-52 (T) *S*, *I*, *W*, *E*, *F*, 1953 *A* (4)
Van Vollenhoven, K T (Northern Transvaal) 1955 *BI* (4), 1956 *A* (2), *NZ*
Van Vuuren, T F (Eastern Province) 1912-13 (T) *S*, *I*, *W*, *E*, *F*
Van Wyk, C J (Transvaal) 1951-52 (T) *S*, *I*, *W*, *E*, *F*, 1953 *A* (4), 1955 *BI*
Van Wyk, J F B (Northern Transvaal) 1970 *NZ* (4), 1971 *F* (2), *A* (3), 1972 *E*, 1974 *BI* (3), 1976 *NZ* (2)
Van Wyk, S P (Western Province) 1928 *NZ* (2)
Van Zyl, B P (Western Province) 1961 *I*
Van Zyl, C G P (Orange Free State) 1965 *NZ* (4)
Van Zyl, G H (Western Province) 1958 *F*, 1960 *S*, *NZ* (4), 1960-61 (T) *W*, *I*, *E*, *S*, *F*, 1961 *I*, *A* (2), 1962 *BI* (3)
Van Zyl, H J (Transvaal) 1960 *NZ* (4), 1960-61 (T) *I*, *E*, *S*, 1961 *I*, *A* (2)
Van Zyl, P J (Boland) 1961 *I*
Veldsman, P E (Western Province) 1977 Wld
Venter, F D (Transvaal) 1931-32 (T) *W*, *S*, 1933 *A*
Versfeld, C (Western Province) 1891 *BI*
Versfeld, M (Western Province) 1891 *BI* (3)
Vigne, J T (Transvaal) 1891 *BI* (3)
Viljoen, J F (Griqualand West) 1971 *F* (2), *A* (3), 1972 *E*
Viljoen, J T (Natal) 1971 *A* (3)
Visagie, P J (Griqualand West) 1967 *F* (4), 1968 *BI* (4), 1968-69 (ST) *F* (2), 1969 *A* (4), 1969-70 (T) *S*, *E*, 1970 *NZ* (4), 1971 *F* (2), *A* (3)
Visser, J de V (Western Province) 1981 *NZ*, *US*
Visser, P J (Transvaal) 1933 *A*
Viviers, S S (Orange Free State) 1956 *A* (2), *NZ* (3)
Vogel, M L (Orange Free State) 1974 *BI* (R)

Wagenaar, C (Northern Transvaal) 1977 Wld
Wahl, J J (Western Province) 1949 *NZ*
Walker, A P (Natal) 1921 *NZ* (2), 1924 *BI* (4)
Walker, H N (Orange Free State) 1953 *A*, 1956 *A*, *NZ* (2)
Walker, H W (Transvaal) 1910 *BI* (3)
Walton, D C (Natal) 1964 *F*, 1964-65 (ST) *I*, *S*, 1965 *NZ* (2), 1969 *A* (2), 1969-70 (T) *E*
Waring, F W (Western Province) 1931-32 (T), *I*, *E*, 1933 *A* (5)
Wessels, J J (Western Province) 1896 *BI* (3)
Whipp, P J M (Western Province) 1974 *BI* (2), 1975 *F*, 1976 *NZ* (3), 1980 *S Am* (2)
White, J (Border) 1931-32 (T) *W*, 1933 *A* (5), 1937 *A* (2), *NZ* (2)
Williams, A E (Griqualand West) 1910 *BI*
Williams, D O (Western Province) 1937 *A* (2), *NZ* (3), 1938 *BI* (3)
Williams, J G (Northern Transvaal) 1971 *F* (2), *A* (3), 1972 *E*, 1974 *BI* (3), 1974 (ST) *F* (2), 1976 *NZ* (2)
Wilson, L G (Western Province) 1960 *NZ* (2), 1960-61 (T) *W*, *I*, *E*, *F*, 1961 *I*, *A* (2), 1962 *BI* (4), 1963 *A* (4), 1964 *W*, *F*, 1964-65 (ST) *I*, *S*, 1965 *A* (2), *NZ* (4)
Wolmarans, B J (Orange Free State) 1977 Wld
Wyness, M R K (Western Province) 1962 *BI* (4), 1963 *A*

Zeller, W C (Natal) 1921 *NZ* (2)
Zimerman, M (Western Province) 1931-32 (T) *W*, *I*, *E*, *S*

SOUTH AFRICAN INTERNATIONAL RECORDS

From 1890-91, when uniform points-scoring was first adopted by International Board countries, to 30 April 1984, except in the case of matches against British Isles. These date from 1910, when Lions' teams first became representative of the Four Home Unions. Both team and individual records are against or on tour in International Board countries and British Isles only, unless otherwise stated.

TEAM RECORDS

Highest score
44 v Scotland (44-0) 1951 Murrayfield
S Africa beat France 55-6 at Parc des Princes (Paris) on 3 January 1907, but it is not regarded as an official international match

v individual countries
9 v England { (9-3) 1913 Twickenham / (9-18) 1972 Johannesburg }
44 v Scotland (44-0) 1951 Murrayfield
38 v Ireland (38-0) 1912 Dublin
24 v Wales (24-3) 1964 Durban
38 v France { (38-5) 1913 Bordeaux / (38-25) 1975 Bloemfontein }
24 v N Zealand (24-12) 1981 Wellington
30 v Australia (30-11) 1969 Johannesburg
34 v B Isles (34-14) 1962 Bloemfontein

Biggest winning points margin
44 v Scotland (44-0) 1951 Murrayfield
v individual countries
7 v England (7-0) 1932 Twickenham
44 v Scotland (44-0) 1951 Murrayfield
38 v Ireland (38-0) 1912 Dublin
21 v Wales (24-3) 1964 Durban
33 v France (38-5) 1913 Bordeaux
17 v N Zealand (17-0) 1928 Durban
25 v Australia (28-3) 1961 Johannesburg
20 v B Isles (34-14) 1962 Bloemfontein

Highest score by opposing team
28 B Isles (9-28) 1974 Pretoria
by individual countries
18 England (9-18) 1972 Johannesburg
10 Scotland (18-10) 1960 Port Elizabeth
15 Ireland (23-15) 1981 Cape Town
6 Wales (6-6) 1970 Cardiff
25 France (38-25) 1975 Bloemfontein
25 N Zealand (22-25) 1981 Auckland
21 Australia (6-21) 1933 Durban
28 B Isles (9-28) 1974 Pretoria

Biggest losing points margin
19 v B Isles (9-28) 1974 Pretoria
v individual countries
9 v England (9-18) 1972 Johannesburg
6 v Scotland (0-6) 1906 Glasgow
3 v Ireland (6-9) 1965 Dublin
No defeat v Wales
5 v France (14-19) 1967 Johannesburg
17 v N Zealand (3-20) 1965 Auckland
15 v Australia (6-21) 1933 Durban
19 v B Isles (9-28) 1974 Pretoria

Most tries by South Africa in an international
10 v Ireland (38-0) 1912 Dublin
S Africa scored 13 tries in the 'unofficial' match v France in Paris in 1907

Most tries against South Africa in an international
5 { by B Isles (22-23) 1955 Johannesburg / by N Zealand (3-20) 1965 Auckland / by B Isles (9-28) 1974 Pretoria }

Most points on overseas tour (all matches)
753 in Australia/N Zealand (26 matches) 1937

Most tries on overseas tour (all matches)
161 in Australia/N Zealand (26 matches) 1937

INDIVIDUAL RECORDS

Most capped player
F C H du Preez } 38 { 1960-71
J H Ellis } 38 { 1965-76

in individual positions

Full-back
L G Wilson 27 1960-65

Wing
J P Engelbrecht 33 1960-69

Centre
J L Gainsford 33 1960-67

Fly-half
P J Visagie 25 1967-71

Scrum-half
D J de Villiers 25 1962-70

Prop
J F K Marais 35 1963-74

Hooker
G F Malan 18 1958-65

Lock
F C H du Preez 31(38)* 1960-71

Flanker
J H Ellis 38 1965-76

No 8
D J Hopwood 22† 1960-65

**du Preez won 7 caps as a flanker*
†T P Bedford, 25 caps, won 19 at No 8 and 6 as a flanker

Most internationals as captain – 22
D J de Villiers 1965-70

Most points in internationals – 130
P J Visagie (25 appearances) 1967-71
H E Botha [17 appearances] has scored 173 points, but only 102 in 10 appearances against I B countries or British Isles

---

Most points in international series – 43
P J Visagie (4 appearances) v Australia 1969

Most points in an international – 22
G R Bosch v France 1975 Pretoria
D Mare scored 22 points in the 'unofficial' match v France in Paris in 1907

Most tries in internationals – 8
J L Gainsford (33 appearances) 1960-67
J P Engelbrecht (33 appearances) 1960-69
J S Germishuys has scored 12 tries, but only 6 against I B coutries or British Isles

---

Most tries in an international – 3
E E McHardy v Ireland 1912 Dublin
J A Stegmann v Ireland 1912 Dublin
K T van Vollenhoven v B Isles 1955 Cape Town
H J van Zyl v Australia 1961 Johannesburg
R H Mordt v New Zealand 1981 Auckland

Most conversions in an international – 7
A Geffin v Scotland 1951 Murrayfield

Most points for South Africa on overseas tour – 190
G H Brand (20 appearances) 1937 Australia/N Zealand

Most tries for South Africa on overseas tour – 22
J A Loubser (20 appearances) 1906-07 B Isles/France

Most points for South Africa in international series on tour – 35
H E Botha (3 appearances) 1981 N Zealand

Most tries for South Africa in international series on tour – 6
E E McHardy (5 appearances) 1912-13 B Isles/France

Most points for South Africa in any match on tour – 31
H E Botha v Nelson Bays 1981 Nelson
W J de W Ras scored 35 points against British Schools Old Boys in a match at Montevideo in 1980, but this was not in an International Board country

---

Most tries for South Africa in any match on tour – 6
R G Drysburgh v Queensland 1956 Brisbane

THE 1983 SEASON IN NEW ZEALAND

Donald Cameron *New Zealand Herald*

Seldom has the rugby pasture of New Zealand been so heavily cultivated as in 1983 and seldom has the harvest been so fruitful. The British Lions came and went, New Zealand made a brief and successful one-Test tour to Australia, Canterbury brought a new, stylish dimension to the business of defending the Ranfurly Shield and near the end of the year the All Blacks, with rather too many seedlings in the side, were in England and Scotland, drawing at Murrayfield and losing at Twickenham. In the background all this time was the waning threat of Mr David Lord's professional rugby plans, and so much murmuring about the modest financial return to leading players that the New Zealand Rugby Union went off hopefully to the International Board meeting with an expansive plan embracing more tour money for players and a scheme for a World Cup in the near future.

Much has been written and said about the Lions' unfortunate expedition, that this was a touring team of modest ability. But the tour did tend to confirm a trend already noticeable when the Wallabies toured New Zealand in 1982 – that the general level of provincial rugby in New Zealand continues to improve; that the tighter competition of the first division of the national championship is breeding a higher quality of competitive play, and that even the more modest sides of the second division are playing the running, positive game as well as they can.

This lift in quality was no more evident than in the later matches Canterbury played for the Ranfurly Shield. The famous shield produces, perhaps once a year, a game of memorable quality. In 1983 the last four challenges, by Hawkes Bay, Wellington, Auckland and Manawatu, all produced rugby which tingled the nerve-ends and had 30,000 or 40,000 feverish Lancaster Park spectators yelling their heads off, either in alarm or exultation. Canterbury won them all, beating Hawkes Bay 32-3, Wellington 20-16, Auckland 31-9 and Manawatu 26-15, with a sweeping, confident flow to their rugby matched only by the All Blacks' withering display in the fourth Test against the Lions.

So Canterbury, even more than the All Blacks, put the hallmark on the New Zealand season. They did not have a ball-winning pack of vast size, nor backs of lightning speed. But they did have a superbly fit, well-drilled unit which emphasised the old-fashioned virtues of backing-up, of the blindside variation, of the simple art that three backs running at pace will defeat two defenders. It was like a refresher course in the simple basics of rugby, and set the example for other New Zealand rugby teams to follow. Canterbury accepted the high number of nine challenges, won them all, and it will be some time before the rest of the country reaches up to the Canterbury standard.

The tour of Scotland and England in October-November will rank among the most forgettable of All Black expeditions, but it was a sobering and timely reminder that there is still a gap between the real international player and the promising novice, that the All Black jersey is not in itself an impenetrable armour. It also emphasies that the Lions provided only one aspect of British rugby, and that when British sides at division or international level are well-organised they are more formidable than starry-eyed New Zealanders may think. In other words the tour, which really did not reveal too many new players of high quality, brought New Zealand firmly back to earth.

Yet it was on solid earth, at the tap-roots of the game leading up to the quality of Canterbury, that New Zealand had a fruitful year. The flow of young players back to the game, slowed by the controversy of the 1981 Springbok tour and the concurrent love affair with soccer as New Zealand headed for the last World Cup, resumed in full spate. At least among the major Unions the attendances at club and representative matches showed a marked increase. This buoyant attitude permeated the Lions tour for, whatever their quality, they played before big crowds. By the end of the tour the NZRU had a profit of £296,774 from the Lions, from gross gate-takings of £1,050,689. Various other NZRU enterprises were less successful, and an eight-match tour by Tonga which cost the NZRU £49,686 must cause New Zealand to wonder whether it can afford any more missionary enterprises.

The rumblings of professionalism did not ripple the New Zealand water quite as much as what are believed here to be the unrealistic attitudes of the International Board toward payment of players and the World Cup. In turn, most of this dissent is focussed on the four home Unions, for it is obvious that France and Australia have more liberal views, and that South Africa must follow the prevalent trend. In the event the discontent with the IRB was stopped short of complete rebellion, and there was never any real prospect that New Zealand would leave the fold.

However, there remains a communication gap. I mentioned earlier that the All Blacks tour of Scotland and England closed the credibility gap between New Zealand and British rugby, playing-wise, that the Lions seemed to open. One of the lessons of 1983 was, I feel, that the communication gap at the hierarchy level still remains. Just as the All Blacks learned some facts of rugby-playing life at Murrayfield and Leicester and Twickenham, some senior British officials might glean some valuable information if they spent a few weeks in New Zealand next winter and gave their ideas on rugby a different dimension.

NEW ZEALAND INTERNATIONAL PLAYERS *(up to 30 April 1984)*

ABBREVIATIONS

A	Australia
AW	Anglo-Welsh
BI	British Isles teams
E	England
F	France
I	Ireland
R	Romania
S	Scotland
SA	South Africa
US	United States of America
W	Wales
(T)	Tour to Northern Hemisphere
(ST)	Short tour to Northern Hemisphere
(R)	Replacement – (2[1R]) denotes two appearances, one as a replacement

Abbott, H L (Taranaki) 1905-06 (T) *F*
Aitken, G G (Wellington) 1921 *SA* (2)
Allen, F R (Auckland) 1946 *A* (2), 1947 *A* (2), 1949 *SA* (2)
Allen, N H (Counties) 1980 *A*, 1980 (ST) *W*
Alley, G T (Canterbury) 1928 *SA* (3)
Anderson, A (Canterbury) 1983 (ST) *S, E*
Archer, W R (Otago, Southland) 1955 *A* (2), 1956 *SA* (2)
Argus, W G (Canterbury) 1946 *A* (2), 1947 *A* (2)
Arnold, D A (Canterbury) 1963-64 (T) *I, W, E, F*
Arnold, K D (Waikato) 1947 *A* (2)
Ashby, D L (Southland) 1958 *A*
Asher, A A (Auckland) 1903 *A*
Ashworth, B G (Auckland) 1978 *A* (2)
Ashworth, J C (Canterbury) 1978 *A* (3), 1980 *A* (3), 1981 *SA* (3), 1982 *A* (2), 1983 *BI* (4), *A*
Atkinson, H (West Coast) 1913 *A*
Avery, H E (Wellington) 1910 *A* (3)

Badeley, C E O (Auckland) 1921 *SA* (2)
Baird, J (Otago) 1913 *A*
Ball, N (Wellington) 1931 *A*, 1932 *A* (2), 1935-36 (T) *W, E*
Barrett, J (Auckland) 1913 *A* (2)
Barry, E F (Wellington) 1934 *A*
Batty, G B (Wellington, Bay of Plenty) 1972-73 (T) *W, S, E, I, F*, 1973 *E*, 1974 *A* (2), 1974 (ST) *I*, 1975 *S*, 1976 *SA* (4) 1977 *BI*
Batty, W (Auckland) 1930 *BI* (3), 1931 *A*
Beatty, G E (Taranaki) 1950 *BI*
Bell, R H (Otago) 1951 *A*, 1952 *A (2)*
Belliss, E A (Wanganui) 1921 *SA* (3)
Bennet, R (Otago) 1905 *A*
Berghan, T (Otago) 1938 *A* (3)
Bevan, V D (Wellington) 1949 *A* (2), 1950 *BI* (4)
Birtwistle, W M (Canterbury) 1965 *SA* (4), 1967-68 (T) *E, W, S*
Black, J E (Canterbury) 1977 (ST) *F*, 1979 *A*, 1980 *A*
Black, N W (Auckland) 1949 *SA*
Black, R S (Otago) 1914 *A*
Blake, A W (Wairarapa) 1949 *A*
Boggs, E G (Auckland) 1946 *A*, 1949 *SA*
Bond, J G (Canterbury) 1949 *A*
Booth, E E (Otago) 1905-06 (T) *F*, 1907 *A* (2)
Bowden, N J G (Taranaki) 1952 *A*
Bowers, R G (Wellington) 1953-54 (T) *I, F*
Bowman, A W (Hawke's Bay) 1938 *A* (3)
Braid, G J (Bay of Plenty) 1983 (ST) *S, E*
Bremner, S G (Auckland, Canterbury) 1952 *A*, 1956 *SA*
Briscoe, K C (Taranaki) 1959 *BI*, 1960 *SA* (4), 1963-64 (T) *I, W, E, S*
Brown, C (Taranaki) 1913 *A* (2)
Brown, R H (Taranaki) 1955 *A*, 1956 *SA* (4), 1957 *A* (2), 1958 *A* (3), 1959 *BI* (2), 1961 *F* (3), 1962 *A*
Brownlie, C J (Hawke's Bay) 1924-25 (T) *W, E, F*
Brownlie, M J (Hawke's Bay) 1924-25 (T) *I, W, E, F*, 1928 *SA* (4)
Bruce, J A (Auckland) 1914 *A* (2)
Bruce, O D (Canterbury) 1976 *SA* (3), 1977 *BI* (3), 1977 (ST) *F* (2), 1978 *A* (2), 1978 (T) *I, W, E, S*
Bryers, R F (King Country) 1949 *A*
Budd, T A (Southland) 1946 *A*, 1949 *A*
Bullock-Douglas, G A H (Wanganui) 1932 *A* (3), 1934 *A* (2)
Burgess, G A J (Auckland) 1981 *SA*
Burgess, G F (Southland) 1905 *A*
Burgess, R E (Manawatu) 1971 *BI* (3), 1972 *A*, 1972-73 (T) *W, I, F*
Burke, P S (Taranaki) 1955 *A*, 1957 *A* (2)
Burns, P J (Canterbury) 1908 *AW*, 1910 *A* (3), 1913 *A*
Bush, R G (Otago) 1931 *A*
Bush, W K (Canterbury) 1974 *A* (2), 1975 *S*, 1976 *I, SA* (2), 1977 *BI* (3[1R]), 1978 (T) *I, W*, 1979 *A*
Buxton, J B (Canterbury) 1955 *A*, 1956 *SA*

Cain, M J (Taranaki) 1913 *US*, 1914 *A* (3)
Callesen, J A (Manawatu) 1974 *A* (3), 1975 *S*
Cameron, D (Taranaki) 1908 *AW* (3)
Cameron, L M (Manawatu) 1980 *A*, 1981 *SA* (3[1R]), 1981 (ST) *R*
Carleton, S R (Canterbury) 1928 *SA* (3), 1929 *A* (3)
Carrington, K R (Auckland) 1971 *BI* (3)
Casey, S T (Otago) 1905-06 (T) *S, I, E, W*, 1907 *A* (3), 1908 *AW*
Catley, E H (Waikato) 1946 *A*, 1947 *A* (2), 1949 *SA* (4)
Caughey, T H C (Auckland) 1932 *A* (2), 1934 *A* (2), 1935-36 (T) *S, I, E*, 1936 *A*, 1937 *SA*
Caulton, R W (Wellington) 1959 *BI* (3), 1960 *SA* (2), 1961 *F*, 1963 *E* (2), 1963-64 (T) *I, W, E, S, F*, 1964 *A* (3)
Cherrington, N P (North Auckland) 1950 *BI*
Christian, D L (Auckland) 1949 *SA*
Clark, D W (Otago) 1964 *A* (2)
Clark, W H (Wellington) 1953-54 (T) *W, I, E, S*, 1955 *A* (2), 1956 *SA* (3)
Clarke, A H (Auckland) 1958 *A*, 1959 *BI*, 1960 *SA*
Clarke, D B (Waikato) 1956 *SA* (2), 1957 *A* (2), 1958 *A* (2), 1959 *BI* (4), 1960 *SA* (4), 1961 *F* (3), 1962 *A* (5), 1963 *E* (2), 1963-64 (T) *I, W, E, S, F*, 1964 *A* (2)
Clarke, I J (Waikato) 1953-54 (T) *W*, 1955 *A* (3), 1956 *SA* (4), 1957 *A* (2), 1958 *A* (2), 1959 *BI* (2), 1960 *SA* (2), 1961 *F* (3), 1962 *A* (3), 1963 *E* (2)
Clarke, R L (Taranaki) 1932 *A* (2)
Cobden, D G (Canterbury) 1937 *SA*
Cockerill, M S (Taranaki) 1951 *A* (3)
Cockroft, E A P (South Canterbury) 1913 *A*, 1914 *A* (2)
Codlin, B W (Counties) 1980 *A* (3)

Collins, A H (Taranaki) 1932 *A* (2), 1934 *A*
Collins, J L (Poverty Bay) 1964 *A*, 1965 *SA* (2)
Colman, J T H (Taranaki) 1907 *A* (2), 1908 *AW* (2)
Connor, D M (Auckland) 1961 *F* (3), 1962 *A* (5), 1963 *E* (2), 1964 *A* (2)
Conway, R J (Otago, Bay of Plenty) 1959 *BI* (3), 1960 *SA* (3), 1965 *SA* (4)
Cooke, A E (Auckland, Wellington) 1924-25 (T), *I*, *W*, *E*, *F*, 1930 *BI* (4)
Cooke, R J (Canterbury) 1903 *A*
Corner, M M N (Auckland) 1930 *BI* (3), 1931 *A*, 1934 *A*, 1935-36 (T) *E*
Cossey, R R (Counties) 1958 *A*
Cottrell, A I (Canterbury) 1929 *A* (3), 1930 *BI* (4), 1931 *A*, 1932 *A* (3)
Cottrell, W D (Canterbury) 1968 *A* (2), *F* (2), 1970 *SA*, 1971 *BI* (4)
Couch, M B R (Wairarapa) 1947 *A*, 1949 *A*, (2)
Coughlan, T D (South Canterbury) 1958 *A*
Creighton, J N (Canterbury) 1962 *A*
Crichton, S A (Wellington) 1983 (ST) *S*, *E*
Cross, T (Canterbury) 1904 *BI*, 1905 *A*
Crowley, P J B (Auckland) 1949 *SA* (2), 1950 *BI* (4)
Cummings, W (Canterbury) 1913 *A* (2)
Cundy, R T (Wairarapa) 1929 *A* (R)
Cunningham, G R (Auckland) 1979 *A*, 1979 (ST) *S*, *E*, 1980 *A* (2)
Cunningham, W (Auckland) 1905-06 (T) *S*, *I*, *F*, 1907 *A* (3), 1908 *AW* (3)
Cupples, L F (Bay of Plenty) 1924-25 (T) *I*, *W*
Currie, C J (Canterbury) 1978 (T) *I*, *W*
Cuthill, J E (Otago) 1913 *A*, *US*

Dalley, W C (Canterbury) 1924-25 (T) *I*, 1928 *SA* (4)
Dalton, A G (Counties) 1977 (ST) *F*, 1978 *A* (3), 1978 (T) *I*, *W*, *E*, *S*, 1979 *F* (2), 1979 (ST) *S*, 1981 *S* (2), *SA* (3), 1981 (ST) *R*, *F* (2), 1982 *A* (3), 1983 *BI* (4), *A*
Dalton, D (Hawke's Bay) 1935-36 (T) *I*, *W*, 1936 *A* (2), 1937 *SA* (3), 1938 *A* (2)
Dalton, R A (Wellington) 1947 *A* (2)
Dalzell, G N (Canterbury) 1953-54 (T) *W*, *I*, *E*, *S*, *F*
Davie, M G (Canterbury) 1983 (ST) *E* (R)
Davies, W A (Auckland, Otago) 1960 *SA*, 1962 *A* (2)
Davis, K (Auckland) 1952 *A*, 1953-54 (T) *W*, *I*, *E*, *S*, *F*, 1955 *A*, 1958 *A* (3)
Davis, L J (Canterbury) 1976 *I*, 1977 *BI* (2)
Davis, W L (Hawke's Bay) 1967 *A*, 1967-68 (T) *E*, *W*, *F*, *S*, 1968 *A* (2), *F*, 1969 *W* (2), 1970 *SA*
Deans, R G (Canterbury) 1905-06 (T) *S*, *I*, *E*, *W*, 1908 *AW*
Deans, R M (Canterbury) 1983 (ST) *S*, *E*
Delamore, G W (Wellington) 1949 *SA*
Dewar, H (Taranaki) 1913 *A*, *US*
Diack, E S (Otago) 1959 *BI*
Dick, J (Auckland) 1937 *SA* (2), 1938 *A*
Dick, M J (Auckland) 1963-64 (T) *I*, *W*, *E*, *S*, *F*, 1965 *SA*, 1966 *BI*, 1967 *A*, 1967-68 (T) *E*, *W*, *F*, 1969 *W* (2), 1970 *SA* (2)
Dixon, M J (Canterbury) 1953-54 (T) *I*, *E*, *S*, *F*, 1956 *SA* (4), 1957 *A* (2)
Dobson, R L (Auckland) 1949 *A*
Dodd, E H (Wellington) 1905 *A*
Donald, A J (Wanganui) 1983 (ST) *S*, *E*
Donald, J G (Wairarapa) 1921 *SA* (2)
Donald, Q (Wairarapa) 1924-25 (T) *I*, *W*, *E*, *F*
Donaldson, M W (Manawatu) 1977 (ST) *F* (2), 1978 *A* (3), 1978 (T) *I*, *E*, *S*, 1979 *F* (2), *A*, 1979 (ST) *S* (R), 1981 *SA* (R)

Wanganui's Andy Donald, a new cap on New Zealand's tour to England and Scotland, rounds Colin Deans in the outstanding victory over the South of Scotland at Gala.

Dougan, J P (Wellington) 1972 *A*, 1973 *E*
Downing, A J (Auckland) 1913 *A*, *US*, 1914 *A* (3)
Duff, R H (Canterbury) 1951 *A* (3), 1952 *A* (2), 1955 *A* (2), 1956 *SA* (4)
Duncan, J (Otago) 1903 *A*
Duncan, M G (Hawke's Bay) 1971 *BI* (2[1R])
Duncan, W D (Otago) 1921 *SA* (3)
Dunn, E (North Auckland) 1979 *A*, 1979 (ST) *S*, *1981 S*
Dunn, I T (North Auckland) 1983 *BI* (2) *A*
Dunn, J M (Auckland) 1946 *A*

Eastgate, B P (Canterbury) 1952 *A* (2), 1953-54 (T) *S*
Elliot, K G (Wellington) 1946 *A* (2)
Elsom, A E G (Canterbury) 1952 *A* (2), 1953-54 (T) *W*, 1955 *A* (3)
Elvidge, R R (Otago) 1946 *A* (2), 1949 *SA* (4), 1950 *BI* (3)
Erceg, C P (Auckland) 1951 *A* (3), 1952 *A*
Evans, D A (Hawke's Bay) 1910 *A*
Eveleigh, K A (Manawatu) 1976 *SA* (2), 1977 *BI* (2)

Fanning, A H N (Canterbury) 1913 *A*
Fanning, B J (Canterbury) 1903 *A*, 1904 *BI*
Farrell, C P (Auckland) 1977 *BI* (2)
Fawcett, C L (Auckland) 1976 *SA* (2)
Fea, W R (Otago) 1921 *SA*
Finlay, B E L (Manawatu) 1959 *BI*
Finlay, J (Manawatu) 1946 *A*
Finlayson, I (North Auckland) 1928 *SA* (4), 1930 *BI* (2)
Fitzgerald, J T (Wellington) 1952 *A*
Fitzpatrick, B B J (Wellington) 1953-54 (T) *W*, *I*, *F*
Fleming, J K (Wellington) 1979 (ST) S, E, 1980 *A* (3)
Fletcher, C J C (North Auckland) 1921 *SA*
Fogarty, R (Taranaki) 1921 *SA* (2)
Ford, B R (Marlborough) 1977 *BI* (2), 1978 (T) *I*, 1979 (ST) *E*
Francis, A R H (Auckland) 1905 *A*, 1907 *A* (3), 1908 *AW* (3), 1910 *A* (3)
Francis, W C (Wellington) 1913 *A* (2), 1914 *A* (3)
Fraser, B G (Wellington) 1979 (ST) *S*, *E*, 1980 *A*, 1980 (ST) *W*, 1981 *S* (2), *SA* (3), 1981 (ST) *R*, *F* (2), 1982 *A* (3), 1983 *BI* (4), *A*, 1983 (ST) *S*, *E*
Frazer, H F (Hawke's Bay) 1946 *A* (2), 1947 *A* (2), 1949 *SA*
Fryer, F C (Canterbury) 1907 *A* (3), 1908 *AW*
Fuller, W B (Canterbury) 1910 *A* (2)
Furlong, B D M (Hawke's Bay) 1970 *SA*

Gallaher, D (Auckland) 1903 *A*, 1904 *BI*, 1905-06 (T) *S*, *E*, *W*, *F*
Gard, P C (North Otago) 1971 *BI*
Gardiner, A J (Taranaki) 1974 *A*
Geddes, J H (Southland) 1929 *A*
Geddes, W McK (Auckland) 1913 *A*
Gemmell, B McL (Auckland) 1974 *A* (2)
George, V L (Southland) 1938 *A* (3)
Gilbert, G D M (West Coast) 1935-36 (T), *S*, *I*, *W*, *E*
Gillespie, C T (Wellington) 1913 *A*
Gillespie, W D (Otago) 1958 *A*
Gillett, G A (Canterbury, Auckland) 1905-06 (T) *S*, *I*, *E*, *W*, 1907 *A* (2), 1908 *AW* (2)
Gillies, C C (Otago) 1936 *A*
Gilray, C M (Otago) 1905 *A*
Glasgow, F T (Taranaki, Southland) 1905-06 (T) *S*, *I*, *E*, *W*, *F*, 1908 *AW*
Glenn, W S (Taranaki) 1904 *BI*, 1905-06 (T) *F*
Goddard, M P (South Canterbury) 1946 *A*, 1947 *A* (2), 1949 *SA* (2)
Going, S M (North Auckland) 1967 *A*, 1967-68 (T) *F*, 1968 *F*, 1969 *W* (2), 1970 *SA* (2[1R]), 1971 *BI* (4), 1972 *A* (3), 1972-73 (T) *W*, *S*, *E*, *I*, *F*, 1973 *E*, 1974 (ST) *I*, 1975 *S*, 1976 *I* (R), *SA* (4), 1977 *BI* (2)
Graham, D J (Canterbury) 1958 *A* (2), 1960 *SA* (2), 1961 *F* (3), 1962 *A* (5), 1963 *E* (2), 1963-64 (T) *I*, *W*, *E*, *S*, *F*, 1964 *A* (3)
Graham, J B (Otago) 1913 *US*, 1914 *A* (2)
Graham, W G (Otago) 1979 *F* (R)
Grant, L A (South Canterbury) 1947 *A* (2), 1949 *SA* (2)
Gray, G D (Canterbury) 1908 *AW*, 1913 *A*, *US*
Gray, K F (Wellington) 1963-64 (T) *I*, *W*, *E*, *S*, *F*, 1964 *A* (3), 1965 *SA* (4), 1966 *BI* (4), 1967-68 (T) *W*, *F*, *S*, 1968 *A*, *F* (2), 1969 *W* (2)
Gray, W N (Bay of Plenty) 1955 *A* (2), 1956 *SA* (4)
Green, C I (Canterbury) 1983 (ST) *S* (R), *E*
Grenside, B A (Hawke's Bay) 1928 *SA* (4), 1929 *A* (2)
Griffiths, J L (Wellington) 1934 *A*, 1935-36 (T) *S*, *I*, *W*, 1936 *A* (2), 1938 *A*
Guy, R A (North Auckland) 1971 *BI* (4)

Haden, A M (Auckland) 1977 *BI* (4), 1977 (ST) *F* (2), 1978 *A* (3), 1978 (T) *I*, *W*, *E*, *S*, 1979 *F* (2), *A*, 1979 (ST) *S*, *E*, 1980 *A* (3), 1980 (ST) *W*, 1981 *S*, *SA* (3), 1981 (ST) *R*, *F* (2), 1982 *A* (3), 1983 *BI* (4), *A*
Hadley, S (Auckland) 1928 *SA* (4)
Hadley, W E (Auckland) 1934 *A* (2), 1935-36 (T) *S*, *I*, *W*, *E*, 1936 *A* (2)
Haig, J S (Otago) 1946 *A* (2)
Haig, L S (Otago) 1950 *BI* (3), 1951 *A* (3), 1953-54 (T) *W*, *E*, *S*
Hales, D A (Canterbury) 1972 *A* (3), 1972-73 (T) *W*
Hamilton, D C (Southland) 1908 *AW*
Hammond, I A (Marlborough) 1952 *A*
Harper, E T (Canterbury) 1904 *BI*, 1905-06 (T) *F*
Harris, P C (Manawatu) 1976 *SA*
Hart, A H (Taranaki) 1924-25 (T) *I*
Hart, G F (Canterbury) 1930 *BI* (4), 1931 *A*, 1934 *A*, 1935-36 (T) *S*, *I*, *W*, 1936 *A* (2)
Harvey, I H (Wairarapa) 1928 *SA*
Harvey, L R (Otago) 1949 *SA* (4), 1950 *BI* (4)
Harvey, P (Canterbury) 1904 *BI*
Hasell, E W (Canterbury) 1913 *A* (2)
Hayward, H (Auckland) 1908 *AW*
Hazlett, E J (Southland) 1966 *BI* (4), 1967 *A*, 1967-68 (T) *E*
Hazlett, W E (Southland) 1928 *SA* (4), 1930 *BI* (4)
Heeps, T R (Wellington) 1962 *A* (5)
Heke, W R (North Auckland) 1929 *A* (3)
Hemi, R C (Waikato) 1953-54 (T) *W*, *I*, *E*, *S*, *F*, 1955 *A* (3), 1956 *SA* (3), 1957 *A* (2), 1959 *BI* (3)
Henderson, P (Wanganui) 1949 *SA* (4), 1950 *BI* (3)
Herewini, M A (Auckland) 1962 *A*, 1963-64 (T) *I*, *S*, *F*, 1965 *SA*, 1966 *BI* (4), 1967 *A*
Hewson, A R (Wellington) 1981 *S* (2), *SA* (3), 1981 (ST) *R*, *F* (2), 1982 *A* (3), 1983 *BI* (4), *A*
Higginson, G (Canterbury, Hawke's Bay) 1980 (ST) *W*, 1981 *S*, *SA*, 1982 *A* (2), 1983 *A*
Hill, S F (Canterbury) 1955 *A*, 1956 *SA* (3), 1957 *A* (2), 1958 *A*, 1959 *BI* (4)
Hines, G R (Waikato) 1980 *A*
Hobbs, M J B (Canterbury) 1983 *BI* (4), *A*, 1983 (ST) *S*, *E*
Holder, E C (Buller) 1934 *A*
Hook, L S (Auckland) 1929 *A* (3)
Hooper, J A (Canterbury) 1937 *SA* (3)
Hopkinson, A E (Canterbury) 1967-68 (T) *S*, 1968 *A*, *F* (3), 1969 *W*, 1970 *SA* (3)
Hore, J (Otago) 1930 *BI* (3), 1932 *A* (3), 1934 *A* (2), 1935-36 (T) *S*, *E*
Horsley, R H (Wellington) 1960 *SA* (3)
Hotop, J (Canterbury) 1952 *A* (2), 1955 *A*
Hughes, A M (Auckland) 1949 *A* (2), 1950 *BI* (4)
Hughes, E (Southland, Wellington) 1907 *A* (3), 1908 *AW*, 1921 *SA* (2)
Hunter, B A (Otago) 1971 *BI* (3)
Hunter, J (Taranaki) 1905-06 (T) *S*, *I*, *E*, *W*, *F*, 1907 *A* (3), 1908 *AW* (3)
Hurst, I A (Canterbury) 1972-73 (T) *I*, *F*, 1973 *E*, 1974 *A* (2)

Ifwersen, K D (Auckland) 1921 *SA*
Innes, G D (Canterbury) 1932 *A*
Irvine, I B (North Auckland) 1952 *A*
Irvine, J G (Otago) 1914 *A* (3)
Irvine, W R (Hawke's Bay, Wairarapa) 1924-25 (T) *I*, *W*, *E*, *F*, 1930 *BI*
Irwin, M W (Otago) 1955 *A* (2), 1956 *SA*, 1958 *A*, 1959 *BI* (2), 1960 *SA*

Jackson, E S (Hawke's Bay) 1936 *A* (2), 1937 *SA* (3), 1938 *A*
Jaffray, J L (Otago, South Canterbury) 1972 *A*, 1975 *S*, 1976 *I*, *SA*, 1977 *BI*, 1979 *F* (2)
Jarden, R A (Wellington) 1951 *A* (2), 1952 *A* (2), 1953-54 (T) *W*, *I*, *E*, *S*, *F*, 1955 *A* (3), 1956 *SA* (4)
Jefferd, A C R (East Coast) 1981 *S* (2), *SA*
Jessep, E M (Wellington) 1931 *A*, 1932 *A*

Johnson, L M (Wellington) 1928 *SA* (4)
Johnston, W (Otago) 1907 *A* (3)
Johnstone, B R (Auckland) 1976 *SA*, 1977 *BI* (2), 1977 (ST) *F* (2), 1978 (T) *I*, *W*, *E*, *S*, 1979 *F* (2), 1979 (ST) *S*, *E*
Johnstone, P (Otago) 1949 *SA* (2), 1950 *BI* (4), 1951 *A* (3)
Jones, M G (North Auckland) 1973 *E*
Jones, P F (North Auckland) 1953-54 (T) *E*, *S*, 1955 *A* (2), 1956 *SA* (2), 1958 *A* (3), 1959 *BI*, 1960 *SA*
Joseph, H T (Canterbury) 1971 *BI* (2)

Karam, J F (Wellington, Horowhenua) 1972-73 (T) *W*, *S*, *E*, *I*, *F*, 1974 *A* (3), 1974 (ST) *I*, 1975 *S*
Katene, T (Wellington) 1955 *A*
Kearney, J C (Otago) 1947 *A*, 1949 *SA* (3)
Kelly, J W (Auckland) 1949 *A* (2)
Kember, G F (Wellington) 1970 *SA*
Ketels, R C (Counties) 1980 (ST) *W*, 1981 *S* (2), 1981 (ST) *R*, *F*
Kiernan, H A D (Auckland) 1903 *A*
Kilby, F D (Wellington) 1932 *A* (3), 1934 *A*
Killeen, B A (Auckland) 1936 *A*
King, R R (West Coast) 1934 *A*, 1935-36 (T) *S*, *I*, *W*, *E*, 1936 *A* (2), 1937 *SA* (3), 1938 *A* (3)
Kingstone, C N (Taranaki) 1921 *SA* (3)
Kirkpatrick, I A (Canterbury, Poverty Bay) 1967-68 (T) *F*, 1968 *A* (2[1R]), *F* (3), 1969 *W* (2), 1970 *SA* (4), 1971 *BI* (4), 1972 *A* (3), 1972-73 (T) *W*, *S*, *E*, *I*, *F*, 1973 *E*, 1974 *A* (3), 1974 (ST) *I*, 1975 *S*, 1976 *I*, *SA* (4), 1977 *BI* (4)
Kirton, E W (Otago) 1967-68 (T) *E*, *W*, *F*, *S*, 1968 *A* (2), *F* (3), 1969 *W* (2), 1970 *SA* (2)
Kivell, A L (Taranaki) 1929 *A* (2)
Knight, A (Auckland) 1934 *A*
Knight, G A (Manawatu) 1977 (ST) *F* (2), 1978 *A* (3), 1978 (T) *E*, *S*, 1979 *F* (2), *A*, 1980 *A* (3), 1980 (ST) *W*, 1981 *S* (2), *SA* (2), 1982 *A* (3), 1983 *BI* (4), *A*
Knight, L G (Poverty Bay) 1977 *BI* (4), 1977 (ST) *F* (2)
Koteka, P T (Waikato) 1981 (ST) *F*, 1982 *A*
Kreft, A J (Otago) 1968 *A*

Laidlaw, C R (Otago, Canterbury) 1963-64 (T) *F*, 1964 *A*, 1965 *SA* (4), 1966 *BI* (4), 1967-68 (T) *E*, *W*, *S*, 1968 *A* (2), *F* (2), 1970 *SA* (3)
Laidlaw, K F (Southland) 1960 *SA* (3)
Lambert, K K (Manawatu) 1972-73 (T) *S* (R), *E*, *I*, *F*, 1973 *F*, 1974 (ST) *I*, 1976 *SA* (3), 1977 *BI* (2)
Lambourn, A (Wellington) 1934 *A* (2), 1935-36 (T) *S*, *I*, *W*, *E*, 1937 *SA* (3), 1938 *A*
Le Lievre, J M (Canterbury) 1962 *A*
Lendrum, R N (Counties) 1973 *E*
Leslie, A R (Wellington) 1974 *A* (3), 1974 (ST), *I*, 1975 *S*, 1976 *I*, *SA* (4)
Leys, E T (Wellington) 1929 *A*
Lilburne, H T (Canterbury, Wellington) 1928 *SA* (2), 1929 *A* (3), 1930 *BI* (2), 1931 *A*, 1932 *A*, 1934 *A*
Lindsay, D F (Otago) 1928 *SA* (3)
Lineen, T R (Auckland) 1957 *A* (2), 1958 *A* (3), 1959 *BI* (4), 1960 *SA* (3)
Lister, T N (South Canterbury) 1968 *A* (2), *F*, 1969 *W* (2), 1970 *SA* (2), 1971 *BI*
Little, P F (Auckland) 1961 *F* (2), 1962 *A* (3), 1963-64 (T) *I*, *W*, *E*, *S*, *F*
Loader, C J (Wellington) 1953-54 (T) *I*, *E*, *S*, *F*
Lochore, B J (Wairarapa) 1963-64 (T) *E*, *S*, 1965 *SA* (4), 1966 *BI* (4), 1967 *A*, 1967-68 (T) *E*, *W*, *F*, *S*, 1968 *A*, *F* (2), 1969 *W* (2), 1970 *SA* (4), 1971 *BI*
Long, A J (Auckland) 1903 *A*
Loveridge, D S (Taranaki) 1978 (T) *W*, 1979 (ST) *S*, *E*, 1980 *A* (3), 1980 (ST) *W*, 1981 *S* (2), *SA* (3), 1981 (ST) *R*, *F* (2), 1982 *A* (3), 1983 *BI* (4), *A*
Lucas, F W (Auckland) 1924-25 (T) *I*, *F*, 1928 *SA*, 1930 *BI* (4)
Lunn, W A (Otago) 1949 *A* (2)
Lynch, T W (South Canterbury) 1913 *A*, 1914 *A* (3)
Lynch, T W (Canterbury) 1951 *A* (3)

McAtamney, F S (Otago) 1956 *SA*
McCaw, W A (Southland) 1951 *A* (3), 1953-54 (T) *W*, *F*
McCool, M J (Wairarapa-Bush) 1979 *A*
McCormick, W F (Canterbury) 1965 *SA*, 1967-68 (T) *E*, *W*, *F*, *S*, 1968 *A* (2), *F* (3), 1969 *W* (2), 1970 *SA* (3), 1971 *BI*
McCullough, J F (Taranaki) 1959 *BI* (3)
McDonald, A (Otago) 1905-06 (T) *S*, *I*, *E*, *W*, 1907 *A*, 1908 *AW*, 1913 *A*, *US*
Macdonald, H H (Canterbury, North Auckland) 1972-73 (T) *W*, *S*, *E*, *I*, *F*, 1973 *E*, 1974 (ST) *I*, 1975 *S*, 1976 *I*, *SA* (3)
McEldowney, J T (Taranaki) 1977 *BI* (2)
MacEwan, I N (Wellington) 1956 *SA*, 1957 *A* (2), 1958 *A* (3), 1959 *BI* (3), 1960 *SA* (4), 1961 *F* (3), 1962 *A* (4)
McGrattan, B (Wellington) 1983 (ST) *S*, *E*
McGregor, A J (Auckland) 1913 *A*, *US*
McGregor, D (Canterbury, Southland) 1903 *A*, 1904 *BI*, 1905-06 (T) *E*, *W*
McGregor, N P (Canterbury) 1924-25 (T) *W*, *E*
McGregor, R W (Auckland) 1903 *A*, 1904 *BI*
McHugh, M J (Auckland) 1946 *A* (2), 1949 *SA*
McIntosh, D N (Wellington) 1956 *SA* (2), 1957 *A* (2)
McKay, D W (Auckland) 1961 *F* (3), 1963 *E* (2)
McKechnie, B J (Southland) 1977 (ST) *F* (2), 1978 *A* (2[1R]), 1978 (T) *W* (R), *E*, *S*, 1979 *A*, 1981 *SA* (R), 1981 (ST) *F*
McKellar, G F (Wellington) 1910 *A* (3)
McKenzie, R J (Wellington) 1913 *A*, *US*, 1914 *A* (2)
McKenzie, R McC (Manawatu) 1934 *A*, 1935-36 (T) *S*, 1936 *A*, 1937 *SA* (3), 1938 *A* (3)
McLachlan, J S (Auckland) 1974 *A*
McLaren, H C (Waikato) 1952 *A*
McLean, A L (Bay of Plenty) 1921 *SA* (2)
McLean, H F (Wellington, Auckland) 1930 *BI* (2), 1932 *A* (3), 1934 *A*, 1935-36 (T) *I*, *W*, *E*
McLean, J K (King Country, Auckland) 1947 *A*, 1949 *A*
McLeod, B E (Counties) 1964 *A* (3), 1965 *SA* (4), 1966 *BI* (4), 1967-68 (T) *E*, *W*, *F*, *S*, 1968 *A* (2), *F* (3), 1969 *W* (2), 1970 *SA* (2)
McMinn, A F (Wairarapa, Manawatu) 1903 *A*, 1905 *A*
McMinn, F A (Manawatu) 1904 *BI*
McMullen, R F (Auckland) 1957 *A* (2), 1958 *A* (3), 1959 *BI* (3), 1960 *SA* (3)
McNab, J R (Otago) 1949 *SA* (3), 1950 *BI* (3)
McNaughton, A M (Bay of Plenty) 1971 *BI* (3)
McNeece, J (Southland) 1913 *A* (2), 1914 *A* (3)
McPhail, B E (Canterbury) 1959 *BI* (2)
Macpherson, D G (Otago) 1905 *A*
MacRae, I R (Hawke's Bay) 1966 *BI* (4), 1967 *A*, 1967-68 (T) *E*, *W*, *F*, *S*, 1968 *F* (2), 1969 *W* (2), 1970 *SA* (4)
McRae, J A (Southland) 1946 *A* (2[1R])
McWilliams, R G (Auckland) 1928 *SA* (3), 1929 *A* (3), 1930 *BI* (4)
Mackrell, W H C (Auckland) 1905-06 (T) *F*
Macky, J V (Auckland) 1913 *A*
Maguire, J R (Auckland) 1910 *A* (3)
Mahoney, A (Bush) 1935-36 (T) *S*, *I*, *W*, *E*
Mains, L W (Otago) 1971 *BI* (3), 1976 *I*
Major, J (Taranaki) 1967 *A*
Manchester, J E (Canterbury) 1932 *A* (3), 1934 *A* (2), 1935-36 (T) *S*, *I*, *W*, *E*
Mason, D F (Wellington) 1947 *A* (R)
Masters, R R (Canterbury) 1924-25 (T) *I*, *W*, *E*, *F*
Mataira, H K (Hawke's Bay) 1934 *A*
Matheson, J D (Otago) 1972 *A* (3), 1972-73 (T) *W*, *S*
Max, D S (Nelson) 1931 *A*, 1934 *A* (2)
Meads, C E (King Country) 1957 *A* (2), 1958 *A* (3), 1959 *BI* (3), 1960 *SA* (4), 1961 *F* (3), 1962 *A* (4), 1963 *E* (2), 1963-64 (T) *I*, *W*, *E*, *S*, *F*, 1964 *A* (3), 1965 *SA* (4), 1966 *BI* (4), 1967 *A*, 1967-68 (T) *E*, *W*, *F*, *S*, 1968 *A* (2), *F* (3), 1969 *W* (2), 1970 *SA* (2), 1971 *BI* (4)
Meads, S T (King Country) 1961 *F*, 1962 *A* (2), 1963-64 (T) *I*, 1964 *A* (3), 1965 *SA* (4), 1966 *BI* (4)
Meates, K F (Canterbury) 1952 *A* (2)
Meates, W A (Otago) 1949 *SA* (3), 1950 *BI* (4)
Metcalfe, T C (Southland) 1931 *A*, 1932 *A*
Mexted, G G (Wellington) 1950 *BI*
Mexted, M G (Wellington) 1979 (ST) *S*, *E*, 1980 *A* (3), 1980 (ST) *W*, 1981 *S* (2), *SA* (3), 1981 (ST) *R*, *F* (2), 1982 *A* (3), 1983 *BI* (4), *A*, 1983 (ST) *S*, *E*
Mill, J J (Hawke's Bay, Wairarapa) 1924-25 (T) *W*, *E*, *F*, 1930 *BI*
Milliken, H M (Canterbury) 1938 *A* (3)
Milner, H P (Wanganui) 1970 *SA*
Mitchell, N A (Southland, Otago) 1935-36 (T) *S*, *I*, *W*, *E*, 1936 *A*, 1937 *SA*, 1938 *A* (2)
Mitchell, T W (Canterbury) 1976 *SA* (R)

Mitchell, W J (Canterbury) 1910 *A* (2)
Mitchinson, F E (Wellington) 1907 *A* (3), 1908 *AW* (3), 1910 *A* (3), 1913 *A* (R), *US*
Moffitt, J E (Wellington) 1921 *SA* (3)
Moore, G J T (Otago) 1949 *A*
Moreton, R C (Canterbury) 1962 *A* (2), 1964 *A* (3), 1965 *SA* (2)
Morgan, J E (North Auckland) 1974 *A*, 1974 (ST) *I*, 1976 *SA* (3)
Morris, T J (Nelson Bays) 1972 *A* (3)
Morrison, T C (South Canterbury) 1938 *A* (3)
Morrison, T G C (Canterbury) 1962 *A* (2), 1964 *A* (3), 1965 *SA* (2)
Morgan, J E (North Auckland) 1974 *A*, 1974 (ST) *I*, (2), 1978 (T) *I*, *W*, *E*, *S*, 1979 *F* (2), *A*, 1979 (ST) *S*, *E*, 1980 (ST) *W*, 1981 *S* (2), 1981 (ST) *F* (2), 1982 *A* (3)
Muller, B L (Taranaki) 1967 *A*, 1967-68 (T) *E*, *W*, *F*, 1968 *A*, *F* 1969 *W*, 1970 *SA* (3), 1971 *BI* (4)
Mumm, W J (Buller) 1949 *A*
Murdoch, K (Otago) 1970 *SA*, 1972 *A*, 1972-73 (T) *W*
Murdoch, P H (Auckland) 1964 *A* (2), 1965 *SA* (3)
Murray, H V (Canterbury) 1913 *A*, *US*, 1914 *A* (2)
Murray, P C (Wanganui) 1908 *AW*
Myers, R G (Waikato) 1978 *A*
Mynott, H J (Taranaki) 1905-06 (T), *I*, *W*, *F*, 1907 *A* (3), 1910 *A* (2)

Nathan, W J (Auckland) 1962 *A* (5), 1963 *E* (2), 1963-64 (T) *W*, *F*, 1966 *BI* (4), 1967 *A*
Nelson, K A (Otago) 1962 *A* (2)
Nepia, G (Hawke's Bay, East Coast) 1924-25 (T) *I*, *W*, *E*, *F*, 1929 *A*, 1930 *BI* (4)
Nesbit, S R (Auckland) 1960 *SA* (2)
Newton, F (Canterbury) 1905-06 (T) *E*, *W*, *F*
Nicholls, H E (Wellington) 1921 *SA*
Nicholls, M F (Wellington) 1921 *SA* (3), 1924-25 (T) *I*, *W*, *E*, *F*, 1928 *SA*, 1930 *BI* (2)
Nicholson, G W (Auckland) 1903 *A*, 1904 *BI*, 1907 *A* (2)
Norton, R W (Canterbury) 1971 *BI* (4), 1972 *A* (3), 1972-73 (T) *W*, *S*, *E*, *I*, *F*, 1973 *E*, 1974 *A* (3), 1974 (ST) *I*, 1975 *S*, 1976 *I*, *SA* (4), 1977 *BI* (4)

O'Brien, J G (Auckland) 1914 *A*
O'Callaghan, M W (Manawatu) 1968 *F* (3)
O'Callaghan, T R (Wellington) 1949 *A*
O'Donnell, D H (Wellington) 1949 *A*
Old, G H (Manawatu) 1981 *SA*, 1981 (ST) *R* (R), 1982 *A* (R)
O'Leary, M J (Auckland) 1910 *A* (2), 1913 *A* (2)
Oliver, C J (Canterbury) 1929 *A* (2), 1934 *A*, 1935-36 (T), *S*, *I*, *W*, *E*
Oliver, D J (Wellington) 1930 *BI* (2)
Oliver, D O (Otago) 1953-54 (T) *I*, *F*
Oliver, F J (Southland, Otago, Manawatu) 1976 *SA*, 1977 *BI* (4), 1977 (ST) *F* (2), 1978 *A* (3), 1978 (T) *I*, *W*, *E*, *S*, 1979 *F* (2), 1981 *SA*
Orr, R W (Otago) 1949 *A*
Osborne, W M (Wanganui) 1975 *S*, 1976 *SA* (2[2R]), 1977 *BI* (4), 1977 (ST) *F* (2[1R]), 1978 (T), *I*, *W*, *E*, *S*, 1980 (ST) *W*, 1982 *A* (2)
O'Sullivan, J M (Taranaki) 1905-06 (T) *S*, *I*, *E*, *W*, 1907 *A*
O'Sullivan, T P A (Taranaki) 1960 *SA*, 1961 *F*, 1962 *A* (2)

Page, J R (Wellington) 1931 *A*, 1932 *A* (3), 1934 *A* (2)
Palmer, B P (Auckland) 1929 *A*, 1932 *A* (2)
Parker, J H (Canterbury) 1924-25 (T) *I*, *W*, *E*
Parkhill, A A (Otago) 1937 *SA* (3), 1938 *A* (3)
Parkinson, R M (Poverty Bay) 1972 *A* (3), 1972-73 (T) *W*, *S*, *E*, 1973 *E*
Paterson, A M (Otago) 1908 *AW* (2), 1910 *A* (3)
Paton, H (Otago) 1910 *A* (2)
Phillips, W J (King Country) 1937 *SA*, 1938 *A* (2)
Pickering, E A R (Waikato) 1958 *A*, 1959 *BI* (2)
Pokere, S T (Southland) 1981 *SA*, 1982 *A* (3), 1983 *BI* (4), *A*, 1983 (ST) *S*, *E*
Pollock, H R (Wellington) 1932 *A* (3), 1936 *A* (2)
Porter, C G (Wellington) 1924-25 (T) *F*, 1929 *A* (2), 1930 *BI* (4)
Proctor, A C (Otago) 1932 *A*
Purdue, C A (Southland) 1905 *A*
Purdue, E (Southland) 1905 *A*
Purdue, G B (Southland) 1931 *A*, 1932 *A* (3)
Purvis, N A (Otago) 1976 *I*

Quaid, C E (Otago) 1938 *A* (2)

Rangi, R E (Auckland) 1964 *A* (2), 1965 *SA* (4), 1966 *BI* (4)
Rankin, J G (Canterbury) 1936 *A* (2), 1937 *SA*
Reedy, W J (Wellington) 1908 *AW* (2)
Reid, A R (Waikato) 1952 *A*, 1956 *SA* (2), 1957 *A* (2)
Reid, H R (Bay of Plenty) 1980 *A* (2), 1980 (ST) *W*, 1983 (ST) *S*, *E*
Reid, K H (Wairarapa) 1929 *A* (2)
Reid, S T (Hawke's Bay) 1935-36 (T) *S*, *I*, *W*, *E*, 1936 *A* (2), 1937 *SA* (3)
Reside, W B (Wairarapa) 1929 *A*
Rhind, P K (Canterbury) 1946 *A* (2)
Richardson, J (Otago, Southland) 1921 *SA* (3), 1924-25 (T) *I*, *W*, *E*, *F*
Rickit, H (Waikato) 1981 *S* (2)
Ridland, A J (Southland) 1910 *A* (3)
Roberts, E J (Wellington) 1914 *A* (3), 1921 *SA* (2)
Roberts, F (Wellington) 1905-06 (T) *S*, *I*, *E*, *W*, 1907 *A* (3), 1908 *AW* (2), 1910 *A* (3)
Roberts, R W (Taranaki) 1913 *A*, *US*, 1914 *A* (3)
Robertson, B J (Counties) 1972 *A* (2), 1972-73 (T) *S*, *E*, *I*, *F* 1974 *A* (3), 1974 (ST) *I*, 1976 *I*, *SA* (4), 1977 *BI* (3), 1977 (ST) *F* (2), 1978 *A* (3), 1978 (T) *W*, *E*, *S*, 1979 *F* (2), *A*, 1980 *A* (2), 1980 (ST) *W*, 1981 *S* (2)
Robertson, D J (Otago) 1974 *A* (3), 1974 (ST) *I*, 1975 *S*, 1976 *I*, *SA* (3), 1977 *BI*
Robilliard, A C C (Canterbury) 1928 *SA* (4)
Robinson, C E (Southland) 1951 *A* (3), 1952 *A* (2)
Rollerson, D L (Manawatu) 1980 (ST) *W*, 1981 *S*, *SA* (3), 1981 (ST) *R*, *F* (2[1R])
Roper, R A (Taranaki) 1949 *A*, 1950 *BI* (4)
Rowley, H C B (Wanganui) 1949 *A*
Rutledge, L M (Southland) 1978 *A* (3), 1978 (T) *I*, *W*, *E*, *S*, 1979 *F* (2), *A*, 1980 *A* (3)
Ryan, J (Wellington) 1910 *A*, 1914 *A* (3)

Sadler, B S (Wellington) 1935-36 (T) *S*, *I*, *W*, 1936 *A* (2)
Salmon, J L B (Wellington) 1981 (ST) *R*, *F* (2[1R])
Savage, L T (Canterbury) 1949 *SA* (3)
Saxton, C K (South Canterbury) 1938 *A* (3)
Scott, R W H (Auckland) 1946 *A* (2), 1947 *A* (2), 1949 *SA* (4), 1950 *BI* (4), 1953-54 (T) *W*, *I*, *E*, *S*, *F*
Scown, A I (Taranaki) 1972 *A* (3), 1972-73 (T) *W* (R), *S*
Scrimshaw, G (Canterbury) 1928 *SA*
Seear, G A (Otago) 1977 (ST) *F* (2), 1978 *A* (3), 1978 (T) *I*, *W*, *E*, *S*, 1979 *F* (2), *A*
Seeling, C E (Auckland) 1904 *BI*, 1905-06 (T) *S*, *I*, *E*, *W*, *F*, 1907 *A* (2), 1908 *AW* (3)
Sellars, G M V (Auckland) 1913 *A*, *US*
Shaw, M W (Manawatu) 1980 *A* (3[1R]), 1980 (ST) *W*, 1981 *S* (2), *SA* (2), 1981 (ST) *R*, *F* (2), 1982 *A* (3), 1983 *BI* (4), *A*, 1983 (ST) *S*, *E*
Shelford, F K (Bay of Plenty) 1981 *SA*, 1981 (ST) *R*
Siddells, S K (Wellington) 1921 *SA*
Simon, H J (Otago) 1937 *SA* (3)
Simpson, J G (Auckland) 1947 *A* (2), 1949 *SA* (4), 1950 *BI* (3)
Sims, G S (Otago) 1972 *A*
Skeen, J R (Auckland) 1952 *A*
Skinner, K L (Otago, Counties) 1949 *SA* (4), 1950 *BI* (4), 1951 *A* (3), 1952 *A* (2), 1953-54 (T) *W*, *I*, *E*, *S*, *F*, 1956 *SA* (2)
Skudder, G R (Waikato) 1969 *W*
Sloane, P H (North Auckland) 1979 (ST) *E*
Smith, A E (Taranaki) 1969 *W* (2), 1970 *SA*
Smith, G W (Auckland) 1905-06 (T) *S*, *I*
Smith, I S T (Otago, North Otago) 1964 *A* (3), 1965 *SA* (3), 1966 *BI* (3)
Smith, J B (North Auckland) 1946 *A*, 1947 *A*, 1949 *A* (2)
Smith, R M (Canterbury) 1955 *A*
Smith, W E (Nelson) 1905 *A*
Smith, W R (Canterbury) 1980 *A*, 1982 *A* (3), 1983 *BI* (2), 1983 (ST) *S*, *E*
Snow, E M (Nelson) 1929 *A* (3)
Solomon, F (Auckland) 1931 *A*, 1932 *A* (2)
Sonntag, W T C (Otago) 1929 *A* (3)
Spencer, J C (Wellington) 1905 *A*, 1907 *A* (R)
Spiers, J E (Counties) 1979 (ST) *S*, *E*, 1981 (ST) *R*, *F* (2)

Spillane, A P (South Canterbury) 1913 *A* (2)
Stead, J W (Southland) 1904 *BI*, 1905-06 (T) *S*, *I*, *E*, *F*, 1908 *AW* (2)
Steel, A G (Canterbury) 1966 *BI* (4), 1967 *A*, 1967-68 (T) *F*, *S*, 1968 *A* (2)
Steel, J (West Coast) 1921 *SA* (3), 1924-25 (T) *W*, *E*, *F*
Steele, L B (Wellington) 1951 *A* (3)
Steere, E R G (Hawke's Bay) 1930 *BI* (4), 1931 *A*, 1932 *A*
Stephens, O G (Wellington) 1968 *F*
Stevens, I N (Wellington) 1972-73 (T) *S*, *E*, 1974 *A*
Stewart, A J (Canterbury, South Canterbury) 1963 *E* (2), 1963-64 (T) *I*, *W*, *E*, *S*, *F*, 1964 *A*
Stewart, J D (Auckland) 1913 *A* (2)
Stewart, K W (Southland) 1973 *E*, 1974 *A* (3), 1974 (ST) *I*, 1975 *S*, 1976 *I*, *SA* (2), 1979 (ST) *S*, *E*, 1981 *SA* (2)
Stewart, R T (South Canterbury, Canterbury) 1928 *SA* (4) 1930 *BI*
Stohr, L B (Taranaki) 1910 *A* (3)
Stone, A M (Waikato) 1981 (ST) *F* (2), 1983 *BI* (R)
Storey, P W (South Canterbury) 1921 *SA* (2)
Strahan, S C (Manawatu) 1967 *A*, 1967-68 (T) *E*, *W*, *F*, *S*, 1968 *A* (2), *F* (3), 1970 *SA* (3), 1972 *A* (3), 1973 *E*
Strang, W A (South Canterbury) 1928 *SA* (2), 1930 *BI* (2), 1931 *A*
Stringfellow, J C (Wairarapa) 1929 *A* (2[1R])
Stuart, K C (Canterbury) 1955 *A*
Stuart, R C (Canterbury) 1949 *A* (2), 1953-54 (T) *W*, *I*, *E*, *S*, *F*
Stuart, R L (Hawke's Bay) 1977 (ST) *F* (R)
Sullivan, J L (Taranaki) 1937 *SA* (3), 1938 *A* (3)
Sutherland, A R (Marlborough) 1970 *SA* (2), 1971 *BI*, 1972 *A* (3), 1972-73 (T) *W*, *E*, *I*, *F*
Svenson, K S (Wellington) 1924-25 (T) *I*, *W*, *E*, *F*
Swain, J P (Hawke's Bay) 1928 *SA* (4)

Tanner, J M (Auckland) 1950 *BI*, 1951 *A* (3), 1953-54 (T) *W*
Tanner, K J (Canterbury) 1974 *A* (3), 1974 (ST) *I*, 1975 *S*, 1976 *I*, *SA*
Taylor, H M (Canterbury) 1913 *A*, *US*, 1914 *A* (3)
Taylor, J M (Otago) 1937 *SA* (3), 1938 *A* (3)
Taylor, M B (Waikato) 1979 *F* (2), *A*, 1979 (ST) *S*, *E*, 1980 *A* (2)
Taylor, N M (Bay of Plenty, Hawke's Bay) 1977 *BI* (2[1R]), 1977 (ST) *F* (2), 1978 *A* (3), 1978 (T) *I*, 1982 *A*
Taylor, R (Taranaki) 1913 *A* (2)
Taylor, W T (Canterbury) 1983 *BI* (4), *A*, 1983 (ST) *S*
Tetzlaff, P L (Auckland) 1947 *A* (2)
Thimbleby, N W (Hawke's Bay) 1970 *SA*
Thomas, B T (Auckland, Wellington) 1962 *A*, 1964 *A* (3)
Thomson, H D (Wellington) 1908 *AW*
Thorne, G S (Auckland) 1968 *A* (2), *F* (3), 1969 *W*, 1970 *SA* (4)
Thornton, N H (Auckland) 1947 *A* (2), 1949 *SA*
Tilyard, J T (Wellington) 1913 *A*
Tindill, E W T (Wellington) 1935-36 (T) *E*
Townsend, L J (Otago) 1955 *A* (2)
Tremain, K R (Canterbury, Hawke's Bay) 1959 *BI* (3), 1960 *SA* (4), 1961 *F* (2), 1962 *A* (3), 1963 *E* (2), 1963-64 (T) *I*, *W*, *E*, *S*, *F*, 1964 *A* (3), 1965 *SA* (4), 1966 *BI* (4), 1967 *A*, 1967-68 (T) *E*, *W*, *S*, 1968 *A*, *F* (3)
Trevathan, D (Otago) 1937 *SA* (3)
Tuck, J M (Waikato) 1929 *A* (3)
Turtill, H S (Canterbury) 1905 *A*
Twigden, T M (Auckland) 1980 *A* (2)
Tyler, G A (Auckland) 1903 *A*, 1904 *BI*, 1905-06 (T) *S*, *I*, *E*, *W*, *F*

Udy, D K (Wairarapa) 1903 *A*
Urbahn, R J (Taranaki) 1959 *BI* (3)
Urlich, R A (Auckland) 1970 *SA* (2)
Uttley, I N (Wellington) 1963 *E* (2)

Vincent, P B (Canterbury) 1956 *SA* (2)
Vodanovich, I M H (Wellington) 1955 *A* (3)

Wallace, W J (Wellington) 1903 *A*, 1904 *BI*, 1905-06 (T) *S*, *I*, *E*, *W*, *F*, 1907 *A* (3), 1908 *AW*
Walsh, P T (Counties) 1955 *A* (3), 1956 *SA* (3), 1957 *A* (2), 1958 *A* (3), 1959 *BI*, 1963 *E*
Ward, R H (Southland) 1936 *A*, 1937 *SA* (2)
Waterman, A C (North Auckland) 1929 *A* (2)
Watkins, E L (Wellington) 1905 *A*
Watt, B A (Canterbury) 1962 *A* (2), 1963 *E* (2), 1963-64 (T) *W*, *E*, *S*, 1964 *A*
Watt, J M (Otago) 1936 *A* (2)
Watt, J R (Wellington) 1958 *A*, 1960 *SA* (4), 1961 *F* (2), 1962 *A* (2)
Watts, M G (Taranaki) 1979 *F* (2), 1980 *A* (3[1R])
Webb, D S (North Auckland) 1959 *BI*
Wells, J (Wellington) 1936 *A* (2)
West, A H (Taranaki) 1921 *SA* (2)
Whetton, G W (Auckland) 1981 *SA*, 1981 (ST) *R*, *F* (2), 1982 *A*, 1983 *BI* (4)
Whineray, W J (Canterbury, Waikato, Auckland) 1957 *A* (2), 1958 *A* (3), 1959 *BI* (4), 1960 *SA* (4), 1961 *F* (3), 1962 *A* (5), 1963 *E* (2), 1963-64 (T) *I*, *W*, *E*, *S*, *F*, 1965 *SA* (4)
White, A (Southland) 1921 *SA*, 1924-25 (T) *I*, *E*, *F*
White, H L (Auckland) 1953-54 (T) *I*, *E*, *F*, 1955 *A*
White, R A (Poverty Bay) 1949 *A* (2), 1950 *BI* (4), 1951 *A* (3), 1952 *A* (2), 1953-54 (T) *W*, *I*, *E*, *S*, *F*, 1955 *A* (3), 1956 *SA* (4)
White, R M (Wellington) 1946 *A* (2), 1947 *A* (2)
Whiting, G J (King Country) 1972 *A* (2), 1972-73 (T) *S*, *E*, *I*, *F*
Whiting, P J (Auckland) 1971 *BI* (3), 1972 *A* (3), 1972-73 (T) *W*, *S*, *E*, *I*, *F*, 1974 *A* (3), 1974 (ST) *I*, 1976 *I*, *SA* (4)
Williams, B G (Auckland) 1970 *SA* (4), 1971 *BI* (3), 1972 *A* (3), 1972-73 (T) *W*, *S*, *E*, *I*, *F*, 1973 *E*, 1974 *A* (3), 1974 (ST) *I*, 1975 *S*, 1976 *I*, *SA* (4), 1977 *BI* (4), 1977 (ST) *F*, 1978 *A* (3), 1978 (T) *I* (R), *W*, *E*, *S*
Williams, G C (Wellington) 1967-68 (T) *E*, *W*, *F*, *S*, 1968 *A*
Williams, P (Otago) 1913 *A*
Williment, M (Wellington) 1964 *A*, 1965 *SA* (3), 1966 *BI* (4), 1967 *A*
Willocks, C (Otago) 1946 *A* (2), 1949 *SA* (3)
Wilson, B W (Otago) 1977 *BI* (2), 1978 *A* (3), 1979 *F* (2), *A*
Wilson, D D (Canterbury) 1953-54 (T) *E*, *S*
Wilson, H W (Otago) 1949 *A*, 1950 *BI*, 1951 *A* (3)
Wilson, N A (Wellington) 1908 *AW* (2), 1910 *A* (3), 1913 *A* (2), 1914 *A* (3)
Wilson, N L (Otago) 1951 *A* (3)
Wilson, R G (Canterbury) 1979 (ST) *S*, *E*
Wilson, S S (Wellington) 1977 (ST) *F* (2), 1978 *A* (3), 1978 (T) *I*, *W*, *E*, *S*, 1979 *F* (2), *A*, 1979 (ST) *S*, *E*, 1980 *A*, 1980 (ST) *W*, 1981 *S* (2), *SA* (3), 1981 (ST) *R*, *F* (2), 1982 *A* (3), 1983 *BI* (4), *A*, 1983 (ST) *S*, *E*
Wolfe, T N (Wellington, Taranaki) 1961 *F* (3), 1962 *A* (2), 1963 *E*
Wood, M E (Canterbury, Auckland) 1903 *A*, 1904 *BI*
Woodman, F A (North Auckland) 1981 *SA* (2), 1981 (ST) *F*
Wrigley, E (Wairarapa) 1905 *A*
Wylie, J T (Auckland) 1913 *A*, *US*
Wyllie, A J (Canterbury) 1970 *SA* (2), 1971 *BI* (3), 1972-73 (T) *W*, *S*, *E*, *I*, *F*, 1973 *E*

Yates, V M (North Auckland) 1961 *F* (3)
Young, D (Canterbury) 1956 *SA*, 1958 *A* (3), 1960 *SA* (4), 1961 *F* (3), 1962 *A* (4), 1963 *E* (2), 1963-64 (T) *I*, *W*, *E*, *S*, *F*

NEW ZEALAND INTERNATIONAL RECORDS

From 1890-91, when uniform points-scoring was first adopted by International Board countries, to 30 April 1984, except in the case of matches against British Isles. These date from 1910, when British Isles teams first became representative of the Four Home Unions. Both team and individual records are against International Board countries and British Isles only, unless otherwise stated.

TEAM RECORDS

Highest score
40 v Scotland (40-15) 1981 Auckland
v individual countries
23 v England (23-11) 1967 Twickenham
40 v Scotland (40-15) 1981 Auckland
17 v Ireland (17-9) 1935 Dublin
33 v Wales (33-12) 1969 Auckland
38 v France (38-8) 1906 Parc des Princes
25 v S Africa (25-22) 1981 Auckland
38 v Australia (38-3) 1972 Auckland
38 v B Isles (38-6) 1983 Auckland

Biggest winning points margin
35 v Australia (38-3) 1972 Auckland
v individual countries
15 v England (15-0) 1905 Crystal Palace (London)
25 v Scotland (40-15) 1981 Auckland
15 v Ireland (15-0) 1905 Dublin
21 v Wales (33-12) 1969 Auckland
30 v France (38-8) 1906 Parc des Princes
17 v S Africa (20-3) 1965 Auckland
35 v Australia (38-3) 1972 Auckland
32 v B Isles (38-6) 1983 Auckland

Highest score by opposing team
30 Australia (16-30) 1978 Auckland
by individual countries
16 England (10-16) 1973 Auckland
25 Scotland (25-25) 1983 Murrayfield
10 Ireland (10-10) 1973 Dublin
16 Wales (19-16) 1972 Cardiff
24 France (19-24) 1979 Auckland
24 S Africa (12-24) 1981 Wellington
30 Australia (16-30) 1978 Auckland
17 B Isles (18-17) 1959 Dunedin

Biggest losing points margin
17 v South Africa (0-17) 1928 Durban
v individual countries
13 v England (0-13) 1936 Twickenham
No defeat v Scotland
No defeat v Ireland
5 v Wales (8-13) 1953 Cardiff
7 v France (6-13) 1973 Parc des Princes
17 v S Africa (0-17) 1928 Durban
16 v Australia (10-26) 1980 Sydney
10 v B Isles (3-13) 1971 Wellington

Most tries by New Zealand in an international
10 v France (38-8) 1906 Parc des Princes

Most tries against New Zealand in an international
5 by { S Africa (6-17) 1937 Auckland
Australia (16-30) 1978 Auckland }

Most points on overseas tour (all matches)
868 in B Isles/France (33 matches) 1905-06

Most tries on overseas tour (all matches)
215 in B Isles/France (33 matches) 1905-06

INDIVIDUAL RECORDS

Most capped player
C E Meads 55 1957-71
in individual positions
Full-back
D B Clarke 31 1956-64

Wing
B G Williams 36(38)** 1970-78
Centre (includes 2nd five-eighth)
B J Robertson 34 1972-81
1st five-eighth
O D Bruce 14 1976-78
Scrum-half
S M Going 29 1967-77
Prop
W J Whineray 32 1957-65
Hooker
R W Norton 27 1971-77
Lock
C E Meads 48(55)* 1957-71
Flanker
K R Tremain 36(38)† 1959-68
I A Kirkpatrick 36(39)†† 1967-77
No 8
B J Lochore 24(25)‡ 1963-71

**Meads won 5 caps as a flanker, 2 as a No 8*
***Williams won 2 caps as a centre*
†Tremain won 2 caps as a No 8
††Kirkpatrick won 3 caps as a No 8
‡Lochore won 1 cap as a lock
Note: A G Dalton and M G Mexted have played in the same number of matches as the most capped hooker and No 8 respectively. However, each won one cap against Romania.

Most internationals as captain – 30
W J Whineray 1958-65

Most points in internationals – 207
D B Clarke (31 appearances) 1956-64

Most points in an international – 26
A R Hewson v Australia 1982 Auckland

Most tries in internationals – 19
S S Wilson (33* appearances) 1977-83
**excludes one match against Romania*

Most tries in an international – 4
D McGregor v England 1905 Crystal Palace

Most conversions in an international – 6
A R Hewson v Scotland 1981 Auckland

Most points for New Zealand on overseas tour – 230
W J Wallace (25 appearances) 1905-06 B Isles/France

Most tries for New Zealand on overseas tour – 42
J Hunter (23 appearances) 1905-06 B Isles/France

Most points in international series – 46
A R Hewson (4 appearances) v B Isles 1983

Most points for New Zealand in international series on tour – 32
W F McCormick (4 appearances) 1967 B Isles/France

Most tries for New Zealand in international series on tour – 5
K S Svenson (4 appearances) 1924-25 B Isles/France

Most points for New Zealand in any match on tour – 41
J F Karam v South Australia 1974 Adelaide

Most tries for New Zealand in any match on tour – 8
T R Heeps v Northern NSW 1962 Quirindi

THE 1983 SEASON IN AUSTRALIA

Jim Woodward *Sydney Daily Telegraph*

While Australia maintained a policy of trying to play attractive rugby football, it is ironic that 1983 will not be remembered as a vintage year in the international arena because of the lack of a more basic component – goal-kicking. Two wins and a draw – 15-all with France – from six internationals is about the success ratio Australia has come to expect in recent times. But coach Bob Dwyer and his fellow selectors could have boasted a far better record had they not gambled in this critical area.

Since 1974 Australia has gained a fair percentage of success from the goal-kicking talents of Queensland's utility back, Paul McLean. To round off a career of 30 caps which yielded an Australian record of 260 international points, McLean, in 1982, landed five penalties and three conversions to help sink Scotland 33-9 at the Sydney Cricket Ground. But following his retirement, the Australian selectors decided not to seek a specialist goal-kicker, instead electing to use the reluctant, and sometimes unsuccessful, talent of Roger Gould or David Campese.

With no pressure on him due to a nine-try glut against the USA in Sydney, Gould landed four conversions from six attempts and Campese one from five as Australia scored a 49-3 victory. Later in the season, however, with far more at stake, the lack of a 'nerves-of-steel' kicker cost Australia dearly; for example, when a bumper crowd of 44,100 packed the Sydney Cricket Ground in August to watch Australia try to wrest the Bledisloe Cup from the All Blacks, as they had done in an similar one-off match at the same ground in 1979. At the finish Dwyer was left lamenting an 18-8 defeat after his side had scored two tries to one but failed with too many kicks.

Four times Campese lined up crucial shots at goal, including a conversion from almost right in front, and four times he missed. During the same 80 minutes New Zealand full-back Allan Hewson rubbed salt in the wound by landing four penalty goals and a conversion from six attempts. Then, with Campese again the goal-kicker, Australian breakaway Chris Roche scored the only try of the game as the Wallabies had to settle for a 15-15 draw against France at Clermont-Ferrand. How much rosier the Australian season would have been with wins in those two games. On return from France, Dwyer vowed to find a goal-kicker who could function under pressure.

The United States, on their first tour to Australia, had every reason to feel confident on the eve of the Test match after excellent lead-up form. During the earlier games, the Americans did not come across either Campese or the elusive Australian captain and fly-half Mark Ella. When the Test was over the tourists must have felt they had still only gained a fleeting glimpse of the pair. Campese, his goose-step in top working order, raced in for four tries to equal the Australian international record set by flanker Greg Cornelsen against the All Blacks at Eden Park in 1978. Mark Ella was a brilliant link-man at fly-half.

Making his Test debut in that match was Warringah (Sydney) half-back Dominic Vaughan, who got his chance following the severe knee injury Phil Cox suffered in a club match. Vaughan was the half-back in the Australian schoolboy team which took Britain by storm in 1977.

Hugo Porta's Argentinians were next to arrive, hell-bent on at least drawing a series against Australia – as they had done at home in 1979. The Pumas took the first Test, 18-3, after a frightening display of forward power at Brisbane's Ballymore Park. Twice Argentina crossed for push-over tries on Australian feeds, the first time after the Australian scrum disintegrated.

Basic alterations to the front row, including the recall of veteran loose-head prop John Meadows, saw Australia hold their own and record a 29-13 win in the second Test at the Sydney Cricket Ground, a victory which also included an early and bewildering penalty try awarded to Australia by Welsh referee Clive Norling. It was a remarkable come-back by Meadows who, only a few months previously, had been purely concerned with staying alive after having a cancerous growth removed from his groin.

The Australian provincial crown Queensland has worn so proudly in recent times slipped a little in 1983. Their coach, Bob Templeton, has always claimed his side takes a while to warm up and Sydney certainly caught them on the hop when they made an April trip to Brisbane and won 27-22. But come 5 June, Queensland were on the boil to record a 15-10 win against NSW, at Ballymore. Then the return match at the Sydney Cricket Ground saw NSW knock holes in Templeton's earlier theory when Queensland went down 6-7.

The Sydney Cricket Ground was also the venue for the downfall of Sydney – unbeaten by touring international sides since 1974. Since going down to the All Blacks that winter, Sydney had remained undefeated against England, Japan, Fiji, Wales, Ireland, New Zealand, France, a World XV and Scotland. But another World XV was invited to play Sydney in 1983. It took the efforts of Andy Dalton, Gary Knight, Gary Whetton, Andy Haden, Graham Mourie, Mark Shaw, Mark Donaldson and Steve Pokere plus Jean-Pierre Rives, Hugo Porta and Rafael Madero before the home side was finally beaten, 33-16.

The Australian selectors again sent a fully representative team to the annual Hong Kong Sevens tournament and came away with a second successive win, this time beating Fiji in deep mud in the final.

On the club scene, Manly won their first Sydney premiership since 1950 and prevented Randwick from winning six in a row by beating them 12-10 at the Sports Ground. In Brisbane the powerful Brothers Club took another Queensland championship with a 30-15 win over University.

AUSTRALIAN INTERNATIONAL PLAYERS *(up to 30 April 1984)*

ABBREVIATIONS

Arg	Argentina
BI	British Isles teams
E	England
F	France
Fj	Fiji
I	Ireland
It	Italy
J	Japan
M	Maoris
NZ	New Zealand
S	Scotland
SA	South Africa
Tg	Tonga
US	United States of America
W	Wales
(R)	Replacement – (2[1R]) denotes two appearances, one as a replacement
(T)	Tour to Northern Hemisphere
(ST)	Short tour to Northern Hemisphere
NB	*Australia awards 'caps' for matches against Fiji, Italy, the Maoris, Tonga, Japan, Argentina, and America, in addition to the International Board countries and the British Isles*

Abrahams, A M F (New South Wales) 1967 *NZ*, 1968 *NZ*, 1969 *W*
Adams, N J (New South Wales) 1955 *NZ*
Adamson, R W (New South Wales) 1912 *US*
Allan, T (New South Wales) 1946 *NZ* (2), *M*, 1947 *NZ*, 1947-48 (T) *S, I, W, E, F*, 1949 *M* (3), *NZ* (2)
Anlezark, E A (New South Wales) 1905 *NZ*
Austin, L R (New South Wales) 1963 *E*

Baker, R L (New South Wales) 1904 *BI* (2)
Baker, W H (New South Wales) 1914 *NZ* (3)
Ballesty, J P (New South Wales) 1968 *NZ* (2), *F*, 1968-69 (ST) *I, S*, 1969 *W, SA* (3)
Bannon D P (New South Wales) 1946 *M*
Barker, H S (New South Wales) 1952 *Fj* (2), *NZ* (2), 1953 *SA*, 1954 *Fj* (2)
Barnett, J T (New South Wales) 1907 *NZ* (3), 1908-09 (T), *W, E*
Barry, M J (Queensland) 1971 *SA*
Barton, R F D (New South Wales) 1899 *BI*
Batch, P G (Queensland) 1975-76 (T), *S, W, E*, 1976 *Fj* (3), 1976-77 (ST) *F* (2), 1978 *W* (2), *NZ* (3), 1979 *Arg*
Batterham, R P (New South Wales) 1967 *NZ*, 1970 *S*
Battishall, B R (New South Wales) 1973-74 (ST) *E*
Baxter, A J (New South Wales) 1949 *M* (3), *NZ* (2), 1951 *NZ* (2), 1952 *NZ* (2)
Baxter, T J (Queensland) 1958 *NZ*
Beith, B McN (New South Wales) 1914 *NZ*
Bell, K R (Queensland) 1968-69 (ST) *S*
Bennett, W G (Queensland) 1931 *M*, 1933 *SA* (3)
Bermingham, J V (Queensland) 1934 *NZ* (2), 1937 *SA*
Berne, J E (New South Wales) 1975-76 (T) *S*
Besomo, K S (New South Wales) 1979 *I*
Betts, T N (Queensland) 1951 *NZ* (2), 1954 *Fj*
Biilmann, R R (New South Wales) 1933 *SA* (4)
Birt, R (Queensland) 1914 *NZ*
Blair, M R (New South Wales) 1931 *M, NZ*
Bland, G V (New South Wales) 1932 *NZ* (3), 1933 *SA* (4)
Blomley, J (New South Wales) 1949 *M* (3), *NZ* (2), 1950 *BI* (2)
Boland, S B (Queensland) 1899 *BI* (2), 1903 *NZ*
Bonis, E T (Queensland) 1929 *NZ* (3), 1930 *BI*, 1931 *M, NZ*, 1932 *NZ* (3), 1933 *SA* (5), 1934 *NZ* (2), 1936 *NZ* (2), *M*, 1937 *SA*, 1938 *NZ*
Bosler, J M (New South Wales) 1953 *SA*
Bouffler, R G (New South Wales) 1899 *BI*
Bourke, T K (Queensland) 1947 *NZ*
Boyce, E S (New South Wales) 1962 *NZ* (2), 1964 *NZ* (3), 1965 *SA* (2), 1966-67 (T) *W, S, E, I, F*, 1967 *I*
Boyce, J S (New South Wales) 1962 *NZ* (3), 1963 *E, SA* (4), 1964 *NZ* (2), 1965 *SA* (2)
Boyd, A (New South Wales) 1899 *BI*
Boyd, A F McC (Queensland) 1958 *M*
Brass, J E (New South Wales) 1966 *BI*, 1966-67 (T) *W, S, E, I, F*, 1967 *I, NZ*, 1968 *NZ, F*, 1968-69 (ST) *I, S*
Breckenridge, J W (New South Wales) 1929 *NZ* (3), 1930 *BI*
Bridle, O L (Victoria) 1931 *M*, 1932 *NZ* (3), 1933 *SA* (3), 1934 *NZ* (2), 1936 *NZ* (2), *M*
Broad, E G (Queensland) 1949 *M*
Brockhoff, J D (New South Wales) 1949 *M* (2), *NZ* (2), 1950 *BI* (2), 1951 *NZ* (2)
Brown, B R (Queensland) 1972 *NZ* (2)
Brown, J V (New South Wales) 1956 *SA* (2), 1957 *NZ* (2), 1957-58 (T) *W, I, E, S, F*
Brown, R C (New South Wales) 1975 *E* (2)
Brown, S W (New South Wales) 1953 *SA* (3)
Buchan, A J (New South Wales) 1946 *NZ* (2), 1947 *NZ* (2), 1947-48 (T) *S, I, W, E, F*, 1949 *M*
Burdon, A (New South Wales) 1903 *NZ*, 1904 *BI* (2), 1905 *NZ*
Burge, A B (New South Wales) 1907 *NZ*, 1908-09 (T) *W*
Burge, P H (New South Wales) 1907 *NZ* (3)
Burke, C T (New South Wales) 1946 *NZ*, 1947 *NZ* (2), 1947-48 (T), *S, I, W, E, F*, 1949 *M* (2), *NZ* (2), 1950 *BI* (2), 1951 *NZ* (3), 1953 *SA* (3), 1954 *Fj*, 1955 *NZ* (3), 1956 *SA* (2)
Burnet, D R (New South Wales) 1972 *F* (2), *NZ* (3), *Fj*
Butler, O F (New South Wales) 1969 *SA* (2), 1970 *S*, 1971 *SA* (2), 1971-72 (ST) *F* (2)

Cameron, A S (New South Wales) 1951 *NZ* (3), 1952 *Fj* (2), *NZ* (2), 1953 *SA* (4), 1954 *Fj* (2), 1955 *NZ* (3), 1956 *SA* (2), 1957 *NZ*, 1957-58 (T) *I*
Campbell, J D (New South Wales) 1910 *NZ* (3)
Campese, D I (Australian Capital Territory) 1982 *NZ* (3), 1983 *US, Arg* (2), *NZ*, 1983 (ST) *It, F* (2)
Canniffe, W D (Queensland) 1907 *NZ*
Carberry, C M (New South Wales, Queensland) 1973 *Tg*, 1973-74 (ST) *E*, 1975-76 (T) *I, US*, 1976 *Fj* (3), 1981 *F* (2), 1981-82 (T) *I, W, S, E*
Cardy, A M (New South Wales) 1966 *BI* (2), 1966-67 (T) *W, S, E, I, F*, 1968 *NZ* (2)
Carew, P J (Queensland) 1899 *BI* (4)
Carmichael, P P (Queensland) 1904 *BI*, 1907 *NZ*, 1908-09 (T) *W, E*
Carpenter, M G (Victoria) 1938 *NZ* (2)

Carr, E T A (New South Wales) 1913 *NZ* (3), 1914 *NZ* (3)
Carroll, D B (New South Wales) 1908-09 (T) *W*, 1912 *US*
Carroll, J C (New South Wales) 1953 *SA*
Carroll, J H (New South Wales) 1958 *M* (2), *NZ* (3), 1959 *BI* (2)
Carson, J (New South Wales) 1899 *BI*
Carson, P J (New South Wales) 1979 *NZ*, 1980 *NZ*
Casey, T V (New South Wales) 1963 *SA* (3), 1964 *NZ* (3)
Catchpole, K W (New South Wales) 1961 *Fj* (3), *SA* (2), *F*, 1962 *NZ* (3), 1963 *SA* (3), 1964 *NZ* (3), 1965 *SA* (2), 1966 *BI* (2), 1966-67 (T) *W, S, E, I, F*, 1967 *I, NZ*, 1968 *NZ*
Cawsey, R M (New South Wales) 1949 *M, NZ* (2)
Cerutti, W H (New South Wales) 1929 *NZ* (3), 1930 *BI*, 1931 *M, NZ*, 1932 *NZ* (3), 1933 *SA* (5), 1936 *M*, 1937 *SA* (2)
Challoner, R L (New South Wales) 1899 *BI*
Chapman, G A (New South Wales) 1962 *NZ* (3)
Clark, J G (Queensland) 1931 *M, NZ*, 1932 *NZ* (2), 1933 *SA*
Clarken, J C (New South Wales) 1905 *NZ*, 1910 *NZ* (3)
Cleary, M A (New South Wales) 1961 *Fj* (3), *SA* (2), *F*
Clements, P (New South Wales) 1982 *NZ*
Clifford, M (New South Wales) 1938 *NZ*
Cobb, W G (New South Wales) 1899 *BI* (2)
Cocks, M R (New South Wales and Queensland) 1972 *F* (2), *NZ* (2), *Fj*, 1973 *Tg* (2), 1973-74 (ST) *W, E*, 1975 *J*
Codey, D (NSW Country) 1983 *Arg*
Cody, E W (New South Wales) 1913 *NZ* (3)
Colbert, R (New South Wales) 1952 *Fj, NZ* (2), 1953 *SA* (3)
Cole, J W (New South Wales) 1968 *NZ* (2), *F*, 1968-69 (ST), *I, S*, 1969 *W, SA* (4), 1970 *S*, 1971 *SA* (3), 1971-72 (ST) *F* (2), 1972 *NZ* (3), 1973 *Tg* (2), 1974 *NZ* (3)
Collins, P K (New South Wales) 1937 *SA*, 1938 *NZ* (2)
Colton, A J (Queensland) 1899 *BI* (2)
Colton, T (Queensland) 1904 *BI* (2)
Connor, D M (Queensland) 1957-58 (T) *W, I, E, S, F*, 1958 *M* (2), *NZ* (3), 1959 *BI* (2)
Cooke, B P (Queensland) 1979 *I*
Cooke, G M (Queensland) 1932 *NZ* (3), 1933 *SA* (3), 1946 *NZ*, 1947 *NZ*, 1947-48 (T) *S, I, W, E, F*
Coolican, J E (New South Wales) 1982 *NZ*, 1983 (ST) *It, F* (2)
Corfe, A C (Queensland) 1899 *BI*
Cornelsen, G (New South Wales) 1974 *NZ* (2), 1975 *J*, 1975-76 (T) *S, W, E*, 1976-77 (ST) *F* (2), 1978 *W* (2), *NZ* (3), 1979 *I* (2), *NZ, Arg* (2), 1980 *NZ* (3), 1981-82 (T) *I, W, S, E*
Cornes, J R (Queensland) 1972 *Fj*
Cornforth, R G W (New South Wales) 1947 *NZ*, 1950 *BI*
Costello, P P S (Queensland) 1950 *BI*
Cottrell, N V (Queensland) 1949 *M* (3), *NZ* (2), 1950 *BI* (2), 1951 *NZ* (3), 1952 *Fj* (2), *NZ* (2)
Cowper, D L (Victoria) 1931 *NZ*, 1932 *NZ* (3), 1933 *SA* (5)
Cox, B P (New South Wales) 1952 *Fj* (2), *NZ* (2), 1954 *Fj*, 1955 *NZ*, 1956 *SA*, 1957 *NZ* (2)
Cox, M H (New South Wales) 1981-82 (T) *W, S*
Cox, P A (New South Wales) 1979 *Arg* (2), 1980 *Fj, NZ* (2), 1981-82 (T) *W* (R), *S*, 1982 *S* (2), *NZ* (3)
Craig, R R (New South Wales) 1908-09 (T) *W*
Cremin, J F (New South Wales) 1946 *NZ* (2), 1947 *NZ*
Crittle, C P (New South Wales) 1962 *NZ* (2), 1963 *SA* (3), 1964 *NZ* (3), 1965 *SA* (2), 1966 *BI* (2), 1966-67 (T) *S, E, I*
Cross, J R (New South Wales) 1955 *NZ* (3)
Cross, K A (New South Wales) 1949 *M, NZ* (2), 1950 *BI* (2), 1951 *NZ* (2), 1952 *NZ*, 1953 *SA* (4), 1954 *Fj* (2), 1955 *NZ*, 1956 *SA* (2), 1957 *NZ* (2)
Crossman, O C (New South Wales) 1929 *NZ*, 1930 *BI*
Crowe, P J (New South Wales) 1976-77 (ST) *F*, 1978 *W* (2), 1979 *I, NZ, Arg*
Curley, T G P (New South Wales) 1957 *NZ* (2), 1957-58 (T) *W, I, E, S, F*, 1958 *M, NZ* (3)
Curran, D J (New South Wales) 1980 *NZ*, 1981 *F* (2), 1981-82 (T) *W*, 1983 *Arg*
Currie, E W (Queensland) 1899 *BI*
Cutler, S A G (New South Wales) 1982 *NZ* (R)

D'Arcy, A M (Queensland) 1980 *Fj, NZ*, 1981 *F* (2), 1981-82 (T) *I, W, S, E*, 1982 *S* (2)
Darveniza, P (New South Wales) 1969 *W, SA* (3)
Davidson, R A L (New South Wales) 1952 *Fj* (2), *NZ* (2), 1953 *SA*, 1957 *NZ* (2), 1957-58 (T) *W, I, E, S, F*, 1958 *M*
Davis, C C (New South Wales) 1949 *NZ*, 1951 *NZ* (3)
Davis, E H (Victoria) 1947-48 (T) *S, W*, 1949 *M* (2)
Davis, G V (New South Wales) 1963 *E, SA* (4), 1964 *NZ* (3), 1965 *SA*, 1966 *BI* (2), 1966-67 (T) *W, S, E, I, F*, 1967 *I, NZ*, 1968 *NZ* (2), *F*, 1968-69 (ST) *I, S*, 1969 *W, SA* (4), 1970 *S*, 1971 *SA* (3), 1971-72 (ST) *F* (2), 1972 *F* (2), *NZ* (3)
Davis, G W G (New South Wales) 1955 *NZ* (2)
Davis, R A (New South Wales) 1974 *NZ* (3)
Davis, W (New South Wales) 1899 *BI* (3)
Dawson, W L (New South Wales) 1946 *NZ* (2)
Diett, L J (New South Wales) 1959 *BI* (2)
Dix, W (New South Wales) 1907 *NZ* (3), 1908-09 (T) *E*
Dixon, E J (Queensland) 1904 *BI*
Donald, K J (Queensland) 1957 *NZ*, 1957-58 (T) *W, I, E, S*, 1958 *M* (2), 1959 *BI* (2)
Dore, E (Queensland) 1904 *BI*
Dore, M J (Queensland) 1905 *NZ*
Dorr, R W (Victoria) 1936 *M*, 1937 *SA*
Douglas, J A (Victoria) 1962 *NZ* (3)
Dowse, J H (New South Wales) 1961 *Fj* (2), *SA* (2)
Dunbar, A R (New South Wales) 1910 *NZ* (3), 1912 *US*
Dunlop, E E (Victoria) 1932 *NZ*, 1934 *NZ*
Dunn, P K (New South Wales) 1958 *NZ* (3), 1959 *BI* (2)
Dunworth, D A (Queensland) 1971-72 (ST) *F* (2), 1972 *F* (2), 1976 *Fj*
Dwyer, L J (New South Wales) 1910 *NZ* (3), 1912 *US*, 1913 *NZ*, 1914 *NZ* (3)

Eastes, C C (New South Wales) 1946 *NZ* (2), 1947 *NZ* (2), 1949 *M* (2)
Ella, G A (New South Wales) 1982 *NZ* (2), 1983 (ST) *F* (2)
Ella, G J (New South Wales) 1982 *S*, 1983 (ST) *It*
Ella, M G (New South Wales) 1980 *NZ* (3), 1981 *F*, 1981-82 (T) *S, E*, 1982 *S, NZ* (3), 1983 *US, Arg* (2), *NZ*, 1983 (ST) *It, F* (2)
Ellem, M A (New South Wales) 1976 *Fj* (R)
Elliott, F M (New South Wales) 1957 *NZ*
Ellis, C S (New South Wales) 1899 *BI* (4)
Ellis, K J (New South Wales) 1958 *NZ* (3), 1959 *BI* (2)
Ellwood, B J (New South Wales) 1958 *NZ* (3), 1961 *Fj* (2), *SA, F*, 1962 *NZ* (5), 1963 *SA* (4), 1964 *NZ*, 1965 *SA* (2), 1966 *BI*
Emanuel, D M (New South Wales) 1957 *NZ*, 1957-58 (T) *W, I, E, S, F*, 1958 *M* (3)
Emery, N A (New South Wales) 1947 *NZ*, 1947-48 (T) *S, I, W, E, F*, 1949 *M* (2), *NZ* (2)
Evans, L J (Queensland) 1903 *NZ*, 1904 *BI* (2)
Evans, W T (Queensland) 1899 *BI* (2)

Fahey, E J (New South Wales) 1912 *US*, 1913 *NZ* (2), 1914 *NZ*
Fairfax, R L (New South Wales) 1971-72 (ST) *F* (2), 1972 *F* (2), *NZ, Fj* 1973-74 (ST) *W, E*
Farmer, E H (Queensland) 1910 *NZ*
Fay, G (New South Wales) 1971 *SA*, 1972 *NZ* (3), 1973 *Tg* (2), 1973-74 (ST) *W, E*, 1974 *NZ* (3), 1975 *E* (2), *J*, 1975-76 (T) *S, W, I, US*, 1978 *W* (2), *NZ* (3), 1979 *I*
Fenwicke, P T (New South Wales) 1957 *NZ*, 1957-58 (T) *W, I, E*, 1959 *BI* (2)
Fihelly, J A (Queensland) 1907 *NZ* (2[1R])
Finlay, A N (New South Wales) 1929 *NZ* (3), 1930 *BI*
Finley, F G (New South Wales) 1904 *BI*
Finnane, S C (New South Wales) 1975 *E, J* (2), 1975-76 (T) *E*, 1978 *W* (2)
Flanagan, P (Queensland) 1907 *NZ* (2)
Flynn, J P (Queensland) 1914 *NZ* (2)
Fogarty, J R (Queensland) 1949 *M* (2)
Forbes, C F (Queensland) 1953 *SA* (3), 1954 *Fj*, 1956 *SA* (2)
Ford, B (Queensland) 1957 *NZ*
Ford, E E (New South Wales) 1929 *NZ* (2)
Ford, J A (New South Wales) 1929 *NZ* (3), 1930 *BI*
Forman, T R (New South Wales) 1968-69 (ST) *I, S*,

1969 *W*, *SA* (4)
Fox, O G (New South Wales) 1957-58 (T) *F*
Francis, E (Queensland) 1914 *NZ* (2)
Freedman, J E (New South Wales) 1962 *NZ* (3), 1963 *SA*
Freeman, E (New South Wales) 1946 *NZ* (R), *M*
Freney, M E (Queensland) 1972 *NZ* (3), 1973 *Tg*, 1973-74 (ST) *W*, *E*, (R)
Furness, D C (New South Wales) 1946 *M*
Futter, F C (New South Wales) 1904 *BI*

Gardner, W C (New South Wales) 1950 *BI*
Garner, R L (New South Wales) 1949 *NZ* (2)
Gavin, K A (New South Wales) 1908-09 (T) *E*
Gelling, A M (New South Wales) 1972 *NZ*, *Fj*
George, H W (New South Wales) 1910 *NZ* (3), 1912 *US*, 1913 *NZ* (2), 1914 *NZ* (2)
Gibbons, E de C (New South Wales) 1936 *NZ* (2) *M*
Gibbs, P R (Victoria) 1966-67 (T) *S*
Gilbert, H (New South Wales) 1910 *NZ* (3)
Gordon, G C (New South Wales) 1929 *NZ*
Gordon, K M (New South Wales) 1950 *BI* (2)
Gould, R G (Queensland) 1980 *NZ* (3), 1981-82 (T) *I*, *W*, *S*, 1982 *S*, *NZ* (3), 1983 *US*, *Arg*, 1983 (ST) *F* (2)
Graham, C S (Queensland) 1899 *BI*
Graham, R (New South Wales) 1973 *Tg* (2), 1973-74 (ST), *W*, *E*, 1974 *NZ* (2), 1975 *E*, *J* (2), 1975-76 (T) *S*, *W*, *I*, *US*, 1976 *Fj* (3), 1976-77 (ST) *F* (2)
Gralton, A S I (Queensland) 1899 *BI* (2), 1903 *NZ*
Graves, R H (New South Wales) 1907 *NZ* (R)
Gregory, S C (Queensland) 1968 *NZ*, *F*, 1968-69 (ST) *I*, *S*, 1969 *SA* (2), 1971 *SA* (2), 1971-72 (ST) *F* (2) 1972 *F* (2), 1973 *Tg* (2), 1973-74 (ST) *W*, *E*
Grey, G O (New South Wales) 1972 *F* (R), *NZ* (3), *Fj* (R)
Griffin, T S (New South Wales) 1907 *NZ* (2), 1908-09 (T) *W*, 1910 *NZ* (2), 1912 *US*
Grigg, P C (Queensland) 1980 *NZ*, 1982 *S*, *NZ* (3), 1983 *Arg*, *NZ*
Grimmond, D N (New South Wales) 1964 *NZ*
Gudsell, K E (New South Wales) 1951 *NZ* (3)
Guerassimoff, J (Queensland) 1963 *SA* (3), 1964 *NZ* (3), 1965 *SA*, 1966 *BI* (2), 1966-67 (T) *E*, *I*, *F*
Gunther, W J (New South Wales) 1957 *NZ*

Hall, D (Queensland) 1980 *Fj*, *NZ* (3), 1981 *F* (2), 1982 *S* (2), *NZ* (2), 1983 *US*, *Arg* (2), *NZ*, 1983 (ST) *It*
Hamalainen, H A (Queensland) 1929 *NZ* (3)
Hamilton, B G (New South Wales) 1946 *M*
Hammand, C A (New South Wales) 1908-09 (T), *W*, *E*
Hammon, J D C (Victoria) 1937 *SA*
Handy, C B (Queensland) 1978 *NZ*, 1979 *NZ*, *Arg* (2), 1980 *NZ* (2)
Hanley, R G (Queensland) 1983 *US* (R), 1983 (ST) *It* (R)
Hardcastle, P A (New South Wales) 1946 *NZ* (2), M, 1947 *NZ*, 1949 *M*
Hardcastle, W R (New South Wales) 1899 *BI*, 1903 *NZ*
Harding, M A (New South Wales) 1983 (ST) *It*
Harvey, P B (Queensland) 1949 *M* (2)
Harvey, R M (New South Wales) 1957-58 (T) *F*, 1958 *M*
Hatherell, W I (Queensland) 1952 *Fj* (2)
Hauser, R G (Queensland) 1975 *J* (2[1R]), 1975-76 (T) *W* (R), *E*, *I*, *US*, 1976 *Fj* (3), 1976-77 (ST) *F* (2), 1978 *W* (2), 1979 *I* (2)
Hawker, M J (New South Wales) 1980 *Fj*, *NZ* (3), 1981 *F* (2), 1981-82 (T) *I*, *W*, *E*, 1982 *S* (2), *NZ* (3), 1983 *US*, *Arg* (2), *NZ*, 1983 (ST) *It*, *F* (2)
Hawthorne, P F (New South Wales) 1962 *NZ* (3), 1963 *E*, *SA* (4), 1964 *NZ* (3), 1965 *SA* (2), 1966 *BI* (2), 1966-67 (T) *W*, *E*, *I*, *F*, 1967 *I*, *NZ*
Hayes, E S (Queensland) 1934 *NZ* (2), 1938 *NZ* (3)
Heinrich, E L (New South Wales) 1961 *Fj* (3), *SA*, *F*, 1962 *NZ* (3), 1963 *E*, *SA*
Henrich, V W (New South Wales) 1954 *Fj* (2)
Heming, R J (New South Wales) 1961 *Fj* (2), *SA* (2), *F*, 1962 *NZ* (4), 1963 *SA* (3), 1964 *NZ* (3), 1965 *SA* (2), 1966 *BI* (2), 1966-67 (T) *W*, *F*
Hemingway, W H (New South Wales) 1931 *M*, *NZ*, 1932 *NZ*
Henry, A R (Queensland) 1899 *BI*
Herd, H V (New South Wales) 1931 *M*
Hickey, J (New South Wales) 1908-09 (T) *W*, *E*
Hillhouse, D W (Queensland) 1975-76 (T) *S*, *E*, 1976 *Fj* (3), 1976-77 (ST) *F* (2), 1978 *W* (2), 1983 *US*, *Arg* (2), *NZ*, 1983 (ST) *It*, *F* (2)
Hills, E F (Victoria) 1950 *BI* (2)
Hindmarsh, J A (Queensland) 1904 *BI*
Hindmarsh, J C (New South Wales) 1975 *J*, 1975-76 (T) *S*, *W*, *US*, 1976 *Fj* (3), 1976-77 (ST) *F* (2)
Hipwell, J N B (New South Wales) 1968 *NZ* (2[1R]), *F*, 1968-69 (ST) *I*, *S*, 1969 *W*, *SA* (4), 1970 *S*, 1971 *SA* (2), 1971-72 (ST) *F* (2), 1972 *F* (2), 1973 *Tg*, 1973-74 (ST) *W*, *E*, 1974 *NZ* (3), 1975 *E* (2), *J*, 1975-76 (T) *S*, *W*, 1978 *NZ* (3), 1981 *F* (2), 1981-82 (T) *I*, *W*, *E*
Hirschberg, W A (New South Wales) 1905 *NZ*
Hodgins, C H (New South Wales) 1910 *NZ* (3)
Hodgson, A J (New South Wales) 1933 *SA* (3), 1934 *NZ*, 1936 *NZ* (2), *M*, 1937 *SA*, 1938 *NZ* (3)
Honan, B D (Queensland) 1968 *NZ* (2[1R]), *F*, 1968-69 (ST) *I*, *S*, 1969 *SA* (4)
Honan, R E (Queensland) 1964 *NZ* (2)
Horodam, D J (Queensland) 1913 *NZ*
Horsley, G R (Queensland) 1954 *Fj*
Horton, P A (New South Wales) 1974 *NZ* (3), 1975 *E* (2), *J* (2), 1975-76 (T) *S*, *W*, *E*, 1976-77 (ST) *F* (2), 1978 *W* (2), *NZ* (3), 1979 *NZ*, *Arg*
How, R A (New South Wales) 1967 *I*
Howard, J (Queensland) 1938 *NZ* (2)
Howard, J L (New South Wales) 1970 *S*, 1971 *SA*, 1972 *NZ*, *F* (R), 1973 *Tg* (2), 1973-74 (ST) *W*
Howell, M L (New South Wales) 1946 *NZ* (R), 1947 *NZ*, 1947-48 (T) *S*, *I*, *W*
Hughes, B D (New South Wales) 1913 *NZ* (2)
Hughes, J C (New South Wales) 1907 *NZ* (2)
Hughes, N McL (New South Wales) 1953 *SA* (4), 1955 *NZ* (3), 1956 *SA* (2), 1957-58 (T) *W*, *I*, *E*, *S*, *F*
Hutchinson, E E (New South Wales) 1937 *SA* (2)
Hutchinson, F E (New South Wales) 1936 *NZ* (2), 1938 *NZ* (2)

Ide, W P J (Queensland) 1938 *NZ* (2)
Ives, W N (New South Wales) 1929 *NZ*

James, P M (Queensland) 1958 *M* (2)
Jessep, E M (Victoria) 1934 *NZ* (2)
Johnson, A P (New South Wales) 1946 *NZ*, *M*
Johnson, B B (New South Wales) 1952 *Fj* (2), *NZ* (2), 1953 *SA* (3), 1955 *NZ* (2)
Johnson, P G (New South Wales) 1959 *BI* (2), 1961 *Fj* (3), *SA* (2), *F*, 1962 *NZ* (5), 1963 *E*, *SA* (4), 1964 *NZ* (3), 1965 *SA* (2), 1966 *BI* (2), 1966-67 (T) *W*, *S*, *E*, *I*, *F*, 1967 *I*, *NZ*, 1968 *NZ* (2), *F*, 1968-69 (ST) *I*, *S*, 1970 *S*, 1971 *SA* (2), 1971-72 (ST) *F* (2)
Jones, G G (Queensland) 1952 *Fj* (2), 1953 *SA* (4), 1954 *Fj* (2), 1955 *NZ* (3), 1956 *SA*
Jones, H (New South Wales) 1913 *NZ* (3)
Jones, P A (New South Wales) 1963 *E*, *SA*
Joyce, J E (New South Wales) 1903 *NZ*
Judd, H A (New South Wales) 1903 *NZ*, 1904 *BI* (3), 1905 *NZ*
Judd, P B (New South Wales) 1931 *M*, *NZ*

Kay, A R (Victoria) 1958 *NZ*, 1959 *BI*
Kearney, K H (New South Wales) 1947 *NZ* (2), 1947-48 (T) *S*, *I*, *W*, *E*, *F*
Kelaher, J D (New South Wales) 1933 *SA* (5), 1934 *NZ* (2), 1936 *NZ* (2), *M*, 1937 *SA* (2), 1938 *NZ*
Kelleher, R J (Queensland) 1969 *SA* (2)
Keller, D H (New South Wales) 1947 *NZ*, 1947-48 (T) *S*, *I*, *W*, *E*, *F*
Kelly, A J (New South Wales) 1899 *BI*
Kelly, R L F (New South Wales) 1936 *NZ* (2), *M*, 1937 *SA* (2), 1938 *NZ* (2)
Kent, A (Queensland) 1912 *US*
Kerr, F R (Victoria) 1938 *NZ*
King, S C (New South Wales) 1929 *NZ* (3), 1930 *BI*, 1932 *NZ* (2)
Knight, M (New South Wales) 1978 *W* (2), *NZ*
Knight, S O (New South Wales) 1969 *SA* (2), 1970 *S*, 1971 *SA* (3)
Kraefft, D F (New South Wales) 1947 *NZ*, 1947-48 (T) *S*, *I*, *W*, *E*, *F*
Kreutzer, S D (Queensland) 1914 *NZ*

Lambie, J K (New South Wales) 1974 *NZ* (3), 1975-76 (T) *W*

Peter Lucas, the Wallaby flanker who has become a regular in the Australian back row as well as in the successful New South Wales side.

Lang, C W P (Victoria) 1938 *NZ* (2)
Larkin, E R (New South Wales) 1903 *NZ*
Larkin, K K (Queensland) 1958 *M* (2)
Latimer, N B (New South Wales) 1957 *NZ*
Lawton, T (Queensland) 1929 *NZ* (3), 1930 *BI*, 1932 *NZ* (2)
Lawton, T A (Queensland) 1983 (ST) *F* (2[1R])
Lenehan, J K (New South Wales) 1957-58 (T) *W, E, S, F*, 1958 *M* (3), 1959 *BI* (2), 1961 *SA* (2), *F*, 1962 *NZ* (4), 1965 *SA* (2), 1966-67 (T) *W, S, E, I, F*, 1967 *I*
L'Estrange, R D (Queensland) 1971-72 (ST) *F* (2), 1972 *NZ* (3), 1973 *Tg* (2), 1973-74 (ST) *W, E*, 1974 *NZ* (3), 1975-76 (T) *S, W, I, US*
Lewis, L S (Queensland) 1934 *NZ* (2), 1936 *NZ*, 1938 *NZ*
Lindsay, R T G (Queensland) 1932 *NZ*
Lisle, R J (New South Wales) 1961 *Fj* (3), *SA*
Livermore, A E (Queensland) 1946 *NZ, M*
Loane, M E (Queensland) 1973 *Tg* (2), 1974 *NZ*, 1975 *E* (2), *J*, 1975-76 (T) *E, I*, 1976 *Fj* (3), 1976-77 (ST) *F* (2), 1978 *W* (2), 1979 *I* (2), *NZ, Arg* (2), 1981 *F* (2), 1981-82 (T) *I, W, S, E*, 1982 *S* (2)
Logan, D L (New South Wales) 1958 *M*
Loudon, R B (New South Wales) 1929 *NZ*, 1933 *SA* (4), 1934 *NZ*
Love, E W (New South Wales) 1932 *NZ* (3)
Lowth, D R (New South Wales) 1958 *NZ*
Lucas, B C (Queensland) 1905 *NZ*
Lucas, P W (New South Wales) 1982 *NZ* (3)
Lutge, D (New South Wales) 1903 *NZ*, 1904 *BI* (3)

McArthur, M (New South Wales) 1908-09 (T) *E*
McBain, M I (Queensland) 1983 (ST) *It, F*
MacBride, J W T (New South Wales) 1946 *NZ* (2), *M*, 1947 *NZ* (2), 1947-48 (T) *S, I, W, E, F*
McCabe, A J M (New South Wales) 1908-09 (T) *E*
McCarthy, F J C (Queensland) 1950 *BI*
McCowan, R H (Queensland) 1899 *BI* (3)
McCue, P A (New South Wales) 1907 *NZ* (2), 1908-09 (T) *W, E*
McDermott, L C (Queensland) 1962 *NZ* (2)
McDonald, B S (New South Wales) 1969 *SA*, 1970 *S*
McDonald, J C (Queensland) 1938 *NZ* (2)
Macdougall, D G (New South Wales) 1961 *Fj, SA*
Macdougall, S G (New South Wales and Australian Capital Territory) 1971 *SA*, 1973-74 (ST) *E*, 1974 *NZ* (3), 1975 *E* (2), 1975-76 (T) *E*
McGhie, G H (Queensland) 1929 *NZ* (2), 1930 *BI*
McGill, A N (New South Wales) 1968 *NZ* (2), *F*, 1969 *W, SA* (4), 1970 *S*, 1971 *SA* (3), 1971-72 (ST) *F* (2), 1972 *F* (2), *NZ* (3), 1973 *Tg* (2)
McIntyre, A J (Queensland) 1982 *NZ* (3), 1983 (ST) *F* (2)
McKid, W A (New South Wales) 1975-76 (T) *E*, 1976 *Fj*, 1978 *NZ* (2), 1979 *I* (2)
McKinnon, A (Queensland) 1904 *BI*
McKivat, C H (New South Wales) 1907 *NZ* (2), 1908-09 (T) *W, E*
McLaughlin, R E M (New South Wales) 1936 *NZ* (2)
McLean, A D (Queensland) 1933 *SA* (5), 1934 *NZ* (2), 1936 *NZ* (2), *M*
McLean, J D (Queensland) 1904 *BI* (2), 1905 *NZ*
McLean, J J (Queensland) 1971 *SA* (2), 1971-72 (ST) *F* (2), 1972 *F* (2), *NZ* (3), *Fj*, 1973-74 (ST) *W, E*, 1974 *NZ*
McLean, P E (Queensland) 1974 *NZ* (3), 1975 *J* (2), 1975-76 (T) *S, W, E, I*, 1976 *Fj* (3), 1976-77 (ST) *F* (2), 1978 *W* (2), *NZ*, 1979 *I* (2), *NZ, Arg* (2), 1980 *Fj*, 1981 *F* (2), 1981-82 (T) *I, W, S, E*, 1982 *S*
McLean, P W (Queensland) 1978 *NZ* (3), 1979 *I* (2), *NZ, Arg* (2), 1980 *Fj* (R), *NZ*, 1981-82 (T) *I, W, S, E*, 1982 *S* (2)
McLean, R A (New South Wales) 1971 *SA* (3), 1971-72 (ST) *F* (2)
McLean, W M (Queensland) 1946 *NZ* (2), *M*, 1947 *NZ* (2)
McMahon, M J (Queensland) 1913 *NZ*
McMaster, R E (Queensland) 1946 *NZ* (2), *M*, 1947 *NZ* (2), 1947-48 (T) *I, W*
MacMillan, D I (Queensland) 1950 *BI* (2)
McMullen, K V (New South Wales) 1962 *NZ* (2), 1963 *E, SA*
McShane, J M S (New South Wales) 1937 *SA* (2)
Mackney, W A R (New South Wales) 1933 *SA* (2), 1934 *NZ* (2)
Magrath, E (New South Wales) 1961 *Fj, SA, F*
Malcolm, S J (New South Wales) 1929 *NZ* (3), 1930 *BI*, 1931 *NZ*, 1932 *NZ* (3), 1933 *SA* (2), 1934 *NZ* (2)
Malone, J H (New South Wales) 1936 *NZ* (2), *M*, 1937 *SA*
Malouf, B P (New South Wales) 1982 *NZ*
Mandible, E F (New South Wales) 1907 *NZ* (2), 1908-09 (T) *W*
Manning, J (New South Wales) 1904 *BI*
Manning, R C S (Queensland) 1967 *NZ*
Mansfield, B W (New South Wales) 1975 *J*
Marks, H (New South Wales) 1899 *BI* (2)
Marks, R J P (Queensland) 1962 *NZ* (2), 1963 *E, SA* (3), 1964 *NZ* (3), 1965 *SA* (2), 1966-67 (T) *W, S, E, I, F*, 1967 *I*
Marshall, J S (New South Wales) 1949 *M*
Martin, M C (New South Wales) 1980 *Fj, NZ* (2), 1981 *F* (2), 1981-82 (T) *W* (R)
Massey-Westropp, M (New South Wales) 1914 *NZ*
Mathers, M J (New South Wales) 1980 *Fj, NZ* (R)
Maund, J W (New South Wales) 1903 *NZ*
Meadows, J E C (Victoria, Queensland) 1974 *NZ*,

1975-76 (T) *S, W, I, US*, 1976 *Fj* (2), 1976-77 (ST) *F* (2), 1978 *NZ* (3), 1979 *I* (2), 1981-82 (T) *I, S, E*, 1982 *NZ* (2), 1983 *US, Arg, NZ*
Meadows, R W (New South Wales) 1958 *M* (3), *NZ* (3)
Meibusch, J H (Queensland) 1904 *BI*
Meibusch, L S (Queensland) 1912 *US*
Melrose, T C (New South Wales) 1978 *NZ*, 1979 *I* (2), *NZ, Arg* (2)
Messenger, H H (New South Wales) 1907 *NZ* (2)
Middleton, S A (New South Wales) 1908-09 (T) *E*, 1910 *NZ* (3)
Miller, A R (New South Wales) 1952 *Fj* (2), *NZ* (2), 1953 *SA* (4), 1954 *Fj* (2), 1955 *NZ* (3), 1956 *SA* (2), 1957 *NZ* (2), 1957-58 (T) *W, E, S, F*, 1958 *M* (3), 1959 *BI* (2), 1961 *Fj* (3), *SA, F* 1962 *NZ* (2), 1966 *BI* (2), 1966-67 (T) *W, S, I, F*, 1967 *I, NZ*
Miller, J M (New South Wales) 1962 *NZ*, 1963 *E, SA*, 1966-67 (T) *W, S, E*
Miller, S W J (New South Wales) 1899 *BI*
Monaghan, L E (New South Wales) 1973-74 (ST) *E*, 1974 *NZ* (3), 1975 *E* (2), 1975-76 (T) *S, W, E, I, US*, 1976-77 (ST) *F*, 1978 *W* (2), *NZ* 1979 *I* (2)
Monti, C I A (Queensland) 1938 *NZ*
Moon, B J (Queensland) 1978 *NZ* (2), 1979 *I* (2), *NZ, Arg* (2), 1980 *Fj, NZ* (3), 1981 *F* (2), 1981-82 (T) *I, W, S, E*, 1982 *S* (2), 1983 *US, Arg* (2), *NZ*, 1983 (ST) *It, F* (2)
Mooney, T P (Queensland) 1954 *Fj* (2)
Moran, H M (New South Wales) 1908-09 (T) *W*
Morrissey, W (Queensland) 1914 *NZ*
Morton, A R (New South Wales) 1957 *NZ* (2), 1957-58 (T) *F*, 1958 *M* (3), 1959 *BI* (2)
Mossop, R P (New South Wales) 1949 *NZ* (2), 1950 *BI* (2), 1951 *NZ*
Moutray, I E (New South Wales) 1963 *SA*
Murphy, P J (Queensland) 1910 *NZ* (3), 1913 *NZ* (3), 1914 *NZ* (3)
Murphy, W (Queensland) 1912 *US*

Nicholson, F C (Queensland) 1904 *BI*
Nicholson, F V (Queensland) 1903 *NZ*, 1904 *BI*

O'Brien, F W H (New South Wales) 1937 *SA*, 1938 *NZ*
O'Connor, M D (Australian Capital Territory, Queensland) 1979 *Arg* (2), 1980 *Fj, NZ* (3), 1981 *F* (2), 1981-82 (T) *I, E*, 1982 *S* (2)
O'Donnell, C (New South Wales) 1913 *NZ* (2)
O'Donnell, I C (New South Wales) 1899 *BI* (2)
O'Donnell, J M (New South Wales) 1899 *BI*
O'Gorman, J F (New South Wales) 1961 *Fj, SA* (2), *F*, 1962 *NZ*, 1963 *E, SA* (4), 1965 *SA* (2), 1966-67 (T) *W, S, E, I, F*, 1967 *I*
O'Neill, D J (Queensland) 1964 *NZ* (2)
O'Neill, J M (Queensland) 1952 *NZ* (2), 1956 *SA* (2)
Osborne, D H (Victoria) 1975 *E* (2), *J*
Outterside, R (New South Wales) 1959 *BI* (2)
Oxenham, A McE (Queensland) 1904 *BI*, 1907 *NZ*
Oxlade, A M (Queensland) 1904 *BI* (2), 1905 *NZ*, 1907 *NZ*
Oxlade, B D (Queensland) 1938 *NZ* (3)

Palfreyman, J R L (New South Wales) 1929 *NZ*, 1930 *BI*, 1931 *NZ*, 1932 *NZ*
Parker, A J (Queensland) 1983 *Arg* (2[1R]), *NZ*
Parkinson, C E (Queensland) 1907 *NZ*
Pashley, J J (New South Wales) 1954 *Fj* (2), 1958 *M* (3)
Pauling, T P (New South Wales) 1936 *NZ*, 1937 *SA*
Pearse, G K (New South Wales) 1975-76 (T) *W* (R), *I, US*, 1976 *Fj* (3), 1978 *NZ* (3)
Penman, A P (New South Wales) 1905 *NZ*
Perrin, P D (Queensland) 1962 *NZ*
Perrin, T D (New South Wales) 1931 *M, NZ*
Phelps, R (New South Wales) 1955 *NZ* (2), 1956 *SA* (2), 1957 *NZ* (2), 1957-58 (T) *W, I, E, S, F*, 1958 *M, NZ* (3), 1961 *Fj* (3), *SA* (2), *F*, 1962 *NZ* (2)
Phipps, J A (New South Wales) 1953 *SA* (4), 1954 *Fj* (2), 1955 *NZ* (2), 1956 *SA* (2)
Phipps, P J (New South Wales) 1955 *NZ*
Pilecki, S J (Queensland) 1978 *W* (2), *NZ* (2), 1979 *I* (2), *NZ, Arg* (2), 1980 *Fj, NZ* (2), 1982 *S* (2), 1983 *US, Arg* (2), *NZ*
Piper, B J C (New South Wales) 1946 *NZ* (2), *M*, 1947 *NZ*, 1947-48 (T) *S, I, W, E, F*, 1949 *M* (3)
Poidevin, S P (New South Wales) 1980 *Fj, NZ* (3), 1981 *F* (2), 1981-82 (T) *I, W, S, E*, 1982 *NZ* (3), 1983 *US, Arg* (2), *NZ*, 1983 (ST) *It, F* (2)
Potter, R T (Queensland) 1961 *Fj*
Pope, A M (Queensland) 1968 *NZ* (R)
Potts, J M (New South Wales) 1957 *NZ* (2), 1957-58 (T) *W, I*, 1959 *BI*
Prentice, C W (New South Wales) 1914 *NZ*
Prentice, W S (New South Wales) 1908-09 (T) *W, E*, 1910 *NZ* (3), 1912 *US*
Price, R A (New South Wales) 1974 *NZ* (3), 1975 *E* (2), *J* (2), 1975-76 (T) *US*
Primmer, C J (Queensland) 1951 *NZ* (2)
Proctor, I J (New South Wales) 1967 *NZ*
Prosser, R B (New South Wales) 1966-67 (T) *E, I*, 1967 *I, NZ*, 1968 *NZ* (2), *F*, 1968-69 (ST) *I, S*, 1969 *W, SA* (4), 1971 *SA* (3), 1971-72 (ST) *F* (2), 1972 *F* (2), *NZ* (3), *Fj*
Pugh, G H (New South Wales) 1912 *US*
Purcell, M P (Queensland) 1966-67 (T) *W, S*, 1967 *I*
Purkis, E M (New South Wales) 1957-58 (T) *S*, 1958 *M*

Ramalli, C (New South Wales) 1938 *NZ* (2)
Ramsay, K M (New South Wales) 1936 *M*, 1937 *SA*, 1938 *NZ* (2)
Rankin, R (New South Wales) 1936 *NZ* (2), *M*, 1937 *SA* (2), 1938 *NZ* (2)
Rathie, D S (Queensland) 1972 *F* (2)
Redwood, C (Queensland) 1903 *NZ*, 1904 *BI* (3)
Reid, T W (New South Wales) 1961 *Fj* (3), *SA*, 1962 *NZ*
Reilly, N P (Queensland) 1968 *NZ* (2), *F*, 1968-69 (ST) *I, S*, 1969 *W, SA* (4)
Reynolds, L J (New South Wales) 1910 *NZ* (2[1R])
Richards, E W (Queensland) 1904 *BI* (2), 1905 *NZ*, 1907 *NZ*
Richards, G (New South Wales) 1978 *NZ* (2[1R]), 1981 *F*
Richards, T J (Queensland) 1908-09 (T) *W, E*, 1912 *US*
Richards, V S (New South Wales) 1936 *NZ* (2[1R]), *M*, 1937 *SA*, 1938 *NZ*
Richardson, G C (Queensland) 1971 *SA* (3), 1972 *NZ* (2), *Fj*, 1973 *Tg* (2), 1973-74 (ST) *W*
Riley, S A (New South Wales) 1903 *NZ*
Roberts, B T (New South Wales) 1956 *SA*
Roberts, H F (Queensland) 1961 *Fj* (2), *SA, F*
Robertson, I J (New South Wales) 1975 *J* (2)
Roche, C (Queensland) 1982 *S* (2), *NZ* (3), 1983 *US, Arg* (2), *NZ*, 1983 (ST) *It, F* (2)
Rose, H A (New South Wales) 1967 *I, NZ*, 1968 *NZ* (2), *F*, 1968-69 (ST) *I, S*, 1969 *W, SA* (4), 1970 *S*
Rosenblum, R G (New South Wales) 1969 *SA* (2), 1970 *S*
Rosewell, J S H (New South Wales) 1907 *NZ* (2)
Ross, A W (New South Wales) 1929 *NZ*, 1930 *BI*, 1931 *M, NZ*, 1932 *NZ* (2), 1933 *SA*, 1934 *NZ* (2)
Ross, W S (Queensland) 1979 *I* (2), *Arg*, 1980 *Fj, NZ* (3), 1982 *S* (2), 1983 *US, Arg* (2), *NZ*
Rothwell, P R (New South Wales) 1951 *NZ* (3), 1952 *Fj*
Row, F L (New South Wales) 1899 *BI* (3)
Row, N E (New South Wales) 1907 *NZ* (2), 1908-09 (T) *E*, 1910 *NZ* (3)
Rowles, P G (New South Wales) 1972 *Fj*, 1973-74 (ST) *E*
Roxburgh, J R (New South Wales) 1968 *NZ* (2), *F*, 1969 *W, SA* (4), 1970 *S*
Ruebner, G (New South Wales) 1966 *BI* (2)
Russell, C J (New South Wales) 1907 *NZ* (3), 1908-09 (T) *W, E*
Ryan, J R (New South Wales) 1975 *J*, 1975-76 (T) *I, US*, 1976 *Fj* (3)
Ryan, K J (Queensland) 1957-58 (T) *E*, 1958 *M, NZ* (3)
Ryan, P F (New South Wales) 1963 *E, SA* 1966 *BI* (2)

Sampson, J H (New South Wales) 1899 *BI*
Sayle, J L (New South Wales) 1967 *NZ*
Schulte, B G (Queensland) 1946 *NZ, M*
Scott, P R I (New South Wales) 1962 *NZ* (2)
Shambrook, G G (Queensland) 1976 *Fj* (2)
Shaw, A A (Queensland) 1973-74 (ST) *W, E*, 1975 *E* (2), *J*, 1975-76 (T) *S, W, E, I, US*, 1976 *Fj* (3), 1976-77 (ST) *F* (2), 1978 *W* (2), *NZ* (3), 1979 *I* (2), *NZ, Arg* (2), 1980 *Fj, NZ* (3), 1981 *F* (2), 1981-82 (T) *I, W, S*, 1982 *S* (2)

Shaw, G A (New South Wales) 1969 *W, SA* (R), 1970 *S*, 1971 *SA* (3), 1971-72 (ST) *F* (2), 1973-74 (ST) *W, E*, 1974 *NZ* (3), 1975 *E* (2), *J* (2), 1975-76 (T) *W, E, I, US*, 1976 *Fj* (3), 1976-77 (ST) *F* (2), 1979 *NZ*
Shehadie, N M (New South Wales) 1947 *NZ*, 1947-48 (T) *E, F*, 1949 *M* (3), *NZ* (2), 1950 *BI* (2), 1951 *NZ* (3), 1952 *Fj* (2), *NZ*, 1953 *SA* (4), 1954 *Fj* (2), 1955 *NZ* (3), 1956 *SA* (2), 1957 *NZ*, 1957-58 (T) *W, I*
Sheil, A G R (Queensland) 1956 *SA*
Shepherd, D J (Victoria) 1964 *NZ*, 1965 *SA* (2), 1966 *BI* (2)
Simpson, R J (New South Wales) 1913 *NZ*
Skinner, A J (New South Wales) 1969 *W, SA*, 1970 *S*
Slack, A G (Queensland) 1978 *W* (2), *NZ* (2), 1979 *NZ, Arg* (2), 1980 *Fj*, 1981-82 (T) *I, W, S, E*, 1982 *S, NZ*, 1983 *US, Arg* (2), *NZ*, 1983 (ST) *It*
Slater, S H (New South Wales) 1910 *NZ*
Smith, F B (New South Wales) 1905 *NZ*, 1907 *NZ* (3)
Smith, L M (New South Wales) 1905 *NZ*
Smith, P V (New South Wales) 1967 *NZ*, 1968 *NZ* (2), *F*, 1968-69 (ST) *I, S*, 1969 *W, SA*
Smith, R A (New South Wales) 1971 *SA* (2), 1972 *F* (2), *NZ* (3[1R]), *Fj*, 1975 *E* (2), *J* (2), 1975-76 (T) *S, W, E, I, US*, 1976 *Fj* (3), 1976-77 (ST) *F* (2)
Solomon, H J (New South Wales) 1949 *M, NZ*, 1950 *BI* (2), 1951 *NZ* (2), 1952 *Fj* (2), *NZ* (2), 1953 *SA* (3), 1955 *NZ*
Spragg, S A (New South Wales) 1899 *BI* (4)
Stapleton, E T (New South Wales) 1951 *NZ* (3), 1952 *Fj* (2), *NZ* (2), 1953 *SA* (4), 1954 *Fj*, 1955 *NZ* (3), 1958 *NZ*
Steggall, J C (Queensland) 1931 *M, NZ*, 1932 *NZ* (3), 1933 *SA* (5)
Stegman, T R (New South Wales) 1973 *Tg* (2)
Stephens, O G (New South Wales) 1973 *Tg* (2), 1973-74 (ST) *W*, 1974 *NZ* (2)
Stewart, A A (New South Wales) 1979 *NZ, Arg* (2)
Stone, A H (New South Wales) 1937 *SA*, 1938 *NZ* (2)
Stone, C G (New South Wales) 1938 *NZ*
Stone, J M (New South Wales) 1946 *M, NZ*
Storey, G P (New South Wales) 1929 *NZ* (R), 1930 *BI*
Storey, K P (New South Wales) 1936 *NZ*
Storey, N J D (New South Wales) 1962 *NZ*
Strachan, D J (New South Wales) 1955 *NZ* (2)
Street, N O (New South Wales) 1899 *BI*
Streeter, S F (New South Wales) 1978 *NZ*
Stuart, R (New South Wales) 1910 *NZ* (2)
Stumbles, B D (New South Wales) 1972 *NZ* (3[1R]), *Fj*
Sturtridge, G S (Victoria) 1929 *NZ*, 1932 *NZ* (3), 1933 *SA* (5)
Sullivan, P D (New South Wales) 1971 *SA* (3), 1971-72 (ST) *F* (2), 1972 *F* (2), *NZ* (2), *Fj*, 1973 *Tg* (2), 1973-74 (ST) *W*
Summons, A J (New South Wales) 1957-58 (T) *W, I, E, S*, 1958 *M, NZ* (3), 1959 *BI* (2)
Suttor, D C (New South Wales) 1913 *NZ* (3)
Swannell, B I (New South Wales) 1905 *NZ*
Sweeney, T L (Queensland) 1953 *SA*

Taafe, B S (New South Wales) 1969 *SA*, 1972 *F* (2)
Tanner, W H (Queensland) 1899 *BI* (2)
Tasker, W G (New South Wales) 1913 *NZ* (3), 1914 *NZ* (3)
Tate, M J (New South Wales) 1951 *NZ*, 1952 *Fj* (2), *NZ* (2), 1953 *SA*, 1954 *Fj* (2)
Taylor, D A (Queensland) 1968 *NZ* (2), *F*, 1968-69 (ST) *I, S*
Taylor, J I (New South Wales) 1971 *SA*, 1972 *F* (2), *Fj*
Teitzel, R G (Queensland) 1966-67 (T) *W, S, E, I, F*, 1967 *I, NZ*
Thompson, E G (Queensland) 1929 *NZ* (3), 1930 *BI*
Thompson, F (New South Wales) 1913 *NZ* (3), 1914 *NZ* (2)
Thompson, J (Queensland) 1914 *NZ* (2)
Thompson, P D (Queensland) 1950 *BI*
Thompson, R J (Western Australia) 1971 *SA*, 1971-72 (ST) *F* (R), 1972 *Fj*
Thornett, J E (New South Wales) 1955 *NZ* (3), 1956 *SA* (2), 1957-58 (T) *W, I, S, F*, 1958 *M* (2), *NZ* (2), 1959 *BI* (2), 1961 *Fj* (2), *SA* (2), *F*, 1962 *NZ* (4), 1963 *E, SA* (4), 1964 *NZ* (3), 1965 *SA* (2), 1966 *BI* (2), 1966-67 (T) *F*
Thornett, R N (New South Wales) 1961 *Fj* (3), *SA* (2), *F*, 1962 *NZ* (5)
Thorpe, A C (New South Wales) 1929 *NZ* (R)
Timbury, F R V (Queensland) 1910 *NZ* (2)
Tindall, E N (New South Wales) 1973 *Tg*
Tolhurst, H A (New South Wales) 1931 *M, NZ*
Tonkin, A E J (New South Wales) 1947-48 (T) *S, I, W, E, F*, 1950 *BI*
Tooth, R M (New South Wales) 1951 *NZ* (3), 1954 *Fj* (2), 1955 *NZ* (3), 1957 *NZ* (2)
Towers, C H T (New South Wales) 1929 *NZ* (2), 1930 *BI*, 1931 *M, NZ*, 1934 *NZ* (2), 1937 *SA* (2)
Trivett, R K (Queensland) 1966 *BI* (2)
Turnbull, A (Victoria) 1961 *Fj*
Turnbull, R V (New South Wales) 1968-69 (ST) *I*
Tuynman, S N (New South Wales) 1983 (ST) *F* (2)
Tweedale, E (New South Wales) 1946 *NZ* (2), 1947 *NZ*, 1947-48 (T) *S, I, E, F*, 1949 *M* (3)

Vaughan, D (New South Wales) 1983 *US, Arg*, 1983 (ST) *It, F* (2)
Vaughan, G N (Victoria) 1957-58 (T) *E, S, F*, 1958 *M* (3)
Verge, A (New South Wales) 1904 *BI* (2)

Walden, R J (New South Wales) 1934 *NZ*, 1936 *NZ* (2), *M*
Walker, A K (New South Wales) 1947 *NZ*, 1947-48 (T) *E, F*, 1950 *BI* (2)
Walker, A S B (New South Wales) 1912 *US*
Walker, L R (New South Wales) 1982 *NZ* (2)
Wallach, C (New South Wales) 1913 *NZ* (2), 1914 *NZ* (3)
Walsh, J J (New South Wales) 1953 *SA* (4)
Walsh, P B (New South Wales) 1904 *BI* (3)
Walsham, K P (New South Wales) 1962 *NZ*, 1963 *E*
Ward, P G (New South Wales) 1899 *BI* (4)
Ward, T (Queensland) 1899 *BI*
Watson, G W (Queensland) 1907 *NZ*
Watson, W T (New South Wales) 1912 *US*, 1913 *NZ* (3), 1914 *NZ*
Weatherstone, L J (Australian Capital Territory) 1975 *E* (2), *J* (2), 1975-76 (T) *S* (R), *E, I*
Webb, W (New South Wales) 1899 *BI* (2)
Wells, B G (New South Wales) 1958 *M*
Westfield, R E (New South Wales) 1929 *NZ* (2)
White, C J B (New South Wales) 1899 *BI*, 1903 *NZ*, 1904 *BI*
White, J M (New South Wales) 1904 *BI*
White, J P L (New South Wales) 1958 *NZ* (3), 1961 *Fj* (3), *SA* (2), *F*, 1962 *NZ* (5), 1963 *E, SA* (4), 1964 *NZ* (3), 1965 *SA* (2)
White, M C (Queensland) 1931 *M, NZ*, 1932 *NZ* (2), 1933 *SA* (5)
White, S W (New South Wales) 1956 *SA* (2), 1957-58 (T) *I, E, S*, 1958 *M* (2)
White, W G S (Queensland) 1933 *SA* (5), 1934 *NZ* (2), 1936 *NZ* (2), *M*
White, W J (New South Wales) 1932 *NZ*
Wickham, S M (New South Wales) 1903 *NZ*, 1904 *BI* (3), 1905 *NZ*
Williams, D (Queensland) 1913 *NZ*, 1914 *NZ* (3)
Williams, J L (New South Wales) 1963 *SA* (3)
Williams, S A (New South Wales) 1980 *Fj, NZ* (2), 1981 *F* (2), 1981-82 (T) *E*, 1982 *NZ* (3), 1983 *US, Arg* (2[1R]), *NZ*, 1983 (ST) *It, F* (2)
Wilson, B J (New South Wales) 1949 *NZ* (2)
Wilson, C R (Queensland) 1957 *NZ*, 1958 *NZ* (3)
Wilson, V W (Queensland) 1937 *SA* (2), 1938 *NZ* (3)
Windon, C J (New South Wales) 1946 *NZ* (2), 1947 *NZ*, 1947-48 (T) *S, I, W, E, F*, 1949 *M* (3), *NZ* (2), 1951 *NZ* (3), 1952 *Fj* (2), *NZ* (2)
Windon, K S (New South Wales) 1937 *SA* (2), 1946 *M*
Windsor, J C (Queensland) 1947 *NZ*
Winning, K C (Queensland) 1951 *NZ*
Wogan, L W (New South Wales) 1913 *NZ* (3), 1914 *NZ* (3)
Wood, F (New South Wales) 1907 *NZ* (3), 1910 *NZ* (3), 1913 *NZ* (3), 1914 *NZ* (3)
Wood, R N (Queensland) 1972 *Fj*
Wright, K J (New South Wales) 1975 *E* (2), *J*, 1975-76 (T) *US*, 1976-77 (ST) *F* (2), 1978 *NZ* (3)

Yanz, K (New South Wales) 1957-58 (T) *F*

AUSTRALIAN INTERNATIONAL RECORDS

From 1890-91, when uniform points-scoring was first adopted by International Board countries, to 30 April 1984, except in the case of matches against British Isles. These date from 1910, when British Isles teams first became officially representative of the Four Home Unions. Both team and individual records are against International Board countries and British Isles only, unless otherwise stated.

TEAM RECORDS

Highest score

33 v Scotland (33-9) 1982 Sydney

Australia scored 50 against Japan at Brisbane in 1975, but this was not against an IB country

v individual countries

30 v England (30-21) 1975 Brisbane
33 v Scotland (33-9) 1982 Sydney
20 v Ireland (20-10) 1976 Dublin
19 v Wales (19-17) 1978 Sydney
24 v France (24-14) 1981 Sydney
30 v N Zealand (30-16) 1978 Auckland
21 v S Africa (21-6) 1933 Durban
8 v B Isles (8-11) 1966 Sydney

Biggest winning points margin

24 v Scotland (33-9) 1982 Sydney

Australia beat US by 46 points (49-3) at Sydney in 1983, but this was not against an IB country

v individual countries

12 v England (23-11) 1967 Twickenham
24 v Scotland (33-9) 1982 Sydney
13 v Ireland (16-3) 1947 Dublin
10 v Wales (18-8) 1978 Brisbane
10 v France (24-14) 1981 Sydney
16 v N Zealand (26-10) 1980 Sydney
15 v S Africa (21-6) 1933 Durban
1 v B Isles (6-5) 1930 Sydney

Highest score by opposing team

38 { N Zealand (13-38) 1936 Dunedin
N Zealand (3-38) 1972 Auckland }

by individual countries

23 England (6-23) 1976 Twickenham
24 Scotland (15-24) 1981 Murrayfield
27 Ireland (12-27) 1979 Brisbane
28 Wales (3-28) 1975 Cardiff
34 France (6-34) 1976 Paris (Parc des Princes)
38 { N Zealand (13-38) 1936 Dunedin
N Zealand (3-38) 1972 Auckland }
30 S Africa (11-30) 1969 Johannesburg
31 B Isles (0-31) 1966 Brisbane

Biggest losing points margin

35 v N Zealand (3-38) 1972 Auckland

v individual countries

17 v England { (3-20) 1973 Twickenham
(6-23) 1976 Twickenham }
9 v Scotland (15-24) 1981 Murrayfield
15 v Ireland (12-27) 1979 Brisbane
25 v Wales (3-28) 1975 Cardiff
28 v France (6-34) 1976 Parc des Princes
35 v N Zealand (3-38) 1972 Auckland
25 v S Africa (3-28) 1961 Johannesburg
31 v B Isles (0-31) 1966 Brisbane

Most tries by Australia in an international

6 v Scotland (23-3) 1970 Sydney

Australia scored 9 against US at Sydney in 1983, but this was not against an IB country

---

Most tries against Australia in an international

8 by South Africa (3-28) 1961 Johannesburg

Most points on overseas tour (all matches)

500 in B Isles/France (35 matches) 1947-48

Most tries on overseas tour (all matches)

115 in B Isles/France (35 matches) 1947-48

INDIVIDUAL RECORDS

Most capped players

P G Johnson 39 1959-71
G V Davis 39 1963-72

in individual positions
Full-back
A N McGill 19* 1968-72
Wing
J W Cole 22‡ 1968-74
Centre
G A Shaw 21** 1969-79
Fly-half
P F Hawthorne 21* 1962-67
Scrum-half
J N B Hipwell 34 1968-82
Prop
R B Prosser 24 1967-72
Hooker
P G Johnson 39 1959-71
Lock
G Fay 20† 1971-79
Flanker
G V Davis 39 1963-72
No 8
M E Loane 20 1974-82

**P E McLean, 22 caps, has won 8 at full back, one at centre, and 13 at fly-half*
†A R Miller, 31 caps, won 12 as a prop, 19 as lock
‡B J Moon has won 26 caps as a wing, but only 19 against IB nations
***M J Hawker, 21 caps, has won 15 as a centre and one as a wing against IB nations. In his other matches, he has played as a centre four times and once as a fly-half*

Most internationals as captain – 16
J E Thornett 1962-67
G V Davis 1969-72

Most points in internationals – 162
P E McLean (22 appearances)* 1974-82
**excludes 8 appearances against Japan, Fiji and Argentina, in which McLean scored 98 points*

Most points in an international – 21
P E McLean v Scotland 1982 Sydney

Most tries in internationals – 7
C J Windon (15 appearances)* 1946-52
**excludes 5 appearances against Maoris and Fiji, in which Windon scored 4 tries*
B J Moon has scored 12 tries, but only 6 in 19 appearances against IB countries

---

Most tries in an international – 4
G Cornelsen v N Zealand 1978 Auckland
D I Campese scored 4 against US at Sydney in 1983, but this was not against an IB country

---

Most conversions in an international – 3*
R R Biilmann v SA 1933 Durban
P F Ryan v England 1963 Sydney
P E McLean v Scotland 1982 Sydney
**P E McLean kicked 6 against Japan at Brisbane in 1975, but this was not against an IB country*

Most points on overseas tour – 154
P E McLean (18 appearances) B Isles 1975-76

Most tries on overseas tour – 23
C J Russell B Isles 1908-09

Most points in international series on tour – 34
R G Gould (3 appearances) 1982 New Zealand

Most points in any match on tour – 23
J C Hindmarsh v Glamorgan 1975 Neath

Most tries in any match on tour – 6
J S Boyce v Wairarapa (NZ) 1962 Masterton

LEADING CAP-WINNERS
(up to 30 April 1984)

ENGLAND

A Neary	43
J V Pullin	42
P J Wheeler	41
D J Duckham	36
D P Rogers	34
W B Beaumont	34
J P Scott	32
W W Wakefield	31
F E Cotton	31
M A C Slemen	31
E Evans	30
R Cove-Smith	29
C R Jacobs	29
M P Weston	29
P J Squires	29
J Butterfield	28
S J Smith	28
A T Voyce	27
J S Tucker	27
C N Lowe	25
J D Currie	25
M S Phillips	25
C B Stevens	25
P W Dodge	25
J Carleton	25
R E G Jeeps	24
P J Larter	24
A G Ripley	24
J MacG K Kendall-Carpenter	23
R W D Marques	23
R M Uttley	23
W H Hare	23
W J A Davies	22
P E Judd	22
C W Ralston	22
P J Dixon	22
J G G Birkett	21
H G Periton	21
C R Woodward	21
M J Colclough	21
P B Jackson	20
N E Horton	20

SCOTLAND

J M Renwick	51
A R Irvine	51
A B Carmichael	50
A F McHarg	44
J McLauchlan	43
H F McLeod	40
D M D Rollo	40
J MacD Bannerman	37
A J Tomes	37
C T Deans	34
A R Smith	33
I S Smith	32
F A L Laidlaw	32
I R McGeechan	32
N S Bruce	31
I H P Laughland	31
G L Brown	30
W I D Elliot	29
W M Simmers	28
P K Stagg	28
D G Leslie	28
J W Y Kemp	27
K J F Scotland	27
P C Brown	27
R J Laidlaw	27
J Y Rutherford	27
D Drysdale	26
J C McCallum	26
G P S Macpherson	26
K W Robertson	26
W E Maclagan	25
J B Nelson	25
J P Fisher	25
J W Telfer	25

G D Stevenson	24
M A Biggar	24
I G Milne	24
M C Morrison	23
J A Beattie	23
M J Campbell-Lamerton	23
J N M Frame	23
W C C Steele	23
B H Hay	23
J Aitken	23
J H Calder	23
D R Bedell-Sivright	22
A Robson	22
S Wilson	22
R J Arneil	22
R G MacMillan	21
W P Scott	21
W E Kyle	21
J M B Scott	21
J R Paterson	21
W B Welsh	21
P W Kininmonth	21
A J W Hinshelwood	21
D W Morgan	21
D I Johnston	21
C Reid	20
D S Davies	20
J C Dykes	20
W R Logan	20
J C Dawson	20
J T Greenwood	20
J W C Turner	20
N A MacEwan	20
W Cuthbertson	20

Jim Renwick, Scotland's joint most-capped player, who was hampered by injury during the season and unable to play a part in the Grand Slam.

IRELAND

C M H Gibson	69
W J McBride	63
J F Slattery	61
T J Kiernan	54
M I Keane	51
J W Kyle	46
K W Kennedy	45
P A Orr	43
G V Stephenson	42
N A A Murphy	41
W P Duggan	41
N J Henderson	40
R J McLoughlin	40
S Millar	37
J R Kavanagh	35
W A Mulcahy	35
E O'D Davy	34
A C Pedlow	30
G T Hamlet	30
W E Crawford	30
J D Clinch	30
J L Farrell	29
B G M Wood	29
A J F O'Reilly	29
M Sugden	28
J S McCarthy	28
L M Magee	27
A R Dawson	27
M G Molloy	27
J J Moloney	27
J C Walsh	26
R M Young	26

J B O'Driscoll	26
G R Beamish	25
K D Mullen	25
F P K Bresnihan	25
A T A Duggan	25
B J McGann	25
T O Grace	25
S A McKinney	25
J A E Siggins	24
A Tedford	23
J W McKay	23
F Gardiner	22
J A O'Meara	22
A A Mulligan	22
M K Flynn	22
A H Ensor	22
S O Campbell	22
C E Allen	21
R Roe	21
P O'Callaghan	21
J C Parke	20
J McVicker	20
C J Hanrahan	20
D J O'Brien	20
N H Brophy	20
M G Doyle	20

WALES

J P R Williams	55
G O Edwards	53
T G R Davies	46
K J Jones	44
G Price	41
T M Davies	38
D Williams	36
R M Owen	35
B V Meredith	34
D I E Bebb	34
W D Morris	34
A J Martin	34
W J Bancroft	33
B Price	32
J R G Stephens	32
G A D Wheel	32
J J Williams	30
S P Fenwick	30
W J Trew	29
C I Morgan	29
P Bennett	29
J Squire	29
R W Windsor	28
A J Gould	27
W C Powell	27
M C Thomas	27
H J Morgan	27
R C C Thomas	26
A E I Pask	26
S J Watkins	26
J Taylor	26
G Travers	25
H Tanner	25
B John	25
N R Gale	25
W D Thomas	25
E Gwyn Nicholls	24
R T Gabe	24
D J Lloyd	24
J J Hodges	23
E C Davey	23
J A Gwilliam	23
R H Williams	23
J Young	23
D L Quinnell	23
R W R Gravell	23
T R Prosser	22
B L Williams	22
W O G Williams	22
S J Dawes	22
T J Davies	21
E M Jenkins	21
B Thomas	21
W R Willis	21
D Watkins	21
W Llewellyn	20
A F Harding	20
J Webb	20
A Skym	20
T D Holmes	20

FRANCE

NB Matches against International Board countries only

R Bertranne	52
B Dauga	50
J-P Rives	47
M Crauste	43
W Spanghero	42
R Paparemborde	42
J-P Lux	40
J Prat	38
M Celaya	35
A Boniface	34
A Domenech	34
J-C Skréla	34
G Dufau	33
J-L Joinel	31
M Vannier	30
E Cester	30
P Villepreux	29
C Darrouy	28
J Dupuy	28
C Dourthe	28
J Iraçabal	28
J-M Aguirre	28
A Cassayet	27
J Bouquet	27
G Basquet	26
P Dintrans	26
A Jauréguy	25
R Biénès	25
E Ribère	25
M Prat	25
L Mias	25
J Gachassin	25
J-P Bastiat	25
A Paco	25
P Albaladejo	24
C Lacaze	24
R Bénésis	24
J Trillo	24
A Roques	23
G Boniface	23
C Carrère	23
G Cholley	23
M Pomathios	22
J-P Romeu	22
M Communeau	21
F Moncla	21
J-L Azarète	21
B Chevallier	20
P Lacroix	20
C Spanghero	20
J-L Averous	20
S Blanco	20
D Codorniou	20

SOUTH AFRICA

F C H Du Preez	38
J H Ellis	38
J F K Marais	35
J P Engelbrecht	33
J L Gainsford	33
J T Claassen	28
F du T Roux	27
L G Wilson	27
T P Bedford	25
D J de Villiers	25
P J F Greyling	25
S H Nomis	25
P J Visagie	25
D J Hopwood	22
A C Koch	22
M Du Plessis	22
J A du Rand	21

NEW ZEALAND

C E Meads	55
I A Kirkpatrick	39
K R Tremain	38
B G Williams	38
A M Haden	37
B J Robertson	34
S S Wilson	34
W J Whineray	32
D B Clarke	31
S M Going	29
R W Norton	27
A G Dalton	27

G A Knight	26
B J Lochore	25
B E McLeod	24
K F Gray	24
I J Clarke	24
M G Mexted	24
R A White	23
D S Loveridge	23
D J Graham	22
D Young	22
B G Fraser	22
G N K Mourie	21
M W Shaw	21
K L Skinner	20
C R Laidlaw	20
I N MacEwan	20
P J Whiting	20

AUSTRALIA

P G Johnson	42
A R Miller	41
G V Davis	39
J E Thornett	37
J N B Hipwell	36
A A Shaw	36
N M Shehadie	30
P E McLean	30
M E Loane	28
K W Catchpole	27
G A Shaw	27
C T Burke	26
B J Moon	26
R B Prosser	25
G Cornelsen	25
J K Lenehan	24
J P L White	24
J W Cole	24
G Fay	24
R Phelps	23
R A Smith	22
J E C Meadows	22
E T Bonis	21
P F Hawthorne	21
R J Heming	21
A N McGill	21
M J Hawker	21
A S Cameron	20
B J Ellwood	20
C J Windon	20
S P Poidevin	20

WORLD'S LEADING CAP-WINNERS
(up to 30 April 1984)

For purposes of comparison, the following list includes only caps won for individual countries against the International Board countries and the British Isles, and in special centenary or celebration matches. Where additional caps have been given for other matches, the player's total number of caps is shown in brackets.

C M H Gibson (Ireland)	69
W J McBride (Ireland)	63
J F Slattery (Ireland)	61
C E Meads (New Zealand)	55
J P R Williams (Wales)	55
T J Kiernan (Ireland)	54
G O Edwards (Wales)	53
R Bertranne (France)	52 (69)
M I Keane (Ireland)	51
B Dauga (France)	50 (63)
A B Carmichael (Scotland)	50
A R Irvine (Scotland)	50 (51)
J M Renwick (Scotland)	50 (51)
J-P Rives (France)	47 (59)
J W Kyle (Ireland)	46
T G R Davies (Wales)	46
K W Kennedy (Ireland)	45
K J Jones (Wales)	44
A F McHarg (Scotland)	44
J McLauchlan (Scotland)	43
A Neary (England)	43
M Crauste (France)	43 (62)

P A Orr (Ireland)	43	**P J Wheeler** (England)	41
R Paparemborde (France)	42 (55)	**W P Duggan** (Ireland)	41
W Spanghero (France)	42 (51)	**N J Henderson** (Ireland)	40
J V Pullin (England)	42	**H F McLeod** (Scotland)	40
G V Stephenson (Ireland)	41 (42)	**D M D Rollo** (Scotland)	40
N A A Murphy (Ireland)	41	**R J McLoughlin** (Ireland)	40
G Price (Wales)	41	**J-P Lux** (France)	40 (47)

Australia's leading cap-winners, on the same basis, are P G Johnson 39 (42) and G V Davis 39. A R Miller has 41 Australian caps, but only 31 against the International Board countries and the British Isles.

The following list incorporates appearances by home countries' players for British Isles teams (the Lions) in international matches against New Zealand, Australia and South Africa (up to 30 April 1984). The number of Lions' appearances is shown in brackets.

C M H Gibson (Ireland)	81 (12)	**J-P Rives** (France)	47
W J McBride (Ireland)	80 (17)	**S Millar** (Ireland)	46 (9)
J F Slattery (Ireland)	65 (4)	**H F McLeod** (Scotland)	46 (6)
G O Edwards (Wales)	63 (10)	**T M Davies** (Wales)	46 (8)
J P R Williams (Wales)	63 (8)	**W P Duggan** (Ireland)	45 (4)
T J Kiernan (Ireland)	59 (5)	**A F McHarg** (Scotland)	44
A R Irvine (Scotland)	59 (9)	**A Neary** (England)	44 (1)
C E Meads (New Zealand)	55	**P A Orr** (Ireland)	44 (1)
G Price (Wales)	53 (12)	**M Crauste** (France)	43
J W Kyle (Ireland)	52 (6)	**R J McLoughlin** (Ireland)	43 (3)
R Bertranne (France)	52	**B V Meredith** (Wales)	42 (8)
M I Keane (Ireland)	52 (1)	**D I E Bebb** (Wales)	42 (8)
T G R Davies (Wales)	51 (5)	**W Spanghero** (France)	42
J McLauchlan (Scotland)	51 (8)	**R Paparemborde** (France)	42
J M Renwick (Scotland)	51 (1)	**G V Stephenson** (Ireland)	41
B Dauga (France)	50	**N J Henderson** (Ireland)	41 (1)
A B Carmichael (Scotland)	50	**W A Mulcahy** (Ireland)	41 (6)
N A A Murphy (Ireland)	49 (8)	**D Williams** (Wales)	41 (5)
K W Kennedy (Ireland)	49 (4)	**D M D Rollo** (Scotland)	40
J V Pullin (England)	49 (7)	**J-P Lux** (France)	40
P J Wheeler (England)	48 (7)	**I R McGeechan** (Scotland)	40 (8)
K J Jones (Wales)	47 (3)		

Most appearances for the Lions are by W J McBride 17, R E G Jeeps (England) 13, C M H Gibson 12, G Price 12, and A J F O'Reilly (Ireland), R H Williams (Wales), and G O Edwards 10 each, up to 30 April 1984.

INTERNATIONAL REFEREES AND OFFICIALS 1983-84

Leading Referees

Up to 30 April 1984, in matches between International Board countries, v British Isles and in special centenary or celebration matches for which caps were awarded. Figures in brackets show appointments in other major internationals for which an IB country has awarded caps.

10 or more Internationals

K D Kelleher	Ireland	21 (2)	**C H Gadney**	England	13 (2)
D G Walters	Wales	21 (2)	**J P Murphy**	New Zealand	13 (0)
R C Williams	Ireland	20 (1)	**T H Vile**	Wales	12 (1)
M Joseph	Wales	19 (3)	**N R Sanson**	Scotland	12 (1)
M J Dowling	Ireland	18 (0)	**R G Byres**	Australia	12 (1)
A M Hosie	Scotland	18 (1)	**M A Allan**	Scotland	11 (0)
B S Cumberlege	England	16 (0)	**A I Dickie**	Scotland	11 (0)
A E Freethy	Wales	16 (1)	**N H Lambert**	Ireland	11 (0)
J R West	Ireland	16 (1)	**R F Johnson**	England	11 (1)
F Palmade	France	15 (0)	**T N Pearce**	England	10 (0)
I David	Wales	14 (0)	**Air Cdre G C Lamb**	England	10 (1)
D P D'Arcy	Ireland	14 (3)	**Dr I R Vanderfield**	Australia	10 (4)

Referees – International Match Appearances 1983-84

Matches controlled between 30 April 1983 and 30 April 1984

1983	
NZ v BI (2)	**F Palmade** (France)
NZ v BI (2)	**R G Byres** (Australia)
A v NZ	**J B Anderson** (Scotland)
S v NZ	***R Hourquet** (France)
E v NZ	**A M Hosie** (Scotland)
F v A (2)	**G Harrison** (NZ)
1984	
W v S	***O Doyle** (Ireland)
F v I	**C Norling** (Wales)
I v W	**R G Byres** (Australia)
S v E	**D I H Burnett** (Ireland)
W v F	**R G Byres** (Australia)
E v I	**R Hourquet** (France)
I v S	***F A Howard** (England)
F v E	**A M Hosie** (Scotland)
E v W	**J B Anderson** (Scotland)
S v F	***W Jones** (Wales)

**denotes debut in matches between International Board Countries.*

Rugby Union Officials 1983-84

ENGLAND
President C R Jacobs
Hon Treasurer A A Grimsdell
Secretary
Air Cdre R H G Weighill CBE DFC

SCOTLAND
President A Robson
Treasurer I A Forbes
Secretary I A L Hogg

IRELAND
President G F Reidy
Hon Treasurer J E Nelson
Sec/Treasurer R FitzGerald

WALES
President E B Davies
Hon Treasurer K M Harris OBE
Secretary R Williams

FRANCE
President A J R Ferrasse
Treasurer General R Conchon
Secretary J-C Bourrier

SOUTH AFRICA
President Dr D H Craven
Sec/Treasurer A Kellermann

NEW ZEALAND
President N H Stanley
Chairman C A Blazey OBE
Sec/Treasurer B R Usmar

AUSTRALIA
President Sir Nicholas Shehadie OBE
Hon Treasurer L J Howard
Secretary J D Dedrick

INTERNATIONAL REFEREES

From the 1919-20 season onwards, up to 30 April 1984. The list is confined to matches between the International Board countries v British Isles and to special centenary or celebration matches for which caps were awarded. Where a referee has officiated at five or more international matches the totals are shown at the end of his entry in brackets.

ABBREVIATIONS

A	Australia	*S*	Scotland
BI	British Isles	*SA*	South Africa
E	England	*W*	Wales
F	France	*Wld*	World Invitation XV
I	Ireland	(C)	Centenary
NZ	New Zealand	(R)	Replacement
Pres XV	President's XV		

Ackermann, C J (South Africa) 1953 *SA v A* (2), 1955 *SA v BI*, 1958 *SA v F*
Acton, W H (Ireland) 1926 *W v E, E v S*
Allan, M A (Scotland) 1931 *I v W, I v SA*, 1933 *E v I, I v W*, 1934 *I v E*, 1935 *E v I, I v W*, 1936 *I v E*, 1937 *I v W*, 1947 *I v E*, 1948 *I v W* **(11)**
Anderson, C (Scotland) 1928 *I v F*
Anderson, J B (Scotland) 1981 *W v E, I v A*, 1983 *I v E, A v NZ*, 1984 *E v W* **(5)**
Angus, A W (Scotland) 1924 *W v E*
Austin, A W C (Scotland) 1952 *W v F*, 1953 *I v E*, 1954 *I v W*
Austry, R (France) 1972 *E v I*

Baise, M (South Africa) 1967 *SA v F* (2), 1968 *SA v BI* (2), 1969 *SA v A*, 1974 *SA v BI* (2) **(7)**
Baise, S (South Africa) 1969 *SA v A*
Barnes, P (Australia) 1938 *A v NZ*
Baxter, J (England) 1920 *S v I*, 1921 *W v S, I v S*, 1923 *W v S*, 1925 *W v S, I v W* **(6)**
Bean, A S (England) 1939 *W v S*, 1947 *F v W, W v A*, 1948 *S v F, W v F*, 1949 *F v S, S v I* **(7)**
Beattie, R A (Scotland) 1937 *E v W*, 1938 *W v E*, 1947 *W v E, I v A*, 1948 *E v W*, 1949 *I v E*, 1950 *E v I, I v W* **(8)**
Bell, T (Ireland) 1932 *S v W*, 1933 *E v W*
Bezuidenhout, G P (South Africa) 1976 *SA v NZ* (3), 1977 *SA v Wld*
Bonnet, J-P (France) 1979 *W v E*, 1980 *S v E, SA v BI* (2), 1981 *I v E*, 1982 *W v S* **(6)**
Bott, J G (England) 1931 *W v S*, 1933 *W v S*
Boundy, L M (England) 1955 *S v I*, 1956 *W v S*, 1957 *F v S, I v F, S v I*, 1958 *S v F*, 1959 *S v I*, 1961 *S v SA* **(8)**
Brook, P G (England) 1963 *F v W*, 1964 *W v S*, 1965 *W v I, I v SA*, 1966 *F v I* **(5)**
Brown, D A (England) 1960 *I v W*
Brunton, J (England) 1924 *W v NZ*
Burmeister, R D (South Africa) 1949 *SA v NZ* (2), 1953 *SA v A*, 1955 *SA v BI* (2), 1960 *SA v NZ* (2), 1961 *SA v A* **(8)**
Burnett, D I H (Ireland) 1977 *W v E*, 1979 *F v W*, 1980 *E v W*, 1981 *S v W, E v S*, 1982 *W v F*, 1983 *E v F*, 1984 *S v E* **(8)**
Burnett, R T (Australia) 1974 *A v NZ*, 1975 *A v E*, 1978 *A v W*
Burnett, W (Scotland) 1932 *I v E*, 1934 *W v I*
Burrell, G (Scotland) 1958 *E v I*, 1959 *W v I*
Burrell, R P (Scotland) 1966 *I v W*, 1967 *I v F, F v NZ*, 1969 *I v E, F v W* **(5)**
Byres, R G (Australia) 1978 *A v W*, 1979 *A v I* (2), *A v NZ*, 1980 *A v NZ*, 1981 *NZ v S*, 1982 *A v S* (2), 1983 *NZ v BI* (2), 1984 *I v W, W v F* **(12)**

Calitz, M (South Africa) 1961 *SA v I*
Calmet, R (France) 1970 *E v W*
Carlson, K R V (South Africa) 1962 *SA v BI*
Chapman, W S (Australia) 1938 *A v NZ* (2)
Chevrier, G (France) 1980 *I v S*
Clark, K H (Ireland) 1973 *E v F*, 1974 *S v F*, 1976 *F v E*
Collett, C K (Australia) 1981 *NZ v S*
Cooney, R C (Australia) 1929 *A v NZ*, 1930 *A v BI*, 1932 *A v NZ*, 1934 *A v NZ*
Cooney, W M (Australia) 1972 *A v F*, 1975 *A v E*
Cooper, Dr P F (England) 1952 *I v W*, 1953 *S v W, W v I, W v NZ*, 1954 *I v NZ, W v S*, 1956 *F v I, W v F*, 1957 *F v W* **(9)**
Craven, W S D (England) 1920 *F v W*
Crawford, S H (Ireland) 1920 *S v W*, 1921 *S v E*
Crowe, K J (Australia) 1965 *A v SA*, 1966 *A v BI*, 1968 *A v NZ*
Cumberlege, B S (England) 1926 *S v I, W v I*, 1927 *S v F, I v S, I v W*, 1928 *S v I*, 1929 *F v I, S v F, I v S*, 1930 *I v F, S v I*, 1931 *I v S*, 1932 *S v SA, S v I*, 1933 *I v S*, 1934 *S v I* **(16)**
Cunningham, J G (Scotland) 1921 *F v I*
Cuny, Dr A (France) 1976 *W v S*

D'Arcy, D P (Ireland) 1967 *E v F, E v S, F v W*, 1968 *E v W, S v E, F v SA*, 1969 *E v F, W v E*, 1970 *W v S*, 1971 *W v E*, 1973 *F v NZ, F v W*, 1975 *E v S, W v A* **(14)**
David, I (Wales) 1938 *E v S*, 1939 *S v E*, 1947 *E v S*, 1952 *S v F, I v S, E v I*, 1953 *S v I*, 1954 *S v F, E v NZ, S v NZ, F v NZ, F v E*, 1955 *I v F*, 1956 *F v E* **(14)**
Day, H L V (England) 1934 *S v W*
De Bruyn, C J (South Africa) 1969 *SA v A*, 1974 *SA v BI* (2)
Dickie, A I (Scotland) 1954 *F v I, E v I, W v F*, 1955 *I v E, W v I*, 1956 *E v I, I v W*, 1957 *W v E, I v E*, 1958 *W v A, W v F* **(11)**
Domercq, G (France) 1972 *S v NZ*, 1973 *W v E*, 1976 *E v W*, 1977 *S v W*, 1978 *I v W* **(5)**
Donaldson, S (Ireland) 1937 *S v E*
Doocey, T F (New Zealand) 1976 *NZ v I*, 1983 *E v S, F v W*
Dowling, M J (Ireland) 1947 *S v W*, 1950 *W v S, S v E, W v F*, 1951 *W v E, S v W, F v W, E v S, S v SA*, 1952 *W v S, F v SA, S v E*, 1953 *W v E, E v S*, 1954 *E v W*, 1955 *S v W*, 1956 *S v F, S v E* **(18)**
Doyle, O E (Ireland) 1984 *W v S*
Duffy, B (New Zealand) 1977 *NZ v BI*
Durand, C (France) 1969 *E v S*, 1970 *I v S*, 1971 *E v S*

Elliott, H B (England) 1955 *F v S*, 1956 *I v S*
Engelbrecht, Dr G K (South Africa) 1964 *SA v W*
Evans, W J (Wales) 1958 *F v E, I v A*

Farquhar, A B (New Zealand) 1961 *NZ v F* (3), 1962 *NZ v A* (2), 1964 *NZ v A* **(6)**
Faull, J W (Wales) 1936 *S v I, E v NZ*, 1937 *E v I*
Ferguson, C F (Australia) 1963 *A v E*, 1965 *A v SA*, 1968 *A v F*, 1969 *A v W*, 1971 *A v SA* (2) **(6)**
Finlay, A K (Australia) 1962 *A v NZ*
Fleury, A L (New Zealand) 1959 *NZ v BI*
Fong, A S (New Zealand) 1946 *NZ v A*, 1950 *NZ v BI*
Forsyth, R A (New Zealand) 1958 *NZ v A*
Freeman, W L (Ireland) 1932 *E v SA*
Freethy, A E (Wales) 1924 *E v F, I v NZ*, 1925 *E v NZ, I v S, S v E, F v E*, 1926 *E v F*, 1927 *F v E*, 1928 *I v E, E v F*, 1929 *E v I, F v E*, 1930 *I v E, E v F*, 1931 *E v I, F v E* **(16)**
Fright, W H (New Zealand) 1956 *NZ v SA* (2)
Frood, J (New Zealand) 1952 *NZ v A*

Gadney, C H (England) 1935 *S v NZ, W v NZ*, 1936 *S v W, W v I*, 1937 *W v S, I v S*, 1938 *S v W, S v I*, 1939 *I v S*, 1947 *F v S, S v I*, 1948 *F v A, I v S* **(13)**
Garling, A F (Australia) 1981 *A v NZ* (2)
Gillies, C R (New Zealand) 1958 *NZ v A* (2), 1959 *NZ v BI* (2)
Gilliland, R W (Ireland) 1965 *S v W, E v F, F v W*, 1966 *E v W*, 1967 *F v A* **(5)**
Gillmore, W N (England) 1958 *I v S*
Glasgow, O B (Ireland) 1953 *F v S, F v W*, 1954 *S v E*, 1955 *W v E, F v W* **(5)**
Gourlay, I W (South Africa) 1976 *SA v NZ*
Grierson, T F E (Scotland) 1970 *I v SA*, 1972 *F v E*, 1973 *W v I*, 1975 *E v F*
Griffiths, A A (New Zealand) 1952 *NZ v A*

Harland, R W (Ireland) 1922 *F v W*, 1925 *W v F*, 1926 *F v W*, 1928 *W v E, S v W, F v W*, 1929 *E v W*, 1931 *W v F* **(8)**
Harrison, G (New Zealand) 1981 *A v F*, 1983 *F v A* (2)
Harrison, H C (England) 1922 *F v S*
Haslett, F W (Ireland) 1934 *W v E, E v S*, 1935 *E v W, W v S*, 1936 *W v E* **(5)**
Haydon, N V (Australia) 1957 *A v NZ*
Helliwell, D (England) 1926 *S v W*, 1929 *W v S*, 1930 *F v S, W v I, F v W* **(5)**
Hill, E D (New Zealand) 1949 *NZ v A*
Hinton, W P (Ireland) 1921 *S v F*
Hofmeyr, E W (South Africa) 1949 *SA v NZ* (2), 1961 *SA v A*, 1963 *SA v A*
Hollander, S (New Zealand) 1930 *NZ v BI* (3), 1931 *NZ v A*
Holmes, E (England) 1931 *W v SA*, 1932 *W v I*
Horak, A M (South Africa) 1938 *SA v BI*
Hosie, A M (Scotland) 1973 *I v E*, 1974 *F v I*, 1975 *W v E*, 1976 *E v I, F v A*, 1977 *F v W, I v F*, 1979 *W v I, I v E*, 1980 *W v F, F v I*, 1981 *E v F*, 1982 *E v I, NZ v A* (2), 1983 *I v F, E v NZ*, 1984 *F v E* **(18)**
Hourquet, R (France) 1983 *S v NZ*, 1984 *E v I*
Howard, F A (England) 1984 *I v S*
Hughes, D M (Wales) 1966 *S v F, I v S*, 1967 *I v E, S v I*
Hughes, J (England) 1935 *I v S*
Hughes, P E (England) 1978 *I v S*

Ireland, J C H (Scotland) 1938 *W v I, I v E*, 1939 *E v W, E v I, I v W* **(5)**
Irving, A L C (Australia) 1934 *A v NZ*, 1937 *A v SA*

Jackson, W H (England) 1927 *W v S, W v F*
Jamieson, G A (Ireland) 1972 *W v S*
Jeffares, R W (Ireland) 1930 *W v E, E v S*, 1931 *S v F*, 1935 *S v E, I v NZ* **(5)**
Johnson, R F (England) 1970 *F v I, E v W* (R), 1971 *W v I*, 1972 *I v F, W v NZ*, 1973 *I v F*, 1974 *W v S, I v NZ, F v SA*, 1975 *S v I, S v A* **(11)**
Jones, T (Wales) 1947 *E v F*, 1948 *E v I, F v E*, 1949 *E v F*, 1950 *S v F*, 1951 *I v E* **(6)**
Jones, W (Wales) 1984 *S v F*
Jones, W K M (Wales) 1968 *I v A*, 1970 *F v E*, 1971 *S v I*
Joseph, M (Wales) 1966 *S v A*, 1967 *I v A*, 1968 *I v S, E v I*, 1969 *S v I, S v SA*, 1970 *S v E*, 1971 *I v E, S v E* (C), 1972 *S v F, S v E*, 1973 *I v NZ, S v Pres XV* (C), 1974 *E v I*, 1976 *E v A, F v A*, 1977 *E v S, S v I, F v S* **(19)**
Joynson, D C (Wales) 1955 *E v S*

Keenan, H (England) 1963 *I v NZ*
Kelleher, J C (Wales) 1973 *E v S*, 1974 *F v E*, 1977 *E v F*
Kelleher, K D (Ireland) 1960 *W v S*, 1961 *W v E, E v S*, 1962 *S v E, W v F*, 1963 *W v E*, 1964 *E v W*, 1965 *F v S, W v E*, 1966 *S v E, W v F, W v A*, 1967 *E v A, F v S, S v W, S v NZ*, 1968 *S v F*, 1969 *S v W, E v SA*, 1970 *W v F*, 1971 *F v S* **(21)**
Kilner, W F B (Australia) 1937 *A v SA*
King, J S (New Zealand) 1937 *NZ v SA* (2)
King, M H R (England) 1961 *S v I*

Laidlaw, H B (Scotland) 1963 *I v E*, 1964 *W v F*, 1965 *I v E*, 1968 *F v E, W v F* **(5)**
Lamb, G C (England) 1968 *F v I, W v S, F v SA*, 1969 *F v S, I v F*, 1970 *S v F, W v SA, I v W*, 1971 *I v F, F v A* **(10)**
Lambert, N H (Ireland) 1947 *S v A*, 1948 *E v A, S v E*, 1949 *W v E, S v W, E v S, F v W*, 1950 *E v W, F v E*, 1951 *W v SA*, 1952 *E v W* **(11)**
Larkin, F A (Australia) 1932 *A v NZ*
Lawrie, A A (Scotland) 1924 *I v F*, 1925 *E v W*, 1926 *I v F*
Lewis, A R (Wales) 1970 *E v I*, 1971 *E v F*, 1972 *F v I*, 1973 *S v I, E v A* **(5)**
Lewis, E M (Wales) 1971 *F v A*
Lewis, M S (Wales) 1975 *F v S*, 1976 *I v S*
Llewellyn, V S (Wales) 1951 *E v F*
Llewellyn, W J (Wales) 1926 *F v S, I v E*
Lloyd, D M (Wales) 1975 *I v F*, 1976 *S v E*
Lloyd, R A (Ireland) 1922 *E v S, S v W*
Louw, L L (South Africa) 1953 *SA v A*
Luff, A C (England) 1963 *W v I*, 1964 *I v S, I v W*

Macassey, L E (New Zealand) 1937 *NZ v SA*
McAuley, C J (New Zealand) 1962 *NZ v A*
McDavitt, P A (New Zealand) 1972 *NZ v A*, 1975 *NZ v S*, 1977 *NZ v BI*
McGill, J (Scotland) 1925 *F v I*, 1929 *I v W*
McGowan, J B (Ireland) 1923 *W v F*, 1924 *S v W*
McGrath, R (Ireland) 1928 *F v S*
McKenzie, E (New Zealand) 1921 *NZ v SA*
McKenzie, H J (New Zealand) 1936 *NZ v A*
McMahon, D C J (Scotland) 1961 *W v I*, 1963 *E v F*, 1964 *E v NZ*, 1967 *E v NZ, W v E*, 1969 *W v I* **(6)**
McMullen, R F (New Zealand) 1973 *NZ v E*
Malan, Dr W C (South Africa) 1970 *SA v NZ*, 1971 *SA v F* (2)
Marie, B (France) 1965 *F v W* (R), 1966 *E v I*
Matheson, A M (New Zealand) 1946 *NZ v A*
Mayne, A V (Australia) 1929 *A v NZ* (2), 1932 *A v NZ*
Millar, D H (New Zealand) 1965 *NZ v SA*, 1968 *NZ v F*, 1977 *NZ v BI* (2), 1978 *NZ v A* (3) **(7)**
Millar, W A (South Africa) 1924 *SA v BI* (2)
Mitchell, R (Ireland) 1955 *E v F*, 1956 *E v W*, 1957 *E v S*
Moffat, F J C (Scotland) 1932 *W v E*
Moffitt, J (New Zealand) 1936 *NZ v A*
Moolman, Dr J (South Africa) 1972 *SA v E*
Moore, T W (Australia) 1947 *A v NZ*, 1950 *A v BI*, 1951 *A v NZ*, 1956 *A v SA*
Murdoch, W C W (Scotland) 1951 *W v I, I v SA*, 1952 *E v SA, F v E*
Murphy, J P (New Zealand) 1959 *NZ v BI*, 1963 *NZ v E*, 1964 *NZ v A* (2), 1965 *NZ v SA* (3), 1966 *NZ v BI* (3), 1968 *NZ v F*, 1969 *NZ v W* (2) **(13)**
Myburgh, P A (South Africa) 1962 *SA v BI*, 1963 *SA v A* (3)

Neilson, A E (New Zealand) 1921 *NZ v SA* (2)
Neser, V H (South Africa) 1924 *SA v BI*, 1928 *SA v NZ* (4), 1933 *SA v A* (4) **(9)**
Norling, C (Wales) 1978 *I v NZ*, 1979 *E v S*, 1980 *F v E*, 1981 *I v F, NZ v SA* (2), *F v NZ*, 1982 *I v S*, 1984 *F v I* **(9)**

Oakley, C D (South Africa) 1924 *SA v BI*
O'Callaghan, B J (Australia) 1959 *A v BI*

Palmade, F (France) 1973 *F v S* (R), *S v W*, 1974 *I v S*, 1975 *I v E*, 1977 *I v E*, 1978 *E v I*, 1979 *S v W*, 1980 *SA v BI* (2), 1981 *W v I, SA v I* (2), 1982 *E v W*, 1983 *NZ v BI* (2) **(15)**

Parfitt, V J (Wales) 1953 *E v F*, 1954 *I v S*
Parkes, Dr N M (England) 1958 *W v S, F v A, I v W, F v I*, 1959 *F v W*, 1960 *W v F*, 1961 *F v W*, 1962 *W v S, I v S* **(9)**
Parkinson, F G M (New Zealand) 1955 *NZ v A*, 1956 *NZ v SA* (2)
Pattinson, K A (England) 1973 *F v S, W v A*, 1974 *I v W*, 1975 *F v W*, 1976 *S v F* **(5)**
Pearce, T N (England) 1948 *F v I, W v S*, 1949 *I v F, W v I*, 1950 *F v I, I v S*, 1951 *F v S, I v F, S v I*, 1952 *F v I* **(10)**
Phillips, T H (Wales) 1936 *E v S*
Potter-Irwin, F C (England) 1920 *W v I, F v S*
Pretorius, N F (South Africa) 1938 *SA v BI*
Price, F G (Wales) 1963 *I v F*
Prideaux, L M (England) 1980 *W v S, I v W*, 1981 *S v I, NZ v SA*
Priest, T E (England) 1953 *I v F*
Pring, J P G (New Zealand) 1966 *NZ v BI*, 1967 *NZ v A*, 1968 *NZ v F*, 1971 *NZ v BI* (4), 1972 *NZ v A* **(8)**
Purcell, N (Ireland) 1927 *S v E*

Quittenton, R C (England) 1978 *W v NZ*, 1979 *I v F, F v S, S v NZ*, 1981 *S v A*, 1982 *NZ v A*, 1983 *S v W* **(7)**

Rea, M D M (Ireland) 1982 *F v E*
Reilly, J R (Australia) 1972 *A v F*
Richards, A (Wales) 1981 *A v F*, 1982 *E v A*, 1983 *F v S*
Robbertse, P (South Africa) 1967 *SA v F*, 1969 *SA v A*, 1970 *SA v NZ* (2)
Roberts, E (Wales) 1924 *F v S*
Roberts, R A (England) 1924 *F v W*
Robertson, W A (Scotland) 1920 *I v E, E v F*
Robson, C F (New Zealand) 1963 *NZ v E*
Rowlands, K (Wales) 1981 *F v S*, 1982 *S v E*
Royds, P M R (England) 1921 *W v F*, 1923 *F v I*

St Guilhem, J (France) 1974 *S v E*, 1975 *W v I*
Sanson, N R (Scotland) 1974 *W v F, F v SA*, 1975 *I v Pres XV* (C), *SA v F* (2), 1976 *I v A, I v W*, 1977 *W v I*, 1978 *F v E, E v W, E v NZ*, 1979 *E v NZ* **(12)**
Schoeman, J P J (South Africa) 1968 *SA v BI*
Schofield, T D (Wales) 1920 *E v S*, 1921 *E v I*, 1922 *S v I*
Scott, J M B (Scotland) 1923 *E v W*
Scott, R L (Scotland) 1927 *F v I, E v W*
Short, J A (Scotland) 1982 *I v W*
Slabber, M J (South Africa) 1955 *SA v BI*, 1960 *SA v NZ*
Strasheim, Dr E A (South Africa) 1958 *SA v F*, 1960 *SA v S, SA v NZ*, 1962 *SA v BI* (2), 1964 *SA v F*, 1967 *SA v F*, 1968 *SA v BI* **(8)**
Strasheim, Dr J J (South Africa) 1938 *SA v BI*
Sturrock, J C (Scotland) 1921 *E v W, F v E*, 1922 *W v I*
Sullivan, G (New Zealand) 1950 *NZ v BI*
Sutherland, F E (New Zealand) 1930 *NZ v BI*

Taylor, A R (New Zealand) 1965 *NZ v SA* (R), 1972 *NZ v A*
Taylor, J A S (Scotland) 1957 *W v I*, 1960 *E v W, F v E, W v SA*, 1962 *E v W, F v I, I v W* **(7)**
Tennant, J M (Scotland) 1920 *I v F*, 1921 *I v W*, 1922 *W v E, E v F, I v F, I v E*, 1923 *I v W* **(7)**
Thomas, C (Wales) 1979 *S v I*, 1980 *E v I*
Thomas, C G P (Wales) 1977 *F v NZ*, 1978 *S v F, F v I*
Tierney, A T (Australia) 1957 *A v NZ*, 1959 *A v BI*
Tindill, E W T (New Zealand) 1950 *NZ v BI* (2), 1955 *NZ v A*
Titcomb, M H (England) 1966 *W v S*, 1967 *W v I, W v NZ*, 1968 *I v W, S v A*, 1971 *S v W, E v Pres XV* (C), 1972 *W v F* **(8)**
Tolhurst, H A (Australia) 1951 *A v NZ* (2)
Tomalin, L C (Australia) 1947 *A v NZ*, 1950 *A v BI*
Treharne, G J (Wales) 1960 *I v SA*, 1961 *E v SA, I v E, I v F*, 1963 *S v I* **(5)**
Trigg, J A F (England) 1982 *S v F*, 1983 *W v I*
Tulloch, J L (Scotland) 1920 *W v E*, 1924 *W v I*

Vanderfield, Dr I R (Australia) 1956 *A v SA*, 1961 *A v F*, 1962 *A v NZ*, 1966 *A v BI*, 1967 *A v I*, 1968 *A v NZ*, 1970 *A v S*, 1971 *A v SA*, 1974 *A v NZ* (2) **(10)**
Van der Horst, A W (South Africa) 1933 *SA v A*
Vile, T H (Wales) 1923 *S v F, E v I, I v S, S v E, F v E*, 1924 *I v E, S v I, E v S*, 1925 *E v I*, 1927 *E v I*, 1928 *E v S*, 1931 *F v I* **(12)**

Walsh, L (New Zealand) 1949 *NZ v A*
Walters, D G (Wales) 1959 *F v S, I v E, E v S, I v F*, 1960 *S v F, E v I, I v S, F v I*, 1961 *F v SA, E v F*, 1962 *E v I, F v E*, 1963 *E v S*, 1964 *E v I, F v E, F v I*, 1965 *I v F, S v I, E v S, S v SA*, 1966 *F v E* **(21)**
Warren, T H H (Scotland) 1928 *W v I*
Welsby, A (England) 1976 *F v I*, 1978 *W v F*, 1981 *F v W*, 1982 *F v I*
West, J R (Ireland) 1974 *E v W*, 1975 *S v W*, 1976 *W v F*, 1977 *F v NZ*, 1978 *W v S, S v E, S v NZ*, 1979 *E v F, NZ v F* (2), 1980 *S v F, SA v F, W v NZ*, 1981 *F v NZ, W v A*, 1983 *W v E* **(16)**
Wheeler, Dr E de C (Ireland) 1925 *S v F*
Wheeler, Dr J R (Ireland) 1929 *S v E*, 1930 *S v W*, 1931 *E v W, S v E*, 1932 *E v S*, 1933 *S v E* **(6)**
Whittaker, J B G (England) 1947 *I v F, W v I*
Wilkins, H E B (England) 1925 *F v NZ*, 1929 *W v F*
Williams, R C (Ireland) 1957 *S v W, E v F*, 1958 *E v W, E v A, S v A, S v E*, 1959 *W v E, S v W, E v F*, 1960 *S v E*, 1961 *F v S, S v W*, 1962 *S v F*, 1963 *F v S, S v W, W v NZ*, 1964 *S v F, S v NZ, F v NZ, S v E* **(20)**
Wolstenholme, B H (New Zealand) 1955 *NZ v A*
Woolley, A (South Africa) 1970 *SA v NZ*

Yché, J-C (France) 1983 *S v I*
Young, J (Scotland) 1971 *F v W*, 1972 *E v W*, 1973 *E v NZ*

INTERNATIONAL MATCH APPEARANCES FOR BRITISH ISLES TEAMS *(up to 30 April 1984)*

*From 1910 onwards, when British Isles teams first became officially representative of the Four Home Unions. (*Uncapped when first chosen to tour.)*

ABBREVIATIONS

A	Australia
NZ	New Zealand
SA	South Africa
(R)	Replacement – (2[1R]) denotes two appearances, one of them as a replacement

CLUB ABBREVIATIONS

NIFC	North of Ireland Football Club
CIYMS	Church of Ireland Young Men's Society

Aarvold, C D (Cambridge U, Blackheath and England) 1930 *NZ* (4), *A*
Ackerman, R A (L Welsh and Wales) 1983 *NZ* (2[1R])
Alexander, R (NIFC and Ireland) 1938 *SA* (3)
Arneil, R J (Edinburgh Acads and Scotland) 1968 *SA* (4)
Ashcroft, A (Waterloo and England) 1959 *A*, *NZ*

Bainbridge, S J (Gosforth and England) 1983 *NZ* (2)
Baird, G R T (Kelso and Scotland) 1983 *NZ* (4)
Baker, D G S (Old Merchant Taylors and England) 1955 *SA* (2)
Bassett, J (Penarth and Wales) 1930 *NZ* (4), *A*
Beamish, G R (Leicester, RAF and Ireland) 1930 *NZ* (4), *A*
Beattie, J R (Glasgow Acads and Scotland) 1983 *NZ* (R)
Beaumont, W B (Fylde and England) 1977 *NZ* (3), 1980 *SA* (4)
Bebb, D I E (Swansea and Wales) 1962 *SA* (2), 1966 *A* (2), *NZ* (4)
Bennett, P (Llanelli and Wales) 1974 *SA* (4), 1977 *NZ* (4)
Bevan, J C (Cardiff Coll of Ed, Cardiff and Wales) 1971 *NZ*
Black, A W (Edinburgh U and Scotland) 1950 *NZ* (2)
Black, B H (Oxford U, Blackheath and England) 1930 *NZ* (4), *A*
Blakiston, A F (Northampton and England) 1924 *SA* (4)
Bowcott, H M (Cambridge U, Cardiff and Wales) 1930 *NZ* (4), *A*
Boyle, C V (Dublin U and Ireland) 1938 *SA* (2)
Brand, T N (NIFC and *Ireland) 1924 *SA* (2)
Bresnihan, F P K (UC Dublin and Ireland) 1968 *SA* (3)
Brophy, N H (UC Dublin and Ireland) 1962 *SA* (2)
Brown, G L (W of Scotland and Scotland) 1971 *NZ* (2), 1974 *SA* (3), 1977 *NZ* (3)
Budge, G M (Edinburgh Wands and Scotland) 1950 *NZ*
Burcher, D H (Newport and Wales) 1977 *NZ*
Butterfield, J (Northampton and England) 1955 *SA* (4)

Calder, J H (Stewart's-Melville FP and Scotland) 1983 *NZ*
Cameron, A (Glasgow HSFP and Scotland) 1955 *SA* (2)
Campbell, S O (Old Belvedere and Ireland) 1980 *SA* (3[1R]), 1983 *NZ* (4)
Campbell-Lamerton, M J (Halifax, Army and Scotland) 1962 *SA* (4), 1966 *A* (2), *NZ* (2)
Carleton, J (Orrell and England) 1980 *SA* (3), 1983 *NZ* (3)
Cleaver, W B (Cardiff and Wales) 1950 *NZ* (3)
Clifford, T (Young Munster and Ireland) 1950 *NZ* (3), *A* (2)
Cobner, T J (Pontypool and Wales) 1977 *NZ* (3)
Colclough, M J (Angoulême and England) 1980 *SA* (4), 1983 *NZ* (4)
Connell, G C (Trinity Acads and Scotland) 1968 *SA*
Cotton F E (Loughborough Colls, Coventry, and England) 1974 *SA* (4), 1977 *NZ* (3)
Coulman, M J (Moseley and England) 1968 *SA*
Cove-Smith, R (Old Merchant Taylors and England) 1924 *SA* (4)
Cowan, R C (Selkirk and Scotland) 1962 *SA*
Cromey, G E (Queen's U, Belfast and Ireland) 1938 *SA*
Cunningham, W A (Lansdowne and Ireland) 1924 *SA*

Dancer, G T (Bedford) 1938 *SA* (3)
Davies, C (Cardiff and Wales) 1950 *NZ*
Davies, D M (Somerset Police and Wales) 1950 *NZ* (2), *A*
Davies, D S (Hawick and Scotland) 1924 *SA* (4)
Davies, H J (Newport and Wales) 1924 *SA*
Davies, T G R (Cardiff, London Welsh and Wales) 1968 *SA*, 1971 *NZ* (4)
Davies, T J (Llanelli and Wales) 1959 *NZ* (2)
Davies, T M (London Welsh, Swansea and Wales) 1971 *NZ* (4), 1974 *SA* (4)
Davies, W G (Cardiff and Wales) 1980 *SA*
Davies, W P C (Harlequins and England) 1955 *SA* (3)
Dawes, S J (London Welsh and Wales) 1971 *NZ* (4)
Dawson, A R (Wanderers and Ireland) 1959 *A* (2), *NZ* (4)
Dixon, P J (Harlequins and England) 1971 *NZ* (3)
Dodge, P W (Leicester and England) 1980 *SA* (2)
Doyle, M G (Blackrock Coll and Ireland) 1968 *SA*
Drysdale, D (Heriot's FP and Scotland) 1924 *SA* (4)
Duckham, D J (Coventry and England) 1971 *NZ* (3)
Duggan, W P (Blackrock Coll and Ireland) 1977 *NZ* (4)
Duff, P L (Glasgow Acads and Scotland) 1938 *SA* (2)

Edwards, G O (Cardiff and Wales) 1968 *SA* (2), 1971 *NZ* (4), 1974 *SA* (4)
Evans, G (Maesteg and Wales) 1983 *NZ* (2)
Evans, G L (Newport and Wales) 1977 *NZ* (3)
Evans, R T (Newport and Wales) 1950 *NZ* (4), *A* (2)
Evans, T P (Swansea and Wales) 1977 *NZ*
Evans, W R (Cardiff and Wales) 1959 *A*, *NZ* (3)

Farrell, J L (Bective Rangers and Ireland) 1930 *NZ* (4), *A*
Faull, J (Swansea and Wales) 1959 *A*, *NZ* (3)
Fenwick, S P (Bridgend and Wales) 1977 *NZ* (4)
Fitzgerald, C F (St Mary's Coll and Ireland) 1983 *NZ* (4)
Foster, A R (Queen's Univ, Belfast and Ireland) 1910 *SA* (3)

Gibson, C M H (Cambridge U, NIFC and Ireland) 1966, *NZ* (4), 1968 *SA* (4[1R]), 1971 *NZ* (4)
Giles, J L (Coventry and England) 1938 *SA* (2)
Gravell, R W R (Llanelli and Wales) 1980 *SA* (4[1R])
Graves, C R A (Wanderers and Ireland) 1938 *SA* (2)
Greenwood, J T (Dunfermline and Scotland) 1955 *SA* (4)
Grieve, C F (Oxford U and Scotland) 1938 *SA* (2)
Griffiths, G M (Cardiff and Wales) 1955 *SA* (3)
Griffiths, V M (Newport and Wales) 1924 *SA* (2)

Handford, F G (Manchester and England) 1910 *SA* (3)
Harding, W Rowe (Cambridge U, Swansea and Wales) 1924 *SA* (3)
Harris, S W (Blackheath and England) 1924 *SA* (2)
Hay, B H (Boroughmuir and Scotland) 1980 *SA* (3)
Hayward, D J (Newbridge and Wales) 1950 *NZ* (3)
Henderson, N J (Queen's U, Belfast, NIFC and Ireland) 1950 *NZ*
Henderson, R G (Northern and Scotland) 1924 *SA* (2)
Hendrie K G P (Heriot's FP and Scotland) 1924 *SA*
Hewitt, D (Queen's U, Belfast, Instonians and Ireland) 1959 *A* (2), *NZ* (3), 1962 *SA*
Higgins, R (Liverpool and England) 1955 *SA*
Hinshelwood, A J W (London Scottish and Scotland) 1966 *NZ* (2), 1968 *SA*
Hodgson, J McD (Northern and *England) 1930 *NZ* (2)
Holmes, T D (Cardiff and Wales) 1983 *NZ*
Hopkins, R (Maesteg and Wales) 1971 *NZ* (R)
Horrocks-Taylor, J P (Leicester and England) 1959 *NZ*
Horton, A L (Blackheath and England) 1968 *SA* (3)
Howard, W G (Old Birkonians) 1938 *SA*
Howie, R A (Kirkcaldy and Scotland) 1924 *SA* (4)

Irvine, A R (Heriot's FP and Scotland) 1974 *SA* (2), 1977 *NZ* (4), 1980 *SA* (3)
Irwin, D G (Instonians and Ireland) 1983 *NZ* (3)
Isherwood, G A M (Old Alleynians and Sale) 1910 *SA* (3)

Jackson, P B (Coventry and England) 1959 *A* (2), *NZ* (3)
Jarman, H (Newport and Wales) 1910 *SA* (3)
Jeeps, R E G (Northampton and *England) 1955 *SA* (4), 1959 *A* (2), *NZ* (3), 1962 *SA* (4)
Jenkins, V G J (Oxford U, London Welsh and Wales) 1938 *SA*
John B (Cardiff and Wales) 1968 *SA*, 1971 *NZ* (4)
John, E R (Neath and Wales) 1950 *NZ* (4), *A* (2)
Jones, B L (Devonport Services, Llanelli and Wales) 1950 *NZ*, *A* (2)
Jones, D K (Llanelli, Cardiff, and Wales) 1962 *SA* (3), 1966 *A* (2), *NZ*
Jones, E L (Llanelli and *Wales) 1938 *SA* (2)
Jones, Ivor (Llanelli and Wales) 1930 *NZ* (4), *A*
Jones, J P (Pontypool, Newport and Wales) 1910 *SA* (3)
Jones, K D (Cardiff and Wales) 1962 *SA* (4)
Jones, K J (Newport and Wales) 1950 *NZ* (3)
Jones, S T (Pontypool and Wales) 1983 *NZ* (3)

Keane, M I (Lansdowne and Ireland) 1977 *NZ*
Kennedy, K W (CIYMS, London Irish and Ireland) 1966 *A* (2), *NZ* (2)
Kiernan, M J (Dolphin and Ireland) 1983 *NZ* (3)
Kiernan, T J (Cork Const and Ireland) 1962 *SA*, 1968 *SA* (4)
Kinnear, R M (Heriot's FP and *Scotland) 1924 *SA* (4)
Kininmonth, P W (Oxford U, Richmond and Scotland) 1950 *NZ* (3)
Kyle, J W (Queen's U Belfast, NIFC and Ireland) 1950 *NZ* (4), *A* (2)

Laidlaw, F A L (Melrose and Scotland) 1966 *NZ* (2)
Laidlaw, R J (Jedforest and Scotland) 1983 *NZ* (4[1R])
Lamont, R A (Instonians and Ireland) 1966 *NZ* (4)
Lane, M F (UC Cork and Ireland) 1950 *NZ*, *A*
Larter, P J (Northampton, RAF and England) 1968 *SA*
Lewis, A R (Abertillery and Wales) 1966 *NZ* (3)
Lynch, J F (St Mary's Coll and Ireland) 1971 *NZ* (4)

McBride, W J (Ballymena and Ireland) 1962 *SA* (2), 1966 *NZ* (3), 1968 *SA* (4), 1971 *NZ* (4), 1974 *SA* (4)
Macdonald, R (Edinburgh U and Scotland) 1950 *NZ*, *A*
McFadyean, C W (Moseley and England) 1966 *NZ* (4)
McGeechan, I R (Headingley and Scotland) 1974 *SA* (4), 1977 *NZ* (4[1R])
McKay, J W (Queen's U, Belfast and Ireland) 1950 *NZ* (4), *A* (2)
McKibbin, H R (Queen's U, Belfast and Ireland) 1938 *SA* (3)
McLauchlan, J (Jordanhill and Scotland) 1971 *NZ* (4), 1974 *SA* (4)
McLeod, H F (Hawick and Scotland) 1959 *A* (2), *NZ* (4)
McLoughlin, R J (Gosforth, Blackrock Coll and Ireland) 1966 *A* (2), *NZ*
MacNeill, H P (Oxford U and Ireland) 1983 *NZ* (3[1R])
Macpherson, N C (Newport and Scotland) 1924 *SA* (4)
Macrae, D J (St Andrew's U and Scotland) 1938 *SA*
McVicker, J (Collegians and Ireland) 1924 *SA* (3)
Martindale, S A (Kendal and England) 1930 *A*
Marsden-Jones, D (London Welsh and Wales) 1924 *SA* (2)
Marques, R W D (Harlequins and England) 1959 *A*, *NZ*
Martin, A J (Aberavon and Wales) 1977 *NZ*
Matthews, J (Cardiff and Wales) 1950 *NZ* (4), *A* (2)
Maxwell, R B (Birkenhead Park) 1924 *SA*
Mayne, R B (Queen's U, Belfast and Ireland) 1938 *SA* (3)
Meredith, B V (Newport and Wales) 1955 *SA* (4), 1962 *SA* (4)
Meredith, C C (Neath and Wales) 1955 *SA* (4)
Millar, S (Ballymena and Ireland) 1959 *A* (2), *NZ*, 1962 *SA* (4), 1968 *SA* (2)
Milliken, R A (Bangor and Ireland) 1974 *SA* (4)
Morgan, C I (Cardiff and Wales) 1955 *SA* (4)
Morgan, D W (Stewart's-Melville FP and Scotland) 1977 *NZ* (2[1R])
Morgan, G J (Clontarf and Ireland) 1938 *SA*
Morgan, H J (Abertillery and Wales) 1959 *NZ* (2), 1962 *SA* (2)
Morgan, M E (Swansea and Wales) 1938 *SA* (2)
Morley, J C (Newport and Wales) 1930 *NZ* (3)
Mulcahy, W A (U C Dublin and Ireland) 1959 *A*, *NZ*, 1962 *SA* (4)
Mullen, K D (Old Belvedere and Ireland) 1950 *NZ* (2), *A*
Mulligan, A A (Wanderers, London Irish and Ireland), 1959 *NZ*
Murphy, N A A (Cork Const and Ireland) 1959 *A*, *NZ* (3), 1966 *A* (2), *NZ* (2)
Murray, P F (Wanderers and Ireland) 1930 *NZ* (3), *A*

Neale, M E (Bristol, Blackheath and *England) 1910 *SA* (3)
Neary, A (Broughton Park and England) 1977 *NZ*
Nelson, J E (Malone and Ireland) 1950 *NZ* (2), *A* (2)
Nicholson, B E (Harlequins and England) 1938 *SA*
Norris, C H (Cardiff and Wales) 1966 *NZ* (3)
Norster, R L (Cardiff and Wales) 1983 *NZ* (2)
Novis, A L (Blackheath and England) 1930 *NZ* (2), *A*

O'Donnell, R C (St Mary's Coll and Ireland) 1980 *SA*
O'Driscoll, J B (London Irish and Ireland) 1980 *SA* (4), 1983 *NZ* (2)
O'Neill, H O'H (Queen's U, Belfast and Ireland) 1930 *NZ* (4), *A*
O'Reilly, A J F (Old Belvedere and Ireland) 1955 *SA* (4), 1959 *A* (2), *NZ* (4)
Orr, P A (Old Wesley and Ireland) 1977 *NZ*
O'Shea, J P (Cardiff and Wales) 1968 *SA*

Parker, D (Swansea and Wales) 1930 *NZ* (4), *A*
Pask, A E I (Abertillery and Wales) 1962 *SA* (3), 1966 *A* (2), *NZ* (3)
Patterson, C S (Instonians and Ireland) 1980 *SA* (3)
Patterson, W M (Sale and *England) 1959 *NZ*
Paxton, I A M (Selkirk and Scotland) 1983 *NZ* (4)
Pedlow, A C (CIYMS and Ireland) 1955 *SA* (2)
Pillman, C H (Blackheath and England) 1910 *SA* (2)
Piper, O J S (Cork Const and Ireland) 1910 *SA*
Poole, H (Cardiff) 1930 *NZ*
Preece, I (Coventry and England) 1950 *NZ*
Prentice, F D (Leicester and England) 1930 *NZ*, *A*
Price, B (Newport and Wales) 1966 *A* (2), *NZ* (2)
Price, G (Pontypool and Wales) 1977 *NZ* (4), 1980 *SA* (4), 1983 *NZ* (4)

Price, M J (Pontypool and Wales) 1959 *A* (2), *NZ* (3)
Prosser, T R (Pontypool and Wales) 1959 *NZ*
Pullin, J V (Bristol and England) 1968 *SA* (3), 1971 *NZ* (4)

Quinnell, D L (Llanelli and *Wales) 1971 *NZ*, 1977 *NZ* (2), 1980 *SA* (2)

Ralston, C W (Richmond and England) 1974 *SA*
Rees, H E (Neath and *Wales) 1977 *NZ*
Reeve, J S R (Harlequins and England) 1930 *NZ* (3), *A*
Reid, T E (Garryowen and Ireland) 1955 *SA* (2)
Renwick, J M (Hawick and Scotland) 1980 *SA*
Rew, H (Blackheath, Army and England) 1930 *NZ* (4)
Reynolds, F J (Old Cranleighans and England) 1938 *SA* (2)
Richards, D S (Swansea and Wales) 1980 *SA*
Richards, M C R (Cardiff and Wales) 1968 *SA* (3)
Richards, T J (Bristol) 1910 *SA* (3)
Rimmer, G (Waterloo and England) 1950 *NZ*
Ringland, T M (Ballymena and Ireland) 1983 *NZ*
Risman, A B W (Loughborough Colls and England) 1959 *A* (2), *NZ* (2)
Robbie, J C (Greystones and Ireland) 1980 *SA*
Robins, J D (Birkenhead Park and Wales) 1950 *NZ* (3), *A* (2)
Robins, R J (Pontypridd and Wales) 1955 *SA* (4)
Rogers, D P (Bedford and England) 1962 *SA* (2)
Rowlands, K A (Cardiff and Wales) 1962 *SA* (3)
Rutherford, D (Gloucester and England) 1966 *A*
Rutherford, J Y (Selkirk and Scotland) 1983 *NZ*

Savage, K F (Northampton and England) 1968 *SA* (4)
Scotland, K J F (Cambridge U, Heriot's FP and Scotland) 1959 *A* (2), *NZ* (3)
Sharp, R A W (Oxford U, Redruth and England) 1962 *SA* (2)
Slattery, J F (Blackrock Coll and Ireland) 1974 *SA* (4)
Slemen, M A C (Liverpool and England) 1980 *SA*
Smith, A R (Edinburgh Wands, London Scottish and Scotland) 1962 *SA* (3)
Smith, D F (Richmond and England) 1910 *SA* (3)
Smith, D W C (London Scottish and Scotland) 1950 *A*
Smith, G K (Kelso and Scotland) 1959 *A* (2), *NZ* (2)
Smith, I S (Oxford U, London Scottish and Scotland) 1924 *SA* (2)
Smyth, T (Malone, Newport and Ireland) 1910 *SA* (2)
Spong, R S (Old Millhillians and England) 1930 *NZ* (4) *A*
Spoors, J A (Bristol) 1910 *SA* (3)
Squire, J (Newport, Pontypool and Wales) 1977 *NZ*, 1980 *SA* (4), 1983 *NZ*
Squires, P J (Harrogate and England) 1977 *NZ*
Stagg, P K (Oxford U, Sale and Scotland) 1968 *SA* (3)
Steele, W C C (Bedford, RAF and Scotland) 1974 *SA* (2)
Stephens, I (Bridgend and Wales) 1983 *NZ*
Stephens, J R G (Neath and Wales) 1950 *A* (2)
Stevenson, R C (St Andrew's U and Scotland) 1910 *SA* (3)

Tanner, H (Swansea and Wales) 1938 *SA*
Taylor, A R (Cross Keys and Wales) 1938 *SA* (2)
Taylor, J (London Welsh and Wales) 1971 *NZ* (4)
Taylor, R B (Northampton and England) 1968 *SA* (4)
Telfer, J W (Melrose and Scotland) 1966 *A* (2), *NZ* (3), 1968 *SA* (3)
Thomas, M C (Devonport Services, Newport and Wales) 1950 *NZ* (2), *A*, 1959 *NZ*
Thomas, R C C (Swansea and Wales) 1955 *SA* (2)
Thomas, W D (Llanelli and *Wales) 1966 *NZ* (2), 1968 *SA* (2[1R]), 1971 *NZ* (2)
Thompson, R H (Instonians, London Irish and Ireland) 1955 *SA* (3)
Travers, W H (Newport and Wales) 1938 *SA* (2)
Tucker, C C (Shannon and Ireland) 1980 *SA* (2)
Turner, J W C (Gala and Scotland) 1968 *SA* (4)

Unwin, E J (Rosslyn Park, Army and England) 1938 *SA* (2)
Uttley, R M (Gosforth and England) 1974 *SA* (4)

Voyce, A T (Gloucester and England) 1924 *SA* (2)

Waddell, G H (Cambridge U, London Scottish and Scotland) 1962 *SA* (2)
Waddell, H (Glasgow Acads and Scotland) 1924 *SA* (3)
Walker, S (Instonians and Ireland) 1938 *SA* (3)
Wallace, W (Percy Park) 1924 *SA*
Waller, P D (Newport and Wales) 1910 *SA* (3)
Ward, A J P (Garryowen and Ireland) 1980 *SA*
Waters, J A (Selkirk and Scotland) 1938 *SA*
Watkins, D (Newport and Wales) 1966 *A* (2), *NZ* (4)
Watkins, S J (Newport and Wales) 1966 *A* (2), *NZ*
Webb, J (Abertillery and Wales) 1910 *SA* (3)
Welsh, W B (Hawick and Scotland) 1930 *NZ*
Weston, M P (Richmond, Durham City and England) 1962 *SA* (4), 1966 *A* (2)
Wheeler, P J (Leicester and England) 1977 *NZ* (3), 1980 *SA* (4)
Whitley, H (Northern and *England) 1924 *SA* (3)
Willcox, J G (Oxford U, Harlequins and England) 1962 *SA* (3)
Williams, B L (Cardiff and Wales) 1950 *A* (2), *NZ* (3)
Williams, C (Swansea and Wales) 1980 *SA* (4)
Williams, D (Ebbw Vale and Wales) 1966 *A* (2), *NZ* (3)
Williams, D B (Cardiff and *Wales) 1977 *NZ* (3)
Williams, J J (Llanelli and Wales) 1974 *SA* (4), 1977 *NZ* (3)
Williams, J P R (London Welsh and Wales) 1971 *NZ* (4), 1974 *SA* (4)
Williams, R H (Llanelli and Wales) 1955 *SA* (4), 1959 *A* (2), *NZ* (4)
Williams, S H (Newport and *England) 1910 *SA* (3)
Williams, W O G (Swansea and Wales) 1955 *SA* (4)
Willis, W R (Cardiff and Wales) 1950 *NZ*, *A* (2)
Windsor, R W (Pontypool and Wales) 1974 *SA* (4), 1977 *NZ*
Winterbottom, P J (Headingley and England) 1983 *NZ* (4)
Wilson, S (London Scottish and Scotland) 1966 *A*, *NZ* (4)
Wood, B G M (Garryowen and Ireland) 1959 *NZ* (2)
Wood, K B (Leicester) 1910 *SA*
Woodward, C R (Leicester and England) 1980 *SA* (2)

Young, A T (Cambridge U, Blackheath and England) 1924 *SA*
Young, J (Harrogate, RAF and Wales) 1968 *SA*
Young, J R C (Oxford U, Harlequins and England) 1959 *NZ*
Young, R M (Queen's U, Belfast, Collegians and Ireland) 1966 *A* (2), *NZ*, 1968 *SA*

RESULTS OF BRITISH ISLES MATCHES
(up to 30 April 1984)

From 1910 onwards – the tour to South Africa in that year was the first fully representative one in which the Four Home Unions cooperated.

v SOUTH AFRICA

Played 30 British Isles won 8, South Africa won 18, Drawn 4

1910 *1* Johannesburg
South Africa 1G 4T (14)
to 1DG 2T (10)

2 Port Elizabeth
British Isles 1G 1T (8) to 1T (3)

3 Cape Town
South Africa 3G 1PG 1T (21) to 1G (5)
South Africa won series 2-1

1924 *1* Durban
South Africa 1DG 1T (7) to 1T (3)

2 Johannesburg
South Africa 1G 1PG 3T (17) to 0

3 Port Elizabeth
Drawn 1T (3) each

4 Cape Town
South Africa 1DG 4T (16) to 1PG 2T (9)
South Africa won series 3-0, with 1 draw

1938 *1* Johannesburg
South Africa 4G 2PG (26)
to 4PG (12)

2 Port Elizabeth
South Africa 2G 2PG 1T (19)
to 1T (3)

3 Cape Town
British Isles 1G 1PG 1DG 3T (21)
to 2G 1PG 1T (16)
South Africa won series 2-1

1955 *1* Johannesburg
British Isles 4G 1T (23) to 2G 2PG 2T (22)

2 Cape Town
South Africa 2G 5T (25)
to 1PG 2T (9)

3 Pretoria
British Isles 1PG 1DG 1T (9)
to 2PG (6)

4 Port Elizabeth
South Africa 2G 1DG 3T (22)
to 1G 1T (8)
Series drawn 2-2

1962 *1* Johannesburg
Drawn 1T (3) each

2 Durban
South Africa 1PG (3) to 0

3 Cape Town
South Africa 1G 1PG (8) to 1DG (3)

4 Bloemfontein
South Africa 5G 2PG 1T (34)
to 1G 1PG 2T (14)
South Africa won series 3-0, with 1 draw

1968 *1* Pretoria
South Africa 2G 4PG 1T (25)
to 1G 5PG (20)

2 Port Elizabeth
Drawn 2PG (6) each

3 Cape Town
South Africa 1G 2PG (11) to 2PG (6)

4 Johannesburg
South Africa 2G 1DG 2T (19) to 2PG (6)
South Africa won series 3-0, with 1 draw

1974 *1* Cape Town
British Isles 3PG 1DG (12) to 1DG (3)

2 Pretoria
British Isles 1G 1PG 1DG 4T (28)
to 2 PG 1DG (9)

3 Port Elizabeth
British Isles 1G 2PG 2DG 2T (26)
to 3PG (9)

4 Johannesburg
Drawn British Isles 1G 1PG 1T (13)
South Africa 3PG 1T (13)
British Isles won series 3-0, with 1 draw

1980 *1* Cape Town
South Africa 3G 2T (26)
to 5PG 1DG 1T (22)

2 Bloemfontein
South Africa 2G 2PG 2T (26)
to 1G 3PG 1T (19)

3 Port Elizabeth
South Africa 1G 1PG 1DG (12)
to 2PG 1T (10)

4 Pretoria
British Isles 1G 1PG 2T (17)
to 3PG 1T (13)
South Africa won series 3-1

v NEW ZEALAND

Played 28 British Isles won 5, New Zealand won 21, Drawn 2

1930 *1* Dunedin
British Isles 2T (6) to 1T (3)

2 Christchurch
New Zealand 2G 1GM (13) to 2G (10)

3 Auckland
New Zealand 1G 1DG 2T (15)
to 2G (10)

4 Wellington
New Zealand 2G 4T (22) to 1G 1PG (8)
New Zealand won series 3-1

1950 *1* Dunedin
Drawn 2T 1PG (9) each

2 Christchurch
New Zealand 1G 1T (8) to 0

3 Wellington
New Zealand 1PG 1T (6) to 1PG (3)

4 Auckland
New Zealand 1G 1DG 1T (11)
to 1G 1PG (8)
New Zealand won series 3-0, with 1 draw

1959 *1* Dunedin
New Zealand 6PG (18)
to 1G 1PG 3T (17)

2 Wellington
New Zealand 1G 2T (11) to 1G 1PG (8)

3 Christchurch
New Zealand 2G 1PG 1DG 2T (22)
to 1G 1PG (8)

4 Auckland
British Isles 3T (9) to 2PG (6)
New Zealand won series 3-1

1966 *1* Dunedin
New Zealand 1G 2PG 1DG 2T (20)
to 1PG (3)

2 Wellington
New Zealand 2G 1PG 1T (16)
to 3PG 1DG (12)

3 Christchurch
New Zealand 2G 2PG 1T (19) to 2T (6)

4 Auckland
New Zealand 3G 1PG 1DG 1T (24)
to 1G 1PG 1T (11)
New Zealand won series 4-0

1971 *1* Dunedin
British Isles 2PG 1T (9) to 1PG (3)

2 Christchurch
New Zealand 2G 1PG 3T (22)
to 1PG 1DG 2T (12)

3 Wellington
British Isles 2G 1DG (13) to 1T (3)

4 Auckland
Drawn British Isles 1G 2PG 1DG (14)
New Zealand 1G 2PG 1T (14)
British Isles won series 2-1, with 1 draw

1977 *1* Wellington
New Zealand 2G 1T (16) to 4PG (12)

2 Christchurch
British Isles 3PG 1T (13) to 3PG (9)

3 Dunedin
New Zealand 1G 2PG 1DG 1T (19)
to 1PG 1T (7)

4 Auckland
New Zealand 2PG 1T (10) to 1G 1PG (9)
New Zealand won series 3-1

1983 *1* Christchurch
New Zealand 3PG 1DG 1T (16)
to 3PG 1DG (12)

2 Wellington
New Zealand 1G 1PG (9) to 0

3 Dunedin
New Zealand 1G 3PG (15) to 2T (8)

4 Auckland
New Zealand 4G 2PG 2T (38) to 2PG (6)
New Zealand won series 4-0

v AUSTRALIA

Played 7 British Isles won 6, Australia won 1, Drawn 0

1930 Sydney
Australia 2T (6) to 1G (5)

1950 *1* Brisbane
British Isles 2G 2PG 1DG (19)
to 2PG (6)

2 Sydney
British Isles 3G 1PG 2T (24) to 1T (3)
British Isles won series 2-0

1959 *1* Brisbane
British Isles 1G 2PG 1DG 1T (17)
to 2PG (6)

2 Sydney
British Isles 3G 1PG 2T (24) to 1PG (3)
British Isles won series 2-0

1966 *1* Sydney
British Isles 1G 1PG 1T (11)
to 1G 1PG (8)

2 Brisbane
British Isles 5G 1PG 1DG (31) to 0
British Isles won series 2-0

BRITISH ISLES RECORDS
(up to 30 April 1984)

From 1910 onwards – the tour to South Africa in that year was the first fully representative one in which the Four Home Unions cooperated.

TEAM RECORDS

Highest score
31 v Australia (31-0) 1966 Brisbane
v individual countries
28 v S Africa (28-9) 1974 Pretoria
17 v New Zealand (17-18) 1959 Dunedin
31 v Australia (31-0) 1966 Brisbane

Biggest winning points margin
31 v Australia (31-0) 1966 Brisbane
v individual countries
19 v S Africa (28-9) 1974 Pretoria
10 v New Zealand (13-3) 1971 Wellington
31 v Australia (31-0) 1966 Brisbane

Highest score by opposing team
38 New Zealand (6-38) 1983 Auckland
by individual countries
34 S Africa (14-34) 1962 Bloemfontein
38 New Zealand (6-38) 1983 Auckland
8 Australia (11-8) 1966 Sydney

Biggest losing points margin
32 v New Zealand (6-38) 1983 Auckland
v individual countries
20 v S Africa (14-34) 1962 Bloemfontein
32 v New Zealand (6-38) 1983 Auckland
1 v Australia (5-6) 1930 Sydney

Most tries by B Isles in an international
5 {
v Australia (24-3) 1950 Sydney
v S Africa (23-22) 1955 Johannesburg
v Australia (24-3) 1959 Sydney
v Australia (31-0) 1966 Brisbane
v S Africa (28-9) 1974 Pretoria
}

Most tries against B Isles in an international
7 by South Africa (9-25) 1955 Cape Town

Most points on overseas tour (all matches)
842 in Australia, New Zealand and Canada (33 matches) 1959
(includes 582 points in 25 matches in New Zealand)

Most tries on overseas tour (all matches)
165 in Australia, New Zealand and Canada (33 matches) 1959
(includes 113 tries in 25 matches in New Zealand)

INDIVIDUAL RECORDS

Most capped player
W J McBride 17 1962-74

Most internationals as captain – 6
A R Dawson 1959

Most points in internationals – 44
P Bennett (8 appearances) 1974-77

Most points in an international – 18
A J P Ward v S Africa 1980 Cape Town

Most tries in internationals – 6
A J F O'Reilly (10 appearances) 1955-59

Most tries in an international – 2
C D Aarvold v New Zealand 1930 Christchurch
J E Nelson v Australia 1950 Sydney
M J Price v Australia 1959 Sydney
M J Price v New Zealand 1959 Dunedin
D K Jones v Australia 1966 Brisbane
T G R Davies v New Zealand 1971 Christchurch

J J Williams v S Africa 1974 Pretoria
J J Williams v S Africa 1974 Port Elizabeth

Most conversions in an international – 5
S Wilson v Australia 1966 Brisbane

Most points for B Isles on overseas tour – 188
B John (17 appearances) 1971 Australia/ N Zealand
(includes 180 points in 16 appearances in N Zealand)

Most tries for B Isles on overseas tour – 22*
A J F O'Reilly (23 appearances) 1959 Australia/N Zealand/Canada
(includes 17* tries in 17 appearances in N Zealand)
**Includes one penalty try*

Most points for B Isles in international series – 35
T J Kiernan (4 appearances) 1968 S Africa

Most tries for B Isles in international series – 4
J J Williams (4 appearances) 1974 S Africa

Most points for B Isles in any match on tour – 37
A G B Old v South Western Districts 1974 Mossel Bay, SA

Most tries for B Isles in any match on tour – 6
D J Duckham v West Coast-Buller 1971 Greymouth NZ
J J Williams v South Western Districts 1974 Mossel Bay, SA
(A R Irvine scored 5 tries from full-back v King Country-Wanganui 1977 Taumarunui, NZ)

WORLD INTERNATIONAL RECORDS

From 1890-91, when uniform points-scoring was first adopted by International Board countries, to 30 April 1984. Both team and individual records are for matches between International Board countries, matches for and against British Isles, and for special centenary or other celebration matches for which caps were awarded.

TEAM RECORDS

Highest score – 49
Wales (49-14) v France 1910 Swansea

Biggest winning margin – 44
South Africa (44-0) v Scotland 1951 Murrayfield

Most tries in an international – 11
Wales (47-5) v France 1909 Paris (Colombes)

Most points on an overseas tour (all matches) – 868
New Zealand to B Isles/France (33 matches) 1905-06

Most tries on an overseas tour (all matches) – 215
New Zealand to B Isles/France (33 matches) 1905-06

Most points in an international series – 97
New Zealand v Australia (3 matches) 1972 in NZ

Most tries in an international series – 16
South Africa v B Isles (4 matches) 1955 in SA
New Zealand v Australia (3 matches) 1972 in NZ

Most points in Five Nations Championship in a season – 102
Wales 1975-76

Most tries in Five Nations Championship in a season – 21
Wales 1909-10

Biggest win on a major tour (all matches)
117-6 New Zealand v S Australia 1974 Adelaide

INDIVIDUAL RECORDS

(including appearances for British Isles, shown in brackets)

Most capped player
C M H Gibson (Ireland) 81 (12)*** 1964-79

in individual positions

Full-back
J P R Williams (Wales) 62 (8)* 1969-81

Wing
K J Jones (Wales) 47 (3)** 1947-57

Centre (includes 2nd five-eighth)
J M Renwick (Scotland) 50 (1)† 1972-83

Fly-half (includes 1st five-eighth)
J W Kyle (Ireland) 52 (6) 1947-58

Scrum-half
G O Edwards (Wales) 63 (10) 1967-78

Prop
G Price (Wales) 53 (12) 1975-83

Hooker
K W Kennedy (Ireland) 49 (4) 1965-75
J V Pullin (England) 49 (7) 1966-76

Lock
W J McBride (Ireland) 80 (17) 1962-75

Flanker
J F Slattery (Ireland) 65 (4) 1970-84

No 8
T M Davies (Wales) 46 (8)†† 1969-76

**Williams won 63 caps in all, but was chosen once for Wales as a flanker.*

***T G R Davies (Wales), 51 (5), won 39 caps as a wing and 12 as a centre, one of them for the Lions.*
****Gibson made 40 appearances for Ireland as a centre and 8 for the Lions, making 48 at centre in all. As a fly-half he made 25 appearances for Ireland and 4 for the Lions, making 29 in all. He also made four appearances for Ireland on the wing. His 69 caps for Ireland, out of 81 in all, are the record for an individual country.*
† Renwick has won 51 caps for Scotland and the Lions against IB countries, but played once as a replacement wing. R Bertranne (France) has made most appearances, 52, for an individual country as a threequarter. He played 39 times in the centre and 13 on the wing.
†† B Dauga (France), 50 caps, won 21 at No 8 and 29 at lock.

Most internationals as captain – 30
W J Whineray (NZ) 1958-65
J-P Rives (France) 1979-84
Rives has captained France in four other matches, against non-IB nations.

Most points in internationals – 289*
A R Irvine (Scotland) [59 (9) appearances] 1972-82
**made up of 261 points for Scotland and 28 for British Isles; includes one penalty try and excludes 12 points v Romania.*

Most points in an international – 26
A R Hewson (NZ) v Australia 1982 Auckland

Most tries in internationals – 24
I S Smith (Scotland) (32 appearances) 1924-33

Most tries in an international – 5
D Lambert (England) v France 1907 London (Richmond)

Most penalty goals in an international – 6
D B Clarke (NZ) v B Isles 1959 Dunedin
G R Bosch (SA) v France 1975 Pretoria
G Evans (Wales) v France 1982 Cardiff
S O Campbell (Ireland) v Scotland 1982 Dublin

Most conversions in an international – 8
J Bancroft (Wales) v France 1910 Swansea

Most dropped goals in an international – 3
P Albaladejo (France) v Ireland 1960 Paris (Colombes)
P F Hawthorne (Australia) v England 1967 Twickenham
H E Botha (SA) v Ireland 1981 Durban

Most points in Five Nations Championship in a season – 54
J-P Lescarboura (France) (4 appearances) 1983-84

Most tries in Five Nations Championship in a season – 8
C N Lowe (England) (4 appearances) 1913-14
I S Smith (Scotland) (4 appearances) 1924-25

Most penalty goals in Five Nations Championship in a season – 14
S O Campbell (Ireland) (4 appearances) 1982-83
W H Hare (England) (4 appearances) 1982-83

Most conversions in International Championship in a season – 11
J Bancroft (Wales) (4 appearances) 1908-09

Most dropped goals in International Championship in a season – 5
G Camberabéro (France) (3 appearances) 1966-67
J-P Lescarboura (France) dropped a goal in each championship match 1983-84, a feat never performed before.

Most points on an overseas tour – 230
W J Wallace (NZ) (25 appearances) in B Isles/France 1905-06

Most tries on an overseas tour – 42
J Hunter (NZ) (23 appearances) in B Isles/France 1905-06

Most points in any match on tour – 41
J F Karam (NZ) v South Australia 1974 Adelaide

Most tries in any match on tour – 8
T R Heeps (NZ) v Northern NSW 1962 Quirindi

INTERNATIONAL TOURS
(up to 30 April 1984)

**Indicates replacement during tour, throughout this section*

BRITISH ISLES TEAMS TO AUSTRALIA AND NEW ZEALAND

1888

Full record

in Australia	Played 16	Won 14	Lost 0	Drawn 2	Points for 210	Against 65
in New Zealand	Played 19	Won 13	Lost 2	Drawn 4	Points for 82	Against 33

Players

Full-backs: J T Haslam (Batley), A G Paul (Swinton)
Threequarters: H C Speakman (Runcorn), Dr H Brooks (Edinburgh U, Durham), J Anderton (Salford), A E Stoddart (Blackheath)
Half-backs: W Bumby (Swinton), J Nolan (Rochdale Hornets), W Burnett (Hawick)
Forwards: C Mathers (Bramley), S Williams (Salford), T Banks (Swinton), R L Seddon (Swinton), H Eagles (Swinton), A J Stuart (Dewsbury), W H Thomas (Cambridge U), T Kent (Salford), A P Penketh (Douglas, IOM), R Burnett (Hawick), A J Laing (Hawick), Dr J Smith (Edinburgh U), J P Clowes (Halifax)
Captains †R L Seddon, A E Stoddart **Managers** A Shaw, A Shrewsbury

†*Stoddart took over as captain after Seddon had been drowned in Australia*

1899 (Australia only)

Full record	Played 21	Won 18	Lost 3	Drawn 0	Points for 333	Against 90
International record	Played 4	Won 3	Lost 1			
International details	Jun 24	Australia 13	British Isles 3	(Sydney)		
	Jul 22	Australia 0	British Isles 11	(Brisbane)		
	Aug 5	Australia 10	British Isles 11	(Sydney)		
	Aug 12	Australia 0	British Isles 13	(Sydney)		

Players

Full-backs: E Martelli (Dublin U), C E K Thompson (Lancashire)
Threequarters: A B Timms (Edinburgh U), E T Nicholson (Birkenhead Park), A M Bucher (Edinburgh Acads), E G Nicholls (Cardiff), G P Doran (Lansdowne)
Half-backs: Rev M Mullineux (Blackheath), G Cookson (Manchester), C Y Adamson (Durham)
Forwards: F M Stout (Gloucester), J W Jarman (Bristol), H G S Gray (Scottish Trials), G R Gibson (Northern), W Judkins (Coventry), F C Belson (Bath), J S Francomb (Manchester), B I Swannell (Northampton), G V Evers (Moseley), T M W McGown (N of Ireland), A Ayre-Smith (Guy's Hospital)
Captain and Manager Rev M Mullineux

1904

Full record

in Australia	Played 14	Won 14	Lost 0	Drawn 0	Points for 265	Against 51
in New Zealand	Played 5	Won 2	Lost 2	Drawn 1	Points for 22	Against 33

International record

v Australia	Played 3	Won 3
v New Zealand	Played 1	Lost 1

International details

v Australia	Jul 2	Australia 0	British Isles 17	(Sydney)
	Jul 23	Australia 3	British Isles 17	(Brisbane)
	Jul 30	Australia 0	British Isles 16	(Sydney)
v New Zealand	Aug 13	New Zealand 9	British Isles 3	(Wellington)

Players

Full-back: C F Stanger-Leathes (Northern)
Threequarters: J L Fisher (Hull and E Riding), R T Gabe (Cardiff), W F Jowett (Swansea), W Llewellyn (Llwynypia and Newport), E Morgan (London Welsh and Guy's Hospital), P F McEvedy (Guy's Hospital), A B O'Brien (Guy's Hospital)
Half-backs: P F Bush (Cardiff), F C Hulme (Birkenhead Park), T H Vile (Newport)
Forwards: D R Bedell-Sivright (Cambridge U), T S Bevan (Swansea), S N Crowther (Lennox), J T Sharland (Streatham), D D Dobson (Oxford U), C D Patterson (Malone), R W Edwards (Malone), A F Harding (Cardiff, London Welsh), B S Massey (Hull and E Riding), R J Rogers (Bath), F McK Saunders (Guy's Hospital), D H Traill (Guy's Hospital), B I Swannell (Northampton)
Captain D R Bedell-Sivright **Manager** A B O'Brien

1908 (Anglo-Welsh)

Full record

in Australia	Played 9	Won 7	Lost 2	Drawn 0	Points for 139	Against 48
in New Zealand	Played 17	Won 9	Lost 7	Drawn 1	Points for 184	Against 153

International record

v New Zealand Played 3 Lost 2 Drawn 1

International details

Jun 6	New Zealand 32	British Isles 5	(Dunedin)
Jun 27	New Zealand 3	British Isles 3	(Wellington)
Jul 25	New Zealand 29	British Isles 0	(Auckland)

Players

Full-backs: J C M Dyke (Cardiff), E J Jackett (Falmouth, Leicester)
Threequarters: F E Chapman (Westoe, West Hartlepool), R A Gibbs (Cardiff), J L Williams (Cardiff), R B Griffiths (Newport), J P 'Ponty' Jones (Pontypool, London Welsh), J P 'Tuan' Jones (Guy's Hospital), Dr P F McEvedy (Guy's Hospital), H H Vassall (Oxford U, Blackheath)
Half-backs: J Davey (Redruth), H Laxon (Cambridge U), W L Morgan (Cardiff), G L Williams (Liverpool)
Forwards: H Archer (Guy's Hospital), R Dibble (Bridgwater and Albion), P J Down (Bristol), G V Kyrke (Marlborough Nomads), R K Green (Neath), E Morgan (Swansea), L S Thomas (Penarth), A F Harding (Cardiff, London Welsh), J F Williams (London Welsh), G R Hind (Guy's Hospital), F S Jackson (Leicester), W L Oldham (Coventry), J A S Ritson (Northern), T W Smith (Leicester)
Captain A F Harding **Manager** G H Harnett

1930

Full record

in New Zealand	Played 21	Won 15	Lost 6	Drawn 0	Points for 420	Against 205
in Australia	Played 7	Won 5	Lost 2	Drawn 0	Points for 204	Against 113

International record

v New Zealand	Played 4	Won 1	Lost 3
v Australia	Played 1	Lost 1	

International details

v New Zealand	Jun 21	New Zealand 3	British Isles 6	(Dunedin)
	Jul 5	New Zealand 13	British Isles 10	(Christchurch)
	Jul 26	New Zealand 15	British Isles 10	(Auckland)

	Aug 9	New Zealand 22	British Isles 8	(Wellington)
v Australia	Aug 30	Australia 6	British Isles 5	(Sydney)

Players
Full-backs: J Bassett (Penarth), W G McG Bonner (Bradford)
Threequarters: C D Aarvold (Cambridge U and Blackheath), J S R Reeve (Harlequins), J C Morley (Newport), A L Novis (Blackheath and Army), R Jennings (Redruth), H M Bowcott (Cambridge U and Cardiff), T E Jones-Davies (London Welsh), P F Murray (Wanderers)
Half-backs: R S Spong (Old Millhillians), W H Sobey (Old Millhillians), T C Knowles (Birkenhead Park), H Poole (Cardiff)
Forwards: F D Prentice (Leicester), H Rew (Blackheath and Army), D Parker (Swansea), W B Welsh (Hawick), B H Black (Oxford U and Blackheath), M J Dunne (Lansdowne), G R Beamish (Leicester and RAF), J L Farrell (Bective Rangers), J McD Hodgson (Northern), H O'H O'Neill (Queen's U, Belfast), Ivor Jones (Llanelli), H Wilkinson (Halifax), S A Martindale (Kendal), D A Kendrew (Woodford, Leicester and Army), H C S Jones (Manchester)
Captain F D Prentice **Manager** J Baxter

1950

Full record

in New Zealand	Played 23	Won 17	Lost 5	Drawn 1	Points for 420	Against 162
in Australia	Played 6	Won 5	Lost 1	Drawn 0	Points for 150	Against 52

International record

v New Zealand	Played 4	Lost 3	Drawn 1
v Australia	Played 2	Won 2	

International details

v New Zealand	May 27	New Zealand 9	British Isles 9	(Dunedin)
	Jun 10	New Zealand 8	British Isles 0	(Christchurch)
	Jul 1	New Zealand 6	British Isles 3	(Wellington)
	Jul 29	New Zealand 11	British Isles 8	(Auckland)
v Australia	Aug 19	Australia 6	British Isles 19	(Brisbane)
	Aug 26	Australia 3	British Isles 24	(Sydney)

Players
Full-backs: G W Norton (Bective Rangers), W B Cleaver (Cardiff), B Lewis Jones* (Devonport Services and Llanelli)
Threequarters: D W C Smith (London Scottish), M F Lane (U C Cork), K J Jones (Newport), M C Thomas (Devonport Services and Newport), B L Williams (Cardiff), J Matthews (Cardiff), N J Henderson (Queen's U, Belfast), R Macdonald (Edinburgh U)
Half-backs: J W Kyle (Queen's U, Belfast), I Preece (Coventry), W R Willis (Cardiff), G Rimmer (Waterloo), A W Black (Edinburgh U)
Forwards: V G Roberts (Penryn), J S McCarthy (Dolphin), R T Evans (Newport), J W McKay (Queen's U, Belfast), J R G Stephens (Neath), E R John (Neath), P W Kininmonth (Oxford U and Richmond), J E Nelson (Malone), D J Hayward (Newbridge), J D Robins (Birkenhead Park), T Clifford (Young Munster), C Davies (Cardiff), G M Budge (Edinburgh Wanderers), D M Davies (Somerset Police), Dr K D Mullen (Old Belvedere)
Captain Dr K D Mullen **Manager** Surgeon-Captain (D) L B Osborne (RN)
Assistant Manager E L Savage

1959

Full record

in Australia	Played 6	Won 5	Lost 1	Drawn 0	Points for 174	Against 70
in New Zealand	Played 25	Won 20	Lost 5	Drawn 0	Points for 582	Against 266

International record

v Australia	Played 2	Won 2	
v New Zealand	Played 4	Won 1	Lost 3

International details

v Australia	Jun 6	Australia 6	British Isles 17	(Brisbane)
	Jun 13	Australia 3	British Isles 24	(Sydney)
v New Zealand	Jul 18	New Zealand 18	British Isles 17	(Dunedin)
	Aug 15	New Zealand 11	British Isles 8	(Wellington)
	Aug 29	New Zealand 22	British Isles 8	(Christchurch)
	Sep 19	New Zealand 6	British Isles 9	(Auckland)

Players

Full-backs: T J Davies (Llanelli), K J F Scotland (Cambridge U)
Threequarters: J R C Young (Oxford U), P B Jackson (Coventry), A J F O'Reilly (Old Belvedere), N H Brophy (UC Dublin), M J Price (Pontypool), W M Patterson* (Sale), D Hewitt (Queen's U, Belfast), J Butterfield (Northampton), M C Thomas (Newport), G H Waddell (Cambridge U)
Half-backs: J P Horrocks-Taylor* (Leicester), A B W Risman (Manchester U), M A F English (Limerick Bohemians), R E G Jeeps (Northampton), S Coughtrie (Edinburgh Acads), A A Mulligan* (Wanderers, London Irish)
Forwards: B V Meredith (Newport), R Prosser (Pontypool), A R Dawson (Wanderers), H F McLeod (Hawick), G K Smith (Kelso), S Millar (Ballymena), B G M Wood (Garryowen), R H Williams (Llanelli), W A Mulcahy (UC Dublin), W R Evans (Cardiff), R W D Marques (Harlequins), A Ashcroft (Waterloo), N A A Murphy (Cork Constitution), H J Morgan (Abertillery), J Faull (Swansea)
Captain A R Dawson **Manager** A Wilson **Assistant Manager** O B Glasgow

1966

Full record

in Australia	Played 8	Won 7	Lost 0	Drawn 1	Points for 202	Against 48
in New Zealand	Played 25	Won 15	Lost 8	Drawn 2	Points for 300	Against 281

International record

v Australia	Played 2	Won 2
v New Zealand	Played 4	Lost 4

International details

v Australia	May 28	Australia 8	British Isles 11	(Sydney)
	Jun 4	Australia 0	British Isles 31	(Brisbane)
v New Zealand	Jul 16	New Zealand 20	British Isles 3	(Dunedin)
	Aug 6	New Zealand 16	British Isles 12	(Wellington)
	Aug 27	New Zealand 19	British Isles 6	(Christchurch)
	Sep 10	New Zealand 24	British Isles 11	(Auckland)

Players

Full-backs: D Rutherford (Gloucester), S Wilson (London Scottish), T G Price* (Llanelli)
Threequarters: D I E Bebb (Swansea), A J W Hinshelwood (London Scottish), K F Savage (Northampton), S J Watkins (Newport), D K Jones (Cardiff), F P K Bresnihan* (UC Dublin), M P Weston (Durham City), C W McFadyean (Moseley), J C Walsh (Sunday's Well)
Half-backs: C M H Gibson (Cambridge U), D Watkins (Newport), A R Lewis (Abertillery), R M Young (Queen's U, Belfast)
Forwards: R A Lamont (Instonians), A E I Pask (Abertillery), N A A Murphy (Cork Constitution), D Grant (Hawick), G J Prothero (Bridgend), J W Telfer (Melrose), W J McBride (Ballymena), M J Campbell-Lamerton (London Scottish), W D Thomas (Llanelli), B Price (Newport), R J McLoughlin (Gosforth), D L Powell (Northampton), C H Norris (Cardiff), D Williams (Ebbw Vale), K W Kennedy (CIYMS), F A L Laidlaw (Melrose)

Captain M J Campbell-Lamerton **Manager** D J O'Brien
Assistant Manager J D Robins

1971

Full record

in Australia	Played 2	Won 1	Lost 1	Drawn 0	Points for 25	Against 27
in New Zealand	Played 24	Won 22	Lost 1	Drawn 1	Points for 555	Against 204

International record

v New Zealand Played 4 Won 2 Lost 1 Drawn 1

International details

v New Zealand	Jun 26	New Zealand 3	British Isles 9	(Dunedin)
	Jul 10	New Zealand 22	British Isles 12	(Christchurch)
	Jul 31	New Zealand 3	British Isles 13	(Wellington)
	Aug 14	New Zealand 14	British Isles 14	(Auckland)

Players

Full-backs: R Hiller (Harlequins), J P R Williams (London Welsh)
Threequarters: D J Duckham (Coventry), A G Biggar (London Scottish), T G R Davies (London Welsh), J C Bevan (Cardiff Coll of Education), A J Lewis (Ebbw Vale), J S Spencer (Headingley), S J Dawes (London Welsh), C W W Rea (Headingley)
Half-backs: C M H Gibson (North of Ireland), B John (Cardiff), G O Edwards (Cardiff), R Hopkins (Maesteg)
Forwards: T M Davies (London Welsh), P J Dixon (Harlequins), J Taylor (London Welsh, J F Slattery (U C Dublin), M L Hipwell (Terenure Coll), D L Quinnell (Llanelli), R J Arneil* (Leicester), W D Thomas (Llanelli), W J McBride (Ballymena), M G Roberts (London Welsh), G L Brown (West of Scotland), T G Evans* (London Welsh), A B Carmichael (West of Scotland), R J McLoughlin (Blackrock Coll), J McLauchlan (Jordanhill Coll), J F Lynch (St Mary's Coll), C B Stevens* (Harlequins and Penzance-Newlyn), J V Pullin (Bristol), F A L Laidlaw (Melrose)
Captain S J Dawes **Manager** Dr D W C Smith **Assistant Manager** C R James

1977 (New Zealand and Fiji only)

Full record	Played 26	Won 21	Lost 5	Drawn 0	Points for 607	Against 320
in New Zealand	Played 25	Won 21	Lost 4	Drawn 0	Points for 586	Against 295
in Fiji	Played 1	Lost 1	Points for 21	Against 25		

International record

v New Zealand Played 4 Won 1 Lost 3

International details

v New Zealand	Jun 18	New Zealand 16	British Isles 12	(Wellington)
	Jul 9	New Zealand 9	British Isles 13	(Christchurch)
	Jul 30	New Zealand 19	British Isles 7	(Dunedin)
	Aug 13	New Zealand 10	British Isles 9	(Auckland)

Players

Full-backs: A R Irvine (Heriot's FP), B H Hay (Boroughmuir)
Threequarters: P J Squires (Harrogate), H E Rees (Neath), J J Williams (Llanelli), G L Evans (Newport), C M H Gibson (North of Ireland FC), S P Fenwick (Bridgend), D H Burcher (Newport), I R McGeechan (Headingley)
Half-backs: P Bennett (Llanelli), J D Bevan (Aberavon), D W Morgan (Stewart's Melville FP), D B Williams (Cardiff), A D Lewis* (Cambridge U & London Welsh)
Forwards: W P Duggan (Blackrock Coll), J Squire (Newport), T J Cobner (Pontypool), T P Evans (Swansea), A Neary (Broughton Park), D L Quinnell (Llanelli), G L Brown (West of Scotland), N E Horton (Moseley), A J Martin (Aberavon), M I Keane (Lansdowne), W B Beaumont* (Fylde), F E Cotton (Sale), P A Orr (Old Wesley), G Price (Pontypool), C Williams (Aberavon), A G Faulkner* (Pontypool), R W Windsor (Pontypool), P J Wheeler (Leicester)
Captain P Bennett **Manager** G Burrell **Assistant Manager** S J Dawes

1983 (New Zealand only)

Full record Played 18 Won 12 Lost 6 Drawn 0 Points for 478 Against 276

International record	Played 4 Lost 4			
International details	Jun 4	New Zealand 16	British Isles 12	(Christchurch)
	Jun 18	New Zealand 9	British Isles 0	(Wellington)
	Jul 2	New Zealand 15	British Isles 8	(Dunedin)
	Jul 16	New Zealand 38	British Isles 6	(Auckland)

Players

Full-backs: H P MacNeill (Oxford U), W H Hare (Leicester), G Evans (Maesteg)
Threequarters: J Carleton (Orrell), G R T Baird (Kelso), T M Ringland (Ballymena), D G Irwin (Instonians), M J Kiernan (Dolphin), R A Ackerman (London Welsh), C R Woodward (Leicester)
Half-backs: S O Campbell (Old Belvedere), J Y Rutherford (Selkirk), T D Holmes (Cardiff), R J Laidlaw (Jedforest), N D Melville* (Wasps), S J Smith* (Sale)
Forwards: S T Jones (Pontypool), I Stephens (Bridgend), G A J McLoughlin* (Shannon), G Price (Pontypool), I G Milne (Heriot's FP), C T Deans (Hawick), C F Fitzgerald (St Mary's Coll), S B Boyle (Gloucester), R L Norster (Cardiff), M J Colclough (Angoulême), D G Lenihan* (Cork Const), S J Bainbridge (Gosforth), J H Calder (Stewart's-Melville FP), J B O'Driscoll (London Irish), P J Winterbottom (Headingley), J Squire (Pontypool), N C Jeavons* (Moseley), J R Beattie (Glasgow Acads), I A M Paxton (Selkirk), E T Butler* (Pontypool)

Captain C F Fitzgerald **Manager** W J McBride **Assistant Manager** J W Telfer

BRITISH ISLES TEAMS TO SOUTH AFRICA

1891

Full record Played 19 Won 19 Lost 0 Drawn 0 Points for 224 Against 1

International record	Played 3 Won 3			
International details	Jul 30	South Africa 0	British Isles 4	(Port Elizabeth)
	Aug 29	South Africa 0	British Isles 3	(Kimberley)
	Sep 5	South Africa 0	British Isles 4	(Cape Town)

Players

Full-backs: W G Mitchell (Cambridge U and Richmond), E Bromet (Cambridge U)
Threequarters: P R Clauss (Oxford U), R L Aston (Cambridge U), W E Maclagan (London Scottish)
Half-backs: H Marshall (Blackheath), B G Roscoe (Lancashire), A Rotherham (Cambridge U), W Wotherspoon (Cambridge U)
Forwards: W E Bromet (Oxford U), J H Gould (Old Leysians), J Hammond (Cambridge U), P F Hancock (Somerset), W J Jackson (Gloucester), R G MacMillan (London Scottish), E Mayfield (Cambridge U), C P Simpson (Cambridge U), A A Surtees (Cambridge U), R Thompson (Cambridge U), W H Thorman (Cambridge U), T Whittaker (Lancashire)

Captain W E Maclagan **Manager** E H Ash

1896

Full record Played 21 Won 19 Lost 1 Drawn 1 Points for 310 Against 45

International record	Played 4 Won 3 Lost 1			
International details	Jul 30	South Africa 0	British Isles 8	(Port Elizabeth)
	Aug 22	South Africa 8	British Isles 17	(Johannesburg)
	Aug 29	South Africa 3	British Isles 9	(Kimberley)
	Sep 5	South Africa 5	British Isles 0	(Cape Town)

Players
Full-back: J F Byrne (Moseley)
Threequarters: C A Boyd (Dublin U), J T Magee (Bective Rangers), L Q Bulger (Dublin U and Lansdowne), C O Robinson (Northumberland), O G Mackie (Cambridge U and Wakefield Trinity)
Half-backs: Rev M Mullineux (Blackheath), S P Bell (Cambridge U), L M Magee (Bective Rangers and London Irish)
Forwards: J Hammond (Blackheath and Cambridge U), T J Crean (Dublin Wands), A W D Meares (Dublin U), R Johnston (Dublin Wands), A D Clinch (Dublin U), J Sealy (Dublin U), W J Carey (Oxford U), P F Hancock (Blackheath and Somerset), W Mortimer (Marlborough Nomads), A F Todd (Blackheath), R C Mullins (Oxford U), G W Lee* (Rockcliff)
Captain J Hammond **Manager** R Walker

1903

Full record	Played 22 Won 11 Lost 8 Drawn 3 Points for 231 Against 138			
International record	Played 3 Lost 1 Drawn 2			
International details	Aug 26	South Africa 10	British Isles 10	(Johannesburg)
	Sep 5	South Africa 0	British Isles 0	(Kimberley)
	Sep 12	South Africa 8	British Isles 0	(Cape Town)

Players
Full-backs: E M Harrison (Guy's Hospital)
Threequarters: A E Hind (Cambridge U), I G Davidson (North of Ireland), G F Collett (Gloucestershire), R T Skrimshire (Newport and Blackheath), E F Walker (Lennox)
Half-backs: L L Greig (United Services), J I Gillespie (Edinburgh Acads), R M Neill (Edinburgh Acads), P S Hancock (Richmond)
Forwards: M C Morrison (Royal HSFP), W P Scott (West of Scotland), D R Bedell-Sivright (Cambridge U), W T C Cave (Cambridge U), J C Hosack (Edinburgh Wands), A Tedford (Malone), R S Smyth (Dublin U), Joseph Wallace (Dublin Wands), James Wallace (Dublin Wands), F M Stout (Richmond), T A Gibson (Cambridge U)
Captain M C Morrison **Manager** J Hammond

1910

Full record	Played 24 Won 13 Lost 8 Drawn 3 Points for 290 Against 236			
International record	Played 3 Won 1 Lost 2			
International details	Aug 6	South Africa 14	British Isles 10	(Kimberley)
	Aug 27	South Africa 3	British Isles 8	(Port Elizabeth)
	Sep 3	South Africa 21	British Isles 5	(Cape Town)

Players
Full-backs: S H Williams (Newport)
Threequarters: A Melville Baker (Newport), R C S Plummer (Newport), M E Neale (Bristol), A R Foster (Derry), C G Timms (Edinburgh U), J P Jones (Pontypool and Newport), J A Spoors (Bristol), K B Wood (Leicester)
Half-backs: N F Humphreys (Tynedale), A N McClinton (North of Ireland), G A M Isherwood (Cheshire, Sale and Old Alleynians), E Milroy* (Watsonians)
Forwards: Dr T Smyth (Newport), W Tyrrell (Queen's U, Belfast), D F Smith (Richmond), P D Waller (Newport), J Reid-Kerr (Greenock Wands), R Stevenson (St Andrew's U), L M Speirs (Watsonians), E O'D Crean (Liverpool), H Jarman (Newport), O J S Piper (Cork Constitution), Dr W A Roberston (Edinburgh U and Hartlepool Rovers), C H Pillman (Blackheath), W J Ashby (Queen's Coll, Cork), F G Handford* (Kersal), T J Richards* (Bristol), J Webb* (Abertillery)
Captain Dr T Smyth **Managers** W Cail and Walter E Rees

1924

Full record Played 21 Won 9 Lost 9 Drawn 3 Points for 175 Against 155
International record Played 4 Lost 3 Drawn 1

International details				
	Aug 16	South Africa 7	British Isles 3	(Durban)
	Aug 23	South Africa 17	British Isles 0	(Johannesburg)
	Sep 13	South Africa 3	British Isles 3	(Port Elizabeth)
	Sep 20	South Africa 16	British Isles 9	(Cape Town)

Players
Full-backs: D Drysdale (Heriot's FP), W F Gaisford (St Bart's Hospital), T E Holliday (Aspatria)
Threequarters: R Harding (Swansea), I S Smith (Oxford U), S W Harris (Blackheath), W Wallace (Percy Park), R M Kinnear (Heriot's FP), J H Bordass (Cambridge U), R B Maxwell (Birkenhead Park)
Half-backs: H J Davies* (Newport), V M Griffiths (Newport), H Waddell (Glasgow Acads), W A Cunningham* (Lansdowne), A T Young (Blackheath), H Whitley (Northern)
Forwards: Dr R Cove-Smith (Old Merchant Taylors), A F Blakiston (Blackheath), A T Voyce (Gloucester), N C Macpherson (Newport), R G Henderson (Northern), K G P Hendrie (Heriot's FP), D S Davies (Hawick), R A Howie (Kirkcaldy), A Ross (Kilmarnock), J D Clinch (Dublin U), Dr W J Roche (UC Cork, Newport), J McVicker (Belfast Collegians), D Marsden-Jones (Cardiff and London Welsh), M J Bradley (Dolphin), T N Brand (North of Ireland)
Captain Dr R Cove-Smith **Manager** H Packer

1938

Full record Played 23 Won 17 Lost 6 Drawn 0 Points for 407 Against 272
International record Played 3 Won 1 Lost 2

International details				
	Aug 6	South Africa 26	British Isles 12	(Johannesburg)
	Sep 3	South Africa 19	British Isles 3	(Port Elizabeth)
	Sep 10	South Africa 16	British Isles 21	(Cape Town)

Players
Full-backs: V G J Jenkins (London Welsh), C F Grieve (Oxford U)
Threequarters: E J Unwin (Rosslyn Park), W H Clement (Llanelli), E L Jones (Llanelli), C V Boyle (Dublin U), R Leyland (Waterloo), D J Macrae (St Andrews U), H R McKibbin (Queen's U, Belfast), B E Nicholson (Old Whitgiftians and Harlequins)
Half-backs: F J Reynolds (Old Cranleighans), G E Cromey (Queen's U, Belfast), J L Giles (Coventry), H Tanner (Swansea), G J Moran (Clontarf)
Forwards: S Walker (Belfast Instonians), M E Morgan (Swansea), W G Howard (Old Birkonians), W H Travers (Newport), C R A Graves (Dublin Wands), R B Mayne (Queen's U), G T Dancer (Bedford), S R Couchman (Old Cranleighans), A G Purchas (Coventry), J A Waters (Selkirk), P L Duff (Glasgow Acads), I Williams (Cardiff), A R Taylor (Cross Keys), R Alexander (North of Ireland)
Captain S Walker **Manager** Col B C Hartley **Assistant Manager** H A Haigh-Smith

1955

Full record Played 24 Won 18 Lost 5 Drawn 1 Points for 418 Against 271
International record Played 4 Won 2 Lost 2

International details				
	Aug 6	South Africa 22	British Isles 23	(Johannesburg)
	Aug 20	South Africa 25	British Isles 9	(Cape Town)
	Sep 3	South Africa 6	British Isles 9	(Pretoria)
	Sep 24	South Africa 22	British Isles 8	(Port Elizabeth)

Players
Full-backs: A Cameron (Glasgow HSFP), A G Thomas (Llanelli)
Threequarters: A R Smith (Cambridge U), F D Sykes (Northampton), H Morris (Cardiff), A C Pedlow (Queen's U, Belfast), J Butterfield (Northampton), W P C Davies (Harlequins), A J F O'Reilly (Old Belvedere), J P Quinn (New Brighton), G Griffiths* (Cardiff)
Half-backs: C I Morgan (Cardiff), D G S Baker (Old Merchant Taylors), J E Williams (Old Millhillians), R E G Jeeps (Northampton), T Lloyd (Maesteg)
Forwards: R H Thompson (Instonians), C C Meredith (Neath), B V Meredith (Newport), H F McLeod (Hawick), W O Williams (Swansea), R Roe (Lansdowne), T Elliot (Gala), E J S Michie (Aberdeen U), T E Reid (Garryowen), R H Williams (Llanelli), J T Greenwood (Dunfermline), R J Robins (Pontypridd), R Higgins (Liverpool), D S Wilson (Metropolitan Police), R C C Thomas (Swansea)
Captain R H Thompson **Manager** J A E Siggins **Assistant Manager** D E Davies

1962

Full record Played 24 Won 15 Lost 5 Drawn 4 Points for 351 Against 208
International record Played 4 Won 0 Lost 3 Drawn 1

International details				
Jun 23	South Africa 3	British Isles 3	(Johannesburg)
Jul 21	South Africa 3	British Isles 0	(Durban)
Aug 4	South Africa 8	British Isles 3	(Cape Town)
Aug 25	South Africa 34	British Isles 14	(Bloemfontein)

Players
Full-backs: T J Kiernan (UC Cork), J G Willcox (Oxford U)
Threequarters: N H Brophy (Blackrock), D I E Bebb (Swansea), R C Cowan (Selkirk), A R Smith (Edinburgh Wands), J M Dee (Hartlepool Rovers), W R Hunter (CIYMS), M P Weston (Durham City), D K Jones (Llanelli), D Hewitt (Queen's U, Belfast)
Half-backs: R A W Sharp (Oxford U), R E G Jeeps (Northampton), G H Waddell (London Scottish), A O'Connor (Aberavon), H J C Brown* (RAF, Blackheath)
Forwards: S Millar (Ballymena), K D Jones (Cardiff), D M D Rollo (Howe of Fife), T P Wright (Blackheath), B V Meredith (Newport), A E I Pask (Abertillery), S A M Hodgson (Durham City), M J Campbell-Lamerton (Army, Halifax), W J McBride (Ballymena), W A Mulcahy (Bohemians), K A Rowlands (Cardiff), H J Morgan (Abertillery), D P Rogers (Bedford), J Douglas (Stewart's Coll FP), D Nash (Ebbw Vale), H O Godwin* (Coventry), G D Davidge* (Newport)
Captain A R Smith **Manager** Instructor-Commander D B Vaughan RN
Assistant Manager H R McKibbin

1968

Full record Played 20 Won 15 Lost 4 Drawn 1 Points for 377 Against 181
International record Played 4 Lost 3 Drawn 1

International details			
Jun 8	South Africa 25	British Isles 20	(Pretoria)
Jun 22	South Africa 6	British Isles 6	(Port Elizabeth)
Jul 13	South Africa 11	British Isles 6	(Cape Town)
Jul 27	South Africa 19	British Isles 6	(Johannesburg)

Players
Full-backs: T J Kiernan (Cork Constitution), R Hiller (Harlequins)
Threequarters: A J W Hinshelwood (London Scottish), W K Jones (Cardiff), M C R Richards (Cardiff), K F Savage (Northampton), F P K Bresnihan (UC Dublin), T G R Davies (Cardiff), K S Jarrett (Newport), W H Raybould (London Welsh), J W C Turner (Gala)
Half-backs: C M H Gibson (North of Ireland), B John (Cardiff), G O Edwards (Cardiff), R M Young (Queen's U, Belfast), G C Connell* (London Scottish)

Forwards: A L Horton (Blackheath), M J Coulman (Moseley), S Millar (Ballymena), J P O'Shea (Cardiff), P J Larter (Northampton), W J McBride (Ballymena), P K Stagg (Sale), W D Thomas (Llanelli), J V Pullin (Bristol), J Young (Harrogate), M G Doyle (Blackrock Coll), J Taylor (London Welsh), K G Goodall* (City of Derry), R J Arneil (Edinburgh Acads), R B Taylor (Northampton), J W Telfer (Melrose), B R West* (Northampton)
Captain T J Kiernan **Manager** D K Brooks **Assistant Manager** A R Dawson

1974

Full record Played 22 Won 21 Lost 0 Drawn 1 Points for 729 Against 207
International record Played 4 Won 3 Drawn 1

International details	Jun 8	South Africa 3	British Isles 12	(Cape Town)
	Jun 22	South Africa 9	British Isles 28	(Pretoria)
	Jul 13	South Africa 9	British Isles 26	(Port Elizabeth)
	Jul 27	South Africa 13	British Isles 13	(Johannesburg)

Players
Full-backs: A R Irvine (Heriot's FP), J P R Williams (London Welsh)
Threequarters: T O Grace (St Mary's Coll, Dublin), C F W Rees (London Welsh), W C C Steele (Bedford and RAF), J J Williams (Llanelli), A J Morley* (Bristol), R T E Bergiers (Llanelli), G W Evans (Coventry), I R McGeechan (Headingley), R A Milliken (Bangor, N Ireland)
Half-backs: P Bennett (Llanelli), A G B Old (Leicester), C M H Gibson* (North of Ireland FC), G O Edwards (Cardiff), J J Moloney (St Mary's Coll, Dublin)
Forwards: T M Davies (Swansea), A G Ripley (Rosslyn Park), T P David (Llanelli), S A McKinney (Dungannon), A Neary (Broughton Park), J F Slattery (Blackrock Coll), G L Brown (West of Scotland), W J McBride (Ballymena), C W Ralston (Richmond), R M Uttley (Gosforth), M A Burton (Gloucester), A B Carmichael (West of Scotland), F E Cotton (Coventry), J McLauchlan (Jordanhill), K W Kennedy (London Irish), R W Windsor (Pontypool)
Captain W J McBride **Manager** A G Thomas **Assistant Manager** S Millar

1980

Full record Played 18 Won 15 Lost 3 Drawn 0 Points for 401 Against 244
International record Played 4 Won 1 Lost 3

International details	May 31	South Africa 26	British Isles 22	(Cape Town)
	Jun 14	South Africa 26	British Isles 19	(Bloemfontein)
	Jun 28	South Africa 12	British Isles 10	(Port Elizabeth)
	Jul 12	South Africa 13	British Isles 17	(Pretoria)

Players
Full-backs: B H Hay (Boroughmuir), R C O'Donnell (St Mary's Coll, Dublin), A R Irvine* (Heriot's FP)
Threequarters: J Carleton (Orrell), H E Rees (Neath), M A C Slemen (Liverpool), P Morgan (Llanelli), R W R Gravell (Llanelli), J M Renwick (Hawick), D S Richards (Swansea), C R Woodward (Leicester), P W Dodge* (Leicester)
Half-backs: S O Campbell (Old Belvedere), W G Davies (Cardiff), A J P Ward* (Garryowen), T D Holmes (Cardiff), C S Patterson (Instonians), J C Robbie* (Greystones), S J Smith* (Sale)
Forwards: J R Beattie (Glasgow Acads), D L Quinnell (Llanelli), S M Lane (Cardiff), J B O'Driscoll (London Irish), J Squire (Pontypool), C C Tucker (Shannon), G P Williams* (Bridgend), W B Beaumont (Fylde), M J Colclough (Angoulême), A J Martin (Aberavon), A J Tomes (Hawick), P J Blakeway (Gloucester),

G Price (Pontypool), F E Cotton (Sale), C Williams (Swansea), I Stephens* (Bridgend), P A Orr* (Old Wesley), A J Phillips (Cardiff), P J Wheeler (Leicester)
Captain W B Beaumont **Manager** S Millar **Assistant Manager** N A A Murphy

NEW ZEALAND TO BRITISH ISLES AND FRANCE

1888-89 (The Maoris)

Full record	Played 74	Won 49	Lost 20	Drawn 5	Points for 394	Against 188
International record	Played 3	Won 1	Lost 2			
International details	Dec 1	Ireland 4	Maoris 13	(Dublin)		
	Dec 22	Wales 5	Maoris 0	(Swansea)		
	Feb 16	England 7	Maoris 0	(Blackheath)		

Players
Backs: W Elliot (Grafton), D R Gage (Poneke), C Goldsmith (Te Aute Coll), E Ihimaira (Te Aute Coll), P Keogh (Kaikorai), H H Lee (Riverton), C Madigan (Grafton), E McCausland (Gordon), F Warbrick (Tauranga), J A Warbrick (Hawke's Bay), W Warbrick (Matata), H J Wynyard (North Shore), W T Wynyard (North Shore)
Forwards: W Anderson (Hokianga), T R Ellison (Poneke), Wi Karauria (Nelson), R Maynard (North Shore), Wiri Nehua (Te Aute Coll), T Rene (Nelson), D Stewart (Thames), R G Taiaroa (Dunedin), Alfred Warbrick (Matata), Arthur Warbrick (Matata), A Webster (Hokianga), G A Williams (Poneke), G Wynyard (North Shore)
Captain J A Warbrick **Managers** J R Scott and T Eyton

1905-06

Full record	Played 33	Won 32	Lost 1	Drawn 0	Points for 868	Against 47
in B Isles	Played 32	Won 31	Lost 1	Drawn 0	Points for 830	Against 39
in France	Played 1	Won 1	Lost 0	Drawn 0	Points for 38	Against 8
International record	Played 5	Won 4	Lost 1			
International details	Nov 18	Scotland 7	New Zealand 12	(Inverleith)		
	Nov 25	Ireland 0	New Zealand 15	(Dublin)		
	Dec 2	England 0	New Zealand 15	(Crystal Palace)		
	Dec 16	Wales 3	New Zealand 0	(Cardiff)		
	Jan 1	France 8	New Zealand 38	(Parc des Princes)		

Players
Full-backs: G A Gillett (Canterbury), W J Wallace (Wellington)
Threequarters: H L Abbott (Taranaki), E E Booth (Otago), R G Deans (Canterbury), E T Harper (Canterbury), D McGregor (Wellington), G W Smith (Auckland), H D Thomson (Wanganui)
Five-eighths: J Hunter (Taranaki), H J Mynott (Taranaki), J W Stead (Southland)
Scrum-half: F Roberts (Wellington)
Forwards: S Casey (Otago), J Corbett (West Coast), W Cunningham (Auckland), D Gallaher (Auckland), F T Glasgow (Taranaki), W S Glenn (Taranaki), W Johnston (Otago), W H Mackrell (Auckland), A McDonald (Otago), F Newton (Canterbury), G W Nicholson (Auckland), J M O'Sullivan (Taranaki), C E Seeling (Auckland), G A Tyler (Auckland)
Captain D Gallaher **Manager** G H Dixon

1924-25

Full record	Played 30	Won 30	Lost 0	Drawn 0	Points for 721	Against 112
in B Isles	Played 28	Won 28	Lost 0	Drawn 0	Points for 654	Against 98
in France	Played 2	Won 2	Lost 0	Drawn 0	Points for 67	Against 14
International record	Played 4	Won 4				

International details	Nov 1	Ireland 0	New Zealand 6	(Dublin)
	Nov 29	Wales 0	New Zealand 19	(Swansea)
	Jan 3	England 11	New Zealand 17	(Twickenham)
	Jan 18	France 6	New Zealand 30	(Toulouse)

Players
Full-back: G Nepia (Hawke's Bay)
Threequarters: H W Brown (Taranaki), A H Hart (Taranaki), F W Lucas (Auckland), A C C Robilliard (Canterbury), J Steel (West Coast), K S Svenson (Wellington)
Five-eighths: C E O Badeley (Auckland), A E Cooke (Auckland), N P McGregor (Canterbury), M F Nicholls (Wellington), L Paewai (Hawke's Bay)
Scrum-halves: W C Dalley (Canterbury), J J Mill (Hawke's Bay)
Forwards: C J Brownlie (Hawke's Bay), M J Brownlie (Hawke's Bay), L F Cupples (Bay of Plenty), Q Donald (Wairarapa), I H Harvey (Wairarapa), W R Irvine (Hawke's Bay), R R Masters (Canterbury), B V McCleary (Canterbury), H G Munro (Otago), J H Parker (Canterbury), C G Porter (Wellington), J Richardson (Southland), R T Stewart (South Canterbury), A H West (Taranaki), A White (Southland)
Captain C G Porter **Manager** S S M Dean

1926-27 (The Maoris)

Full record	Played 31	Won 22	Lost 7	Drawn 2	Points for 459	Against 194
in England and Wales	Played 16	Won 8	Lost 6	Drawn 2	Points for 126	Against 113
in France	Played 15	Won 14	Lost 1	Drawn 0	Points for 333	Against 81
International record	Played 1	Won 1				
International details	Dec 26	France 3	Maoris 12	(Paris, Colombes)		

Players
Full-backs: R Pelham (Auckland), H Phillips (Marlborough)
Threequarters: W P Barclay (Hawke's Bay), A C Falwasser (Taranaki), L R Grace (Hawke's Bay), W Lockwood (East Coast), E Love (Wellington), W Potaka (Wanganui), T P Robinson (Canterbury)
Five-eighths: J R Bell (Southland), J H MacDonald (Marlborough), M Mete (Manawhenua), D Wi Neera (Wellington)
Scrum-halves: H Kingi (Wanganui), W H Shortland (Hawke's Bay)
Forwards: A Crawford (East Coast), T Dennis (Poverty Bay), J Gemmell (Hawke's Bay), S W Gemmell (Hawke's Bay), P Haupapa (Bay of Plenty), J Manihera (Canterbury), T Manning (South Canterbury), Rev P Matene (North Auckland), O S Olsen (North Auckland), W Rika (North Auckland), J Stewart (Otago), D Tatana (Manawhenua), W H Wilson (Hawke's Bay)
Captain W P Barclay **Managers** W T Parata and H Harris

1935-36 (British Isles only)

Full record	Played 28	Won 24	Lost 3	Drawn 1	Points for 431	Against 180
International record	Played 4	Won 2	Lost 2			
International details	Nov 23	Scotland 8	New Zealand 18	(Murrayfield)		
	Dec 7	Ireland 9	New Zealand 17	(Dublin)		
	Dec 21	Wales 13	New Zealand 12	(Cardiff)		
	Jan 4	England 13	New Zealand 0	(Twickenham)		

Players
Full-back: G D M Gilbert (West Coast)
Threequarters: N Ball (Wellington), H M Brown (Auckland), T H C Caughey (Auckland), G F Hart (Canterbury), N A Mitchell (Southland), C J Oliver (Canterbury)
Five-eighths: J L Griffiths (Wellington), J R Page (Wellington), D Solomon (Auckland), E W T Tindill (Wellington)

Scrum-halves: M M N Corner (Auckland), B S Sadler (Wellington)
Forwards: G T Adkins (South Canterbury), J J Best (Marlborough), W R Collins (Hawke's Bay), D Dalton (Hawke's Bay), W E Hadley (Auckland), J Hore (Otago), R R King (West Coast), A Lambourn (Wellington), A Mahoney (Bush), J E Manchester (Canterbury), R M McKenzie (Manawatu), H F McLean (Auckland), C S Pepper (Auckland), S T Reid (Hawke's Bay), F H Vorrath (Otago), J G Wynyard (Waikato)
Captain J E Manchester **Manager** V R S Meredith

1953-54

Full record	Played 31	Won 25	Lost 4	Drawn 2	Points for 446	Against 129
in B Isles	Played 29	Won 25	Lost 2	Drawn 2	Points for 438	Against 115
in France	Played 2	Won 0	Lost 2	Drawn 0	Points for 8	Against 14

International record Played 5 Won 3 Lost 2

International details				
Dec 19	Wales 13	New Zealand 8	(Cardiff)
Jan 9	Ireland 3	New Zealand 14	(Dublin)
Jan 30	England 0	New Zealand 5	(Twickenham)
Feb 13	Scotland 0	New Zealand 3	(Murrayfield)
Feb 27	France 3	New Zealand 0	(Paris, Colombes)

Players
Full-backs: J W Kelly (Auckland), R W H Scott (Auckland)
Threequarters: M J Dixon (Canterbury), A E G Elsom (Canterbury), W S S Freebairn (Manawatu), R A Jarden (Wellington), J T Fitzgerald (Wellington), J M Tanner (Auckland)
Five-eighths: B B J Fitzpatrick (Wellington), C J Loader (Wellington), D D Wilson (Canterbury), R G Bowers (Wellington), L S Haig (Otago)
Scrum-halves: V D Bevan (Wellington), K Davis (Auckland)
Forwards: W A McCaw (Southland), R C Stuart (Canterbury), W H Clark (Wellington), P F Jones (North Auckland), R J O'Dea (Thames Valley), O D Oliver (Otago), K P Bagley (Manawatu), G N Dalzell (Canterbury), R A White (Poverty Bay), I J Clarke (Waikato), B P Eastgate (Canterbury), K L Skinner (Otago), H L White (Auckland), R C Hemi (Waikato), C A Woods (Southland)
Captain R C Stuart **Manager** N Millard **Assistant Manager** A E Marslin

1963-64

Full record	Played 34	Won 32	Lost 1	Drawn 1	Points for 568	Against 153
in B Isles	Played 30	Won 28	Lost 1	Drawn 1	Points for 508	Against 137
in France	Played 4	Won 4	Lost 0	Drawn 0	Points for 60	Against 16

International record Played 5 Won 4 Drawn 1

International details				
Dec 7	Ireland 5	New Zealand 6	(Dublin)
Dec 21	Wales 0	New Zealand 6	(Cardiff)
Jan 4	England 0	New Zealand 14	(Twickenham)
Jan 18	Scotland 0	New Zealand 0	(Murrayfield)
Feb 8	France 3	New Zealand 12	(Paris, Colombes)

Players
Full-back: D B Clarke (Waikato)
Threequarters: R W Caulton (Wellington), W L Davis (Hawke's Bay), M J Dick (Auckland), I S T Smith (Otago), P F Little (Auckland), I R MacRae (Hawke's Bay)
Five-eighths: D A Arnold (Canterbury), P T Walsh (Counties), M A Herewini (Auckland), E W Kirton (Otago), B A Watt (Canterbury)
Scrum-halves: K C Briscoe (Taranaki), C R Laidlaw (Otago)
Forwards: I J Clarke (Waikato), K F Gray (Wellington), J M Le Lievre (Canterbury),

W J Whineray (Auckland), D Young (Canterbury), J Major (Taranaki), R H Horsley (Manawatu), C E Meads (King Country), A J Stewart (Canterbury), S T Meads (King Country), K E Barry (Thames Valley), D J Graham (Canterbury), W J Nathan (Auckland), K R Tremain (Hawke's Bay), B J Lochore (Wairarapa), K A Nelson (Otago)

Captain W J Whineray **Manager** F D Kilby **Assistant Manager** N J McPhail

1967

Full record	Played 15	Won 14	Lost 0	Drawn 1	Points for 294	Against 129
in B Isles	Played 11	Won 10	Lost 0	Drawn 1	Points for 207	Against 78
in France	Played 4	Won 4	Lost 0	Drawn 0	Points for 87	Against 51

International record Played 4 Won 4

International details	Nov 4	England 11	New Zealand 23	(Twickenham)
	Nov 11	Wales 6	New Zealand 13	(Cardiff)
	Nov 25	France 15	New Zealand 21	(Paris, Colombes)
	Dec 2	Scotland 3	New Zealand 14	(Murrayfield)

Players

Full-back: W F McCormick (Canterbury)

Threequarters: M J Dick (Auckland), W M Birtwistle (Waikato), A G Steel (Canterbury), P H Clarke (Marlborough), G S Thorne (Auckland), W L Davis (Hawke's Bay)

Five-eighths: I R MacRae (Hawke's Bay), G F Kember (Wellington), W D Cottrell (Canterbury), E W Kirton (Otago), M A Herewini (Auckland)

Scrum-halves: C R Laidlaw (Otago), S M Going (North Auckland)

Forwards: B J Lochore (Wairarapa), I A Kirkpatrick (Canterbury), W J Nathan (Auckland), K R Tremain (Hawke's Bay), G C Williams (Wellington), M C Wills (Taranaki), C E Meads (King Country), A G Jennings (Bay of Plenty), S C Strahan (Manawatu), A E Smith (Taranaki), A E Hopkinson (Canterbury), E J Hazlett (Southland), B L Muller (Taranaki), K F Gray (Wellington), B E McLeod (Counties), J Major (Taranaki)

Captain B J Lochore **Manager** C K Saxton **Assistant Manager** F R Allen

1972-73

Full record	Played 30	Won 23	Lost 5	Drawn 2	Points for 568	Against 254
in Britain and Ireland	Played 26	Won 20	Lost 4	Drawn 2	Points for 521	Against 227
in France	Played 4	Won 3	Lost 1	Drawn 0	Points for 47	Against 27

International record Played 5 Won 3 Lost 1 Drawn 1

International details	Dec 2	Wales 16	New Zealand 19	(Cardiff)
	Dec 16	Scotland 9	New Zealand 14	(Murrayfield)
	Jan 6	England 0	New Zealand 9	(Twickenham)
	Jan 20	Ireland 10	New Zealand 10	(Dublin)
	Feb 10	France 13	New Zealand 6	(Parc des Princes)

Players

Full-backs: J F Karam (Wellington), T J Morris (Nelson-Bays)

Threequarters: B G Williams (Auckland), G B Batty (Wellington), D A Hales (Canterbury), G R Skudder (Waikato), B J Robertson (Counties), I A Hurst (Canterbury)

Five-eighths: R M Parkinson (Poverty Bay), M Sayers (Wellington), R E Burgess (Manawatu), I N Stevens (Wellington)

Scrum-halves: S M Going (North Auckland), G L Colling (Otago)

Forwards: A R Sutherland (Marlborough), A J Wyllie (Canterbury), B Holmes (North Auckland), I A Kirkpatrick (Poverty Bay), K W Stewart (Southland), A I Scown (Taranaki), H H Macdonald (Canterbury), I M Eliason (Taranaki), A M Haden (Auckland), P J Whiting (Auckland), K Murdoch (Otago),

J D Matheson (Otago), K K Lambert (Manawatu), G J Whiting (King Country), R A Urlich (Auckland), R W Norton (Canterbury), L A Clark* (Otago), A L R McNicol* (Wanganui)
Captain I A Kirkpatrick **Manager** E L Todd **Assistant Manager** R H Duff

1974 (to Ireland and UK)

Full record	Played 8	Won 7	Lost 0	Drawn 1	Points for 127	Against 50
in Ireland	Played 6	Won 6	Lost 0	Drawn 0	Points for 102	Against 34
International record	Played 1	Won 1				
International details	Nov 23	Ireland 6	New Zealand 15	(Dublin)		

Players
Full-backs: J F Karam (Wellington), K T Going (North Auckland)
Threequarters: T W Mitchell (Canterbury), B G Williams (Auckland), G Batty (Wellington), B J Robertson (Counties), I A Hurst (Canterbury), J E Morgan (North Auckland), G M Kane (Waikato)
Half-backs: D J Robertson (Otago), O D Bruce (Canterbury), S M Going (North Auckland), I N Stevens (Wellington)
Forwards: A R Leslie (Wellington), L G Knight (Auckland), I A Kirkpatrick (Poverty Bay), K W Stewart (Southland), K A Eveleigh (Manawatu), P J Whiting (Auckland), H H Macdonald (Canterbury), J A Callesen (Manawatu), K J Tanner (Canterbury), A J Gardiner (Taranaki), W K Bush (Canterbury), K K Lambert (Manawatu), R W Norton (Canterbury), G M Crossman (Bay of Plenty)
Captain A R Leslie **Manager** N H Stanley **Assistant Manager** J J Stewart

1977 (France only, except for one match in Italy)

Full record	Played 9	Won 8	Lost 1	Drawn 0	Points for 216	Against 86
in Italy	Played 1	Won 1	Lost 0	Drawn 0	Points for 17	Against 9
in France	Played 8	Won 7	Lost 1	Drawn 0	Points for 199	Against 77
International record	Played 2	Won 1	Lost 1			
International details	Nov 11	France 18	New Zealand 13	(Toulouse)		
	Nov 19	France 3	New Zealand 15	(Parc des Princes)		

Players
Full-back: B W Wilson (Otago)
Threequarters: B G Williams (Auckland), B R Ford (Marlborough), B J Robertson (Counties), S S Wilson (Wellington), N M Taylor (Bay of Plenty), W M Osborne (Wanganui), B Hegarty* (Wellington & Biarritz)
Half-backs: O D Bruce (Canterbury), B J McKechnie (Southland), M W Donaldson (Manawatu), K M Green (Waikato)
Forwards: G N K Mourie (Taranaki), K A Eveleigh (Manawatu), L G Knight (Poverty Bay), G A Seear (Otago), R G Myers (Waikato), R L Stuart (Hawke's Bay), F J Oliver (Southland), A M Haden (Auckland), G A Knight (Manawatu), B R Johnstone (Auckland), J C Ashworth (Canterbury), J T McEldowney (Taranaki), A G Dalton (Counties), J E Black (Canterbury)
Captain G N K Mourie **Manager** R M Don **Assistant Manager** J Gleeson

1978 (no matches in France)

Full record	Played 18	Won 17	Lost 1	Drawn 0	Points for 364	Against 147
International record	Played 4	Won 4				
International details	Nov 4	Ireland 6	New Zealand 10	(Dublin)		
	Nov 11	Wales 12	New Zealand 13	(Cardiff)		
	Nov 25	England 6	New Zealand 16	(Twickenham)		
	Dec 9	Scotland 9	New Zealand 18	(Murrayfield)		

Players
Full-backs: C J Currie (Canterbury), B J McKechnie (Southland),

R G Wilson* (Canterbury)
Threequarters: B R Ford (Marlborough), B G Williams (Auckland), S S Wilson (Wellington), R Kururangi (Counties), B J Robertson (Counties),
Five-eighths: J L Jaffray (Otago), W M Osborne (Wanganui), N M Taylor (Bay of Plenty), O D Bruce (Canterbury), E J Dunn (North Auckland),
Scrum-halves: M W Donaldson (Manawatu), D S Loveridge (Taranaki)
Forwards: G A Seear (Otago), A A McGregor (Southland), G N K Mourie (Taranaki), B G Ashworth (Auckland), L M Rutledge (Southland), W G Graham (Otago), A M Haden (Auckland), F J Oliver (Otago), J K Loveday (Manawatu), J K Fleming (Wellington), W K Bush (Canterbury), J C Ashworth (Canterbury), G A Knight (Manawatu), B R Johnstone (Auckland), A G Dalton (Counties), J E Black (Canterbury)
Captain G N K Mourie **Manager** R W Thomas **Assistant Manager** J Gleeson

1979 (to England and Scotland only, except for one match in Italy)

Full record Played 11 Won 10 Lost 1 Drawn 0 Points for 192 Against 95
International record (in UK) Played 2 Won 2 Points for 30 Against 15
International details

Nov 10	Scotland 6	New Zealand 20	(Murrayfield)
Nov 24	England 9	New Zealand 10	(Twickenham)

Players
Full-backs: R G Wilson (Canterbury), A R Hewson (Wellington)
Threequarters: S S Wilson (Wellington), B R Ford (Marlborough), B G Fraser (Wellington), G R Cunningham (Auckland), T M Twigden (Auckland)
Five-eighths: K J Keane (Canterbury), E Dunn (North Auckland), M B Taylor (Waikato)
Scrum-halves: M W Donaldson (Manawatu), D S Loveridge (Taranaki)
Forwards: M G Mexted (Wellington), G N K Mourie (Taranaki), K W Stewart (Southland), M Burgoyne (North Auckland), V E Stewart (Canterbury), A M Haden (Auckland), J K Fleming (Wellington), B R Johnstone (Auckland), B A Thompson (Canterbury), R C Ketels (Counties), J E Speirs (Counties), A G Dalton (Counties), P H Sloane (North Auckland)
Captain G N K Mourie **Manager** R W Thomas **Assistant Manager** E A Watson

1980 (to Wales only, except for two matches in North America)

Full record Played 7 Won 7 Lost 0 Drawn 0 Points for 197 Against 41
in Wales Played 5 Won 5 Points for 101 Against 25
International record Played 1 Won 1
International details Nov 1 Wales 3 New Zealand 23 (Cardiff)
Players
Full-backs: B W Codlin (Counties), D L Rollerson (Manawatu)
Threequarters: S S Wilson (Wellington), B G Fraser (Wellington), F A Woodman (North Auckland), B J Robertson (Counties)
Five-eighths: W M Osborne (Wanganui), M B Taylor (Waikato), N H Allen (Counties)
Scrum-halves: M W Donaldson (Manawatu), D S Loveridge (Taranaki)
Forwards: G H Old (Manawatu), M G Mexted (Wellington), G N K Mourie (Taranaki), G R Hines (Waikato), M W Shaw (Manawatu), G Higginson (Canterbury), F J Oliver (Manawatu), A M Haden (Auckland), R C Ketels (Counties), G A Knight (Manawatu), J E Spiers (Counties), J C Ashworth (Canterbury), H R Reid (Bay of Plenty), A G Dalton (Counties)
Captain G N K Mourie **Manager** R A Harper **Assistant Manager** E A Watson

1981 (to France only, except for two matches in Romania)

Full record Played 10 Won 8 Lost 1 Drawn 1 Points for 170 Against 108

in Romania	Played 2	Won 2	Lost 0	Drawn 0	Points for 39	Against 15
in France	Played 8	Won 6	Lost 1	Drawn 1	Points for 131	Against 93

International record

v Romania	Played 1	Won 1
v France	Played 2	Won 2

International details

v Romania	Oct 24	Romania 6	New Zealand 14	(Bucharest)
v France	Nov 14	France 9	New Zealand 13	(Toulouse)
	Nov 21	France 6	New Zealand 18	(Parc des Princes)

Players
Full-back: A R Hewson (Wellington)
Threequarters: B G Fraser (Wellington), S S Wilson (Wellington), F A Woodman (North Auckland), J L B Salmon (Wellington), A M Stone (Waikato), L M Cameron (Manawatu)
Five-eighths: S T Pokere (Southland), D L Rollerson (Manawatu), B J McKechnie (Southland), J Boe* (Waikato)
Scrum-halves: D S Loveridge (Taranaki), A Donald (Wanganui)
Forwards: M G Mexted (Wellington), G H Old (Manawatu), G N K Mourie (Taranaki), F K Shelford (Bay of Plenty), M W Shaw (Manawatu), B Morrissey* (Waikato), A M Haden (Auckland), G W Whetton (Auckland), J Ross (Mid-Canterbury), R C Ketels (Counties), W Neville (North Auckland), J E Spiers (Counties), P T Koteka (Waikato), H R Reid (Bay of Plenty), A G Dalton (Counties)
Captain G N K Mourie **Manager** P Gill **Assistant Manager** P Burke

1983 (to England and Scotland only)

Full record Played 8 Won 5 Lost 2 Drawn 1 Points for 162 Against 116
International record Played 2 Lost 1 Drawn 1
International details

Nov 12	Scotland 25	New Zealand 25	(Murrayfield)
Nov 19	England 15	New Zealand 9	(Twickenham)

Players
Full-backs: K J Crowley (Taranaki), R M Deans (Canterbury)
Threequarters: S S Wilson (Wellington), B G Fraser (Wellington), B W Smith (Waikato), C I Green (Canterbury), S T Pokere (Southland), W T Taylor (Canterbury)
Half-backs: I T Dunn (North Auckland), W R Smith (Canterbury), A J Donald (Wanganui), D E Kirk (Otago)
Forwards: K G Boroevich (King Country), S A Crichton (Wellington), M G Davie (Canterbury), B McGrattan (Wellington), H R Reid (Bay of Plenty), B H Wilson (Counties), A Anderson (Canterbury), G J Braid (Bay of Plenty), A G Robinson (North Auckland), M J Hobbs (Canterbury), M W Shaw (Manawatu), F N K Shelford (Hawke's Bay), M G Mexted (Wellington), G H Old (Manawatu)
Captain S S Wilson **Manager** P W Mitchell **Assistant Manager** D B Rope

NEW ZEALAND TO SOUTH AFRICA

1928

Full record Played 22 Won 16 Lost 5 Drawn 1 Points for 339 Against 144
International record Played 4 Won 2 Lost 2
International details

Jun 30	South Africa 17	New Zealand 0	(Durban)
Jul 21	South Africa 6	New Zealand 7	(Johannesburg)
Aug 18	South Africa 11	New Zealand 6	(Port Elizabeth)
Sep 1	South Africa 5	New Zealand 13	(Cape Town)

Players
Full-back: H T Lilburne (Canterbury)
Threequarters: S R Carleton (Canterbury), B A Grenside (Hawke's Bay), D F Lindsay (Otago), F W Lucas (Auckland), A C C Robilliard (Canterbury), C A Rushbrook (Wellington), T R Sheen (Auckland)
Five-eighths: L M Johnson (Wellington), N P McGregor (Canterbury), M F Nicholls (Wellington), W A Strang (South Canterbury)
Scrum-halves: W C Dalley (Canterbury), F D Kilby (Wellington)
Forwards: G T Alley (Canterbury), C J Brownlie (Hawke's Bay), M J Brownlie (Hawke's Bay), J T Burrows (Canterbury), I H Finlayson (North Auckland), S Hadley (Auckland), I H Harvey (Wairarapa), W E Hazlett (Southland), J Hore (Otago), R G McWilliams (Auckland), G Scrimshaw (Canterbury), E M Snow (Nelson), R T Stewart (South Canterbury), J P Swain (Hawke's Bay), E P Ward (Taranaki)
Captain M J Brownlie **Manager** W F Hornig

1949

Full record Played 24 Won 14 Lost 7 Drawn 3 Points for 230 Against 146
International record Played 4 Lost 4

International details			
Jul 16	South Africa 15	New Zealand 11	(Cape Town)
Aug 13	South Africa 12	New Zealand 6	(Johannesburg)
Sep 3	South Africa 9	New Zealand 3	(Durban)
Sep 17	South Africa 11	New Zealand 8	(Port Elizabeth)

Players
Full-backs: J W Goddard (South Canterbury), R W H Scott (Auckland)
Threequarters: E G Boggs (Auckland), I J Botting (Otago), P Henderson (Wanganui), W A Meates (Otago), Dr R R Elvidge (Otago), M P Goddard (South Canterbury)
Five-eighths: F R Allen (Auckland), K E Gudsell (Wanganui), N W Black (Auckland), G W Delamore (Wellington), J C Kearney (Otago)
Scrum-halves: W J Conrad (Waikato), L T Savage (Canterbury)
Forwards: L A Grant (South Canterbury), N H Thornton (Auckland), P J B Crowley (Auckland), P Johnstone (Otago), J R McNab (Otago), H F Frazer (Hawke's Bay), L R Harvey (Otago), M J McHugh (Auckland), C Willocks (Otago), D L Christian (Auckland), R A Dalton (Otago), J G Simpson (Auckland), K L Skinner (Otago), E H Catley (Waikato), N L Wilson (Otago)
Captain F R Allen **Manager** J H Parker **Assistant Manager** A McDonald

1960

Full record Played 26 Won 20 Lost 4 Drawn 2 Points for 441 Against 164
International record Played 4 Won 1 Lost 2 Drawn 1

International details			
Jun 25	South Africa 13	New Zealand 0	(Johannesburg)
Jul 23	South Africa 3	New Zealand 11	(Cape Town)
Aug 13	South Africa 11	New Zealand 11	(Bloemfontein)
Aug 27	South Africa 8	New Zealand 3	(Port Elizabeth)

Players
Full-backs: D B Clarke (Waikato), W A Davies (Auckland)
Threequarters: D H Cameron (Mid-Canterbury), R W Caulton (Wellington), K F Laidlaw (Southland), R F McMullen (Auckland), T P A O'Sullivan (Taranaki), J R Watt (Wellington)
Five-eighths: S G Bremner (Canterbury), A H Clarke (Auckland), T R Lineen (Auckland), S R Nesbit (Auckland)
Scrum-halves: K C Briscoe (Taranaki), R J Urbahn (Taranaki)

Forwards: E J Anderson (Bay of Plenty), R J Boon* (Taranaki), Dr H C Burry (Canterbury), I J Clarke (Waikato), R J Conway (Otago), W D Gillespie (Otago), D J Graham (Canterbury), R C Hemi (Waikato), R H Horsley (Wellington), M W Irwin (Otago), P F Jones (North Auckland), I N MacEwan (Wellington), C E Meads (King Country), E A R Pickering (Waikato), K R Tremain (Canterbury), W J Whineray (Auckland), D Young (Canterbury)
Captain W J Whineray **Manager** T H Pearce **Assistant Manager** J L Sullivan

1970

Full record Played 24 Won 21 Lost 3 Drawn 0 Points for 687 Against 228
International record Played 4 Won 1 Lost 3
International details

Jul 25	South Africa	17	New Zealand	6	(Pretoria)
Aug 8	South Africa	8	New Zealand	9	(Cape Town)
Aug 29	South Africa	14	New Zealand	3	(Port Elizabeth)
Sep 12	South Africa	20	New Zealand	17	(Johannesburg)

Players
Full-back: W F McCormick (Canterbury)
Threequarters: M J Dick (Auckland), B A Hunter (Otago), B G Williams (Auckland), G S Thorne (Auckland), W L Davis (Hawke's Bay), H P Milner (Wanganui)
Five-eighths: I R MacRae (Hawke's Bay), W D Cottrell (Canterbury), E W Kirton (Otago), B D M Furlong (Hawke's Bay), G F Kember (Wellington)
Scrum-halves: C R Laidlaw (Otago), S M Going (North Auckland)
Forwards: B J Lochore (Wairarapa), A R Sutherland (Marlborough), I A Kirkpatrick (Poverty Bay), A J Wyllie (Canterbury), T N Lister (South Canterbury), B Holmes (North Auckland), C E Meads (King Country), S C Strahan (Manawatu), A E Smith (Taranaki), J F Burns (Canterbury), B L Muller (Taranaki), K Murdoch (Otago), A E Hopkinson (Canterbury), N W Thimbleby (Hawke's Bay), B E McLeod (Counties), R A Urlich (Auckland)
Captain B J Lochore **Manager** R L Burk **Assistant Manager** I M H Vodanovich

1976

Full record Played 24 Won 18 Lost 6 Drawn 0 Points for 610 Against 291
International record Played 4 Won 1 Lost 3
International details

Jul 24	South Africa	16	New Zealand	7	(Durban)
Aug 14	South Africa	9	New Zealand	15	(Bloemfontein)
Sep 4	South Africa	15	New Zealand	10	(Cape Town)
Sep 18	South Africa	15	New Zealand	14	(Johannesburg)

Players
Full-backs: L W Mains (Otago), C L Fawcett (Auckland)
Threequarters: B G Williams (Auckland), N A Purvis (Otago), B J Robertson (Counties), W M Osborne (Wanganui), G B Batty (Bay of Plenty), T W Mitchell (Canterbury)
Five-eighths: J E Morgan (North Auckland), J L Jaffray (Otago), D J Robertson (Otago), O D Bruce (Canterbury)
Scrum-halves: L J Davis (Canterbury), S M Going (North Auckland)
Forwards: A R Leslie (Wellington), A R Sutherland (Marlborough), K A Eveleigh (Manawatu), L G Knight (Poverty Bay), I A Kirkpatrick (Poverty Bay), K W Stewart (Southland), P J Whiting (Auckland), G A Seear (Otago), F J Oliver (Southland), H H Macdonald (North Auckland), K K Lambert (Manawatu), W K Bush (Canterbury), K J Tanner (Canterbury), B R Johnstone (Auckland), P C Harris* (Manawatu), R W Norton (Canterbury), G M Crossman (Bay of Plenty)
Captain A R Leslie **Manager** N H Stanley **Assistant Manager** J J Stewart

SOUTH AFRICA TO BRITISH ISLES AND FRANCE

1906-07 (British Isles only)

Full record Played 28 Won 25 Lost 2 Drawn 1 Points for 553 Against 79
International record Played 4 Won 2 Lost 1 Drawn 1

International details

Nov 17	Scotland 6	South Africa 0	(Glasgow)
Nov 24	Ireland 12	South Africa 15	(Belfast)
Dec 1	Wales 0	South Africa 11	(Swansea)
Dec 8	England 3	South Africa 3	(Crystal Palace)

Players
Full-backs: A R Burmeister (WP), A F Marsberg (GW), S Joubert* (WP)
Threequarters: A C Stegmann (WP), J A Loubser (WP), J le Roux (WP), A Morkel (TVL), J D Krige (WP), H A de Villiers (WP), J G Hirsch (EP), S C de Melker (GW)
Half-backs: H W Carolin (WP), F J Dobbin (GW), D C Jackson (WP), D Mare (WP)
Forwards: P J Roos (WP), W A Burger (B), D Brooks (B), W A Neill (B), H J Daneel (WP), P A le Roux (WP), D J Brink (WP), W C Martheze (GW), J W E Raaff (GW), W S Morkel (TVL), D F T Morkel (TVL), H G Reid (TVL), W A Millar (WP), A F Burdett (WP)
Captain P J Roos **Manager** J C Carden

1912-13

Full record	Played 27	Won 24	Lost 3	Drawn 0	Points for 441	Against 101
in B Isles	Played 26	Won 23	Lost 3	Drawn 0	Points for 403	Against 96
in France	Played 1	Won 1	Lost 0	Drawn 0	Points for 38	Against 5

International record Played 5 Won 5

International details

Nov 23	Scotland 0	South Africa 16	(Inverleith)
Nov 30	Ireland 0	South Africa 38	(Dublin)
Dec 14	Wales 0	South Africa 3	(Cardiff)
Jan 4	England 3	South Africa 9	(Twickenham)
Jan 11	France 5	South Africa 38	(Bordeaux)

Players
Full-backs: P G Morkel (WP), J J Meintjies (GW)
Threequarters: J Stegmann (WP), A van der Hoff (TVL), E E McHardy (OFS), W J Mills (WP), R R Luyt (WP), G M Wrentmore (WP), W A Krige (WP), J Morkel (WP)
Half-backs: J D McCulloch (GW), F P Luyt (WP), J Immelman (WP), F J Dobbin (GW)
Forwards: E H Shum (TVL), D F T Morkel (TVL), T F van Vuuren (EP), G Thompson (WP), A S Knight (TVL), S N Cronje (TVL), E T Delaney (GW), W H Morkel (WP), S H Ledger (GW), L H Louw (WP), J A J Francis (TVL), J S Braine (GW), W A Millar (WP), J D Luyt (EP)
Captain W A Millar **Manager** M Honnet

1931-32 (British Isles only)

Full record Played 26 Won 23 Lost 1 Drawn 2 Points for 407 Against 124
International record Played 4 Won 4

International details

Dec 5	Wales 3	South Africa 8	(Swansea)
Dec 19	Ireland 3	South Africa 8	(Dublin)
Jan 2	England 0	South Africa 7	(Twickenham)
Jan 16	Scotland 3	South Africa 6	(Murrayfield)

Players
Full-backs: J C Tindall (WP), G H Brand (WP)
Threequarters: J van Niekerk (WP), M Zimerman (WP), J H van der Westhuizen (WP), F D Venter (TVL), J C van der Westhuizen (WP), B G Gray (WP), F W Waring (WP), J White (B), D O Williams* (Villagers)

Half-backs: B L Osler (WP), M G Francis (OFS), P de Villiers (WP), D H Craven (Stellenbosch U)
Forwards: M M Louw (WP), S R du Toit (WP), A van der Merwe (Worcester), S C Louw (WP), P J Mostert (WP), A J McDonald (WP), L C Strachan (TVL), J N Bierman (TVL), H G Kipling (GW), G M Daneel (TVL), V Geere (TVL), P J Nel (N), W F Bergh (SWD), H M Forrest (TVL), J B Dold (EP)
Captain B L Osler **Manager** T B Pienaar

1951-52

Full record	Played 31	Won 30	Lost 1	Drawn 0	Points for 562	Against 167
in B Isles	Played 27	Won 26	Lost 1	Drawn 0	Points for 499	Against 143
in France	Played 4	Won 4	Lost 0	Drawn 0	Points for 63	Against 24

International record	Played 5	Won 5		
International details	Nov 24	Scotland 0	South Africa 44	(Murrayfield)
	Dec 8	Ireland 5	South Africa 17	(Dublin)
	Dec 22	Wales 3	South Africa 6	(Cardiff)
	Jan 5	England 3	South Africa 8	(Twickenham)
	Feb 16	France 3	South Africa 25	(Paris, Colombes)

Players
Full-backs: J Buchler (TVL), A C Keevy (E TVL)
Threequarters: J K Ochse (WP), F P Marais (Boland), M J Saunders (B), P Johnstone (WP), M T Lategan (WP), R A M van Schoor (R), D J Sinclair (TVL), S S Viviers (OFS)
Half-backs: J D Brewis (N TVL), D J Fry (WP), J S Oelofse (TVL), P A du Toit (N TVL)
Forwards: P W Wessels (OFS), W H Delport (EP), A C Koch (Boland), A Geffin (TVL), H P J Bekker (N TVL), F E van der Ryst (TVL), E E Dinkelmann (N TVL), J A Pickard (WP), G Dannhauser (TVL), W H M Barnard (GW), S P Fry (WP), C J van Wyk (TVL), B Myburgh (E TVL), J A du Rand (R), B J Kenyon (B), H S Muller (TVL)
Captain B J Kenyon **Manager** F W Mellish **Assistant Manager** Dr D H Craven

1960-61

Full record	Played 34	Won 31	Lost 1	Drawn 2	Points for 567	Against 132
in B Isles	Played 30	Won 28	Lost 1	Drawn 1	Points for 476	Against 110
in France	Played 4	Won 3	Lost 0	Drawn 1	Points for 91	Against 22

International record	Played 5	Won 4	Drawn 1	
International details	Dec 3	Wales 0	South Africa 3	(Cardiff)
	Dec 17	Ireland 3	South Africa 8	(Dublin)
	Jan 7	England 0	South Africa 5	(Twickenham)
	Jan 21	Scotland 5	South Africa 12	(Murrayfield)
	Feb 18	France 0	South Africa 0	(Paris, Colombes)

Players
Full-backs: L G Wilson (WP), G J Wentzel (EP)
Threequarters: H J van Zyl (TVL), M J G Antelme (TVL), J P Engelbrecht (WP), F du T Roux (WP), B P van Zyl* (WP), A I Kirkpatrick (GW), J L Gainsford (WP), D A Stewart (WP), B B van Niekerk (OFS)
Half-backs: K Oxlee (N), C F Nimb (WP), R J Lockyear (GW), P de W Uys (N TVL)
Forwards: P S du Toit (WP), S P Kuhn (TVL), J L Myburgh (N TVL), D N Holton (EP), G F Malan (WP), R A Hill (R), R G Johns* (WP), A S Malan (TVL), J T Claassen (W TVL), H S van der Merwe (N TVL), P J van Zyl (Boland), H J M Pelser (TVL), G H van Zyl (WP), J P F Botha (N TVL), F C H du Preez (N TVL), D J Hopwood (WP), A P Baard (WP)
Captain A S Malan **Manager** W F Bergh **Assistant Manager** M M (Boy) Louw

1965 (Ireland and Scotland only)

Full record	Played 5 Won 0 Lost 4 Drawn 1 Points for 37 Against 53				
International record	Played 2 Lost 2				
International details	Apr 10	Ireland	9	South Africa 6	(Dublin)
	Apr 17	Scotland	8	South Africa 5	(Murrayfield)

Players
Full-back: L G Wilson (WP)
Threequarters: C D Cilliers (OFS), C W Dirksen (N TVL), J P Engelbrecht (WP), J L Gainsford (WP), W J Mans (WP), D A Stewart (WP)
Half-backs: J H Barnard (TVL), K Oxlee (N), S C Conradie* (WP), D J de Villiers (WP), D J J de Vos (WP)
Forwards: S P Kuhn (TVL), J F K Marais (WP), J B Neethling (WP), D C Walton (N), J W Wessels (OFS), G Carelse (EP), F C H du Preez (N TVL), A S Malan (TVL), J Schoeman (WP), M R Suter (N), T P Bedford (N), D J Hopwood (WP)
Captain A S Malan **Manager** B M Medway **Assistant Manager** M M Louw

1968 (France only)

Full record	Played 6 Won 5 Lost 1 Drawn 0 Points for 84 Against 43				
International record	Played 2 Won 2				
International details	Nov 9	France	9	South Africa 12	(Bordeaux)
	Nov 16	France	11	South Africa 16	(Paris, Colombes)

Players
Full-backs: H O de Villiers (WP), R L Gould (N)
Threequarters: J P Engelbrecht (WP), S H Nomis (TVL), E Olivier (WP), F du T Roux (WP), O A Roux (N TVL)
Half-backs: P J Visagie (GW), M A Menter (N TVL), D J de Villiers (WP), P de W Uys (N TVL)
Forwards: J F K Marais (WP), J L Myburgh (N TVL), J B Neethling (WP), G Pitzer (N TVL), D C Walton (N), F C H du Preez (N TVL), J P Naude (WP), G Carelse (EP), J H Ellis (SWA), P J F Greyling (OFS), M J Lourens (N TVL), T P Bedford (N)
Captain D J de Villiers **Manager** F C Eloff **Assistant Manager** J T Claassen

1969-70 (British Isles only)

Full record	Played 24 Won 15 Lost 5 Drawn 4 Points for 323 Against 157				
International record	Played 4 Lost 2 Drawn 2				
International details	Dec 6	Scotland	6	South Africa 3	(Murrayfield)
	Dec 20	England	11	South Africa 8	(Twickenham)
	Jan 10	Ireland	8	South Africa 8	(Dublin)
	Jan 24	Wales	6	South Africa 6	(Cardiff)

Players
Full-backs: H O de Villiers (WP), P J Durand (WP)
Threequarters: R N Grobler (N TVL), G H Muller (WP), S H Nomis (TVL), A E van der Watt (WP), E Olivier (WP), O A Roux (N TVL), J P van der Merwe (WP), P J van der Schyff (W TVL), F du T Roux* (GW)
Half-backs: M J Lawless (WP), P J Visagie (GW), D J de Villiers (Boland), D J J de Vos (W TVL)
Forwards: J L Myburgh (N TVL), J B Neethling (WP), J F K Marais (EP), R Potgieter (N TVL), G Carelse (EP), A E de Wet (WP), F C H du Preez (N TVL), G Pitzer (N TVL), D C Walton (N), M C J van Rensburg (N), A J Bates (W TVL), J H Ellis (SWA), P J F Greyling (TVL), P I van Deventer (GW), T P Bedford (N), M W Jennings (Boland), I J de Klerk* (TVL), C H Cockrell* (WP), R Barnard* (TVL)
Captain D J de Villiers **Manager** C A J Bornman **Assistant Manager** A S Malan

1974 (France only)

Full record Played 9 Won 8 Lost 1 Drawn 0 Points for 170 Against 74
International record Played 2 Won 2
International details Nov 23 France 4 South Africa 13 (Toulouse)
Nov 30 France 8 South Africa 10 (Paris, Parc des Princes)
Players
Full-backs: I W Robertson (R), D S L Snyman (WP)
Threequarters: C Fourie (EP), W P Stapelberg (N TVL), C F Pope (WP), P J M Whipp (WP), J J Oosthuizen (WP), J A van Staden (N TVL)
Half-backs: J C P Snyman (OFS), G R Bosch (TVL), P C R Bayvel (TVL), R J McCallum (WP)
Forwards: M du Plessis (WP), J L Kritzinger (TVL), J H Ellis (SWA), T T Fourie (SE TVL), C J Grobler (OFS), J L van Heerden (N TVL), J G Williams (N TVL), K B H De Klerk (TVL), J De Bruyn (OFS), J F K Marais (EP), N S E Bezuidenhoudt (N TVL), J C J Stander (OFS), D S van Den Berg (N), A Bestbier (OFS), R J Cockrell (WP)
Captain J F K Marais **Managers** J Z le Roux
Assistant Managers J T Claassen and A I Kirkpatrick*

SOUTH AFRICA TO AUSTRALIA AND NEW ZEALAND

1921

Full record
in Australia Played 4 Won 4 Lost 0 Drawn 0 Points for 83 Against 38
in New Zealand Played 19 Won 15 Lost 2 Drawn 2 Points for 244 Against 81
International record
v New Zealand Played 3 Won 1 Lost 1 Drawn 1
International details Aug 13 New Zealand 13 South Africa 5 (Dunedin)
Aug 27 New Zealand 5 South Africa 9 (Auckland)
Sep 17 New Zealand 0 South Africa 0 (Wellington)
Players
Full-backs: P G Morkel (WP), I B de Villiers (TVL)
Threequarters: A J van Heerden (TVL), W C Zeller (N), J S Weepner (WP), Henry Morkel (WP), W D Sendin (GW), W A Clarkson (N), S S Strauss (GW), C du P Meyer (WP)
Half-backs: J S de Kock (WP), J C Tindall (WP), J P Michau (WP), W H Townsend (N)
Forwards: T B Pienaar (WP), W H (Boy) Morkel (WP), M Ellis (TVL), N J du Plessis (W TVL), G W van Rooyen (TVL), J M Michau (TVL), T L Kruger (TVL), A P Walker (N), Royal Morkel (WP), F W Mellish (WP), Harry Morkel (WP), J S Olivier (WP), L B Siedle (N), P J Mostert (WP), H H Scholtz (WP)
Captain T B Pienaar **Manager** H C Bennett

1937

Full record
in Australia Played 9 Won 8 Lost 1 Drawn 0 Points for 342 Against 65
in New Zealand Played 17 Won 16 Lost 1 Drawn 0 Points for 411 Against 104
International record
in Australia Played 2 Won 2
in New Zealand Played 3 Won 2 Lost 1

International details

v Australia	Jun 26	Australia	5	South Africa	9	(Sydney)
	Jul 17	Australia	17	South Africa	26	(Sydney)
v New Zealand	Aug 14	New Zealand	13	South Africa	7	(Wellington)
	Sep 4	New Zealand	6	South Africa	13	(Christchurch)
	Sep 25	New Zealand	6	South Africa	17	(Auckland)

Players

Full-backs: G H Brand (WP), F G Turner (TVL)
Threequarters: D O Williams (WP), P J Lyster (N), J A Broodryk (TVL), A D Lawton (WP), L Babrow (WP), J L A Bester (Gardens), S R Hofmeyr (WP), J White (B), G P Lochner (EP)
Half-backs: D F van de Vyver (WP), T A Harris (TVL), D H Craven (EP), P du P de Villiers (WP)
Forwards: W E Bastard (N), W G Bergh (TVL), B A du Toit (TVL), C B Jennings (B), J W Lotz (TVL), M M Louw (WP), S C Louw (TVL), H J Martin (TVL), P J Nel (N), A R Sheriff (TVL), L C Strachan (TVL), M A van den Berg (WP), G L van Reenen (WP), H H Watt (WP)
Captain P J Nel **Manager** P W Day **Assistant Manager** A de Villiers

1956

Full record

in Australia	Played 6	Won 6	Lost 0	Drawn 0	Points for 150	Against 26
in New Zealand	Played 23	Won 16	Lost 6	Drawn 1	Points for 370	Against 177

International record

in Australia	Played 2	Won 2	
in New Zealand	Played 4	Won 1	Lost 3

International details

v Australia	May 26	Australia	0	South Africa	9	(Sydney)
	Jun 2	Australia	0	South Africa	9	(Brisbane)
v New Zealand	Jul 14	New Zealand	10	South Africa	6	(Dunedin)
	Aug 4	New Zealand	3	South Africa	8	(Wellington)
	Aug 18	New Zealand	17	South Africa	10	(Christchurch)
	Sep 1	New Zealand	11	South Africa	5	(Auckland)

Players

Full-backs: J U Buchler (TVL), S S Viviers (OFS)
Threequarters: K T van Vollenhoven (N TVL), P G Johnstone (TVL), R G Dryburgh (N), J du Preez (WP), T P Briers* (WP), W Rosenberg (TVL), P E Montini (WP), A I Kirkpatrick (GW), J J Nel (WP)
Half-backs: C A Ulyate (TVL), B F Howe (B), B D Pfaff (WP), T A Gentles (WP), C F Strydom (OFS)
Forwards: H P J Bekker (N TVL), A C Koch (Boland), P S du Toit (WP), H N Walker (W TV), A J van der Merwe (Boland), M Hanekom (Boland), J A du Rand (N TVL), J T Claassen (W TVL), C J de Nysschen (N), J A J Pickard (WP), C J van Wyk (TVL), D S P Ackermann (WP), C J De Wilzem (OFS), G P Lochner (WPI), D F Retief (N TVL), J J Starke* (Stellenbosch)
Captain S S Viviers **Manager** Dr D H Craven **Assistant Manager** D J de Villiers

1965

Full record

in Australia	Played 6	Won 3	Lost 3	Drawn 0	Points for 184	Against 53
in New Zealand	Played 24	Won 19	Lost 5	Drawn 0	Points for 485	Against 232

International record

v Australia	Played 2	Lost 2	
v New Zealand	Played 4	Won 1	Lost 3

International details

v Australia	Jun 19	Australia	18	South Africa 11	(Sydney)
	Jun 26	Australia	12	South Africa 8	(Brisbane)
v New Zealand	Jul 31	New Zealand	6	South Africa 3	(Wellington)
	Aug 21	New Zealand	13	South Africa 0	(Dunedin)
	Sep 4	New Zealand	16	South Africa 19	(Christchurch)
	Sep 18	New Zealand	20	South Africa 3	(Auckland)

Players

Full-backs: L G Wilson (WP), C G Mulder (E TVL)
Threequarters: J P Engelbrecht (WP), F du T Roux (GW), J L Gainsford (WP), E Olivier* (WP), G Brynard (WP), J T Truter (N), S H Nomis (TVL), W J Mans (WP), C J C Cronje (E TVL)
Half-backs: K Oxlee (N), J H Barnard (TVL), D J de Villiers (WP), C M Smith (OFS)
Forwards: D J Hopwood (WP), J A Nel (W TVL), J Schoeman (WP), F C H du Preez (N TVL), J P Naude (WP), J H Ellis (SWA), A W MacDonald (Rho), G F Malan (TVL), C P van Zyl (OFS), D C Walton (N), C P Goosen (OFS), T P Bedford (N), L J Slabber* (OFS), P H Botha (TVL), A Janson (WP), W H Parker (EP), J F Marais (EP)
Captain D J de Villiers **Manager** J F Louw **Assistant Manager** H S (Hennie) Muller

1971 (Australia only)

Full record Played 13 Won 13 Lost 0 Drawn 0 Points for 396 Against 102
International record Played 3 Won 3
International details

Jul 17	Australia 11	South Africa 19	(Sydney)
Jul 31	Australia 6	South Africa 14	(Brisbane)
Aug 7	Australia 6	South Africa 18	(Sydney)

Players

Full-backs: I D McCallum (WP), O A Roux (N TVL)
Threequarters: G H Muller (WP), S H Nomis (TVL), J T Viljoen (N), P A Cronje (TVL), J S Jansen (OFS), P S Swanson (TVL), A E van der Watt* (WP)
Half-backs: P J Visagie (GW), D S L Snyman (WP), J F Viljoen (GW), D J J de Vos (W TVL)
Forwards: J F K Marais (EP), M J Louw (TVL), J T Sauermann (TVL), J F B van Wyk (N TVL), R W Barnard (TVL), F C H du Preez (N TVL), J J Spies (N TVL), J G Williams (N TVL), J H Ellis (SWA), P J F Greyling (TVL), M J Lourens (N TVL), T P Bedford (N), M du Plessis (WP), A J Bates* (W TVL),
Captain J F K Marais **Manager** G P Lochner **Assistant Manager** J T Claassen

1981 (New Zealand only, except for three matches in USA)

Full record	Played 17	Won 14	Lost 2	Drawn 1	Points for 535	Against 190
in New Zealand	Played 14	Won 11	Lost 2	Drawn 1	Points for 410	Against 171
in USA	Played 3	Won 3	Lost 0	Drawn 0	Points for 125	Against 19

International record

v New Zealand	Played 3	Won 1	Lost 2
v USA	Played 1	Won 1	

International details

v New Zealand	Aug 15	New Zealand 14	South Africa 9	(Christchurch)
	Aug 29	New Zealand 12	South Africa 24	(Wellington)
	Sep 12	New Zealand 25	South Africa 22	(Auckland)
v USA	Sep 26	USA 7	South Africa 38	(Glenville, NY)

Players

Full-backs: Z M J Pienaar (OFS), J W Heunis (N TVL)
Threequarters: J S Germishuys (TVL), D S Botha (N TVL) E F W Krantz (OFS), R H Mordt (TVL), C J du Plessis (WP), W du Plessis (WP), E G Tobias (Boland),

D M Gerber (EP)
Half-backs: H E Botha (N TVL), J J Beck (WP), D J Serfontein (WP), B J Wolmarans (OFS), G Visagie* (Natal)
Forwards: W Claassen (Natal), J H Marais (N TVL), M B Burger (N TVL), S B Geldenhuys (N TVL), E Jansen (OFS), R J Louw (WP), H J Bekker (WP), L C Moolman (N TVL), M T S Stofberg (N TVL), J de V Visser (WP), P G du Toit (WP), O W Oosthuizen (N TVL), H J van Aswegen (WP), P R van der Merwe (S W Districts), R J Cockrell (WP), W J H Kahts (N TVL), S Povey* (WP)
Captain W Claassen **Manager** J T Claassen
Assistant Managers C M Smith, A Williams

AUSTRALIA TO BRITISH ISLES AND FRANCE

1908-09 (England and Wales only)

Full record	Played 31	Won 25	Lost 5	Drawn 1	Points for 438	Against 149
International record	Played 2	Won 1	Lost 1			
International details	Dec 12	Wales 9	Australia 6	(Cardiff)		
	Jan 9	England 3	Australia 9	(Blackheath)		

Players
Full-backs: P P Carmichael (Queensland), W Dix (Armidale)
Threequarters: C Russell (Newtown), F B Smith (Central West), H Daly (Central West), D B Carroll (St George), J Hickey (Glebe), E Mandible (Sydney), E Parkinson (Queensland)
Five-eighths: W Prentice (West Suburbs), A J McCabe (Sydney), J M Stevenson (Northern)
Scrum-halves: F Wood (Glebe), C H McKivat (Glebe)
Forwards: Dr H M Moran (Newcastle), T S Griffen (Glebe), S A Middleton (Glebe), E McIntyre (Central West), K Gavin* (Central West), P A McCue (Newtown), J T Barnett (Newtown), P H Burge (S Sydney), A B Burge* (S Sydney), C E Murnin (Eastern Suburbs), N E Row (Eastern Suburbs), M McArthur (Eastern Suburbs), P Flanagan (Queensland), T J Richards (Queensland), C H McMurtrie (Orange), R R Craig (Balmain), C A Hammand (University)
Captain Dr H M Moran **Manager** J McMahon **Assistant Manager** S Wickham

1927-28 (New South Wales, 'The Waratahs')

Full record	Played 31	Won 24	Lost 5	Drawn 2	Points for 432	Against 207
in B Isles	Played 28	Won 22	Lost 4	Drawn 2	Points for 400	Against 177
in France	Played 3	Won 2	Lost 1	Drawn 0	Points for 32	Against 30
International record	Played 5	Won 3	Lost 2			
International details	Nov 12	Ireland 3	New South Wales 5	(Dublin)		
	Nov 26	Wales 8	New South Wales 18	(Cardiff)		
	Dec 17	Scotland 10	New South Wales 8	(Murrayfield)		
	Jan 7	England 18	New South Wales 11	(Twickenham)		
	Jan 22	France 8	New South Wales 11	(Paris, Colombes)		

Players
Full-back: A W Ross (Sydney U)
Threequarters: E E Ford (Glebe-Balmain), A C Wallace (University and Glebe-Balmain), A J A Bowers (Randwick), G C Gordon (YMCA), W H Mann (University), C H T Towers (Randwick), W B J Sheehan (University), S C King (Western Suburbs), J B Egan (Eastern Suburbs)
Half-backs: T Lawton (Western Suburbs), S J Malcolm (Newcastle),

F W Meagher (Randwick), J L Duncan (Randwick)
Forwards: J A Ford (Glebe-Balmain), A J Tancred (Glebe-Balmain), J W Breckenridge (Glebe-Balmain), E N Greatorex (YMCA), A N Finlay (University), G P Storey (Western Suburbs), G Bland (Manly), E J Thorn (Manly), C L Fox (North Sydney), B Judd (Randwick), M R Blair (Western Suburbs), J G Blackwood (Eastern Suburbs), H F Woods (YMCA), K Tarleton (YMCA), J L Tancred (Glebe-Balmain)
Captain A C Wallace **Manager** E Gordon Shaw

1947-48

Full record	Played 35	Won 29	Lost 6	Drawn 0	Points for 500	Against 243
in B Isles	Played 30	Won 25	Lost 5	Drawn 0	Points for 429	Against 197
in France	Played 5	Won 4	Lost 1	Drawn 0	Points for 71	Against 46

International record Played 5 Won 3 Lost 2

International details				
Nov 22	Scotland 7	Australia 16	(Murrayfield)	
Dec 6	Ireland 3	Australia 16	(Dublin)	
Dec 20	Wales 6	Australia 0	(Cardiff)	
Jan 3	England 0	Australia 11	(Twickenham)	
Jan 11	France 13	Australia 6	(Paris, Colombes)	

Players
Full-backs: B J C Piper (NSW), C J Windsor (Queensland)
Threequarters: C C Eastes (NSW), A E J Tonkin (NSW), J W T MacBride (NSW), T K Bourke (Queensland), T Allan (NSW), M L Howell (NSW), A K Walker (NSW)
Five-eighths: J F Cremin (NSW), N A Emery (NSW), E G Broad (Queensland)
Scrum-halves: C T Burke (NSW), R M Cawsey (NSW)
Forwards: W M McLean (Queensland), A J Buchan (NSW), C J Windon (NSW), J O Stenmark (NSW), K C Winning (Queensland), J G Fuller (NSW), G M Cooke (Queensland), P A Hardcastle (NSW), D F Kraefft (NSW), N Shehadie (NSW), R E McMaster (Queensland), E Tweedale (NSW), D H Keller (NSW), E H Davis (Victoria), K H Kearney (NSW), W L Dawson (NSW)
Captain W M McLean **Manager** A J Tancred **Assistant Manager** J Noseda

1957-58

Full record	Played 34	Won 16	Lost 15	Drawn 3	Points for 285	Against 244
in B Isles	Played 30	Won 14	Lost 13	Drawn 3	Points for 248	Against 203
in France	Played 4	Won 2	Lost 2	Drawn 0	Points for 37	Against 41

International record Played 5 Lost 5

International details			
Jan 4	Wales 9	Australia 3	(Cardiff)
Jan 18	Ireland 9	Australia 6	(Dublin)
Feb 1	England 9	Australia 6	(Twickenham)
Feb 15	Scotland 12	Australia 8	(Murrayfield)
Mar 9	France 19	Australia 0	(Paris, Colombes)

Players
Full-backs: T G Curley (NSW), J K Lenehan (NSW)
Threequarters: K J Donald (Queensland), R Phelps (NSW), A R Morton (NSW), O G Fox (NSW), J A Phipps (NSW), G D Bailey (NSW), J M Potts (NSW), S W White (NSW)
Half-backs: R Harvey (NSW), A Summons (NSW), D Logan (NSW), D M Connor (Queensland)
Forwards: R A L Davidson (NSW), P T Fenwicke (NSW), N M Hughes (NSW), W J Gunther (NSW), J E Thornett (NSW), K Yanz (NSW), E M Purkis (NSW), A R Miller (NSW), A S Cameron (NSW), D M Emanuel (NSW), S Scotts (NSW),

N Shehadie (NSW), G N Vaughan (Victoria), K J Ryan (Queensland), J V Brown (NSW), R Meadows (NSW)
Captain R A L Davidson **Manager** T H McClenaghan
Assistant Manager D L Cowper

1966-67

Full record	Played 34	Won 17	Lost 14	Drawn 3	Points for 348	Against 322
in B Isles	Played 30	Won 15	Lost 13	Drawn 2	Points for 303	Against 280
in France	Played 4	Won 2	Lost 1	Drawn 1	Points for 45	Against 42

International record Played 5 Won 2 Lost 3

International details					
Dec 3	Wales	11	Australia	14	(Cardiff)
Dec 17	Scotland	11	Australia	5	(Murrayfield)
Jan 7	England	11	Australia	23	(Twickenham)
Jan 21	Ireland	15	Australia	8	(Dublin)
Feb 11	France	20	Australia	14	(Paris, Colombes)

Players
Full-backs: J K Lenehan (NSW), P F Ryan (NSW)
Threequarters: E S Boyce (NSW), P V Smith (NSW), R Webb (Victoria) R J Marks (Queensland), J E Brass (NSW), A M Cardy (NSW), J A Francis (NSW)
Five-eighths: P R Gibbs (Victoria), A M C Moore (NSW), P F Hawthorne (NSW)
Scrum-halves: J N B Hipwell (NSW), K W Catchpole (NSW)
Forwards: J E Thornett (NSW), R Cullen (Queensland), R B Prosser (NSW), R G Teitzel (Queensland), R J Heming (NSW), R D Tulloch (Victoria), J O'Gorman (NSW), G V Davis (NSW), C P Crittle (NSW), P G Johnson (NSW), A R Miller (NSW), J M Miller (NSW), D A O'Callaghan (NSW), D A Taylor (Queensland), M P Purcell (Queensland), J Guerassimoff (Queensland), R Taylor* (NSW)
Captain J E Thornett **Manager** R E M McLaughlin **Assistant Manager** A S Roper

1968 (Ireland and Scotland only)

Full record	Played 5	Won 2	Lost 3	Drawn 0	Points for 38	Against 40

International record Played 2 Lost 2

International details					
Oct 26	Ireland	10	Australia	3	(Dublin)
Nov 2	Scotland	9	Australia	3	(Murrayfield)

Players
Full-back: A N McGill (NSW)
Threequarters: T R Forman (NSW), R P Batterham (NSW), J W Cole (NSW), B D Honan (Queensland), A M Pope (Queensland), P V Smith (NSW), J E Brass (NSW)
Five-eighth: J P Ballesty (NSW)
Scrum-halves: M J Barry (Queensland), J N B Hipwell (NSW)
Forwards: P G Johnson (NSW), P Darveniza (NSW), R B Prosser (NSW), R V Turnbull (NSW), N P Reilly (Queensland), S C Gregory (Queensland), K R Bell (Queensland), A J Skinner (NSW), D A Taylor (Queensland), H A Rose (NSW), G V Davis (NSW)
Captain P G Johnson **Manager** J H Lord **Assistant Manager** D M Connor

1971 (France only)

Full record	Played 8	Won 4	Lost 4	Drawn 0	Points for 110	Against 101

International record Played 2 Won 1 Lost 1

International details					
Nov 20	France	11	Australia	13	(Toulouse)
Nov 27	France	18	Australia	9	(Paris, Colombes)

Players
Full-back: A N McGill (NSW)
Threequarters: J W Cole (NSW), R P Batterham (NSW), L Monaghan (NSW), J J McLean (Queensland), D L'Estrange (Queensland), D Rathie (Queensland), G A Shaw (NSW)
Half-backs: G C Richardson (Queensland), R L Fairfax (NSW), J N B Hipwell (NSW), G Grey (NSW)
Forwards: G V Davis (NSW), M Flynn (Queensland), P D Sullivan (NSW), R McLean (NSW), O Butler (NSW), S Gregory (Queensland), B Stumbles (NSW), R Smith (NSW), D Dunworth (Queensland), R B Prosser (NSW), B Brown (Queensland), P G Johnson (NSW), R Thompson (WA)
Captain G V Davis **Manager** J French **Assistant Manager** R I Templeton

1973 (England and Wales only)

Full record	Played 8	Won 2	Lost 5	Drawn 1	Points for 85	Against 131
International record	Played 2	Lost 2				
International details	Nov 10	Wales	24	Australia 0	(Cardiff)	
	Nov 17	England	20	Australia 3	(Twickenham)	

Players
Full-backs: A N McGill (NSW), R L Fairfax (NSW) (utility back)
Threequarters: L E Monaghan (NSW), O Stephens (NSW), J J McLean (Queensland), D R Burnet (NSW), R D L'Estrange (Queensland), G A Shaw (NSW)
Half-backs: G C Richardson (Queensland), P G Rowles (NSW), J N B Hipwell (NSW), R G Hauser (South Australia)
Forwards: K G McCurrach (NSW), A A Shaw (Queensland), P D Sullivan (NSW), B R Battishall (NSW), M R Cocks (Queensland), G Fay (NSW), R A Smith (NSW), S C Gregory (NSW), J L Howard (NSW), R Graham (NSW), S G Macdougall (NSW), M E Freney (Queensland), C M Carberry (NSW)
Captain P D Sullivan **Manager** J E Freedman **Assistant Manager** R I Templeton

1975-76 (including one match in USA)

Full record	Played 26	Won 19	Lost 6	Drawn 1	Points for 496	Against 349
in B Isles	Played 25	Won 18	Lost 6	Drawn 1	Points for 472	Against 337
in USA	Played 1	Won 1	Lost 0	Drawn 0	Points for 24	Against 12
International record	Played 5	Won 2	Lost 3			
International details	Dec 6	Scotland 10	Australia 3	(Murrayfield)		
	Dec 20	Wales 28	Australia 3	(Cardiff)		
	Jan 3	England 23	Australia 6	(Twickenham)		
	Jan 17	Ireland 10	Australia 20	(Dublin)		
	Jan 31	USA 12	Australia 24	(Los Angeles)		

Players
Full-back: M A Fitzgerald (NSW)
Threequarters: J R Ryan (NSW), L E Monaghan (NSW), P G Batch (Queensland), L J Weatherstone (ACT), G A Shaw (NSW), W A McKid (NSW), R D L'Estrange (Queensland), J Berne (NSW)
Half-backs: K J Wright (NSW), P E McLean (Queensland), J C Hindmarsh (NSW), J N B Hipwell (NSW), R G Hauser (Queensland), G O Grey* (NSW)
Forwards: A A Shaw (Queensland), M E Loane (Queensland), R A Price (NSW), G K Pearse (NSW), J K Lambie (NSW), G Cornelsen (NSW), R A Smith (NSW), B W Mansfield (NSW), D W Hillhouse (Queensland), G S Eisenhauer (NSW[C]), G Fay* (NSW), J E C Meadows (Victoria), S G Macdougall (ACT), S C Finnane (NSW), R Graham (NSW), P A Horton (NSW), C M Carberry (NSW)
Captain J N B Hipwell **Manager** R V Turnbull **Assistant Manager** J D Brockhoff

1976 (France only, except for one match in Italy)

Full record	Played 10	Won 4	Lost 6	Drawn 0	Points for 114	Against 163
in France	Played 9	Won 3	Lost 6	Drawn 0	Points for 98	Against 148
in Italy	Played 1	Won 1	Lost 0	Drawn 0	Points for 16	Against 15

International record Played 2 Lost 2

International details	Oct 24	France 18	Australia 15	(Bordeaux)
	Oct 30	France 34	Australia 6	(Paris, Parc des Princes)

Players
Full-back: P E McLean (Queensland)
Threequarters: P G Batch (Queensland), L E Monaghan (NSW), J R Ryan (NSW), P J Crowe (NSW), G A Shaw (NSW), W A McKid (NSW), G G Shambrook (Queensland)
Half-backs: K J Wright (NSW), J C Hindmarsh (NSW), R G Hauser (Queensland), G O Grey (NSW)
Forwards: M E Loane (Queensland), A A Shaw (Queensland), G Cornelsen (NSW), G K Pearse (NSW), B R Battishall (NSW), R A Smith (NSW), D W Hillhouse (Queensland), G S Eisenhauer (NSW), K S Besomo (NSW), R Graham (NSW), S C Finnane (NS), J E C Meadows (Victoria), D A Dunworth (Queensland), C M Carberry (NSW), P A Horton (NSW), A M Gelling* (NSW)
Captain G A Shaw **Manager** J G Bain **Assistant Manager** R I Templeton

1981-82

Full record	Played 23	Won 16	Lost 6	Drawn 1	Points for 431	Against 219

International record Played 4 Won 1 Lost 3

International details	Nov 21	Ireland	12	Australia 16	(Dublin)
	Dec 5	Wales	18	Australia 13	(Cardiff)
	Dec 19	Scotland	24	Australia 15	(Murrayfield)
	Jan 2	England	15	Australia 11	(Twickenham)

Players
Full-backs: R G Gould (Queensland), G J Ella (NSW)
Threequarters: B J Moon (Queensland), M C Martin (NSW), P C Grigg (Queensland), G A Ella (NSW), A G Slack (Queensland), M D O'Connor (Queensland), M H Cox (NSW), M J Hawker (NSW)
Half-backs: P E McLean (Queensland), M G Ella (NSW), J N B Hipwell (NSW), A J Parker (Queensland), P A Cox* (NSW)
Forwards: M E Loane (Queensland), D Hall (Queensland), A A Shaw (Queensland), C Roche (Queensland), S P Poidevin (NSW), G Cornelsen (NSW), P W Lucas (NSW), S A Williams (NSW), M J Mathers (NSW), P W McLean (Queensland), S J Pilecki (Queensland), J E C Meadows (Victoria), A M D'Arcy (Queensland), D J Curran (NSW), B P Malouf (NSW), C M Carberry (Queensland), L R Walker* (NSW)
Captain A A Shaw **Manager** Sir Nicholas Shehadie, OBE
Assistant Manager R I Templeton

1983 (to France only, except for two matches in Italy)

Full record	Played 11	Won 6	Lost 3	Drawn 2	Points for 190	Against 157
in Italy	Played 2	Won 2	Lost 0	Drawn 0	Points for 55	Against 7
in France	Played 9	Won 4	Lost 3	Drawn 2	Points for 135	Against 150

International record Played 3 Won 1 Lost 1 Drawn 1

International details	Oct 22	Italy	7	Australia 29	(Rovigo)
	Nov 13	France	15	Australia 15	(Clermont-Ferrand)
	Nov 19	France	15	Australia 6	(Parc des Princes)

Players
Full-backs: G J Ella (NSW), R G Gould (Queensland)
Threequarters: D I Campese (ACT), R G Hanley (Queensland), B J Moon (Queensland), G A Ella (NSW), M J Hawker (NSW), A G Slack (Queensland)
Half-backs: M G Ella (NSW), A J Parker (Queensland), D Vaughan (NSW), M Lynagh (Queensland), T A Lane* (Queensland)
Forwards: J E Coolican (NSW), O B Hall (NSW), M A Harding (NSW), A J McIntyre (Queensland), T A Lawton (Queensland), M I McBain (Queensland), S A G Cutler (NSW), D W Hillhouse (Queensland), N C Holt (Queensland), S A Williams (NSW), J S Miller (Queensland), S P Poidevin (NSW), C Roche (Queensland), D Hall (Queensland), S N Tuynman (NSW), R Crerar* (NSW)
Captain M G Ella **Manager** Dr C R Wilson **Assistant Manager** R Dwyer

AUSTRALIA TO SOUTH AFRICA

1933

Full record	Played 23 Won 12 Lost 10 Drawn 1 Points for 299 Against 195			
International record	Played 5 Won 2 Lost 3			
International details	Jul 8	South Africa 17	Australia 3	(Cape Town)
	Jul 22	South Africa 6	Australia 21	(Durban)
	Aug 12	South Africa 12	Australia 3	(Johannesburg)
	Aug 26	South Africa 11	Australia 0	(Port Elizabeth)
	Sep 2	South Africa 4	Australia 15	(Bloemfontein)

Players
Full-backs: Dr A W Ross (NSW), F G McPhillips (NSW)
Threequarters: W J Warlow (Queensland), B A Grace (NSW), A D McLean (Queensland), J Kelaher (NSW), J B Young (NSW), Dr G S Sturtridge (Victoria), D L Cowper (Victoria), J C Steggall (Queensland)
Half-backs: R R Biilmann (NSW), C N Campbell (NSW), S J Malcolm (NSW), W G Bennett (Queensland)
Forwards: O L Bridle (Victoria), J B T Doneley (Queensland), G M Cooke (Queensland), W A Mackney (NSW), W Ritter (Queensland), W G S White (Queensland), A J Hodgson (NSW), E Love (NSW), J G Clark (Queensland), G Bland (NSW), R B Loudon (NSW), M C White (Queensland), M F Morton (NSW), W H Cerutti (NSW), E T Bonis (Queensland)
Captain A W Ross **Manager** Dr W F Mathews

1953

Full record	Played 27 Won 16 Lost 10 Drawn 1 Points for 450 Against 413			
International record	Played 4 Won 1 Lost 3			
International details	Aug 22	South Africa 25	Australia 3	(Johannesburg)
	Sep 5	South Africa 14	Australia 18	(Cape Town)
	Sep 19	South Africa 18	Australia 8	(Durban)
	Sep 26	South Africa 22	Australia 9	(Port Elizabeth)

Players
Full-backs: T Sweeney (Queensland), R Colbert (NSW)
Threequarters: E Stapleton (NSW), G Jones (Queensland), S W White (NSW), G Horsley (Queensland), H S Barker (NSW), J Blomley (NSW), H J Solomon (NSW), J A Phipps (NSW)
Half-backs: S W Brown (NSW), M Tate (NSW), C T Burke (NSW), J Bosler (NSW)
Forwards: N Shehadie (NSW), E Morey (NSW), A S Cameron (NSW), A R Miller (NSW), C F Forbes (Queensland), R A L Davidson (NSW), J C Carroll (NSW), F M Elliott (NSW), J J Walsh (NSW), J Bain (NSW), K A Cross (NSW), R Outterside (NSW), C Windon (NSW), D Brockhoff (NSW),

B B Johnson (NSW), N McL Hughes (NSW)
Captain H J Solomon **Manager** J W Breckenridge **Assistant Manager** A C Wallace

1961 (Short)

Full record Played 6 Won 3 Lost 2 Drawn 1 Points for 90 Against 80
International record Played 2 Lost 2
International details

Aug 5	South Africa 28	Australia 3	(Johannesburg)
Aug 12	South Africa 23	Australia 11	(Port Elizabeth)

Players
Full-back: J Lenehan (NSW)
Threequarters: M Cleary (NSW), F Magrath (NSW), R Phelps (NSW), B Ellwood (NSW), J Lisle (NSW)
Half-backs: J Dowse (NSW), H Roberts (Queensland), O Edwards (Queensland), K Catchpole (NSW)
Forwards: T Reid (NSW), E Heinrich (NSW), J O'Gorman (NSW), R Heming (NSW), J Thornett (NSW), R Thornett (NSW), G Macdougall (NSW), A Miller (NSW), J White (NSW), D McDeed (NSW), P Johnson (NSW)
Captain K Catchpole **Manager** B J Halvorsen

1963

Full record Played 24 Won 15 Lost 8 Drawn 1 Points for 303 Against 233
International record Played 4 Won 2 Lost 2
International details

Jul 13	South Africa 14	Australia 3	(Pretoria)
Aug 10	South Africa 5	Australia 9	(Cape Town)
Aug 24	South Africa 9	Australia 11	(Johannesburg)
Sep 7	South Africa 22	Australia 6	(Port Elizabeth)

Players
Full-backs: T Casey (NSW), P Ryan (NSW)
Threequarters: K Walsham (NSW), J Williams (NSW), J Boyce (NSW), J Wolfe (Queensland), R Marks (Queensland), I Moutray (NSW), P Jones (NSW), B Ellwood (NSW)
Half-backs: P Hawthorne (NSW), J Klem (NSW), K Catchpole (NSW), K McMullen (NSW)
Forwards: J Guerassimoff (Queensland), D O'Neill (Queensland), G Davis (NSW), D Shepherd (Victoria), E Heinrich (NSW), J O'Gorman (NSW), R Heming (NSW), J M Miller (NSW), P Crittle (NSW), J Thornett (NSW), J White (NSW), L Austin (NSW), J Freedman (NSW), B Bailey (NSW), P Johnson (NSW), M Jenkinson (NSW)
Captain J Thornett **Manager** R E M McLaughlin **Assistant Manager** A S Roper

1969

Full record Played 26 Won 15 Lost 11 Drawn 0 Points for 465 Against 353
International record Played 4 Lost 4
International details

Aug 2	South Africa 30	Australia 11	(Johannesburg)
Aug 16	South Africa 16	Australia 9	(Durban)
Sep 6	South Africa 11	Australia 3	(Cape Town)
Sep 20	South Africa 19	Australia 8	(Bloemfontein)

Players
Full-backs: A N McGill (NSW), B A Weir (NSW)
Threequarters: T R Forman (NSW), R P Batterham (NSW), J W Cole (NSW), P D Moore (Queensland), S O Knight (NSW), P V Smith (NSW), B D Honan (Queensland), G A Shaw (NSW)
Half-backs: J P Ballesty (NSW), R G Rosenblum (NSW), J N B Hipwell (NSW), M J Barry (Queensland)

Forwards: J R Roxburgh (NSW), J L Howard (NSW), R B Prosser (NSW), S S Sullivan (Queensland), B S Taafe (NSW), P Darveniza (NSW), S C Gregory (Queensland), A M Abrahams (NSW), N P Reilly (Queensland), O F Butler (NSW), G V Davis (NSW), M R Cocks (NSW), B McDonald (NSW), R J Kelleher (Queensland), H A Rose (NSW), A J Skinner (NSW), R Wood* (Queensland)

Captain G V Davis **Manager** C C Eastes **Assistant Manager** D M Connor

ENGLAND TO AUSTRALIA, NEW ZEALAND AND FIJI

1963 (New Zealand and Australia only)

Full record

in New Zealand	Played 5	Won 1	Lost 4	Drawn 0	Points for 45	Against 73
in Australia	Played 1	Won 0	Lost 1	Drawn 0	Points for 9	Against 18

International record

v New Zealand	Played 2	Lost 2
v Australia	Played 1	Lost 1

International details

May 25	New Zealand	21	England	11	(Auckland)
Jun 1	New Zealand	9	England	6	(Christchurch)
Jun 4	Australia	18	England	9	(Sydney)

Players

Full-back: R W Hosen (Northampton)

Threequarters: M S Phillips (Fylde), F D Sykes (Northampton), M P Weston (Durham City), J C Gibson (United Services), J M Ranson (Rosslyn Park), J M Dee (Hartlepool Rovers)

Half-backs: R F Read (Harlequins), J P Horrocks-Taylor (Leicester), T C Wintle (St Mary's Hospital), S J S Clarke (Cambridge U)

Forwards: P E Judd (Coventry), J E Highton (United Services), C R Jacobs (Northampton), H O Godwin (Coventry), J D Thorne (Bristol), J E Owen (Coventry), T A Pargetter (Coventry), A M Davis (Torquay Athletic), D P Rogers (Bedford), D G Perry (Bedford), B J Wightman (Coventry), V R Marriott (Harlequins)

Captain M P Weston **Manager** J T W Berry

Assistant Manager M R Steele-Bodger

1973 (Fiji and New Zealand only)

Full record

in Fiji	Played 1	Won 1	Lost 0	Drawn 0	Points for 13	Against 12
in New Zealand	Played 4	Won 1	Lost 3	Drawn 0	Points for 47	Against 60

International record

v New Zealand	Played 1	Won 1

International details Sep 15 New Zealand 10 England 16 (Auckland)

Players

Full-backs: P A Rossborough (Coventry), A M Jorden (Blackheath)

Threequarters: D J Duckham (Coventry), P M Knight (Bristol), P J Squires (Harrogate), J P A G Janion (Richmond), G W Evans (Coventry), P S Preece (Coventry)

Half-backs: A G B Old (Leicester), M J Cooper (Moseley), S J Smith (Sale), J G Webster (Moseley)

Forwards: M A Burton (Gloucester), C B Stevens (Penzance-Newlyn), F E Cotton (Loughborough Colls and Coventry), J V Pullin (Bristol), J White (Bristol), C W Ralston (Richmond), N O Martin (Bedford), R M Uttley (Gosforth), R M Wilkinson (Cambridge U and Bedford), P J Hendy (St Ives), A Neary (Broughton Park), J A Watkins (Gloucester), A G Ripley (Rosslyn Park)

Captain J V Pullin **Manager** D L Sanders **Assistant Manager** J Elders

1975 (Australia only)

Full record Played 8 Won 4 Lost 4 Drawn 0 Points for 217 Against 110
International record Played 2 Lost 2
International details May 24 Australia 16 England 9 (Sydney)
May 31 Australia 30 England 21 (Brisbane)

Players
Full-backs: P E Butler (Gloucester), A J Hignell (Cambridge U)
Threequarters: P J Squires (Harrogate), A J Morley (Bristol), D M Wyatt (Bedford), P S Preece (Coventry), K Smith (Roundhay), A W Maxwell (New Brighton), J P A G Janion* (Richmond)
Half-backs: W N Bennett (Bedford), A J Wordsworth (Cambridge U), A G B Old* (Middlesbrough), W B Ashton (Orrell), P Kingston (Gloucester), I N Orum* (Roundhay)
Forwards: A G Ripley (Rosslyn Park), D M Rollitt (Bristol), A Neary (Broughton Park), S R Callum (Upper Clapton), P J Dixon* (Gosforth), R M Uttley (Gosforth), W B Beaumont (Fylde), R M Wilkinson (Bedford), N D Mantell (Rosslyn Park), F E Cotton (Coventry), M A Burton (Gloucester), P J Blakeway (Gloucester), B G Nelmes* (Cardiff), J V Pullin (Bristol), J A G D Raphael (Northampton)
Captain A Neary **Manager** A O Lewis **Assistant Manager** J Burgess

ENGLAND TO SOUTH AFRICA

1972

Full record Played 7 Won 6 Lost 0 Drawn 1 Points for 166 Against 58
International record Played 1 Won 1
International details Jun 3 South Africa 9 England 18 (Johannesburg)

Players
Full-backs: S A Doble (Moseley), D F Whibley (Leicester)
Threequarters: P M Knight (Bristol), A A Richards (Fylde), J P A G Janion (Bedford), A J Morley (Bristol), J S Spencer (Headingley), P S Preece (Coventry)
Half-backs: A G B Old (Middlesbrough), T Palmer (Gloucester), L E Weston (West of Scotland), J G Webster (Moseley), S J Smith* (Loughborough Colls)
Forwards: M A Burton (Gloucester), F E Cotton (Loughborough Colls), C B Stevens (Harlequins and Penzance-Newlyn), J V Pullin (Bristol), A V Boddy (Metropolitan Police), P J Larter (RAF and Northampton), C W Ralston (Richmond), D E J Watt (Bristol), T A Cowell (Rugby), A Neary (Broughton Park), J A Watkins (Gloucester), J Barton (Coventry), A G Ripley (Rosslyn Park)
Captain J V Pullin **Manager** A O Lewis **Assistant Manager** J Elders

SCOTLAND TO SOUTH AFRICA

1960

Full record Played 3 Won 2 Lost 1 Drawn 0 Points for 61 Against 45
International record Played 1 Lost 1
International details May 1 South Africa 18 Scotland 10 (Port Elizabeth)

Players
Full-back: R W T Chisholm (Melrose)
Threequarters: A R Smith (Cambridge U, Edinburgh Wands), R H Thomson (London Scottish), R C Cowan (Selkirk), G D Stevenson (Hawick), T McClung (Edinburgh Acads), P J Burnet (London Scottish)
Half-backs: G H Waddell (London Scottish), R B Shillinglaw (Gala and Army), A J Hastie (Melrose)

Forwards: H F McLeod (Hawick), J B Neill (Edinburgh Acads), D M D Rollo (Howe of Fife), N S Bruce (Blackheath), T O Grant (Hawick), J W Y Kemp (Glasgow HSFP), F H ten Bos (Oxford U, London Scottish), W Hart (Melrose), D B Edwards (Heriot's FP), R M Tollervey (Heriot's FP), C E B Stewart (Kelso)
Captain G H Waddell **Managers** R W Shaw and C W Drummond

SCOTLAND TO AUSTRALIA

1970

Full record Played 6 Won 3 Lost 3 Drawn 0 Points for 109 Against 94
International record Played 1 Lost 1
International details Jun 6 Australia 23 Scotland 3 (Sydney)
Players
Full-back: I S G Smith (London Scottish)
Threequarters: M A Smith (London Scottish), J N M Frame (Gala), J W C Turner (Gala), C W Rea (West of Scotland), A G Biggar (London Scottish), A D Gill (Gala)
Half-backs: I Robertson (Watsonians), C M Telfer (Hawick), D S Paterson (Gala), G C Connell (London Scottish)
Forwards: F A L Laidlaw (Melrose), D T Deans (Hawick), N Suddon (Hawick), J McLauchlan (Jordanhill Coll), A B Carmichael (West of Scotland), P K Stagg (Sale), G L Brown (West of Scotland), P C Brown (Gala), T G Elliott (Langholm), W Lauder (Neath), G K Oliver (Gala), R J Arneil (Leicester)
Captain F A L Laidlaw **Managers** H S P Monro and G Burrell

1982

Full record Played 9 Won 6 Lost 3 Drawn 0 Points for 220 Against 113
International record Played 2 Won 1 Lost 1
International details Jul 4 Australia 7 Scotland 12 (Brisbane)
Jul 10 Australia 33 Scotland 9 (Sydney)
Players
Full-backs: P W Dods (Gala), A R Irvine (Heriot's FP)
Threequarters: G R T Baird (Kelso), J A Pollock (Gosforth), R J Gordon (London Scottish), D I Johnston (Watsonians), K W Robertson (Melrose), C J Williamson (West of Scotland)
Half-backs: B M Gossman (West of Scotland), J Y Rutherford (Selkirk), I G Hunter (Selkirk), R J Laidlaw (Jedforest)
Forwards: J Aitken (Gala), G M McGuinness (West of Scotland), I G Milne (Heriot's FP), N A Rowan (Boroughmuir), R F Cunningham (Bath), C T Deans (Hawick), W Cuthbertson (Kilmarnock), I D McKie (Sale), A J Tomes (Hawick), F Calder (Stewart's Melville FP), J H Calder (Stewart's Melville FP), I A M Paxton (Selkirk), D B White (Gala), R E Paxton (Kelso), John Calder* (Stewart's Melville FP)
Captain A R Irvine **Manager** I A A MacGregor **Assistant Manager** J W Telfer

SCOTLAND TO NEW ZEALAND

1975

Full record Played 7 Won 4 Lost 3 Drawn 0 Points for 157 Against 104
International record Played 1 Lost 1
International details Jun 14 New Zealand 24 Scotland 0 (Auckland)
Players
Full-backs: A R Irvine (Heriot's FP), B H Hay (Boroughmuir)
Threequarters: W C C Steele (RAF and London Scottish), L G Dick (Jordanhill),

J N M Frame (Gala), D L Bell (Watsonians), G A Birkett (Harlequins), J M Renwick (Hawick)
Half-backs: I R McGeechan (Headingley), C M Telfer (Hawick), A J M Lawson (London Scottish), D W Morgan (Stewart's Melville FP)
Forwards: D G Leslie (Dundee HSFP), G Y Mackie (Highland), W S Watson (Boroughmuir), W Lauder (Neath), M A Biggar (London Scottish), A J Tomes (Hawick), I A Barnes (Hawick), A F McHarg (London Scottish), N A K Pender (Hawick), A B Carmichael (West of Scotland), J McLauchlan (Jordanhill), D F Madsen (Gosforth), C D Fisher (Waterloo)
Captain J McLauchlan **Manager** G Burrell **Assistant Manager** W Dickinson

1981

Full record	Played 8	Won 5	Lost 3	Drawn 0	Points for 189	Against 125
International record	Played 2	Lost 2				
International details	Jun 13	New Zealand 11	Scotland 4	(Dunedin)		
	Jun 20	New Zealand 40	Scotland 15	(Auckland)		

Players
Full-backs: A R Irvine (Heriot's FP), P W Dods (Gala)
Threequarters: S Munro (Ayr), B H Hay (Boroughmuir), G R T Baird (Kelso), R W Breakey (Gosforth), A G Cranston (Hawick), J M Renwick (Hawick)
Half-backs: J Y Rutherford (Selkirk), R Wilson (London Scottish), R J Laidlaw (Jedforest), I G Hunter (Selkirk), A J M Lawson* (London Scottish, Heriot's FP)
Forwards: D B White (Gala), I A M Paxton (Selkirk), P M Lillington* (Durham U), J H Calder (Stewart's Melville FP), G Dickson (Gala), D G Leslie (Gala), W Cuthbertson (Kilmarnock), T J Smith (Gala), A J Tomes (Hawick), J Aitken (Gala), G M McGuinness (West of Scotland), I G Milne (Heriot's FP), N A Rowan (Boroughmuir), C T Deans (Hawick), K G Lawrie (Gala)
Captain A R Irvine **Manager** G K Smith **Assistant Manager** J W Telfer

IRELAND TO SOUTH AFRICA

1961

Full record	Played 4	Won 3	Lost 1	Drawn 0	Points for 59	Against 36
International record	Played 1	Lost 1				
International details	May 13	South Africa 24	Ireland 8	(Cape Town)		

Players
Full-back: T J Kiernan (UC Cork, Cork Constitution)
Threequarters: A J F O'Reilly (Old Belvedere, Leicester), N H Brophy (UC Dublin), J C Walsh (UC Cork, Sunday's Well), K J Houston (London Irish, Oxford U), W J Hewitt (Instonians), J F Dooley (Galwegians)
Half-backs: W G Tormey (UC Dublin), D C Glass (Belfast Collegians), A A Mulligan (Cambridge U, London Irish), T J Cleary (Limerick)
Forwards: S Millar (Ballymena), B G M Wood (Garryowen), J N Thomas (Blackrock), A R Dawson (Wanderers), J S Dick (Queen's U, Belfast), W A Mulcahy (UC Dublin, Bective Rangers), M G Culliton (Wanderers), C J Dick (Ballymena), N A A Murphy (Cork Constitution), D Scott (Malone), J R Kavanagh (UC Dublin, Wanderers), T McGrath (Garryowen)
Captain A R Dawson **Manager** N F Murphy **Assistant Manager** T A O'Reilly

1981

Full record	Played 7	Won 3	Lost 4	Drawn 0	Points for 207	Against 90
International record	Played 2	Lost 2				

International details	May 30	South Africa 23	Ireland 15	(Cape Town)
	Jun 6	South Africa 12	Ireland 10	(Durban)

Players

Full-backs: J J Murphy (Greystones), K A O'Brien (Broughton Park)
Threequarters: K D Crossan (Instonians), T J Kennedy (St Mary's Coll), M J Kiernan (Dolphin), A C McLennan (Wanderers), J A Hewitt (North of Ireland FC), A W Irwin (Queen's U, Belfast), D G Irwin (Queen's U, Belfast)
Half-backs: S O Campbell (Old Belvedere), P M Dean (St Mary's Coll), M A M Quinn* (Lansdowne), J C Robbie (Greystones), R J M McGrath (Wanderers), J B O'Connor* (Palmerston)
Forwards: W P Duggan (Blackrock Coll), R K Kearney (Wanderers), J F Slattery (Blackrock Coll), J B O'Driscoll (London Irish), A F O'Leary (Cork Constitution), B O Foley (Shannon), J J Holland (Wanderers), G H Wallace (Old Wesley), D C Fitzgerald (Dublin U), G A J McLoughlin (Shannon), P A Orr (Old Wesley), J L Cantrell (Blackrock Coll), H T Harbison (UC Dublin)
Captain J F Slattery **Manager** P F Madigan **Assistant Manager** T J Kiernan

IRELAND TO AUSTRALIA

1967

Full record	Played 6	Won 4	Lost 2	Drawn 0	Points for 119	Against 80
International record	Played 1	Won 1				
International details	May 13	Australia 5	Ireland 11	(Sydney)		

Players

Full-backs: T J Kiernan (Cork Constitution)
Threequarters: A T A Duggan (Lansdowne), F P K Bresnihan (UC Dublin), J C Walsh (UC Cork), N H Brophy (UC Dublin), P J McGrath (UC Cork), J B Murray (UC Dublin)
Half-backs: C M H Gibson (NIFC), B F Sherry (Terenure), L Hall (UC Cork)
Forwards: S A Hutton (Malone), K W Kennedy (London Irish), S MacHale (Lansdowne), P O'Callaghan (Dolphin), W J McBride (Ballymena), M G Molloy (UC Galway), K G Goodall (City of Derry), T A Moore (Highfield), M G Doyle (UC Dublin), L G Butler (Blackrock), J M Flynn (Wanderers), D J Hickie (St Mary's College)
Captain T J Kiernan **Manager** E O'D Davy **Assistant Manager** D McKibbin

1979

Full record	Played 8	Won 7	Lost 1	Drawn 0	Points for 184	Against 75
International record	Played 2	Won 2				
International details	Jun 3	Australia 12	Ireland 27	(Brisbane)		
	Jun 16	Australia 3	Ireland 9	(Sydney)		

Players

Full-backs: F N G Ennis (Wanderers), R C O'Donnell (St Mary's Coll)
Threequarters: C M H Gibson (North of Ireland FC), T J Kennedy (St Mary's Coll), A C McLennan (Wanderers), P A J Andreucetti (St Mary's Coll), D G Irwin (Queen's U, Belfast), P P McNaughton (Greystones)
Half-backs: S O Campbell (Old Belvedere), A J P Ward (Garryowen), J J Moloney (St Mary's Coll), C S Patterson (Instonians)
Forwards: W P Duggan (Blackrock Coll), C D Cantillon (Cork Constitution), A J McLean (Ballymena), J B O'Driscoll (London Irish), J F Slattery (Blackrock Coll), B O Foley (Shannon), M I Keane (Lansdowne), H W Steele (Ballymena), E M J Byrne (Blackrock Coll), M P Fitzpatrick* (Wanderers), G A J McLoughlin (Shannon), P A Orr (Old Wesley), C F Fitzgerald (St Mary's Coll), P C Whelan (Garryowen)
Captain J F Slattery **Manager** J F Coffey **Assistant Manager** N A A Murphy

IRELAND TO NEW ZEALAND AND FIJI

1976

Full record	Played 8	Won 5	Lost 3	Drawn 0	Points for 96	Against 68
in New Zealand	Played 7	Won 4	Lost 3	Drawn 0	Points for 88	Against 68
in Fiji	Played 1	Won 1	Lost 0	Drawn 0	Points for 8	Against 0
International record	Played 1	Lost 1				

International details Jun 5 New Zealand 11 Ireland 3 (Wellington)

Players

Full-backs: A H Ensor (Wanderers), L A Moloney (Garryowen)
Threequarters: T O Grace (St Mary's Coll), A W McMaster (Ballymena), J A Brady (Wanderers), C M H Gibson (North of Ireland FC), J A McIlrath (Ballymena)
Half-backs: B J McGann (Cork Constitution), M A Quinn (Lansdowne), D M Canniffe (Lansdowne), J C Robbie (Dublin U), R J M McGrath* (Wanderers)
Forwards: W P Duggan (Blackrock Coll), H W Steele (Ballymena), S A McKinney (Dungannon), S M Deering (Garryowen), J C Davidson* (Dungannon), R F Hakin (CIYMS), M I Keane (Lansdowne), B O Foley (Shannon), E J O'Rafferty (Wanderers), T A O Feighery (St Mary's Coll), P O'Callaghan (Dolphin), P A Orr (Old Wesley), R J Clegg (Bangor), J L Cantrell (UC Dublin), P C Whelan (Garryowen)
Captain T O Grace **Manager** K J Quilligan **Assistant Manager** T W Meates

WALES TO SOUTH AFRICA

1964

Full record	Played 4	Won 2	Lost 2	Drawn 0	Points for 43	Against 58
International record	Played 1	Lost 1				

International details May 23 South Africa 24 Wales 3 (Durban)

Players

Full-backs: G T R Hodgson (Neath), H J Davies (London Welsh)
Threequarters: D I Bebb (Carmarthen TC, Swansea), S J Watkins (Newport), P M Rees (Newport), K Bradshaw (Bridgend), D K Jones (London Welsh, Cardiff), S J Dawes (London Welsh)
Half-backs: D Watkins (Newport), M Young (Bridgend), D C T Rowlands (Pontypool), A R Lewis (Abertillery)
Forwards: L J Cunningham (Aberavon), D Williams (Ebbw Vale), R G Waldron (Neath), N R Gale (Llanelli), J Isaacs (Swansea), B E Thomas (Neath), B Price (Newport), J T Mantle (Loughborough Colls), D J Hayward (Cardiff), H J Morgan (Abertillery), G J Prothero (Bridgend), A E I Pask (Abertillery)
Captain D C T Rowlands **Manager** D J Phillips
Assistant Manager Alun G Thomas

WALES TO AUSTRALIA, NEW ZEALAND AND FIJI

1969

Full record						
in New Zealand	Played 5	Won 2	Lost 2	Drawn 1	Points for 62	Against 76
in Australia	Played 1	Won 1	Lost 0	Drawn 0	Points for 19	Against 16
in Fiji	Played 1	Won 1	Lost 0	Drawn 0	Points for 31	Against 11
International record						
v New Zealand	Played 2	Lost 2				
v Australia	Played 1	Won 1				

International details

v New Zealand	May 31	New Zealand 19	Wales 0	(Christchurch)
	Jun 14	New Zealand 33	Wales 12	(Auckland)
v Australia	Jun 21	Australia 16	Wales 19	(Sydney)

Players

Full-back: J P R Williams (London Welsh)
Threequarters: S J Watkins (Newport), A P Skirving (Newport), M C R Richards (Cardiff), S J Dawes (London Welsh), T G R Davies (Cardiff), K S Jarrett (Newport)
Half-backs: B John (Cardiff), P Bennett (Llanelli), G O Edwards (Cardiff), R Hopkins (Maesteg)
Forwards: T M Davies (London Welsh), D Hughes (Newbridge), W D Morris (Neath), J Taylor (London Welsh), B Price (Newport), B E Thomas (Neath), W D Thomas (Llanelli), D B Llewelyn (Newport), D J Lloyd (Bridgend), D Williams (Ebbw Vale), N R Gale (Llanelli), J Young (Harrogate), V C Perrins* (Newport)
Captain B Price **Manager** H C Rogers **Assistant Manager** D C T Rowlands

1978 (Australia only)

Full record Played 9 Won 5 Lost 4 Drawn 0 Points for 227 Against 106
International record Played 2 Lost 2
International details

Jun 11	Australia 18	Wales 8	(Brisbane)
Jun 17	Australia 19	Wales 17	(Sydney)

Players

Full-back: J P R Williams (Bridgend)
Threequarters: T G R Davies (Cardiff), G L Evans (Newport), J J Williams (Llanelli), P C T Daniels (Cardiff), A J Donovan (Swansea), S P Fenwick (Bridgend), R W R Gravell (Llanelli)
Half-backs: W G Davies (Cardiff), D S Richards (Swansea), T D Holmes (Cardiff), D B Williams (Newport)
Forwards: C Davis (Newbridge), D L Quinnell (Llanelli), J Squire (Newport), T J Cobner (Pontypool), S M Lane (Cardiff), B G Clegg (Swansea), A J Martin (Aberavon), G A D Wheel (Swansea), A G Faulkner (Pontypool), G Price (Pontypool), S J Richardson (Aberavon), M J Watkins (Cardiff), R W Windsor (Pontypool)
Captain T J Cobner **Manager** D C T Rowlands **Assistant Manager** S J Dawes

FRANCE TO SOUTH AFRICA

1958

Full record Played 10 Won 5 Lost 3 Drawn 2 Points for 137 Against 124
International record Played 2 Won 1 Drawn 1
International details

Jul 26	South Africa 3	France 3	(Cape Town)
Aug 16	South Africa 5	France 9	(Johannesburg)

Players

Full-backs: M Vannier (Racing Club de France), P Lacaze (FC Lourdais)
Threequarters: J Dupuy (S Tarbais), H Rancoule (FC Lourdais), J Lepatey (SC Mazamet), L Rogé (AS Béziers), A Marquesuzaa (Racing Club de France), G Stener (Paris U), L Casaux (S Tarbais)
Half-backs: R Martine (FC Lourdais), A Haget (Paris UC), P Danos (AS Béziers), P Lacroix (S Montois)
Forwards: J Barthe (FC Lourdais), M Celaya (Biarritz), J Carrère (RC Toulonnais), L Mias (SC Mazamet), B Mommejat (S Cadurcien), R Baulon (A Bayonnais), F Moncla (Racing Club de France), L Echavé (SU Agen), A Roques (S Cadurcien), R Barrière (AS Béziers), A Quaglio (SC Mazamet), R Vigier (AS Montferrand),

A Fremaux (Paris U), J de Gregorio (FC Grenoble)
Captain M Celaya **Manager** S Saulnier **Assistant Manager** M Laurent

1964

Full record Played 6 Won 5 Lost 1 Drawn 0 Points for 117 Against 55
International record Played 1 Won 1
International details Jul 25 South Africa 6 France 8 (Springs)
Players
Full-back: P Dedieu (AS Béziers)
Threequarters: J Gachassin (FC Lourdais), C Darrouy (S Montois), M Arnaudet (FC Lourdais), R Halçaren (FC Lourdais), J Dupuy (S Tarbais), J Piqué (S Paloise)
Half-backs: P Albaladejo (US Dacquoise), J Capdouze (S Paloise), J-C Hiquet (SU Agen), J-C Lasserre (US Dax), C Laborde (RCF)
Forwards: W Spanghero (RC Narbonne), M Crauste (FC Lourdais), M Lira (La Voulte S), M Sitjar (SU Agen), J-J Rupert (US Tyrosse), B Dauga (S Montois), E Cester (Toulouse OEC), A Herrero (RC Toulonnais), A Gruarin (RC Toulonnais), J C Berejnoi (SC Tulle), M Etcheverry (S Paloise), Y Menthiller (US Romans), J M Cabanier (US Montauban)
Captain M Crauste **Manager** S Saulnier **Assistant Manager** J Prat

1967

Full record Played 13 Won 8 Lost 4 Drawn 1 Points for 209 Against 161
International record Played 4 Won 1 Lost 2 Drawn 1
International details

Jul 15	South Africa 26	France 3	(Durban)
Jul 22	South Africa 16	France 3	(Bloemfontein)
Jul 29	South Africa 14	France 19	(Johannesburg)
Aug 12	South Africa 6	France 6	(Cape Town)

Players
Full-backs: C Lacaze (SC Angoulême), P Villepreux (S Toulousain), J Crampagne (CA Beglais)
Threequarters: C Darrouy (S Montois), J Londios (US Montauban), B Duprat (A Bayonnais), J-P Lux (US Tyrosse), C Dourthe (US Dax), J Trillo (CA Beglais), J Saby (SC Graulhet), J-P Mir (FC Lourdais)
Half-backs: G Camberabero (La Voulte S), J-L Dehez (SU Agen), J-C Roques (CA Brive), M Puget (CA Brive), G Sutra (RC Narbonne)
Forwards: A Abadie (SC Graulhet), J-M Esponda (Racing Club de France), M Lasserre (SU Agen), B Cardebat (US Montauban), J-M Cabanier (US Montauban), J-C Malbet (SU Agen), B Dauga (S Montois), W Spanghero (RC Narbonne). J Fort (SU Agen), A Plantefol (Racing Club de France), C Carrère (RC Toulonnais), M Sitjar (SU Agen), A Quilis (RC Narbonne), G Viard (RC Narbonne)
Captain C Darrouy **Manager** M Laurent **Assistant Manager** A Garrigues

1971

Full record Played 9 Won 7 Lost 1 Drawn 1 Points for 228 Against 92
International record Played 2 Lost 1 Drawn 1
International details

Jun 12	South Africa 22	France 9	(Bloemfontein)
Jun 19	South Africa 8	France 8	(Durban)

Players
Full-back: P Villepreux (S Toulousain)
Threequarters: R Bertranne (S Bagnerais), R Bourgarel (S Toulousain), J Cantoni (AS Béziers), C Dourthe (US Dax), A Marot (CA Brive), J Maso (RC Narbonne), J Sillières (S Tarbais), J Trillo (CA Beglais)
Half-backs: M Barrau (S Beaumontois), J-L Berot (S Toulousain),

G Pardiès* (SU Agen), M Pebeyre (AS Montferrand)
Forwards: J-L Azarète (St Jean-de-Luz Ol), J-P Bastiat (US Dax), P Biemouret (SU Agen), C Carrère (RC Toulonnais), B Dauga (S Montois), A Estève (AS Béziers), M Etcheverry (S Paloise), J Iraçabal (A Bayonnais), M Lasserre (SU Agen), J le Droff (FC Auch), J-C Skrela (S Toulousain), C Spanghero (RC Narbonne), W Spanghero (RC Narbonne), C Swierczinski (CA Beglais), M Yachvili (CA Brive)
Captain C Carrère **Manager** E Pebeyre
Assistant Managers F Cazenave and M Celaya

1975

Full record Played 11 Won 6 Lost 4 Drawn 1 Points for 282 Against 190
International record Played 2 Lost 2
International details Jun 21 South Africa 38 France 25 (Bloemfontein)
Jun 28 South Africa 33 France 18 (Pretoria)
Players
Full-backs: J M Aguirre (S Bagnerais), M Droitecourt (AS Montferrand)
Threequarters: J-C Amade (Biarritz Ol), J-L Averous (La Voulte Sp), D Harize (S Cahors), M Dupey (FC Auch), C Badin (CA Brive), R Bertranne (S Bagnerais), J-M Etchenique (Biarritz Ol), F Sangalli (RC Narbonne)
Half-backs: J-P Romeu (AS Montferrand), J P Pesteil (AS Béziers), R Astre (AS Béziers), J Fouroux (La Voulte Sp)
Forwards: Y Brunet (USA Perpignan), J Costantino (AS Montferrand), D Revallier (UA Gaillac), R Paparemborde (S Paloise), B Forestier (CA Beglais), G Cholley (Castres Ol), J-P Decrae (Racing Club de France), F Haget (SU Agen), A Guilbert (RC Toulon), M Julian (Castres Ol), M Yachvili (CA Brive), J-C Skréla (S Toulousain), P Peron (Racing Club de France), S Lassoujade (SU Agen), G Rousset (AS Béziers), J-L Joinel (CA Brive), M Palmie* (AS Béziers)
Captains (joint) R Astre and J Fouroux **Manager** M Batigne
Assistant Managers M Celaya and F Cazenave

1980

Full record Played 4 Won 3 Lost 1 Drawn 0 Points for 90 Against 95
International record Played 1 Lost 1
International details Nov 8 South Africa 37 France 15 (Pretoria)
Players
Full-backs: S Gabernet (Toulouse), S Blanco (Biarritz)
Threequarters: D Bustaffa (Carcassonne), C Martinez (Béziers), J-C Castagnet (Pau), L Pardo (Bayonne), R Bertranne (Bagnères), P Mesny (Grenoble)
Half-backs: B Viviès (Agen), P Fort (Béziers), J Gallion (Toulon), J-P Elissalde (La Rochelle)
Forwards: J-L Joinel (Brive), M Carpentier (Lourdes), T Sinico (Valence), J-P Rives (Toulouse), P Lacans (Béziers), J-P Wolff (Béziers), A Maleig (Tarbes), J-P Fauvel (SC de Tulle), D Dubroca (Agen), R Paparemborde (Pau), P Dospital (Bayonne), B Herrero (Nice), P Dintrans (Tarbes)
Captain J-P Rives **Manager** Y Noe **Assistant Managers** M Celaya, J Piqué

FRANCE TO AUSTRALIA AND NEW ZEALAND

1961

Full record

in New Zealand	Played 13	Won 6	Lost 7	Drawn 0	Points for 150	Against 149
in Australia	Played 2	Won 2	Lost 0	Drawn 0	Points for 30	Against 20

International record
v New Zealand Played 3 Lost 3
v Australia Played 1 Won 1

International details

v New Zealand	Jul 22	New Zealand	13	France	6	(Auckland)
	Aug 5	New Zealand	5	France	3	(Wellington)
	Aug 19	New Zealand	32	France	3	(Christchurch)
v Australia	Aug 26	Australia	8	France	15	(Sydney)

Players
Full-backs: M Vannier (RC Chalon), J Meynard (US Cognac)
Threequarters: S Plantey (Racing Club de France), G Boniface (S Montois), H Rancoule (RC Toulon), J Dupuy (S Tarbais), G Calvo (FC Lourdais), J Piqué (S Paloise), J Bouquet (CS Vienne), A Boniface (S Montois)
Half-backs: C Lacaze (FC Lourdais), G Camberabero (La Voulte S), P Albaladejo (US Dacquoise), P Lacroix (SU Agen), L Camberabero (La Voulte S), J Serin (SC Mazamet)
Forwards: M Celaya (S Bordelais), S Meyer (CA Perigueux), R Lefèvre (CA Brive), M Crauste (FC Lourdais), F Moncla (S Paloise), C Vidal (SC Mazamet), M Cassiede (US Dax), J P Saux (S Paloise), A Domenech (CA Brive), A Bianco (FC Auch), G Bouguyon (FC Grenoble) P Cazals (S Montois), J Laudouar (AS Soustons), J Rollet (A Bayonnais)
Captain F Moncla **Manager** M Laurent **Assistant Manager** G Basquet

1968

Full record

in New Zealand	Played 12	Won 8	Lost 4	Drawn 0	Points for 154	Against 120
in Australia	Played 2	Won 1	Lost 1	Drawn 0	Points for 41	Against 22

International record
v New Zealand Played 3 Lost 3
v Australia Played 1 Lost 1

International details

v New Zealand	Jul 13	New Zealand	12	France	9	(Christchurch)
	Jul 27	New Zealand	9	France	3	(Wellington)
	Aug 10	New Zealand	19	France	12	(Auckland)
v Australia	Aug 17	Australia	11	France	10	(Sydney)

Players
Full-backs: P Villepreux (S Toulousain), C Lacaze (Angoulême)
Threequarters: A Campaes (FC Lourdais), J M Bonal (S Toulousain), P Besson (CA Brive), A Piazza (US Montauban), J-P Lux (US Tyrosse), C Dourthe (US Dax), J Trillo (CA Beglais), J Maso (US Perpignan)
Half-backs: J Andrieu (SC Graulhet), C Boujet (Grenoble), J-L Berot (S Toulousain), M Puget (CA Brive)
Forwards: M Greffe (Grenoble), W Spanghero (RC Narbonne), M Billiere (S Toulousain), J Salut (Toulouse, OEC), C Carrère (RC Toulonnais), B Dutin (Mont de Marsan), C Chenevay (Grenoble), B Dauga (Mont de Marsan), A Plantefol (SU Agen), E Cester (Toulouse OEC), J-M Esponda (US Perpignan), M Lasserre (SU Agen), J-C Noble (La Voulte S), J Iraçabal (A Bayonnais), M Yachvili (SC Tulle), J-P Baux (CA Lannemezan)
Captain C Carrère **Manager** J-C Bourrier **Assistant Manager** A Garrigues

1972 (Australia only)

Full record Played 9 Won 8 Lost 0 Drawn 1 Points for 254 Against 122
International record Played 2 Won 1 Drawn 1
International details

Jun 17	Australia	14	France	14	(Sydney)
Jun 25	Australia	15	France	16	(Brisbane)

Players
Full-backs: P Villepreux (S Toulousain), H Cabrol (AS Béziers)
Threequarters: B Duprat (A Bayonnais), J Cantoni (AS Béziers), G Lavagne (AS Béziers), J Trillo (CA Beglais), C Dourthe (US Dax), J-P Lux (US Dax), J Maso (RC Narbonne)
Half-backs: J-L Berot (S Toulousain), A Marot (CA Briviste), M Barrau (S Beaumontois) J Fouroux (La Voulte Sp)
Forwards: J-C Skrela (S Toulousain), P Biemouret (SU Agen), O Saisset (AS Béziers), W Spanghero (RC Narbonne), B Vinsonneau (US Dax), C Spanghero (RC Narbonne), J-P Bastiat (US Dax), A Estève (AS Béziers), J Iraçabal (A Bayonnais), J-L Azarète (St Jean de Luz), A Vaquerin (AS Béziers), J-C Rossignol (CA Briviste), A Lubrano (AS Béziers), R Bénésis (SU Agen)
Captain W Spanghero **Manager** R Dasse
Assistant Managers M Celaya and F Cazenave

1979 (New Zealand only, except one match in Fiji)

Full record	Played 9	Won 6	Lost 3	Drawn 0	Points for 168	Against 116
in New Zealand	Played 8	Won 5	Lost 3	Drawn 0	Points for 155	Against 112

International record (in NZ)
Played 2 Won 1 Lost 1

International details	Jul 7	New Zealand 23	France 9	(Christchurch)
	Jul 14	New Zealand 19	France 24	(Auckland)

Players
Full-backs: J-M Aguirre (Bagnères), S Blanco (Biarritz)
Threequarters: F Costes (Montferrand), J-L Averous (La Voulte), D Bustaffa (Carcassonne), D Codorniou (Narbonne), P Mesny* (Racing Club de France), M Duffranc (Tyrosse), L Pardo (Tarbes)
Half-backs: A Caussade (Lourdes), G Laporte (Graulhet), J Gallion (Toulon), Y Laffarge (Montferrand)
Forwards: Y Malquier (Narbonne), C Beguerie (Agen), J-L Joinel (Brive), J-P Rives (Toulouse), F Haget (Biarritz), P Salas (Narbonne), J-F Marchal (Lourdes), A Maleig (Oloron), G Colomine (Narbonne), D Dubroca (Agen), R Paparemborde (Pau), P Dintrans (Tarbes), J-F Perche (Bourg)
Captain J-P Rives **Manager** Y Noé **Assistant Managers** F Cazenave, J Desclaux

1981 (Australia only)

Full record	Played 9	Won 6	Lost 3	Drawn 0	Points for 189	Against 112

International record Played 2 Lost 2

International details	Jul 5	Australia 17	France 15	(Brisbane)
	Jul 11	Australia 24	France 14	(Sydney)

Players
Full-backs: S Gabernet (Toulouse), S Blanco (Biarritz)
Threequarters: M Bruel (Pau), M Fabre (Béziers), J-L Averous (La Voulte), P Chadebech (Brive), D Codorniou (Narbonne), P Mesny (Grenoble), L Pardo (Bayonne)
Half-backs: B Viviès (Agen), M Sallefranque (Dax), P Berbizier (Lourdes), J-P Elissalde (La Rochelle), A Mournet* (Bagnères)
Forwards: M Carpentier (Lourdes), D Erbani (Agen), J-P Rives (Toulouse), P Lacans (Béziers), L Rodriguez (Mont-de-Marsan), O Derghali (Bagnères), D Revallier (Graulhet), A Lorieux (Grenoble), P Salas (Narbonne), R Paparemborde (Pau), M Crémaschi (Lourdes), J-P Wolff (Béziers), J-L Dupont (Agen), P Dintrans (Tarbes)
Captain J-P Rives **Manager** Y Noé **Assistant Managers** J Fouroux, J Piqué

CLUB SECTION

ENGLAND

Bath

Year of formation 1865
Grounds Recreation Ground, Bath Tel: Bath 25192
Horse Show Ground, London Road, Bath Tel: Bath 310548
Colours Blue, white, and black
Most capped player R A Gerrard (England) 14 caps
Captain 1983-84 R Spurrell
1st XV 1983-84 P39 W29 D0 L10 F850 A468
Review of the season Bath proudly advanced to their first John Player Cup triumph, beating Bristol, the holders and favourites, in a frantic final. Their back row – captain Roger Spurrell, rugged No 8 Paul Simpson and the talented John Hall – performed extremely well, both on the day and throughout the season. Bath played some excellent open rugby during the season, with John Horton and the explosive David Trick outstanding. Trick scored 17 tries and John Palmer 184 points.

Bedford

Year of formation 1886
Ground Goldington Road, Bedford Tel: Bedford 59160/54619
Colours Wide hoops in Oxford and Cambridge blues
Most capped player D P Rogers (England) 34 caps
Captain 1983-84 I G Peck
1st XV 1983-84 P42 W17 D0 L25 F549 A797
Review of the season Bedford conceded a record number of tries (115) and points, overtaking the 740 scored against them during 1975-76. Their eight successive defeats in January and February were the longest losing sequence in any season but, nevertheless, an air of optimism for the Centenary season in 1986-87 pervaded the club under the influence of Ian Peck, a dedicated captain. Leicester (twice) and Bridgend topped 60 points against Bedford, whose consolation was wins over Swansea, Neath, Gosforth and Gloucester, together with a last-minute defeat at Pontypool (27-25). Simon Smith scored 223 points, despite being restricted to 26 appearances by a knee injury. George Philip and Kevin Canning, the wings, each scored seven tries.

Birkenhead Park

Year of formation 1871
Ground Upper Park, Park Road North, Birkenhead, Merseyside Tel: 051 652 4646
Colours Red, white and navy blue hoops
Most capped player J R Paterson (Scotland) 21 caps
Captain 1983-84 K McGovern
1st XV 1983-84 P43 W21 D1 L21 F664 A778
Review of the season This was a frustrating season in that the club showed an overall improvement and did enough to have challenged for promotion to the northern merit table, had it been an average year. Unfortunately for Park, 1983-84 was a season in which a handful of qualifiers fared better than in the past and, as consequence, they finished out of contention, in fifth place despite four wins. Sale and Orrell were among their scalps, along with London Scottish and Wasps. They lost skipper Kevin McGovern during the season and Clive Plummer took over the task of leading the side. Fly-half Phil Dobbing was the club's leading scorer with 219 points to his credit and wing Peter Kolokotroni topped the try scoring with 13.

Birmingham

Year of formation 1911
Ground Forshaw Heath Lane, Earlswood, Solihull, W Midlands B94 5LH
Tel: Wythall (0564) 822955
Colours Red jerseys, white shorts, red, black and white stockings
Captain 1983-84 D L Read
1st XV 1983-84 P35 W9 D1 L25 F366 A764
Review of the season Birmingham had young and talented backs but lacked forward strength, despite the influence of John Griffiths, a former Moseley prop who made most appearances (34) and captained the side in the long-term absence of David Read through knee ligament trouble and a dislocated ankle. The team was restricted, partly through injuries, to nine wins, which included two over Rugby and one at Penarth. Hooker Ian Bletcher, outside half Martin Smith and wing Peter Turnbull showed skill and leading scorers were wing Simon Furze (10 tries), Smith (8 tries) and Fraser Hemming-Allen, whose 81 points in 13 games included 21 in the 25-3 win over Birkenhead Park.

Blackheath

Year of formation 1858
Ground Rectory Field, Blackheath, London SE3 Tel: 01-858 1578/3677
Colours Red and black hoops
Most capped player C N Lowe (England) 25 caps
Captain 1983-84 C Kibble
1st XV 1983-84 P41 W20 D2 L19 F852 A468
Review of the season Despite a period of improvement for Blackheath at the end of the season, they finished with a record somewhat inferior to that of the previous season. They could play notably well, as they showed when beating Leicester at home with some ease, but they lost heavily to Bath in the John Player Cup. Nick Collyer scored 119 points. The club, as usual, had an excellent run in the late-season sevens tournaments.

Bradford and Bingley

Year of formation 1982 (on amalgamation of Bradford and Bingley)
Ground Wagon Lane, Bingley, W Yorks Tel: Bingley (0274 56) 0468
Colours Red, amber and black hoops, dark blue shorts, black stockings with red and amber tops
Most capped player E Myers (England) 18 caps (while playing for Bradford)
Captain 1983-84 R Hood
1st XV 1983-84 P42 W22 D2 L18 F527 A573
Review of the season It was a period of consolidation for the club, in its second season following the merger between Bradford and Bingley. They were fortunate in having flanker Robert Hood to lead them and the club started the season very well, fading only after a fairly heavy defeat at the hands of Wakefield. If they had a bogey team it must have been Wakefield, who also knocked them out of the Yorkshire Cup in the early stages. There were county honours for second row pair Sid Burnhope and Paul Wood who both played for Yorkshire 'B' in the annual tussle with Lancashire 'B'. Centre Duncan Barr, a former Oxford University player, also had a good season and there were some good performances from the enigmatic Nick Cummins at scrum-half.

Bristol

Year of formation 1888
Ground Memorial Ground, Filton Avenue, Horfield, Bristol BS7 0AG
Tel: Bristol 48360
Colours Blue and white

Most capped player J V Pullin (England) 42 caps
Captain 1983-84 M J Rafter
1st XV 1983-84 P49 W32 D3 L14 F1,209 A696
Review of the season Bristol scored 1,209 points, a club record. Alan Morley passed the world record number of tries and continued to score at a prodigious rate. Bristol played some superb rugby, fielded one of the outstanding players of the season in fly-half Stuart Barnes, and made a large contribution to the Gloucestershire county team. Yet Bristol failed to cap it all – they lost narrowly to Bath in the John Player Cup final. Barnes (218) was the leading scorer and Morley (42) scored most tries.

Broughton Park

Year of formation 1882
Ground Chelsfield Grove, Chorlton, Manchester 21 Tel: 061-881 2481
Colours Black and white hooped jerseys, black shorts
Most capped player A Neary (England) 43 caps
Captain 1983-84 J Wilde
1st XV 1983-84 P37 W25 D2 L10 F738 A444
Review of the season It was an extremely good season for Broughton Park under Jimmy Wilde's leadership. The club recovered confidence after dropping out of the northern merit table the previous season and it was perhaps significant that they beat northern champions, West Hartlepool, to ensure a speedy return, finishing runners-up to Morley in the qualifying table. In keeping with tradition they had a solid pack but this time they also displayed rare flair and adventure behind the scrum. Apart from the regular sorties of experienced full-back Kevin O'Brien, the players who caught the eye were wing Steve Brown and centres Lindsay Renwick and Chris Morgan. The club's former Lancashire hooker, Keith Pacey, retired at the end of the season.

Cambridge University

Year of formation 1872
Ground Grange Road, Cambridge Tel: Cambridge 54131
Colours Light blue and white hoops
Most capped player C M H Gibson (Ireland) 69 caps
Captain 1983-84 M D Balley
1st XV 1983-84 P20 W9 D1 L11 F442 A359
Review of the season Cambridge duly proceeded to their ninth win in 11 'Varsity matches in a lively match at Twickenham, where the clever play of the likes of Kevin Simms, at centre, and wing Mark Bailey delighted their supporters. Yet it was by no means a vintage Cambridge team. Success came rarely against the major clubs and in a hard-working pack only Ellison, at No 8, played with real authority. The University made a successful pre-season tour to Japan.

Coventry

Year of formation 1874
Ground Coundon Road, Coventry Tel: Coventry 591274
Colours Navy and white hoops, navy shorts
Most capped player D J Duckham (England) 36 caps
Captain 1983-84 S P Thomas
1st XV 1983-84 P41 W27 D1 L13 F736 A534
Review of the season Coventry, casting aside their worst injury list in post-war years, reached the John Player Special Cup quarter-finals and won eight of nine games after being eliminated by Harlequins. Powerful forward play, featuring Mal Malik (who played in all 41 games), Steve Brain and Lee Johnson, a prop and joint leading try-scorer with eight, was marred by a woeful lack of penetration in the backs. Steve Thomas, who

stepped down after two season as captain, was absent for 14 weeks after fracturing a wrist in December but still scored 154 points. John Cooke, a centre, and flanker Paul Thomas each scored eight tries.

Fylde

Year of formation 1919
Ground The Woodlands Memorial Ground, Blackpool Road, Ansdell, Lytham St Annes
Tel: Lytham 734733
Colours Claret, gold and white
Most capped player W B Beaumont (England) 34 caps
Captain 1983-84 M J Weir
1st XV 1983-84 P41 W13 D4 L24 F541 A805
Review of the season This was one of Fylde's worst seasons although they managed to hang on to a northern merit table place thanks to a late season flourish. In that sense the pattern had been much the same as that of the previous season. Injuries took their toll and two key forwards, Cumbria No 8 Andy Macfarlane and former England Under-23 hooker Mike Dixon, missed a great deal of the season along with flanker Mark Hesketh. New Zealander Paul Turner filled the full-back berth and topped the scoring with 104 points, and Colin Dickinson finished up as leading try-scorer with 13 to his credit.

Gloucester

Year of formation 1873
Ground Kingsholm, Kingsholm Road, Gloucester GL1 3AX
Tel: Gloucester 20901 (office) 28385 (club)
Colours Cherry and white
Most capped player A T Voyce (England) 27 caps
Captain 1983-84 G A F Sargent
1st XV 1983-84 P49 W33 D1 L15 F1,022 A623
Review of the season Gloucester's final record was much improved, although they often infuriated their supporters by their inconsistency. Their was nothing much wrong with their forwards, who were, to a man, in contention for higher honours – indeed, Malcom Preedy, Mike Teague, Steve Mills and John Fidler toured South Africa with England. The club qualified for the next John Player Cup after being absent in 1983-84. Sadly, their half-backs did not always cash in on the good work up front, though Nick Price, the wing, scored 27 tries.

Gosforth

Year of formation 1877
Ground New Ground, Great North Road, Gosforth, Newcastle upon Tyne NE3 2DT
Tel: Newcastle 856915
Colours Green and white hoops, white shorts, green and white hooped stockings
Most capped player R J McLoughlin (Ireland) 40 caps
Captain 1983-84 R Anderson
1st XV 1983-84 P43 W29 D3 L11 F860 A457
Review of the season By the standards of most clubs it was a good season but, for a club of Gosforth's eminence, it can be regarded only as moderately successful. Alnwick surprisingly stopped them from winning their 14th consecutive Northumberland Cup, and they lost out to Wasps in the third round of the John Player Cup. Nevertheless, Gosforth finished comfortably in the top four of the northern merit table yet again and locals were delighted to see popular prop Colin White follow Steve Bainbridge into the England team. Wing Jim Pollock played for Scotland and prop John Curry for the England under-23s. Scoring machine David Johnson scored 334 points at fly-half.

Halifax

Year of formation 1873
Ground Ovenden Park, Halifax   Tel: Halifax 65926
Colours Dark blue, light blue and white narrow hoops
Most capped player J P Horrocks-Taylor (England) and G T Thomson (England) 9 caps each
Captain 1983-84 A Davidson
1st XV 1983-84   P38   W15   D3   L20   P481   A490
Review of the season Halifax managed just one win and one draw in the northern merit qualifying table, but while it was a fairly disappointing season in this respect it was one that gave hope for the future. Under the leadership of Alan Davidson the side started to adopt a much more positive role towards the end of the season. With greater confidence they went out to attack rather than contain: in their match against northern champions West Hartlepool they had led at half-time. But this was a fairly young side – especially in the back division – and lack of experience told in the end. The fact that six members of the team got into the Yorkshire Under-21 squad supports the club view that the future has more of a rosy hue.

Harlequins

Year of formation 1866
Grounds Stoop Memorial Ground, Craneford Way, Twickenham, Middlesex and RFU Ground, Twickenham   Tel: 01-892 3080 (Stoop)
Colours Light blue, magenta, chocolate, French grey, black and light green
Most capped player W W Wakefield (England) 31 caps
Captain 1983-84 D H Cooke
1st XV 1983-84   P40   W27   D0   L13   F797   A550
Review of the season Harlequins got off to a slow start in the season but eventually they found a team spirit and a cohesion, becoming one of the most effective teams in the country at the end. They lost to Bristol in the semi-finals of the John Player Cup. They were well-served by the All Blacks centre Jamie Salmon – now a 'reinstated' Englishman – and also by the colourful American wing, Willie Jefferson. Chris Butcher and David Cooke, the respected captain, were outstanding. Ray Dudman (223) scored most points.

Harrogate

Year of formation 1871
Ground Claro Road, Harrogate   Tel: Harrogate 66966/64933
Colours Red, amber and black
Most capped player P J Squires (England) 29 caps
Captain 1983-84 C Simmonds
1st XV 1983-84   P38   W14   D3   L21   F424   A547
Review of the season Having finished close to the foot of the northern merit table the previous season, Harrogate were prime candidates to take the drop – and they did. It was a season in which the club failed to make any real impact and they were defeated heavily in the Yorkshire Cup by beaten finalists, Wakefield. They lost the services of skipper Colin Simmons and the vastly experienced Peter Squires took over his role. Harrogate were also hampered by the absence of centre Robert Booth, who had set a new club scoring record the previous season.

Hartlepool Rovers

Year of formation 1897
Ground The Friarage, West View Road, Hartlepool   Tel: Hartlepool 67741
Colours White jerseys, black shorts, red stockings

Most capped player G S Conway (England) 18 caps
Captain 1983-84 A Calvert
1st XV 1983-84 P44 W28 D0/1 aban L15 F836 A502
Review of the season Rovers had a very satisfactory season on their return to the northern merit table and twice lost narrowly to old rivals West Hartlepool, who went on to win the northern title. One of those defeats was in the Durham Senior Cup. Skipper Alan Calvert had another fine campaign, amassing 273 points and passing the 2,000 points mark for the club during the season. Gary Dinsdale did well with 20 tries to his credit and there was another fine contribution from 6ft 7ins lock John Howe, already in his second season at just 20 years of age.

Headingley

Year of formation 1878
Ground Bridge Road, Kirkstall, Leeds 5 Tel: Leeds 755029
Colours Green, black and white jerseys, blue shorts
Most capped player I R McGeechan (Scotland) 32 caps
Captain 1983-84 T Sinclair
1st XV 1983-84 P47 W29 D2 L16 F801 A513
Review of the season It was very nearly another record-breaking season for the Yorkshire club. Tim Sinclair, the hooker, led the side well in their first season back in the northern merit table and Headingley grew in strength and confidence as the season progressed, finishing in sixth place in the table. They also won the Yorkshire Cup for the second successive year and the only disappointment was losing to eventual winners Bath in the third round of the John Player Cup. Their British Lions flanker Peter Winterbottom had another fine season. The front row comprised three Yorkshire players in Sinclair, Adam Machell and Paul Huntsman.

Huddersfield

Year of formation 1909
Ground Tandem, Waterloo, Huddersfield Tel: Huddersfield 23864
Colours White, claret and gold
Most capped player N M Hall (England) 17 caps
Captain 1983-84 M Birch
1st XV 1983-84 P38 W9 D0 L29 F329 A808
Review of the season A glance at their playing record would lead anyone to think Huddersfield had had a pretty dismal season but, encouragingly, it was a 100 per cent improvement on the previous season when they only managed to win four games. The improvement came about despite troublesome injuries, the main victim being skipper Mark Birch. The previous season skipper Martin Szostak had broken his wrist in the first half of the season and when Mark Birch took over he first broke his jaw and then a leg. He returned to take over the captaincy permanently at the start of the season but was again put out of action by damaged knee ligaments.

Hull and East Riding

Year of formation 1901
Ground The Circle, Anlaby Road, Kingston-upon-Hull, North Humberside
Tel: Hull 507098/507918
Colours Cherry and white hoops, navy shorts
Most capped player R D Sangwin (England) 2 caps
Captain 1983-84 I Furlong
1st XV 1983-84 P42 W27 D1 L14 F681 A575
Review of the season It was the second best season in the club's history, the first team winning nearly twice as many games as they lost. Unfortunately their success wasn't

reflected in terms of earning promotion to the northern merit table, but they were constantly on the heels of the three front runners, Broughton Park, Morley and Preston Grasshoppers. The side was well led by policeman Ian Furlong and officials are confident the players can build on the success. It is a pity, therefore, that they have lost the services of key players like Steve Harris, who moved to Bedford and John Buckton who has taken a job in London.

Leicester

Year of formation 1880
Ground The Clubhouse, Aylestone Road, Leicester LE2 7LF Tel: Leicester 540276
Colours Scarlet, green and white
Most capped player P J Wheeler (England) 41 caps
Captain 1983-84 I Smith
1st XV 1983-84 P41 W28 D1 L12 F1,030 A577
Review of the season Leicester failed to reach the John Player Special Cup semi-finals for the first time in seven years but scored a club record points total and topped the Midlands Merit Table. They also supplied eight players for England against Ireland, a feat without parallel in modern times. Injury and unavailability restricted leading players to infrequent appearances and 41 players were called upon, including nine newcomers. Dusty Hare, the leading points-scorer with 239, played in only 20 games. Wing Barry Evans scored 24 of the 144 tries (five short of equalling the club's best overall total), with Kevin Williams (14 tries), Underwood (12) and Dean Richards (10) featuring prominently. Les Cusworth dropped nine goals, a club record, and Leicester beat Zimbabwe and the Barbarians as well as topping 60 points against Bedford (twice) and Saracens.

Liverpool

Year of formation 1857
Ground St Michael's, Church Road, Liverpool L17 7BD
Tel: Liverpool (051) 727 6330
Colours Red, blue and black horizontal stripes, white shorts
Most capped player M A C Slemen (England) 31 caps
Captain 1983-84 A Askew
1st XV 1983-84 P44 W27 D2 L15 F798 A540
Review of the season It was a case of peaks and troughs for the Merseyside club, who finished further down the northern merit table than is their custom. They made a good start to the season, and again found form later to win the Lancashire Cup. In between, the club lost the services of Ken Moss, who joined Wasps, and hooker Paul Dadswell who retired from the game. Both were good players with representative experience but the remaining players were not short on representative honours either. Mike Slemen was recalled to the England side, although he eventually lost his place to Rory Underwood. Peter Buckton captained the England Under-23 touring party to Spain and was accompanied there by the exciting Cambridge University centre Kevin Simms who, along with his brother, plays for Liverpool when home from college.

London Irish

Year of formation 1898
Ground The Avenue, Sunbury-on-Thames, Middlesex Tel: Sunbury-on-Thames 83034
Colours Emerald green jerseys, white shorts
Most capped player K W Kennedy (Ireland) 45 caps
Captain 1983-84 G Beringer
1st XV 1983-84 P29 W12 D1 L16 F491 A439
Review of the season It was a mediocre season for the Irish despite the driving leadership of hooker Guy Beringer and the excellence of Barry Murphy and Hugh Condon at

half-back. The Irish beat Bedford in their first John Player match but failed against Coventry in the next round. Horner and Christopher were effective flankers but there is still rebuilding to be done. Paul O'Donnell scored 118 points.

London Scottish

Year of formation 1878
Ground Richmond Athletic Ground, Richmond, Surrey Tel: 01-940 0397
Colours Blue jerseys, red lion on left breast, white shorts, red stockings
Most capped player A F McHarg (Scotland) 44 caps
Captain 1983-84 J Fraser
1st XV 1983-84 P30 W14 D0 L16 F435 A418
Review of the season The Scottish finally said goodbye to Alastair McHarg, their magnificent forward whose skill and enterprise in the second row has served the club and the Scottish national team so well. The club welcomed Duncan Bruce-Lockhart to the centre and fielded a penetrative back division; but there was little authority in the forwards. Sadly, Ron Wilson, the fly-half, had to retire following a serious knee-injury. The Scottish reached the quarter-finals of the Cup, losing to Nottingham. Stewart Irvine (146) was leading points-scorer.

London Welsh

Year of formation 1885
Ground Old Deer Park, Kew Road, Richmond, Surrey Tel: 01-940 2420/0706
Colours Scarlet jerseys and white shorts
Most capped player J P R Williams (Wales) 55 caps
Captain 1983-84 B Bradley
1st XV 1983-84 P38 W16 D3 L19 F592 A637
Review of the season At their best, the Welsh were a very good team indeed. They had a powerful scrummaging unit, and three internationals appeared behind the scrum when Mark Douglas arrived from Llanelli to join Bob Ackerman and Clive Rees. Yet the Welsh often lapsed into mediocrity, notably when they were heavily defeated by Bristol in the John Player Cup quarter-finals. Two occasions which delighted the club were the appearance of the tireless Kevin Bowring for the Barbarians and their superb display in the Middlesex Sevens, which the Welsh won for the first time since 1973. Ian George scored 158 points before departing for Northampton.

Manchester

Year of formation 1860
Ground Grove Park, Grove Lane, Cheadle Hulme, Cheshire Tel: 061-485 1115
Colours Red and white hooped jerseys, white shorts, red stockings
Most capped player G S Conway (England) 18 caps
Captain 1983-84 D Cotter
1st XV 1983-84 P32 W3 D2 L27 F244 A827
Review of the season It was a disastrous season for one of the oldest clubs in the game, and one they will be eager to erase from memory. Nothing went right for them – their troubles started even before the season began when skipper Dennis Cotter was injured on a warm-up tour. He was plagued by injury problems all season and was never able to command his place in the side – partly because one of the few successes was Roger Smith, who replaced him at scrum-half. The club was also dealt a blow when they lost four key players to other clubs – Terry and Peter Broughton to Sale along with prop Nick Wheeler, and Steve Burnage to Orrell. With British Lion John O'Driscoll opting to play for London Irish, the Manchester cupboard was left bare of talent. There was little on the credit side but, towards the end of the season, the team was strengthened by the arrival of

wing Steve Parrott, front row forwards Tex and Greg Birch from Broughton Park and flanker Dave Hall from Sale.

Metropolitan Police

Year of formation 1923
Ground Police Sports Club, Imber Court, Embercourt Road, East Molesey, Surrey
Tel: 01-398 1267
Colours Dark blue jerseys, navy blue shorts (alt. sky blue jerseys)
Most capped player A M Rees (Wales) 13 caps
Captain 1983-84 S Jones
1st XV 1983-84 P36 W13 D1 L22 F419 A509
Review of the season The Police had won two thirds of their matches in the previous season, but in 1983-84 they won barely a third. It was a disappointing season. They had powerful forwards in Paul Ackford and Phil de Lacey at lock and Gordon Raybould at No 8. Tim Bryan marshalled the side well from fly-half. But injury and working duties often weakened the side.

Middlesbrough

Year of formation 1872
Ground Acklam Park, Green Lane, Middlesbrough, Cleveland
Tel: Middlesbrough 88567
Colours Maroon jerseys, white shorts, maroon stockings
Most capped player A G B Old (England) 16 caps
Captain 1983-84 A Robinson
1st XV 1983-84 P42 W18 D2 L22 F601 A592
Review of the season After narrowly missing promotion to the northern merit table the previous season, Middlesbrough were never in the hunt in 1983-84. Their cause wasn't helped by the absence for the first half of the season of fly-half Paul Wood, the Yorkshire 'B' player, who damaged knee ligaments in only the second game. It is perhaps a telling statistic that with Paul in the side, Middlesbrough lost only one of their last nine games, against Morley in the Yorkshire Cup. The fly-half finished with a points tally of 193 from just 17 outings and the club was left to ponder what might have been.

Morley

Year of formation 1878
Ground Scatcherd Lane, Morley, Leeds Tel: Leeds 533487
Colours Maroon
Most capped player G H Marsden (England) 3 caps
Captain 1983-84 K Plant
1st XV 1983-84 P39 W31 D1 L7 F821 A345
Review of the season By losing to Wakefield in the semi-finals of the Yorkshire Cup, Morley missed out on a John Player Cup place. But this was their only set-back – the club roared back into the northern merit table by winning a fascinating three-cornered fight between themselves, Broughton Park and Preston Grasshoppers. The turning point came, ironically, after they had been beaten 6-4 by West Hartlepool in the second round of the John Player Cup. They then swept into an impressive run of victories, losing only two matches between Christmas and the end of the season.

Moseley

Year of formation 1873
Ground The Reddings, Reddings Road, Moseley, Birmingham B13 8IW
Tel: Birmingham (021) 449 2149

Colours Black and red
Most capped player N E Horton (England) 20 caps
Captain 1983-84 G N J Cox
1st XV 1983-84 P48 W25 D2 L21 F760 A744
Review of the season Moseley improved slightly on their record of the previous season, which had been their worst in 18 years. Their 107 tries, 21 by John Goodwin, a promising left wing, surpassed those conceded by one. Best wins were over Blackheath (38-0), Llanelli, Swansea, Newport and Wasps, who suffered their first defeat by an English club in 10 months. Victory at Sale in the John Player Special Cup led to a disappointing home elimination by Nottingham. Moseley celebrated 100 years of playing at The Reddings by meeting a Midlands XV, who won 42-26. Clive Meanwell scored 142 points, Ian Metcalfe 100, and Simon Hunter ran in nine tries.

Northampton

Year of formation 1880
Ground Franklins Gardens, Northampton Tel: Northampton 51543
Colours Black, green and gold
Most capped player C R Jacobs (England) 29 caps
Captains 1983-84 J A G D Raphael, G S Pearce (from 1 April)
1st XV 1983-84 P43 W26 D1 L16 F689 A627
Review of the season Northampton recovered from their worst post-war season in 1982-83 to finish with their best record in eight years, aided by a heavy programme of home games. Jon Raphael was an inspiring captain until he retired on medical advice after neck trouble, and Dick Tilley brought other benefits in his first season as coach. Injuries to David Caplan, the former England full-back, and Steve Worrall, the Combined Services scrum-half (who was absent for the final three months with a broken jaw), detracted from Northampton's performances. Worrall was leading points scorer with 173, and wing Frank Packman scored most tries, 18, including five against Rugby.

Northern

Year of formation 1876
Ground McCracken Park, Great North Road, Newcastle upon Tyne 3
Tel: Newcastle upon Tyne 363369
Colours White jerseys, navy blue shorts, red stockings
Most capped player J D Currie (England) 25 caps
Captain 1983-84 G Longstaffe
1st XV 1983-84 P43 W15 D1 L27 F459 A661
Review of the season In their first season down in the northern merit qualifying table, Northern were unable to make a serious challenge for an early return to the senior table. Their cause was not helped by the loss of yet more players to the side just across the road – Gosforth. Alistair Tindle and Simon Tilley made the switch, but the biggest loss was their former captain and talented back row player, Giles Smallwood. The result of the departures was the development of a good young side that might well help the club back into the merit table in future.

Nottingham

Year of formation 1877
Ground Ireland Avenue, Beeston, Nottingham Tel: Nottingham 254238
Colours Green and white jerseys, green shorts
Most capped player V H Cartwright (England) 14 caps
Captain 1983-84 P Cook
1st XV 1983-84 P40 W30 D1 L9 F833 A374
Review of the season Nottingham's memorable season brought a first appearance in the John Player Special Cup semi-finals and a club record points total, overtaking the 803 of

nine years earlier. An expansive approach, instilled by Alan Davies in his seventh season as coach, and by Peter Cook, the captain, yielded 108 tries, with only 40 conceded. Keiron Murphy, a former England Colts scrum-half, scored four tries in the defeat of Harlequins (42-10). Other outstanding wins were over Llanelli (45-3), Bristol, Moseley (twice), Richmond, London Scottish, Blackheath and at Maesteg and Rosslyn Park (36-4). Simon Hodgkinson scored 396 points and Steve Holdstock ran in 18 tries.

Nuneaton

Year of formation 1879
Ground Harry Cleaver Ground, Attleborough Road, Nuneaton Tel: Nuneaton 383206
Colours Black, red, white hoops, black shorts
Most capped player W A Holmes (England) 16 caps
Captain 1983-84 G Mumford
1st XV 1983-84 P42 W24 D1 L17 F771 A596
Review of the season Nuneaton enjoyed their best season for 30 years, scoring 118 tries, playing attractive rugby and recovering swiftly from losing their opening three matches to Halifax, Leicester (59-4) and Hull and East Riding. Wins over Walsall and Fylde brought a John Player Special Cup third round appearance for only the second time, but a 9-6 home defeat by Richmond proved a major disappointment. Selwyn Brewster, a speedy wing, scored 22 tries to complement the efforts of a stalwart pack in which Terry McCarthy, scorer of 21 tries, George Mumford and Paul Griffiths impressed. Andy Savage, the scrum-half, scored 199 points. A striking improvement in away form brought wins at Manchester, New Brighton and Oxford (61-13) but finest victories were over Northampton, Bedford, London Irish, and Plymouth Albion at the home ground.

Orrell

Year of formation 1927
Ground Edge Hall Road, Orrell, nr Wigan, Greater Manchester, Lancs WN5 8TL
Tel: Upholland (0695) 623193
Colours Amber and black hoops, black shorts and stockings
Most capped player J Carleton (England) 25 caps
Captain 1983-84 D Southern
1st XV 1983-84 P47 W36 D4 L7 F1,126 A427
Review of the season After a tremendous start Orrell fell away badly, and while most clubs would be delighted with 36 victories and a points haul in excess of 1,000, it was not a good season by this club's standards. They romped undefeated through the first half of the season, thanks to some powerhouse pack play and accurate goal-kicking by Steve Burnage and Ged Glynn. But they were never quite the same side after losing to Wasps in the fourth round of the John Player Cup. They slipped down a merit table they had led and finished out of the top four.

Otley

Year of formation 1865 Re-formed 1907
Ground Cross Green, Otley, West Yorkshire Tel: Otley 461180
Colours Black and white hoops, black shorts, black stockings
Most capped player A H Bateson (England) 4 caps
Captain 1983-84 J Dracup
1st XV 1983-84 P40 W17 D4 L19 F567 A484
Review of the season This was a difficult season for a club in only its second season in the northern merit table. It was clear from quite early on in the campaign that they were going to have to fight to steer clear of the relegation zone. Although the season generally was mixed they struggled in merit games and were relegated with only two victories to their credit. Injuries did not help their cause and skipper and full-back James Dracup suffered

more than most. Injury kept him out until after Christmas and when he did return to the side he was promptly injured again, prop Russell Stead taking over the reins.

Oxford University

Year of formation 1869
Ground University Rugby Ground, Iffley Road, Oxford Tel: Oxford 242017
Colours Dark blue
Most capped player J M Bannerman (Scotland) 37 caps
Captain 1983 H P MacNeill **1984** T S O'Brien
1st XV 1983-84 P24 W5 D1 L18 F320 A508
Review of the season Despite the presence of the illustrious British Lion, Hugo MacNeill, at full-back and of Stuart Barnes at fly-half, Oxford had a poor season and subsided to their ninth defeat in 11 'Varsity matches – albeit with a consistently brave and imaginative display. Tim O'Brien appeared for them at Twickenham, thus becoming the first man to win a rugby blue for both universities. The team lacked a snappy service from the base of the scrum and only Martin Gargan, an outstanding No 8, was a real force in the pack.

Richmond

Year of formation 1861
Ground Athletic Ground, Richmond, Surrey Tel: 01-940 0397
Colours Old gold, red and black
Most capped player C W Ralston (England) 22 caps
Captain 1983-84 M Slagter
1st XV 1983-84 P35 W16 D1 L18 F530 A624
Review of the season Richmond had slightly improved and were well led by lock Martin Slagter. They had trouble beating Nuneaton in the third round of the John Player Cup, and lost at Waterloo in the fourth round. On the credit side there were signs of an emerging new generation of useful players. The club's sevens team, usually so successful, were knocked out of the Middlesex Sevens in the second round proper – ironically, by their own second string. Andy Janes was top scorer with 110 points and Bruce Roxburgh scored most tries (11).

Rosslyn Park

Year of formation 1879
Ground Priory Lane, Upper Richmond Road, Roehampton, London SW15
Tel: 01-876 1879
Colours Red and white hoops
Most capped player A G Ripley (England) 24 caps
Captain 1983-84 T Allchurch
1st XV 1983-84 P35 W16 D1 L18 F430 A524
Review of the season The Park won their first five games, showing promise, but it was a false dawn. Their run ended with a hammering at Orrell and for all the prompting of Toby Allchurch, the flanker and new captain, and the hard work of Rad Montgomery, Mark Jermyn and Simon Henderson, the Park ended with more defeats than victories. They also had problems with their re-seeded pitch, occasionally having to play away from Roehampton. Cedric Carr, the promising wing, scored 19 tries.

Roundhay

Year of formation 1924
Ground Chandos Park, Chandos Avenue, Lidgett Lane, Leeds LS8 1QX
Tel: Leeds 661815
Colours Emerald, scarlet and white, white shorts

Most capped player D T Wilkins (England) 13 caps
Captain 1983-84 B Willis
1st XV 1983-84 P45 W24 D2 L19 F701 A488
Review of the season It was a difficult season for the Yorkshire club, who only just survived in the northern merit table. Their first problem came before the start of the season when they lost the previous year's skipper, Simon Tipping, to Sale. Barry Willis took over the captaincy but he damaged a shoulder in mid-season and that kept him sidelined for the remainder of the matches. The brightest note for the club was the success of centre Steve Burnhill, who played for Yorkshire in the absence of Bryan Barley and was then chosen to tour South Africa with England.

Sale

Year of formation 1861
Ground Heywood Road, Brooklands, Sale, Cheshire Tel: 061 973 6348
Colours Blue and white hoops, blue shorts, blue stockings
Most capped player F E Cotton (England) 31 caps
Captain 1983-84 A M Bond
1st XV 1983-84 P42 W34 D1 L7 F1,058 A365
Review of the season For the second successive year, Sale passed the 1,000 points mark, setting another club record in the process. They failed to hang on to the northern merit table title but finished in second position to retain their place in the forefront of northern rugby. They also won the Cheshire Cup for the 13th time in as many attempts and are still undefeated in the competition. Unfortunately, they didn't fare quite so well in the John Player Cup – they were knocked out at home by Moseley. Once again Sale displayed both fitness and style and the player who took most honours was Yorkshire flanker Simon Tipping, who joined the club from Roundhay. Sid Lowdon continued to impress at full-back and reached a personal 1,000 points for the club during the season.

Saracens

Year of formation 1876
Ground Bramley Sports Ground, Green Road, Southgate, London N14
Tel: 01-449 3770
Colours Black jerseys with red star and crescent, black shorts, red stockings
Most capped player V S Harding (England) 6 caps
Captain 1983-84 A Keay
1st XV 1983-84 P39 W16 D2 L21 F481 A608
Review of the season Saracens tried to pull themselves out of the doldrums but injuries and lack of consistency prevented them from making a real impression. Andy Keay was a brave and committed captain and Jaszcak, Grier and Sherriff also played well in the forwards. A win over London Welsh at Southgate was a satisfying result but there were not too many others. Dave Gregory was the leading scorer with 167 points, while Andy Phillips scored ten tries.

Sheffield

Year of formation 1902
Ground Abbeydale Park, Totley Rise, Sheffield
Tel: Sheffield 362040 (steward), 360992 (groundsman)
Colours Blue and white bands, red stockings
Most capped player A G B Old (England) 16 caps
Captain 1983-84 W M Reichwald
1st XV 1983-84 P43 W27 D2 L14 F737 A563
Review of the season Sheffield had a satisfactory season, finishing just in the top half of the northern merit table – a special achievement as the club actually played all the other 27

clubs in the merit and qualifying tables. The major disappointment was losing to the eventual winners, Headingley, in the semi-finals of the Yorkshire Cup. The sides finished level on points but Headingley advanced by virtue of having scored more tries. Bill Reichwald again led the side well and also played for Yorkshire against Surrey in the county championship. Scrum-half David Holmes also played for Yorkshire at the start of the season and Grant Treece showed a good deal of class during the campaign, whether at wing, centre or full-back.

Vale of Lune

Year of formation 1900
Ground Powderhouse Lane, Lancaster   Tel: Lancaster (0524) 64029
Colours Cherry and white hoops, navy shorts, red stockings
Captain 1983-84 J Ashworth
1st XV 1983-84   P48   W34   D1   L13   F942   A469
Review of the season A record-breaking season for Vale, who gained 34 victories and, for the first time in the club's history, reached the semi-final of the Lancashire Cup in which they were beaten 12-6 by Liverpool. It was also the club's best-ever season in the northern merit table, and for a time they led the field only to fall away after Christmas, eventually finishing in mid-table. Wing Mark Nelson set a new club try-scoring record with 36 to his credit and he also went on to play for Lancashire 'B' along with promising full-back Andy Higgin. Back row forward Sam Hodgson played for the North against New Zealand at Gateshead and scrum-half Mark Hancock played for the county's under-21 team. Mick Curran, who returned to Vale after a spell at Sale topped the scoring with 284 points.

Wakefield

Year of formation 1901
Ground College Grove, Wakefield, West Yorks   Tel: Wakefield 72038/63431
Colours Black and gold
Most capped player B Barley (England) 3 caps
Captain 1983-84 M Shuttleworth
1st XV 1983-84   P43   W28   D1   L14   F850   A466
Review of the season In terms of the northern merit table it was a season of mixed fortunes and the club's greatest claim to fame was ending Orrell's unbeaten run. Generally, however, results were good, despite the disappointment of being beaten by Headingley in the final of the Yorkshire Cup. Full-back Martin Shuttleworth captained the side for the fourth successive season, stepping down after the last game, and his presence caused an interesting positional switch for young Ray Adamson, a full-back who joined at the start of the campaign. Adamson was moved to fly-half from where he broke the club's scoring record with 303 points. He also played for Yorkshire 'B' and a number of players played for the county at different levels. Mike Harrison, Neil Bennett, Steve Townend and Bryan Barley all played for the senior side.

Wasps

Year of formation 1867
Ground Repton Avenue (off Rugby Avenue), Sudbury (Wembley), Middlesex
Tel: 01-902 4220
Colours Black jerseys with golden wasp on left breast, black shorts, black stockings with gold hoop on turnover
Most capped player R M Uttley (England) 23 caps
Captain 1983-84 N D Melville
1st XV 1983-84   P41   W31   D4   L6   F952   A434
Review of the season Wasps began the season well, having recruited some excellent players and obviously relishing the wise coaching of Alan Black. Many people felt they

would not last the pace, but in fact they kept up their momentum almost to the end. They were hit by injury, notably to their captain, Nigel Melville. They went through from two tough ties in the cup at Gosforth and Orrell before losing at Bath. Mark Williams and John Cullen at half-back and Alan Isichei and Ken Moss in the forwards were outstanding. Nick Stringer scored 161 points.

Waterloo

Year of formation 1882
Ground St Anthony's Road, Blundellsands, Liverpool L23 8TW Tel: 051 924 4552
Colours Green, red and white hoops
Most capped player H G Periton (England) 21 caps
Captain 1983-84 L Connor
1st XV 1983-84 P43 W34 D2 L7 F916 A431
Review of the season It was Waterloo's best ever-season with 34 victories and only one heavy defeat, which was inflicted by Pontypool upon a weakened side. The club finished third in the northern merit table to ensure a place in the John Player Cup, a competition in which they would have beaten Bristol but for a late penalty goal by Stuart Barnes. They had wins over Nottingham, Richmond, Wasps, Orrell, London Irish, Liverpool, Coventry, London Scottish and Northampton, and held Leicester to a draw. All this was achieved without international lock Jim Syddall and Wales 'B' flanker Mick Leach for much of the season. Wing Maurice Cotter – the leading scorer with 349 points – played for Lancashire along with skipper Laurie Connor, who also played for the Barbarians.

West Hartlepool

Year of formation 1881
Ground Brierton Lane, Hartlepool Tel: Hartlepool 72640
Colours Green, red and white hoops, white shorts, green and red stockings
Most capped player C D Aarvold (England) 16 caps
Captain 1983-84 C E Bentley
1st XV 1983-84 P43 W32 D4 L7 F801 A429
Review of the season West Hartlepool won just one game fewer than the previous season but they won't much mind missing out on that record, for they still managed to win the northern merit title. The crucial game was their first in the merit table early in the season when they beat Sale, the side that chased them all the way to a tight finish. West really clinched the title when they won three merit games, against Wakefield, Headingley and Roundhay, in a week. They also won the Durham Cup for the third successive season but lost narrowly to Orrell in the John Player Cup. The outstanding contribution of the season came from scrum-half Ivan Waterson, from New Zealand, who scored 11 tries in the campaign.

Wilmslow

Year of formation 1886 Re-formed 1923
Ground Memorial Ground, Pownall Park, Wilmslow, Cheshire
Tel: Wilmslow 22274/24148
Colours Sky blue, maroon and white jerseys, white shorts, maroon stockings
Captain 1983-84 M Hamlin
1st XV 1983-84 P39 W15 D2 L22 F502 A574
Review of the season The Cheshire club had a very mixed campaign which could have turned out rather differently had they had fewer injuries and more backs capable of utilising possession won by a useful pack. It was very late into the season before the club could claim to have fielded the same side in successive games, so serious were the injury problems. Skipper Mike Hamlin was a tower of strength and he was well supported by a pack that held its own against most sides and dominated the remainder.

SCOTLAND

Aberdeen Grammar School FP

Year of formation 1893
Ground Rubislaw Field, Aberdeen
Colours White jerseys with blue collar, navy shorts
Most capped player E J S Michie (Scotland) 15 caps
Captain 1983-84 I Gilbert
1st XV 1983-84 P27 W13 D0 L14 F367 A378
Review of the season It was a disappointing season in which Aberdeen Grammar were relegated from the second division after having been champions of the third the previous year. Only three league games were won, including their visit to their Aberdeen neighbours, Gordonians. Jim Cargill was top scorer with 90 points, and back row forward Kevin Wyness had most tries (6).

Ayr

Year of formation 1897
Ground Millbrae, Alloway, Ayr Tel: Alloway 41944
Colours Pink and black
Most capped player S Munro (Scotland) 10 caps
Captain 1983-84 A D Brown
1st XV 1983-84 P35 W22 D2 L11 F563 A500
Review of the season Ayr stayed in the first division of the club championship for a second season, escaping from trouble only by taking five points from their last three matches – a draw against local rivals Kilmarnock and wins against Selkirk and West of Scotland. Grant Steel, who scored 23 of Ayr's 33 points in those three crucial games, was top scorer with 185, taking over the front-line kicking role when John Brown retired because of recurring shoulder injury. No 8 John Young was top try scorer with 10. Ayr regained the Glasgow and District Cup but lost the Ayrshire Cup.

Boroughmuir

Year of formation 1919 ('Boroughmuir FP' until 1974)
Ground Meggetland, Colinton Road, Edinburgh EH14 IAS
Tel: Edinburgh (031) 443 7571
Colours Navy blue and emerald green
Most capped player B H Hay (Scotland) 23 caps
Captain 1983-84 P A Black
1st XV 1983-84 P31 W21 D0 L10 F646 A430
Review of the season Boroughmuir finished seventh in the first division, their lowest position in the championship since the competition's first season. Grant Russell was top scorer with 139 points, Mike Hall also reached three figures with 109, and Mike DeBusk topped the try list with 14. He scored three of these in the 50-16 win against Haddington, Boroughmuir's biggest league score at Meggetland. The following week they fell heavily to Hawick 4-45. These contrasting results summed up the season.

Clarkston

Year of formation 1937
Ground Braidholm, Giffnock, Glasgow Tel: Glasgow (041) 637 5850
Colours Scarlet, white and green
Captain 1983-84 K Fairbairn
1st XV 1983-84 P35 W18 D1 L16 F522 A448

Review of the season Clarkston had a typically mixed season in which they won their league match against Edinburgh Academicals (second division runners-up) and the Glasgow and District Cup tie against first division Kilmarnock. However, they lost to relegated Aberdeen Grammar. In many games they relied heavily on the goal-kicking of fly-half Trevor Brannan, who finished top scorer with 211 points. Bill Hoellrich topped the try list with 15.

Edinburgh Academicals

Year of formation 1857
Ground Raeburn Place, Edinburgh Tel: Edinburgh (031) 322 1070
Colours Blue and white stripes
Most capped player W I D Elliot (Scotland) 29 caps
Captain 1983-84 W K Dodds
1st XV 1983-84 P30 W16 D0 L14 F374 A480
Review of the season Overall it was an average season in which Academicals lost almost as many games as they won. But they had victories in the major matches – they won all six of their league fixtures in the 1984 half of the season, earning promotion to the first division for the first time, and finishing runners-up to their Glasgow namesakes. Victories included a satisfying win against Glasgow Academicals. Ewan Drummond was top scorer with 103 points, and Stewart Howgate again topped the try list, this time with eight.

Gala

Year of formation 1875
Ground Netherdale, Galashiels Tel: Galashiels 3811
Colours Maroon jerseys, white shorts
Most capped player P C Brown (Scotland) 27 caps
Captain 1983-84 K G Lawrie
1st XV 1983-84 P32 W27 D0 L5 F914 A331
Review of the season Gala lost the national title to their old rivals Hawick, but this was their only defeat in the championship. They also lost to Hawick in the Border League, an April defeat that ended a run of 21 successive victories in all matches. But no other Scottish club beat them. International full-back Peter Dods was top scorer with 210 points for the club (plus 193 in other matches), and Dougie Wilson had most tries (31).

Glasgow Academicals

Year of formation 1886
Ground New Anniesland, Anniesland Road, Glasgow Tel: 041-959 1101/1323
Colours Navy blue and white
Most capped player J B Nelson (Scotland) 25 caps
Captain 1983-84 A G Ker
1st XV 1983-84 P32 W19 D2 L11 F743 A488
Review of the season Academicals had their best season since the official leagues started in 1973, winning the second division title. Their success was based on a big, mobile pack in which the best-known member was John Beattie, the British Lion of 1980 and 1983. Club records were set in the 82-3 win over Hutchesons': it was the club's highest score and biggest margin, and Fraser MacNaughton had an individual best with 38 points (five tries, nine conversions). MacNaughton was top scorer with 255 points and David Hunter had 25 tries.

Glasgow High/Kelvinside

Year of formation 1982 (on amalgamation of Glasgow HSFP and Kelvinside Academicals)
Ground Old Anniesland, Glasgow Tel: 959 1154

Colours Chocolate and gold
Most capped player None (Prior to amalgamation J M Bannerman (Glasgow High) was capped 37 times and D M White (Kelvinside) 4 times – both for Scotland)
Captain 1983-84 D Hogg
1st XV 1983-84 P33 W11 D1 L21 F425 A630
Review of the season Winning only three league matches, Glasgow High/Kelvinside slipped back to the third division. They failed to win any of their six matches in a disastrous second half of the league programme, though the season had started hopefully with a win against their neighbours, Glasgow Academicals, who went on to take the Division 2 title. John Hodgkinson, though missing in mid-season because of injury, was still top scorer with 101 points, and Donald Wilson ran in 14 tries.

Gordonians

Year of formation 1903
Ground Seafield, Thorngrove Avenue, Aberdeen Tel: Aberdeen 37027
Colours Blue jerseys with gold hoops, blue shorts
Most capped player I G McCrae (Scotland) 6 caps
Captain 1983-84 J S P Hutcheson
1st XV 1983-84 P25 W9 D1 L15 F305 A358
Review of the season Gordonians' middle-of-the-table position in the second division summed up their season. They would have preferred to have relied less on their goal-kickers and more on try-scoring. More than half of the first XV's points were scored by two players, Callum MacGregor with 83 and Alastair Morgan with 79, while their leading try-scorer, Alan Reid, totalled only five. The highlight of the league season was a 31-14 away win against Glasgow High/Kelvinside.

Haddington

Year of formation 1911
Ground Neilson Park, Haddington Tel: Haddington 3702
Colours Scarlet jerseys and stockings, black shorts
Captain 1983-84 N M Morrison
1st XV 1983-84 P32 W11 D1 L20 F369 A763
Review of the season Losing all 12 league matches, Haddington dropped back to the second division. The signs were there from the beginning of the season, when they lost to Hawick by 0-82 in their opening league match, and three weeks later they fell to Stewart's-Melville by 0-70. With a good number of youngsters round an experienced core, however, Haddington have hope for the future. Finlay Duncan scored 83 points, seven more than Ian Clark, and David Thorne topped the try list with 10.

Hawick

Year of formation 1873
Ground Mansfield Park, Mansfield Road, Hawick Tel: Hawick 4291
Colours Green jerseys, white shorts
Most capped player J M Renwick (Scotland) 51 caps
Captain 1983-84 R W Murray
1st XV 1983-84 P34 W28 D0 L6 F1,061 A250
Review of the season For the seventh time in 11 years Hawick took the national championship, winning all 13 games, and for the first time in their history they scored more than 1,000 points in all games. Their top scores were in league games: 82-0 against Haddington and 73-3 against West of Scotland. They also regained the Border League title. Colin Gass was again top scorer, this time with 319 points, and Keith Mitchell had 27 tries, six more than his captain, Billy Murray. Gass and Mitchell were also top scorers in the first division, with 178 points and 12 tries.

Heriot's FP

Year of formation 1890
Ground Goldenacre, Ferry Road, Edinburgh
Tel: Edinburgh (031) 552 5925 (pavilion) 552 4097 (groundsman)
Colours Blue and white horizontal stripes
Most capped player A R Irvine (Scotland) 51 caps
Captain 1983-84 A R Irvine
1st XV 1983-84 P34 W27 D1 L6 F910 A387
Review of the season Heriot's finished only fifth in the first division, upset by losing to Watsonians and drawing with Melrose as well as falling to the top two, Hawick and Gala. Defeat by Watsonians was followed by 21 successive games without losing, including a friendly win over Hawick, and their run of successes ended only in the last match of the season, when Heriot's lost to Stewart's-Melville in the Murrayfield Cup final. Peter Steven, the Scotland 'B' wing, was top scorer with 198 points and 26 tries.

Highland

Year of formation 1922
Ground Northern Meeting Park, Inverness; clubhouse at Canel Park
Tel: Inverness 38644
Colours Green jerseys with red band, red and green hooped stockings, black shorts
Most capped player N A MacEwan (Scotland) 20 caps
Captain 1983-84 A D G Mackenzie
1st XV 1983-84 P24 W14 D0 L10 F345 A302
Review of the season After a promising start to the league programme Highland slipped away, winning only two of their last eight second division matches, but they still finished comfortably in the middle of the table. Their best result was a 42-6 win over Langholm in Inverness. David Graham was again top scorer (95 points).

Howe of Fife

Year of formation 1922
Ground Duffins Park, Cupar; clubhouse 15 Provis Wind, Cupar Tel: Cupar 52819
Colours Blue and white hoops
Most capped player D M D Rollo (Scotland) 40 caps
Captain 1983-84 B H Bell
1st XV 1983-84 P35 W15 D3 L17 F413 A474
Review of the season Howe of Fife again escaped relegation from the second division, though they lost three of their last five league matches. Their crucial win was against Glasgow High/Kelvinside, who ultimately dropped to the third division. In all matches Howe almost broke even, and they proved themselves best in their district by winning the Midlands Cup, beating Dundee High School FP by 10-9 in the final. Robbie Rutherford was top scorer with 92 points, 12 ahead of Tom Macaskill, and back row forward Ian Kirkhope had most tries (6).

Jedforest

Year of formation 1885
Ground Riverside Park, Jedburgh Tel: Jedburgh 2232 and 2486
Colours Royal blue jerseys and stockings, white shorts
Most capped player R J Laidlaw (Scotland) 27 caps
Captain 1983-84 D Miller
1st XV 1983-84 P30 W14 D1 L15 F452 A407
Review of the season Victories against Ayr, Haddington, and Melrose were enough to ensure that Jedforest stayed up in the first division, and they gave a good account of

themselves even against Hawick, the eventual champions. Jedforest lost that game only by two penalty goals. Gordon Jackson topped the points list with 75, and experienced back row forward Robbie Lindores scored most tries (9), but their outstanding player was once again international scrum-half Roy Laidlaw.

Jordanhill

Year of formation 1972 (on amalgamation of College and School FP clubs)
Ground Kilmardinny Playing Fields, Milngavie Road, Bearsden, Glasgow G61 3TB Tel: Glasgow (041) 942 8980
Colours Red jersey, green shorts
Most capped player J (Ian) McLauchlan (Scotland) 43 caps
Captain 1983-84 H Campbell
1st XV 1983-84 P26 W10 D2 L14 F284 A396
Review of the season Handicapped by the absence through injury of captain Hugh Campbell for much of the season, Jordanhill finished in the bottom half of the second division, though their worst result was in the Glasgow and District Cup competition, when Ayr beat them 33-0. Peter Brown was top scorer with 99 points.

Kelso

Year of formation 1876
Ground Poynder Park, Kelso, Roxburghshire Tel: 2300
Colours Black and white
Most capped player G K Smith (Scotland) 18 caps
Captain 1983-84 R E Paxton
1st XV 1983-84 P30 W21 D0 L9 F721 A316
Review of the season Kelso looked certain to finish third behind Hawick and Gala in the first division, having lost only to the top two. In the event, they fell against Heriot's and Stewart's-Melville in the last two matches and had to share third place with the latter club. Outside the national championship, Kelso's most notable result was a Border League win against Hawick, and their biggest competitive score was in beating Langholm 52-0. Colin Flannigan, who set the Scottish scoring record the previous season, again had most points (308). Wings Sandy Thomson and Douglas Robeson shared the try-scoring honours, each with 15.

Kilmarnock

Year of formation 1868
Ground Bellsland, Queens Drive, Kilmarnock Tel: Kilmarnock 22314
Colours White with red hoop surmounted by white Maltese cross
Most capped player W Cuthbertson (Scotland) 20 caps
Captain 1983-84 H Hamilton
1st XV 1983-84 P37 W20 D3 L14 F630 A475
Review of the season Kilmarnock won only two league matches and dropped back to the second division, beaten by Melrose in the relegation decider, but they had the small consolation of taking the Ayrshire Cup from Ayr. Stephen Martin was top scorer with 110 points, following in the footsteps of his brother, Derek, who missed the entire season with a broken leg. Wing John Robertson was again leading try-scorer, with 10.

Langholm

Year of formation 1872
Ground Milntown, Langholm, Dumfriesshire Tel: Langholm 80386
Colours Crimson jerseys and blue shorts
Most capped player C Elliot (Scotland) 12 caps

Captain 1983-84 B J Mackay
1st XV 1983-84 P28 W11 D1 L16 F250 A529
Review of the season Langholm suffered the ignominy of being warned by the SRU as a result of indiscipline on and off the field, and one of their players, Hector Barnfather, was suspended *sine die*. After winning all four October league matches Langholm fell away, with only two more wins, and in nine successive matches they failed to score a try. Stephen Little was again top scorer (101 points).

Melrose

Year of formation 1877
Ground Greenyards, Melrose Tel: Melrose 2559/2993
Colours Yellow and black
Most capped player F A L Laidlaw (Scotland) 32 caps
Captain 1983-84 K W Robertson
1st XV 1983-84 P32 W12 D1 L19 F397 A558
Review of the season Melrose escaped relegation by winning their last match against Kilmarnock 6-3, but their most incredible victory in competitive rugby was 19-18 against Kelso in the Border League, David Shiel kicking three dropped goals, all from long range, in the closing minutes. In all Shiel scored 19 dropped goals, two more than he had in the previous season, and a total of 99 points. Rob Moffat and Colin Ruthven each scored eight tries.

Portobello FP

Year of formation Reformed in 1954
Ground Cavalry Park, Duddingston Road West, Edinburgh
Tel: Edinburgh (031) 661 4554
Colours Navy blue and old gold hoops
Captain 1983-84 A T I Denham
1st XV 1983-84 P29 W16 D1 L12 F421 A347
Review of the season Portobello finished in a highly creditable third place in the second division, having been only second in the third the previous season. Only four league games were lost, including one against Edinburgh Academicals, which ended Portobello's record of not having lost a championship match since their entry in 1977. The McIntyre clan dominated the try-scoring, Steve and Russell totalling 14 apiece. Eddie Henderson, the former Gala and South of Scotland back, was top scorer with 84 points.

Preston Lodge

Year of formation 1929
Ground Pennypit Park, Prestonpans, East Lothian
Colours Black with maroon and white hoops
Captain 1983-84 R Dickson
1st XV 1983-84 P35 W23 D1 L11 F635 A358
Review of the season Preston Lodge lost their unbeaten home record, which they had maintained in the championship since November 1981, in losing to Jordanhill. Overall it was not quite as successful a season as the previous one. Preston Lodge lost more than twice as many matches as before, which reflected their strengthening fixture list, but in the second division they still stayed well up in the table, finishing joint fifth. Brian Palmer, for the second successive year, was top scorer (178 points), and Derek Kerr was leading try-scorer with 21, 10 of which came in league matches.

Royal High

Year of formation 1867
Ground Jock's Lodge, Edinburgh Tel: Edinburgh (031) 556 2033

Colours Black and white hoops
Most capped player J P Fisher (Scotland) 25 caps
Captain 1983-84 A G Sneddon
1st XV 1983-84 P32 W17 D0 L15 F412 A532
Review of the season Royal High were in danger of relegation to the third division until they won three of their last four matches. Their fortunes were transformed by the introduction of Andy Middlemiss, who scored 65 points in seven games. Peter Thom was top scorer with 84 points and 10 tries.

Selkirk

Year of formation 1907
Ground Philiphaugh, Selkirk Tel: Selkirk 20403
Colours Navy blue jerseys, white shorts
Most capped player J Y Rutherford (Scotland) 27 caps
Captain 1983-84 J Y Rutherford
1st XV 1983-84 P32 W19 D0 L13 F621 A435
Review of the season Selkirk had a good opening run in the first division, winning five games in a row, but they lost all the remaining seven once they ran into injury troubles, first with John Rutherford and then with Gordon Hunter. Rutherford broke his jaw playing in the international against New Zealand, and Hunter fractured a cheekbone earning his debut cap in Dublin. These two players were still the leading scorers, Hunter with 104 points and Rutherford with 102. Iwan Tukalo ran in 24 tries for Selkirk as well as seven in other matches and was a late choice for Scotland's visit to Romania.

Stewart's-Melville FP

Year of formation 1973 (on amalgamation of Daniel Stewart's College FP and Melville College FP)
Grounds Inverleith and Ferryfield, Ferry Road, Edinburgh EH5 2DW
Tel: Edinburgh (031) 522 3004 and 552 2112
Colours Scarlet jerseys with broad blacks bands divided by narrow gold bands, white shorts, black stockings
Most capped player J H Calder (Scotland) 23 caps
Captain 1983-84 A K Brewster
1st XV 1983-84 P31 W21 D0 L10 F833 A445
Review of the season Stewart's-Melville had an incredible opening run, scoring 453 points in winning their first 11 matches – including a 94-0 victory with 17 tries against Leith Academicals – but home defeats by Heriot's and Hawick in successive league games took the impetus out of their campaign. They finished joint third in the first division with Kelso, having lost only two more championship matches, and completed their season by beating Heriot's in the Murrayfield Cup final, which was Douglas Morgan's last game for the club. Morgan scored 301 points, and Dave Lister and Malcolm Lowes were joint top try-scorers with 18 each, one more than Chris Spence.

Stirling County

Year of formation 1904
Ground Bridgehaugh Park, Stirling Tel: Stirling 4827
Colours Red, white and black
Most capped player W H Welsh (Scotland) 8 caps
Captain 1983-84 E T N Pollock
1st XV 1983-84 P34 W21 D0 L13 F513 A447
Review of the season Stirling County were challenging for promotion from the second division until they lost to Glasgow Academicals, the eventual champions, but they still finished in a very creditable fourth position. Sid House, formerly with Highland and

Greenock, proved a welcome recruit at fly-half, scoring 131 points. Matt Stevenson topped the try list with 11.

Watsonians

Year of formation 1875
Ground Myreside, Edinburgh Tel: Edinburgh (031) 447 1395
Colours Maroon and white
Most capped player J C MacCallum (Scotland) 26 caps
Captain 1983-84 G N Buchan
1st XV 1983-84 P28 W18 D0 L10 F541 A354
Review of the season For the second successive season, Watsonians won more league games than they lost. They gave themselves a good start to the championship with five victories in six matches, and finished in fifth place. Their game was again based on a mobile pack and fast backs, including international centres David Johnston and Euan Kennedy, as well as Scotland 'B' full-back Gavin Hastings. Outside the league they twice topped 50 points, including a 54-6 win against Leith Academicals in the Murrayfield Cup. Hastings was top scorer with 119 points, and Johnston had most tries, 14, including 4 against Leith.

West of Scotland

Year of formation 1865
Ground Burnbrae, Glasgow Road, Milngavie, Glasgow G62 6HX
Tel: Glasgow (041) 956 2891/1960
Colours Red and yellow hooped jerseys and navy blue shorts
Most capped player A B Carmichael (Scotland) 50 caps
Captain 1983-84 D Gray
1st XV 1983-84 P26 W13 D0 L13 F433 A497
Review of the season It was a thoroughly disappointing season for West of Scotland. Only four league games were won, all of them against clubs below them in the championship, and the lowest point was their record 73-3 defeat by Hawick. Injuries and retirement left West short of key personnel in the middle five. Colin Mair and Matt Duncan were the top scorers with 109 points and nine tries respectively.

IRELAND

Academy

Year of formation 1975 (formerly Belfast Royal Academy FP)
Ground Hydepark, Mallusk, Co Antrim, N Ireland Tel: Glengormley 3085
Colours Maroon jerseys, navy shorts, maroon and white stockings
Most capped player K J Houston (Ireland) 6 caps
Captain 1983-84 W Lockhead
1st XV 1983-84 P24 W8 D2 L14 F266 A356
Review of the season Not an auspicious season for the club – they managed only eight wins and are looking forward to a vast improvement in the coming season. Their final record was almost exactly the same as that of the previous season.

Ballymena

Year of formation 1922
Ground Eaton Park, Ballymena Tel: Ballymena 6746
Colours Black jerseys, white shorts, black stockings with white turnover
Most capped player W J McBride (Ireland) 63 caps
Captain 1983-84 F Allen
1st XV 1983-84 P32 W19 D1 L12 F581 A420
Review of the season The Lions wing, Trevor Ringland, who had probably his best season, and Peter Millar, a young prop and son of the legendary Syd Millar, were among the best performers in a reasonable season. Ballymena are a young side with great ambitions and can be expected to become one of Ireland's better sides in a short while. Ringland had performed with distinction on the Lions tour.

Bangor

Year of formation 1885
Ground Upritchard Park, Bloomfield Road South, Bangor, Co Down, N Ireland
Colours Old gold, royal blue and black
Most capped player R A Milliken (Ireland) 14 caps
Captain 1983-84 D Morrow
1st XV 1983-84 P30 W25 D1 L4 F558 A257
Review of the season Bangor's playing record was once again the best among Ireland's clubs. It was ironic, therefore, that their four defeats in the season included the semi-final of the Ulster League and the second round of the Ulster Cup – so apart from the floodlight Bass Boston Cup they won no senior trophies. But they are a very good side and they play a highly entertaining brand of football. They had the misfortune to lose their Ulster lock, John Rogers, with a broken leg near the end of the season. A promising player is their full-back or wing, Terry McMaster.

Bective Rangers

Year of formation 1881
Ground Donnybrook, Dublin 4 Tel: Dublin 693894
Colours Red, green and white striped jerseys, white shorts
Most capped player J L Farrell (Ireland) 29 caps
Captain 1983-84 H Harbison
1st XV 1983-84 P29 W9 D4 L16 F374 A393
Review of the season As has been the case over the past few seasons, Bective Rangers' most polished player in a disappointing year was full-back Brendan Murphy. He scored 186 points, which made him the eighth-highest scorer in Leinster rugby, even though his club had the worst record of Leinster's 15 senior clubs with only nine wins. But Bective

did supply the hooker to take over from Ciaran Fitzgerald in the national team, in the very competent Harry Harbison.

Blackrock College

Year of formation 1882
Ground Stradbrook Road, Blackrock Tel: Dublin 805697
Colours Narrow royal blue and white striped jerseys, navy shorts, navy stockings
Most capped player J F Slattery (Ireland) 61 caps
Captain 1983-84 Job Langbroek
1st XV 1983-84 P30 W20 D3 L7 F528 A328
Review of the season Although Blackrock College lost both the Leinster Cup and League, titles which they had won the season before, they still managed to finish the season with the best record in Leinster. Once again their pack, with Willie Duggan and Fergus Slattery so prominent, took some mastering, but Wanderers succeeded in taming them in the Leinster Cup in one of the best club matches of the season. Daragh Coakley, Blackrock's diminutive fly-half, scored 273 points, which made him the highest scorer in the province.

Bohemians

Year of formation 1922
Ground Thomond Park, Limerick Tel: Limerick 51877
Colours Red and white
Most capped player M A F English (Ireland) 16 caps
Captain 1983-84 M Wixted
1st XV 1983-84 P33 W17 D2 L14 F348 A347
Review of the season A reasonably good season in which the team scored 44 tries – the fourth highest total among Munster clubs. Tommy Lenihan scored seven of these. While none of the major trophies in Munster came the way of Bohemians, the overall reaction to the season was one of quiet satisfaction.

CIYMS

Year of formation 1922
Ground Circular Road, Belfast Tel: Belfast 768225/760120
Colours Black and white hooped jerseys, black shorts, blue stockings
Most capped player A C Pedlow (Ireland) 30 caps
Captain 1983-84 G McFadden
1st XV 1983-84 P25 W9 D0 L16 F273 A366
Review of the season Not the happiest season for 'CI', so often among Ireland's club elite. They have a fine lock in the Ulster player, Colin Morrison, and the club believes that their under-20 team is the best in Ireland – these assets augur well for the future. However their final record last season was vastly inferior to that of 1982-83.

Clontarf

Year of formation 1876
Ground Castle Avenue, Clontarf, Dublin Tel: Dublin 336214
Colours Red and blue jerseys, white shorts, red and blue striped stockings
Most capped player G J Morgan (Ireland) 19 caps
Captain 1983-84 N Gaffney
1st XV 1983-84 P29 W11 D1 L17 F301 A421
Review of the season Clontarf struggled for most of the season even though they were enthusiastically led by Niall Gaffney and had the services of a nationally famous Gaelic

footballer, Brian Mullins, at No 8. Their final record was slightly inferior to that of the previous season.

Collegians

Year of formation 1890
Ground Deramore Park, Belfast, N Ireland Tel: Belfast 665943
Colours White and maroon, navy stockings with maroon tops
Most capped player J McVicker (Ireland) 20 caps
Captain 1983-84 A Campbell
1st XV 1983-84 P29 W18 D0 L11 F433 A311
Review of the season Collegians, the Ulster Cup holders, lost to City of Derry in the first round, thus reversing very early on the result of the Cup final the previous season. Still, it was a fairly good season overall, with Roy Palmer, usually the full-back, getting an Irish Trial and a 'B' cap against Scotland, and lock Maurice Dawson and scrum-half Ricky Stewart also adding distinction to the club.

Corinthians

Year of formation 1932
Ground Corinthian Park, Tuam Road, Galway
Colours Blue, black and white
Captain 1983-84 J O'Dea
1st XV 1983-84 P31 W17 D2 L12 F381 A270
Review of the season Corinthians won the Connacht Cup, beating Athlone 10-9 in the final, but that triumph was somewhat muted by their defeat in the League at the hands of old Galway city rivals, Galwegians. It was Corinthians' first loss in six seasons in the League and they were going for their 41st consecutive League win when Galwegians called a halt to their successful run. Noel Mannion at No 8 and flanker Declan Greaney were their most consistent forwards, and the half-back combination of Cammie Gallagher and Ciaran Smyth was cool and efficient.

Cork Constitution

Year of formation 1892
Ground Temple Hill, Ballintemple, Cork Tel: Cork 32563
Colours White, black and blue
Most capped player T J Kiernan (Ireland) 54 caps
Captain 1983-84 Moss Finn
1st XV 1983-84 P27 W23 D0 L4 F445 A212
Review of the season With international Moss Finn, in excellent form in the centre, and ace line-out player, Donal Lenihan, having a splendid season, Constitution lost only four matches. But like Bangor in Ulster and Blackrock College in Leinster – the other leading clubs in Ireland – they failed in the Cup at an early stage. However, they did win the Munster League and the Cork Charity Cup. John Barry, the 'B' international full-back, was their highest scorer with 180 points and Ian O'Leary was their top try-scorer with 10.

Dolphin

Year of formation 1902
Ground Musgrave Park, Cork Tel: Cork 22069
Colours Navy blue
Most capped player J S McCarthy (Ireland) 28 caps
Captain 1983-84 P Aherne
1st XV 1983-84 P27 W13 D2 L12 F352 A273

Review of the season International Michael Kiernan, who had played for Dolphin, moved to Dublin and joined Lansdowne, depriving Dolphin of much-needed dash in their back division. Considering this sad loss, Dolphins had a satisfactory season.

Dublin University

Year of formation 1854
Ground College Park, Trinity College, Dublin 2 Tel: 778423
Colours White jerseys and shorts, black stockings with red bands
Most capped player J D Clinch (Ireland) 30 caps
Captain 1983-84 P Clinch
1st XV 1983-84 P28 W13 D0 L15 F439 A413
Review of the season Trinity produced some of the most exciting young backs and it was surprising that Brendan Mullin, their 20-year-old centre, was not capped for Ireland. Perhaps the Irish selectors felt that it would be wiser to wait a while but there seems no doubt that he is an oustanding talent. But overall, the youth and inexperience of the forwards tended to make the going difficult. Trinity won 13 of their 28 matches in an average season and their leading scorer was fly-half Cedric Cruess-Callaghan, who totalled 166 points.

Dungannon

Year of formation 1873
Ground Stevenson Park, Dungannon, N Ireland Tel: Dungannon 22387
Colours Royal blue and white hoops, white shorts
Most capped player S A McKinney (Ireland) 25 caps
Captain 1983-84 J McCoy
1st XV 1983-84 P23 W6 D1 L16 F199 A374
Review of the season The captain and tight-head prop, Jim McCoy, played for Ireland in 1984 but generally, Dungannon did not have much to celebrate. Willie Anderson continued to play for Ulster at No 8 and served Dungannon well. However, they won only six matches during 1983-84, a record which illustrates that the club is going through a transitional stage.

Galwegians

Year of formation 1922
Ground Glenina, Galway, Co Galway Tel: Galway (091) 62484
Colours Sky blue jerseys, white shorts, sky blue stockings with black tops
Most capped player P J A O'Sullivan (Ireland) 15 caps
Captain 1983-84 J Kelly
1st XV 1983-84 P30 W10 D4 L16 F304 A374
Review of the season The highlight of the season was the victory over Corinthians in the Connacht League, which gave Galwegians the title. But the local rivalry, always intense, was heightened when Corinthians beat them in the Cup. Colin Hitchcock, a young doctor beginning his rugby career, did not turn out as often as he and the club would have wished, but there were good displays throughout the season from full-back Mick Quaid and lock Mick Tarpey.

Garryowen

Year of formation 1884
Ground Dooradoyle, Limerick Tel: Limerick 46094
Colours Light blue jerseys with white star on breast
Most capped player B G M Wood (Ireland) 29 caps
Captain 1983-84 D Madden

1st XV 1983-84 P28 W14 D2 L12 F317 A317
Review of the season Perhaps the most noteworthy feature of a less-than-outstanding season was that Garryowen, the famed Limerick club for whom Tony Ward used to play, scored exactly the same total of points – 317 – as they conceded. They failed, for once, to win any of the Munster senior trophies but victories for their under-20 team in both the Limerick Cup and League suggest that they will soon regain their former eminence among Ireland's clubs.

Instonians

Year of formation 1919
Ground Shane Park, Stockmans Lane, Belfast BT9 7JD Tel: Belfast 660629
Colours Yellow, black and purple
Most capped player D Hewitt (Ireland) 18 caps
Captain 1983-84 J McKim
1st XV 1983-84 P29 W14 D2 L13 F428 A379
Review of the season With two internationals in their back division – Keith Crossan on the wing and David Irwin in the centre – Instonians enjoyed only a mediocre season by their own high standards. They failed to win any of the Ulster Senior trophies. Irwin eventually lost his Ireland place.

Lansdowne

Year of formation 1872
Ground Lansdowne Road, Dublin 4 Tel: Dublin 689292/689300
Colours Red, yellow and black
Most capped player M I Keane (Ireland) 51 caps
Captain 1983-84 V Becker
1st XV 1983-84 P30 W14 D3 L13 F487 A438
Review of the season Lansdowne were disappointing despite all the talent at their disposal. They had much speed in their threequarter line-centres Michael Kiernan and Rory Moroney, both capped during the season, plus the captain and former international Vincent Becker and the other wing, John McGeady, performed well when they got possession. Although they had Moss Keane and Des Fitzgerald, both current internationals, in the pack, they finished with almost as many losses as wins, which really was way below expectations.

Malone

Year of formation 1892
Ground Gibson Park Avenue, Cregagh Road, Belfast BT6 9GL
Tel: Belfast 57819/51312 (office)
Colours White shirts, blue shorts, red stockings
Most capped player W E Crawford (Ireland) 30 caps
Captain 1983-84 H Williamson
1st XV 1983-84 P31 W15 D1 L15 F401 A370
Review of the season Malone, the club that fields more teams at the weekend than any other club in Ireland, had the distinction of winning the Ulster Senior Cup in 1984. They owed their success to their pack, which included Irish flanker Willie Duncan, and to the half-backs, Stephen Cowan and Ian Brown. Brown was a resourceful fly-half for Ulster and young Cowan gained a senior cup medal one season after winning an Ulster Schools Senior Cup medal with Grosvenor High School.

Monkstown

Year of formation 1883
Ground Sydney Parade, Dublin 4 Tel: Dublin 691794

Colours Royal blue and gold
Most capped player J C Parke (Ireland) 20 caps
Captain 1983-84 F Condon
1st XV 1983-84 P40 W14 D4 L22 F442 A462
Review of the season Monkstown, one of Ireland's oldest clubs, celebrated their centenary by playing 40 matches against all kinds of opposition. But while they played with great spirit and enjoyed much goodwill from all their opponents, they only managed to win 14 of their matches.

North of Ireland (NIFC)

Year of formation 1859
Ground Shaftesbury Avenue, Belfast BT7 2ES Tel: Belfast 21096/23342
Colours Red, black, and blue jerseys, navy shorts, black stockings with red, black and blue turnover
Most capped player C M H Gibson (Ireland) 69 caps
Captain 1983-84 A Creighton
1st XV 1983-84 P26 W12 D0 L14 F280 A310
Review of the season 'North' finished the season well, appearing in the Ulster Cup final, but they were beaten by Malone at Ravenhill. They had some injury problems at one stage and brought back to action the great Mike Gibson, who, at the age of 41, was still turning out for various junior teams in the club. He played at fly-half in the Ulster Final, but even his presence was not enough to win the match.

Old Belvedere

Year of formation 1930
Ground Anglesea Road, Ballsbridge, Dublin 4 Tel: Dublin 689748
Colours Black and white hooped jerseys, black shorts
Most capped player A J F O'Reilly (Ireland) 29 caps
Captain 1983-84 J Walsh
1st XV 1983-84 P31 W15 D1 L15 F415 A477
Review of the season This was not one of Old Belvedere's better seasons. The absence of Ollie Campbell, who suffered from a virus, obviously had a bad effect even though the Australian, Michael Broad, filled the fly-half position adequately in most respects. 'Belvo' are by tradition one of Ireland's more skilful teams, but they lacked resources last season, and defensively they did not do too well, conceding an average of over two tries per match.

Old Wesley

Year of formation 1891
Ground Donnybrook, Dublin 4 Tel: Dublin 689149
Colours White jerseys with red and white band, white shorts
Most capped player P A Orr (Ireland) 39 caps
Captain 1983-84 C Callan
1st XV 1983-84 P29 W14 D5 L10 F324 A316
Review of the season For some seasons now Old Wesley have had one of the strongest packs of forwards in Irish rugby, with the brothers George and Bob Wallace at lock and Phil Orr at loose-head prop. Unfortunately, the quality of their back play has not really been on a par with that of the forward play. Only Stephen Hennessey, at full-back, has been outstanding and the 193 points he scored during the season made him the fifth-highest scorer in Leinster.

Palmerston

Year of formation 1899
Ground Milltown Road, Clonskeagh, Dublin 6 Tel: Dublin 973126
Colours Black, green and white jerseys, black shorts
Captain 1983-84 T Leggett
1st XV 1983-84 P30 W15 D3 L12 F391 A344
Review of the season Palmerston had one of their best seasons for a long time and much of the credit goes to their fly-half, Gerry Browner, who scored 192 points. This total was made up of good place-kicking, which yielded some 40 penalty goals, together with the conversion of 20 of his team's 49 tries. Otherwise, it was team-work rather than any outstanding individual ability which provided success.

Queen's University, Belfast

Year of formation 1869
Ground Upper Malone Playing Fields, Upper Malone Road, Belfast
Tel: Belfast 611662
Colours Royal blue jerseys, white shorts, green, blue and black stockings
Most capped player J W Kyle (Ireland) 46 caps
Captain 1983-84 J Alexander
1st XV 1983-84 P34 W12 D0 L22 F355 A522
Review of the season Queen's, like all the Irish university teams, are finding the going tough against more mature opponents. Nowadays, students seem to be less experienced than of yore. Queen's had Ulster players in scrum-half Rab Brady and flanker Peter Matthews but they sorely missed flanker Nigel Carr, who did not play during the season because of injury.

St Mary's College

Year of formation 1900
Ground Templeville Road, Dublin 6 Tel: Dublin 900440
Colours Royal blue jerseys with white star, white shorts, royal blue stockings
Most capped player J J Moloney (Ireland) 27 caps
Captain 1983-84 D Fanning
1st XV 1983-84 P36 W18 D6 L12 F479 A370
Review of the season St Mary's enjoyed a rather mixed season by their own high standards. They were knocked out of the Leinster Senior Cup at the semi-final stage by the eager students of UCD, and even though veteran performers in their pack like captain Declan Fanning and flanker Shay Deering tried hard, the pack as a unit was not just strong enough. It was a pity that such backs as Tony Ward and Paul Dean, who could have dominated, were not better served.

Sunday's Well

Year of formation 1924
Ground Musgrave Park, Cork Tel: Cork 25926
Colours Red, white and green
Most capped player J C Walsh (Ireland) 25 caps
Captain 1983-84 J Joyce
1st XV 1983-84 P26 W6 D3 L17 F226 A381
Review of the season Not a very happy season for Sunday's Well, who finished lowest in the merit table of the 11 senior clubs in Munster, managing a mere six victories. They made no impression, either, in the Senior Cup.

Terenure College

Year of formation 1941
Ground Lakelands Park, Terenure, Dublin 6 Tel: Dublin 907572
Colours Purple, black and white
Most capped player M L Hipwell (Ireland) 12 caps
Captain 1983-84 N O'Kelly
1st XV 1983-84 P31 W18 D2 L11 F513 A382
Review of the season Terenure College won the Leinster Senior League title with a most consistent performance. They owed a lot to their captain and scrum-half, Niall O'Kelly, who partnered his brother Michael at half-back. Ray Hopkins at full-back and Paul Haycock on the right wing were other notable contributors, and a young and spirited pack laid the groundwork. But the energy they put into the League seemed to take a lot of steam out of Terenure and they fell to Skerries in the first round of the Cup. Nevertheless, it was a good season.

University College, Cork

Year of formation 1872
Ground Mardyke, Western Road, Cork Tel: 45772
Colours Red jersey with black bar, white skull-and-crossbones on chest
Most capped player J Russell (Ireland) 19 caps
Captain 1983-84 O Crotty
1st XV 1983-84 P24 W8 D0 L16 F332 A420
Review of the season UCC were the most successful of the university teams, winning the Dudley Cup for inter-varsity competition. Although their overall record was patchy, they still produced the two top try-scorers in Munster in the brothers Owen and Jim Crotty, their wings. Owen, the club captain, scored 17 tries and Jim managed 14.

University College, Dublin

Year of formation 1910
Ground University College Dublin, Belfield, Dublin 4 Tel: Dublin 693616
Colours St Patrick's blue jerseys, white shorts, navy blue stockings with St Patrick's blue tops
Most capped player R J McLoughlin (Ireland) 40 caps
Captain 1983-84 W Burns
1st XV 1983-84 P29 W19 D3 L7 F484 A391
Review of the season UCD started slowly but built up to a good season, which ended with a hard-earned place in the Leinster Cup final. But the young side, much of their energy having been dissipated in two strenuous matches against St Mary's in the semi-final, were no match for Wanderers in the final. They showed themselves to be a lively and talented side that will improve further with experience. Willie Burns was an inspiring captain and hooker and their best forward was flanker Derek McGrath, who forged his way into the Irish team.

Wanderers

Year of formation 1870
Ground Lansdowne Road, Dublin 4 Tel: Dublin 689277
Junior ground Merrion Road, Dublin Tel: Dublin 693227/695272
Colours Blue, black and white hooped jerseys, navy shorts, black stockings with blue and white turnover
Most capped player J R Kavanagh (Ireland) 35 caps
Captain 1983-84 F Ennis
1st XV 1983-84 P32 W21 D0 L11 F591 A391

Review of the season Wanderers had an excellent season, winning 65 per cent of their matches and gaining the top honour of the Leinster season in taking the Leinster Cup in sparkling style. They beat UCD 27-4 in the final with a superb display. Frank Ennis, their full-back and captain, had to drop out of the team before the Cup due to injury but Ian Burns, the fly-half deputised most efficiently. Ronan Kearney, Pat Kenny, Jerry Holland and Mick Fitzpatrick were fine forwards, and with Robbie McGrath and Ian Burns at half-back and the versatile John Duffy in the centre the possession was used expertly. Their best performance was in eliminating Blackrock College in a fine game in the semi-final.

WALES

Aberavon

Year of formation 1876
Ground Talbot Athletic Ground, Manor Street, Port Talbot, Glamorgan
Tel: Port Talbot 882427/886038
Colours Red and black hoops, white shorts, and red stockings
Most capped player A J Martin (Wales) 34 caps
Captain 1983-84 A Owen
1st XV 1983-84 P50 W27 D2 L21 F845 A721
Review of the season Another disappointing season for the Wizards, although they reached the semi-final stage of the Cup. There, they went out 12-3 to Neath, whom they had trounced 31-7 three months earlier, and ironically defeated again, 23-12 after the cup-tie. Scrum-half Ray Giles was capped against Romania. Mike Lewis was top scorer with 201 points while 20-year-old newcomer Andrew Jones registered 143. But the lack of try-scoring power was borne out by the end-of-season tally – the top try-scorer, wing Kevin James, accumulated only 12. A significant statistic is that opponents kicked 94 penalty goals against them.

Abertillery

Year of formation 1884
Ground The Park, Abertillery, Gwent Tel: Abertillery 212226
Colours Green and white hoops
Most capped player H J Morgan (Wales) 27 caps
Captain 1983-84 M Cairns
1st XV 1983-84 P57 W27 D4 L26 F812 A755
Review of the season Abertillery launched their centenary season by reaching the August final of the Snelling Sevens, and though they failed against Cardiff it was a memorable start. Mike Cairns' side fought valiantly before losing to Japan 17-13, having defeated Cardiff 9-3 in the first match of the season. They also defeated Newport and Swansea and gave Pontypool a fright before losing 27-22. Kevin Clarke's 233 points included 12 tries and Nigel Paul secured 158 points. Adrian Parry scored 14 tries. Malcolm Lewis, the only secretary/player among major Welsh clubs, broke Ray Gladwyn's 17-year-old record of 494 appearances. Cairns was out for a long spell with a broken leg and missed the Japan match.

Bridgend

Year of formation 1878
Ground Brewery Field, Tondu Road, Bridgend, Mid-Glamorgan
Tel: Bridgend 2707/59032
Colours Blue and white stripes
Most capped player J P R Williams (Wales) 55 caps
Captain 1983-84 M James
1st XV 1983-84 P52 W40 D3 L9 F1,596 A536
Review of the season Always exciting attackers, Bridgend finished as runners-up in the Welsh club championship, piling up a world record 269 tries, of which 107 were scored by their wings, Mark Titley (who won his first cap) with a post-war Bridgend record of 42, Glen Webbe (34) and Tony Lewis (31). Five players passed a century of points for the season: Howell Davies (390), Titley (168), Webbe and Jeff Stephenson (136 each) and Tony Lewis (124). Full-back Davies won his first cap and set a Welsh record with 39 points in four Five Nations' matches. Davies' 40 points in the 100-7 victory over Penarth was a British record – and Bridgend's score was the biggest ever in a first-class match in Wales.

Cardiff

Year of formation 1876
Ground Cardiff Arms Park, Westgate Street, Cardiff Tel: Cardiff 23546
Colours Cambridge blue and black
Most capped player G O Edwards (Wales) 53 caps
Captain 1983-84 J P Scott
1st XV 1983-84 P47 W36 D1 L10 F1,214 A649
Review of the season Cardiff won the WRU/Schweppes Cup for the third time in four years, John Scott setting an all-time record for the club with four consecutive seasons of captaincy. Gareth Davies improved his record points total in a season to 383 as the team registered their highest aggregate of points. Hooker Alan Phillips' total of 24 tries was a record for a forward in one season. Adrian Hadley (20 tries) became a new cap, but Terry Holmes did not play until the end of February, having suffered a serious knee injury in New Zealand with the 1983 Lions. Cardiff were the only team to win at Pontypool, and they finished third in the Welsh club championship.

Cross Keys

Year of formation 1885
Ground Pandy Park, Cross Keys, Gwent Tel: Cross Keys 270289
Colours Black and white hoops
Most capped player S Morris (Wales) 19 caps
Captain 1983-84 D Church
1st XV 1983-84 P47 W21 D0 L26 F687 A695
Review of the season A record aggregate of 687 points in all matches gave the Pandy Park club some consolation in another season when defeats outnumbered victories. Mike Avery became the fastest century-scorer in the club's history, reaching that target in just 11 games, and went on to pass Alf Wainfur's record for a season with 223 points. Fly-half Colin Watkins supplied 82 points. New wing Mike Robinson scored nine tries and wing forward Mark Whitlock eight. Derek Church, despite injury, set an inspiring example while Chris Booker impressed as a line-out specialist, though John Collins, another line-out star, joined London Welsh.

Ebbw Vale

Year of formation 1880
Ground Eugene Cross Park, Ebbw Vale Tel: Ebbw Vale 302157/302995
Colours Red, white, and green hoops
Most capped player Denzil Williams (Wales) 36 caps
Captain 1983-84 C Dennehy
1st XV 1983-84 P54 W21 D1 L32 F685 A948
Review of the season Ebbw Vale slumped from eighth in the Welsh championship to 17th, the lowest finishing spot in their history, with 31 defeats plus failure in the cup. Mike Morgan, joining from Newport, reached a century of points in record time, just 10 games, and was top scorer with 110 despite transferring to Tredegar. Richard Owen's 64 was next best while skipper Carl Dennehy, a Wales 'B' back row selection, collected nine tries. Ebbw Vale were crushed 61-18 by Cardiff and 57-0 by Pontypool. Ian Watkins proved an outstanding hooker while David Bidgood played with consistent expertise in the second row.

Glamorgan Wanderers

Year of formation 1893
Ground The Memorial Ground, Stirling Road, Ely, Cardiff Tel: Cardiff 591039
Colours Cambridge blue, black and white

Captain 1983-84 J Davies
1st XV 1983-84 P50 W28 D0 L22 F854 A865
Review of the season Under the energetic leadership of lock John Davies, the Wanderers made quite an impression. Steve Williams, who had been coaching at Cross Keys, joined John Richards in January and their work together saw the team win 16 of the last 20 games. Victories were registered over Aberavon, Maesteg and at Bath. Mark Hembury broke the club scoring record in his first season with 273 points from 37 appearances while Eammon Holland's total of 23 tries was another club record. Nick Ward scored 75 points. Prop Paul Prickett missed only one game. Skipper Davies and Mike Thomas formed an excellent second row and Paul Marney, recruited from Aberavon, a useful No 8.

Llanelli

Year of formation 1872
Ground Stradey Park, Llanelli, Dyfed Tel: Llanelli 4060
Colours Scarlet jerseys with white collars, club crest on left breast
Most capped player J J Williams (Wales) 30 caps
Captain 1983-84 P May
1st XV 1983-84 P52 W32 D2 L18 F1,282 A784
Review of the season Llanelli slipped from fourth to seventh place in the Welsh club championship, winning only one of their last seven games, during which, remarkably, they scored just 19 points while conceding 114. Phil May was the outstanding all-round line-out forward in Wales, especially proficient on the short throw or against anyone in the mini-line. They drew with Pontypool at Stradey in the quarter-final of the Cup but put the holders out on try ruling. Gary Pearce topped the score-chart with 293, and Martin Gravelle had 212. Wing Phil Lewis scored 34 tries in 39 appearances. Only Neath and Maesteg won at Stradey. There was a first cap for Mark Douglas.

Maesteg

Year of formation 1882
Ground Llynvi Road, Maesteg, Mid-Glamorgan Tel: Maesteg 732283
Colours Black and amber
Most capped player G Evans (Wales) 10 caps
Captain 1983-84 D Arthur
1st XV 1983-84 P55 W30 D3 L22 F1,034 A865
Review of the season The Old Parish slipped from fifth to 12th in the Welsh championship despite the dynamic leadership of Dai Arthur, one of the finest pack-leaders on the Welsh scene. Gwyn Evans, who lost his place in the Welsh team following the defeat in Romania, provided most points with 190 in 25 games; Peter Jones on the wing scored 21 tries and Andrew Taylor, 14. Derek Brown (12 tries) and Robbie Llewellyn (11) were lively back row forwards while prop Peter Francis played in 47 games. A home draw with Pontypool was a notable feat, and Maesteg gained their first double over Llanelli for more than 30 years.

Neath

Year of formation 1871
Ground The Gnoll, Gnoll Park Road, Neath, West Glamorgan Tel: Neath 4420
Colours Black with white Maltese cross
Most capped player W D Morris (Wales) 34 caps
Captain 1983-84 H E Rees
1st XV 1983-84 P52 W31 D2 L19 F846 A630
Review of the season With the motivation of team-manager Brian Thomas, the ex-Wales lock, very much in evidence, Neath climbed to ninth in the Welsh championship, their best finishing position for seven years. They reached the final of the Cup and fought

valiantly against Cardiff, whom they defeated two days later at the Gnoll, Neale Harris improved his record aggregate for a season to 299 points and David Jacob raised 15 tries. Gareth Jones was an exciting new scrum-half and Lyn Jones a dynamic openside flanker. Neath defeated Pontypool 10-8, at the Gnoll.

Newbridge

Year of formation 1890
Ground Welfare Ground, Bridge Street, Newbridge, Gwent Tel: Newbridge 243247
Colours Blue and black hoops (alternate, red)
Most capped player D Hayward (Wales) 15 caps
Captain 1983-84 J T Stokes
1st XV 1983-84 P52 W37 D2 L13 F1,129 A744
Review of the season Inevitably, Paul Turner figured prominently in another highly successful season. He improved his record for a season to 405 points and the club recorded their highest aggregate. Alan Glasson, a powerful wing, supplied 92 points from 23 tries and fellow wing Chris Phillips crossed for 17. Japan pipped them 19-14 in a memorable match, but Jim Stokes's team gained the double over Swansea. The 30-year-old hooker nearly died when he contracted paratyphoid in October, but returned to play in the New Year. Terry Shaw won his first cap for Wales while Martin Short proved an excellent No 8. Simon Harris, in the summer a fast bowler for the local Rogerstone CC, joined from Risca to play well at lock.

Newport

Year of formation 1874
Ground Rodney Parade, Newport, Gwent Tel: Newport 58193
Colours Black and amber
Most capped player K J Jones (Wales) 44 caps
Captain 1983-84 M J Watkins
1st XV 1983-84 P50 W31 D2 L17 F1,110 A711
Review of the season Newport, registering a record aggregate of points as they passed 1,000 for the first time, climbed to sixth in the Welsh championship – their best finishing place for seven years – under the inspiring leadership of Mike Watkins. Watkins, who took over the captaincy of the national team as a new cap after the Scottish defeat, led them to victories over Ireland and England. Andy Phillips, who missed the second half of the season with injury, was top scorer with 174 points while Tony Coombs' 22 made him the club's highest try-scoring scrum-half. Marc Batten crossed for 21 tries and flanker Richard Collins (from Pontypridd) and Roger Powell accumulated 15 apiece. Rhys Morgan won his first cap at prop.

Penarth

Year of formation 1880
Ground Athletic Grounds, Lavernock Road, Penarth, South Glamorgan
Tel: Penarth 708402
Colours Royal blue (alternative with white hoops)
Most capped player J Bassett (Wales) 15 caps
Captain 1983-84 V Crane
1st XV 1983-84 P46 W11 D1 L34 F518 A1,097
Review of the season Outside half Roddy Crane's 259 in 45 games was a points record for the Seasiders. Peter Goodfellow joined from Cardiff and was a star performer, mostly at full-back. Rob MacPherson scored five tries as a purposeful No 8 and fellow back row man Chris Williams played in 34 games, travelling from Camborne on each occasion. Paul Adams, a convert from soccer, played excellently in the second row. A 12-6 home win over Aberavon proved a great boost and Penarth fought doggedly before losing 32-21

to the Barbarians. Sadly, the Seasiders went down to a record defeat in a major club match in Wales in the final match of the season, 100-7 at Bridgend.

Pontypool

Year of formation 1901
Ground Pontypool Park, Pontypool Tel: Pontypool 3492 (ground) 2524 (HQ)
Colours Red, white, and black hoops
Most capped player G Price (Wales) 41 caps
Captain 1983-84 E T Butler
1st XV 1983-84 P50 W46 D2 L2 F1,607 A483
Review of the season Pontypool, winning the Welsh club championship for the fourth time in post-war years, set a world record aggregate in all matches of 1,607 points. Peter Lewis scored 472 of them – the second highest total in Welsh rugby history surpassed only by another Pontypool full-back, Robin Williams, who notched up 517 in 1974-75. Scrum-half David Bishop totalled 256 points including 39 tries, a post-war record, and Chris Huish's 100 points from 25 tries made him the club's record try-scoring forward. Only Cardiff (at Pontypool) and Neath defeated Pontypool, while Maesteg and Llanelli (in the Cup) forced draws. Mark Brown won his first cap, but Graham Price and Jeff Squire withdrew from international consideration.

Pontypridd

Year of formation 1876
Ground Sardis Road Ground, Pwllgwaun, Pontypridd Tel: Pontypridd 405006
Colours Black and white hoops
Most capped player R J Robins (Wales) 13 caps
Captain 1983-84 R Dyer
1st XV 1983-84 P50 W17 D0 L33 F604 A948
Review of the season Another season in the doldrums was a keen disappointment for Pontypridd supporters, who watched a total of 33 defeats, including one by a 12-17 margin against little Ynysybwl at Sardis Road. Coach Eddie Jones stressed that the club lacked quality players and that an extensive rebuilding policy was necessary. They lost 60-0 at Pontypool, 44-0 away to South Wales Police and 55-8 to Bridgend, but managed a 19-14 win over Swansea. Rhys Williams was top scorer with 76 points while Phil Jones supplied 50 points and Carl Groves 12 tries.

South Wales Police

Year of formation 1969
Ground Police Recreation Ground, Waterton Cross, Bridgend, Mid-Glamorgan
Tel: Bridgend 55555 ext 218/Bridgend 4481
Colours Red jerseys, white shorts, royal blue stockings
Most capped player I Hall (Wales) 8 caps
Captain 1983-84 P Noble
1st XV 1983-84 P52 W40 D1 L11 F1,321 A712
Review of the season Fifth place in the Welsh club championship was the highest finishing place ever for the Police who, captained by scrum-half Phil Noble, raised a record aggregate in all matches of 1,321 points and another record of 226 tries. Amazingly, wing Mark Brinkworth scored 54 tries in 40 games, the largest tally by a major club player since Neath's Dan Jones totalled 59 in 1928-29. Brinkworth scored six in the match against Metropolitan Police. In retaining the British Police Cup, Noble's team crushed Wiltshire 70-0 in the early stages and toppled Lancashire 45-3 in the final. They defeated Bristol 20-19. Bleddyn Bowen won his first cap.

Swansea

Year of formation 1874
Ground St Helen's Ground, Swansea, West Glamorgan Tel: Swansea 464918/466593
Colours All white
Most capped player T M Davies (Wales) 38 caps
Captain 1983-84 D S Richards
1st XV 1983-84 P51 W32 D0 L19 F1,229 A751
Review of the season Champions the previous season, Swansea unaccountably slipped to eighth in the Welsh championship, their lowest spot for five years. Robert Jones, the Cwmtawe schoolboy, looks a scrum-half for the future, but the talent behind the scrum was often shackled by lack of authority in the pack. Skipper David Richards announced his retirement from international rugby while Richard Moriarty was recalled by Wales in the new and unexpected role of blindside flanker. Mark Wyatt, dogged by injuries, was nevertheless the top scorer with 294 points and Roger Blyth supplied 163. Tony Swift scored 21 tries to pass 100 for the club.

Tredegar

Year of formation 1899
Ground Tredegar Recreation Ground, Park Hill, Tredegar, Gwent
Tel: Tredegar 2879
Colours Red, black and white
Captain 1983-84 I Lewis
1st XV 1983-84 P48 W28 D2 L18 F903 A518
Review of the season Ian Lewis, always a resourceful and consistent scrum-half, and Nick Hunt as his partner, helped Tredegar climb to tenth place in the Welsh table and they registered their first-ever double over Ebbw Vale, though losing to them in the cup 10-9. Steve Giles scored the most points (109), while Mike Morgan, who had scored 110 points for Ebbw Vale, joined Tredegar and contributed 107 points. A third centurion was Gary Moses with 104. Centre Howard Dwyer scored 18 tries in a club record of 145 – the club also registered a record aggregate in all games. A double over South Wales Police was an achievement, and they pipped Newbridge 8-7 at Tredegar.

FIXTURES 1984-85
Compiled by John Griffiths

Venues and fixtures understood to be correct at time of going to press, but subject to alteration. The compiler thanks all those officials who assisted him in his efforts, especially those at the various Union headquarters.

Saturday, 1 September

Harlequins v French Barbarians (Twickenham)
Collegians Tournament
Carmarthern Athletic v Crawshay's Welsh
Aberavon v Glamorgan Wands
Aberdeen GSFP v Preston Lodge
Abertillery v Neath
Ayr v Kilmarnock
Birmingham v Hull ER
Bristol v Northampton
Boroughmuir v Jedforest
Cardiff v East District RU
Clarkston v West of Scotland
Colwyn Bay v London Welsh
Cork Const v Galwegians
Cross Keys v S Wales Police
Durham City v Wakefield
Edinburgh Wands v Corstorphine
Exeter v Liverpool
Fylde v Blackheath
Gala v Gosforth
Glasgow High v Glasgow Acads
Gloucester v Swansea
Greystones v Malone
Harrogate v Selkirk
Hartlepool Rovers v Watsonians
Headingley v Saracens
Heriot's FP v London Scottish
Highfield v Dolphin
Kendal v Middlesbrough
Lansdowne v Old Belvedere
Leicester v Bedford
Llanelli v Pontypridd
London Irish v Pontypool
Lydney v Penarth
Maesteg v Wasps
Manchester v Waterloo
Moseley v Nottingham
Newbridge v Ebbw Vale
Newport v Coventry
Northern v Huddersfield
Nuneaton v Halifax
Orrell v New Brighton
Palmerston v Garryowen
Penzance-Newlyn v St Ives
Percy Park v Westoe
Plymouth Albion v Bath
Rosslyn Park v Vale of Lune
Roundhay v Hawick
Rugby v Birkenhead Park
Sale v Morley
Skerries v Clontarf
Terenure Coll v Bective Rangers
Torquay Ath v Richmond
Trinity Acads v Stewart's-Melville FP
Wanderers v Old Wesley
West Hartlepool v Preston Grasshoppers
Wigton v Stirling County
Young Munster v Sunday's Well

Sunday, 2 September

Harlequins/Lord's Taverners Tournament (Stoop Ground)
Northern Sevens (Northern RFC, Newcastle)
Bohemians v Shannon
Falmouth v Stockwood Park
Llangennech v Llanelli
North Wales XV v London Welsh

Monday, 3 September

Pembrokeshire v Crawshay's Welsh (Pembroke Dock)
Middlesbrough v Watsonians
Nelson v Newport

Tuesday, 4 September

Bangor v CIYMS
Esher v Rosslyn Park
Gosforth v Durham City
Greenock Wands v Glasgow High
Haddington v Heriot's FP
Marr v Kilmarnock
Melrose v Preston Lodge
Musselburgh v Selkirk
Nuneaton v Leicester
Portobello v Boroughmuir
Stirling County v Glasgow Acads

Wednesday, 5 September

Bath v S Wales Police
Birkenhead Park v Davenport
Blackheath v Maidstone
Bristol v Cheltenham
Broughton Park v Monkstown
Cardiff v Glamorgan Wands
Collegians v Instonians
Coventry v Birmingham

Dolphin v Cork Const
Falmouth v Camborne
Huddersfield v Wakefield
Maesteg v Llanelli
Malone v Coleraine
Merthyr v Newbridge
New Brighton v Ruthin
Newton Abbot v Taunton
Northern v Hawick
Pill Harriers v Newport
Pontypool v Tredegar
Pontypridd v Eastern RU (US)
Ripon v Otley
Rugby v Bedford
Stafford v Manchester
Stroud v Gloucester
Taibach v Aberavon
Vale of Lune v Halifax
Waterloo v Chester
Ystalyfera v Swansea

Thursday, 6 September

Jedforest v Cooptimists
St Mary's Coll v Clontarf

Saturday, 8 September

Schweppes/WRU Cup: *1st prelim round (Welsh fixtures subject to rearrangement)*
Blackrock Festival
Abertillery v S Wales Police
Academy v CIYMS
Ards v Skerries
Bath v Leicester
Bective Rangers v Galwegians
Bedford v London Irish
Bohemians v Garryowen
Boroughmuir v Sale
Bridgend v Newbridge
Cardiff v Neath
Cheltenham v Maesteg
Cork Const v Old Wesley
Coventry v Gloucester
Dolphin v Sunday's Well
Dunfermline v Selkirk
Ebbw Vale v Pontypool
Edinburgh Acads v Ayr
Falmouth v Penarth
Gala v Jedforest
Gosforth v Liverpool
Haddington v Glenrothes
Harlequins v Northampton
Hawick v Headingley
Heriot's FP v Northern
Highland v Kirkcaldy
Howe of Fife v Glasgow High
Huddersfield v Sheffield
Hull ER v Hartlepool Rovers
Hutchesons' v Edinburgh Wands
Instonians v NIFC
Kilmarnock v Alnwick
Kendal v Durham City
Langholm v Melrose
Lansdowne v Bangor
Llanelli v Aberavon
London Scottish v Orrell
Malone v Ballymena
Manchester v Wrexham
Middlesbrough v Bradford
Morley v West Hartlepool
New Brighton v Birkenhead Park
Newport v Bristol
Nottingham v Blackheath
Percy Park v Carlisle
Preston Lodge v Trinity Acads
Rosslyn Park v Met Police
Roundhay v Redcar
Royal High v Leith Acads
St Ives v Lydney
Saracens v London Welsh
Stewart's-Melville FP v Kelso
Stirling County v Ryton
Swansea v Moseley
Torquay Ath v Launceston
Tredegar v Birmingham
Vale of Lune v Otley
Wakefield v Broughton Park
Wasps v Richmond
Waterloo v Plymouth Albion
Watsonians v Tynedale
West of Scotland v Fylde
Weston-super-Mare v Nuneaton

Sunday, 9 September

New Brighton v Plymouth Albion
Norwich v Wasps

Monday, 10 September

Northumberland v South of Scotland
Harlequins v Old Gaytonians

Tuesday, 11 September

Askeans v Blackheath
Dunbar v Haddington
Edinburgh Wands v Melrose
Glasgow High v Allan Glen's
Headingley v West Hartlepool
Heriot's FP v Portobello
Huddersfield v Halifax
Northampton v Nottingham
Old Wesley v St Mary's Coll
Penarth v Eastern RU (US)
Perthshire v Stirling County
Preston Grasshoppers v Orrell

Wednesday, 12 September

Bridgend v Glamorgan Wands
Bristol v Cardiff
Broughton v Royal High
Broughton Park v Sale

Collegians v Lisburn
Ebbw Vale v Blaina
Gloucester v Maesteg
Instonians v Armagh
Lansdowne v Skerries
Leicester v Birmingham
Liverpool v New Brighton
Llanelli v Tredegar
Lymm v Manchester
Moseley v Nuneaton
Newbridge v Abertillery
Pontypool v Newport
Rugby v Coventry
S Wales Police v Pontypridd
Stockton v Middlesbrough
Swansea v Cross Keys
Waterloo v St Helens
Wellington v Taunton

Friday, 14 September

NIFC v Cork Const

Saturday, 15 September

Cornwall v Ulster
South of Scotland v Leinster
Aberavon v Newbridge
Aberdeen GSFP v Highland
Ayr v Academy
Bangor v Monkstown
Birkenhead Park v Sale
Blackheath v London Irish
Bridgwater Albion v St Ives
Bristol v Swansea
Broughton Park v Cheltenham
Cardiff v Coventry
CIYMS v Sunday's Well
Collegians v City of Derry
Cross Keys v Eastern RU (US)
Dolphin v Greystones
Durham City v Stockton
Edinburgh Acads v Sunderland
Exeter v Orrell
Exmouth v Falmouth
Fylde v Hartlepool Rovers
Galwegians v Ballymena
Garryowen v Corinthians
Glamorgan Wands v Ebbw Vale
Gosforth v Rosslyn Park
Guy's H v Nuneaton
Haddington v Alnwick
Harlequins v Llanelli
Harrogate v Rugby
Hawick v Melrose
Headingley v London Scottish
Heriot's FP v Lansdowne
Jedforest v Otley
Jordanhill v Stewart's-Melville FP
Kelso v Boroughmuir
Leicester v London Welsh
Liverpool v Wasps
Lydney v Torquay Ath
Maesteg v Plymouth Albion
Malone v Terenure Coll
Met Police v Birmingham
Morley v Middlesbrough
Moseley v Bath
New Brighton v St Mary's Coll
Newport v Neath
Northampton v Richmond
Nottingham v Bedford
Old Belvedere v Clontarf
Old Wesley v Highfield
Percy Park v Royal High
Perthshire v Edinburgh Wands
Pontypool v Penarth
Pontypridd v Gloucester
Roundhay v Gala
Saracens v Bridgend
Selkirk v Langholm
Skerries v Instonians
S Wales Police v Launceston
Stirling County v Hutchesons'
Taunton v Tiverton
Tynedale v Kilmarnock
UC Cork v Bohemians
Vale of Lune v Wakefield
Waterloo v Hull ER
Watsonians v Preston Lodge
West Hartlepool v Northern
West of Scotland v Glasgow High
Weston-super-Mare v Abertillery
Wilmslow v Manchester

Sunday, 16 September

Surrey v Munster (London Irish RFC)
Bective Rangers v Blackrock Coll
Brixham v Orrell
Norwich v Saracens

Monday, 17 September

Harlequins v Maidstone
Jedforest v Broughton
Selkirk v Edinburgh Wands

Tuesday, 18 September

South of Scotland v Durham
Hawick v Gosforth
Melrose v U of Victoria (BC)
Northern v Blaydon
Wakefield v Halifax
West of Scotland v Stirling County

Wednesday, 19 September

Ystalyfera v Crawshay's Welsh
Buckinghamshire v Oxfordshire (Marlow)
Cornwall v Royal Navy
Eastern Counties v Berkshire
Middlesex v Munster (Rosslyn Park RFC)

Birkenhead Park v Chester
Bridgend v Llanelli
Cardiff v Penarth
Cross Keys v Pontypridd
Cwmbran v Pontypool
Heaton Moor v Manchester
London Welsh v Met Police
Monkstown v Palmerston
Newbridge v Gloucester
Newport v Bath
Sale v Kendal
Swansea v Ebbw Vale
Taunton v Weston-super-Mare
Tredegar v Abertillery
Watsonians v Royal High
Ystrad Rhondda v Maesteg

Saturday, 22 September

John Player/RFU Cup: *1st round*
(English fixtures subject to rearrangement)
Aberavon v Cardiff
Abertillery v Maesteg
Armagh v Academy
Ayr v Sunderland
Bedford v Richmond
Bradford v Edinburgh Acads
Bridgend v Pontypool
Broughton Park v Gosforth
Cambuslang v Highland
CIYMS v Clontarf
Durham City v West Hartlepool
Edinburgh Wands v Kirkcaldy
Falmouth v Newquay Hornets
Fylde v Waterloo
Garryowen v Bangor
Glamorgan Wands v Weston-super-Mare
Gloucester v Bristol
Greystones v City of Derry
Harlequins v Leicester
Heriot's FP v Hawick
Highfield v Cork Const
Hillhead v Watsonians
Jedforest v Glasgow Acads
Leith Acads v Kilmarnock
Llanelli v Bath
London Irish v Rosslyn Park
London Scottish v London Welsh
Manchester v Birkenhead Park
Melrose v Harrogate
Met Police v Newbridge
Middlesbrough v Rugby
Morley v Hull ER
Neath v Pontypridd
New Brighton v Sheffield
NIFC v West of Scotland
Northampton v Moseley
Northern v Boroughmuir
Old Wesley v Old Belvedere
Orrell v Blackheath
Otley v Huddersfield
Palmerston v Malone
Penarth v Cross Keys
Percy Park v Tynedale
Roundhay v Vale of Lune
St Ives v Redruth
St Mary's Coll v Galwegians
Sale v Coventry
Saracens v Cheltenham
Selkirk v Royal High
Skerries v Bohemians
S Wales Police v Clifton
Stewart's-Melville FP v Ballymena
Stirling County v Gordonians
Sunday's Well v Bective Rangers
Swansea v Newport
Terenure Coll v Monkstown
Torquay Ath v Ebbw Vale
Wakefield v Liverpool
Wanderers v Instonians
Wasps v Headingley
Wolverhampton v Taunton

Sunday, 23 September

Blackrock Coll v Dublin U

Monday, 24 September

Somerset v British Police (Bath)
Hawick v Glasgow Acads
Kelso v Glasgow High
Selkirk v Allan Glen's

Tuesday, 25 September

St Helens v Orrell

Wednesday, 26 September

Rest of England v RFU President's XV (Leicester)
Hampshire v Sussex (Havant RFC)
Kent v Anglo-Scots
Blaina v Abertillery
Ebbw Vale v S Wales Police
Llanelli v Gloucester
Maesteg v Tredegar
Moseley v Rugby
Newbridge v Neath
Pontypool Dist v Pontypool
Pontypridd v Cardiff

Saturday, 29 September

ENGLAND v RFU PRESIDENT'S XV (Twickenham)
Aberavon v Torquay Ath
Abercynon v S Glam Inst
Abertillery v Pontypool
Academy v Athlone
Bangor v Old Wesley
Bective Rangers v Dublin U
Bedford v Wasps

Bristol v Nottingham
CIYMS v Terenure Coll
Collegians v Greystones
Cork Const v Instonians
Coventry v Blackheath
Cross Keys v Bridgend
Falmouth v Devonport Services
Fylde v Roundhay
Galwegians v Sunday's Well
Garryowen v Cardiff
Gloucester v Waterloo
Halifax v Manchester
Harlequins v London Welsh
Highfield v Old Belvedere
Hull ER v Harrogate
Leicester v Saracens
Liverpool v Wilmslow
Llanelli v Newport
London Scottish v London Irish
Maesteg v Exeter
Malone v UC Dublin
Neath v Bath
Newbridge v S Wales Police
New Brighton v Broughton Park
Northampton v Headingley
Northern v Sale
Pontypridd v Ebbw Vale
Rosslyn Park v Richmond
Rugby v Birmingham
Sandal v Huddersfield
St Mary's Coll v Skerries
Shannon v Monkstown
Sheffield v Gosforth
Stroud v St Ives
Swansea v Lansdowne
Taunton v Newbury
Tredegar v Nuneaton
Vale of Lune v Durham City
Wakefield v Moseley
Wanderers v Dolphin
Young Munster v UC Cork

SRU Championship
Division 1
Boroughmuir v Stewart's-Melville FP
Edinburgh Acads v Heriot's FP
Gala v Glasgow Acads
Kelso v Jedforest
Melrose v Hawick
Selkirk v Ayr
Watsonians v West of Scotland
Division 2
Dunfermline v Preston Lodge
Edinburgh Wands v Kilmarnock
Haddington v Gordonians
Howe of Fife v Portobello
Jordanhill v Royal High
Langholm v Clarkston
Stirling County v Highland

Sunday, 30 September

Glengarth Sevens

Tuesday, 2 October

Newport v Barbarians
Penarth v Ebbw Vale
Roundhay v Huddersfield

Wednesday, 3 October

Bridgend v Crawshay's Welsh
Berkshire v Hampshire (Bracknell)
Aberavon v Cross Keys
Abertillery v Pontypridd
Gloucester v Glamorgan Wands
Harlequins v West London Inst
Maesteg v Bath
Newbridge v Bristol
Nottingham v Coventry
Orrell v Moseley
Swansea v Pontypool

Saturday, 6 October

Ulster v Yorkshire (Ravenhill, Belfast)
Abertillery v Plymouth Albion
Academy v Bangor
Ards v Malone
Ballinasloe v Galwegians
Bath v Aberavon
Bective Rangers v Athlone
Birkenhead Park v West Hartlepool
Birmingham v Huddersfield
Blackheath v Wasps
Bridgwater Albion v Cross Keys
Bristol v London Irish
Cardiff v Newport
Clifton v Glamorgan Wands
Cork Const v Young Munster
Coventry v Leicester
Dublin U v Collegians
Ebbw Vale v Bridgend
Esher v Penarth
Exeter U v Taunton
Exeter v Nottingham
Garryowen v Blackrock Coll
Gloucester v Bedford
Gosforth v Fylde
Greystones v CIYMS
Harlequins v Swansea
Harrogate v Middlesbrough
Hull ER v Vale of Lune
Instonians v Bohemians
Liverpool v Broughton Park
Manchester v New Brighton
Monkstown v St Mary's Coll
Morley v Durham City
Moseley v Sale
Neath v Llanelli
Newbridge v Saracens
Northampton v London Scottish
Nuneaton v Rugby
Old Belvedere v Skerries
Old Crescent v Highfield

Oxford U v Henley
Palmerston v Clontarf
Penzance-Newlyn v Falmouth
Pontypool v Maesteg
Pontypridd v Wakefield
Preston Grasshoppers v Otley
Richmond v London Welsh
Rosslyn Park v Orrell
Roundhay v Met Police
St Ives v Hayle
S Glam Inst v Abercarn
S Wales Police v Cheltenham
Terenure Coll v UC Cork
Torquay Ath v Camborne
UC Dublin v Old Wesley
Waterloo v Wanderers
Wilmslow v Northern

SRU Championship
Division 1
Ayr v Gala
Glasgow Acads v Heriot's FP
Hawick v Edinburgh Acads
Selkirk v Boroughmuir
Stewart's-Melville FP v Jedforest
Watsonians v Melrose
West of Scotland v Kelso
Division 2
Gordonians v Clarkston
Highland v Edinburgh Wands
Kilmarnock v Howe of Fife
Portobello v Dunfermline
Preston Lodge v Langholm
Royal High v Haddington
Stirling County v Jordanhill

Sunday, 7 October

Cambridge U v Cambridge City

Monday, 8 October

Selkirk v Gala

Tuesday, 9 October

Neath v S Glam Inst
Northampton v Birmingham
Orrell v West Park

Wednesday, 10 October

Bridgend v Cardiff
Bristol v Met Police
Cambridge U v St Mary's H
Harlequins v Loughborough Students
Newport v Newport Dist RU
Nuneaton v Burton
Pontypool v Gloucester
Tredegar v Pontypridd

Saturday, 13 October

County Championship
Division 1
Gloucestershire v Kent (Bristol)
Middlesex v Notts, Lincs and Derbys (Stoop Ground)
Northumberland v Surrey (County Ground, Gosforth)
Somerset v Yorkshire (Bath)
Division 2
Cornwall v Durham (Camborne)
Cumbria v Cheshire (Kendal)
Eastern Counties v Lancashire (Southend)
Warwickshire v Devon (Rugby)
Division 3
Hampshire v Dorset/Wilts (US Portsmouth)
Hertfordshire v Buckinghamshire (Croxley Green)
Leicester v Sussex (Stoneygate, Leicester)
Staffordshire v North Midlands (Burton)
Division 4
Berkshire v East Midlands (Newbury)

Schweppes/WRU Cup: *2nd prelim round*
(Welsh fixtures subject to rearrangement)
Aberavon v Maesteg
Abertillery v Newbridge
Academy v NIFC
Bedford v Pontypool
Birmingham v Blackheath
Bridgwater Albion v Nuneaton
Broughton Park v Manchester
CIYMS v Armagh
Cambridge U v Guy's H
Cheltenham v Nottingham
Chester v Otley
Clontarf v Corinthians
Coventry v Wanderers
Dublin U v Palmerston
Fylde v Northern
Galwegians v Old Crescent
Gloucester v Harlequins
Halifax v Orrell
Harrogate v Vale of Lune
Huddersfield v Headingley
Hull ER v Preston Grasshoppers
Instonians v Collegians
Lansdowne v Greystones
Leicester v Richmond
Liverpool v Bath
Llanelli v Swansea
London Scottish v Rosslyn Park
London Welsh v Bridgend
Malone v Bangor
Met Police v Birkenhead Park
Middlesbrough v Roundhay
Monkstown v Bective Rangers
Neath v Sale

New Brighton v Loughborough Students
Newport v Penarth
Northampton v Cardiff
Old Wesley v Terenure Coll
Oxford U v Ebbw Vale
Pontypridd v Moseley
St Mary's Coll v Old Belvedere
Sheffield v Rugby
S Wales Police v S Glam Inst
Taunton v Falmouth
Torquay Ath v Barnstaple
Truro v St Ives
Tynedale v Gosforth
Wakefield v Wilmslow
Wasps v Bristol
West Hartlepool v Kendal
Young Munster v Skerries

SRU Championship
Division 1
Boroughmuir v Ayr
Glasgow Acads v Hawick
Heriot's FP v Gala
Jedforest v Selkirk
Kelso v Melrose
Stewart's-Melville FP v West of Scotland
Watsonians v Edinburgh Acads
Division 2
Clarkston v Royal High
Dunfermline v Howe of Fife
Edinburgh Wands v Jordanhill
Kilmarnock v Highland
Portobello v Langholm
Preston Lodge v Gordonians
Stirling County v Haddington

Sunday, 14 October

Garryowen v Shannon
Saracens v London Irish
UC Galway v Bohemians
Waterloo v Hartlepool Rovers

Wednesday, 17 October

London Division v Australians (Twickenham)
Combined Services v Public School Wands (Aldershot)
Abertillery v Newport
Bridgend v Swansea
Bristol v Clifton
Cardiff v Pontypool
Ebbw Vale v Gloucester
Maesteg v S Glam Inst
Pembrokeshire v S Wales Police
Pontypridd v Aberavon
Rosslyn Park v Cambridge U
Tredegar v Newbridge

Saturday, 20 October

South and South West Division v Australians (Exeter)
Academy v Ards
Ballymena v CIYMS
Bective Rangers v Palmerston
Blackheath v London Scottish
Blackrock Coll v St Mary's Coll
Bohemians v Cork Const
Bradford v Huddersfield
Bridgend v Coventry
Cambridge U v Cardiff
Cheltenham v Loughborough Students
Collegians v Portadown
Dolphin v Sunday's Well
Dungannon v Bangor
Ebbw Vale v Bedford
Falmouth v Redruth
Garryowen v UC Dublin
Glamorgan Wands v S Glam Inst
Greystones v Old Wesley
Harlequins v Rosslyn Park
Hartlepool Rovers v Vale of Lune
Hull ER v Stafford
Instonians v Malone
Lansdowne v Terenure Coll
Leicester v Northampton
Liverpool v Harrogate
London Irish v Wasps
London Welsh v Llanelli
Maesteg v Cross Keys
Manchester v Manchester U
Met Police v Nuneaton
Middlesbrough v Halifax
Monkstown v Clontarf
Moseley v Aberavon
Newbridge v Pontypridd
New Brighton v Birmingham
Newport v Gloucester
Nottingham v Waterloo
Old Belvedere v Wanderers
Orrell v Gosforth
Otley v Wakefield
Penarth v Lydney
Penryn v St Ives
Plymouth Albion v Torquay Ath
Pontypool v Abertillery
Preston Grasshoppers v Birkenhead Park
Richmond v Oxford U
Roundhay v Wilmslow
Rugby v Fylde
Sale v West Hartlepool
Saracens v Sheffield
Skerries v Dublin U
S Wales Police v Tredegar
Swansea v Neath
Taunton v Esher
Tynedale v Northern
Waterpark v UC Cork
Young Munster v Highfield

SRU Championship
Division 1
Ayr v Heriot's FP
Edinburgh Acads v Kelso
Glasgow Acads v Watsonians
Hawick v Gala
Jedforest v Boroughmuir
Melrose v Stewart's-Melville FP
Selkirk v West of Scotland
Division 2
Gordonians v Portobello
Haddington v Edinburgh Wands
Howe of Fife v Highland
Jordanhill v Kilmarnock
Langholm v Dunfermline
Royal High v Preston Lodge
Stirling County v Clarkston

Sunday, 21 October

Galwegians v Westport

Monday, 22 October

Bristol v Bath

Tuesday, 23 October

Combined Services v British Police (Portsmouth)
Kilmarnock v Hutchesons'
Neath v Ebbw Vale

Wednesday, 24 October

Cardiff v Australians
County Championship
Division 4
East Midlands v Oxfordshire (Northampton)

Cambridge U Past/Present v Invitation XV
Cheltenham v Glamorgan Wands
Cross Keys v Exeter U
Durham City v Headingley
Leicester v Oxford U
Newport v Newbridge
Swansea v Pontypridd

Saturday, 27 October

Combined Services v Australians (Aldershot)
Munster v Connacht (Cork)
Ulster v Leinster (Ravenhill, Belfast)

County Championship
Division 1
Middlesex v Northumberland (Saracens RFC)
Notts, Lincs and Derbys v Surrey (Beeston)
Somerset v Gloucestershire (Bath)
Yorkshire v Kent (Otley)
Division 2
Cheshire v Durham (Chester)
Cumbria v Cornwall (Kendal)
Eastern Counties v Warwickshire (Grange Rd, Cambridge)
Lancashire v Devon (Vale of Lune)
Division 2
Buckinghamshire v Dorset/Wilts (Marlow)
Hertfordshire v Hampshire (Croxley Green)
North Midlands v Sussex (Stourbridge)
Staffordshire v Leicestershire (Burton)
Division 4
Oxfordshire v Berkshire

Aberavon v Bridgend
Bath v US Portsmouth
Bedford v Roundhay
Birkenhead Park v Blackheath
CIYMS v NIFC
Cardiff v Harlequins
Collegians v Old Wesley
Coventry v Moseley
Durham City v Middlesbrough
Durham U v Percy Park
Ebbw Vale v Cross Keys
Esher v London Irish
Fylde v London Scottish
Glamorgan Wands v Newport
Gloucester v Clifton
Gosforth v Hull ER
Halifax v New Brighton
Harrogate v Sale
Headingley v Loughborough Students
Instonians v Academy
Maesteg v Newbridge
Malone v Skerries
Manchester v Macclesfield
Met Police v Nottingham
Neath v London Welsh
Newbold-on-Avon v Taunton
Newton Abbot v Falmouth
Northern v Alnwick
Nuneaton v Liverpool
Oxford U v Northampton
Pontypool v S Wales Police
Queen's U, Belfast v Old Belvedere
Richmond v Cambridge U
Rosslyn Park v St Mary's H
Rugby v Tredegar
Saracens v Bristol
Sheffield v Orrell
S Glam Inst v Berry Hill
Stroud v Penarth
Sunday's Well v Portadown
Swansea v Leicester
Torquay Ath v Newbury
Tynedale v Otley
UC Dublin v Monkstown
Wakefield v Preston Grasshoppers

Wasps v Pontypridd
Waterloo v Vale of Lune
West Hartlepool v Huddersfield

SRU Championship
Division 1
Ayr v Jedforest
Gala v Watsonians
Heriot's FP v Hawick
Kelso v Glasgow Acads
Selkirk v Melrose
Stewart's-Melville FP v Edinburgh Acads
West of Scotland v Boroughmuir
Division 2
Clarkston v Edinburgh Wands
Dunfermline v Gordonians
Highland v Jordanhill
Howe of Fife v Langholm
Kilmarnock v Haddington
Portobello v Royal High
Preston Lodge v Stirling County

Sunday, 28 October

Blackrock Coll v Bangor
Bohemians v Corinthians
Clontarf v Bective Rangers
Old Crescent v Garryowen
Shannon v Galwegians
Terenure Coll v St Mary's Coll
UC Cork v Dolphin

Monday, 29 October

Dublin U v Wanderers
Greystones v Skerries
Monkstown v Lansdowne

Tuesday, 30 October

Swansea v Australians
Headingley v Roundhay
Northampton v Cambridge U
Penarth v Bridgend

Wednesday, 31 October

County Championship
Division 4
East Midlands v Berkshire (Bedford)

Gloucester v Abertillery
Lydney v Glamorgan Wands
Maesteg v S Wales Police
Newbridge v Cardiff
Newport v Ebbw Vale
Rosslyn Park v Saracens

Saturday, 3 November

ENGLAND v AUSTRALIA
(Twickenham)

Belgium v Welsh Districts Union
(Brussels)
Llanelli v Leinster
Abertillery v Glamorgan Wands
Armagh v Bangor
Ballymena v Instonians
Bath v Newbridge
Blackheath v Swansea
Bridgend v Bristol
Broughton Park v Huddersfield
Cambridge U v London Scottish
Cardiff v Leicester
CIYMS v Malone
Clontarf v Palmerston
Collegians v Ards
Cross Keys v Penarth
Durham City v Redcar
Ebbw Vale v Cheltenham
Falmouth v Hayle
Fylde v Otley
Gosforth v West Hartlepool
Greystones v Bective Rangers
Headingley v Hull ER
Highfield v Cork Const
Lansdowne v Dublin U
London Welsh v Coventry
Loughborough Students v St Mary's H
Lydney v Pontypridd
Manchester v Harrogate
Monkstown v Galwegians
Moseley v Newport
Neath v Pontypool
New Brighton v Rugby
Northampton v Aberavon
Nottingham v Maesteg
Old Belvedere v Corinthians
Old Crescent v Bohemians
Old Wesley v Blackrock Coll
Oxford U v Bedford
Percy Park v Workington
Plymouth Albion v Met Police
Portadown v Academy
Preston Grasshoppers v Roundhay
Queen's U, Belfast v Terenure Coll
Richmond v Exeter
Rosslyn Park v Gloucester
St Mary's Coll v Wanderers
Sale v Orrell
Shannon v Dolphin
Skerries v UC Dublin
Sheffield v Middlesbrough
S Glam Inst v S Wales Police
Streatham-Croydon v Saracens
Sunday's Well v UC Cork
Taunton v Devonport Services
Vale of Lune v Northern
Wasps v Wakefield
Waterloo v Liverpool
Waterpark v Garryowen
Wilmslow v Birkenhead Park

SRU Championship
Division 1
Boroughmuir v Melrose
Edinburgh Acads v Selkirk
Gala v Kelso
Glasgow Acads v Stewart's-Melville FP
Hawick v Ayr
Jedforest v West of Scotland
Watsonians v Heriot's FP
Division 2
Clarkston v Kilmarnock
Edinburgh Wands v Preston Lodge
Haddington v Highland
Jordanhill v Howe of Fife
Langholm v Gordonians
Royal High v Dunfermline
Stirling County v Portobello

Sunday, 4 November

Falmouth v St Bart's H
London Irish v Harlequins
UC Galway v Monkstown

Tuesday, 6 November

Midland Division v Australians (Leicester)
Orrell v Warrington

Wednesday, 7 November

Aberavon v Pontypool
Abertillery v Bristol
Cardiff v Oxford U
Ebbw Vale v S Glam Inst
Glamorgan Wands v Tredegar
Gloucester v S Wales Police
Maesteg v Swansea
Pontypridd v Newport

Friday, 9 November

Bangor v Queen's U, Belfast
Old Belvedere v Waterpark

Saturday, 10 November

IRELAND v AUSTRALIA (Dublin)
Wales B v France B (Newport)

County Championship
Division 1
Gloucestershire v Yorkshire (Gloucester)
Kent v Somerset (Blackheath)
Northumberland v Notts, Lincs and Derbys (County Ground, Gosforth)
Surrey v Middlesex (Rosslyn Park RFC)
Division 2
Cornwall v Cheshire (Redruth)
Devon v Eastern Counties (Exeter)
Durham v Cumbria
Warwickshire v Lancashire (Nuneaton)
Division 3
Dorset/Wilts v Hertfordshire (Dorchester)
Hampshire v Buckinghamshire (Trojans RFC)
Leicestershire v North Midlands (Hinckley RFC)
Sussex v Staffordshire (Worthing)
Division 4
Oxfordshire v East Midlands
Bath v Cheltenham
Bective Rangers v Old Wesley
Bedford v Aberavon
Birkenhead Park v Orrell
Bridgend v Neath
Bristol v Stroud
Clontarf v Collegians
Coventry v Northampton
Durham City v Hull ER
Ebbw Vale v Cardiff
Falmouth v Paignton
Harlequins v Richmond
Huddersfield v Sale
Leicester v Cambridge U
Liverpool v Loughborough Students
London Scottish v US Portsmouth
London Welsh v Moseley
Maesteg v Abertillery
Manchester v Preston Grasshoppers
Middlesbrough v Blaydon
Monkstown v Malone
Morley v Broughton Park
Morpeth v Gosforth
NIFC v Dublin U
Newbridge v S Glam Inst
Newport v Rosslyn Park
Otley v Northern
Oxford U v Blackheath
Penarth v Glamorgan Wands
Plymouth Albion v Gloucester
Pontypool v Cross Keys
Pontypridd v Nuneaton
Roundhay v Halifax
Rugby v Met Police
St Ives v Cornwall Police
Saracens v Wasps
Swansea v Llanelli
Taunton v Camborne
UC Dublin v Cork Const
Vale of Lune v CIYMS
Waterloo v New Brighton
West Hartlepool v Wilmslow

SRU Championship
Division 1
Edinburgh Acads v Boroughmuir
Hawick v Watsonians
Kelso v Heriot's FP
Melrose v Jedforest
Selkirk v Glasgow Acads
Stewart's-Melville FP v Gala

West of Scotland v Ayr
Division 2
Dunfermline v Stirling County
Gordonians v Howe of Fife
Highland v Clarkston
Jordanhill v Haddington
Kilmarnock v Preston Lodge
Portobello v Edinburgh Wands
Royal High v Langholm

Sunday, 11 November

Bohemians v Garryowen
Greystones v Blackrock Coll
Highfield v Sunday's Well
Old Crescent v Dolphin
St Mary's Coll v Lansdowne
Skerries v Palmerston
UC Galway v Galwegians
Wanderers v Terenure Coll

Tuesday, 13 November

Leicester v Nottingham
Rosslyn Park v Exeter U

Wednesday, 14 November

Ulster v Australians (Ravenhill, Belfast)
Cambridge U v Bedford
Coventry v Nuneaton
Gloucester v Cheltenham
Hartlepool Rovers v Percy Park

Saturday, 17 November

Munster v Australians (Limerick)
Schweppes/WRU Cup: *1st Round Proper*
(Welsh fixtures subject to rearrangement)
Academy v Collegians
Alnwick v Durham City
Athlone v Clontarf
Bangor v CIYMS
Bath v Coventry
Bradford v Wakefield
Bridgwater Albion v Torquay Ath
Bristol v London Welsh
Burton v Huddersfield
Cambridge U v Blackheath
Cheltenham v Rugby
Dublin U v Old Belvedere
Falmouth v Bideford
Gloucester v Broughton Park
Gosforth v Headingley
Harlequins v Oxford U
Harrogate v Orrell
Hull ER v Wilmslow
Instonians v City of Derry
Launceston v St Ives
Liverpool v Roundhay
London Scottish v Richmond
Loughborough Students v Fylde
Malone v Armagh
Manchester U v Manchester
Middlesbrough v New Brighton
Monkstown v Blackrock Coll
Morley v Nuneaton
Moseley v Rosslyn Park
Northampton v Bedford
Northern v Durham U
Otley v Sheffield
Palmerston v Bective Rangers
Preston Grasshoppers v Birmingham
St Mary's Coll v UC Dublin
Sale v Nottingham
S Wales Police v Penarth
Streatham-Croydon v Met Police
Terenure Coll v Greystones
US Portsmouth v Saracens
Wanderers v Skerries
Wasps v Leicester
Waterloo v London Irish
West Hartlepool v Vale of Lune

SRU Championship
Division 1
Ayr v Watsonians
Boroughmuir v Glasgow Acads
Gala v Selkirk
Heriot's FP v Stewart's-Melville FP
Jedforest v Edinburgh Acads
Kelso v Hawick
Melrose v West of Scotland
Division 2
Clarkston v Jordanhill
Dunfermline v Edinburgh Wands
Gordonians v Royal High
Howe of Fife v Haddington
Langholm v Stirling County
Portobello v Kilmarnock
Preston Lodge v Highland

Sunday, 18 November

Bohemians v Galwegians
Clontarf v Highfield
Dolphin v UC Galway
Garryowen v Cork Const
Old Wesley v Lansdowne
UC Cork v Shannon

Tuesday, 20 November

Llanelli v Australians
Neath v Cross Keys
Rosslyn Park v Loughborough Students
Roundhay v Leeds Poly

Wednesday, 21 November

Oxford U v Major R V Stanley's XV
Aberavon v Penarth
Abertillery v S Glam Inst
Gloucester v Exeter U

Maesteg v Mid District RU
Pontypridd v Pontpool

Friday, 23 November

S Wales Police v Bristol

Saturday, 24 November

WALES v AUSTRALIA (Cardiff)
Leinster v Munster (Lansdowne Road)
Ulster v Connacht (Ravenhill, Belfast)
Scottish North and Midland v Edinburgh District
Glasgow District v South of Scotland (Hughenden)

County Championship: Semi Finals *(Division 1, 2 and 3)*
Division 4
Berkshire v Oxfordshire (Abbey RFC)

Bedford v Coventry
Birkenhead Park v Morley
Blackheath v Neath
Boroughmuir v Glasgow High
Broughton Park v Otley
Collegians v Coleraine
Cross Keys v Glamorgan Wands
Dungannon v Monkstown
Durham City v Instonians
Durham U v West Hartlepool
Ebbw Vale v Northampton
Exeter U v S Glam Inst
Gala v Haddington
Glasgow Acads v Watsonians
Gosforth v Preston Grasshoppers
Halifax v Sale
Harlequins v Cambridge U
Highfield v Athlone
Highland v Ayr
Kilmarnock v West of Scotland
Leicester v Moseley
Liverpool v Hull ER
London Irish v Gloucester
London Scottish v Oxford U
London Welsh v Newport
Loughborough Students v Middlesbrough
Malone v Academy
Manchester v Bradford
Newbridge v Bridgend
Nottingham v Guy's H
Nuneaton v Stroud
Old Wesley v CIYMS
Orrell v Chester
Palmerston v Bangor
Panmure v Edinburgh Wands
Penarth v Pontypridd
Rosslyn Park v Waterloo
Roundhay v Northern
Rugby v Lydney
St Helens v Huddersfield
St Ives v Truro
Taunton v Torquay Ath
Tiverton v Falmouth
Tredegar v Maesteg
Vale of Lune v New Brighton
Wakefield v Fylde
Wasps v Met Police
Weston-super-Mare v Birmingham

Sunday, 25 November

Bective Rangers v Clontarf
Cork Const v Waterpark
Garryowen v Dolphin
Greystones v Bohemians
Highfield v UC Cork
Nenagh v Galwegians
Old Belvedere v St Mary's Coll
Saracens v Abertillery
Swansea v Richmond
Terenure Coll v Skerries

Monday, 26 November

Bath v Exeter

Tuesday, 27 November

Blaydon v Gosforth
Glamorgan Wands v Neath
Penarth v Maesteg
Percy Park v Northern

Wednesday, 28 November

Northern Division v Australians (Waterloo)
Cambridge U v M R Steele-Bodger's XV (provisional)
Bridgend v S Glam Inst
Cardiff v Llanelli
Ebbw Vale v Aberavon
Exeter v Royal Navy
Gloucester v Loughborough Students
Moseley v Newbridge

Saturday, 1 December

Ireland B v Scotland B (Galway)
South of Scotland v Australia (Hawick)
John Player/RFU Cup: *2nd round*
(English fixtures subject to rearrangement)
Academy v City of Derry
Ayr v Portobello
Bective Rangers v Old Crescent
Birmingham v Penarth
Blackheath v Harlequins
Bohemians v Young Munster
Bridgend v Abertillery
Bristol v Newport
Cambridge U v Nottingham
CIYMS v Blackrock Coll

Clontarf v Sunday's Well
Collegians v Palmerston
Cork Const v Old Belvedere
Coventry v Richmond
Dolphin v Old Wesley
Dungannon v Greystones
Durham City v Huddersfield
Edinburgh Wands v Watsonians
Falmouth v Bridgwater Albion
Fylde v Birkenhead Park
Gloucester v Leicester
Halifax v Rugby
Headingley v Moseley
Heriot's FP v Edinburgh Acads
Highfield v Monkstown
Hull ER v Manchester
Instonians v Lansdowne
Jedforest v Langholm
Jordanhill v Glasgow High
Liverpool v Saracens
London Scottish v Bath
London Welsh v Aberavon
Loughborough Students v Preston Grasshoppers
Maesteg v Ebbw Vale
Melrose v Kelso
Met Police v London Irish
Middlesbrough v Broughton Park
Newbridge v Cross Keys
Northampton v Llanelli
Northern v Gala
Otley v Percy Park
Pontypool v Glamorgan Wands
Queen's U, Belfast v Malone
Rosslyn Park v Wasps
Roundhay v Waterloo
Royal High v Boroughmuir
St Ives v Somerset Police
St Mary's Coll v Bangor
Sale v Pontypridd
Selkirk v Alnwick
Shannon v Skerries
S Glam Inst v Tredegar
S Wales Police v Torquay Ath
Stewart's-Melville FP v Hartlepool Rovers
Stirling County v Kilmarnock
Streatham-Croydon v Nuneaton
Swansea v Cardiff
Terenure Coll v Ballymena
Tynedale v Hawick
US Portsmouth v Taunton
Vale of Lune v Cheltenham
Wakefield v Morley
West of Scotland v Gosforth

Sunday, 2 December

Galwegians v Sligo
Garryowen v Combined U's

Tuesday, 4 December

Glasgow District v Australians (Hughenden)

Wednesday, 5 December

Dublin U v UC Dublin (Colours Match)
Ebbw Vale v Neath
Newbridge v Glamorgan Wands

Saturday, 8 December

SCOTLAND v AUSTRALIA (Murrayfield)
England Trial (Twickenham) (provisional)
Connacht v Leinster (Galway)
Munster v Ulster (Limerick)
Schweppes/WRU Cup: *2nd round*
(Welsh fixtures subject to rearrangement)
Ballymena v Old Wesley
Bath v Gloucester
Bedford v Harlequins
Birkenhead Park v Headingley
Blackrock Coll v Clontarf
Bohemians v Collegians
Boroughmuir v Stirling County
Broughton Park v Bradford
CIYMS v Queen's U, Belfast
Coventry v Liverpool
Dunfermline v West of Scotland
Durham City v Jedforest
Edinburgh Wands v Percy Park
Fylde v Hawick
Glamorgan Wands v Penarth
Glasgow High v Heriot's FP
Gosforth v Harrogate
Haddington v Selkirk
Highfield v Academy
Instonians v Bective Rangers
Kendal v Vale of Lune
Kilmarnock v Highland
Leicester v Blackheath
London Irish v Northampton
Melrose v Tynedale
Monkstown v Athlone
Moseley v Bristol
Musselburgh v Royal High
New Brighton v Met Police
Nottingham v Saracens
Nuneaton v Hull ER
Old Belvedere v NIFC
Orrell v Northern
Otley v Manchester
Plymouth Albion v S Wales Police
Portadown v Bangor
Preston Lodge v Ayr
Richmond v Rosslyn Park
Roundhay v Loughborough Students
Rugby v Streatham-Croydon
St Austell v Falmouth

Sale v Waterloo
Skerries v City of Derry
Stewart's-Melville FP v Clarkston
Taunton v St Ives
Torquay Ath v Clifton
Wakefield v Middlesbrough
Wasps v London Scottish
Watsonians v Edinburgh Acads
Young Munster v Malone

Sunday, 9 December

Galwegians v Terenure Coll
Greystones v St Mary's Coll
Sunday's Well v Shannon
UC Cork v Garryowen
Young Munster v Dolphin

Tuesday, 11 December

Oxford U v Cambridge U (Twickenham)
Hillhead v Kilmarnock
Newport v Aberavon

Wednesday, 12 December

Pontypool v Australians
Hampshire v Royal Navy (Portsmouth RFC)
Abertillery v Cheltenham
Bedford v RAF
Edinburgh Wands v Howe of Fife
Lydney v S Glam Inst

Friday, 14 December

Maesteg v Pontypridd
Neath v Bridgend
Queen's U, Belfast v UC Cork
Tredegar v Cross Keys

Saturday, 15 December

Barbarians v Australians (Cardiff)
Anglo Scots v Scottish North and Midland
South of Scotland v Edinburgh District
Scotland Schools v New Zealand Schools (18 group)
Academy v Portadown
Bangor v Skerries
Bective Rangers v Wanderers
Bedford v Moseley
Birkenhead Park v London Scottish
Birmingham v Stroud
Blackrock Coll v Terenure Coll
Blaydon v Durham City
Bristol v Leicester
Broughton Park v Halifax
Camborne v St Ives
Civil Service v Monkstown
Clontarf v Dublin U
Cork Const v Old Crescent
Dolphin v Waterpark
Edinburgh Acads v Trinity Acads
Exeter v Met Police
Falmouth v Penzance-Newlyn
Garryowen v Sunday's Well
Glasgow High v Edinburgh Wands
Gloucester v Coventry
Gosforth v Nottingham
Greystones v Young Munster
Harlequins v Bath
Hawick v Boroughmuir
Heriot's FP v Glasgow Acads
Highfield v Bohemians
Highland v Moray
Huddersfield v Preston Grasshoppers
Hull ER v Kendal
Instonians v UC Cork
Kelso v Selkirk
Kilmarnock v Jordanhill
Langholm v Gala
Lansdowne v CIYMS
Leith Acads v Jedforest
Liverpool v Manchester
London Irish v London Welsh
Malone v Collegians
NIFC v St Mary's Coll
Northampton v Wasps
Northern v Melrose
Nuneaton v New Brighton
Orrell v Wakefield
Palmerston v Old Wesley
Portobello v Stirling County
Richmond v Blackheath
Rosslyn Park v Plymouth Albion
Roundhay v Sheffield
Royal High v Jedforest
Sale v Headingley
Saracens v Rugby
Shannon v Old Belvedere
S Glam Inst v Blaina
S Wales Police v Glamorgan Wands
Stewart's-Melville FP v Preston Lodge
Taunton v Penarth
Vale of Lune v Fylde
Waterloo v Middlesbrough
Watsonians v Ayr
West Hartlepool v Otley
Westoe v Percy Park
West of Scotland v Tynedale

Sunday, 16 December

Newbridge v Swansea

Monday, 17 December

Tredegar v Pontypool

Tuesday, 18 December

Glamorgan Wands v Pontypridd
Nottingham v RAF

Saturday, 22 December

Ireland Trial (Lansdowne Road)
Edinburgh District v Anglo Scots
Glasgow District v Scottish North and Midland
Wales Schools v New Zealand Schools (18 group)
France Schools v Scotland Schools (18 group)
Athlone v Garryowen
Ayr v Clarkston
Ballymena v Greystones
Bath v Sale
Bedford v Orrell
Blackrock Coll v Skerries
Bohemians v Dolphin
Boroughmuir v Heriot's FP
Bradford v Waterloo
Cambuslang v Kilmarnock
Cardiff v Bridgend
CIYMS v Academy
Clontarf v Lansdowne
Coventry v Rosslyn Park
Dungannon v Instonians
Durham City v Tynedale
Edinburgh Wands v Edinburgh Acads
Fylde v Sheffield
Glamorgan Wands v Bristol
Glasgow Acads v Highland
Glasgow High v Leith Acads
Gloucester v Newport
Haddington v Stewart's-Melville FP
Hawick v Langholm
Headingley v Wakefield
Huddersfield v Morley
Jedforest v Melrose
Jordanhill v West of Scotland
Kelso v Gala
Liverpool v Birkenhead Park
Llanelli v S Wales Police
London Welsh v Leicester
Lydney v Cross Keys
Maesteg v Aberavon
Malone v Portadown
Manchester v Davenport
Middlesbrough v Gosforth
Morpeth v Northern
Moseley v Ebbw Vale
New Brighton v Hartlepool Rovers
Newquay Hornets v Falmouth
Nottingham v Rugby
Nuneaton v Northampton
Old Wesley v Monkstown
Penarth v Newbridge
Queen's U, Belfast v Collegians
Richmond v Harlequins
Roundhay v Harrogate
St Mary's Coll v Bective Rangers
Saracens v Exeter
Selkirk v Preston Lodge
Sidmouth v Taunton
Stirling County v Dunfermline
Streatham-Croydon v Birmingham
Swansea v Abertillery
Terenure Coll v Palmerston
UC Cork v Corinthians
Vale of Lune v Broughton Park
Wasps v Blackheath
Watsonians v Portobello
West Hartlepool v Hull ER

Sunday, 23 December

Shannon v Cork Const
Wanderers v Bangor

Wednesday, 26 December

Aberavon v Neath
Abertillery v Ebbw Vale
Bath v Clifton
Bedford v Old Paulines
Bridgend v Maesteg
Bristol v Newbridge
Cardiff v Pontypridd
Clanwilliam v Dolphin
Cork Const v UC Cork
Cross Keys v Pontypool
Durham City v Sunderland
Exeter v Torquay Ath
Falmouth v Penryn
Fylde v Preston Grasshoppers
Gala v Melrose
Gloucester v Lydney
Gosforth v Northern
Glasgow Acads v Glasgow High
Hayle v St Ives
Heriot's FP v Royal High
Instonians v Old Campbellians
Jedforest v Hawick
Kelso v Haddington
Llanelli v London Welsh
London Irish v Old Millhillians
Manchester v Wilmslow
Middlesbrough v Redcar
Morley v Otley
Moseley v Coventry
New Brighton v Old Birkonians
Newport v S Glam Inst
Northampton v Saracens
Rockcliff v Percy Park
Roundhay v West Park
Rugby v Nuneaton
Sale v Broughton Park
Swansea v Glamorgan Wands
Taunton v Bridgwater Albion
Vale of Lune v Kendal
Waterloo v Birkenhead Park
West Hartlepool v Hartlepool Rovers

Thursday, 27 December

Leicester v Barbarians
Hillhead v West of Scotland
Swansea v London Welsh

Saturday, 29 December

Northern Division v Romanians (Birkenhead Park)
Anglo Scots v Glasgow District
Scottish North and Midland v South of Scotland
Festive Sevens (Highland RFC)
Aberavon v Abertillery
Academy v Ballymena
Armagh v Instonians
Ayr v Stirling County
Bangor v NIFC
Birmingham v Glamorgan Wands
Blackheath v Sidcup
Blaydon v Jedforest
Bohemians v Shannon
Broughton v Preston Lodge
Clontarf v Terenure Coll
Collegians v CIYMS
Coventry v Cardiff
Davenport v Hull ER
Ebbw Vale v Tredegar
Dolphin v Highfield
Dungannon v Malone
Fylde v Sale
Gala v Langholm
Garryowen v St Mary's Coll
Glasgow Acads v Melrose
Glasgow High v Hutchesons'
Gloucester v Bridgend
Greystones v Ards
Harrogate v Wakefield
Heriot's FP v Watsonians
Huddersfield v Vale of Lune
Kilmarnock v Clarkston
Llanelli v Bristol
London Scottish v Harlequins
Madras v Royal High
Middlesbrough v West Hartlepool
Neath v Maesteg
Newport v Torquay Ath
Northampton v Bath
Northern v Morley
Nottingham v Wasps
Nuneaton v Manchester
Old Belvedere v Bective Rangers
Old Wesley v Dublin U
Otley v Liverpool
Penarth v S Wales Police
Percy Park v Durham City
Pontypool v Newbridge
Portobello v Haddington
Rosslyn Park v Bedford
Rugby v Roundhay
St Ives v Penzance-Newlyn
Saracens v Richmond
Selkirk v Hawick
Skerries v Monkstown
Stewart's-Melville FP v Boroughmuir
Taunton v Barnstaple
Truro v Falmouth
Waterloo v Moseley
West of Scotland v Edinburgh Academy
Weston-super-Mare v Cross Keys
Widnes v Orrell
Wigton v Edinburgh Wands
Wilmslow v Broughton Park
Young Munster v Cork Const

Sunday, 30 December

Galwegians v Athlone

Monday, 31 December

Swansea v S Glam Inst

Tuesday, 1 January

South and South-West Division v Romanians (Gloucester)
Cardiff v Crawshay's Welsh
Clifton v Bristol
Falmouth v St Austell
Fylde v St Helens
Glamorgan Wands v Maesteg
Gosforth v Novocastrians
Liverpool v Bradford
London Welsh v Bedford
Lydney v Penarth
Moseley v Gloucester
Nottingham v Wakefield
Nuneaton v Edwardians
Otley v Headingley
Percy Park v Rockcliff
Pontypool v Bath
Pontypridd v Aberavon
Roundhegians v Roundhay
Sale v Manchester
Saracens v Blackheath
Wasps v Rosslyn Park

Wednesday, 2 January

Glasgow High v Melrose
Greenock Wands v Ayr
Haddington v Musselburgh
Hawick v Heriot's FP
Jedforest v Kelso
Kirkcaldy v Stirling County
Newport v Llanelli
North Berwick v Preston Lodge
Royal High v Gala
Shannon v UC Cork

Thursday, 3 January

Bangor v Ballymena

Saturday, 5 January

ENGLAND v ROMANIA (Twickenham)
Wales Trial (Cardiff) (provisional)

Edinburgh District v Glasgow District
South of Scotland v Anglo Scots
Scotland Schools v Wales Schools (18 group)
Abertillery v Penarth
Ayr v Howe of Fife
Birkenhead Park v Birmingham
Blackrock Coll v Instonians
Bohemians v Palmerston
Bridgend v Newport
Bristol v Bedford
Cardiff v Moseley
CIYMS v City of Derry
Clontarf v Greystones
Ebbw Vale v Saracens
Exeter v S Wales Police
Fylde v Liverpool
Gala v Edinburgh Acads
Garryowen v Dublin U
Gloucester v London Scottish
Haddington v Royal High
Harlequins v Army
Hawick v Kelso
Highland v Morgan FP
Hull ER v Tynedale
Langholm v Jedforest
Llanelli v Newbridge
London Irish v Rugby
London Welsh v Northampton
Maesteg v Pontypool
Manchester v Vale of Lune
Melrose v Selkirk
Met Police v Cross Keys
Monkstown v Old Belvedere
Morley v Orrell
Morpeth v Durham City
Musselburgh v Kilmarnock
NIFC v Collegians
Neath v Coventry
New Brighton v Sale
Northern v Middlesbrough
Nottingham v Broughton Park
Nuneaton v Roundhay
Old Wesley v Wanderers
Percy Park v Sunderland
Perthshire v Glasgow High
Preston Lodge v Heriot's FP
Richmond v Wasps
Rosslyn Park v Blackheath
St Ives v Falmouth
St Mary's Coll v Dolphin
Sheffield v West Hartlepool
Stirling County v Watsonians
Sunday's Well v Skerries
Swansea v Aberavon
Taunton v Sidcup
Terenure Coll v Academy
Torquay Ath v Pontypridd
UC Cork v Lansdowne
UC Dublin v Bective Rangers
Wakefield v Gosforth
Waterloo v Bath
West of Scotland v Edinburgh Wands
Weston-super-Mare v Glamorgan Wands

Sunday, 6 January

Cork Const v Highfield

Wednesday, 9 January

Army v Hampshire (Aldershot)
Blaina v S Glam Inst
Llanelli v Glamorgan Wands

Saturday, 12 January

Abertillery v Bridgend
Ballymena v Malone
Bath v London Welsh
Bective Rangers v Northampton
Bedford v Sale
Bristol v Coventry
Cardiff v Aberavon
Cheltenham v Torquay Ath
Chester v Huddersfield
City of Derry v Bangor
Clontarf v Blackrock Coll
Collegians v Queen's U, Belfast
Corinthians v Highfield
Cork Const v St Mary's Coll
Cross Keys v Tredegar
Dolphin v Curragh
Dungannon v Academy
Ebbw Vale v Maesteg
Falmouth v Launceston
Fylde v Nuneaton
Galwegians v UC Dublin
Garryowen v Old Belvedere
Glamorgan Wands v Newbridge
Gosforth v London Scottish
Harlequins v Blackheath
Instonians v CIYMS
Leicester v Gloucester
Liverpool v Lansdowne
Manchester v Headingley
Met Police v Saracens
Middlesbrough v Birmingham
Morley v Roundhay
Moseley v Neath
Newport v Swansea
Northern v Hartlepool Rovers
Old Wesley v Bohemians
Orrell v Nottingham
Otley v Hull ER
Palmerston v Dublin U
Penryn v Taunton
Percy Park v Morpeth
Pontypool v Pontypridd
Preston Grasshoppers v Vale of Lune
Richmond v London Irish
Rosslyn Park v Exeter
Rugby v Harrogate
St Ives v Camborne
Shannon v Greystones

Sheffield v Wakefield
Skerries v Terenure Coll
S Glam Inst v Penarth
UC Cork v Wanderers
Wasps v Llanelli
Waterloo v Broughton Park
Waterpark v Sunday's Well
West Hartlepool v Bradford
Wilmslow v New Brighton
Young Munster v Monkstown

SRU Championship
Division 1
Ayr v Melrose
Boroughmuir v Gala
Glasgow Acads v Jedforest
Hawick v Stewart's-Melville FP
Selkirk v Heriot's FP
Watsonians v Kelso
West of Scotland v Edinburgh Acads
Division 2
Edinburgh Wands v Langholm
Haddington v Clarkston
Highland v Portobello
Jordanhill v Preston Lodge
Kilmarnock v Dunfermline
Royal High v Howe of Fife
Stirling County v Gordonians

Wednesday, 16 January

Abertillery v Llanelli
Blaenavon v Pontypool
Musselburgh v Watsonians
Oxford U v Army
Royal Navy v Met Police
Treorchy v S Glam Inst

Friday, 18 January

Aberavon v Ebbw Vale
Bedford v Leicester
Exeter v Bristol
Maesteg v Taibach
Neath v Penarth
Old Belvedere v Dolphin
Tredegar v S Wales Police

Saturday, 19 January

IRELAND v ENGLAND
(Lansdowne Road)
FRANCE v WALES (Paris)
Scotland B v France B (Aberdeen)
Alnwick v West of Scotland
Ards v Collegians
Aspatria v Percy Park
Birmingham v Rugby
Boroughmuir v Clarkston
Broughton Park v Preston Grasshoppers
Cambridge U v Exeter U
Clontarf v Dungannon
Coventry v Newbridge
Davenport v Otley
Dublin U v Bangor
Durham City v Bradford
Edinburgh Acads v Broughton
Edinburgh Wands v Cambuslang
Gala v Middlesbrough
Glamorgan Wands v Bridgend
Glasgow High v Watsonians
Gosforth v Richmond
Harlequins v Birkenhead Park
Harrogate v Loughborough Students
Headingley v Waterloo
Heriot's FP v Kelso
Hull ER v Westoe
Jedforest v Hartlepool Rovers
London Scottish v Northern
London Welsh v Sale
Manchester v Huddersfield
Met Police v Bath
Monkstown v Old Crescent
New Brighton v Kendal
Newport v Cross Keys
Newquay Hornets v St Ives
Nottingham v Rosslyn Park
Nuneaton v Cheltenham
Old Wesley v Queen's U, Belfast
Orrell v West Hartlepool
Oxford U v Durham U
Preston Lodge v Kilmarnock
Stewart's-Melville FP v Melrose
Stirling County v Selkirk
Taunton v Paignton
Torquay Ath v Devonport Services
Trinity Acads v Royal High
UC Dublin v CIYMS
Vale of Lune v Liverpool
Wakefield v Roundhay
Wasps v Gloucester
Wilmslow v Fylde

Sunday, 20 January

Bohemians v Waterpark
Greystones v Wanderers
Highfield v Shannon
Northampton v Blackheath
Palmerston v St Mary's Coll
Redruth v Falmouth
Saracens v Moseley
Skerries v Bective Rangers
Terenure Coll v Garryowen
Young Munster v Galwegians

Wednesday, 23 January

Surrey v Army (Roehampton)
England Schools v New Zealand Schools
(Twickenham) (18 group)
Bath v Royal Navy
Cambridge U v RAF
Combined Old Boys v Oxford U

Saturday, 26 January

John Player/RFU Cup: *3rd round*
Schweppes/WRU Cup: *3rd round*
(English and Welsh fixtures subject to rearrangement)
Bangor v Instonians
Bath v Saracens
Bective Rangers v Shannon
Blackheath v Royal Navy
Bradford v New Brighton
Bristol v Gosforth
Broughton Park v Wilmslow
Chester v Hull ER
CIYMS v Ards
Clifton v Penarth
Clontarf v Old Belvedere
Dolphin v Lansdowne
Dungannon v Collegians
Durham City v Halifax
Garryowen v Old Wesley
Harrogate v Fylde
Kendal v Otley
London Welsh v Liverpool
Loughborough Students v Streatham-Croydon
Malone v City of Derry
Met Police v US Portsmouth
Middlesbrough v Birkenhead Park
Monkstown v Cork Const
Northern v Headingley
Old Crescent v Sunday's Well
Orrell v Huddersfield
Oxford U v Nuneaton
Penzance-Newlyn v Taunton
Percy Park v Blaydon
Queen's U, Belfast v Academy
Richmond v Waterloo
Rugby v West Hartlepool
St Helens v Vale of Lune
Sheffield v Sale
Skerries v Highfield
S Glam Inst v Glamorgan Wands
S Wales Police v Lydney
Torquay Ath v Exeter U
UC Cork v Blackrock Coll
Wakefield v Hartlepool Rovers
Wasps v Harlequins
Waterpark v Galwegians
West Park v Manchester
Weston-super-Mare v St Ives

SRU Championship
Division 1
Edinburgh Acads v Melrose
Glasgow Acads v West of Scotland
Hawick v Selkirk
Heriot's FP v Boroughmuir
Jedforest v Gala
Kelso v Ayr
Stewart's-Melville FP v Watsonians
Division 2
Dunfermline v Highland
Gordonians v Edinburgh Wands
Howe of Fife v Clarkston
Langholm v Kilmarnock
Portobello v Jordanhill
Preston Lodge v Haddington
Royal High v Stirling County

Sunday, 27 January

Bradford v Vale of Lune
Greystones v Dublin U
St Mary's Coll v Terenure Coll

Tuesday, 29 January

Edinburgh Wands v Heriot's FP

Wednesday, 30 January

Bridgend v S Wales Police
Cambridge U v Royal Navy
Clifton v Bath
Cross Keys v Newbridge
Glamorgan Wands v Swansea
Moseley v Loughborough Students
RAF v Oxford U

Friday, 1 February

Ayr v CIYMS
Bath v Rosslyn Park
Bristol v Gloucester
Kelso v Old Wesley
Kilmarnock v City of Derry
Maesteg v Neath
Newbridge v Pontypool
Selkirk v Ards
Wasps v Moseley
Watsonians v Old Belvedere
West of Scotland v Clontarf

Saturday, 2 February

SCOTLAND v IRELAND (Murrayfield)
ENGLAND v FRANCE (Twickenham)
Abertillery v Aberavon
Army v Cambridge U
Bective Rangers v Queen's U, Belfast
Birkenhead Park v Otley
Cardiff v Ebbw Vale
Coleraine v Instonians
Corinthians v Skerries
Cork Const v Dublin U
Dunfermline v Glasgow High
Dungannon v St Mary's Coll
Edinburgh Acads v Old Wesley
Falmouth v Brixham
Garryowen v Wanderers
Glamorgan Wands v Plymouth Albion
Greystones v Old Crescent
Haddington v Boroughmuir
Hartlepool Rovers v Durham City

Headingley v Richmond
Heaton Moor v Huddersfield
Highfield v Waterpark
Hull ER v Middlesbrough
Kilmarnock v Hillhead
Liverpool v Sale
Llanelli v Bridgend
London Scottish v Leicester
London Welsh v Beziers
Loughborough Students v Wakefield
Manchester v Sheffield
Melrose v Langholm
Musselburgh v Gala
New Brighton v West Hartlepool
Newcastle U v Percy Park
Nottingham v Northern
Nuneaton v Bradford
Orrell v Broughton Park
Penarth v Tredegar
Perthshire v Highland
Preston Lodge v Leith Acads
Roundhay v Gosforth
Royal High v Hawick
Rugby v Weston-super-Mare
St Ives v Exeter U
S Glam Inst v Cross Keys
Stewart's-Melville FP v Glasgow Acads
Stirling County v Bangor
Sunday's Well v Bohemians
Swansea v Bedford
Taunton v Solihull
UC Galway v UC Cork
Vale of Lune v Birmingham
Waterloo v Coventry

Sunday, 3 February

Harlequins v Met Police
London Irish v Blackheath
Monkstown v Terenure Coll
Saracens v Northampton

Tuesday, 5 February

Aberavon v Pontypridd

Wednesday, 6 February

Civil Service v Army (Chiswick)
Cheltenham v S Wales Police
Glamorgan Wands v Lydney
Llanelli v S Glam Inst
Newbridge v Newport
Oxford U v Royal Navy

Saturday, 9 February

Aberavon v S Wales Police
Abertillery v Nuneaton
Academy v Ballinasloe
Bective Rangers v Waterpark
Bedford v Headingley
Birmingham v Wilmslow
Blackheath v Richmond
Bohemians v Clontarf
Bridgend v London Welsh
Cambridge U v Wasps
Cardiff v Bristol
Civil Service v Highfield
CIYMS v Palmerston
Collegians v Bangor
Coventry v London Scottish
Cross Keys v Torquay Ath
Dublin U v UC Galway
Dungannon v Galwegians
Durham U v Middlesbrough
Ebbw Vale v Penarth
Edwardians v Taunton
Exeter v Newbridge
Falmouth v Sidmouth
Garryowen v Greystones
Glamorgan Wands v Pontypool
Gloucester v Bath
Gosforth v Waterloo
Halifax v Birkenhead Park
Harrogate v West Hartlepool
Hull ER v Wakefield
Lansdowne v Cork Const
Leicester v Newport
Llanelli v Harlequins
London Irish v Liverpool
Manchester v Rugby
Met Police v Maesteg
Middlesbrough v Saracens
Moseley v Northampton
Neath v Swansea
Northern v New Brighton
Orrell v Fylde
Otley v Durham City
Pontypridd v Nottingham
Roundhay v Bradford
St Ives v Devonport Services
St Mary's Coll v Malone
Sale v Rosslyn Park
Shannon v Terenure Coll
Sheffield v Broughton Park
Skerries v Old Wesley
Sunday's Well v Monkstown
UC Cork v UC Dublin
Vale of Lune v Morley

SRU Championship
Division 1
Ayr v Edinburgh Acads
Boroughmuir v Hawick
Gala v West of Scotland
Heriot's FP v Jedforest
Kelso v Stewart's-Melville FP
Melrose v Glasgow Acads
Watsonians v Selkirk
Division 2
Clarkston v Preston Lodge
Dunfermline v Jordanhill
Edinburgh Wands v Royal High
Haddington v Portobello

Howe of Fife v Stirling County
Kilmarnock v Gordonians
Langholm v Highland

Sunday, 10 February

Dolphin v Blackrock Coll
Nenagh v Terenure Coll

Wednesday, 13 Februrary

Army v Public School Wands (Aldershot)
Bath v RAF
Coventry v Cheltenham
Edinburgh Wands v Edinburgh U
Glamorgan Wands v Royal Navy
Llanelli v Breconshire
Maesteg v Lydney
Old Belvedere v Terenure Coll

Friday, 15 February

Aberavon v Rosslyn Park
Bristol v Richmond
Cardiff v London Welsh
Cross Keys v Abertillery
Exeter v Blackheath
Llanelli v Army
Newbridge v Tredegar
Nottingham v Gloucester
Pontypridd v Neath
Swansea v S Wales Police

Saturday, 16 February

WALES v ENGLAND (Cardiff)
FRANCE v SCOTLAND (Paris)
Birkenhead Park v Broughton Park
Blackrock Coll v Liverpool
Blaydon v Otley
Bohemians v St Mary's Coll
Boroughmuir v Gala
Bradford v Hull ER
Bridgend v Bath
Cambuslang v Stirling County
Clifton v Taunton
Collegians v Wanderers
Edinburgh Acads v Melrose
Fylde v Wasps
Galwegians v Dolphin
Garryowen v Bective Rangers
Glamorgan Wands v Cambridge U
Glasgow High v Ayr
Greystones v Bangor
Halifax v Huddersfield
Hartlepool Rovers v Roundhay
Hawick v Sale
Hayle v St Ives
Headingley v Harlequins
Heriot's FP v Selkirk
Highfield v Young Munster
Instonians v Old Belvedere
Kelso v Kilmarnock
Kirkcaldy v Haddington
Leicester v Orrell
London Irish v West Hartlepool
London Scottish v Bedford
Loughborough Students v Nuneaton
Lydney v Birmingham
Malone v Clontarf
Met Police v Sidcup
Monkstown v CIYMS
Musselburgh v Edinburgh Wands
New Brighton v Wakefield
Northampton v Coventry
Northern v West of Scotland
Old Wesley v Shannon
Oxford U v Oxford
Palmerston v Academy
Penryn v Falmouth
Preston Lodge v Corstorphine
Rugby v Cheltenham
Skerries v NIFC
Stoke v Manchester
Sunday's Well v Athlone
UC Cork v Dublin U
Vale of Lune v Tynedale
Waterloo v Harrogate
Watsonians v Stewart's-Melville FP
Wilmslow v Middlesbrough

Sunday, 17 February

Dorset and Wilts v Southern Universities
Moseley v Gosforth
Saracens v London U
Vale of Lune v Wasps

Tuesday, 19 February

Swansea v Penarth

Wednesday, 20 February

Royal Navy v Civil Service
Territorial Army v Army
United Banks v Kent (Lloyds Bank Club)
Glamorgan Wands v S Wales Police
Northern v Newcastle U
Pontypridd v Penarth
Tredegar v S Glam Inst

Friday, 22 February

Wales Youth v Wales Colleges

Saturday, 23 February

John Player/RFU Cup: ***4th round***
Schweppes/WRU Cup: ***4th round***
(English and Welsh fixtures subject to rearrangement)
Aberavon v Exeter
Abertillery v Moseley

Academy v Skerries
Athlone v Bohemians
Bangor v City of Derry
Bath v Wasps
Bedford v Bridgend
Birkenhead Park v Waterloo
Birmingham v Plymouth Albion
Blackheath v Army
Cambridge U v Saracens
Clontarf v Old Crescent
Coleraine v CIYMS
Coventry v Fylde
Cross Keys v Ebbw Vale
Dolphin v Palmerston
Dublin U v Monkstown
Durham City v Roundhay
Falmouth v St Ives
Galwegians v Highfield
Garryowen v Lansdowne
Harlequins v Orrell
Harrogate v Broughton Park
Hull ER v Blaydon
Instonians v Queen's U, Belfast
Liverpool v Gloucester
London Irish v Richmond
London Scottish v Met Police
London Welsh v Neath
Loughborough Students v Esher
NIFC v Malone
Newbridge v Maesteg
Northampton v Leicester
Northern v Halifax
Nuneaton v Glamorgan Wands
Old Wesley v Bective Rangers
Otley v New Brighton
Oxford U v Nottingham
Penarth v S Glam Inst
Preston Grasshoppers v Middlesbrough
Rugby v Morley
St Mary's Coll v Ballymena
Sale v Bristol
Sunday's Well v Corinthians
Taunton v Guy's H
Terenure Coll v Dungannon
Torquay Ath v Stroud
Upper Wharfedale v Huddersfield
Vale of Lune v Wilmslow
Wakefield v Cheltenham
Waterpark v Greystones
West Hartlepool v Manchester

SRU Championship
Division 1
Ayr v Stewart's-Melville FP
Edinburgh Acads v Glasgow Acads
Hawick v Jedforest
Melrose v Gala
Selkirk v Kelso
Watsonians v Boroughmuir
West of Scotland v Heriot's FP
Division 2
Haddington v Dunfermline
Highland v Gordonians
Jordanhill v Langholm
Portobello v Clarkston
Preston Lodge v Howe of Fife
Royal High v Kilmarnock
Stirling County v Edinburgh Wands

Sunday, 24 February

UC Galway v Highfield

Tuesday, 26 February

Bridgend v Penarth
Nottingham v Loughborough Students
Roundhay v Leeds U

Wednesday, 27 February

United Hospitals v Hampshire
Bath v Exeter U
Cambridge U v Anti-Assassins
Cardiff v S Glam Inst
Cross Keys v Llanelli
Moseley v Birmingham
Newport v Abertillery
Queen's U, Belfast v Dublin U

Thursday, 28 February

Ayr v Jordanhill
Bangor v Academy

Friday, 1 March

Gloucester v Northampton
Haddington v Kenfig Hill
Musselburgh v Heriot's FP
Old Belvedere v Collegians
Pontypridd v Bristol
Preston Lodge v Llandaff
Rosslyn Park v London Irish
West of Scotland v Neath

Saturday, 2 March

SCOTLAND v WALES (Murrayfield)
IRELAND v FRANCE (Lansdowne Road)
Army v Royal Navy (Twickenham)
Barnstaple v Falmouth
Birkenhead Park v Bedford
Birmingham v Roundhay
Boroughmuir v Highland
Bridgwater Albion v Taunton
Broughton Park v Loughborough Students
Clarkston v Selkirk
Clontarf v Waterpark
Coventry v Wasps
Dublin U v Instonians
Durham City v Sheffield
Edinburgh Wands v Jedforest
Esher v Met Police
Fylde v Langholm

Gala v Vale of Lune
Glasgow High v Greenock Wands
Hull ER v New Brighton
Kendal v Huddersfield
Leicester v Harlequins
Liverpool v Northern
Manchester v Morley
Melrose v Alnwick
Middlesbrough v Hartlepool Rovers
Nottingham v Headingley
Nuneaton v Saracens
Old Wesley v UC Cork
Otley v Bradford
Portadown v Malone
Richmond v London Scottish
Royal High v Percy Park
Rugby v Oxford U
St Ives v Penryn
Sale v Gosforth
Stewart's-Melville FP v Hawick
Stirling County v Lampeter
Waterloo v Wakefield
West Hartlepool v Tynedale
Wilmslow v Orrell

Sunday, 3 March

Blackheath v Moseley
Blackrock Coll v Bective Rangers
Galwegians v Garryowen
Highfield v Old Crescent
Monkstown v Skerries
Northern v London Welsh
St Mary's Coll v Greystones
Terenure Coll v Cork Const

Monday, 4 March

Bath v Pontypridd
Cross Keys v Aberavon
Maesteg v Glamorgan Wands
Pontypool v Neath

Tuesday, 5 March

Edinburgh U v Preston Lodge

Wednesday, 6 March

East Midlands v Barbarians
(Northampton)
Oxford U v Oxfordshire
Bristol v Llanelli
Ebbw Vale v Newport
Rugby v RAF
Swansea v Bridgend

Saturday, 9 March

John Player/RFU Cup: *Quarter-finals*
(English fixtures subject to rearrangement)
Wales Youth v France Youth
(Abertillery)
Abertillery v Torquay Ath
Bath v Swansea
Bective Rangers v UC Cork
Birkenhead Park v Manchester
Bohemians v Lansdowne
Bridgend v Aberavon
Bristol v London Scottish
Broughton Park v Fylde
Camborne v Falmouth
Clifton v S Glam Inst
Corinthians v Monkstown
Dublin U v St Mary's Coll
Durham City v Durham U
Ebbw Vale v Glamorgan Wands
Exeter v Maesteg
Galwegians v Blackrock Coll
Gosforth v Bradford
Greystones v Cork Const
Harlequins v Bedford
Hartlepool Rovers v Otley
Hull ER v Roundhay
Leicester v Coventry
Liverpool v Moseley
Llanelli v Wakefield
London Irish v Nuneaton
London Welsh v Blackheath
Loughborough Students v Wilmslow
Met Police v Stroud
Middlesbrough v Vale of Lune
Newbridge v Cheltenham
New Brighton v Harrogate
Newport v Pontypridd
Nottingham v Birmingham
Orrell v Headingley
Pontypool v Cardiff
Redruth v St Ives
Richmond v Gloucester
Rosslyn Park v Northampton
Rugby v Huddersfield
Saracens v Neath
Skerries v Old Belvedere
S Wales Police v Plymouth Albion
Sunday's Well v Terenure Coll
UC Galway v Old Wesley
Walsall v Taunton
Wasps v Sale
Waterloo v Northern
West Hartlepool v Halifax

SRU Championship
Division 1
Boroughmuir v Kelso
Gala v Edinburgh Acads
Glasgow Acads v Ayr
Heriot's FP v Melrose
Jedforest v Watsonians
Stewart's-Melville FP v Selkirk
West of Scotland v Hawick
Division 2
Clarkston v Dunfermline
Edinburgh Wands v Howe of Fife
Gordonians v Jordanhill
Highland v Royal High

Kilmarnock v Stirling County
Langholm v Haddington
Preston Lodge v Portobello

Sunday, 10 March

Dolphin v Clontarf
Highfield v Garryowen

Tuesday, 12 March

Leicester v Loughborough Students
Llanelli v Penarth

Wednesday, 13 March

United Hospitals v Army
Clifton v S Wales Police
Ebbw Vale v Bath
Llangennech v Swansea
Maesteg v Newport
Moseley v Combined Old Boys
Wasps v London Welsh

Friday, 15 March

England Colts v Italy Colts
Aberavon v Newport
Bangor v Collegians
Bedford v Saracens
Cardiff v Bective Rangers
Ebbw Vale v Bohemians
Glamorgan Wands v Abertillery
Gloucester v Orrell
Leicester v RAF
Neath v Newbridge
Pontypridd v Cross Keys

Saturday, 16 March

ENGLAND v SCOTLAND
(Twickenham)
WALES v IRELAND (Cardiff)
Alnwick v Ayr
Boroughmuir v Edinburgh Acads
Cheltenham v Nuneaton
CIYMS v Portadown
Clontarf v Wanderers
Cork Const v Sunday's Well
Dolphin v UC Cork
Dublin U v Oxford U
Dunfermline v Watsonians
Edinburgh Wands v Leith Acads
Falmouth v Truro
Gosforth v Vale of Lune
Harrogate v Birkenhead Park
Headingley v Liverpool
Heriot's FP v Stirling County
Highfield v Dungannon
Huddersfield v Blaydon
Hull ER v Broughton Park
Jedforest v Tynedale
Langholm v Hawick
London Scottish v Nottingham
London Welsh v Rosslyn Park
Malone v Ards
Manchester v Roundhay
Melrose v Haddington
Monkstown v Ballymena
Moseley v Richmond
New Brighton v Morley
Northampton v Sale
Northern v London Irish
Otley v Middlesbrough
Penarth v Cheltenham
Plymouth Albion v Bristol
Portobello v Kelso
St Helens v Durham City
St Ives v Launceston
St Mary's Coll v Old Wesley
Selkirk v Kilmarnock
Sheffield v Birmingham
Stewart's-Melville FP v Royal High
US Portsmouth v Wasps
West Hartlepool v Wakefield
Wilmslow v Waterloo

Sunday, 17 March

Blackheath v Met Police
Galwegians v Corinthians
Greystones v Old Belvedere
Harlequins v Coventry
Redruth v Bristol
Terenure Coll v Blackrock Coll

Monday, 18 March

Bohemians v Garryowen
Bristol v Pontypool
Monkstown v Oxford U
Old Wesley v Clontarf

Tuesday, 19 March

Northampton v Met Police

Wednesday, 20 March

British Polytechnics v UAU
Coventry v Bedford
Ebbw Vale v Newbridge
Leicester v Royal Navy
Pontypridd v S Glamorgan Inst

Thursday, 21 March

Cheltenham v Gloucester

Saturday, 23 March

Army v Royal Air Force (Twickenham)
John Player/RFU Cup: *Semi-finals*
Schweppes/WRU Cup: *Semi-finals*

(English and Welsh fixtures subject to rearrangement)
Scotland Schools v Scotland Youth (Murrayfield)
Abertillery v Cross Keys
Armagh v CIYMS
Ayr v Edinburgh Wands
Bath v Richmond
Bective Rangers v Lansdowne
Birkenhead Park v Nuneaton
Birmingham v Cheltenham
Blackheath v Bedford
Boroughmuir v Watsonians
Bridgend v Ebbw Vale
Broughton Park v St Helens
City of Derry v Malone
Clarkston v Melrose
Clifton v St Ives
Clontarf v UC Dublin
Collegians v NIFC
Darlington v Durham City
Dublin U v Greystones
Edinburgh Acads v Dunfermline
Esher v Torquay Ath
Exeter v Glamorgan Wands
Falmouth v Weston-super-Mare
Fylde v Middlesbrough
Gala v Hawick
Gosforth v Otley
Haddington v Stirling County
Huddersfield v Hartlepool Rovers
Hull ER v Halifax
Kelso v Tynedale
Kilmarnock v Howe of Fife
Liverpool v Nottingham
Llanelli v Neath
London Scottish v Moseley
London Welsh v Harlequins
Maesteg v Coventry
Met Police v S Wales Police
Monkstown v Portadown
Musselburgh v Preston Lodge
Newbridge v Aberavon
New Brighton v Headingley
Newport v Cardiff
Orrell v Wasps
Palmerston v Old Belvedere
Penarth v Pontypool
Pontypridd v London Irish
Queen's U, Belfast v Bangor
Rosslyn Park v Bristol
Roundhay v West Hartlepool
Rugby v Preston Grasshoppers
Sale v Leicester
Saracens v Gloucester
Selkirk v Jedforest
Skerries v St Mary's Coll
Stewart's-Melville FP v Heriot's FP
Sunday's Well v Waterpark
Terenure Coll v Old Wesley
Tredegar v Taunton
UC Cork v Highfield
Vale of Lune v Sheffield
Wakefield v Northern
Waterloo v Northampton
West of Scotland v Royal High
Young Munster v Cork Const

Sunday, 24 March

Galwegians v UC Galway

Tuesday, 26 March

Penarth v Newport

Wednesday, 27 March

Aberavon v Bristol
Cross Keys v Maesteg
Ebbw Vale v Swansea
Manchester v Orrell
Nuneaton v Coventry
Plymouth Albion v Royal Navy
Pontypool v Bridgend
S Glam Inst v Treorchy
Taunton v Brixham

Friday, 29 March

Wales Schools v Scotland Schools (18 group)

Saturday, 30 March

County Championship: Final (Twickenham)
England Colts v Wales Colts (Moseley)
Abertillery v Met Police
Ards v Academy
Armagh v Galwegians
Ayr v City of Derry
Bangor v Dungannon
Bedford v Vale of Lune
Bridgend v Rosslyn Park
Bristol v Harlequins
Coventry v Ebbw Vale
Cross Keys v Rugby
Dolphin v Collegians
Dublin U v Ballymena
Dunfermline v Preston Lodge
Fylde v Manchester
Gloucester v Moseley
Guy's H v Blackheath
Haddington v Kilmarnock
Harrogate v Kelso
Highland v Alloa
Huddersfield v Hull ER
Instonians v West of Scotland
Jedforest v New Brighton
Leicester v Headingley
Llanelli v Cardiff
London Irish v Bath
London Welsh v Swansea
Lydney v Falmouth

Malone v CIYMS
Melrose v Glasgow High
Middlesbrough v Boroughmuir
Monkstown v Greystones
Musselburgh v Stirling County
Neath v Newport
Northampton v Liverpool
Northern v Saracens
Nuneaton v Nottingham
Orrell v Roundhay
Otley v Halifax
Plymouth Albion v Maesteg
Pontypool v Aberavon
Pontypridd v Newbridge
Royal High v Hartlepool Rovers
Sale v Wakefield
Sheffield v Birkenhead Park
Stewart's-Melville FP v Portobello
Stroud v Taunton
Torquay Ath v S Wales Police
Tredegar v Glamorgan Wands
Tynedale v Selkirk
Wasps v Gosforth
Waterloo v London Scottish
Watsonians v Leith Acads
West Hartlepool v Broughton Park

Monday, 1 April

Selkirk v Langholm

Wednesday, 3 April

Abertillery v Newbridge
Burton v Nuneaton
Coventry v Rugby
Cross Keys v Swansea
Ebbw Vale v Llanelli
Talywain v Pontypool

Thursday, 4 April

Lydney v Gloucester

Friday, 5 April

Penarth v Barbarians
France Schools v Wales Schools
(18 group)
Aberavon v Northampton
Blackheath v West Hartlepool
Camborne v Wasps
Pontypridd v Tredegar
Saracens v Broughton Park
Taunton v Old Millhillians
Vale of Lune v Sale

Saturday, 6 April

Cardiff v Barbarians
Gala Sevens
Royal Navy v Royal Air Force
(Twickenham)
Ireland Schools v Scotland Schools
(18 group)
Aberavon v London Welsh
Armagh v Skerries
Ballymena v Bohemians
Bangor v Portadown
Bath v Bristol
Bedford v Waterloo
Blackheath v Liverpool
Collegians v Academy
Dungannon v CIYMS
Durham City v Malone
Ebbw Vale v Abertillery
Glamorgan Wands v Cross Keys
Gloucester v New Brighton
Gosforth v Coventry
Harrogate v Northern
Headingley v Rugby
Leicester v Neath
Llanelli v Northampton
Maesteg v Bridgend
Malone v Omagh
Met Police v Broughton Park
Middlesbrough v Huddersfield
Newport v Moseley
Nottingham v Fylde
Old Belvedere v Sale
Orrell v West of Scotland
Penzance-Newlyn v Wasps
Pontypool v Nuneaton
Pontypridd v S Wales Police
Roundhay v Otley
Saracens v Manchester
Sheffield v Hull ER
Swansea v Harlequins
Taunton v Henley
Torquay Ath v Plymouth Albion
Vale of Lune v Birkenhead Park
Wakefield v Newbridge
Waterpark v Monkstown

Monday, 8 April

Swansea v Barbarians
Bath v West Hartlepool
Bedford v Northampton
Birkenhead Park v Nottingham
Bridgend v Pontypridd
Bristol v Abertillery
Broughton Park v Kendal
Cardiff v S Wales Police
Coventry v Headingley
Cross Keys v Newbridge
Durham City v Monkstown
Gloucester v Fylde
Hull ER v Northern
Leicester v Pontypool
Llanelli v Moseley
Maesteg v Maesteg Celtic
Neath v Aberavon
Newport v London Welsh
Nuneaton v Wilmslow
Otley v Orrell

Preston Grasshoppers v New Brighton
Redruth v Wasps
St Ives v St Mary's H
Sheffield v Liverpool
Taunton v OMT
Torquay Ath v Glamorgan Wands
Tredegar v Ebbw Vale
Vale of Lune v West of Scotland
Waterloo v Morley

Tuesday, 9 April

England Schools v France Schools
(Torquay) (18 group)

Wednesday, 10 April

Taibach v Crawshay's Welsh
London Scottish v Saracens
Pontypool v Ebbw Vale

Saturday, 13 April

Melrose Sevens
Highland Sevens
England Schools v Scotland Schools
(18 group)
Wales Schools v Ireland Schools
(18 group)
Aberavon v Llanelli
Academy v Queen's U, Belfast
Ards v Bangor
Bath v Newport
Birkenhead Park v Hull ER
Bridgend v Cross Keys
Brixham v Ebbw Vale
Cardiff v Swansea
Cheltenham v New Brighton
CIYMS v Ballymena
Collegians v Sligo
Coventry v Pontypridd
Exeter v Northampton
Fylde v Halifax
Glasgow High v Instonians
Gosforth v Bedford
Hayle v Falmouth
Headingley v Vale of Lune
Huddersfield v Wilmslow
Leicester v Bristol
Lichfield v Manchester
Liverpool v Orrell
Moseley v London Irish
Neath v Gloucester
Newbridge v London Welsh
Northern v Preston Grasshoppers
Nuneaton v Birmingham
Otley v Harrogate
Penarth v Abertillery
Richmond v Nottingham
Rosslyn Park v Harlequins
Roundhay v Broughton Park
Rugby v Oxford
St Ives v Newquay Hornets
Sale v Pontypool
Saracens v Wakefield
Skerries v Portadown
S Wales Police v Maesteg
Taunton v Stafford
Tynedale v Middlesbrough
Wasps v Waterloo
West of Scotland v West Hartlepool
Weston-super-Mare v Torquay Ath

Tuesday, 16 April

Llanelli v Maesteg
Rugby v Northampton
S Wales Police v Newbridge
Vale of Lune v Furness

Wednesday, 17 April

Bristol v Exeter
Newport v Pontypool
Pontypridd v Abertillery

Saturday, 20 April

Munster Cup Final
Ulster Cup Final
Kirkcaldy Sevens
Wales Schools v England Schools
(18 group)
Aberavon v Swansea
Ballymena v Bangor
Bath v Llanelli
Birmingham v Bedford
Bridgend v Moseley
Bristol v Maesteg
Broughton Park v West of Scotland
Cross Keys v Newport
Ebbw Vale v Pontypridd
Falmouth v Stroud
Fylde v New Brighton
Glamorgan Wands v Cheltenham
Gloucester v Sale
Gosforth v Leicester
Hull ER v St Helens
Manchester v Wakefield
Met Police v Northampton
Neath v Cardiff
Newbridge v Nottingham
Northern v Sheffield
Plymouth Albion v Nuneaton
Pontypool v Coventry
Preston Grasshoppers v Durham City
Roundhay v Birkenhead Park
Rugby v Vale of Lune
Skerries v Queen's U, Belfast
Sligo v Monkstown
Tredegar v Penarth
Waterloo v Orrell
West Hartlepool v Liverpool
Weston-super-Mare v Taunton
Wilmslow v Otley

Monday, 22 April

Maesteg v Penarth

Tuesday, 23 April

Pontypridd v Llanelli

Wednesday, 24 April

Abertillery v Tredegar
Bath v Cardiff
Bedford v Nuneaton
Birkenhead Park v New Brighton
S Wales Police v Pontypool

Friday, 26 April

Newbridge v Penarth
Penzance-Newlyn v Ebbw Vale
Pontypridd v Maesteg

Saturday, 27 April

John Player/RFU Cup Final (Twickenham)
Schweppes/WRU Cup Final (Cardiff)
Leinster Cup Final
Bedford v Bath
Birkenhead Park v Bradford
Birmingham v Manchester
Coventry v Bristol
Exeter v Gloucester
Fylde v Headingley
Huddersfield v Harrogate
Launceston v Falmouth
Morley v Gosforth
Moseley v Leicester
New Brighton v Widnes
Northampton v Cheltenham
Northern v Broughton Park
Nottingham v Newport
Nuneaton v West Hartlepool
Otley v Rugby
Percy Park v Hull ER
Pontypool v Waterloo
Redruth v Ebbw Vale
Ryton v Durham City
St Ives v Barnstaple
Sale v Roundhay
S Wales Police v Abertillery
Tredegar v Torquay Ath
Vale of Lune v Orrell
West of Scotland v Wakefield

Sunday, 28 April

Connacht Cup Final

Tuesday, 30 April

Llanelli v Pontypool
New Brighton v St Helens
Pontypridd v Glamorgan Wands

Saturday, 4 May

Middlesex Sevens: Finals (Twickenham)

MAJOR FIXTURES IN BRITAIN, IRELAND AND FRANCE, 1984-85

September 1984

29 **ENGLAND v PRESIDENT'S XV** (Twickenham)

November

3 **ENGLAND v AUSTRALIA** (Twickenham)
10 **IRELAND v AUSTRALIA** (Dublin)
Wales B v France B (Newport)
24 **WALES v AUSTRALIA** (Cardiff)

December

1 **Ireland B v Scotland B** (Galway)
8 **SCOTLAND v AUSTRALIA** (Murrayfield)
England Trial (Twickenham) *(provisional)*
11 **Oxford University v Cambridge University** (Twickenham)
15 **Barbarians v Australians** (Cardiff)
22 **Ireland Trial** (Lansdowne Road)

January 1985

5 **ENGLAND v ROMANIA** (Twickenham)
Wales Trial (Cardiff) *(provisional)*
19 **IRELAND v ENGLAND** (Dublin)
FRANCE v WALES (Paris)
Scotland B v France B (Aberdeen)

February

2 **SCOTLAND v IRELAND** (Murrayfield)
ENGLAND v FRANCE (Twickenham)
16 **WALES v ENGLAND** (Cardiff)
FRANCE v SCOTLAND (Paris)

March

2 **SCOTLAND v WALES** (Murrayfield)
IRELAND v FRANCE (Dublin)
Army v Royal Navy (Twickenham)
16 **ENGLAND v SCOTLAND** (Twickenham)
WALES v IRELAND (Cardiff)
23 **Army v Royal Air Force** (Twickenham)
30 **County Championship Final** (Twickenham)

April

6 **Royal Navy v Royal Air Force** (Twickenham)
27 **John Player/RFU Cup Final** (Twickenham)
Schweppes/WRU Cup Final (Cardiff)

May

4 **Middlesex Sevens Finals** (Twickenham)

MAJOR TOURS

AUSTRALIANS TO BRITISH ISLES

October 1984

17 **London Division** (Twickenham)
20 **South and South West Division** (Exeter)
24 **Cardiff**
27 **Combined Services** (Aldershot)
30 **Swansea**

November

3 **ENGLAND** (Twickenham)
6 **Midland Division** (Leicester)
10 **IRELAND** (Dublin)
14 **Ulster** (Belfast)
17 **Munster** (Limerick)
20 **Llanelli**
24 **WALES** (Cardiff)
28 **Northern Division** (Waterloo)

December

1 **South of Scotland** (Hawick)
4 **Glasgow District** (Hughenden)
8 **SCOTLAND** (Murrayfield)
12 **Pontypool**
15 **Barbarians** (Cardiff)

ROMANIANS TO ENGLAND

December 1984

29 **Northern Division** (Birkenhead Park)

January 1985

1 **South and South West Division** (Gloucester)
5 **ENGLAND** (Twickenham)